LUNNEY & OLIPHANT'S
TORT LAW

LUNNEY & OLIPHANT'S TORT LAW

Text and Materials

SEVENTH EDITION

Donal Nolan

Professor of Private Law, University of Oxford
Francis Reynolds and Clarendon Fellow and Tutor in Law,
Worcester College, Oxford

and

Ken Oliphant

Professor of Tort Law, University of Bristol

Great Clarendon Street, Oxford, OX2 6DP,
United Kingdom

Oxford University Press is a department of the University of Oxford.
It furthers the University's objective of excellence in research, scholarship,
and education by publishing worldwide. Oxford is a registered trade mark of
Oxford University Press in the UK and in certain other countries

© Donal Nolan and Ken Oliphant 2023

The moral rights of the authors have been asserted

First edition 2000
Second edition 2003
Third edition 2008
Fourth edition 2010
Fifth edition 2013
Sixth edition 2017

All rights reserved. No part of this publication may be reproduced, stored in
a retrieval system, or transmitted, in any form or by any means, without the
prior permission in writing of Oxford University Press, or as expressly permitted
by law, by licence or under terms agreed with the appropriate reprographics
rights organization. Enquiries concerning reproduction outside the scope of the
above should be sent to the Rights Department, Oxford University Press, at the
address above

You must not circulate this work in any other form
and you must impose this same condition on any acquirer

Public sector information reproduced under Open Government Licence v3.0
(http://www.nationalarchives.gov.uk/doc/open-government-licence/ open-government-licence.htm)

Published in the United States of America by Oxford University Press
198 Madison Avenue, New York, NY 10016, United States of America

British Library Cataloguing in Publication Data
Data available

Library of Congress Control Number: 2022950246

ISBN 978–0–19–886511–7

Printed in the UK by
Bell & Bain Ltd., Glasgow

Links to third party websites are provided by Oxford in good faith and
for information only. Oxford disclaims any responsibility for the materials
contained in any third party website referenced in this work.

PREFACE TO SEVENTH EDITION

The time gap between this new edition, once again prepared by Donal Nolan and Ken Oliphant, and the previous one is rather longer than we would have liked. The challenges posed by the COVID-19 pandemic and demanding institutional roles, combined with a major overhaul of many parts of the book, significantly slowed the pace of our progress. However, we hope that the changes we have made for the new edition will make use of the book as enjoyable, informative and rewarding as possible.

We remain committed to the aims set out in the preface to the first edition: to produce a stimulating resource for use in the teaching of tort law and a work worthy of scholarly attention. But to keep the work current we have made significant changes for the new edition, with the intention of better reflecting the current state of the law and of highlighting issues and debates that are of the most topical interest.

The most obvious of those changes are structural. The biggest of them has been the removal of the chapter on the negligence liability of public bodies, and the redistribution of material previously to be found there to Chapter 3 (introduction to negligence) and Chapter 9 (omissions and acts of third parties). This change was made in the light of the courts' recent move away from the application of special liability rules to claims against public bodies, in favour of the application of general negligence principles. Another important structural change is the recasting of Chapter 10 as 'Statutory Liability Regimes' (previously 'Special Liability Regimes'), dealing as before with occupiers' liability, product liability and breach of statutory duty, but no longer covering employers' liability as a separate topic. Significant structural changes that we have made to other chapters are set out below.

We have endeavoured to state the law on the materials known to us on 1 June 2022, though it was also possible to make selective reference to a few subsequent developments.

New in the Seventh Edition

- New 'feature' extracts from major recent cases, including: *R (Jalloh) v Secretary of State for the Home Department* [2021] AC 762 (false imprisonment); *Robinson v Chief Constable of West Yorkshire Police* [2018] AC 736 (duty of care); *Henderson v Dorset Healthcare University NHS Foundation Trust* [2021] AC 563 (defence of illegality); *N v Poole Borough Council* [2020] AC 780 (nonfeasance of public authority); *Williams v Network Rail Infrastructure Ltd* [2019] QB 601 (private nuisance); *Lachaux v Independent Print Ltd* [2020] AC 612 and *Stocker v Stocker* [2020] AC 593 (defamation); *ZXC v Bloomberg LP* [2022] UKSC 5 (misuse of private information); and *Various Claimants v Barclays Bank* [2020] AC 973 and *Various Claimants v Wm Morrison Supermarkets plc* [2020] AC 989 (vicarious liability).
- Detailed coverage of recent legislation, including a new feature extract from the Automated and Electric Vehicles Act 2018, and discussion of the implications of the Civil Liability Act 2018 and Building Safety Act 2022.

- Extensive reference to recent scholarship and reports, including a new feature extract from the European Commission's *Report on the Safety and Liability Implications of Artificial Intelligence, the Internet of Things and Robotics* (COM (2020) 64 final).
- Chapter 3 (Introduction to Negligence) has been extensively rewritten and sections II and III reorganised, with the addition to the former of a new subsection on the implications of the decision in *Robinson v Chief Constable of West Yorkshire Police* for the duty of care enquiry (and including an overview of the 'assumption of responsibility' concept), along with the renaming of section III as 'Negligence and Public Law' (previously, 'Negligence in the Human Rights Era') to reflect the inclusion there of material on the negligence liability of public authorities, a topic previously covered in the former Chapter 10.
- Significant cuts have been made to some of the extracts and commentary in Chapter 5 (Causation and Scope of Liability), which also includes coverage of recent decisions such as *Clay v TUI Ltd* [2018] 4 All ER 672 and *Meadows v Khan* [2022] AC 852.
- Chapter 6 (Defences to Negligence) has been significantly overhauled, with cuts and rationalisation of the sections on *volenti* and exclusion of liability and a significant expansion and reorganisation of the section on illegality in the light of the recent case law on that defence.
- Chapter 7 (Psychiatric Illness) has been reorganised, with the order in which we address primary and secondary victims reversed, so that the former (more logically) now come first.
- Significant cuts have been made to Chapter 8 (Economic Loss), where the discussion of the exceptions to the general no-recovery rule has also been reorganised in order to streamline the analysis.
- A new section has been added to Chapter 9 (Omissions and Acts of Third Parties) on the liability of public authorities for omissions, a topic previously covered in the former Chapter 10 on the liability of public bodies. The incorporation of the discussion of the nonfeasance of public bodies into this chapter has also enabled us to streamline the treatment of key cases such as *Michael v Chief Constable of South Wales* [2015] 2 AC 1732. A new section of commentary addresses the topical issue of parent company liability for the harmful activities of a subsidiary, including extended discussion of *Lungowe v Vedanta Resources plc* [2020] AC 1045 and *Okpabi v Royal Dutch Shell plc* [2021] 1 WLR 1294.
- The rebranded Chapter 10 (now 'Statutory Liability Regimes'), previously Chapter 11, has been overhauled, with some of the changes necessitated by the removal of the previous section on employers' liability and the incorporation of some of the material therein into the discussion of breach of statutory duty. The treatment of product liability has been expanded, with a more extensive discussion of the rationales for strict product liability and a topical new sub-section on the future of product liability in the light of technological developments such as artificial intelligence. The section on breach of statutory duty has also been rewritten and reorganised, with the incorporation of additional extracts from the scholarly literature to illuminate key debates.
- Chapter 11 (Nuisance), previously Chapter 12, has been reorganised throughout, with the structure of the discussion of private nuisance and (to a lesser extent) the rule in *Rylands v Fletcher* overhauled in order to streamline it and highlight the significance of recent developments.

- Significant changes have been made to parts of Chapter 12 (Defamation), previously Chapter 13, in the light of the Supreme Court decisions in *Lachaux v Independent Print Ltd* [2020] AC 612 and *Stocker v Stocker* [2020] AC 593.
- Chapter 14 (Vicarious Liability), previously Chapter 15, has been extensively reorganised so as to better match the current state of the law in this area. In the discussion of vicarious liability, the key modern concepts of relationships 'akin to employment' and the 'close connection' test have thereby been emphasised, while the final section of the chapter is now focused exclusively on the 'non-delegable duty of care', and incorporates some of the discussion of the operation of that concept in the employers' liability context from the former Chapter 11.
- In Chapter 16 (Death and Damages), previously Chapter 17, the analysis of loss of dependency and bereavement claims has been separated out, so that each now has its own section (Ch. 16.III. 2 and 3).

Thanks and Acknowledgements

There is a host of people to whom we should record our thanks, beginning with our current and former colleagues, and our friends elsewhere in the academic world, who have helped to shape our ideas through their published writings and discussions in public and private forums. Our thanks also go to generations of law students in numerous places around the world for their valuable feedback on previous editions and for helping us to refine our ideas in the course of seminar and tutorial debate. We are also grateful for thoughtful comments supplied by OUP's anonymous reviewers and to readers who have emailed with remarks and suggestions. At OUP we extend our thanks to Helen Swann, our publishing editor, and Emily Cunningham, our editorial contact, for their considerable efforts in seeing this new edition onto the shelves, as well as to our excellent copyeditor, Fiona Tatham, proofreader, Ian Pickett, and Seemadevi Sekar at Straive, our production manager. Donal Nolan would also like to thank Eleni Katsampouka for again providing outstanding research assistance. We would like in addition to give special thanks to Maria and Annelise for the sort of support that cannot be summarised in a few short words.

Donal Nolan
Ken Oliphant

FROM THE PREFACE TO THE FIRST EDITION

Our aim in preparing this book has been to produce a stimulating resource for use in the teaching of tort law and a work worthy of scholarly attention. It is more than simply a casebook as traditionally conceived. On the one hand, a high proportion of materials extracted in it are not cases but (for example) the diagnoses and prescriptions of law reformers or the critical analyses of academic commentators. The law of tort has generated a rich secondary literature, and we have endeavoured to provide students with easy access to a selection of the best and most interesting examples of that literature. On the other hand, the extent of our own authorial contribution is very considerable. In addition to the short introductions at the beginning of each new chapter (and many of the subsections within each chapter), we have written substantial commentaries following on from each extract (or series of extracts). These are designed to shed light on the significance of the material extracted and to identify further, related issues for consideration. Frequently, we have expressed personal views about the topic under discussion (hoping thereby to provoke debate rather than to foreclose it). On a number of occasions, we have developed what we believe to be original analyses worthy of consideration as contributions to scholarly debate.

Tort law cannot be viewed simply as a self-contained collection of legal rules, and we have sought to explore the law from a variety of perspectives that are external to it (amongst them the comparative, the socio-legal, the theoretical, the feminist and the economic). We believe that each has something to add to our understanding of the law.

LIST OF ABBREVIATIONS

ABI	Association of British Insurers
ABS	Alternative Business Structure
AC	Law Reports: Appeal Cases
Admin LR	Administrative Law Reports
AHA	Area Health Authority
AI	Artificial Intelligence
AJDA	Actualité Juridique: Droit Administratif
ALJ	Australian Law Journal
ALJR	Australian Law Journal Reports
All ER	All England Law Reports
ALR	Australian Law Reports
Am JLH	American Journal of Legal History
Am L Rev	American Law Review
Am U LR	American University Law Review
APIL	Association of Personal Injury Lawyers
ASHE	Annual Survey of Hours and Earnings
ATE	After-the-Event (Insurance)
B & Ad	Barnewall & Adolphus Reports
B & S	Best & Smith Reports
BC	Borough Council
BCCI	Bank of Credit and Commerce International
BCLC	Butterworths Company Law Cases
BGB	*Bürgerliches Gesetzbuch* (German Civil Code)
BGHZ	Entscheidungen des Bundesgerichtshofes in Zivilsachen
BLR	Building Law Reports
BMLR	Butterworths Medico-Legal Reports
Br Col R	British Columbia Reports (Canada)
BWCC	Butterworth's Workmen's Compensation Cases
C & P	Carrington & Payne Reports
Can Bar Rev	Canadian Bar Review
Car & Kir	Carrington & Kirwan Reports
CC	County Council
CCLT	Canadian Cases on the Law of Torts
CFA	Conditional Fee Agreement
Ch D	Chancery Division
CICA	Criminal Injuries Compensation Authority
CJEU	Court of Justice of the European Union
CLC	Commercial Law Cases
CLJ	Cambridge Law Journal
CLP	Current Legal Problems
CLR	Commonwealth Law Reports (Australia)

CLSA	Courts and Legal Services Act 1990
CMC	Claims Management Company
CMLR	Common Market Law Reports
CMO	Chief Medical Officer
Col LR	Columbia Law Review
Comm L World Rev	Common Law World Review
Con LR	Construction Law Reports
Consumer L Jnl	Consumer Law Journal
Conv	Conveyancer
Cornell L Rev	Cornell Law Review
CP	Consultation Paper
CPD	Common Pleas Division
CPR	Civil Procedure Rules
CPS	Crown Prosecution Service
Cr App R	Criminal Appeal Reports
Cr App R(S)	Criminal Appeal Reports (Sentencing)
Crim LR	Criminal Law Review
CRU	Compensation Recovery Unit
CUP	Cambridge University Press
DBA	Damages-based agreement
DCA	Department for Constitutional Affairs
DHSS	Department of Health and Social Security
DLR	Dominion Law Reports (Canada)
DR	Decisions and Reports of the European Commission of Human Rights
E & B	Ellis & Blackburn Reports
EC	European Community
ECHR	European Convention for the Protection of Human Rights and Fundamental Freedoms
ECJ	European Court of Justice
ECR	European Court Reports
ECtHR	European Court of Human Rights
Edin LR	Edinburgh Law Review
EEC	European Economic Community
EG	Estates Gazette
EGLR	Estates Gazette Law Reports
EHRR	European Human Rights Reports
EL	Employers' liability
EMLR	Entertainment and Media Law Reports
Env L Rev	Environmental Law Review
ER	English Reports
EU	European Union
EUP	Edinburgh University Press
Eur Rev Priv Law	European Review of Private Law
EWCA Civ	England & Wales Court of Appeal, Civil Division
EWHC	England & Wales High Court
Ex D	Exchequer Division

FCFCA	Full Court of the Federal Court (Australia)
FCR	Family Court Reporter
FL Rev	Federal Law Review
FLR	Family Law Reports
FRCs	Fixed recoverable costs
FSR	Fleet Street Reports
Georgetown LJ	Georgetown Law Journal
GLC	Greater London Council
GM	genetically modified
H & N	Hurlstone & Norman Reports
Harv L Rev	Harvard Law Review
Hawaii L Rev	Hawaii Law Review
HCA	High Court of Australia
HL Cas	House of Lords Cases
HLR	Housing Law Reports
HMSO	Her Majesty's Stationery Office
HRA	Human Rights Act 1998
ICLQ	International and Comparative Law Quarterly
ICR	Industrial Cases Reports
ILGS	Index-Linked Government Stock
ILJ	Industrial Law Journal
Imm AR	Immigration Appeal Reports
IoT	Internet of Things
Iowa L Rev	Iowa Law Review
IRLR	Industrial Relations Law Reports
JEL	Journal of Environmental Law
JETL	Journal of European Tort Law
J Leg Ed	Journal of Legal Education
J Leg His	Journal of Legal History
J Leg St	Journal of Legal Studies
J Soc Pol	Journal of Social Policy
JLE	Journal of Law and Economics
JLS	Journal of Law and Society
JPIL	Journal of Personal Injury Law
JSPTL	Journal of the Society of Public Teachers of Law
KB	King's Bench
KCLJ/KLJ	King's College Law Journal/King's Law Journal
KIR	Knight's Industrial Reports
LASPOA	Legal Aid, Sentencing and Punishment of Offenders Act 2012
Law Com	Law Commission
LBC	Law Book Company
LCD	Lord Chancellor's Department

LEA	Local Education Authority
Leg His	Legal History
LGR	Local Government Reports
Lloyd's Rep Med	Lloyd's Medical Law Reports
LMCLQ	Lloyd's Maritime and Commercial Law Quarterly
LQR	Law Quarterly Review
LS	Legal Studies
LS Gaz	Law Society Gazette
LT	Law Times Reports
M & W	Meeson and Welsby Reports
ME	Myalgic encephalomyelitis
Med L Rev	Medical Law Review
Med LR	Medical Law Reports
MIB	Motor Insurers' Bureau
Mich LR	Michigan Law Review
Minn LR	Minnesota Law Review
MLR	Modern Law Review
MOD	Ministry of Defence
NAO	National Audit Office
NHBC	National House Building Council
NHS	National Health Service
NILQ	Northern Ireland Law Quarterly
NJW	Neue Juristische Wochenschrift
NLJ	New Law Journal
NSR	Nova Scotia Reports (Canada)
NSWCA	New South Wales Court of Appeal (Australia)
NSWR	New South Wales Reports (Australia)
NTLR	Northern Territory Law Reports (Australia)
NZLR	New Zealand Law Reports
NZ L Rev	New Zealand Law Review
OJLS	Oxford Journal of Legal Studies
OR	Ontario Reports (Canada)
Osgoode Hall LJ	Osgoode Hall Law Journal
OUP	Oxford University Press
PACE	Police and Criminal Evidence Act 1984
PCT	Primary Care Trust
PD	Probate Division *or* Practice Direction
PI	Personal injury
PIQR	Personal Injuries and Quantum Reports
PL	Public Law
PN	Professional Negligence
PPO	Periodical payment order
PSLA	Pain, suffering and loss of amenity
PTSD	Post-traumatic stress disorder
QB	Queen's Bench

RIA	Regulatory Impact Assessment
RPC	Reports of Patent Cases
RPI	Retail Price Index
RSC	Rules of the Supreme Court
RTA	Road traffic accident
RTR	Road Traffic Reports
SASR	South Australian State Reports
SCR	Supreme Court Reports (Canada)
SI	Statutory Instrument
Sing Comp L Rev	Singapore Comparative Law Review
SLC	Scottish Law Commission
SLT	Scots Law Times
Sol J	Solicitors' Journal
SR (NSW)	State Reports New South Wales (Australia)
Stan L Rev	Stanford Law Review
Stat Law	Statute Law Review
Syd L Rev	Sydney Law Review
TEC	Treaty establishing the European Community
TEU	Treaty on European Union
Tex L Rev	Texas Law Review
TFEU	Treaty on the Functioning of the European Union
TLJ	Torts Law Journal
TLR	Times Law Reports
Tort LR	Tort Law Review
U Chi L Rev	University of Chicago Law Review
U of Toronto LJ	University of Toronto Law Journal
UAE	United Arab Emirates
UCTA	Unfair Contract Terms Act 1977
UCLA	University of California Los Angeles
UCLA L Rev	UCLA Law Review
UKHL	United Kingdom House of Lords
U L Rev	University Law Review
UN	United Nations
UNELJ	University of New England Law Journal
VAT	Value Added Tax
VR	Victorian Reports (Australia)
VUWLR	Victoria University of Wellington Law Review
WALR	Western Australian Law Reports
WASCA	Western Australia Court of Appeal
WLR	Weekly Law Reports
WWR	Western Weekly Reports (Canada)
Yale LJ	Yale Law Journal
YB	Yearbook
ZEuP	Zeitschrift für Europäisches Privatrecht

LIST OF ABBREVIATIONS OF COMMONLY CITED WORKS

Atiyah	*Atiyah's Accidents, Compensation and the Law*, 9th edn by P. Cane and J. Goudkamp (Cambridge: CUP, 2018)
Baker	J. Baker, *An Introduction to English Legal History*, 5th edn (Oxford: OUP, 2019)
Barendt	E. Barendt et al., *Libel and the Media: The Chilling Effect* (Oxford: Clarendon Press, 1997)
Beever	A. Beever, *Rediscovering the Law of Negligence* (Oxford: Hart, 2007)
Blackstone	W. Blackstone, *Commentaries on the Laws of England* (originally published 1765–69; facsimile edition by University of Chicago Press, 1979)
Challenging Orthodoxy	S. Pitel, J. Neyers and E. Chamberlain (eds), *Tort Law: Challenging Orthodoxy* (Oxford: Hart, 2013)
Clerk & Lindsell	*Clerk & Lindsell on the Law of Torts*, 23rd edn ed. by M. Jones (London: Sweet & Maxwell, 2020)
Conaghan & Mansell	J. Conaghan and W. Mansell, *The Wrongs of Tort*, 2nd edn (London: Pluto Press, 1999)
Cornish & Clark	W. Cornish et al., *Law and Society in England 1750–1950,* 2nd edn (Oxford: Hart, 2019)
Defences in Tort	A. Dyson, J. Goudkamp and F. Wilmot-Smith (eds), *Defences in Tort* (Oxford: Hart, 2015)
Dobbs, Heyden & Bublick	D.B. Dobbs, P.T. Heyden and E.M. Bublick, *The Law of Torts*, 2nd edn (St. Paul, Minn.: Thomson West, 2011)
European Tort Law	Annual, beginning with H. Koziol and B. Steininger (eds), *European Tort Law 2001: Tort and Insurance Law Yearbook* (Vienna: Springer-Verlag, 2002)
Fairgrieve and Goldberg	D. Fairgrieve and R. Goldberg, *Product Liability*, 3rd edn (Oxford: OUP, 2020)
Fleming	*Fleming's The Law of Tort*, 10th edn ed. by C. Sappideen and P. Vines (Sydney: Lawbook Co, 2011)
Gatley	*Gatley on Libel and Slander*, 13th edn ed. by R. Parkes et al. (London: Sweet & Maxwell, 2022)
Giliker	P. Giliker, *The Europeanisation of English Tort Law* (Oxford: Hart, 2014)
Hart & Honoré	H.L.A. Hart and Tony Honoré, *Causation in the Law*, 2nd edn (Oxford: Clarendon Press, 1985)
Hoffmann Festschrift	P. Davies and J. Pila (eds), *The Jurisprudence of Lord Hoffmann: A Festschrift in Honour of Lord Leonard Hoffmann* (Oxford: Hart, 2015)

Ibbetson	D. Ibbetson, *An Historical Introduction to the Law of Obligations* (Oxford: OUP, 1999)
Jackson Report	The Right Honourable Lord Justice Jackson, *Review of Civil Litigation Costs: Final Report* (The Stationery Office, 2010)
Leveson	The Right Honourable Lord Justice Leveson, *An Inquiry into the Culture, Practices and Ethics of the Press: Report* (HC 780, 2012)
McBride & Bagshaw	N.J. McBride and R. Bagshaw, *Tort Law*, 6th edn (Harlow: Pearson, 2018)
Mitchell	P. Mitchell, *A History of Tort Law 1900–1950* (Cambridge: CUP, 2015)
Mitchell & Mitchell	C. Mitchell and P. Mitchell (eds), *Landmark Cases in the Law of Tort* (Oxford: Hart, 2010)
North	P. North, *Occupiers' Liability*, 2nd edn (Oxford: OUP, 2014)
Oliphant	K. Oliphant (ed.), *The Law of Tort*, 3rd edn (London: LexisNexis, 2015)
Pearson Commission	Royal Commission on Civil Liability and Compensation for Personal Injury, Chairman: Lord Pearson, *Report*, Cmnd 7054, 1978
Plunkett	J. Plunkett, *The Duty of Care in Negligence* (Oxford: Hart, 2018)
Private Law in the 21st Century	K. Barker, K. Fairweather and R. Grantham (eds), *Private Law in the 21st Century* (Oxford: Hart, 2017)
Rights and Private Law	D. Nolan and A. Robertson (eds), *Rights and Private Law* (Oxford: Hart, 2012)
Salmond & Heuston	*Salmond & Heuston on the Law of Torts*, 21st edn by R. Buckley (London: Sweet & Maxwell, 1996)
Stanton	K. Stanton et al., *Statutory Torts* (London: Sweet & Maxwell, 2003)
Stapleton	J. Stapleton, *Three Essays on Torts* (Oxford: OUP, 2021)
Stevens	R. Stevens, *Torts and Rights* (Oxford: OUP, 2007)
Tort Law and the Legislature	T.T. Arvind and J. Steele (eds), *Tort Law and the Legislature: Common Law, Statute and the Dynamics of Legal Change* (Oxford: Hart, 2013)
van Dam	C. van Dam, *European Tort Law*, 2nd edn (Oxford: OUP, 2013)
van Gerven	W. van Gerven et al., *Cases, Materials and Text on National, Supranational and International Tort Law* (Oxford: Hart, 2000)
Weir	T. Weir, *A Casebook on Tort*, 10th edn (London: Sweet & Maxwell, 2004)
Winfield & Jolowicz	*Winfield & Jolowicz on Tort*, 20th edn by J. Goudkamp and D. Nolan (London: Sweet & Maxwell, 2020)

ACKNOWLEDGEMENTS

We are grateful to all authors and publishers of copyright material used in this book and in particular to the following for permission to reprint from the sources indicated.

Extracts from Crown copyright material are reproduced under the terms of the Open Government Licence v3.0; Parliamentary copyright material is reproduced under the Open Parliament Licence v3.0; and court judgments in which Crown copyright subsists are reproduced under the Open Justice Licence v1.0.

The American Law Institute for extract from *Restatement of the Law Third, Torts: Liability for Physical and Emotional Harm*, copyright © 2009, 2012 by The American Law Institute. All rights reserved. Reproduced with permission.

Cambridge Law Journal and the authors for extracts from R. Dias, 'Trouble on Oiled Waters: Problems of the Wagon Mound (No 2)' [1967] *Cambridge Law Journal* 62; Conor Gearty, 'The Place of Private Nuisance in a Modern Law of Torts' [1989] *Cambridge Law Journal* 214; and Anthony J.E. Jaffey, '*Violenti Non Fit Injuria*' [1985] *Cambridge Law Journal* 87.

Cambridge University Press for extracts from P. Cane and J. Goudkamp, *Atiyah's Accidents, Compensation and the Law* (9th edn, Cambridge, 2018); R. Lewis, 'Insurance and the Tort System' (2005) 25 *Legal Studies* 85; K. Williams, 'State of Fear: Britain's "compensation culture" reviewed' (2005 25 *Legal Studies* 499; R. Kidner, 'Vicarious Liability: For Whom Should the "Employer" be Liable?' (1995) 15 *Legal Studies* 47; and D. Harris, I. D. Campbell and R. Halson, *Remedies in Contract and Tort* 2nd edn (London: Butterworths, 2002) pp.315-16. Reproduced with permission of the Licensor through PLSclear.

European Commission, Report on the Safety and Liability Implications of Artificial Intelligence, the Internet of Things and Robotics COM(2020) 64 final, licensed under the Creative Commons Attribution 4.0 International licence.

Hart Publishing, an imprint of Bloomsbury Plc for extracts from P. S. Atiyah: *The Damages Lottery* (Hart, 1997); R. Lewis, 'Structural Factors Affecting the Number and Cost of Personal Injury Claims in the Tort System', in E. Quill and R.J. Friel, *Damages and Compensation Culture: Comparative Perspectives* (Oxford: Hart, 2016); and A Morris 'Deconstructing Policy on Costs and the Compensation Culture', in E. Quill and R.J. Friel, *Damages and Compensation Culture: Comparative Perspectives* (Oxford: Hart, 2016).

David Ibbetson for 'The Tort of Negligence in the Common Law in the 19th and 20th Centuries' first published in the first edition of this book and subsequently in *Negligence: the comparative legal history of the law of torts* edited by E.J.H. Schrage (Berlin: Duncker & Humblot, 2001).

The Incorporated Council of Law Reporting for extracts from *Appeal Court Reports* (AC), *Queen's Bench Reports* (QB), *King's Bench Reports* (KB), and *Weekly Law Reports* (WLR).

Oxford University Press for extracts from J.H. Baker, *Introduction to English Legal History* (5th edn, Oxford: OUP, 2019); J. Baker & S. Milson, 'Rattlesdene v Grunestone' and 'The Farrier's Case' in *Sources of English Legal History: Private Law to 1750* (2nd edn, Butterworths, 2010); E. Barendt et al., *Libel and the Media: The Chilling Effect* (OUP, 1997); and D. Harris et al., *Compensation and Support for Illness and Injury* (OUP, 1984).

RELX (UK) Ltd trading as LexisNexis for extracts from *All England Law Reports* (All ER).

Sweet & Maxwell Ltd for extracts from ; from *Law Quarterly Review:* W. Bishop, 'Negligent Representation through Economist's Eyes' (1980) 96 *LQR* 360; B.S. Markesinis, 'Negligence, Nuisance and Affirmative Duties of Action' (1989) 105 *LQR* 104; and from *Road Traffic Reports* and *Fleet Street Reports*.

Thomson-Reuters for extracts from *Commonwealth Law Reports* and from C. Sappideen & P. Vines (eds), *Fleming's The Law of Tort*, 10th edn (Sydney: Lawbook Co, 2011), reproduced with permission of Thomson Reuters (Professional) Australia Limited.

Thomas Reuters Canada Limited for extracts from *Bazley v Curry* (1999) 174 D.L.R. (4th) 45 (S.C.C.). Reproduced by permission of Thomson Reuters Canada Limited.

University of Chicago Law School via Copyright Clearance Center for extract from James A. Henderson, 'The New Zealand Accident Compensation Reform' (1981) 48 *University of Chicago Law Review* 781, copyright © 1981 by the University of Chicago Law School.

Wiley-Blackwell Publishers via Copyright Clearance Center for extracts from *Modern Law Review*: R. Lewis, 'The Politics and Economics of Tort Law: Judicially Imposed Periodical Payments of Damages' (2006) 69 MLR 418; and P.S. Atiyah, 'Res Ipsa Loquitur in England and Australia' (1972) 35 MLR 337.

R.B.G. Williams and Oxford University Press for extracts from Glanville Williams, 'The Aims of the Law of Tort' (1951) 4 *Current Legal Problems* 137.

Every effort has been made to trace and contact copyright holders but this has not been possible in every case. If notified, the publisher will undertake to rectify any errors or omissions at the earliest opportunity.

CONTENTS

Table of Cases — xxvii
Table of Legislation — liii

1. General Introduction — 1

I. Historical Development of Tort Law — 1
1. Origins of Tort Law — 1
2. The Forms of Action — 2
3. The Development of Fault-Based Liability — 7
4. Eighteenth-Century Developments — 8
5. The Classification of Obligations — 9
6. The Modern Pre-Eminence of Negligence — 12

II. Theories of Tort — 17
1. The Aims of the Law of Tort — 18
2. Doctrinal Classifications: Tort Law and other Legal Categories — 23

III. Modern Influences on Tort Law — 24
1. The Influence of Insurance — 25
2. The Influence of Human Rights — 28
3. Concerns about 'Compensation Culture' — 32

2. Intentional Interference with the Person — 42

I. Introduction — 42
1. Historical Background — 42
2. Trespass and Fault — 43

II. Assault — 49

III. Battery — 53

IV. False Imprisonment — 58
1. Elements of the Tort — 58
2. Directness — 62

V. Intentional Infliction of Physical or Emotional Harm — 65

VI. Defences — 79
1. Introduction — 79
2. Lawful Arrest and Detention — 81

	3. Consent	86
	4. Necessity	92
	5. Self-Defence and Related Defences	101

3 Negligence—Introduction 106

I. Formulation of a General Duty of Care — 106
1. Historical Introduction — 106
2. *Donoghue v Stevenson* — 110
3. *Donoghue v Stevenson* in Action—The Development of Liability for Defective Products — 115

II. The Duty of Care in the Modern Law — 121
1. Introduction: 'Notional Duty' — 122
2. The Foreseeable Claimant — 126
3. The *Caparo* Three-Stage Approach to Duty — 134
4. The *Robinson* Decision and the Duty of Care — 143

III. Negligence and Public Law — 157
1. The Negligence Liability of Public Authorities — 157
2. Negligence and Human Rights — 166

4 Breach of Duty 171

I. Introduction — 171

II. Reasonable Care: Relevant Considerations — 182
1. Gravity of the Potential Harm — 183
2. The Cost of Precautions — 185
3. Utility of the Defendant's Conduct — 188

III. Negligence Judged from the Defendant's Standpoint — 194

IV. The Objective Standard of Care — 200
1. Lack of Skill and Experience — 202
2. Physical and Mental Disability — 206
3. Age — 210
4. Special Skills — 213

V. Common Practice — 215
1. Common Industrial Practice — 215
2. Professional Standards — 216

VI. *Res Ipsa Loquitur* — 221
1. Purpose and Effect — 221
2. Application of the Maxim — 223

5 Causation and Scope of Liability — 227

- I. Factual Causation — 227
  1. The But-For Test — 227
  2. Challenges to the Orthodox But-For Approach — 229
  3. Multiple Sufficient Causes — 265
- II. Intervening Acts — 273
- III. Remoteness — 283
  1. *Wagon Mound* and the Scope of Risk Approach — 284
  2. The *SAAMCO* decision — 289

6 Defences to Negligence — 296

- I. Introduction — 296
- II. *Volenti Non Fit Injuria* — 296
  1. Introduction — 296
  2. The Operation of the Defence — 298
  3. Evaluation — 305
- III. Contributory Negligence — 307
  1. Historical Background — 307
  2. The 1945 Act — 308
  3. Apportionment — 312
- IV. Exclusion of Liability — 320
- V. Illegality (*Ex Turpi Causa Non Oritur Actio*) — 326
  1. Claimants Seeking to Avoid the Consequences of Criminal Sanctions — 329
  2. Claimants not Recovering for the Consequences of their Own Criminal Acts — 330
  3. *Patel* and *Henderson* — 334
  4. The Rationale of the Illegality Defence — 347

7 Negligence: Duty of Care—Psychiatric Illness — 349

- I. Introduction — 349
- II. Primary Victims or Participants — 351
- III. Secondary Victims or Witnesses — 363
- IV. Other Types of Case — 377
- V. Evaluation and Reform — 386
  1. Criticisms of the Current Law — 386
  2. Proposals for Reform — 389

8 Negligence: Duty of Care—Economic Loss 394

   I. The Basic Exclusionary Rule 394
      1. Introduction 394
      2. Case Law 395
      3. Justifications for the Exclusionary Rule 400
   II. Defective Product Economic Loss 403
   III. The *Hedley Byrne* Exception 421
      1. The *Hedley Byrne* Decision 421
      2. *Hedley Byrne* and the Supply of Information 431
      3. *Hedley Byrne* and the Provision of Services 445
   IV. Economic Loss Recovery Beyond *Hedley Byrne* 452
   V. The Duty of Care and Pure Economic Loss—Evaluation 464
      1. Economic Analysis and Negligent Misrepresentation 464
      2. Rights-Based and Policy-Based Analyses of the Current Law 467

9 Negligence: Duty of Care—Omissions and Acts of Third Parties 472

   I. Acts and Omissions 472
   II. Liability for Omissions 476
   III. Liability for the Acts of a Third Party 491
   IV. Nonfeasance by Public Bodies 506

10 Statutory Liability Regimes 524

   I. Occupiers' Liability 525
      1. The Law pre-1957 525
      2. The 1957 Act 527
      3. The 1984 Act 544
   II. Product Liability 555
      1. Rationales for Strict Liability for Defective Products 556
      2. The Consumer Protection Act 1987 562
      3. The Future of Product Liability 592
   III. Breach of Statutory Duty 601
      1. The Development of the Tort 602
      2. The Indicators of Parliamentary Intent 607

3. The Scope of Protection	617
4. Evaluation and Reform	619

11 Nuisance and the Rule in *Rylands v Fletcher* — 625

I. Public and Private Nuisance — 626

II. Private Nuisance — 629
1. The Nature of Private Nuisance — 629
2. Unreasonable Interference — 635
3. Nuisance, Negligence and Fault — 649
4. Who Can Sue — 658
5. Defences — 665
6. Remedies — 673

III. The Rule in *Rylands v Fletcher* — 681
1. The *Rylands v Fletcher* Case — 681
2. Nuisance and *Rylands v Fletcher* — 683
3. The Elements of a *Rylands v Fletcher* Claim — 686
4. Defences — 692
5. *Rylands v Fletcher* and Liability for Fire — 694
6. The Future of *Rylands v Fletcher* — 696

12 Defamation — 698

I. Introduction — 698

II. Libel and Slander — 699
1. The Distinction between Libel and Slander — 699
2. Slander: General Requirement of Special Damage — 700

III. Defamation: Elements of the Cause of Action — 704
1. The Statement must be Defamatory — 704
2. The Statement must Refer to the Claimant — 726
3. The Statement must be Published — 732

IV. Defamation: Defences — 737
1. Truth — 738
2. Honest Opinion — 742
3. Privilege — 746
4. Publication on Matter of Public Interest — 755
5. Offers of Amends — 760
6. Innocent Dissemination — 763

v.	Remedies	766
	1. Damages	766
	2. Injunctions	771
vi.	Defamation, Free Speech and the Press	774

13 Privacy — 782

i.	Introduction	782
ii.	Misuse of Private Information	794

14 Vicarious Liability — 816

i.	Development of and Justification for Vicarious Liability	817
ii.	Relationships Triggering Vicarious Liability	823
	1. Employee or Independent Contractor?	823
	2. Lending of Employees	829
	3. Relationships 'Akin to Employment'	833
	4. Vehicle Drivers	844
iii.	The Course of Employment	845
	1. The Close Connection Test	846
	2. Carelessness of the Employee	862
	3. Employee's Use of Vehicles on Unauthorised Journeys	865
	4. Criminal Acts of the Employee	868
iv.	Non-delegable Duty of Care	871
	1. Introduction	871
	2. Traditional Categories of Non-delegable Duty	872
	3. A General Principle?	877

15 Damages for Personal Injury — 885

i.	Introduction	885
ii.	Different Types of Damages	885
	1. Compensatory Damages	885
	2. Restitutionary Damages	885
	3. Exemplary or Punitive Damages	886
	4. Aggravated Damages	896
	5. Nominal Damages	897
	6. Contemptuous Damages	897

III.	Lump Sums and Periodical Payments	898
IV.	Damages for Personal Injury	906
	1. Non-Pecuniary Losses	906
	2. Loss of Earnings	915
	3. Medical Care	925
	4. Deductions	934

16 Death and Damages — 940

I.	The Effect of Death on Existing Causes of Action	940
II.	Death as a Cause of Action	944
	1. Common Law	944
	2. The Background to Statutory Reform	946
III.	Current Legislation	948
	1. Loss of Dependency	948
	2. Who May Claim and for What?	951
	3. Bereavement Damages	961

17 How Tort Works — 964

I.	Tort Law in Operation	964
	1. When are Claims for Compensation Made?	964
	2. The Personal Injury Claims Process	975
	3. The Settlement of Personal Injury Claims	984
	4. The Cost and Adequacy of Tort Damages	990
	5. Who Pays Damages?	993
II.	Tort and the Fault Principle Evaluated	996
	1. The Moral Basis of the Fault Principle	996
	2. Alternatives to Tort Law	1000

Index — 1015

TABLE OF CASES

United Kingdom

A v A Health and Social Services Trust [2012] NI 77 ... 134

A v B plc [2003] QB 195 ... 796, 811

A v Bottrill [2003] 1 AC 449 ... 893

A v Health and Social Services Trust [2011] NICA 28 ... 126

A v Hoare [2008] 1 AC 844 (HL); [2006] EWCA Civ 395 ... 46, 68

A v National Blood Authority [2001] EWHC 446 (QB); [2001] 3 All ER 289 ... 562, 568, 571–4, 576, 577, 578, 580, 581, 586, 590

A (A Child) v Ministry of Defence [2005] QB 183 ... 879

A (Conjoined Twins), Re [2001] Fam 147 ... 98

AAA v Unilever plc [2018] EWCA Civ 1532 ... 499

AB v Ministry of Defence (2011) 117 BMLR 101 ... 246

AB v South West Water Services Ltd [1993] QB 507 ... 888, 891

AB v Tameside & Glossop Health Authority [1997] 8 Med LR 91 ... 377, 384

ABC v St George's Healthcare NHS Trust [2020] PIQR P13 ... 138

Abernethy v Hutchinson (1824) 1 H & Tw 28 ... 803

Abouzaid v Mothercare (UK) Ltd (2001) *The Times*, 20 February ... 562, 582, 583

Adam v Ward [1917] AC 309 ... 748

Adams v Rhymney Valley DC (2001) 33 HLR 41 ... 217

Admiralty Commissioners v Owners of Steamship Amerika [1917] AC 38 ... 921

Admiralty Commissioners v Susquehanna (Owners), *The Susquehanna* [1926] AC 655 ... 910

Admiralty Commissioners v Volute [1922] 1 AC 129 ... 308

Adorian v Metropolitan Police Commissioner [2009] 1 WLR 1859 ... 105

Ahmed v Shafique [2009] EWHC 618 (QB) ... 64

Airedale NHS Trust v Bland [1993] AC 789 ... 98

Al Saudi Banque v Clark Pixley (a firm) [1990] Ch 313 ... 437, 440

Al-Fagih v HH Saudi Research and Marketing (UK) Ltd [2002] EMLR 215 ... 760

Al-Kandari v J.R. Brown & Co [1988] QB 665 (CA); [1987] QB 514 (QBD) ... 384

Albazero, The [1977] AC 774 ... 399

Alcock v Chief Constable of the South Yorkshire Police [1992] 1 AC 310 ... 148, 350, 351, 352, 353, 357, 359, 360, 362, 367–70, 371, 372, 373, 374, 375, 379, 382, 383, 386, 393

Alexander v North Eastern Railway Co (1865) 6 B & S 340, 122 ER 1221 ... 739

Alexandrou v Oxford [1993] 4 All ER 328 ... 511

Alfred McAlpine Construction Ltd v Panatown Ltd [2001] 1 AC 518 ... 399

Ali v Luton BC [2022] EWHC 132 (QB) ... 861

Allen v British Rail Engineering [2001] PIQR Q10 ... 244

Allen v Gulf Oil Refining Limited [1981] AC 1001 ... 671

Allied Maples v Simmons & Simmons [1995] 1 WLR 1602 ... 242

Allin v City & Hackney Health Authority [1996] 7 Med LR 167 ... 377, 384

Allison v London Underground [2008] ICR 719 ... 602

Alphacell Ltd v Woodward [1972] AC 824 ... 274

American Cyanamid Co v Ethicon Ltd [1975] AC 396 ... 772, 773, 786

Amin v Imran Khan & Partners [2011] EWHC 2958 (QB) ... 944

AMP v Persons Unknown [2011] EWHC 3454 (QB) ... 78

An Informer v A Chief Constable [2013] QB 579 ... 514

Anchor Brewhouse Developments Ltd v Berkley House (Docklands Developments) Ltd (1987) 38 BLR 82 ... 793

Anderson v Imrie [2016] CSOH 171, 2017 Rep LR 21 ... 320

Anderson v Newham College of Higher Education [2003] ICR 212 ... 319

Anderson v Oppenheimer (1880) 5 QBD 602 ... 688

Andreae v Selfridge & Co Ltd [1938] Ch 1 ... 674

Andrews v Schooling [1991] 1 WLR 783 ... 416

Andrews v Secretary of State for Health (1998), unreported, 19 June ... 385

Anglian Water Services Ltd v Crawshaw Robbins & Co Ltd [2001] BLR 173 ... 656

Anns v Merton London Borough Council [1978] AC 728 ... 136, 137, 145, 149, 159, 160, 161, 162, 367, 402, 403, 404, 405, 407, 408, 409, 410, 411, 412, 413, 418, 420, 454, 462, 507

Ansell v Waterhouse (1817) 6 M & S 385 ... 107

Appleton v Garrett (1995) 34 BMLR 23 ... 87

Armes v Nottinghamshire County Council [2018] AC 355 . . . 816, 822, 839, 840, 841, 842, 870, 872, 881, 882, 883, 884
Arthur J.S. Hall v Simons [2002] 1 AC 615 . . . 142
Ashby v White (1703) 2 Ld Raym 938 . . . 945
Ashdown v Samuel Williams & Sons Ltd [1957] 1 QB 409 . . . 321, 543
Ashley v Chief Constable of Sussex Police [2008] 1 AC 962 (HL); [2007] 1 WLR 398 (CA) . . . 86, 88, 101–3, 104, 897
Ashmore v British Coal Corp [1990] 2 QB 338 . . . 176
Ashton v Turner [1981] QB 137 . . . 314
Aspro Travel Ltd v Owners Abroad Group [1996] 1 WLR 132 . . . 732, 741
Associated Provincial Picture Houses Ltd v Wednesbury Corp [1948] 1 KB 223 . . . 161
Aston v Imperial Chemical Industries Group (1992), unreported, 21 May . . . 384
Aswan Engineering Establishment Co v Lupdine Ltd [1987] 1 WLR 1 . . . 415
AT v Dulghieru [2009] EWHC 225 (QB) . . . 888
Atkinson v Newcastle & Gateshead Waterworks Co (1877) LR 2 Ex D 441 . . . 602–3, 604
Attia v British Gas [1988] QB 304 . . . 351
Attorney General v Corke [1933] Ch 89 . . . 687
Attorney General v Cory Bros & Co Ltd [1921] 1 AC 521 . . . 688
Attorney General v Gastonia Coaches [1977] RTR 219 . . . 628
Attorney General v Guardian Newspapers Ltd (No 2) [1990] 1 AC 109 . . . 778, 795–6, 804
Attorney General v Hartwell [2004] 1 WLR 1273 . . . 289
Attorney General v PYA Quarries Ltd [1957] 2 QB 169 . . . 627–8
Attorney General of the British Virgin Islands v Hartwell [2004] 1 WLR 1273 . . . 147
Attorney General of Trinidad and Tobago v Ramanoop [2006] 1 AC 328 . . . 897
Austin v Commissioner of the Police of the Metropolis [2009] 1 AC 564 (HL); [2008] 1 All ER 564 (CA) . . . 31, 85, 92
Austin v Culpepper (1684) 2 Show 313 . . . 707

B (Adult: Refusal of Treatment), Re [2002] 2 All ER 449 . . . 99
Baddeley v Earl Granville (1887) 19 QBD 423 . . . 603
Badger v Ministry of Defence [2006] 3 All ER 173 . . . 312
BAE Systems (Operations) Ltd v Konczak [2018] ICR 1 . . . 245
Bagley v North Herts Health Authority (1986) 136 NLJ 1014 . . . 232
Bailey v Ministry of Defence [2009] 1 WLR 1052 . . . 246, 247, 248

Baker v Bolton (1808) 1 Camp 493 . . . 940, 945
Baker v Crow Carrying Co Ltd (1960), unreported, (CA) . . . 397
Baker v Quantum Clothing Group Ltd [2011] 1 WLR 1003 . . . 196, 216
Baker v T.E. Hopkins [1959] 1 WLR 966 . . . 283
Baker v Willoughby [1970] AC 467 . . . 266–8, 269, 270, 271, 272, 273, 318
Balfour v Barty King [1957] 1 QB 496 . . . 873
Bamford v Turnley (1862) 3 B & S 66, 122 ER 27 . . . 647–8, 684
Banca Nazionale del Lavoro SPA v Playboy Club London Ltd [2018] 1 WLR 4041 . . . 444, 455
Bank voor Handel en Scheepvaart NV v Slatford [1953] 1 QB 248 . . . 825
Barber v Somerset County Council [2004] 1 WLR 1089 . . . 381, 383
Barclays Bank see Various Claimants v Barclays Bank plc
Barker v Corus UK Ltd [2006] 2 AC 572 . . . 239, 251–2, 254, 255, 256, 257, 258, 260, 261, 262, 265
Barlow v Wigan Metropolitan Borough Council [2021] 3 All ER 223 . . . 554
Barnes v Flucker 1985 SLT 142 . . . 320
Barnes v Hants CC [1969] 1 WLR 1563 . . . 486, 497
Barnes v Nayer (1986) *The Times*, 19 December . . . 80
Barnes v Scout Association [2010] EWCA Civ 1476 . . . 193
Barnett v Chelsea and Kensington Hospital Management Committee [1969] 1 QB 428 . . . 228–9, 238, 489
Baron Bernstein of Leigh v Skyviews Ltd [1978] QB 479 . . . 793, 794
Barr v Biffa Waste Services Ltd [2013] QB 455 . . . 631, 635, 672
Barrett v London Borough of Enfield [2001] 2 AC 550 (HL); [1998] QB 367 (CA) . . . 69, 146, 161, 163, 490, 519, 881
Barrett v Ministry of Defence [1995] 1 WLR 1217 . . . 155, 482–4, 485, 486
Barron v Vines [2016] EWHC 1226 (QB) . . . 768–9, 770
Baten's Case (1610) 9 Co Rep 53b . . . 630
Baturina v Times Newspapers Ltd [2011] 1 WLR 1526 . . . 726, 730
Baxter v Camden London Borough Council (No. 2) [2001] 1 AC 1 (HL); [2001] QB 1 (CA) . . . 641
Baxter v Ford Motor Co (1932) 12 P 2d 409 . . . 560
Beach v Freeson [1972] 1 QB 14 . . . 749
Beard v London General Omnibus Company [1900] 2 QB 530 . . . 864
Beaulieu v Fingham (1401) . . . 7, 694
Beaumont v Ferrer [2017] PIQR P1 . . . 331, 333

Beaumont Business Centres Ltd v Florala Properties Ltd [2020] EWHC 550 (Ch) . . . 680
Bell v Great Northern Railway Co of Ireland (1890) 26 LR Ir 428 . . . 349
Bellefield Computer Services Ltd v E Turner & Sons [2000] BLR 97 . . . 415
Bellman v Northampton Recruitment Ltd [2019] 1 All ER 1133 . . . 851, 854, 869
Benham v Gambling [1941] AC 157 . . . 909, 921, 923, 943
Benmax v Austin Motor Co Ltd [1955] AC 370 . . . 175
Berkoff v Burchill [1996] 4 All ER 1008 . . . 706
Bernard v Attorney General of Jamaica [2005] IRLR 398 . . . 857, 860
Best v Samuel Fox & Co Ltd [1952] AC 716 . . . 395
Bhamra v Dubb [2010] EWCA Civ 13 . . . 185
Bici v Ministry of Defence [2004] EWHC 786 (QB) . . . 49, 52, 68
Biffa Waste Services Ltd v Maschinenfabrik Ernst Hese GmbH [2009] QB 725 . . . 832, 873
Billings (AC) & Sons Ltd v Riden [1958] AC 240 . . . 532
Bilta (UK) Ltd v Nazir [2016] AC 1 . . . 347
Bilta (UK) Ltd v Nazir (No 2) [2016] AC 1 . . . 335
Bird v Holbrook (1828) 4 Bing 628 . . . 11
Bird v Jones (1845) 7 QB 742, 115 ER 668 . . . 58–9, 60
Bird v Pearce [1979] RTR 369 . . . 521
Blacker v Lake & Elliot Ltd (1912) 107 LT 533 . . . 110
Blackpool Football Club Ltd v DSN [2021] EWCA Civ 1352 . . . 835, 840, 843
Blake v Barnard (1840) 9 C & P 626 . . . 52
Blake v Galloway [2004] 1 WLR 2844 . . . 199
Blake v Midland Railway Company (1852) 18 QB 93 . . . 947, 952
Bland v Morris [2006] RTR 31 . . . 282
Bland v Moseley (Aldred's Case) (1610) 9 Co Rep 57b . . . 634
Bicc v London and North Eastern Rly Co [1938] AC 126 . . . 866
Bliss v Hall (1838) 4 Bing NC 183 . . . 667
Bloodworth v Gray (1844) 7 Man & G 334 . . . 703
Blue Circle Industries plc v Ministry of Defence [1999] Ch 289 . . . 242
Blyth v Birmingham Waterworks Co (1856) 11 Ex 781 . . . 171, 173
Bogle v McDonald's Restaurants Ltd [2002] EWHC 490 (QB) . . . 38, 578, 582
Bolam v Friern Hospital Management Committee [1957] 1 WLR 582 . . . 216–17, 218
Bole v Huntsbuild Ltd (2009) 127 Con LR 154 . . . 416
Bolitho v City and Hackney Health Authority [1998] AC 232 . . . 217–18, 229

Bolton v Stone [1951] AC 850 . . . 171–4, 176, 179, 180, 182, 187, 199, 549
Bone v Seale [1975] 1 WLR 797 . . . 673
Bonnard v Perryman [1891] 2 Ch 269 . . . 741, 772–3
Bonnington Castings Ltd v Wardlaw [1956] AC 613 . . . 243–4, 245, 246, 257
Bookbinder v Tebbit [1989] 1 WLR 640 . . . 740
Bordin v St Mary's NHS Trust [2000] Lloyd's Rep 287 . . . 960
Boson v Sandford (1691) 2 Salk 440 . . . 853
Bottomley v Todmorden Cricket Club [2004] PIQR P18 . . . 535
Bourhill v Young [1943] AC 92 . . . 127–9, 287, 353, 363, 364, 367, 389
Bourne Leisure Ltd v Marsden [2009] EWCA Civ 671 . . . 537
Bowater v Mayor, Aldermen and Burgesses of the Borough of Rowley Regis [1944] KB 476 . . . 298
Bradburn v Great Western Railway Co (1874) LR 10 Exch 1 . . . 935
Bradford Corporation v Pickles [1895] AC 587 . . . 634, 635, 646, 647
Bradford-Smart v West Sussex County Council [2002] 1 FCR 425 . . . 384
Branson v Bower [2002] QB 737 . . . 744, 746
Brayshaw v Partners of Apsley Surgery [2019] 2 All ER 997 . . . 77, 868
Breslin v McKevitt [2011] NICA 33 . . . 48, 57
Brett Wilson LLP v Person(s) Unknown [2016] 1 All ER 1006 . . . 766
Bridlington Relay v Yorkshire Electricity Board [1965] Ch 436 . . . 637
Britannic Merthyr Coal Co v David [1910] AC 74 . . . 610
British Celanese Ltd v A H Hunt (Capacitors) Ltd [1969] 1 WLR 959 . . . 397, 656
British Chiropractic Association v Singh [2011] 1 WLR 133 . . . 744
British Coal Corporation v National Union of Mineworkers (1996), unreported, 28 June (QBD) . . . 778
British Columbia Electric Railway v Loach [1916] 1 AC 719 . . . 308
British Railways Board v Herrington [1972] AC 877 . . . 544, 547, 550, 551, 552, 554
Brooke v Bool [1928] 2 KB 578 . . . 872
Brooks v Commissioner of Police of the Metropolis [2005] 1 WLR 1495 . . . 153
Brown v Robinson [2004] UKPC 56; (2004) 65 WIR 258 . . . 857, 869
Brown v Rolls Royce [1960] 1 WLR 210 . . . 216
Browne v Associated Newspapers Ltd [2008] QB 103 . . . 804, 812
Browne v DC Thomson & Co 1912 SC 359 . . . 731
Brumder v Motornet Service and Repairs Ltd [2013] 1 WLR 2783 . . . 319

BTC v Gourley [1956] AC 185 . . . 934
Bunt v Tilley [2007] 1 WLR 1243 . . . 735, 765
Burgess v Lejonvarn [2017] BLR 277 (CA); [2016] EWHC 40 (TCC) . . . 430
Burns v Edman [1970] 2 QB 541 . . . 347, 952
Burrows v March Gas & Coke Co (1872) LR 7 Ex 96 . . . 120
Burstein v Times Newspapers Ltd [2001] 1 WLR 579 . . . 769, 771
Burton v Islington Health Authority [1993] QB 204 . . . 132
Butterfield v Forrester (1809) 11 East 60, 103 ER 926 . . . 307–8
BXB v Watch Tower and Bible Tract Society of Pennsylvania [2021] 4 WLR 42 . . . 870, 871
Bybrook Barn Centre Ltd v Kent County Council [2001] BLR 55 . . . 655
Byrne v Deane [1937] 1 KB 818 . . . 713–15, 727, 732

C v D [2006] EWHC 166 (QB) . . . 68
C v MGN [2013] 1 WLR 1015 . . . 769
C v WH [2016] PIQR Q2 . . . 75
Cadam v Beaverbrook Newspapers Ltd [1959] 1 QB 413 . . . 742
Cairns v Modi [2013] 1 WLR 1015 . . . 734, 769
Caldwell v Maguire [2002] PIQR P6 . . . 199
Callery v Gray [2002] 1 WLR 2000 . . . 980
Calvert v William Hill Credit Ltd [2009] Ch 330 . . . 312
Cambridge Water Co v Eastern Counties Leather plc [1994] 2 AC 264 . . . 649–50, 656, 683–5, 686, 688, 689, 690, 691, 696
Campbell v Advantage Insurance Co Ltd [2021] EWCA Civ 1698 . . . 310
Campbell v MGN Ltd [2004] 2 AC 457 (HL); [2003] QB 633 (CA) . . . 32, 795–803, 804, 805, 806, 807, 809, 813, 814
Campbell v Northern Ireland Housing Executive [1995] NI 167 . . . 554
Campbell v Peter Gordon Joiners Ltd [2016] AC 1513 . . . 608, 612
Camrose v Action Press (1937) *The Times*, 14–16 October . . . 707
Canadian Pacific Rly Co v Kelvin Shipping Co Ltd (1927) 138 LT 369 . . . 277
Candler v Crane, Christmas & Co [1951] 2 KB 164 . . . 422, 423, 424, 425, 433, 434, 435
Candlewood Navigation Corp Ltd v Mitsui OSK Lines [1986] AC 1 . . . 437
Cann v Wilson (1888) 39 Ch D 39 . . . 433
Caparo Industries plc v Dickman [1990] 2 AC 605 . . . 135–7, 138, 139, 143, 144, 145, 146, 148, 149, 291, 436–41, 442, 443, 444, 445, 448, 449, 452, 453, 454, 458, 459, 466, 470
Capital & Counties plc v Hampshire County Council [1997] QB 1004 . . . 140, 477–9, 480, 488, 489, 511, 514

Capital and Counties Bank v Henty (1882) 7 App Cas 741 . . . 706
Capps v Miller [1989] 1 WLR 839 . . . 315
Carder v Secretary of State for Health [2017] ICR 392 . . . 244
Carmarthenshire County Council v Lewis [1955] AC 549 . . . 496, 497
Carr-Glynn v Frearsons (a firm) [1999] Ch 326 (CA); [1997] 2 All ER 614 (ChD) . . . 462
Carstairs v Taylor (1871) LR 6 Ex 217 . . . 688
Carty v Croydon London Borough Council [2005] 1 WLR 2312 . . . 162
Cass v Edinburgh & District Tramways Co Ltd 1909 SC 1068 . . . 320
Cassel v Riverside Health Authority [1992] PIQR Q168 . . . 919
Cassell v Broome [1972] AC 1027 . . . 888, 890–1, 892, 893, 906
Cassidy v Daily Mirror Newspapers Ltd [1929] 2 KB 331 . . . 716, 724–6, 727, 732, 760
Cassidy v Ministry of Health [1951] 2 KB 343 . . . 478, 825
Cattle v Stockton Waterworks Co (1875) LR 10 QB 453 . . . 395, 396, 946
Cattley v St John's Ambulance Brigade (1988), unreported, 25 November (QBD) . . . 215
Cavalier v Pope [1906] AC 428 . . . 532, 534
CBS Songs Ltd v Amstrad Consumer Electronics plc [1988] AC 1013 . . . 33–4
Century Insurance Company Limited v Northern Ireland Transport Board [1942] AC 509 . . . 862
CGL Group Ltd v Royal Bank of Scotland plc [2018] 1 WLR 2137 . . . 160, 455
Chadwick v British Railways Board [1967] 1 WLR 912 . . . 359, 361
Chadwick v Continental Tyres [2008] ScotCS CSOH 24 . . . 584
Chandler v Cape plc [2012] 1 WLR 3111 . . . 499
Chaplin v Hicks [1911] 2 KB 786 . . . 230, 234, 235, 239, 923
Charleston v News Group Newspapers Ltd [1995] 2 AC 65 . . . 706
Chase v News Group Newspapers Ltd [2003] EMLR 11 . . . 724, 742
Chattell v Daily Mail (1901) 18 TLR 165 . . . 707
Chatterton v Gerson [1981] QB 432 . . . 86, 87
Chatterton v Secretary of State for India [1895] 2 QB 189 . . . 747
Chaudhury v Prabhaker [1989] 1 WLR 29 . . . 430
Chell v Tarmac Cement and Lime Ltd [2020] EWHC 2613 (QB) . . . 860, 870
Chief Constable of Essex Police v Transport Arendonk BVBA [2020] EWHC 212 (QB) . . . 155
Christian Brothers case *see* Various Claimants v Catholic Child Welfare Society
Christie v Davey [1893] 1 Ch 316 . . . 645–6, 647

Church of Jesus Christ of Latter-Day Saints (Great Britain) v West Yorkshire Fire and Civil Defence Authority see Capital & Counties plc v Hampshire County Council

Clare v Perry [2005] EWCA Civ 39 . . . 295

Clark v Farley [2018] PIQR P15 . . . 331, 345

Clark v London General Omnibus Company Limited [1906] 2 KB 648 . . . 944–5

Clark Fixing Ltd v Dudley Metropolitan Borough Council [2001] EWCA Civ 1898 . . . 506

Clarke v Devon County Council [2005] 2 FLR 747 . . . 920

Clay v TUI Ltd [2018] 4 All ER 672 . . . 280

Clift v Slough BC [2011] 1 WLR 1774 . . . 750

Clunis v Camden & Islington Health Authority [1998] QB 978 . . . 328, 329, 330, 337, 338, 339, 343

Coco v A N Clark (Engineers) Ltd [1969] RPC 41 . . . 795, 796, 803, 804

Cole v Turner (1704) 6 Mod Rep 149, 90 ER 958 . . . 55

Collett v Smith (2009) 106(26) LSG 18 . . . 199

Collins v Wilcock [1984] 1 WLR 1172 . . . 53, 54, 55, 56, 81

Colls v Home and Colonial Stores Ltd [1904] AC 179 . . . 633

Color Quest Ltd v Total Downstream UK plc [2009] EWHC 540 (Comm); sub nom Shell UK Ltd v Total UK Ltd [2011] QB 86 (CA) . . . 697

Conarken Group Ltd v Network Rail Infrastructure Ltd [2011] 2 CLC 1 . . . 398

Condon v Basi [1985] 1 WLR 866 . . . 199, 206

Conway v George Wimpey & Co Ltd [1951] 2 KB 266 . . . 864

Cook v Broderip [1968] EG 128 . . . 542

Cook v Swinfen [1967] 1 WLR 457 . . . 379

Cooke v Midland Great Western Railway of Ireland [1909] AC 229 . . . 526

Cooke v Mirror Group Newspapers [2015] 1 WLR 895 . . . 712

Cooke v United Bristol Healthcare NHS Trust [2004] 1 WLR 251 . . . 925

Cookson v Knowles [1979] AC 556 . . . 906, 953

Corby Group Litigation, In Re [2009] QB 335 . . . 626, 628

Corr v IBC Vehicles Ltd [2008] 1 AC 884 . . . 208, 280, 310

Costello v Chief Constable of Northumbria Police [1999] ICR 730 . . . 514

Couch v Steel (1854) 3 E & B 402, 23 LJ (QB) 121 . . . 602, 603

Coulson (William) & Sons v James Coulson & Co (1887) 3 TLR 846 . . . 773, 786, 787

Cox v Feeney (1863) 4 F & F 13 . . . 755

Cox v Hockenhull [2000] 1 WLR 750 . . . 952

Cox v Ministry of Justice [2016] AC 660 . . . 822, 824, 835–8, 839, 840, 841, 842, 852

Coxall v Goodyear Great Britain Ltd [2003] 1 WLR 536 . . . 188

Crawford Adjusters Ltd v Sagicor Insurance Ltd [2014] AC 366 . . . 140

Crédit Lyonnais Bank Nederland NV v Export Credit Guarantee Corporation [2000] 1 AC 486 . . . 872

Creswell v Eaton [1991] 1 WLR 1113 . . . 953

Creutzfeldt-Jakob Disease Litigation, Re [1998] 41 BMLR 157 . . . 385

Croke v Wiseman [1982] 1 WLR 71 (A) . . . 919, 920, 924

Cross v Kirkby [2000] EWCA Civ 426 . . . 332

Cruise v Express Newspapers plc [1999] QB 931 . . . 707

CTB v News Group Newspapers Ltd [2011] EWHC 1232 (QB) . . . 811

Cullen v Chief Constable of the Royal Ulster Constabulary [2003] 1 WLR 1763 . . . 614

Cullin v London Fire & Civil Defence Authority [1999] PIQR P314 . . . 361

Culnane v Morris [2006] 1 WLR 2880 . . . 779

Cunningham v Harrison [1973] QB 942 . . . 930, 931

Cunningham v Reading Football Club Ltd [1992] PIQR P141 . . . 535

Cunningham v Rochdale MBC [2021] EWCA Civ 1719 . . . 125

Curwen v James [1963] 1 WLR 748 . . . 266

Customs and Excise Commissioners v Barclays Bank plc [2007] 1 AC 181 . . . 435–6, 449, 452–4, 455, 470, 508

Cutler v Wandsworth Stadium Ltd [1949] AC 398 . . . 607, 608, 612, 615

D v Commissioner of Police of the Metropolis [2019] AC 196 (SC); [2016] QB 161 (CA) . . . 31, 141, 168, 169, 515

D v East Berkshire Community Health NHS Trust [2005] 2 AC 373 (HL); [2004] QB 558 (CA) . . . 75, 123–4, 141, 168, 169, 170, 516, 519

D & F Estates Ltd v Church Comrs for England [1989] AC 177 . . . 404–6, 407, 408, 409, 410, 411, 412, 413, 414, 415, 418, 420, 469, 841

Daborn v Bath Tramways Motor Co Ltd & Trevor Smithey [1946] 2 All ER 333 . . . 189

Dacas v Brook Street Bureau (UK) Ltd [2004] ICR 1436 . . . 828, 834

Daiichi UK Ltd v Stop Huntingdon Animal Cruelty [2005] 1 BCLC 27 . . . 78

Daly v General Steam Navigation Ltd [1981] 1 WLR 120 . . . 933

Daniels v R. White & Sons Ltd [1938] 4 All ER 258 . . . 560

Dann v Hamilton [1939] 1 KB 509 . . . 299, 302, 306

Danns v Department of Health (1995) 25 BMLR 121 . . . 163

Darby v National Trust [2001] PIQR P27 ... 540, 548
Darker v Chief Constable of West Midlands Police [2001] 1 AC 435 ... 142
Darnley v Croydon Health Services NHS Trust [2019] AC 831 ... 150, 151, 155
Davidson v Chief Constable of North Wales [1994] 2 All ER 597 ... 62–3, 64, 85
Davie v New Merton Board Mills Ltd [1959] AC 604 (HL); [1958] 1 QB 210 (CA) ... 26, 532, 874, 875
Davies v Mann (1842) 10 M & W 547, 152 ER 588 ... 308
Davies v Solomon (1871) LR 7 QB 112 ... 701
Davies v Swan Motor Co (Swansea) Ltd [1949] 2 KB 326 ... 311, 313
Davies v Taylor [1974] AC 207 ... 953
Daw v Intel Incorporation (UK) Ltd [2007] 2 All ER 126 ... 381
Day v Edwards (1794) 5 TR 648 ... 9
Day v High Performance Sports Ltd [2003] EWHC 197 (QB) ... 475
De Buse v McCarthy [1942] 1 KB 156 ... 749
Dean v Allin & Watts [2001] 2 Lloyd's Rep 249 ... 450
Delaney v Pickett [2012] 1 WLR 2149 ... 332
Delaware Mansions Ltd v Westminster City Council [2002] 1 AC 321 ... 631, 655
Denham v Midland Employers' Mutual Assurance Ltd [1955] 2 QB 437 ... 830
Dennis v Ministry of Defence [2003] EWHC 793 (QB) ... 677
Department of the Environment v Thomas Bates and Son Ltd [1991] 1 AC 499 ... 412, 414
Derbyshire County Council v Times Newspapers [1993] AC 534 ... 774, 776–8, 791
Derry v Peek (1889) 14 App Cas 337 ... 109, 421, 422, 424, 425, 426
Dews v National Coal Board [1988] AC 1 ... 934
Dickins v O2 plc [2009] IRLR 58 ... 381
Dobson v Thames Water Utilities [2009] 3 All ER 319 ... 664, 665, 673
Dobson v Thames Water Utilities (No 2) (2011) 140 Con LR 135 ... 665
Dodds v Dodds [1978] QB 543 ... 951
Doe d. Murray, Bishop of Rochester v Bridges (1831) B & Ad 847 ... 602, 608, 614
Donachie v Chief Constable of Greater Manchester [2004] EWCA Civ 405 ... 350
Donaghey v Boulton & Paul Ltd [1968] AC 1 ... 618
Donnelly v Joyce [1974] QB 454 ... 930, 931
Donoghue v Folkstone Properties Ltd [2003] QB 1008; [2003] 3 All ER 1101 ... 536, 547, 549
Donoghue v Stevenson; McAlister v Stevenson [1932] AC 562 ... 11, 12, 15, 110–15, 116, 117, 118, 119, 120, 121, 128, 134, 135, 136, 138, 156, 171, 173, 199, 297, 366, 368, 395, 403, 405, 408, 409, 410, 411, 413, 420, 421, 423, 425, 429, 453, 493, 494, 507, 544, 555, 556, 560, 654
Dooley v Cammell Laird & Co Ltd [1951] 1 Lloyd's Rep 271 ... 352, 362
Dorset Yacht case see Home Office v Dorset Yacht Co Ltd
Doughty v Turner Manufacturing Co Ltd [1964] 1 QB 518 ... 288
Douglas v Hello! Ltd [2001] 1 FLR 982; [2001] QB 967 ... 800, 804
Douglas v Hello! Ltd (No 3) [2006] QB 125 (CA); [2003] 3 All ER 996 (Ch D), sub nom OBG Ltd v Allan [2008] 1 AC 1 (HL) ... 804, 805
DPP v K [1990] 1 WLR 1067 ... 57
Drake v Foster Wheeler Ltd [2011] 1 All ER 63 ... 933
Dryden v Johnson Matthey plc [2019] AC 403 ... 126
Dubai Aluminium Co Ltd v Salaam [2003] 2 AC 366 ... 837, 854, 856, 857, 858, 859, 869
Duchess of Argyll v Duke of Argyll [1967] Ch 302 ... 803
Duke v University of Salford [2013] EWHC 196 (QB) ... 778
Dulieu v White & Sons [1901] 2 KB 669 ... 66, 349, 350, 352, 356, 363
Dunnage v Randall [2016] QB 639 ... 207–9, 210
Dunster v Abbott [1954] 1 WLR 58 ... 534
Durham v BAI (Run-Off) Ltd [2012] 1 WLR 867 ... 258, 260
Dutton v Bognor Regis Urban District Council [1972] 1 QB 373 ... 403, 405, 411, 412, 413

E v English Province of Our Lady of Charity [2013] QB 722 ... 824, 829, 833, 838, 840
E Hulton & Co v Jones [1910] AC 20 ... 726, 727–8, 729, 730
E Warnink BV v J Townend & Sons (Hull) Ltd [1979] AC 731 ... 788
East Dorset District Council v Eaglebeam Ltd [2006] EWHC 2378 (QB) ... 628
East Suffolk Rivers Catchment Board v Kent [1941] AC 74 ... 479, 507
Eastern and South African Telegraph Company Ltd v Cape Town Tramways Companies Ltd [1902] AC 381 ... 637
Eastwood v Holmes (1858) 1 F & F 347 ... 730
Eastwood v Magnox Electric plc [2005] 1 AC 503 ... 383
Edward Wong Finance Co Ltd v Johnson Stokes & Master (a firm) [1984] AC 296 ... 217
Edwards v Bell (1824) 1 Bing 403 ... 738
Edwards v Chesterfield Royal Hospital NHS Foundation Trust [2012] 2 AC 22 ... 383
Edwards v London Borough of Sutton [2017] PIQR P2 ... 551

Eggar v Viscount Chelmsford [1965] 1 QB 248 . . . 754
Elliott v Saunders (1994), unreported, 10 June (QBD) . . . 206
Elliott Steam Tug Co v Shipping Controller [1922] 1 KB 127 . . . 396
Emeh v Kensington & Chelsea Area Health Authority [1984] 3 All ER 1044 . . . 280
Employers' Liability Insurance 'Trigger' Litigation see Durham v BAI (Run Off) Ltd
Empress Car Co (Abertillery) Ltd v National Rivers Authority [1999] 2 AC 22 . . . 274–6
Entick v Carrington (1765) 19 State Tr 1029, 95 ER 807 . . . 81, 886
Equitas Insurance Ltd v Municipal Mutual Insurance Ltd [2020] 1 All ER 16 . . . 261, 264
Esso Petroleum v Mardon [1976] QB 801 . . . 430
Evans v Triplex Safety Glass Co Ltd [1936] 1 All ER 283 . . . 120
F (Mental Patient: Sterilisation), Re [1990] 2 AC 1 . . . 55, 88, 93–5, 97, 98, 100
Fagan v Metropolitan Police Commissioner [1969] 1 QB 439 . . . 57
Fairchild v Glenhaven Funeral Services Ltd [2003] 1 AC 32 (HL); [2002] 1 WLR 1052 (CA) . . . 235, 249–51, 252, 253, 254, 255, 256, 257, 258, 259, 260, 261, 262, 263, 264, 265, 535, 542
Fairman v Perpetual Investment Building Society [1923] AC 74 . . . 532
Fardon v Harcourt-Rivington [1932] All ER Rep 81; (1932) 146 LT 391 . . . 179
Farraj v King's Healthcare NHS Trust [2010] 1 WLR 2139 . . . 882
Farrell v Merton, Sutton and Wandsworth Health Authority (2001) 57 BMLR 158 . . . 384
Farrier's Case, The (1372) . . . 6
Fay v Prentice (1845) 1 CB 828 . . . 630
FB v Rana [2017] PIQR P17 . . . 205
Fearn v Board of Trustees of the Tate Gallery [2020] Ch 621 (CA); [2019] Ch 369 (ChD) . . . 634, 635, 637, 665, 793
Ferdinand v MGN Ltd [2011] EWHC 2454 (QB) . . . 812
Ferguson v British Gas Trading [2010] 1 WLR 785 . . . 78
Ferguson v John Dawson & Partners (Contractors) Ltd [1976] 1 WLR 1213 . . . 828
Ferguson v Welsh [1987] 1 WLR 1553 . . . 530, 535, 542
Fetter v Beal (1701) 1 Ld Raym 339 . . . 899
Fielding v Variety Incorporated [1967] 2 QB 841 . . . 767
Fish v Kelly (1864) 17 CBNS 194 . . . 428
Fish & Fish Ltd v Sea Shepherd UK [2015] AC 1229 . . . 872

Fishenden v Higgs & Hill Ltd (1935) 153 LT 128 . . . 678
Fitzgerald v Lane [1987] QB 781 . . . 263
Fleming v Hislop (1886) 11 App Cas 686 . . . 668
Fletcher v Rylands (1866) LR 1 Exch 265 . . . 681–2, 688, 689, 692
Flewster v Role (1808) 1 Camp 187 . . . 63
Flint v Tittensor [2015] 1 WLR 4370 . . . 104, 332
Flood v Times Newspapers Ltd [2012] 2 AC 273 . . . 757, 758, 760, 774
Flora v Wakom (Heathrow) Ltd [2007] 1 WLR 482 . . . 917, 919
Forde v Skinner (1830) 4 Car & P 239, 172 ER 687 . . . 55
Forrester v Tyrrell (1893) 9 TLR 257 . . . 700
Forsikringsaktieselskapet Vesta v Butcher [1988] 3 WLR 565 . . . 309
Fowler v Lanning [1959] 1 QB 426 . . . 43, 44, 45
Francome v News Group Newspapers Ltd [1984] 1 WLR 892 . . . 804
Franklin v South Eastern Railway (1858) 3 H & N 211, 157 ER 448 . . . 952
Fraser v Evans [1969] 1 QB 349 . . . 773
Freeman v Home Office (No 2) [1984] QB 524 . . . 86, 87
Froom v Butcher [1976] QB 286 . . . 313–14
Frost v Chief Constable of South Yorkshire Police see White v Chief Constable of South Yorkshire Police
Fryer v Pearson (2000) The Times, 4 April . . . 225, 226
Furmedge v Chester-Le-Street DC [2011] EWHC 1226 (QB) . . . 536
Fytche v Wincanton Logistics plc [2004] ICR 975 . . . 618

G4S Care and Justice Services (UK) v Manley [2016] EWHC 2355 (QB) . . . 537
Galli-Atkinson v Seghal [2003] Lloyd's Rep Med 285 . . . 372
Galt v British Railways Board (1983) 133 NLJ 870 . . . 352
Gammell v Wilson [1982] AC 27 . . . 924, 943
Garrett v London Borough of Camden [2001] EWCA Civ 395 . . . 379
Gaunt v Fynney (1873) LR 8 Ch App 8 . . . 646
Gawler v Raettig [2007] EWCA Civ 1560 . . . 314
GB v Home Office [2015] EWHC 819 (QB) . . . 881, 882, 884
Geary v JD Wetherspoon Plc [2011] EWHC 1506 (QB) . . . 536
Geddis v Proprietors of Bann Reservoirs (1878) 3 App Cas 430 . . . 670–1
Gee v DePuy International Ltd [2018] Med LR 347 . . . 569, 580, 581, 582, 585

TABLE OF CASES

George v Eagle Air Services Ltd [2009] 1 WLR 2133 ... 225
George v Skivington (1869) LR 5 Ex 1 ... 108
Gerrard v Eurasian Natural Resources Corporation Ltd [2020] EWHC 3241 ... 77
Giles v Walker (1890) 24 QBD 656 ... 656
Gillick v Brook Advisory Centres [2001] EWCA Civ 1263 ... 719
Gillick v West Norfolk Health Authority [1986] AC 112 ... 88, 100
Gillingham Borough Council v Medway (Chatham) Dock Co Ltd [1993] QB 343 ... 628, 641, 643, 644, 645
Glaister v Appleby-in-Westmoreland Town Council [2010] PIQR P6 ... 543
Glasgow Corpn v Taylor [1922] 1 AC 44 ... 538
Glasgow Corporation v Muir [1943] AC 448 ... 200
Godfrey v Demon Internet Ltd [2001] QB 201 ... 735, 765
Gogay v Hertfordshire County Council [2000] IRLR 703 ... 383
Gold v Haringey Health Authority [1988] QB 481 ... 217
Goldman v Hargrave [1967] 1 AC 645 ... 487–8, 505, 631, 632, 650, 655, 656
Goldsmith v Bhoyrul [1998] QB 459 ... 778
Goodenough v Chief Constable of Thames Valley Police [2020] EWHC 1428 (QB) ... 103
Goodwill v British Pregnancy Advisory Service [1996] 1 WLR 1397 ... 463
Gore v Stannard (t/a Wyvern Tyres) [2014] QB 1 ... 687, 694, 695, 696, 873
Gorham v British Telecommunications plc [2000] 1 WLR 2129 ... 463
Gorringe v Calderdale Metropolitan Borough Council [2004] 1 WLR 1057 (HL); [2002] RTR 446 (CA) ... 34, 158, 161, 507, 508, 518, 521
Gorris v Scott (1874) LR 9 Exch 125 ... 291, 605, 617–18
Gough v Thorne [1966] 1 WLR 1387 ... 211, 320
Governors of the Peabody Donation Fund v Sir Lindsay Parkinson & Co Ltd [1985] AC 210 ... 407
Graham v Commercial Bodyworks Ltd [2015] ICR 665 ... 869, 870
Gran Gelato v Richcliff (Group) Ltd [1992] Ch 560 ... 450
Grant v Australian Knitting Mills Ltd [1936] AC 85 ... 115–17, 118, 119, 120, 555, 587
Gravil v Carroll [2008] ICR 1222 ... 869
Gray v Barr [1971] 2 QB 554 ... 80, 951
Gray v Jones [1939] 1 All ER 795 ... 702
Gray v Thames Trains Limited [2009] 1 AC 1339 ... 327–9, 330, 332, 333, 336, 337, 338, 339, 340, 341, 342, 343, 344, 345, 348
Graysim Holdings Limited v P & O Property Holdings Ltd [1996] AC 329 ... 534

Greatorex v Greatorex [2000] 1 WLR 1970 ... 375, 376
Green v Fibreglass Ltd [1958] 2 QB 245 ... 542
Green v Goddard (1702) 2 Salk 641 ... 104
Greene v Associated Newspapers Ltd [2005] QB 972 ... 773
Greene v Chelsea Borough Council [1954] 2 QB 127 ... 532, 533
Greenman v Yuba Power Products Inc (1963) 377 P 2d 897 ... 560
Greenock Corporation v Caledonian Railway [1917] AC 556 ... 693
Gregg v Scott [2005] 2 AC 176 ... 232–8, 239, 240, 241, 242, 251, 260, 262, 924, 943, 951
Griffiths v Arch Engineering Co Ltd [1968] 3 All ER 217 ... 118
Griffiths v Williams (1995) The Times, 24 November ... 61
Grobbelaar v News Group Newspapers Ltd [2002] 1 WLR 3024 (HL); [2001] 2 All ER 437 (CA) ... 739, 740, 770, 898
Grondona v Stoffel & Co [2021] AC 540 ... 345, 346, 347
Groom v Crocker [1939] 1 KB 194 ... 707
Group Seven Ltd v Notable Services LLP [2019] PNLR 22 ... 854
Groves v Lord Wimborne [1898] 2 QB 402 ... 604–5, 606, 608, 610, 611, 613, 616
Gujra v Roath [2018] 1 WLR 3208 ... 332, 345
Gulati v MGN Ltd [2017] QB 149 ... 815
Gwilliam v West Hertfordshire Hospitals NHS Trust [2003] QB 443 ... 27, 541, 542, 543
Gwynn v SE Railway (1868) 18 LT 738 ... 739

H v Commissioner of Police of the Metropolis [2013] 1 WLR 3021 ... 100
H v Ministry of Defence [1991] 2 QB 103 ... 175
H v News Group Newspapers Ltd [2011] 1 WLR 1645 ... 811
H v S [2003] QB 965 ... 959, 960
H. & N. Emanuel v Greater London Council [1971] 2 All ER 835 ... 694
H. West & Son Ltd v Shephard [1964] AC 326 ... 906, 910–13
Hale v Jennings Bros [1938] 1 All ER 579 ... 686
Haley v London Electricity Board [1965] AC 778 ... 130, 185
Hall (Inspector of Taxes) v Lorimer [1994] 1 All ER 250 ... 828
Halsey v Esso Petroleum [1961] 1 WLR 683 ... 628, 640
Hambrook v Stokes Bros [1925] 1 KB 141 ... 363, 365, 374
Harakas v Baltic Mercantile and Shipping Exchange Ltd [1982] 1 WLR 958 ... 773
Hargroves, Aronson & Co v Hartopp [1905] 1 KB 472 ... 532

Harman v Delany (1731) 2 Strange 898, Fitzgibbon 253 . . . 701

Harnett v Bond [1925] AC 669 (HL); [1924] 2 KB 517 (CA) . . . 63, 474

Harris v Empress Motors [1984] 1 WLR 212 . . . 924

Harris v Evans [1998] 1 WLR 1285 . . . 430, 431, 432

Harris v Wyre Forest District Council see Smith v Eric S Bush (a firm)

Harrison v Jagged Globe (Alpine) Ltd [2012] EWCA Civ 835 . . . 882

Hartley v Mayoh & Co [1954] 1 QB 383 . . . 619

Hartman v South Essex Mental Health NHS Trust [2005] ICR 782 . . . 382

Hartwell v Grayson, Rollo and Clover Docks Ltd [1947] KB 901 . . . 532

Harvey v Cairns 1989 SLT 107 . . . 320

Harvey v Plymouth City Council [2010] PIQR P18 . . . 530

Harvey v RG O'Dell [1958] 2 QB 78 . . . 868

Harwood v Wyken Colliery Co [1913] 2 KB 158 . . . 269

Haseldine v CA Daw & Sons Ltd [1941] 2 KB 343 . . . 118, 532, 541, 542

Hastings v (First) Finsbury Orthopaedics Ltd 2019 SLT 1411 . . . 569, 581, 583

Hatton v Sutherland [2002] 2 All ER 1 . . . 185, 245, 374, 378–81, 382, 385

Hawkins v Coulsdon and Purley UDC [1954] 1 QB 319 . . . 532

Hawley v Luminar Leisure Ltd [2006] IRLR 817 . . . 832

Hay v Hughes [1975] QB 790 . . . 956, 957, 958

Hay (or Bourhill) v Young see Bourhill v Young

Hayden v Hayden [1992] 1 WLR 986 . . . 955, 956, 957, 958, 959

Haynes v Harwood [1935] 1 KB 146 . . . 277, 503

Haystead v Chief Constable of Derbyshire [2000] 3 All ER 890 . . . 57

Heath v Mayor of Brighton (1908) 98 LT 718 . . . 637

Heaven v Pender (t/a West India Graving Dock Co) (1883) 11 QBD 503 . . . 109, 110, 111, 112, 510

Hedley Byrne & Co Ltd v Heller & Partners Ltd [1964] AC 465 . . . 136, 148, 154, 377, 394, 396, 406, 407, 412, 421–31, 432, 433, 434, 435, 437, 440, 444, 445, 447, 448, 449, 450, 451, 452, 453, 455, 456, 457, 458, 459, 460, 461, 463, 466, 468, 469, 478, 510, 511, 520

Heil v Rankin [2001] QB 272 . . . 907, 991

Heilbut, Symons & Co v Buckleton [1913] AC 30 . . . 427

Hemmens v Wilson Browne [1995] Ch 223 . . . 462

Henderson v Dorset Healthcare University NHS Foundation Trust [2021] AC 563 . . . 330, 334, 336–44, 345, 346, 347

Henderson v Henry E. Jenkins & Sons [1970] AC 282 . . . 222, 224

Henderson v Merrett Syndicates Ltd [1995] 2 AC 145 . . . 24, 291, 445–8, 449, 450, 451, 452, 453, 460, 470, 478, 486

Heneghan v Manchester Dry Docks Ltd [2016] 1 WLR 2036 . . . 246, 259, 262

Henningsen v Bloomfield Motors (1960) 161 A 2d 69 . . . 560

Herbage v Pressdram Ltd [1984] 1 WLR 1160 . . . 773

Herd v Weardale Steel, Coal and Coke Co [1915] AC 67 (HL); [1913] 3 KB 771 (CA) . . . 90, 91, 92

Hern v Nichols (1708) 1 Salk 289 . . . 853

Herring v Boyle (1834) 1 Cr M R 377, 149 ER 1126 . . . 61

Hewson v Downs [1970] 1 QB 73 . . . 938

Hicks v Chief Constable of the South Yorkshire Police [1992] 2 All ER 65 . . . 792, 941–2, 943, 944

Higgins v Butcher (1607) Yelv 89, 80 ER 61 . . . 946

Hill v Chief Constable of West Yorkshire [1989] AC 53 . . . 140, 144, 145, 152, 153, 154, 513

Hilton v Burton (Rhodes) Ltd [1961] 1 WLR 705 . . . 868

Hinz v Berry [1970] 2 QB 40 . . . 350

Hird v Wood (1894) 38 Sol J 234 . . . 732

Hirose Electrical UK Ltd v Peak Ingredients Ltd [2011] Env LR 34 . . . 643

Hoare v Silverlock (1848) 12 QB 630 . . . 707

Hobbs (Farms) v Baxenden [1992] 1 Lloyd's Rep 54 . . . 485

Holbeck Hall Hotel Ltd v Scarborough Borough Council [2000] QB 836 . . . 657

Hollywood Silver Fox Farm v Emmett [1936] 1 All ER 825 . . . 646

Holtby v Brigham & Cowan (Hull) Ltd [2000] 3 All ER 421 . . . 244, 245

Home Office v Butchart [2006] 1 WLR 1155 . . . 378, 383

Home Office v Dorset Yacht Co Ltd [1970] AC 1004 . . . 136, 147, 160, 161, 162, 277, 278, 491–5, 496, 497, 502, 503, 510, 513

Honeywill & Stein v Larkin Bros [1934] 1 KB 102 . . . 873

Hopkins v Akramy [2021] QB 564 . . . 883

Hopper v Reeve (1817) 7 Taunt 698, 129 ER 278 . . . 57

Hopps v Mott MacDonald Ltd [2009] EWHC 1881 (QB) . . . 193

Horrocks v Lowe [1975] AC 135 (HL); [1972] 1 WLR 1625 (CA) . . . 752–4

Hotson v East Berkshire Area Health Authority [1987] AC 750 . . . 229–32, 234, 235, 236, 238, 239, 240, 241, 242, 262

Hounga v Allen [2014] 1 WLR 2889 . . . 332, 335, 340, 341

Housecroft v Burnett [1986] 1 All ER 332 . . . 924, 926
Howmet Ltd v Economy Devices Ltd (2016) 168 Con LR 27 . . . 120, 121
HRH Duchess of Sussex v Associated Newspapers Ltd [2021] EWCA Civ 1810 . . . 803, 805, 809
HRH Prince of Wales v Associated Newspapers Ltd [2008] Ch 57 . . . 804
Huckle v Money (1763) 2 Wils 205 . . . 886
Hucks v Cole [1993] 4 Med LR 393 . . . 218
Hugh v National Coal Board, 1972 SC 252 . . . 305
Hughes v Lord Advocate [1963] AC 837 . . . 288
Hughes v Percival (1883) 8 App Cas 443 . . . 878
Hughes v Rattan [2021] EWHC 2032 (QB) . . . 882
Hughes v Williams [2012] EWHC 1078 (QB) . . . 315
Hughes-Holland v BPE Solicitors [2018] AC 599 . . . 293
Humphrey v Aegis Defence Services [2017] 2 All ER 235 . . . 190
Hunt v Severs [1994] 2 AC 350 . . . 26, 929–32, 933, 960
Hunter v British Coal [1999] QB 140 . . . 362, 363
Hunter v Butler [1996] RTR 396 . . . 953
Hunter v Canary Wharf Ltd [1997] AC 655 (HL); [1996] 1 All ER 482 (CA) . . . 67, 125, 489, 625, 628, 630, 631, 632, 634, 635, 639, 658–63, 664, 665, 673, 675, 685, 790, 794
Huntingdon Life Sciences v Curtin (1997) The Times, 11 December . . . 78
Hussain v Lancaster City Council [2000] QB 1 . . . 655
Hussain v New Taplow Paper Mills Ltd [1988] AC 514 . . . 934
Huth v Huth [1915] 3 KB 32 . . . 733
HXA v Surrey County Council [2021] EWHC 250 (QB) . . . 150

Ide v ATB Sales [2008] PIQR P13 . . . 585
Ilford UDC v Beal [1925] 1 KB 671 . . . 651
Ilkiw v Samuels [1963] 1 WLR 991 . . . 863, 864
Imerman v Tchenguiz [2011] Fam 116 . . . 803, 804
Imperial Chemical Industries Ltd v Shatwell [1965] AC 656 . . . 297, 299, 302–5, 306, 604
Imperial Gas Light and Coke Company v Broadbent (1859) 7 HLC 600 . . . 675
Indermaur v Dames (1866) LR 1 CP 274 . . . 525, 541
Inland Revenue Comrs v Hambrook [1956] 2 QB 656 . . . 395
Innes v Wylie (1844) 1 Car & Kir 257, 174 ER 800 . . . 56
International Energy Group Ltd v Zurich Insurance plc [2016] AC 509 . . . 258, 261, 264
Invercargill CC v Hamlin [1996] AC 624 . . . 415

Iqbal v London Transport Executive (1973) The Times, 6 June . . . 864
Iqbal v Prison Officers Association [2010] QB 732 . . . 62, 85, 90
Iqbal v Whipps Cross University Hospital NHS Trust [2008] PIQR P9 . . . 924
Island Records Ltd, ex p [1978] 1 Ch 122 . . . 609
Islington LBC v University College London Hospital NHS Trust [2006] PIQR P3 . . . 398, 927

J Lyons & Sons v Wilkins [1899] 1 Ch 255 . . . 635
J Trevor & Sons v Solomon (1977) 248 EG 779 . . . 773
Jackson v Murray [2015] UKSC 5, [2015] 2 All ER 805; [2012] CSIH 100, 2013 SCLR 429; [2012] CSOH 100, 2012 SCLR 605 . . . 315–18, 319
Jacobs v London County Council [1950] AC 361 . . . 532
Jaggard v Sawyer [1995] 1 WLR 269 . . . 675
Jain v Trent Strategic Health Authority [2009] 1 AC 853 . . . 141
Jameel v Wall Street Journal Europe Sprl [2007] 1 AC 359 . . . 758, 760, 779
Jameel (Yousef) v Dow Jones & Co Inc [2005] QB 946 . . . 705, 709, 710, 711
James v Campbell (1832) 5 C & P 372 . . . 49
James v White Lion Hotel [2021] QB 1153 . . . 551
James-Bowen v Commissioner of Police of the Metropolis [2018] 1 WLR 4021 . . . 141, 150
Jan de Nul (UK) Ltd v NV Royale Belge [2002] EWCA Civ 209 . . . 629
Janvier v Sweeney [1919] 2 KB 316 . . . 66, 67, 71, 72, 73
Jebson v Ministry of Defence [2000] 1 WLR 2055 . . . 485
Jensen v Faux [2011] 1 WLR 3038 . . . 416
Jeynes v News Magazines Ltd [2008] EWCA Civ 130 . . . 718, 719
Job Edwards Ltd v Birmingham Navigations [1924] 1 KB 341 . . . 487
Jobling v Associated Dairies Ltd [1982] AC 794 . . . 269–72, 273
Joel v Morison (1834) 6 C & P 501 . . . 867
John v Associated Newspapers [2006] EWHC 1611 (QB) . . . 813
John v MGN Ltd [1997] QB 586 . . . 767–8, 769, 770, 771, 778
John Munroe (Acrylics) Ltd v London Fire and Civil Defence Authority see Capital & Counties plc v Hampshire County Council
Johnson v Coventry Churchill International Ltd [1992] 3 All ER 14 . . . 876
Johnson v Unisys Ltd [2003] 1 AC 518 . . . 383
Johnson (t/a Johnson Butchers) v BJW Property Developments Ltd [2002] 3 All ER 574 . . . 695

Johnstone v Bloomsbury Health Authority [1992] QB 333 ... 326
Jolley v Sutton London Borough Council [2000] 1 WLR 1082 ... 289
Jones v Department of Employment [1989] 1 QB 1 ... 163
Jones v Jones [1916] 2 AC 481 ... 699, 703
Jones v Kaney [2011] 2 AC 398 ... 142
Jones v Livox Quarries [1952] 2 QB 608 ... 310–11
Jones v Ministry of Defence [2021] EWHC (QB) 2276 ... 640, 648, 670
Jones v Tower Boot Co [1997] 2 All ER 395 ... 845
Jones v Wright [1991] 3 All ER 88 ... 369
Joseph v Spiller [2011] 1 AC 852 ... 744, 745
Joyce v O'Brien [2014] 1 WLR 70 ... 332
JR v Sheffield Teaching Hospitals NHS Foundation Trust [2017] 1 WLR 4847 ... 924
JR38, In re [2016] AC 1131 ... 807
JT v First-Tier Tribunal [2019] 1 WLR 1313 ... 1005
Junior Books Co Ltd v Veitchi Co Ltd [1983] 1 AC 520 ... 137
JXJ v The Province of Great Britain of the Institute of Brothers of the Christian Schools [2020] ELR 579 ... 843, 870

K v News Group Newspapers Ltd [2011] 1 WLR 1827 ... 807, 812
K v Secretary of State for the Home Department [2002] EWCA Civ 775 ... 496
Kadir v Mistry [2014] EWCA Civ 1177 ... 909
Kafagi v JBW Group Ltd [2018] EWCA Civ 1157 ... 829, 842
Kalma v African Minerals Ltd [2020] EWCA Civ 144 ... 150, 496
Karagozlu v Metropolitan Police Officer [2007] 1 WLR 1881 ... 84
Kasapis v Laimos [1959] 2 Lloyd's Rep 378 ... 486
Kay v ITW Ltd [1968] 1 QB 140 ... 862
Kaye v Robertson [1991] FSR 62 ... 55, 773, 782, 785–8, 789, 793, 794
Kelsen v Imperial Tobacco Co (of Great Britain and Ireland) Ltd [1957] 2 QB 334 ... 630, 632
Kemsley v Foot [1952] AC 345 ... 745
Kennaway v Thompson [1981] QB 88 ... 675
Kennedy v Cordia (Services) LLP [2016] 1 WLR 597 ... 607
Kent v Griffiths [2001] QB 36 ... 189, 480–1, 482, 511, 514, 521
Keown v Coventry Healthcare NHS Trust [2006] 1 WLR 953 ... 536
Kerr v Kennedy [1942] 1 KB 409 ... 703
Khashoggi v IPC Magazines Ltd [1986] 1 WLR 1412 ... 741
Khorasandjian v Bush [1993] QB 727 ... 67, 658, 660, 661, 662, 663, 664, 790, 793

Killick v PricewaterhouseCoopers [2001] 1 Lloyd's Rep PN 18 ... 436
King v Lake (1667) 1 Hardres 470 ... 700, 701
King v Phillips [1953] 1 QB 429 ... 287, 396
King v Sussex Ambulance NHS Trust [2002] ICR 1413 ... 189
Kirkham v Boughey [1958] 2 QB 338 ... 395
Kirkham v Chief Constable of Greater Manchester Police [1990] 2 QB 283 ... 281
Kitchen v Royal Air Force Association [1958] 1 WLR 563 ... 230
Knapp v Railway Executive [1949] 2 All ER 508 ... 619
Knauer v Ministry of Justice [2016] AC 908 ... 953
Knightley v Johns [1982] 1 WLR 349 ... 276–8
Knuppfer v London Express [1944] AC 116 ... 726, 730–1
Kolasa v Ealing Hospital NHS Trust [2015] EWHC 289 (QB) ... 536
KR v Bryn Alyn Community (Holdings) Ltd [2003] QB 1441 ... 46
Kralj v McGrath [1986] 1 All ER 54 ... 896
Kuddus v Chief Constable of Leicestershire [2002] 2 AC 122 ... 888, 889, 890, 891–2, 893, 894

L (A Child) v Reading Borough Council [2001] 1 WLR 1575 ... 142
L (Medical Treatment: Gillick Competency), Re [1998] 2 FLR 810 ... 100
Lachaux v Independent Print Ltd [2020] AC 612 (SC); [2016] QB 402 (QBD) ... 699, 704, 706, 708–11, 712
Lachaux v Independent Print Ltd [2021] EWHC 1797 (QB) ... 711
Lamb v Camden London Borough Council [1981] QB 625 ... 27, 279, 502, 504
Lane v Holloway [1968] 1 QB 379 ... 80, 88, 104
Langridge v Levy (1837) 2 M & W 519, 150 ER 863 ... 108
Latimer v AEC Ltd [1953] AC 643 ... 185–7
Launchbury v Morgans [1971] 2 QB 245 ... 845
Lavery v Ministry of Defence [1984] NI 99 ... 892
Law Society v KPMG Peat Marwick [2000] 1 WLR 1921 ... 442
Lawrence v Fen Tigers Ltd [2014] AC 822 (SC); [2012] 1 WLR 2127 (CA); [2011] 4 All ER 1314 (QBD) ... 636, 640, 641–4, 645, 648, 668–9, 670, 671, 672, 677–9, 680, 681
Lawrence v Fen Tigers Ltd (No. 2) [2015] AC 106 ... 655
Lawrence v Obee (1814) 3 Camp 514, 170 ER 1465 ... 668
Laws v Florinplace [1981] 1 All ER 659 ... 633
Le Fanu v Malcolmson (1848) 1 HLC 637 ... 731, 732

Le Lievre v Gould [1893] 1 QB 491 ... 109, 110, 112
Leach v Chief Constable of Gloucestershire [1999] 1 WLR 1421 ... 377, 382
Leakey v National Trust for Places of Historic Interest or Natural Beauty [1980] QB 485 ... 631, 632, 657
Leame v Bray (1803) 3 East 593 ... 9
Lear v Hickstead Ltd [2016] 4 WLR 73 ... 289
Lee Ting Sang v Chung Chi-Keung [1990] 2 AC 374 ... 828
Leigh v Gladstone (1909) 26 TLR 139 ... 98
Lemmon v Webb [1894] 3 Ch 1 ... 656
Les Laboratoires Servier v Apotex Inc [2015] AC 430 ... 333, 335, 340
Lessees and Management Co of Herons Court v Heronslea Ltd [2019] 1 WLR 5849 ... 416
Letang v Cooper [1965] QB 232 ... 44–5, 46
Levi v Bates [2016] QB 91 ... 78
Lewis v Daily Telegraph [1964] AC 234 ... 716, 721–3, 724, 741, 742
Lewis v Wandsworth London Borough Council [2020] EWHC 3205 (QB) ... 176
Lim Poh Choo v Camden and Islington Area Health Authority [1980] AC 174 ... 885, 898, 909, 910, 913, 926
Limpus v London General Omnibus Co (1862) 1 H&C 542, 158 ER 993 ... 864, 865
Linden Gardens Trust Ltd v Lenesta Sludge Disposals Ltd [1994] 1 AC 85 ... 399, 458
Lindsay v Berkeley Homes (Capital) plc [2018] EWHC 2042 (TCC) ... 697
Linklaters Business Services v Sir Robert McAlpine Ltd (No 2) (2010) 133 Con LR 211 ... 415
Lippiatt v South Gloucestershire Council [2000] QB 51 ... 655, 687
Lister v Hesley Hall Ltd [2002] 1 AC 215 ... 846–50, 851, 852, 853, 854, 855, 856, 857, 859, 868, 869, 870, 871
Liverpool Corporation v Coghill & Son Ltd [1918] 1 Ch 307 ... 670
Livingstone v Ministry of Defence [1984] NI 356 ... 49
LMS International Ltd v Styrene Packaging and Insulation Ltd [2006] Build LR 50 ... 691, 695
Logdon v DPP [1976] Crim LR 121 ... 52
London Association for Protection of Trade v Greenlands Ltd [1916] 2 AC 15 ... 748
London Graving Dock Co Ltd v Horton [1951] AC 151 ... 539
London Passenger Transport Board v Upson [1949] AC 155 ... 601, 611
Longden v British Coal Corporation [1998] AC 653 ... 935
Longmeid v Holliday (1851) 6 Ex 761, 155 ER 752 ... 108

Lonrho Ltd v Shell Petroleum Co. Ltd (No. 2) [1982] AC 173 ... 607, 608
Lord v Pacific Steam Navigation Co Ltd, The Oropesa [1943] P 32 ... 278, 283, 492
Losinjska Plovidba v Transco Overseas, The Orjula [1995] 2 Lloyd's Rep 395 ... 414
Loutchansky v Times Newspapers Ltd (No 2) [2002] QB 783 ... 736, 779
Lownds v Home Office [2002] 1 WLR 2450 ... 977
Lungowe v Vedanta Resources plc [2020] AC 1045 ... 499, 500, 501
Lyon v Daily Telegraph [1943] KB 746 ... 742

MA v St George's Healthcare NHS Trust [2015] EWHC 1866 (QB) ... 754
McAleer v Chief Constable of the PSNI [2014] NIQB 53 ... 80
McAlister v Stevenson see Donoghue v Stevenson
McAlpine v Bercow [2013] EWHC 1342 (QB) ... 719
McCarten Turkington Breen v Times Newspapers [2001] 2 AC 277 ... 752
McCarthy v Chief Constable of South Yorkshire Police (1996), noted in Daily Telegraph, 12 December ... 371
McCluskey v Wallace 1998 SC 711 ... 318
McCord v Swansea Football Club (1997) The Times, 11 February ... 199
McCoy v East Midlands Strategic Health Authority (2011) 118 BMLR 107 ... 132
McCracken v Smith [2015] PIQR P19 ... 331, 333
McDermid v Nash Dredging & Reclamation Co Ltd [1987] AC 906 ... 875–6
McDonald v National Grid Electricity Transmission Plc [2015] AC 1128 ... 619
McFarlane v E.E. Caledonia Ltd [1994] 2 All ER 1 ... 353, 355, 356, 371
McFarlane v Tayside Health Authority [2000] 2 AC 59 ... 133, 146
McGeown v Northern Ireland Housing Executive [1995] 1 AC 233 ... 554
McGhee v National Coal Board [1973] 1 WLR 1 ... 248–9, 257, 258, 261, 262, 263
McGlinchey v General Motors (UK) Ltd [2012] CSIH 91 ... 585
McKay v Essex Area Health Authority [1982] QB 1166 ... 133
McKenna v British Aluminium Ltd [2002] Env LR 30 ... 665
McKennitt v Ash [2008] QB 73 ... 803, 804
McKew v Holland and Hannen and Cubitts (Scotland) Ltd [1969] 3 All ER 1621 ... 279, 280
McKinnell v White 1971 SLT 61 ... 320
MacLaren v Robertson (1859) 21 D 183 ... 707

McLoughlin v Jones [2002] QB 1312 ... 378, 379, 380

McLoughlin v O'Brian [1983] 1 AC 410 ... 353, 364–6, 367, 368, 369, 370, 372, 373, 387

McManus v Beckham [2002] 1 WLR 2982 ... 734

McMillan v Crown Prosecution Service [2008] EWHC 1457 (Admin) ... 56

McNaghten's case (1843) 10 C & F 200 ... 340, 639

McTear v Imperial Tobacco Ltd [2005] CSOH 69, 2005 2 SC 1 ... 296–7, 306, 583

McWilliams v Sir William Arrol [1962] 1 WLR 295 ... 242

Maga v Birmingham Roman Catholic Archdiocese Trustees [2010] 1 WLR 1441 ... 851, 870

Maguire v Harland and Wolff [2005] PIQR P21 ... 196

Maguire v Sefton Metropolitan Borough Council [2006] 1 WLR 2550 ... 535

Majrowski v Guy's and St Thomas's NHS Hospital Trust [2007] 1 AC 224 ... 34, 77, 818, 857, 877

Mallett v McMonagle [1970] AC 166 ... 231

Malone v Laskey [1907] 2 KB 141 ... 658, 662

Manchester Building Society v Grant Thornton UK LLP [2022] AC 783 ... 294

Mansfield v Weetabix Ltd [1998] 1 WLR 1263 ... 206–7, 209

Marc Rich and Co AG v Bishop Rock Marine Co Ltd [1996] AC 211 ... 135, 139, 140

Margarine Union GmbH v Cambay Prince Steamship Co Ltd [1969] 1 QB 219 ... 396

Margereson v J.W. Roberts Ltd [1996] PIQR P358 ... 196

Market Investigations v Minister of Social Security [1969] 2 QB 173 ... 824–6, 829, 834

Marsden v Bourne Leisure Ltd [2009] EWCA Civ 671 ... 538

Marshall v Osmond [1983] 2 All ER 225 ... 154

Martin v Watson [1996] 1 AC 74 ... 64

Mason v Lovy Auto Parts [1967] 2 QB 530 ... 695

Massey-Harris-Ferguson v Piper [1956] 2 QB 396 ... 619

Mattis v Pollock [2003] 1 WLR 2158 ... 860, 869

Mawe v Pigott (1869) Ir R 4 CL 54 ... 715

Maynard v West Midlands Regional Health Authority [1984] 1 WLR 634 ... 214, 217, 218

MB, Re [1997] 2 FLR 426 ... 99

Mbasogo v Logo Ltd [2007] QB 846 ... 52, 68

Mead v Clarke Chapman & Co Ltd [1956] 1 WLR 76 ... 266

Meade's and Belt's Case (1823) 1 Lew CC 184, 168 ER 1006 ... 50, 51

Meadows v Khan [2022] AC 852 ... 125, 293, 294

Mediterranean Freight Services Ltd v BP Oil International Ltd, *The Fiona* [1994] 2 Lloyd's Rep 506 ... 276

Meering v Grahame-White Aviation Co Ltd (1919) 122 LT 44 ... 61, 82

Mersey Docks and Harbour Board v Coggins & Griffith [1947] AC 1 ... 826, 831, 832

Mersey Docks and Harbour Board Trustees v Gibbs (1866) LR 1 HL 93 ... 158

Metropolitan International Schools Ltd v Designtechnica Corp [2011] 1 WLR 1743 ... 735, 765

Metropolitan Properties Ltd v Jones [1939] 2 All ER 202 ... 646

Michael v Chief Constable of South Wales Police [2015] AC 1732 ... 31, 139, 140, 143, 144, 145, 146, 148, 154, 158, 168, 480, 482, 505, 508–12, 513, 515, 516, 517, 518, 520, 523

Middleweek v Chief Constable of the Merseyside Police [1992] 1 AC 179n ... 83, 84

Midland Bank Trust Co Ltd v Hett, Stubbs & Kemp [1979] Ch 384 ... 448, 450

Miles v Forest Rock Granite Co (1918) 34 TLR 500 ... 686, 687

Miller v Hancock [1893] 2 QB 177 ... 532

Miller v Jackson [1977] QB 966 ... 176, 665–7, 668, 676

Milne v Express Newspapers Ltd [2005] 1 WLR 772 ... 763

Ministry of Housing and Local Government v Sharp [1970] 2 QB 223 ... 454, 455

Mirza v Bhandal (1999), unreported, 27 April (QBD) ... 416

Mitchell v Glasgow City Council [2009] 1 AC 874 ... 279, 498, 505, 510, 523

Mitchil v Alestree (1676) 1 Vent 295 ... 8

MM (An Adult), Re [2007] EWHC 2003 (Fam) ... 99

Mohammed v Home Office [2011] 1 WLR 2862 ... 165

Mohamud v Wm Morrison Supermarkets plc [2016] AC 677 (SC); [2014] 2 All ER 990 (CA) ... 823, 835, 836, 846, 850, 852–3, 854, 855, 856, 857, 858, 860, 861, 868, 869

Moloney v Lambeth Borough Council (1966) 64 LGR 440 ... 538

Monk v PC Harrington Ltd [2009] PIQR P3 ... 362

Monk v Warbey [1935] 1 KB 75 ... 611

Monroe v Hopkins [2017] EWHC 433 (QB), [2017] 4 WLR 68 ... 720

Monson v Tussauds Ltd [1894] 1 QB 671 ... 700, 706, 737

Montgomery v Lanarkshire Health Board [2015] AC 1430 ... 219–20, 221

Moore v Meagher (1807) 1 Taunt 39 ... 701

Morgan v Odhams Press Ltd [1971] 1 WLR 1239 ... 728

TABLE OF CASES

Morgan Crucible Co plc v Hill Samuel Bank Ltd [1991] 1 All ER 148 (CA); [1990] 3 All ER 330 (QBD) . . . 442, 443, 444

Morgans v Launchbury [1973] AC 127 . . . 26, 844

Morren v Swinton and Pendlebury Borough Council [1965] 1 WLR 576 . . . 825

Morris v CW Martin & Sons Ltd [1966] 1 QB 716 . . . 851, 859

Morris v Murray [1991] 2 QB 6 . . . 299–302, 306, 307

Morris v Redland Bricks Ltd [1970] AC 652 . . . 772

Morrison Sports Ltd v Scottish Power UK plc [2010] 1 WLR 1934 . . . 616

Morrison Steamship Co Ltd v Greystoke Castle (cargo owners) [1947] AC 265 . . . 396

Morrison Supermarkets see Various Claimants v Wm Morrison Supermarkets plc

Morriss v Marsden [1952] 1 All ER 925 . . . 209

Morse v Barratt (Leeds) Ltd (1992) 9 Constr LJ 158 . . . 414

Morton v William Dixon 1909 SC 807 . . . 215

Mosley v News Group Newspapers Ltd [2008] EMLR 20 . . . 811, 889

Mowan v Wandsworth London Borough Council (2001) 33 HLR 56 . . . 655

Mulcahy v Ministry of Defence [1996] QB 732 . . . 135, 142

Mulholland v McCrea [1961] NI 135 . . . 951

Mullen v AG Barr [1929] SC 461 . . . 114

Muller v King's College London NHS Foundation Trust [2017] QB 987 . . . 219

Mullin v Richards [1998] 1 WLR 1304 . . . 210–12

Murphy v Brentwood District Council [1991] 1 AC 398 . . . 137, 406–13, 414, 415, 416, 417, 418, 420, 469, 507

Murphy v Culhane [1977] 1 QB 94 . . . 79–80, 310

Murray v Express Newspapers plc [2009] Ch 481 . . . 805, 806, 807, 813

Murray v Ministry of Defence [1988] 1 WLR 692 . . . 61, 62

Musgrove v Pandelis [1919] 2 KB 43 . . . 694, 695

Mutual Life & Citizens Assurance Co Ltd v Evatt [1971] AC 793 . . . 430, 449

Muuse v Secretary of State for the Home Department [2010] EWCA Civ 45 . . . 890

Myroft v Sleight (1921) 90 LJKB 883 . . . 715

N v Poole Borough Council [2020] AC 780 . . . 149, 155, 160, 170, 475, 482, 516–20, 521, 522

N (a child) v Newham LBC [2007] CLY 2931 . . . 320

Napier v Pressdram Ltd [2010] 1 WLR 934 . . . 70

National Coal Board v England [1954] AC 403 . . . 331

Naylor v Payling [2004] PIQR P615 . . . 543

Neale v Queen Mary's Sidcup NHS Trust [2003] EWHC 1471 (QB) . . . 924

Neame v Johnson (1992), unreported, 24 November (CA) . . . 539

Nettleship v Weston [1971] 2 QB 691 . . . 26, 202–4, 206, 207, 209, 213, 214, 998

Network Rail Infrastructure Ltd v C.J. Morris [2004] Env LR 41 . . . 637

Neville v Fine Arts Co [1897] AC 68 . . . 719

Newstead v London Express Newspaper Ltd [1940] 1 KB 377 . . . 727, 729

Ng Chun Pui v Lee Chuen Tat [1988] RTR 298 . . . 222, 223–4

Nichols v Marsland (1876) 2 Ex D 1 . . . 692, 693

Nocton v Lord Ashburton [1914] AC 932 . . . 421, 422, 424, 425, 426, 434, 459, 461

Northumbrian Water Ltd v Sir Robert McAlpine Ltd [2014] BLR 605 . . . 656

Norwich City Council v Harvey [1989] 1 WLR 828 . . . 135

Nottingham v Aldridge [1971] 2 QB 739 . . . 868

NRAM Ltd v Steel [2018] 1 WLR 1190 . . . 450, 455

O (A Child) v Rhodes [2016] AC 219 (SC); [2015] EMLR 4 (CA); [2014] EWHC 2468 (QB) . . . 43, 48, 69–74, 75

OBG Ltd v Allan see Douglas v Hello! Ltd (No 3)

O'Connell v Jackson [1972] 1 QB 270 . . . 315

Officer L, In Re [2007] 1 WLR 2135 . . . 522

Ogwo v Taylor [1988] AC 431 . . . 362, 535

O'Hare v Coutts & Co [2016] EWHC 2224 (QB) . . . 221

Okpabi v Royal Dutch Shell plc [2021] 1 WLR 1294 . . . 499, 500, 501

Oliver v Ashman [1962] 2 QB 210 . . . 921, 922

OLL Ltd v Secretary of State for Transport [1997] 3 All ER 897 . . . 480

One Step (Support) Ltd v Morris-Garner [2019] AC 649 . . . 681

Orchard v Lee [2009] PIQR P16 . . . 199

O'Reilly v Mackman [1983] 2 AC 237 . . . 616

Ormrod v Crosville Motor Services Ltd [1953] 1 WLR 1120 . . . 844

Oropesa, The see Lord v Pacific Steam Navigation Co Ltd

O'Rourke v Camden London Borough Council [1998] AC 188 . . . 608, 614–16, 617

Orr-Ewing v Colquhoun (1877) 2 App Cas 839 . . . 635

O'Shea v MGN Ltd [2001] EMLR 40 . . . 32, 729, 730, 779

Overseas Tankship (UK) Ltd v Morts Dock & Engineering Co Ltd, *The Wagon Mound* (No 1) [1961] AC 388 . . . 177, 178, 179, 181, 284–7, 288, 357, 492, 650

Overseas Tankship (UK) Ltd v The Miller Steamship Co Pty Ltd, *The Wagon Mound* (No 2) [1967] 1 AC 617; [1963] 1 Ll Rep 402 . . . 175, 177–80, 181, 650

Owen v Martin [1992] PIQR Q151 . . . 954
Owens v Brimmell [1977] QB 859 . . . 314

P Perl (Exporters) Ltd v Camden London Borough [1984] 1 QB 342 . . . 503, 504
Page v Smith [1996] 1 AC 155 . . . 289, 349, 352–4, 355, 356, 357, 358, 367, 379, 385, 386, 392
Page v Smith (No 2) [1996] 3 All ER 272 . . . 355
Palmer v Boyer (1594) Cro Eliz 342 . . . 706
Palmer v Palmer [2006] EWHC 1284 (QB) . . . 584
Palmer v Tees Health Authority [2000] PIQR P1 . . . 373, 497
Pamplin v Express Newspapers Ltd (No 2) [1988] 1 WLR 116 . . . 770
Paris v Stepney Borough Council [1951] AC 367 (HL); [1950] 1 KB 320 (CA) . . . 183–4, 185, 380
Parkinson v St James and Seacroft University Hospital NHS Trust [2002] QB 266 . . . 133
Parmiter v Coupland (1840) 6 M & W 105 . . . 705
Parry v Cleaver [1970] AC 1 . . . 934, 935
Pasley v Freeman (1789) 3 TR 51 . . . 421
Patchett v Swimming Pool & Allied Trades Association Ltd [2010] 2 All ER (Comm) 138 . . . 431
Patel v Mirza [2017] AC 467 . . . 334–5, 336, 337, 338, 339, 340, 341, 342, 343, 344, 345, 346, 348
Paul v Royal Wolverhampton NHS Trust [2022] PIQR P8 . . . 372, 373
Peabody Donation Fund v Sir Lindsay Parkinson & Co [1985] AC 210 . . . 138
Pearce v United Bristol Healthcare NHS Trust [1999] PIQR P53 . . . 220
Penney v East Kent Health Authority [2000] PNLR 323 . . . 219
Pennington v Brinsop Hall Coal Co (1877) 5 Ch D 769 . . . 676
Performance Cars Ltd v Abraham [1962] 1 QB 33 . . . 268, 269
Perrett v Collins [1998] 2 Lloyd's Rep 255; [1999] PNLR 77 . . . 140, 146
Perry v Kendricks Transport Ltd [1956] 1 WLR 85 . . . 693
Petch v Commissioners of Customs and Excise [1993] ICR 789 (CA) . . . 379
Peters v East Midlands Strategic Health Authority [2010] QB 48 . . . 926
Pettigrew v Northern Ireland Office [1990] NI 179 . . . 892
Phelps v Hillingdon London Borough Council [2001] 2 AC 619 . . . 161, 163, 516, 519, 520, 617
Philips v Whiteley (William) Ltd [1938] 1 All ER 566 . . . 213–14
Phillips v Britannia Hygienic Laundry Co Ltd [1923] 2 KB 832 . . . 603, 609–10, 611, 614, 616
Phipps v Rochester Corporation [1955] 1 QB 450 . . . 537, 538

Photo Production Ltd v Securicor Transport Ltd [1980] AC 827 . . . 878
Pickett v British Rail Engineering [1980] AC 136 . . . 920, 921–3, 924, 943
Pile v Chief Constable of Merseyside Police [2020] EWHC 2472 (QB) . . . 56
Piper v JRI (Manufacturing) Ltd (2006) 92 BMLR 141 . . . 586, 587
Pitts v Hunt [1991] 1 QB 24 . . . 319, 331, 332
PJS v News Group Newspapers Ltd [2016] AC 1081 . . . 803, 809, 811
Platt v Liverpool City Council [1997] CLY 4864 . . . 552
Plumb v Cobden Flour Mills Co Ltd [1914] AC 62 . . . 864
Poland v John Parr [1927] 1 KB 236 . . . 869
Polemis and Furness, Withy & Co Ltd, Re [1921] 3 KB 560 . . . 285, 286, 287, 492
Pollard v Tesco Stores Ltd [2006] EWCA Civ 393 . . . 583
Polly Peck (Holdings) plc v Trelford [1986] 1 QB 1000 . . . 741
Pope v D. Murphy & Son Ltd [1961] 1 QB 222 . . . 923
Pratley v Surrey County Council [2004] ICR 159 . . . 289, 382
Prebble v Television New Zealand Ltd [1995] 1 AC 321 . . . 747
Prendergast v Sam & Dee Ltd (1989) *The Times*, 14 March . . . 282
Pride of Derby and Derbyshire Angling Associations Ltd v British Celanese Ltd [1953] 1 Ch 149 . . . 675
Priestley v Fowler (1837) 3 M & W 1, 150 ER 1030 . . . 947
Prince Albert v Strange (1849) 1 McN & G 23 . . . 784, 785, 803
Pritchard v Co-operative Group Ltd [2012] QB 320 . . . 48, 80, 104, 310
Pursell v Horn (1838) 8 AD & E 602, 112 ER 966 . . . 55

Qualcast (Wolverhampton) Ltd v Haynes [1959] AC 743 . . . 175
Quarman v Burnett (1840) 6 M & W 499 . . . 841
Quartz Hill Consolidated Mining Co v Beal (1882) 20 Ch D 501 . . . 773

R, Re [1992] Fam 11 . . . 100
R v B [2007] 1 WLR 1567 . . . 87, 88
R v Bournewood Community and Mental Health NHS Trust, ex *p* L [1999] 1 AC 458 . . . 61, 62, 92
R v Brown [1994] 1 AC 212 . . . 88
R v Cheshire [1991] 1 WLR 844 . . . 282
R v Comr of Police of the Metropolis, ex *p* Nahar (1983) *The Times*, 28 May . . . 83, 84

R v Cotesworth (1704) 3 Mod 172, 87 ER 928 ... 57

R v Criminal Injuries Compensation Board, *ex p* K [1999] QB 1131 ... 955–8

R v Deputy Governor of Parkhurst Prison, *ex p* Hague [1992] 1 AC 58 (HL); [1990] 3 WLR 1210 (CA) ... 81–4, 85, 608, 612–14

R v Devonald [2008] EWCA Crim 527 ... 87

R v Governor of Brockhill Prison, *ex p* Evans [2001] 2 AC 19 ... 47, 85

R v Ireland; R v Burstow [1998] AC 147 ... 50–1, 52

R v Jheeta [2007] EWCA Crim 1699 ... 87

R v Jogee [2017] AC 387 ... 331

R v Richardson [1999] QB 444 ... 87

R v Rimmington; R v Goldstein [2006] 1 AC 459 ... 628

R v St George (1840) 9 C & P 483 ... 52

R v Spratt [1990] 1 WLR 1073 ... 57

R v Sutton [1977] 1 WLR 1086 ... 53

R v Tabassum [2000] 4 Lloyd's Rep Med 404 ... 87

R v Williams [1923] 1 KB 340 ... 87

R v Williams (Gladstone) [1987] 3 All ER 411 ... 101

R v Wilson [1955] 1 WLR 493 ... 51

R (Jalloh) v Secretary of State for the Home Department [2021] AC 262 (SC); [2019] 1 WLR 394 (CA) ... 31, 59–60, 61, 62, 85

R (Lumba) v Secretary of State for the Home Department [2012] 1 AC 245 ... 60, 62, 85, 897

R (M) v Hackney London Borough Council [2011] 1 WLR 2873 ... 64

R (Wood) v Comr of Police of the Metropolis [2010] 1 WLR 123 ... 807

Rabone v Pennine Care NHS Trust [2012] 2 AC 72 ... 523, 962, 963

Radclyffe v Ministry of Defence [2009] EWCA Civ 635 ... 305

Rahman v Arearose Ltd [2001] QB 351 ... 245, 246, 273, 282

Rainham Chemical Works v Belvedere Fish Guano Co Ltd [1921] 2 AC 465 ... 688, 689

Rantzen v Mirror Group Newspapers (1986) Ltd [1994] QB 670 ... 769

Rapier v London Tramways Co [1893] 2 Ch 588 ... 649

Ratcliff v McConnell [1999] 1 WLR 670 ... 551–2

Ratcliffe v Evans [1892] 2 QB 524 ... 699

Ratcliffe v Plymouth & Torbay Health Authority [1998] PIQR P170 ... 225

Rattlesdene v Grunestone (1317) ... 5–6

Ravenscroft v Rederiaktiebolaget Transatlantic [1992] 2 All ER 470n ... 373, 377

Razumas v Ministry of Justice [2018] PIQR P10 ... 882, 884

RE (A Minor) v Calderdale and Huddersfield NHS Foundation Trust (2017) 156 BMLR 204 ... 371, 384

Read v Coker (1853) 13 CB 850, 138 ER 1437 ... 52

Read v J Lyons & Company Ltd [1947] AC 156 ... 684, 686, 689, 691

Ready Mixed Concrete (South East) v Minister of Pensions & National Insurance [1968] 2 QB 497 ... 824

Redland Bricks v Morris [1970] AC 652 ... 675

Reedie v The London & North Western Railway Company (1849) 4 Exch 244, 154 ER 1201 ... 817

Rees v Commissioner of Police of the Metropolis [2021] EWCA Civ 49 ... 890

Rees v Darlington Area Health Authority [2004] 1 AC 309 ... 133

Reeves v Commissioner of Police of the Metropolis [2000] 1 AC 360 (HL); [1999] QB 169 (CA) ... 99, 281, 310, 326, 489, 550

Regan v Paul Properties Ltd [2007] Ch 135 ... 677

Rendlesham Estates plc v Barr Ltd [2015] 1 WLR 3663 ... 416

Revill v Newbery [1996] QB 567 ... 535, 546

Reynolds v Clarke (1725) 1 Str 634 ... 8

Reynolds v Times Newspapers Ltd [2001] 2 AC 127 ... 32, 746, 747–8, 755–6, 757, 758, 759, 760, 774, 778, 781, 796, 808

Rhind v Astbury Water Park Ltd [2004] EWCA Civ 756 ... 536

Ribee v Norrie [2001] PIQR P128 ... 694

Richard v BBC [2019] Ch 169 ... 810

Richardson v Pitt-Stanley [1995] QB 123 ... 611, 612

Riches v News Group Newspapers [1986] QB 256 ... 732

Rickards v Lothian [1913] AC 263 ... 684, 689, 690, 692–3

Rigby v Chief Constable of Northamptonshire [1985] 1 WLR 1242 ... 154, 163

Riverstone Meat Co Pty Ltd v Lancashire Shipping Co Ltd [1961] AC 807 ... 542

Riyad Bank v Ahli United Bank plc [2006] 2 Lloyd's Rep 292 ... 451

Robert Addie & Sons (Collieries) Ltd v Dumbreck [1929] AC 358 ... 525, 526, 544

Roberts v Gable [2008] QB 502 ... 760

Roberts v Ramsbottom [1980] 1 WLR 823 ... 206, 207, 209

Roberts v Secretary of State for the Home Department [2006] 1 WLR 843 ... 85

Robertson v Balmain New Ferry Co *see* Robinson v Balmain New Ferry Company

Robinson v Balmain New Ferry Company [1910] AC 295 ... 61, 90, 91, 92

Robinson v Chief Constable of West Yorkshire Police [2018] AC 736 (SC); [2014] PIQR P14 (CA) ... 138, 142, 144–8, 149, 150, 151, 152, 153, 154, 155, 156, 157, 158, 455, 470, 489, 517, 518, 861

Robinson v Kilvert (1889) 41 Ch D 88 ... 636

Robinson v National Bank of Scotland [1916] SC (HL) 154 ... 421, 424, 425

Robinson v PE Jones (Contractors) Ltd [2012] QB 44 ... 450

Robson v News Group Newspapers [1996] CLY 5660 ... 740

Roe v Minister of Health [1954] 2 QB 66 ... 181, 194–5

Roles v Nathan [1963] 1 WLR 1117 ... 538, 540

Ronayne v Liverpool Women's Hospital NHS Foundation Trust [2015] PIQR P20 ... 374

Rondel v Worsley [1969] 1 AC 191 ... 142

Rookes v Barnard [1964] AC 1129 ... 886–8, 889, 891, 892, 893, 896

Rose v Ford [1937] AC 826 ... 911, 921

Rose v Plenty [1976] 1 WLR 141 ... 847, 862–3

Ross v Caunters [1980] Ch 297 ... 456, 457

Ross v Fedden (1872) 26 LT 966 ... 684, 688

Rothschild v Associated Newspapers Ltd [2013] EMLR 18 ... 741

Rothwell v Chemical & Insulating Co Ltd [2008] 1 AC 281 ... 125, 357, 358, 385, 393, 899, 943

Rouse v Squires [1973] QB 889 ... 277, 282

Rowe v Dolman [2008] EWCA Civ 1040 ... 903

Rowlands v Chief Constable of Merseyside Police [2007] 1 WLR 1065 ... 894, 896

Rowley v Secretary of State for Work and Pensions [2007] 1 WLR 2861 ... 163, 455

Rowling v Takaro Properties Ltd [1988] AC 473 ... 137, 162, 163, 409

Royal Opera House Covent Garden Foundation v Goldscheider [2019] PIQR P15 ... 289

Rufus v Elliott [2015] EWCA Civ 121 ... 719

Rushbond plc v The JS Design Partnership LLP [2021] EWCA Civ 1889 ... 125, 506

Rust v Victoria Graving Dock Co (1887) 36 Ch D 113 ... 674

Rylands v Fletcher (1868) LR 3 HL 330 ... 487, 569, 619, 652, 681–97, 889, 996, 999

S (A Child) (Identification: Restrictions on Publication), In re [2005] 1 AC 593 ... 808

SAAMCO case see South Australia Asset Management Corp v York Montague Ltd

Sadgrove v Hole [1901] 2 KB 1 ... 733

Saif Ali v Sidney Mitchell & Co [1980] AC 198 ... 142

St George v Home Office [2009] 1 WLR 1670 ... 312

St George's Healthcare NHS Trust v S [1999] Fam 26 ... 99

St Helen's Smelting Co v Tipping (1865) 11 HL Cas 642, 11 ER 1483 ... 625, 638–9, 640, 660, 661

St John Poulton's Trustee in Bankruptcy v Ministry of Justice [2011] Ch 1 ... 616

Salsbury v Woodland [1970] 1 QB 324 ... 841

Sampson v Hodson-Pressinger [1981] 3 All ER 710 ... 641

Sandhar v Department of Transport, Environment and the Regions [2005] 1 WLR 1632 ... 521

Savage v South Essex Partnership NHS Foundation Trust [2009] 1 AC 681 ... 489, 523

Savory v Holland & Hannen & Cubitts (Southern) Ltd [1964] 1 WLR 1158 ... 188

Sayers v Harlow UDC [1958] 1 WLR 623 ... 280

SCM (UK) Ltd v W.J. Whittall & Son Ltd [1971] 1 QB 337 (CA); [1970] 1 WLR 1017 (QBD) ... 397, 656

Scott v London and St Katherine Docks Co (1865) 3 H & C 596 ... 221, 224

Scott v Sampson (1882) 8 QBD 491 ... 769, 770

Scott v Shepherd (1773) 2 W Bl 892 ... 8

Scullion v Bank of Scotland [2011] 1 WLR 3212 ... 436

Sebry v Companies House [2016] 1 WLR 2499 ... 455, 461, 462

Secretary of State for the Home Department v Robb [1995] Fam 127 ... 98, 490

Seddon v Driver and Vehicle Licensing Agency [2019] 1 WLR 4593 ... 436, 442

Sedleigh-Denfield v O'Callaghan [1940] AC 880 ... 488, 505, 631, 650, 651–3, 654, 655

Selwood v Durham County Council [2012] PIQR P20 ... 498

Serafin v Malkiewicz [2020] 1 WLR 2455 (SC); [2017] EWHC 2992 (QB) ... 738, 759

Shah v Akram (1981) 79 LS Gaz 814 ... 715

Shah v Standard Chartered Bank [1999] QB 241 ... 724, 742

Shakoor v Situ [2001] 1 WLR 410 ... 205

Shelbourne v Cancer Research UK [2019] PIQR P16 ... 854

Shelfer v City of London Electric Lighting Company [1895] 1 Ch 287 ... 648, 674–5, 676, 677, 679, 680, 681

Shoreham-by-Sea UDC v Dolphin Canadian Proteins Ltd (1972) 71 LGR 261 ... 639

Shortor v Surrey and Sussex Healthcare NHS Trust (2015) 144 BMLR 136 ... 371, 375

Shtern v Cummings [2014] UKPC 18 ... 534

Sicri v Associated Newspapers Ltd [2020] EWHC 3541 (QB) ... 806, 810

Sidaway v Board of Governors of Bethlem Royal Hospital [1985] AC 871 ... 217, 219, 220

Siddorn v Patel [2007] EWHC 1248 (QB) ... 551

Sienkiewicz v Greif (UK) Ltd [2011] 2 AC 229 ... 253–7, 258, 259, 261, 262, 263

Sim v Stretch [1936] 2 All ER 1237; (1936) 52 TLR 669 ... 704, 705, 706

Simaan General Contracting Co v Pilkington Glass Ltd (No 2) [1988] QB 758 ... 451

Simkiss v Rhondda Borough Council (1983) 81 LGR 460 . . . 538
Simmons v British Steel plc [2004] ICR 585 . . . 245
Simmons v Castle [2013] 1 WLR 1239 . . . 908, 977, 982, 991
Simmons v Mitchell (1880) 6 App Cas 156 . . . 703
Simpson v Thompson (1877) 3 App Cas 279 . . . 395
Sinfield v London Organising Committee of the Olympic and Paralympic Games [2018] PIQR P8 . . . 974
Sion v Hampstead Health Authority [1994] 5 Med LR 170 . . . 374
Sirros v Moore [1975] QB 118 . . . 142
SKX v Manchester City Council [2021] 4 WLR 56 . . . 843, 851, 884
Slater v Clay Cross Co Ltd [1956] 2 QB 264 . . . 531
Slazenger Ltd v Gibbs (1916) 33 TLR 35 . . . 707
Slim v Daily Telegraph [1968] 2 QB 157 . . . 715, 718
Slipper v British Broadcasting Corporation [1991] 1 QB 283 . . . 712, 734
Smeaton v Equifax plc [2013] 2 All ER 959 . . . 455
Smith v Austin Lifts Ltd [1959] 1 WLR 100 . . . 540
Smith v Baker & Sons [1891] AC 325 . . . 134, 297, 298
Smith v Blackburn [1974] RTR 533 . . . 313
Smith v Cawdle Fen Commissioners [1938] 4 All ER 64 . . . 273
Smith v Chief Constable of Sussex Police [2009] 1 AC 225 . . . 153, 511, 513, 515
Smith v Chief Superintendent, Woking Police Station (1983) 76 Cr App R 234 . . . 52
Smith v Eric S Bush (a firm); Harris v Wyre Forest District Council [1990] 1 AC 831 . . . 27, 431–5, 440, 441, 442, 443, 444, 448, 453, 466, 469
Smith v Finch [2009] EWHC 53 (QB) . . . 315
Smith v Giddy [1904] 2 KB 448 . . . 656
Smith v Lancashire Teaching Hospitals NHS Trust [2018] QB 804 . . . 962
Smith v Leech Brain & Co [1962] 2 QB 405 . . . 288
Smith v Littlewoods Organisation Ltd [1987] AC 241 . . . 121, 501–5, 506, 509, 655
Smith v Ministry of Defence [2014] AC 52 . . . 142, 152
Smith v P & O Bulk Shipping Ltd [1998] 2 Lloyd's Rep 81 . . . 195
Smith v Scott [1973] Ch 314 . . . 655
Smith v Secretary of State of Health [2002] Lloyd's Rep Med 333 . . . 163
Smith v Stages [1989] AC 928 . . . 865–7
Smith v Storey (1980), unreported, 26 June (CA) . . . 542
Smith v Stratton [2015] EWCA Civ 1413 . . . 332
Smoker v London Fire & Civil Defence Authority [1991] 2 AC 502 . . . 935
Smoldon v Whitworth [1997] PIQR P133 . . . 199
Sobrinho v Impresa Publishing SA [2016] EWHC 66 (QB); [2016] EMLR 12 . . . 711
Société Remorquage à Hélice v Bennetts [1911] 1 KB 243 . . . 396
South Australia Asset Management Corp v York Montague Ltd (SAAMCO) [1997] AC 191 (HL) . . . 283, 289–95
Spartan Steel and Alloys Ltd v Martin & Co Ltd [1973] QB 27 . . . 394, 395–7, 398, 399, 400, 467, 469
Spencer v Wincanton Holdings Ltd [2010] PIQR P8 . . . 280
Spittle v Bunney [1988] 1 WLR 847 . . . 953
Spring v Guardian Assurance plc [1995] 2 AC 296 . . . 430, 448, 449, 454, 510, 511, 520
Standard Chartered Bank v Pakistan National Shipping (Nos 2 & 4) [2003] 1 AC 959 . . . 310
Stanley v Saddique (Mohammed) [1992] QB 1 . . . 955, 956, 957, 958, 959
Stannard v Gore see Gore v Stannard (t/a Wyvern Tyres)
Stansbie v Troman [1948] 2 KB 48 . . . 275, 503, 506
Stanton v Collinson [2010] RTR 284 . . . 314
Stapley v Gypsum Mines Ltd [1953] AC 663 . . . 203, 312, 314
Stennett v Hancock [1939] 2 All ER 578 . . . 118
Stephens v Myers (1830) 4 C & P 349, 172 ER 735 . . . 49–50, 52
Stern v Piper [1997] QB 123 . . . 741, 742
Stocker v Stocker [2020] AC 593 . . . 716–20, 721
Stokes v GKN [1968] 1 WLR 1776 . . . 216
Stone & Rolls Ltd v Moore Stephens (a firm) [2009] 1 AC 1391 . . . 332
Stovin v Wise [1996] AC 923 . . . 138, 161, 163, 472–3, 474, 507, 508, 522
Stuart v Bell [1891] 2 QB 341 . . . 749
Stubbings v Webb [1993] AC 498 . . . 46
Sturges v Bridgman (1879) 11 Ch D 852 . . . 641, 667, 668, 669, 670
Sube v News Group Newspapers [2020] EMLR 25 . . . 77, 78
Sumner v Colborne [2019] QB 430 . . . 135, 150, 521
Sumner v William Henderson & Sons Ltd [1963] 1 WLR 823 (CA); [1964] 1 QB 450 (QBD) . . . 874
Sunbolf v Alford (1838) 3 M & W 247, 150 ER 1135 . . . 81
Surtees v Kingston-upon-Thames Borough Council [1992] PIQR P101 . . . 881

Sutcliffe v Clients Investment Co Ltd [1924] 2 KB 746 . . . 532
Sutherland v Stopes [1925] AC 47 . . . 738
Sutradhar (FC) v National Environment Research Council [2006] 4 All ER 490 (HL); [2004] PNLR 30 (CA) . . . 429, 474, 486
Sutton v Syston Rugby Football Club Ltd [2011] EWCA Civ 1182 . . . 193
Swain v Puri [1996] PIQR P442 . . . 547
Swift v Secretary of State for Justice [2014] QB 373 . . . 951, 963
Swinney v Chief Constable of Northumbria [1997] QB 464 . . . 153, 514
Swinney v Chief Constable of Northumbria (No 2) (1999) 11 Admin LR 811 . . . 514

Taberna Europe v Selskabet AF 1 September 2008 [2017] QB 633 . . . 431, 441, 442
Tai Hing Cotton Mill Ltd v Liu Chong Hing Bank Ltd [1986] AC 80 . . . 450
Tamiz v Google Inc [2013] 1 WLR 2151 . . . 735, 765
Target Holdings v Redferns (a firm) [1996] AC 421 . . . 24
Targett v Torfaen Borough Council [1992] 3 All ER 27 . . . 420
Tate & Lyle Industries v GLC [1983] 2 AC 509 . . . 628
Taylor v Novo [2014] QB 150 . . . 372
Taylor v Rover Co Ltd [1966] 1 WLR 1491 . . . 874
Taylorson v Shieldness Produce Ltd [1994] PIQR P329 . . . 374
Telnikoff v Matusevich [1991] 2 AC 343 . . . 744
Tennent v Earl of Glasgow (1864) 2 M (HL) 22 . . . 693
Tesco Stores Ltd v Pollard [2006] EWCA Civ 393 . . . 583
Tetley v Chitty [1986] 1 All ER 663 . . . 655
Theaker v Richardson [1962] 1 WLR 151 . . . 732, 733
Theakston v MGN Ltd [2002] EMLR 22 . . . 810
Theedom v Nourish Trading (t/a CSP Recruitment) [2016] EMLR 10 . . . 767
The Thelma (Owners) v The Endymion (Owners) [1953] 2 Lloyd's Rep 613 . . . 845
Thomas v News Group Newspapers [2002] EMLR 78 . . . 78
Thomas v NUM [1986] Ch 20 . . . 52, 793
Thomas v Taylor Wimpey Developments Ltd [2019] PNLR 26 . . . 414
Thomas v Thomas (1835) 2 Cr M&R 34 . . . 670
Thompson v Arnold [2008] PIQR P1 . . . 943, 951
Thompson v Commissioner of Police of the Metropolis [1998] QB 498 . . . 889, 890, 896
Thompson v Smith Shiprepairers [1984] QB 405 . . . 196, 215, 216
Thompson-Schwab v Costaki [1956] 1 WLR 335 . . . 633

Thompstone v Tameside and Glossop Acute Services NHS Trust [2008] 1 WLR 2207 . . . 916, 919
Thomson v Christie Manson & Woods Limited [2005] EWCA Civ 555 . . . 430
Thomson v Cremin [1956] 1 WLR 103n . . . 532
Thorley v Lord Kerry (1812) 4 Taunton 355, 128 ER 367 . . . 701–2
Thornton v Kirklees Metropolitan Borough Council [1979] QB 626 . . . 616
Thornton v Telegraph Media Group Ltd [2011] 1 WLR 1985 . . . 705, 709, 710, 711
Tilbrook v Parr [2012] EWHC 1946 (QB) . . . 732
Tindall v Chief Constable of Thames Valley Police [2022] EWCA Civ 25 . . . 522
Tinsley v Milligan [1994] 1 AC 340 . . . 332, 336, 338
Todd v Hawkins (1837) 8 C & P 88 . . . 749
Tolley v Carr [2011] RTR 7 . . . 283
Tolley v JS Fry & Sons Ltd [1931] AC 333 (HL); [1930] 1 KB 467 (CA) . . . 713, 786, 787, 794
Tomlinson v Congleton Borough Council [2004] 1 AC 46 . . . 32–3, 190, 192, 193, 535, 536, 548–50, 551, 553, 555
Toombes v Mitchell [2021] QB 622 . . . 133
Toumia v Evans (Secretary General of the Prison Officers' Association) (1999) *The Times*, 1 April . . . 84
TP and KM v United Kingdom [2001] 2 FLR 549 . . . 170
Transco plc v Stockport Metropolitan Borough Council [2004] 2 AC 1 . . . 651, 664, 685, 686, 687, 688–90, 691, 692, 695, 696
Transport Arendonk v Chief Constable of Essex Police [2020] RTR 22 . . . 522
Tremain v Pike [1969] 1 WLR 1556 . . . 288
Trotman v North Yorkshire County Council [1999] LGR 584 . . . 850
Trustees of the Barry Congregation of Jehovah's Witnesses v BXB [2021] 4 WLR 42 . . . 843, 870, 871
'Truth' (NZ) Ltd v Holloway [1960] 1 WLR 997 . . . 741
Tuberville v Savage (1669) 1 Mod Rep 3, 86 ER 684 . . . 52, 54
Turberville v Stampe (1697) 1 Ld Raym 264, 91 ER 1072 . . . 694, 853
Turner v Metro-Goldwyn-Mayer Pictures Ltd [1950] 1 All ER 449 . . . 746, 749
Turner v News Group Newspapers [2006] 1 WLR 3469 . . . 771
Tutton v Walter [1986] QB 61 . . . 553
TVZ v Manchester City Football Club Ltd [2022] EWHC 7 (QB) . . . 843
Twine v Bean's Express Ltd (1946) 175 LT 131 . . . 818, 864

Undre v Harrow LBC [2017] EMLR 8 . . . 763

Vacwell Engineering Co Ltd v BDH Chemicals Ltd [1971] 1 QB 88 . . . 288, 485

Vaickuviene v J Sainsbury plc 2014 SC 147 . . . 869

Van Colle v Chief Constable of the Hertfordshire Police [2009] 1 AC 225 (HL) . . . 168, 169, 511, 522

Vanderpant v Mayfair Hotels [1930] 1 Ch 138 . . . 628

Various Claimants v Barclays Bank plc [2020] AC 973 . . . 829, 834, 840–2, 843, 844, 861

Various Claimants v Catholic Child Welfare Society (Christian Brothers case) [2013] 2 AC 1 . . . 821, 832, 833, 835, 836, 837, 838, 839, 840, 841, 843, 852, 857, 858, 868, 870, 871, 877

Various Claimants v Wm Morrison Supermarkets plc [2020] AC 989 . . . 855–9, 860, 861, 868, 869, 870, 871

Veakins v Kier Islington Ltd [2010] IRLR 132 . . . 78

Vellino v Chief Constable of Greater Manchester Police [2002] 1 WLR 218 . . . 328, 332, 333

Vernon v Bosley [1997] 1 All ER 577 . . . 350, 374

Viasystems (Tyneside) Ltd v Thermal Transfer (Northern) Ltd [2006] QB 510 . . . 822, 829–31, 832, 833, 838

Victorian Railways Comrs v Coultas (1888) 13 App Cas 222 . . . 66, 67, 75, 349, 350, 354

Videan v British Transport Commission [1963] 2 QB 650 . . . 544

Villers v Monsley (1769) 1 Bos & P 331, 2 Wils 403, 95 ER 886 . . . 705, 706

Vizetelly v Mudie's Select Library Ltd [1900] 2 QB 170 . . . 763

Vowles v Evans [2003] 1 WLR 1607 . . . 27, 199, 206, 215

W, Re [1993] Fam 64 . . . 100

W v Essex County Council [2001] 2 AC 592 . . . 355, 363, 373, 384

W v Home Office [1997] Imm AR 302 . . . 62

Wagon Mound, The see Overseas Tankship (UK) Ltd

Wainwright v Home Office [2004] 2 AC 406 (HL); [2002] QB 1334 (CA) . . . 31–2, 43, 65–8, 69, 74, 75, 77, 789–92, 793, 795

Wakley v Cooke (1849) 4 Exch 511 . . . 740

Walker v Commissioner of Police of the Metropolis [2015] 1 WLR 312 . . . 61, 85

Walker v Northumberland County Council [1995] 1 All ER 737 . . . 378, 379, 380

Wallett v Vickers [2019] PIQR P6 . . . 331, 333, 345

Walter v Selfe (1851) 4 De G & Sm 315 . . . 635

Walters v North Glamorgan NHS Trust [2003] PIQR P16 . . . 372, 374

Ward v James [1966] 1 QB 273 . . . 175

Warnes v Forge [2020] 4 WLR 91 . . . 708

Warren v Henlys Ltd [1948] 2 All ER 932 . . . 869

Warriner v Warriner [2002] 1 WLR 1703 . . . 925

Wasserman v Freilich [2016] EWHC 312 (QB) . . . 744

Waters v Commissioner of Police of the Metropolis [2000] 1 WLR 1607 . . . 384

Watson v British Boxing Board [2001] QB 1134 . . . 486

Watson v Croft Promosport Ltd [2009] 3 All ER 249 . . . 641, 643, 676, 677

Watson v Gray (1998) *The Times*, 26 November . . . 199

Watt v Hertfordshire County Council [1954] 1 WLR 835 . . . 188–9

Watt v Longsdon [1930] 1 KB 130 . . . 749, 750

Watts v Fraser (1835) 1 M & Rob 449 . . . 767

Watts v Times Newspapers Ltd [1997] QB 650 . . . 749

Wattson v Port of London Authority [1969] 1 Lloyd's Rep 95 . . . 930

Waugh v James Allan Ltd [1964] 2 Lloyd's Rep 1 . . . 207, 209

Weaver v Lloyd (1824) 1 B & C 678, 130 ER 162 . . . 739

Webb v Barclays Bank plc [2001] EWCA Civ 1141 . . . 282

Webb v Bird (1862) 13 CBNS 841 . . . 634

Webster v Burton Hospitals NHS Foundation Trust [2017] EWCA Civ 62 . . . 221

Weddall v Barchester Healthcare Limited [2012] IRLR 307 . . . 869

Weld-Blundell v Stephens [1920] AC 956 . . . 275, 279, 286, 493

Weldon v Home Office [1992] 1 AC 58 (HL); [1990] 3 WLR 465 (CA) . . . 82, 84

Weller v Associated Newspapers Ltd [2016] 1 WLR 1541 . . . 813

Wells v Cooper [1958] 2 QB 265 . . . 215

Wells v Wells [1999] 1 AC 345 . . . 916, 917, 925, 992

Welton v North Cornwall District Council [1997] 1 WLR 570 . . . 430, 431, 507

Wennhak v Morgan (1880) 20 QBD 637 . . . 732

West v T. Clarke Ltd, 20 May 1982 (QBD) . . . 539

Westcott v Westcott [2009] QB 407 . . . 747

Western Steamship Co Ltd v NV Konninklijke Rotterdamsche Lloyd, *The Empire Jamaica* [1955] P 259 . . . 292

Westwood v Post Office [1974] 1 AC 1 . . . 552

Wheat v E. Lacon & Co Ltd [1966] AC 552 . . . 531–3, 534

Wheeler v Copas [1981] 3 All ER 405 . . . 536

Wheeler v JJ Saunders Ltd [1996] Ch 19 . . . 641, 643, 671

Wheeler v New Merton Board Mills [1933] 2 KB 669 . . . 603

White v Bayley (1861) 10 CB (NS) 227 . . . 793

White v Blackmore [1972] 2 QB 651 . . . 321, 543
White v Chief Constable of South Yorkshire Police sub nom Frost v Chief Constable of South Yorkshire Police [1999] 2 AC 455 . . . 352, 357, 358–60, 361, 362, 363, 367, 379, 382, 386, 392, 393
White v City of St Albans (1990), unreported, 2 March (CA) . . . 547
White v Jones [1995] 2 AC 207 (HL); [1993] 3 WLR 730 (CA) . . . 24, 399, 456–60, 461, 462, 463, 464, 466, 486
Widdowson v Newgate Meat Corporation [1998] PIQR P138 . . . 224
Wigg v British Railways Board (1986) 136 NLJ 446 . . . 352
Wild v Southend University Hospital NHS Foundation Trust [2016] PIQR P3 . . . 384
Wilkes v DePuy International Ltd [2016] EWHC 3096 (QB) . . . 569, 574–80, 581, 582, 583
Wilkes v Wood (1763) Lofft 1 . . . 886
Wilkin-Shaw v Fuller [2012] ELR 575 . . . 193
Wilkinson v Downton [1897] 2 QB 57; [1895–9] All ER Rep 267 . . . 11, 12, 43, 65, 66, 67, 68, 69, 70, 71, 72, 73, 74, 75, 77, 79, 791, 793
Williams v Bermuda Hospitals Board [2016] AC 888 . . . 246, 247, 248, 259
Williams v Department of the Environment, 30 November 1981 (QBD) . . . 539
Williams v Holland (1833) 2 LJCP (NS) 190 . . . 9, 134
Williams v Humphrey (1975), unreported, 12 February . . . 53
Williams v Natural Life Health Foods Ltd [1998] 1 WLR 830 . . . 449, 453, 463
Williams v Network Rail Infrastructure Ltd [2019] QB 601 . . . 629–32, 633, 637
Williams v Reason [1988] 1 WLR 96 . . . 740
Williamson v John I Thornycroft & Co. Ltd [1940] 2 KB 658 . . . 266
Wilsher v Essex Area Health Authority [1988] AC 1074 (HL); [1987] QB 730 (CA) . . . 204, 235, 236, 257, 261, 262
Wilson v Exel UK Ltd 2010 SLT 671 . . . 869
Wilson v Pringle [1987] QB 237 . . . 47, 53–5, 56
Wilsons & Clyde Coal Co Ltd v English [1938] AC 57 . . . 379, 871
Winch v Mid Bedfordshire District Council [2002] All ER (D) 380 . . . 655
Winterbottom v Wright (1842) 10 M & W 109 . . . 107–8, 114, 119
Wise v Kay [1962] 1 QB 638 . . . 910, 912
Withers v Perry Chain [1961] 1 WLR 1314 . . . 185, 187
Wong v Parkside Health NHS Trust [2001] EWCA Civ 1721; [2003] 3 All ER 932 . . . 67, 71
Woodland v Swimming Teachers Association [2014] AC 537 (SC); [2011] EWHC 2631 (QB) . . . 871, 872, 873, 877–81, 882, 883, 884

Woodley v Metropolitan District Railway Co (1877) 2 Ex D 384 . . . 298, 299
Woodrup v Nicol [1993] PIQR Q104 . . . 926
Woodward v Mayor of Hastings [1945] KB 174 . . . 542
Wooldridge v Sumner [1963] 2 QB 43 . . . 196–8, 199, 305
Woollins v British Celanese Ltd [1966] 1 KIR 438 . . . 539
Worsley v Tambrands Ltd [2000] PIQR P95 . . . 584
Worthington v Metropolitan Housing Trust [2018] HLR 32 . . . 79
Wright v British Railways Board [1983] 2 AC 773 . . . 906
Wright v Cambridge Medical Group [2013] QB 312 . . . 229, 282
Wright v Lodge [1993] 4 All ER 299 . . . 282

X v Y [1988] 2 All ER 648 . . . 809
X (Minors) v Bedfordshire CC [1995] 2 AC 633 . . . 160, 161, 169, 170, 515, 516, 518, 519, 607–8, 615, 616, 617, 623
XA v YA [2011] PIQR P1 . . . 490

YAH v Medway NHS Foundation Trust [2019] 1 WLR 1413 . . . 375, 384
Yearworth v North Bristol NHS Trust [2010] QB 1 . . . 351
Yetkin v Mahmood [2011] QB 827 . . . 521, 522
Young v Charles Church (1997) 39 BMLR 146 . . . 356
Young v Downey [2020] EWHC 3457 (QB) . . . 371
Young v Post Office [2002] IRLR 660 . . . 382
Youssoupoff v Metro-Goldwyn-Mayer Pictures Ltd (1934) 50 TLR 581 . . . 708
Yuen Kun Yeu v Attorney General of Hong Kong [1988] AC 175 . . . 142, 472

Zeromska-Smith v United Lincolnshire Hospitals NHS Trust [2019] EWHC 980 (QB) . . . 384
ZXC v Bloomberg LP [2022] UKSC 5; [2021] QB 28 (CA) . . . 806–8, 810

Australia
Adeels Palace Pty Ltd v Moubarak (2009) 239 CLR 420 . . . 506
Alcan Gove Pty Ltd v Zabic [2015] 89 ALJR 845 . . . 125
Allen v Chadwick (2015) 256 CLR 148 . . . 302
Australian Broadcasting Corpn v Lenah Game Meats Pty Ltd (2001) 208 CLR 199 . . . 797

Balmain New Ferry Company v Robertson (1906) 4 CLR 379 . . . 88–89
Barclay v Penberthy (2012) 246 CLR 258 . . . 398, 399

TABLE OF CASES

Barnes v Commonwealth (1937) SR (NSW) 511 ... 377

Benson v Lee [1972] VR 879 ... 371

Bevan v Coolahan (2019) 101 NSWLR 86 ... 331

Binsaris v Northern Territory (2020) 380 ALR 1 ... 48, 92

Braverus Maritime Inc v Port Kembla Coal Terminal Ltd [2005] FCAFC 25 ... 312

Brookfield Multiplex Ltd v Owners–Strata Plan No 61288 (2014) 254 CLR 185 ... 394, 419, 420

Bryan v Maloney (1995) 182 CLR 609 ... 419, 420

Burnie Port Authority v General Jones Pty Ltd (1994) 179 CLR 520 ... 691, 692, 696

CAL No 14 Pty Ltd v Motor Accidents Insurance Board; CAL No 14 Pty Ltd v Scott (2009) 239 CLR 390 ... 485

Caltex Oil (Australia) v The Dredge 'Willemstad' (1976) 136 CLR 529 ... 399

Campbelltown City Council v Mackay (1989) 15 NSWLR 501 ... 351

Carrier v Bonham [2002] 1 Qd R 474 ... 210

Cattanach v Melchior (2003) 215 CLR 1 ... 134

Chester v Waverley Municipal Council (1939) 62 CLR 1 ... 365

Cole v South Tweed Heads Rugby League Football Club Ltd (2004) 217 CLR 469 ... 485

Cook v Cook (1986) 162 CLR 376 ... 204

Crimmins v Stevedoring Industry Finance Committee (1999) 200 CLR 1 ... 157

CSR v Eddy (2005) 226 CLR 1 ... 933

De Jager v Payneham and Magill Lodges Hall Inc (1984) 36 SASR 498 ... 655

De Sales v Ingrilli (2002) 212 CLR 338 ... 954

Dimitrelos v 14 Martin Place Pty Ltd [2007] NSWCA 85 ... 542

Esanda Finance Corporation Ltd v Peat Marwick Hungerfords (1997) 188 CLR 241 ... 444, 445, 466

FAI General Insurance Co Ltd v Lucre (2000) 50 NSWLR 261 ... 376

Graham Barclay Oysters Pty Ltd v Ryan (2001) 211 CLR 540 ... 590

Gray v Motor Accident Commission (1998) 196 CLR 1 ... 894

Hackshaw v Shaw (1984) 155 CLR 614 ... 43

Hahn v Conley (1971) 126 CLR 276 ... 490

Harriton v Stephens (2006) 226 CLR 52 ... 133

Hill v Van Erp (1997) 188 CLR 159 ... 461, 463, 466

Homsi v Homsi (2016) 51 VR 694 ... 376

Hunter Area Health Service v Presland (2005) 63 NSWLR 22 ... 330

Imbree v McNeilly (2008) 236 CLR 510 ... 204

Insurance Comr v Joyce (1948) 77 CLR 39 ... 203

Jaensch v Coffey (1984) 155 CLR 549 ... 372, 374

Johnson Tiles v Esso Australia [2003] VSC 27 ... 470, 471

Kars v Kars (1996) 187 CLR 354 ... 932

Kenny & Good Pty Ltd v MGICA (1999) 199 CLR 413 ... 293

King v Philcox (2015) 255 CLR 304 ... 371

Koehler v Cerebos (Australia) Ltd (2005) 222 CLR 44 ... 383

Kondis v State Transport Authority (1984) 154 CLR 672 ... 882

Kozarov v Victoria (2022) 273 CLR 115 ... 382, 383

Lange v Australian Broadcasting Corporation (1997) 189 CLR 520 ... 32

Lewis v Australian Capital Territory (2020) 381 ALR 375 ... 60, 897

Lipman v Clendinnen (1932) 46 CLR 550 ... 525, 526

McFadzean v Construction, Forestry, Mining and Energy Union (2007) 20 VR 250 ... 60

McHale v Watson (1964) 111 CLR 384; (1966) 115 CLR 199 ... 43, 211, 212

March v E. & M. H. Stramare Pty Ltd (1991) 171 CLR 506 ... 312

Marsh v Baxter (2015) 49 WAR 1 ... 637

Miller v Miller (2011) 242 CLR 446 ... 332

Mulligan v Coffs Harbour City Council (2005) 223 CLR 486 ... 551

New South Wales v Ibbett (2006) 229 CLR 638 ... 894

Perre v Apand Pty Ltd (1999) 198 CLR 180 ... 399

Prince Alfred College Inc v ADC (2016) 258 CLR 134 ... 821, 845, 851, 854, 870

Queensland Stations Pty v Federal Comr of Taxation (1945) 70 CLR 539 ... 825

Rixon v Star City Pty Ltd [2001] NSWCA 265 ... 56

Rogers v Whitaker (1992) 175 CLR 479 ... 220

Schellenberg v Tunnel Holdings (2000) 200 CLR 121 ... 226

Scott v Davis (2000) 204 CLR 333 ... 845

Sellars v Adelaide Petroleum NL (1994) 179 CLR 332 ... 242

Skelton v Collins (1966) 115 CLR 94 . . . 915, 923
Smith v Leurs (1945) 70 CLR 256 . . . 493, 503
Stingel v Clark (2006) 226 CLR 442 . . . 43, 46
Sutherland Shire Council v Heyman (1985) 60 ALR 1 . . . 136, 137, 439

Tabet v Gett (2010) 242 CLR 537 . . . 241
Tame v New South Wales (2002) 211 CLR 317 . . . 375, 377, 393
The Age Co Ltd v YZ [2019] VR 189 . . . 382

Vairy v Wyong Shire Council (2005) 223 CLR 422 . . . 551
Venning v Chin (1974) 10 SASR 299 . . . 43
Victoria Park Racing and Recreation Grounds Ltd v Taylor (1937) 58 CLR 479 . . . 633

Wallace v Kam (2013) 250 CLR 375 . . . 227, 283
Wilkinson v Sporting Life (1933) 49 CLR 365 . . . 715
Woolcock Street Investments Pty Ltd v CDG Pty Ltd (2004) 216 CLR 515 . . . 419

Canada

1688782 Ontario Inc v Maple Leaf Foods Inc (2020) 450 DLR (4th) 181 . . . 155, 402, 414, 419, 469

Andrews v Grand & Toy Alberta Ltd (1978) 83 DLR (3d) 452 . . . 270, 913, 914
Arnold v Teno (1978) 83 DLR (3d) 609 . . . 914
Aubry v Éditions Vice-Versa Inc [1998] 1 SCR 591 . . . 801

Bazley v Curry (1999) 174 DLR (4th) 45 . . . 819–21, 822, 846, 847, 848, 849, 850, 854, 868
Bell Canada v Cope (Sarnia) Ltd (1980) 11 CCLT 170 . . . 44
Blackwater v Plint [2005] 3 SCR 3 . . . 833
Brooks v Canadian Pacific Railway Ltd (2007) 283 DLR (4th) 540 . . . 686

Canadian National Railway Co v Norsk Pacific Steamship Co [1992] 1 SCR 1021 . . . 399, 400–2, 403
Childs v Desormeaux [2006] 1 SCR 643 . . . 485, 506
City of Kamloops v Nielsen [1984] 2 SCR 2 . . . 402, 418
Clements v Clements [2012] 2 SCR 181 . . . 262, 263
Cook v Lewis [1951] SCR 830 . . . 44, 263
Crocker v Sundance Northwest Resorts Ltd (1988) 51 DLR (4th) 321 . . . 484

Deloitte & Touche v Livent Inc [2017] 2 SCR 855 . . . 443, 445, 455

Fenn v City of Peterborough (1976) 73 DLR (3d) 177 . . . 372
Fontaine v Loewen Estate [1998] 1 SCR 424 . . . 226

Hall v Hebert [1993] 2 SCR 159 . . . 334, 347
Hercules Management Ltd v Ernst & Young [1997] 2 SCR 165 . . . 444, 445
Horsley v Maclaren (1972) 22 DLR (3d) 545 . . . 475

Jacobi v Griffiths (1999) 174 DLR (4th) 71 . . . 846, 847, 849, 850, 868
Jordan House Ltd v Menow (1973) 38 DLR (3d) 105 . . . 484, 485

KLB v British Columbia [2003] 2 SCR 403 . . . 840

Larin v Goshen (1975) 56 DLR 3d 719 . . . 44
Lawson v Laferriere [1991] 1 SCR 541 . . . 241
London Drugs v Kuehne & Nagel International [1992] 3 SCR 299 . . . 820

Marshall v Curry [1933] 3 DLR 260 . . . 94
Montreal Locomotive Works v Montreal and A-G for Canada [1947] 1 DLR 161 . . . 825
Motherwell v Motherwell (1976) 73 DLR (3d) 62 . . . 660, 662
Murray v McMurchy [1949] 2 DLR 442 . . . 94

Non-Marine Underwriters, Lloyds of London v Scalera [2000] 1 SCR 551 . . . 53, 56, 86

Penner v Mitchell [1978] 5 WWR 328 . . . 270
Plains Engineering Ltd v Barnes Security Services Ltd (1987) 43 CCLT 129 (Alta. QB) . . . 821

Queen in the Right of Canada, The v Saskatchewan Wheat Pool [1983] 1 SCR 205 . . . 607, 619, 623

R v Dyment [1988] 2 SCR 417 . . . 795
R v Imperial Tobacco Canada Ltd [2011] 3 SCR 45 . . . 163, 474
Reibl v Hughes (1981) 114 DLR 3d 1 (Supreme Court of Canada); (1978) 21 OR (2d) 14 (Ontario CA) . . . 87
Rivtow Marine Ltd v Washington Iron Works [1974] SCR 1189 . . . 486

Saadati v Moorhead [2017] 1 SCR 543 . . . 350
Stewart v Pettie [1995] 1 SCR 131 . . . 506

Thornton v Board of School Trustees of School District No 57 (1978) 83 DLR (3d) 480 . . . 913–14

Walmsley v Humenick [1954] 2 DLR 232 . . . 44
Winnipeg Condominium Corporation No 36 v Bird Construction Co [1995] 1 SCR 85 . . . 402, 418–19, 420
Wolfenden v Giles (1892) 2 Br Col R 284 . . . 707

TABLE OF CASES

European Court of Human Rights

A v United Kingdom (2003) 36 EHRR 51 ... 747

Axel Springer AG v Germany (Application No 39954/08) [2012] EMLR 15 ... 808

Bladet Tromsø and Stensaas v Norway (2000) 29 EHRR 125 ... 808

Earl Spencer v United Kingdom (1998) 25 EHRR CD 105 ... 791

Europapress Holding d.o.o. v Croatia (2011) 53 EHRR 27 ... 776

HL v United Kingdom (2004) 40 EHRR 761 ... 61

Jain v United Kingdom [2010] ECHR 411 ... 141

Khatun v United Kingdom (1998) 26 EHRR CD 212 ... 664

Lingens v Austria (1986) 8 EHRR 407 ... 776

MAK and RK v United Kingdom [2010] 2 FLR 451 ... 170

Osman v United Kingdom [1999] 1 FLR 193 ... 31, 522, 523

Peck v United Kingdom (App No 44647/98) (2003) 36 EHRR 41 ... 791, 813, 814

Pedersen v Denmark (2006) 42 EHRR 24 ... 808

Reynolds v United Kingdom (2012) 55 EHRR 35 ... 962

Steel and Morris v United Kingdom (2004) 41 EHRR 22 ... 768

Times Newspapers Ltd v United Kingdom [2009] EMLR 14 ... 736

Tolstoy Miloslavsky v United Kingdom (1995) 20 EHRR 442 ... 776

von Hannover v Germany (App No 59320/00) (2005) 40 EHRR 1; [2004] EMLR 21 ... 808, 811, 812

von Hannover v Germany (App Nos 40660/08 and 60641/08) (2012) 55 EHRR 388 ... 813

Weber v Switzerland (1990) 12 EHRR 508 ... 776

Z v United Kingdom [2001] 2 FLR 612 ... 31, 170

European Court of Justice

Boston Scientific Medizintechnik GmbH v AOK Sachsen-Anhalt–Die Gesundheitskasse (Cases C-503–504/13) [2015] 3 CMLR 173 ... 581, 583

Commission v France (Case C-52/00) [2002] ECR I-3827 ... 561

Commission v Greece (Case C-154/00) [2002] ECR I-3879 ... 561

Commission v United Kingdom (Case C-300/95) [1997] ECR I-2649 ... 587–9

O'Byrne v Sanofi (Case C-127/04) [2006] ECR I-1313 ... 586

Sanchez v Medicina Asturiana SA (Case C-183/00) [2002] ECR I-3901 ... 562

Skov AEG v Bilka Lavprisvarehus A/S (Case C-402/03) [2006] ECR I-199 ... 561

Veedfald v Arhus Amtskommune (Case C-203/99) [2001] ECR I-3569 ... 586

VI v Krone-Verlag Gesellschaft mbH & Co KG (Case C-65/20) ... 570, 571

France

Football Club de Metz v Wiroth, Colmar, Ch. dét. à Metz, 20 avril 1955 ... 399

Germany

BGHZ 29, 65, NJW, 479 ... 398

OLG Düsseldorf, 20 December 2002, 14 U 99/02 ... 583

Hong Kong

Blakeney-Williams v Cathay Pacific Airways Ltd [2013] EMLR 6 ... 770

Oriental Daily Publisher Ltd v Ming Pao Holdings Ltd [2013] EMLR 7 ... 718

Ireland

GE v The Commissioner of An Garda Síochána, Irish CA, 16 April 2021, unreported ... 61

Moynihan v Moynihan [1975] IR 192 ... 845

Italy

Torino Calcio SpA v Romero, Cass. civ., SU, 26.1.1971, no 174 ... 399

Netherlands

Baby Kelly case ... 133

Scholten v Sanquin Bloedvoorziening, Rb. Amsterdam, 3 February 1999, NJ 1999, 621 ... 590

New Zealand

Beals v Hayward [1960] NZLR 131 ... 44

Body Corporate No 207624 v North Shore City Council [2013] 2 NZLR 297 ... 415, 420

Couch v Attorney-General [2010] NZSC 27 ... 893

Ellis v Counties Manukau District Health Board [2007] 1 NZLR 196 ... 330

Gartside v Sheffield Young & Ellis [1983] NZLR 37 ... 457

Invercargill CC v Hamlin [1994] 3 NZLR 513 ... 415

McCallion v Dodd [1966] NZLR 710 ... 490

Police v Greaves [1964] NZLR 295 ... 52

Rolls Royce New Zealand Ltd v Carter Holt Harvey Ltd [2005] 1 NZLR 324 ... 451

S v Attorney General [2003] 3 NZLR 450 ... 840

Thompson v Police [2012] NZAR 741 ... 56

van Soest v Residual Health Management Unit [2000] 1 NZLR 179 ... 350, 393

Singapore

ACB v Thomson Medical Pte Ltd [2017] 1 SLR 918 ... 134

JU v See Tho Kai Yin [2005] 4 SLR 96 ... 133

Man Mohan Singh v Zurich Insurance (Singapore) Pte Ltd [2008] 3 SLR(R) 735 ... 350

Ng Huat Seng v Munib Mohammad Madni [2017] 2 SLR 1074 ... 842, 873

RSP Architects Planners & Engineers v Management Corporation Strata Title Plan No 1075 [1999] 2 SLR(R) 134 ... 420

United States of America

Barber v Time Inc, 159 SW 2d 291 (1942) ... 789

BMW of North America Inc v Gore, 116 S Ct 1589 (1996) ... 895

Boronkay v Robinson & Carpenter (1928) 160 NE 400 ... 618

City of Chicago v Tribune Co (1923) 139 NE 86 ... 777

Dillon v Twin State Gas (1932) 163 A 111 ... 273

Escola v Coca Cola Bottling Co of Fresno, 150 P 2d 436 (1944) ... 556, 559, 561, 1000

Greenman v Yuba Power Products Inc, 377 P 2d 897 (1963) ... 1000

Grimshaw v Ford Motors (1981) 119 Cal App 3d 757 ... 183

Hewellette v George, 68 Miss 703, 9 So 885 (1891) ... 490

Higginbotham v Mobil Oil Corpn (1977) 545 F 2d 422 ... 225

McDonald's coffee case ... 35, 37, 38

MacPherson v Buick Motor Co, 217 NY 382 (1916) ... 556

Natchez Times v Dunigan, 72 So 2d 681 (1954) ... 707

New York Times Co v Sullivan, 376 US 254 (1964) ... 32, 774, 777, 779, 780, 781

Palsgraf v Long Island Railway Co, 162 NE 99 (1928) ... 126, 127

Peck v Tribune Clo, 214 US 185 (1909) ... 715

Rousey v Rousey, 528 A2d 416 (1987) ... 490

St Amant v Thompson, 390 US 727 (1968) ... 780

Sindell v Abbot Laboratories, 607 P 2d 924 (1980) ... 264

Southern Air Transport Inc v American Broadcasting Co, 877 F 2d 1010 (US App DC, 1989) ... 708

State Farm v Campbell, 538 US 408 (2003) ... 895

Summers v Tice, 199 P 2d 1 (1948) ... 263

Talmage v Smith (1894) 101 Mich 370 ... 48

Tarasoff v University of California, 551 P 2d 334 (1976) ... 497

Ultramares Corp v Touche, Niven & Co, 255 NY 170; 174 NE 441 (1931) ... 140, 437, 466

United States v Carroll Towing Co (1947) 159 F 2d 169 ... 182

US v Silk (1946) 331 US 704 ... 825

Vincent v Lake Erie Transportation Co, 124 NW 221 (Minn. 1910) ... 92

Wagner v International Rly Co (1921) 232 NY 176 ... 352

TABLE OF LEGISLATION

Table of United Kingdom Statutes

Access to Justice Act 1999 . . . 980
  s. 27 . . . 980
Administration of Justice Act 1982
  s. 1(1)(a) . . . 909, 943
  s. 1(1)(b) . . . 909, 941, 943
  s. 3 . . . 961
  s. 3(1) . . . 955
  s. 4 . . . 943
  s. 5 . . . 925
  s. 6 . . . 899
Administration of Justice (Miscellaneous Provisions) Act 1933
  s. 6 . . . 907
Animals Act 1971 . . . 601
  s. 2 . . . 999
Automated and Electric Vehicles Act 2018 . . . 597–601
  s. 2 . . . 600
  s. 2(1) . . . 597, 600
  s. 2(2) . . . 597
  s. 2(3) . . . 597–8
  s. 2(5) . . . 598
  s. 2(6) . . . 598
  s. 2(7) . . . 598, 600
  s. 3 . . . 598
  s. 3(1) . . . 598, 600
  s. 3(2) . . . 598, 600
  s. 4 . . . 598–9, 600
  s. 4(1) . . . 598
  s. 4(2) . . . 598
  s. 4(3) . . . 598
  s. 4(4) . . . 598
  s. 4(5) . . . 599
  s. 4(6) . . . 599
  s. 5 . . . 600
  s. 5(1) . . . 599
  s. 5(2) . . . 599
  s. 5(3) . . . 599
  s. 5(4) . . . 599
  s. 6(3) . . . 599
  s. 8(1) . . . 599
  s. 8(3) . . . 599

Bill of Rights 1688
  Art. IX . . . 747
Broadcasting Act 1990
  s. 166 . . . 700
Building Act 1984
  s. 38 . . . 417
Building Safety Act 2022 . . . 416–17
  s. 134 . . . 416
  s. 135 . . . 416

  s. 148 . . . 417
  s. 149 . . . 417

Chancery Amendment Act 1858 see Lord Cairns' Act
Children Act 1989 . . . 517
Civil Aviation Act 1982
  s. 76(2) . . . 999
Civil Evidence Act 1968
  s. 13 . . . 742
Civil Liability Act 2018 . . . 975
  s. 1 . . . 908
  s. 3 . . . 908
  ss. 3–5 . . . 40
  s. 6 . . . 975
  ss. 7–8 . . . 975
  s. 10 . . . 916
Civil Liability (Contribution) Act 1978 . . . 281, 831, 832
Civil Partnership Act 2004 . . . 962
Clean Air Act 1993 . . . 626
Companies Act 1985 . . . 291, 438
Companies Act 2006
  Pt 16 (ss. 475–539) . . . 442
  ss. 534–538 . . . 443
  s. 1157 . . . 443
Compensation Act 2006 . . . 39
  s. 1 . . . 39, 191, 192, 193, 551
  s. 2 . . . 39
  s. 3 . . . 253, 254, 256, 258, 261
  s. 3(1) . . . 253, 254, 258
  s. 3(2) . . . 253
  s. 3(3) . . . 253
  s. 3(3)(b) . . . 258
  s. 3(4) . . . 253
Congenital Disabilities (Civil Liability) Act 1976 . . . 130–2, 133, 1003
  s. 1 . . . 130–1, 566
  s. 1(1) . . . 130
  s. 1(2) . . . 130, 132
  s. 1(2)(a) . . . 133
  s. 1(2)(b) . . . 133
  s. 1(3) . . . 130, 132
  s. 1(4) . . . 130, 132
  s. 1(5) . . . 130
  s. 1(6) . . . 130, 132
  s. 1(7) . . . 131, 132
  s. 1A . . . 131, 132, 133
  s. 1A(1) . . . 131
  s. 1A(2) . . . 131
  s. 1A(3) . . . 131

Congenital Disabilities (Civil Liability) Act 1976 *(Cont.)*
   s. 1A(4) ... 131
   s. 2 ... 131, 132
   s. 4(1) ... 131
   s. 4(2) ... 131
   s. 4(3) ... 132
   s. 4(5) ... 132
Consumer Protection Act 1987 ... 119, 524, 555, 560, 562–92, 597, 600, 601
   Pt I (ss. 1–9) ... 591
   s. 1 ... 563
   s. 1(1) ... 562, 563
   s. 1(2) ... 563, 569, 570
   s. 1(3) ... 563
   s. 2 ... 569
   s. 2(1) ... 563, 575
   s. 2(2) ... 563, 569, 575
   s. 2(3) ... 563–4, 570
   s. 2(5) ... 564
   s. 2(6) ... 564
   s. 3 ... 564, 571, 575, 576
   s. 3(1) ... 564, 576
   s. 3(1)(a) ... 577
   s. 3(2) ... 564, 577
   s. 3(2)(a) ... 571, 577
   s. 3(2)(b) ... 584
   s. 4 ... 564–5, 586
   s. 4(1) ... 564–5
   s. 4(1)(a) ... 586
   s. 4(1)(c) ... 586
   s. 4(1)(d) ... 586, 596
   s. 4(1)(e) ... 587, 588, 589, 590
   s. 4(2) ... 565
   s. 5 ... 565, 584
   s. 5(1) ... 565
   s. 5(2) ... 565, 584
   s. 5(3) ... 565, 584
   s. 5(4) ... 565, 585
   s. 5(5) ... 565
   s. 5(6) ... 565
   s. 5(7) ... 566
   s. 6(1) ... 566
   s. 6(2) ... 566
   s. 6(3) ... 566
   s. 6(4) ... 566, 584
   s. 6(5) ... 566
   s. 7 ... 326, 566
   s. 45(1) ... 567
   s. 46 ... 570, 584
   s. 46(1) ... 567
   s. 46(3) ... 567
   s. 46(4) ... 567
   s. 46(8) ... 567
   s. 46(9) ... 567
Consumer Rights Act 2015 ... 296, 321, 323–6, 543, 553
   s. 2 ... 325
   s. 2(2) ... 323
   s. 2(3) ... 323
   s. 2(4) ... 323
   s. 2(7) ... 323
   ss. 9–11 ... 560
   Pt 2 (ss. 61–76) ... 543
   s. 61 ... 323, 324, 325, 543
   s. 61(1) ... 324
   s. 61(2) ... 324
   s. 61(3) ... 324
   s. 61(4) ... 324
   s. 61(5) ... 324
   s. 61(6) ... 324
   s. 61(7) ... 324
   s. 61(8) ... 324
   s. 62 ... 322, 325, 543
   s. 62(1) ... 324
   s. 62(2) ... 324
   s. 62(3) ... 324
   s. 62(4) ... 324
   s. 62(5) ... 324
   s. 62(8) ... 324
   s. 65 ... 322, 324–5, 543
   s. 65(1) ... 324
   s. 65(2) ... 324
   s. 65(3) ... 325
   s. 65(4) ... 325
   s. 65(5) ... 325
   s. 65(6) ... 325
   s. 66(4) ... 325, 326, 543
   s. 68 ... 325
   s. 68(1) ... 325
   s. 68(2) ... 325
   s. 69(1) ... 325
Contagious Diseases (Animals) Act 1869 ... 617
   s. 75 ... 618
Contracts (Rights of Third Parties) Act 1999 ... 464
   s. 1(1)(b) ... 464
Copyright, Designs and Patents Act 1988
   Pt I (ss. 1–179) ... 764
Countryside and Rights of Way Act 2000 ... 554–5
   Pt 1 (ss. 1–46) ... 545, 546
   s. 2 ... 555
   s. 2(1) ... 528, 545, 546
   s. 16 ... 546
   s. 20 ... 546
County Courts Acts (1846–) ... 13
County Courts Act 1984
   s. 51 ... 899
   s. 51(1)–(2) ... 899
Courts Act 2003 ... 899, 903, 917, 918
   s. 100 ... 901
Courts and Legal Services Act 1990
   s. 8 ... 776
   s. 58 ... 982
   s. 58A ... 982
   s. 58AA ... 983
   s. 58C ... 982
Crime and Courts Act 2013
   s. 34 ... 889, 893
   ss. 34–38 ... 767
   s. 34(1)(c) ... 889
   s. 34(6) ... 889
   ss. 41–42 ... 767

Criminal Injuries Compensation Act
1995 ... 1005
Criminal Justice Act 2003
   s. 329 ... 80, 104, 105
   s. 329(8)(b) ... 104
Criminal Justice and Courts Act 2015
   s. 33 ... 78
   s. 57 ... 974
   s. 57(1) ... 974
   s. 57(2) ... 974
   s. 57(3) ... 974
   s. 57(4) ... 974
   s. 57(5) ... 974
Criminal Law Act 1967
   s. 3 ... 105
Crown Proceedings Act 1947 ... 159

Damages Act 1996 ... 901–2, 916
   s. 1 ... 916, 925
   s. 1(2) ... 925
   s. 2 ... 903, 917, 953
   s. 2(1) ... 901, 903
   s. 2(2) ... 901, 903
   s. 2(3) ... 902, 903
   s. 2(4) ... 903
   s. 2(6) ... 904
   s. 2(8) ... 902, 919
   s. 2(9) ... 902, 919
   s. 7 ... 953
Damages (Scotland) Act 2011 (ASP 7) ... 563
   s. 4 ... 961
Data Protection Act 1998 ... 790, 855
Defamation Act 1952
   s. 2 ... 703
   s. 3(1) ... 787
   s. 4 ... 726, 762
   s. 5 ... 738, 740
   s. 6 ... 743, 745
   s. 7 ... 751
Defamation Act 1996 ... 750, 751, 769, 772
   s. 1 ... 733, 763, 764, 765, 766
   s. 1(1) ... 764
   s. 1(2) ... 764
   s. 1(3) ... 764
   s. 1(4) ... 764
   s. 1(5) ... 764
   s. 2 ... 726, 729, 761
   s. 2(1) ... 761
   s. 2(2) ... 761
   s. 2(3) ... 761
   s. 2(4) ... 761
   s. 3(1) ... 761
   s. 3(2) ... 761
   s. 3(3) ... 761
   s. 3(4) ... 761
   s. 3(5) ... 762, 763
   s. 3(6) ... 762
   s. 3(10) ... 762
   s. 4 ... 762
   s. 4(1) ... 762
   s. 4(2) ... 762
   s. 4(3) ... 762, 763
   s. 4(4) ... 762
   s. 4(5) ... 762
   ss. 8–9 ... 772
   s. 14 ... 743, 747
   ss. 14–15 ... 742
   s. 15 ... 743, 747, 751, 772
   s. 15(1) ... 751
   s. 15(2) ... 751
   s. 15(3) ... 751, 752
   s. 15(4) ... 751
   Sch. 1 ... 751
      Pt I ... 751
      Pt II ... 751
Defamation Act 2013 ... 32, 698, 702, 703, 704, 705, 706, 709, 710, 711, 712, 740, 745, 746, 751, 755, 766, 772, 775, 779, 781
   s. 1 ... 704, 705, 708, 709, 710, 711, 763, 767
   s. 1(1) ... 705, 708, 709, 726
   s. 1(2) ... 708, 709, 710, 713, 779
   s. 2 ... 738
   s. 2(1) ... 738, 741
   s. 2(2) ... 738, 740
   s. 2(3) ... 738, 740
   s. 2(4) ... 738
   s. 3 ... 743
   s. 3(1) ... 743
   s. 3(2) ... 743
   s. 3(3) ... 743
   s. 3(4) ... 743
   s. 3(4)(b) ... 746
   s. 3(5) ... 743, 746
   s. 3(6) ... 743, 746
   s. 3(7) ... 743, 757
   s. 3(8) ... 743
   s. 4 ... 746, 757
   s. 4(1) ... 757
   s. 4(1)(b) ... 758, 759, 760
   s. 4(2) ... 757, 759, 760
   s. 4(3) ... 757, 760
   s. 4(4) ... 757
   s. 4(5) ... 757
   s. 4(6) ... 757
   s. 5(1) ... 766
   s. 5(2) ... 766
   s. 5(3) ... 766
   s. 5(4) ... 766
   s. 5(6) ... 766
   s. 6 ... 752
   s. 6(1) ... 752
   s. 6(2) ... 752
   s. 6(3) ... 752
   s. 6(6) ... 752
   s. 7 ... 751
   s. 7(1) ... 747
   s. 8 ... 737
   s. 8(1) ... 737
   s. 8(2) ... 737
   s. 8(3) ... 737
   s. 8(4) ... 737
   s. 8(5) ... 737
   s. 10 ... 765, 766
   s. 10(1) ... 765

Defamation Act 2013 (Cont.)
    s. 10(2)...765
    s. 11...61, 706, 718, 721, 770
    s. 12...772
    s. 14...699
    s. 14(1)...703
    s. 14(2)...703
Defective Premises Act 1972...405, 409, 412, 415–17
    s. 1...412, 416
    s. 1(1)...416
    s. 1(4)...416
    s. 1(5)...416
    s. 2...412, 416
    s. 2A...416
    s. 4...534
    s. 4(1)...534

Employers' Liability Act 1880...603
Employers' Liability (Compulsory Insurance) Act 1969...16, 611, 612
Employers' Liability (Defective Equipment) Act 1969...874
    s. 1(2)...326
Enterprise and Regulatory Reform Act 2013
    s. 69...606, 999
Environmental Protection Act 1990...626
    s. 73(6)...690
    s. 79(1)...626
Equality Act 2010...706
    s. 109...845
European Union (Withdrawal) Act 2018
    s. 6...562

Factory and Workshop Act 1878...605, 614
    s. 5...604, 605
    s. 5(3)...604
    s. 5(4)...613
    s. 6(3)...613
    s. 81...605
    s. 82...604, 605
    s. 86...605
    s. 87...605
Factory and Workshop Act 1891
    s. 6(2)...604
    s. 6(4)...604
Family Law Act 1996...659
    s. 30...662
    s. 31...662
Family Law Reform Act 1969...100
Fatal Accidents Act 1846 (Lord Campbell's Act)...940, 944, 947, 948, 950, 952
    s. 1...922
Fatal Accidents Acts 1846–1908...283, 531
Fatal Accidents Acts 1846–1976...80, 921, 941
Fatal Accidents Act 1976...79, 281, 563, 566, 924, 925, 929, 933, 935, 940, 943, 944, 948–63
    s. 1...922, 948–9
    s. 1(1)...943, 948, 950, 951
    s. 1(2)...948, 951, 962

    s. 1(3)...948–9, 962
    s. 1(4)...949
    s. 1(4A)...949
    s. 1(5)...949
    s. 1(6)...949
    s. 1A...940, 943, 961, 962
    s. 1A(1)...961
    s. 1A(2)...961
    s. 1A(2)(aa)...962
    s. 1A(2A)...961, 962
    s. 1A(3)...961
    s. 1A(4)...961
    s. 1A(5)...961
    s. 2...949
    s. 2(1)...949
    s. 2(2)...949
    s. 2(3)...949
    s. 2(4)...949
    s. 3...949–50, 956
    s. 3(1)...949
    s. 3(2)...949
    s. 3(3)...950, 954
    s. 3(4)...950
    s. 3(5)...950, 953
    s. 3(6)...950
    s. 4...950, 954, 955, 956, 957, 958, 959, 960
    s. 4(1)...958
    s. 5...566, 599, 950
    ss. 7–8...962
Financial Services Act 2012
    s. 25...142
    s. 33...142
Financial Services and Markets Act 2000
    s. 150...607
Fire Services Act 1947
    s. 30(2)–(3)...479
Forfeiture Act 1982...337, 344

Gas Act 1965
    s. 14...999
Gulf Oil Refining Act 1965...671

Health and Safety at Work etc. Act 1974...606
    s. 47(2)...606
Health and Social Care (Community Health and Standards) Act 2003...927–9
    s. 150(1)...927
    s. 150(2)...928
    s. 150(3)...928
    s. 150(3)(b)...929
    s. 150(4)...928
    s. 150(5)...928, 929
    s. 150(6)...928
    s. 153(3)...929
    Sch. 10...928
Highways Act 1980...554
    s. 41...508, 554
    s. 58...554
Housing Act 1977...616
Housing Act 1985...615
    Pt III (ss. 58–78)...615
    s. 62...614

TABLE OF LEGISLATION

s. 62(1) ... 615
s. 63(1) ... 614, 615
s. 65 ... 615
Housing (Homeless Persons) Act 1977 ... 616
Human Fertilisation and Embryology Act 1990 ... 132
  s. 1 ... 131
  s. 1(6) ... 131
Human Fertilisation and Embryology Act 2008
  s. 43 ... 949
Human Rights Act 1998 ... 28–32, 78, 85, 158, 166–70, 477, 498, 508, 515, 516, 522, 523, 626, 655, 664, 665, 726, 729, 730, 736, 750, 769, 774, 775, 778, 779, 782, 789, 791, 794, 795, 799, 814, 815, 962
  s. 1(1) ... 28
  s. 1A ... 963
  s. 2 ... 30
  s. 2(1) ... 28–9, 814
  s. 3 ... 29, 30, 671, 963
  s. 3(1) ... 29
  s. 3(2) ... 29
  s. 4 ... 962
  s. 6 ... 30, 166, 167, 791, 792, 796, 799
  s. 6(1) ... 29, 814
  s. 6(2) ... 29
  s. 6(3) ... 29, 814
  s. 6(5) ... 29
  s. 6(6) ... 29
  s. 7 ... 30, 522, 664, 791, 792, 962
  s. 7(1) ... 29, 167, 962
  s. 7(6) ... 29
  s. 8 ... 30, 522, 665
  s. 8(1) ... 30, 167
  s. 8(2) ... 30
  s. 8(3) ... 30
  s. 9 ... 30, 982
  s. 11 ... 30
  s. 12 ... 32, 773
  s. 12(3) ... 773, 812
  s. 12(4) ... 806, 807, 808
  s. 12(4)(b) ... 802
  Sch. 1 ... 982

Immigration Act 1971 ... 60
Imprisonment (Temporary Provisions) Act 1980
  s. 6 ... 83

Judicature Act 1873 ... 2, 3, 9, 11, 13, 674
Judicature Act 1875 ... 2, 3, 9, 13, 674

Latent Damage Act 1986 ... 416
Law of Libel Amendment Act 1888 ... 751
Law Reform (Contributory Negligence) Act 1945 ... 80, 279, 281, 308–12, 315, 317, 566, 599
  s. 1 ... 314
  s. 1(1) ... 80, 308–9, 310, 311, 317, 319, 950
  s. 1(2) ... 309
  s. 1(4) ... 80
  s. 1(5) ... 309
  s. 1(6) ... 309
  s. 4 ... 80, 309
Law Reform (Limitation of Actions, etc) Act 1954
  s. 2(1) ... 44, 45, 46
Law Reform (Miscellaneous Provisions) Act 1934 ... 531, 566, 921, 940–1, 943–4, 950
  s. 1 ... 944
  s. 1(1) ... 940, 941
  s. 1(1A) ... 940
  s. 1(2) ... 940–1
  s. 1(2)(c) ... 943
  s. 1(4) ... 941
  s. 1(5) ... 941
Law Reform (Personal Injuries) Act 1948 ... 605
  s. 1 ... 874
  s. 1(3) ... 326
  s. 2(1) ... 938
  s. 2(4) ... 926
Legal Aid, Sentencing and Punishment of Offenders Act 2012 ... 908, 976, 982
  s. 44 ... 982
  s. 45 ... 983
  s. 46 ... 982
  s. 55 ... 989
  ss. 56–60 ... 972
Legal Services Act 2007
  Pt V (ss. 71–111) ... 973
Limitation Act 1939 ... 44
Limitation Act 1975 ... 46
Limitation Act 1980
  s. 2 ... 46
  s. 4A ... 737
  s. 11 ... 46
  s. 11(4)(b) ... 46
  s. 11A(4) ... 585, 586
  s. 14 ... 46
  s. 14A ... 416
  s. 14B ... 416
  s. 33 ... 46, 586
Limited Liability Partnerships Act 2000 ... 443
Local Government Act 1972
  s. 222 ... 626
Locomotives on Highways Act 1896 ... 610
  s. 6 ... 609
  s. 6(1) ... 609
  s. 7 ... 609
Lord Cairns' Act 1858 ... 675
  s. 2 ... 674
Lord Campbell's Act see Fatal Accidents Act 1846

Maritime Conventions Act 1911 ... 308
Matrimonial Homes Act 1983 ... 659, 661
Mental Capacity Act 2005 ... 95–101
  s. 1 ... 95
  s. 1(1) ... 95
  s. 1(2) ... 95
  s. 1(3) ... 95
  s. 1(4) ... 95

Mental Capacity Act 2005 *(Cont.)*
    s. 1(5)...95
    s. 1(6)...95
    s. 2(1)...95
    s. 2(2)...95
    s. 2(3)...95
    s. 2(4)...95
    s. 3...95–6
    s. 3(1)...95–6, 99
    s. 3(2)...96
    s. 3(3)...96
    s. 3(4)...96
    s. 4...61, 96–7
    s. 4(1)...96
    s. 4(2)...96
    s. 4(3)...96, 100
    s. 4(3)(a)...97
    s. 4(4)...96
    s. 4(5)...96
    s. 4(6)...96
    s. 4(6)(a)...98
    s. 4(7)...96–7
    s. 4(8)...97
    s. 4(9)...97
    s. 4(10)...97
    s. 4(11)...97
    s. 4A...61
    s. 5...97, 98, 100
    s. 5(1)...97
    s. 5(2)...97
    s. 5(3)...97
    s. 5(4)...97
    Sch. A1...62
Mental Health Act 1983...99, 336
    s. 37...336, 337
    s. 41...336, 337
Mesothelioma Act 2014...265
Misrepresentation Act 1967
    s. 3...322
Misrepresentation Act (Northern Ireland) 1967
    s. 3...322

National Health Service Act 1977...480
    s. 1...480
    s. 3(1)...480
National Health Service Act 2006...926
National Parks and Access to the Countryside Act 1949...528
NHS Redress Act 2006...926, 1006
    s. 3(3)(a)...927
Northern Ireland (Emergency Provisions) Act 1987
    s. 15...614
Nuclear Installations Act 1965...999
    s. 7...690

Occupiers' Liability Act 1957...190, 191, 321, 489, 524, 525, 527–43, 544, 546, 548, 550, 553, 554, 555, 569, 601
    s. 1...527–8, 530
    s. 1(1)...527, 534, 536
    s. 1(2)...527
    s. 1(3)...528, 536
    s. 1(3)(a)...536
    s. 1(3)(b)...536
    s. 1(4)...528
    s. 2...528–9, 530, 545, 551, 552
    s. 2(1)...326, 528, 543
    s. 2(2)...528, 535, 537, 540, 548, 550
    s. 2(3)...528, 537
    s. 2(3)(a)...537
    s. 2(3)(b)...538, 539
    s. 2(4)...528, 532, 537, 540
    s. 2(4)(a)...539
    s. 2(4)(b)...540
    s. 2(5)...528, 543
    s. 2(6)...529, 530
    s. 3...529
    s. 3(1)...529
    s. 3(2)...529
    s. 3(3)...529
    s. 3(4)...529
    s. 3(5)...529
    s. 4...532, 534
    s. 5...529, 530
    s. 5(1)...529
    s. 5(2)...529
    s. 5(3)...529
    s. 5(4)...529
Occupiers' Liability Act 1984...190, 191, 489, 524, 525, 530, 535, 544–55, 569, 601
    s. 1(1)...545, 546
    s. 1(1)(a)...536, 551
    s. 1(2)...545
    s. 1(3)...536, 545, 547, 551, 552
    s. 1(3)(a)...547
    s. 1(3)(b)...547
    s. 1(3)(c)...547, 550, 551, 553
    s. 1(4)...545, 547, 551
    s. 1(5)...545, 550, 552
    s. 1(6)...545, 552
    s. 1(6A)...545, 555
    s. 1(6AA)...546
    s. 1(6B)...546
    s. 1(6C)...546
    s. 1(7)...546, 554
    s. 1(8)...546, 553
    s. 1(9)...546
    s. 1A...546, 555
Occupiers' Liability Act (Northern Ireland) 1957...321
Offences Against the Person Act 1861...51
    ss. 44–45...79
    s. 47...57

Parliamentary Papers Act 1840
    s. 1...747
Planning Act 2008...672
    s. 158...671, 672
Police and Criminal Evidence Act 1984...64, 81
    s. 1...81
    s. 24...63, 81
    s. 24A...81
    s. 117...81

Prescription Act 1832 ... 667
Prison Act 1952
   s. 12 ... 83
   s. 12(1) ... 81, 82, 83
   s. 13 ... 82
Protection from Harassment Act 1997 ... 67, 76–9, 664, 790, 793
   s. 1 ... 76, 77
   s. 1(1) ... 68, 76
   s. 1(1A) ... 76, 78, 79
   s. 1(2) ... 76
   s. 1(3) ... 76
   s. 1(3)(c) ... 78
   s. 3(1) ... 76
   s. 3(2) ... 68, 76, 78
   s. 3(3)–(9) ... 78
   s. 3A(1) ... 76
   s. 3A(2) ... 76
   s. 7 ... 76–7, 79
   s. 7(1) ... 76
   s. 7(2) ... 76, 77
   s. 7(3) ... 68, 77
   s. 7(3A) ... 77
   s. 7(4) ... 77
   s. 7(5) ... 77, 78
Public Health Act 1936 ... 406, 407, 408

Race Relations Act 1976 ... 845
Rehabilitation of Offenders Act 1974 ... 738
   s. 8 ... 742
Road Traffic Act 1930 ... 16
   s. 35 ... 611
   s. 35(1) ... 611
Road Traffic Act 1972
   s. 148 ... 301
Road Traffic Act 1988
   s. 39 ... 508
   s. 143 ... 16, 597, 600
   s. 149 ... 326
   s. 157 ... 927
   ss. 158–159 ... 927
Road Traffic (NHS Charges) Act 1999 ... 927

Sale of Goods Act 1979 ... 323, 570
   ss. 13–15 ... 560
Senior Courts Act 1981
   s. 32A ... 899
   s. 50 ... 674
   s. 69 ... 175, 706
   s. 69(1) ... 718
Sexual Offences Act 2003 ... 87
Slander of Women Act 1891 ... 699, 703
   s. 1 ... 703
Social Action, Responsibility and Heroism Act 2015 ... 39, 191–4
   s. 1 ... 191, 475
   s. 2 ... 192, 193
   s. 3 ... 192, 193
   s. 4 ... 192, 193, 475

Social Security (Recovery of Benefits) Act 1997 ... 936–9
   s. 1 ... 936
   s. 1(1) ... 936
   s. 1(1)(b) ... 938
   s. 1(2) ... 936, 939
   s. 1(3) ... 936
   s. 1(4) ... 936
   s. 1(4)(c) ... 938
   s. 3 ... 936–7, 938
   s. 3(1) ... 936
   s. 3(2) ... 936
   s. 3(3) ... 936
   s. 3(4) ... 937
   s. 4 ... 939
   s. 4(1) ... 937, 939
   s. 6 ... 939
   s. 6(1) ... 937, 939
   s. 8 ... 937, 938
   s. 8(1) ... 937
   s. 8(2) ... 937
   s. 8(3) ... 937
   s. 8(4) ... 937
   s. 8(5) ... 937
   Sch. 1 ... 939
   Sch. 2 ... 938, 939
Street Offences Act 1959 ... 53

Theatres Act 1968
   s. 4(1) ... 700

Unfair Contract Terms Act 1977 ... 296, 321–3, 325–6, 432, 543, 553
   s. 1(1) ... 321
   s. 1(3) ... 321–2, 325
   s. 1(3)(b) ... 325, 543
   s. 1(4) ... 322
   s. 2 ... 322, 325, 543
   s. 2(1) ... 322, 325, 326, 543
   s. 2(2) ... 322, 325, 543
   s. 2(3) ... 322
   s. 2(4) ... 322
   s. 11 ... 322–3
   s. 11(1) ... 322
   s. 11(2) ... 322
   s. 11(3) ... 322
   s. 11(4) ... 322–3
   s. 11(5) ... 323
   s. 13(1) ... 323
   s. 13(2) ... 323
   s. 14 ... 323

Water Industry Act 1991
   s. 209 ... 690
Water Resources Act 1991
   s. 85(1) ... 274
Waterworks Clauses Act 1847
   s. 35 ... 603
   s. 42 ... 603
Workmen's Compensation Act 1897 ... 603, 606, 1001

Table of Statutes from Other Jurisdictions

Australia
Civil Liability Act 1936 (South Australia) . . . 371
Civil Liability Act 2002 (NSW)
  s. 5L . . . 41
  s. 5M . . . 41
  s. 15B . . . 933
  s. 16 . . . 909
  Pt 3 (ss. 27–33) . . . 393
  s. 42 . . . 41
  s. 45 . . . 41
  ss. 70–71 . . . 134

France
Code civil . . . 1, 122, 475
Code pénal
  Art. 222-6 . . . 475

Germany
Bürgerliches Gesetzbuch (BGB) (Civil Code) . . . 1, 120, 122, 394
  Art. 823 I . . . 120, 122, 394

New Zealand
Accident Compensation Act 2001 . . . 1008
Accident Insurance Act 1998 . . . 1008
Accident Rehabilitation and Compensation Insurance Act 1992 . . . 1008, 1010, 1011

Social Security Act 1938 . . . 1007

Workers' Compensation Act 1900 . . . 1007

Trinidad & Tobago
Constitution . . . 897

United States of America
Constitution of the United States . . . 777, 780
  1st Amendment . . . 780, 788
  14th Amendment . . . 780, 895

Restatement of the Law of Torts, 2d (1977) . . . 794
  § 402A(1) . . . 560
  § 652A . . . 792
  § 652D . . . 797
Restatement of the Law of Torts, 3d: Liability for Physical and Emotional Harm (2010) . . . 47–8
  § 1 . . . 47
  § 29 . . . 283
  § 38 . . . 475
  § 46 . . . 74

Table of Statutory Instruments

Civil Procedure (Amendment) Rules 2013 (SI 2013/262) . . . 982, 989
Civil Procedure Rules 1998 (SI 1998/3132) . . . 902, 975, 976, 978
  Pt 26
    r. 26.6(1)ff . . . 975, 984
  Pt 27
    PD 27B . . . 975, 984
  Pt 28, r. 28 . . . 979
  Pt 36 . . . 989
    r. 36.17 . . . 989
  Pt 41 . . . 903
    r. 41.2 . . . 899
    r. 41.3 . . . 899
    r. 41.3(2) . . . 899
    r. 41.3A . . . 953
    r. 41.7 . . . 903
    r. 41.8(2) . . . 925
    r. 41.8(3) . . . 904
    PD 41 . . . 899
    PD 41B . . . 903
  Pt 44
    r. 44.14 . . . 989
    r. 44.14(1) . . . 982
  Pt 45
    Section III (rr. 45.16–45.29L) . . . 983
    r. 45.19(2A) . . . 973
    Section VI (rr. 45.37–45.40) . . . 983
  Pt 53, PD 53, para. 2.3 . . . 724
Criminal Injuries Compensation Scheme 2012 (Amendment) Instrument 2019 . . . 1005

Damages for Bereavement (Variation of Sum) (England and Wales) Order 2020 (SI 2020/316) . . . 961
Damages (Personal Injury) Order 2001 (SI 2001/2301) . . . 916
Damages (Personal Injury) Order 2017 (SI 2017/206) . . . 916
Damages (Personal Injury) Order 2019 (SI 2019/1126) . . . 916
Damages (Variation of Periodical Payments) Order 2005 (SI 2005/841) . . . 902–3, 904
  Art. 1(2) . . . 902
  Art. 2 . . . 902, 904
  Art. 5 . . . 902
  Art. 7 . . . 903
  Art. 9 . . . 904
Diffuse Mesothelioma Payment Scheme Regulations 2014 (SI 2014/916) . . . 265

Electronic Commerce (EC Directive) Regulations 2002 (SI 2002/2013) . . . 766
  regs. 17–19 . . . 735

TABLE OF LEGISLATION

European Communities (Rights against Insurers) Regulations 2002 (SI 2002/3061)... 26

Fatal Accidents Act 1976 (Remedial) Order 2020 (SI 2020/1023)... 962

Management of Health and Safety at Work Regulations 1999 (SI 1999/3242)
reg. 22... 606
Motor Cars (Use and Construction) Order 1904
Art. II
cl. 6... 609

National Health Service (Concerns, Complaints and Redress Arrangements) (Wales) Regulations 2011 (SI 2011/704) (W.108)... 927, 1006

Personal Injuries (NHS Charges) (Amounts) Regulations 2007 (SI 2007/115)
reg. 2... 929
Sch. 1... 929
Prison Rules 1964 (SI 1964/388)... 81, 82, 613
r. 8(1)... 613
r. 43... 613
r. 43(2)... 612, 613

Quarries (Explosives) Regulations 1959 (SI 1959/2259)... 303

Whiplash Injury Regulations 2021 (SI 2021/642)... 975
r. 2... 908
r. 3... 908

Table of European Legislation

Directive 85/374/EEC (Product Liability Directive)... 555, 561, 562, 563, 569, 570, 571, 572, 573, 575, 576, 577, 578, 579, 580, 581, 583, 586, 587, 590, 591, 592, 593, 594, 595, 596, 999
Art. 1... 568
Art. 2... 568, 570
Art. 4... 568, 573
Art. 6... 568, 572, 573, 574, 576
Art. 7... 568, 587, 589
Art. 7(e)... 588, 589
Art. 8... 568
Art. 8(1)... 585
Art. 9... 584
Directive 99/34/EC (amending the Product Liability Directive)... 570
Directive 2009/103/EC (Motor Insurance Directive)... 595

Table of International Treaties and Conventions

European Convention for the Protection of Human Rights and Fundamental Freedoms 1950... 28, 30, 31, 32, 65, 78, 166, 167, 168, 169, 170, 516, 665, 671, 773, 774, 775–6, 778, 791, 794, 796, 799, 802, 804, 808, 814, 951, 962
Art. 2... 30, 31, 168, 522, 962, 963
Arts. 2–12... 28
Art 3... 31, 168, 791
Art. 5... 30, 31, 85
Art. 6... 30, 747
Art. 8... 30, 31, 170, 626, 664, 665, 671, 698, 744, 747, 750, 782, 789, 791, 792, 796, 797, 798, 799, 804, 805, 806, 807, 809, 812, 815, 889, 951, 962
Art. 8(1)... 782, 791, 796
Art. 8(2)... 31, 782, 791, 796, 797
Art. 10... 30, 31, 32, 78, 698, 726, 729, 736, 775–6, 778, 779, 796, 798, 804, 806, 807, 809, 812, 815, 889
Art. 10(1)... 78, 775, 797
Art. 10(2)... 729, 775–6, 797
Art. 11... 78
Art. 13... 814
Art. 14... 28, 951, 962
Arts. 16–18... 28
Art. 26... 28
Art. 27(2)... 28
Art. 31... 28
Art 41... 963
Art. 46... 28
Protocol 1
Art. 1... 671
Arts. 1–3... 28
Protocol 6
Arts. 1–2... 28

Hague Rules 1924... 139

Table of Court Rules and Practice Guidance

Practice Guidance (Interim Non-disclosure Orders) [2012] 1 WLR 1003... 812

Rules of the Supreme Court
Ord 53... 616

1 GENERAL INTRODUCTION

I. Historical Development of Tort Law

1. Origins of Tort Law

The law of tort—the word derives from the French for 'wrong'—is the law of civil liability for wrongfully inflicted injury, or at least a very large part of it. (Breach of contract and breach of trust are perhaps the other two most important civil wrongs.) Tort itself is a very old legal concept, older even than the concept of crime. According to Sir Henry Maine, 'the penal law of ancient communities is not the law of crimes; it is the law of wrongs, or, to use the English technical word, of torts' (*Ancient Law* (1861), p. 328). It developed in the days before states were sufficiently organised to have a centralised prosecuting authority; the only alternative was to leave the task of punishing wrongful conduct to private individuals. The existence of such remedies was necessary for the maintenance of public order, for in their absence feuds and acts of unrestrained vengeance would no doubt have been common. Tort was a form of legalised self-help. For the injured party, the incentive was often not only the award of compensation, but also the entitlement to an additional punitive element of damages. Under Roman law's action for theft (*actio furti*), for instance, the plaintiff was entitled to recover at least 'double damages', i.e. twice the worth of the thing stolen. Indeed, where the defendant was caught red-handed (in a case of 'manifest theft') fourfold damages would be awarded. As the temptation to take the law into one's own hands would be at its strongest in such a case, a greater than usual incentive was required to ensure that the matter was resolved by lawful means.

Although the Roman law of tort—or 'delict', as it is more usually called—developed in piecemeal fashion, the civilian jurisdictions which took it as their model sought to systematise the principles of tortious liability, eliminating its anomalies and diminishing its complexity (following the analysis of the great natural lawyers such as Grotius). Their Codes—which mainly date from the Napoleonic era and thereafter—reduce the law of tort to its bare essentials. Until recently, it could be said that '[a]lmost the whole of the French law of delict rests on a mere five articles in the *Code Civile* which have remained in force virtually unchanged for 195 years' (K. Zweigert and H. Kötz, *An Introduction to Comparative Law*, 3rd edn, trans. T. Weir (Oxford: OUP, 1998), p. 615). Those articles remain substantially unchanged, but are now incorporated in a revised Code of 2016, which adds additional provisions to make a whopping thirteen articles in all. The revised code retains a broad general clause imposing liability for all damage caused by fault. By contrast, the German *Bürgerliches Gesetzbuch* (BGB) has a more intricate structure, with no single liability for fault; instead, tortious liability primarily rests on three 'more limited but still broad' principles. The other civilian jurisdictions in Europe (not including Scotland whose law of delict is in many respects very close to the English law of tort) take varying positions, some more closely aligned with the French approach, some with the German.

The English law of tort stands in stark contrast. 'The Common Law of Torts started out by having specific types of liability just like Roman law, but, whereas on the Continent legal scholars ironed out the old distinctions between the several delicts to the point where a general principle of delictual liability became not only a possibility but an actuality in most legal systems, Anglo-American lawyers have largely adhered to the separate types of case and separate torts which developed under the writ system' (Zweigert and Kötz, *op. cit.*, p. 605). It is perhaps this lack of principle which led the great American judge and jurist, Oliver Wendell Holmes, to pronounce: 'Torts is not a proper subject for a law book' ((1871) 5 Am L Rev 340). Holmes nevertheless overcame his early prejudice, and wrote—in his masterly analysis *The Common Law* (originally published in 1881)—an account of the law of torts which remains a rewarding and insightful read today.

Holmes set himself the task of discovering 'whether there is any common ground at the bottom of all liability in tort, and if so, what that ground is' (*The Common Law*, p. 77). He considered that this was not an easy task: 'The law did not begin with a theory. It has never worked one out' (*ibid.*). He found that discussions of general principle had been 'darkened' by historical controversies that had no contemporary relevance (*ibid.*, p. 78). Nevertheless, he felt that a full account of the law required a knowledge of its history, asserting at the beginning of his great work that '[i]n order to know what it is, we must know what it has been' (*ibid.*, p. 1). Accordingly it is with the historical development of the English law of torts through the forms of action that we begin.

2. The Forms of Action

For most of its history, English common law developed through the procedural mechanisms used to bring an action before the courts. These were known as the forms of action, the writs that it was necessary to purchase from the Chancery so that an action could be commenced in the royal courts. At the very beginnings of the common law these writs were drawn up on an ad-hoc basis, but this soon became impractical and standard-form writs began to develop. Writs set out in a formulaic style the gist of the plaintiff's complaint and instructed the local sheriff to summon the defendant to answer the allegation. There were different writs for different actions within what later became known as the law of tort. It was during this period that the foundations of modern tort law were set down. Although the forms of action were abolished by the Judicature Acts of 1873 and 1875, an understanding of modern tort law is impossible without an appreciation of the writ system and of the most important forms of action that developed under it. Amongst these, undisputed pride of place goes to the writ of trespass—'that fertile mother of actions', to use Maitland's phrase—from which developed the more flexible writ of trespass on the plaintiff's special case (the action on the case or—more simply—'case').

(a) The Writ of Trespass

The writ of trespass was one of the original royal writs (issued in the Crown's name) and it became relatively common after 1250. Trespass was a writ of wrong rather than a writ of right: it complained of a wrong rather than demanded the reinstatement of a right. The mode of trial was by jury and the remedy was damages. A number of different forms of trespass were recognised. The writ of trespass *quare clausum fregit* corresponds to the modern tort of trespass to land; that of trespass *de bonis asportatis* to the modern trespass to goods. The writs dealing with trespass to the person took various forms, corresponding to the modern torts of assault, battery and false imprisonment. What all of them had in common was a requirement that the defendant had acted *vi et armis* ('with force and arms') and *contra pacem* ('in breach of the [king's] peace'). The writ of trespass *vi et armis* for battery, for example, required the defendant 'to show why with force and arms he made assault on the [plaintiff] at [a particular place] and beat, wounded and ill-treated him so that his life was despaired of, and offered other outrages against him, to the grave damage of the self-same [plaintiff] and against our peace' (see *Baker*, p. 585). These requirements were imposed in order to prevent the King's Courts being overwhelmed with business; cases not involving violence and a threat to public safety were left to be dealt with in the local courts.

F. Maitland, *The Forms of Action at Common Law* (Cambridge: CUP, 1909)

What was a form of action? Already owing to modern reforms [the Judicature Acts of 1873 and 1875] it is impossible to assume that every law student must have heard or read or discovered for himself an answer to that question, but it is still one which must be answered if he is to have more than a very superficial knowledge of our law as it stands even at the present day. The forms of action we have buried, but they still rule us from their graves. Let us then for a while place ourselves in Blackstone's day, or, for this matters not, some seventy years later in 1830, and let us look for a moment at English civil procedure.

Let it be granted that one man has been wronged by another; the first thing that he or his advisers have to consider is what form of action he shall bring. It is not enough that in some way or another he should compel his adversary to appear in court and should then state in the words that naturally occur to him the facts on which he relies and the remedy to which he thinks himself entitled. No, English law knows a certain number of forms of action, each with its own uncouth name, a writ of right, an assize of novel disseisin or of *mort d'ancestor*, a writ of entry *sur disseisin* in the *per* and *cui*, a writ of besaiel, of *quare impedit*, an action of covenant, debt, detinue, replevin, trespass, assumpsit, ejectment, case. This choice is not merely a choice between a number of queer technical terms, it is a choice between methods of procedure adapted to cases of different kinds.

[Maitland then discusses a number of procedural differences between the different actions.]

These remarks may be enough to show that the differences between the several forms of action have been of very great practical importance—'a form of action' has implied a particular original process, a particular mesne process, a particular final process, a particular mode of pleading, of trial, of judgment. But further to a very considerable degree the substantive law administered in a given form of action has grown up independently of the law administered in other forms. Each procedural pigeon-hole contains its own rules of substantive law, and it is with great caution that we may argue from what is found in one to what will probably be found in another; each has its own precedents. It is quite possible that a litigant will find that his case will fit some two or three of these pigeon-holes. If that be so he will have a choice, which will often be a choice between the old, cumbrous, costly, on the one hand, the modern, rapid, cheap, on the other. Or again he may make a bad choice, fail in his action and take such comfort as he can from the hints of the judges that another form of action might have been more successful. The plaintiff's choice is irrevocable; he must play the rules of the game that he has chosen. Lastly he may find that, plausible as his case may seem, it just will not fit any one of the receptacles provided by the courts and he may take to himself the lesson that where there is no remedy there is no wrong.

[Maitland then proceeds to a chronological survey of the major developments in the history of the forms of action.]

1189–1272

The most important phenomenon is the appearance of Trespass—that fertile mother of actions. Instances of what we can not but call actions of trespass are found even in John's reign, but I think it clear that the writ of trespass did not become a writ of course until very late in Henry III's reign. Now trespass is to start with a semi-criminal action. It has its roots in criminal law, and criminal procedure. The historical importance of trespass is so great that we may step aside to look at the criminal procedure out of which it grew. The old criminal action (yes, action) was the Appeal of Felony (*appellum de felonia*). It was but slowly supplanted by indictment—the procedure of the common accuser set going by Henry II, the appeal on the other hand being an action brought by a person aggrieved by the crime. The appellant had to pronounce certain accusing words. In each case he must say of the appellee '*fecit hoc* (the murder, rape, robbery or mayhem) *nequitur et in felonia, vi et armis et contra pacem Domini Regis*' [he did this—the murder, etc—wickedly and feloniously, with force and arms and contrary to the King's Peace].

He charges him with a wicked deed of violence to be punished by death, or in the twelfth century by mutilation. The procedure is stringent with outlawry in default of appearance. The new phenomenon appears about the year 1250, it is an action which might be called an attenuated appeal based on an act of violence. The defendant is charged with a breach of the king's peace, though with one that does not amount to felony. Remember that throughout the Middle Ages there is no such word as misdemeanour—the crimes that do not amount to felony are trespasses (Latin *transgressiones*). The action of trespass is founded on a breach of the king's peace:—with force and arms the defendant has assaulted and beaten the plaintiff, broken the plaintiff's close, or carried off the plaintiff's goods; he is sued for damages. The plaintiff does not seek violence but compensation, but the unsuccessful plaintiff will also be punished and pretty severely. In other actions the unsuccessful party has to pay an amercement for making an unjust, or resisting a just claim; the defendant found guilty of trespass is fined and imprisoned. What is more, the action for trespass shows its semi-criminal nature in the process that can be used against a defendant who will not appear—if he will not appear, his body can be seized and imprisoned; if he can not be found, he may be outlawed. We thus can see that the action of trespass is one that will become very popular with plaintiffs because of the stringent process against defendants. I very much doubt whether in Henry III's day the action could as yet be used save where there really had been what we might fairly call violence and breach of the peace; but gradually the convenience of this new action showed itself. In order to constitute a case for 'Trespass *vi et armis*', it was to the last necessary that there should be some wrongful application of physical force to the [plaintiff's] lands or goods or person—but a wrongful step on his land, a wrongful touch to his person or chattels was held to be force enough and an adequate breach of the king's peace. This action then has the future before it.

COMMENTARY

Each form of action had its own procedure. The dominant role played by the action of trespass depended greatly upon the convenience of its procedure. A defendant who did not appear could be fined or outlawed (an aspect of 'mesne' or middle process—the procedure for bringing a defendant to justice—whereby the defendant forfeited his chattels and was subject to other civil disabilities). The mode of adjudication was trial by jury. This was much preferable to the older modes of trial, such as trial by ordeal (in which the defendant was subjected to a physical test, e.g. ducking in water to see if they would sink) or trial by battle (in which the parties might have to—literally—'fight it out'). No wonder trespass rapidly proved very popular!

(b) Trespass on the Case

The unsatisfactory nature of the requirement that the defendant should have acted 'with force and arms' (*vi et armis*) soon became apparent. Local courts were generally forbidden to entertain suits for more than 40 shillings without royal sanction, and there would have been a failure of justice if non-violent trespasses involving larger sums were excluded from the King's Courts as well. Baker writes (p. 68): 'The pressure for change is first seen in attempts to use *vi et armis* writs fictitiously, or at least by taking an elastic view of "force", in the hope that no exception would be taken.' Throughout the first part of the fourteenth century there are examples of actions against blacksmiths for killing horses *vi et armis* and *contra pacem* but it seems more likely these are actions for carelessness in shoeing the horse rather than that they indicate a group of equicidal tradesmen. By the middle of the fourteenth century the Chancery clerks had begun drawing up a new writ of trespass. This writ required the plaintiff to plead his special 'case'. If the defendant's act had not been *vi et armis*, the plaintiff had to explain why it was nonetheless wrongful. The earliest forms of this writ involved situations where the parties were in a pre-existing relationship in the course of which the defendant had 'assumed responsibility' to the plaintiff. If the plaintiff had asked the defendant to shoe his horse or to hold a chattel on the plaintiff's behalf, any contact with the animal or chattel could not be *vi et armis*, but it could be wrongful if the shoeing was done carelessly or the chattel lost. The modern law of contract derives from the action on the case for *assumpsit* ('undertaking' or 'assumption of responsibility'), and today a party who has undertaken to do something under a contract and has done it carelessly may be liable in both contract and tort. The following extracts provide examples of the courts' willingness, first, to stretch the writ of trespass *vi et armis* and subsequently to sanction the later action on the case.

Rattlesdene v Grunestone (1317)
J. H. Baker and S. F. C. Milsom *Sources of English Legal History: Private Law to 1750*, 2nd edn (Oxford: OUP, 2009)

Suffolk. Richard de Grunestone and his wife Mary were attached to answer Simon de Rattlesdene on a plea why, whereas the same Simon had lately bought from the aforesaid Richard at Orford a certain tun of wine for 6 marks 6s 8d and had left that tun in the same place until he should require delivery, the aforesaid Richard and Mary with force and arms drew off a great part of the wine from the aforesaid tun, and instead of the wine so drawn off they filled the tun up with salt water so that all the wine became rotten and was altogether destroyed to the grave damage of this Simon and against the [king's] peace.

And as to this the same Simon by his attorney complains that whereas the same Simon had bought from the aforesaid Richard at Orford the aforesaid tun, and had left it in the same place until etc, the aforesaid Richard and Mary on the Thursday in the octave of St John the Baptist in the ninth year of the present king's reign [1 July 1316] with force and arms, namely with swords and bows and arrows, drew off a great part of the wine from the aforesaid tun and instead of the wine so drawn off they filled the tun with salt water so that all the aforesaid wine was destroyed etc, to the grave damage etc, and against [the king's] peace etc whereby he says that he is the worse off and has suffered damage to the value of £10; and therefore he produces suit etc.

And Richard and Mary come by . . . their attorney and they deny force and wrong [and will deny it] when [and where they should] etc. And well do they deny that on the day and in the year aforesaid they ever drew off the aforesaid wine with force and arms or instead of the wine put in salt water or did him any other wrong as the aforesaid Simon complains. And of this [they] put themselves upon the countryside, and so does Simon. And so the sheriff is told to cause to come [a jury on such a day].

COMMENTARY

So vital was the allegation of *vi et armis* that claims that injury was inflicted 'with force and arms'—and often, for good measure, 'with swords, bows, arrows and clubs' (see Milsom 'Trespass from Henry III to Edward III' (1958) 74 LQR 195)—were made in the most unlikely circumstances. Can it really have been the case in this action that the defendants drew off a quantity of wine 'with force and arms, namely with swords and bows and arrows'? More likely, this was an action by a disgruntled purchaser of the wine for loss caused by an accident in the course of shipping.

The Farrier's Case (1372)

J. H. Baker and S. F. C. Milsom, *Sources of English Legal History: Private Law to 1750*, 2nd edn (Oxford: OUP, 2009)

Trespass was brought against a farrier for injuring a horse with a nail; and the writ said to show why, at a certain place, he drove a nail into the quick of the horse's hoof, whereby the plaintiff lost the profit from his horse for a long time.

Percy [for the defendant]. He has brought a writ of trespass against us, and does not say 'with force and arms'. We pray judgment of the writ.

Fyncheden CJ. He has brought his writ according to his case. (So he thought the writ good.)

Percy. The writ should be 'with force and arms', or should say that he drove the nail maliciously; and since there is neither the one nor the other, we pray judgment . . .

Then the writ was held good. And the defendant took issue that he shod the horse, without this that he injured it with a nail . . . etc.

COMMENTARY

This is an early example of an action on the case. The court holds that it is not necessary to include the allegation, as would be required in trespass, that the defendant acted *vi et armis*. Rather than relying upon evasive fiction, the court openly accepts that the action in trespass has been stretched beyond its earlier limits and become something new and different.

3. The Development of Fault-Based Liability

(a) Writs of Trespass and Fault

To a contemporary observer it is inconceivable that the law of tort could exist without the fault-based law of negligence. In historical terms, however, the development of negligence as a separate tort is a relatively recent event. To have talked to a medieval or early modern lawyer about the law of 'negligence' would have resulted in a short and puzzled conversation. This is not because notions of fault were unimportant, but rather that its role was obscured by the writ system that dominated the early common law. The formulaic language used on the writs meant that it was not necessary to plead the state of mind or culpability of the defendant. No doubt, if the allegation was that the defendant 'assaulted the plaintiff with force and arms and beat, wounded and ill-treated him so that his life was despaired of', it could safely be assumed that the harm was inflicted intentionally and that the defendant was culpable. But as the writ of trespass was stretched to include cases of accidental injury—a trend that, as was noted earlier, led to the development of trespass on the case—the defendant's fault could not be taken for granted. It is difficult today to ascertain precisely what role was played in such cases by the concept of fault, but it seems likely that the taking of all reasonable care to avoid the injury of which the plaintiff complained was regarded as a defence. This does not necessarily appear from the language of the early law reports ('Year Books'), however, as the reporters were primarily interested in the form of the writ (and legal challenges to its form) and the pleadings. Even later law reporters, who might note the jury's verdict on the facts, frequently said nothing about the likely reason for the verdict. There was thus no record of the evidence put to the jury by defendants 'pleading the general issue', i.e. entering a plea of Not Guilty. Nevertheless, respected authorities conjecture that the issue of fault was often raised at this stage (*Baker*, p. 429; S. F. C. Milsom, *Historical Foundations of the Common Law*, 2nd edn (London: Butterworths, 1981), pp. 296–300; cf. *Ibbetson*, p. 59, who argues that questions of fault might be reflected in the jury's deliberation as to whether the defendant *caused* the plaintiff's injury).

(b) Negligence and the Action on the Case

Liability for negligently inflicted injuries was first recognised by stretching the scope of trespass, but it found a more natural home in the action on the case. As already noted, the earliest examples of actions on the case involved parties in a pre-existing relationship with each other, e.g. the relationship between vendor and purchaser. Most of these cases would today be regarded as falling under the law of contract, not tort. Tort concerns itself primarily with parties who are strangers to one another. Liability here was slower to develop than in the case of pre-existing relationships.

Two of the earliest examples of liability imposed in the absence of a pre-existing relationship were for harm caused by the escape of fire and by dangerous animals (the *scienter* action). The liability was premised on the allegation that it was a custom of the realm that a particular activity should be pursued so as not to cause harm. Customs of this nature were also held to apply to innkeepers and common carriers but never developed much further as 'the common custom of this realm is common law and need not be pleaded' (*Beaulieu v Fingham* (1401), in Baker and Milsom, *op. cit.*, p. 610). Liability under these customs was probably stricter than under the modern conception of negligence, although, as noted earlier, it is difficult to ascertain whether it was wholly independent of fault.

Actions for pure negligence were rare, but, as *Baker* points out (p. 436), this was probably because the existing law covered most situations. Forcible wrongs could be remedied in trespass, but if the wrong was non-forcible it was probably because there had been careless performance of an undertaking, remediable by *assumpsit* (which laid the foundations for the modern law of contract) or because the harm had been caused indirectly. Indirect harm normally involved the escape of something dangerous, like fire or an animal, which was covered by existing actions in case. There was no perceived need to develop a distinct general liability for negligence and the satisfactory nature of the existing remedies made any such development unlikely.

4. Eighteenth-Century Developments

(a) The Beginnings of Negligence

As with much of the development of the common law, the impetus for change came with the attempt of lawyers to modify legal rules for the benefit of their own clients. From the latter half of the seventeenth century, writs began to appear from which the development of the modern tort of negligence can be traced. However, a general liability for negligence did not sit easily with the forms of action in which it would need to be pleaded. The beginning of the problem can probably be traced to *Mitchil v Alestree* (1676) 1 Vent 295. The plaintiff had been injured in Little Lincoln's Inn Fields when one of the horses the defendants were trying to break in escaped and kicked her. Prima facie this was a forcible wrong, remediable in trespass *vi et armis*. However, it was a defence to trespass to show that the contact had been against the defendant's will, so that in *Mitchil*, if the jury could be convinced that the contact was the result of the independent action of the horse, it might find for the defendant. This encouraged the plaintiff to plead the action in case, by alleging that the defendant's wrong was to break in the horses 'improvidently, rashly and without due consideration of the unsuitability of the place for the purpose'. She was successful. Another reason why the plaintiff might want to choose case instead of trespass *vi et armis* was the development of vicarious liability. It was during the course of the eighteenth century that case became the appropriate form of action in which to sue an employer 'vicariously', i.e. for a tort committed by an employee. Again, case was the correct action even where the employee's act had been forcible *vis-à-vis* the plaintiff.

(b) The Direct/Indirect Distinction

If the forms of action were to mean anything at all, there needed to be some guidance on the circumstances in which trespass *vi et armis* or case was the appropriate form. It was this need that led to the introduction of the infamous direct/indirect distinction between actions of trespass and case. In *Reynolds v Clarke* (1725) 1 Str 634 at 636, Fortescue J ruled:

> [I]f a man throws a log into the highway, and in that act it hits me; I may maintain trespass, because it is an immediate wrong; but if, as it lies there, I tumble over it, and receive an injury, I must bring an action upon the case; because it is only prejudicial in consequence, for which originally I could have no action at all.

This distinction proved difficult to operate in practice. In the famous case of *Scott v Shepherd* (1773) 2 W Bl 892 the defendant threw a lighted squib (firework) into a crowded market, where it was twice thrown on before striking the plaintiff in the face and exploding. The plaintiff pleaded in trespass *vi et armis* and this was ultimately held to be the correct form.

Although the distinction was problematic throughout the history of the two actions of trespass and case, the increase in the number of running-down cases towards the end of the eighteenth century caused particular difficulties. If the plaintiff was hit by a horse-drawn stagecoach, this was a forcible act and hence trespass was the appropriate form of action. However, if the horses had bolted contrary to the intention of the driver this might be a defence to trespass. But, in case, liability might well be imposed if the allegation was that the defendant had carelessly attempted to control the horses. Further, if the coach had been driven by an employee rather than its owner, case had to be brought as this was the proper form for vicarious liability. None of this mattered much if courts were prepared to turn a blind eye to whether or not an action was in the correct form, but in *Day v Edwards* (1794) 5 TR 648, Lord Kenyon CJ held that, in a running-down case, the plaintiff complained of an immediate act and hence trespass was the required form of action. This was reaffirmed by his successor, Lord Ellenborough CJ (see *Leame v Bray* (1803) 3 East 593), but the practical difficulties with a rigid distinction between trespass and case proved insurmountable.

The solution lay in allowing the plaintiff to 'waive' the trespass and sue instead in case. In *Williams v Holland* (1833) 2 LJCP (NS) 190, the Court of Common Pleas decided that this would be permitted where the plaintiff's injury was occasioned by the 'carelessness and negligence' of the defendant, notwithstanding the act was immediate, so long as it was not a wilful act. It thus became the norm to bring case whether the negligence of the defendant produced immediate or consequential damage. The independent action in negligence was thus well and truly established by the time the last vestiges of the forms of action were abolished by the Judicature Acts 1873–5, and the direct/indirect distinction was effectively jettisoned in favour of a new classification: intention and negligence.

For more detailed discussion on the historical development of the tort of negligence see: A. Kiralfy, *The Action on the Case* (London: Sweet & Maxwell, 1951); Milsom, 'Not Doing is No Trespass: A View of the Boundaries of Case' [1954] CLJ 105 and 'Trespass from Henry III to Edward III', *op. cit.*, 195–224, 407–36, 561–90; Baker, 'Introduction' (1977) 94 Selden Society 23 (Spelman's Reports, vol. II), ch. VIII; Prichard, 'Trespass, Case and the Rule in *Williams v Holland*' [1964] CLJ 234 and '*Scott v Shepherd* and the Emergence of the Tort of Negligence', Selden Society Lecture (1976); Ibbetson, chs 8 and 9.

5. The Classification of Obligations

The task of classifying the various forms of action under the headings we recognise in the modern law—the law of tort, the law of contract, the law of property, etc—began in England in the early seventeenth century. In the category of those actions imposing personal obligations, as opposed to recognising rights over property, contract (*assumpsit*) came to be regarded as distinct. (Equity, which imposed obligations on trustees and fiduciaries, was always a separate entity.) This left behind a miscellaneous collection of actions in trespass and case which resisted easy classification. These actions were lumped together in books as 'torts', but little thought was given to how they should be rationalised, or whether the law could be simplified, or whether obligations recognised in the courts of equity should be introduced to the classification. The development of general principles of liability had to wait until the period after the abolition of the forms of action in 1875, and many would argue that the task is yet to be completed. The most important advance was the recognition of a generalised liability for negligently inflicted injuries. No such rationalisation has occurred in the case of liability for intentional wrongdoing, which remains governed by a diverse set of more specific causes of action applicable in different circumstances.

> **J, Baker, *Introduction to English Legal History***
> 5th edn (Oxford: OUP, 2019)
>
> The law of torts, or civil wrongs, is extensive and its boundaries are not fixed by any unifying general principle. The very word 'tort', which has long been appropriated by lawyers, was far from technical in origin. The nearest medieval equivalent was 'trespass', whereas the old French word *tort* (*injuria* in Latin) denoted any kind of legal injury and is best translated as 'wrong' . . . [I]n the early sixteenth century there was nothing incongruous about describing a breach of contract as a tort or trespass. But when the action of *assumpsit* became a truly contractual remedy, based on a promise in return for consideration, breaches of contract came to be seen as legally different in a number of ways from other kinds of trespass . . . By the middle of the seventeenth century, contract and tort were seen as being so different that claims in tort and contract could not be joined in the same action. Thus, when an action was brought in 1665 against the hirer of a horse for misusing the animal and not paying the hire, counsel argued that the joinder of the two causes of action was erroneous because one sounded in tort and the other in 'breach of promise only'. In another case the same year, counsel treated contract and tort as mutually exclusive: 'tort can never be done where there is a special agreement, unless there be duty by statute or common law incumbent'. This is near the modern understanding of the word . . . Already by the same period legal indexes were classifying 'tort' in the modern sense, as a subheading under 'actions on the case'.
>
> As different kinds of trespass action acquired separate characteristics in the sixteenth and seventeenth centuries, further subdivisions of the law of torts were made, some of which survived the abolition of the writ system itself. Since the eighteenth century, however, the law of torts has undergone a gradual rearrangement as a result of the rapid expansion of the tort of negligence. Liability for negligence alone—that is, without reference to other factors such as contract—was rarely imposed before 1700, and even at the beginning of the twentieth century Sir John Salmond was denying the existence of a separate tort of negligence. In the practitioners' book, *Clerk and Lindsell on Torts*, negligence did not reach the status of a separate chapter until as late as 1947. It would be easy to conclude from this that negligence has a short history; but this would be misleading. The negligence approach of the modern law determines liability by focusing on the quality of the defendant's act rather than on the kind of harm done to the plaintiff. The reordering of so much of the modern law of tort around the concept of negligence is a consequence of that shift of focus, which was partly a result of abolishing the forms of action. But there is nothing modern about the concept of negligence in itself; what has changed is its primacy. Negligence and fault have always been familiar ideas, and for at least four centuries before 1700 they played a role in law and legal terminology, but their role was subsidiary. A plaintiff might allege negligence alongside other factors, to reinforce liability, or a defendant might rely on the absence of negligence to show that he was not at fault. The concept was not tied to a particular form of action. It was not even confined to actions in tort, in the modern sense of the term . . .

G. Williams and B. Hepple, *Foundations of the Law of Tort*
2nd edn (London: Butterworths, 1984)

Since the Judicature Act [1873] judges have been slowly emancipating themselves from the forms of action; they have begun to think in terms of broad rules of law which are not related to the old categories. An outstanding example is the case of *Wilkinson v Downton* [1897] 2 QB 57, decided by an eminent judge of the Victorian era, Wright J:

> Mr Downton, in jest, told Mrs Wilkinson that her husband had been 'smashed up' in an accident and had both his legs broken. The lady suffered a serious shock entailing weeks of suffering and incapacity. At the risk of seeming to have no sense of humour she sued Downton for damages. Wright J held that the action well lay.

There was no precedent for this decision before the Judicature Act. The plaintiff could not have brought an action for trespass, which lay only for the direct physical infliction of harm (or the threat of it). Here the plaintiff had been physically injured, but only as a result of her mental shock following upon the words spoken. She could not have sued for this mental suffering in deceit, because an action for deceit could be brought only where the defendant had made a fraudulent statement on which the plaintiff was intended to rely, and did rely to his detriment; here the plaintiff was not claiming in respect of damage resulting from any conduct on her part in reliance upon the truth of the statement. The damage resulted merely from her belief in its truth, and from the effect that that belief had upon her mind. Notwithstanding these difficulties, the judge felt able to assert the existence of a principle of law without the attempt to relate his decision to any of the ancient writs, as by saying that the concept of trespass to the person could be extended to a 'psychological assault'. Instead, he assumed the existence of a general principle of law according to which a person who intends without justification to cause fear or anxiety to another, in circumstances where grave effects are likely to follow, is responsible if such effects do follow . . . The decision is an outstanding example of the greater readiness of the courts at the present day to lay down general principles of liability instead of indulging in mere historical research.

COMMENTARY

As we shall see in Chapter 2, the imposition of liability for an intentional act causing indirect harm was not unknown under the forms of action (see *Bird v Holbrook* (1828) 4 Bing 628) but the rationalisation of the result by way of a wide general principle was predominantly a nineteenth-century development. Even then, the courts stopped short of integrating the old writs of trespass to the person—assault, battery and false imprisonment—within the new scheme, and these remained the primary remedy for injuries caused intentionally and directly. Wright J's general principle was effectively side-lined: in the next 100 years, it was applied on only a handful of occasions (see further in Ch. 2.V). Perhaps this was just as well, for there is considerable doubt whether Wright J ever intended his judgment to form the basis for a broad principle of liability (see Lunney, 'Practical Joking and Its Penalty: *Wilkinson v Downton* in Context' (2002) 10 Tort L Rev 168).

A later and more influential example of the introduction of a broad principle of liability was the opinion of Lord Atkin in *Donoghue v Stevenson* [1932] AC 562, in which his Lordship identified a single principle—the 'neighbour principle'—running through all the instances of liability for negligently inflicted harm (see Ch. 3.I.2). If *Wilkinson v Downton* provides a rule for intentionally inflicted harm, and *Donoghue v Stevenson* a rule for negligently inflicted harm, is the rest of the law of tort necessary at all?

6. The Modern Pre-Eminence of Negligence

Without doubt, the tort that has dominated all others since the early twentieth century is negligence; according to one writer it has attained a 'majestic pre-eminence' (M. Millner, *Negligence in Modern Law* (London: Butterworths, 1967), p. 227). However, as we have seen, negligence as an independent action is a relatively modern phenomenon, and the main period of its growth has been in the last ninety years. Why should negligence, as opposed to other torts, have achieved this position? The following extract suggests some possible reasons.

> **D. Ibbetson, 'The Tort of Negligence in the Common Law in the Nineteenth and Twentieth Centuries' in E. Schrage (ed.), *Negligence: The Comparative Legal History of the Law of Torts***
> (Berlin: Duncker & Humblot, 2001)
>
> **Transformative Factors in the Twentieth-Century Tort of Negligence**
>
> From around the beginning of the twentieth century a number of factors combined to alter the nature and structure of negligence liability.
>
> First of all, there were a number of economic changes which altered the basis on which negligence liability operated. Most obvious of these was the increasing preponderance of corporate defendants. This was, of course, not a new phenomenon, as the frequency of actions against railway companies in the nineteenth century amply demonstrates; but the increasingly corporate nature of industrial enterprise by the early twentieth century meant that actions were ever more commonly brought against companies rather than individuals. This undoubtedly brought about a more plaintiff-centred approach to liability, equivalent to that found in actions by railway passengers after the 1850s. As well as the prejudice against wealthy defendants—the maxim of natural jurisprudence, 'It is no sin to rob an apparently rich man'—large corporate defendants were undoubtedly better able to spread losses across their business and so pass them on to customers or shareholders than were individual capitalists or small partnerships. Moreover, in so far as the nineteenth-century legal thinking was built on a moral principle that individuals should only be liable for their own shortcomings, the justification for this in a world of corporate defendants was rather more difficult to see. Added to this there was the increasing availability of liability insurance. Whereas in the nineteenth century individuals might only insure against their losses, from the late nineteenth century it became possible to insure against legal liability; and well into the twentieth century there were doubts about the legality of insuring against the consequence of one's own wrongdoing. Moreover, as the century progressed it became compulsory to take out such liability insurance in respect of certain activities, such as driving a motor vehicle. The same arguments came into play here as in the case of corporate defendants: as between an injured plaintiff and an anonymous (and wealthy) insurance company it was easy to have sympathy with the plaintiff; and losses could be spread widely and relatively painlessly rather than borne by the individual plaintiff or defendant.
>
> Secondly, there was an intellectual shift. The acute individualism which had characterised Victorian England began to give way to a more communitarian approach: no longer was it

obvious that an individual who caused harm to another while pursuing his own economic self-interest should be liable only if it could be shown that he had not taken reasonable care. Alongside this, legal commentators began to stress that negligence liability did not depend on a moral principle but on a social one; it was not based on something internal to the defendant but on a failure to live up to an external standard, and that external standard was something which could be determined by public policy. The American jurist Oliver Wendell Holmes was the principal proponent of this view, and even before 1900 it had become so much part of common learning that it was being misunderstood by examination candidates. As corporate and insured defendants became the norm judges and scholars, especially in America, came to formulate the principles of liability in wholly economic, non-moral terms.

Thirdly, this time affecting more the structure of liability than its incidence, the jury disappeared from the trial of negligence actions. This occurred in three stages. First of all, the County Courts Acts [dating from 1846] provided that trial would be without jury in small cases, and might be without jury in other cases within the jurisdiction of the court (though either party had a right to demand a jury). In practice, jury trials in County Courts were very uncommon in any form of action, including negligence actions; they were abolished in 1934. Secondly, after the Judicature Acts 1873–1875 it was possible for some negligence cases to be assigned to the Chancery Division of the High Court; such cases would be heard without a jury. Thirdly, and most significantly, after a prolonged stutter, the jury was to all intents and purposes made optional after the Judicature Acts of 1873–1875, though in actions sounding in tort the option generally appears to have been exercised; temporary provisions restricting the right to trial by jury to a small number of situations (not including negligence) were in force from 1918 to 1925; new rules of procedure were introduced in 1932; and in 1933 the right to trial by jury in negligence actions was effectively abolished. After this, practically all cases were tried by judge alone. In so far as the classic structure of the tort of negligence had been largely generated by the separation between judge and jury, the reintegration of the trial process brought about a reintegration of the elements of the tort of negligence.

COMMENTARY

Ibbetson provides a useful corrective to those tempted to view tort law's development in purely doctrinal terms, as the progressive rationalisation of disparate pockets of liability driven only by legal logic. While tort law's 'intellectual history' should not be disregarded (see G. E. White, *Tort Law in America: An Intellectual History* (expanded edn, New York: OUP, 2003); J. Goudkamp and D. Nolan (eds), *Scholars of Tort Law* (Oxford: Hart, 2019)), it is important to explicate the link between tort law and the social, economic and political environment in which it operates, and to consider how, over the passage of time, tort has responded to changes in that environment. In fact, the influence of external, societal factors upon the law of tort can be traced back a very long way. The writ of trespass *vi et armis*, it may plausibly be argued, was introduced as a means of maintaining the authority of the sovereign and the security of the realm: the writ enabled the King's courts to deal with outbreaks of violent behaviour which would previously have ended up only in the local courts. But it is with the Industrial Revolution that the influence of extra-legal factors becomes most interesting, above all in the development of a generalised liability for negligence.

Tort Law and the Industrial Revolution

According to the very influential but highly controversial thesis of Morton J. Horwitz (*The Transformation of American Law 1780–1860* (New York: OUP, 1977)), tort law was transformed in the nineteenth century in order to provide a subsidy to the industrial concerns that had sprung up in the aftermath of the Industrial Revolution. (Horwitz concentrated on America, but believed his thesis equally applicable to England.) Horwitz claimed that the courts of the time abandoned the erstwhile general principle of strict liability (i.e. liability without fault), as expressed by the Latin maxim *sic utere tuo ut alienum non laedas* (use your own only in such a way that you do not harm anyone else's), and adopted instead the fault-based standard of negligence (p. 99):

> At the beginning of the nineteenth century there was a general private law presumption in favour of compensation, expressed by the oft-cited common law maxim *sic utere*. For Blackstone, it was clear that even an otherwise lawful use of one's property that caused injury to the land of another would establish liability in nuisance, 'for it is incumbent on him to find some other place to do that act, where it will be less offensive.' In 1800, therefore, virtually all injuries were still conceived of as nuisances, thereby invoking a standard of strict liability which tended to ignore the specific character of the defendant's acts. By the time of the [American] Civil War [1861–65], however, many types of injuries had been reclassified under a 'negligence' heading, which had the effect of substantially reducing entrepreneurial liability ... [T]he law of negligence became a leading means by which the dynamic and growing forces in American society were able to challenge and eventually overwhelm the weak and relatively powerless segments of the American economy. After 1840 the principle that one could not be held liable for socially useful activity exercised with due care became a commonplace of American law.

The thesis is not without its difficulties. Horwitz's apparent ascription of conscious agency to the judiciary fails to deal with the very wide range of different attitudes evident in the decisions of different judges. It ignores the likely hostility to industrial expansion of those many judges who were members of the landed gentry. And its depiction of a straightforward change from strict liability to negligence liability fails to fit the facts. As Rabin, 'The Historical Development of the Fault Principle: A Reinterpretation' (1981) 15 Ga L Rev 925 points out, we should regard 'the view that the industrial era was dominated by a comprehensive theory of fault liability for unintended harm as largely a myth ... Along similar lines ... [it is] a serious mistake to characterize the pre-industrial era as one of strict liability' (p. 927). Far from replacing strict liability, 'fault liability emerged out of a worldview dominated largely by no-liability thinking' (p. 928), as was evident in the continuing denial—until well into the twentieth century—of any general duty to consumers of products and trespassers, and significant limitations placed on employers' liability to their employees. For further criticism of the Horwitz thesis in its application to tort law, see Schwartz, 'Tort Law and Economy in Nineteenth Century America' (1981) 90 Yale LJ 1717, and, for more nuanced views on the relationship between free market economics and negligence liability generally, see Freyer, 'Legal Innovation and Market Capitalism 1790–1820' in M. Grossberg and C. Tomlins (eds), *Cambridge History of Law in America, Volume II: The Long Nineteenth Century* (New York: CUP, 2008) and G. E. White, *Law in American History, Volume I: From the Colonial Years Through the Civil War* (New York: OUP, 2012), pp. 8–9.

Yet there is no denying that industrialisation had a significant influence on tort law, both as a catalyst for expansion and as a cause for circumspection. As regards the former, it seems clear that '[a]dvances in transportation and industry—mills, dams, carriages, ships—made injuries involving strangers more common', and as a result forced the courts to move beyond a conception of negligence liability as peculiar to certain pre-existing relationships and to adopt a generalised theory of liability: 'the modern negligence principle in tort law seems to have been an intellectual response to the increased number of accidents involving persons who had no pre-existing relationship with one another' (White, *Tort Law in America*, p. 16). However, the seemingly unstoppable development of negligence into a generalised liability was a cause of alarm to at least some members of the judiciary, who urged caution and sought ways to limit the new liabilities to which entrepreneurs were exposed. This 'backlash' was most apparent in relation to accidents in the workplace, in which context a number of very effective defences were developed by the courts so as to safeguard the interests of employers (see further Ch. 6). However, industrial concerns were never granted an immunity from suit in negligence, and in some areas negligence liability flourished. Consider especially the large number of actions by passengers against railway companies from the mid-nineteenth century on: 'Mass transportation ... [gave] rise to mass litigation' (R. Kostal, *Law and English Railway Capitalism 1825–1875* (Oxford: OUP, 1994), p. 255). This was, says Kostal (p. 290), 'the first wave of personal injury litigation in English legal history'.

From Laissez-Faire Individualism to the Welfare State

By the end of the nineteenth century, the prevailing political mood was beginning to change. There was a recognition both that the courts had too jealously protected employers from negligence actions brought by injured employees and that the tort system as a whole was inadequate to the task of providing compensation for the victims of industrial (and other) accidents. In 1897, a no-fault Workmen's Compensation Scheme was introduced by legislation. It was not just a response to the inadequacies of the law of employer's liability; more significantly, it was the first step on the road towards the welfare state. In the twentieth century, the principal burden of providing compensation for the victims of accident, illness or other misfortune was to fall upon taxpayers, not tortfeasors. And it became trite to observe a shift from the laissez-faire individualism of the nineteenth century to the more community-spirited outlook of the twentieth.

Tort law could not remain immune to the changing mood of the times, and the courts sought to adapt its principles in an effort to broaden the scope of tort compensation. Duties of care were recognised in many new types of case, expanding still further the scope of liability in negligence, a development which culminated in Lord Atkin's enunciation of his 'neighbour principle' in *Donoghue v Stevenson* [1932] AC 562 (see further in Ch. 3). And fault came to be determined by reference to an external or objective standard, the standard of the reasonable person (see Ch. 4.IV), thereby divorcing legal notions of fault from the moral notions of the ordinary person. As W. Cornish et al., *Law and Society in England 1750–1950*, 2nd edn (Oxford: Hart, 2019), p. 507 point out: 'Liability for personal fault had undoubtedly appealed to the strongly individualistic strain in Victorian moralising; but as a basis for a workable system of accident compensation it had required significant compromise.' Its moral trappings stripped away, tort law came to be seen as no more than a component part of the compensation system: it was 'simply a complex of legal rules, largely devoid of moral content and of penal or deterrent effect, the function of which is to mark off the field of recoverable damage' (Millner, *op. cit.*, p. 4). Whether tort law could ever be a satisfactory system of accident compensation remained to be tested.

Tort Law and Insurance

It was only with the underpinning of the insurance system that tort law could even aspire to act as a major source of compensation to the victims of accidents. The development of liability insurance in the late nineteenth century, initially as a mechanism for protecting employers against the risk of lawsuits from employees, came to be seen as a justification for tapping the compensation potential of tort law still further (see White, *Tort Law in America*, pp. 147–50). By the middle of the twentieth century, tort law's function was identified as the transfer of losses away from the victims of accidents and the distribution or spreading of those losses throughout society by means (especially) of the liability insurance system (see James, 'Accident Liability Reconsidered: The Impact of Liability Insurance' (1948) 57 Yale LJ 549). The buck no longer stopped with the negligent actor, but was passed on to their insurer and thereafter spread amongst the class of premium-payers as a whole. So vital was insurance thought to be to the effectiveness of the tort compensation system that legislation was introduced to require the commonest targets of negligence litigation—car owners and employers—to take out compulsory insurance against their potential liabilities (see, respectively, the Road Traffic Act 1930 (now Road Traffic Act 1988, s. 143ff) and the Employers' Liability (Compulsory Insurance) Act 1969).

Insurers no doubt play a major role in the operation of tort law, but whether insurance considerations have brought about change in the substantive doctrines of tort law is another, more disputed matter. Certainly, the predominant judicial attitude is that the insurance position of the parties should have no influence on the adjudication of individual cases. The issue is considered in more detail later in this chapter (see III.1).

The Modern Tort Crisis

As the twentieth century progressed, tort law in general—and negligence liability in particular—were stretched further and further (see P. Atiyah, *The Damages Lottery* (Oxford: Hart, 1997), chs 2 and 3). It increasingly came to be seen as falling between two stools. On the one hand, it sought to fulfil compensation objectives for which it was fundamentally ill-suited. Compared with social security, tort law was a very expensive method of providing compensation, and, notwithstanding the breadth of the negligence principle, it compensated a very small proportion of all accident victims, namely those injured by another's fault. At the same time, tort law offended against principles of equality as successful claimants received disproportionately high awards compared with those left to rely upon the social security system. By the 1960s and 70s, the notion that tort law could be justified in terms of accident compensation was thoroughly discredited (see especially the first edition of Patrick Atiyah's *Accidents, Compensation and the Law*, published in 1970). The greater the success of the negligence principle in expanding the reach of tort law, the more its inadequacies were exposed: 'in the very moment of its triumph, the shadow of its decline' was falling upon the tort of negligence (Millner, *op. cit.*, p. 234). Reformers, including Atiyah, sought to pursue compensation objectives by other means, for example by the introduction of universal no-fault compensation paid by the state. The high-water mark of such efforts came in 1974, on the other side of the world, when New Zealand abolished its system of tort compensation for personal injuries and replaced it with a no-fault Accident Compensation Scheme (see further in Ch. 17.II.2(b)). However, similar reform proposals in Australia were never implemented, while in the United Kingdom the idea never really got off the ground at all: a Royal Commission on *Civil Liability and Compensation for Personal Injury*, chaired by Lord Pearson, confounded the hopes and expectations of advocates of the no-fault endeavour by refusing even to contemplate universal no-fault compensation (Cmnd 7054, 1978). Such is the rhetorical appeal of the notion of fault-based liability that it now seems highly unlikely that it will ever be abolished in order to make way for any alternative compensation mechanism (see further Ch. 17.II).

At the same time, tort law came under attack from those who believed it had betrayed its moral purpose of promoting justice between individuals. In their eyes, tort law could only be seen as a part of private law, and it risked incoherence if it sought to pursue 'public' goals, for example, the provision of accident compensation, which were inconsistent with the bipartite nature of legal proceedings (see, e.g., E. Weinrib, *The Idea of Private Law* (Oxford: Oxford University Press, revised edn, 2012); A. Beever, *A Theory of Tort Liability* (Oxford: Hart, 2016)). In short, tort law was about individual, not social, responsibility. Subscribers to this position believed that tort law had over-stretched itself in an effort to be something it could not, and should not, become. In particular, it had extended liability to losses that were better left to lie where they fell (e.g. because they were entrepreneurial risks: see the discussion of pure economic loss in Ch. 8); it had encouraged a 'pass the buck' mentality whereby individuals sought someone else to blame for every misfortune that befell them (often on the basis that someone else, often the state, had a duty to take positive steps for their benefit: see Ch. 9); and it had overburdened business and the insurance industry by 'opening the floodgates' of liability. This last concern was particularly highlighted by various 'crises' said to have afflicted the insurance industry at regular intervals since the late 1980s, exemplified by the near collapse of the Lloyds of London insurance market in 1990. Although it was conceded that a number of other factors played a role in these crises (e.g. general economic conditions and a succession of natural disasters), it was also alleged that tort law had played a contributory role by encouraging the spread of (risky) third-party or liability insurance at the expense of (comparatively safe) first-party or loss insurance: it is much easier to predict the potential losses of a single insured person than it is to predict the potential losses of all those other people—who knows how many there could be?—to whom the insured might be held liable (see generally Priest, 'The Current Insurance Crisis and Modern Tort Law' (1987) 96 Yale LJ 1521). To this day the problem of the increasing cost, and sometimes unavailability, of liability insurance has been a common cry of those who bemoan the 'compensation culture' (see further in III.3).

These tensions show no signs of resolution. The past several decades have seen, in society as a whole, a return to nineteenth-century values of individual responsibility and self-reliance, and fears that tort law might undermine these by 'going too far' have caused the courts to cut back the scope of liability in negligence in certain notable respects (see Chs 3 and 7–9). But tort law has not shed all traces of the loss-distribution ideology which prompted its spectacular growth throughout the greater part of the twentieth century: consider, in particular, the doctrine of an employer's vicarious liability for torts committed by their employees (see Ch. 14). It has been argued that the attempt to reconcile the nineteenth-century requirement of individual fault with the idea of a wider social responsibility for accident victims has led to a lack of coherence in the law of tort in general and negligence in particular (see Hepple, 'Negligence: The Search for Coherence' (1997) CLP 69). Yet tort law continues to muddle on, seeking what can only be an uneasy compromise between notions of loss-distribution on the one hand and individualised justice on the other.

II. Theories of Tort

Having looked at this history, let us now consider current views as to the nature and functions of tortious liability. We shall consider two issues. First, what are the aims of tort law—what purposes might it pursue, how effectively does it pursue them? Secondly, how do the aims of tort law differ from those of other branches of the law, and how in doctrinal terms are torts to be distinguished from, say, crimes, contracts and trusts?

1. The Aims of the Law of Tort

G. Williams, 'The Aims of the Law of Tort' [1951] CLP 137

An intelligent approach to the study of law must take account of its purpose, and must be prepared to test the law critically in the light of its purpose. The question that I shall propound is the end or social function or *raison d'etre* of the law of tort, and particularly of the action in tort for damages.

It is commonly said that the civil action for damages aims at compensation, as opposed to the criminal prosecution which aims at punishment. This, however, does not look below the surface of things. Granted that the immediate object of the tort action is to compensate the plaintiff at the expense of the tortfeasor, why do we wish to do this? Is it to restore the *status quo ante*?—but if so, why do we want to restore the *status quo ante*? And could we not restore this status in some other and better way, for instance by a system of national insurance? Or is it really that we want to deter people from committing torts? Or, again, is it that the payment of compensation is regarded as educational, or as a kind of expiation for a wrong?

. . . There are four possible bases of the action for damages in tort: appeasement, justice, deterrence and compensation.

Appeasement.—Crime and tort have common historical roots. The object of early law is to prevent the disruption of society by disputes arising from the infliction of injury. Primitive law looks not so much to preventing crime in general as to preventing the continuance of this squabble in particular. The victim's vengeance is bought off by compensation, which gives him satisfaction in two ways: he is comforted to receive the money himself, and he is pleased that the aggressor is discomfited by being made to pay. By this means the victim is induced to 'let off steam' within the law rather than outside it.

In modern times the safety-valve function of the law of tort probably takes a subordinate place. We do not reckon on the recrudescence of family feuds as a serious possibility, or even that of duelling. However, it may be thought that unredressed torts would be regarded as a canker in society, and to that extent the law can still be regarded as having a pacificatory aim . . .

Justice.—With the growth of moral ideas it came to be thought that the law of tort was the expression of a moral principle. One who by his fault has caused damage to another ought as a matter of justice to make compensation. Two variants of this theory may be perceived: (1) The first places emphasis upon the fact that the payment of compensation is an evil for the offender, and declares that justice requires that he should suffer this evil. This is the principal of ethical retribution, exemplified (in criminal law) by Kant's dictum about the moral necessity of executing even the last murderer. (2) The second variant looks at the same situation from the point of view of the victim; it emphasises the fact that the payment of compensation is a benefit to the victim of the wrong, and declares that justice requires that he should receive this compensation.

It may be thought that these two variants are simply two different ways of stating the same thing, but that is not entirely true. (1) Many people who would not subscribe generally to the principle of ethical retribution would nevertheless assert the principle of ethical compensation. Again, (2) one who asserts the principle of ethical compensation does not necessarily say that the wrongdoer must himself be afflicted. If no one else will pay the compensation, the wrongdoer must; but if someone (such as the State or an insurance company) steps in and pays for him, the requirement of recuperation is satisfied even though there is no ethical retribution against the offender.

Those who adopt the doctrine of ethical retribution do not, and cannot, refer it to any other principle. It is a postulate—an ultimate value-judgment which can only be accepted or rejected . . .

The case is far different with ethical compensation. This does serve a social purpose, independently of any doctrine of punishment or (for that matter) of deterrence. Imagine a small community of comparatively moral people who hardly need a deterrent legal system but who do occasionally commit acts of negligence or even of unruly temper. Even such a community would find educational value in a rule requiring the making of reparation for harm caused by fault. Whereas people do not voluntarily accept punishment for themselves (except for religious reasons by way of penance), good people do accept for themselves the necessity of paying compensation for harm that they have caused. It is not a question of punishment, but of showing in a practical way one's solicitude and contrition, and of obeying the golden rule that we should do as we would be done by . . .

Deterrence.—Ranged against the theory of tort as part of the moral order are those who believe that it is merely a regime of prevention. The action in tort is a 'judicial parable', designed to control the future conduct of the community in general. In England this view seems to have been first expounded by Bentham. Blackstone had expressed the opinion that civil injuries are 'immaterial to the public', but Bentham thought that such a contrast with criminal law could not be maintained, and that the underlying object of civil and criminal law was the same. Both criminal punishment and tort damages were sanctions and therefore evils: the only difference was in the degree of evil. The purpose of threatening them was to secure obedience to rules . . .

Whatever the imperfections of the moral interpretation of tort, the deterrent theory itself fails to provide a perfect rationale. For one thing, it offends against the principle that deterrent punishment must be kept to the effective minimum. According to utilitarian philosophy, of which the deterrent theory is an application, a punishment must not be greater than is necessary to repress the mischief in question. Damages in tort, however, may be far greater than are needful as a warning . . .

Compensation.—Finally there is the compensatory or reparative theory, according to which one who has caused injury to another must make good the damage whether he was at fault or not. This is the same as the theory of ethical compensation except that it does not require culpability on the part of the defendant. If valid, it justifies strict liability [i.e. liability independent of fault], which the theory of ethical compensation does not. The difficulty is, however, to state it in such a form as to make it acceptable. If it is said that a person who has been damaged by another ought to be compensated, we readily assent, moved as we are by sympathy for the victim's loss. But what has to be shown is not merely that the sufferer ought to be compensated, but that he ought to be compensated by the defendant. In the absence of any moral blame of the defendant, how is this demonstration possible?

It is fashionable to say that the question is simply one of who ought to bear the risk. This, however, is a restatement of the problem rather than a solution to it. A more satisfactory version is that known as the entrepreneur theory or, to speak English, the enterprise theory. This regards liability for torts connected with an enterprise as a normal business expense. Nothing can be undertaken without some risk of damage to others, and if the risk eventuates it must be shouldered by the undertaker in the same way as the cost of his raw materials. That this attitude has come into prominence in the present century, though not unknown in the last, is symptomatic of the general search for security at the cost, if need be, of freedom of enterprise . . .

[Williams proceeds to consider whether the rules of the law of tort are consistent or inconsistent with the principal theories of liability. He concludes:]

Our attempt to find a coherent purpose in the present law of tort cannot be said to have met with striking success . . . Where possible the law seems to like to ride two or three horses at once; but occasionally a situation occurs where one must be selected. The tendency then is to choose the deterrent purpose for the torts of intention, and the compensatory purpose for other torts.

COMMENTARY

Of the four possible functions of tort law canvassed by Williams, we can place on one side appeasement (which 'takes a subordinate place' in the modern law) and compensation (which we have already considered in some detail, and will consider further in Ch. 17). It is necessary, however, to say something more on the topics of deterrence and justice.

Deterrence

Notwithstanding Williams's scepticism as to whether deterrence can be seen as one of the functions of tort law, some very sophisticated attempts have been made, especially by members of the law and economics movement in the United States, to demonstrate just that. It is a basic tenet of the economic analysis of law that the incentive provided by the threat of tort liability by and large promotes economic efficiency, and that it is its function to do so. Economic efficiency does not entail the making of as great a reduction in the accident rate as is possible, but only such a reduction as is efficient. In the language of Guido Calabresi, one of the founding fathers of the law and economics movement, the aim is to reduce not the number of accidents, but the costs of accidents, taking into account also the cost of safety measures (see *The Cost of Accidents* (New Haven, Conn.: Yale University Press, 1970)). Perhaps the most influential figure in the movement over recent decades has been the judge and scholar Richard Posner, who argues that tort law's general reliance upon principles of fault-based liability makes it the best mechanism available for ensuring that all efficient precautions are taken in order to reduce the risk of accidental injury (see especially 'A Theory of Negligence' (1972) 1 J Leg St 29). Posner summarises his approach as follows (p. 33):

> [T]he dominant function of the fault system is to generate rules of liability that if followed will bring about, at least approximately, the efficient—cost-justified—level of accidents and safety. Under this view, damages are assessed against the defendant as a way of measuring the costs of accidents, and the damages so assessed are paid over to the plaintiff (to be divided with his lawyer) as the price of enlisting their participation in the operation of the system. Because we do not like to see resources squandered, a judgment of negligence has inescapable overtones of moral disapproval, for it implies that there was a cheaper alternative to the accident.

In other published writing, Posner has gone beyond the claim made in this extract, namely that economic inefficiency attracts moral disapproval, to argue that economic efficiency is the foundation of all moral imperatives and hence the main meaning of 'justice' itself (see *The Economics of Justice* (Cambridge, Mass.: Harvard University Press, 1981)). This somewhat implausible claim is subjected to convincing criticism by Ronald Dworkin in 'Is Wealth A Value?', ch. 12 of *A Matter of Principle* (London: Duckworth, 1985) and in ch. 8 of *Law's Empire* (London: Fontana, 1986). Dworkin accuses Posner of 'moral monstrousness' in suggesting that wealth is a value of intrinsic, or even instrumental, worth.

Even ignoring such extravagant claims about its normative foundations, the descriptive elements of the economic analysis of tort law have attracted a sceptical response from several quarters. S. Sugarman, *Doing Away with Personal Injury Law* (New York: Quorum, 1989), for instance, argues that tort law's role in reducing levels of excessively dangerous activity has been exaggerated. He points to a number of other behavioural controls apart from the law of tort that might exercise such a deterrent effect: '[s]elf-preservation instincts, market forces, personal morality, and governmental regulation (criminal and administrative) combine to control unreasonably dangerous actions independently of tort law' (p. 128). And he claims that, seen in terms of deterrence, tort's record has largely been one of a conspicuous lack of success: 'successful lawsuits represent a catalog of tort failures; people behaved in unacceptable ways notwithstanding the threat of liability' (p. 130). For further criticism, see Abel, 'Torts' in D. Kairys (ed.), *The Politics of Law*, 3rd edn (New York: Basic Books, 1998).

Justice

The depiction of tort law as designed to serve instrumental goals, for example the compensation of accident victims or the deterrence of accidents, has been disputed by a number of recent commentators. Their view is that tort law does not look forward to the achievement of instrumental goals of this nature, but backwards to a wrong that needs to be redressed. The central idea in tort law, then, is corrective justice. In Aristotle's classic account, corrective justice is contrasted with distributive justice: the former makes good a wrong without any regard to the needs, character or worth of the individuals concerned; the latter is concerned only with the distribution of goods throughout society as a whole, having regard to every person's needs and desert (*Nichomachean Ethics*, revised edn (London: Penguin Classics, 1976), pp. 176–7, 180). In terms of this scheme, tort law would be a system of corrective justice, social security a system of distributive justice. The idea that the function of tort law is to achieve (corrective) justice is perhaps the longest-standing of all theories of tort—it is considered by Williams (see earlier) under the name of 'ethical compensation'—but it has received a particular stimulus in recent decades, largely by way of a backlash to the vogue enjoyed by the instrumentalist accounts of tort law considered earlier. In particular, it has gained ground as a result of the increasing perception that tort law is ill-suited as a mechanism for achieving a rational system of compensation for incapacity.

One of the leading modern-day proponents of the corrective justice theory is Ernest J. Weinrib, who, in the following passage, describes the elements of tort law and procedure (and of the doctrine and procedure of private law more generally) that support his analysis (*The Idea of Private Law*, revised edn (Oxford: OUP, 2012), p. 1ff):

> The most striking feature about private law is that it directly connects two particular parties through the phenomenon of liability. Both procedure and doctrine express this connection. Procedurally, litigation in private law takes the form of a claim that a particular plaintiff presses against a particular defendant. Doctrinally, requirements such as the causation of harm attest to the dependence of the plaintiff's claim on a wrong suffered at the defendant's hands. In singling out the two parties and bringing them together in this way, private law looks neither to the litigants individually nor to the interests of the community as a whole, but to a bipolar relationship of liability.

Weinrib argues that instrumental accounts of tort law cannot make sense of these features because they look only to a desired outcome across society as a whole. In his view, tort law can perform a rational function only if it abstains from all attempts to achieve instrumental goals, and tort lawyers should give up evaluating tort law in terms of such external (social rather than legal) goals and seek an 'internal' understanding of the law in the notion of corrective justice. As he puts it in his more recent monograph, *Corrective Justice* (Oxford: OUP, 2012), the relational structure that underpins corrective justice excludes considerations 'such as a party's deep pocket or insurability against loss, that refer to the position of only one of the parties. Similarly excluded are instrumental considerations such as the promotion of economic efficiency, for although these may refer to both of the parties, they relate the two parties not to each other but to the goal that both parties serve' (p. 4).

Weinrib's point about the unsuitability of tort law for the pursuit of instrumental goals is well taken (at least in relation to compensation for incapacity). However, as a blueprint for action his account is flawed. Over time, the tort system has come to play a role in our overall system of compensation for incapacity—largely through the 'stretching' of certain of its key doctrines, notably the concept of fault. This role may be, by and large, only limited, but in some areas it is very significant, for example in respect of accidents at work and on the roads. If, as Weinrib suggests, the courts should abandon those doctrines which were the product of the stretching of tort law to make it fulfil compensation goals, and should ignore such instrumental concerns in applying the law, then surely this cannot be done without putting in tort law's place some mechanism for ensuring adequate compensation for those who are to lose out. Weinrib is right to consider tort law from an internal perspective, but wrong to look at it in a vacuum, in isolation from its social context.

Even if it is conceded that tort law's only concern is corrective justice, the question arises of what sort of wrongs it should attempt to redress, and how it should redress them. Aristotle's account of corrective justice was purely formal. It entailed neither a particular conception of 'wrongful conduct' sufficient to give rise to injustice, nor a particular response by way of remedying that injustice. It may thus be regarded as an empty receptacle into which different conceptions of 'wrong' and 'remedy' can be placed. As Posner has pointed out, the concept of corrective justice is compatible with a number of different understandings of the wrongful conduct whose outcome is to be corrected (see 'The Concept of Corrective Justice in Recent Theories of Tort Law' (1981) 10 J Leg St 187). Similarly, there is a wide range of different remedies that might appropriately be employed to redress a wrong. Admittedly, it is tempting to think that redress must entail the payment of compensation to restore the victim as nearly as possible to the position they would have been in if the injustice had not occurred; this indeed is the principle of the modern law of tort. But there is no reason for thinking that this is necessarily the just outcome. If a very poor person were to cause some small financial injury to a billionaire, would it really be just to demand that they pay compensation in respect of the full extent of that loss, at the cost of personal financial ruin, or would we think that justice had been secured by a sincere apology? It is no doubt true (as Aristotle held) that the wealth, character and desert of an individual are irrelevant in considering whether an injury inflicted or sustained is wrongful, but these factors may be very pertinent to the question of how in justice the wrong should be put right.

There is nothing then in the notion of corrective justice that requires the remedying of wrongful conduct through the law of tort. Nevertheless, the idea that tort law ought to perform such a function has strong intuitive appeal. Those interested in reading further should consult Fletcher, 'Fairness and Utility in Tort Theory' (1972) 85 Harv L Rev 537, Epstein, 'A Theory of Strict Liability' (1973) 2 J Leg St 151, D. Owens (ed.), *Philosophical Foundations of Tort Law* (Oxford: Clarendon Press, 1995), J. Oberdiek (ed.), *Philosophical Foundations of the Law of Torts* (Oxford: OUP, 2014) and A. Ripstein, *Private Wrongs* (Cambridge, Mass.: Harvard University Press, 2016). An interesting attempt to analyse the English law of negligence in corrective justice terms may be found in *Beever*; the same author's more recent *A Theory of Tort Liability* (cited previously) adapts that analysis to make the argument that tort law's fundamental concern is with freedom. Sharing the antipathy of the corrective justice scholars to instrumentalist theories of tort law is the explicitly rights-based account provided by R. Stevens, *Torts and Rights* (Oxford: OUP, 2007). For critical responses to (amongst others) Weinrib, Beever and Stevens, see Priel, 'Torts, Rights and Right-wing Ideology' (2011) 19 TLJ 1 and P. Cane, 'Rights in Private Law', in *Rights and Private Law*.

Can the existence of compulsory liability insurance regimes in respect of road accidents and accidents at work be reconciled with a corrective justice theory of tort law?

2. Doctrinal Classifications: Tort Law and other Legal Categories

C. Sapideen and P. Vines (eds), *Fleming's Law of Torts*, 10th edn
(Sydney: Lawbook Co., 2011)

Perhaps the most profitable method of delimiting the field of tort liability is to describe it in terms of the policies which have brought it into existence and contrast these with the policies underlying other forms of liability. Broadly speaking, the entire field of liability may be divided according to its purposes into criminal, tortious, contractual and restitutionary. Each of these is distinguishable by the nature of the conduct or its consequences and the purpose for which legal remedies are given.

The law of tort and crime, despite their common origin in revenge and deterrence, long ago parted company and assumed distinctly separate functions. A crime is an offence against the state, as representative of the public, which will vindicate its interests by punishing the offender. A criminal prosecution is not concerned with repairing an injury that may have been done to an individual, but with exacting a penalty in order to protect society as a whole. In other words, criminal law has state purposes which may not apply to tort; Tort liability, on the other hand, exists primarily to compensate the victim by compelling the wrongdoer to pay for the damage done. Its paradigm is the conflict between two individuals, even though not all tort cases only concern individuals. Some traces of its older link with punishment and crime have survived to the present day, most prominently exemplary damages to punish and deter contumelious and outrageous wrongdoing. Yet the principal concern of the law of torts nowadays is with casualties of accidents, that is, of unintended harm . . . In the law of accidents, the law is concerned chiefly with distributing losses which are an inevitable by-product of modern living, and, in allocating the risk, makes less and less allowance to ideas of punishment, admonition and deterrence . . .

The law of contract exists, at least in its most immediate reach, for the purpose of vindicating a single interest, that of having promises of others performed. This it does either by specifically compelling the promisor to perform or by awarding the promisee damages to put him in as good a position as if the promise had been kept. Thus while contract law as a rule assures the promisee the benefit of the bargain, tort law has the different function of primarily compensating injuries or losses. Moreover, by comparison the interests vindicated by the law of torts are much more numerous. They may be interests in personal security, reputation or dignity, as in actions for assault, personal injuries and defamation. They may be interests in property, as in actions for trespass and conversion; or interests in unimpaired relations with others, as in causing injury or death to relatives. Hence the field covered by the law of torts is much broader, and certainly more diverse, than that of contract.

According to another distinction, tort duties are said to be 'primarily fixed by law', in contrast to contractual obligations which can arise only from voluntary agreement. Certainly, in classical theory, the function of contract is to promote voluntary allocation of risks (typically, but not exclusively, commercial risks) in a self-regulating society, while tort law allocates risks collectively in accordance with community values by the fiat of court or legislature. But this distinction, though still fundamentally sound, has become somewhat blurred as the area of self-regulation by contract is being progressively narrowed by regulatory legislation and judicial policing for fairness inspired by collectivist and egalitarian ideals. Besides, contractual terms (where not expressly spelled out) are 'implied' (imposed) by law and [are] usually identical with tort duties arising from one party's 'undertaking' to act for another, as in the case of professional and other services.

> The third field of legal liability calling for demarcation from tort, restitution, serves the idea that justice requires the restitution of unintended benefits so as to prevent unjustified enrichment. Common illustrations are the return of money paid under mistake or the recovery of a bribe or profit (rather than loss) from misappropriation. Unlike the law of contract, it has nothing to do with promises and, unlike tort, with losses.
>
> To summarise, criminal liability is distinguished from tort by the fact its object is to punish for the purposes of the state, not to compensate; contractual liability by reason of the different interests protected and the fact that risks are allocated primarily voluntarily rather than collectively; and restitution because it is concerned with the restitution of benefits, not compensation for losses.

COMMENTARY

The analysis of tort liability put forward here is similar to that found in other leading tort works (*Winfield & Jolowicz*, ch. 1; *Clerk & Lindsell*, paras 1-01 to 1-10). However, it should be noted that the distinction between tort, on the one hand, and other forms of civil liability, on the other, has been challenged. Attempts have been made to find general principles of liability for the law of obligations, of which the current law of tort, contract and restitution form part (see, e.g., Patrick Atiyah's efforts to find a common foundation for all types of civil liability in the notion of reliance: P. S. Atiyah, *Promises, Morals, and Law* (Oxford: Clarendon Press, 1981), cf. Hedley (1988) 8 LS 137; McBride (1994) 14 LS 35). This may be going too far, but it is certainly true that the distinction between tort and other forms of liability has become somewhat blurred in certain respects. Damages for loss of an expectation of gain under a contract have been awarded in tort (*White v Jones* [1995] 2 AC 207); it has been affirmed that a defendant may be concurrently liable in contract and tort (*Henderson v Merrett Syndicates* [1995] 2 AC 145; see Stapleton (1997) 113 LQR 257); common law causation concepts associated with the law of tort have been imported into the law of trusts (*Target Holdings v Redferns (a firm)* [1996] AC 421); and causes of action like breach of confidence, historically recognised as equitable, are now re-classified as torts. In so far as the result is the abandonment of old distinctions between different heads of liability based only on historical chance (e.g. the historical distinction between common law and equitable wrongs), then they can only be applauded. But it may confidently be asserted that there will always be a need for the separate exposition of the principles of tortious liability (perhaps including, in time, wrongs whose origins are in equity), if for no other reason than that tort is the general law, while contracts and trusts (for example) are institutional arrangements entered into by consent and the conditions for their formation, dissolution, etc. themselves merit independent analysis (see also K. Stanton, *The Modern Law of Tort* (London: Sweet & Maxwell, 1994), p. 10).

III. Modern Influences on Tort Law

In this final section of our general introduction, we highlight a number of external factors that have had a particular influence on the development of tort law in recent years, and can be expected to shape its future.

1. The Influence of Insurance

R. Lewis, 'Insurance and the Tort System' (2005) 25 LS 85

There is no doubt that insurance profoundly influences the practical operation of the law of tort. Liability is not merely an ancillary device to protect the insured, but is the 'primary medium for the payment of compensation, and tort law [is] a subsidiary part of the process' (P. Cane, *Atiyah's Accidents, Compensation and the Law*). Although the majority of defendants in tort are individual people, they are almost all insured. In nine out of ten cases the real defendants are insurance companies, with the remainder comprising large self-insured organisations or public bodies. Only rarely are individuals the real defendants. Instead, policyholders cede control over their case to their insurer and thereafter usually play little or no part in the litigation process. Insurers determine how the defence is to be conducted and, for example, commonly make admissions without the consent of the insured, and settle cases in spite of the policyholder's objection.

Insurers pay out 94 per cent of tort compensation. Classic studies reveal that it is their bureaucracy that dictates much litigation procedure, and determines when, and for how much, claims are settled. It is their buildings, rather than courts of law, or even solicitors' offices, that are the important centres of tort practice . . . Because insurers dominate the system, it is very difficult to view any tort case in isolation: each and every case is affected, no matter whether determined in court or out of it . . . Insurers are the paymasters of the tort system: they process the routine payments and they decide which elements of damage they will accept or contest . . . Insurers determine the extent that lawyers become involved in disputes, and the tactics that are used in the proceedings. Increasingly cases are being settled at an early stage, and without resort to the issue of court documents. Insurers decide, in particular, whether a case merits the very exceptional treatment of being taken to a court hearing. In effect, they allow trial judges to determine only 1 per cent of all the claims made. Only a few of these are appealed with the result that the senior judiciary are left to adjudicate upon a small fraction of what are, by then, very untypical cases. Whether an appeal court is to be given an opportunity to examine a point of tort law may depend upon the insurer for, if it serves the insurer's purpose for doubt to remain, the claimant can be paid in full and threatened with a costs award if the action is continued. In this sense tort principles themselves have been shaped by and for insurers . . .

The importance of insurers to the tort system is reflected in the fact that the claims which are brought closely match the areas where liability insurance is to be found. Thus road and work accidents predominate partly because those are the two major areas where tort insurance is compulsory. They constitute 86 per cent of all the claims brought for personal injury. They dominate the practice of tort even though they are relatively minor causes of disability and incapacity for work. Those suffering injury in areas not covered by insurance are extremely unlikely to obtain compensation. According to one study [for the Pearson Commission, 1078], whereas 1 in 4 road accident victims and 1 in 10 work accident victims gain compensation from tort, only 1 in 67 injured elsewhere do so . . .

This influence of insurance upon the general pattern of tort liability is matched by its effect upon the level of compensation awarded. The principles upon which damages are assessed implicitly recognise that it is a company with a deep pocket that will pay and not an individual. Although most awards in tort are for very limited sums—little more than £2,500—there are very few individuals who could afford to pay the amounts required in serious injury cases . . . If it were not for insurance there would be little hope of restoring the claimant to the pre-accident position in a serious injury case. It is doubtful whether we would even wish to attempt to place full responsibility for the damage on most defendants. The very nature of the tort system would have to change. Without insurance, it is probable that tort liability itself could not survive . . .

Whether the rules of tort themselves have been changed to reflect insurance is more difficult to establish. On the one hand, it is certainly true that the foundations of tort remain largely unchanged. Formally, liability still depends upon proof of fault and, even where rules have been revised more in favour of claimants, it is too easy to suggest that insurance is the cause. On the other hand, some judges have acknowledged that they have concerned themselves with who has the deeper pocket, or who was in the better position to distribute, or absorb, a loss.

It is difficult to conclude that loss distribution arguments have influenced only the facts found and not, to some degree, the rules applied. However, substantial change in tort rules has not occurred. Instead it is the overall involvement of insurers with the system which leads us to conclude that insurance has had a major effect.

COMMENTARY

The type of insurance we are concerned with here is liability (or third-party) insurance, which is to be contrasted with loss (first-party) insurance in which the insured pays to be indemnified in the event of some adverse event (e.g. illness or injury), or for someone else to be indemnified (e.g. on the insured's death), usually whether or not another person is liable for the adversity. Liability insurance is essentially parasitic on the tort system as it is triggered only where there is a liability to pay damages to someone else. Loss insurance is largely independent of the tort system—it is concerned simply with loss, not liability—but a loss insurer may get involved in tort litigation where it has a right ('the right of subrogation') to bring a claim in the insured's name, after paying him under the policy, for an injury for which another person is liable. In fact, a tort claim—recorded under the names of two private individuals—could well be in reality between two insurers, the claimant's loss insurer and the defendant's liability insurer. The latter usually has full control over the defence by virtue of an express term of the contract of insurance, and need not seek approval from or even consult the defendant about either litigation strategy or settlement.

The courts too are usually unaware whether either or both the parties before them were insured at the relevant time, so they do not know who is really going to pay the damages, or who will actually benefit from them. (In road traffic accident cases, however, it is possible for the claimant to proceed directly, and by name, against the defendant's liability insurer: European Communities (Rights against Insurers) Regulations 2002, SI 2002/3061.) The traditional judicial view is that the insurance position of the parties should not be disclosed in case it influences the court in deciding questions of liability or damages (see, e.g., *Davie v New Merton Board Mills Ltd* [1959] AC 604 at 626–7, per Viscount Simonds, *Morgans v Launchbury* [1973] AC 127 at 136–7, per Lord Wilberforce, and *Hunt v Severs* [1994] 2 AC 350 at 363, per Lord Bridge). However, in a small but not insignificant set of cases, there has been express discussion of the insurance position. A notable example is provided by Lord Denning who—in a typically candid moment—openly approved of judges demanding a higher standard of care from parties (specifically, drivers of motor vehicles) known to be insured in order to secure compensation for the injured person (*Nettleship v Weston* [1971] 2 QB 691 at 699):

[A] person injured by a motor-car should not be left to bear the loss on his own, but should be compensated out of the insurance fund. The fund is better able to bear it than he can. But the injured person is only able to recover if the driver is liable in law. So the judges see to it that he is liable, unless he can prove care and skill of a high standard.

It must be admitted that such expressions of opinion are very rare, and that many judges would doubtless disapprove of Lord Denning's sentiments, especially as they entail a move away from the purported basis of liability for tortious negligence—i.e. fault—in favour of considerations of loss distribution. There is perhaps greater judicial willingness to admit to the influence of insurance considerations in contexts where 'policy' is a relevant factor, e.g. in determining whether it is fair, just and reasonable to recognise a duty of care. In *Vowles v Evans* [2003] 1 WLR 1607, a case considering the liability of a rugby referee to a player, the Court of Appeal expressly acknowledged (at 1614) that the availability of insurance—to both defendant and claimant—could bear on this crucial question of policy. (See also, in slightly different contexts, *Smith v Eric S. Bush* [1990] 1 AC 831 at 859, per Lord Griffiths, and *Gwilliam v West Hertfordshire Hospitals NHS Trust* [2003] QB 443.)

More recently, some scholars have argued for greater engagement with the insurance position of the parties but only where that position is definitely known to the court. If parties to a contract agree that certain risks will be allocated to one of them with an express or implied obligation to insure against that risk, does it make sense to ignore these insurance arrangements in determining the scope of any tort liability owed by the contracting parties to each other? (See Merkin, 'Tort, Insurance and Ideology: Further Thoughts' (2012) 75 MLR 301.)

A broader question is whether the development and spread of liability insurance has been instrumental in bringing about major structural changes in tort law doctrine (e.g. extensions in the application of the duty of care concept) in the interests of loss distribution. In a subsequent section of his article, Lewis identifies two diametrically opposed points of view, both well-represented in the literature: on the one hand, that insurance has been the 'hidden hand' that has pulled legal liability rules along with it (see, in the American context, K. Abraham, *The Liability Century: Insurance and Tort Law from the Progressive Era to 9/11* (Cambridge, Mass.: Harvard University Press, 2008); on the other, that the influence of insurance has been overstated and actually rather limited. A leading representative of the latter school of thought is Jane Stapleton, who argues that 'neither actual insurance nor insurability are or should be relevant to the reach and shape of tort liability' ('Tort, Insurance and Ideology' (1995) 58 MLR 820 at 820). One important point that she makes is that the courts very rarely point to the *claimant's* ability to protect themselves by purchasing first-party (loss) insurance as a reason for absolving the defendant from liability. (For a much-criticised example, see *Lamb v Camden Borough Council* [1981] 1 QB 625 at 637–8, per Lord Denning MR.) And rightly so: the result would be the shifting of accident costs—mediated through the pricing of insurance premiums—from tortfeasors to victims, and the diminution of whatever deterrent effect that tort law possesses (cf. Merkin, *op. cit.*).

As Lewis argues, the main impact of insurance on the substantive rules of tort may actually have been on the law of damages—an area mostly ignored by other scholars—rather than the principles of liability. In fact, a number of recent reforms relating to the assessment of damages—e.g. the new judicial power to order that damages be paid periodically rather than in the traditional lump sum—could not have been contemplated were it not possible to draw upon the insurance industry's technology and financial resources. (See further Ch. 15.) The impact of insurance on liability rules is much more difficult to establish—at least in the United Kingdom, where tort remains largely fault-based. But the influence is perhaps easier to discern in systems such as the French, which over the course of the twentieth century moved decisively in the direction of strict liability, a development which many French commentators have associated directly with the growth of liability insurance (see, e.g., G. Viney, *Introduction à la responsabilité*, 2nd edn (Paris: LGDJ, 1995), para. 25, translated in *van Gerven*, pp. 23–4).

Insurers themselves are not always happy with reforms which purport to have an insurance rationale, as they may increase insurers' costs and falsify the assumptions grounding their past and present premium rates. Other things being equal, however, more liability means more business for liability insurers. Yet insurers have increasingly sought to influence the tort reform agenda by contributing to public debate and applying pressure in the political sphere to curb the scope of liability. Their role in the current debate about 'compensation culture' is considered later.

For further analysis of tort law's insurance context, see Chapter 17. For additional discussion of some of the points addressed in this section, see Davies, 'The End of the Affair: Duty of Care and Liability Insurance' (1989) 9 LS 67, Morgan, 'Tort, Insurance and Incoherence' (2004) 67 MLR 384 and R. Merkin and J. Steele, *Insurance and the Law of Obligations* (Oxford: OUP, 2013).

2. The Influence of Human Rights

A topic of contemporary importance, and no little controversy, has been the effect upon the law of tort of the incorporation of human rights standards into English law. By the Human Rights Act 1998, the courts have an obligation to act compatibly with many of the rights recognised in the European Convention on Human Rights and Fundamental Freedoms (ECHR). That will change if government proposals to replace the Act with a British Bill of Rights come to fruition. Until such time, though, the 1998 Act will continue to impact on tortious liability, albeit in ways that are not always easy to pin down.

Human Rights Act 1998

1. The Convention rights

(1) In this Act 'the Convention rights' means the rights and fundamental freedoms set out in—

    (a) Articles 2 to 12 and 14 of the Convention;
    (b) Articles 1 to 3 of the First Protocol; and
    (c) Articles 1 and 2 of the Sixth Protocol

as read with Articles 16 to 18 of the Convention . . .

2. Interpretation of Convention rights

(1) A court or tribunal determining a question which has arisen in connection with a Convention right must take into account any—

    (a) judgment, decision, declaration or advisory opinion of the European Court of Human Rights;
    (b) opinion of the Commission given in a report adopted under Article 31 of the Convention;
    (c) decision of the Commission in connection with Article 26 or 27(2) of the Convention; or
    (d) decision of the Committee of Ministers taken under Article 46 of the Convention

whenever made or given, so far as, in the opinion of the court or tribunal, it is relevant to the proceedings in which that question has arisen . . .

3. Interpretation of legislation

(1) So far as it is possible to do so, primary legislation and subordinate legislation must be read and given effect in a way which is compatible with the Convention rights.

(2) This section—
   (a) applies to primary legislation and subordinate legislation whenever enacted;
   (b) does not affect the validity, continuing operation or enforcement of any incompatible primary legislation; and
   (c) does not affect the validity, continuing operation or enforcement of any incompatible subordinate legislation if (disregarding any possibility of revocation) primary legislation prevents removal of the incompatibility . . .

6. Acts of public authorities

(1) It is unlawful for a public authority to act in a way which is incompatible with a Convention right.

(2) Subsection (1) does not apply to an act if—
   (a) as the result of one or more provisions of primary legislation, the authority could not have acted differently; or
   (b) in the case of one or more provisions of, or made under, primary legislation which cannot be read or given effect in a way which is compatible with the Convention rights, the authority was acting so as to give effect to or enforce those provisions.

(3) In this section 'public authority' includes—
   (a) a court or tribunal; and
   (b) any person certain of whose functions are functions of a public nature

but does not include either House of Parliament or a person exercising functions in connection with proceedings in Parliament . . .

(5) In relation to a particular act, a person is not a public authority by virtue only of subsection (3)(b) if the nature of the act is private.

(6) 'An act' includes a failure to act but does not include a failure to—
   (a) introduce in, or lay before, Parliament a proposal for legislation; or
   (b) make any primary legislation or remedial order.

7. Proceedings

(1) A person who claims that a public authority has acted (or proposes to act) in a way which is made unlawful by section 6(1) may—
   (a) bring proceedings against the authority under this Act in the appropriate court or tribunal; or
   (b) rely on the Convention right or rights concerned in any legal proceedings but only if he is (or would be) a victim of the unlawful act . . .

(6) In subsection (1)(b) 'legal proceedings' includes—
   (a) proceedings brought by or at the instigation of a public authority; and
   (b) an appeal against the decision of a court or tribunal.

8. Judicial remedies

(1) In relation to any act (or proposed act) of a public authority which the court finds is (or would be) unlawful, it may grant such relief or remedy, or make such order, within its powers as it considers just and appropriate.

(2) But damages may be awarded only by a court which has power to award damages, or to order the payment of compensation, in civil proceedings.

(3) No award of damages is to be made unless, taking account of all the circumstances of the case, including—

    (a) any other relief or remedy granted, or order made, in relation to the act in question (by that or any other court); and

    (b) the consequences of any decision (of that or any other court) in respect of that act,

the court is satisfied that the award is necessary to afford just satisfaction to the person in whose favour it is made . . .

11. Safeguard for existing human rights

A person's reliance on a Convention right does not restrict—

    (a) any other right or freedom conferred on him by or under any law having effect in any part of the United Kingdom; or

    (b) his right to make any claim or bring any proceedings which he could make or bring apart from section 7 to 9.

COMMENTARY

The Human Rights Act 1998 (hereinafter HRA) came into force in October 2000. Not all of the Convention rights are incorporated by the HRA, but some of the most important that are incorporated are Article 2 (right to life), Article 5 (right to liberty and security), Article 6 (right to a fair trial), Article 8 (right to respect for private and family life) and Article 10 (right to freedom of expression).

There are several ways in which the HRA may have an impact upon the law of tort. First, s. 3 of the HRA requires a court or tribunal to interpret legislation, as far as possible, in accordance with the Convention rights. Secondly, s. 6 makes it unlawful for a public authority (as defined) to act in a manner that is incompatible with the Convention rights. As courts are public authorities for the purpose of the HRA, it seems that a court must give a judgment which is compatible with the Convention rights even in an action between two private individuals (see A. Young, 'Mapping Horizontal Effect' in D. Hoffman (ed.), *The Impact of the UK Human Rights Act on Private Law* (Cambridge: CUP, 2011)). If a public authority does breach s. 6, the 'victim' may bring proceedings under the Act (s. 7) and, if successful, may be awarded compensation or granted some other remedy at the discretion of the court (s. 8) (although note that s. 9, not extracted, limits the remedies available where it is alleged that a judicial act is in breach of a Convention right: see further Bamforth [1999] CLJ 159). Also important is s. 2, which requires a court or tribunal, when considering any question which has arisen in connection with a Convention right, to take account of, amongst other things, decisions of the European Commission and Court of Human Rights.

The effects of the Act have been considerable in some areas of tort law, but less significant in others. One question, which is addressed in more detail later in this book, is how the statutory remedy against public authorities impacts on the liabilities of public authorities at common law (see Ch. 3.III.2). How other common law liabilities have been affected by the HRA is considered at relevant points of later chapters, but some particular issues of interest are identified in outline here.

Trespass to the Person (Assault, Battery and False Imprisonment) and Articles 2 and 5

Trespass to the person protects interests in personal security and freedom: assault and battery protect against unwanted or threatened interferences with the person, whilst false imprisonment protects the liberty interest of the individual. Article 2 (right to life) and Article 5 (right to liberty and security) are concerned with similar subject-matter, and the question arises whether the remedies provided in tort are sufficient to satisfy the obligations thereby imposed upon the state. It is important to note that the obligation imposed may be one of positive action. Thus the state might be liable under the Convention not only for breaching the Convention itself but also for failing to take steps to ensure that a third party did not contravene another's Convention rights. For example, the estate of a person who was stabbed to death by another would have a civil action against the actual perpetrator in battery, but might also be able to sue the state for breach of Article 2 if it failed to take reasonable steps to safeguard the deceased's right to life (cf. *Osman v United Kingdom* [1999] 1 FLR 193 and *Michael v Chief Constable of South Wales Police* [2015] AC 1732). Such obligations might be imposed in respect of other Convention rights (see, e.g., *Z v United Kingdom* [2001] 2 FLR 612 and *D v Commissioner of Police of the Metropolis* [2016] QB 161, both on Article 3), but in the tort context are especially relevant in relation to Articles 2 and 5.

Article 5 may also be relevant where there is a challenge to the lawfulness of a person's detention by the state. The concept of deprivation of liberty under Article 5 is somewhat less absolute than the concept of imprisonment in the common law tort of false imprisonment, but the latter allows the imprisoner to rely on a variety of defences (e.g. lawful authority or necessity), whereas the former does not. Circumstances that might justify an imprisonment at common law are wrapped into the assessment of whether there is a deprivation of liberty contrary to Article 5. It follows that a claimant challenging their detention by the state may well plead the causes of action in false imprisonment and under the HRA as alternatives because their scope is not identical and it may be difficult to predict which will prove to be more advantageous. See further *Austin v Commissioner of Police of the Metropolis* [2009] AC 564, considered in Chapter 2. Also considered in Chapter 2 is *R (Jalloh) v Secretary of State for the Home Department* [2021] AC 262, where the Home Secretary argued unsuccessfully that the scope of the common law tort should be restricted by aligning the concept of imprisonment with deprivation of liberty under Article 5. That, according to Lady Hale at [33], would be 'a retrograde step': 'There is ... every reason for the common law to continue to protect those whom it has protected for centuries against unlawful imprisonment, whether by the state or private persons.'

Defamation, Privacy and Articles 8 and 10

Defamation is a tort that protects one's reputation, usually by an award of damages and, if required, an injunction. Most commonly, defendants in defamation cases are members of the media, sued for a false allegation that lowers the reputation of the claimant in the eyes of the general public. Two Convention rights are clearly relevant in this context. Article 8 guarantees a right to privacy, subject to the derogations set out in Article 8(2). Such a right is wider than the tort of defamation, which protects only reputation. Traditionally, English law does not recognise a liability for invasion of privacy as such, and that approach has been affirmed by the House of Lords even post-HRA (*Wainwright v Home Office* [2004] 2 AC

406). Nevertheless, under the influence of the Convention right, the courts have manipulated established principles of the equitable law of confidence to a very considerable extent, creating what is effectively a tort applying to the wrongful disclosure of private information (*Campbell v MGN Ltd* [2004] 2 AC 457). See further Chapter 13.

The right to privacy has to be balanced against the competing right to freedom of expression in Article 10 of the Convention, which HRA, s. 12 explicitly directs the courts to heed when considering the grant of any relief that might affect its exercise. In other common law jurisdictions, the highest courts have balanced these competing concerns in ways that contrast with the traditional approach of the English law of defamation (see *New York Times v Sullivan* 376 US 254 (1964), *Lange v Australian Broadcasting Corporation* (1997) 189 CLR 520). On occasion, the English courts have shown themselves prepared to modify existing rules to ensure that the principles of defamation law are compatible with the Convention (see especially *Reynolds v Times Newspapers* [2001] 2 AC 127 and *O'Shea v MGN Ltd* [2001] EMLR 40) but a recent analysis of the first decade of defamation cases under the Act concluded that '[t]he post-HRA changes to the law of defamation have been more subtle and less extensive than the monumental changes that have occurred in the law of privacy' (Oliphant, 'Defamation' in Hoffman, *op. cit.*). The legislative changes under the Defamation Act 2013 have been much more significant than those effected by the courts. See further Chapter 12.

Conclusion

The preceding discussion is merely a sample of the effects the HRA has had—and may have in future—on the law of tort. Though uncertainties remain about the Act's future, it is already clear that the ECHR has played a more significant role in the English law of tort than was the case before the HRA, and it seems likely that at least some of the consequent development of common law principles will endure even if the Act itself (as has been proposed) should be repealed.

For further discussion and analysis, see J. Wright, *Tort Law and Human Rights*, 2nd edn (Oxford: Hart, 2017).

3. Concerns about 'Compensation Culture'

Tomlinson v Congleton Borough Council [2004] 1 AC 46

The claimant waded into the defendant council's lake, threw himself forward into a dive, and hit his head on the sandy bottom, suffering serious injuries. The lake was on the site of an old quarry, which the council had transformed into a beauty spot. Various water sports were pursued on the lake, and sand had been deposited around it to create a beach, which was a popular place to picnic and sunbathe. As the result of a risk assessment, the council decided to prohibit swimming as unduly dangerous—for example, because a swimmer might be injured by windsurfers. Because warning signs proved ineffective, the council concluded that the only way of dealing with the problem was to make the water less accessible and less inviting. Shortly before the claimant's accident, it allocated a sum in its budget to a scheme to remove or cover over the beaches and replace them with muddy reed beds. The beach off which the claimant was injured was destroyed a few months after the accident. The claimant sued the council under the law of occupiers' liability (see Ch. 10.I), and the case eventually came before the House of Lords.

Lord Hobhouse

[81] . . . [I]t is not, and should never be, the policy of the law to require the protection of the foolhardy or reckless few to deprive, or interfere with, the enjoyment by the remainder of society of the liberties and amenities to which they are rightly entitled. Does the law require that all trees be cut down because some youths may climb them and fall? Does the law require the coastline and other beauty spots to be lined with warning notices? Does the law require that attractive waterside picnic spots be destroyed because of a few foolhardy individuals who choose to ignore warning notices and indulge in activities dangerous only to themselves? The answer to all these questions is, of course, no. But this is the road down which your Lordships, like other courts before, have been invited to travel and which the councils in the present case found so inviting. In truth, the arguments for the claimant have involved an attack upon the liberties of the citizen which should not be countenanced. They attack the liberty of the individual to engage in dangerous, but otherwise harmless, pastimes at his own risk and the liberty of citizens as a whole fully to enjoy the variety and quality of the landscape of this country. The pursuit of an unrestrained culture of blame and compensation has many evil consequences and one is certainly the interference with the liberty of the citizen.

Lord Scott

[94] . . . [The claimant] was simply sporting about in the water with his friends, giving free rein to his exuberance. And why not? And why should the council be discouraged by the law of tort from providing facilities for young men and young women to enjoy themselves in this way? Of course there is some risk of accidents arising out of the joie-de-vivre of the young. But that is no reason for imposing a grey and dull safety regime on everyone.

COMMENTARY

This is one of the emblematic decisions of the modern law of tort, and we shall encounter it again (see further extracts in Ch. 4.II.3 and Ch. 10.I.3). In the passages extracted, Lord Hobhouse and Lord Scott explicitly addressed concerns that the deterrent effect of potential tort liability might lead to the undesirable withdrawal of services and amenities of value to the community at large, and the imposition of (in Lord Scott's words) 'a grey and dull safety regime on everyone'. No doubt the decision reduced the anxiety previously experienced by councils and other landowners—indeed potential defendants in general—about their potential liabilities, and made it less likely that they would go to such extreme lengths in the interests of risk reduction. The Law Lords also struck out against the dilution of individual responsibility that can result if tort law is too ready to accord the injury victim a remedy. In an official report shortly afterwards (*Better Routes to Redress*, extracted later), the Better Regulation Task Force stated that the decision was 'an important legal precedent . . . which should make people understand that they need to be responsible for their own actions and should anticipate risk'.

Though *Tomlinson* addressed concerns of compensation in a particularly direct and explicit fashion, it was far from being the first case to contain expressions of judicial concern about the supposed excesses of the tort system. Lord Templeman anticipated the modern 'compensation culture' debate as early as 1986, deriding the assumption 'that for every mischance in an accident-prone world someone solvent must be liable in damages' (*CBS Songs*

Ltd v Amstrad Consumer Electronics plc [1988] AC 1013 at 1059). His words were echoed almost twenty years later by Lord Steyn in *Gorringe v Calderdale Metropolitan Borough Council* [2004] 1 WLR 1057 at [2]: 'the courts must not contribute to the creation of a society bent on litigation, which is premised on the illusion that for every misfortune there is a remedy'.

In *Majrowski v Guy's and St Thomas's NHS Trust* [2007] 1 AC 224 at [69], Lady Hale attempted to explain why the increased scope for claiming compensation in the modern law had raised concern: 'The fear is that, instead of learning to cope with the inevitable irritations and misfortunes of life, people will look to others to compensate them for all their woes, and those others will then become unduly defensive or protective.' Do you think that such fears *ought* to influence how the courts develop and apply the law? In particular, do the courts have sufficient evidence on which to determine whether or not the fears have any foundation in fact?

The factual evidence for the existence of a 'compensation culture' is considered in the following extracts.

Better Regulation Task Force, *Better Routes to Redress* (2004)

Almost every day there is a report in the media—newspaper, radio or television, suggesting that the United Kingdom is in the grip of a compensation culture. Headlines shout about people trying to claim what appear to be large sums of money for what are portrayed as dubious reasons. But what is not always reported is the outcome. The reality is often very different. Litigating is not easy. Many claims never reach court. Some will, of course, be settled out-of-court; others disappear because the claim had little chance of succeeding in the first place. For a claimant to succeed they have to be able to prove that first someone else owed them a duty of care and then that the same person was negligent.

The term 'compensation culture' is not used to describe a society where people are able to seek compensation. Rather a 'compensation culture' implies that a decision to seek compensation is wrong. 'Compensation culture' is a pejorative term and suggests that those that seek to 'blame and claim' should be criticised. It suggests greed; rather than people legitimately enforcing their rights. Few would oppose the principle that if people's rights are infringed, appropriate action should be available to the injured party to gain compensation from the guilty party. So why the double standards? . . .

Developments in recent years, principally the introduction of 'no win no fee' arrangements—where the claimant only pays their lawyer's fees in the event of success—and the emergence of claims management companies have increased access to justice. But they have also meant that more people have been encouraged to 'have a go' at claiming redress for a wrong they feel they have suffered.

We live in a much richer, but more risk averse, society than ever before. We are also much better informed about our rights, which means we are more aware when there is a case to answer. However some people may be persuaded, by what they have read in the papers or through the contact they have had with claims management companies, to look for compensation where none is available and therefore decide to 'have a go'. This has had both positive and negative impacts. On the positive side the public sector, such as schools, rather than cancelling trips and activities as the media would have us believe, have become much better at assessing and managing risks. Local authorities have put sophisticated systems in place to manage, for example, repairs to their pathways and highways.

However, on the negative side, the 'have a go' culture that encourages people to pursue misconceived or trivial claims:

- has put a drain on public sector resources;
- may make businesses and other organisations more cautious for fear of litigation;
- contributes to higher insurance premiums; and
- clogs up the system for those with indisputable claims . . .

However the so-called 'compensation culture' cannot be blamed for all these problems. Some have arisen from poor operational practices by companies . . .

The compensation culture: it's all in the mind . . .

Almost everyone we spoke to in the course of this study told us that they did not believe that there is a compensation culture in the UK. They argued that the reality is somewhat different, because the number of accident claims, including personal injury claims, is going down . . . , and that this proves the absence of a compensation culture in the UK. However, it ignores the fact that . . . people believe that there is a 'compensation culture' in the UK.

It is this perception, and the impact it is having on the UK as a whole, which needs to be tackled. Quoting statistics will not win the argument whilst the papers run 'compensation culture' stories. There is undoubtedly a perception that the public have a greater tendency now than ever before to seek redress if they suffer an injustice or injury, which they believe was someone else's fault. People look for someone else to blame for their misfortune. Advances in science and technology also mean that links between cause and effect are better understood. In the health arena, for example in areas such as passive smoking or occupational exposure to asbestos, this has led to a large increase in claims . . .

Don't believe everything you read

Regardless of perception, the truth behind the 'compensation culture' is somewhat different to how it is portrayed by the media and commentators. Many of the stories we read and hear either are simply not true or only have a grain of truth about them. The truth behind the famous, or rather infamous, McDonald's coffee case, which is often held up as a shining example of the 'compensation culture', is different to how it is reported or quoted. Newspapers readily use the incident to highlight the 'compensation culture'.

Litigating is not easy

Litigating, or pursuing a case to court, is only one form of redress. The majority of claims never make it to court. In order to litigate successfully the party who accuses (the claimant) another of acting in a negligent manner has to be able to prove that the other party (the defendant) owed them a duty of care and was negligent. This is the tort of negligence . . . The shift in recent years has been over what kinds of experiences are now appropriate to try to litigate against. Whole new types of claims that were simply not considered by lawyers 20 or 30 years ago are now being pursued. However, despite what the media would lead us to believe such claims do not always succeed . . .

Keeping the perception alive: the media

The perception of the 'compensation culture' is largely, though not entirely, perpetuated by the media. Whilst appearing to despise the phenomenon, it fills many column inches in newspapers. The media regularly report claims for apparently exorbitant sums, without later reporting the final outcome, which may have been very different. They also report stories from other parts of the world without pointing out that such cases would be unlikely to succeed here . . .

Impact of the 'compensation culture' perception

The threat of litigation, or just a complaint or claim, can have some positive effects. We have already mentioned improved risk assessments in the case of schools and maintenance work by local authorities. It can also help to improve the provision of goods and services without the need for Government intervention. Those who complain loudest about the current system need to think about the alternatives. However, there are also negative aspects of the 'have a go' culture. Dealing with complaints and claims costs a great deal of money . . . Of course, some of the claims each local authority handles will be genuine but a large number will be vexatious or frivolous. Dealing with these puts an enormous drain on local authority resources; resources which come from local residents and businesses and which could be better spent for the benefit of the same residents and businesses. Fear of litigation does change behaviour. Reporting incidents that appear trivial, and may be urban myths, will encourage others to change their behaviour. There are more serious examples of an overly cautious approach being taken. Pharmaceutical companies are more wary about developing new drugs for fear of litigation, and some doctors prefer to carry out a caesarean section to a natural birth because it is perceived as less risky (despite caesarean section not being risk free). Excessive risk aversion is not helpful to the UK's prosperity nor well-being.

K. Williams, 'State of Fear: Britain's "compensation culture" reviewed' (2005) 25 LS 499

Claims that Britain is in the grip of a 'compensation culture' and, consequently, a 'litigation crisis' are asserted with increased frequency. Concerns of this kind can be found in the columns of newspapers, in official reports, political discourse, legislative debate, and judicial decisions . . .

Is there a problem?

The answer to this question is hotly disputed, depending as it does on what exactly is thought to constitute the 'problem', as well as on who is asked. The growth of a 'compensation culture' implies an increased and unreasonable willingness to seek legal redress when things go wrong, whilst 'litigation crisis' implies that this shift in social attitudes has been translated into undesirable (perhaps unbearable) levels of formal disputing . . .

It seems there may be a number of different problems. Frequently it appears that there are too many (successful) claims; at other times that compensation payouts are too costly, quite commonly that lawyers' fees are excessive; sometimes a mixture of all of these . . . [But] the statistical evidence is both incomplete and somewhat equivocal . . . And, of course, even if we could establish with certainty how many claims there are, that would not tell us how many claims is too many. It often seems to be assumed, implicitly at least, that any increase is a cause for concern whilst a fall is to be applauded . . .

There are two other considerations connected with the numbers issue. First, claimant lawyers often point out with considerable (if self-interested) justification that the great majority of injured persons never resort to the law; that it is precisely the absence of a compensation culture that characterises our liability system . . . A second point is whether legitimate, well-founded claims should be counted as part of the 'problem'. After all, one reason why 'compensation crisis' stories find such ready audiences seems to be related to the ways in which they reflect public anxieties about the decline of social and moral values, such as self-reliance and personal responsibility; anxieties that are represented here by tales of greedy lawyers egging on grasping claimants chasing compensation for trivial harms which in an earlier era would have been stoically shouldered without public complaint. Accordingly, any attempt to test for the existence of a 'crisis' should, arguably, look beyond the absolute numbers of injury claims to whether there has been an increase in those that are substantially without merit or are bought off simply for their nuisance value. Unfortunately, there is no direct or reliable evidence to answer this crucial question either . . .

The 'real' problem and some of its causes

The idea that defendants are beset by ever-increasing numbers of doubtful claims is not proven. Indeed, the 'problem' we started with seems to have come down to this: that whatever may be the actual likelihood of irresponsible litigation, many believe themselves to be at heightened risk of being unfairly sued. According to the Task Force, this critical misperception or 'urban myth' induces socially and economically damaging risk-averse behaviour. Reputedly, organisations become less innovative, scarce resources that would be better applied elsewhere are unproductively diverted, unnecessarily costly safety precautions are taken, sometimes beneficial activities are fearfully abandoned altogether . . .

[T]he Task force . . . make anxious reference to an expanding liability regime . . . [They] say that new types of claims 'that were simply not considered by lawyers twenty or thirty years ago are now being pursued'—the implication being that the judiciary must take the blame to the extent that novel claims are admitted. Of course, quite how expansions of tort liability affect (insured) defendants or society more broadly is uncertain and disputed . . . No doubt the great bulk of claims will continue to be based on conventional legal principles applied to perfectly ordinary road traffic and workplace injury cases. On the other hand, the psychological impact of new, especially uncertain liabilities on defendants (and on their insurers' underwriting and pricing policies) may be marked, even where the development in question initially appears to advantage relatively few claimants. In fact, some recent judicial decisions have the potential to affect large numbers (albeit we can only guess how many) and destabilise some (particularly public sector) budgets.

COMMENTARY

A man driving his new Winnebago motor home set it on cruise control, then went into the back to make himself a cup of coffee; the vehicle left the highway, crashed and overturned—and the man successfully sued the manufacturers for failing to advise him not to leave the driving seat! More evidence of the excesses of our compensation culture? Well, no: just one of the myths, often perpetuated by an uncritical news media, that have grown up about the tort system, and which are exposed in the Better Regulation Task Force (BRTF) report. In fact, there is no truth in the story at all: 'Winnebago man' did not exist. But this has not prevented his story being reported as fact in numerous national newspapers (including *The Express*, the *Daily Star*, the *Daily Record*, *The People* and *The Mirror*, plus the London *Evening Standard*).

Not quite belonging in the category of pure myth are 'myth-representations'—stories that have some basis in truth but are told in such a way as to present a wholly misleading picture. The famous 'McDonald's coffee case' is the pre-eminent example. Eighty-one-year-old Stella Liebeck got a cup of coffee from a McDonald's drive-through restaurant and suffered third-degree burns after spilling it on her lap in the front seat of her car. She was awarded $2.9 million in damages by a New Mexico jury. Her case has become perhaps *the* emblem of the excesses of the US tort system, and by implication *our* tort system too, and of modern tort law's alleged subversion of traditional values of individual responsibility. But how accurate has the case's representation been in the media and in public debate?

The truth is that the reporting of the case has been sensationalised, partial, misleading and sometimes inaccurate (see W. Haltom and M. McCann, *Distorting the Law* (Chicago: University of Chicago Press, 2004), ch. 6). The plaintiff has been castigated for trying to profit from a trivial accident that was really her own fault; the tort process has been called into question for ignoring her own responsibility for the accident, and for awarding compensation going far beyond her losses. In fact, the truth is much more complex than such media portrayals, and rather different in key respects. Mrs Liebeck was not driving the car, merely a passenger, and the car was not in fact being driven at all at the material time, but parked up. Her injuries were far from trivial: she sustained third-degree burns, was in hospital for more than a week, suffered partial disability for two years after the accident, and was left with permanent scarring on 16 per cent of her body. The jury found McDonald's at fault because the coffee was not just hot—as, of course, it had to be—but excessively hot (considerably hotter than that produced by (e.g.) a domestic coffee machine). The jury did not ignore Mrs Liebeck's share of responsibility for the accident, but found her guilty of contributory negligence and reduced her damages by 20 per cent. After the reduction, the compensatory component of her award was only $160,000, a significant part of this attributable to her medical fees. The rest was punitive damages, the (very large) figure said to represent two days' profits for McDonald's from sales of coffee. In fact, Mrs Liebeck never received anything like the $2.9 million still quoted in news reports. As very commonly occurs in the United States, the award for punitive damages was subsequently reduced very considerably by the judge—to $480,000. Even the combined sum of $640,000 is unlikely to have been what Mrs Liebeck actually received, because—to forestall an appeal— she then accepted an undisclosed sum in final settlement of her claim.

Mrs Liebeck was commemorated—fairly or not—by the institution of an annual Stella Award for America's most frivolous or outrageous lawsuits of the year: see www.stellaawards.com. While this may seem just a bit of fun, Haltom and McCann, *op. cit.*, argue that a more serious intent lies behind such interventions: the production of, and saturation of the media with, popular narratives ('pop torts') that advance the cause of tort reform.

However the McDonald's coffee case is interpreted, its lessons are not easily applied to England and Wales. Our tort law is very different from that in the United States: no jury determination of liability or assessment of damages for personal injury; no punitive damages for negligence; and, until 2013, no contingency fees to feed the lawyers who drive the process. Even the 2013 introduction of 'damages-based agreements', by which the lawyers take a percentage of the damages, subject to a statutory cap, rather than an uplift of their usual fee (as under the longer-standing system of conditional fees), does not seem to have resulted in the excesses associated with contingency fees in the United States. For now, it is still pertinent to note that, when similar coffee cases were brought against McDonald's on this side of the Atlantic, they failed (see *Bogle v McDonald's Restaurants Ltd* [2002] EWHC 490, noted in Ch. 10.II.2). Why do you think the media has not given the same prominence to the claims that failed as to Mrs Liebeck's claim in the United States?

For further discussion of the tort system in the United States, highlighting differences with England and Wales, see J. Fleming, *The American Tort Process* (Oxford: OUP, 1988) and see further in Chapter 17.I.3(c).

Legislative Intervention in the UK

The official response to concerns about compensation culture may be traced back to December 2002, when the Department of Work and Pensions established an official review of employers' liability compulsory insurance after significant rises in premiums had raised concerns that the costs of the system were too high and that employers were finding it difficult to secure affordable cover. The review's recommendations (*Review of Employers' Liability Compulsory Insurance: Second Stage Report*, 2003) were conspicuously lacking in substance and did little to settle public fears; consequently, a 'media and political frenzy' developed (Morris, 'Spiralling or Stabilising? The Compensation Culture and Our Propensity to Claim Damages for Personal Injury' (2007) 70 MLR 349 at 350), with contributions from across the political spectrum. The insurance industry itself engaged in substantial lobbying and made frequent interventions in the public debate, seeking (according to Morris, p. 365):

> to create a sense of moral and political panic . . . [and] to undermine the legitimacy of those using the tort system and even the tort system itself . . . Insurers have also used the compensation culture as a smokescreen to hide their own role in the sudden and significant increases in liability insurance premiums.

The latter proposition finds some support in an analysis by the Office of Fair Trading (OFT), which noted 'a tendency (perhaps understandable) on the part of the insurance industry, to exaggerate the effect of some drivers of liability insurance premiums, such as changes in tort law' (*An analysis of current problems in the UK liability insurance market* (2003), para. 10.4). In fact, said the OFT, there was 'a consistent pattern of substantial losses and under-pricing of liability risks over many years' in which a significant explanatory factor was '[t]he failure of the market as a whole to anticipate and accurately quantify the effect of a number of emergent risks, including a variety of gradually developing diseases' (paras 10.11–10.12).

Other groups also sought to influence the political process because of concerns about their potential liabilities and the rising costs of liability insurance, amongst them teachers responsible for the organisation of school trips, and companies and volunteer groups engaged in outdoor pursuits. (On the latter, see in particular J. Fulbrook, *Outdoor Activities, Negligence and the Law* (Aldershot: Ashgate Publishing, 2005).) The Labour government of the day decided to legislate to address the public concern about compensation culture and the result was the Compensation Act 2006. Section 1 (extracted in Chapter 4), was evidently an attempt to change public perceptions and reassure volunteer groups by restating the well-established common law rule that the deterrent effect of potential liability should be considered in assessing the level of care that would have been exercised by a reasonable person when engaging in a desirable activity. Section 2 also restated existing principle: 'An apology, an offer of treatment or other redress, shall not of itself amount to an admission of negligence or breach of statutory duty.' The government hoped that the provision would reduce the number of cases in which adversarial disputes prevent the early rehabilitation of the accident victim (Hansard, HC vol. 447 col. 422, 8 June 2006). The Social Action, Responsibility and Heroism Act 2015 returned to the topic of desirable activities and made further legislative provision for persons engaging in 'social action' with the aspiration of preventing them from being deterred from volunteering or otherwise participating due to worries about liability.

In turn, some commentators have questioned whether valuable legislative time should have been devoted to these simple restatements of existing law, and have voiced concern that the Acts will promote new litigation about the meaning of their constituent terms. For extracts and further discussion, see Chapter 4.II.3.

In the first years of the new millennium, recorded numbers of personal injury claims in the United Kingdom were relatively stable, and even fell for a while, notwithstanding the then-recent introduction of 'no win no fee' litigation and the rise of the claims management companies (see Morris (2007) 70 MLR 349 at 357–8). After 2006, however, the number of recorded claims rose quite substantially, prompting a reform of the 'no win no fee' regime in 2012 (see Ch. 17.I.3(c)). Increases in the numbers of motor claims were especially pronounced, leading to concerns about rising motor insurance premiums (see House of Commons Transport Committee, *The Cost of Motor Insurance* (HC 2010–11, 591) and several follow-up reports). A particular focus of disquiet has been the proportion of claims relating to whiplash injuries, which may be hard to diagnose and (it is said) easy to fake or exaggerate; though the public rhetoric has sometimes been overblown, it has prompted a set of changes in the rules governing the claims process as well as the introduction of a new statutory tariff of damages intended to moderate the level of compensation paid for minor whiplash injury and so to reduce the incentive to sue (see the Civil Liability Act 2018, ss. 3–5 and the further analysis in Chs 15 and 17).

To put these concerns in context, however, it may be noted that, according to an estimate endorsed by the BRTF (p. 15), overall tort costs in the United Kingdom represent a surprisingly low percentage of gross domestic product (0.6 per cent), and are significantly lower than the comparable figures for most other developed countries, including France (0.8 per cent), Germany (1.3 per cent), Italy (1.7 per cent) and the United States (1.9 per cent). Other estimates have put the figure a little higher—at around 1 per cent. See further in Chapter 17.I.4.

Compensation Culture and Tort Reform in Other Countries

As these figures suggest, the issue of compensation culture is certainly not unique to the United Kingdom, and several other countries have embarked upon legislative reform with a view to constraining the costs of the tort system.

It is in the United States that tort law has been the focus of the most intense political scrutiny and the subject of the most divisive debate. The titles of two books published at the height of the discussion give a strong flavour of the positions taken on either side: C. Bogus, *Why Lawsuits are Good for America* (New York: New York University Press, 2001), and P. Howard, *The Collapse of the Common Good: How America's Lawsuit Culture Undermines our Freedom* (Ballantyne Books, 2002). In general, tort reform is constitutionally a matter for the state legislatures, with only limited scope for federal intervention. Amongst the reforms that have been adopted in different states are caps on the level of damages for non-pecuniary loss, caps on punitive damages, the introduction of proportionate liability for secondary defendants (in place of joint and several liability in full), restrictions on the scope for class actions and adoption of the (English) 'loser pays' costs rule. As already noted, it must always be remembered, when considering tort law in the United States, that many of the most problematic and controversial matters—e.g. jury assessment of damages, the availability of punitive damages, class actions—are either not to be found at all in England and Wales or only present in a very watered-down form. For further analysis, see Rabin, 'Some Reflections on the Process of Tort Reform' (1988) 25 San Diego L Rev 13; Galanter, 'Real World Torts: An Antidote to Anecdote' (1996) 55 Md L Rev 1093.

Another country to have embarked upon extensive tort reform is Australia. In 2002, the Federal Government convened an expert panel to review the law of negligence in response to the collapse of a leading liability insurer and general concerns about the cost and availability of public liability insurance (*Review of the Law of Negligence: Final Report*, 2002, https://treasury.gov.au/sites/default/files/2019-03/R2002-001_Law_Neg_Final.pdf ('the Ipp report')). The major part of the review's recommendations related to the restatement of existing principles in statutory form, with a view to correcting alleged misunderstandings of the law, promoting greater clarity and certainty and giving the courts more guidance as to the application of rules and principles that are open to various interpretations (paras 1.12–1.13). As in the United States, tort reform falls constitutionally within the competence of the states, some of whom considered that the Ipp review had not gone far enough and went considerably further in their own legislation (e.g. by introducing greater protection for certain sorts of defendants including public authorities and providers of recreational services: see Civil Liability Act 2002 (NSW), ss. 5L, 5M, 42, 45). However, the extent to which these reforms were needed, or have themselves been responsible for any reduction in insurance costs, has been questioned (Wright, 'National trends in personal injury litigation: Before and after "Ipp"' (2006) 14 TLJ 233). Indeed, Ipp JA—the chair of the expert panel mentioned earlier—has himself questioned the breadth of the reforms and commented: 'It is difficult to accept that public sentiment will allow all these changes to remain long-term features of the law' ('Themes in the Law of Tort' (2007) 81 ALJ 609). For discussion of the reforms, see J. Goudkamp, 'Reforming English Tort Law: Lessons from Australia', in E. Quill and R. J. Friel (eds), *Damages and Compensation Culture: Comparative Perspectives* (Oxford: Hart, 2016), Keeler, 'Personal Responsibility and the Reforms Recommended By the Ipp Report: "Time Future Contained in Time Past"' (2006) 14 TLJ 48, and McDonald, 'The Impact of the Civil Liability Legislation On Fundamental Policies and Principles on the Common Law Of Negligence' (2006) 14 TLJ 268.

More recently, and closer to home, Ireland presents us with another model for possible reform. Since 2004, a new statutory body, the Personal Injuries Assessment Board (PIAB), has had the task of assessing compensation in most cases of personal injury where liability is not contested. Claimants must submit to the procedure and cannot initiate a claim in court without the PIAB's authorisation. Proceedings are conducted entirely on paper, with no oral hearing. Claimants can get assistance from the PIAB's own telephone advice line, but if they want to be represented by a solicitor they must make arrangements at their own expense; they usually also have to bear a significant part of the cost of any medical report. The parties can choose whether to accept or reject the Board's assessment of the compensation, but, if both accept, it has the same legal effect as a court judgment. If either party rejects the assessment, the case has to be pursued through the courts. The reform aims to allow the resolution of personal injury claims quickly (an average of seven months, as opposed to four years for personal injury claims in the courts pre-PIAB) and without the legal expenses and experts fees associated with traditional tort litigation. Perhaps predictably, the new scheme has proved controversial, but an independent analysis of its functioning concluded that the 'bureaucratisation' effects of the claims settlement process have resulted in greater rationality and transparency than in traditional pre-hearing settlements, and brought improvements in economy and speed of resolution, while advocating the increased involvement of lawyers to promote greater equity in outcomes (Ilan, 'Four Years of the Personal Injuries Assessment Board: Assessing Its Impact' [2009:1] JSIJ 54). See further Dowling, 'Personal Injuries Assessment Board: A Decade of Delivery?', in Quill and Friel (eds), *op. cit.*

It can be seen that, in the United States, Australia and Ireland, 'tort reform' generally refers to *restrictions* on the scope of liability in tort or the ability to sue for damages. That is increasingly true in the United Kingdom as well, but it should be noted that some of the recent tort reforms here have actually *increased* compensation entitlements, or at least effected a significant transfer of the cost from the public to the private sector (see Lewis, 'The Politics of Tort Reform' (2006) 69 MLR 418). These issues are considered in more detail in Chapters 15 and 17.

2. INTENTIONAL INTERFERENCE WITH THE PERSON

I. Introduction

1. Historical Background

The civil wrongs now classified as intentional interference with the person are amongst the oldest causes of action known to the common law. From the early days of the common law, it was undoubtedly a wrong intentionally to cause someone injury, either by hitting them directly or doing some forcible act which had the immediate consequence of injury to another (e.g. throwing a stone). These wrongs were generally remedied in local courts. But the lawlessness that accompanied the reign of Stephen (1135–54), together with the reforms of the legal system made by Henry II (1154–89), encouraged litigants to bring claims before the central (royal) courts. By 1250 the royal writ of trespass had acquired two formal requirements: that the defendant acted *vi et armis* (with force and arms) and *contra pacem* (against the king's peace). The first requirement is self-explanatory: what was targeted was violent or threatening behaviour. The second was included to prevent the royal courts from being flooded with business; only if the force was such as to breach the king's peace would the royal courts have an interest in the case.

However, as Chapter 1 has made apparent, these allegations were only formal, and it became standard practice for a party who wanted the benefits of trial in the royal courts (in terms of mode of trial and procedure) to insert these allegations as a matter of course. Once the case was before the court, evidence as to what actually happened could be presented to the jury; hence the limitation could be overcome. This ultimately led to the creation of a new form of trespass writ, trespass on the case, which did not require the wrong to be *vi et armis* or *contra pacem*. Unlike trespass *vi et armis*, case was not actionable *per se*, that is, it required proof of damage flowing from the interference with the claimant. The development of this action and its relationship with trespass was considered in Chapter 1, but it is important to remember that, although there was controversy in the late eighteenth and early nineteenth centuries relating to which form of action should be used for unintentional wrongs causing direct harm, it was never doubted that the proper form of action for intentional wrongs causing direct harm was trespass *vi et armis*.

The old form of action for trespass to the person was classified into three separate causes of action—assault, battery and false imprisonment—all of which survive in the modern law. These torts were of more everyday significance in former, more violent, times, but remain important today as mechanisms by which the common law protects our most fundamental rights. As we shall see, most of the recent case law on trespass to the person consists of actions against the security apparatus of the state, particularly the police and prison authorities, though battery also plays an important background role in modern medical law. Apart from these actions, there is also in the modern law a more general cause of action for intentional infliction of physical or emotional harm deriving from *Wilkinson v Downton* [1897] 2 QB 57. That cause of action can be regarded as a descendant of the action on the case, since damage is a prerequisite of liability, and that liability extends to indirect consequences of the defendant's conduct. However, the *Wilkinson v Downton* tort has come to be overshadowed by negligence—another tort derived from the action on the case—while its scope of operation has been considerably curtailed by the decisions in *Wainwright v Home Office* [2004] 2 AC 406 and in *O (A Child) v Rhodes* [2016] AC 219 (both extracted in V). In this chapter we will consider the elements of each of these causes of action, as well as the most recent arrival in the stable of intentional torts, the statutory tort of harassment, before turning to look at defences to these torts.

2. Trespass and Fault

As previously noted, the writ of trespass *vi et armis* lay only for direct interferences. This requirement of directness was, in theory, capable of being satisfied by either intentional or unintentional conduct. By the time the forms of action were abolished in the 1870s, however, it was generally accepted that unintentional wrongs causing direct harm (in modern parlance, negligence) were actionable in case. Thus the substantive, as opposed to procedural, distinction between trespass and negligence was that trespass dealt with intentional wrongs and negligence with unintentional wrongs. But what if the claimant pleaded neither intention nor negligence but merely directness, for example, 'the defendant shot me'? Such a pleading may have been acceptable for the old writ of trespass *vi et armis*, but after the forms of action had been abolished, did that pleading disclose a substantive cause of action? While the issue had a practical significance (as we shall see in the next section) it also raised important questions about the relationship between trespass and negligence.

(a) General

In *Fowler v Lanning* [1959] 1 QB 426, the statement of claim alleged that at a certain time and date 'the defendant shot the plaintiff', and that as a result the plaintiff sustained personal injuries and had suffered loss and damage. The defendant objected that the statement of claim disclosed no cause of action, since the plaintiff had not alleged that the shooting was either intentional or negligent, and this point of law was ordered to be disposed of before trial of the action on the facts. Diplock J agreed with the defendant: it was up to the plaintiff to prove intention or negligence on the defendant's part, and so 'he must allege either intention on the part of the defendant, or, if he relies on negligence, he must state the facts which he alleges constitute negligence' ([1959] 1 QB 426 at 440). The approach of Diplock J has much to commend it. It forces the claimant to allege facts which constitute intention or negligence, allowing the defendant to know the exact nature of the claim. The defendant does not have to come to trial blindfold, ready to defend evidence of intention and negligence, whichever is raised. The decision may therefore be thought to promote procedural fairness. It also promotes efficiency, as the purpose of the pleadings is to limit the issues in dispute between the parties.

However, the decision in *Fowler v Lanning* has not won universal support elsewhere. There remains doubt in Australia over whether it represents the law in that jurisdiction (compare *McHale v Watson* (1964) 111 CLR 384, per Windeyer J; *Venning v Chin* (1974) 10 SASR 299; *Hackshaw v Shaw* (1984) 155 CLR 614 at [5] per Deane J; *Stingel v Clark* (2006) 226

CLR 442 at [47] per Gummow J). In Canada, *Walmsley v Humenick* [1954] 2 DLR 232 took the same line as *Fowler v Lanning*, but later cases have followed an earlier Canadian Supreme Court decision (*Cook v Lewis* [1951] SCR 830) which suggests the onus of disproving intent or negligence lies with the defendant (*Larin v Goshen* (1975) 56 DLR 3d 719; *Bell Canada v Cope (Sarnia) Ltd* (1980) 11 CCLT 170). New Zealand appears to follow *Fowler v Lanning* (*Beals v Hayward* [1960] NZLR 131).

Letang v Cooper [1965] QB 232

The plaintiff was sunbathing in the car park of a hotel when she was run over by the defendant's car. As the time for her to bring an action in negligence had expired, she framed her action in trespass, seeking to benefit from the longer limitation period for this cause of action. She was successful before Elwes J but the Court of Appeal reversed the decision.

Lord Denning MR

The sole question is whether the action is statute barred. The plaintiff admits that the action for negligence is barred after three years, but she claims that the action for trespass to the person is not barred until six years have elapsed. The judge has so held and awarded her £575 damages for trespass to the person.

Under the Limitation Act 1939, the period of limitation was six years in all actions founded 'on tort'; but in 1954 Parliament reduced it to three years in actions for damages for personal injuries, provided that the actions come within these words of s. 2(1) of the Law Reform (Limitation of Actions, etc) Act 1954:

> . . . in the case of actions for damages for negligence, nuisance or breach of duty (whether the duty exists by virtue of a contract or of a provision made by or under a statute or independently of any contract or any such provision) where the damages claimed by the plaintiff for the negligence, nuisance or breach of duty consist of or include damages in respect of personal injuries to any person . . .

The plaintiff says that these words do not cover an action for trespass to the person, and that, therefore, the time bar is not the new period of three years, but the old period of six years.

The argument, as it was developed before us, became a direct invitation to this court to go back to the old forms of action and to decide this case by reference to them.

[Lord Denning considered the distinction between trespass and case, and identified a number of difficulties with relying on it in this context. He continued:]

I must decline, therefore, to go back to the old forms of action in order to construe this statute . . .

The truth is that the distinction between trespass and case is obsolete. We have a different sub-division altogether. Instead of dividing actions for personal injuries into trespass (direct damage) or case (consequential damage), we divide the causes of action now according as the defendant did the injury intentionally or unintentionally. If one man intentionally applies force directly to another, the plaintiff has a cause of action in assault and battery, or, if you so please to describe it, in trespass to the person. 'The least touching of another in anger is a battery.' If he does not inflict injury intentionally, but only unintentionally, the plaintiff has no cause of action today in trespass. His only cause of action is in negligence, and then only on proof of want of reasonable care. If the plaintiff cannot prove want of reasonable care, he may have no cause of action at all. Thus, it is not enough nowadays for the plaintiff to plead that 'the defendant shot the plaintiff'. He must also allege that he did it intentionally or negligently. If intentional, it is the tort of assault and battery. If negligent and causing damage, it is the tort of negligence.

The modern law on this subject was well expounded by my brother Diplock J in *Fowler v Lanning* with which I fully agree. But I would go this one step further: when the injury is not inflicted intentionally, but negligently, I would say that the only cause of action is negligence and not trespass. If it were trespass, it would be actionable without proof of damage; and that is not the law today.

[Lord Denning went on to decide that, even if he was wrong about this, the words 'breach of duty' in the Law Reform (Limitation of Actions, etc) Act 1954, s. 2(1) were wide enough to encompass the cause of action for trespass to the person as well as negligence, and hence that the three-year limitation period in that section applied.]

Danckwerts LJ, in a short concurring judgment, agreed with Lord Denning MR. **Diplock LJ** held that the plaintiff's action was for 'negligence, nuisance, or breach of duty' under s. 2(1) of the 1954 Act, and was therefore subject to a three-year limitation period where damages for personal injury were claimed.

Appeal allowed.

COMMENTARY

As the extract shows, Lord Denning MR favoured abolition of the action for 'negligent trespass', because trespass connotes intention. In his concurring judgment, Diplock LJ was more circumspect, holding that the label did not matter as long as no procedural consequences attached to it. Nevertheless, he accepted that in cases where intention was lacking, the language of 'negligence' was to be preferred, and he also made it clear that in cases of unintentional trespass to the person actual damage would (as in negligence) be a necessary ingredient of the cause of action. Beever ('The Form of Liability in the Torts of Trespass' (2011) 40 *Common Law World Review* 378, 386–7) argues that in reality there is little difference between the two positions:

Diplock LJ's position was not: when a defendant unintentionally causes a claimant's injury, the claimant is able to sue under the set of principles associated with the law of negligence and, with certain modifications, under the set of principles relevant to the law of trespass; his Lordship's position was: when a defendant unintentionally causes a claimant's injury, the claimant is able to sue only under the set of principles associated with the law of negligence, but we can, if we want, nevertheless describe the relevant fact pattern ('cause of action') as negligence or trespass. Accordingly, the disagreement between Lord Denning and Diplock LJ is of no substantive consequence at all.

Hence, although it might still be possible to describe certain facts as giving rise to a cause of action in 'negligent trespass' (see *Salmond & Heuston*, p. 7), a claimant will obtain no benefit from framing their action in such a way.

According to Lord Denning, the modern distinction between the causes of action for trespass and negligence lay in the concept of intention. Intentional harms were remediable in trespass; negligent harms in negligence. A claimant would not be allowed to 'dress up' a negligence claim as an intentional tort and seek a longer limitation period. However, any strict dichotomy between intention and negligence is obviously false, since intentional conduct can of course amount to negligence, as the courts have recognised in other contexts (see, for example, the discussion of intentional infliction of harm in V). The difficulties this false dichotomy gave rise to were revealed when it came to the converse question of whether a claimant should be permitted to bring an action for intentional harm in negligence for the purpose of obtaining a more favourable limitation period. In *Stubbings v Webb* [1993] AC 498 the House of Lords considered the legislative history of the special limitation period of three years (as opposed to the normal six for tort actions) prescribed for actions in 'negligence, nuisance or breach of duty' where damages are claimed for personal injury, which is currently to be found in s. 11 of the Limitation Act 1980. (The court in *Letang v Cooper* was considering the corresponding provision in the now repealed Limitation of Actions Act 1954, s. 2(1).) The House of Lords in *Stubbings* refused to interpret the words 'negligence, nuisance or breach of duty' as including deliberate sexual or physical abuse, with the result that the provisions of the 1980 Act allowing for the discretionary extension of the limitation period for personal injury claims (s. 33) did not apply. It followed that the plaintiff's abuse claims were subject to the normal six-year limitation period for actions in tort under s. 2 of the 1980 Act, which commenced from the date of the abuse and, as the abuse had taken place between sixteen and twenty-eight years earlier, her claims were statute-barred. The decision attracted few admirers (see McGee (1993) 109 LQR 356; Jones (1994) 110 LQR 31; Lunney (1993–94) 4 KCLJ 79; Conaghan, 'Tort Litigation in the Context of Intra-familial Abuse' (1998) 61 MLR 132), but although the Law Commission (*Limitation of Actions*, Law Com. No. 270, para. 4.33) recommended that the same limitation regime should govern claims for personal injury whether founded on an intentional tort or negligence, no legislative change was made. Attempts to avoid the problem by pleading negligence in relation to conduct that was in essence a deliberate sexual or physical assault were severely criticised by the Court of Appeal in *KR v Bryn Alyn Community (Holdings) Ltd* [2003] QB 1441, which held that in most cases they were impermissible attempts to avoid the reasoning in *Stubbings*. In the end, the House of Lords in *A v Hoare* [2008] 1 AC 844 reconsidered its earlier decision and unanimously declined to follow it (as had a majority of the High Court of Australia, applying similarly worded legislation, in *Stingel v Clark* (2006) 226 CLR 442), holding that the phrase 'negligence, nuisance or breach of duty' was wide enough to encompass personal injury arising out of a deliberate assault. Lord Hoffmann noted (at [14]) that the Limitation Act 1975 had introduced a more favourable limitation regime for personal injuries caused by negligence, by providing for a later commencement date ('the date of knowledge... of the person injured') in cases of latent harm (see now Limitation Act 1980, ss. 11(4)(b), 14), and said that in his view there could 'be no moral or other ground' for denying recourse to this regime to a victim of intentional injury. With this decision, Handford commented, the House of Lords 'corrected a long-standing anomaly and considerably eased the burden on sexual abuse victims who wish to obtain justice from the courts' ((2008) 16 Tort L Rev 61, 63).

For discussion of the role of the intentional torts in child abuse cases, see P. Case, *Compensating Child Abuse in England and Wales* (Cambridge: CUP, 2007) and L. Hoyano and C. Keenan, *Child Abuse: Law and Policy Across Boundaries* (Oxford: OUP, 2007).

(b) The Concept of Intention

The distinction between intentional and negligent wrongs is fundamental to the law of torts. Two questions arise in this context: what does 'intention' mean, and what must the defendant have intended? The latter question is the easier to answer: as far as the intentional torts against the person are concerned the defendant must intend the consequences of his conduct that constitute the wrongful interference. In the case of battery, this means that the unlawful contact must be intended (see *Wilson v Pringle*, discussed later) whilst, for assault, the defendant must intend the acts that, objectively, cause apprehension of an imminent infliction of force. So the mere act of intentionally firing a gun will not amount to a battery if there is no-one in sight, but it will be sufficient if the gun is aimed at another who is consequently hit by a bullet. Similarly, throwing a punch when alone is no assault, but may be so if another is in range of the blow. Note, however, that intention does not necessarily connote fault. It is not a condition of liability in trespass to the person that the defendant intended to cause harm to the claimant or to act in any way unlawfully. For example, a surgeon who amputates the wrong leg because of an error made by someone else commits battery, and a prison governor who acted in accordance with the law as generally understood at the relevant time was held liable for false imprisonment when the courts subsequently decided that that general understanding had been wrong (*R v Governor of Brockhill Prison, ex p. Evans* [2001] 2 AC 19, discussed in VI.2). In this sense, it has correctly been noted that liability in the trespass torts is strict (see, e.g., Beever, *op. cit.*).

The concept of intention is further analysed in the next extract from the *Restatement of the Law (Third), Torts: Liability for Physical and Emotional Harm* (2010). The *Restatement* is published by the American Law Institute and is a summary of the law which applies in the majority of the states of the United States. Although the extract sometimes refers to an intention to cause harm, the intentional torts against the person require only an intention to bring about the wrongful interference in question (e.g. in battery, the unlawful contact). The extract should be read with this in mind.

American Law Institute, *Restatement Third, Torts: Liability for Physical and Emotional Harm* (2010)

Chapter 1—Intent, Recklessness, and Negligence: Definitions

§ 1 Intent

A person acts with the intent to produce a consequence if:
(a) the person acts with the purpose of producing that consequence; or
(b) the person acts knowing that the consequence is substantially certain to result.

Illustration:
1. In a forest area Ken deliberately pulls the trigger of a rifle. He hopes to hit a wild deer, and he is unaware that any person is in the vicinity. The gun discharges. In fact, Nancy is nearby and is struck by the bullet. Ken has intentionally shot his gun. Yet he has not intentionally caused the harm to Nancy; he did not act with the purpose to produce that harm nor did he know that the harm was substantially certain to occur . . .
2. Wendy throws a rock at Andrew, someone she dislikes, at a distance of 100 feet, wanting to hit Andrew. Given the distance, it is far from certain Wendy will succeed in this; rather, it is probable that the rock will miss its target. In fact, Wendy's aim is true, and Andrew is struck by the rock. Wendy has purposely, and hence intentionally, caused this harm.
3. The Jones Company runs an aluminum smelter, which emits particulate fluorides as part of the industrial process. Jones knows that these particles, carried by the air, will land on neighboring property, and in doing so will bring about a range of harms. Far from desiring

this result, Jones in fact regrets it. Despite its regret, Jones has knowingly, and hence intentionally, caused the resulting harms.

4. When Steve, a police officer, seeks to pull to the side of the road a car that has made an illegal turn, the car speeds away. Steve undertakes a chase, and continues the chase even though the car is making every effort to escape, driving rapidly and somewhat wildly. Steve is well aware there is a significant likelihood that someone will suffer physical harm, either personal injury or at least property damage, in the course of the chase. In fact, the escaping car strikes the car owned by Ruth, which she is driving carefully on the highway. Steve, in initiating and continuing the chase, has not intentionally harmed Ruth or her car. Steve did not harbor a purpose that Ruth (or anyone else) suffer any harm; while Steve knew there was a significant likelihood of such harm, the harm was not substantially certain to occur.

5. Joanne, a physician, provides medication to her patient, Mark. Because Joanne has confused one medication with another, the medication she gives Mark is certain to cause harm to Mark. Such harm ensues. Joanne has not intentionally harmed Mark. While Joanne's conduct was substantially certain to cause him harm, Joanne lacked the knowledge that this would happen.

COMMENTARY

As the extract makes clear, intention is not to be equated with motive: when the authorities in an Australian prison fired CS gas to incapacitate a rioting prisoner, knowing that other inmates would inevitably be exposed to the fumes, that exposure was intentional, even though not desired (*Binsaris v Northern Territory* (2020) 380 ALR 1). A more difficult question is whether recklessness as to consequences can amount to 'intention' for the purpose of the intentional torts. The US *Restatement* suggests it does not, and the Supreme Court held in *O (A Child) v Rhodes* [2016] AC 219 (extracted in V) that recklessness is not sufficient for liability to arise in the tort of intentional infliction of physical or emotional harm. However, the Northern Ireland Court of Appeal held in a case against a number of individuals allegedly involved in the 1998 terrorist bombing in Omagh that recklessness could satisfy the intention requirement for battery (*Breslin v McKevitt* [2011] NICA 33), and Aikens LJ assumed in *Pritchard v Co-operative Group Ltd* [2012] QB 320 that recklessness would satisfy the mental element in both assault and battery. The practical significance of the issue may be diminished because, where a claimant has suffered physical injury, his reckless conduct might be categorised as negligent and thus a remedy provided. Nonetheless, there might be procedural advantages in having reckless conduct categorised as intentional rather than negligent (e.g. in terms of limitation periods), and the issue awaits resolution by the courts. On the relationship between intention and recklessness in tort law more generally, see Cane, 'Mens Rea in Tort Law' (2000) 20 OJLS 533, 535–8.

Another difficulty arises when A, seeking to hit B, actually hits C. In the American case of *Talmage v Smith* (1894) 101 Mich 370, the defendant threw a stick towards a group of boys, and there was evidence that it was directed at a particular boy. However, the stick missed that boy and instead struck the plaintiff, who successfully sued in trespass. According to the Supreme Court of Michigan: 'The right of the plaintiff was made to depend upon the intention on the part of the defendant to hit somebody, and to inflict an unwarranted injury upon some one. Under these circumstances, the fact that the injury resulted to another than was intended does not relieve the defendant from responsibility....' This principle of 'transferred intent' appears to have been applied in *James v Campbell* (1832) 5 C & P 372 where the defendant was held liable in battery for hitting the plaintiff, even though he intended to hit a third person and did not know he had struck the plaintiff, the judge holding that this went to damages and not to liability (see also *Livingstone v Ministry of Defence* [1984] NI 356; *Bici v Ministry of Defence* [2004] EWHC 786 (QB)). Would these actions be better treated as actions in negligence? See Beever, 'Transferred Malice in Tort Law' (2009) 29 LS 400.

II. Assault

Assault is defined in the following terms by *Blackstone*, vol. III, 'Of Private Wrongs', ch. 8, I, 2–3:

> [A]ssault ... is an attempt or offer to beat another, without touching him: as if one lifts up his cane, or his fist, in a threatening manner; or strikes at him, but misses him; this is an assault, insultus, which Finch describes to be 'an unlawful setting upon one's person'. This also is an inchoate violence, amounting considerably higher than bare threats; and therefore, though no actual suffering is proved, yet the party injured may have redress by action of trespass vi et armis; wherein he shall recover damages as a compensation for the injury.

The claimant must establish that the conduct of the defendant created a reasonable apprehension of an imminent battery. These issues are considered in the following extracts.

Stephens v Myers (1830) 4 C & P 349, 172 ER 735

Assault. The declaration stated that the defendant threatened and attempted to assault the plaintiff. Plea—Not Guilty.

It appeared that the plaintiff was acting as chairman, at a parish meeting, and sat at the head of a table, at which table the defendant also sat, there being about six or seven persons between him and the plaintiff. The defendant having, in the course of some angry discussion, which took place, been very vociferous, and interrupted the proceedings of the meeting, a motion was made, that he should be turned out, which was carried by a very large majority. Upon this, the defendant said, he would rather pull the chairman out of the chair, than be turned out of the room; and immediately advanced with his fist clenched towards the chairman, but was stopt by the churchwarden who sat next but one to the chairman, at a time when he was not near enough for any blow he might have meditated to have reached the chairman; but the witness said, that it seemed to them that he was advancing with an intention to strike the chairman.

Spankie, Serjt, for the defendant, upon this evidence, contended, that no assault had been committed, as there was no power in the defendant, from the situation of the parties, to execute his threat—there was not a present ability—he had not the means of executing his intention at the time he was stopt.

Tindal CJ, summing up to the jury:

It is not every threat, when there is no actual personal violence that constitutes an assault, there must, in all cases, be the means of carrying the threat into effect. The question I shall leave to you will be, whether the defendant was advancing at the time, in a threatening attitude, to strike the chairman so that his blow would almost immediately have reached the chairman, if he had not been stopt; then, though he was not near enough at the time to have struck him, yet if he was advancing with that intent, I think it amounts to an assault in law. If he was so advancing, that, within a second or two of time, he would have reached the plaintiff, it seems to me it is an assault in law. If you think he was not advancing to strike the plaintiff, then only can you find for the defendant; otherwise you must find it for the plaintiff, and give him such damages, as you think the nature of the case requires.

Verdict for the plaintiff, damages 1 shilling.

COMMENTARY

Would the plaintiff have succeeded if, being a particularly timid soul, he had feared being thrown out of his chair even though the defendant had been threatening him from outside the hall? It seems the jury thought him fairly timorous, for even in 1830 an award of one shilling as damages was paltry.

R v Ireland; R v Burstow [1998] AC 147

A number of issues arose in these appeals, one of which was whether the maker of silent telephone calls could be convicted of a criminal offence which required the accused to have committed an assault against the victim.

Lord Steyn

It is to assault in the form of an act causing the victim to fear an immediate application of force to her that I must turn. Counsel argued that as a matter of law an assault can never be committed by words alone and therefore it cannot be committed by silence. The premise depends on the slenderest authority, namely an observation by Holroyd J to a jury that 'no words or singing are equivalent to an assault' (see *Meade's and Belt's Case* (1823) 1 Lew CC 184 at 185, 168 ER 1006). The proposition that a gesture may amount to an assault, but that words can never suffice, is unrealistic and indefensible. A thing said is also a thing done. There is no reason why something said should be incapable of causing an apprehension of immediate personal violence, e.g. a man accosting a woman in a dark alley saying 'come with me or I will stab you'. I would, therefore, reject the proposition that an assault can never be committed by words.

That brings me to the critical question whether a silent caller may be guilty of an assault. The answer to this question seems to me to be 'Yes, depending on the facts'. It involves questions of fact within the province of the jury. After all, there is no reason why a telephone caller who says to a woman in a menacing way 'I will be at your door in a minute or two' may not be guilty of an assault if he causes his victim to apprehend immediate personal violence. Take now the case of the silent caller. He intends by his silence to cause fear and he is so understood. The victim is assailed by uncertainty about his intentions. Fear may dominate her emotions, and it may be the fear that the caller's arrival at her door may be imminent. She may fear the possibility of immediate personal violence. As a matter of law the caller may be guilty of an assault: whether he is or not will depend on the circumstance and in particular on the impact of the caller's potentially menacing call or calls on the victim. Such a prosecution case . . . may be fit to leave to the jury. . . .

Lord Hope of Craighead

[I]t has been recognised for many centuries that putting a person in fear may amount to what in law is an assault. This is reflected in the meaning which is given to the word 'assault' in Archbold's *Criminal Pleading, Evidence and Practice* (1997) p 1594 para 19–66, namely that an assault is any act by which a person intentionally or recklessly causes another to apprehend immediate and unlawful violence. . . .

The question is whether such an act can include the making of a series of silent telephone calls. Counsel for the appellant said that such an act could not amount to an assault under any circumstances, just as words alone could not amount to an assault. He also submitted that, in order for there to be an assault, it had to be proved that what the victim apprehended was immediate and unlawful violence, not just a repetition of the telephone calls. It was not enough to show merely that the victim was inconvenienced or afraid. . . .

There is no clear guidance on this point either in the statute [Offences Against the Person Act 1861] or in the authorities. On the one hand in *Meade's and Belt's Case* (1823) 1 Lew CC 184, 168 ER 1006 Holroyd J said that no words or singing can amount to an assault. On the other hand in *R v Wilson* [1955] 1 WLR 493 at 494 Lord Goddard CJ said that the appellant's words, 'Get out knives' would itself be an assault. . . .

The fact is that the means by which a person of evil disposition may intentionally or recklessly cause another to apprehend immediate and unlawful violence will vary according to the circumstances. Just as it is not true to say that every blow which is struck is an assault—some blows, which would otherwise amount to battery, may be struck by accident or in jest or may otherwise be entirely justified—so also it is not true to say that mere words or gestures can never constitute an assault. It all depends on the circumstances. If the words or gestures are accompanied in their turn by gestures or by words which threaten immediate and unlawful violence, that will be sufficient for an assault. The words or gestures must be seen in their whole context.

In this case the means which the appellant used to communicate with his victims was the telephone. While he remained silent, there can be no doubt that he was intentionally communicating with them as directly as if he was present with them in the same room. But whereas for him merely to remain silent with them in the same room, where they could see him and assess his demeanour, would have been unlikely to give rise to any feelings of apprehension on their part, his silence when using the telephone in calls made to them repeatedly was an act of an entirely different character. He was using his silence as a means of conveying a message to his victims. This was that he knew who and where they were, and that his purpose in making contact with them was as malicious as it was deliberate. In my opinion silent telephone calls of this nature are just as capable as words or gestures, said or made in the presence of the victim, of causing an apprehension of immediate and unlawful violence.

Whether this requirement, and in particular that of immediacy, is in fact satisfied will depend on the circumstances. This will need in each case, if it is disputed, to be explored in evidence.

COMMENTARY

The latter of the two extracts is from a criminal case, and it should be noted that assault (like battery and false imprisonment) is a crime as well as a tort. The elements of the crime of assault are similar, if not identical, to the tort of assault (although the subjective mental element of *mens rea* is not required in a civil claim) so that criminal assault cases can generally be used as authority in civil cases, although the different context of the decisions should be recognised.

Any successful action for assault requires the claimant to have apprehended the direct and immediate application of force to their person. As the extracts from *Ireland* show, the question of immediacy is one of fact for the judge or jury. In *Mbasogo v Logo Ltd* [2007] QB 846, the claimant, the President of Equatorial Guinea, alleged assault against a group of mercenaries. The mercenaries were an advance party of a larger group whose aim was to overthrow the government but the plot was foiled. The striking out of the claim was upheld by the Court of Appeal: it was not clear that the advance group was even armed, still less that it had the capacity to carry out an immediate attack (see also *Thomas v NUM* [1986] Ch 20).

Although the possibility that mere words can amount to an assault was only finally confirmed in *Ireland*, it has long been the law that words accompanied by actions can, even if the words amount to a merely conditional threat and the claimant could avoid danger simply by complying with the defendant's demand. In *Read v Coker* (1853) 13 CB 850, 138 ER 1437, the plaintiff was told to leave premises where he conducted his business. He refused, whereupon the defendant collected together some of his workmen, who stood near the plaintiff with their sleeves and aprons tucked up, and told the plaintiff they would break his neck if he did not leave. He did leave, but later brought a successful action for assault. In the course of proceedings brought by the defendant for a mistrial Jervis CJ stated: '[T]he facts here clearly showed that the defendant was guilty of an assault. There was a threat of violence exhibiting an intention to assault, and a present ability to carry the threat into execution.' (See also *Police v Greaves* [1964] NZLR 295.)

However, not every conditional threat will be actionable. In *Tuberville v Savage* (1669) 1 Mod Rep 3, 86 ER 684, the defendant put his hand on his sword and said to the plaintiff: 'If it were not assize time I would not take such language from you.' The court held that this amounted to a declaration that the plaintiff would not be assaulted; hence there was no action. While the principle is sound, it should be remembered that the main question is whether the conduct creates an apprehension of immediate force, and one wonders whether the plaintiff, confronted by a man obviously angry and drawing a sword, would really have been calmed by the defendant's words.

A further question that arises is whether the defendant must intend the claimant to apprehend an imminent application of force. It has been suggested that this is so (*Bici v Ministry of Defence* [2004] EWHC 786 (QB)), though it may be difficult for a defendant to persuade a judge or jury that his subjective intention was not to cause the claimant any apprehension if, viewing his conduct objectively, this is exactly what it did. Thus it has been held that pointing an unloaded gun at another may amount to an assault as long as the claimant does not know the gun is unloaded (see *R v St George* (1840) 9 C & P 483; *Logdon v DPP* [1976] Crim LR 121; contra, *Blake v Barnard* (1840) 9 C & P 626). Any apprehension of an imminent battery must also be reasonable. There is no assault if there is no means to put the threat into effect but whether this is so should not be governed solely by hindsight. In *Stephens v Myers*, it turned out that the defendant was stopped before he was in a position to hit the plaintiff, but the latter, watching nervously from his seat, was in no position to know this. This is supported by the decision in *Ireland*, which clearly focuses attention on the position of the victim in answering the reasonable apprehension question. The victims did not know whether the silent callers were close enough to apply immediate force, but the possibility that they might be was sufficient. Similarly, in another criminal case, *Smith v Chief Superintendent, Woking Police Station* (1983) 76 Cr App R 234, an intruder who looked through the victim's closed window was found guilty of assault, because it was perfectly reasonable for the elderly victim to have feared the application of immediate force.

III. Battery

Battery is the unlawful touching of another. *Blackstone*, vol. III, 'Of Private Wrongs', ch. 8, I, 2–3 describes a battery as follows:

> Battery is the unlawful beating of another. The least touching of another's person wilfully, or in anger, is a battery; for the law cannot draw the line between different degrees of violence, and therefore totally prohibits the first and lowest stage of it: every man's person being sacred, and no other having a right to meddle with it, in any the slightest manner . . . But battery is, in some cases, justifiable or lawful . . . On account of these causes of justification, battery is defined to be the unlawful beating of another . . .

Battery is unquestionably one of the most important torts known to the common law, for the interest it protects is so fundamental: as McLachlin J said in *Non-Marine Underwriters, Lloyds of London v Scalera* [2000] 1 SCR 551 at [12], it recognises 'the right of each person to control his or her body and who touches it'. The defences to a prima facie battery will be considered later in the chapter. Here we focus on what touchings might be considered unlawful.

Wilson v Pringle [1987] QB 237

Two schoolboys were involved in an incident in a school corridor as a result of which one fell and was injured. The boy who fell claimed damages, alleging a battery by the other boy. The defendant admitted that he had indulged in horseplay with the plaintiff but claimed that this was insufficient, as the ingredients of trespass to the person were a deliberate touching, hostility and an intention to inflict injury, and therefore horseplay in which there was no intention to inflict injury could not amount to a trespass to the person. The plaintiff contended that there merely had to be an intentional application of force, such as horseplay involved, regardless of whether it was intended to cause injury.

Croom-Johnson LJ

[W]hat does entitle an injured plaintiff to sue for the tort of trespass to the person? Reference must be made to one further case: *Williams v Humphrey* (12 February 1975, unreported), decided by Talbot J. There the defendant, a boy just under 16, pushed the plaintiff into a swimming pool and caused him physical injury. The judge found the defendant acted negligently and awarded damages. But there was another claim in trespass. Talbot J rejected the submission that the action would not lie unless there was an intent to injure. He held that it was sufficient, if the act was intentional, that there was no justification for it. . . .

The reasoning in *Williams v Humphrey* is all right as far as it goes, but it does not go far enough. It did not give effect to the reasoning of the older authorities . . . that for there to be either an assault or a battery there must be something in the nature of hostility. It may be evinced by anger, by words or gesture. Sometimes the very act of battery will speak for itself, as where somebody uses a weapon on another. What, then, turns a friendly touching (which is not actionable) into an unfriendly one (which is)? . . .

[His Lordship considered *R v Sutton* [1977] 1 WLR 1086 and continued:]

A more recent authority is *Collins v Wilcock* [1984] 1 WLR 1172. . . . The facts were that a woman police officer, suspecting that a woman was soliciting contrary to the Street Offences Act 1959, tried to question her. The woman walked away, and was followed by the police officer. The officer took hold of her arm in order to restrain her. The woman scratched the officer's arm. She was arrested, charged with assaulting a police officer in the execution of her duty, and convicted. On appeal by case stated, the appeal was allowed, on the ground that the officer had gone beyond the scope of her duty in detaining the woman in circumstances short of arresting her. The officer had accordingly committed a battery.

The judgment of the Divisional Court was given by Robert Goff LJ. It is necessary to give a long quotation to do full justice to it. He said (at 1177–8):

> . . . The fundamental principle, plain and incontestable, is that every person's body is inviolate . . . The effect is that everybody is protected not only against physical injury but against any form of physical molestation. But so widely drawn a principle must inevitably be subject to exceptions. For example, children may be subjected to reasonable punishment; people may be subjected to the lawful exercise of the power of arrest; and reasonable force may be used in self-defence or for the prevention of crime. But, apart from these special instances where the control or constraint is lawful, a broader exception has been created to allow for the exigencies of everyday life. Generally speaking, consent is a defence to battery; and most of the physical contacts of ordinary life are not actionable because they are impliedly consented to by all who move in society and so expose themselves to the risk of bodily contact. So nobody can complain of the jostling which is inevitable from his presence in, for example, a supermarket, an underground station or a busy street; nor can a person who attends a party complain if his hand is seized in friendship, or even if his back is (within reason) slapped (see *Tuberville v Savage* (1669) 1 Mod Rep 3, 86 ER 684). Although such cases are regarded as examples of implied consent, it is more common nowadays to treat them as falling within a general exception embracing all physical contact which is generally acceptable in the ordinary conduct of daily life. . . . Among such forms of conduct, long held to be acceptable, is touching a person for the purpose of engaging his attention, though of course using no greater degree of physical contact than is reasonably necessary in the circumstances for that purpose. . . .

This rationalisation by Robert Goff LJ draws the so-called 'defences' to an action for trespass to the person (of which consent, self-defence, ejecting a trespasser, exercising parental authority, and statutory authority are some examples) under one umbrella of 'a general exception embracing all physical contact which is generally acceptable in the ordinary conduct of daily life'. . . .

Nevertheless, it still remains to indicate what is to be proved by a plaintiff who brings an action for battery. Robert Goff LJ's judgment is illustrative of the considerations which underlie such an action, but it is not practicable to define a battery as 'physical contact which is not generally acceptable in the ordinary conduct of daily life'.

In our view, the authorities lead one to the conclusion that in a battery there must be an intentional touching or contact in one form or another of the plaintiff by the defendant. That touching must be proved to be a hostile touching. That still leaves unanswered the question, when is a touching to be called hostile? Hostility cannot be equated with ill-will or malevolence. It cannot be governed by the obvious intention shown in acts like punching, stabbing or shooting. It cannot be solely governed by an expressed intention, although that may be strong evidence. But the element of hostility, in the sense in which it is now to be considered, must be a question of fact for the tribunal of fact. It may be imported from the circumstances. Take the example of the police officer in *Collins v Wilcock*. She touched the woman deliberately, but without an intention to do more than restrain her temporarily. Nevertheless, she was acting unlawfully and in that way was acting with hostility. She was acting contrary to the woman's legal right not to be physically restrained. We see no more difficulty in establishing what she intended by means of question and answer, or by inference from the surrounding circumstances, than there is in establishing whether an apparently playful blow was struck in anger. The rules of law governing the legality of arrest may require strict application to the facts of appropriate cases, but in the ordinary give and take of everyday life the tribunal of fact should find no difficulty in answering the question, 'was this, or was it not, a battery?' Where the immediate act of touching does not itself demonstrate hostility, the plaintiff should plead the facts which are said to do so.

Although we are all entitled to protection from physical molestation, we live in a crowded world in which people must be considered as taking on themselves some risk of injury (where it occurs) from the acts of others which are not in themselves unlawful. If negligence cannot be proved, it may be that an injured plaintiff who is also unable to prove a battery, will be without redress . . .

Appeal allowed.

COMMENTARY

Battery is the unlawful application of force to another. The concept of 'an application of force' is construed broadly to include things like pouring water on a person (*Pursell v Horn* (1838) 8 AD & E 602, 112 ER 966), or cutting their hair (*Forde v Skinner* (1830) 4 Car & P 239, 172 ER 687), and is generally free from difficulty, though there can be tricky cases at the margins (e.g. could taking a flash photograph amount to a battery? See *Kaye v Robertson* [1991] FSR 62). By contrast, the question of what constitutes unlawfulness in this context has proven more troublesome. Holt CJ in *Cole v Turner* (1704) 6 Mod Rep 149, 90 ER 958 said that the least touching of another 'in anger' constituted a battery, but this is clearly too narrow. Battery is concerned with the protection of physical integrity, and the defendant's motive cannot be the sole determinant of whether this integrity has been breached. Hence giving someone an unwanted kiss, or touching a sleeping person, may be a battery despite the absence of any animus towards the person touched.

Nonetheless, it is clear that some forms of touching do not constitute a battery (e.g. a congratulatory pat on the back, forcing past another to exit a crowded bus or train or tapping another to gain their attention). The rationalisation for this non-actionability is more difficult. One possible rationale, considered in *Wilson*, is that there is implied consent to such touchings (see also Beever, *op. cit.*, p. 391, referring to an 'implied licence' in the case of 'ordinary touching'), while in *Collins v Wilcock* [1984] 1 WLR 1172, Robert Goff LJ referred to a general exception embracing all physical contact which is generally acceptable in the ordinary conduct of daily life. In *Wilson* Robert Goff LJ's test was dismissed as 'not practicable', and instead it was said that the contact needed to be 'hostile' to be actionable, but Lord Goff (as he had by then become) reiterated his earlier approach in *Re F (Mental Patient: Sterilisation)* [1990] 2 AC 1, where he also disapproved of the 'hostility' requirement as being 'difficult to reconcile with the principle that any touching of another's body is, in the absence of lawful excuse, capable of amounting to a battery and trespass'. Implied consent was also dismissed as a governing principle: it could not apply where a person was not capable of giving consent (e.g. in the case of a child or a mentally disabled person) but it could not be right that every touching of such a person amounted to a battery. There is much to be said for Lord Goff's view. Hostility is inapposite because many touchings that are unlawful are not 'hostile' in the ordinary sense of that word. The only example of a hostile touching given in *Wilson* was the case of *Collins v Wilcock*, where it was suggested that because the contact made by the police constable was 'unlawful' it was hostile. But this is surely circular: because the touching is unlawful it is hostile, and hence it is unlawful. By contrast, it seems eminently sensible for the law to permit touchings on the basis that they are 'the casual, accidental or inevitable consequence of general human activity and interaction' (*Non-Marine Underwriters, Lloyds of London v Scalera* [2000] 1 SCR 551 at [21], per McLachlin J). It is therefore unsurprising that Lord Goff's views have proved persuasive in other parts of the Commonwealth (*Rixon v Star City Pty Ltd* [2001] NSWCA 265; *Thompson v Police* [2012] NZAR 741; cf. the *Scalera* case, where McLachlin J did not find it necessary to decide between the implied consent or Goff approaches). However, it must be recognised that the boundary of the exception identified by Lord Goff is not always easy to draw. In *McMillan v Crown Prosecution Service* [2008] EWHC 1457 (Admin) the intoxicated appellant had been engaged in anti-social behaviour in a garden outside the entrance to a house. A police constable, who had warned the appellant about her behaviour earlier in the evening, took hold of her arm, without her consent, for the purpose of helping her down the stairs to speak to her in the street. Once in the street her disorderly conduct continued and she was then arrested. There was no suggestion that the police constable intervened to protect the appellant from harm; rather, the constable was attempting a 'negotiated solution' to the problem of removing her from the garden. It was held that the conduct of the police constable fell within the exception. Where there is no consent, nor any lawful arrest, do you think forcibly leading a person from one place to another goes beyond contact that is acceptable in daily life?

Another difficult case involving the police and an intoxicated claimant is *Pile v Chief Constable of Merseyside Police* [2020] EWHC 2472 (QB), where it was held that police officers who had changed the soiled clothing of a female detainee rendered insensible by drink had not committed battery, as there was a presumption of implied consent to the removal of clothing in these circumstances. Turner J was obviously outraged at the claim that the police had wronged the claimant by seeking to preserve her dignity in this way, commenting sarcastically (at [1]) that 'Cheryl Pile brings this appeal to establish the liberty of inebriated English subjects to be allowed to lie undisturbed overnight in their own vomit soaked clothing', and noting (at [38]) that 'some members of the public may well have found it to have been a grotesque result' if she had been awarded compensation in these circumstances. Do you think that his outrage was justified? If so, was implied consent a better explanation of the outcome than that the touching was generally acceptable in the ordinary conduct of daily life?

Innes v Wylie (1844) 1 Car & Kir 257, 174 ER 800

The plaintiff was a member of a society which attempted to expel him. Under orders from the defendant, a policeman stopped the plaintiff entering the room in which the society was dining. The question of assault was dealt with in the summing up to the jury.

Lord Denman CJ

You will say, whether, on the evidence, you think that the policeman committed an assault on the plaintiff, or was merely passive. If the policeman was entirely passive like a door or a wall put to prevent the plaintiff from entering the room, and simply obstructing the entrance of the plaintiff, no assault has been committed on the plaintiff, and your verdict will be for the defendant. The question is, did the policeman take any active measures to prevent the plaintiff from entering the room, or did he stand in the door-way passive, and not move at all. . . .

Verdict for the plaintiff, damages 40 shillings.

COMMENTARY

This extract shows that battery requires a positive act on the defendant's part. As in other areas of law, the distinction between misfeasance and nonfeasance is not an easy one. In *Fagan v Metropolitan Police Commissioner* [1969] 1 QB 439, a criminal case, Fagan was parking his car under instruction from a police officer. Unbeknownst to him, the car came to rest on the officer's foot, at which point he was asked to move the car. He responded with verbal abuse, and he turned off the car's engine before complying with the officer's request. The majority of the Court of Appeal held that Fagan was guilty of a criminal assault (which for this purpose included a battery) as his act was a continuing one. Accordingly, the offence was complete once he had knowledge of his car's position because at that point he was still acting (i.e. there was a continuing positive act). Bridge J dissented, holding that 'the car rested on the foot by its own weight and remained stationary by its own inertia. The appellant's fault was that he omitted to manipulate the controls to set it in motion again.' In Bridge J's view, this was simply a failure to act, not sufficient to constitute the offence.

Not only must the defendant act positively, but the contact or apprehension of contact must be the direct result of the act. This is a hangover from the old forms of action where trespass *vi et armis* could only be brought for direct interferences. Contact may still be direct even if achieved through the use of an intervening object—hence hitting or touching another with a stick will be sufficient. In the criminal law this has been extended so that a person may be guilty of battery if he strikes another with the result that a third person suffers a forcible blow. In *Haystead v Chief Constable of Derbyshire* [2000] 3 All ER 890, the accused struck a woman holding a 12-month-old child with the result that she dropped the child onto the floor. It was held that he was correctly convicted of a criminal assault of the child, as the movement by which the woman had lost hold of the child was entirely and immediately the result of the accused's action in punching her.

Direct does not here mean instantaneous; a person who fires a bullet at another is liable in battery even though there is a gap between the act and the contact. The question is one of degree, but it has been held that spitting (*R v Cotesworth* (1704) 3 Mod Rep 172, 87 ER 928), throwing water (*Hopper v Reeve* (1817) 7 Taunt 698, 129 ER 278), or throwing a chair so as to make contact with another person all amount to batteries. What if there is a significant time period between the defendant's conduct and the application of force? In *DPP v K* [1990] 1 WLR 1067, a criminal case, a 15-year-old boy placed sulphuric acid in a hand dryer, which caused injury to another pupil when he later used the dryer. It was held that the perpetrator could be guilty of an assault occasioning actual bodily harm contrary to s. 47 of the Offences against the Person Act 1861. (It may be noted that *DPP v K* has been held to be wrongly decided as a matter of criminal law (see *R v Spratt* [1990] 1 WLR 1073), but not on this point.) At least as a matter of civil law, liability in such a case should depend on the length of time between the act and the contact, assuming the requisite intention (*vis-à-vis* the contact) could be shown. A short time between the act and the contact might be sufficient to satisfy the directness requirement of battery.

Could terrorists who planted a bomb be liable in battery to the victims injured when it exploded forty minutes later? See *Breslin v McKevitt* [2011] NICA 33, where the Court of Appeal of Northern Ireland held that those responsible for the Omagh terrorist bombing of 1998 committed a battery on the victims because '[a] deliberate planting of a bomb with intent to kill or injure someone clearly constitutes a battery' (at [17]). Does this approach leave any scope for a directness requirement in battery?

IV. False Imprisonment

1. Elements of the Tort

Blackstone, *Commentaries on the Law of England*, vol. III, 'Of Private Wrongs', ch. 8, II

We are next to consider the violation of the right of personal liberty. This is effected by the injury of false imprisonment, for which the law has not only decreed a punishment, as a heinous public crime, but has also given a private reparation to the party; as well by removing the actual confinement for the present, as, after it is over, by subjecting the wrongdoer to a civil action, on account of the damage sustained by the loss of time and liberty.

To constitute the injury of false imprisonment there are two points requisite: 1. The detention of the person; and, 2. The unlawfulness of such detention. Every confinement of the person is an imprisonment, whether it be in a common prison, or in a private house, or in the stocks, or even by forcibly detaining one in the public streets. Unlawful, or false, imprisonment consists in such confinement or detention without sufficient authority. . . .

Bird v Jones (1845) 7 QB 742, 115 ER 668

The defendant's employer had appropriated part of Hammersmith Bridge for seating to view a rowing regatta on the river. The plaintiff attempted to pass through the appropriated part of the bridge and managed to enter the enclosure, whereupon the defendant stationed two policemen to block his path and prevent him from entering further into the enclosure. He was told he could freely go back the way he came, but after waiting for over half an hour the plaintiff attempted to push past the policemen, whereupon he committed an assault upon the defendant and was arrested. The plaintiff's case was for wrongful arrest upon a breach of peace. Because of the way the case had been pleaded by the parties, one question the court had to consider was whether the plaintiff had been falsely imprisoned during the period he was obstructed by the policemen.

Patteson J

I have no doubt that, in general, if one man compels another to stay in any given place against his will, he imprisons that other just as much as if he locked him in a room: and I agree that it is not necessary, in order to constitute an imprisonment, that a man's person should be touched. I agree, also, that the compelling a man to go in a given direction against his will may amount to imprisonment. But I cannot bring my mind to the conclusion that, if one man merely obstructs the passage of another in a particular direction, whether by threat of personal violence or other wise, leaving him at liberty to stay where he is or to go in any other direction if he pleases, he can be said thereby to imprison him. He does him wrong, undoubtedly, if there was a right to pass in that direction, and would be liable to an action on the case for obstructing the passage or of assault, if, on the party persisting in going in that direction, he touched his person, or so threatened him as to amount to an assault. But imprisonment is, as I apprehend, a total restraint of the liberty of the person, for however short a time, and not a partial obstruction of his will, whatever inconvenience it may bring on him. . . .

Coleridge J

And I am of opinion that there was no imprisonment. To call it so appears to me to confound partial obstruction and disturbance with total obstruction and detention. A prison may have its boundaries large or narrow, visible and tangible, or, though real, still in the conception only; it may itself be moveable or fixed but a boundary it must have; and that boundary the party imprisoned must be prevented from passing; he must be prevented from leaving that place within the ambit of which the party imprisoning him would confine him, except by prison-breach. Some confusion seems to me to arise from confounding imprisonment of the body with mere loss of freedom: it is one part of the definition of freedom to be able to go whithersoever one pleases: but imprisonment is something more than the mere loss of this power; it includes the notion of restraint within some limits defined by a will or power exterior to our own. . . .

Denman CJ dissented.

R (on the application of Jalloh) v Secretary of State for the Home Department [2021] AC 262

The claimant was a foreign national against whom a deportation order had been made following his conviction for several criminal offences. The defendant Secretary of State served him with a notice of restriction under which a curfew was imposed on him pending his deportation whereby he was required to be present at his home between 11 pm and 7 am every day. The claimant was warned that breach of the notice without reasonable excuse would attract serious criminal sanctions, and his compliance with it was monitored by an electronic tag. It was subsequently determined that the defendant had had no power to impose the curfew and the claimant was awarded damages of £4,000 for false imprisonment. The Court of Appeal dismissed an appeal against that award. The defendant appealed to the Supreme Court on the ground that the curfew did not amount to imprisonment of the claimant.

Baroness Hale (with whom Lord Kerr, Lord Carnwath, Lord Briggs and Lord Sales agreed)

24. . . . The essence of imprisonment is being made to stay in a particular place by another person. The methods which might be used to keep a person there are many and various. They could be physical barriers, such as locks and bars. They could be physical people, such as guards who would physically prevent the person leaving if he tried to do so. They could also be threats, whether of force or of legal process. . . . The point is that the person is obliged to stay where he is ordered to stay whether he wants to do so or not.

25. In this case there is no doubt that the defendant defined the place where the claimant was to stay between the hours of 11.00 p m and 7.00 a m. There was no suggestion that he could go somewhere else during those hours without the defendant's permission. This is not a case like *Bird v Jones* 7 QB 742 where the claimant could cross the bridge by another route . . .

27. There is, of course, a crucial difference between voluntary compliance with an instruction and enforced compliance with that instruction. The Court of Appeal held that this was a case of enforced not voluntary compliance and I agree. It is not to be compared with those cases in which the claimant went voluntarily with the sheriff's order. There can be no doubt that the claimant's compliance was enforced. He was wearing an electronic tag which meant that leaving his address would be detected. The monitoring company would then telephone him to find out where he was. He was warned in the clearest possible terms that breaking the

> curfew could lead to a £5,000 fine or imprisonment for up to six months or both. He was well aware that it could also lead to his being detained again under the [Immigration Act 1971]. All of this was backed up by the full authority of the state, which was claiming to have the power to do this. The idea that the claimant was a free agent, able to come and go as he pleased, is completely unreal. . . .
>
> *Appeal dismissed.*

COMMENTARY

One of the reasons that Denman CJ gave for dissenting in *Bird v Jones* was that the requirement of total constraint favoured by the majority meant that no action would lie for false imprisonment where the plaintiff could find some means of escape, such as through a window. In later cases, the courts have confirmed that this is correct, though with the caveat that the means of escape must be reasonable, so that, for example, a claimant would be falsely imprisoned if the only way out of his or her confinement would be swimming through a lake infested with crocodiles. In the Court of Appeal in *Jalloh*, Davis LJ confirmed that the key to this issue was reasonableness and said that it could not be considered reasonable for the claimant to circumvent the curfew instruction by acting in a way which would necessarily attract a criminal sanction ([2019] 1 WLR 394 at [82]; see also [2021] AC 262 at [21]–[22], per Lady Hale, citing *McFadzean v Construction, Forestry, Mining and Energy Union* (2007) 20 VR 250, where the defendants were held not to have imprisoned the plaintiff anti-logging protesters by blocking the exits from their camp as the protesters could have escaped along a track through the bush). Lady Hale regarded the fact that the claimant in *Jalloh* occasionally violated the curfew as irrelevant to the position when he was complying with it. But what if it was unclear whether the 'compliance' was for fear of sanction or voluntary? And would he have been imprisoned if he knew that non-compliance would never in fact attract the threatened sanction?

The blocking of the public right of passage by the defendant in *Bird v Jones* was a public nuisance, but to bring a claim for that the plaintiff would have had to have suffered special damage over and above that suffered by the public generally (see Ch. 11.I). By contrast, as a form of trespass to the person, false imprisonment is actionable without damage, as the Supreme Court confirmed in *R (Lumba) v Secretary of State for the Home Department* [2012] 1 AC 245. This case involved two appeals by claimants whose detention was tainted by public law illegality because of a failure to follow correct procedures in reaching the decision to detain them. However, it was accepted that it would have been inevitable that they would have been detained if the correct procedures had been followed. By a majority of 6:3, the Supreme Court held that the fact that the imprisonment might have been lawfully procured was irrelevant to the question of whether the tort of false imprisonment had been committed, though the inevitability of a lawful exercise of the relevant power was 'a powerful reason for concluding that the detainee has suffered no loss and is entitled to no more than nominal damages' (per Lord Dyson at [70]). On similar facts, the High Court of Australia in *Lewis v Australian Capital Territory* (2020) 381 ALR 375 also awarded the plaintiff nominal damages. Liability was not contested, it being assumed that for these purposes there was 'no role for a counterfactual analysis that would seek to replace what did in fact happen with what would otherwise have happened' (at [45], per Gordon J). According to Gageler J (at [25]):

[A] person whose status or prior conduct renders that person especially vulnerable to detention in the exercise of lawful authority is not an outlaw. The person is entitled to expect that if, when, and for so long as, detention occurs in fact it will occur only in accordance with law. If the person is in fact detained for any period otherwise than in the exercise of lawful authority, the person is entitled to maintain an action for wrongful imprisonment . . .

False imprisonment is one of the three remaining civil causes of action where the claimant is prima facie entitled to trial by jury, the others being fraud and malicious prosecution (defamation used to be such a cause of action but this was changed by the Defamation Act 2013, s. 11). In *Griffiths v Williams* (*The Times*, 24 November 1995) the Court of Appeal upheld a jury's award of £50,000 damages to a victim of rape. Rape is not itself a civil cause of action, and so a damages claim by a rape victim must be framed in terms of a tort (or torts) which is, e.g. assault, battery and false imprisonment. Of these, only false imprisonment carries with it a prima facie right to a jury trial, so it must have been on that basis that the trial in this case was by jury.

The features of the tort as it has developed 'reflect the critical importance historically attached by the law not only to personal liberty, but to the principle of legality' (*GE v The Commissioner of An Garda Síochána*, unreported, Irish CA, 16 April 2021, at [71], per Murray J). Hence, any unlawful and intentional interference with liberty, even for a short period, is sufficient to amount to false imprisonment. In *Walker v Commissioner of Police of the Metropolis* [2015] 1 WLR 312, for example, nominal damages of £5 were awarded to a man who had been detained in a doorway for a matter of seconds by a police officer. Applying that logic, it would seem obvious that being forced to wait twenty minutes on a wharf for a ferry, as in *Robinson v Balmain New Ferry Company* [1910] AC 295 (discussed later in this chapter), would amount to imprisonment. And yet in the Court of Appeal in *Jalloh*, Davis LJ said that there had been 'no complete restraint' in *Robinson* as the plaintiff 'had a perfectly viable means of lawfully exiting the wharf' ([2019] 1 WLR 394 at [74]; see also [2021] AC 262 at [16], where Lady Hale said that there was no imprisonment 'as there was an exit route and [the plaintiff] had agreed to the terms'). However, the decision of the Privy Council in *Robinson* does not seem to rest on the absence of total restraint, and while it is true that the plaintiff had entered the wharf subject to the condition that he would exit by ferry (see the discussion of the case later in this chapter), that surely points towards a defence of consent rather than the conclusion that he was not imprisoned in the first place. After all, if I lock you in a room with an exit that will open automatically in twenty minutes are you not imprisoned until it does?

Some early authorities suggested that the claimant's knowledge of the imprisonment was necessary to bring an action (*Herring v Boyle* (1834) 1 Cr M & R 377, 149 ER 1126) but this was disapproved in obiter dicta of Atkin LJ in *Meering v Grahame-White Aviation* (1919) 122 LT 44 and Lord Griffiths in *Murray v Ministry of Defence* [1988] 1 WLR 692 (although the latter recognised it would be relevant to the question of damages). The correctness of this view was cast into doubt by the decision of the House of Lords in *R v Bournewood Mental Health Trust (ex p L)* [1999] 1 AC 458 where a majority held that a mentally ill patient who was held in an unlocked ward and did not leave it, but who would have been detained if he had, was not imprisoned. This reasoning—which appears inconsistent with that in *Meering* and *Murray*—was used to justify the treatment regime applied to a certain category of mentally ill patients but the *Bournewood* solution was roundly criticised when the applicant took his case to the ECtHR: *HL v United Kingdom* (2004) 40 EHRR 761. In response to the adverse findings of the ECtHR, the Mental Capacity Act 2005 was amended to regulate deprivations of liberty for mentally ill patients in the *Bournewood* situation (see ss. 4, 4A and Sch. A1) thus removing uncertainty over when such patients may be detained. Given the statutory regime now in place, there is little to recommend the majority reasoning in *Bournewood*, which seems to have been motivated in part by a desire to find that the treatment of patients in Bournewood's situation was lawful. In *R (Lumba) v Secretary of State for the Home Department* [2012] 1 AC 245 the majority of the Supreme Court cited Lord Griffiths' views in *Murray* with approval and although *Bournewood* was not discussed it seems clear that it remains the law that the claimant's knowledge of the imprisonment is not necessary to found an action in false imprisonment. As for the authority of *Bournewood* itself, in *Jalloh* (at [23]) Lady Hale appeared sympathetic to the argument of counsel for the claimant that the case 'might well be decided differently today' and that it was 'not easy to grasp' the rationale of the majority. (See also Martin [2020] CLJ 211, 214, questioning why, '[i]f the essence of imprisonment is being made to stay in a particular place by another', that requirement was not met in *Bournewood*.)

Finally, regarding the intention requirement of the tort, it was held in *Iqbal v Prison Officers Association* [2010] QB 732 that it is the imprisonment (as opposed to the act which amounts to it) that must be intended, although Smith LJ considered that recklessness as to whether conduct would result in imprisonment would satisfy the intention requirement. The victim of a merely negligent imprisonment, although probably without a remedy in false imprisonment, may well be able to sue in negligence instead. It has been held that loss of liberty, even in the absence of any physical injury, constitutes damage sufficient for liability in the tort of negligence: see *W v Home Office* [1997] Imm AR 302, noted (1998) 61 MLR 573, and Nolan, 'New Forms of Damage in Negligence' (2007) 70 MLR 59, 62–70.

2. Directness

The curtailment of the claimant's liberty must be direct if it is to amount to false imprisonment. Where the defendant's own act is responsible for the imprisonment (e.g. where it is he who locks a door), this requirement is easily satisfied. But what if the defendant acts through an intermediary? If A tells B to arrest C and B does so, can A be held to have imprisoned C? This issue is considered in the following extract.

Davidson v Chief Constable of North Wales [1994] 2 All ER 597

The plaintiff's friend, H, bought a music cassette in a shop and then joined the plaintiff who was waiting by the cassette counter; they talked for a while before leaving. A store detective (a Mrs Yates) formed the impression that the cassette had been stolen and called the police. When the police officers arrived the store detective told them that H and the plaintiff had stolen the cassette and pointed them out, whereupon the officers arrested them on suspicion of shoplifting. The accusation was denied, but neither H nor the plaintiff could produce the receipt and they were taken to the police station. They were released after two hours when a shop assistant affirmed that the cassette had been paid for. At the trial of the plaintiff's action for false imprisonment against the police and the store detective, the store detective said that she intended and expected the police officers to act upon the information she gave them, and that she had never known of any occasion when they had failed to do so. The police officers gave evidence that they had exercised their own judgement in arresting the plaintiff based on the information given by the store detective. The judge withdrew the case against both defendants from the jury on the grounds that: (1) the police officers had acted lawfully because they had had reasonable grounds to make the arrest; and (2) as the officers had acted independently of the store detective the latter had no case to answer. The plaintiff appealed.

Sir Thomas Bingham MR

[T]he question which arose for the decision of the learned judge in this case was whether there was information properly to be considered by the jury as to whether what Mrs Yates did went beyond laying information before police officers for them to take such action as they thought fit and amounted to some direction, or procuring, or direct request, or direct encouragement that they should act by way of arresting these defendants. He decided that there was no evidence which went beyond the giving of information. Certainly there was no express request. Certainly there was no encouragement. Certainly there was no discussion of any kind as to what action the police officers should take.

The crux of Mr Clover's submission is that this case is different from the case in which an ordinary member of the public gives information to a police officer because this is a store detective, somebody better informed than an ordinary member of the public as to what was likely to happen upon making a complaint, and somebody with a very clear intention and expectation as to what would happen. No doubt the store detective did have an intention and expectation as to what would happen. The fact remains that the learned judge to my mind quite correctly held that what Mrs Yates did and said in no way went beyond the mere giving of information, leaving it to the officers to exercise a discretion which on their unchallenged evidence they did as to whether they should take any action or not.

In those circumstances the learned judge was, as I think, entirely correct to withdraw the matter from the jury . . .

Staughton LJ

Whether a request by itself is sufficient to make a person liable does not arise in this case. What is clear . . . is that merely giving information is not enough. That does not give rise to false imprisonment. Mrs Yates did no more than that. However much one may look at evidence and analyse what possible consequences might or would arise from the information which she gave, the fact is that all she did was give the information. . . .

Waite LJ agreed with Sir Thomas Bingham MR and Staughton LJ.

Appeal dismissed.

COMMENTARY

Although the imprisonment must result directly from the defendant's act, there can still be liability where the claimant is detained by a third party, but only if the third party has acted as an agent or without exercising an independent discretion (*Flewster v Role* (1808) 1 Camp 187; *Harnett v Bond* [1925] AC 669). In *Davidson*, the third party was the police, who have statutory authority to arrest in such circumstances, subject to reasonable suspicion of certain matters (Police and Criminal Evidence Act 1984 (PACE) s. 24). It is likely that police officers will say that an independent discretion was exercised before deciding to arrest, since if an arrest was made solely on the advice of another it could be argued that they did not in fact act on the basis of their reasonable suspicions. As *Davidson* shows, the result will be that a person who gave the information on which the police acted cannot be liable in false imprisonment because the arrest has not been caused 'directly' by that person. It follows that in many arrest cases success against one defendant will lead to success against both (because if the police are not entitled to the defence under PACE they are liable, and if they have not exercised any discretion of their own the informant is liable as they have merely acted as her agents). Conversely, in such a case failure against one defendant will often be fatal to both claims (as in *Davidson*), although this may not be so where the informant can be said to have gone beyond merely providing information on which the arresting party acted. Hence in *R(M) v Hackney London Borough Council* [2011] 1 WLR 2873 the Court of Appeal had no difficulty in finding that the medical health practitioner who wrote to an NHS Trust to request that the claimant be detained had procured his detention: the very purpose of writing the letter was to allow the Trust to exercise its powers to detain those suspected of being mentally ill for treatment. See also *Ahmed v Shafique* [2009] EWHC 618 (QB) and more generally Spencer [1994] CLJ 433.

The decision in *Davidson* should be seen in the light of a number of related torts that require proof of malice if they are to be actionable. The most important of these is malicious prosecution, which was historically an action on the case, requiring for that reason no element of directness. Even though no liability would arise in false imprisonment if the arrest was made by a party exercising discretion, an action might lie in malicious prosecution if a prosecution was later carried on by the person procuring the arrest. In this action the claimant must establish four elements, three of which are that the defendant acted with malice, that the claimant was 'prosecuted' by the defendant and that the prosecution was without reasonable and probable cause. The 'prosecution' requirement (that the defendant set the law in motion against the claimant) has been difficult to prove in modern times where the charge sheet or other originating document is usually signed by the police. An exception is *Martin v Watson* [1996] 1 AC 74. The plaintiff was arrested and charged with exposing his person with intent to insult after the defendant had complained to the police. The charge sheet was signed by a police officer. At the hearing the prosecution offered no evidence and the magistrates dismissed the charge. Subsequently, the plaintiff sued the defendant for malicious prosecution. The Court of Appeal held that a person who made an allegation to the police, knowing that it was untrue and intending that the police should act against the person accused, did not thereby 'set the law in motion' and was not the prosecutor for the purposes of the tort of malicious prosecution. But the House of Lords held that this requirement could be satisfied even though the defendant had not taken any formal steps to charge the plaintiff but had merely provided false or malicious information on which the charge was based, as in those circumstances no real discretion could be exercised by the prosecutor. This would not have helped the plaintiff in *Davidson* because no charge was ever made (nor was there any evidence that the information given by the store detective was deliberately false), but Trindade, 'The Modern Tort of False Imprisonment', in N. Mullany (ed.), *Torts in the Nineties* (Sydney: LBC, 1997), has suggested that:

> The courts may therefore conclude in the future that a deprivation of liberty brought about by a police officer acting on the basis of deliberately false information supplied by the defendant is a deprivation brought about directly by the defendant for which an action in false imprisonment would lie against the defendant who supplied the wrong information.

Some support for Trindade's view can be derived from *Ahmed v Shafique* [2009] EWHC 618 (QB). While recognising that the state of mind of an informant should arguably be irrelevant to the (apparently) objective question of whether or not they had procured an arrest, Sharp J thought (at [86]) 'there are obviously sound reasons why a malicious informant who knowingly gives false information to the police (which they are not in a position to check) with the intention of bringing about an innocent person's prosecution and conviction should be held to account'.

v. Intentional Infliction of Physical or Emotional Harm

Trespass to the person requires the intentional interference with the claimant to be direct. Is any remedy provided in respect of intentionally inflicted harm caused indirectly to the claimant? Under the old forms of action, trespass on the case lay for indirectly inflicted damage, and by the late nineteenth century negligence had evolved out of that action to become the standard remedy for personal injury except where there was direct interference that would ground a claim in trespass to the person. But there might be a reason for seeking a different cause of action, based on intention, if negligence was unavailable and the harm indirect. In the nineteenth century negligence did not recognise injury caused by psychiatric means as compensatable. If the claimant could show that the defendant intended to cause her emotional distress would the courts decide this was sufficient damage to found a cause of action?

In *Wilkinson v Downton* [1897] 2 QB 57 the defendant told the plaintiff, presumably as a practical joke, that her husband had been injured in an accident and that she should go to him immediately. In fact, he was not injured but, unsurprisingly, the plaintiff did not find it amusing and sued for the adverse health consequences she suffered from the shock of believing, at least for a short time, that the statement was true. Wright J stated:

> The defendant has, as I assume for the moment, wilfully done an act calculated to cause physical harm to the female plaintiff, i.e., to infringe her right to personal safety, and has thereby in fact caused physical harm to her. That proposition, without more, appears to me to state a good cause of action, there being no justification alleged for the act.

The scope of the so-called *Wilkinson v Downton* tort in modern law was considered by the House of Lords in *Wainwright v Home Office* [2004] 2 AC 406.

> ### Wainwright v Home Office [2004] 2 AC 406
>
> The claimants, a mother and son, were visiting in a prison. Because of concerns over the presence of drugs in the prison, they were required to submit to a strip-search before being allowed to enter. Although the searches were conducted in good faith, the prison officers who carried them out failed to comply with the statutory guidelines governing such searches. The claimants brought an action alleging that the conduct of the officers amounted to a tort, whether it be breach of privacy, liability under *Wilkinson v Downton* or an extension of trespass to the person, and that the failure to recognise the conduct as tortious would lead to a further breach of the claimant's rights under the ECHR. The claimants succeeded at first instance but, apart from some contact that the Home Office conceded amounted to a battery, failed before the Court of Appeal and the House of Lords. The extract deals with the *Wilkinson v Downton* issue.

Lord Hoffmann

[36] I turn next to the alternative argument based upon *Wilkinson v Downton* [1897] 2 QB 57. This is a case which has been far more often discussed than applied. Thomas Wilkinson, landlord of the Albion public house in Limehouse, went by train to the races at Harlow, leaving his wife Lavinia behind the bar. Downton was a customer who decided to play what he would no doubt have described as a practical joke on Mrs Wilkinson. He went into the Albion and told her that her husband had decided to return in a horse-drawn vehicle which had been involved in an accident in which he had been seriously injured. The story was completely false and Mr Wilkinson returned safely by train later that evening. But the effect on Mrs Wilkinson was dramatic. Her hair turned white and she became so ill that for some time her life was thought in danger. The jury awarded her £100 for nervous shock and the question for the judge on further consideration was whether she had a cause of action.

[37] The difficulty in the judge's way was the decision of the Privy Council in *Victorian Railways Comrs v Coultas* (1888) 13 App Cas 222, in which it had been said that nervous shock was too remote a consequence of a negligent act (in that case, putting the plaintiff in imminent fear of being run down by a train) to be a recoverable head of damages. Wright J distinguished the case on the ground that Downton was not merely negligent but had intended to cause injury. Quite what the judge meant by this is not altogether clear; Downton obviously did not intend to cause any kind of injury but merely to give Mrs Wilkinson a fright. The judge said, however ([1897] 2 QB 57 at 59), that as what he said could not fail to produce grave effects 'upon any but an exceptionally indifferent person', an intention to cause such effects should be 'imputed' to him.

[38] The outcome of the case was approved and the reasoning commented upon by the Court of Appeal in *Janvier v Sweeney* [1919] 2 KB 316. During the First World War Mlle Janvier lived as a paid companion in a house in Mayfair and corresponded with her German lover who was interned as an enemy alien on the Isle of Man. Sweeney was a private detective who wanted secretly to obtain some of her employer's documents and sent his assistant to induce her to co-operate by pretending to be from Scotland Yard and saying that the authorities wanted her because she was corresponding with a German spy. Mlle Janvier suffered severe nervous shock from which she took a long time to recover. The jury awarded her £250.

[39] By this time, no one was troubled by the *Victorian Railways Comrs* case. In *Dulieu v White & Sons* [1901] 2 KB 669, the Divisional Court had declined to follow it; Phillimore J said ([1901] 2 KB 669 at 683) that in principle 'terror wrongfully induced and inducing physical mischief gives a cause of action'. So on that basis Mlle Janvier was entitled to succeed whether the detectives intended to cause her injury or were merely negligent as to the consequences of their threats. Duke LJ observed ([1919] 2 KB 316 at 326) that the case was stronger than *Wilkinson v Downton* because Downton had intended merely to play a practical joke and not to commit a wrongful act. The detectives, on the other hand, intended to blackmail the plaintiff to attain an unlawful object.

[40] By the time of *Janvier's* case, therefore, the law was able comfortably to accommodate the facts of *Wilkinson v Downton* in the law of nervous shock caused by negligence. It was unnecessary to fashion a tort of intention or to discuss what the requisite intention, actual or imputed, should be. Indeed, the remark of Duke LJ to which I have referred suggests that he did not take seriously the idea that Downton had in any sense intended to cause injury.

[41] Commentators and counsel have nevertheless been unwilling to allow *Wilkinson v Downton* to disappear beneath the surface of the law of negligence. Although, in cases of actual psychiatric injury, there is no point in arguing about whether the injury was in

some sense intentional if negligence will do just as well, it has been suggested (as the claimants submit in this case) that damages for distress falling short of psychiatric injury can be recovered if there was an intention to cause it. This submission was squarely put to the Court of Appeal in *Wong v Parkside Health NHS Trust* [2001] EWCA Civ 1721 and rejected. Hale LJ said that before the passing of the Protection from Harassment Act 1997 there was no tort of intentional harassment which gave a remedy for anything less than physical or psychiatric injury. That leaves *Wilkinson v Downton* with no leading role in the modern law.

[42] In *Khorasandjian v Bush* [1993] QB 727 the Court of Appeal, faced with the absence of a tort of causing distress by harassment, tried to press into service the action for private nuisance. In *Hunter v Canary Wharf Ltd, Hunter v London Docklands Development Corp* [1997] AC 655, as I have already mentioned, the House of Lords regarded this as illegitimate and, in view of the passing of the 1997 Act, unnecessary. I did however observe ([1997] AC 655 at 707) that:

> The law of harassment has now been put on a statutory basis . . . and it is unnecessary to consider how the common law might have developed. But as at present advised, I see no reason why a tort of intention should be subject to the rule which excludes compensation for mere distress, inconvenience or discomfort in actions based on negligence . . . The policy considerations are quite different.

[43] Mr Wilby said that the Court of Appeal in *Wong*'s case should have adopted this remark and awarded Ms Wong damages for distress caused by intentional harassment before the 1997 Act came into force. Likewise, the prison officers in this case did acts calculated to cause distress to the Wainwrights and therefore should be liable on the basis of imputed intention as in *Wilkinson v Downton*.

[44] I do not resile from the proposition that the policy considerations which limit the heads of recoverable damage in negligence do not apply equally to torts of intention. If someone actually intends to cause harm by a wrongful act and does so, there is ordinarily no reason why he should not have to pay compensation. But I think that if you adopt such a principle, you have to be very careful about what you mean by intend. In *Wilkinson v Downton* Wright J wanted to water down the concept of intention as much as possible. He clearly thought, as the Court of Appeal did afterwards in *Janvier*'s case, that the plaintiff should succeed whether the conduct of the defendant was intentional or negligent. But the *Victorian Railway Comrs* case prevented him from saying so. So he devised a concept of imputed intention which sailed as close to negligence as he felt he could go.

[45] If, on the other hand, one is going to draw a principled distinction which justifies abandoning the rule that damages for mere distress are not recoverable, imputed intention will not do. The defendant must actually have acted in a way which he knew to be unjustifiable and either intended to cause harm or at least acted without caring whether he caused harm or not. Lord Woolf CJ, as I read his judgment ([2002] QB 1334 at [50]–[51]), might have been inclined to accept such a principle. But the facts did not support a claim on this basis. The judge made no finding that the prison officers intended to cause distress or realised that they were acting without justification in asking the Wainwrights to strip. He said that they had acted in good faith and that:

> The deviations from the procedure laid down for strip searches were, in my judgment, not intended to increase the humiliation necessarily involved but merely sloppiness.

[46] Even on the basis of a genuine intention to cause distress, I would wish, as in *Hunter v Canary Wharf Ltd*, to reserve my opinion on whether compensation should be recoverable.

In institutions and workplaces all over the country, people constantly do and say things with the intention of causing distress and humiliation to others. This shows lack of consideration and appalling manners but I am not sure that the right way to deal with it is always by litigation. The Protection from Harassment Act 1997 defines harassment in s. 1(1) as a 'course of conduct' amounting to harassment and provides by s. 7(3) that a course of conduct must involve conduct on at least two occasions. If these requirements are satisfied, the claimant may pursue a civil remedy for damages for anxiety: see s. 3(2). The requirement of a course of conduct shows that Parliament was conscious that it might not be in the public interest to allow the law to be set in motion for one boorish incident. It may be that any development of the common law should show similar caution.

[47] In my opinion, therefore, the claimants can build nothing on *Wilkinson v Downton* [1897] 2 QB 57, [1895–9] All ER Rep 267. It does not provide a remedy for distress which does not amount to recognised psychiatric injury and so far as there may be a tort of intention under which such damage is recoverable, the necessary intention was not established. I am also in complete agreement with Buxton LJ ([2002] QB 1334 at [67]–[72]) that *Wilkinson v Downton* has nothing to do with trespass to the person.

Lords Bingham, **Hope** and **Hutton** agreed with Lord Hoffmann; **Lord Scott**, in a short concurring speech, also agreed with Lord Hoffmann.

Appeal dismissed.

COMMENTARY

Is there now any scope for the rule in *Wilkinson v Downton* to operate? As far as claims for psychiatric injury are concerned, Lord Hoffmann thought that *Wilkinson* had no role as liability in negligence would provide a satisfactory remedy, but it has been suggested in some later cases that there might still be a role for the separate liability: see *Bici v Ministry of Defence* [2004] EWHC 786 (QB) and *C v D* [2006] EWHC 166 (QB), the latter being a successful post-*Wainwright* claim for psychiatric injury under *Wilkinson* (cf. the Court of Appeal's later observation, with reference to *C v D*, that it would be preferable for the law to develop along conventional modern lines rather than through recourse to this obscure tort, whose jurisprudential basis remained unclear: *A v Hoare* [2006] EWCA Civ 395 at [136]; the point was not discussed in the House of Lords). More broadly, Johnston [2004] CLJ 15, 18, commenting on *Wainwright*, notes: 'Lord Hoffmann's analysis on this point may have consigned *Wilkinson v Downton* to the category of historical interest, although the "tort of intention" that he discussed may yet resurface in the future' (see also Lunney, 'Practical Joking and Its Penalty: *Wilkinson v Downton* in Context' (2002) 10 Tort L Rev 168). However, that tort will not encompass claims for mental distress; although Lord Hoffmann did not rule definitively against such a claim, in a passage not extracted, Lord Scott was unequivocally opposed to the idea that the infliction of humiliation and distress by conduct calculated to humiliate and cause distress was, without more, tortious at common law (see also *Mbasogo*, discussed earlier, where a claim for the intentional infliction of mental distress was struck out as unarguable). Whether the intentional infliction of other types of harm might of itself give rise to an action seems to be an unanswered question; Lord Hoffmann hinted (at [44]) that such claims might exist but he had earlier suggested that there would be no such claim for psychiatric injury and no other examples were given.

O (A Child) v Rhodes [2016] AC 219

The defendant, a concert pianist, author and television filmmaker, wrote a memoir in which he gave graphic accounts of sexual abuse he had suffered as a child, and the profound effect this had had on his life. The publication of the memoir was opposed by his ex-wife, on the grounds that it would be likely to cause psychological harm to their son (now aged 12), who lived with his mother in the United States, and who already suffered from a range of conditions and disorders, including Asperger's syndrome. She brought proceedings against the defendant and his publishers in the son's name, seeking an injunction to prevent publication of the book in its present form, and relying (inter alia) on the tort of intentional infliction of physical or psychological harm. Bean J ([2014] EWHC 2468 (QB)) struck out the proceedings on the ground that the *Wilkinson v Downton* tort did not extend beyond false and threatening words. This decision was reversed by the Court of Appeal ([2015] EMLR 4), which held that the claimant had sufficiently strong prospects of establishing liability at trial to justify the grant of an interim injunction restraining the defendant and his publishers from publishing the book without first deleting passages detailing the abuse and its consequences. The defendant appealed to the Supreme Court.

Baroness Hale and Lord Toulson

1. By these proceedings, a mother seeks to prevent a father from publishing a book about his life containing certain passages which she considers risk causing psychological harm to their son who is now aged 12 . . . [T]hese proceedings have been brought in his name . . . alleging that publication would constitute a tort against him. The tort in question is that recognised in *Wilkinson v Downton* [1897] 2 QB 57 and generally known as intentionally causing physical or psychological harm. What, then, is the proper scope of the tort in the modern law? In particular, can it ever be used to prevent a person from publishing true information about himself? . . .

Subsequent case law

51. *Wilkinson v Downton* [1897] 2 QB 57 has been a source of much discussion and debate in legal textbooks and academic articles but seldom invoked in practice. This may be due to the development of the law of negligence in the area of recognised illness resulting from nervous shock. But a distinctive feature of the present case is that the courts below have held that there is no arguable case against the father in negligence (applying *Barrett v Enfield London Borough Council* [2001] 2 AC 550), and the claimant has therefore been constrained to rely on *Wilkinson v Downton*. . . .

Analysis

72. The order made by the Court of Appeal was novel in two respects. The material which the father was banned from publishing was not deceptive or intimidatory but autobiographical; and the ban was principally directed, not to the substance of the autobiographical material, but to the vivid form of language used to communicate it. The appeal therefore raises important questions about freedom of speech and about the nature and limits of liability under *Wilkinson v Downton* [1897] 2 QB 57.

73. In *Wilkinson v Downton* Wright J recognised that wilful infringement of the right to personal safety was a tort. It has three elements: a conduct element, a mental element and a consequence element. The issues in this case relate to the first and second elements. It is common ground that the consequence required for liability is physical harm or recognised psychiatric illness. In *Wainwright v Home Office* [2004] 2 AC 406 Lord Hoffmann discussed and

left open (with expressions of caution) the question whether intentional causation of severe distress might be actionable, but no one in this case has suggested that it is.

74. The conduct element requires words or conduct directed towards the claimant for which there is no justification or reasonable excuse, and the burden of proof is on the claimant. We are concerned in this case with the curtailment of freedom of speech, which gives rise to its own particular considerations. We agree with the approach of the Court of Appeal in regarding the tort as confined to those towards whom the relevant words or conduct were directed, but they may be a group. A person who shouts 'fire' in a cinema, when there is no fire, is addressing himself to the audience. In the present case the Court of Appeal treated the publication of the book as conduct directed towards the claimant and considered that the question of justification had therefore to be judged vis-à-vis him. In this respect we consider that they erred.

75. The book is for a wide audience and the question of justification has to be considered accordingly, not in relation to the claimant in isolation. In point of fact, the father's case is that although the book is dedicated to the claimant, he would not expect him to see it until he is much older. Arden LJ said that the father could not be heard to say that he did not intend the book to reach the child, since it was dedicated to him and some parts of it are addressed to him. We have only found one passage addressed to him, which is in the acknowledgments, but more fundamentally we do not understand why the father may not be heard to say that the book is not intended for his eyes at this stage of his life. Arden LJ also held that there could be no justification for the publication if it was likely to cause psychiatric harm to him. That approach excluded consideration of the wider question of justification based on the legitimate interest of the defendant in telling his story to the world at large in the way in which he wishes to tell it, and the corresponding interest of the public in hearing his story.

76. When those factors are taken into account, as they must be, the only proper conclusion is that there is every justification for the publication. A person who has suffered in the way that the father has suffered, and has struggled to cope with the consequences of his suffering in the way that he has struggled, has the right to tell the world about it. And there is a corresponding public interest in others being able to listen to his life story in all its searing detail. Of course vulnerable children need to be protected as far as reasonably practicable from exposure to material which would harm them, but the right way of doing so is not to expand *Wilkinson v Downton* [1897] 2 QB 57 to ban the publication of a work of general interest. But in pointing out the general interest attaching to this publication, we do not mean to suggest that there needs to be some identifiable general interest in the subject matter of a publication for it to be justified within the meaning of *Wilkinson v Downton*.

77. Freedom to report the truth is a basic right to which the law gives a very high level of protection (see, for example, *Napier v Pressdram Ltd* [2010] 1 WLR 934, para 42). It is difficult to envisage any circumstances in which speech which is not deceptive, threatening or possibly abusive, could give rise to liability in tort for wilful infringement of another's right to personal safety. The right to report the truth is justification in itself. That is not to say that the right of disclosure is absolute, for a person may owe a duty to treat information as private or confidential. But there is no general law prohibiting the publication of facts which will cause distress to another, even if that is the person's intention. The question whether (and, if so, in what circumstances) liability under *Wilkinson v Downton* [1897] 2 QB 57 might arise from words which are not deceptive or threatening, but are abusive, has not so far arisen and does not arise for consideration in this case.

80. Our conclusion that the publication of the father's book is not within the scope of the conduct element of the tort is enough to decide this case. However, the issue of the mental element required for the tort has been argued before us and it is right that we should address it. The Court of Appeal found that the necessary intention could be imputed to the father.

The court cannot be criticised for doing so, since it was bound by previous decisions of the court which upheld that approach (in particular, *Janvier v Sweeney* [1919] 2 KB 316 and *Wong v Parkside Health NHS Trust* [2003] 3 All ER 932).

81. There is a critical difference, not always recognised in the authorities, between imputing the existence of an intention as a matter of law and inferring the existence of an intention as a matter of fact. Imputation of an intention by operation of a rule of law is a vestige of a previous age and has no proper role in the modern law of tort. It is unsound in principle. It was abolished in the criminal law nearly 50 years ago and its continued survival in the tort of wilful infringement of the right to personal safety is unjustifiable . . . The doctrine was created by the courts and it is high time now for this court to declare its demise.

82. The abolition of imputed intent clears the way to proper consideration of two important questions about the mental element of this particular tort.

83. First, where a recognised psychiatric illness is the product of severe mental or emotional distress, (a) is it necessary that the defendant should have intended to cause illness or (b) is it sufficient that he intended to cause severe distress which in fact results in recognisable illness? . . .

84. Secondly, is recklessness sufficient and, if so, how is recklessness to be defined for this purpose? Recklessness is a word capable of different shades of meaning. In everyday usage it may include thoughtlessness about the likely consequences in circumstances where there is an obvious high risk, or in other words gross negligence . . .

87. Our answer to the first question is that of option (b): para 83 above. Our answer to the second question is not to include recklessness in the definition of the mental element. To hold that the necessary mental element is intention to cause physical harm or severe mental or emotional distress strikes a just balance . . . It means that a person who actually intends to cause another to suffer severe mental or emotional distress (which should not be understated) bears the risk of legal liability if the deliberately inflicted severe distress causes the other to suffer a recognised psychiatric illness . . . This formulation of the mental element is preferable to including recklessness as an alternative to intention. Recklessness was not a term used in *Wilkinson v Downton* [1897] 2 QB 57 or *Janvier v Sweeney* [1919] 2 KB 316 and it presents problems of definition . . .

88. It would be possible to limit liability for the tort to cases in which the defendant's conduct was 'extreme, flagrant, or outrageous', as in Canada. But this argument has not so far been advanced in this country, and, although Arden LJ adverted to it as a possibility, the father has not sought to pursue it. We are inclined to the view, which is necessarily obiter, that the tort is sufficiently contained by the combination of (a) the conduct element requiring words or conduct directed at the claimant for which there is no justification or excuse, (b) the mental element requiring an intention to cause at least severe mental or emotional distress, and (c) the consequence element requiring physical harm or recognised psychiatric illness.

89. In the present case there is no basis for supposing that the father has an actual intention to cause psychiatric harm or severe mental or emotional distress to the claimant.

90. We conclude that there is no arguable case that the publication of the book would constitute the requisite conduct element of the tort or that the father has the requisite mental element. On both grounds the appeal must be allowed and the order of Bean J restored.

Lord Neuberger

[Lord Neuberger expressed his agreement with the judgment of Baroness Hale and Lord Toulson. He continued:]

97. . . . . [I]t would, I think, be an inappropriate restriction on freedom of expression, an unacceptable form of judicial censorship, if a court could restrain publication of a book written by

a defendant, whose contents could otherwise be freely promulgated, only refer in general and unobjectionable terms to the claimant, and are neither intended nor expected by the defendant to harm the claimant, simply because the claimant might suffer psychological harm if he got to read it (or extracts from it). Whatever the nature and ingredients of the tort whose origin can be traced to *Wilkinson v Downton* [1897] 2 QB 57, it therefore cannot possibly apply in this case. And that, at least in a narrow sense, is in my view the beginning and the end of this case.

101. It would not, however, be right to leave matters there, in the light of the decision in *Wilkinson v Downton* (on which the Court of Appeal relied) and the subsequent cases in this and other common law jurisdictions . . . Given that there was a valid claim in that case and there is none in this case, it raises the question as to the characterisation of the tort in question, which could perhaps be characterised as the tort of making distressing statements.

103. While I would certainly accept that an action not otherwise tortious which causes a claimant distress could give rise to a cause of action, I would be reluctant to decide definitively that liability for distressing actions and distressing words should be subject to the same rules, at this stage at any rate. There is of course a substantial overlap between words and actions: after all, words can threaten or promise actions, and freedom of expression can in some respects extend to actions as well as words. And, in the light of what I say below, it might be the case that the tort of making distressing statements is to be limited to statements which are the verbal equivalent of physical assaults. However, there are relevant differences between words and actions . . .

104. In order to decide when a statement, which is not otherwise tortious, and which causes a claimant distress, should be capable of founding a cause of action, it is necessary to bear in mind five points, some of which are in tension. First, that there must be circumstances in which such a cause of action should exist: the facts of *Wilkinson v Downton* [1897] 2 QB 57 and *Janvier v Sweeney* [1919] 2 KB 316, 322 make that point good. Secondly, given the importance of freedom of expression, which includes the need to avoid constraining ordinary (even much offensive) discourse, it is vital that the boundaries of the cause of action are relatively narrow. Thirdly, because of the importance of legal certainty, particularly in the area of what people can say, the tort should be defined as clearly as possible. Fourthly, in the light of the almost literally infinite permutations of possible human interactions, it is realistic to proceed on the basis that it may well be that no set of parameters can be devised which would cater for absolutely every possibility. Fifthly, given all these factors, there will almost inevitably be aspects of the parameters on which it would be wrong to express a concluded view, and to let the law develop in a characteristic common law way, namely on a case-by-case basis.

105. In other words, the tort exists, and should be defined narrowly and as clearly as possible, but it would be dangerous to say categorically that each ingredient of the tort must always be present. None the less, it seems to me that it is worth identifying what are, at least normally, and hopefully almost always, the essential ingredients of the tort.

106. *Wilkinson v Downton* and *Janvier v Sweeney* were cases where the statement made by the defendant was untrue, gratuitous, intended to distress the plaintiff, directed at the plaintiff, and caused the plaintiff serious distress amounting to psychiatric illness. Clearly, where all these ingredients are present, the tort would be established, but the question is whether they are all strictly required.

107. First, if it is possible at all, it will be a very rare case where a statement which is not untrue could give rise to a claim, save, perhaps where the statement was a threat or (possibly) an insult.

110. This does not, of course, mean that every untruthful statement, threat or insult could give rise to a claim. Because of the importance of freedom of expression and of the law not impeding ordinary discourse, there must be a second and demanding requirement which has to

be satisfied before liability can attach to an untruth, an insult or a threat which was intended to, and did, cause distress, but would not otherwise be civilly actionable. Baroness Hale DPSC and Lord Toulson JSC have suggested a test of 'justification or reasonable excuse' in paras 74–76 above, and I have used the adjective 'gratuitous' in para 106 above. Neither description is ideal as it can be said to be question-begging (virtually every threat, untruth or insult can be said to be unjustified, inexcusable and gratuitous), and it involves a subjective assessment. There may be something to be said for the adjectives 'outrageous', 'flagrant' or 'extreme', which seem to have been applied by the US and Canadian courts . . . Of course, even with a test of outrageousness a subjective judgment will be involved to some extent, but that cannot be avoided.

111. As mentioned, it seems to me to be vital that the tort does not interfere with the give and take of ordinary human discourse (including unpleasant, heated arguments, whether in domestic, social, business or other contexts, sometimes involving the trading of insults or threats), or with normal, including trenchant, journalism and other writing. Inevitably, whether a particular statement is gratuitous must depend on the context. An unprompted statement made simply because the defendant wanted to say it or because he was inspired by malice, as in *Janvier v Sweeney*, or something very close to malice, as in *Wilkinson v Downton*, may be different from the same statement made in the course of a heated argument, especially if provoked by a series of wounding statements by the defendant. Similarly, it would be wrong for this tort to be invoked to justify relief against a polemic op-ed newspaper article or a strongly worded and antipathetic biography, save in the most unusual circumstances. The tort should not somehow be used to extend or supplement the law of defamation.

112. Thirdly, I consider that there must be an intention on the part of the defendant to cause the claimant distress. This requirement might seem at first sight to be too narrow, not least because it might appear that it would not have caught the defendant in *Wilkinson v Downton*: he merely intended his cruel statement as a joke. However, the fact that a statement is intended to be a joke is not inconsistent with the notion that it was intended to upset. How, it might be asked rhetorically, could Mr Downton not have intended to cause the apparently happily married Mrs Wilkinson significant distress by falsely telling her that her husband had been very seriously injured? That was the very purpose of the so-called joke. There are statements (and indeed actions) whose consequences or potential consequences are so obvious that the perpetrator cannot realistically say that those consequences were unintended.

113. Intentionality may seem to be a fairly strict requirement, as it excludes not merely negligently harmful statements, but also recklessly harmful statements. However, in agreement with Baroness Hale DPSC and Lord Toulson JSC, I consider that recklessness is not enough. In truth, I doubt it would add much. Further, in practice, recklessness is a somewhat tricky concept. Quite apart from this, bearing in mind the importance of freedom of expression and of the law not sticking its nose into human discourse except where necessary, it appears to me that the line should be drawn at intentionality.

114. I am inclined to think that distressing the claimant has to be the primary purpose, but I do not consider that it need be the sole purpose. The degree of distress which is actually intended must be significant, and not trivial, and it can amount to feelings such as despair, misery, terror, fear or even serious worry. But it plainly does not have to amount to a recognised psychiatric disease (even if such disease is an essential ingredient, as to which see below). It is, I think, hard to be more specific than that.

115. Fourthly, the statement must, I think, be directed at the claimant in order to be tortious. In most cases this will add nothing to the requirements already mentioned. However, I would have thought that a statement which is aimed at upsetting a large group of addressees, without any particular individual (or relatively small group of individuals) in mind, should not be caught.

116. Then there is the question as to whether a claimant can only bring an action if he suffers distress to a sufficient degree to amount to a recognised illness or condition (whether psychological or physiological-assuming that the distinction is a valid one). Like Lord Hoffmann in *Wainwright v Home Office* [2004] 2 AC 406, I consider that there is much to be said for the view that the class of potential claimants should not be limited to those who can establish that they suffered from a recognised psychiatric illness as a result of the actionable statement of the defendant.

119. As I see it, therefore, there is plainly a powerful case for saying that, in relation to the instant tort, liability for distressing statements, where intent to cause distress is an essential ingredient, it should be enough for the claimant to establish that he suffered significant distress as a result of the defendant's statement. It is not entirely easy to see why, if an intention to cause the claimant significant distress is an ingredient of the tort and is enough to establish the tort in principle, the claimant should have to establish that he suffered something more serious than significant distress before he can recover any compensation. Further, the narrow restrictions on the tort should ensure that it is rarely invoked anyway.

122. In all these circumstances, it seems to me clear, even at this interlocutory stage, that the claimant's case plainly fails all but one of the requirements of the tort on which it is said to be based. While there is some (disputed) evidence that they could cause the claimant serious distress, the contents of the defendant's book are not untrue, threatening or insulting, they are not gratuitous or unjustified, let alone outrageous, they are not directed at the claimant, and they are not intended to distress the claimant . . .

Lord Clarke agreed with Baroness Hale and Lord Toulson. **Lord Wilson** agreed with Baroness Hale and Lord Toulson, and also with Lord Neuberger.

Appeal allowed.

COMMENTARY

The decision of the Court of Appeal in *O (A Child)* was subject to stinging criticism by commentators who saw it as a dangerous attack on freedom of speech: see e.g. Liew (2015) 78 MLR 359. According to Dickinson (2015) 131 LQR 542, 543, '[i]n granting the injunction, by an overly mechanical application of what it perceived to be the individual elements of the tort, the Court of Appeal created a common law basis for censoring graphic or disturbing works of literature'. By contrast, the decision of the Supreme Court has been welcomed: see Dickinson, *op. cit.*; Hunt [2015] CLJ 392.

Liew, *op. cit.*, pointed out (at 359) that the previous structure of the rule in *Wilkinson v Downton* left 'no analytical room' for taking into account the defendant's freedom of expression, and suggested the development of a control mechanism of 'justifiability' to enable policy considerations to be taken into account. Such an approach commended itself to the Supreme Court, with Lady Hale and Lord Toulson making it clear that liability in the *Wilkinson v Downton* tort requires words or conduct directed towards the claimant for which there was no justification or reasonable excuse. It followed that there was no liability on the facts, as the defendant's interest in telling his own life story provided adequate justification for his actions. However, they rejected (at [88]) the possibility of limiting the tort to 'extreme and outrageous' conduct (as in the United States: see the *Restatement of the Law (Third), Torts: Liability for Physical and Emotional Harm* (2010) § 46). By contrast, Lord Neuberger (at [110]) preferred to ask whether the statement was 'gratuitous', and thought that an 'extreme and outrageous' conduct test might be preferable to an exculpatory test of justification or reasonable excuse.

The broader implications of the Court of Appeal's decision for freedom of expression were of great concern to the Supreme Court. According to Lady Hale and Lord Toulson (at [78]), the interlocutory injunction granted by the court below, which permitted publication of the defendant's book only in a 'bowdlerised' version, presented problems 'both as a matter of principle and in the form of the injunction'. The court had 'taken editorial control over the manner in which the father's story' was expressed. A right to convey information to the public carried with it 'a right to choose the language in which it is expressed in order to convey the information most effectively'. If freedom of expression is such an important consideration, should a distinction be drawn between distressing conduct and distressing words in this context (as suggested by Lord Neuberger at [103])?

According to Hunt, (*op. cit.*, 394), the result of the new 'no justification or reasonable excuse' requirement is that the *Wilkinson v Downton* tort 'may not be used to restrain a person from publishing true information about himself, unless, perhaps, in extreme cases where the words are also threatening or abusive'. The requirement could also prove determinative in other types of case, as where a young man's fiancée leaves him for his best friend (see *D v East Berkshire Community Health NHS Trust* [2005] 2 AC 373 at [100]; Liew, *op. cit.*, 359–60).

O (A Child) confirms that the mental element of the tort is intention to cause physical harm or severe mental or emotional distress, a test which was held to be satisfied where a teacher at a special needs school engaged in inappropriate sexual behaviour with a vulnerable pupil, since the likely negative consequences of this for the pupil were obvious (*C v WH* [2016] PIQR Q2). It might be thought logical to extend the tort to cases where the claimant has suffered severe mental or emotional distress falling short of a psychiatric illness, so that the damage requirement and the mental element of the cause of action coalesce, but we have seen that such an extension did not commend itself to Lord Hoffmann and Lord Scott in *Wainwright*. Lord Neuberger in the instant case was more attracted to such an extension, but ultimately left the point open (at [116]–[119]). Dickinson, *op. cit.*, 546, supports such an extension, asking '[w]hy, if it suffices for C to prove that D *intended* consequence *x* or *y* in the alternative, should C be required to prove that consequence *y* has eventuated (or is likely to eventuate) in order to secure relief?' Can you think of a reason why?

In the courts below, the claimant in *O (A Child)* had also relied on negligence, but the Court of Appeal held that it would not be fair, just and reasonable to impose on parents a general common law duty to protect the emotional and psychological wellbeing of their children. Although this ruling was not challenged in the Supreme Court, Lord Neuberger (at [94]) made a point of signalling his approval of it. Coupled with the possibility that the *Wilkinson v Downton* tort might in future be extended to forms of harm (such as mental distress) not actionable in negligence, the outcome of this litigation in the Court of Appeal demonstrates that the cause of action still has a sphere of operation independent of negligence, if admittedly a somewhat limited one.

Finally, it is noteworthy that Lady Hale and Lord Toulson were critical in their judgment of the historical analysis of Lord Hoffmann in *Wainwright*, which they said (at [62]) showed the 'pitfalls of interpreting a decision more than a century earlier without a full understanding of jurisprudence and common legal terminology of the earlier period'. In particular, imputed intention was not a novel concept devised by Wright J to circumvent a perceived obstacle in the law of negligence, but was 'in the mainstream of legal thinking' at the time. Furthermore, there was no reason to suppose that Wright J would have felt obliged to follow the decision of the Privy Council in *Victorian Railways Comrs v Coultas* (1888) 13 App Cas 222 unless he could find a way of distinguishing it.

Protection from Harassment Act 1997

1. Prohibition of harassment

(1) A person must not pursue a course of conduct—
 (a) which amounts to harassment of another, and
 (b) which he knows or ought to know amounts to harassment of the other.

(1A) A person must not pursue a course of conduct—
 (a) which involves harassment of two or more persons, and
 (b) which he knows or ought to know involves harassment of those persons, and
 (c) by which he intends to persuade any person (whether or not one of those mentioned above)—
  (i) not to do something that he is entitled or required to do, or
  (ii) to do something that he is not under any obligation to do.

(2) For the purposes of this section, the person whose course of conduct is in question ought to know that it amounts to or involves harassment of another if a reasonable person in possession of the same information would think the course of conduct amounted to [or involved] harassment of the other.

(3) Subsection (1) or (1A) does not apply to a course of conduct if the person who pursued it shows—
 (a) that it was pursued for the purpose of preventing or detecting crime,
 (b) that it was pursued under any enactment or rule of law or to comply with any condition or requirement imposed by any person under any enactment, or
 (c) that in the particular circumstances the pursuit of the course of conduct was reasonable.

3. Civil remedy

(1) An actual or apprehended breach of section 1(1) may be the subject of a claim in civil proceedings by the person who is or may be the victim of the course of conduct in question.

(2) On such a claim, damages may be awarded for (among other things) any anxiety caused by the harassment and any financial loss resulting from the harassment. . . .

3A. Injunctions to protect persons from harassment within section 1(1A)

(1) This section applies where there is an actual or apprehended breach of section 1(1A) by any person ('the relevant person').

(2) In such a case—
 (a) any person who is or may be a victim of the course of conduct in question, or
 (b) any person who is or may be a person falling within section 1(1A)(c),
 may apply to the High Court or a county court for an injunction restraining the relevant person from pursuing any conduct which amounts to harassment in relation to any person or persons mentioned or described in the injunction.

7. Interpretation of this group of sections

(1) This section applies for the interpretation of sections 1 to 5A.

(2) References to harassing a person include alarming the person or causing the person distress.

(3) A 'course of conduct' must involve—
   (a) in the case of conduct in relation to a single person (see section 1(1)), conduct on at least two occasions in relation to that person, or
   (b) in the case of conduct in relation to two or more persons (see section 1(1A)), conduct on at least one occasion in relation to each of those persons.

(3A) A person's conduct on any occasion shall be taken, if aided, abetted, counselled or procured by another—
   (a) to be conduct on that occasion of the other (as well as conduct of the person whose conduct it is); and
   (b) to be conduct in relation to which the other's knowledge and purpose, and what he ought to have known, are the same as they were in relation to what was contemplated or reasonably foreseeable at the time of the aiding, abetting, counselling or procuring.

(4) 'Conduct' includes speech.

(5) References to a person, in the context of the harassment of a person, are references to a person who is an individual.

COMMENTARY

One reason for the reluctance of the House of Lords in *Wainwright* to reinvigorate the *Wilkinson v Downton* tort was the existence of the Protection from Harassment Act 1997. The Act imposes both civil and criminal sanctions in respect of conduct that amounts to harassment. As s. 1 makes clear, the tort of harassment is committed when the defendant pursues a course of conduct which amounts to harassment, when they know or should know that it does. Although 'harassment' itself is not defined in the Act, s. 7(2) makes clear that it includes alarming a person or causing a person distress, though the defendant's conduct need not actually have this effect to count as harassment: *Majrowski v Guy's and St Thomas's NHS Trust* [2007] 1 AC 224 at [66]. The defendant's conduct must however be unwelcome, so religious proselytisation to which the claimant responded with enthusiasm was not capable of amounting to harassment (*Brayshaw v Partners of Apsley Surgery* [2019] 2 All ER 997).

The potential scope of the legislation is broad, and to curtail it the courts have sought to distinguish between what Lord Nicholls termed 'unattractive, even unreasonable' conduct and 'oppressive and unacceptable' conduct (*Majrowski* at [30]). Since harassment is a crime as well as a tort, Lord Nicholls also said that when drawing that distinction the courts may find it helpful to ask whether the defendant's conduct is such as to merit criminal sanctions, which clearly puts a heavy burden on the claimant (*Sube v News Group Newspapers* [2020] EMLR 25 at [84]). Ultimately, however, there is much truth in the observation that 'the only test for harassment that emerges [from the case law] is the elephant test: you know it when you see it' (Shmilovits (2019) 135 LQR 27, 28). The focus on the causing of alarm and distress might suggest that there can be no liability under the Act for conduct not intended to come to the victim's attention, such as secret surveillance and monitoring of communications, but that has recently been denied on the ground that this would 'greatly cut down the protection for victims which [the Act] provides' (*Gerrard v Eurasian Natural Resources Corporation Ltd* [2020] EWHC 3241 at [94], per Richard Spearman QC), albeit with the caveat that for the tort to be committed the victim must in the end learn of the harassing conduct. Examples of conduct that have been held to amount to harassment include: workplace bullying (*Veakins v Kier Islington Ltd* [2010] IRLR 132); persistent and unjustified demands for payment by a utility company (*Ferguson v British Gas Trading* [2010] 1 WLR 785); and uploading explicit images of the claimant to the internet (*AMP v Persons Unknown* [2011] EWHC 3454 (QB) (note that this is now a criminal offence in its own right if done with intent to cause distress: Criminal Justice and Courts Act 2015, s. 33)).

To constitute harassment a course of conduct must be targeted at an individual or individuals (see *Thomas v News Group Newspapers* [2002] EMLR 78 at [30]; see also *Levi v Bates* [2016] QB 91), so that behaviour which is not aimed or directed at anyone in particular—such as loud and aggressive shouting in a public place—cannot be harassment, even if it causes alarm and distress. Although corporations cannot bring a claim under the Act (s. 7(5)), the employees of a company can sue if conduct targeted at the company was capable of causing them the requisite alarm or distress (*Daiichi UK Ltd v Stop Huntingdon Animal Cruelty* [2005] 1 BCLC 27). More generally, the ability to bring a claim for harassment extends beyond the targeted person to other persons who are 'foreseeably, and directly, harmed by the course of targeted conduct . . . to the extent that they can properly be described as victims of it' (*Levi v Bates* [2016] QB 91 at [34], per Briggs LJ). Amendments in 2005 extended the Act to cover harassment for the purpose of influencing the conduct of a third person; in these cases at least two persons must be the subject of the harassing behaviour (s. 1(1A)).

The remedies available to a victim of harassment are damages, including for resultant economic loss (s. 3(2)), and injunctive relief. Breach of an injunction granted under the Act may lead to a warrant for arrest and conviction for a criminal offence (s. 3(3)–(9)). It should be noted that harassment falling under s. 1(1A) is treated differently: the only remedy available to the third party whose conduct the defendant is attempting to influence is an injunction.

The scope of the legislation is potentially very wide, although applying the Human Rights Act 1998, the 1997 Act must be interpreted so as to be consistent with the rights to freedom of expression and association recognised in Articles 10 and 11 of the European Convention on Human Rights. In *Thomas v News Group Newspapers* [2002] EMLR 78, it was accepted by the Court of Appeal that, in principle, publication of press articles was capable of amounting to harassment under the Act. However, the newspaper would normally be able to claim that its conduct was reasonable under s. 1(3)(c) unless the alleged harassment was such as to take the publications outside the scope of Article 10(1) (e.g. because they were defamatory, or, as in *Thomas*, incited racial hatred). In practice, it seems that harassment claims against media organisations are very unlikely to succeed: a recent case involving an immigrant couple vilified in the popular press for allegedly demanding a bigger council house for their large family was said to be the first such claim to make it to trial for eight years, and the action was ultimately unsuccessful: *Sube v News Group Newspapers* [2020] EMLR 25. Even without the influence of the Convention, there had been suggestions that the Act could not be interpreted so as to clamp down on discussion of matters of public interest or rights of political protest and public demonstration 'which was so much a part of our democratic tradition' (*Huntingdon Life Sciences v Curtin, The Times*, 11 December 1997, QBD, per Eady J). See further Mead, 'The Human Rights Act: A Panacea for Peaceful Public Protest?' (1998) 3 *Journal of Civil Liberties* 206. Nevertheless, the uncertainty that besets the law of harassment remains a threat to freedom, according to Shmilovits (*op. cit.*, 31):

This nebulous tort . . . deals with acts that are just bad enough to be illegal. It is the border between impropriety and illegality. The consequence of impropriety is social censure. The consequence of illegality is state sanction. That the tort doubles as a criminal offence . . . underscores its social significance. The boundary between freedom and delinquency should be clear—not least because any uncertainty tends to come at the expense of freedom.

Liability attaches only to a 'course of conduct', which is defined in s. 7 to mean conduct on at least two occasions or, for harassment falling under s. 1(1A), conduct on at least one occasion in respect of the two persons who must be harassed for the section to apply. Thus the plaintiff in *Wilkinson v Downton* could not recover under the Act and would be left to a remedy at common law. However, where there is a course of conduct, it is only the course of conduct which must constitute harassment and not its individual elements, as was reiterated in a case where correspondence from a housing association to two of its tenants threatening to evict them from their homes was held to be actionable under the Act (*Worthington v Metropolitan Housing Trust* [2018] HLR 32; for trenchant criticism of this decision, see Shmilovits, *op. cit.*).

vi. Defences

1. Introduction

Four defences—lawful arrest and detention, consent, necessity and self-defence—will be considered in some detail in the text that follows. A number of other defences—contributory negligence, *volenti non fit injuria* and illegality—are considered in Chapter 6, but, as the following extract from *Murphy v Culhane* shows, they might equally arise in an action for intentional interference with the person. Various other defences of more restricted scope should also be noted, for example the exercise of disciplinary powers by parents over children, and prior institution of criminal proceedings against the defendant (see Offences Against the Person Act 1861, ss. 44–45). An issue that has not been unequivocally resolved is whether provocation acts as a general defence in this context.

Murphy v Culhane [1977] 1 QB 94

The plaintiff was the widow of a man killed in a criminal affray. She claimed damages under a predecessor of the Fatal Accidents Act 1976. The defendant alleged that the plaintiff's husband and others had come to assault him, and that her husband's death had occurred in the course of a criminal attack originated by him. Judgment was given against the defendant on the basis of the admissions made by him, and he appealed.

Lord Denning MR

Apart altogether from damages, however, I think there may well be a defence on liability. If Murphy was one of a gang which set out to beat up Culhane, it may well be that he could not sue for damages if he got more than he bargained for. A man who takes part in a criminal affray may well be said to have been guilty of such a wicked act as to deprive himself of a cause of action or, alternatively, to have taken on himself the risk. I put the case in the course of argument: suppose that a burglar breaks into a house and the householder, finding him there, picks up a gun and shoots him, using more force maybe than is reasonably necessary.

The householder may be guilty of manslaughter and liable to be brought before the criminal courts. But I doubt very much whether the burglar's widow could have an action for damages. The householder might well have a defence either on grounds of *ex turpi causa non oritur actio* or *volenti non fit injuria*. So in the present case it is open to Mr Culhane to raise both those defences. Such defences would go to the whole claim.

There is another point, too, [which is that] even if Mrs Murphy were entitled to damages under the Fatal Accidents Acts, they fall to be reduced under the Law Reform (Contributory Negligence) Act 1945 because the death of her husband might be the result partly of his own fault and partly of the default of the defendant: see s. 1(1) and (4) of the 1945 Act. On this point I must explain a sentence in *Gray v Barr* ([1971] 2 QB 554 at 569) where the widow of the dead man was held to be entitled to full compensation without any reduction. Her husband had not been guilty of any 'fault' within s. 4 of the 1945 Act because his conduct had not been such as to make him liable in an action of tort or, alternatively, was not such that he should be regarded as responsible in any degree for the damage. So also in *Lane v Holloway* ([1968] 1 QB 379 at 393), as Winn LJ pointed out. But in the present case the conduct of Mr Murphy may well have been such as to make him liable in tort.

Orr and **Waller LJJ** agreed with Lord Denning MR.

Appeal allowed.

COMMENTARY

In *Barnes v Nayer, The Times*, 19 December 1986, the Court of Appeal affirmed that, in a claim for damages for assault or battery 'if it was possible on the facts properly to say *ex turpi causa* or *volenti non fit injuria*, then probably the two defences described shortly by those Latin tags, could be relied upon'. The court did not, however, agree with other aspects of Lord Denning's judgment (discussed later). Note also that Lord Denning's comments in relation to a possible reduction of damages under the Law Reform (Contributory Negligence) Act 1945 were not followed in *Pritchard v Co-operative Group Ltd* [2012] QB 320, where it was held that contributory negligence is not a defence to an action in trespass to the person (see further in Ch. 6.III.2).

The traditional view is that, in civil actions, provocation may lead to a reduction in exemplary damages but not in compensatory damages (see *Lane v Holloway* [1968] 1 QB 379). In *Murphy v Culhane*, however, Lord Denning suggested that the level of compensatory damages might be reduced unless the reaction of the defendant was out of all proportion to the provocation of the claimant. This dictum was subsequently criticised by the Court of Appeal in *Barnes v Nayer*, but support for Lord Denning's view was provided by Gillen J in *McAleer v Chief Constable of the PSNI* [2014] NIQB 53, who said (at [28]):

For my own part, I incline to the view that provocation may still serve to reduce compensatory damages in some cases . . . If the law is to maintain public confidence, legal integrity demands that in a case where a plaintiff provokes a defendant into a measure of excessive force he should not be permitted to recover full damages against such a defendant.

Note also that the effect of the Criminal Justice Act 2003, s. 329 (see VI.5) may be to make available a provocation defence in limited circumstances.

2. Lawful Arrest and Detention

Arrest or detention of a person suspected of a criminal offence—but not a civil wrong (see *Sunbolf v Alford* (1838) 3 M & W 247, 150 ER 1135)—may be justified by a variety of different powers. These powers are not exclusive to the police, and there are a number of circumstances in which a private individual may make a 'citizen's arrest'. Nevertheless, the powers available to the police are much more extensive than those available to ordinary people. This is not to say that the police have *carte blanche* to use force against, or restrain the movement of, private individuals. Like other government agencies, the police are subject to the 'rule of law', meaning that they must demonstrate clear legal authority to justify interference with the rights of private citizens (see *Entick v Carrington* (1765) 19 State Tr 1029, 95 ER 807), and that in the absence of such authority, they may face liabilities in trespass to the person (see, e.g., *Collins v Wilcock*, discussed earlier).

Police powers are now extensively catalogued in the Police and Criminal Evidence Act 1984, though other independent powers exist (e.g. the common law power to arrest for breach of the peace). The Act recognises a general power of arrest without warrant for constables (s. 24) and a more limited power of arrest in respect of indictable offences which may be exercised by private individuals in defined circumstances (s. 24A). Also included in the Act is a power to stop and search a person who is suspected of carrying a stolen or prohibited article in a public place (s. 1; prohibited articles include offensive weapons and housebreaking implements). An officer may use reasonable force in exercising any of the powers recognised in the Act (s. 117). For further details of police powers, see R. Clayton and H. Tomlinson, *Civil Actions Against the Police*, 4th edn (London: Sweet & Maxwell, 2021).

In recent times, actions against prison authorities by inmates have become increasingly common. The Prisons Act 1952, s. 12(1) provides that '[a] prisoner, whether sentenced to imprisonment or committed to prison on remand pending trial or otherwise, may be lawfully confined in any prison'. However, it has been argued that solitary confinement and other restrictions of liberty within the prison for disciplinary reasons may give rise to liability for false imprisonment where there is a breach of the Prison Rules, as will be seen from the next extract.

R v Deputy Governor of Parkhurst Prison, Ex parte Hague
[1992] 1 AC 58

In two separate cases the question arose whether a convicted prisoner who had been restrained in a way not permitted by the Prison Rules 1964 while serving his sentence had a cause of action in private law for damages against the prison governor or the Home Office. The causes of action relied upon were breach of statutory duty and false imprisonment. The House of Lords held that no claim for either cause of action was available, but the extract deals only with the false imprisonment issue.

Lord Bridge of Harwich

To ask at the outset whether a convicted prisoner enjoys in law a 'residual liberty', as if the extent of any citizen's right to liberty were a species of right *in rem* or a matter of status, is to ask the wrong question. An action for false imprisonment is an action *in personam*. The tort of false imprisonment has two ingredients: the fact of imprisonment and the absence of lawful authority to justify it. In *Meering v Grahame-White Aviation Co Ltd* (1919) 122 LT 44 at 54 Atkin LJ said that 'any restraint within defined bounds which is a restraint in fact may be an imprisonment.' Thus if A imposes on B a restraint within defined bounds and is sued by B for false imprisonment, the action will succeed or fail according to whether or not A can justify the restraint imposed on B as lawful. A child may be lawfully restrained within defined bounds by his parents or by the schoolmaster to whom the parents have delegated their authority. But if precisely the same restraint is imposed by a stranger without authority, it will be unlawful and will constitute the tort of false imprisonment.

I shall leave aside initially questions arising from the situation where a convicted prisoner serving a sentence is restrained by a member of the prison staff acting in bad faith, by a fellow prisoner or any other third party, or in circumstances where it can be said that the conditions of his detention are intolerable. I shall address first what I believe to be the primary and fundamental issue, *viz* whether any restraint within defined bounds imposed upon a convicted prisoner whilst serving his sentence by the prison governor or by officers acting with the authority of the prison governor and in good faith, but in circumstances where the particular form of restraint is not sanctioned by the Prison Rules, amounts for that reason to the tort of false imprisonment.

The starting point is s. 12(1) of the Prison Act 1952 which provides:

> A prisoner, whether sentenced to imprisonment or committed to prison on remand pending trial or otherwise, may be lawfully confined in any prison.

This provides lawful authority for the restraint of the prisoner within the defined bounds of the prison by the governor of the prison, who has the legal custody of the prisoner under s. 13, or by any prison officer acting with the governor's authority. Can the prisoner then complain that his legal rights are infringed by a restraint which confines him at any particular time within a particular part of the prison? It seems to me that the reality of prison life demands a negative answer to this question. Certainly in the ordinary closed prison the ordinary prisoner will at any time of day or night be in a particular part of the prison, not because that is where he chooses to be, but because that is where the prison regime requires him to be. He will be in his cell, in the part of the prison where he is required to work, in the exercise yard, eating meals, attending education classes or enjoying whatever recreation is permitted, all in the appointed place and at the appointed time and all in accordance with a more or less rigid regime to which he must conform. Thus the concept of the prisoner's 'residual liberty' as a species of freedom of movement within the prison enjoyed as a legal right which the prison authorities cannot lawfully restrain seems to me quite illusory. The prisoner is at all times lawfully restrained within closely defined bounds and if he is kept in a segregated cell, at a time when, if the rules had not been misapplied, he would be in the company of other prisoners in the workshop, at the dinner table or elsewhere, this is not the deprivation of his liberty of movement, which is the essence of the tort of false imprisonment, it is the substitution of one form of restraint for another. . . .

In my opinion, to hold a prisoner entitled to damages for false imprisonment on the ground that he has been subject to a restraint upon his movement which was not in accordance with the Prison Rules would be, in effect, to confer on him under a different legal label a cause of action for breach of statutory duty under the rules. Having reached the conclusion that it was not the intention of the rules to confer such a right, I am satisfied that the right cannot properly be asserted in the alternative guise of a claim to damages for false imprisonment. . . .

I turn next to the question posed by the example given in the judgment of Parker LJ in *Weldon*'s case [1990] 3 WLR 465 at 480, of a prisoner locked in a shed by fellow prisoners.

I think the short answer to this question is given by Taylor LJ who said in *Hague*'s case [1990] 3 WLR 1210 at 1267:

> In such a situation an action for false imprisonment would surely lie (for what it was worth), since the fellow prisoners would have no defence under s. 12 of the Prison Act 1952.

The prisoner locked in the shed is certainly restrained within defined bounds and it is *nihil ad rem* that if he were not locked in the shed, he would be locked in his cell or restrained in accordance with the prison regime in some other part of the prison. The restraint in the shed is unlawful because the fellow prisoners acted without the authority of the governor and it is only the governor, who has the legal custody of the prisoner, and persons acting with the authority of the governor who can rely on the provisions of s. 12(1).

This consideration also leads to the conclusion that a prison officer who acts in bad faith by deliberately subjecting a prisoner to a restraint which he knows he has no authority to impose may render himself personally liable to an action for false imprisonment as well as committing the tort of misfeasance in public office. Lacking the authority of the governor, he also lacks the protection of s. 12(1). But if the officer deliberately acts outside the scope of his authority, he cannot render the governor or the Home Office vicariously liable for his tortious conduct. This no doubt explains why Mr Harris did not seek to sustain the decision of the Court of Appeal in his favour on the ground that the plaintiff's pleading should be read as involving an allegation of bad faith.

There remains the question whether an otherwise lawful imprisonment may be rendered unlawful by reason only of the conditions of detention. In *R v Comr of Police of the Metropolis, ex p Nahar, The Times*, 28 May 1983, two applicants for habeas corpus who had been remanded in custody were held pursuant to the provisions of s. 6 of the Imprisonment (Temporary Provisions) Act 1980 in cells below the Camberwell Green Magistrates' Court which were designed only to enable persons to be held in custody for a few hours at a time and which were obviously deficient in many respects for the purpose of accommodating prisoners for longer periods. They sought their release on the ground that the conditions of their detention rendered it unlawful. The applications were rejected, but Stephen Brown J said in the course of his judgment: 'There must be some minimum standard to render detention lawful.' McCullough J said:

> Despite the temporary nature of the detention there contemplated, there must be implied into s. 6 of the 1980 Act some term which relates to the conditions under which a prisoner may lawfully be detained. I say so because it is possible to conceive of hypothetical circumstances in which the conditions of detention were such as would make that detention unlawful.
>
> I do not propose to offer any formulation of that term. Were it broken in any particular case I would reject emphatically the suggestion that the matter would not be one for the exercise of the court's jurisdiction to grant the writ of habeas corpus.

These observations were considered by the Court of Appeal in *Middleweek v Chief Constable of the Merseyside Police (Note)* [1992] 1 AC 179. The plaintiff had been awarded damages for false imprisonment by the jury on the basis that his otherwise lawful detention at a police station had been rendered unlawful because it was unreasonable in the circumstances to keep him in a police cell. The defendant successfully appealed, but Ackner LJ, delivering the judgment of the court, said (at 487):

> We agree with the views expressed by the Divisional Court that it must be possible to conceive of hypothetical cases in which the conditions of detention are so intolerable as

to render the detention unlawful and thereby provide a remedy to the prisoner in damages for false imprisonment. A person lawfully detained in a prison cell would, in our judgment, cease to be so lawfully detained if the conditions in that cell were such as to be seriously prejudicial to his health if he continued to occupy it, e.g. because it became and remained seriously flooded, or contained a fractured gas pipe allowing gas to escape into the cell. We do not therefore accept as an absolute proposition that, if detention is initially lawful, it can never become unlawful by reason of changes in the conditions of imprisonment.

I sympathise entirely with the view that the person lawfully held in custody who is subjected to intolerable conditions ought not to be left without a remedy against his custodian, but the proposition that the conditions of detention may render the detention itself unlawful raises formidable difficulties. If the proposition be sound, the corollary must be that when the conditions of detention deteriorate to the point of intolerability, the detainee is entitled immediately to go free. It is impossible, I think, to define with any precision what would amount to intolerable conditions for this purpose . . . The examples given by Ackner LJ of a flooded or gas-filled cell are so extreme that they do not, with respect, offer much guidance as to where the line should be drawn. The law is certainly left in a very unsatisfactory state if the legality or otherwise of detaining a person who in law is and remains liable to detention depends on such an imprecise criterion and may vary from time to time as the conditions of his detention change.

The logical solution to the problem, I believe, is that if the conditions of an otherwise lawful detention are truly intolerable, the law ought to be capable of providing a remedy directly related to those conditions without characterising the fact of the detention itself as unlawful. I see no real difficulty in saying that the law can provide such a remedy. Whenever one person is lawfully in the custody of another, the custodian owes a duty of care to the detainee. If the custodian negligently allows, or *a fortiori*, if he deliberately causes, the detainee to suffer in any way in his health he will be in breach of that duty. But short of anything that could properly be described as a physical injury or an impairment of health, if a person lawfully detained is kept in conditions which cause him for the time being physical pain or a degree of discomfort which can properly be described as intolerable, I believe that could and should be treated as a breach of the custodian's duty of care for which the law should award damages. For this purpose it is quite unnecessary to attempt any definition of the criterion of intolerability. It would be a question of fact and degree in any case which came before the court to determine whether the conditions to which a detainee had been subjected were such as to warrant an award of damages for the discomfort he had suffered. In principle I believe it is acceptable for the law to provide a remedy on this basis, but that the remedy suggested in the *Nahar* and *Middleweek* cases is not. In practice, the problem is perhaps not very likely to arise.

Lord Jauncey delivered a separate concurring speech and **Lord Goff**, **Lord Lowry** and **Lord Ackner** agreed generally with Lord Bridge and Lord Jauncey.

Appeal in Hague *case dismissed; Appeal in* Weldon *case allowed.*

COMMENTARY

That a prisoner may bring an action in the tort of misfeasance in public office for 'loss of liberty' was confirmed in *Karagozlu v Metropolitan Police Officer* [2007] 1 WLR 1881. And in *Toumia v Evans (Secretary General of the Prison Officers' Association)*, *The Times*, 1 April 1999, it was held that, following dicta in *Hague*, it was arguable that a prison officer who deliberately locked a prisoner in his cell contrary to the orders of the prison governor would be liable for false imprisonment. By contrast, were an officer to fail to release a prisoner from his cell (e.g. for exercise or education) contrary to the governor's orders, it is now clear that no false imprisonment action would lie for this omission. The claimant in *Iqbal v Prison Officers Association* [2010] QB 732 was a prisoner who was kept in his cell throughout the day because of a strike by prison officers. In the normal course of events he would have been allowed out of his cell for several short periods but, as a result of the strike, the prison governor lawfully ordered that all prisoners be kept in their cells throughout the day. Relying on dicta in *Hague* that there may be some residual liberty against persons not acting with the authority of the prison governor, the claimant argued that the failure of the prison officers to open his cell and release him could found a claim for false imprisonment. A majority of the Court of Appeal rejected the claim for two main reasons. First, in the absence of a special duty to act, false imprisonment required a positive act, not a mere omission (see further in VI.3(b)), and the most that could be said against the prison officers was that they had failed to open the cell. Second, the imprisonment had not been caused directly by the action of the prison officers; the immediate cause of the claimant remaining in his cell was the order of the governor and even though it was foreseeable that the governor might make this order as a result of the strike this did not amount to the prison officers procuring the imprisonment (see *Davidson v Chief Constable of North Wales* [1994] 2 All ER 597, discussed earlier).

The defence is one of lawful authority, not reasonable belief that lawful authority existed. This is graphically illustrated by the decision of the House of Lords in *R v Governor of Brockhill Prison, ex p. Evans* [2001] 2 AC 19. In this case a prison governor who incorrectly calculated the release date of a prisoner was held liable in false imprisonment from the date the prisoner should have been released, even though the governor had calculated the date in accordance with pre-existing judicial authority which was only overruled when the prisoner sought judicial review of the governor's decision. Commenting on the Court of Appeal decision (which the House of Lords upheld), Fordham, 'False Imprisonment in Good Faith' (2000) 8 Tort L Rev 53 at 67, argued: 'As long as the officials responsible for detaining a person actually intend to detain him or her, then the fact that they are unaware that the detention was unauthorised is surely irrelevant. The focus of an action for false imprisonment is, after all, primarily on the plaintiff and the wrongful deprivation of his or her liberty.' Do you agree? For comment on the House of Lords' decision, see Cane (2001) 117 LQR 5.

In cases where the imprisonment is carried out by a 'public authority' under the Human Rights Act 1998, there may be both a claim for false imprisonment and a claim under the 1998 Act for a deprivation of liberty in breach of Article 5, ECHR (the right to liberty and security). However, it is important to note that there are significant differences between the common law and the Convention when it comes to protection of freedom of movement—for example, it is well established that there can be an 'imprisonment' which is not a 'deprivation of liberty': see *Austin v Commissioner of Police of the Metropolis* [2009] AC 564; *Walker v Commissioner of Police of the Metropolis* [2015] 1 WLR 312; *R (Jalloh) v Secretary of State for the Home Department* [2021] AC 262. Discussion of the derogations allowed under Article 5 is beyond the scope of this book, but it is possible that circumstances which would give rise to a defence of lawful authority at common law would not serve to defeat a claim for breach of Article 5 (see *Jalloh* at [31]) and vice versa (*R (Lumba) v Secretary of State for the Home Department* [2012] 1 AC 245 at [199]), although when the issue has arisen in practice the courts have tended to find that, if the defence succeeds for false imprisonment, it succeeds for an HRA claim as well (see, e.g., *Roberts v Secretary of State for the Home Department* [2006] 1 WLR 843 at [41]).

3. Consent

(a) General Principles

It has been held that, strictly speaking, lack of consent is an element of the intentional torts, to be pleaded and proved by the claimant, rather than a defence (*Freeman v Home Office (No. 2)* [1984] QB 524), though the point is not free from difficulty, and was the subject of a spirited disagreement between McLachlin J and Iacobucci J in the context of 'sexual battery' in *Non-Marine Underwriters, Lloyds of London v Scalera* [2000] 1 SCR 551 (see also *Ashley v Chief Constable of Sussex Police* [2007] 1 WLR 398 at 410). In any case, practically speaking the defendant may need to lead evidence from which the court can infer consent, so not much will necessarily turn on the point.

The defendant may still be liable if the claimant's apparent consent was given under duress or without full knowledge of the material facts. The next extracted case considers when consent will be vitiated in this way.

Chatterton v Gerson [1981] QB 432

The plaintiff complained that the defendant surgeon did not advise her as to the possible side effects of the course of treatment he was proposing for her. The plaintiff claimed in both battery and negligence, but her action was dismissed. The extract relates to the dismissal of the cause of action for battery.

Bristow J

It is clear law that in any context in which consent of the injured party is a defence to what would otherwise be a crime or a civil wrong, the consent must be real. Where, for example, a woman's consent to sexual intercourse is obtained by fraud, her apparent consent is no defence to a charge of rape. It is not difficult to state the principle or to appreciate its good sense. As so often, the problem lies in its application. . . .

In my judgment what the court has to do in each case is to look at all the circumstances and say, 'Was there a real consent?' I think justice requires that in order to vitiate the reality of consent there must be a greater failure of communication between doctor and patient than that involved in a breach of duty if the claim is based on negligence. When the claim is based on negligence the plaintiff must prove not only the breach of duty to inform but that had the duty not been broken she would not have chosen to have the operation. Where the claim is based on trespass to the person, once it is shown that the consent is unreal, then what the plaintiff would have decided if she had been given the information which would have prevented vitiation of the reality of her consent is irrelevant.

In my judgment once the patient is informed in broad terms of the nature of the procedure which is intended, and gives her consent, that consent is real, and the cause of the action on which to base a claim for failure to go into risks and implications is negligence, not trespass. Of course, if information is withheld in bad faith, the consent will be vitiated by fraud. Of course, if by some accident, as in a case in the 1940s in the Salford Hundred Court, where a boy was admitted to hospital for tonsillectomy and due to administrative error was circumcised instead, trespass would be the appropriate cause of action against the doctor, though he was as much the victim of the error as the boy. But in my judgment it would be very much against the interests of justice if actions which are really based on a failure by the doctor to perform his duty adequately to inform were pleaded in trespass. . . .

Action dismissed.

COMMENTARY

In his judgment Bristow J mentioned the decision of the Ontario Court of Appeal in *Reibl v Hughes*. This was confirmed by the Supreme Court of Canada (1981) 114 DLR 3d 1, where it was said that, unless there was fraud or misrepresentation to secure the consent, a failure to advise of risks, however serious, went to negligence and not battery. For a discussion of the issue see Tan, 'Failure of Medical Advice: Trespass or Negligence?' (1987) 7 LS 149, and Maclean, 'The Doctrine of Informed Consent: Does It Exist and Has It Crossed the Atlantic?' (2004) 24 LS 386, 398–401.

The Reality of Consent

Consent must be real to be effective, and consent obtained by duress is no defence. Clearly the threat of physical violence will vitiate consent, but the courts have been reluctant to treat lesser forms of pressure in the same way. In *Freeman v Home Office (No. 2)* [1984] QB 524, for example, it was held that the institutional pressures acting upon a prisoner's mind did not affect the genuineness of his consent to medical treatment.

To what extent can consent be vitiated by fraud? In criminal law it was long thought that consent was vitiated only by fraud that went to the essential nature of the contact, as in *R v Williams* [1923] 1 KB 340, where it was held that there was no consent to sexual intercourse when the accused told the victim he was merely performing an exercise to improve her singing voice. According to the Sexual Offences Act 2003 (which only applies where there is a sexual assault as defined by the Act) there is no consent if the victim was deliberately deceived by the defendant 'as to the nature or purpose of the relevant act', wording which, it has been held, did not represent a departure from the previous law (*R v B* [2007] 1 WLR 1567; *R v Jheeta* [2007] EWCA Crim 1699). This suggests that only fraud as to the 'purpose' of the act vitiated consent prior to the 2003 Act but this is hard to reconcile with the decision in *R v Tabassum* [2000] 4 Lloyd's Rep Med 404, where various women who had given the accused consent to examine their breasts for the purpose of conducting medical research said that the only reason they consented was that they thought he was medically qualified when in fact he was not. The Court of Appeal held that the accused was properly convicted of assault, as the women's consent was to touching for a medical procedure, not for indecent assault, but there was no evidence that the accused had a sexual motive for his actions; on the contrary, he touched the victims for the purpose for which he had told them he would touch them. The gist of their complaint was that he did not possess an attribute—a medical qualification—that they thought he possessed. Contrast *R v Richardson* [1999] QB 444, where a dentist who had been suspended from practice but continued to carry out dental treatment on patients was held not guilty of a criminal assault. Although *Richardson* was distinguished in *Tabassum*, the grounds on which this was done are not altogether convincing. Another borderline criminal law case is *R v Devonald* [2008] EWCA Crim 527, where the accused had persuaded his daughter's ex-boyfriend to perform a sexual act in front of a webcam by posing as a 20-year-old woman called 'Cassie'. In a prosecution for procuring a sexual act, could it be said that the defendant's fraud went to the 'nature and purpose' of the act performed by the ex-boyfriend? See further, Elvin, 'The Concept of Consent under the Sexual Offences Act 2003' (2008) 72 J Crim L 519.

It is in any case possible that in private law fraud vitiates consent even when it does not go to the essential nature or purpose of the contact. In *Chatterton*, Bristow J suggested that there might be a battery where information about treatment risks was deliberately withheld in bad faith. This is consistent with the later case of *Appleton v Garrett* (1995) 34 BMLR 23, where the plaintiffs were patients of a dentist who had deliberately and fraudulently performed unnecessary dental work on them. Dyson J held that the defendant's failure to provide any information on whether the treatment was necessary was in bad faith, that this vitiated the plaintiffs' consent and that trespass to the person was established. If this is correct, however, then the position in tort is apparently at odds with that in criminal law, where fraud that goes only to the consequences of the contact does not undermine the reality of a person's consent to that contact, whether in bad faith or not. In the controversial criminal case of *R v B* [2007] 1 WLR 1567, the failure of the accused to tell his sexual partner that he was HIV-positive can hardly have been in good faith but the Court of Appeal held that his omission did not vitiate any consent she had given to the act of sexual intercourse. Should a man be guilty of battery any more than rape if he seduces a woman by telling her untruthfully that he is very rich?

Capacity to Consent

In the case of children and those suffering from a mental disability, the question of capacity to consent may arise. The general rule is that the subject of the proposed interference must have the ability to understand what is involved. This was accepted by the House of Lords in *Gillick v West Norfolk Health Authority* [1986] AC 112 when considering the capacity of teenage girls to consent to contraceptive treatment. Lord Scarman said that the child's understanding would have to go further than a simple appreciation of the doctor's reasons for touching the child and the purposes behind the touching; the child would have to have an understanding of the wider social and moral implications of the contraceptive treatment.

Where a person lacks the capacity to consent, touching (e.g. in the course of medical treatment) may be justified by reference to either the consent of a parent or guardian or the separate defence of necessity (discussed later).

Can Consent be Ineffective for Reasons of Public Policy?

In criminal law, 'nearly everyone agrees that the consent of the victim is not a defence to a charge of inflicting really serious personal injury . . .' (*R v Brown* [1994] 1 AC 212 at 248, per Lord Lowry). Similarly, it has been suggested that injuries inflicted during the course of a mutually agreed fight might be tortious, although damages could not be recovered because the parties were engaged in an illegal activity (*Re F (Mental Patient: Sterilisation)* [1990] 2 AC 1, per Neill LJ). However, this seems extremely doubtful as a matter of principle, and the better view is surely that of Lord Denning, who clearly thought that in such a case consent would operate as a defence provided the injuries were in proportion to the occasion (*Lane v Holloway* [1968] 1 QB 379 at 386). In *Brown*, the House of Lords held by a 3–2 majority that consent was no defence to consensual acts of sado-masochism occasioning actual bodily harm, but it would be a very strange result if a participant in such an activity could sue another in battery despite their having validly consented (see further *Ashley v Chief Constable of Sussex Police* [2008] 1 AC 962 at [18]–[19]; *Fleming*, p. 97; Stevens, 'Private Rights and Public Wrongs', in M. Dyson (ed.), *Unravelling Tort and Crime* (Cambridge: CUP, 2014) pp. 114–18).

(b) Revocation of Consent

Balmain New Ferry Company Ltd v Robertson (1906) 4 CLR 379

The plaintiff entered a wharf to catch a ferry, passing through a turnstile over which was a sign stating that the charge for entry or exit from the wharf was one penny irrespective of whether a ferry had been used. After entering the plaintiff realised he had just missed a ferry, whereupon he sought to leave the wharf. He was restrained by employees of the defendant when he refused to pay the extra penny but finally forced his way out. His action in false imprisonment was successful at first instance, but the defendant appealed to the High Court of Australia.

Griffith CJ

This agreement involves, in my opinion, an implied promise by the plaintiff that he would not ask for egress by land except on payment of one penny, and, further, a consent on his part that the defendant should be entitled to prevent him from departing in that way until he paid the penny. . . .

O'Connor J

[T]he abridgement of a man's liberty is not under all circumstances actionable. He may enter into a contract which necessarily involves the surrender of a portion of his liberty for a certain period, and if the act complained of is nothing more than a restraint in accordance with that surrender he cannot complain. Nor can he, without the assent of the other party, by electing to put an end to the contract, become entitled at once, unconditionally and irrespective of the other party's rights, to regain his liberty as if he had never surrendered it. A familiar instance of such a contract is that between a passenger and a railway company which undertakes to carry him on a journey. If the passenger suddenly during the journey decided to abandon it and to leave the train at the next station, being one at which the train was not timed to stop, he clearly would not be entitled to have the train stopped at that station. However much he might object, the railway company could lawfully carry him on to the next stopping place of that particular train. In such a case the passenger's liberty would be for a certain period restrained, but the restraint would not be actionable, because it is an implied term of such a contract that the passenger will permit the restraint of liberty so far as may be necessary for the performance by the company of the contract of carriage according to the time of that train. . . .

The first question is, what is the contract to be implied from the plaintiff's payment at and passing through the turnstiles under these circumstances? It is that in consideration of that payment the company undertook to carry him as a passenger to Balmain by any of their ferry boats from that wharf. That is the only contract which could be implied from the circumstances, and the plaintiff was permitted to enter the wharf for the purpose of that contract being performed. It is not denied that the company were ready to perform their part, but the plaintiff, as far as one party can do so, rescinded the contract and determined to go back from the wharf to the street. What then were his rights? They were, in my opinion, no more and no less than they would have been if he had landed from his own boat at the company's wharf. He was on private property. He had not been forced or entrapped there. He had entered it of his own free will and with the knowledge that the only exit on the land side was through the turnstile, operated as a part of the company's system of collecting fares in the manner I have mentioned. If he wished to use the turnstile as a means of exit he could only do so on complying with the usual conditions on which the company opened them. The company were lawfully entitled to impose the condition of a penny payment on all who used the turnstiles, whether they had travelled by the company's steamers or not, and they were under no obligation to make an exception in the plaintiff's favour. The company, therefore, being lawfully entitled to impose that condition, and the plaintiff being free to pass out at any time on complying with it, he had only himself to blame for his detention, and there was no imprisonment of which he could legally complain . . .

Appeal allowed.

Robinson v Balmain New Ferry Company [1910] AC 295

The plaintiff unsuccessfully appealed to the Privy Council (where his name was mistakenly recorded as 'Robinson' instead of 'Robertson').

Lord Loreburn LC

[I]n the circumstances admitted it is clear to their Lordships that there was no false imprisonment at all. The plaintiff was merely called upon to leave the wharf in the way which he contracted to leave it. There is no law requiring the defendants to make the exit from their premises gratuitous to people who come there upon a definite contract which involves their leaving the wharf by another way; and the defendants were entitled to resist a forcible passage through another turnstile.

The question whether the notice which was affixed to these premises was brought home to the knowledge of the plaintiff is immaterial, because the notice itself is immaterial. When the plaintiff entered the defendants' premises there was nothing agreed as to the terms on which he might go back, because neither party contemplated his going back. When he desired to do so the defendants were entitled to impose a reasonable condition before allowing him to pass through their turnstile from a place to which he had gone of his own free will. The payment of a penny was a quite fair condition, and if he did not choose to comply with it the defendants were not bound to let him through. He could proceed on the journey he had contracted for. . . .

COMMENTARY

In *Herd v Weardale Steel Coke and Coal Co* [1915] AC 67, the plaintiff miner descended into the pit at the beginning of his shift at 9.30 am, and was due to be returned to the surface at 4 pm. On arriving at the bottom of the pit, he refused to do certain work on the ground that it was unsafe, and at 11 am requested to be taken to the surface. The defendant employer ordered that he not be taken up at that time, and it was not until 1.30 pm that he was returned to the surface. There was evidence that the lift was at the bottom of the shaft at 1.10 pm and could conveniently have been used to bring him up. The employer successfully sued the plaintiff for breach of contract, whilst the plaintiff sued in respect of his underground detention, winning at first instance but losing in the Court of Appeal and in the House of Lords. There, Viscount Haldane LC (at 73) said:

My Lords, under these circumstances I find it wholly impossible to come to the conclusion that the principle to which I have alluded, and on which the doctrine of false imprisonment is based, has any application to the case. *Volenti non fit injuria*. The man chose to go to the bottom of the mine under these conditions—conditions which he accepted. He had no right to call upon the employers to make use of special machinery put there at their cost, and involving cost in its working, to bring him to the surface just when he pleased. . . .

Even though the House of Lords' decision is based on the plaintiff's contractual consent to the deprivation of liberty, could the decision be justified on the basis that there was no positive act by the defendant (essential for liability in trespass) but rather an omission to take him to the surface? (It was treated as authority for this proposition in *Iqbal v Prison Officers Association* [2010] QB 732.) The majority of the Court of Appeal in *Herd v Weardale* thought that if, after the shift had finished, the employer told the employee he would have to wait another hour before being brought to the surface, there would be liability for breach of contract but not false imprisonment (see [1913] 3 KB 771). Vaughan Williams LJ (dissenting) said that 'it is a legitimate conclusion from the admitted facts that the defendants refused permission to the men to use the lift as penalty or punishment for their refusal to obey the order' (at 784), but in the House of Lords Viscount Haldane thought the motive of the defendant irrelevant. Do you agree? (See Williams, 'Two Cases on False Imprisonment', in R. H. C. Holland and G. Schwarzenberger (eds), *Law, Justice and Equity (Essays in Tribute to G.W. Keeton)* (London: Pitman, 1967).)

K. F. Tan, 'A Misconceived Issue in the Tort of False Imprisonment' (1981) 44 MLR 166

It is . . . sufficiently clear that at common law a person cannot restrain the liberty of another to enforce a monetary condition as to exit. Such restraint is false imprisonment unless authorised by law. . . . This is so because the reasonableness of the condition as to exit does not determine whether the restraint of liberty used to enforce the condition is or is not false imprisonment. The basis for this proposition is that no person can by imprisonment force another to abide by or conform to any condition, if that other person does not consent to it, unless such compliance is required by law. If compliance is required by contract that other person can choose to abandon the contract and assume liability for the breach. He cannot then be compelled to perform or comply with the contract, unless specific performance is ordered by the courts. . . .

If there is any issue in such a situation . . . it is whether the defence of consent applies . . . to negate liability for false imprisonment. . . .

[I]n the tort of false imprisonment consent once given to submission of liberty cannot, in certain situations, be withdrawn for a critical period. These situations arise when a person puts himself voluntarily, for whatever purpose, in a position which necessarily involves a temporary surrender of his liberty and some inconvenience in meeting, for a critical duration, the withdrawal of his consent to submission of liberty. The difficulty in the tort is deciding at what stage and for what duration the consent given to submission of liberty is irrevocable. This must be decided according to the particular circumstance of each case. The decision would involve the balancing and adjustment of two competing claims: the claim to personal liberty and the claim of inconvenience entailed in giving in to such claim.

In *Robinson* and *Herd* the withdrawal of the plaintiffs' consent to submission of liberty involved some inconvenience to the defendants. The cases, therefore, necessitated deciding whether the plaintiffs' submission of their liberty could be withdrawn. . . .

[The author proceeds to argue that, to the extent that the two decisions rested on a defence of consent, it was inappropriately applied, since in neither case would meeting the plaintiff's demand for freedom following the revocation of his consent have caused any real inconvenience to the defendant. He concludes:]

Robinson and *Herd* do not stand for the proposition that it is no false imprisonment to restrain the liberty of another to enforce a reasonable condition as to exit from premises. Reasonableness of the condition as to exit is a misconceived issue. The cases merely involved the application of the defence of consent in the tort of false imprisonment.

COMMENTARY

How can *Robinson* and *Herd* be reconciled with the general rule, adverted to earlier, that one cannot imprison to enforce a civil claim without statutory authority? It has been argued that in *Robinson* there was no imprisonment, as the plaintiff could have left the wharf by ferry as he had agreed to do (a point expressly made by Griffith CJ in the High Court of Australia), while *Herd* can perhaps be reconciled with the general rule on the ground that it was a case of omission rather than commission. These explanations are not free from difficulty, however, since in *Robinson* the plaintiff could not leave the wharf by ferry immediately (see further in IV.1), while *Herd* is not a classic omission case since the defendant had in effect imprisoned the plaintiff in its mine in the first place, albeit of course with his consent. In the end, therefore, there is much to be said for Tan's view that the true explanation for these decisions lies in the fact of the plaintiff's initial consent and the consequences of such consent being revoked, though that still leaves open the question of whether the courts arrived at the correct conclusions on the facts of the two cases.

Lunney, 'False Imprisonment, Fare Dodging and Federation—Mr Robertson's Evening Out' (2009) 31 Syd L Rev 537, argues that the High Court and Privy Council in *Robertson/Robinson* were influenced by a commercial imperative, namely that a finding in the plaintiff's favour would have threatened the efficient operation of ferry transport on Sydney Harbour by necessitating costly changes to the system for collecting fares. And according to Tan (at 175–6), *Robinson* and *Herd* were decided at a time when judges were 'perhaps, more sympathetic to the interest and convenience of business enterprise', and this probably played a part in the decisions of the Privy Council and House of Lords. He considers it likely that 'courts today would not, when faced with *Robinson* and *Herd*'s type of situation, give at the expense of personal liberty so much weight to the convenience of enterprise as was given in the two cases'. Do you think that he is right?

4. Necessity

The common law has long recognised necessity as a defence to all forms of trespass (for detailed discussion, see Virgo, 'Justifying Necessity as a Defence in Tort Law', in A. Dyson et al. (eds), *Defences in Tort* (Oxford: Hart, 2015)). This defence is available to a defendant whose otherwise wrongful conduct was reasonably necessary to avert a greater threat to his or her own interests ('private' necessity) or to an important public interest, including the interests of the claimant or a third party ('public' necessity). The threat averted can be to either person or property although in the latter case it may be more difficult to establish that the defendant's conduct was justified. When it comes to trespass to the person, pleas of necessity are most commonly seen in battery cases, but necessity is also a defence to a claim in false imprisonment (see *R v Bournewood Community and Mental Health NHS Trust, ex p. L* [1999] 1 AC 458; *Austin v Commissioner of Police of the Metropolis* [2008] 1 All ER 564 (CA); necessity was not considered on appeal to the House of Lords: [2009] 1 AC 564). A difficult question is whether in cases of necessity the defendant must make compensation for any loss his (justified) conduct causes the claimant. Suppose, for example, that the defendant uses the claimant's boat to save himself from drowning, but that, through no fault of the defendant, the boat is damaged as a result. Must the defendant pay for the damage, even though he has a defence to an action for trespass to goods, and if so, how can this obligation be justified? (See the famous American case of *Vincent v Lake Erie Transportation Co* 124 NW 221 (Minn. 1910), where a duty to compensate was recognised; and see also the observations of Gageler J in the Australian battery case of *Binsaris v Northern Territory* (2020) 380 ALR 1 at [46]–[49]). Stevens, p. 104 argues for a duty to compensate on the basis that the defendant in such cases has an 'incomplete privilege', whereby he is entitled to act in a way that would otherwise be tortious only if he compensates the claimant for any loss caused; cf. Virgo, *op. cit.*, who, while sympathetic to this analysis, denies that a duty to compensate currently exists in English law.

In recent times, the defence of necessity has been used to justify medical treatment given to patients who lack the capacity to consent. *Re F (Mental Patient: Sterilisation)* [1990] 2 AC 1 concerned the legality of the sterilisation of an adult woman who, because of a mental disability, was in this position. A unanimous House of Lords held that in these circumstances treatment that was in the best interests of the patient was lawful. For Lords Goff and Brandon, this was because it was necessary that the treatment be provided. In the extract below, Lord Goff explains why he arrived at this conclusion. That extract is followed by the relevant provisions of the Mental Capacity Act 2005, which has now superseded the common law in this area.

In Re F (Mental Patient: Sterilisation) [1990] 2 AC 1

The facts are noted in the previous paragraph.

Lord Goff

On what principle can medical treatment be justified when given without consent? We are searching for a principle on which, in limited circumstances, recognition may be given to a need, in the interests of the patient, that treatment should be given to him in circumstances where he is (temporarily or permanently) disabled from consenting to it. It is this criterion of a need which points to the principle of necessity as providing justification.

That there exists in the common law a principle of necessity which may justify action which would otherwise be unlawful is not in doubt. But historically the principle has been seen to be restricted to two groups of cases, which have been called cases of public necessity and cases of private necessity. The former occurred when a man interfered with another man's property in the public interest, for example (in the days before we could dial 999 for the fire brigade) the destruction of another man's house to prevent the spread of a catastrophic fire, as indeed occurred in the Great Fire of London in 1666. The latter cases occurred when a man interfered with another's property to save his own person or property from imminent danger, for example when he entered on his neighbour's land without his consent in order to prevent the spread of fire onto his own land.

There is, however, a third group of cases, which is also properly described as founded on the principle of necessity and which is more pertinent to the resolution of the problem in the present case. These cases are concerned with action taken as a matter of necessity to assist another person without his consent . . .

We are concerned here with action taken to preserve the life, health or well-being of another who is unable to consent to it. Such action is sometimes said to be justified as arising from an emergency . . . Doubtless, in the case of a person of sound mind, there will ordinarily have to be an emergency before such action taken without consent can be lawful; for otherwise there would be an opportunity to communicate with the assisted person and to seek his consent. But this is not always so; and indeed the historical origins of the principle of necessity do not point to emergency as such as providing the criterion of lawful intervention without consent . . . In truth, the relevance of an emergency is that it may give rise to a necessity to act in the interests of the assisted person without first obtaining his consent. Emergency is however not the criterion or even a prerequisite; it is simply a frequent origin of the necessity which implies intervention. The principle is one of necessity, not of emergency . . .

We can derive some guidance as to the nature of the principle of necessity from the cases on agency of necessity in mercantile law . . . [F]rom them can be derived the basic requirements, applicable in these cases of necessity, that, to fall within the principle, not only (1) must there be a necessity to act when it is not practicable to communicate with the assisted person, but also (2) the action taken must be such as a reasonable person would in all the circumstances take, acting in the best interests of the assisted person.

On this statement of principle, I wish to observe that officious intervention cannot be justified by the principle of necessity. So intervention cannot be justified when another more appropriate person is available and willing to act; nor can it be justified when it is contrary to the known wishes of the assisted person, to the extent that he is capable of rationally forming such a wish . . . [A]s a general rule, if the above criteria are fulfilled, interference with the assisted person's person or property (as the case may be) will not be unlawful. Take the example of a railway accident, in which injured passengers are trapped in the wreckage. It is this principle which may render lawful the actions of other citizens, railway staff, passengers or outsiders, who rush to give aid and comfort to the victims: the surgeon who amputates the limb of an unconscious passenger to free him from the wreckage; the ambulance man who conveys him to hospital; the doctors and nurses who treat him and care for him while he is still unconscious. Take the example of an elderly person who suffers a stroke which renders him incapable of speech or movement. It is by virtue of this principle that the doctor who treats him, the nurse who cares for him, even the relative or friend or neighbour who comes in to look after him will commit no wrong when he or she touches his body.

The two examples I have given illustrate, in the one case, an emergency and, in the other, a permanent or semi-permanent state of affairs. Another example of the latter kind is that of a mentally disordered person who is disabled from giving consent. I can see no good reason why the principle of necessity should not be applicable in his case as it is in the case of the victim of a stroke. Furthermore, in the case of a mentally disordered person, as in the case of a stroke victim, the permanent state of affairs calls for a wider range of care than may be requisite in an emergency which arises from accidental injury. When the state of affairs is permanent, or semi-permanent, action properly taken to preserve the life, health or well-being of the assisted person may well transcend such measures as surgical operation or substantial medical treatment and may extend to include such humdrum matters as routine medical or dental treatment, even simple care such as dressing and undressing and putting to bed.

The distinction I have drawn between cases of emergency and cases where the state of affairs is (more or less) permanent is relevant in another respect. We are here concerned with medical treatment, and I limit myself to cases of that kind. Where, for example, a surgeon performs an operation without his consent on a patient temporarily rendered unconscious in an accident, he should do no more than is reasonably required, in the best interests of the patient, before he recovers consciousness. I can see no practical difficulty arising from this requirement, which derives from the fact that the patient is expected before long to regain consciousness and can then be consulted about longer term measures. The point has however arisen in a more acute form where a surgeon, in the course of an operation, discovers some other condition which, in his opinion, requires operative treatment for which he has not received the patient's consent. In what circumstances he should operate forthwith, and in what circumstances he should postpone the further treatment until he has received the patient's consent, is a difficult matter which has troubled the Canadian courts (see *Marshall v Curry* [1933] 3 DLR 260 and *Murray v McMurchy* [1949] 2 DLR 442), but which it is not necessary for your Lordships to consider in the present case.

But where the state of affairs is permanent or semi-permanent, as may be so in the case of a mentally disordered person, there is no point in waiting to obtain the patient's consent. The need to care for him is obvious; and the doctor must then act in the best interests of his patient, just as if he had received his patient's consent so to do. Were this not so, much useful treatment and care could, in theory at least, be denied to the unfortunate . . .

Lord Bridge, **Lord Brandon**, **Lord Jauncey** and **Lord Griffiths** delivered separate concurring speeches.

Appeal dismissed.

Mental Capacity Act 2005

1. The principles

(1) The following principles apply for the purposes of this Act.

(2) A person must be assumed to have capacity unless it is established that he lacks capacity.

(3) A person is not to be treated as unable to make a decision unless all practicable steps to help him to do so have been taken without success.

(4) A person is not to be treated as unable to make a decision merely because he makes an unwise decision.

(5) An act done, or decision made, under this Act for or on behalf of a person who lacks capacity must be done, or made, in his best interests.

(6) Before the act is done, or the decision is made, regard must be had to whether the purpose for which it is needed can be as effectively achieved in a way that is less restrictive of the person's rights and freedom of action.

2. People who lack capacity

(1) For the purposes of this Act, a person lacks capacity in relation to a matter if at the material time he is unable to make a decision for himself in relation to the matter because of an impairment of, or a disturbance in the functioning of, the mind or brain.

(2) It does not matter whether the impairment or disturbance is permanent or temporary.

(3) A lack of capacity cannot be established merely by reference to—
  (a) a person's age or appearance, or
  (b) a condition of his, or an aspect of his behaviour, which might lead others to make unjustified assumptions about his capacity.

(4) In proceedings under this Act or any other enactment, any question whether a person lacks capacity within the meaning of this Act must be decided on the balance of probabilities . . .

3. Inability to make decisions

(1) For the purposes of section 2, a person is unable to make a decision for himself if he is unable—
  (a) to understand the information relevant to the decision,
  (b) to retain that information,

(c) to use or weigh that information as part of the process of making the decision, or
(d) to communicate his decision (whether by talking, using sign language or any other means).

(2) A person is not to be regarded as unable to understand the information relevant to a decision if he is able to understand an explanation of it given to him in a way that is appropriate to his circumstances (using simple language, visual aids or any other means).

(3) The fact that a person is able to retain the information relevant to a decision for a short period only does not prevent him from being regarded as able to make the decision.

(4) The information relevant to a decision includes information about the reasonably foreseeable consequences of—
(a) deciding one way or another, or
(b) failing to make the decision . . .

4. Best interests

(1) In determining for the purposes of this Act what is in a person's best interests, the person making the determination must not make it merely on the basis of —
(a) the person's age or appearance, or
(b) a condition of his, or an aspect of his behaviour, which might lead others to make unjustified assumptions about what might be in his best interests.

(2) The person making the determination must consider all the relevant circumstances and, in particular, take the following steps.

(3) He must consider—
(a) whether it is likely that the person will at some time have capacity in relation to the matter in question, and
(b) if it appears likely that he will, when that is likely to be.

(4) He must, so far as reasonably practicable, permit and encourage the person to participate, or to improve his ability to participate, as fully as possible in any act done for him and any decision affecting him.

(5) Where the determination relates to life-sustaining treatment he must not, in considering whether the treatment is in the best interests of the person concerned, be motivated by a desire to bring about his death.

(6) He must consider, so far as is reasonably ascertainable—
(a) the person's past and present wishes and feelings (and, in particular, any relevant written statement made by him when he had capacity),
(b) the beliefs and values that would be likely to influence his decision if he had capacity, and
(c) the other factors that he would be likely to consider if he were able to do so.

(7) He must take into account, if it is practicable and appropriate to consult them, the views of—
(a) anyone named by the person as someone to be consulted on the matter in question or on matters of that kind,
(b) anyone engaged in caring for the person or interested in his welfare,
(c) any donee of a lasting power of attorney granted by the person, and
(d) any deputy appointed for the person by the court,

as to what would be in the person's best interests and, in particular, as to the matters mentioned in subsection (6).

(8) The duties imposed by subsections (1) to (7) also apply in relation to the exercise of any powers which—
   (a) are exercisable under a lasting power of attorney, or
   (b) are exercisable by a person under this Act where he reasonably believes that another person lacks capacity.

(9) In the case of an act done, or a decision made, by a person other than the court, there is sufficient compliance with this section if (having complied with the requirements of subsections (1) to (7)) he reasonably believes that what he does or decides is in the best interests of the person concerned.

(10) 'Life-sustaining treatment' means treatment which in the view of a person providing health care for the person concerned is necessary to sustain life.

(11) 'Relevant circumstances' are those—
   (a) of which the person making the determination is aware, and
   (b) which it would be reasonable to regard as relevant.

5. Acts in connection with care or treatment

(1) If a person ('D') does an act in connection with the care or treatment of another person ('P'), the act is one to which this section applies if—
   (a) before doing the act, D takes reasonable steps to establish whether P lacks capacity in relation to the matter in question, and
   (b) when doing the act, D reasonably believes—
      (i) that P lacks capacity in relation to the matter, and
      (ii) that it will be in P's best interests for the act to be done.

(2) D does not incur any liability in relation to the act that he would not have incurred if P—
   (a) had had capacity to consent in relation to the matter, and
   (b) had consented to D's doing the act.

(3) Nothing in this section excludes a person's civil liability for loss or damage, or his criminal liability, resulting from his negligence in doing the act.

(4) Nothing in this section affects the operation of sections 24 to 26 (advance decisions to refuse treatment).

COMMENTARY

The Mental Capacity Act 2005, which came into full effect in October 2007, now determines whether a person has capacity to consent to medical treatment and, if not, what treatment would be in his or her best interests. Nonetheless, the pre-existing law as set out in *Re F* is relevant in interpreting the legislation. For example, in interpreting the significance to be given to s. 4(3)(a)—that capacity might exist at some time in the future—Lord Goff's view that necessity does not encompass 'officious intervention', so that the treatment of a non-urgent condition of a temporarily incapacitated patient should await that patient's consent, is clearly relevant. Do you agree with his view? If the vast majority of patients would have wished the condition to be treated at the same time as the urgent surgery, does it make any sense to force them into another surgical operation, together with its associated risks, and, in the case of the NHS, at the public's expense, rather than treating the problem at once? If the need for surgical treatment exceeds the capacity to provide it (undoubtedly the position in the NHS), can this rule be justified? Conversely, do such utilitarian concerns have any place when considering rights of personal autonomy?

In the case of those whose lack of capacity is permanent, a decision must be made as to what is in the patient's best interests. In *Re F*, the conclusion that the sterilisation operation was in fact in the patient's best interests was reached (after consultation) by the medical practitioners involved in her care and treatment. Not everyone agrees that this group is the best one to make such decisions. Commenting on *Re F*, Shaw (1990) 53 MLR 91 at 103 writes:

The supposed absence of maternal feelings in mentally handicapped women, their assumed inability to care for any potential offspring and the pain that they might suffer if they were separated from a child are common themes in recent English cases although in the absence of definite criteria for decision making it is hard to tell what weight is placed upon them. Is it acceptable that judges should make public policy choices about the relevance of such factors to the presumed best interests of mentally handicapped people in the closed forum of the courtroom? More, is it appropriate that the basis for such choices, which essentially determine the content of the claim which mentally handicapped people may make upon the resources of society, should be made by reference for the most part only to the clinical judgement of doctors and in isolation from wide questions of resource allocation?

The common law defence of necessity may extend beyond situations where the claimant is unable to consent to an activity the aim of which is to benefit the claimant. In the tragic case of *Re A (Conjoined Twins)* [2001] Fam 147, the Court of Appeal held that it would be lawful to operate on conjoined twins for the purpose of saving one of them, even if the operation would cause the death of the other. The decision of Brooke LJ was partly based on the defence of necessity available to the surgeons who performed the surgery. Although the case dealt with the question of criminal liability, there seems little doubt that necessity could also have been invoked as a defence to any battery claim made by the estate of the dead child. Under the 2005 Act, any defence would have to fall within s. 5 which requires the treatment to be in the best interests of the patient. Whether such treatment could fall within s. 5 is an open question (cf. *Airedale NHS Trust v Bland* [1993] AC 789, holding that it may be lawful to turn off the life support system of a patient in a persistent vegetative state).

The 2005 Act also requires that the person's past and present wishes be considered in determining what is in their best interests: s. 4(6)(a). In *Re F*, Lord Goff stated that the principle of necessity would not be operative where the treatment was contrary to the known wishes of the claimant but what if following those wishes would result in the claimant's suffering injury or even death? The following section considers this issue.

Consent, Capacity, Necessity and Best Interests

Early in the twentieth century it was held that prison staff had a 'duty' to prevent a prisoner from conducting a hunger strike where it caused a risk to the prisoner's health (*Leigh v Gladstone* (1909) 26 TLR 139). However, a greater recognition of personal autonomy in modern times has led to a different conclusion. In *Secretary of State for the Home Department v Robb* [1995] Fam 127, a declaration was obtained by prison officials that they might lawfully abstain from providing hydration and nutrition to a prisoner on a hunger strike as long as he retained the capacity to refuse to receive nutrition. Thorpe J accepted that an adult of sound mind had a right of self-determination which entitled them to refuse nutrition and hydration. However, the House of Lords has ruled that the police may be liable in negligence for failing to take reasonable steps to prevent a prisoner of sound mind committing suicide (*Reeves v Commissioner of Police of the Metropolis* [2000] 1 AC 360). The result of these cases seems to be that the police have a duty to take steps to prevent the suicide but that these steps cannot amount to a battery as this would infringe the right of self-determination. Is this a defensible position for the law to take?

Autonomy is a value worth protecting only if decisions relating to it are made with full capacity. Section 3(1) of the 2005 Act sets out the test for determining whether a person has capacity but it has been held that there is 'no relevant distinction between the test in s. 3(1) of the Act and the pre-existing common law' (*Re MM* (An Adult) [2007] EWHC 2003 (Fam) at [74] per Munby J) with the result that pre-Act cases remain useful guides to determining how s. 3(1) will be applied. The leading pre-Act case is *Re MB* [1997] 2 FLR 426, where a health authority obtained a declaration that it would be lawful to perform a caesarean section on a pregnant woman who had refused to consent to the administration of anaesthetic by needle or mask. According to Butler-Sloss LJ, the woman's fear of needles was so overpowering that she was not capable of making a decision at all at the relevant time. Was it relevant that the failure to undergo the procedure might have endangered the life of the child? After considering the relevant authorities, Butler-Sloss LJ concluded that it was not, holding that a competent woman who had the capacity to decide may choose not to have medical intervention, even though the consequence may be the death or serious disability of the child she bears or her own death. As the foetus did not have separate legal personality until it was born alive, it did not have any separate interests (from its mother) capable of being taken into account when a court was asked to grant a declaration in respect of a caesarean section operation. Whether a pregnant woman should be subject to controls for the benefit of her unborn child was a matter for Parliament. This reasoning, which was obiter, was confirmed in *St George's Healthcare NHS Trust v S* [1999] Fam 26, where the Court of Appeal held that a pregnant woman of sound mind had the right to refuse medical treatment even where this would result in the death of the foetus, commenting (at 50): 'In our judgment while pregnancy increases the personal responsibilities of a woman it does not diminish her entitlement to decide whether or not to undergo medical treatment.' It was also held in this case that the Mental Health Act 1983 could not be used to achieve the detention and subsequent treatment of an individual because her thinking process is 'unusual, even apparently bizarre and irrational, and contrary to the views of the overwhelming majority of the community at large' (at 51).

This latter point was taken up by Butler-Sloss P in *Re B (Adult: Refusal of Treatment)* [2002] 2 All ER 449. In this case the applicant, a tetraplegic patient, sought a declaration that the failure of hospital staff to turn off the ventilator to which she was attached was unlawful. The consequence of turning off the ventilator was almost certain death. In finding that the applicant had capacity, and granting the declaration, Butler-Sloss P gave the following guidance in respect of a patient's competence to make such a decision:

If there are difficulties in deciding whether the patient has sufficient mental capacity, particularly if the refusal may have grave consequences for the patient, it is most important that those considering the issue should not confuse the question of mental capacity with the nature of the decision made by the patient, however grave the consequences. The view of the patient may reflect a difference in values rather than an absence of competence and the assessment of capacity should be approached with this firmly in mind. The doctors must not allow their emotional reaction to or strong disagreement with the decision of the patient to cloud their judgment in answering the primary question whether the patient has the mental capacity to make the decision.

Butler-Sloss P thought that this case illustrated the serious danger of 'benevolent paternalism which does not embrace recognition of the personal autonomy of the severely disabled patient'. Do you agree? On the role of autonomy and the potentially different ways it is recognised in the distinct contexts of consent and capacity see Coggon and Miola, 'Autonomy, Liberty and Medical Decision-Making' [2011] CLJ 523.

These cases dealt with capacity to refuse consent to medical treatment, but the House of Lords' decision in *Gillick v West Norfolk Health Authority* [1986] AC 112 (see earlier) concerned the converse question of the capacity to give consent to such treatment. The two situations are not strictly comparable, however, as the ability of children to refuse consent to treatment is limited. In *Re R* [1992] Fam 11, a 15-year-old girl in local authority care suffered bouts of suicidal and violent behaviour, but during periods of lucidity she refused antipsychotic drugs. In the exercise of its wardship jurisdiction, the Court of Appeal declared that the drugs could nonetheless be administered, Lord Donaldson MR holding that a *Gillick* competent child could give an effective consent to medical treatment, but that, if treatment was refused, consent could be given by anyone exercising parental rights. A similar conclusion was reached in *Re W* [1993] Fam 64, where the appellant had the power to consent to treatment under the Family Law Reform Act 1969, but this was held not to give her a corresponding right to refuse treatment where the court, in the exercise of its inherent jurisdiction, considered it to be in her best interests. Commenting on these cases, Bainham argues that they show little respect for the autonomy of the child in these situations and that 'unbridled paternalism reigns' ([2006] CLJ 285, 287). Do these decisions leave any scope for *Gillick* competent children to refuse treatment if persons exercising parental authority consent on their behalf? (See *Re L (Medical Treatment: Gillick Competency)* [1998] 2 FLR 810.) For further discussion of consent in the context of medical procedures see M. Brazier and E. Cave, *Medicine, Patients and the Law*, 6th edn (Manchester: Manchester UP, 2016), chs 5–6, and A. Maclean, *Autonomy, Informed Consent and Medical Law* (Cambridge: CUP, 2009), pp. 154–56.

Although the Mental Capacity Act 2005 in many ways codifies the common law position, s. 5, which provides a defence to battery in respect of acts done in connection with the care or treatment of an incapacitated person, differs from the common law defence of necessity set out in *Re F*. The s. 5 defence applies if the defendant (1) has taken reasonable steps to ascertain if the person has capacity in relation to the matter in question; (2) reasonably believes that the person does not have capacity; and (3) reasonably believes that it will be in the person's best interests for the act to be done. By contrast, at common law the defendant's reasonable belief to the contrary afforded no defence if the person did not in fact lack capacity or if the acts were not in fact in their best interests. However, even the more generous statutory defence was not available in *H v Commissioner of Police of the Metropolis* [2013] 1 WLR 3021, where the Court of Appeal upheld the trial judge's conclusion that s. 5 could not be relied upon by police officers in respect of their treatment of an autistic child, because their failure to consult the child's carers before acting meant that they had not *reasonably* believed that their intervention was in his best interests. This was despite the fact that the situation facing the officers was described as difficult and unusual and their belief that the child might injure himself if no action was taken. *H* may alleviate any fear that the s. 5 defence will protect the kind of officious intervention which Lord Goff thought was not covered by the defence of necessity at common law: as noted earlier, in determining what is in the person's best interests the defendant must consider, amongst other things, the likelihood that the person may have capacity in the future (s. 4(3)) and a failure to do so is likely to lead to the conclusion that any belief that the treatment is in the patient's best interests is not reasonable.

For further details about the Act see P. Bartlett, *Blackstone's Guide to the Mental Capacity Act 2005*, 2nd edn (Oxford: OUP, 2008).

5. Self-Defence and Related Defences

Ashley v Chief Constable of Sussex Police [2008] 1 AC 962

The deceased was shot dead by a police officer during an early morning raid on his flat pursuant to a drug trafficking investigation. Although the deceased was naked and unarmed at the time, the officer who shot him maintained that the shooting was an act of self-defence. The officer was tried and acquitted of murder, and subsequently the personal representatives of the deceased sought damages from the defendant chief constable for assault and battery, negligence and false imprisonment. One issue for the House of Lords was whether a mistaken but reasonable belief of the officer that he was under attack could found a defence of self-defence to battery. The other issue (not discussed here) was whether the claim in battery should be allowed to proceed even though the defendant had admitted liability in negligence and false imprisonment and agreed to pay all damages flowing from the incident. By a bare majority, their Lordships agreed that the battery claim should be allowed to proceed.

Lord Scott of Foscote

Issue 1: the self-defence criteria

16 In para 37 of his judgment [in the Court of Appeal] Sir Anthony Clarke MR identified three possible approaches to the criteria requisite for a successful plea of self-defence, namely, (1) the necessity to take action in response to an attack, or imminent attack, must be judged on the assumption that the facts were as the defendant honestly believed them to be, whether or not he was mistaken and, if he made a mistake of fact, whether or not it was reasonable for him to have done so (solution 1); (2) the necessity to take action in response to an attack or imminent attack must be judged on the facts as the defendant honestly believed them to be, whether or not he was mistaken, but, if he made a mistake of fact, he can rely on that fact only if the mistake was a reasonable one for him to have made (solution 2); (3) in order to establish the relevant necessity the defendant must establish that there was in fact an imminent and real risk of attack (solution 3). It was common ground that, in addition, based on whatever belief the defendant is entitled to rely on, the defendant must, in a civil action, satisfy the court that it was reasonable for him to have taken the action he did. Of the three solutions the Court of Appeal held that solution 2 was the correct one. On this appeal the chief constable has contended, as he did below, that solution 1 is the correct one. The claimants have not cross-appealed in order to contend that solution 3 should be preferred.

17 It was held in *R v Williams (Gladstone)* [1987] 3 All ER 411 and is now accepted that, for the purposes of the criminal law, solution 1 is the correct one . . . It is urged upon your Lordships that the criteria for self-defence in civil law should be the same as in criminal law. In my opinion, however, this plea for consistency between the criminal law and the civil law lacks cogency for the ends to be served by the two systems are very different. One of the main functions of the criminal law is to identify, and provide punitive sanctions for, behaviour that is

categorised as criminal because it is damaging to the good order of society. It is fundamental to criminal law and procedure that everyone charged with criminal behaviour should be presumed innocent until proven guilty and that, as a general rule, no one should be punished for a crime that he or she did not intend to commit or be punished for the consequences of an honest mistake . . .

18 The function of the civil law of tort is different. Its main function is to identify and protect the rights that every person is entitled to assert against, and require to be respected by, others. The rights of one person, however, often run counter to the rights of others and the civil law, in particular the law of tort, must then strike a balance between the conflicting rights. Thus, for instance, the right of freedom of expression may conflict with the right of others not to be defamed. The rules and principles of the tort of defamation must strike the balance. The right not to be physically harmed by the actions of another may conflict with the rights of other people to engage in activities involving the possibility of accidentally causing harm. The balance between these conflicting rights must be struck by the rules and principles of the tort of negligence. As to assault and battery and self-defence, every person has the right in principle not to be subjected to physical harm by the intentional actions of another person. But every person has the right also to protect himself by using reasonable force to repel an attack or to prevent an imminent attack. The rules and principles defining what does constitute legitimate self-defence must strike the balance between these conflicting rights. The balance struck is serving a quite different purpose from that served by the criminal law when answering the question whether the infliction of physical injury on another in consequence of a mistaken belief by the assailant of a need for self-defence should be categorised as a criminal offence and attract penal sanctions. To hold, in a civil case, that a mistaken and unreasonably held belief by A that he was about to be attacked by B justified a pre-emptive attack in believed self-defence by A on B would, in my opinion, constitute a wholly unacceptable striking of the balance. It is one thing to say that if A's mistaken belief was honestly held he should not be punished by the criminal law. It would be quite another to say that A's unreasonably held mistaken belief would be sufficient to justify the law in setting aside B's right not to be subjected to physical violence by A. I would have no hesitation whatever in holding that for civil law purposes an excuse of self-defence based on non existent facts that are honestly but unreasonably believed to exist must fail. This is the conclusion to which the Court of Appeal came in preferring solution 2 . . .

20 I would, therefore, dismiss the chief constable's appeal against the Court of Appeal's adoption of solution 2. It has not been contended on behalf of the Ashleys that solution 3 might be the correct solution in a civil case but, speaking for myself, I think that that solution would have a good deal to be said for it, as appears to have been the view also of Sir Anthony Clarke MR [2007] 1 WLR 398, paras 63–78. I would start with the principle that every person is prima facie entitled not to be the object of physical harm intentionally inflicted by another. If consent to the infliction of the injury has not been given and cannot be implied why should it be a defence in a tort claim for the assailant to say that although his belief that his victim had consented was a mistaken one nonetheless it had been a reasonable one for him to make? Why, for civil law purposes, should not a person who proposes to make physical advances of a sexual nature to another be expected first to make sure that the advances will be welcome? Similarly, where there is in fact no risk or imminent danger from which the assailant needs to protect himself, I find it difficult to see on what basis the right of the victim not to be subjected to physical violence can be set at naught on the ground of mistake made by the assailant, whether or not reasonably made . . . However, and in my view, unfortunately, solution 3 has not been contended for on this appeal, its pros and cons have not been the subject of argument, and your Lordships cannot, therefore, conclude that it is the correct solution. But I would, for my part, regard the point as remaining open.

Lord Neuberger of Abbotsbury

89 . . . Thirdly, there is the argument that the inflictor of an alleged battery has to go further than the Court of Appeal held, and show that he was in fact under imminent threat of attack. The point appears to me to be difficult, and the authorities are not entirely clear on the point: see Sir Anthony Clarke MR's analysis, in paras 63 to 78. Like him, I think that the balance of authority favours the conclusion that a defendant does not have to go that far, although the point is plainly open for reconsideration in your Lordships' House.

90 There are powerful arguments both ways. It is easy to conceive of circumstances where it would be inevitable that either the inflictor or the victim would have a thoroughly understandable sense of great grievance if, as the case may be, there was or was not a valid claim for damages for the infliction of severe violence in circumstances where the inflictor reasonably, but wrongly, believed he was under imminent threat of attack. As the Ashleys have not challenged the Court of Appeal's conclusion on this issue, it appears to me that in this case it should be left open in your Lordships' House.

91 Fourthly, if a reasonable but mistaken belief will do, other questions may need to be considered. One such question is whether, when seeking to justify the reasonableness of his belief, a defendant can rely on factors which were not the claimant's responsibility. There is obviously a strong argument for saying that a defendant can rely on such factors. Otherwise, one would be getting close to holding that the belief must be correct. Further, it could lead to difficulties if one had to decide whether the claimant was responsible for the defendant's belief, especially if only some of the factors which influenced the defendant could be taken into account. However, it can also be said to be unfair on the claimant if matters for which he had no responsibility can serve to justify the reasonableness of the defendant's mistaken belief. The answer may ultimately depend on whether one judges the issue of reasonableness from the claimant's point of view or from that of the defendant . . .

Lords Rodger, **Bingham** and **Carswell** delivered speeches agreeing with Lord Scott on this issue.

COMMENTARY

Their Lordships were agreed in *Ashley* that to rely on self-defence the defendant would have to show at the very least that they had an honest and reasonable belief in the existence of an imminent threat to them. In the Court of Appeal in *Ashley*, Sir Anthony Clarke MR held that it was not necessary for the defendant also to establish that there was *in fact* such a threat ([2007] 1 WLR 398 at [61]), with the result that the defence could be founded on a mistaken yet reasonable belief, a holding that has since been treated as binding on a first instance judge (see *Goodenough v Chief Constable of Thames Valley Police* [2020] EWHC 1428 (QB)). However, in the House of Lords, Lords Scott, Rodger and Neuberger left this point open, and Lord Scott considered (at [19]) that the position in the defence of consent weighed in favour of the view that an actual threat was required, for where the claimant is not consenting, it is no defence to a claim in battery that the defendant reasonably thought that they were (although of course, since consent is objectively determined, it will be sufficient that it reasonably appeared from the claimant's conduct that they were consenting: *Winfield & Jolowicz*, para. 16–009). Suppose that, because of an administrative error, a surgeon operates on a patient in the mistaken but reasonable belief that the patient has consented to the operation. Despite not being at fault in any way, the surgeon commits battery. So why should the position be different when a police officer shoots a suspect in the mistaken but reasonable belief that the officer is under attack?

A potentially significant consideration in this context is where the responsibility lies for the forming of the reasonable but mistaken belief. If it lies with the claimant, then that militates in favour of allowing the defendant the protection of the defence, particularly because it is now clear that contributory negligence—the solution to this scenario suggested by Lord Scott (at [20])—is not a defence to an action in trespass to the person (*Pritchard v Co-operative Group Ltd* [2012] QB 320; see further in Ch. 6.III.2). But what if the mistake is induced by the conduct of third parties? If, for example, a police briefing was responsible for creating the reasonable belief in an officer that they were under attack, would this suffice to found the defence? Although Lord Neuberger pointed out the problem (at [90]) he provided no solutions, and both Lord Rodger in the House of Lords and Arden LJ in the Court of Appeal expressly left open the question of whether the defence could be based on a mistake which was not induced by the claimant. (Again, as the surgery example from the previous paragraph shows, the defence of consent cannot be founded on such a mistake.) For further comment on *Ashley*, see Palmer and Steele (2008) 71 MLR 801.

Apart from the presence of a reasonable belief that the victim was threatening the claimant, the claimant must also show that the response to the threat was proportionate. In *Lane v Holloway* [1968] 1 QB 379, the 64-year-old plaintiff struck the 23-year-old defendant on the shoulder, and the defendant responded by hitting the plaintiff in the eye with such severity that he was in hospital for a month. The Court of Appeal held that the blow was out of all proportion to the original act of the plaintiff so that no defence of consent or self-defence was applicable (see also *Flint v Tittensor* [2015] 1 WLR 4370, where Edis J held that, even if the defendant had been acting in self-defence when he drove towards a man who had deliberately damaged his car, his response would have been disproportionate).

Analogous principles govern the defence of property and of other persons. In the context of the defence of property, it is generally the case that a warning should be given before any force is applied, but if actual force has already been applied to one's property such a warning may be unnecessary 'for it is but returning violence with violence' (*Green v Goddard* (1702) 2 Salk 641).

Aspects of self-defence and defence of property form part of the statutory defence set out in the Criminal Justice Act 2003, s. 329. The section may provide a defence to an action for trespass to the person where the claimant was convicted of an imprisonable offence committed on the same occasion as the allegedly tortious conduct of the defendant. In these circumstances there is a defence if the defendant did the act said to constitute the trespass only because they believed (1) that the claimant was about to commit an offence, was in the course of committing an offence, or had committed an offence immediately beforehand; and (2) that the act was necessary to defend themselves or another person, protect or recover property, prevent the commission or continuation of an offence, or apprehend, or secure the conviction of, the claimant after they had committed an offence, or necessary to assist in achieving any of these things. The defence is not available where, in all the circumstances, the defendant's conduct was grossly disproportionate. In such a case the claimant must seek the permission of the court to bring proceedings and permission is to be given only if there is evidence that the requirements of the defence are not met. In many ways the provision merely codifies the common law relating to self-defence and illegality but there are some differences, most notably that for the purposes of this defence the defendant's belief need only be honest rather than reasonable (s. 329(8)(b)). It is important to note that s. 329 applies to the police as well as to private individuals. Should the police be given this special statutory protection against actions in trespass to the person just because the claimant is ultimately convicted of an imprisonable offence? For criticism of the section as it applies to police, see *Adorian v Metropolitan Police Commissioner* [2009] 1 WLR 1859 at [7], and Spencer [2010] CLJ 19.

One way in which s. 329 might be avoided is for the claimant to bring the civil claim before any criminal prosecution is launched. Whether the courts would allow this to occur is open to doubt: the court hearing the civil claim has power to stay (suspend) those proceedings until after the criminal prosecution is complete. Although such a course is not mandated by the legislation, s. 329 would be rendered otiose if the civil claim could simply precede the criminal prosecution (albeit the practical delays in getting the civil case to court may make this scenario more hypothetical than real). On the power to stay civil proceedings associated with criminal conduct, and on the relationship between tort and criminal actions more generally, see Dyson, 'The Timing of Tortious and Criminal Actions for the Same Wrong' [2012] CLJ 86.

Note also the power to use reasonable force in the prevention of crime under Criminal Law Act 1967, s. 3.

3 NEGLIGENCE—INTRODUCTION

I. Formulation of a General Duty of Care

1. Historical Introduction

Because of the piecemeal development of civil liability under the forms of action, little thought was given by early common lawyers to the existence of any general principle underlying the various examples of liability. As late as the latter half of the eighteenth century, Blackstone in his *Commentaries on the Laws of England* described trespass on the case as a 'universal remedy given for all personal wrongs and injuries without force' (vol. III, ch. 8, para. 4); he thought in terms only of the form of action, not of the substantive grounds for allowing the action. Similarly, the authors of Digests and Abridgements (early types of practitioner texts) were concerned only to provide examples of factual situations where liability had been held to exist, and to state the correct form of action in which to plead those facts. As *Baker* points out (p. 413), even though *Comyns Digest* (published in 1762) might have had a heading 'Action upon the Case for Negligence', many examples of what would today be considered negligence were included under 'Actions upon the Case for Misfeasance' and no attempt was made to rationalise the specific examples under a general theory of liability. For parties in a pre-existing relationship, liability came to be associated with the assumption of an obligation by promise (*assumpsit*), and this provided the unifying basis for the law of contract. But it was not until a good deal later that the idea of obligation or duty was to play a similar role in the development of a general theory of tortious liability (applicable to parties who had no prior relationship). 'Duty' was first put forward as a unifying concept in this regard in Buller's *Nisi Prius* ('An Institute of the Law Relative to Trials at Nisi Prius'), published in 1768, in which it was suggested that:

> Every man ought to take reasonable care that he does not injure his neighbour; therefore, wherever a man receives hurt through the default of another, though the same were not wilful, yet if it be occasioned by negligence or folly the law gives him an action to recover for the injury so sustained . . . However, it is proper in such cases to prove that the injury was such as would probably follow from the act done.

The notion that liability in negligence was based on the existence of a duty owed by the defendant to the claimant was slow to take hold (see Winfield, 'Duty in Tortious Negligence' (1934) Col LR 41; M. J. Prichard, '*Scott v Shepherd* and the Emergence of the Tort of Negligence' (London: Selden Society, 1976); Plunkett, 'The Historical Foundations of the Duty of Care' (2015) 41 Monash UL Rev 716), but by the early nineteenth century it was said that damages could be sought for 'the negligent or wilful conduct of the party sued, in doing or omitting something contrary to the duty which the law casts on him in the particular case' (*Ansell v Waterhouse* (1817) 6 M & S 385). This still left the question when such a duty would be imposed, and the earliest 'discussions' of the tort of negligence usually consisted of nothing more than lists of factual situations where a duty had been held to exist.

Particular problems arose where the defendant acted pursuant to a contractual obligation. By the beginning of the nineteenth century a contracting party might be able to sue the other party for breach of a tortious duty imposed by law. In addition, it was clear that a stranger to the contract might, in certain circumstances, sue for injury caused by negligent behaviour where the activity was undertaken pursuant to a contract; pedestrians injured by the negligence of a coachman were an obvious example. But the recognition of a duty where the parties were bound by a chain of contracts (e.g. between manufacturer, supplier and consumer of goods) was a much slower process. The initial tendency was to limit the plaintiff to a claim under their contract, and to rule out any attempt to rely on an obligation arising under a contract to which he was not party. Each party was expected to protect their own interests by securing appropriate warranties in the contracts to which they were party. Many of the early authorities dealt with the liability of the manufacturer or supplier of defective goods or equipment, and raised the question whether a plaintiff who was not a party to the initial contract of sale or supply should be able to claim the benefit of a warranty given thereunder by the manufacturer or supplier.

Winterbottom v Wright (1842) 10 M & W 109

The plaintiff entered into a contract with the Postmaster General to drive a mail coach. The coach had been supplied by the defendant to the Postmaster General under a contract which provided that during the term of the contract the coach was to be kept in a fit, proper, safe and secure state. The plaintiff alleged that the defendant 'negligently conducted himself, and so utterly disregarded his aforesaid contract and so wholly neglected and failed to perform his duty in this behalf' that the plaintiff was injured when the coach collapsed throwing him from his seat.

Lord Abinger CB

I am clearly of opinion that the defendant is entitled to our judgment . . . Here the action is brought simply because the defendant was a contractor with a third person; and it is contended that thereupon he became liable to every body who might use the carriage . . . There is no privity of contract between these parties; and if the plaintiff can sue, every passenger, or even any person passing along the road, who was injured by the upsetting of the coach, may bring a similar action. Unless we confine the operation of such contracts as this to the parties who entered into them, the most absurd and outrageous consequences, to which I can see no limit, would ensue . . .

There is . . . a class of cases in which the law permits a contract to be turned into a tort; but unless there has been some public duty undertaken, or a public nuisance committed, they are all cases in which an action might have been maintained on the contract . . .

Alderson B

If we were to hold that the plaintiff could sue in such a case, there is no point at which such actions would stop. The only safe rule is to confine the right to recover to those who enter into the contract; if we go one step beyond that, there is no reason why we should not go fifty . . .

> **Rolfe B**
>
> The duty, therefore, is shewn to have arisen solely from the contract; and the fallacy consists in the use of the word 'duty'. If a duty to the Postmaster General be meant, that is true; but if a duty to the plaintiff be intended (and in that sense the word is evidently used), there was none . . .
>
> Judgment for the defendant.

COMMENTARY

In *Langridge v Levy* (1837) 2 M & W 519, 150 ER 863, the plaintiff's father bought a gun for his own and his son's use. The defendant falsely told him it was made by a reputable gun-maker; it was not and when the plaintiff fired it, it exploded, causing him injury. The Court of Exchequer allowed the plaintiff's claim because of the fraudulent misrepresentation but refused to found liability on the basis of a breach of a contractual duty owed to a third party. The plaintiff in *Winterbottom v Wright* attempted to use this case as an authority in support of his claim, but, as the court noted, *Langridge* was decided on a narrower ground.

The judges in *Winterbottom v Wright* were clearly influenced by a form of what would today be called the 'floodgates' argument, namely a concern that imposing liability in the instant case would lead to countless more extensions in the scope of the duty. Allied to this was a concern over the proper limits of liability in contractual settings. Once a contractual obligation was held to give rise to a duty in tort which extended beyond the parties to the contract, what other limitation was there? (See Palmer, 'Why Privity Entered Tort—An Historical Re-examination of *Winterbottom v Wright*' (1983) 27 Am JLH 85.)

With hindsight, it seems odd that the common law would allow a claim by the pedestrian injured by the negligent driving of a coachman, but not a claim by the coachman injured by the negligent maintenance of the coach (see Winfield, 'Duty in Tortious Negligence' (1934) Col LR 41). Given this anomaly, it is not surprising that the alignment of tortious product liability with contractual liability was periodically challenged. An exception was developed to the general rule of no liability in tort, resulting in the recognition of a potential liability in respect of articles 'dangerous in themselves' (*Longmeid v Holliday* (1851) 6 Ex 761, 155 ER 752). And a more direct challenge was mounted in *George v Skivington* (1869) LR 5 Ex 1. In that case, the first plaintiff was injured after using hair wash which had been sold to her husband, but for her use, by the defendant. (The husband was the second plaintiff in the action.) There was no fraud; nor did the case fit into the exception for articles 'dangerous in themselves'. Nonetheless, the Court of Exchequer went out of its way to hold that the wife had a good cause of action (see Ibbetson, '*George v Skivington* (1869)' in *Mitchell & Mitchell*). Kelly CB expressly noted that the action was not upon a contract, and hence no question of warranty arose; rather, an action on the case was brought for 'unskilfulness and negligence in the manufacture of it whereby the person who used it was injured'.

The attempt to clarify the law of liability for defective products brought with it the common law's first attempt at a normative explanation of the duty of care (see the following extract).

Heaven v Pender (1883) 11 QBD 503

The plaintiff was painting a ship when one of the ropes holding up the staging on which he was working broke; he fell and was injured. The staging had been erected by the defendant dock owner under contract with the plaintiff's employer. It was found that the rope which snapped was unfit for use at the time it was supplied by the defendant. The plaintiff succeeded in recovering damages in the county court, but the Queen's Bench Division on appeal ordered that judgment be entered for the defendant. The plaintiff appealed to the Court of Appeal.

Brett MR

Actionable negligence consists in the neglect of the use of ordinary care or skill towards a person to whom the defendant owes the duty of observing ordinary care and skill, by which neglect the plaintiff, without contributory negligence on his part, has suffered injury to his person or property. . . .

If a person contracts with another to use ordinary care and skill towards him or his property the obligation need not be considered in the light of a duty; it is an obligation of contract. It is undoubted, however, that there may be the obligation of such a duty from one person to another although there is no contract between them with regard to such duty. . . .

The questions which we have to solve in this case are—what is the proper definition of the relation between two persons other than the relation established by contract, or fraud, which imposes on the one of them a duty towards the other to observe, with regard to the person or property of such other, such ordinary care or skill as may be necessary to prevent injury to his person or property. . . .

The proposition which [the cases] suggest, and which is, therefore, to be deduced from them, is that whenever one person is by circumstances placed in such a position with regard to another that everyone of ordinary sense who did think would at once recognise that if he did not use ordinary care and skill in his own conduct with regard to those circumstances he would cause danger of injury to person or property of the other, a duty arises to use ordinary care and skill to avoid such danger. . . .

Bowen and **Cotton LJJ** delivered separate judgments in favour of allowing the appeal.

Appeal allowed.

COMMENTARY

The attempt of Brett MR to enunciate a general principle defining when a duty of care exists was rejected by the other two judges in the case, who confined their reasoning to the particular facts. And shortly afterwards, the House of Lords affirmed that there was no general principle of liability for negligent misstatements causing monetary loss (*Derry v Peek* (1889) 14 App Cas 337). Brett MR (as Lord Esher) subsequently attempted to resuscitate his general principle by suggesting that it would only arise where there was physical proximity between the parties. In *Le Lievre v Gould* [1893] 1 QB 491, an action by a mortgagee against a surveyor who had prepared certificates for the mortgagor, he stated:

> A man is entitled to be as negligent as he pleases towards the whole world if he owes no duty to them. The case of *Heaven v Pender* has no bearing upon the present question. That case established that, under certain circumstances, one man may owe a duty to another, even though there is no contract between them. If one man is near to another, or is near to the property of another, a

duty lies upon him not to do that which may cause a personal injury to that other, or may injure his property. For instance, if a man is driving along a road, it is his duty not to do that which may injure another person whom he meets on the road, or to his horse or his carriage. In the same way it is the duty of a man not to do that which will injure the house of another which he is near. . . . That is the effect of the decision in *Heaven v Pender*, but it has no application to the present case. . . .

Notwithstanding Lord Esher's efforts, the general principle enunciated in *Heaven v Pender* did not result in more extensive liability in the product liability context, as can be seen from Lord Sumner's statement in *Blacker v Lake & Elliot Ltd* (1912) 107 LT 533 at 536 that 'the breach of the defendant's contract with A to use care and skill in and about the manufacture or repair of an article does not of itself give any cause of action to B when he is injured by reason of the article proving to be defective'. The courts continued to think in terms of a general rule of no liability, to which only limited exceptions were made (in respect of articles dangerous in themselves and also, eventually, articles which were not normally dangerous but had become so because of a defect known to the manufacturer). However, the case for a unified approach to liability for negligence continued to be made by academics, in particular the author of an influential textbook on tort, Frederick Pollock (see Lobban, 'Common Law Reasoning and the Foundation of Modern Private Law' (2007) 32 *Australian Journal of Legal Philosophy* 39, 62–3), though it was not until 1932 that the limited notion of duty explained in *Le Lievre v Gould* was expanded into the notions of closeness, proximity and neighbourhood—used in a metaphorical rather than literal sense—that underlie the modern concept of the duty of care.

2. Donoghue v Stevenson

> **Lord Atkin of Aberdovey, 'Law as an Educational Subject'** [1932] JSPTL 27
>
> It is quite true that law and morality do not cover identical fields. No doubt morality extends beyond the more limited range in which you can lay down the definite prohibitions of law; but, apart from that, the British law has always necessarily ingrained in it moral teaching in this sense: that it lays down standards of honesty and plain dealing between man and man. . . .
>
> [A man] is not to injure his neighbour by acts of negligence; and that certainly covers a very large field of the law. I doubt whether the whole law of tort could not be comprised in the golden maxim to do unto your neighbour as you would that he should do unto you. It imposes standards . . . and it is of the utmost importance to the community that those standards should be maintained; and it teaches a man to respect his neighbour's right of property and person. . . .

> **Donoghue v Stevenson** [1932] AC 562
>
> The pursuer alleged that she and a friend had entered a café in Paisley, near Glasgow, and her friend had purchased a bottle of ginger beer manufactured by the defender for her consumption. The opaque glass of the bottle made it impossible to see its contents. The pursuer drank some of the ginger beer, and as she was pouring more into her glass the partly decomposed

remains of a snail came out of the bottle. She alleged that she suffered shock and severe gastro-enteritis as a result. The defender's argument that the pursuer's claim against him for damages disclosed no cause of action was accepted by the Second Division of the Court of Session. The pursuer appealed to the House of Lords.

Lord Atkin

My Lords, the sole question for determination in this case is legal: Do the averments made by the pursuer in her pleading, if true, disclose a cause of action? I need not restate the particular facts. The question is whether the manufacturer of an article of drink sold by him to a distributor, in circumstances which prevent the distributor or the ultimate purchaser from discovering by inspection any defect, is under any legal duty to the ultimate purchaser or consumer to take reasonable care that the article is free from defects likely to cause injury to health. I do not think a more important problem has occupied your Lordships in your judicial capacity: important both because of its bearing on public health and because of the practical test which it applies to the system under which it arises. The case has to be determined in accordance with Scots law; but it has been a matter of agreement between the experienced counsel who argued this case, and it appears to be the basis of the judgments of the learned judges of the Court of Session, that for the purposes of determining this problem the laws of Scotland and of England are the same. I speak with little authority on this point, but my own research, such as it is, satisfies me that the principles of the law of Scotland on such a question as the present are identical with those of English law; and I discuss the issue on that footing. The law of both countries appears to be that in order to support an action for negligence the complainant has to show that he has been injured by the breach of a duty owed to him in the circumstances by the defendant to take reasonable care to avoid such injury. In the present case we are not concerned with the breach of the duty; if a duty exists, that would be a question of fact which is sufficiently averred and for present purposes must be assumed. We are solely concerned with the question whether, as a matter of law in the circumstances alleged, the defender owed any duty to the pursuer to take care.

It is remarkable how difficult it is to find in the English authorities statements of general application defining the relations between parties that give rise to the duty. The courts are concerned with the particular relations which come before them in actual litigation, and it is sufficient to say whether the duty exists in those circumstances. The result is that the courts have been engaged upon an elaborate classification of duties as they exist in respect of property, whether real or personal, with further divisions as to ownership, occupation or control, and distinctions based on the particular relations of the one side or the other, whether manufacturer, salesman, landlord, customer, tenant, stranger, and so on. In this way it can be ascertained at any time whether the law recognises a duty, but only where the case can be referred to some particular species which has been determined and classified. And yet the duty which is common to all cases where liability is established must logically be based upon some element common to the cases where it is found to exist. To seek a complete logical definition of the general principle is probably to go beyond the function of the judge, for the more general the definition the more likely it is to omit essentials or to introduce non-essentials. The attempt was made by Brett MR in *Heaven v Pender* (1883) 11 QBD 503, in a definition to which I will later refer. As framed, it was demonstrably too wide, though it appears to me, if properly limited, to be capable of affording a valuable practical guide.

At present I content myself with pointing out that in English law there must be, and is, some general conception of relations giving rise to a duty of care, of which the particular cases found in the books are but rare instances. The liability for negligence, whether you style it such or treat it as in other systems as a species of 'culpa', is no doubt based upon a general public sentiment of moral wrongdoing for which the offender must pay. But acts or omissions which any moral code would censure cannot in a practical world be treated so as to give a right to every person injured by them to demand relief. In this way rules of law arise which limit the range of complainants and the extent of their remedy. The rule that you are to love your neighbour becomes in law, you must not injure your neighbour; and the lawyer's question, Who is my neighbour? receives a restricted reply. You must take reasonable care to avoid acts or omissions which you can reasonably foresee would be likely to injure your neighbour. Who, then, in law is my neighbour? The answer seems to be—persons who are so closely and directly affected by my act that I ought reasonably to have them in contemplation as being so affected when I am directing my mind to the acts or omissions which are called in question. This appears to me to be the doctrine of *Heaven v Pender*, as laid down by Lord Esher (then Brett MR) when it is limited by the notion of proximity introduced by Lord Esher himself and AL Smith LJ in *Le Lievre v Gould*. Lord Esher says: 'That case established that, under certain circumstances, one man may owe a duty to another, even though there is no contract between them. If one man is near to another, or is near to the property of another, a duty lies upon him not to do that which may cause a personal injury to that other, or may injure his property'. . . . I think that this sufficiently states the truth if proximity be not confined to mere physical proximity but be used, as I think it was intended, to extend to such close and direct relations that the act complained of directly affects a person whom the person alleged to be bound to take care would know would be directly affected by his careless act. . . .

With this necessary qualification of proximate relationship as explained in *Le Lievre v Gould*, I think the judgment of Lord Esher expresses the law of England; without the qualification I think the majority of the court in *Heaven v Pender* were justified in thinking the principle was expressed in too general terms. There will no doubt arise cases where it will be difficult to determine whether the contemplated relationship is so close that the duty arises. But in the class of case now before the court I cannot conceive any difficulty to arise. A manufacturer puts up an article of food in a container which he knows will be opened by the actual consumer. There can be no inspection by any purchaser and no reasonable preliminary inspection by the consumer. Negligently, in the course of preparation, he allows the content to be mixed with poison. It is said that the law of England and Scotland is that the poisoned consumer has no remedy against the negligent manufacturer. If this were the result of the authorities, I should consider the result a grave defect in the law, and so contrary to principle that I should hesitate long before following any decision to that effect which had not the authority of this House. . . .

. . . I venture to say that in the branch of the law which deals with civil wrongs, dependent in England at any rate entirely upon the application by judges of general principles also formulated by judges, it is of particular importance to guard against the danger of stating propositions of law in wider terms than is necessary, lest essential factors be omitted in the wider survey, and the inherent adaptability of English law be unduly restricted. For this reason it is very necessary in considering reported cases in the law of torts that the actual decision alone should carry authority, proper weight, of course, being given to the dicta of the judges. . . .

[His Lordship considered various decided cases, including *Winterbottom v Wright*, and continued:]

I do not find it necessary to discuss at length the cases dealing with duties where the thing is dangerous, or, in the narrower category, belongs to a class of things which are dangerous in themselves. I regard the distinction as an unnatural one so far as it is used to serve as a logical differentiation by which to distinguish the existence or non-existence of a legal right. . . . The nature of the thing may very well call for different degrees of care, and the person dealing with it may well contemplate persons as being within the sphere of his duty to take care who would not be sufficiently proximate with less dangerous goods; so that not only the degree of care but the range of persons to whom a duty is owed may be extended. But they all illustrate the general principle . . .

My Lords, if your Lordships accept the view that this pleading discloses a relevant cause of action you will be affirming the proposition that by Scots and English law alike a manufacturer of products, which he sells in such a form as to show that he intends them to reach the ultimate consumer in the form in which they left him with no reasonable possibility of intermediate examination, and with the knowledge that the absence of reasonable care in the preparation or putting up of the products will result in an injury to the consumer's life or property, owes a duty to the consumer to take that reasonable care.

It is a proposition which I venture to say no one in Scotland or England who was not a lawyer would for one moment doubt. It will be an advantage to make it clear that the law in this matter, as in most others, is in accordance with sound common sense. I think that this appeal should be allowed.

Lord Macmillan

On the one hand, there is the well established principle that no one other than a party to a contract can complain of a breach of that contract. On the other hand, there is the equally well established doctrine that negligence apart from contract gives a right of action to the party injured by that negligence—and here I use the term negligence, of course, in its technical legal sense, implying a duty owed and neglected. The fact that there is a contractual relationship between the parties which may give rise to an action for breach of contract, does not exclude the co-existence of a right founded on negligence as between the same parties, independently of the contract, though arising out of the relationship in fact brought about by the contract. Of this the best illustration is the right of the injured railway passenger to sue the railway company either for breach of the contract of safe carriage or for negligence in carrying him. And there is no reason why the same set of facts should not give one person a right of action in contract and another person a right of action in tort . . .

If . . . you disregard the fact that the circumstances of the case at one stage include the existence of a contract of sale between the manufacturer and the retailer and approach the question by asking whether there is evidence of carelessness on the part of the manufacturer, and whether he owed a duty to be careful in a question with the party who has been injured in consequence of his want of care, the circumstance that the injured party was not a party to an incidental contract of sale becomes irrelevant, and his title to sue the manufacturer is unaffected by that circumstance. The appellant in the present instance asks that her case be approached as a case of delict [i.e. tort], not as a case of breach of contract. She does not require to invoke the exceptional cases in which a person not a party to a contract has been held entitled to complain of some defect in the subject matter of the contract which has caused him harm. . . .

The law takes no cognisance of carelessness in the abstract. It concerns itself with carelessness only where there is a duty to take care and where failure in that duty has caused damage. In such circumstances carelessness assumes the legal quality of negligence and entails the consequences in law of negligence. What, then, are the circumstances which give rise to this duty to take care? In the daily contacts of social and business life human beings are thrown into, or place themselves, in an infinite variety of relations with their fellows; and the law can refer only to the standards of the reasonable man in order to determine whether any particular relation gives rise to a duty to take care as between those who stand in that relation to each other. The grounds of action may be as various and manifold as human errancy; and the conception of legal responsibility may develop in adaptation to altering social conditions and standards. The criterion of judgment must adjust and adapt itself to the changing circumstances of life. The categories of negligence are never closed. The cardinal principle of liability is that the party complained of should owe the party complaining a duty to take care, and that the party complaining should be able to prove that he has suffered damage in consequence of a breach of that duty. Where there is room for diversity of view, it is in determining what circumstances will establish such a relationship between the parties as to give rise, on the one side, to a duty to take care, and on the other side to a right to have care taken. . . .

Now I have no hesitation in affirming that a person who for gain engages in the business of manufacturing articles of food and drink intended for consumption by members of the public in the form in which he issues them is under a duty to take care in the manufacture of these articles. That duty, in my opinion, he owes to those whom he intends to consume his products. He manufactures his commodities for human consumption; he intends and contemplates that they shall be consumed. By reason of that very fact he places himself in a relationship with all potential consumers of his commodities, and that relationship which he assumes and desires for his own ends imposes upon him a duty to take care to avoid injuring them. . . .

Lord Thankerton delivered a speech in favour of allowing the appeal, whilst **Lord Buckmaster** and **Lord Tomlin** delivered speeches in favour of dismissing the appeal.

Appeal allowed.

COMMENTARY

Readers who take for granted the wide scope of the tort of negligence in the modern law may well underestimate the importance of *Donoghue v Stevenson*. Its immediate importance was to impose a duty of care on manufacturers in respect of the production of certain types of goods, i.e. those which could not be inspected before consumption or use. A similar case had only recently been dismissed in Scotland (*Mullen v AG Barr* 1929 SC 461—ginger beer bottle containing a mouse) so the result of this action was hardly a foregone conclusion when it reached the House of Lords. That the case ever made it to the House of Lords was due to the perseverance of the pursuer's lawyers, who successfully petitioned the House to allow Mrs Donoghue to proceed as a pauper. The development of the law of products liability from this beginning will be considered briefly below.

The 'Privity Fallacy'

On a wider doctrinal level, the majority of the House of Lords held that the existence of a contract between the defendant and a third party did not prevent the defendant owing a duty to the plaintiff in tort in relation to the performance of that contract. Hence the 'privity of contract' fallacy was exposed. *Winterbottom v Wright* was distinguished on the ground that the plaintiff in that case had sought to found his claim on the defendant's breach of contract with a third party, not his breach of an independent tortious duty owed directly to the plaintiff ('no duty was alleged other than the duty arising out of the contract': [1932] AC 562 at 589, per Lord Atkin). Following *Donoghue*, the existence of a contract between the defendant and a third party has rarely affected the defendant's tort liability to a claimant who suffers personal injury (though the position may be otherwise where the claim is for pure economic loss: see Ch. 8).

The 'Neighbour Principle'

Despite the achievements discussed already, *Donoghue* is probably best known for Lord Atkin's neighbour principle. As can be seen from the majority speeches, it does not form part of the ratio of the case, but the decision has nevertheless been regarded as introducing into the law a general moral principle of 'good neighbourliness'. To answer the question whether A owes B a duty of care necessarily requires a consideration of whether A ought to take care to look after B's interests. Knowledge of Lord Atkin's personal views helps to explain his conviction that we all have a duty to take care of our 'neighbours'. His biographer has described his Christian faith as a 'strong constant in his life', and a speech he gave to an audience at King's College London in October 1931 (less than two months before *Donoghue v Stevenson* was argued) is replete with references to the relationship between law and morality (see 'Law as an Educational Subject', extracted earlier, and more generally Chamberlain, 'Lord Atkin's Opinion in *Donoghue v Stevenson*: Perspectives from Biblical Hermenuetics' (2010) 4 Law and Humanities 91). In addition, it is known that Lord Atkin discussed the concept of 'neighbour' with his family and guests over the summer of 1931 (see generally G. Lewis, *Lord Atkin* (London: Butterworths, 1983)).

Lord Atkin's reliance upon a broad moral principle should be contrasted with the more pragmatic approach of Lord Macmillan. Lord Macmillan had originally drafted a speech deciding the case by reference to Scottish law, but it seems likely that Lord Atkin persuaded him to widen the decision to cover English law as well (see Rodger, 'Lord Macmillan's Speech in *Donoghue v Stevenson*' (1992) 108 LQR 236), a not unreasonable suggestion as the case had been argued on the basis that English and Scottish law were the same. For Lord Macmillan, the 'categories of negligence are never closed' and 'the conception of legal responsibility may develop in adaptation to altering social conditions and standards'. This gives little guidance as to when a duty of care should be owed and leaves the issue to be decided as particular factual scenarios come before the courts. This more cautious, case-by-case approach, which eschews generalisation, is similar to that currently favoured by the courts.

Further historical background on the *Donoghue* decision can be found in Rodger, 'Mrs Donoghue and Alfenus Varus' (1988) CLP 1; P. Burns (ed.), *Donoghue v Stevenson and the Modern Law of Negligence* (Vancouver: CLE, 1991); McBryde, '*Donoghue v Stevenson*: The Story of the "Snail in the Bottle" Case', in A. Gamble (ed.), *Obligations in Context* (Edinburgh: EUP, 1990); and M. Chapman, *The Snail and the Ginger Beer: The Singular Case of Donoghue v Stevenson* (London: Wildy, Simmonds & Hill, 2010). It was never actually determined whether there was a snail in the ginger beer bottle; the defender died before proofs were required and the matter was settled with his estate in December 1934 (see (1955) 71 LQR 472). On the (considerable) folklore surrounding the case, see Conn, 'Gingerlore: The Legends of *Donoghue v Stevenson*' [2013] Jur Rev 265.

3. *Donoghue v Stevenson* in Action—The Development of Liability for Defective Products

Grant v Australian Knitting Mills Ltd [1936] AC 85

The plaintiff bought two pairs of underwear manufactured by the defendants from a retail shop. After he had worn one of the pairs for a couple of days, the plaintiff's legs began to itch and appeared red. After a week he sent that pair for washing and wore the second pair, and by the time he visited a dermatologist and was advised to dispose of the garments one pair had been washed twice and the other once. Despite this the rash worsened and spread; he was in bed for seventeen weeks and spent a further three months in hospital after a relapse. His dermatologist at one stage feared he might die. He sued the retailers for breach of contract and the manufacturers in negligence. He was successful against both at first instance, but the High Court of Australia overturned the decision, holding that there was no breach of contract and no evidence of negligence. The manufacturers provided details of the precautions they took to ensure that no chemicals remained in the clothes they supplied. The plaintiff appealed to the Privy Council.

Lord Wright

[W]hen the position of the manufacturers is considered, different questions arise; there is no privity of contract between the appellant and the manufacturers; between them the liability, if any, must be in tort, and the gist of the cause of action is negligence. The facts set out in the foregoing show in their Lordships' judgment negligence in manufacture. According to the evidence, the method of manufacture was correct; the danger of excess sulphites being left was recognised and was guarded against; the process was intended to be foolproof. If excess sulphites were left in the garment, that could only be because someone was at fault. The appellant is not required to lay his finger on the exact person in all the chain who was responsible or to specify what he did wrong. Negligence is found as a matter of inference from the existence of the defects taken in connection with all the known circumstances; even if the manufacturers could by apt evidence have rebutted that inference they have not done so. . . .

[It was argued on behalf of the manufacturers] that the present case fell outside the decision of the House of Lords in *Donoghue (or McAlister) v Stevenson* [1932] AC 562. Their Lordships, like the judges in the courts in Australia, will follow that decision, and the only question here can be what that authority decides and whether this case comes within its principles. . . .

It is clear that the decision treats negligence, where there is a duty to take care, as a specific tort in itself, and not simply as an element in some more complex relationship or in some specialised breach of duty, and still less as having any dependence on contract. All that is necessary as a step to establish the tort of actionable negligence is to define the precise relationship from which the duty to take care is to be deduced. It is, however, essential in English law that the duty should be established; the mere fact that a man is injured by another's act gives in itself no cause of action; if the act is deliberate, the party injured will have no claim in law even though the injury is intentional, so long as the other party is merely exercising a legal right; if the act involves lack of due care, again no case of actionable negligence will arise unless the duty to be careful exists. In *Donoghue's* case, the duty was deduced simply from the facts relied on, namely, that the injured party was one of a class for whose use, in the contemplation and intention of the makers, the article was issued to the world, and the article was used by that party in the state in which it was prepared and issued without it being changed in any way and without there being any warning of, or means of detecting, the hidden danger; there was, it is true, no personal intercourse between the maker and the user; but though the duty is personal, because it is inter partes, it needs no interchange of words, spoken or written, or signs of offer or assent; it is thus different in character from any contractual relationship; no question of consideration between the parties is relevant; for these reasons the use of the word 'privity' in this connection is apt to mislead because of the suggestion of some overt relationship like that in contract, and the word 'proximity' is open to the same objection; if the term proximity is to be applied at all, it can only be in the sense that the want of care and the injury are in essence directly and intimately connected; though there may be intervening transactions of sale and purchase and intervening handling between these two events, the events are themselves unaffected by what happened between them; proximity can only properly be used to exclude any element of remoteness, or of some interfering complication between the want of care and the injury, and, like 'privity', may mislead by introducing alien ideas. . . .

It is obvious that the principles thus laid down involve a duty based on the simple facts detailed above, a duty quite unaffected by any contracts dealing with the thing, for instance, of sale by maker to retailer, and again by retailer to consumer or to the consumer's friend. . . .

If the foregoing are the essential features of *Donoghue's* case they are also to be found, in their Lordships' judgment, in the present case. The presence of the deleterious chemical in the pants, due to negligence in manufacture, was a hidden and latent defect, just as much as were the remains of the snail in the opaque bottle: it could not be detected by any examination that could reasonably be made. Nothing happened between the making of the garments and their being worn to change their condition. The garments were made by the manufacturers for the purpose of being worn exactly as they were worn in fact by the appellant; it was not contemplated that they should be first washed. It is immaterial that the appellant has a claim in contract against the retailers; because that is a quite independent cause of action, based on different considerations, even though the damage may be the same. Equally irrelevant is any question of liability between the retailers and the manufacturers on the contract of sale between them. The tort liability is independent of any question of contract . . .

Counsel for the respondents, however, sought to distinguish *Donoghue's* case from the present on the ground that in the former the makers of the ginger beer had retained 'control' over it in the sense that they had placed it in stoppered and sealed bottles, so that it would not be tampered with until it was opened to be drunk, whereas the garments in question were merely put into paper packets, each containing six sets, which in ordinary course would be taken down by the shopkeeper and opened and the contents handled and disposed of separately so that they would be exposed to the air. He contended that, though there was no reason to think that the garments, when sold to the appellant were in any other condition, least of all as regards sulphur contents, than when sold to the retailers by the manufacturers, still the mere possibility and not the fact of their condition having been changed was sufficient to distinguish *Donoghue's* case; there was no 'control' because nothing was done by the manufacturers to exclude the possibility of any tampering while the goods were on their way to the user. Their Lordships do not accept that contention. The decision in *Donoghue's* case did not depend on the bottle being stoppered and sealed; the essential point in this regard was that the article should reach the consumer or user subject to the same defect it had when it left the manufacturer. That this was true of the garment is in their Lordships opinion beyond question. At most there might in other cases be a greater difficulty of proof of the fact. . . .

In their Lordships' opinion it is enough for them to decide this case on its actual facts. No doubt, many difficult problems will arise before the precise limits of the principle are defined: many qualifying conditions and many complications of fact may in the future come before the courts for decision. It is enough to say that their Lordships hold the present case to come within the principle of *Donoghue's* case and they think that the judgment of the Chief Justice was right and should be restored as against both respondents . . .

Appeal allowed.

COMMENTARY

Unlike *Donoghue v Stevenson*, this appeal was about the correctness of a judgment on the merits, and not a decision on a preliminary issue of law. Hence the court was required to consider whether all the elements of a cause of action in negligence were complete: there had to be a duty of care, and a breach of that duty which had caused the claimant damage. We shall consider each of the elements in turn in order to provide a general overview of the most important issues that arise in negligence litigation.

Duty

The existence of a duty of care is an indispensable requirement for a successful claim in negligence. If there is no duty, the failure to take reasonable care cannot give rise to liability. The chief significance of *Donoghue v Stevenson* was in providing a generalised concept of duty which was applicable to a wide range of different situations. Gradually, with the passage of time, the circumstances in which duties of care were recognised moved further and further from the specific factual context of the leading case. And potential limitations on the scope of liability under the principle of *Donoghue v Stevenson* in cases where the plaintiff suffered physical injury were rejected.

The early stages of this process are evident in *Grant*. One question for the Privy Council was whether *Donoghue v Stevenson* applied only to products which the manufacturer supplied in a sealed and opaque container (like the bottle of ginger beer in the earlier case). This was a plausible interpretation of certain passages of their Lordship's speeches in *Donoghue*, but it was rejected by the Privy Council, who ruled that the essential question was whether the product reached the consumer subject to the same defect it had when it left the manufacturer. Another question for the Privy Council was whether the fact that the defect might have been discovered precluded the imposition of a duty of care on the manufacturer, given that Lord Atkin had stated in *Donoghue* that there should be 'no reasonable possibility of intermediate examination'. On the facts, the Privy Council ruled that the presence of the chemicals in the pants could not have been detected by any examination that could reasonably have been made, and so the limitation—which arose only where there was a reasonable possibility of discovering the defect—did not apply. Subsequently, it has been made clear that Lord Atkin's words did not lay down a separate requirement of liability under *Donoghue v Stevenson* and that liability can arise even if a third party did have a reasonable opportunity of inspecting the goods (*Griffiths v Arch Engineering Co Ltd* [1968] 3 All ER 217). It seems therefore that the possibility of intermediate examination goes to the question of legal causation rather than to the existence of a duty.

Later decisions take the process of 'stretching' the principle still further. It has been recognised, for instance, that a manufacturer owes a duty of care not only to the consumer of the product in question, but to anyone who is foreseeably injured by the product (*Stennett v Hancock* [1939] 2 All ER 578). And the range of potential defendants has also been extended, for example, to the repairer of a product who negligently leaves it in a dangerous state (*Haseldine v Daw & Sons Ltd* [1941] 2 KB 343). The result has been a rapid expansion in the scope of the tort of negligence such that, where physical injury to person or property is caused by a positive act, it is now generally safe to assume the existence of a duty of care.

Admittedly, where the type of loss that the claimant has suffered is purely economic or psychiatric, or where the alleged negligence consists of an omission rather than a positive act, the circumstances in which a duty of care will arise are more limited (see Chs 7–9). Nevertheless, the restrictive approach to the imposition of liability in these 'problematic' cases should not mask the broad scope of the duty of care applying to 'simple' cases (as defined earlier). It is quite unthinkable, for instance, that anyone would ever deny the existence of a duty of care in respect of physical injury caused by accidents in the workplace, collisions on the roads or railways, or dangerously defective products.

Breach

The *Grant* decision case also raises the question of breach of duty (i.e. unreasonable conduct) by the defendant. All the plaintiff could do was point to the existence of the sulphur in the clothing; he could not show how or why it had come to be there or who was responsible for its presence. In response the manufacturer gave evidence that they had received no complaints about the 4,737,600 other garments treated the same way. If these figures are to be believed, the percentage chance that sulphur would remain in a garment was 0.000021. *Weir* (p. 26) suggests that such a low rate of failure should have entitled the manufacturer to a prize rather than a finding of negligence.

If such a high standard of performance can amount to negligence, one might question the extent to which the resultant liability is really fault-based. In the United States, the common law liability of the manufacturer to the ultimate consumer developed beyond negligence to strict liability, that is, liability without fault, and a similar regime of strict liability for defective products was introduced into the United Kingdom by the Consumer Protection Act 1987 (see Ch. 10.II.2). In a strict liability regime the issue is not whether the defendant has exercised reasonable care in manufacturing the product in question but whether the product was defective. The possible rationales for imposing strict liability for defective products are set out in Chapter 10.II.1, while the question of whether other strict liabilities should be introduced into English law is considered in Chapter 17.II.1.

It is worth noting at this point that it was the English common law's preference for a tort—rather than contract—based analysis of the manufacturer's liability that led it to rest that liability on a finding of fault. If the courts had recognised a contractual warranty as to quality or fitness for purpose owed to the ultimate consumer of the product then the resultant liability would have been strict, for the taking of all reasonable care is no defence to an action for breach of warranty. It was perhaps open to the House of Lords in *Donoghue* to set the law along this course by straightforwardly overruling *Winterbottom v Wright*, rather than distinguishing it on the basis that the plaintiff in the earlier action had pleaded his case in contract, not tort. This solution would undoubtedly have required a significant modification of the contractual doctrines of privity and consideration, but it would have accorded consumers the benefits associated with strict liability. Professor Milsom has commented: 'At the time [of *Donoghue*] it seemed a triumph to reach the manufacturer purely on the basis of wrong, and to exclude any trace of contractual analysis. But perhaps it was the contractual position that really needed reconsidering' (*Historical Foundations of the Common Law*, 2nd edn (London: Butterworths, 1981), p. 400). However, as *Grant* illustrates, the malleability of the fault concept allows tribunals of fact to impose liability even where the manufacturer appears to have done all that could reasonably be expected of it.

Damage

Unlike trespass to the person, negligence (descended from the action on the case) is not actionable *per se*: it is necessary to prove that the claimant suffered legally recognised damage as a result of the defendant's breach of duty. However, not all kinds of damage receive equal treatment from the law of negligence. The law reserves its most general protection for interests in the physical integrity of property and the person. But purely financial interests, for example, are protected only exceptionally. So if a negligently manufactured product causes physical injury or property damage, there is generally no obstacle to recovery, but if the claim is simply that the product does not work—and so has caused the claimant to incur repair costs or to lose trade or business—this purely economic loss is unlikely to give rise to liability (see Ch. 8). Financial interests are of a lesser order than interests in physical integrity, and so the law by and large leaves individuals to make their own (contractual) arrangements for the protection of these interests.

It is crucial to note that in English law the classification of the claimant's damage has important implications for the existence of a duty of care. The existence of the duty must be ed separately in respect of each different type of damage suffered by the claimant; that the defendant owed a duty of care in respect of one type of damage does not [mean] that there is a duty in respect of others. Other legal systems address the nature of the [claimant]'s damage more directly. Under the German civil code, the *Bürgerliches Gesetzbuch* (BGB), for example, the most general principle of liability for negligence, under Article 823 I BGB, applies only in respect of certain 'protected interests' which, for the most part, are set out in the code itself (see II.1). English law's rather indirect way of attaching significance to the type of damage suffered by the claimant should nevertheless not be allowed to obscure the vital role played by that factor in determining liability in negligence.

Causation

There must be a causal link between the claimant's damage and the defendant's breach of his duty of care. The concept of causation brings together a number of discrete principles, which are well illustrated by the product liability cases. First, it must be established that the defendant's negligent conduct was the factual cause of the claimant's loss, in the sense that the loss would not have occurred but for the negligence. In *Evans v Triplex Safety Glass Co Ltd* [1936] 1 All ER 283, the plaintiffs sued in respect of an allegedly defective windscreen which had broken and showered them with shards of glass. The claim failed because, even assuming negligence on the defendants' part, there was no evidence that this rather than various other possible causes was the actual cause of the windscreen's disintegration: the damage might very well have occurred even if the defendants had taken all reasonable care. (Additionally, the court ruled that the allegation that the defendants had failed to take reasonable care could not be substantiated.) Secondly, there is the question of the effect of intervening acts. Even if the hurdle of but-for or factual causation is overcome, the court may have to consider whether acts or omissions occurring between the defendant's breach of duty and the claimant's damage operate so as to negate the defendant's responsibility for the injury. In *Burrows v March Gas & Coke Co* (1872) LR 7 Ex 96, the defendants supplied the plaintiff with a defective pipe; when a gas-fitter who had been called in to look for the source of an escape of gas from the pipe searched for it with a lighted candle, he caused an explosion which did damage to the plaintiff. Although the explosion would not have happened but for the defendants' earlier breach of duty, they could not be regarded as responsible for a loss the immediate cause of which was a third party's reckless conduct. Although the case (which pre-dated *Donoghue v Stevenson*) was in fact decided in contract, there is no doubt that the court would have adopted the same analysis even if it had recognised a tortious duty (albeit that a modern court might find both parties to be responsible for the accident: see Ch. 5.II). A third question is that of remoteness. A defendant is only responsible for types of loss that are the reasonably foreseeable consequence of his negligence. If the claimant sustains a loss of a different type, that is too remote.

What if the claimant makes use of a product which obviously has a dangerous defect? If he does so deliberately, then his doing so may be held to have 'broken the chain of causation' between the producer's negligence and his damage, with the result that the producer is relieved of any liability (see, e.g., *Howmet Ltd v Economy Devices Ltd* (2016) 168 Con LR 27). As Lord Wright said in *Grant*, 'the man who consumes or uses a thing which he knows to be noxious cannot complain in respect of whatever mischief follows because it follows from his own conscious volition in choosing to incur the risk or certainty of mischance'. By contrast, where the claimant has not consciously adverted to the danger, but is nevertheless at fault in not identifying it, the more appropriate solution is likely to be the application of the partial defence of contributory negligence, which provides for a reduction in the damages award in proportion to the claimant's own responsibility for the injury. (Even where the claimant consciously runs the risk of injury, it may sometimes be thought preferable to make a deduction for contributory negligence rather than to bar the claim altogether, although rather surprisingly in *Howmet* a majority of the Court of Appeal ruled out this possibility in cases where the claimant had freely chosen to make use of a chattel known to be dangerous.) The interaction of principles of causation with the various defences that can be raised to a negligence action is considered further in Chapter 5.II.

II. The Duty of Care in the Modern Law

As we have seen, *Donoghue v Stevenson* established the central role of the 'duty of care' concept in the tort of negligence. Fault, damage and causation are all irrelevant if the defendant is under no duty to the claimant. Although the Roman lawyer Buckland wrote in 1935 that the duty of care was 'an unnecessary fifth wheel on the coach, incapable of sound analysis and possibly productive of injustice' ('The Duty to Take Care' (1935) 51 LQR 637), the modern law treats the duty concept as an indispensable tool with which to denote when a person should be held responsible for the consequences of their negligence—and when they should be safeguarded against liability in respect of those consequences. In fact, it is helpful to regard the duty concept as primarily concerned with cases of the latter sort, or in other words to conceive of this element of the negligence enquiry as essentially negative or exclusionary in character (see *Smith v Littlewoods Organisation Ltd* [1987] AC 241 at 280, per Lord Goff).

Despite the centrality of the duty of care to the modern law of negligence, it remains controversial. One of us has argued that the duty concept is now obscuring understanding of negligence law and hindering its rational development, and has therefore proposed its 'deconstruction', a process whereby the disparate issues currently subsumed under the duty umbrella are separated out and reclassified under the other components of the negligence enquiry, namely fault (or 'breach of duty'), damage, causation, remoteness and defences (Nolan, 'Deconstructing the Duty of Care' (2013) 129 LQR 559). Other scholars have been similarly critical of the concept (see Howarth, 'Negligence after *Murphy*: Time to Re-think' [1991] CLJ 67; and Hepple, 'Negligence: The Search for Coherence' (1997) 50 CLP 69, 93). For a helpful overview of the debate, see *Plunkett*, pp. 164–73.

By contrast, McBride has defended the duty of care concept, but argued that there is not a single 'duty of care'; rather there are numerous 'duties of care' of a relatively high degree of specificity—a duty to do *x* rather than a general duty to exercise reasonable care in the circumstances (see McBride, 'Duties of Care—Do they Really Exist?' (2004) 24 OJLS 417). One difficulty with this approach is that it tends to conflate the 'duty of care' question with the 'breach of duty' question. As Howarth, 'Many Duties of Care—Or a Duty of Care? Notes from the Underground' (2006) 26 OJLS 449, 466 says:

> Judges who follow the 'many duties' path tend to use the phrase 'there was no duty' even where the defendant's case is that they acted reasonably, not that there was no legal requirement for them to act reasonably. These judges tend to claim that the question is whether there was a duty to take precisely the precaution the defendant is accused of failing to take. But that view collapses the distinction between the two arguments. Indeed, if such a way of thinking were taken to its logical conclusion, there would never be any separate consideration of breach of duty since the issue would already have been resolved in setting the precise 'duty' involved. The concept of fault would disappear.

In our view, the duty of care concept is best understood as playing a dual role in the modern law of negligence, such that there are two different duty of care questions: first, whether there is a rule of law that either allows or bars recovery in this category of case (the legal, or 'notional', duty question); and secondly, whether damage to someone in the claimant's position was a reasonably foreseeable consequence of the defendant's negligence (the factual duty, or 'foreseeable claimant', question). See further on this distinction, Nolan, *op. cit.*, 564–6, and—seeking to reframe the debate about the duty of care in terms of its *protective scope* rather than its *existence*—Oliphant, 'Rationalising Tort Law for the Twenty-First Century', in *Private Law in the 21st Century*, pp. 59–64.

1. Introduction: 'Notional Duty'

The role of the notional duty question can be illuminated by comparing the approach of English law with that of other jurisdictions that do without any concept of 'duty' at all. In France, the *Code civil* imposes a general obligation to pay compensation for losses caused by the fault of another. The control mechanism used to limit liability is the law of causation (van Dam, para. 605–3) but this control is exerted in a much less systematic fashion than in English law, and it is apparent that French law has a much more expansive conception of liability for fault than that to be found in the common law. Conversely, Article 823 I of the German BGB provides for compensation to be paid where any of a list of protected interests is infringed intentionally or negligently; these include life, body, health, freedom and property (see further B. S. Markesinis, J. Bell and A. Janssen, *Markesinis's German Law of Torts*, 5th edn (Oxford: Hart, 2019), ch. 2). In German law, it is these protected interests (*Rechtsgüter*) that provide the principal limitation on the scope of liability for negligence (and indeed for intentional injury). In English law, that function is performed by the concept of the duty of care, though the set of protected interests is nowhere set out in explicit fashion, while the related question of what constitutes actionable 'damage' has been neglected to a very considerable extent (see further Nolan, 'New Forms of Damage in Negligence' (2007) 70 MLR 59 and Nolan, 'Damage in the English Law of Negligence' (2013) 4 JETL 259). Additionally, the duty concept's role in delimiting the interests protected by the tort of negligence may be obscured by the sheer variety of factors that may affect the decision whether or not a duty of care arises on the facts. To the advantage of the English practice, however, is the possibility of taking account of the protected interests in a more nuanced fashion—allowing for greater or lesser protection according to the perceived importance of the interest infringed in the individual case. A different approach is therefore possible depending on whether the damage takes the form of personal injury, property damage, pure economic loss or some other type of actionable harm.

The *Principles of European Tort Law* (Vienna: Springer, 2005) elaborated by the European Group on Tort Law—a group of tort law experts from different jurisdictions—attempt a synthesis of the best elements of common law and civil law tort traditions. Their 'general conditions of liability', applicable (as in most European systems) to both intentional and negligent conduct, state that '[d]amage requires material or immaterial harm to a legally protected interest' (Article 2:101). The protected interests are then introduced in a fashion which seeks to combine explicit statement (as in the German civil code) with flexibility of treatment (as under the common law).

Principles of European Tort Law, Article. 2:102: Protected Interests

(1) The scope of protection of an interest depends on its nature; the higher its value, the precision of its definition and its obviousness, the more extensive is its protection.

(2) Life, bodily or mental integrity, human dignity and liberty enjoy the most extensive protection.

(3) Extensive protection is granted to property rights, including those in intangible property.

(4) Protection of pure economic interests or contractual relationships may be more limited in scope. In such cases, due regard must be had especially to the proximity between the actor and the endangered person, or to the fact that the actor is aware of the fact that he will cause damage even though his interests are necessarily valued lower than those of the victim.

Some academics go further than the protected interests approach, arguing that private law duties, including the duty of care in negligence, are necessarily correlative to a right possessed by the claimant. For example, as the claimant has a right to bodily safety, a defendant owes a duty not negligently to cause bodily injury (see, e.g., R. Stevens, *Torts and Rights* (Oxford: OUP, 2007)). On this view, the classification of damage is only relevant in so far as it helps to determine whether an underlying right of the claimant has been infringed. For some proponents of rights-based approaches to negligence law part of their appeal is the belief that they can generate a law of negligence that is not affected by the policy considerations referred to earlier (see *Beever*). The extent to which the law of negligence, or the law of tort more generally, can or should be based on this approach is controversial and it is likely that policy factors will continue to play a role, along with the type of harm suffered by the claimant, in determining the duty of care question.

The function of the duty of care concept in English law was considered by Lord Rodger in the next extract.

D v East Berkshire Community Health NHS Trust [2005] 2 AC 373

The claimants alleged negligence on the part of the defendant's child welfare professionals (doctors and social workers) who had formed the opinion, subsequently shown to be erroneous, that the claimants had been guilty of abusing their children. For present purposes, it is enough to note that one argument advanced for the claimants was that the duty concept was an inappropriate mechanism for determining whether liability could arise in these circumstances, and that the relevant considerations were better taken into account in determining whether or not there had been a breach of duty.

Lord Rodger

100. . . . [T]he world is full of harm for which the law furnishes no remedy. For instance, a trader owes no duty of care to avoid injuring his rivals by destroying their long-established businesses. If he does so and, as a result, one of his competitors descends into a clinical depression and his family are reduced to penury, in the eyes of the law they suffer no wrong and the law will provide no redress—because competition is regarded as operating to the overall good of the economy and society. A young man whose fiancée deserts him for his best friend may become clinically depressed as a result, but in the circumstances the fiancée owes him no duty of care to avoid causing this suffering. So he too will have no right to damages for his illness. The same goes for a middle-aged woman whose husband runs off with a younger

woman. Experience suggests that such intimate matters are best left to the individuals themselves. However badly one of them may have treated the other, the law does not get involved in awarding damages.

101. Other relationships are also important. We may have children, parents, grandparents, brothers, sisters, uncles and aunts—not to mention friends, colleagues, employees and employers—who play an essential part in our lives and contribute to our happiness and prosperity. We share in their successes, but are also affected by anything bad which happens to them. So it is—and always has been—readily foreseeable that if a defendant injures or kills someone, his act is likely to affect not only the victim but many others besides. To varying degrees, these others can plausibly claim to have suffered real harm as a result of the defendant's act. For the most part, however, the policy of the law is to concentrate on compensating the victim for the effects of his injuries while doing little or nothing for the others. In technical language, the defendants owe a duty of care to the victim but not to the third parties, who therefore suffer no legal wrong.

COMMENTARY

The extract highlights a number of important points. First, one of the important functions of the duty of care in English law (but not its only function) is to determine whether or not the claimant has suffered a form of harm that is capable of grounding a claim in negligence. Lord Rodger's examples are of cases where the loss in question may be styled *damnum* but not *injuria*, following a famous distinction made in Roman law: i.e. a loss that the law does not recognise as actionable damage. Secondly, the duty concept allows not just for a distinction between actionable and non-actionable damage, but also for an intermediate category of damage actionable under a limited set of circumstances. The 'ricochet' losses considered by Lord Rodger in [100] provide examples. The relatives of the victim may, in certain limited circumstances, have a claim against the injurer for their own losses that are consequential on the victim's injury, e.g. their mental suffering or their loss of economically valuable services. English law identifies such claims as falling in areas of 'limited duty', and prescribes specific requirements that they must satisfy (e.g. requirements of proximity or assumption of responsibility) if a duty of care is in fact to be recognised. Thirdly, whether or not a duty of care arises depends not only on the nature of the claimant's damage, but also on a variety of other 'complexities'. Depending on the circumstances of the case, the court may take account of *how* the damage was caused (positive act or omission?) and whether it was caused directly by the defendant or through a third party, as well as policy factors relevant to the 'fairness, justice and reasonableness' of imposing a duty of care.

In *D*, Lord Bingham stated, at [49], that he would regard a shift of emphasis from consideration of duty to consideration of breach as 'welcome', adding that 'the concept of duty has proved itself a somewhat blunt instrument for dividing claims which ought reasonably to lead to recovery from claims which ought not'. And Lord Nicholls also admitted that the idea was 'not without attraction', while ultimately rejecting it on the ground that it would create too much uncertainty. (For an appraisal of the advantages and disadvantages of modifying the standard of care in response to liability concerns, as opposed to employing a no-duty or limited duty rule, see Nolan, 'Varying the Standard of Care in Negligence' [2013] CLJ 651, 680–7.)

One of us ('New Forms of Damage', *op. cit.*) has argued that it would be conducive to greater clarity in the law if the question of actionable damage were considered separately, and proposed a further distinction between 'never actionable' and 'sometimes actionable' harm:

[I]t seems preferable to deal with the question of whether a given harm is ever actionable under the heading of actionable damage, and to deal with the question of whether a sometimes actionable harm is actionable in this particular case under the separate heading of duty of care, since doing so draws attention to the distinction we have identified, and makes it more likely that the important issues raised by the former question will be addressed openly and comprehensively. Unfortunately, however, there is a tendency to subsume the damage issue into the duty of care question.

Furthermore, in *Meadows v Khan* [2022] AC 852 a plurality of the Supreme Court recently put forward a new six-part roadmap for negligence analysis, in which the damage issue was expressly separated out from the issue of duty and turned into the first of six questions (the 'actionability' question) that a court should ask in a negligence case. By contrast, Lord Burrows—who, along with Lord Leggatt, was not persuaded by the new roadmap—considered (at [80]) that the damage issue could 'be conveniently treated as a sub-issue under the duty of care enquiry'. Which approach do you think is preferable? As to the new roadmap more generally, it is critically analysed by Nolan and Plunkett (2022) 138 LQR 175, and note that so far it seems that the lower courts are reluctant to employ it: see *Cunningham v Rochdale MBC* [2021] EWCA Civ 1719 at [23]; *Rushbond plc v The JS Design Partnership LLP* [2021] EWCA Civ 1889 at [74].

Logically, the question whether a particular interest is protected is distinct from the question whether it has been damaged on the facts. (Cf. *Principles of European Tort Law*, Article 2:101: 'Damage requires material or immaterial harm to a legally protected interest'.) In practice, 'damage' more often emerges as a matter of proof (i.e. did the claimant in fact suffer the harm) rather than as a legal issue. In some cases, however, it may be questioned whether the type of harm admittedly suffered by the claimant amounts to damage sufficient to ground a negligence action at all. One such case was *Rothwell v Chemical & Insulating Co Ltd* [2008] 1 AC 281, a test case in which a number of nominated claimants sued their employers in respect of the appearance of harmless pleural plaques (fibrous tissues on the membrane of the lung) as a consequence of their exposure to asbestos in the workplace. A unanimous House of Lords held that the development of pleural plaques did not constitute personal injury in itself, Lord Hoffmann commenting at [11]:

It was not merely that the plaques caused no immediate symptoms . . . The important point was that, save in the most exceptional case, the plaques would never cause any symptoms, did not increase the susceptibility of the claimants to other diseases or shorten their expectation of life.

In his Lordship's view, 'damage' was an abstract concept of being worse off, physically or economically. It was not merely a physical change as this might be consistent with an improvement (a successful operation) or with having a neutral effect. Nor could the change be trivial, but exactly how much of a change was necessary before the change amounted to actionable damage was a matter of degree.

Applying analogous reasoning, do you think that property covered in dust by nearby building works is or could be 'damaged'? (See *Hunter v Canary Wharf Ltd* [1996] 1 All ER 482 (CA).) Has a worker whose mesothelial cells have undergone molecular changes after asbestos inhalation, such that the later onset of mesothelioma is inevitable, suffered a personal injury? (See *Alcan Gove Pty Ltd v Zabic* [2015] 89 ALJR 845.) And could being born with a different coloured skin from that which was anticipated, as a result of a medical mix-up, amount to damage for which a legal action could be brought? (See *A v Health and Social Services Trust* [2011] NICA 28.)

For a recent case exploring the limits of damage in the personal injury context, where the Supreme Court took a more expansive view of the concept than the first instance judge and the Court of Appeal, see *Dryden v Johnson Matthey plc* [2019] AC 403 (noted by Morgan [2018] CLJ 461; Huang (2019) 82 MLR 737), and for a more detailed discussion of the requirement of damage in negligence, see *Winfield & Jolowicz*, para. 7–003ff.

2. The Foreseeable Claimant

An important early step in the process of limiting a wrongdoer's liability for the consequences of his negligence came with the recognition that the 'duty' recognised by the tort of negligence is a relative concept. The duty is owed not to the world at large (as a duty in criminal law would be), but only to an individual within the scope of the risk created, that is, to a foreseeable victim. This idea was explored in the well-known American case of *Palsgraf v Long Island Railroad Co*, 162 NE 99 (1928). The plaintiff was standing on a platform of the defendant's railroad when a train stopped at the station. A man carrying a package tried to get on the train, but appeared to be having difficulties, so a railway guard on the train, who had held the door open, reached forward to help him in, and another guard on the platform pushed him from behind. As a result of the alleged negligence of the guards, the package was dislodged, and fell on the track. Although the package appeared to be innocuous, it contained fireworks which then exploded. The explosion caused a set of weighing scales at the other end of the platform to fall onto the plaintiff, injuring her. The New York Court of Appeals rejected the plaintiff's claim, though their reasoning was not uniform. Cardozo J held that the guards had not owed the plaintiff a duty of care because it had not been foreseeable that their alleged lack of care would create a risk of harm *to the plaintiff*. The fact that the guards might have owed a duty to others (such as the passenger they were assisting) was irrelevant:

> What the plaintiff must show is 'a wrong' to herself, i.e. a violation of her own right, and not merely a wrong to someone else, nor conduct 'wrongful' because unsocial, but not 'a wrong' to anyone . . . Negligence, like risk, is thus a term of relation. Negligence in the abstract, apart from things related, is surely not a tort, if indeed it is understandable at all. Negligence is not a tort unless it results in the commission of a wrong, and the commission of a wrong imports the violation of a right, in this case, we are told, the right to be protected against interference with one's bodily security. But bodily security is protected, not against all forms of interference or aggression, but only against some.
>
> One who seeks redress at law does not make out a cause of action by showing without more that there has been damage to his person. If the harm was not wilful, he must show that the act as to him had possibilities of danger so many and so apparent as to entitle him to be protected against the doing of it though the harm was unintended. . . . The victim does not sue derivatively, or by right of subrogation, to vindicate an interest invaded in the person of another. Thus to view his cause of action is to ignore the fundamental difference between tort and crime. . . . He sues for breach of a duty owing to himself.

A different approach was taken by Andrews J:

> The proposition is this: Every one owes to the world at large the duty of refraining from those acts that may unreasonably threaten the safety of others. Such an act occurs. Not only is he

wronged to whom harm might reasonably be expected to result, but he also who is in fact injured, even if he be outside what would generally be thought the danger zone. There needs be duty due the one complaining, but this is not a duty to a particular individual, because as to him harm might be expected. Harm to someone being the natural result of the act, not only that one alone, but all those in fact injured may complain. . . . Unreasonable risk being taken, its consequences are not confined to those who might probably be hurt. . . .

Andrews J went on to hold that the defendant's negligence was not in fact the 'proximate cause' of the plaintiff's injury. So, despite the fact that he espoused a very different theory of negligence from that of Cardozo J, he reached the same conclusion as to liability on the facts of the case. In his judgment, the concept of 'proximate cause' does the work that the concept of 'duty' does in Cardozo J's. Andrews J's approach has appealed to some English commentators: Buckland (*op. cit.*) wrote that the majority view in *Palsgraf* seems 'only to be another way of saying that a man ought not to be responsible for unforeseeable consequences' (at p. 648).

Doubts have been expressed whether the events described in the judgments in the *Palsgraf* decision could have occurred in the manner envisaged. Although the court accepted that it was the shock of the explosion which threw down the scales, injuring the plaintiff, it has been suggested that the more likely explanation is that the scales were knocked down by people running about in a panic following the explosion (see Prosser, '*Palsgraf* Revisited' (1953) 52 Mich L Rev 1; cf. G. E. White, *Tort Law in America: An Intellectual History,* expanded edn (New York: OUP, 2003), pp. 357–8, n. 117). If this version of the facts had been accepted by the court, do you think the plaintiff would have been more likely to have succeeded?

The rule that a duty of care is owed only to a foreseeable claimant was considered by the House of Lords in the next extracted case.

Bourhill v Young [1943] AC 92

The pursuer, described in the opinions as a fishwife (i.e. a woman who sells fish), was a passenger on an Edinburgh tram. After she had alighted at a stop, and as she was lifting her fish-basket from the driver's platform, she heard the sound of a collision between a motor-cycle and a car. The motorcyclist, a certain John Young, had been travelling at excessive speed and had been unable to avoid the car when it had crossed his path while making a right turn. He was thrown on the street and sustained injuries from which he died. The accident occurred some 45 or 50 feet away from where the pursuer was standing, but out of her line of sight. After Mr Young's body had been removed, the pursuer approached the site of the accident and saw the blood left on the roadway. She alleged that, as an immediate result of the violent collision and the extreme shock of the occurrence, she wrenched and injured her back and sustained a severe nervous shock. At the time of the accident, she was eight months pregnant and five weeks later she gave birth to a baby which was still-born. Having failed in her action against the estate of Mr Young before the Scottish courts, she appealed to the House of Lords.

Lord Macmillan

The duty to take care is the duty to avoid doing or omitting to do anything the doing or omitting to do which may have as its reasonable and probable consequence injury to others and the duty is owed to those to whom injury may reasonably and probably be anticipated if the duty is not observed.

There is no absolute standard of what is reasonable and probable. It must depend on circumstances and must always be a question of degree. In the present instance the late John Young was clearly negligent in a question with the occupants of the motor car with which his cycle collided. He was driving at an excessive speed in a public thoroughfare and he ought to have foreseen that he might consequently collide with any vehicle which he might meet in his course, for such an occurrence may reasonably and probably be expected to ensue from driving at a high speed in a street. But can it be said that he ought further to have foreseen that his excessive speed, involving the possibility of collision with another vehicle, might cause injury by shock to the pursuer? The pursuer was not within his line of vision, for she was on the other side of a tramway car which was standing between him and her when he passed and it was not until he had proceeded some distance beyond her that he collided with the motor car. The pursuer did not see the accident and she expressly admits that her 'terror did not involve any element of reasonable fear of immediate bodily injury to herself.' She was not so placed that there was any reasonable likelihood of her being affected by the deceased's careless driving.

In these circumstances I am of opinion . . . that the late John Young was under no duty to the pursuer to foresee that his negligence in driving at an excessive speed and consequently colliding with a motor car might result in injury to the pursuer, for such a result could not reasonably and probably be anticipated. He was, therefore, not guilty of negligence in a question with the pursuer.

Lord Wright quoted Lord Atkin's 'well-known aphorism' in *Donoghue v Stevenson*—'You must take reasonable care to avoid acts or omissions which you can reasonably foresee would be likely to injure your neighbour'—and continued:

This general concept of reasonable foresight as the criterion of negligence or breach of duty (strict or otherwise) may be criticised as too vague; but negligence is a fluid principle, which has to be applied to the most diverse conditions and problems of human life. It is a concrete not an abstract idea. . . . It is also always relative to the individual affected. This raises a serious additional difficulty in the cases where it has to be determined not merely whether the act itself is negligent against someone but whether it is negligent vis-à-vis the plaintiff. This is a crucial point in cases of nervous shock. Thus in the present case John Young was certainly negligent in an issue between himself and the owner of the car which he ran into, but it is another question whether he was negligent vis-à-vis the appellant.

In such cases terms like 'derivative' and 'original' and 'primary' and 'secondary' have been applied to define and distinguish the type of the negligence. If, however, the appellant has a cause of action, it is because of a wrong to herself. She cannot build on a wrong to someone else. Her interest, which was in her own bodily security, was of a different order from the interest of the owner of the car. . . .

The present case, like many others of this type, may, however, raise the different question whether the appellant's illness was not due to her peculiar susceptibility. She was 8 months gone in pregnancy. Can it be said, apart from everything else, that it was likely that a person of normal nervous strength would have been affected in the circumstances by illness as the appellant was? Does the criterion of reasonable foresight extend beyond people of ordinary health or susceptibility, or does it take into account the peculiar susceptibilities or infirmities of those affected which the defendant neither knew of nor could reasonably be taken to have foreseen? Must the manner of conduct adapt itself to such special individual peculiarities? If extreme cases are taken, the answer appears to be fairly clear, unless, indeed, there is knowledge of the extraordinary risk. One who suffers from the terrible tendency to bleed on slight contact, which is denoted by the term 'a bleeder;' cannot complain if he mixes with the crowd and suffers severely, perhaps fatally, from being merely brushed against. There is no actionable wrong done there. A blind or deaf man who crosses the traffic on a busy street cannot complain if he is run over by a careful driver who does not know of and could not be expected to observe and guard against the man's infirmity. These questions go to 'culpability, not compensation'. . . . No doubt it has long ago been stated and often restated that, if the wrong is established, the wrongdoer must take the victim as he finds him. That, however, is only true . . . on the condition that the wrong has been established or admitted. The question of liability is anterior to the question of the measure of the consequences which go with the liability.

What is now being considered is the question of liability, and this, I think, in a question whether there is a duty owing to members of the public who come within the ambit of the act, must generally depend on a normal standard of susceptibility. This, it may be said, is somewhat vague. That is true; but definition involves limitation, which it is desirable to avoid further than is necessary in a principle of law like negligence which is widely ranging and is still in the stage of development. It is here, as elsewhere, a question of what the hypothetical reasonable man, viewing the position, I suppose *ex post facto*, would say it was proper to foresee. What danger of particular infirmity that would include must depend on all the circumstances; but generally, I think, a reasonably normal condition, if medical evidence is capable of defining it, would be the standard. The test of the plaintiff's extraordinary susceptibility, if unknown to the defendant, would in effect make the defendant an insurer. The lawyer likes to draw fixed and definite lines and is apt to ask where the thing is to stop. I should reply it should stop where in the particular case the good sense of the jury, or of the judge, decides.

However, when I apply the considerations which I have been discussing to the present appeal, I come to the conclusion that the judgment should be affirmed. The case is peculiar, as indeed, though to a varying extent, all these cases are apt to be. There is no dispute about the facts. Upon these facts, can it be said that a duty is made out, and breach of that duty, so that the damage which is found is recoverable? I think not. The appellant was completely outside the range of the collision. She merely heard a noise, which upset her, without her having any definite idea at all. As she said: 'I just got into a pack of nerves and I did not know whether I was going to get it or not.' She saw nothing of the actual accident, or indeed any marks of blood until later. I cannot accept that John Young could reasonably have foreseen, or, more correctly, the reasonable hypothetical observer could reasonably have foreseen, the likelihood that anyone placed as the appellant was, could be affected in the manner in which she was. In my opinion John Young was guilty of no breach of duty to the appellant and was not in law responsible for the hurt she sustained. I may add that the issue of duty or no duty is indeed a question for the court, but it depends on the view taken of the facts. In the present case both courts below have taken the view that the appellant has, on the facts of the case, no redress and I agree with their view.

Lord Russell of Killowen, **Lord Thankerton** and **Lord Porter** delivered separate concurring opinions.

Appeal dismissed.

COMMENTARY

The law relating to 'nervous shock' has moved on significantly since this decision, albeit that the reluctance to compensate for harm caused by psychiatric means persists, at least in 'secondary victim' cases such as *Bourhill*, where the claimant suffers the harm because of something that happens to another person. See Chapter 7 for the current law on this topic.

In the instant case, Lord Wright said that 'the question of liability . . . must generally depend on a normal standard of susceptibility'. He admitted, however, that what the reasonable person would foresee was a matter that was 'somewhat vague' and accepted that some kind of infirmity might be reasonably foreseeable. (See also *Haley v London Electricity Board* [1965] AC 778, where the House of Lords held that the duty of care owed by persons excavating a highway was to ensure the reasonable safety of all persons whose use of the highway was reasonably foreseeable, including the blind or infirm.)

See further on the 'factual duty' question, *Plunkett*, ch. 4.

If the House of Lords had held that the deceased motorcyclist owed a duty of care to Mrs Bourhill, might he also have owed a duty to her child *in ventro*? Consider the following extract.

Congenital Disabilities (Civil Liability) Act 1976

1. Civil liability to child born disabled

(1) If a child is born disabled as the result of such an occurrence before its birth as is mentioned in subsection (2) below, and a person (other than the child's own mother) is under this section answerable to the child in respect of the occurrence, the child's disabilities are to be regarded as damage resulting from the wrongful act of that person and actionable accordingly at the suit of the child.

(2) An occurrence to which this section applies is one which—

  (a) affected either parent of the child in his or her ability to have a normal, healthy child; or

  (b) affected the mother during her pregnancy, or affected her or the child in the course of its birth, so that the child is born with disabilities which would not otherwise have been present.

(3) Subject to the following subsections, a person (here referred to as 'the defendant') is answerable to the child if he was liable in tort to the parent or would, if sued in due time, have been so; and it is no answer that there could not have been such liability because the parent suffered no actionable injury, if there was a breach of legal duty which, accompanied by injury, would have given rise to the liability.

(4) In the case of an occurrence preceding the time of conception, the defendant is not answerable to the child if at that time either or both of the parents knew the risk of their child being born disabled (that is to say, the particular risk created by the occurrence); but should it be the child's father who is the defendant, this subsection does not apply if he knew of the risk and the mother did not . . .

(5) The defendant is not answerable to the child, for anything he did or omitted to do when responsible in a professional capacity for treating or advising the parent, if he took reasonable care having due regard to then received professional opinion applicable to the particular class of case; but this does not mean that he is answerable only because he departed from received opinion.

(6) Liability to the child under this section may be treated as having been excluded or limited by contract made with the parent affected, to the same extent and subject to the same restrictions as liability in the parent's own case; and a contract term which could have been set up by the defendant in an action by the parent, so as to exclude or limit his liability to him or her, operates in the defendant's favour to the same, but no greater, extent in an action under this section by the child.

(7) If in the child's action under this section it is shown that the parent affected shared the responsibility for the child being born disabled, the damages are to be reduced to such extent as the court thinks just and equitable having regard to the extent of the parent's responsibility. . . .

1A. Extension of section 1 to cover infertility treatments

(1) In any case where—
   (a) a child carried by a woman as the result of the placing in her of an embryo or of sperm and eggs or her artificial insemination is born disabled,
   (b) the disability results from an act or omission in the course of the selection, or the keeping or use outside the body, of the embryo carried by her or of the gametes used to bring about the creation of the embryo, and
   (c) a person is under this section answerable to the child in respect of the act or omission, the child's disabilities are to be regarded as damage resulting from the wrongful act of that person and actionable accordingly at the suit of the child.

(2) Subject to subsection (3) below and the applied provisions of section 1 of this Act, a person (here referred to as 'the defendant') is answerable to the child if he was liable in tort to one or both of the parents (here referred to as 'the parent or parents concerned') or would, if sued in due time, have been so; and it is no answer that there could not have been such liability because the parent or parents concerned suffered no actionable injury, if there was a breach of legal duty which, accompanied by injury, would have given rise to the liability.

(3) The defendant is not under this section answerable to the child if at the time the embryo, or the sperm and eggs, are placed in the woman or the time of her insemination (as the case may be) either or both of the parents knew the risk of their child being born disabled (that is to say, the particular risk created by the act or omission).

(4) Subsections (5) to (7) of section 1 of this Act apply for the purposes of this section as they apply for the purposes of that but as if references to the parent or the parent affected were references to the parent or parents concerned.

2. Liability of woman driving when pregnant

A woman driving a motor vehicle when she knows (or ought reasonably to know) herself to be pregnant is to be regarded as being under the same duty to take care for the safety of her unborn child as the law imposes on her with respect to the safety of other people; and if in consequence of her breach of that duty her child is born with disabilities which would not otherwise have been present, those disabilities are to be regarded as damage resulting from her wrongful act and actionable accordingly at the suit of the child. . . .

4. Interpretation and other supplementary provisions

(1) References in this Act to a child being born disabled or with disabilities are to its being born with any deformity, disease or abnormality, including predisposition (whether or not susceptible of immediate prognosis) to physical or mental defect in the future.

(2) In this Act—
   (a) 'born' means born alive (the moment of a child's birth being when it first has a life separate from its mother), and 'birth' has a corresponding meaning; and
   (b) 'motor vehicle' means a mechanically propelled vehicle intended or adapted for use on roads and

references to embryos shall be construed in accordance with section 1 of the Human Fertilisation and Embryology Act 1990 and any regulations made under s. 1(6) of that Act.

(3) Liability to a child under section 1, 1A or 2 of this Act is to be regarded—

(a) as respects all its incidents and any matters arising or to arise out of it; and

(b) subject to any contrary context or intention, for the purpose of construing references in enactments and documents to personal or bodily injuries and cognate matters as liability for personal injuries sustained by the child immediately after its birth . . .

(5) This Act applies in respect of births after (but not before) its passing, and in respect of any such birth it replaces any law in force before its passing, whereby a person could be liable to a child in respect of disabilities with which it might be born; but in section 1(3) of this Act the expression 'liable in tort' does not include any reference to liability by virtue of this Act, or to liability by virtue of any such law . . .

COMMENTARY

Before this legislation was passed there was some doubt as to whether a child in this position had an action, and hence the Law Commission recommended legislation to put the matter beyond doubt. The Commission's recommendations formed the basis of the 1976 Act (*Injuries to Unborn Children* (Law Com. 60, 1974)). The Court of Appeal subsequently held that a child had a cause of action in respect of pre-natal injuries even at common law (*Burton v Islington Health Authority* [1993] QB 204) but this is of little practical importance as the Act replaces the existing common law in respect of congenital disabilities suffered after its enactment.

The Act only allows a claim where the child is born alive, so that negligently killing a previously healthy foetus will not attract liability under the Act. Three injury-causing situations are covered by s. 1(2). The first relates to a period prior to conception, and deals with the ability of either parent to produce a healthy child. The second situation deals with conduct that affects the mother during pregnancy in respect of her ability to have a healthy child. The third situation covers negligence relating to the birth of the child. The Human Fertilisation and Embryology Act 1990 extended the Act's coverage to include injury caused by the selection, storage and use of embryos and gametes during fertility treatment (see s. 1A of the Act). However, the defendant is liable to the child only if they would have been liable in tort to either parent (or, in the second and third situations, to the mother). The child's claim is therefore derivative to some extent, but, as the defendant's conduct may not cause any damage to the parent, s. 1(3) provides that the actionability of the parent's claim depends upon breach of a legal duty rather than resultant damage (as would generally be required in a negligence action). The derivative nature of the claim is further demonstrated by s. 1(4), (6) and (7), which ensure that the duty owed to the child is no greater than that owed to the relevant parent. The child must also establish that the negligence caused the injury, which can be extremely difficult in medical negligence cases (see, e.g., *McCoy v East Midlands Strategic Health Authority* (2011) 118 BMLR 107, and more generally Ch. 5). Unless the mother's tortious conduct relates to the driving of a motor vehicle (s. 2), the child cannot bring a claim against its own mother. The Law Commission took the view that this immunity should not extend to the father and this is the position under the Act. Do you think that mother and father should be treated differently?

The child may claim in respect of 'disabilities', which are defined so as to cover any deformity, disease or abnormality with which the child is born. However, what if the child's claim relates to the fact that it was born at all? Suppose, for example, that a doctor negligently advises that the foetus is healthy when, in fact, it has a serious disease which will render it severely disabled when born. Can the child claim damages from the doctor for the pain and suffering it suffers because the pregnancy was not terminated? A 'wrongful life' claim of this kind was rejected by the Court of Appeal at common law in *McKay v Essex Area Health Authority* [1982] QB 1166 on public policy grounds: the claim entailed that the child would have been better off not being born at all. Furthermore, the Law Commission had clearly intended that the 1976 Act would bar such a claim, and it was held in *McKay*, obiter, that the wording of s. 1(2)(b) did indeed have this effect (this was also taken as read in *Toombes v Mitchell* [2021] QB 622). Note, however, first, that s. 1A appears to allow for a wrongful life action to be brought where the negligence relates to the selection of embryos and gametes (see Scott, 'Reconsidering "Wrongful Life" in England After Thirty Years: Legislative Mistakes and Unjustifiable Anomalies' [2013] CLJ 115), and, second, that in *Toombes* it was held that because the rider in s. 1(2)(b) is not reproduced in s. 1(2)(a), the legislative bar on wrongful life claims is limited to cases where *the pregnancy was not terminated* because of the defendant's negligence, and does not apply where the relevant 'occurrence' was pre-conception, so that the negligence *led to the conception* of a child with a disability. The decision in *McKay* is consistent with the position in France and Germany (see *van Dam*, para. 708-2), and also in Australia and Singapore (*Harriton v Stephens* (2006) 226 CLR 52; *JU v See Tho Kai Yin* [2005] 4 SLR 96), although a wrongful life claim was allowed in the Netherlands in the 'Baby Kelly' case (Hoge Raad, 18 March 2005). For an analysis of the treatment of such claims in a range of jurisdictions, see Ruda, '"I Didn't Ask to be Born": Wrongful Life from a Comparative Perspective' (2010) 1 JETL 204, and for critical discussion of the issues raised by such claims, see Perry, 'It's a Wonderful Life' (2008) 93 Cornell L Rev 329; and Scott, *op. cit.*

The rejection of wrongful life claims may not produce much hardship where the parents can bring a 'wrongful conception' or 'wrongful birth' action. Such claims allege that, but for the negligence, the parents would not have conceived the child, or would have had a termination, with the main head of damages being the cost of bringing up the child. However, in *McFarlane v Tayside Health Authority* [2000] 2 AC 59 the House of Lords held that the cost of raising a healthy but unplanned child was not recoverable in a wrongful conception or wrongful birth action. Soon after *McFarlane* was decided the Court of Appeal recognised an exception to that rule, by holding that where the child was born with disabilities, the *additional* costs of rearing the child attributable to those disabilities were recoverable (see *Parkinson v St James and Seacroft University Hospital NHS Trust* [2002] QB 266). The Court of Appeal subsequently sought to recognise a second exception, by permitting recovery in such a case of the additional costs of raising a *healthy* child attributable to *the disability of its mother* but on appeal the claim was rejected by a four to three majority of the House of Lords (*Rees v Darlington Area Health Authority* [2004] 1 AC 309). In obiter dicta, three members of the majority cast doubt on the correctness of *Parkinson*, but the final member of the majority appeared to agree with the minority that the additional costs attributable to the child's disability should be recoverable, while a different member of the majority thought it arguable that the costs associated with the child's disability should be recoverable where the purpose of the procedure that had been carried out negligently was to prevent the birth of a disabled child. In addition, the majority in *Rees* held that, in any case where negligence resulted in the birth of an unplanned child, a fixed sum award of £15,000 should be made, seemingly to the parents jointly, to compensate for the interference with their autonomy caused by their having an unplanned child. The minority in *Rees* expressed grave concerns about the use of a conventional award of this kind, while the precise nature and purpose of the award is contested (see Nolan, 'New Forms of Damage in Negligence', *op. cit.*, 77–80).

Cases of so-called 'reproductive negligence' are increasingly common, and a variety of approaches are evident in the Commonwealth case law. In Australia, for example, the High Court split four to three in *Cattanach v Melchior* (2003) 215 CLR 1 in favour of allowing a claim for the cost of upkeep of a healthy child in a wrongful conception claim, only for a number of states to pass legislation reversing that decision, while leaving open the possibility of a *Parkinson*-type claim (see, e.g., Civil Liability Act 2002 (NSW), ss. 70–71). More recently, the Singapore Court of Appeal held in *ACB v Thomson Medical Pte Ltd* [2017] 1 SLR 918 that claims for the cost of upkeep of an unplanned child would not be permitted in that jurisdiction, while allowing a claim for 'loss of genetic affinity' where a fertility clinic had negligently fertilised the plaintiff's ovum with the sperm of a stranger instead of her husband. (Cf. *A v A Health and Social Services Trust* [2012] NI 77.) A variety of approaches to these issues may also be observed in the rest of Europe (see *van Dam*, para. 707-2).

For further discussion of reproductive negligence, see N. Priaulx, *The Harm Paradox: Tort Law and the Unwanted Child in an Era of Choice* (Oxford: Routledge-Cavendish, 2007), chs 2, 4; J. K. Mason, *The Troubled Pregnancy: Legal Wrongs and Rights in Reproduction* (Cambridge: CUP, 2007), chs 3–6; Fox, 'Reproductive Negligence' (2017) 117 Col LR 149; and Todd, 'Common Law Protection for Injury to a Person's Reproductive Autonomy' (2019) 135 LQR 635.

3. The *Caparo* Three-Stage Approach to Duty

We have seen that a duty of care is owed only to those who might foreseeably suffer damage as a result of the defendant's negligence. Foreseeability may be regarded as the factual aspect of the duty of care inquiry, though it must be admitted that its role in the duty of care analysis is controversial (see, e.g., Scott, 'The History of Foreseeability' (2019) 72 CLP 287). In any case, the existence of a duty is not simply a matter of factual investigation into the risks foreseeably arising out of the defendant's conduct, as the court must also consider what may be termed the legal aspect of the duty of care inquiry. By emphasising that the recognition of a duty is ultimately a legal as well as a factual question, the courts have been able to introduce restrictions on the scope of liability in what they consider to be particularly problematic areas.

The result is that the existence of a duty of care may still be a live issue despite the fact that the foreseeability of damage to the claimant has been established, but that this will generally be so only in those 'battlegrounds' of the modern law of negligence where the legitimacy of holding a negligent party liable for foreseeable damage suffered by another is disputed. The major such battlegrounds are in liability for psychiatric illness, pure economic loss, omissions and acts of third parties. Detailed consideration of these problem areas can be found in Chapters 7–9. By contrast, in the traditional heartland of the negligence tort—which is to say claims for physical injury to person or property caused by positive acts—the existence of a duty will generally be indisputable, and little or no consideration need be given to the issue once the foreseeability hurdle has been crossed. By the time that *Donoghue v Stevenson* imposed a duty of care on manufacturers of products to their end users, it was already well established, for example, that one road-user owed a duty of care to another (e.g. *Williams v Holland* (1833) 2 LJCP (NS) 190) and that an employer owed a duty of care to their employees (*Smith v Baker & Sons* [1891] AC 325). Indeed, we can go so far as to say that in the modern law of negligence there is a strong presumption that a duty of care will be recognised where a positive act of the defendant foreseeably causes physical harm to the person or property of the claimant, a presumption which can be traced back to the influence of the *Donoghue* decision, even if the ratio of that case was much narrower (see *Stapleton*, pp. 14–15, describing this as 'a well-settled fundamental principle of the common law'). This is only a presumption rather than a rule, however, and there are certain exceptional cases where the courts have denied the existence of a duty of care even where foreseeable physical injury was caused by positive conduct (e.g. where allowing a claim would upset a prior allocation of risks as between parties to a commercial venture: see *Norwich City Council v Harvey* [1989] 1 WLR 828; and see also *Marc Rich and Co AG v Bishop Rock Marine Co Ltd* [1996] AC 211 and *Mulcahy v Ministry of Defence* [1996] QB 732, both noted later, and *Sumner v Colborne* [2019] QB 430, holding that an owner of land adjoining the highway owes no duty of care in respect of vegetation on that land which obstructs the visibility of road users).

Where duty is a live issue, the question of how the courts should determine whether a duty of care was owed is controversial and difficult (see *Plunkett*, ch. 3). In the next extracted case, Lord Bridge summarised the competing approaches to that issue and laid the foundations for an analytical structure that has proven influential.

Caparo Industries plc v Dickman [1990] 2 AC 605

The facts of this case are not relevant for present purposes. They are set out, along with additional extracts, in Chapter 8.III.2.

Lord Bridge of Harwich

In determining the existence and scope of the duty of care which one person may owe to another in the infinitely varied circumstances of human relationships there has for long been a tension between two different approaches. Traditionally the law finds the existence of the duty in different specific situations each exhibiting its own particular characteristics. In this way the law has identified a wide variety of duty situations, all falling within the ambit of the tort of negligence, but sufficiently distinct to require separate definition of the essential ingredients by which the existence of the duty is to be recognised. Commenting on the outcome of this traditional approach, Lord Atkin, in his seminal speech in *Donoghue v Stevenson* [1932] AC 562 at 579–80 observed:

> The result is that the Courts have been engaged upon an elaborate classification of duties. . . . In this way it can be ascertained at any time whether the law recognises a duty, but only where the case can be referred to some particular species which has been examined and classified. And yet the duty which is common to all the cases where liability is established must logically be based upon some element common to the cases where it is found to exist.

It is this last sentence which signifies the introduction of the more modern approach of seeking a single general principle which may be applied in all circumstances to determine the existence of a duty of care. Yet Lord Atkin himself sounds the appropriate note of caution by adding:

> To seek a complete logical definition of the general principle is probably to go beyond the function of the judge, for the more general the definition the more likely it is to omit essentials or to introduce non-essentials.

Lord Reid gave a large impetus to the modern approach in *Home Office v Dorset Yacht Co Ltd* [1970] AC 1004 at 1026–7, where he said:

> In later years there has been a steady trend towards regarding the law of negligence as depending on principle so that, when a new point emerges, one should ask not whether it is covered by authority but whether recognised principles apply to it. *Donoghue v Stevenson* may be regarded as a milestone, and the well-known passage in Lord Atkin's speech should I think be regarded as a statement of principle. It is not to be treated as if it were a statutory definition. It will require qualification in new circumstances. But I think that the time has come when we can and should say that it ought to apply unless there is some justification or valid explanation for its exclusion.

The most comprehensive attempt to articulate a single general principle is reached in the well-known passage from the speech of Lord Wilberforce in *Anns v Merton London Borough* [1978] AC 728 at 751–2:

> Through the trilogy of cases in this House, *Donoghue v Stevenson* [1932] AC 562, *Hedley Byrne & Co Ltd v Heller & Partners Ltd* [1964] AC 465, and *Home Office v Dorset Yacht Co Ltd* [1970] AC 1004, the position has now been reached that in order to establish that a duty of care arises in a particular situation, it is not necessary to bring the facts of that situation within those of previous situations in which a duty of care has been held to exist. Rather the question has to be approached in two stages. First one has to ask whether, as between the alleged wrongdoer and the person who has suffered damage there is a sufficient relationship of proximity or neighbourhood such that, in the reasonable contemplation of the former, carelessness on his part may be likely to cause damage to the latter, in which case a prima facie duty of care arises. Secondly, if the first question is answered affirmatively, it is necessary to consider whether there are any considerations which ought to negative, or to reduce or limit the scope of the duty or the class of person to whom it is owed or the damages to which a breach of it may give rise (see the *Dorset Yacht* case [1970] AC 1004 at 1027, per Lord Reid).

But since *Anns's* case a series of decisions of the Privy Council and of your Lordships' House, notably in judgments and speeches delivered by Lord Keith, have emphasised the inability of any single general principle to provide a practical test which can be applied to every situation to determine whether a duty of care is owed and, if so, what is its scope. . . . What emerges is that, in addition to the foreseeability of damage, necessary ingredients in any situation giving rise to a duty of care are that there should exist between the party owing the duty and the party to whom it is owed a relationship characterised by the law as one of 'proximity' or 'neighbourhood' and that the situation should be one in which the court considers it fair, just and reasonable that the law should impose a duty of a given scope on the one party for the benefit of the other. But it is implicit in the passages referred to that the concepts of proximity and fairness embodied in these additional ingredients are not susceptible of any such precise definition as would be necessary to give them utility as practical tests, but amount in effect to little more than convenient labels to attach to the features of different specific situations which, on a detailed examination of all the circumstances, the law recognises pragmatically as giving rise to a duty of care of a given scope. Whilst recognising, of course, the importance of the underlying general principles common to the whole field of negligence, I think the law has now moved in the direction of attaching greater significance to the more traditional categorisation of distinct and recognisable situations as guides to the existence, the scope and the limits of the varied duties of care which the law imposes. We must now, I think, recognise the wisdom of the words of Brennan J in the High Court of Australia in *Sutherland Shire Council v Heyman* (1985) 60 ALR 1 at 43–4, where he said:

> It is preferable in my view, that the law should develop novel categories of negligence incrementally and by analogy with established categories, rather than by a massive extension of a prima facie duty of care restrained only by indefinable 'considerations which ought to negative, or to reduce or limit the scope of the duty or the class of person to whom it is owed'.

Lord Oliver

> I think it has to be recognised that to search for any single formula which will serve as a general test of liability is to pursue a will-o'-the wisp. The fact is that once one discards, as it is now clear that one must, the concept of foreseeability of harm as the single exclusive test, even a prima facie test, of the existence of the duty of care, the attempt to state some general principle which will determine liability in an infinite variety of circumstances serves not to clarify the law but merely to bedevil its development in a way which corresponds with practicality and common sense . . .

COMMENTARY

Although in *Caparo* Lord Bridge denied that any simple formula could offer assistance as a test of liability, his analysis (contrary to his intentions?) has been understood as laying down a 'three-stage test' for the existence of a duty of care, the ingredients of which are (1) foreseeability, (2) proximity and (3) the fairness, justice and reasonableness of recognising such a duty.

This threefold 'test' should be compared with that of Lord Wilberforce in *Anns* (considered by Lord Bridge in the extract). Taken literally, Lord Wilberforce's approach effectively recognised a presumption of liability in every case where injury to the claimant was reasonably foreseeable, and put on the defendant the onus of identifying reasons of public policy which militated against the imposition of such a duty. For a brief period in the late 1970s and early 1980s, the *Anns* approach was interpreted as giving the courts licence to overturn long-established authorities denying the existence of a duty (e.g. in the area of pure economic loss) on the basis that the mere foreseeability of injury gave rise to a prima facie duty of care (see especially *Junior Books Co Ltd v Veitchi Co Ltd* [1983] 1 AC 520). Eventually, there arose a concern amongst the members of the senior judiciary that 'a too literal application of the well-known observation of Lord Wilberforce in *Anns* . . . may be productive of a failure to have regard to, and to analyse and weigh, all the relevant considerations in considering whether it is appropriate that a duty of care should be imposed' (*Rowling v Takaro Properties Ltd* [1988] AC 473 at 501 per Lord Keith). The result was the so-called 'retreat from *Anns*', in which the courts reverted to a more cautious and pragmatic approach to the recognition of duties of care and re-established many of the old rules denying the existence of any duty at all in particular circumstances. (Especially notable in this regard was *Murphy v Brentwood District Council* [1991] 1 AC 398, which overruled *Anns* itself on the economic loss issue in that case: see further Ch. 8.II.)

Lord Bridge's three-stage 'test' should not be read simply as a new, improved version of the two-stage test in *Anns*, for Lord Bridge added the crucial qualification that the law should be developed only incrementally, by analogy with existing duty situations (see especially his reliance on the passage from the judgment of Brennan J in the High Court of Australia in *Sutherland Shire Council v Heyman* (1985) 60 ALR 1 at 43–4, which he cites in the extract). Hence whereas *Anns* invited courts to disregard previously established limits on the number and breadth of duty situations, the *Caparo* approach gave a crucial role to consideration of precisely how far the authorities have already gone.

In *Robinson v Chief Constable of West Yorkshire Police* [2018] AC 736 (extracted later) the Supreme Court signalled a move away from reliance on the *Caparo* three-stage 'test', while at the same time endorsing the incremental approach to the duty of care question approved by Lord Bridge. At the time of writing, the precise implications of the *Robinson* decision for the way in which courts determine duty of care questions remain uncertain, but there is plenty of evidence that the lower courts are (rightly or wrongly) continuing to use the framework provided by Lord Bridge in *Caparo* to organise their reasoning when faced with duty of care questions (see, e.g., the focus on the 'proximity' of the relationship between the claimant and the defendants in *ABC v St George's Healthcare NHS Trust* [2020] PIQR P13). For that reason, it remains important to understand what the courts have meant—and continue to mean—when they refer to questions of 'proximity' and 'fair, just and reasonableness' in duty cases, even if the significance of these labels is somewhat diminished in the aftermath of *Robinson*.

Proximity

Where Lord Wilberforce's two-stage approach had appeared to treat proximity as no more than a synonym for foreseeability (there was a relationship of proximity if harm was foreseeable), it later came to be viewed as conceptually distinct (see, e.g., *Peabody Donation Fund v Sir Lindsay Parkinson & Co* [1985] AC 210 at 240–1). The effect was to reverse the expansion of duty situations prompted by *Anns* by placing an additional hurdle in the way of a successful claim. Yet the nature of proximity remained elusive. In *Stovin v Wise* [1996] AC 923 at 932, Lord Nicholls observed:

> The *Caparo* tripartite test elevates proximity to the dignity of a separate heading. This formulation tends to suggest that proximity is a separate ingredient, distinct from fairness and reasonableness, and capable of being identified by some other criteria. This is not so. Proximity is a slippery word. Proximity is not legal shorthand for a concept with its own, objectively identifiable characteristics. Proximity is convenient shorthand for a relationship between two parties which makes it fair and reasonable that one should owe the other a duty of care. This is only another way of saying that when assessing the requirements of fairness and reasonableness regard must be had to the relationship of the parties.

Yet it may be argued that 'proximity' has acquired a conventional (though not universal) usage as the umbrella term denoting certain particular types of restriction on the scope of the duty of care. Notable amongst these are restrictions on liability for certain types of loss or damage (e.g. pure economic loss and psychiatric illness) and for nonfeasance (omissions) as opposed to misfeasance (positive acts). Judicial reluctance to recognise a duty of care in these contexts is frequently expressed in legal terms by a finding of no proximity. However, the absence of proximity is frequently asserted in conclusory fashion and is effectively treated as a label to be attached to a conclusion reached on grounds of principle or policy that no liability ought to be imposed in the light of the restrictions considered appropriate in the type of case in question. Certain commentators have however contested the dismissal of proximity as a conclusory label, and have argued that the concept plays an autonomous, and more substantive, role in determining whether a duty of care is owed: see, e.g., Witting, 'Duty of Care: An Analytical Approach' (2005) 25 OJLS 33, arguing that the function of the proximity requirement is to identify those persons most appropriately placed to take care to avoid damage to the claimant, whom he defines—drawing on *Donoghue*—as those whose acts or omissions most closely and directly affect the claimant. (For another sophisticated analysis of the concept, see Kramer, 'Proximity as principles: directness, community norms and the tort of negligence' (2003) 11 Tort L Rev 70; and for a recent judicial defence of proximity see the judgment of Lord Kerr, dissenting, in *Michael v Chief Constable of South Wales Police* [2015] AC 1732.)

More recently, Robertson has argued that the duty of care enquiry involves both interpersonal justice considerations, which focus on the relationship between the parties, and community welfare considerations, which look to the interests of the broader community ('Justice, Community Welfare and the Duty of Care' (2011) 127 LQR 370; 'Rights, Pluralism and the Duty of Care' in *Rights and Private Law*). In this 'pluralist' approach, considerations of justice—broadly, questions relating to autonomy and personal responsibility—are considered under the heading of 'proximity', where the focus is on whether the defendant ought to have had the claimant's interests in mind in determining whether and how to act. Robertson does not deny that making this assessment may sometimes be difficult, but he argues that 'difficult cases call for the exercise of judgment according to certain specified criteria, which focus the court's attention on the particular elements involved in determining this question of interpersonal justice ('Rights, Pluralism and the Duty of Care', p. 451).

Robertson's argument draws on the philosophical distinction between corrective and distributive justice, discussed in Chapter 1.II.1. He accepts that policy—as represented by community welfare considerations—can influence the duty of care question but his argument rests on there being a clear distinction between considerations of interpersonal justice and general welfare. While it may be doubted whether it is possible to draw the boundary as starkly as Robertson does—and he admits it can be blurred at the margins—we agree with him that, at least in broad terms, such a distinction is useful in understanding the nature of 'proximity' and its role relative to 'fairness, justice and reasonableness' as and when these concepts are employed by the courts. (See further on the distinction between principle and policy in this context, Plunkett, 'Principle and Policy in Private Law Reasoning' [2016] CLJ 366; and for a helpful discussion of the proximity concept by the same author, see *Plunkett*, pp. 48–53.)

Fairness, Justice and Reasonableness

Whereas the tendency is to use proximity to limit liability for certain kinds of damage and for nonfeasance and damage caused by acts of third parties, the third stage of the *Caparo* framework serves as a repository for a miscellaneous set of policy arguments, undefined in nature and unlimited in number, which have been invoked in a somewhat ad hoc fashion by the courts. An example that demonstrates the varied nature of the concerns which can be raised under this heading is *Marc Rich and Co AG v Bishop Rock Marine Co Ltd* [1996] AC 211. The defendants, a shipping classification society, were alleged to have been negligent in certifying a particular ship as seaworthy after it had undergone temporary repairs. Shortly after it left port, the vessel sank, causing the plaintiff's cargo to be lost. Despite the fact that the harm suffered was property damage—in respect of which a duty of care is usually owed provided the foreseeability requirement is met—a majority of the House of Lords held that the defendants had owed the plaintiff no duty of care. An international convention ('the Hague Rules') limited the liability of carriers to cargo owners in respect of the loss of cargo, and Lord Steyn argued that to impose a duty of care in negligence on these facts would upset the balance of rights and liabilities struck by the convention. Furthermore, the defendant was an independent and non-profit entity, created and operated for the sole purpose of promoting collective welfare interests, namely the safety of lives and ships at sea, and his Lordship considered that this status might be endangered if a duty of care was recognised. Do you find these reasons convincing? Do you think that the House of Lords would have reached the same result if the sinking of the ship had caused loss of life? (See *Perrett v Collins* [1998] 2 Lloyd's Rep 255 at 264, where Hobhouse LJ said that *Marc Rich* 'should not be regarded as an authority which has a relevance to cases of personal injury'.)

As in *Marc Rich*, considerations of fairness, justice, and reasonableness are usually invoked where it is thought to be undesirable to impose a duty of care because of some policy concern (or concerns). Over the course of time, the most important such concern has been the fear of 'opening up the floodgates of liability'. The 'floodgates argument' has several different dimensions (see generally J. Bell, *Policy Arguments in Judicial Decisions* (Oxford: OUP, 1983), ch. 3), but when it has been deployed in the modern law the main worry has been the risk of overburdening potential defendants with 'liability in an indeterminate amount for an indeterminate time to an indeterminate class' (*Ultramares Corp v Touche, Niven & Co* 174 NE 441 (1931) at 444, per Cardozo J). This version of the floodgates argument has been particularly significant in situations where large numbers of claims could potentially arise out of a single incidence of negligence (consider, for example, the treatment of the 'nervous shock' claims arising out of the Hillsborough stadium disaster: see Ch. 7.III). The underlying concern here may to some extent be a question of fairness: it might be thought unreasonable to expose a defendant to liability grossly disproportionate to their fault. But there is also a worry that the imposition of large and/or indeterminate liabilities might in certain circumstances have detrimental effects on society as a whole (e.g. because it would result in the curtailment of certain socially useful activities which come to be seen as carrying a risk of excessive liabilities).

The floodgates argument often overlaps with a separate argument known as 'overkill', namely the concern that imposing a duty of care might result in detrimentally defensive conduct on the part of potential defendants (see, e.g., *Hill v Chief Constable of West Yorkshire* [1989] AC 53). Although one of the purposes of negligence liability may be to encourage careful behaviour, the fear of liability can also cause potential defendants to take *too much* care, in the form of precautions that are not objectively justified. The most familiar example of 'overkill' is the phenomenon of defensive medicine, whereby it is claimed that health professionals perform unnecessary tests and undertake unnecessary procedures—thereby adding to treatment costs and perhaps exposing patients to new or different risks—for the sole purpose of reducing the likelihood of litigation if the patient comes to harm. The overkill concern has some plausibility, although it may be doubted whether the courts have adequate empirical evidence, or sufficient expertise, to enable them to evaluate these sorts of claims with any degree of scientific rigour, and such judicial reliance as there is on the argument tends to be based on little more than conjecture. As Lord Kerr pointed out in *Crawford Adjusters Ltd v Sagicor Insurance Ltd* [2014] AC 366 at [94], policy conclusions in the legal context 'are not usually the product of empirical research', but are usually 'formed instinctually and constitute, at most, informed guesswork about the impact that the selection of a particular policy course will have'. It followed, his Lordship argued, that where possible policy choices should be 'aligned with principle'. Similarly, in *Michael v Chief Constable of South Wales Police* [2015] AC 1732, Lady Hale (dissenting) highlighted the lack of empirical evidence to support public policy objections to otherwise sound claims, and Lord Toulson admitted (at [121]) that the court had 'no way of judging the likely operational consequences of changing the law of negligence as it applied to the police'.

It is certainly true that empirical studies of overkill effects are few in number and somewhat inconclusive in outcome. For example, one study investigated the impact on fire brigades of the decision in *Capital & Counties plc v Hampshire County Council* [1997] QB 1004, extracted in Chapter 9.II, insofar as it recognised liability for a fire officer's positive act of misfeasance aggravating the damage caused by the fire (Hartshorne, Smith and Everton, '"*Caparo* Under Fire": A Study into the Effects upon the Fire Service of Liability in Negligence' (2000) 63 MLR 502). Only a minority (18 per cent) of local fire brigades altered their practices as a result of this decision, and almost all came to view its impact as beneficial or at least neutral. Research into the response of highway authorities in Ireland and Scotland to the threat of liability for accidents on their roads (Halliday, Ilan and Scott, 'The Public Management of Liability Risks' (2011) 31 OJLS 527) found evidence that they adapted their behaviour in order to comply with their duties of care (e.g. by adopting policies on highway inspection), rather than defensively curtailing their activities, which might in any case be contrary to their statutory responsibilities.

At a general level, it seems that the overkill argument is now on the wane (see, e.g., the sceptical response of a majority of the Supreme Court in the human rights case of *D v Commissioner of Police of the Metropolis* [2019] AC 196). However, one particular version of the argument which retains some force is the 'conflict of interests' concern (sometimes referred to as 'conflict of duties', though this is misleading as any legal duties involved cannot logically conflict). In *D v East Berkshire*, for example, the ruling that welfare professionals owed no duty of care to the parents of children suspected of having been abused was in part based on the potential conflict of interest between child and parent, and the concomitant fear that recognising such a duty might undermine child protection. Had a duty of care been recognised, it would of course only have required the professionals to exercise reasonable care when investigating suspected abuse, which would seem to be in the interests of suspected victims as well as suspected abusers. However, the worry seems to have been that a duty to the parent might subconsciously induce potential defendants to adopt detrimentally defensive practices. The conflict of interests concern was also paramount in *Jain v Trent Strategic Health Authority* [2009] 1 AC 853 (noted by Bagshaw (2009) 17 TLJ 295). The claimants in *Jain* lost their nursing home business after the defendant local health authority made an ex parte, without notice application to a magistrate for cancellation of their registration. By the time the claimants were able to present their side of the story, in the appeal hearing six months later, their business had suffered irreversible damage. Their action for damages failed for lack of a duty of care. According to Lord Scott (delivering the leading opinion) (at [28]):

[W]here action is taken by a state authority under statutory powers designed for the benefit or protection of a particular class of persons, a tortious duty of care will not be held to be owed by the state authority to others whose interests may be adversely affected by an exercise of the statutory power. The reason is that the imposition of such a duty would or might inhibit the exercise of the statutory powers and be potentially adverse to the interests of the class of persons the powers were designed to benefit or protect, thereby putting at risk the achievement of their statutory purpose . . .

Note, however, (1) that the loss suffered by the claimants in *Jain* was purely economic, which arguably provided a quite separate explanation for the no-duty holding (see Ch. 8); and (2) that if the facts of *Jain* occurred today then the claimants might well obtain redress under the Human Rights Act (indeed, the claimants in *Jain* subsequently took their complaint to Strasbourg, where their claim was finally settled for £733,500: *Jain v United Kingdom* [2010] ECHR 411). In *James-Bowen v Commissioner of Police of the Metropolis* [2018] 1 WLR 4021 (noted by Morgan [2019] CLJ 15), the Supreme Court held that the stark differences between the interests of employer and employee strongly suggested that it would not be fair, just and reasonable for the former to owe the latter a duty of care to defend legal proceedings brought by a third party so as to protect the employee's economic or reputational interests. Lord Lloyd-Jones said (at [28]) that '[t]he fact that a duty of care may give rise to conflicting interests will often be a weighty consideration against its imposition', while also cautioning that it was not necessarily conclusive against a duty of care being owed. (See further on the conflict of interests issue, Wilberg, 'Defensive Practice or Conflict of Duties? Policy Concerns in Public Authority Negligence Claims' (2010) 126 LQR 420.)

Policy concerns have underlain the recognition at various times of a number of specific immunities to negligence liability by the courts, albeit that many of the immunities of old have now been abolished. One of the most important of these was that enjoyed by barristers and solicitors in respect of their conduct of litigation, as well as of preliminary matters intimately connected with the conduct of a case in court (see *Rondel v Worsley* [1969] 1 AC 191; *Saif Ali v Sidney Mitchell & Co* [1980] AC 198), which was scrapped in *Arthur J.S. Hall v Simons* [2002] 1 AC 615. Whilst an immunity in favour of witnesses giving evidence as to facts within their knowledge continues to be recognised, albeit with limited scope (*L (A Child) v Reading Borough Council* [2001] 1 WLR 1575; *Darker v Chief Constable of West Midlands Police* [2001] 1 AC 435), expert witnesses instructed by a party to litigation no longer enjoy immunity from liability in negligence to that person (*Jones v Kaney* [2011] 2 AC 398). However, there remain a number of areas where the public policy reasons for denying a duty of care are considered to outweigh other considerations so as to justify an effective immunity from negligence liability. Those acting in a judicial or quasi-judicial capacity, for example, owe no duty of care to persons foreseeably affected by their conduct (see *Sirros v Moore* [1975] QB 118; *Yuen Kun Yeu v Attorney General for Hong Kong* [1988] AC 175), and there is also statutory immunity for financial regulators acting in good faith (Financial Services Act 2012, ss. 25, 33; see Nolan, 'The Liability of Financial Supervisory Authorities' (2013) 4 JETL 190). And it has also been held that members of the armed forces benefit from a so-called 'combat immunity' with regard to acts and omissions in the course of military operations against an enemy in time of war or when armed conflict is imminent (*Mulcahy v Ministry of Defence* [1996] QB 732; *Smith v Ministry of Defence* [2014] AC 52). The principal concern here is that the threat of liability might take soldiers' minds off the task in hand.

Some commentators have argued that the weighing of competing policy interests is not something that the courts, as opposed to the legislature, ought to be doing at all. For example, a leading corrective justice theorist has commented that, if judges insist on making policy choices, 'the legislatures should seize control of the law of negligence, replace the common law with statute, and supplant judges with democratically accountable officials' (*Beever*, p. 8; see also *Stevens*, ch. 14). By contrast, in *Smith v Ministry of Defence* [2014] AC 52 at [170], Lord Carnwath defended the judicial invocation of policy arguments, arguing that 'it remains a proper function of the court, faced with a potential clash between public and private interests, to determine as a matter of policy the limits of any actionable duty of care'. As Plunkett demonstrates in a careful evaluation of the arguments for and against the use of policy arguments in private law reasoning ('Principle and Policy in Private Law Reasoning' [2016] CLJ 366), there is no easy answer to the question of the proper role for policy concerns in the duty of care enquiry, and the debate looks set to continue for some time (see II.4 for the discussion of this issue in the *Robinson* decision). It should in any case be noted that policy arguments may be less central to decisions on duty than is commonly supposed. According to an empirical study of duty determinations in England and Canada, community welfare considerations 'play a relatively minor role in the determination of duty cases at the first instance and intermediate appeal levels' (Robertson, 'Policy-based Reasoning in Duty of Care Cases' (2013) 33 LS 119, 121).

4. The *Robinson* Decision and the Duty of Care

Although the speech of Lord Bridge in *Caparo* has often been interpreted as laying down a three-stage test for the existence of a duty of care, whether any meaningful general duty test is possible is open to question, and Lord Oliver in *Caparo* is not alone in decrying the search for such a test as futile and counter-productive. According to *Plunkett*, p. 214:

> Much of the present difficulty surrounding the duty enquiry can be traced to the persistent belief . . . that a general duty formula, capable of explaining *all* the duty cases, exists. . . . The search for a workable general test has, however, borne little fruit, and the various general duty tests that have been proposed have been subject to considerable limitations, generally due to their highly abstract nature. . . . Despite this, the belief that general duty tests are the way forward persists, and such tests continue to be widely used . . .

Nolan argues that there are two reasons why a general duty test cannot work ('The Duty of Care After *Robinson v Chief Constable of West Yorkshire Police*', in D. Clarry (ed.), *The UK Supreme Court Yearbook, Volume 9: 2017–2018 Legal Year* (London, Appellate Press, 2019) at p. 199):

> The first is that in order to encompass the very wide range of different issues that fall under the notional duty umbrella, the concepts that make up a general duty test must by definition be so abstract ('neighbourhood', 'proximity' etc) that in themselves they provide little or no guidance to the court as to whether a duty of care ought to be recognised. And the other reason why such tests inevitably fail is that their relationship with precedent is problematic and obscure. Taken literally, they seem to leave no room for the doctrine of precedent at all. The judge simply applies the test to the facts, or the 'duty situation', and the test itself produces the right answer. Earlier authority simply goes by the board, as in the worst excesses of the *Anns* era. In practice, of course, a more nuanced approach is taken, but the basic question of how the general test is to be reconciled with the doctrine of precedent never receives a satisfactory answer, because no such answer can be given. Hence the use of a general test in combination with traditional precedent-based reasoning necessarily generates irresolvable tensions and the law inevitably becomes unclear and incoherent.

(For a critique of the *Caparo* three-stage 'test' in particular, see Morgan, 'The Rise and Fall of the General Duty of Care' (2006) 22 PN 206, 209–11.)

It is also noteworthy that (unlike the *Anns* two-stage test) the three-stage *Caparo* test failed to achieve real dominance, particularly at the level of the House of Lords/Supreme Court, where it was used in only 30 per cent of duty of care determinations in the quarter century after *Caparo* was decided (*Plunkett*, p. 186). The apparent scepticism of at least some members of the UK's highest court towards the idea of a *Caparo* three-stage 'test' was confirmed in *Michael v Chief Constable of South Wales Police* [2015] AC 1732 (extracted in Ch. 9.IV) at [102]–[106], when Lord Toulson, giving the majority judgment, launched a scathing attack on the interpretation of *Caparo* as laying down a test for the existence of a duty of care:

> The development of the law of negligence has been by an incremental process rather than giant steps. The established method of the court involves examining the decided cases to see how far the law has gone and where it has refrained from going. From that analysis it looks to see whether there is an argument by analogy for extending liability to a new situation, or whether an earlier limitation is no longer logically or socially justifiable. In doing so it pays regard to the need for overall coherence. Often there will be a mixture of policy considerations to take into account.

From time to time the courts have looked for some universal formula or yardstick, but the quest has been elusive. And from time to time a court has used an expression in explaining its reasons for reaching a particular decision which has then been squashed and squeezed in other cases where it does not fit so aptly . . .

[After referring to the passage from the speech of Lord Bridge in *Caparo* extracted earlier, Lord Toulson continued:] Paradoxically, this passage in Lord Bridge's speech has sometimes come to be treated as a blueprint for deciding cases, despite the pains which the author took to make clear that it was not intended to be any such thing.

Commenting on *Michael*, Goudkamp (2015) 131 LQR 519 argued that the case 'arguably signals a major shift in the approach to determining when a duty of care exists generally' and claimed that Lord Toulson's analysis had given the *Caparo* 'test' 'a very significant knock'. In the next extracted case, Lord Reed took further Lord Toulson's criticism of the way in which the *Caparo* framework was being used 'as a blueprint for deciding cases' and put forward an alternative vision of how duty of care questions should be approached by the courts.

Robinson v Chief Constable of West Yorkshire Police [2018] AC 736

A police officer (DS Willan) had seen a suspect (Williams) apparently dealing drugs in a park in Huddersfield and called for backup with a view to making an arrest. By the time the backup (DC Green, DS Roebuck and PC Dhurmea) arrived, Williams was standing in a busy street in front of a bookmakers he had just visited. DS Willan and PC Dhurmea attempted to effect an arrest, but Williams resisted, and in the ensuing tussle, a passer-by (Mrs Robinson), who was described as a 'relatively frail' woman of 76, was knocked over and injured. When Mrs Robinson sued the police for her injuries, the Recorder found that in the circumstances the decision to arrest Williams at the time and place in question had involved a foreseeable risk that the claimant would be injured and that the officers had acted negligently in the way they had gone about the arrest. However, the Recorder also held that the officers had not owed the claimant a duty of care, since *Hill v Chief Constable of West Yorkshire* [1989] AC 53 conferred on them an immunity from suit in negligence. The Court of Appeal dismissed the claimant's appeal from that decision and also expressed the view that, had it been necessary, they would have overturned the Recorder's finding of negligence on the part of the police. The claimant appealed to the Supreme Court.

Lord Reed

3. As will appear, the simple facts of this case have given rise to proceedings raising issues of general importance. Most of those issues can be decided by applying long-established principles of the law of negligence. The fact that the issues have reached this court reflects the extent to which those principles have been eroded in recent times by uncertainty and confusion. . . .

The proceedings in the Court of Appeal

15. In the Court of Appeal [2014] PIQR P14, para 40, Hallett LJ considered that 'the *Caparo* test [*Caparo Industries plc v Dickman* [1990] 2 AC 605, 617–8] applies to all claims in the modern law of negligence'. In consequence, 'The court will only impose a duty where it considers it right to do so on the facts'. The general principle was that (para 46)

> most claims against the police in negligence for their acts or omissions in the course of investigating and suppressing crime and apprehending offenders will fail the third stage of the *Caparo* test.

That is to say, 'It will not be fair, just and reasonable to impose a duty': para 46. That is because 'the courts have concluded that the interests of the public will not be best served by imposing a duty [on] to individuals': para 46. The answer to counsel's rhetorical question, what would the public think if the police, in the process of arresting criminals, could injure innocent members of the public with impunity, was that 'provided the police act within reason, the public would prefer to see them doing their job and taking drug dealers off the street': para 47. . . .

The issues

20. The issues arising from the judgments below and the parties' submissions can be summarised as follows:

(1) Does the existence of a duty of care always depend on the application of 'the *Caparo* test' to the facts of the particular case?
(2) Is there a general rule that the police are not under any duty of care when discharging their function of investigating and preventing crime? Or are the police generally under a duty of care to avoid causing reasonably foreseeable personal injuries, when such a duty would arise in accordance with ordinary principles of the law of negligence? If the latter is the position, does the law distinguish between acts and omissions: in particular, between causing injury, and protecting individuals from injury caused by the conduct of others?
(3) If the latter is the position, is this an omissions case, or a case of a positive act?
(4) Did the police officers owe a duty of care to Mrs Robinson?
(5) If so, was the Court of Appeal entitled to overturn the recorder's finding that the officers failed in that duty?
(6) If there was a breach of a duty of care owed to Mrs Robinson, were her injuries caused by that breach?

(1) Caparo

21. The proposition that there is a *Caparo* test which applies to all claims in the modern law of negligence, and that in consequence the court will only impose a duty of care where it considers it fair, just and reasonable to do so on the particular facts, is mistaken. As Lord Toulson JSC pointed out in his landmark judgment in *Michael v Chief Constable of South Wales Police* [2015] AC 1732, para 106, that understanding of the case mistakes the whole point of the *Caparo* case, which was to repudiate the idea that there is a single test which can be applied in all cases in order to determine whether a duty of care exists, and instead to adopt an approach based, in the manner characteristic of the common law, on precedent, and on the development of the law incrementally and by analogy with established authorities. . . .

24. In the *Caparo* case [1990] 2 AC 605, 617, Lord Bridge of Harwich noted that, since the *Anns* case, a series of decisions of the Privy Council and the House of Lords, notably in judgments and speeches delivered by Lord Keith of Kinkel (including his speech in *Hill v Chief Constable of West Yorkshire* [1989] AC 53), had emphasised 'the inability of any single general principle to provide a practical test which can be applied to every situation to determine whether a duty of care is owed and, if so, what is its scope'. It is ironic that the immediately following passage in Lord Bridge's speech has been treated as laying down such a test, despite, as Lord Toulson JSC remarked in *Michael's* case, the pains which he took, at 617–8, to make clear that it was not intended to be any such thing . . .

[After quoting from the speech of Lord Bridge in *Caparo*, extracted earlier, and highlighting Lord Bridge's adoption of an incremental approach, 'based on the use of established authorities to provide guidance as to how novel questions' of duty should be decided, his Lordship continued:]

26. Applying the approach adopted in the *Caparo* case, there are many situations in which it has been clearly established that a duty of care is or is not owed: for example, by motorists to other road users, by manufacturers to consumers, by employers to their employees, and by doctors to their patients. As Lord Browne-Wilkinson explained in *Barrett v Enfield London Borough Council* [2001] 2 AC 550, 559–60:

> Once the decision is taken that, say, company auditors though liable to shareholders for negligent auditing are not liable to those proposing to invest in the company . . . that decision will apply to all future cases of the same kind.

Where the existence or non-existence of a duty of care has been established, a consideration of justice and reasonableness forms part of the basis on which the law has arrived at the relevant principles. It is therefore unnecessary and inappropriate to reconsider whether the existence of the duty is fair, just and reasonable (subject to the possibility that this court may be invited to depart from an established line of authority). Nor, a fortiori, can justice and reasonableness constitute a basis for discarding established principles and deciding each case according to what the court may regard as its broader merits. Such an approach would be a recipe for inconsistency and uncertainty, as Hobhouse LJ recognised in *Perrett v Collins* [1999] PNLR 77, 90–1:

> It is a truism to say that any case must be decided taking into account the circumstances of the case, but where those circumstances comply with established categories of liability, a defendant should not be allowed to seek to escape from liability by appealing to some vaguer concept of justice or fairness; the law cannot be re-made for every case. Indeed, the previous authorities have by necessary implication held that it is fair, just and reasonable that the plaintiff should recover in the situations falling within the principles they have applied.

27. It is normally only in a novel type of case, where established principles do not provide an answer, that the courts need to go beyond those principles in order to decide whether a duty of care should be recognised. Following the *Caparo* case, the characteristic approach of the common law in such situations is to develop incrementally and by analogy with established authority. The drawing of an analogy depends on identifying the legally significant features of the situations with which the earlier authorities were concerned. The courts also have to exercise judgement when deciding whether a duty of care should be recognised in a novel type of case. It is the exercise of judgement in those circumstances that involves consideration of what is 'fair, just and reasonable'. As Lord Millett observed in *McFarlane v Tayside Health Board* [2000] 2 AC 59, 108, the court is concerned to maintain the coherence of the law and the avoidance of inappropriate distinctions if injustice is to be avoided in other cases. But it is also 'engaged in a search for justice, and this demands that the dispute be resolved in a way which is fair and reasonable and accords with ordinary notions of what is fit and proper'.

28. . . . . It was in any event made clear in *Michael's* case that the idea that the *Caparo* case established a tripartite test is mistaken.

29. Properly understood, the *Caparo* case thus achieves a balance between legal certainty and justice. In the ordinary run of cases, courts consider what has been decided previously and follow the precedents (unless it is necessary to consider whether the precedents should be departed from). In cases where the question whether a duty of care arises has not previously been decided, the courts will consider the closest analogies in the existing law, with a view to maintaining the coherence of the law and the avoidance of inappropriate distinctions. They will also weigh up the reasons for and against imposing liability, in order to decide whether the existence of a duty of care would be just and reasonable. In the present case, however, the court is not required to consider an extension of the law of negligence. All that

is required is the application to particular circumstances of established principles governing liability for personal injuries.

30. Addressing, then, the first of the issues identified in para 20 above, the existence of a duty of care does not depend on the application of a '*Caparo* test' to the facts of the particular case. In the present case, it depends on the application of established principles of the law of negligence. . . .

[After considering the authorities on the negligence liability of public authorities in general, and of the police in particular, his Lordship continued:]

70. Returning, then, to the second of the issues identified in para 20 above, it follows that there is no general rule that the police are not under any duty of care when discharging their function of preventing and investigating crime. They generally owe a duty of care when such a duty arises under ordinary principles of the law of negligence, unless statute or the common law provides otherwise. Applying those principles, they may be under a duty of care to protect an individual from a danger of injury which they have themselves created, including a danger of injury resulting from human agency, as in the *Dorset Yacht* case [1970] AC 1004 and *Attorney General of the British Virgin Islands v Hartwell* [2004] 1 WLR 1273. Applying the same principles, however, the police are not normally under a duty of care to protect individuals from a danger of injury which they have not themselves created, including injury caused by the conduct of third parties, in the absence of special circumstances such as an assumption of responsibility.

71. In the light of that conclusion, the remaining issues in the case are relatively straightforward and can be dealt with comparatively briefly. . . .

(3) *Is this case concerned with an omission or with a positive act?*

. . . 73. In the present case, the ground of action is liability for damage caused by carelessness on the part of the police officers in circumstances in which it was reasonably foreseeable that their carelessness would result in Mrs Robinson's being injured. Her complaint is not that the police officers failed to protect her against the risk of being injured, but that their actions resulted in her being injured. In short, this case is concerned with a positive act, not an omission.

(4) *Did the police officers owe a duty of care to Mrs Robinson?*

74. It was not only reasonably foreseeable, but actually foreseen by the officers, that Williams was likely to resist arrest by attempting to escape. That is why Willan summoned assistance in the first place, before attempting to arrest Williams, and why it was decided that DS Roebuck and DC Green should be positioned on the opposite side of Williams from Willan and Dhurmea, so as to block his escape route. The place where the officers decided to arrest Williams was a moderately busy shopping street in a town centre. Pedestrians were passing in close vicinity to Williams. In those circumstances, it was reasonably foreseeable that if the arrest was attempted at a time when pedestrians—especially physically vulnerable pedestrians, such as a frail and elderly woman—were close to Williams, they might be knocked into and injured in the course of his attempting to escape. That reasonably foreseeable risk of injury was sufficient to impose on the officers a duty of care towards the pedestrians in the immediate vicinity when the arrest was attempted, including Mrs Robinson.

[After concluding in response to question 5 that the Recorder had been entitled to make a finding of negligence on the part of the police officers and in response to question 6 that Mrs Robinson's injuries had been caused by that negligence, his Lordship continued:]

Conclusion

81. For these reasons, I would allow the appeal, hold that the chief constable is liable in damages to Mrs Robinson, and remit the case for the assessment of damages.

Lord Mance

83. As Lord Reed JSC demonstrates, it is unnecessary in every claim of negligence to resort to the three-stage analysis (foreseeability, proximity and fairness, justice and reasonableness) identified in *Caparo Industries plc v Dickman* [1990] 2 AC 605. There are well-established categories, including (generally) liability for causing physical injury by positive act, where the latter two criteria are at least assumed. The concomitant is that there is, absent an assumption of responsibility, no liability for negligently omitting to prevent damage occurring to a potential victim. This also provides a rationale for the general rule that the police and [Crown Prosecution Service] have no liability for failure, by efficient investigation or pursuit of an actual or potential offence, to prevent a subsequent victim from suffering physical injury at the hands of a third party for whose acts the state is not responsible: *Michael v Chief Constable of South Wales Police (Refuge intervening)* [2015] AC 1732, paras 114–30, 137. Economic loss also falls outside the established category of liability for physical injury, but an assumption of responsibility for economic loss will, as discussed in *Hedley Byrne & Co Ltd v Heller & Partners Ltd* [1964] AC 465, likewise satisfy the latter two *Caparo* criteria. Outside any established category, the law will proceed incrementally, and all three stages of the *Caparo* analysis will be material.

84. It would be unrealistic to suggest that, when recognising and developing an established category, the courts are not influenced by policy considerations. . . .

85. The key to the application of the above principles is to ascertain whether or not a particular situation falls within an established category. Lord Reed JSC treats physical loss resulting foreseeably from positive conduct as constituting axiomatically such a category, whatever the precise circumstances. I accept that principle as generally correct: see e.g. *Alcock v Chief Constable of South Yorkshire Police* [1992] 1 AC 310, 396, per Lord Keith of Kinkel. But I am not persuaded that it is always a safe guide at the margins. I note that Lord Oliver of Aylmerton went no further in the *Caparo* case [1990] 2 AC 605, 632 than to say that, 'in the context of loss caused by physical damage', 'the existence of the nexus between the careless defendant and the injured plaintiff can rarely give rise to any difficulty'. . . .

97. . . . The present case concerns . . . a quite delicate operational decision involving co-ordination between four officers, with a view to the arrest of suspected drug dealers, in a public place. It can be suggested that this raises special considerations, negativing any duty of care. But in my view we should not accept that suggestion. Rather we should now recognise the direct physical interface between the police and the public, in the course of an arrest placing an innocent passer-by or bystander at risk, as falling within a now established area of general police liability for positive negligent conduct which foreseeably and directly inflicts physical injury on the public. On that basis, I would also allow this appeal and restore the judge's judgment.

Lord Hughes gave a concurring judgment. **Baroness Hale** and **Lord Hodge** agreed with Lord Reed.

Appeal allowed.

COMMENTARY

Robinson 'is a landmark in the tort of negligence' (Tofaris [2018] CLJ 454, 454). Of the many significant aspects of the decision, the most important is Lord Reed's discussion of how a court should go about determining whether a duty of care was owed in a particular negligence case. Indeed, it would be no exaggeration to say that Lord Reed's judgment is the most important judicial consideration of the general duty issue since the 1990s, even if, as Tofaris points out (*op. cit.*, 455), his analysis 'was not original, and nor was it meant to be'. According to Cameron (2019) 23 Edin LR 82, 86, Lord Reed's treatment of the question 'amounts to a conscious attempt to bring an end to some serious misconceptions and a fair measure of confusion consequent on *Anns* and arising in the retreat from *Anns*'. Nolan ('The Duty of Care After *Robinson v Chief Constable of West Yorkshire Police*', pp. 174–5) commends the judgment as representing 'a golden opportunity to place future duty of care reasoning on a secure, settled and defensible footing', and argues that 'Lord Reed's approach to the duty question is not only the best of the alternatives available, but the only approach that is consistent with common law method and the rule of law'. Similarly, Tofaris maintains that the judgment 'has resolved several ambiguities in the law of negligence and has provided a blueprint for its future development' (*op. cit.*, 457).

Robinson appears to represent a decisive break with the *Caparo* three-stage test. It seems clear that Lord Reed intended the courts not to use the three-stage framework at all, and instead to use the approach set out in his judgment, which focuses on incremental development of the law by analogy with established authority. Nolan (*op. cit.*, p. 181) emphasises that in his view 'Lord Reed was not merely rejecting the notion that . . . the three-stage test should be used to decide all duty cases', and that he made it 'crystal clear' that he disapproved of the very idea that Lord Bridge had intended to lay down a test, 'or that the supposed test could be of use in deciding *any* duty case' (see also Morgan, 'Nonfeasance and the End of Policy? Reflections on the Revolution in Public Authority Liability' (2019) 35 PN 32, 34). Unfortunately, however some commentators seem to have confused Lord Reed's references to the '*Caparo* approach' to the duty of care issue (namely, the use of precedent-based analogical reasoning) with the three-stage *Caparo* 'test', which leads them to draw the surprising conclusion that in spite of Lord Reed's rather damning dismissal of the three-stage test the correct interpretation of his judgment is that he was merely saying that that test should not be used in *all* negligence cases, but only where a 'novel' duty of care issue arose (see, e.g., Chng, Chan and Goh (2019) 25 TLJ 184, 185). Quite apart from the difficulty of reconciling this view with what Lord Reed actually said, it rests more weight on his references to 'novel cases' than that concept can possibly bear, and if adopted by the courts will doubtless lead to endless arguments as to whether the facts of a given case are 'novel'. After all, whether a case is novel 'depends on how one interprets the existing precedents and draws categories of liability' (*ibid.*, 190), and indeed one can go further, and argue that no meaningful line can be drawn between cases that are novel and those that are not, apart from the usual rules of binding precedent. For these reasons, even the more limited reliance which Lord Reed does in fact place on the idea of a 'novel' case—as one where policy arguments can be invoked—is not free from difficulty, as Morgan points out (*op. cit.*, 41).

According to Lord Reed himself in *N v Poole Borough Council* [2020] AC 780 at [30], '[c]larification of the general approach to establishing a duty of care in novel situations was provided by [*Caparo*] but the decision was widely misunderstood as establishing a general tripartite test'. If in Lord Reed's own opinion *Caparo* did not establish a general test for the duty of care *at all*, then how plausible do you think it is to interpret his judgment in *Robinson* as endorsing the use of a supposed *Caparo* test in novel cases?

In his judgment in *Robinson*, Lord Mance was somewhat less dismissive of the *Caparo* three-stage test than Lord Reed. Although he accepted (at [83]) that it was 'unnecessary in every claim of negligence to resort to the three-stage analysis', this was because there were 'well-established categories, including (generally) liability for causing physical injury by positive act', where the elements of proximity and 'fair, just and reasonableness' were 'at least assumed'. And while he agreed with Lord Reed that outside these categories the law proceeded 'incrementally', he tied this process of incremental development to the *Caparo* test, saying that in such cases 'all three stages of the *Caparo* analysis will be material'.

Nolan (*op. cit.*, p. 175) considers that 'the real question' is not whether *Robinson* is a 'welcome return to orthodoxy, but whether courts at all levels will be prepared to abandon other ways of reasoning'. In particular, he warns that 'the allure of general duty tests is such that some resistance' to Lord Reed's approach is to be expected. But while it is possible to identify decisions in which the *Caparo* test has been used post-*Robinson*, whether as a result of ignorance of that decision and its implications or otherwise (e.g. *Kalma v African Minerals Ltd* [2020] EWCA Civ 144 at [138]), so far it seems that for the most part the courts are following Lord Reed's lead. The incremental approach laid down in *Robinson* has been employed by the lower courts in cases such as *Sumner v Colborne* [2019] QB 430 and *HXA v Surrey County Council* [2021] EWHC 250 (QB), and was unanimously endorsed by the Supreme Court itself in *James-Bowen v Commissioner of Police of the Metropolis* [2018] 1 WLR 4021 at [23] and *Darnley v Croydon Health Services NHS Trust* [2019] AC 831 at [15]–[16], where Lord Lloyd-Jones reaffirmed that English law 'has abandoned the search for a general principle capable of providing a practical test applicable in every situation in order to determine whether a duty of care is owed'.

The decision in *Darnley* is a useful supplement to *Robinson* insofar as it provides guidance to the lower courts as to what amounts to a duty of care issue in the first place and illustrates how the *Robinson* approach works in cases that fall within established categories. The claimant had attended the Accident and Emergency Department (A&E) of the defendant's hospital complaining of a headache after being hit on the head by an unknown assailant. Although he told the receptionist who booked him in what had happened and that he thought that he had suffered a head injury, she told him that he would have to wait for up to four to five hours to be seen. The claimant waited for twenty minutes, after which he left without telling anybody that he was doing so. Later that same evening, he collapsed and was taken back to the same hospital. Despite being operated on as an emergency case, he suffered grave and disabling brain damage. Had the claimant not left A&E, then the hospital's triage system meant that he should in fact have been seen by a nurse within thirty minutes, and he sought damages on the ground that the receptionist had negligently misled him as to the likely waiting time, and that if she had given him accurate information he would have remained in A&E and been seen by a doctor earlier and hence made a complete or near-complete recovery.

Both the trial judge and a majority of the Court of Appeal had held as a matter of law that an A&E receptionist did not owe a patient a duty of care to protect them against injury caused by their failure to wait to be seen. The receptionist's job was to take the details of patients and to show them where to wait. Although they might provide information about waiting times to patients, this was just as a courtesy and it would not be fair, just and reasonable to impose a duty of care in this regard as it would probably mean that hospitals instructed their receptionists not to give such information at all. On appeal to the Supreme Court the reasoning in the lower courts was subjected to stinging criticism, which echoed a note on the decision of the Court of Appeal in which Goudkamp [2017] CLJ 481 had argued that *Darnley* was not a case on duty of care at all, but a case on breach. Applying *Robinson*, Lord Lloyd-Jones, who gave the sole judgment, said that the case fell squarely within an established duty of care category. It was well established that hospitals with A&E departments owed a duty of care to patients who presented themselves complaining of illness or injury and in the instant case that duty had arisen after the claimant had been booked in by the receptionist.

The duty in question was to take reasonable care not to cause physical injury to the patient and this extended to the provision of information which might (if inaccurate) foreseeably cause injury. And while the distinction between medical and non-medical staff might be highly pertinent when deciding whether that duty had been breached, the courts below had been mistaken in attaching significance to it when deciding whether a duty of care was owed in the first place, as the obligations of hospitals had to be considered in the round. On the facts, the Supreme Court held that the receptionist had been negligent and that this had caused the brain damage, so that the claimant was entitled to recover. (It was argued, plausibly enough, that the claimant's decision to leave had been a *novus actus interveniens*, but this possibility was rather summarily dismissed.)

Do you agree with the Supreme Court's criticisms of the reasoning of the lower courts in *Darnley*? In particular, do you think that they were wrong to countenance the possibility that as a matter of law a hospital should not be liable for information provided to a patient by a receptionist where it was not the receptionist's job to provide such information? Would the result have been different if the information had been given by a hospital porter in response to a query from the claimant, or by someone working in the hospital café?

The Relevance of Policy

Robinson is also important because of its implications for the role of policy arguments in duty of care cases. As we saw in II.3, this is a controversial question on which judges and commentators have sometimes violently disagreed. In *Robinson*, Lord Reed sought to explain away earlier decisions in which policy arguments had been deployed to exclude liability—in particular in cases brought against public authorities—as straightforward examples of the application of general negligence principles, such as the omissions rule. And in a section of his judgment not extracted above, where he was responding to some of Lord Hughes's observations, Lord Reed made the following more general comment about the role of policy in negligence adjudication (at [69]):

[I]t is important to understand that [discussions of policy considerations] are not a routine aspect of deciding cases in the law of negligence, and are unnecessary when existing principles provide a clear basis for the decision, as in the present appeal . . . The absence of a duty towards victims of crime, for example, does not depend merely on a policy devised by a recent generation of judges in relation to policing: it is based on the application of a general and long-established principle that the common law imposes no liability to protect persons against harm caused by third parties, in the absence of a recognised exception such as a voluntary assumption of responsibility.

At the same time, Lord Reed made it clear that he was not saying that policy concerns had no place in the duty of care enquiry: on the contrary, while the courts were not 'policy-making bodies in the sense in which that can be said of the Law Commission or government departments', he accepted that 'the exercise of judgement about the potential consequences of a decision' had a part to play when a court was asked to decide whether a novel duty of care existed (*ibid.*), at least where 'established principles' did not provide a clear answer to the duty question (at [42]).

It was this aspect of Lord Reed's analysis that provoked the strongest reaction from Lord Mance and Lord Hughes. According to Lord Mance (at [84]), the reality was that 'in recognising the existence of any generalised duty in particular circumstances [the courts] are making policy choices'. Similarly, Lord Hughes said (at [113]) that earlier judicial reliance on policy considerations was 'simply too considered, too powerful and too authoritative in law to be consigned to history', and that it was not possible to treat such considerations as 'no more than supporting arguments'.

There is a good deal of truth in Lord Reed's point that many of the cases in which policy considerations were mentioned by the judges either were, or could have been, decided in the same way by reference to general negligence principles, so that the discussion of policy was otiose. This insight is borne out by recent empirical research into the use of policy reasoning by the House of Lords/Supreme Court in the period 1985–2015, which shows that only in a small minority of duty of care cases in which reliance was placed upon policy considerations were they solely determinative of the outcome of the duty enquiry (*Plunkett*, p. 203). Perhaps the best example of this phenomenon is *Hill v Chief Constable of West Yorkshire* [1989] AC 53 (see later), where the discussion of policy in Lord Keith's speech consisted of a single paragraph, which began with the words 'That is sufficient for the disposal of the appeal' (at 63). On the other hand, the same empirical research also accords with Lord Mance's observation in *Robinson* that there are undoubtedly *some* earlier cases at the highest level where it was accepted that a duty of care could be denied on policy grounds, even if established principles pointed to the existence of a duty. A good example of such a decision is *Smith v Ministry of Defence*, where (as we saw in II.3) the House of Lords upheld the existence of a 'combat immunity' on the ground that imposing a duty of care on members of the armed forces might hamper military operations in wartime. This immunity means that even in cases where a defendant combatant causes foreseeable physical injury or physical damage to property by their positive conduct (and where one would therefore expect there to be a duty of care in accordance with the general principles upheld in *Robinson*) no liability in negligence can arise. With respect, therefore, Lord Reed's dismissal of *Smith* (at [28]) as a case that raised 'a novel legal issue' and which 'did not concern an established category of liability' rings rather hollow.

Turning to the 'ought' question of the role that policy should play in duty of care determinations, it is noteworthy that Lord Reed's treatment of policy concerns as legitimate, but of secondary significance, accords with much current academic thinking on that question (see, e.g., S. Perry, 'The Role of Duty of Care in a Rights-Based Theory of Negligence Law' in A. Robertson and H.W. Tang (eds), *The Goals of Private Law* (Oxford: Hart, 2009) 83–91; and Robertson, 'Justice, Community Welfare and the Duty of Care' (2011) 127 LQR 370). Having said that, the concurring justices clearly considered that a more expansive role for policy was appropriate, and their objections to Lord Reed's analysis have been echoed by Morgan (*op. cit.*, 32–3), who describes it as a 'dessicated approach' to the duty of care issue which represents a 'radical departure from three decades of case law' by rendering policy reasoning 'unnecessary and even impermissible' within established categories of case. In particular, he expresses concern that:

> [I]f overt consideration of factors for and against liability (policy) is prohibited it may nevertheless continue to exert unacknowledged influence over the development of the formal (principled) legal categories. This would reduce the transparency of legal development. . . . Let us accept that there is no need for elaborate policy reasoning in routine negligence cases. Also, policy reasoning can be done badly and perhaps it often is. The solution is to criticise bad policy reasoning and call for a more rigorous approach. Seeking to prohibit it altogether across a very wide class of cases risks throwing out baby, bathwater, cradle and all.

By contrast, Chng, Chan and Goh (*op. cit.*, 190) are more welcoming of this aspect of Lord Reed's judgment, commenting that the 'key advantage of limiting policy considerations in this fashion is consistency and certainty in legal reasoning, which will in turn contribute to the legitimacy of adjudicative outcomes'. Do you agree?

It will be some time before the full significance of *Robinson* for the role of policy in duty cases becomes clear, and much is likely to rest on what the courts regard as 'novel' cases.

In Morgan's opinion (at 53) 'such cases are more common' than Lord Reed contemplates, and hence 'the apparent attempt to limit policy reasoning may not change much in the end'.

Negligence Actions against the Police

More narrowly, the *Robinson* decision is also a significant authority on the liability of public authorities (on which see III.1) and in particular actions against the police. A key earlier authority on such claims is *Hill v Chief Constable of West Yorkshire* [1989] AC 53, where the House of Lords dismissed an action by the parents of the last victim of the 'Yorkshire Ripper', Peter Sutcliffe. The action alleged that there had been negligence in the conduct of the police investigation of earlier murders committed by Sutcliffe and that this had resulted in the police failing to apprehend Sutcliffe at an earlier date, which would have prevented the murder of the claimants' daughter. The primary basis on which their Lordships struck out the claim as disclosing no cause of action was that there was no proximity between the parties, since it was a case involving the deliberate criminal conduct of a third party (and also an omissions case, although this latter aspect was not emphasised in the reasoning). However, a number of policy grounds were also said to militate against a duty of care being owed. Lord Keith expressed these as follows (at 63):

In some instances the imposition of liability may lead to the exercise of a function being carried on in a detrimentally defensive frame of mind . . . Further it would be reasonable to expect that if potential liability were to be imposed it would be not uncommon for actions to be raised against police forces on the ground that they had failed to catch some criminal as soon as they might have done, with the result that he went on to commit further crimes. While some such actions might involve allegations of a simple and straightforward type of failure . . . others would be likely to enter deeply into the general nature of a police investigation, as indeed the present action would seek to do. The manner of conduct of such an investigation must necessarily involve a variety of decisions to be made on matters of policy and discretion, for example as to which particular line of inquiry is most advantageously to be pursued and what is the most advantageous way to deploy the available resources. Many such decisions would not be regarded by the courts as appropriate to be called in question, yet elaborate investigation of the facts might be necessary to ascertain whether or not this was so. A great deal of police time, trouble and expense might be expected to have to be put into the preparation of the defence to the action and the attendance of witnesses at the trial. The result would be a significant diversion of police manpower and attention from their most important function, that of the suppression of crime.

The *Hill* decision was subsequently interpreted as authority for a principle that the police could not in general be held liable for careless conduct in investigating crime (see, e.g., *Brooks v Commissioner of Police of the Metropolis* [2005] 1 WLR 1495). In *Smith v Chief Constable of Sussex Police* [2009] 1 AC 225, the limits of this principle were tested. The claimant was the victim of a violent assault by his former partner and suffered serious physical injuries as a result. Prior to the attack, the claimant had been in contact with the police about a stream of violent, abusive and threatening messages, including death threats, which had been sent to him by his ex-partner, but it was alleged that the police had failed to respond to his concerns in an appropriate manner. A majority of the House of Lords held that the judge at first instance had been right to strike out the claim in negligence as having no real prospect of success. While Lord Brown (at [125]–[126]) accepted that the facts in the *Smith* case were 'really very strong', his Lordship could find 'no satisfactory basis upon which to distinguish this class of case' from *Hill* and *Brooks*. Conversely, in *Swinney v Chief Constable of Northumbria* [1997] QB 464, it was held that the police *were* under a duty of care in respect of the physical wellbeing of an informer to whom they had assumed a specific responsibility in this regard. Nor did the *Hill* principle apply in cases of positive acts of misfeasance which directly caused physical injury to the claimant (see, e.g., *Marshall v Osmond* [1983] 2 All ER 225; *Rigby v Chief Constable of Northamptonshire* [1985] 1 WLR 1242). Indeed, this had been made clear by Lord Keith in the *Hill* case itself (at 59), when he said that '[t]here is no question that a police officer, like anyone else, may be liable in tort to a person who is injured as a direct result of his acts or omissions'.

In *Michael*, Lord Toulson played down the policy aspect of the *Hill* principle and justified it by reference to the fact that English negligence law rarely imposes positive obligations in the absence of a prior assumption of responsibility (see Ch. 9.IV). It followed that the principle was not an 'immunity', which his Lordship defined (at [44]) as 'an exemption based on a defendant's status from a liability imposed by the law on others', but simply the application of ordinary private law principles to the police, to whom the general law of tort applied as much as to anyone else.

Since the decision of the Court of Appeal in *Robinson* had preceded *Michael* and was difficult to square with Lord Toulson's denial that the *Hill* principle conferred an immunity on the police, the success of the claimant's appeal was not altogether surprising. In the Supreme Court, Lord Reed reiterated (at [45]) that 'the police are subject to liability for causing personal injury in accordance with the general law of tort'. It followed, with reference to negligence in particular, that the police were 'generally under a duty of care to avoid causing personal injury where such a duty would arise according to ordinary principles of the law of negligence' (at [67]). Hence the police could be liable in negligence where by their positive conduct they had caused reasonably foreseeable personal injury or property damage. However, it also followed from the application of those ordinary principles to the police that their public duty to enforce the law and investigate crime did not generate a private law duty to protect individual members of the public from the criminal conduct of third parties. It was this rule that explained the ruling in the *Hill* case and Lord Keith's reliance on public policy arguments had been unnecessary to the decision in the case, which had 'now to be understood in the light of the later authorities' (at [54]). It followed that *Hill* was not 'authority for the proposition that the police enjoy a general immunity from suit in respect of anything done by them in the course of investigating or preventing crime' (at [55]). Although this principle is itself simple enough, Lord Reed's efforts to reconcile it with all of the earlier authorities were not always persuasive (see Nolan, *op. cit.*, at pp. 187–8).

Assumption of Responsibility

We have already come across the idea that a duty of care can be based on an 'assumption of responsibility', and the importance of this concept was reiterated in *Robinson*. The concept will be discussed in more detail in later chapters dealing with the types of case in which an assumption of responsibility is capable of generating a duty of care, namely pure economic loss cases (see Ch. 8.III); cases involving omissions and third parties (Ch. 9); and, perhaps, claims for psychiatric injury (see Ch. 7.IV). Nevertheless, it will be useful at this point to provide a brief overview of the concept.

Assumption of responsibility first came to prominence in *Hedley Byrne & Co Ltd v Heller & Partners Ltd* [1964] AC 465 (extracted in Ch. 8.III), a case of alleged negligent misstatement causing pure economic loss, but the concept is now of more general significance, and extends beyond the provision of information and advice to encompass the negligent provision of services. The basic idea of an assumption of responsibility is that the defendant has taken on a task or job of some kind for the claimant, such as, for example, giving the claimant investment advice, or looking after the claimant's house while they are away.

Where the defendant has taken on a task for the claimant in this way, the law presumes that the defendant is also implicitly taking on the legal duty to perform that task with due care, unless there is a good reason to rebut this presumption, such as that the defendant took on the task or job in an informal or social context, or that the defendant expressly disclaimed legal responsibility. Whether reliance on the part of the claimant is also required for an assumption of responsibility to arise is a contested question, but the balance of authority suggests that, while assumptions of responsibility are in fact often accompanied by some form of reliance, this is not necessary, and that the claimant may even be unaware of the fact that a responsibility has been assumed. Hence, for example, if a doctor stops to treat a person who has collapsed in the street, the doctor comes under a duty of care even if the person is unconscious and so entirely oblivious to their presence (see by analogy *Barrett v Ministry of Defence* [1995] 1 WLR 1217, extracted in Ch. 9.II).

This summary of the concept (which draws on Nolan, 'Assumption of Responsibility: Four Questions' (2019) 72 CLP 123) is broadly consistent with the analysis of Lord Reed in *N v Poole Borough Council* [2020] AC 780, a case decided after *Robinson* and concerned with the negligence liability of child protection agencies (extracted in Ch. 9.IV). According to Lord Reed in *Poole* (at [68]):

[T]he principle [of assumption of responsibility] has been applied in a variety of situations in which the defendant provided information or advice to the claimant with an undertaking that reasonable care would be taken as to its reliability (either express or implied, usually from the reasonable foreseeability of the claimant's reliance upon the exercise of such care) . . . or undertook the performance of some other task or service for the claimant with an undertaking (express or implied) that reasonable care would be taken.

(Cf. *1688782 Ontario Inc v Maple Leaf Foods Inc* (2020) 450 DLR (4th) 181 at [33].)

Lord Reed made it clear in *Poole* that it is no bar to the finding of an assumption of responsibility in a claim against a public authority that at the relevant time the authority was exercising a statutory function. On the contrary, it would frequently be the case that a public body which offered a service to the public assumed a responsibility to those using the service in question. Examples included an education authority accepting a pupil into one of its schools, or a National Health Service hospital admitting a patient who had presented themselves at the hospital's A&E department, as in the *Darnley* case (noted earlier).

It will be apparent that the assumption of responsibility concept has some obvious parallels with contractual obligations, in that an obligation that arises out of an assumption of responsibility is voluntarily incurred, and such an obligation is owed to a particular person, rather than to the world in general. However, there are also important differences between contract and assumption of responsibility, such as that no consideration is required for an assumption of responsibility to generate a legal obligation, and that while breach of contract is actionable per se (i.e. without proof of loss or damage), the breach of an assumed obligation of care is—as in other negligence cases—actionable only if it causes loss or damage of some kind to the claimant.

Two final observations should be made about assumption of responsibility. One is that it is a 'somewhat elastic' concept (*Chief Constable of Essex Police v Transport Arendonk BVBA* [2020] EWHC 212 (QB) at 92), and the outcome of its application to particular facts can therefore be difficult to predict. And the other is that the concept is a fiercely contested one. In particular, many commentators have questioned the coherence and utility of the concept when employed in duty of care cases, arguing that it generally serves to obfuscate rather than illuminate. (See, e.g., A. Robertson and J. Wang, 'The Assumption of

Responsibility' in K. Barker et al. (eds), *The Law of Misstatements: 50 Years on from Hedley Byrne v Heller* (Oxford: Hart, 2015).) In Nolan (*op. cit.*) one of us has defended assumption of responsibility against the criticisms made of it—which, it is argued, are generally based on misunderstandings of the idea—and sought to demonstrate that the concept is a meaningful and distinctive basis on which to impose negligence liability. However, in an article published in the wake of *Robinson*, Morgan renewed the attack, expressing regret that the Supreme Court had not considered the criticisms of the concept, and reiterating them in stringent terms (*op. cit.*, 50):

It might seem sensible enough for tort law to recognise exceptional liabilities when a defendant expressly assumes them. But 'assumption of responsibility' extends way beyond that narrow literal meaning. Application of the doctrine shows frequent judicial willingness to 'infer' such 'voluntary assumption'. The real question becomes when and why such an inference will take place: any idea that the defendant has actually, voluntarily accepted liabilities fades into the background. This is not a harmless fiction. It conceals the real reasons for the decision, and obfuscates the basis of liability. Like other tort duties the ones in this area are typically *imposed* by law—yet they masquerade as 'voluntarily assumed'.

It is difficult to form an opinion on the value of assumption of responsibility as a ground for the imposition of a duty of care without an understanding of its detailed operation in particular duty contexts, but when encountering discussion of it in later chapters, it would be a good idea to keep these debates in mind, and to consider which of the competing views of the concept you find most persuasive.

See further on the role of assumption of responsibility in the duty of care enquiry, the essays in Barker et al. (*op. cit.*) and Plunkett, pp. 58–65; 131–9.

Applying the *Robinson* Approach to Duty

The approach to the determination of duty of care questions in *Robinson* is standard common law reasoning, working with the relevant authorities to determine whether the case is covered by binding precedent, and, if not, reasoning by analogy and by reference to relevant considerations in order to decide whether or not a duty of care is owed. Of course the reasoning process may be more or less straightforward in a particular case, and there are bound to be legitimate disagreements about the considerations that a court should take into account, and how much weight should be accorded to them (see the earlier discussion of policy considerations). But there is nothing particularly mysterious about the task that the courts have been given, and nor is there any reason why they should not be able to perform it successfully.

For that to happen, the authorities must in our view be organised into categories (cf. Cameron, *op. cit.*, 87, arguing that Lord Reed's approach deliberately eschews the language of categories; but is it really possible to reason by analogy without some form of categorisation?). And to understand how the process of categorisation works, reference must be made to the key case types that fall outside the *Donoghue v Stevenson* paradigm of positive conduct directly causing physical harm, where we saw (in III.2) that a duty of care is presumed. These key case types concern omissions, deliberate intervening acts, psychiatric injury and pure economic loss. Although these four types of case give rise to the most general categories of earlier authority, the process of categorisation does not stop there. In a psychiatric injury case, for example, different rules apply to primary victims, secondary victims, victims of work stress and so on (see Ch. 7). And where a case raises a duty issue that does not fall within any of the four key categories (such as the 'combat immunity' question), then a narrower line of authority relating to that particular problem will constitute the relevant body of case law.

Once the relevant category or sub-category has been identified, the judge must then turn to the case law in that category and engage in the process of reasoning from precedent, and by the use of analogy. If a case falls into more than one category (e.g. because it concerns an omission that caused pure economic loss), then the precedents in each category must be considered before a duty determination can be made. As McHugh J said in the Australian case of *Crimmins v Stevedoring Industry Finance Committee* (1999) 200 CLR 1 at [72]–[73], '[i]n determining whether the instant case is analogous to existing precedents, the reasons why the material facts in the precedent cases did or did not found a duty will ordinarily be controlling', and 'the precedent cases have to be examined to reveal their bases in principle and policy'. To the extent that the precedents do not show the way forward, an exercise of judgement will need to be made as to whether negligence liability ought to be extended to the new situation. In an analysis that predates *Robinson*, but which is largely consistent with it, Plunkett argues that the notional element of the duty enquiry is best understood as consisting of two discrete stages (*Plunkett*, pp. 215–6):

> The first stage requires the identification of a broad 'situation' or 'category of case' that the facts of the case fall within. . . . the situations should reference the kind of harm suffered, the way it occurred, and the relationship of the parties to each other. The various duty situations are best understood as consisting of five broad categories, three inclusionary [meaning that the starting assumption is that a duty is owed] (physical injury, property damage, and psychiatric injury) and two exclusionary [meaning that the starting assumption is that a duty is not owed] (omissions and pure economic loss), subject to a number of narrow exclusionary and inclusionary exceptions. . . . If the court determines that the relevant situation does not give rise to a notional duty, it must still ascertain whether, despite reasons why the broad situation should not attract a notional duty, a notional duty should nevertheless exist because, on the facts of the case, the defendant assumed a responsibility towards the claimant. . . . [If so], the claimant will overcome the otherwise exclusionary nature of the category and a notional duty will exist.

Again, it will be difficult for you to assess how convincing this suggested approach to the determination of notional duty questions is at this point, but it may be useful to keep it in mind when you encounter more detailed discussion of the four key case types in Chapters 7–9 of this book.

III. Negligence and Public Law

1. The Negligence Liability of Public Authorities

(a) The Equality Principle

A central tenet of the English legal tradition, most commonly associated with the constitutional scholar Dicey, is the idea that public authorities and public officials are subject to the ordinary law as administered in the ordinary courts. Indeed, for Dicey, this 'equality principle' was one of the three pillars of the rule of law (A. V. Dicey, *Introduction to the Study of the Law of the Constitution*, 8th edn (London: Macmillan, 1915), p. 114):

> [W]hen we speak of the 'rule of law' as a characteristic of our country, [we mean] not only that with us no man is above the law, but (what is a different thing) that here every man, whatever be his rank or condition, is subject to the ordinary law of the realm and amenable to the jurisdiction of the ordinary tribunals.

An early example of the operation of the equality principle is *Mersey Docks and Harbour Board Trustees v Gibbs* (1866) LR 1 HL 93, where a ship had been damaged when it collided with a mud bank at the entrance to the defendants' dock. The defendants were held liable for the damage in negligence, and appealed to the House of Lords on the ground that they were a public body entrusted by Parliament with the task of maintaining the docks. It was held that the defendants' status did not absolve them from their common law duty to exercise reasonable care. According to Blackburn J, who delivered the opinion of the learned judges advising the House ((1866) LR 1 HL 93 at 110):

> The proper rule of construction of such statutes is that, in the absence of something to shew a contrary intention, the Legislature intends that the body, the creature of the statute, shall have the same duties, and that its funds shall be rendered subject to the same liabilities as the general law would impose on a private person doing the same things.

It follows that English law begins from the starting point that when exercising its public law functions a public authority is subject to the same private law obligations as any other legal actor, and so can be liable in tort if in the course of its performance of those functions it violates a private law right. Examples of the operation of this principle include many cases in which the police have been sued for battery and/or false imprisonment after making an unlawful arrest (see Ch. 2), but the principle also applies in negligence, as the Supreme Court forcefully reiterated in *Robinson v Chief Constable of West Yorkshire* [2018] AC 736 (extracted in II.4), where Lord Reed said (at [32]–[33]):

> At common law, public authorities are generally subject to the same liabilities in tort as private individuals and bodies . . . Accordingly, if conduct would be tortious if committed by a private person or body, it is generally tortious if committed by a public authority . . . It follows that public authorities are generally under a duty of care to avoid causing actionable harm in situations where a duty of care would arise under ordinary principles of the law of negligence, unless the law provides otherwise.

Furthermore, after a period of doubt, it is now clear from decisions such as *Gorringe v Calderdale Metropolitan Borough Council* [2004] 1 WLR 1057 and *Michael v Chief Constable of South Wales Police* [2015] AC 1732 that the equality principle cuts both ways, at least in the United Kingdom (the position is otherwise in Australia and Canada). It follows that as a matter of private law analysis, public bodies and officials are, generally speaking, not subject to any *additional* liabilities by virtue of their status, so that 'public authorities, like private individuals and bodies, are generally under no duty of care to prevent the occurrence of harm' (*Robinson* at [34], per Lord Reed). Hence, for example, the police are no more liable in negligence for failing to protect a person from criminal conduct than a private individual would be (see the *Michael* decision; but note that, as we shall see in III.2, in such a case the police might be liable in damages under the Human Rights Act 1998). This 'negative' aspect of the equality principle is very controversial and is discussed in more detail in Chapter 9. In any case the end result is that, as things now stand, 'the law of negligence generally applies to public authorities in the same way that it applies to private individuals and bodies' (*Robinson* at [40], per Lord Reed).

The equality principle has never been absolute and there are a number of exceptions to it. One is the tort of misfeasance in public office, a cause of action which lies only against a 'public officer', in cases where such an officer acts in bad faith (see further, *Winfield & Jolowicz*, paras 8–024ff). Furthermore, we saw in II.3 that there are several instances in which the courts have recognised a special immunity from negligence liability, and some of these—most notably judicial immunity and 'combat immunity'—are by their very nature limited to public defendants. Nor should it be forgotten that historically English law adopted the maxim that 'the King can do no wrong', with the result that those exercising governmental functions in the name of the Crown (i.e. the central government) benefitted from a general immunity from tortious liability, although this immunity was almost completely abolished by the Crown Proceedings Act 1947. (For other exceptions to the equality principle, see K. Oliphant, 'The Liability of Public Authorities in England and Wales' in K. Oliphant (ed.), *The Liability of Public Authorities in Comparative Perspective* (Cambridge: Intersentia, 2016), p. 128.)

(b) Public Law Controls

Although in recent times the English courts have reasserted both aspects of the equality principle, this followed a period in which they departed from the negative aspect of the principle in order to impose liability in negligence on public authorities in cases where a private individual would not have been liable, generally because the defendant was being sued for an omission. This period began with the landmark decision in *Anns* (discussed in II.3), where the House of Lords held that a local authority could be liable for negligence in the exercise of its statutory powers to inspect the foundations of buildings under construction. The *Anns* ruling heralded the recognition of so-called 'unique public duties' in English negligence law, which is to say, common law duties owed by a public authority which are grounded on a statutory power conferred (or a statutory duty imposed) on the authority, and which are not analogous to the common law duties owed by private parties. Coupled with the relatively liberal approach to duties of care more generally that was ushered in by *Anns*, this opened the door to extensive litigation against public authorities, who were particularly attractive targets for negligence actions, since their pockets were deep enough to bear substantial awards of damages, and the array of powers and duties under which they operated made them vulnerable to a wide variety of allegations of both misfeasance and nonfeasance. Fearing the depletion of public funds, a detrimental impact on the performance of public functions and undue interference in matters of government, the courts responded to the opening up of potentially very extensive public authority liability by borrowing a range of control mechanisms from public law in order to limit the scope of the private law duties of care owed by public bodies. With the revival of the negative aspect of the equality principle in recent decades, coupled with a more general retrenchment of negligence liability in areas such as economic loss, some of these special limits on public authority liability have now passed into history, while the practical significance of those that remain is much reduced. Nevertheless, a brief account of these controls is appropriate, both because it is difficult to understand the development of negligence law over the course of last fifty years or so without an appreciation of them, and because some of the restrictions in question are still capable of affecting the outcome of negligence actions against public bodies.

Before we turn to consider these controls, however, two preliminary points should be made. The first is that there are many cases in which negligence claims against public bodies do not raise issues of a specifically public character, such as an action by a public sector worker against their employer alleging a dangerous workplace environment, or an action arising out of the negligent driving of a local government employee. In cases of this kind, the fact that the defendant happens to be a public authority is simply irrelevant. Hence it was only where the claim arose out of the performance of a specifically public function—typically involving allegations of either negligent exercise of, or failure to exercise, a statutory duty or power—that the control mechanisms borrowed from public law had any traction. And the second point is that, quite regardless of these control mechanisms, it is a truism that when considering whether to impose a duty of care on a public authority applying the general approach to duty outlined earlier, the court may find that its analysis is to some extent shaped by the special position occupied by the defendant, since 'the question whether there is such a common law duty and if so its ambit, must be profoundly influenced by the statutory framework within which the acts complained of were done' (*X (Minors) v Bedfordshire CC* [1995] 2 AC 633 at 739, per Lord Browne-Wilkinson). For instance, the statutory framework under which the defendant operates may make it plausible to argue that it has a relationship of proximity with those whom the legislation is intended to benefit such as to give rise to affirmative obligations towards such persons. Conversely, however, where a duty of care *would* ordinarily be owed, it may be excluded or restricted 'where it would be inconsistent with the scheme of the legislation under which the public authority is operating' (*N v Poole Borough Council* [2020] AC 780 at [75], per Lord Reed; see the reliance placed on this argument in *CGL Group Ltd v Royal Bank of Scotland* [2018] 1 WLR 2137). Hence, many of the cases in which the 'overkill' argument (discussed in II.3) has proven decisive have involved public defendants, with the courts expressing concern that the imposition of a duty of care on a public agency such as the police or social services might have a detrimental effect on the performance of their statutory functions, and that the financial burden of litigation will soak up scarce resources that would be better applied to the discharge of those functions in the first place. Since these sorts of arguments operate within the general framework for determining whether a duty of care exists, they are not the subject of further consideration here, although it is important to note that where the defendant is a public authority there is inevitably a degree of overlap or interplay between these sorts of policy considerations and the control mechanisms discussed in this section. (On the role of policy considerations in public authority negligence cases, see D. Fairgrieve and D. Squires, *The Negligence Liability of Public Authorities*, 2nd edn (Oxford: OUP, 2019), ch. 4.)

The control mechanisms that the English courts developed specifically in connection with the liability of public authorities can be grouped into three main categories: first, ideas of *vires*, discretion and irrationality; secondly, notions of justiciability and the distinction between policy and operational matters; and thirdly, the availability of alternative public law remedies.

(i) Vires, Discretion and Irrationality

During the period immediately before and subsequent to *Anns*, it appeared that a negligence action arising out of the exercise of a public function could succeed only if the decision of the public authority under attack was unlawful as a matter of public law, which generally meant showing that it was irrational. The explicit reliance on public law concepts in this connection is traceable to *Home Office v Dorset Yacht Co Ltd* [1970] AC 1004, where Lord Diplock went so far as to maintain that (at 1067):

> The public law concept of ultra vires has replaced the civil law concept of negligence as the test of the legality, and consequently of the actionability, of acts or omissions of government departments or public authorities done in the exercise of a discretion conferred on them by Parliament . . .

In the same case, Lord Reid also drew upon the public concept of discretion when seeking to identify the limits of public authority liability in negligence (at 1031):

> Where Parliament confers a discretion . . . there may, and almost certainly will, be errors of judgment in exercising such a discretion and Parliament cannot have intended that members of the public should be entitled to sue in respect of such errors. But there must come a stage when the discretion is exercised so carelessly or unreasonably that there has been no real exercise of the discretion which Parliament has conferred. The person purporting to exercise his discretion has acted in abuse or excess of his power.

On the facts of *Dorset Yacht*, it was held that the carelessness of officers at a young offenders' institution in leaving their charges unattended was indeed in excess of any discretion that had been conferred on them. It would have been different, suggested Lord Pearson, '[i]f the defendants had, in the exercise of their discretion, released some of these boys, taking them on shore and putting them on trains or buses with tickets to their homes' (at 1053). The matter being a valid exercise of the defendants' discretion, no liability could arise. This analysis was subsequently approved in *Anns*, where Lord Wilberforce accepted that a claimant bringing a negligence action against a public body must prove that the conduct in question 'was not within the limits of a discretion bona fide exercised, before he can begin to rely upon a common law duty of care' ([1978] AC 728 at 755).

In *X (Minors) v Bedfordshire CC* [1995] 2 AC 633, Lord Browne-Wilkinson criticised Lord Diplock's reliance on the concept of ultra vires in this context, but he agreed with Lord Reid and Lord Wilberforce that if the decision complained of fell within the ambit of a discretion conferred by statute, then it could not be actionable at common law. It followed that, in order to establish that a public authority was liable for negligence in the exercise of such a discretion, the first requirement was to show that the decision was so unreasonable that it fell altogether outside the ambit of the discretion. This amounted, in effect, to the adoption of a test of '*Wednesbury* unreasonableness' or 'irrationality' (see *Associated Provincial Picture Houses Ltd v Wednesbury Corp* [1948] 1 KB 223) as a precondition of the liability of a public body. A test of irrationality was also employed by Lord Hoffmann in *Stovin v Wise* [1996] AC 923 (noted in Ch. 9.IV) when identifying the circumstances in which exceptionally a public authority could be held liable in negligence for failing to exercise a statutory power, albeit that while Lord Browne-Wilkinson had applied his test to the defendant's actual conduct (was it irrational of the defendant to have done this?), Lord Hoffmann applied his to the conduct that the claimant was alleging the defendant ought to have engaged in (was it irrational of the defendant not to have done this?).

More recently, however, the courts have abandoned this express dependence on public law concepts in favour of a private law approach, whereby the issues raised by discretionary decision-making are accommodated at the breach of duty stage of the negligence enquiry. The key decision in this regard was *Barrett v Enfield London Borough Council* [2001] 2 AC 550, where Lord Hutton said that, provided the decisions under attack did not involve policy issues, it was preferable for the courts to decide the validity of the claimant's claim by direct application of the concept of negligence, rather than by applying the public law concept of irrationality as a preliminary test to determine whether the decision fell outside the ambit of the statutory discretion. It did not follow, however, that the discretionary nature of a public authority's decision-making was to be ignored altogether, since it would be taken into account at the breach stage of the negligence enquiry. For example, in *Barrett* itself, where a local authority was being sued for alleged defects in its child welfare provision, the House of Lords held that the standard of care expected of the defendant would have to be judged in the light of the fact that it was given discretions to exercise by Parliament in an area involving difficult decisions in relation to the welfare of children. The abandonment of public law controls was confirmed in *Phelps v Hillingdon London Borough Council* [2001] 2 AC 619, where Lord Slynn said that the fact that acts claimed to be negligent were carried out within the ambit of a statutory discretion was not in itself a reason why it should be held that no claim for negligence could be brought in respect of them, and in *Gorringe v Calderdale Metropolitan Borough Council* [2004] 1 WLR 1057, where Lord Hoffmann abandoned his earlier reliance on an irrationality exception in cases of public authority nonfeasance.

(ii) Justiciability and the Policy/Operational Dichotomy

A distinct concern in public authority negligence cases is the fact that it would not be right to hold every decision made by a public body open to judicial scrutiny. Public bodies are part of a political matrix, and it may therefore be more appropriate for them to be held to account by political mechanisms ranging from the ballot box to the obligation to report to Parliament. Furthermore, the legality of their actions can be challenged in public law proceedings for judicial review, which feature safeguards designed to protect their ability to function effectively. Public bodies are also frequently entrusted with the task of balancing broad concerns of social or economic policy, and the interests of different sections of the public. Such matters are 'not of a kind which can be satisfactorily elicited by the adversary procedure and rules of evidence adopted in English courts of law or of which judges are suited by their training and experience to assess the probative value' (*Dorset Yacht* at 1067, per Lord Diplock).

In the negligence context, the courts have responded to this 'justiciability' concern by seeking to carve out a 'no-go' area whereby certain types of public authority decision are excluded from the scope of negligence law altogether, on the footing that the reasonableness of the decision under attack is not a matter appropriate for judicial resolution in private law proceedings. In the early case law on this issue, this control mechanism was expressed in terms of a distinction between 'policy' and 'operational' decisions. According to Lord Wilberforce in *Anns* (at 754), statutes conferring powers on public authorities contained a large area of policy, and decisions on these policy issues were a matter for the public authority to make, and not the courts. By contrast, when it came to the practical execution of these policy decisions—which his Lordship referred to as the 'operational area'—liability might be imposed. It is important to note that Lord Wilberforce was not using the term 'policy' here to refer to the various public policy concerns that may be thought relevant when determining whether a duty of care should be imposed (discussed in II.3), but rather to identify a particular sphere of a public body's activity. His point was that, when a public body was acting in the policy sphere (e.g. in assessing budgetary priorities), the courts should refrain—wholly or in part—from interfering with their decisions by subjecting them to a duty of care.

The distinction between policy and operational matters was, however, felt by many commentators to be unhelpful (see, e.g., Bailey and Bowman, 'The Policy/Operational Dichotomy: A Cuckoo in the Nest' [1986] CLJ 430), and when delivering the advice of the Privy Council in *Rowling v Takaro Properties Ltd* [1988] AC 473 at 501, Lord Keith switched the focus to the question of 'justiciability' itself:

> [The distinction between the policy and operational spheres] does not provide a touchstone of liability, but rather is expressive of the need to exclude altogether those cases in which the decision under attack is of such a kind that a question whether it has been made negligently is unsuitable for judicial resolution, of which notable examples are discretionary decisions on the allocation of scarce resources or the distribution of risks . . .

This shift in terminology proved significant, since while the policy/operational dichotomy was capable of biting relatively low on the decision-making scale, the justiciability requirement appears to exclude only a small category of determinations at the top of that scale (hence in *Carty v Croydon London Borough Council* [2005] 1 WLR 2312 at [21], Dyson LJ observed that cases of non-justiciability 'are comparatively rare'). Nevertheless, some judges have gone further, and questioned the need to employ the concept of justiciability at all. According to Lord Nicholls in *Stovin v Wise* (at 938), for example, it is 'undesirable in principle that in respect of certain types of decisions the possibility of a concurrent common law duty should be absolutely barred, whatever the circumstances', and it should instead be recognised that no bright line can be drawn between the justiciable and the non-justiciable.

There are in any case very few English authorities where the justiciability requirement has been deployed by the courts, perhaps because 'true' policy decisions rarely give rise to claims in negligence in the first place. One example where the requirement was engaged is *Rigby v Chief Constable of Northamptonshire* [1985] 1 WLR 1242, where Taylor J ruled that a negligence action could not be used to challenge a police force's decision to continue its use of flammable CS gas (although on the facts he found operational negligence in using the flammable gas without having adequate fire-fighting equipment nearby). Similarly, the courts have held that the government owes no duty of care when devising strategies to counter disease or deciding what health information to provide to the public: see *Danns v Department of Health* (1995) 25 BMLR 121 (dissemination of newly discovered information about the possibility of natural reversals of vasectomy procedures); and *Smith v Secretary of State of Health* [2002] Lloyd's Rep Med 333 (decision to postpone issuing a general public warning against giving aspirin to children under 12); and see also the analogous Canadian decision in *R v Imperial Tobacco Canada* [2011] 3 SCR 45 that a government decision to promote low tar cigarettes fell within the realm of non-justiciable policy. These cases demonstrate that justiciability continues to operate as a genuine pre-condition of public authority negligence liability, but their rarity also shows that this particular control mechanism is of limited significance in practice.

(iii) Alternative Public Law Remedies

A third example of the influence of public law on the tort of negligence in the post-*Anns* era was the principle that, in cases concerning public authority defendants, the fact that the claimant had an alternative public law remedy available counted against imposition of a duty of care. In *Jones v Department of Employment* [1989] 1 QB 1, for example, the Court of Appeal held that an adjudication officer who had turned down the claimant's claim for unemployment benefit had owed him no common law duty of care, since there was a statutory right of appeal against the officer's decision. Similarly, in *Rowling v Takaro*, the availability of a public law remedy by way of judicial review was said to militate against the imposition of negligence liability.

Once again, however, as the law has moved back towards the Diceyan equality principle, the courts have distanced themselves from the emphasis in the earlier case law on the availability of alternative public law remedies. Hence in *Phelps* the House of Lords emphasised that the availability of alternative methods of obtaining redress ought not to bar a claim for damages at common law where the latter is the only way of securing compensation for past losses, and an argument from alternative remedies also met with a sceptical response in *Barrett*. Indeed, even where Parliament has provided a specific alternative remedy in the relevant legislation, it has been said that it does not automatically follow that claims in negligence were intended to be excluded, as much will depend on how comprehensive a remedy has been provided, and the wider statutory context (*Rowley v Secretary of State for Work and Pensions* [2007] 1 WLR 2861 at [73], per Dyson LJ).

(c) Evaluation and Reform

Law Commission, *Administrative Redress: Public Bodies and the Citizen*, Consultation Paper (Law Com. No. 187, 2008)

3.118 The underlying rationale of the tort of negligence in all cases is to provide compensation for those who suffer loss as a result of the negligence of others. As a matter of basic principle, courts consider that this standard model applies equally whether the defendant is an individual or private organisation, or a public body.

3.119 At the same time, however, courts have come to accept that claims against public bodies frequently raise particular difficulties of their own. Where the defendant is a public body, the traditional goal of ensuring compensation must be weighed against competing public interest factors, which may for one reason or another militate against liability. Of particular concern has been the potential for state liability to expand uncontrollably. This is acutely apparent in cases where the claimant has been injured as an indirect result of a public body's conduct and where the injury has consisted of pure economic loss . . .

4.2 . . . [T]he 'modified corrective justice' principle . . . suggests that where an aggrieved citizen cannot obtain just redress for substandard administrative action through alternative, non-court based mechanisms, they should be able to access the courts to obtain redress, within certain parameters . . .

4.3 These parameters are expressed as a package that attempts to balance the interests of aggrieved claimants against the danger that liability might create an undue burden on resources. The consequence of this is to modify the availability of damages in judicial review and create more certainty and predictability in the tortious liability of public bodies.

4.4 In judicial review, it is suggested that damages should be available as a remedy alongside the prerogative remedies where the administrative decision involved 'serious fault' and where the claimant suffers loss. This would essentially harmonise the system with that which already exists for a 'sufficiently serious' breach of EU law.

4.5 In tort, a similar 'serious fault' scheme would apply to the sphere of public action that can be described as 'truly public'. Action undertaken by public bodies that is not 'truly public' would be subject to the ordinary law of tort. It is not proposed that our suggested scheme would replace the current regime in areas such as medical negligence. Within the 'truly public' sphere the tortious standard of negligence would be replaced by a higher standard of 'serious fault'.

4.6 Within both of these schemes, potential liability would only be imposed where it could be demonstrated that the relevant legal regime 'conferred' a benefit on the claimant. Furthermore, the package would entail modifying the blanket rule on joint and several liability in this area of public body liability . . .

4.9 . . . '[M]odified corrective justice' . . . is the principle on which to base the liability of public bodies in those residual cases that require the court's attention. To summarise . . .

(1) In general, the principle of corrective justice underpins the relationship between the state and individual claimants;
(2) However, in certain circumstances the normal principle of corrective justice needs to be modified. This is in order to take into account certain features of the relationship between the state and potential claimants;

(3) In relation to monetary compensation, the relationship between the state and an individual claimant has a different moral complexion to the relationship between private individual claimants;
(4) An individual's relationship with and expectations of the state are such that they should look first to non-monetary remedies against the state;
(5) However, where compensation is in issue, there is a moral case for limiting it to particularly serious conduct where the state is the respondent;
(6) This modification only applies where the state is undertaking 'truly public' activity. Therefore, it does not apply where the impugned activity could equally have been carried out by a private individual.

COMMENTARY

The Law Commission subsequently announced that because 'the key stakeholder—Government—was firmly opposed' to its recommendations, it would be 'impractical to attempt to pursue the reform of state liability any further at this time': *Administrative Redress: Public Bodies and the Citizen* (Law Com. No. 322, 2010), paras 1.3 and 1.6. Commenting judicially on this 'debacle', Sedley LJ observed: 'it is a troubling comment on the functioning of the separation of powers that the state's independent law reform advisory body has had to abandon a project affecting the liability of government to governed principally because the control exercised by government over Parliament would frustrate any reform, however wise or necessary, which would make government's life more difficult' (*Mohammed v Home Office* [2011] 1 WLR 2862 at [23]).

The enactment of the Law Commission's proposals would have amounted to a clear repudiation of the Diceyan equality principle, and a move towards a public law model of government liability of the kind that can be found in some civilian jurisdictions, such as France (for a comparison of the English and French law in this area, see D. Fairgrieve, *State Liability in Tort: A Comparative Law Study* (Oxford: OUP, 2003)). Another advocate of a public law model is T. Cornford, *Towards a Public Law of Tort* (Abingdon: Ashgate, 2008), who argues that, where a duty arising in public law is intended to benefit particular persons, corrective justice demands that there should be a prima facie right to reparation for damage caused by breach of that duty, with the caveat that compensation may be withheld if its award would unduly affect the public interest or the interests of other citizens. The repeated references to corrective justice in the extract suggest that the Law Commission was itself attracted to this approach, albeit within limits.

The Law Commission's Proposals for Reform

The gist of the Law Commission's own proposal for reform was that the liability of public bodies for 'truly public' acts or omissions should be limited by a new requirement of 'serious fault' and restricted to situations where the underlying legislative scheme was intended to confer rights or benefits on the claimant. The intention was to expand the range of cases in which damages are potentially available, but at the same time to counteract any increase in liability costs by raising the threshold of fault. The latter consideration also underpinned the Commission's further recommendation that there should be a departure from the ordinary English rule of 'joint and several' liability by which any party liable in tort for the same damage may be ordered to compensate the victim in full, albeit with the right to seek contribution or indemnity from other responsible parties. It was felt that joint and several liability could operate harshly in the present context, as the state—always an attractive target for litigation because of its 'deep pockets'—would be left to bear the full cost of compensating the victim if other responsible parties were insolvent or could not be traced, even if its culpability was comparatively small (paras 4.64ff). The Law Commission's recommendation was that there should be a judicial discretion to apportion the liability of a public body for a truly public act or omission when this would be equitable in a given situation.

The Commission's proposals received a rather hostile reception from academic commentators, who criticised a perceived lack of clarity and coherence in the key concepts of 'serious fault', 'truly public' and 'conferral of benefit', and objected to the state setting itself above the citizen by excluding its liability for 'mere' negligence: see, for example, Cornford [2009] PL 70 and Mullender (2009) 72 MLR 961.

Beyond Tort Law

One final point that ought to be made concerns the provision of remedies for public authority failures independently of tort law. The Law Commission's view (paras 2.3ff) was that the vast majority of complaints against public bodies are handled effectively without involving the civil courts, namely by internal redress mechanisms (e.g. formal complaint procedures), alternative external avenues of redress (e.g. public inquiries and tribunals) and the public sector ombudsmen. Only in a comparatively small number of 'residual' complaints is the involvement of the courts necessary—and many of these could be addressed in proceedings for judicial review if (as the Commission recommended: paras 4.31ff) damages were made available as a remedy. In a similar vein, Bailey, 'Public Authority Liability in Negligence: The Continued Search for Coherence' (2006) 26 LS 155, 162 observes:

Apart from the law of tort, compensation for losses caused through the maladministration of a public authority may be paid on an ex gratia basis, commonly but not invariably following an adverse report by an ombudsman . . . By contrast with tort claims, it can be seen that such schemes are broader in scope, not being confined to claimants who suffered losses of a kind covered by tort law or to acts or omissions that would constitute breach of a legal duty. The transaction costs are likely to be much lower, especially where a factual basis for a claim has been established by an ombudsman's report . . . [G]iven the notoriously high administrative and legal costs in obtaining tort damages, this [approach] is likely to be more satisfactory as a method of securing compensation for the victims of maladministration than an expansion of the law of tort.

Bearing these observations in mind, should any reform of the law in this area focus on eliminating *all* negligence claims against public bodies in favour of providing a general remedy for public maladministration by way of a statutory compensation scheme? See further C. Harlow, *State Liability: Tort Law and Beyond* (Oxford: OUP, 2004).

The literature on the liability of public authorities is voluminous, but for a comprehensive and up-to-date analysis see Fairgrieve and Squires, *op. cit.*, and for a comparative survey, see Oliphant, *The Liability of Public Authorities in Comparative Perspective, op. cit.*

2. Negligence and Human Rights

The relationship between the Human Rights Act 1998 (HRA) and the law of negligence is both complex and controversial. (As to the HRA's impact on tort law more generally, see Ch. 1.III.2, where the relevant provisions of the Act are extracted.) It will be recalled that s. 6 of the HRA imposes an obligation on public authorities to respect Convention rights, and that a public authority that fails to comply with this obligation may be the subject of proceedings under s. 7(1). Under s. 8(1), in such proceedings the court has the power to grant whatever remedy within its powers it considers 'just and appropriate', including an award of damages where this is necessary to afford 'just satisfaction' to the victim. The HRA potentially has both 'vertical' and 'horizontal' effects (i.e. it may enable claimants to rely upon specified rights under the European Convention in litigation both against the state and against other private parties). For present purposes, the most notable consequence of this vertical effect is that failures on the part of public authorities (e.g. local councils, the emergency services, government departments and regulators) to safeguard life, physical integrity, private and family life and personal property may give rise to awards of damages to the victims of those failures under the Act (see Ch. 9.IV). The Act's horizontal effect stems from the fact that the courts are 'public authorities' within the meaning of s. 6, and hence (it seems) must reach decisions compatible with Convention rights even in litigation between private parties. This horizontal effect is relatively straightforward in, say, a defamation case where the decision of the court may itself directly implicate the defendant's freedom of expression (see Ch. 12.VI). However, any horizontal effect of the HRA in negligence is necessarily more involved, since it relies on the idea that in certain circumstances a court's failure to develop the common law of negligence in a particular way could itself amount to a violation of the claimant's Convention rights, an idea which is far from universally accepted. (For critical analysis of this idea, see R. Bagshaw, 'Tort Design and Human Rights Thinking', in D. Hoffman (ed.), *The Impact of the UK Human Rights Act on Private Law* (Cambridge: CUP, 2011), pp. 117–28.)

In any case, the reality is that the courts have not responded to the purported horizontal effect of the HRA in negligence cases in a systematic or conceptually consistent manner. The extent to which the courts have considered it appropriate to adapt the law of negligence in response to the Act is considered in the following extract.

Lady Justice Arden, 'Human Rights and Civil Wrongs: Tort Law Under the Spotlight' [2010] PL 140

Early expectations

Before the HRA came into force, there was much debate about the implications of the statutory duty imposed by s. 6 on courts not to act incompatibly with Convention rights. Many people expressed the belief that s. 6 would lead the courts to develop the law of tort to make it consistent with Convention rights. Our tort law is largely case law, and its development is often policy-driven. Convention jurisprudence reflects the values of the Convention, and thus could provide inspiration for decisions about developing tort law.

Since the commencement of the HRA

The courts have indeed in some cases proceeded to develop the common law by reference to Convention rights. Certainly the law of breach of confidence has been transformed by using Convention rights and values. Undoubtedly, the lack of a remedy at common law for invasions of privacy was widely regarded as a deficiency. In actions for disclosure of information in breach of confidence, English law now 'mirrors' the Strasbourg jurisprudence.

But the developments have been subtler than forecast, and it is clear that s. 6 does not have the full effect mooted before the HRA came into force. The law of England and Wales that public bodies should not in general owe a duty of care in the performance of statutory powers has not been qualified so as to provide a remedy where Convention rights have been violated . . .

Is there a principle?

The position would seem to be that the English courts are not necessarily going to develop the common law in the field of tort by reference to Convention rights and values but will do so only in specific cases where that is appropriate for domestic law reasons. It will not be appropriate where the Convention goes against the grain of some established principle of domestic law. The disappointed litigant will then be confined to his statutory remedy for violation of Convention rights. At the moment this is in general distinctly less generous than a tort law remedy in English law but if the Strasbourg jurisprudence on damages were to change there might well be a reason to reconsider the position in tort in domestic law rather than persist in the system of parallel remedies.

COMMENTARY

As Lady Arden explains in the extract, English courts have developed the common law in line with Convention rights 'where that is appropriate for domestic law reasons'. In negligence the overall pattern has been described by one of us (Nolan, 'Negligence and Human Rights Law: The Case for Separate Development' (2013) 76 MLR 286) as 'separate development', meaning that liability in negligence and under the HRA have generally developed independently of each other, so that for the most part the law of negligence has not been affected by the HRA, and in particular the HRA has not 'generated an expansion of remedies under the common law' (J. Wright, *Tort Law and Human Rights*, 2nd edn (Oxford: Hart, 2017), p. 310).

A good example of this general tendency is the decision of a majority of the House of Lords in *Van Colle v Chief Constable of Hertfordshire* [2009] 1 AC 225. According to Lord Hope and Lord Brown, there was no need to extend the common law to provide a remedy for breach of a Convention right, since liability at common law and remedial redress under the HRA could operate as parallel routes to redress. Indeed, for Lord Hope (at [82]), the presence of a possible remedy under the HRA was a ground for *refusing* to extend the common law, since 'any perceived shortfall' in the way that negligence law responded to a case of egregious failure by a public authority to protect the right to life could 'now be dealt with in domestic law under the 1998 Act' (see also *D v East Berkshire Community Health NHS Trust* [2005] 2 AC 373 at [94], per Lord Nicholls). Furthermore, the degree of fault required to be established for a public authority to be held to have violated Article 2 of the Convention by virtue of its failure to protect life was greater than would be required in a negligence claim, with the result that extending negligence law to such cases would actually result in more extensive liability at common law than under the HRA. More fundamentally, Lord Brown argued that actions in tort and under the HRA served different purposes: tort claims provided compensation for loss, while claims for breach of Convention rights were aimed at upholding minimum human rights standards and providing vindication of those rights (see also *D v Commissioner of Police of the Metropolis* [2016] QB 161 at [65]–[68], per Laws LJ). Similarly, *Michael v Chief Constable of South Wales Police* [2015] AC 1732 at [130], Lord Toulson said that the creation of a statutory cause of action under the HRA did not 'itself provide a sufficient reason for the common law to duplicate or extend it'. According to his Lordship (at [125]):

On orthodox common law principles I cannot see a legal basis for fashioning a duty of care limited in scope to that of [Articles 2 and 3 of the Convention], or for gold plating the claimant's Convention rights by providing compensation on a different basis from the [HRA]. Nor do I see a principled legal basis for introducing a wider duty in negligence than would arise either under orthodox common law principles or under the Convention.

The view that claims in negligence and under the HRA serve different purposes, such that the two areas of law should largely develop independently of each other, has also garnered a measure of academic support (see, e.g., Du Bois, 'Human Rights and the Tort Liability of Public Authorities' (2011) 127 LQR 588, and Nolan, *op. cit.*). And as Grušić, 'Tort Law and State Accountability for Overseas Violations of International Human Rights Law and International Humanitarian Law: The UK Perspective' (2021) 36 Utrecht J of Int and Eur L 152, 155 points out:

> The different objectives of tort law and the HRA are reflected in the different content of the rules and principles of the two bodies of law. This can be illustrated by the way the two bodies of law approach the issues of legally relevant harm, limitation, remedies, . . . attribution, duty to confer benefits and causation, and by the modes of reasoning in the two bodies of law. Admittedly, some of these differences are based on contingent factors that have changed in the past and can change again in the future. Nevertheless, these differences are consequences of the different objectives of tort law and the HRA, and, therefore, support the argument that tort law and the HRA are distinct bodies of law.

(See further on these differences, *ibid.* at 155–6, Nolan, *op. cit.*, at 302–11; and on causation specifically, see Turton, 'Causation and Risk in Negligence and Human Rights Law' [2020] CLJ 148.) Nevertheless, influential voices have also been raised *against* the separate development of negligence and human rights law, and in support of a degree of convergence between the two. Lord Bingham was an advocate of this position, for example, arguing in *Van Colle* that there was a strong case for developing the common law of negligence in the light of the Convention, such that, where negligence covered the same ground as a Convention right, it should, so far as practicable, develop in harmony with it. (See also academic proponents of convergence, such as Steele, 'Damages in Tort and under the Human Rights Act: Remedial or Functional Separation?' [2008] CLJ 606.) Furthermore, it is important to remember that the argument for separate development can cut both ways: in *D v Commissioner of Police of the Metropolis* [2019] AC 196, the Supreme Court rejected a submission that the policy concerns which had previously been held to militate against a duty of care being imposed on the police in respect of their conduct of criminal investigations should also be taken into account when considering claims for damages under the HRA, since the bases of the two liability regimes were different, and it could not be assumed that the policy considerations had equal force when it came to liability for breach of Convention rights.

In any case, the current judicial orthodoxy is that negligence and human rights law are two quite distinct remedial regimes that operate on parallel tracks. In any given case, a claimant may choose to rely on one or the other track, or on both, depending on the circumstances (and subject to the caveat that if both causes of action are made out, the claimant will not be entitled to recover twice for essentially the same loss). However, it does not follow from the fact that negligence and human rights law operate on parallel tracks that the HRA may not sometimes affect the outcome of a negligence case. A good example is *D v East Berkshire Community Health NHS Trust* [2004] QB 558, where the Court of Appeal relied on the passage of the HRA to justify its departure from an earlier decision of the House of Lords. The issue was whether social and medical care workers owed a duty of care to children when deciding whether to separate them from their parents for reasons of suspected child abuse. In *X (Minors) v Bedfordshire CC* [1995] 2 AC 633, the House of Lords had previously held that it would not be fair, just and reasonable to recognise a duty of care in such circumstances, but in *D v East Berkshire* the Court of Appeal ruled that the HRA had altered the balance of policy considerations as assessed by the House of Lords. This was because the failure to protect children from abuse could amount to a violation of their rights under the Convention (*Z v United Kingdom* [2001] 2 FLR 612), and hence the agencies involved were now subject to potential liability under the HRA regardless of the position in negligence. In these circumstances, it was considered unlikely that recognising a common law remedy would have any additional chilling effect on the conduct of care professionals, so that in effect the HRA had pulled the rug out from underneath the policy considerations that had proved decisive in *X v Bedfordshire*. (Note that the HRA was not in force when the events that were the subject of the claims in *D v East Berkshire* took place, so that there was no possibility of an action under the Act itself.)

That aspect of the Court of Appeal's decision was not challenged on appeal to the House of Lords (*D v East Berkshire Community Health NHS Trust* [2005] 2 AC 373, extracted in II.1), where their Lordships upheld the ruling below that when exercising their child protection functions the agencies involved had owed no duty of care to the parents of the children thought to be at risk. Intriguingly, *that* decision was also based on the possible chilling effect of such a duty of care, which it was considered might cause child protection agencies to act in a defensive manner, to the possible detriment of victims of abuse. However, the ECtHR had held in *TP and KM v United Kingdom* [2001] 2 FLR 549—which, like *Z v United Kingdom*, arose out of the same facts as the appeals in *X v Bedfordshire*—that child protection professionals might in some circumstances violate the Convention rights of parents whose children had been taken into care, a decision confirmed when the same court held that the unsuccessful parent claimant in *D v East Berkshire* had suffered a violation of his right to respect for private and family life under Article 8 (see *MAK and RK v United Kingdom* [2010] 2 FLR 451). But if, applying those authorities, the parents in such a case would now have a potential claim under the HRA, then the question arises of why the courts have not recognised here the same decisive change in the balance of policy considerations as they have in relation to the claim by the child. (Note that in the most recent Supreme Court decision on the liability of child protection agencies, *N v Poole Borough Council* [2020] AC 780, the policy considerations that were regarded as decisive in *X v Bedfordshire* and *D v East Berkshire* were downplayed, with the focus instead moving to the act/omission distinction: see Ch. 9.IV.)

4 BREACH OF DUTY

I. Introduction

Liability in the tort of negligence is premised on fault. It must be shown that the defendant was in breach of their duty to take reasonable care of the claimant—assuming such a duty to exist. The inquiry is into the content of the duty of care, as opposed to its existence (the topic of Ch. 3). The classic definition is Alderson B's in *Blyth v Birmingham Waterworks Co* (1856) 11 Ex 781 at 784:

> Negligence is the omission to do something which a reasonable man, guided upon those considerations which ordinarily regulate the conduct of human affairs, would do, or doing something which a prudent and reasonable man would not do.

How the courts apply this test in practice is the subject of the present chapter.

The chapter begins by looking at the key cases in which the idea of negligence as conduct falling below the standard of the reasonable person was judicially elaborated (I). In the period after the decision in *Donoghue v Stevenson* [1932] AC 562, establishing negligence as an independent tort, there was a mistaken tendency to treat the foreseeability of the risk attributable to the defendant's conduct as the exclusive test of whether there was a breach of the duty of care. The question was put whether the foreseeability of the claimant's injury was 'reasonable', as if this referred to some absolute standard. In fact, whether or not the defendant's conduct gave rise to a reasonably foreseeable risk of harm is truly relevant only in addressing the question, what would the reasonable person have done in the circumstances? In that context, it is the foreseeable *probability* of the risk materialising that is crucial—a matter of degree, rather than a fixed threshold—and the effect it would have had on a reasonable person's conduct in the circumstances. As is explored further in II of this chapter, a reasonable person decides how to act not by considering the probability of harm in isolation, but with reference to a basket of other factors, including the gravity of the harm if it should occur, the cost of taking precautions against it and the utility of the conduct posing the risk.

Subsequent sections of this chapter address the rule that negligence must be judged from the defendant's standpoint (III), the 'objective' nature of the standard of care (IV), the relevance of 'common practice' in applying that standard (V) and, lastly, the doctrine known by the Latin maxim *res ipsa loquitur* ('the thing speaks for itself', VI).

> **Bolton v Stone** [1951] AC 850
>
> The plaintiff, Miss Stone, was injured when a cricket ball struck her. The ball, which had been hit by a batsman playing in a cricket match at a local cricket club, travelled approximately 100 yards

before it hit her, clearing a fence some 78 yards from the pitch which, at the point where the ball left the ground, was 17 feet high. The evidence suggested that balls had not been hit out of the ground more than six times in thirty years. The plaintiff sued the committee and members of the club, alleging negligence and nuisance in not taking steps to avoid the danger of a ball being hit out of their ground. Oliver J at first instance found for the defendants, but the Court of Appeal reversed his decision, ruling that the defendants were guilty of negligence. On the defendants' appeal to the House of Lords, the only issues in dispute related to the action in negligence.

Lord Oaksey

My Lords, I have come to the conclusion in this difficult case that the decision of Oliver J ought to be restored. Cricket has been played for about ninety years on the ground in question and no ball has been proved to have struck anyone on the highways near the ground until the respondent was struck, nor has there been any complaint to the appellants. In such circumstances was it the duty of the appellants, who are the committee of the club, to take some special precautions other than those they did take to prevent such an accident as happened? The standard of care in the law of negligence is the standard of an ordinarily careful man, but, in my opinion, an ordinarily careful man does not take precautions against every foreseeable risk. He can, of course, foresee the possibility of many risks, but life would be almost impossible if he were to attempt to take precautions against every risk which he can foresee. He takes precautions against risks which are reasonably likely to happen. Many foreseeable risks are extremely unlikely to happen and cannot be guarded against except by almost complete isolation. The ordinarily prudent owner of a dog does not keep his dog always on a lead on a country highway for fear it may cause injury to a passing motor cyclist, nor does the ordinarily prudent pedestrian avoid the use of the highway for fear of skidding motor cars. It may very well be that after this accident the ordinarily prudent committee man of a similar cricket ground would take some further precaution, but that is not to say that he would have taken a similar precaution before the accident . . . There are many footpaths and highways adjacent to cricket grounds and golf courses on to which cricket and golf balls are occasionally driven, but such risks are habitually treated both by the owners and committees of such cricket and golf courses and by the pedestrians who use the adjacent footpaths and highways as negligible, and it is not, in my opinion, actionable negligence not to take precautions to avoid such risks.

Lord Reid

My Lords, it was readily foreseeable that an accident such as befell the respondent might possibly occur during one of the appellants' cricket matches. Balls had been driven into the public road from time to time, and it was obvious that if a person happened to be where a ball fell that person would receive injuries which might or might not be serious. On the other hand, it was plain that the chance of that happening was small. The exact number of times a ball has been driven into the road is not known, but it is not proved that this has happened more than about six times in about thirty years. If I assume that it has happened on the average once in three seasons I shall be doing no injustice to the respondent's case. Then there has to be considered the chance of a person being hit by a ball falling in the road. The road appears to be an ordinary side road giving access to a number of private houses, and there is no evidence to suggest that the traffic on this road is other than what one might expect on such a road. On the whole of that part of the road where a ball could fall there would often be nobody and seldom any great number of people. It follows that the chance of a person ever being struck even in a long period of years was very small.

This case, therefore, raises sharply the question what is the nature and extent of the duty of a person who promotes on his land operations which may cause damage to persons on an adjoining highway. Is it that he must not carry out or permit an operation which he knows or ought to know clearly can cause such damage, however improbable that result may be, or is it that he is only bound to take into account the possibility of such damage if such damage is a likely or probable consequence of what he does or permits, or if the risk of damage is such that a reasonable man, careful of the safety of his neighbour, would regard that risk as material? I do not know of any case where this question has had to be decided or even where it has been fully discussed. Of course there are many cases in which somewhat similar questions have arisen, but, generally speaking, if injury to another person from the defendants' acts is reasonably foreseeable the chance that injury will result is substantial and it does not matter in which way the duty is stated. In such cases I do not think that much assistance is to be got from analysing the language which a judge has used. More assistance is to be got from cases where judges have clearly chosen their language with care in setting out a principle, but even so, statements of the law must be read in light of the facts of the particular case. Nevertheless, making all allowances for this, I do find at least a tendency to base duty rather on the likelihood of damage to others than on its foreseeability alone.

The definition of negligence which has, perhaps, been most often quoted is that of Alderson B in *Blyth v Birmingham Waterworks Co* (1856) 11 Ex 781 at 784:

> Negligence is the omission to do some thing which a reasonable man, guided upon those considerations which ordinarily regulate the conduct of human affairs, would do, or doing something which a prudent and reasonable man would not do.

I think that reasonable men do, in fact, take into account the degree of risk and do not act on a bare possibility as they would if the risk were more substantial. A more recent attempt to find a basis for a man's legal duty to his neighbour is that of Lord Atkin in *Donoghue v Stevenson*. I need not quote the whole passage: for this purpose the important part is (p. 580):

> You must take reasonable care to avoid acts or omissions which you can reasonably foresee would be likely to injure your neighbour.

Parts of Lord Atkin's statement have been criticised as being too wide, but I am not aware that it has been stated that any part of it is too narrow. Lord Atkin does not say 'Which you can reasonably foresee could injure your neighbour': he introduces the limitation 'would be likely to injure your neighbour' . . .

Counsel for the respondent in the present case had to put his case so high as to say that, at least as soon as one ball had been driven into the road in the ordinary course of a match, the appellants could and should have realised that that might happen again, and that, if it did, someone might be injured, and that that was enough to put on the appellants a duty to take steps to prevent such an occurrence. If the true test is foreseeability alone I think that must be so. Once a ball has been driven on to a road without there being anything extraordinary to account for the fact, there is clearly a risk that another will follow and if it does there is clearly a chance, small though it may be, that somebody may be injured. On the theory that it is foreseeability alone that matters it would be irrelevant to consider how often a ball might be expected to land in the road and it would not matter whether the road was the busiest street or the quietest country lane. The only difference between these cases is in the degree of risk. It would take a good deal to make me believe that the law has departed so far from the standards which guide ordinary careful people in ordinary life. In the crowded conditions of modern life even the most careful person cannot avoid creating some risks and accepting others. What a man must not do, and what I think a careful man tries not to do, is to create a risk which is substantial . . . In my judgment, the test to be applied here is whether the risk of damage to a person on the road was so small that a reasonable man in the position of the appellants, considering the matter from the point of views of safety, would have thought it right to refrain from taking steps to prevent the danger. In considering that matter I think that it would be right to take into account not only how remote is the chance that a person might be struck, but also how serious the consequences are likely to be if a person is struck, but I do not think that it would be right to take into account the difficulty of remedial measures. If cricket cannot be played on a ground without creating a substantial risk, then it should not be played there at all. I think that this is in substance the test which Oliver J applied in this case. He considered whether the appellants' ground was large enough to be safe for all practical purposes and held that it was. This is a question, not of law, but of fact and degree. It is not an easy question, and it is one on which opinions may well differ. I can only say that, having given the whole matter repeated and anxious consideration, I find myself unable to decide this question in favour of the respondent.

I think, however, that this case is not far from the border-line. If this appeal is allowed, that does not, in my judgment, mean that in every case where cricket has been played on a ground for a number of years without accident or complaint those who organise matches there are safe to go on in reliance on past immunity. I would have reached a different conclusion if I had thought that the risk here had been other than extremely small because I do not think that a reasonable man, considering the matter from the point of view of safety, would or should disregard any risk unless it is extremely small . . .

In my judgment, the appeal should be allowed.

Lord Radcliffe

My Lords, I agree that this appeal must be allowed. I agree with regret, because I have much sympathy with the decision that commended itself to the majority of the members of the Court of Appeal. I can see nothing unfair in the appellants being required to compensate the respondent for the serious injury that she has received as a result of the sport that they have organised on their cricket ground at Cheetham Hill, but the law of negligence is concerned less with what is fair than with what is culpable, and I cannot persuade myself that the appellants have been guilty of any culpable act or omission in this case . . .

It seems to me that a reasonable man, taking account of the chances against an accident happening, would not have felt himself called on either to abandon the use of the ground for cricket or to increase the height of his surrounding fences. He would have done what the appellants did. In other words, he would have done nothing. Whether, if the unlikely event of an accident did occur and his play turn to another's hurt, he would have thought it equally proper to offer no more consolation to his victim than the reflection that a social being is not immune from social risks, I do not say, for I do not think that that is a consideration which is relevant to legal liability.

I agree with the others of your Lordships that, if the respondent cannot succeed in negligence, she cannot succeed on any other head of claim.

Lord Porter and **Lord Normand** delivered separate concurring speeches.

Appeal allowed.

COMMENTARY

This is a pivotal case in the modern law of negligence. It broaches the crucial issue of the proper approach to determining whether there has been a breach of the duty to take reasonable care. Three possible approaches may be considered: (1) it is a breach of this duty for the defendant to run the risk of *foreseeable* injury to the claimant, however improbable that result might be; (2) *a greater probability* of harm is required before the duty is breached; and (3) the magnitude of the risk is not the ultimate test of breach of duty, but only a component of a wider inquiry.

Their Lordships clearly rejected the first of these possible approaches. In places they could be read as adopting the second approach, which focuses upon *the degree of probability* as the crucial factor in determining whether there was negligence. But, looking at the judgment as a whole, it is clear that it is the third approach that was taken. It is wrong to look at the probability of harm in isolation; rather, it is only one of the factors which bear upon what is really the crucial question, namely whether the risk was such as would make a reasonable person take precautions to guard against it. This question emphasises not so much the magnitude of the risk but *the practical response* to the risk expected from a reasonable person. As Lord Reid states: 'the test to be applied is whether the risk of damage to a person on the road was so small that a reasonable man in the position of the appellants, considering the matter from the point of view of safety, would have thought it right to refrain from taking steps to prevent the danger.' This analysis is confirmed in the next case extracted, *The Wagon Mound (No 2)*.

Having dealt with the key point to come out of the decision of the House of Lords, it is worth addressing a number of other issues raised by the case which should be borne in mind throughout the rest of this chapter.

Questions of Fact and Law

Whether or not there is a breach of duty is a question of fact; whether or not the defendant owes the claimant a duty of care is a question of law (at least in so far as 'notional' as opposed to 'factual' duty is concerned: as to the distinction, see Ch. 3.II). Nevertheless, the distinction between questions of fact and law still has important practical consequences, for example in relation to appeals and the application of the rules on precedent. Questions of fact were once questions for the jury rather than the judge, but jury trial has been effectively abolished for most tort actions, including actions in negligence (see Senior Courts Act 1981, s. 69; *Ward v James* [1966] 1 QB 273; *H v Ministry of Defence* [1991] 2 QB 103).

Whilst there are of course no limits to an appellate court's power to review disputed questions of law, questions of fact are treated differently. The basic approach of the appellate courts in relation to questions of fact was set out by the House of Lords in *Benmax v Austin Motor Co Ltd* [1955] AC 370, a case on the infringement of letters of patent. Their Lordships drew a distinction between *primary facts* and *inferences* drawn from primary facts. An appellate court should not interfere with a trial judge's finding of primary facts (e.g. as to the sequence of events leading up to an accident) unless it appears perverse or against all the evidence. But inferences from those facts are treated differently. In *Benmax*, Lord Reid stated: 'in cases where the point in dispute is the proper inference to be drawn from proved facts, an appeal court is generally in as good a position to evaluate the evidence as the trial judge, and ought not to shrink from that task, though it ought, of course, to give weight to his opinion' (at 376). In *Qualcast (Wolverhampton) Ltd v Haynes* [1959] AC 743 at 762, Lord Denning commented:

> Since *Benmax v Austin Motor Co Ltd* [1955] AC 370, the Court of Appeal no longer takes refuge in that most unsatisfactory formula: 'Although we should not have come to the same conclusion ourselves, we do not think we can interfere.' If the Court of Appeal would not have come to the same conclusion themselves, it does what the Court of Appeal ought to do—what it is there for—it overrules the decision. But, short of that, it should accept the conclusions of fact of the tribunal of fact.

This means that questions such as whether the injury to the claimant was reasonably foreseeable and whether the defendant took reasonable care in view of the risk of injury are fully open to review by an appellate court.

Precedential Value of Decisions on Breach

As a decision whether the standard of care has been satisfied in particular circumstances is a decision of a question of fact, and negligence actions almost inevitably have slightly different facts, it follows that the ruling in one case has no precedential value in another case, even if the facts are superficially the same. Hence, *Bolton v Stone* does not decide that cricket clubs can never be held responsible for injuries sustained from a ball hit out of the ground, as Lord Reid indicated in the previous extract. The point is illustrated clearly by the contrast between *Bolton v Stone* and the later decision of the Court of Appeal in *Miller v Jackson* [1977] QB 966, in which a majority of the Court of Appeal found a cricket club liable in negligence in circumstances in which balls were hit out of the ground into neighbouring gardens several times each season. See also *Lewis v Wandsworth London Borough Council* [2020] EWHC 3205 (QB).

The situation is somewhat different when separate claims arise out of the same basic facts, for example where a number of people are injured by an accident allegedly attributable to the defendant's negligence or by use of an allegedly defective product supplied by the defendant. In such a situation, it is common for one, or a representative sample, of the actions to be brought forward as a 'test case' while the other actions are stayed (i.e. put on hold). Often this results in a 'split trial', with the common issues (e.g. the alleged negligence of the defendant's conduct) ruled upon in an initial hearing and the issues which are peculiar to each individual action (e.g. the quantum of damages) dealt with at a later date if necessary. As English law has not adopted the concept of a class action such as exists in the United States, the decision in the test case is not formally binding upon the other actions in the test case scheme. Nevertheless, the courts have a discretion to strike out any action where it would be an abuse of the process of the court, and they have shown themselves willing to take this course of action where one party seeks to relitigate matters already adjudicated upon in the test case (see *Ashmore v British Coal Corp* [1990] 2 QB 338).

A Note on Terminology—Special and General Duties

Lord Oaksey asked: 'was it the duty of the appellants . . . to take some special precautions other than those they did take to prevent such an accident as happened?' It is important to distinguish questions of this nature—questions whether there was a duty to take specific precautions—from the question whether the defendant owed the claimant a (general) duty of care. The former questions go to *the content* of the duty of care, or—to look at things the other way around—whether there was a *breach of duty*: it is the failure to take the specified precautions which is alleged to be careless. That issue is to be distinguished from the question of *the existence* of a duty of care which allows the defendant to be held legally responsible for the claimant's injury: without such a duty, no liability arises in negligence no matter how carelessly the defendant might have behaved. On the need to keep the two issues distinct, see Howarth, 'Negligence after *Murphy*: Time to Re-think' [1991] CLJ 58 at 72–81; Nolan, 'Deconstructing the Duty of Care' (2013) 129 LQR 559 at 579–80.

Compensation and Culpability

Lastly, in the extract Lord Radcliffe stated that there would be nothing unfair in requiring the appellants to compensate the respondent in respect of her injury even though they were not culpable. In effect, this was to advocate strict liability, that is, liability regardless of fault.

4 BREACH OF DUTY

That was not, however, the law. Nevertheless, it transpires that the cricketing authorities allowed Miss Stone to keep the damages and costs that she had been awarded in the Court of Appeal and did not seek to recover the costs they incurred in their successful appeal against liability in the House of Lords. Despite this goodwill gesture, it is almost certain that Miss Stone was left out of pocket, as she would have had to bear her own costs in the House of Lords (see Goodhart (1952) 68 LQR 3). For further context, see Lunney, 'Six and Out? *Bolton v Stone* after 50 Years' (2003) 24 J Leg Hist 1.

Whether fault on the part of the defendant is the appropriate criterion for determining whether a claimant should be paid compensation is an issue of general importance that we shall return to later on (see Ch. 17.II).

Overseas Tankship (UK) Ltd v The Miller Steamship Co Pty Ltd, The Wagon Mound (No. 2) [1967] 1 AC 617

The facts are set out in the opinion of the Privy Council.

Lord Reid delivered the opinion of the Privy Council:

This is an appeal from a judgment of Walsh J, dated 10 October 1963, in the Supreme Court of New South Wales (Commercial Causes) by which he awarded to the respondents sums of £80,000 and £1,000 in respect of damage from fire sustained by their vessels, Corrimal and Audrey D, on 1 November 1951. These vessels were then at Sheerlegs Wharf, Morts Bay, in Sydney Harbour undergoing repairs. The appellant was charterer by demise of a vessel, the Wagon Mound, which in the early hours of 30 October 1951, had been taking in bunkering oil from Caltex Wharf not far from Sheerlegs Wharf. By reason of carelessness of the Wagon Mound engineers a large quantity of this oil overflowed from the Wagon Mound on to the surface of the water. Some hours later much of the oil had drifted to and accumulated round Sheerlegs Wharf and the respondents' vessels. About 2 pm on 1 November this oil was set alight: the fire spread rapidly and caused extensive damage to the wharf and to the respondents' vessels.

An action was raised against the present appellant by the owners of Sheerlegs Wharf on the ground of negligence. On appeal to the Board it was held that the plaintiffs were not entitled to recover on the ground that it was not foreseeable that such oil on the surface of the water could be set alight (*Overseas Tankship (UK) Ltd v Morts Dock and Engineering Co Ltd* [1961] AC 388). Their Lordships will refer to this case as the *Wagon Mound (No. 1)* . . .

In the present case the respondents sue alternatively in nuisance and in negligence. Walsh J had found in their favour in nuisance but against them in negligence. Before their Lordships the appellant appeals against his decision on nuisance and the respondents appeal against his decision on negligence. Their Lordships are indebted to that learned judge for the full and careful survey of the evidence which is set out in his judgment (see [1963] 1 Ll Rep 402 at 406–8). Few of his findings of fact have been attacked, and their Lordships do not find it necessary to set out or deal with the evidence at any length; but it is desirable to give some explanation of how the fire started before setting out the learned judge's findings.

In the course of repairing the respondents' vessels the Morts Dock Co, the owners of Sheerlegs Wharf, were carrying out oxy-acetylene welding and cutting. This work was apt to cause pieces or drops of hot metal to fly off and fall in the sea. So when their manager arrived on the morning of 30 October and saw the thick scum of oil round the Wharf, he was apprehensive of fire danger and he stopped the work while he took advice. He consulted the manager of Caltex Wharf and, after some further consultation, he was assured that he was safe to proceed: so he did so, and the repair work was carried on normally until the fire broke out on 1 November. Oil of this character with a flash point of 170 °F is extremely difficult to ignite in the open; but we now know that that is not impossible. There is no certainty about how this oil was set alight, but the most probable explanation, accepted by Walsh J, is that there was floating in the oil-covered water some object supporting a piece of inflammable material, and that a hot piece of metal fell on it when it burned for a sufficient time to ignite the surrounding oil.

The findings of the learned trial judge are as follows (see [1963] 1 Ll Rep 402 at 426):

(i) Reasonable people in the position of the officers of the Wagon Mound would regard furnace oil as very difficult to ignite on water.
(ii) Their personal experience would probably have been that this had very rarely happened.
(iii) If they had given attention to the risk of fire from the spillage, they would have regarded it as a possibility, but one which could become an actuality only in very exceptional circumstances.
(iv) They would have considered the chances of the required exceptional circumstances happening whilst the oil remained spread on the harbour waters, as being remote.
(v) I find that the occurrence of damage to [the respondents'] property as a result of the spillage, was not reasonably foreseeable by those for whose acts [the appellant] would be responsible.
(vi) I find that the spillage of oil was brought about by the careless conduct of persons for whose acts [the appellant] would be responsible.
(vii) I find that the spillage of oil was a cause of damage to the property of each of [the respondents].
(viii) Having regard to those findings, and because of finding (v), I hold that the claim of each of [the respondents] framed in negligence fails.

It is now necessary to turn to the respondents' submission that the trial judge was wrong in holding that damage from fire was not reasonably foreseeable. In *Wagon Mound (No. 1)* [1961] AC 388 at 413 the finding on which the Board proceeded was that of the trial judge:

> [the appellants] did not know and could not reasonably be expected to have known that [the oil] was capable of being set afire when spread on water.

In the present case the evidence led was substantially different from the evidence led in *Wagon Mound (No. 1)* and the findings of Walsh J are significantly different. That is not due to there having been any failure by the plaintiffs in *Wagon Mound (No. 1)* in preparing and presenting their case. The plaintiffs there were no doubt embarrassed by a difficulty which does not affect the present plaintiffs. The outbreak of the fire was consequent on the act of the manager of the plaintiffs in *Wagon Mound (No. 1)* in resuming oxy-acetylene welding and cutting while the wharf was surrounded by this oil. So if the plaintiffs in the former case had set out to prove that it was foreseeable by the engineers of the Wagon Mound that this oil could be set alight, they might have had difficulty in parrying the reply that then this must also have been foreseeable by their manager. Then there would have been contributory negligence and at that time contributory negligence was a complete defence in New South Wales.

The crucial finding of Walsh J in this case is in finding (v): that the damage was 'not reasonably foreseeable by those for whose acts the defendant would be responsible'. That is not a primary finding of fact but an inference from the other findings, and it is clear from the learned judge's judgment that in drawing this inference he was to a large extent influenced by his view of the law. The vital parts of the findings of fact which have already been set out in full are (i) that the officers of the Wagon Mound 'would regard furnace oil as very difficult to ignite on water'—not that they would regard this as impossible: (ii) that their experience would probably have been 'that this had very rarely happened'—not that they would never have heard of a case where it had happened, and (iii) that they would have regarded it as a 'possibility, but one which could become an actuality only in very exceptional circumstances'—not, as in *Wagon Mound (No. 1)*, that they could not reasonably be expected to have known that this oil was capable of being set afire when spread on water. The question which must now be determined is whether these differences between the findings in the two cases do or do not lead to different results in law.

In *Wagon Mound (No. 1)* the Board were not concerned with degrees of foreseeability because the finding was that the fire was not foreseeable at all. So Viscount Simonds had no cause to amplify the statement that the 'essential factor in determining liability is whether the damage is of such a kind as the reasonable man should have foreseen' (p. 426). Here the findings show, however, that some risk of fire would have been present to the mind of a reasonable man in the shoes of the ship's chief engineer. So the first question must be what is the precise meaning to be attached in this context to the words 'foreseeable' and 'reasonably foreseeable'.

Before *Bolton v Stone* the cases had fallen into two classes: (i) those where, before the event, the risk of its happening would have been regarded as unreal either because the event would have been thought to be physically impossible or because the possibility of its happening would have been regarded as so fantastic or far-fetched that no reasonable man would have paid any attention to it—'a mere possibility which would never occur to the mind of a reasonable man' (per Lord Dunedin in *Fardon v Harcourt-Rivington* [1932] All ER Rep 81 at 83)—or (ii) those where there was a real and substantial risk or chance that something like the event which happens might occur and then the reasonable man would have taken the steps necessary to eliminate the risk.

Bolton v Stone posed a new problem. There a member of a visiting team drove a cricket ball out of the ground on to an unfrequented adjacent public road and it struck and severely injured a lady who happened to be standing in the road. That it might happen that a ball would be driven on to this road could not have been said to be a fantastic or far-fetched possibility: according to the evidence it had happened about six times in twenty-eight years. Moreover it could not have been said to be a far-fetched or fantastic possibility that such a ball would strike someone in the road: people did pass along the road from time to time. So it could not have been said that, on any ordinary meaning of the words, the fact that a ball might strike a person in the road was not foreseeable or reasonably foreseeable. It was plainly foreseeable; but the chance of its happening in the foreseeable future was infinitesimal. A mathematician given the data could have worked out that it was only likely to happen once in so many thousand years. The House of Lords held that the risk was so small that in the circumstances a reasonable man would have been justified in disregarding it and taking no steps to eliminate it.

It does not follow that, no matter what the circumstances may be, it is justifiable to neglect a risk of such a small magnitude. A reasonable man would only neglect such a risk if he had some valid reason for doing so: e.g., that it would involve considerable expense to eliminate the risk. He would weigh the risk against the difficulty of eliminating it. If the activity which caused the injury to Miss Stone had been an unlawful activity there can be little doubt but that *Bolton v Stone* would have been decided differently. In their Lordships' judgment *Bolton v Stone* did not alter the general principle that a person must be regarded as negligent if he does not take steps to eliminate a risk which he knows or ought to know is a real risk and not a mere possibility which would never influence the mind of a reasonable man. What that decision did was to recognise and give effect to the qualification that it is justifiable not to take steps to eliminate a real risk if it is small and if the circumstances are such that a reasonable man, careful of the safety of his neighbour, would think it right to neglect it.

In the present case there was no justification whatever for discharging the oil into Sydney Harbour. Not only was it an offence to do so, but also it involved considerable loss financially. If the ship's engineer had thought about the matter there could have been no question of balancing the advantages and disadvantages. From every point of view it was both his duty and his interest to stop the discharge immediately.

It follows that in their Lordships' view the only question is whether a reasonable man having the knowledge and experience to be expected of the chief engineer of the Wagon Mound would have known that there was a real risk of the oil on the water catching fire in some way: if it did, serious damage to ships or other property was not only foreseeable but very likely. Their Lordships do not dissent from the view of the trial judge that the possibilities of damage (see [1963] 1 Ll Rep 402 at 411) 'must be significant enough in a practical sense to require a reasonable man to guard against them', but they think that he may have misdirected himself in saying (at 413)

> there does seem to be a real practical difficulty, assuming that some risk of fire damage was foreseeable, but not a high one, in making a factual judgment as to whether this risk was sufficient to attract liability if damage should occur.

In this difficult chapter of the law decisions are not infrequently taken to apply to circumstances far removed from the facts which give rise to them, and it would seem that here too much reliance has been placed on some observations in *Bolton v Stone* and similar observations in other cases.

In their Lordships' view a properly qualified and alert chief engineer would have realised there was a real risk here, and they do not understand Walsh J to deny that; but he appears to have held that, if a real risk can properly be described as remote, it must then be held to be not reasonably foreseeable. That is a possible interpretation of some of the authorities; but this is still an open question and on principle their Lordships cannot accept this view. If a real risk is one which would occur to the mind of a reasonable man in the position of the defendant's servant and which he would not brush aside as far-fetched, and if the criterion is to be what that reasonable man would have done in the circumstances, then surely he would not neglect such a risk if action to eliminate it presented no difficulty, involved no disadvantage and required no expense.

In the present case the evidence shows that the discharge of so much oil on to the water must have taken a considerable time, and a vigilant ship's engineer would have noticed the discharge at an early stage. The findings show that he ought to have known that it is possible to ignite this kind of oil on water, and that the ship's engineer probably ought to have known that this had in fact happened before. The most that can be said to justify inaction is that he would have known that this could only happen in very exceptional circumstances; but that does not mean that a reasonable man would dismiss such risk from his mind and do nothing when it was so easy to prevent it. If it is clear that the reasonable man would have realised or foreseen and prevented the risk, then it must follow that the appellants are liable in damages. The learned judge found this a difficult case: he said that this matter is 'one on which different minds would come to different conclusions' (see [1963] 1 Ll Rep 402 at 424). Taking a rather different view of the law from that of the learned judge, their Lordships must hold that the respondents are entitled to succeed on this issue . . .

Appeal and cross-appeal allowed.

R. W. M. Dias, 'Trouble on Oiled Waters: Problems of *The Wagon Mound (No. 2)*' [1967] CLJ 62

Conduct is careless if it falls short of the standard of the reasonable man's behaviour in the circumstances; and the pattern of his behaviour is determined with reference to the foreseeable likelihood that some harm may occur. Normally if a reasonable man would have foreseen a harmful result as likely to happen, he would have governed his conduct so as to avoid it. If, however, the chance of the happening was remote, he may well have persisted notwithstanding that chance; in which case the reasonableness of his behaviour rests on a balance between the degree of likelihood that the danger will materialise, the cost and practicability of measures needed to avoid it, the gravity of the consequences and the end to be achieved by the activity, including its importance and social utility. A remote likelihood of harm will in some cases be outweighed by one or other of these considerations. Thus, every time that one drives a car or flies an aeroplane it is foreseeable that there is at least a chance of disaster. But it is not for that reason negligent to drive cars or fly aeroplanes, since the balancing considerations outweigh the risk . . .

From all this it will be seen that foreseeability of the likelihood that harm may occur is implicit in the determination of carelessness. With regard to foreseeability of the individual actually affected and the kind of occurrence that actually follows, it has been remarked that this relates to actionability rather than to the careless quality of the defendant's conduct. The two do coalesce whenever the only foreseeable result is harm to a particular person and of a particular kind. The conduct is then said to be careless *qua* that person and *qua* that result simply because no other consideration enters in. Breach of duty and remoteness become, as Denning LJ once said, 'different ways of looking at one and the same problem' (see *Roe v Minister of Health* [1954] 2 QB 66 at 85). Nevertheless it is important to keep the two apart, as when conduct sets up a chain reaction. One consequence might be foreseeable as quite likely to occur, another only as a remote possibility, and yet another not at all. Even though the defendant's conduct is careless with reference to the first, a successful action may or may not lie in respect of the other two. To put it in another way, the question of actionability with regard to these two does not affect the careless quality of the conduct that produces them . . .

COMMENTARY

The Wagon Mound (No. 2) is a very complicated case, not least because of the difference in relation to a crucial matter of fact between it and the earlier case that arose out of the same incident, *The Wagon Mound (No. 1)* [1961] AC 388. In the earlier case, the plaintiffs had conceded that the fire damage for which they sought compensation was not reasonably foreseeable—they had to do so or else they would very likely have been found contributorily negligent and at that time contributory negligence was a *total* defence to liability under New South Wales law.

The real importance of the later case lies in its examination of the nature of the requirement of foreseeability in the modern law of negligence and its role in determining whether the defendant was acting in breach of duty. The reasoning of the Privy Council on these crucial issues can be summarised as follows:

(i) in any case where there is more than a far-fetched possibility of injury to the claimant, the defendant's conduct may amount to a breach of duty if he failed to take such precautions to remove or minimise the risk as would have been taken by the reasonable person;

(ii) there is no precise point on the scale of probabilities that has to be attained before a finding of negligence is justified and, once the trial judge had held that there was a remote but not far-fetched possibility that the oil might catch fire and damage the plaintiff's vessel, it was not necessary to prove additionally that there was any greater degree of probability that damage might result;

(iii) breach of duty is determined rather by looking at the likelihood of the risk relative to all the other circumstances of the case, including the difficulty of taking precautions to guard against the risk; the real issue is the practical question whether the risk was such as to require the taking of such precautions;

(iv) here, given the ease of preventing the oil-spill and the lack of any public benefit associated with the activity (spilling oil into Sydney Harbour served no useful purpose, unlike the playing of cricket in *Bolton v Stone*), it was negligent not to take steps to prevent the oil from leaking because of the (admittedly slight) risk of fire.

The Privy Council's impeccable analysis constitutes confirmation that—in determining breach of duty—the foreseeability of injury is a question of degree, not an absolute threshold, and must be viewed in the light of other factors that would influence the conduct of the reasonable person (see II, immediately following). But, as Dias notes, this does not entail that the same approach to foreseeability should be adopted in other contexts in which the foreseeability of harm is relevant, for example in determining the proper scope of liability for the consequences of negligence. On this, see further in Chapter 5.III.

II. Reasonable Care: Relevant Considerations

In the previous section, we saw that the degree of foreseeability of injury to the claimant does not provide in itself a test of the defendant's negligence. This is to be assessed in the light of a cluster of interlinked considerations, looked at in the round. The court must embark upon a practical inquiry into what (if anything) the reasonable person would have done to eliminate or reduce the risk in question. In the extracts that follow, we see the courts rejecting attempts to limit the range of factors that may impinge upon the inquiry into breach of duty.

One attempt to provide a systematic approach to the factors relevant in assessing the defendant's negligence was provided by the American judge Learned Hand J. In *United States v Carroll Towing Co* (1947) 159 F 2d 169 he held that a decision as to whether particular conduct was negligent required three factors to be considered: the probability that the event would happen ('P'), the gravity of the loss that would be caused if the event occurred ('L') and the burden of preventing the event ('B'). Thus the 'Learned Hand formula' held that there was a breach of the duty of care where B < PL (where the burden of preventing the loss was less than the amount of the loss discounted by the probability of it happening). This formula has been held up by later scholars as an example of the economic analysis of law, imposing liability only where it would be economically efficient to do so (Posner, 'A Theory of Negligence' (1972) 1 J Leg Stud 29). A difficulty with this approach, however, is that it assumes that 'L' (the loss) can be given an accurate value. As is discussed in Chapter 15, this is not necessarily the case: although the law attributes a value even to personal injuries, this cannot be other than a conventional sum. In any event, it may be thought somewhat distasteful to allow the infliction of harm on an individual in the name of economic efficiency

4 BREACH OF DUTY

(see, e.g., the American case of *Grimshaw v Ford Motors* (1981) 119 Cal App 3d 757, awarding punitive damages where Ford had calculated that it would be less expensive to pay off the victims of accidents caused by a defect in their car, which was liable to burst into flames following a collision, than to recall the model and repair the defect). Nonetheless, it cannot be denied that some form of balancing of interests must take place in the breach inquiry, and to that end the Learned Hand formula may be viewed as a useful guide, even if the equation cannot be worked out with scientific accuracy.

(For critical analysis, see Green, 'Negligence = Economic Efficiency: Doubts>' (1997) 75 Tex L Rev 1605; Wright, 'Hand, Posner, and the Myth of the "Hand Formula"' (2003) 4 Theoretical Inquiries in Law 145.)

1. Gravity of the Potential Harm

Paris v Stepney Borough Council [1951] AC 367

The plaintiff was employed as a fitter in a garage owned by the defendant borough council. To the council's knowledge, he had the use of only one eye. While he was using a hammer to remove a bolt on a vehicle, a chip of metal flew off and entered his good eye, so injuring it that he became totally blind. The defendants did not provide him with goggles to wear, and there was evidence that it was not the ordinary practice for employers to supply goggles to men employed in garages on the maintenance and repair of vehicles. The trial judge, Lynskey J, allowed the plaintiff's claim for damages but this decision was reversed in the Court of Appeal for reasons which were clearly stated by Asquith LJ (see [1950] 1 KB 320 at 324):

> The plaintiff's disability could only be relevant to the stringency of the duty owed to him if it increased the risk to which he was exposed. A one-eyed man is no more likely to get a splinter or a chip in his eye than is a two-eyed man. The risk is no greater although the damage may be to a man with only one good eye than to a man with two good eyes. But the quantum of damage is one thing and the scope of duty is another. A greater risk of injury is not the same thing as a risk of greater injury; the first alone is relevant to liability.

The plaintiff appealed to the House of Lords.

Lord Normand

My Lords, this appeal involves a question of general importance affecting the common law duty which an employer owes to his employee. It is this. A workman is suffering, to the employer's knowledge, from a disability which, though it does not increase the risk of an accident's occurring while he is at work, does increase the risk of serious injury if an accident should befall him. Is the special risk of injury a relevant consideration in determining the precautions which the employer should take in fulfilment of the duty of care which he owes to the workman? . . .

It is not disputed that the respondents' duty of care is a duty owed to their employees as individuals. The respondents contend, however, that, though it is not a duty owed to the employees collectively, they must take account in fulfilling the duty only of any disability that increases the risk of an accident's occurring. For that proposition no authority was cited, and, in my opinion, it is contrary to principle. The test is what precautions would the ordinary, reasonable and prudent man take? The relevant considerations include all those facts which could affect the conduct of a reasonable and prudent man and his decision on the precautions to be taken. Would a reasonable and prudent man be influenced, not only by the greater or less probability of an accident occurring but also by the gravity of the consequences if an accident does occur? . . .

The court's task of deciding what precautions a reasonable and prudent man would take in the circumstances of a particular case may not be easy. Nevertheless, the judgment of the reasonable and prudent man should be allowed its common every-day scope, and it should not be restrained from considering the foreseeable consequences of an accident and their seriousness for the person to whom the duty of care is owed. Such a restriction, if it might sometimes simplify the task of the judge or jury, would be an undue and artificial simplification of the problem to be solved. If the court were now to take the narrow view proposed by the respondents the cleavage between the legal conception of the precautions which a reasonable and prudent man would take and the precautions which reasonable and prudent men do in fact take would lessen the respect which the administration of justice ought to command . . .

In the present case . . . the balance of the evidence inclines heavily against the appellant on the question of the usual practice of others, but that evidence necessarily dealt with the normal case when the employee suffers from no special disablement. In the nature of things there could scarcely be proof of what was the usual precaution taken by other employers if the workmen had but one good eye. Since Lynskey J did not deal with the evidence on practice and made no finding about the precautions which should be taken in the ordinary case and without reference to individual disability, I think that his judgment is essentially a finding that the supply of goggles was obviously necessary when a one-eyed man was put to the kind of work to which the appellant was put. The facts on which the learned judge founded his conclusion, the known risk of metal flying when this sort of work was being done, the position of the workman with his eyes close to the bolt he was hammering and on the same level with it or below it, and the disastrous consequences if a particle of metal flew into his one good eye, taken in isolation, seem to me to justify his conclusion. Even for a two-eyed man the risk of losing one eye is a very grievous risk, not to speak of the foreseeable possibility that both eyes might be simultaneously destroyed, or that the loss of one eye might have as a sequel the destruction of vision in the other. It may be said that, if it is obvious that goggles should have been supplied to a one-eyed workman, it is scarcely less obvious that they should have been supplied to all the workmen, and, therefore, that the judgment rests on an unreal or insufficient distinction between the gravity of the risk run by a one-eyed man and the gravity of the risk run by a two-eyed man. I recognise that the argument has some force, but I do not assent to it. Blindness is so great a calamity that even the loss of one of two good eyes is not comparable, and the risk of blindness from sparks of metal is greater for a one-eyed man than for a two-eyed man, for it is less likely that both eyes should be damaged than that one eye should, and the loss of one eye is not necessarily or even usually followed by blindness in the other. What precautions were needed to protect two-eyed men, and whether it could properly be held, in the teeth of the evidence of the usual practice, that goggles should have been supplied for them, were not questions which the learned judge had necessarily to decide. Therefore, though there might have been advantages of lucidity and cogency if the precautions needed for the protection of the two-eyed men had first been considered and the increased risk of damage to which the one-eyed man is exposed had been expressly contrasted, I would allow the appeal and restore the judgment of Lynskey J.

Lord Oaksey and **Lord Macdermott** delivered separate concurring opinions. **Lord Simonds** and **Lord Morton** dissented.

Appeal allowed.

COMMENTARY

Lord Simonds and Lord Morton of Henryton agreed with the majority that the gravity of the injury was a relevant consideration in assessing whether the defendant had acted with due care, but disagreed with the majority's conclusion that there was a breach of duty on the facts of the case. Their dissent was premised on the propositions that the risk to the plaintiff was not materially greater than that to the other workers engaged on the same task—such an accident would be serious in its consequences to any worker whether one-eyed or two-eyed—and it was a risk which could reasonably be run.

The decision of the House of Lords reflects the broader proposition that the content of the defendant's duty of care must be tailored to the known, or reasonably foreseeable, characteristics of the individual claimant. The issue arises not only where the claimant is at risk of more serious injury than other potential victims of the tort, but also where the risk is more likely to eventuate (a question of the foreseeability or probability of harm). A number of the cases involve the claimant's unusual susceptibility to injury, e.g. an allergy (*Withers v Perry Chain* [1961] 1 WLR 1314) or a vulnerability to stress-related illness (*Hatton v Sutherland* [2002] 2 All ER 1 (CA), extracted in Ch. 7.IV). For an interesting application of the same principle, see *Haley v London Electricity Board*, considered in Chapter 3.II.2, and cf. *Bhamra v Dubb* [2010] EWCA Civ 13, where the caterer at a Sikh wedding unintentionally sourced food incorporating eggs, whose consumption the Sikh religion forbids, and thus caused the death of a wedding guest who had a severe egg allergy; the caterer was liable in damages because he had taken insufficient care in obtaining his supplies, and it was foreseeable that a guest might have an egg allergy but would reasonably have assumed that the meal would be egg-free.

It is important to note that the principle applied in such cases is *not* the 'thin skull rule' considered in Chapter 5.III.1. The content of the defendant's duty of care reflects the claimant's susceptibility to injury only when it is known or reasonably foreseeable. The thin skull rule comes into play afterwards—once it has been established that the defendant was in breach of duty—and provides for the liability to extend to the consequences of the claimant's susceptibility even where it was unknown and not reasonably foreseeable.

In *Paris v Stepney*, the Law Lords accepted that the employer had no duty to provide safety goggles to its mechanics generally, but reasonable expectations of safety change over time and failure to provide safety goggles in the same situation today would almost certainly be negligent. On the 'time dimension' of negligence, see later in III.

2. The Cost of Precautions

Latimer v AEC Ltd [1953] AC 643

As the result of an exceptionally heavy rain storm, the defendants' factory was flooded and the water, mixed with an oily liquid ('mystic') which normally collected in channels in the floor, left the floor exceedingly slippery. The defendants spread sawdust on the floor, but there was not enough to cover the floor in its entirety. The plaintiff was injured when he slipped on a portion of the floor which was not covered with sawdust and fell. He sued for damages on grounds that included negligence at common law. The negligence claim was allowed at first instance, but the Court of Appeal allowed the defendant's appeal, holding that a breach of duty had not been established. The House of Lords affirmed the Court of Appeal decision. Their Lordships' consideration of the central question of breach of duty was influenced by the fact that the appellant's allegation that the respondents should have shut down the works did not appear in the initial pleadings and was only advanced at a late stage of the trial, after all the evidence had been introduced.

Lord Porter

[U]ndoubtedly the respondents did their best to get rid of the effects of the flood, employing such of the day workers as could be spared and obtaining volunteers from them for work in the interval between day and night work and from the night shift at a later period, but in the learned judge's opinion it was not possible for them to take any further steps to make the floor less slippery. I understand his view to have been, however, that, inasmuch as the effect of the storm left the gangway in question, and possibly other portions of the works, somewhat slippery and therefore potentially dangerous, they should have shut down the whole works if necessary, or at any rate such portion as was dangerous . . .

On the issue of common law negligence . . . the direction which should be given is not in doubt. It is to determine what action, in the circumstances which have been proved, would a reasonably prudent man have taken. The probability of a workman slipping is one matter which must be borne in mind, but it must be remembered that no one else did so. Nor does the possibility seem to have occurred to anyone at the time. It is true that after the event Mr Milne, one of the respondents' witnesses, expressed the opinion that he would not have gone on to the floor in the condition in which it was and that it would be too dangerous to do so. But this was after the event, and, though he was the respondents' safety engineer and was present until late that night, it seems never to have occurred to him that there was any danger or that any further steps than those actually taken were possible, or required for the safety of the employees. The seriousness of shutting down the works and sending the night shift home and the importance of carrying on the work on which the factory was engaged are all additional elements for consideration, and without adequate information on these matters it is impossible to express any final opinion. Moreover, owing to the course taken at the trial, there is no material for enabling one to judge whether a partial closing of the factory was possible, or the extent to which the cessation of the appellant's activities would have retarded the whole of the work being carried on. In my view, in these circumstances, the appellant has not established that a reasonably careful employer would have shut down the works, or that the respondents ought to have taken the drastic step of closing the factory . . .

Lord Asquith

At common law the question can only be whether, having regard to the nature and extent of the risk created by the slippery patches on the floor, a reasonably careful employer would have suspended all work in this 15-acre factory and sent the night shift home: or whether, having done all he could (and did) do with the sawdust at his disposal, the 40 production service men in the afternoon, and the 24 volunteers between the end of the day shift and the beginning of the night shift, he would have allowed the work to proceed. The learned trial judge concluded that a reasonable employer would have closed down. I agree with practically everything else he said in a most careful judgment. But, of course, this conclusion was crucial . . .

What evidence the learned judge had before him suggests to my mind that the degree of risk was too small to justify, let alone require, closing down. The evidence of the plaintiff himself is that 'you always get a certain amount of grease about' . . . Yet the plaintiff says that except for the accident to himself on this occasion in August, he has never known any accident happen to anyone in the factory through these causes. I cannot resist the conclusion that on this occasion, notwithstanding the extent of the flooding, the risk was inconsiderable, and that the learned judge's conclusion cannot stand. Treated as a finding of fact, it cannot be supported on the evidence, which, as to the onerousness of the suggested of remedial measure, was non-existent. Treated as an inference of fact, it was open to the Court of Appeal and is open to your Lordships' House to draw a different inference, and I would do so.

I agree that the appeal should be dismissed.

Lord Oaksey, **Lord Reid** and **Lord Tucker** delivered separate concurring opinions.

Appeal dismissed.

COMMENTARY

Why were the defendant employers not held to be negligent in failing to have sufficient reserves of sawdust to cover the entire area of the floor?

In *Bolton v Stone* (extracted earlier), at 867, Lord Reid stated that, in determining whether the defendant cricket club had been negligent: 'I do not think that it would be right to take into account the difficulty of remedial measures.' This remark has been seized upon by one well-regarded commentator as evidence that in English law 'the cost of precautions is irrelevant . . . [T]he consideration that the cost to the defendant of precautions would exceed the ex ante quantification of the plaintiff's injury does not exonerate the defendant from liability. The defendant can therefore be liable even for a cost-justified action' (E. Weinrib, *The Idea of Private Law*, revised edn (Oxford: OUP, 2012), p. 149). The present case, not mentioned by Weinrib, makes it clear that his interpretation of the English authorities is quite wrong. But what explanation can be given for Lord Reid's dictum, and his subsequent signing up to the apparently inconsistent decision in *Latimer*? The answer lies in the qualification he gave to the words quoted: 'If cricket cannot be played on a ground without creating a substantial risk, then it should not be played there at all.' It is clear that Lord Reid was saying no more than that, even if it would be impractical for the defendant to pursue their activities in a safer fashion, they can still be found guilty of negligence if the risks associated with those activities were so great as to require them to desist altogether. It must be admitted, however, that cases of this nature will be very rare (though the House of Lords accepted in *Latimer* that there might indeed be cases where a factory would have to be shut down in view of the riskiness of keeping it in operation).

The precautions necessary to protect the claimant may sometimes run counter to the claimant's own wishes. Suppose an employee has an unusual sensitivity to chemicals used in the workplace, and the employer has no alternative work available. Does the latter's duty of care require the employee to be dismissed, or is it enough that the employee is informed of the risks and decides to continue the employment? In *Withers v Perry Chain* [1961] 1 WLR 1314 at 1320,

4 BREACH OF DUTY

Devlin LJ stated: 'there is no legal duty upon an employer to prevent an adult employee from doing work which he or she is willing to do'. But in *Coxall v Goodyear Great Britain Ltd* [2003] 1 WLR 536 at [29] Simon Brown LJ denied that this was an absolute rule, and found that the case before him was one of those exceptional cases in which, despite the employee's desire to remain at work, there was a duty to dismiss him for his own good and to protect him from danger. Brooke LJ agreed the employer was liable on the facts, but only for failing to discuss the employee's options with him once his susceptibility was known. Does Simon Brown LJ's approach give effect to what another judge once derided as 'the nursemaid school of negligence' (*Savory v Holland & Hannen & Cubitts (Southern) Ltd* [1964] 1 WLR 1158 at 1166, per Diplock LJ)?

3. Utility of the Defendant's Conduct

Watt v Hertfordshire County Council [1954] 1 WLR 835

A lifting jack in the defendant's fire station was rarely used. It stood on four wheels, two of which were castored, and it weighed over 100 kg. Only one vehicle at the station was specially fitted to carry it. While that vehicle was properly out on other service, the station received an emergency call to an accident in which a woman had been trapped under a heavy vehicle two or three hundred yards away. The sub-officer in charge ordered the jack to be loaded on a lorry, which was the only other vehicle there capable of carrying it, but on which there was no means of securing it. Whilst carrying a number of firemen employed by the defendants and the jack to the scene of the accident, the driver of the lorry had to brake suddenly and the jack moved inside the lorry and injured one of the firemen. The trial judge, Barry J, dismissed the fireman's claim against the defendant. The fireman appealed.

Singleton LJ

It is not alleged that there was negligence on the part of any particular individual, nor that the driver was negligent in driving too fast, nor that the sub-officer was negligent in giving the order which he did. The case put forward in this court is that, as the defendants had a jack, it was their duty to have a vehicle fitted in all respects to carry that jack, from which it follows, I suppose, that it is said that there must be a vehicle kept at the station at all times, or that, if there is not one, the lifting jack must not be taken out. Indeed [counsel] claimed that, in the case of a happening such as this, if there was not a vehicle fitted to carry the jack, the sub-officer ought to have telephoned to the fire station at St Albans and arranged that they should attend to the emergency. St Albans is some seven miles away, and it was said an extra ten minutes or so would have elapsed if that had been done. I cannot think that is the right way to approach the matter. There was a real emergency; the woman was under a heavy vehicle; these men in the fire service thought they ought to go promptly and to take a lifting jack, and they did so. Most unfortunately this accident happened . . .

The employee in this case was a member of the fire service, who always undertake some risk—but, said [counsel for the plaintiff] not this risk . . .

The purpose to be served in this case was the saving of life. The men were prepared to take that risk. They were not, in my view, called on to take any risk other than that which normally might be encountered in this service. I agree with Barry J that on the whole of the evidence it would not be right to find that the employers were guilty of any failure of the duty which they owed to their workmen. In my opinion, the appeal should be dismissed.

Denning LJ

It is well settled that in measuring due care you must balance the risk against the measures necessary to eliminate the risk. To that proposition there ought to be added this: you must balance the risk against the end to be achieved. If this accident had occurred in a commercial enterprise without any emergency, there could be no doubt that the servant would succeed. But the commercial end to make profit is very different from the human end to save life or limb. The saving of life or limb justifies taking considerable risk, and I am glad to say there have never been wanting in this country men of courage ready to take those risks, notably in the fire service.

In this case the risk involved in sending out the lorry was not so great as to prohibit the attempt to save life. I quite agree that fire engines, ambulances and doctors' cars should not shoot past the traffic lights when they show a red light. That is because the risk is too great to warrant the incurring of the danger. It is always a question of balancing the risk against the end. I agree that this appeal should be dismissed.

Morris LJ delivered a short concurring judgment.

Appeal dismissed.

COMMENTARY

In *Daborn v Bath Tramways Motor Co Ltd & Trevor Smithey* [1946] 2 All ER 333 at 336, Asquith LJ encapsulated the law's approach in such cases in a celebrated dictum:

As has often been pointed out, if all the trains in this country were restricted to a speed of five miles an hour, there would be fewer accidents, but our national life would be intolerably slowed down. The purpose to be served, if sufficiently important, justifies the assumption of abnormal risk.

Does the law's approach unfairly prejudice claimants who are members of the emergency services and daily run substantial risks for the good of society at large? In *King v Sussex Ambulance NHS Trust* [2002] ICR 1413, Buxton LJ expressed some disquiet about the approach taken in *Watt* in the analogous context of injury suffered by an ambulance officer whilst on an urgent call-out. He asked, rhetorically (at [47]):

[W]hy should those who run the risk on behalf of the public, suffer if the risk eventuates? If, as this court held in *Kent v Griffiths* [extracted in Ch. 9.II], the public interest obliges the service to respond to public need, why should it not be equally in the public interest to compensate those who are foreseeably injured in the course of meeting that public need?

In his view, the 'men of courage' that Lord Denning referred to in *Watt* were unduly disadvantaged when compared with workers in the private sector. The latter might very well be able to recover in negligence if exposed to equivalent risks for their employer's commercial benefit rather than the general public good.

Buxton LJ appears to be arguing that compensation should be paid to injured members of the emergency services irrespective of fault. Do you think that the tort system ought to provide compensation in such circumstances, or is this something for which advance provision should be made, if considered desirable, in the service members' contracts of employment?

For a recent Court of Appeal decision accepting that social utility is one of several factors relevant to breach of duty see *Humphrey v Aegis Defence Services* [2017] 2 All ER 235.

For a contrarian view, arguing that utility is not and should not be taken into account in determining negligence, see Beever, 'Negligence and Utility' (2017) 17 OUCLJ 85, whose normative prescription is also accepted by Patten, 'Public Benefit, Private Burden? The Role of Social Utility In Breach of Duty Decisions In Negligence' (2019) 35 PN 230.

Tomlinson v Congleton Borough Council [2004] 1 AC 46

As noted earlier (in Ch. 1.III.3), the claimant suffered serious injuries when he waded into a lake at the defendant council's country park, threw himself forward in a dive and hit his head on the sandy bottom. The lake was a popular public amenity, used for various water sports, and the surrounding beach was used for picnicking and sunbathing. The council prohibited swimming as they regarded it as unduly dangerous, for example because of the risk of collision with windsurfers. They displayed prominent notices which read: 'Dangerous water: no swimming', distributed warning leaflets and employed rangers to enforce the no-swimming policy. Despite these efforts, many visitors continued to swim in the lake and the council concluded that the only way of dealing with the problem was to make the water less accessible and less inviting. Shortly before the claimant's accident, the council approved a scheme to cover over the beaches with soil and establish reed beds in their place, but this was not implemented until after the claimant's accident. The claimant brought an action under the Occupiers' Liability Acts 1957 and 1984 (see Ch. 10.I), failing at first instance, but succeeding (by a majority) before the Court of Appeal. The case then went to the House of Lords.

Lord Hoffmann

46 My Lords . . . I think that there is an important question of freedom at stake. It is unjust that the harmless recreation of responsible parents and children with buckets and spades on the beaches should be prohibited in order to comply with what is thought to be a legal duty to safeguard irresponsible visitors against dangers which are perfectly obvious . . .

47 It is of course understandable that organisations like the Royal Society for the Prevention of Accidents should favour policies which require people to be prevented from taking risks. Their function is to prevent accidents and that is one way of doing so. But they do not have to consider the cost, not only in money but also in deprivation of liberty, which such restrictions entail. The courts will naturally respect the technical expertise of such organisations in drawing attention to what can be done to prevent accidents. But the balance between risk on the one hand and individual autonomy on the other is not a matter of expert opinion. It is a judgment which the courts must make and which in England reflects the individualist values of the common law.

48 As for the council officers, they were obvious[ly] motivated by the view that it was necessary to take defensive measures to prevent the council from being held liable to pay compensation. The borough leisure officer said that he regretted the need to destroy the beaches but saw no alternative if the council was not to be held liable for an accident to a swimmer. So this appeal gives your Lordships the opportunity to say clearly that local authorities and other occupiers of land are ordinarily under no duty to incur such social and financial costs to protect a minority (or even a majority) against obvious dangers.

Lord Browne-Wilkinson, **Lord Hutton**, **Lord Hobhouse** and **Lord Scott** gave separate concurring opinions.

Appeal allowed.

COMMENTARY

It is scarcely credible that the claimant should have succeeded before the Court of Appeal with an argument that entailed the effective destruction of a valuable public amenity enjoyed by thousands of visitors each year. The proposition that 'the exercise of reasonable care requires attractive beaches to be replaced by ballast and muddy reeds justifiably attracts the strong language used by their Lordships in rejecting it' (Lunney (2003) 11 Tort L Rev 140 at 145). Lord Hoffmann was absolutely right to emphasise that the costs of 'compensation culture' are not simply pecuniary—here, the cost of the scheme to destroy the beaches was relatively small—but also the general undermining of personal autonomy and the loss of individual liberty. This accorded entirely with the established law on the relevance of social utility to the determination of whether or not the defendant has exercised due care.

The House of Lords' decision came too late to preserve the beach previously enjoyed by the people of Congleton, but seems to have heralded a more restrictive judicial approach to the resolution of similar claims under the Occupiers' Liability Acts (see Ch. 10.I). The tone of the extract seems to suggest that Lord Hoffmann (like Lord Hobhouse and Lord Scott, extracted in Ch. 1.III.3) was consciously speaking to a wider audience than just the legal profession, and intended his remarks to be given wider publicity—as indeed they were by the general news media.

The particular significance of the case in this context is its very clear recognition that the social utility of an activity extends to such intangible considerations as its contribution to individual flourishing through the scope it allows for autonomous risk-taking. (See also the further extracts in Ch. 10.I.3.) The deprivation of liberty and undermining of personal responsibility that would result from 'a grey and dull safety regime' (as Lord Scott put it, at [94]) must therefore be taken into account in deciding whether the defendant's duty of care required them on the facts to eliminate or reduce the risk in question.

Compensation Act 2006

1. Deterrent effect of potential liability

A court considering a claim in negligence or breach of statutory duty may, in determining whether the defendant should have taken particular steps to meet a standard of care (whether by taking precautions against a risk or otherwise), have regard to whether a requirement to take those steps might—

(a) prevent a desirable activity from being undertaken at all, to a particular extent or in a particular way, or
(b) discourage persons from undertaking functions in connection with a desirable activity.

Social Action, Responsibility and Heroism Act 2015

1. When this Act applies

This Act applies when a court, in considering a claim that a person was negligent or in breach of statutory duty, is determining the steps that the person was required to take to meet a standard of care.

2. Social action

The court must have regard to whether the alleged negligence or breach of statutory duty occurred when the person was acting for the benefit of society or any of its members.

3. Responsibility

The court must have regard to whether the person, in carrying out the activity in the course of which the alleged negligence or breach of statutory duty occurred, demonstrated a predominantly responsible approach towards protecting the safety or other interests of others.

4. Heroism

The court must have regard to whether the alleged negligence or breach of statutory duty occurred when the person was acting heroically by intervening in an emergency to assist an individual in danger.

COMMENTARY

These provisions were direct responses to concerns about 'compensation culture' highlighted in Chapter 1.III.3. Section 1 of the 2006 Act addressed the problem identified by the Better Regulation Task Force in its 2004 report, *Better Routes to Redress* (extracted in Ch. 1.III.3) that the common *misperception* that a compensation culture exists has led to a disproportionate fear of litigation and consequent risk-averse behaviour. The 2015 'SARAH' Act was prompted by specific concerns that worries about liability risk were still deterring people from participating in socially useful activities and formed part of a wider programme to encourage volunteering and involvement in social action. The provisions of both Acts were therefore intended to ease the fear of potential defendants that the courts are too willing to find negligence where there is any evidence that an accident could have been prevented, irrespective of the utility of their actions. Of course, the utility of the defendant's conduct is, in principle, something that should be taken into account at common law, so the real point of these provisions was not to change the law, but only to change perceptions.

As we explained in our earlier discussion, the public debate has often been led astray by the media's uncritical repetition of a number of compensation culture myths, and it is worth highlighting here a particular subset of those myths dealing with risk-averse behaviour induced by liability fears, for example the cancellation of events, the withdrawal of public amenities and the prohibition of traditional activities in public spaces like school playgrounds. Williams, 'Politics, the Media and Refining the Notion of Fault: Section 1 of the Compensation Act 2006' [2006] JPIL 347 at 349–50 exposes as fiction one story that was reported more than thirty times in almost all the national newspapers and repeated even by the then Prime Minister, Tony Blair: that the Bury St Edmunds council had taken down the hanging baskets in the town centre because of fears that they would be sued if the baskets fell down. In fact, the town's traditional floral installations were displayed as usual that year and won the annual Best Large Town award in the regional flower show. The only, very slight basis of truth in the story was that some of the older lamp posts in the town centre had been replaced because they were no longer safe to carry the weight of the baskets. Williams comments (at 349): 'False or exaggerated liability stories of this sort are politically significant, and not just infantilising "infotainment", because they help (indeed, sometimes seem designed) to influence legislative and judicial "tort reform" agendas.' However, *Tomlinson v Congleton*

BC demonstrates that not all the stories are myths: the council did indeed approve a plan to dig up its attractive beach and replace it with muddy reed beds, and had actually implemented the plan in the period between the claimant's accident and the trial. Whether this action was justified is another matter: in retrospect, it looks like a considerable overreaction.

The first case to apply Compensation Act 2006, s. 1 was *Hopps v Mott MacDonald Ltd* [2009] EWHC 1881 (QB). A civilian engineer involved in reconstruction work in Iraq following the invasion of 2003 was injured by an explosive device while travelling in a Land Rover under British army protection. Amongst the issues arising was whether his employers should have ensured he was transported in an armoured vehicle. Applying s. 1, Christopher Clarke J stated (at [93]):

> It seems to me that in determining whether particular steps (e.g. confinement to the airport until armoured vehicles were available for transport) should have been taken I am entitled to have regard to whether such steps would prevent the desirable activity of reconstruction of a shattered infrastructure after a war in a territory occupied by HM forces, particularly when failure to expedite that work would carry with it risks to the safety of coalition forces and civilian contractors in Iraq as a whole.

After weighing the relevant factors, he concluded that the use of an unarmoured vehicle on the occasion in question was not unreasonable. The relevant events occurred in 2003, but the judge rejected an argument that the application of s. 1 entailed impermissibly giving the statute retrospective effect (at [92]):

> Firstly, the section must, as it seems to me, be applicable to this claim since it is a claim which the court is 'considering'. Secondly the purpose of the section is to draw attention to, and to some extent, to expound the principle of the common law expounded by the House of Lords in *Tomlinson v Congleton Borough Council* . . .

Subsequently, s. 1 has been applied in connection with a variety of other 'desirable activities', including sports (*Sutton v Syston Rugby Football Club Ltd* [2011] EWCA Civ 1182), outdoor pursuits (*Wilkin-Shaw v Fuller* [2012] ELR 575) and indoor games (*Barnes v Scout Association* [2010] EWCA Civ 1476). In the last-mentioned case, liability was imposed notwithstanding the invocation of the statute, which merely shows that the social benefit may sometimes be outweighed by the risks involved in the activity undertaken. It was accepted in all the cases that s. 1 adds nothing to the common law.

At the time of writing, there was no substantial case law on the SARAH Act but it seems likely that a number of its terms will require judicial clarification. The Act defines 'social action' as 'acting for the benefit of society or any of its members' (s. 2), which suggests that it should be enough that just one other member of society is to be benefited. Would it therefore encompass acts intended to benefit the defendant's spouse or relative, or a criminal accomplice? (See HL Deb, 4 November 2014 col 1553 (Lord Beecham).) The concept of 'a predominantly responsible approach' (s. 3) also seems problematic. Why should an accident victim be deprived of compensation just because the defendant *otherwise* adequately protected the safety of others? It is just as well, then, that the Act only requires that the court 'have regard to' the specified factors and leaves it open to conclude that the defendant was negligent anyway. This applies even where the defendant was 'acting heroically' (s. 4), so the Act preserves the possibility that even persons who show a selfless disregard for their own personal safety in attempting a rescue might be held liable for harm that results from their intervention if their efforts unreasonably exposed others to risk. Cf. the comically inept superhero Captain Klutz.

Note that the obligation on the court under the 2015 Act is mandatory ('must have regard') rather than merely permissive ('may . . . have regard') as under the earlier statute, though it is hard to see how this make a difference to the court's balancing of the relevant factors in practice. For further analysis of the 2015 Act, see Goudkamp, 'Restating the Common Law? The Social Action, Responsibility and Heroism Act 2015' (2017) 37 LS 577; Mulheron, 'Legislating Dangerously: Bad Samaritans, Good Society, and the Heroism Act 2015' (2017) 80 MLR 88; Peyer and Heywood, 'Walking On Thin Ice: The Perception of Tortious Liability Rules and the Effect on Altruistic Behaviour' (2019) 39 LS 266.

III. Negligence Judged from the Defendant's Standpoint

In determining whether there has been a breach of duty, the court must place itself 'in the shoes' of the defendant: would a reasonable person, in the same circumstances as the defendant found themselves, have acted as the defendant did? This inquiry has a temporal dimension: what could reasonably have been expected from the defendant ought not to be affected by hindsight or by subsequent developments in technological skill or scientific knowledge. Account may however be taken of transient considerations, for example that the defendant had to act in 'the agony of the moment', or in an emergency, a fast-moving sporting contest or some other context demanding a split-second judgement. In these situations, the defendant is not to be judged as if there had been time available for calm reflection.

Roe v Minister of Health [1954] 2 QB 66

The plaintiffs underwent surgical procedures at the first defendant's hospital in 1947. In each case, the plaintiff was administered a spinal anaesthetic consisting of Nupercaine by the second defendant, Dr Graham, a specialist anaesthetist. The Nupercaine was contained in glass ampoules which were, prior to use, immersed in a phenol solution. After the operations the plaintiffs developed spastic paraplegia which resulted in permanent paralysis from the waist downwards. In an action for damages for personal injuries against the first and second defendants, the trial judge found that the injuries to the plaintiffs were caused by the Nupercaine becoming contaminated by the phenol which had percolated into the Nupercaine through molecular flaws or invisible cracks in the ampoules, and that at the date of the operations the risk of percolation through molecular flaws in the glass was not appreciated by competent anaesthetists in general. The trial judge dismissed the plaintiffs' claims. They appealed.

Denning LJ

The only question is whether on the facts as now ascertained anyone was negligent. Leading counsel for the plaintiffs said that the staff were negligent . . . in [amongst other things] not colouring the phenol with a deep dye . . . If the anaesthetists had foreseen that the ampoules might get cracked with cracks that could not be detected on inspection they would, no doubt, have dyed the phenol a deep blue; and this would have exposed the contamination. But I do not think their failure to foresee this was negligence. It is so easy to be wise after the event and to condemn as negligence that which was only a misadventure. We ought always to be on our guard against it, especially in cases against hospitals and doctors. Medical science has conferred great benefits on mankind, but these benefits are attended by considerable risks. Every surgical operation is attended by risks. We cannot take the benefits without taking the risks. Every advance in technique is also attended by risks. Doctors, like the rest of us, have to learn by experience; and experience often teaches in a hard way. Something goes wrong and shows up a weakness, and then it is put right. That is just what happened here. Dr Graham sought to escape the danger of infection by disinfecting the ampoule. In escaping that known danger he, unfortunately, ran into another danger. He did not know that there could be undetectable cracks, but it was not negligent for him not to know it at that time. We must not look at the 1947 accident with 1954 spectacles. The judge acquitted Dr Graham of negligence and we should uphold his decision . . .

This has taught the doctors to be on their guard against invisible cracks. Never again, it is to be hoped, will such a thing happen. After this accident a leading text-book, Professor Macintosh on *Lumbar Puncture and Spinal Anaesthesia*, was published in 1951 which contains the significant warning:

> Never place ampoules of local anaesthetic solution in alcohol or spirit. This common practice is probably responsible for some of the cases of permanent paralysis reported after spinal analgesia.

If the hospitals were to continue the practice after this warning, they could not complain if they were found guilty of negligence. But the warning had not been given at the time of this accident. Indeed, it was the extraordinary accident to these two men which first disclosed the danger. Nowadays it would be negligence not to realise the danger, but it was not then.

One final word. These two men have suffered such terrible consequences that there is a natural feeling that they should be compensated. But we should be doing a disservice to the community at large if we were to impose liability on hospitals and doctors for everything that happens to go wrong. Doctors would be led to think more of their own safety than of the good of their patients. Initiative would be stifled and confidence shaken. A proper sense of proportion requires us to have regard to the conditions in which hospitals and doctors have to work. We must insist on due care for the patient at every point, but we must not condemn as negligence that which is only a misadventure . . . These appeals should be dismissed.

Somerville and **Morris LJJ** delivered concurring judgments.

Appeal dismissed.

COMMENTARY

The 'time dimension' of the inquiry into breach of duty is especially important in actions arising out of the use of dangerous substances whose toxicity is only gradually discovered by medical science. Asbestos is a case in point (see N. Wikeley, *Compensation for Disease* (Aldershot: Dartmouth, 1993)). The risk of various asbestos-related conditions (including the respiratory disease asbestosis, and the invariably fatal cancer mesothelioma) has been known since about 1930, and the Inspector of Factories began warning of the risk to employees handling asbestos in 1945. But the risk to those subject to occasional asbestos exposure only became apparent later. In *Smith v P & O Bulk Shipping Ltd* [1998] 2 Lloyd's Rep 81 the High Court rejected a claim in respect of an employee exposed to asbestos in his workplace environment in the period 1954–71. He did not work directly with asbestos but would often pass others who were working on it and sometimes came into contact with asbestos dust in the air. The High Court held that a reasonable employer would not have known in 1971 that there was a danger to health to those not working directly with or on asbestos, and hence the failure to take precautions against such exposure at that time was not negligent. It will be apparent that much depends in such cases on the nature of the victim's contact with the asbestos, and there is no single date of imputed knowledge that can be relied upon in all cases of asbestos exposure. Similar issues arise in relation to the provision of personal safety equipment (e.g. ear protectors or goggles) to guard against other hazards of the workplace. See, for example, the discussion of the date of imputed knowledge in the context of industrial deafness in *Thompson v Smith Shiprepairers* [1984] QB 405 and *Baker v Quantum Clothing Group Ltd* [2011] 1 WLR 1003.

There can be an interesting interplay in such cases between the breach of duty analysis and principles relating to the existence of a duty of care. A defendant employer, for example, may be in breach of duty to its employees for exposing them to asbestos, but not to residents in the vicinity of its factory who contract an asbestos-related illness because of emissions from the factory (cf. *Margereson v J. W. Roberts Ltd* [1996] PIQR P358, where the plaintiffs succeeded in their action for damages, having been allowed as children to play in loading bays where they were foreseeably at risk from asbestos) or members of an employee's family who contract such illness from asbestos dust on the employee's clothes (*Maguire v Harland and Wolff* [2005] PIQR P21), if the risk to such persons was not foreseeable at the relevant time. Such cases are best analysed as part of the factual aspect of the duty of care inquiry (factual rather than notional duty), rather than in relation to breach of duty. The employer's negligence was a breach of duty to the foreseeable victims (the employees) but not the unforeseeable victims (the local residents and family members) because the employer owed the latter no duty of care.

Wooldridge v Sumner [1963] 2 QB 43

An experienced horse rider, Mr Holladay, competing at the National Horse Show, galloped his horse round a corner of the competition arena. About two feet away from the edge of the arena there was a line of shrubs with a number of benches interspersed between them. Surrounding the arena and behind the shrub and benches was a cinder track. A film cameraman, who had little experience of dealing with horses, was standing about twenty-five yards from the corner by one of the benches, although he had been told by the steward of the course to go outside the competition area while the horses were galloping. The horse went into and behind the line of the shrubs. When the plaintiff saw the horse approaching him, he stepped back or fell into its course and was knocked down and injured. In the cameraman's action against the owner of the horse, the trial judge found that the rider brought the horse into the corner much too fast and that the horse when it crashed into the line of shrubs would have gone out on to the cinder track if its rider had allowed it to do so, where it would not have harmed the plaintiff. He awarded the plaintiff damages for negligence. The defendant appealed.

Diplock LJ

It is a remarkable thing that, in a nation where, during the present century, so many have spent so much of their leisure in watching other people take part in sports and pastimes, there is an almost complete dearth of judicial authority as to the duty of care owed by the actual participants to the spectators . . .

What is reasonable care in a particular circumstance is a jury question, and where, as in a case like this, there is no direct guidance or hindrance from authority, it may be answered by inquiring whether the ordinary reasonable man would say that, in all the circumstances, the defendant's conduct was blameworthy.

The matter has to be looked at from the point of view of the reasonable spectator as well as the reasonable participant . . . because what a reasonable spectator would expect a participant to do without regarding it as blameworthy is as relevant to what is reasonable care as what a reasonable participant would think was blameworthy conduct in himself . . .

A reasonable spectator attending voluntarily to witness any game or competition knows, and presumably desires, that a reasonable participant will concentrate his attention on winning, and if the game or competition is a fast-moving one will have to exercise his judgment and attempt to exert his skill in what, in the analogous context of contributory negligence, is sometimes called 'the agony of the moment'. If the participant does so concentrate his attention and consequently does exercise his judgment and attempt to exert his skill in circumstances of this kind which are inherent in the game or competition in which he is taking part, the question whether any mistake he makes amounts to a breach of duty to take reasonable care must take account of those circumstances.

The law of negligence has always recognised that the standard of care which a reasonable man will exercise depends on the conditions under which the decision to avoid the act or omission relied on as negligence has to be taken. The case of the workman engaged on repetitive work in the noise and bustle of the factory is a familiar example. More apposite for present purposes are the collision cases where a decision has to be made on the spur of the moment . . .

It cannot be suggested that the participant, at any rate if he has some modicum of skill, is by the mere act of participating in breach of his duty of care to a spectator who is present for the very purpose of watching him do so. If, therefore, in the course of the game or competition at a moment when he really has not time to think, a participant by mistake takes a wrong measure, he is not, in my view, to be held guilty of any negligence.

Furthermore, the duty which he owes is a duty of care, not a duty of skill. Save where a consensual relationship exists between a plaintiff and a defendant by which the defendant impliedly warrants his skill, a man owes no duty to his neighbour to exercise any special skill beyond that which an ordinary reasonable man would acquire before indulging in the activity in which he is engaged at the relevant time. It may well be that a participant in a game or competition would be guilty of negligence to a spectator if he took part in it when he knew or ought to have known that his lack of skill was such that, even if he exerted it to the utmost, he was likely to cause injury to a spectator watching him. No question of this arises in the present case. It was common ground that Mr Holladay was an exceptionally skilful and experienced horseman.

The practical result of this analysis of the application of the common law of negligence to participant and spectator would, I think, be expressed by the common man in some such terms as these: 'A person attending a game or competition takes the risk of any damage caused to him by any act of a participant done in the course of and for the purposes of the game or competition, notwithstanding that such act may involve an error of judgment or a lapse of skill, unless the participant's conduct is such as to evince a reckless disregard of the spectator's safety'. The spectator takes the risk because such an act involves no breach of the duty of care owed by the participant to him . . .

As regards the speed at which Mr Holladay went round the bandstand end of the arena, I doubt whether his error of judgment would have amounted to negligence, even if one were to ignore completely the fact that his judgment had to be exercised rapidly in the excitement of the contest although not at a moment of intense crisis. For it does not seem to me that any miscalculation of the speed at which [the horse] could take the corner could be reasonably foreseen to be likely to injure any spectator sitting on or standing by the benches twenty to thirty yards from the point at which a horse taking the corner at too great a speed would cross the line demarcated by the shrubs. The likelihood was that, if a horse was forced by its momentum to go beyond that line, it would run out on to the cinder track without coming into contact with any of the shrubs . . . If it ran out on to the cinder track, there would be no peril to spectators who remained, as reasonably knowledgeable spectators would remain, on the benches in line with the shrubs . . . In fact . . . [t]he horse was deflected from its course before it reached the benches, and no spectator would have been injured had not the plaintiff in a moment of panic stepped or stumbled back out of his proper and safe place among the other spectators in the line of benches into the path of the horse. Such panic in the case of a person ignorant of equine behaviour and, as the judge found, paying little or no attention to what was going on, is understandable and excusable, but, in my view, a reasonable competitor would be entitled to assume that spectators actually in the arena would be paying attention to what was happening, would be knowledgeable about horses, and would take such steps for their own safety as any reasonably attentive and knowledgeable spectator might be expected to take. When due allowance is made for the circumstances in which Mr Holladay had in fact to exercise his judgment as to the speed at which to take the corner, his conduct in taking the corner too fast could not in my view amount to negligence.

As regards the second respect in which the learned judge found Mr Holladay to be negligent, namely, in his attempt to bring back the horse into the arena after it had come into contact with the first shrub . . . here was a classic case where Mr Holladay's decision what to do had to be taken in the 'agony of the moment' when he had no time to think, and if he took the wrong decision that could not in law amount to negligence. The most that can be said against Mr Holladay is that, in the course of, and for the purposes of, the competition he was guilty of an error or errors of judgment or a lapse of skill. That is not enough to constitute a breach of the duty of reasonable care which a participant owes to a spectator. In such circumstances, something in the nature of a reckless disregard of the spectator's safety must be proved, and of this there is no suggestion in the evidence.

Sellers and **Danckwerts LJJ** delivered separate concurring judgments.

Appeal allowed.

COMMENTARY

Their Lordships also found that the plaintiff had failed to prove a causal link between the defendant's negligence (even if that could be established) and the injury he sustained. The accident could just as well have been caused by something the horse saw or thought he saw. Danckwerts LJ (at 59) expressed some regret that the court was 'unable to have the story from the horse's mouth'.

Mr Holladay subsequently won the competition in which he was taking part, causing Sellers LJ to comment: 'there can be no better evidence that Mr Holladay was riding within the rules'. Goodhart, however, in a note in (1962) 78 LQR 490 at 492, advises caution on this point, for the competition judges were assessing the horse, not the rider, and their attention may not have been fixed on the speed at which the corner was rounded.

'A reckless disregard of safety'

According to Diplock LJ, it was necessary to show that the defendant was guilty of something more serious than an error of judgement or a lapse of skill; something in the nature of a reckless disregard of the spectator's safety had to be proved. The correct analysis of this dictum has proved problematic. Does the test of reckless disregard displace the ordinary standard of care in relation to contact sports and certain other activities (on the basis that competitors and spectators are deemed to waive the ordinary standard of care)? Or does it merely attempt to paraphrase, in ordinary language, the trite proposition that, in assessing whether the defendant is in breach of the duty of care, some latitude must be allowed where the alleged negligence arises in the context of a fast-moving sporting activity?

The two different approaches were summarised as follows by Sir John Donaldson MR in *Condon v Basi* [1985] 1 WLR 866 at 868, a successful claim in respect of a leg-breaking tackle in a Sunday-league football match:

> One is to take a more generalised duty of care and to modify it on the basis that the participants in the sport or pastime impliedly consent to taking risks which otherwise would be a breach of the duty of care . . . The other . . . is saying, in effect, that there is a general standard of care, namely the Lord Atkin approach in *Donoghue v Stevenson* [1932] AC 562 that you are under a duty to take all reasonable care taking account of the circumstances in which you are placed, which, in a game of football, are quite different from those which affect you when you are going for a walk in the countryside.

His Lordship conceded that it generally made no difference which approach was preferred. Nevertheless, there are good reasons for preferring the latter. Displacing the ordinary standard of care raises awkward questions as to which activities are to attract the modified standard, and seems to be an unnecessary complication given that the ordinary standard can quite happily accommodate the sporting cases. (See further Kidner, 'The Variable Standard of Care, Contributory Negligence and *Volenti*' (1991) 11 LS 1; Nolan, 'Varying the Standard of Care in Negligence' [2013] CLJ 651 at 655–6.)

On-the-Pitch Incidents

Condon v Basi makes it clear that actions arising out of sporting events may be brought not only by bystanders (as in *Bolton v Stone*) and spectators (as in *Wooldridge*) but also by participants. Such actions have become increasingly common, perhaps because serious injury may deprive those engaged in professional sport of the ever-increasing financial rewards that are on offer. See, e.g., *McCord v Swansea Football Club, The Times*, 11 February 1997; *Watson v Gray, The Times*, 26 November 1998; *Collett v Smith* (2009) 106(26) LSG 18.

Referees have also been the target of tort claims by injured players, for example where they fail to follow standard procedures introduced in the interests of player safety. See *Smoldon v Whitworth* [1997] PIQR P133 and *Vowles v Evans* [2003] 1 WLR 1607, both successful actions for damages in respect of injuries suffered in a collapsed rugby scrum, the former when the referee failed to apply the standard phased sequence of engagement, the latter when the referee allowed a substitute to play in the front row even though he lacked the necessary training and experience.

In *Smoldon v Whitworth*, the Court of Appeal specifically rejected the view that 'reckless disregard' had to be proven in order to establish a breach of duty. The court reiterated its position in *Caldwell v Maguire* [2002] PIQR P6, a claim by one professional jockey against two others whose riding, he alleged, had caused him to fall. The court considered that it was not helpful to say anything other than that something more serious than an error of judgement, oversight or lapse of skill was required. On the facts, however, it was 'not possible to characterise momentary carelessness as negligence' (at [28], per Tuckey LJ) and the claim failed. The same approach was subsequently applied in respect of horseplay between teenage boys (*Blake v Galloway* [2004] 1 WLR 2844; see also *Orchard v Lee* [2009] PIQR P16).

IV. The Objective Standard of Care

Lack of skill or experience is no defence to an action in negligence. The law assesses whether there has been a breach of duty by reference to an objective standard of care. For every activity, there is a certain minimum degree of care and skill that a defendant must exercise on pain of being found guilty of negligence. The question posed by the courts is 'What level of care and skill was required by the activity which the defendant was pursuing?' rather than 'What could this particular defendant have done?'. The objective standard 'eliminates the personal equation and is independent of the idiosyncrasies of the particular person whose conduct is in question' (*Glasgow Corporation v Muir* [1943] AC 448 at 457, per Lord Macmillan). According to Honoré, the effect of such an approach is the imposition of strict liability—by which he means liability without (moral) fault—in cases where the defendant is physically or mentally unable to reach the standards of the reasonable person ('Responsibility and Luck' (1988) 104 LQR 530). Whether or not one accepts that analysis, it is clear that negligence, as defined in law, does not necessarily involve moral culpability.

A rather uncharitable view of the objectively reasonable person is given by the humorist A. P. Herbert in the fictitious case of *Fardell v Potts* (The Reasonable Man), in *Uncommon Law* (London: Methuen, reprinted 1982):

> He is an ideal, a standard, the embodiment of all those qualities which we demand of the good citizen . . . This noble creature stands in singular contrast to his kinsman the Economic Man, whose every action is prompted by the single spur of selfish advantage and directed to the single end of monetary gain . . . All solid virtues are his, save only that peculiar quality by which the affection of other men is won. For it will not be pretended that socially he is much less objectionable than the Economic Man. Though any given example of his behaviour must command our admiration, when taken in the mass his acts create a very different set of impressions . . . Devoid, in short, of any human weakness, with not a single saving vice, sans prejudice, procrastination, ill-nature, avarice and absence of mind, as careful for his own safety as he is for that of others, this excellent but odious creature stands like a monument in our Courts of Justice, vainly appealing to his fellow-citizens to order their lives after his own example.

Tongue in cheek, Herbert has his judge conclude—after a review of the authorities—that 'legally at least there is no reasonable woman' (p. 4). Mayo Moran takes Herbert's 'perceptive mockery' as the starting point of her book, *Rethinking the Reasonable Person* (see the following extract), and argues that he presaged the later insight of various critical commentators who question the use of an idealised person as a legal standard (p. 1).

M. Moran, *Rethinking the Reasonable Person: An Egalitarian Reconstruction of the Objective Standard* (Oxford: OUP, 2003)

The reasonable person—an idealized person—is the common law's characteristically ingenious solution to the complex problem of articulating a standard of appropriate attentiveness to others across an almost infinite variety of individuals and situations. The genius of the reasonable person is largely found in the way he seamlessly weaves together the normative components of the standard—attentiveness to others—with biographical or empirical qualities—age, intelligence, level of education, mode of transportation, etc. Thus constructed, the reasonable person has the undoubted virtue of making an otherwise abstract normative standard seem familiar and knowable. But these very virtues are inextricably linked to his most serious vices. In fact, the use of an idealized person often seems a poor way to capture the idea of what attentiveness to others requires, precisely because it makes it so difficult to distinguish between those qualities of the idealized person that matter normatively and those that do not. Beyond this, the personification of a normative ideal may also incline the decision-maker to read ordinariness into the reasonableness component of the standard . . .

The reasonable person standard purports to derive its objectivity from an appeal to shared rather than individual qualities, and to the extent that it thus relies on customary norms it is essentially a standard of ordinariness. However, if the objective standard draws its notion of what is reasonable in large part from a conception of what is normal or ordinary, then we can expect many problems with these conceptions to 'seep' into determinations under the objective standard. In fact, while in the law of negligence reference to what is customary may seem useful in identifying behaviour long regarded as reasonable, there are also significant dangers here. This is because conceptions of what is normal or ordinary have also exhibited serious and systematic defects: they have consistently located some people beyond the innermost enclave of concern. For many groups including women, those disadvantaged on racial, religious, or ethnic grounds, the poor, and those with mental and physical disabilities, conceptions of what is normal or natural have been and continue to be used to justify discriminatory treatment.

COMMENTARY

Moran's basic argument is that the law's personification of the idea of reasonable care has tended towards a blurring of the distinction between *proper* behaviour and *ordinary* behaviour as the reasonable person is invested with more and more of the defendant's own characteristics and attributes. The only significant check on this process is that the characteristics and attributes must be 'normal', but normality is a slippery and politically contested notion that, as Moran observes, has often been used to justify discriminatory treatment of historically disadvantaged groups. Because the law has been too preoccupied with ordinariness, she argues, it has paid insufficient attention to the question of which characteristics and attributes are normatively relevant. Elsewhere in her book, Moran seeks to substantiate her claims in a detailed analysis of the standard of care demanded of children and the developmentally disabled. She argues—in the case of the former—that gender stereotypes frequently intrude into the inquiry, with the courts particularly inclined to excuse the 'normal' heedlessness of playing boys ('boys will be boys!': see further in IV.3). This gendering of an apparently neutral legal standard is particularly evident, she submits, when the standard of care is considered in the mirror-image context of contributory negligence by the claimant. She explains (at pp. 128–9):

[A]ssumptions about what kind of behaviour is natural for girls as opposed to for boys effectively results in different standards for contributory negligence. The normal boy, it seems, seeks risks and is therefore not chastised for so doing; in contrast, the normal girl seeks safety and avoids risks and is held to that standard.

On the other hand, a recent empirical study of the operation of contributory negligence in first instance courts between 2000 and 2016 found little evidence to support Moran's claims

(J. Goudkamp and D. Nolan, *Contributory Negligence in the Twenty-First Century* (Oxford: OUP, 2019), para. 4.40). The authors found that the success rate of the plea of contributory negligence was slightly higher in cases involving female claimants aged under 18 (73 per cent) than in cases involving male claimants aged under 18 (68 per cent), and that where girls were found guilty of contributory negligence the average discount was also slightly higher (45 per cent) to that in cases involving boy claimants (40 per cent), but these disparities are relatively minor and may well be down to chance.

Other feminist legal scholars have argued, more radically, that the very notion of 'reasonableness' inevitably reflects a male perspective—not just because it is usually interpreted by male judges, but because it is itself a construct of patriarchal society—and should be discarded. See, e.g., Martin, 'A Feminist View of the Reasonable Man: An Alternative Approach to Liability in Negligence for Personal Injury' (1994) 23 Anglo-Am L Rev 334. For Moran, by contrast, it is not the 'reason' part of the reasonable person standard that should be abolished, but the 'person'. Instead of personifying the standard of reasonable care, we would do better to inquire directly into the question of whether the conduct in question betrays that culpable indifference to others that is properly called 'negligence'.

1. Lack of Skill and Experience

Nettleship v Weston [1971] 2 QB 691

The defendant asked the plaintiff, a friend, to teach her to drive. He agreed only after ensuring that he was covered under the defendant's comprehensive car insurance policy. During the course of a lesson and when the defendant was driving, she failed to straighten up the car after having turned a corner, with the result that it mounted the pavement and hit a lamp-post. The plaintiff broke his kneecap as a result of the collision, and sued for negligence. The trial judge dismissed his claim on the basis that the defendant only owed him a duty to do her best, and that she did not fail in that duty.

Lord Denning MR

The Responsibility of the Learner-Driver Towards Persons on or near the Highway

Mrs Weston is clearly liable for the damage to the lamp-post. In the civil law if a driver goes off the road on to the pavement and injures a pedestrian, or damages property, he is prima facie liable. Likewise if he goes on to the wrong side of the road. It is no answer for him to say: 'I was a learner-driver under instruction. I was doing my best and could not help it.' The civil law permits no such excuse. It requires of him the same standard of care as any other driver . . . The learner-driver may be doing his best, but his incompetent best is not good enough. He must drive in as good a manner as a driver of skill, experience and care, who is sound in mind and limb, who makes no errors of judgment, has good eyesight and hearing, and is free from any infirmity . . .

The high standard thus imposed by the judges is, I believe, largely the result of the policy of the Road Traffic Acts. Parliament requires every driver to be insured against third-party risks. The reason is so that a person injured by a motor-car should not be left to bear the loss on his own, but should be compensated out of the insurance fund. The fund is better able to bear it than he can. But the injured person is only able to recover if the driver is liable in law. So the judges see to it that he is liable, unless he can prove care and skill of a high standard . . . Thus we are, in this branch of the law, moving away from the concept: 'No liability without fault'. We are beginning to apply the test: 'On whom should the risk fall?' Morally the learner-driver is not at fault; but legally she is liable to be because she is insured and the risk should fall on her . . .

The Responsibility of the Learner-Driver Towards Passengers in the Car

Mrs Weston took her son with her in the car. We do not know his age. He may have been 21 and have known that his mother was learning to drive. He was not injured. But if he had been injured, would he have had a cause of action? I take it to be clear that, if a driver has a passenger in the car, he owes a duty of care to him. But what is the standard of care required of the driver? Is it a lower standard than he or she owes towards a pedestrian on the pavement? I should have thought not. But, suppose that the driver has never driven a car before, or has taken too much to drink, or has poor eyesight or hearing; and, furthermore, that the passenger knows it and yet accepts a lift from him. Does that make any difference? Dixon J thought it did. In *Insurance Comr v Joyce* (1948) 77 CLR 39 at 56, he said:

> If a man accepts a lift from a car-driver whom he knows to have lost a limb or an eye or to be deaf, he cannot complain if he does not exhibit the skill and competence of a driver who suffers from no defect . . . If he knowingly accepts the voluntary services of a driver affected by drink, he cannot complain of improper driving caused by his condition, because it involves no breach of duty.

We have all the greatest respect for Sir Owen Dixon, but for once I cannot agree with him. The driver owes a duty of care to every passenger in the car, just as he does to every pedestrian on the road; and he must attain the same standard of care in respect of each. If the driver were to be excused according to the knowledge of the passenger, it would result in endless confusion and injustice. One of the passengers may know that the learner-driver is a mere novice. Another passenger may believe him to be entirely competent. One of the passengers may believe the driver to have had only two drinks. Another passenger may know that he has had a dozen. Is the one passenger to recover and the other not? Rather than embark on such enquiries, the law holds that the driver must attain the same standard of care for passengers as for pedestrians. The knowledge of the passenger may go to show that he was guilty of contributory negligence in ever accepting the lift—and thus reduce his damages—but it does not take away the duty of care, nor does it diminish the standard of care which the law requires of the driver . . .

The Responsibility of a Learner-Driver Towards His Instructor

The special factor in this case is that Mr Nettleship was not a mere passenger in the car. He was an instructor teaching Mrs Weston to drive. Seeing that the law lays down, for all drivers of motor cars, a standard of care to which all must conform, I think that even a learner-driver, so long as he is the sole driver, must attain the same standard towards all passengers in the car, including an instructor. But the instructor may be debarred from claiming for a reason peculiar to himself. He may be debarred because he has voluntarily agreed to waive any claim for any injury that may befall him. Otherwise he is not debarred. He may, of course, be guilty of contributory negligence and have his damages reduced on that account. He may, for instance, have let the learner take control too soon, he may not have been quick enough to correct his errors, or he may have participated in the negligent act himself: see *Stapley v Gypsum Mines Ltd* [1953] AC 663. But, apart from contributory negligence, he is not excluded unless it be that he had voluntarily agreed to incur the risk.

[His Lordship proceeded to consider, and reject, the defence of *volenti non fit injuria*, and continued:]

> **Conclusion Thus Far**
>
> In all that I have said, I have treated Mrs Weston as the driver who was herself in control of the car. On that footing, she is plainly liable for the damage done to the lamp-post. She is equally liable for the injury done to Mr Nettleship. She owed a duty of care to each. The standard of care is the same in either case. It is measured objectively by the care to be expected of an experienced, skilled and careful driver.
>
> **Salmon LJ** delivered a separate concurring judgment. **Megaw LJ** concurred on liability but dissented on the question of contributory negligence.
>
> *Appeal allowed.*

COMMENTARY

The Court of Appeal found for the plaintiff but (Megaw LJ dissenting) reduced his damages by 50 per cent for contributory negligence.

The Court of Appeal's approach did not commend itself to the Australian High Court (*Cook v Cook* (1986) 162 CLR 376), which held that, although the standard owed would normally be that of the reasonably competent driver, special circumstances might exist which would alter this standard. An example of such circumstances would be where the driver was, to the knowledge of the passenger, a learner; hence 'the standard of care which arises from the relationship of pupil and instructor is that which is reasonably to be expected of an unqualified and inexperienced driver in the circumstances in which the pupil is placed'. The duty owed to other road users remained that of a careful qualified driver. However, in *Imbree v McNeilly* (2008) 236 CLR 510 the High Court changed its mind and overruled *Cook v Cook*, for reasons both principled and practical. At the level of principle, the variable standard of care recognised in *Cook v Cook* was inconsistent with the essential requirement that the standard of care should be objective and impersonal. Further, the *Cook v Cook* approach required the drawing of difficult distinctions, e.g. between a lack of skill due to inexperience and a lack of care, and left undefined the level of competence that was to be assumed in a learner driver (was it to vary depending on how long the learner had been having lessons?). The decision brings Australian common law into line with English law as established by *Nettleship v Weston*.

Inexperience in the Professions

In *Wilsher v Essex Area Health Authority* [1987] QB 730 (reversed on different grounds at [1988] AC 1074), a majority of the Court of Appeal held that the standard of care required of members of a medical unit was that of the ordinary skilled person exercising and professing to have that special skill, and that the standard was to be determined in the context of particular posts in the unit rather than according to the general rank or status of the people filling the posts. The duty had to be tailored to the acts which the doctor had elected to perform rather than to the doctor themselves. It followed that inexperience was no defence to an action for medical negligence. However, Glidewell LJ held that an inexperienced doctor who was called on to exercise a specialist skill and made a mistake nevertheless satisfied the necessary standard of care if they had sought the advice and help of their superior when necessary. By contrast, the dissenting member of the court, Sir Nicolas Browne-Wilkinson V-C, expressly rejected the view that there was an objective standard which could be determined irrespective of the experience of the individual doctor and the reason why they were occupying the post in question. In his opinion, the ordinary standard of a skilled doctor did not apply to a houseman (a junior doctor) or to a doctor just beginning to train in a speciality. He explained (at 777):

> The houseman has to take up his post in order to gain full professional qualification; anyone who ... wishes to obtain specialist skills has to learn those skills by taking a post in a specialist unit. In my judgment, such doctors cannot in fairness be said to be at fault if, at the start of their time, they lack the very skills which they are seeking to acquire ... In my judgment, so long as the English law rests liability on personal fault, a doctor who has properly accepted a post in a hospital in order to gain necessary experience should only be held liable for acts or omissions which a careful doctor with his qualifications and experience would not have done or omitted.

Cf. *FB v Rana* [2017] PIQR P17 (immaterial that hospital's senior house officer was relatively inexperienced).

Alternative Medicine

Is a practitioner of alternative medicine to be assessed by the standards of orthodox medicine? In *Shakoor v Situ* [2001] 1 WLR 410, the defendant was trained in traditional Chinese herbal medicine and practised with the imprimatur of an association promoting medicine of that type, but he was not qualified as a doctor in the United Kingdom. One of his patients died following a course of treatment prescribed by the defendant for the cure of benign skin blemishes, whose only treatment in western medicine was removal by surgery. The agreed expert evidence was that the death was caused by an extremely rare and unpredictable toxic reaction to the herbal treatment. The question was whether the prescription was negligent. The judge ruled that the defendant's conduct ought not to be assessed by the standards of orthodox medicine, because 'the fact that the patient has chosen to reject the orthodox and prefer the alternative practitioner is something important which must be taken into account'. It was immaterial whether the patient's decision was 'enlightened and informed or based on ignorance and superstition' (at 416). But it was not enough to consider only whether the defendant had exercised the degree of skill appropriate to his 'art', for the fact that he was offering an alternative to orthodox medicine had a number of implications (at 417):

> First of all, the practitioner has to recognise that he is holding himself out as competent to practise within a system of law and medicine which will review the standard of care he has given to a patient. Secondly, where he prescribes a remedy which is taken by a patient it is not enough to say that the remedy is traditional and believed not to be harmful, he has a duty to ensure that the remedy is not actually or potentially harmful. Thirdly ... [a]n alternative practitioner who prescribes a remedy must take steps to satisfy himself that there has not been any adverse report in [orthodox medical] journals on the remedy which ought to affect the use he makes of it. That is not to say that he must take a range of publications himself. It should be enough if he subscribes to an 'association' which arranges to search the relevant literature and promptly report any material publication to him. The relevant literature will be that which would be taken by an orthodox practitioner practising at the level of speciality at which the alternative practitioner holds himself out.

Applying these principles, the judge found that the defendant was not in breach of his duty of care to the deceased since there was nothing in the orthodox medical journals to indicate that his herbal treatment was too hazardous to prescribe, or should have been prescribed only with a warning of the risk of an adverse reaction.

Of course, it is also possible to sue on the basis that the alternative practitioner failed to exercise the skill and care appropriate to his art, though this could be difficult to prove in the case of patient-centred therapies, which are individualised to the particular patient at the particular time, and therapies for which there are no agreed competencies (see J. Stone and J. Matthews, *Complementary Medicine and the Law* (Oxford: OUP, 1996), pp. 167–8).

Sporting Skill

In *Condon v Basi* [1985] 1 WLR 866, one of the football cases summarised earlier, the Court of Appeal rejected what Conor Gearty [1985] CLJ 371 at 373 describes as 'Basi's wonderful argument that he was such a bad footballer he owed no duty not to break his opponents' legs with awful tackles'. Nevertheless Sir John Donaldson MR stated (at 868): 'there will of course be a higher degree of care required of a player in a First Division [now Premier League] football match than of a player in a local league football match . . .'. Gearty queries whether this is desirable, suggesting that it effectively gives rise to a 'Cloggers' Charter' (*ibid.*):

> This gives a new dimension to knock-out competition. Imagine Melchester Rovers, the league leaders, away to non-league Thugs United in the third round of the FA Cup. Must Roy continue to play his immaculate game under threat of a personal injuries action whilst all about him the manicured and expensive legs of his team-mates are hacked to the ground by the legitimately incompetent?

Quite apart from our sympathy for Roy of the Rovers, we should note that Sir John Donaldson's comments on this matter were obiter and were subsequently doubted by Drake J in *Elliott v Saunders*, unreported, QBD, 10 June 1994. Subsequently, in *Vowles v Evans* [2003] 1 WLR 1607 at [28], in an analogous context, the Court of Appeal accepted that there was 'scope for argument' whether the degree of skill to be expected of a referee depends on his grade or that of the match he is refereeing, but stated that a volunteer called to stand in from amongst the spectators when the nominated referee failed to show up or was injured 'cannot reasonably be expected to show the skill of one who holds himself out as referee, or perhaps even to be fully conversant with the laws of the game'. Is the quoted proposition consistent with *Nettleship v Weston*?

2. Physical and Mental Disability

Mansfield v Weetabix Ltd [1998] 1 WLR 1263

The plaintiffs were the owners of a shop that was badly damaged when it was hit by a lorry owned by the first defendant and driven by the second defendant, Mr Tarleton. At the time of the accident, and unbeknownst to him, Tarleton was in a hypoglycaemic state whereby his brain was starved of oxygen and unable to function properly. The trial judge found him to have been negligent. Both defendants appealed.

Leggatt LJ

Mr Tarleton had an impaired degree of consciousness because of the malfunction in his brain caused by the deficiency in glucose.

The judge followed *Roberts v Ramsbottom* [1980] 1 WLR 823. In it a motorist was involved in an accident when unknowingly he was suffering from a stroke and was unaware of his unfitness to drive. Neill J considered several criminal cases about automatism before saying, at p. 832:

> I am satisfied that in a civil action a similar approach should be adopted. The driver will be able to escape liability if his actions at the relevant time were wholly beyond his control.

> The most obvious case is sudden unconsciousness. But if he retained some control, albeit imperfect control, and his driving, judged objectively, was below the required standard, he remains liable.

He gave no reason for being so satisfied. In my judgment, consideration of criminal cases can only introduce confusion. In them the question is whether the defendant was driving. Hence the need, if the defendant is to escape conviction, to show that he was in a state of automatism. In civil cases that is not the test. So Neill J erred when he considered criminal and civil cases indifferently, and assumed that to escape liability in a civil case a defendant must show that he was in a state of automatism . . . Nonetheless, *Roberts's* case was, in my judgment, rightly decided on the alternative ground that the defendant 'continued to drive when he was unfit to do so and when he should have been aware of his unfitness:' see pp. 832–833 . . .

The other case upon which Collins J principally relied was *Nettleship v Weston* [1971] 2 QB 691, in which this court held that the duty of care owed by a learner driver to her instructor is to be judged by the same objective standard as that owed to passengers and other road users by qualified drivers. But although this case shows that there should be no relaxation of the standard of care, it does not refer to cases in which a driver is unaware that he is subject to a disability . . .

There is no reason in principle why a driver should not escape liability where the disabling event is not sudden, but gradual, provided that the driver is unaware of it. A person with Mr Tarleton's very rare condition commonly does not appreciate that his ability is impaired, and he was no exception. Although by the time of trial Mr Tarleton was dead, and there was no direct evidence of his actual state of awareness, the judge held that he 'would not have continued to drive if he had appreciated and was conscious that his ability was impaired.' Of course, if he had known that it was, he would have been negligent in continuing to drive despite his knowledge of his disability. So also if he ought to have known that he was subject to a condition that rendered him unfit to drive: *Waugh v James Allan Ltd* [1964] 2 Lloyd's Rep 1 . . .

In my judgment, the standard of care that Mr Tarleton was obliged to show in these circumstances was that which is to be expected of a reasonably competent driver unaware that he is or may be suffering from a condition that impairs his ability to drive. To apply an objective standard in a way that did not take account of Mr Tarleton's condition would be to impose strict liability. But that is not the law . . . [S]ince in my judgment Mr Tarleton was in no way to blame, he was not negligent. I would therefore allow the appeal.

Aldous LJ

The standard of care that Mr Tarleton was obliged to show was that which is expected of a reasonably competent driver. He did not know and could not reasonably have known of his infirmity which was the cause of the accident. Therefore he was not at fault. His action did not fall below the standard of care required.

Sir Patrick Russell agreed with Leggatt and Aldous LJJ.

Appeal allowed.

Dunnage v Randall [2016] QB 639

While visiting the house of the claimant, his nephew, the deceased had a psychotic episode caused by his florid paranoid schizophrenia. The deceased went outside and came back with a can of petrol from his car, poured the contents over himself and threatened to set himself on fire with a cigarette lighter. The claimant tried to grab the lighter but in the ensuing struggle the deceased succeeded in igniting the fuel and both men were engulfed in flames. The claimant managed to jump to safety from a balcony; the deceased died at the scene. The claimant's action against the estate of the deceased, the first defendant, was defended by the second defendant, the provider of the deceased's household insurance, which provided cover in respect of liability in damages for accidental bodily injury. The judge dismissed the claim but the claimant appealed.

Voss LJ

130. . . . . [I]s there some principle that requires the law to excuse from liability in negligence a defendant who fails to meet the normal standard of care partly because of a medical problem. In my judgment, there is and should be no such principle. The courts have consistently and correctly rejected the notion that the standard of care should be adjusted to take account of personal characteristics of the defendant. The single exception in respect of the liability of children should not, I think, be extended. People with physical and mental health problems should not properly be regarded as analogous to children, even if some commonly and inappropriately speak of adults with mental health problems as having a 'mental age of five' . . .

131. In my judgment, only defendants whose attack or medical incapacity has the effect of entirely eliminating any fault or responsibility for the injury can be excused. It is only defendants in that category that have not actually broken their undoubted duty of care. The actions of a defendant, who is merely impaired by medical problems, whether physical or mental, cannot escape liability if he causes injury by failing to exercise reasonable care.

132. What then does it mean to say that a medical condition entirely eliminates any fault or responsibility for the injury? It simply means that the defendant himself did nothing to cause the injury. Mr Michael Davie QC, leading counsel for the first defendant, gave the example of a person whose arm is holding a knife and who is overcome by another forcing him to stab a victim. The person holding the knife cannot have broken his duty of care because he did nothing himself.

133. In my judgment, however, at all intermediate stages where the defendant does something himself he risks being liable for failing to meet the standards of the reasonable man. This approach avoids the need for medical witnesses to become engaged with difficult and undefined terms such as volition, will, free choice, consciousness, personal autonomy and the like. It is only if the defendant can properly be said to have done nothing himself to cause the injury that he escapes liability. This approach is not directly adopted in any of the authorities, but reflects in large measure, I think, the conceptual analysis favoured by at least three of the justices in *Corr v IBC Vehicles Ltd* [2008] AC 884, per Lord Scott at para 31, per Lord Mance, at paras 51–52, and per Lord Neuberger, at para 65 (who put the matter in terms of asking whether the deceased had 'no real "fault" . . . for his suicide').

134. This approach also has the attraction of not requiring any fine distinction to be made between the effects of physical health problems and mental health problems. Such a distinction seems to me, in the light of modern science, to be outdated and inappropriate. Even mental health problems often have some physical cause or manifestation. There is neither a logical nor a societal reason why the law should differentiate in this area between the two.

135. So where then does that leave this case? The judge held on the basis of the expert evidence that the deceased's 'capacity to think and act rationally and independently was wholly eliminated from the time he took the petrol can out of his car': para 34. It is the use of the word 'rationally' that concerns me. A person can still be acting if he acts irrationally; indeed, it is a matter of regret that even the most intelligent in our society sometimes do act irrationally. Nobody would suggest that they should be excused from liability for their negligence whilst so acting.

136. It is for this reason that it seems to me that the decision of the judge cannot stand . . .

Arden LJ

146. In my judgment, this case is indistinguishable in any material respect from that in *Morriss v Marsden* [1952] 1 All ER 925. In that case, a schizophrenic, who like Vince [the deceased] was deluded, was held liable for assaulting the manager of a hotel where he was staying: like negligence, assault and battery do not require an intention to injure. The attack was unprovoked. His mind directed the attack. It was irrelevant that he did not know that what he was doing was wrong. The court held that the defendant understood the nature and quality of his act even though he was deluded and even though he did not know that what he was doing was wrong.

147. That situation is with respect far removed from the case of a driver who gets into his car or lorry cab mentally and physically fit for the journey but then has an unforeseen episode during the journey which causes him to lose control of the vehicle. It cannot be said that he was negligent because he was acting with due care when he started to drive. This was the situation in *Mansfield v Weetabix Ltd* [1998] 1 WLR 1263. The defendant suffered the onset of a rare form of hypoglaecemic attack. He had no prior experience of this condition which came on gradually, so that he did not perceive the change in his condition. He was held not liable for injuries and damage caused by his inability to control the vehicle due to that episode. *Waugh v James K Allan Ltd* [1964] 2 Lloyd's Rep 1 illustrates the same principle. Vince was not in that position. He was not in control of machinery of which he unforeseeably loses control. Neither party suggests that Vince should have known that he was susceptible to this form of attack, but there is no parallel between *Mansfield* and this case because Vince was never in possession of the petrol can and lighter in the claimant's flat in circumstances when he had performed his duty of care . . .

153. The objective standard of care reflects the policy of the law. It is not a question of the law discriminating unfairly against people with physical or mental illness. The law takes the view as a matter of policy that everyone should owe the same duty of care for the protection of innocent victims. It would after all, in many cases, be open to a person who knows he has reduced abilities to take account of those abilities in what he does: that is why *Mansfield* was decided the other way from *Morriss*. There will be hard cases, as this case may be one, where a person does not know what action to take to avoid injury to others. However, his liability is no doubt treated in law as the price for being able to move freely within society despite his schizophrenia.

Rafferty LJ gave a separate concurring judgment.

Appeal allowed.

COMMENTARY

Are these two decisions consistent with one another? Can either or both of them be satisfactorily reconciled with *Nettleship v Weston* (extracted earlier)?

In *Roberts v Ramsbottom* [1980] 1 WLR 823, Neill J held that the defendant could escape liability only if the incapacity amounted to automatism, as defined in criminal law where the defence requires a *total* loss of consciousness or control over one's actions. This was rejected in *Mansfield* but the decision was approved on the alternative ground that the defendant was at fault for continuing to drive whilst aware of the unfitness, as he had been 'feeling queer' and had earlier hit the back of a parked van. However, the reasoning in *Dunnage* seems to revert to a test of total loss of control of one's actions—as applied by Neill J in *Roberts* but expressly rejected in *Mansfield*. In *Dunnage*, the Court of Appeal thought that *Mansfield* was distinguishable (see [147] per Arden LJ), but it is hard to see the justification for relieving drivers of responsibility for accidents caused by their erratic driving when they are required to carry insurance against the liabilities they incur towards others. On balance, it would be better to adopt the approach taken in *Dunnage* in all cases.

Persuasive support for such an approach may be found in the decision of the Queensland Court of Appeal in *Carrier v Bonham* [2002] 1 Qd R 474, where the claimant bus driver suffered psychiatric injury after the defendant deliberately stepped into the path of his bus in an attempt at committing suicide. The defendant was being treated for schizophrenia, but the court ruled that his mental illness could not be taken into account in deciding whether or not he had been negligent: the ordinary objective standard of a reasonable person was to be applied. One difficulty the court identified with making allowance for the defendant's illness was the impossibility of ascertaining the appropriate standard of care. As McPherson JA remarked (at [35]):

> Unsoundness of mind is not a normal condition in most people, and it is not a stage of development through which all humanity is destined to pass. There is no such thing as a 'normal' condition of unsound mind in those who suffer that affliction. It comes in different varieties and different shades or degrees. For that reason it would be impossible to devise a standard by which the tortious liability of such persons could be judged as a class.

See also McMurdo P at [8]. Another consideration for McPherson JA was that, if mentally ill persons were not to be judged according to the ordinary objective standard of care, there was a risk that society would respond by demanding their confinement ('then it is only a matter of time before there is reversion to the older and less humane practices of the past in the treatment of mental patients': at [36]). See also Arden LJ's comment regarding the deceased in the *Dunnage* case, at [153], that 'his liability is no doubt treated in law as the price for being able to move freely within society despite his schizophrenia'. Do you agree that these considerations provide good reasons for applying the objective standard of care without allowance for those who, because of mental illness, find it difficult or impossible to act with the requisite carefulness? For further analysis of *Dunnage* see Goudkamp and Ihuoma, 'A Tour of the Tort of Negligence' (2016) 32 PN 117; Orchard, 'Liability in Negligence of the Mentally Ill: A Comment on *Dunnage v Randall*' (2016) 45 CLWR 366.

3. Age

Mullin v Richards [1998] 1 WLR 1304

The plaintiff, a 15-year-old schoolgirl, was injured whilst playing at school with the first defendant, another girl of the same age. The two girls were fencing with plastic rulers during a class when one of the rulers snapped and a fragment of plastic entered the victim's right eye, causing her to lose all useful sight in that eye. She brought proceedings for negligence against the other girl and the local education authority. The judge dismissed the claim against the education authority but found that both girls had been guilty of negligence of which the injury was the foreseeable result. Accordingly, he held that the claim against the other schoolgirl succeeded, subject to a reduction of 50 per cent for contributory negligence. The defendant schoolgirl appealed, contending that the judge had erred when considering foreseeability by omitting to take account of the fact that she was not an adult.

Hutchison LJ

By her notice of appeal, the first defendant contends . . . [inter alia] that the judge erred when considering foreseeability by omitting to take account of the fact that the first defendant was not an adult but a 15-year-old schoolgirl. What he should have done, it is contended, was to consider objectively what a normal and reasonable 15-year-old schoolgirl would have foreseen . . .

The argument centres on foreseeability. The test of foreseeability is an objective one; but the fact that the first defendant was at the time a 15-year-old schoolgirl is not irrelevant. The question for the judge is not whether the actions of the defendant were such as an ordinarily prudent and reasonable adult in the defendant's situation would have realised gave rise to a risk of injury, it is whether an ordinarily prudent and reasonable 15-year-old schoolgirl in the defendant's situation would have realised as much. In that connection both counsel referred us to, and relied upon, the Australian decision in *McHale v Watson* (1966) 115 CLR 199, in particular at 213–214 in the judgment of Kitto J. I cite a portion of the passage I have referred to, all of which was cited to us by Mr Lee on behalf of the appellant, and which Mr Stephens has adopted as epitomising the correct approach:

> The standard of care being objective, it is no answer for him [that is a child], any more than it is for an adult, to say that the harm he caused was due to his being abnormally slow-witted, quick-tempered, absent-minded or inexperienced. But it does not follow that he cannot rely in his defence upon a limitation upon the capacity for foresight or prudence, not as being personal to himself, but as being characteristic of humanity at his stage of development and in that sense normal. By doing so he appeals to a standard of ordinariness, to an objective and not a subjective standard.

Mr Stephens also cited to us a passage in the judgment of Owen J (at 234):

> the standard by which his conduct is to be measured is not that to be expected of a reasonable adult but that reasonably to be expected of a child of the same age, intelligence and experience.

I venture to question the word 'intelligence' in that sentence, but I understand Owen J to be making the same point essentially as was made by Kitto J. It is perhaps also material to have in mind the words of Salmon LJ in *Gough v Thorne* [1966] 1 WLR 1387 at 1391, which is cited also by Mr Stephens, where he said:

> The question as to whether the plaintiff can be said to have been guilty of contributory negligence depends on whether any ordinary child of 13½ can be expected to have done any more than this child did. I say 'any ordinary child'. I do not mean a paragon of prudence; nor do I mean a scatter-brained child; but the ordinary girl of 13½.

I need say no more about that principle as to the way in which age affects the assessment of negligence because counsel are agreed upon it and, despite the fact that we have been told that there has been a good deal of controversy in other jurisdictions and that there is no direct authority in this jurisdiction, the approach in *McHale v Watson* seems to me to have the advantage of obvious, indeed irrefutable, logic . . .

The judge, it seems to me, found negligence without there being material on which he could properly do so. He seems indeed from the language he used to have regarded it as axiomatic that if there was a fight going on, such as he found there was, a play fight, that imported that injury was reasonably foreseeable and from his finding that the ruler broke that there was necessarily dangerous or excessive violence. For my part, I would say that in the absence of evidence one simply does not know why the ruler broke, whether because it was unusually weak, unlike other rulers; whether because it had been damaged in some way; or whether because rulers of this sort are particularly prone to break; one does not know. What certainly one cannot infer, and the judge was, I consider, not entitled to infer, was that there was here excessive violence or inappropriate violence over and above that which was inherent in the play fencing in which these two girls were indulging. This was in truth nothing more than a schoolgirls' game such as on the evidence was commonplace in this school and there was, I would hold, no justification for attributing to the participants the foresight of any significant risk of the likelihood of injury. They had seen it done elsewhere with some frequency. They had not heard it prohibited or received any warning about it. They had not been told of any injuries occasioned by it. They were not in any sense behaving culpably. So far as foresight goes, had they paused to think they might, I suppose, have said: 'It is conceivable that some unlucky injury might happen', but if asked if there was any likelihood of it or any real possibility of it, they would, I am sure, have said that they did not foresee any such possibility. Taking the view therefore that the learned judge—who, as I have said, readily and almost without question accepted that on his findings of fact there was negligence on the part of both these young ladies—was wrong in his view and there was no evidence on which he could come to it, I would allow the appeal and direct that judgment be entered for the first defendant.

Sir John Vinelott and **Butler-Sloss LJ** delivered short concurring judgments.

Appeal allowed.

COMMENTARY

Butler-Sloss LJ cited with approval (at 1312) certain additional dicta from the judgment of Kitto J in *McHale v Watson*, including the following ((1966) 115 CLR 199 at 216):

in the absence of relevant statutory provision, children, like everyone else, must accept as they go about in society the risks from which ordinary care on the part of others will not suffice to save them. One such risk is that boys of twelve may behave as boys of twelve . . .

The same applied, she added, to the risk that 'girls of 15 playing together may play as somewhat irresponsible girls of 15'. Whether boys' play is or ought to be distinguished from girls' play may be questioned. Moran (*Rethinking the Reasonable Person*, pp. 80–1, extracted earlier) is particularly troubled by the Australian High Court's nostalgic reconstruction of boyhood in *McHale*, and its celebration of boyish imprudence:

[T]he boy appears as a child of nature—specially responsive to the whims and impulses of the natural world. Beyond this implicit assertion of what the state of boyhood is, however, one can discern a deeper commitment, a commitment to a certain understanding of what is both constitutive and most valuable in the state of boyhood. The characteristic freedom of boyhood is, it seems, defined by the absence of any constraints arising out of the interests of others. So one could not impose liability for boyish imprudence without destroying the most fundamental and valuable characteristic of boyhood as well . . . The delightful freedom of boyhood springs, it seems, from the liberty to ignore the interests of others.

In contrast, Moran finds Butler-Sloss LJ's insistence that girls will be girls 'almost revolutionary' (p. 90). But she doubts the desirability of extending the possibilities of irresponsibility to girls, rather than demanding a reasonable standard of attentiveness to others from both girls and boys.

In the extract, Hutchison LJ seems to question whether it was right to treat the child's intelligence as a relevant factor. In so far as this suggests that the child's *experience* may conversely be taken into account, is this consistent with *Nettleship v Weston*? (Cf. the approach of Owen J in the passage cited by Hutchison LJ.)

It was agreed that, in assessing breach of duty, the foreseeability of injury should be assessed from the point of view of a reasonable child of the defendant's age. Presumably the defendant's age is also relevant in relation to the other elements of the 'breach equation' (e.g. in inquiring how easy it would be for the defendant to take precautions to guard against the risk of harm).

4. Special Skills

Philips v Whiteley (William) Ltd [1938] 1 All ER 566

The plaintiff made an appointment to have her ears pierced at the jewellery department of the defendant's shop. Whiteleys employed a Mr Couzens to perform the operation. For this purpose, he used an instrument he brought with him, having disinfected it by placing it in a flame before leaving his shop. Before actually piercing the ears, he rinsed his fingers in a glass of water into which he had poured a quantity of lysol, a disinfectant. Shortly after the ear piercing, the plaintiff developed an abscess in her neck which required surgery to have it opened and drained. The surgery was skilfully done, leaving only a very small scar. The plaintiff brought an action against the defendant, alleging that the operation was negligently performed and that the abscess was due to that negligence.

Goddard J

In this case, the first thing that I have to consider is the standard of care demanded from Mr Couzens—or, I should say, from Whiteleys, because Whiteleys were the people who undertook to do this piercing. It is not easy in any case to lay down a particular canon or standard by which the care can be judged, but, while it is admitted here, and admitted on all hands, that Mr Couzens did not use the same precautions of procuring an aseptic condition of his instruments as a doctor or a surgeon would use, I do not think that he could be called upon to use that degree of care. Whiteleys have to see that whoever they employ for the operation uses the standard of care and skill that may be expected from a jeweller, and, of course, if the operation is negligently performed—if, for instance, a wholly unsuitable instrument were used so that the ear was badly torn, or something of that sort happened—undoubtedly they would be liable. So, too, if they did not take that degree of care to see that the instruments were clean which one would expect a person of the training and the standing of a jeweller to use. To say, however, that a jeweller warrants or undertakes that he will use instruments which have the degree of surgical cleanliness that a surgeon brings about when he is going to perform a serious operation, or indeed any operation, is, I think, putting the matter too high. The doctors all seem to agree in this case that, if a lady went to a surgeon for the piercing of her ears, he would render his instruments sterile. After all, however, aseptic surgery is a thing of very modern growth. As anybody who has read the life of Lord Lister or the history of medicine in the last fifty or sixty years knows, it is not so many years ago that the best surgeon in the land knew nothing about even antiseptic surgery. Then antiseptic surgery was introduced, and that was followed by aseptic surgery. I do not think that a jeweller holds himself out as a surgeon or professes that he is going to conduct the operation of piercing a lady's ears by means of aseptic surgery, about which it is not to be supposed that he knows anything.

If a person wants to ensure that the operation of piercing her ears is going to be carried out with that proportion of skill and so forth that a Fellow of the Royal College of Surgeons would use, she must go to a surgeon. If she goes to a jeweller, she must expect that he will carry it out in the way that one would expect a jeweller to carry it out. One would expect that he would wash his instruments. One would expect that he would take some means of disinfecting his instrument, just in the same way as one knows that the ordinary layman, when he is going to use a needle to prick a blister or prick a little gathering on a finger, generally takes the precaution to put the needle in a flame, as I think Mr Couzens did. I accept the evidence of Mr Couzens as to what he says he did on this occasion—how he put his instrument in a flame before he left his shop, and how he washed his hands, and so forth. I think that he did. I see no reason to suppose that he is not telling me the absolute truth when he says what he did, and . . . for all practical purposes that is enough. That is to say, for the ordinary every-day matters that would be regarded as enough. It is not a degree of surgical cleanliness, which is a very different thing from ordinary cleanliness. It is not the cleanliness which a doctor would insist upon, because, as I say, Mr Couzens is not a doctor. He was known not to be a doctor. One does not go to a jeweller to get one's ears attended to if one requires to have a doctor in attendance to do it. If one wants a doctor in attendance, one goes to his consulting room or one has him come to see one. I do not see any ground here for holding that Mr Couzens was negligent in the way in which he performed this operation. It might be better, and I think that it probably would, if he boiled his instrument beforehand at his place, or if he took a spirit lamp with him and boiled his instrument at the time, but in view of the medical evidence . . . I see no ground for holding that Mr Couzens departed from the standard of care which you would expect that a man of his position and his training, being what he held himself out to be, was required to possess. Therefore, the charge of negligence fails.

[His Lordship also found for the defendants on the alternative ground that, even if the charge of negligence was proven, it was much more likely that the abscess from which Mrs Philips suffered was due to the subsequent infection of the puncture rather than a dirty needle.]

Judgment for the defendants.

COMMENTARY

Goddard J opted for the lower of the two standards he had to choose between: the standard of a jeweller, not that of a doctor. How can this be reconciled with *Nettleship v Weston* where the court decided to adopt the standard of a qualified driver, instead of the less demanding standard of the average learner driver for which the defendant had argued? The answer seems to be that, in *Nettleship*, the defendant was trying to *lower* the standard *below* that which normally governs driving on the roads, while, in *Philips*, the plaintiff was trying to *raise* the standard *above* that which the court deemed was appropriate to ear-piercing at the time in question. In each case, the court simply re-asserted the 'normal' standard of care required for the activity in question. Of course, where the defendant professes a special skill, then the standard of a person possessed of such skill will be applied (see *Maynard v West Midlands Regional Health Authority* [1984] 1 WLR 634: more is expected of a specialist than of a general practitioner).

An interesting case to consider in this context is *Wells v Cooper* [1958] 2 QB 265. The plaintiff was injured after he slipped and fell when, as he was seeking (with permission) to enter the defendant's house, the door knob he was pulling came away from the door. The door knob had been fixed by the defendant. It was held that the standard expected of him was that of a reasonably competent amateur carpenter, which the court noted was lower than the standard expected of a professional carpenter. The Court of Appeal found that he had not been negligent, noting that the job in question was a 'trivial domestic replacement'; it added that, had the job been something more ambitious, the defendant might have been negligent merely in undertaking the task. What sort of task do you think a competent amateur carpenter would be negligent merely in undertaking?

If a first-aid volunteer attends to an injured person, by what standard should their conduct be judged? Should one distinguish between the standard of care of a first-aider and that of a trained doctor where the aim of first-aid treatment is simply to get the patient into a condition where they can be transported to hospital? (See *Cattley v St John's Ambulance Brigade*, noted by Griffiths (1990) 53 MLR 255, and compare the position of the volunteer stand-in rugby referee considered by the Court of Appeal in *Vowles v Evans*, considered in IV.1.)

First-aiders may be expected to have at least some training. But what of the person professing no special training or skill who is obliged to give emergency medical care through force of circumstances? How would you formulate the standard of care to apply in such a case?

v. Common Practice

The decision whether or not the defendant is in breach of duty must be looked at in the light of other normative systems which regulate the activity in question. In the industrial sphere, the court may attach relevance to the existence of a common practice throughout the industry in question of taking, or not taking, a particular precaution against injury. Similarly, in the case of doctors, architects, lawyers and other professionals, it is necessary to take account of the rules and regulations promulgated by the relevant professional body, and to consider the state of expert opinion in the field. On the one hand, this is a matter of fairness to the defendant: is it reasonable to expect the defendant to 'plough a lone furrow' (to borrow a phrase from Mustill J in *Thompson v Smith Shiprepairers* [1984] QB 405 at 416) when others in the same sector of activity abide by lower standards? On the other hand, it reflects a realistic assessment of the courts' limited expertise in relation to certain technical matters, and of their consequent need to defer to the expert.

1. Common Industrial Practice

In *Morton v William Dixon*, 1909 SC 807 at 809, Lord Dunedin P set out principles which have been applied on many subsequent occasions:

> Where the negligence of the employer consists of what I may call a fault of omission, I think it is absolutely necessary that the proof of that fault of omission should be one of two kinds, either—to show that the thing which he did not do was a thing which was commonly done by

other persons in like circumstances or—to show that it was a thing which was so obviously wanted that it would be folly in anyone to neglect to provide it.

The two propositions Lord Dunedin advances here should be regarded as rules of thumb, not absolutes. First, failure to take a common precaution may indeed be sufficient evidence to warrant a finding of negligence, but it does not necessarily connote negligence. In *Brown v Rolls Royce* [1960] 1 WLR 210, the House of Lords declined to hold the defendant employers liable to a machine-oiler in their factory who had contracted dermatitis. The employee alleged that his condition resulted from contact with oil which would have been avoided had he been supplied with barrier cream. Even though barrier cream was commonly supplied by other employers to men doing work of this kind, there were strong differences of medical opinion about the practice and the defendants had acted throughout with the advice of their medical officer. The House of Lords emphasised that Lord Dunedin's propositions might impose a provisional, evidential burden on the defendants, but they had no compelling legal force (see especially at 215–16, per Lord Denning).

Secondly, the courts will be wary of finding that something which is commonly done by others in like circumstances is negligent unless it amounts to plain folly. In *Stokes v GKN* [1968] 1 WLR 1776 at 1783, Swanwick J stated: 'where there is a recognised and general practice which has been followed for a substantial period in similar circumstances without mishap, [the defendant] is entitled to follow it . . .'. Even where the practice has not been 'without mishap', it may be reasonable to follow it if the risk is 'an inescapable feature of the industry' (*Thompson v Smith Shiprepairers Ltd* [1984] QB 405 at 415, per Mustill J). But a defendant is not entitled to rely upon common practice where 'in the light of common sense or newer knowledge it is clearly bad' and 'where there is developing knowledge, he must reasonably keep abreast of it and not be slow to apply it' (*Stokes* at 1783, per Swanwick J). In *Thompson*, Mustill J (at 416) reinforced this statement by holding that negligence could consist in 'an absence of initiative in seeking out knowledge of facts which are not in themselves obvious'; he added, however, that, while the employer 'must keep up to date . . . the court must be slow to blame him for not ploughing a lone furrow' (quoted approvingly by Lord Mance JSC in *Baker v Quantum Clothing Group Ltd* [2011] 1 WLR 1003 at [10]).

2. Professional Standards

Bolam v Friern Hospital Management Committee [1957] 1 WLR 582

McNair J

[W]here you get a situation which involves the use of some special skill or competence, then the test whether there has been negligence or not is not the test of the man on the top of a Clapham omnibus, because he has not got this special skill. The test is the standard of the ordinary skilled man exercising and professing to have that special skill. A man need not possess the highest expert skill at the risk of being found negligent. It is well established law that it is sufficient if he exercises the ordinary skill of an ordinary competent man exercising that particular art . . . A doctor is not guilty of negligence if he has acted in accordance with a practice accepted as proper by a responsible body of medical men skilled in that particular art. . . . Putting it the other way round, a doctor is not negligent, if he is acting in accordance with such a practice, merely because there is a body of opinion that takes a contrary view. At the same time, that does not mean that a medical man can obstinately and pig-headedly carry on with some old technique if it has been proved to be contrary to what is really substantially the whole of informed medical opinion. Otherwise you might get men today saying: 'I don't believe in anaesthetics. I don't believe in antiseptics. I am going to continue to do my surgery in the way it was done in the eighteenth century'. That clearly would be wrong.

COMMENTARY

The so-called '*Bolam* test' is one of the foundation stones of the modern law of professional negligence (on which, see generally *Jackson and Powell on Professional Liability*, 9th edn (London: Sweet & Maxwell, 2021)). In *Gold v Haringey Health Authority* [1988] QB 481, the Court of Appeal held that it applied to any profession or calling which requires special skill, knowledge or experience. In fact, the test can also be applied to those who are not members of a profession but must nevertheless exercise a special skill (see, e.g., *Adams v Rhymney Valley DC* (2001) 33 HLR 41: selection of window locks by local authority).

The extent to which it should be open to the courts to find that professional judgement was exercised negligently has been a much-disputed question from at least the time of two medical cases reaching the House of Lords in the 1980s. In *Maynard v West Midlands Regional Health Authority* [1984] 1 WLR 634, the House of Lords held that a doctor's exercise of clinical judgement in a manner thought appropriate by a body of competent medical opinion could not be regarded as negligent simply because the trial judge 'preferred' an alternative body of medical opinion. In *Sidaway v Board of Governors of Bethlem Royal Hospital* [1985] AC 871, their Lordships held that the test applied not only to matters of medical diagnosis and treatment, but also to the question of the amount of information that a medical practitioner must give to a patient as to the risks involved in a proposed course of treatment. Dissenting, Lord Scarman (at 881) summarised the result of the *Bolam* test as follows: 'the law imposes the duty of care; but the standard of care is a matter of medical judgment'. This arguably posited an unquestionable proposition of law that medical practice that was in conformity with a body of expert opinion *would not* be reviewed by the courts, and there was certainly a reluctance to review such practice in the subsequent case law, though this was perhaps less marked in claims against other professionals (see, e.g., *Edward Wong Finance Co Ltd v Johnson Stokes & Master (A Firm)* [1984] AC 296, a successful claim against conveyancing solicitors).

Against the backdrop of considerable academic criticism of *Maynard* and *Sidaway*, the nature and extent of the *Bolam* principle was considered again by the House of Lords in *Bolitho v City and Hackney Health Authority* [1998] AC 232, extracted here.

Bolitho v City and Hackney Health Authority [1998] AC 232

Lord Browne-Wilkinson

[T]he court is not bound to hold that a defendant doctor escapes liability for negligent treatment or diagnosis just because he leads evidence from a number of medical experts who are genuinely of opinion that the defendant's treatment or diagnosis accorded with sound medical practice. In the *Bolam* case itself, McNair J [1957] 1 WLR 583, 587 stated that the defendant had to have acted in accordance with the practice accepted as proper by a 'responsible body of medical men.' Later, at p. 588, he referred to 'a standard of practice recognised as proper by a competent reasonable body of opinion.' Again, in . . . *Maynard's* case [1984] 1 WLR 634, 639, Lord Scarman refers to a 'respectable' body of professional opinion. The use of these adjectives—responsible, reasonable and respectable—all show that the court has to be satisfied that the exponents of the body of opinion relied upon can demonstrate that such opinion has a logical basis. In particular in cases involving, as they so often do, the weighing of risks against benefits, the judge before accepting a body of opinion as being responsible, reasonable or respectable, will need to be satisfied that, in forming their views, the experts have directed their minds to the question of comparative risks and benefits and have reached a defensible conclusion on the matter.

There are decisions which demonstrate that the judge is entitled to approach expert professional opinion on this basis . . . [Lord Browne-Wilkinson referred here to *Hucks v Cole* [1993] 4 Med LR 393 amongst other cases.] These decisions demonstrate that in cases of diagnosis and treatment there are cases where, despite a body of professional opinion sanctioning the defendant's conduct, the defendant can properly be held liable for negligence (I am not here considering questions of disclosure of risk). In my judgment that is because, in some cases, it cannot be demonstrated to the judge's satisfaction that the body of opinion relied upon is reasonable or responsible. In the vast majority of cases the fact that distinguished experts in the field are of a particular opinion will demonstrate the reasonableness of that opinion. In particular, where there are questions of assessment of the relative risks and benefits of adopting a particular medical practice, a reasonable view necessarily presupposes that the relative risks and benefits have been weighed by the experts in forming their opinions. But if, in a rare case, it can be demonstrated that the professional opinion is not capable of withstanding logical analysis, the judge is entitled to hold that the body of opinion is not reasonable or responsible.

I emphasise that in my view it will very seldom be right for a judge to reach the conclusion that views genuinely held by a competent medical expert are unreasonable. The assessment of medical risks and benefits is a matter of clinical judgement which a judge would not normally be able to make without expert evidence. As the quotation from Lord Scarman makes clear, it would be wrong to allow such assessment to deteriorate into seeking to persuade the judge to prefer one of two views both of which are capable of being logically supported. It is only where a judge can be satisfied that the body of expert opinion cannot be logically supported at all that such opinion will not provide the benchmark by reference to which the defendant's conduct falls to be assessed.

COMMENTARY

Lord Browne-Wilkinson's apparent modification of the *Bolam* test was applauded by some (e.g. Scott (1998) 148 NLJ 64) as challenging the autonomy of the medical profession. Others were more cautious. Keown [1998] CLJ 248 commented: '*Bolitho* is good as far as it goes, but it does not go as far as it should. For one thing, it is not clear whether medical opinion may be disregarded only if it is illogical. What if the logic is flawless but the premise unsound or unpersuasive?' At the least, though, 'the measured approach now endorsed by the House of Lords in *Bolitho* should reduce the risk of legitimating the lowest common denominator of accepted practice' (Teff, 'The Standard of Care in Medical Negligence—Moving on from *Bolam*' (1998) 18 OJLS 473 at 483). See further Brazier and Miola, 'Bye-bye *Bolam*: A Medical

Litigation Revolution?' (2000) 8 Med L Rev 85; Mulheron, 'Trumping *Bolam*: A Critical Legal Analysis of *Bolitho*'s "Gloss"' [2010] CLJ 609.

For examples of the application of the *Bolitho* principle, see *Penney v East Kent Health Authority* [2000] PNLR 323 (logical inconsistency in the defendant's expert evidence); *Muller v King's College London NHS Foundation Trust* [2017] QB 987 (defence expert's view that mistaken diagnosis was excusable was too lax).

Lord Browne-Wilkinson made clear that he was leaving aside the question of risk disclosure. This was subsequently addressed by a decision of the Supreme Court in 2015, extracted here.

Montgomery v Lanarkshire Health Board [2015] AC 1430

Lord Kerr and Lord Reed (with whom Lord Neuberger, Lord Clarke, Lord Wilson and Lord Hodge agreed)

74. The Hippocratic Corpus advises physicians to reveal nothing to the patient of her present or future condition, 'for many patients through this cause have taken a turn for the worse': *Decorum*, XVI. Around two millennia later, in *Sidaway's* case [1985] AC 871 Lord Templeman said 'the provision of too much information may prejudice the attainment of the objective of restoring the patient's health' (p 904); and similar observations were made by Lord Diplock and Lord Bridge. On that view, if the optimisation of the patient's health is treated as an over-riding objective, then it is unsurprising that the disclosure of information to a patient should be regarded as an aspect of medical care, and that the extent to which disclosure is appropriate should therefore be treated as a matter of clinical judgment, the appropriate standards being set by the medical profession.

75. Since *Sidaway's* case, however, it has become increasingly clear that the paradigm of the doctor-patient relationship implicit in the speeches in that case has ceased to reflect the reality and complexity of the way in which healthcare services are provided, or the way in which the providers and recipients of such services view their relationship. One development which is particularly significant in the present context is that patients are now widely regarded as persons holding rights, rather than as the passive recipients of the care of the medical profession. They are also widely treated as consumers exercising choices . . .

[Lord Kerr and Lord Reed highlighted a number of other social and legal developments, including the courts' increasing consciousness of the extent to which the common law reflects fundamental values, and continued:]

81. The social and legal developments which we have mentioned point away from a model of the relationship between the doctor and the patient based on medical paternalism. They also point away from a model based on a view of the patient as being entirely dependent on information provided by the doctor. What they point towards is an approach to the law which, instead of treating patients as placing themselves in the hands of their doctors (and then being prone to sue their doctors in the event of a disappointing outcome), treats them so far as possible as adults who are capable of understanding that medical treatment is uncertain of success and may involve risks, accepting responsibility for the taking of risks affecting their own lives, and living with the consequences of their choices.

82. In the law of negligence, this approach entails a duty on the part of doctors to take reasonable care to ensure that a patient is aware of material risks of injury that are inherent in treatment. This can be understood, within the traditional framework of negligence, as a duty of care to avoid exposing a person to a risk of injury which she would otherwise have avoided,

but it is also the counterpart of the patient's entitlement to decide whether or not to incur that risk. The existence of that entitlement, and the fact that its exercise does not depend exclusively on medical considerations, are important. They point to a fundamental distinction between, on the one hand, the doctor's role when considering possible investigatory or treatment options and, on the other, her role in discussing with the patient any recommended treatment and possible alternatives, and the risks of injury which may be involved.

83. The former role is an exercise of professional skill and judgment: what risks of injury are involved in an operation, for example, is a matter falling within the expertise of members of the medical profession. But it is a non sequitur to conclude that the question whether a risk of injury, or the availability of an alternative form of treatment, ought to be discussed with the patient is also a matter of purely professional judgment. The doctor's advisory role cannot be regarded as solely an exercise of medical skill without leaving out of account the patient's entitlement to decide on the risks to her health which she is willing to run (a decision which may be influenced by non-medical considerations). Responsibility for determining the nature and extent of a person's rights rests with the courts, not with the medical professions.

87. . . . . An adult person of sound mind is entitled to decide which, if any, of the available forms of treatment to undergo, and her consent must be obtained before treatment interfering with her bodily integrity is undertaken. The doctor is therefore under a duty to take reasonable care to ensure that the patient is aware of any material risks involved in any recommended treatment, and of any reasonable alternative or variant treatments. The test of materiality is whether, in the circumstances of the particular case, a reasonable person in the patient's position would be likely to attach significance to the risk, or the doctor is or should reasonably be aware that the particular patient would be likely to attach significance to it.

88. The doctor is however entitled to withhold from the patient information as to a risk if he reasonably considers that its disclosure would be seriously detrimental to the patient's health. The doctor is also excused from conferring with the patient in circumstances of necessity, as for example where the patient requires treatment urgently but is unconscious or otherwise unable to make a decision . . .

COMMENTARY

In departing decisively from *Sidaway*, though without formally overruling it, the Supreme Court considered that it was adopting what was in substance the approach taken in an earlier decision of the Court of Appeal (*Pearce v United Bristol Healthcare NHS Trust* [1999] PIQR P53) and by the High Court of Australia (*Rogers v Whitaker* (1992) 175 CLR 479). The extent of the information to be disclosed to the patient is now to be assessed by a test of 'materiality', as explained in para. 87 of the judgment. Materiality has two aspects, embracing both an objective, reasonable patient test and a subjective, particular patient test—the latter qualified by the requirement that the doctor is or ought to be aware the patient would attach significance to the information, which may place the onus on the patient to draw relevant circumstances to the doctor's attention (Hobson (2016) 79 MLR 488 at 492). The decision has been praised for its clear recognition of patient decisional autonomy (McGrath [2015] CLJ 211), though it has been doubted whether its impact on medical practice will match its symbolic legal importance: 'the ethics of the medical profession overtook the law some time ago, and in doing so a comprehensive body of professional regulatory standards for pre-operative disclosure and consent are now embedded in clinical practice that are actually far in advance of what the law has ever required' (Heywood (2015) 23 Med L Rev 455 at 466).

In the case itself, the pursuer sought damages on behalf of her son, who was born with cerebral palsy as a result of complications in his birth. The pursuer was diabetic and short of stature, which meant that there was a heightened risk—in the region of 9–10 per cent—of shoulder dystocia where, in the course of birth, the baby's shoulders are unable to pass through the mother's pelvis without medical intervention. Her doctor chose not to inform her of this risk as she anticipated that the pursuer would then ask for a caesarean section, which she did not think was in her best interests. The pursuer's evidence, which the court accepted, was that she would indeed have asked for a caesarean section if she had been informed of the risk, and her baby would then have been born unharmed.

The *Montgomery* principle applies to all information that is material in the sense described, not just (as in *Montgomery* itself) information about the risks of the proposed treatment. It therefore extends to the disclosure of information about alternative treatments and the risks associated with them (see *Webster v Burton Hospitals NHS Foundation Trust* [2017] EWCA Civ 62). The same reasoning has also been considered relevant in cases involving other professionals (see, e.g., *O'Hare v Coutts & Co* [2016] EWHC 2224 (QB): risks associated with investments recommended by defendant bank).

vi. *Res Ipsa Loquitur*

The maxim *res ipsa loquitur* (meaning 'the thing speaks for itself' or, more loosely, 'the accident tells its own story') allows the claimant to succeed in an action for negligence even where there is no evidence as to what caused the accident and, therefore, whether it was attributable to negligence on the part of the defendant. The leading case is *Scott v London and St Katherine Docks Co* (1865) 3 H & C 596 where the principle was stated as follows (at 601, per Erle CJ):

> There must be reasonable evidence of negligence. But where the thing is shown to be under the management of the defendant or his servants, and the accident is such as in the ordinary course of things does not happen if those who have the management use proper care, it affords reasonable evidence, in the absence of explanation by the defendants, that the accident arose from want of care.

The precise nature of the maxim has been the subject of considerable debate.

1. Purpose and Effect

> **P. S. Atiyah, 'Res Ipsa Loquitur in England and Australia'**
> (1972) 35 MLR 337
>
> There are two basic views as to the purpose and effects of the maxim.
>
> 1. The first is that the maxim is not a distinct rule of law (or evidence) in its own right and that in all cases of negligence the ultimate or legal burden of proof rests upon the plaintiff. According to this view the maxim is no more than a summary way of describing a situation in which it is permissible to infer from the occurrence of an accident that it was

probably caused by the negligence of the defendant. However, on this view, the inference of negligence is merely permissible (not obligatory) and if at the conclusion of the case the tribunal of fact is not satisfied that the accident was more probably than not caused by the negligence of the defendant, the plaintiff must fail.

2. The second view is that the maxim involves more than this and that it does represent a distinct rule of law (or evidence) in its own right. According to this view a legal burden of proof may be cast on the defendant in certain circumstances and the maxim therefore represents an exception to the general principle that the legal burden of proof always rests on the plaintiff throughout a negligence action. On this view, once the maxim operates, the plaintiff is entitled to a verdict even though, at the conclusion of the evidence, the tribunal of fact remains in doubt whether the accident was more probably than not caused by the negligence of the defendant. A plaintiff could not, of course, be entitled to a verdict in such a situation unless the legal burden of disproving negligence is upon the defendant . . .

[A] strong case can be made for saying that on policy grounds the second view is preferable and that, so far as English law is concerned, the first view is inconsistent with the actual decision in many recent cases.

The policy grounds for preferring the second view can be simply stated. The normal principle that the legal burden of proof rests on the plaintiff is liable to lead to unjust results in many cases in which the plaintiff does not know but the defendant does know the facts relevant to the issue of negligence or not. In particular, where accidents are caused due to sudden vehicle failure on the roads, or to unexplained disasters (such as explosions) in factories, the plaintiff may be in grave difficulties because he will have no information as to the standards of inspection, maintenance, etc which the defendant has adopted. The defendant may be able to adduce evidence on these matters but the plaintiff will frequently be unable to do so.

COMMENTARY

Though Atiyah prefers the second of the two views he outlines, the weight of modern authority is against him (see especially *Ng v Lee*, in the following extract). Even when the maxim *res ipsa loquitur* applies, the formal burden of proof remains on the claimant. The most that can be said is that, as a purely practical matter, the defendant must at least produce some evidence to counteract the inference of negligence that arises from the maxim's application. In *Henderson v Henry E. Jenkins & Sons* [1970] AC 282 at 301 Lord Pearson helpfully explained the difference between these 'formal' and 'evidential' burdens of proof:

My Lords, in my opinion, the decision in this appeal turns on what is sometimes called 'the evidential burden of proof', which is to be distinguished from the formal (or legal or technical) burden of proof . . . For the purposes of the present case the distinction can be simply stated in this way. In an action for negligence the plaintiff must allege, and has the burden of proving, that the accident was caused by negligence on the part of the defendants. That is the issue throughout the trial, and in giving judgment at the end of the trial the judge has to decide whether he is satisfied on a balance of probabilities that the accident was caused by negligence on the part of the defendants, and if he is not so satisfied the plaintiff's action fails. The formal burden of proof does not shift. But if in the course of the trial there is proved a set of facts which raises a prima facie inference that the accident was caused by negligence on the part of the defendants, the issue will be decided in the plaintiff's favour unless the defendants by their evidence provide some answer which is adequate to displace the prima facie inference. In this situation there is said to be an evidential burden of proof resting on the defendants. I have some doubts whether it is strictly correct to use the expression 'burden of proof' with this meaning, as there is a risk of it being confused with the formal burden of proof, but it is a familiar and convenient usage . . .

Praising Lord Pearson's analysis of the issue, a contemporary commentator observed: 'it would be difficult to find elsewhere a clearer statement of the law on this point' (Goodhart (1970) 86 LQR 145).

2. Application of the Maxim

Ng Chun Pui v Lee Chuen Tat [1988] RTR 298

The first defendant was driving a coach owned by the second defendant westwards in the outer lane of a dual carriageway in Hong Kong. Suddenly the coach crossed the central reservation and collided with a public light bus travelling in the inner lane of the eastbound carriageway. One passenger in the bus was killed, and the driver and three other passengers were injured. The plaintiffs (those injured and the personal representatives of the deceased) commenced an action against the defendants claiming damages for negligence. At the trial the plaintiffs did not call oral evidence and relied on the doctrine of *res ipsa loquitur*, contending that the fact of the accident alone was sufficient evidence of negligence by the first defendant. The defendants called evidence which established that an untraced car being driven in the inner lane of the westbound carriageway had cut into the outer lane in front of the coach, and to avoid hitting the car the first defendant had braked and swerved to the right whereupon the coach had skidded across colliding with the bus. The judge gave judgment for the plaintiffs on liability holding that the defendants had failed to discharge the burden of disproving negligence. On appeal the Court of Appeal of Hong Kong reversed that decision and found that the plaintiffs had failed to prove negligence. The plaintiffs appealed to the Judicial Committee of the Privy Council.

Lord Griffiths delivered the opinion of the Judicial Committee

The plaintiffs called no oral evidence and relied upon the fact of the accident as evidence of negligence or, as the judge put it, the doctrine of *res ipsa loquitur*. There can be no doubt that the plaintiffs were justified in taking this course. In ordinary circumstances if a well maintained coach is being properly driven it will not cross the central reservation of a dual carriageway and collide with on-coming traffic in the other carriageway. In the absence of any explanation of the behaviour of the coach the proper inference to draw is that it was not being driven with the standard of care required by the law and that the driver was therefore negligent. If the defendants had called no evidence the plaintiffs would undoubtedly have been entitled to judgment.

The defendants however did call evidence and gave an explanation of the circumstances that caused the first defendant to lose control of the coach. This evidence was given both by the driver of the coach, i.e. the first defendant, and a passenger sitting in the front of the coach. Their evidence corresponded closely with the contemporary accounts that both of them had given to the police. The judge accepted their evidence and made the following findings of fact:

> The evidence led by the defendants shows clearly that the coach was proceeding along a straight stretch of the road possibly a little in excess of the speed limit of 40 miles per

hour. But the speed of the coach is not alleged to be one of the elements of negligence and I am not particularly concerned with that. The coach was travelling in the fast or outer lane and in that lane there was other traffic about two coach lengths ahead of it. In the inner lane there was a vehicle about 10 to 20 feet ahead and between that vehicle and the coach there was a blue car travelling a little faster than the coach. Suddenly that blue car, which did not subsequently stop and has not been traced, cut into the fast lane some six to eight feet ahead of the coach. That was clearly a very dangerous manoeuvre and the first defendant reacted to it by braking and swerving a little to his right. The coach then skidded across the central reservation, as I have said, colliding with the public light bus.

The judge however was of the view that, despite those findings of fact, because the plaintiffs had originally relied upon the doctrine of *res ipsa loquitur*, the burden of disproving negligence remained upon the defendants and they had failed to discharge it. In their Lordships' opinion this shows a misunderstanding of the so-called doctrine of *res ipsa loquitur*, which is no more than the use of a Latin maxim to describe a state of the evidence from which it is proper to draw an inference of negligence. Although it has been said in a number of cases, it is misleading to talk of the burden of proof shifting to the defendant in a *res ipsa loquitur* situation. The burden of proving negligence rests throughout the case on the plaintiff. Where the plaintiff has suffered injuries as a result of an accident which ought not to have happened if the defendant had taken due care, it will often be possible for the plaintiff to discharge the burden of proof by inviting the court to draw the inference that on the balance of probabilities the defendant must have failed to exercise due care, even though the plaintiff does not know in what particular respects the failure occurred. One of the earliest examples of the operation of this doctrine is *Scott v London and St Katherine Docks Co* (1865) 3 H & C 596 . . .

So in an appropriate case the plaintiff establishes a prima facie case by relying upon the fact of the accident. If the defendant adduces no evidence there is nothing to rebut the inference of negligence and the plaintiff will have proved his case. But if the defendant does adduce evidence that evidence must be evaluated to see if it still reasonable to draw the inference of negligence from the mere fact of the accident. Loosely speaking this may be referred to as a burden on the defendant to show he was not negligent, but that only means that faced with a prima facie case of negligence the defendant will be found negligent unless he produces evidence that is capable of rebutting the prima facie case. Resort to the burden of proof is a poor way to decide a case; it is the duty of the judge to examine all the evidence at the end of the case and decide whether on the facts he finds to have been proved and on the inferences he is prepared to draw he is satisfied that negligence has been established. In so far as resort is had to the burden of proof the burden remains at the end of the case as it was at the beginning upon the plaintiff to prove that his injury was caused by the negligence of the defendants . . .

Appeal dismissed.

COMMENTARY

Lord Griffiths expressly adopted the dictum of Lord Pearson in *Henderson v Henry E. Jenkins & Sons* quoted earlier as clearly expressing the true meaning and effect of *res ipsa loquitur*. An example of the application of the maxim to a road traffic accident, to the plaintiff's benefit, is *Widdowson v Newgate Meat Corporation* [1998] PIQR P138. The plaintiff, who suffered from a serious mental disorder, was injured when struck by a car driven by one of the defendants whilst walking on the edge of the inside lane of a dual carriageway. The plaintiff was not competent to give evidence, and the driver chose not to, although in an earlier statement to police he could offer no explanation for the accident. There was also no evidence of why the plaintiff was on the road at the time or of where he was going. Nonetheless, the Court of Appeal allowed an appeal against the dismissal of the action, holding that there was no absolute rule against invoking the doctrine in road accident cases. Here, there was evidence that the plaintiff had an awareness of road safety, it was a clear night and the driver would have had a long clear view of the road in front. This was sufficient to establish a prima facie case and, in the absence of evidence from *either* of the parties involved in the accident, the defendants could not rebut that inference. However, the plaintiff's damages were reduced by 50 per cent for contributory negligence, because he was not wearing brightly coloured clothing, nor (so it seems) had he moved onto the grass verge as the car approached.

In other cases, the courts have revealed themselves to be more sceptical as to whether the *res* (the happening of the event) is itself evidence of negligence. In *Fryer v Pearson, The Times*, 4 April 2000, noted by Witting (2001) 117 LQR 392, the Court of Appeal doubted whether the presence of a sewing needle in the defendant's carpet was more consistent with fault on the defendant's part than the absence of fault. Where the *res* is more complicated, moreover, it is very unlikely that the maxim will apply as further evidence will be required to ascertain whether the facts are consistent with carelessness or not. Clinical negligence litigation provides a good example. In *Ratcliffe v Plymouth & Torbay Health Authority* [1998] PIQR P170, the Court of Appeal made the point that the maxim may apply in the medical negligence context if the circumstances are sufficient to give rise to an inference of negligence which is supported by ordinary human experience and does not require expert evidence (e.g. surgeon cuts off right foot instead of left, swab is left in operation site or patient wakes up during surgical operation despite general anaesthetic). Such cases will be rare, and more frequently the claimant's case will rely on, or at least be buttressed by, expert evidence adduced on his behalf. Thus, even if the defendant were to call no evidence, the court would be deciding the case on inferences it was entitled to draw from *the whole* of the evidence (including expert evidence), and not on the application of the maxim in its purest form.

A more recent application of the maxim suggests that the policy considerations invoked by Atiyah may exert a strong influence on how the maxim applies, even if one accepts (contrary to Atiyah) that it serves only to raise a factual presumption of negligence rather than formally to shift the burden of proof. In *George v Eagle Air Services Ltd* [2009] 1 WLR 2133, noted by Williams (2009) 125 LQR 567, the defendants' aircraft crashed on landing and the deceased, a passenger, was killed. In the subsequent action for damages for the benefit of the deceased's estate and dependants, it was alleged that the crash was caused by negligence on the part of the pilot, the defendants' employee. The defendants denied negligence, asserted that the aircraft had been serviced by the deceased, who was their mechanic, and was airworthy, but made no attempt to explain the crash. In those circumstances, the Privy Council found that *res ipsa loquitur* was applicable, quoting with approval the view of the US Federal Court of Appeals that '[l]ogic, experience and precedent compel us to reject the argument that airplane crashes ordinarily occur in the absence of default by someone connected with the design, manufacture, or operation of the craft' (*Higginbotham v Mobil Oil Corpn* (1977) 545 F 2d 422 at [19]). Delivering the Privy Council's opinion, Lord Mance explained further (at [13]):

Aircraft, even small aircraft, do not usually crash, and certainly should not do so. And, if they do, then, especially where the crash is on land as here, it is not unreasonable to suppose that their owner/operators will inform themselves of any unusual causes and not unreasonable to place on them the burden of producing an explanation which is at least consistent with absence of fault on their part.

On the facts, as the defendants had provided no such explanation, they failed to displace the inference of negligence which resulted from the crash itself.

The outcome seems correct, but it may be noted that pilot negligence was not the only possible cause of the crash: it might alternatively have resulted from the deceased's own negligent servicing of the aircraft or a manufacturing defect. On the facts, it was not so much the accident that raised an inference that the pilot was to blame, but the defendant's *failure to give any explanation of their own* for the accident when they might reasonably have been expected to provide one, or at least to explain why they could not.

The Future for *Res Ipsa Loquitur*

Because of the uncertainties surrounding its application and effect, there have been calls for the courts to avoid recourse to the maxim (see, e.g., Witting (2001) 117 LQR 392). Such calls have been heeded in Canada (*Fontaine v Loewen Estate* [1998] 1 SCR 424), but, in *Schellenberg v Tunnel Holdings* (2000) 200 CLR 121, the High Court of Australia declined to do away with *res ipsa loquitur*, Gleeson CJ and McHugh J holding that it represented a mode of inferential reasoning, not a rule of law, and viewed in this way was fully consonant with the general body of tort law (at 141). This also appears to be the view taken by the Court of Appeal in *Fryer v Pearson*, although May LJ thought that lawyers should stop using unhelpful Latin phrases to describe straightforward principles of law (at [19]; see also McInnes (2000) 8 Tort L Rev 162 at 164, who notes that the maxim is 'endowed with the seemingly mystical qualities that frequently attend upon Latin appellations'). No matter how this practice is described, however, it seems clear that the court may still infer negligence from the occurrence of the accident itself. If it does so, it is very probable that the defendant will be found liable unless they produce evidence to rebut the inference raised by the *res*. In such circumstances, the practical difference between a reversal in the legal burden of proof, which Atiyah in 1972 contended was the effect of *res ipsa loquitur*, and a reversal of the evidential burden, is more apparent than real.

5 CAUSATION AND SCOPE OF LIABILITY

It is axiomatic that before liability can arise in negligence a causal link must be established between the negligence of the defendant and the damage for which the claimant claims compensation. As in other areas of the law, however, deciding whether this requirement has been satisfied may present considerable difficulties. The 'causation' enquiry in negligence is generally thought to consist of two separate issues (see, e.g., *Wallace v Kam* (2013) 250 CLR 375 at [11]). The claimant must first show a historical connection between the defendant's negligence and the damage ('factual causation'). Whether this requirement is satisfied is usually determined by the application of the but-for test: but for the defendant's negligence, would the claimant have suffered the damage? Difficulties arise when this question cannot be answered because there is insufficient evidence, or where the answer produces a result which seems contrary to common sense, and in such cases the courts have sometimes been willing to apply a different, more claimant-friendly, approach. If factual causation is satisfied, the claimant must then show that the defendant should be legally responsible for the damage the claimant has suffered. This second strand of the causation enquiry (which Stapleton, 'Cause In Fact and the Scope of Liability For Consequences' (2003) 119 LQR 388 terms the 'scope of liability' question) may involve issues of 'legal causation', which is to say consideration of the effect of intervening acts, whether of the claimant or of a third party, occurring between the defendant's negligence and the claimant's damage. It may also involve consideration of whether the defendant should not have to pay for the full extent of the damage because it is considered too remote. Whilst we retain the traditional terminology of legal causation and remoteness in this chapter, it is important to remember, as Stapleton points out, that this second stage is a normative inquiry, and that drawing the line between recoverable and irrecoverable damage inevitably requires, and reflects, a value judgement as to the proper limits of liability.

I. Factual Causation

1. The But-For Test

The default test for establishing factual causation is the but-for test, according to which the claimant must show that without the defendant's negligence, the claimant's damage would not have occurred. Note that while the requirement of factual causation is satisfied by showing that the defendant's negligence was *a* cause of the damage, it need not be the *only* cause. There may in fact be a number of factual causes satisfying the but-for test. For example, if one negligently throws a lighted match on to a newspaper, there are at least two factual causes of the resultant fire—the presence of oxygen in the atmosphere and the negligent act of throwing down the match. And while for negligence purposes, some of these factual causes may be regarded as irrelevant, that determination occurs at the second stage of the causal analysis, under the rubric of 'legal causation'. It follows that the question of factual cause is best understood as a preliminary filter, which is designed to eliminate acts and omissions which bear no relationship with the claimant's damage.

But-for causation is established on the balance of probabilities: if it is more likely than not that an event was a cause, it is treated as if it were one. The application of the balance of probabilities standard of proof as part of the but-for test is considered in the following extracts.

Barnett v Chelsea and Kensington Hospital Management Committee [1969] 1 QB 428

The plaintiff was the wife of one of three nightwatchmen who had gone to the defendant's hospital after drinking some tea and becoming ill. The plaintiff's husband looked particularly unwell, but when the nurse on duty consulted the casualty officer on call, he advised them to go home and consult their own doctors. The men went away but several hours later the plaintiff's husband died from what was held to be arsenical poisoning. In an action against the defendant hospital the judge found that there was evidence of negligence, but that this negligence did not cause the death of the plaintiff's husband.

Nield J

It remains to consider whether it is shown that the deceased's death was caused by that negligence or whether, as the defendants have said, the deceased must have died in any event. In his concluding submission [counsel for the plaintiff] submitted that the casualty officer should have examined the deceased and had he done so he would have caused tests to be made which would have indicated the treatment required and that, since the defendants were at fault in these respects, therefore the onus of proof passed to the defendants to show that the appropriate treatment would have failed . . . I find myself unable to accept that argument, and I am of the view that the onus of proof remains upon the plaintiff . . . However, were it otherwise and the onus did pass to the defendants, then I would find that they have discharged it, as I would proceed to show.

There has been put before me a timetable which I think is of much importance. The deceased attended at the casualty department at five or 10 minutes past eight in the morning. If the casualty officer had got up and dressed and come to see the three men and examined them and decided to admit them, the deceased (and Dr Lockett agreed with this) could not have been in bed in a ward before 11 am. I accept Dr Goulding's evidence that an intravenous drip would not have been set up before 12 noon, and if potassium loss was suspected it could not have been discovered until 12.30 pm. Dr Lockett, dealing with this, said: 'If this man had not been treated until after 12 noon the chances of survival were not good'.

Without going in detail into the considerable volume of technical evidence which has been put before me, it seems to me to be the case that when death results from arsenical poisoning it is brought about by two conditions; on the one hand dehydration and on the other disturbance of the enzyme processes. If the principal condition is one of enzyme disturbance—as I am of the view it was here—then the only method of treatment which is likely to succeed is the use of the specific antidote which is commonly called BAL. Dr Goulding said this in the course of his evidence:

> The only way to deal with this is to use the specific BAL. I see no reasonable prospect of the deceased being given BAL before the time at which he died

and at a later point in his evidence:

> I feel that even if fluid loss had been discovered death would have been caused by the enzyme disturbance. Death might have occurred later.

I regard that evidence as very moderate, and it might be a true assessment of the situation to say that there was no chance of BAL being administered before the death of the deceased. For those reasons, I find that the plaintiff has failed to establish, on the balance of probabilities, that the defendants' negligence caused the death of the deceased.

Judgment for the defendants.

COMMENTARY

The but-for test requires a hypothetical inquiry into what would have happened if the defendant had not been negligent. But can the defendant rely upon the fact that, if they had not been guilty of the negligence of which the claimant complains, they would have caused the injury anyway by negligence of another sort? The issue arose in *Bolitho v City and Hackney Health Authority* [1998] AC 232. In *Bolitho*, a doctor's negligence consisted in not responding to a pager message until a time after the plaintiff's child had died. To prove causation it was therefore necessary to ask what the doctor would have done if she had responded to the pager. Her evidence was that she would not have intubated (i.e. inserted a tube into the child's larynx). It was subsequently accepted that this was the only medical procedure that would have saved the child. The House of Lords held that this was not the end of the causation inquiry, as it was necessary to ask whether the failure to intubate would have been negligent. If it was, causation would have been proved, not on the basis of what the defendant would have done but on what she should have done. This approach was accepted as correct in *Wright v Cambridge Medical Group* [2013] QB 312 on the basis that, if the defendant's argument were allowed to succeed, it would deprive the claimant of the right to claim damages for the (hypothetical) subsequent negligence (see Lord Neuberger MR at [58]).

2. Challenges to the Orthodox But-For Approach

(a) Loss of a Chance

Hotson v East Berkshire Area Health Authority [1987] AC 750

The plaintiff, aged 13, injured his hip in a fall from a tree and was taken to a hospital run by the defendant health authority. His injury was not diagnosed, and after suffering severe pain for five days he was taken back to the hospital. His injuries were then recognised and he was given emergency treatment, but his injury later developed into a medical condition (avascular necrosis) which resulted in a deformity to his hip and left him with limited mobility by the time he was 20. In his action against the health authority negligence was admitted but the authority argued that the delay had not affected the plaintiff's ultimate condition. The trial judge found that there was a 25 per cent chance that with proper medical treatment the plaintiff would have avoided avascular necrosis and awarded him 25 per cent of the damages he would have received if he could have shown on the balance of probabilities that the avascular necrosis was caused by the defendant's negligence. The judgment for the plaintiff was upheld by the Court of Appeal, and the defendant appealed to the House of Lords.

Lord Bridge of Harwich

. . . The plaintiff's claim was for damages for physical injury and consequential loss alleged to have been caused by the authority's breach of their duty of care. In some cases, perhaps particularly medical negligence cases, causation may be so shrouded in mystery that the court can only measure statistical chances. But that was not so here. On the evidence there was a clear conflict as to what had caused the avascular necrosis. The authority's evidence was that the sole cause was the original traumatic injury to the hip. The plaintiff's evidence, at its highest, was that the delay in treatment was a material contributory cause. This was a conflict, like any other about some relevant past event, which the judge could not avoid resolving on a balance of probabilities. Unless the plaintiff proved on a balance of probabilities that the delayed treatment was at least a material contributory cause of the avascular necrosis he failed on the issue of causation and no question of quantification could arise. But the judge's findings of fact . . . are unmistakably to the effect that on a balance of probabilities the injury caused by the plaintiff's fall left insufficient blood vessels intact to keep the epiphysis alive. This amounts to a finding of fact that the fall was the sole cause of the avascular necrosis.

The upshot is that the appeal must be allowed on the narrow ground that the plaintiff failed to establish a cause of action in respect of the avascular necrosis and its consequences. Your Lordships were invited to approach the appeal more broadly and to decide whether, in a claim for damages for personal injury, it can ever be appropriate, where the cause of the injury is unascertainable and all the plaintiff can show is a statistical chance which is less than even that, but for the defendant's breach of duty, he would not have suffered the injury, to award him a proportionate fraction of the full damages appropriate to compensate for the injury as the measure of damages for the lost chance. There is a superficially attractive analogy between the principle applied in such cases as *Chaplin v Hicks* [1911] 2 KB 786 (award of damages for breach of contract assessed by reference to the lost chance of securing valuable employment if the contract had been performed) and *Kitchen v Royal Air Force Association* [1958] 1 WLR 563 (damages for solicitors' negligence assessed by reference to the lost chance of prosecuting a successful civil action) and the principle of awarding damages for the lost chance of avoiding personal injury or, in medical negligence cases, for the lost chance of a better medical result which might have been achieved by prompt diagnosis and correct treatment. I think there are formidable difficulties in the way of accepting the analogy. But I do not see this appeal as a suitable occasion for reaching a settled conclusion as to whether the analogy can ever be applied.

As I have said, there was in this case an inescapable issue of causation first to be resolved. But if the plaintiff had proved on a balance of probabilities that the authority's negligent failure to diagnose and treat his injury promptly had materially contributed to the development of avascular necrosis, I know of no principle of English law which would have entitled the authority to a discount from the full measure of damage to reflect the chance that, even given prompt treatment, avascular necrosis might well still have developed. . . .

Lord Mackay of Clashfern

[W]hat was the plaintiff's condition on being first presented at the hospital? Did he have intact sufficient blood vessels to keep the affected epiphysis alive? The judge had evidence from the authority's expert which amounted to an assertion that the probability was 100 per cent that the fall had not left intact sufficient vessels to keep the epiphysis alive while he had evidence from Mr Bucknill, for the plaintiff, which although not entirely consistent suggested that the probability was perhaps between 40 per cent and 60 per cent, say 50 per cent, that sufficient vessels were left intact to keep the epiphysis alive. The concluding sentence in the judge's fourth finding of fact makes it plain, in my opinion, that he took the view, weighing that testimony along with all the other matters before him, that it was more probable than not that insufficient vessels had been left intact by the fall to maintain an adequate blood supply to the epiphysis and he expressed this balance by saying that it was 75 per cent to 25 per cent, a result reached perhaps as counsel for the plaintiff suggested by going for a figure midway between the competing estimates given by the parties' experts in evidence. Although various statistics were given in evidence, I do not read any of them as dealing with the particular probability which the judge assessed at 75 per cent to 25 per cent. In the circumstances of this case the probable effect of delay in treatment was determined by the state of facts existing when the plaintiff was first presented to the hospital. It is not, in my opinion, correct to say that on arrival at the hospital he had a 25 per cent chance of recovery. If insufficient blood vessels were left intact by the fall he had no prospect of avoiding complete avascular necrosis whereas if sufficient blood vessels were left intact on the judge's findings no further damage to the blood supply would have resulted if he had been given immediate treatment, and he would not have suffered the avascular necrosis.

As I have said, the fundamental question of fact to be answered in this case related to a point in time before the negligent failure to treat began. It must, therefore, be a matter of past fact. It did not raise any question of what might have been the situation in a hypothetical state of facts. To this problem the words of Lord Diplock in *Mallett v McMonagle* [1970] AC 166 at 176 apply:

> In determining what did happen in the past a court decides on the balance of probabilities. Anything that is more probable than not it treats as certain . . .

On the other hand, I consider that it would be unwise in the present case to lay it down as a rule that a plaintiff could never succeed by proving loss of a chance in a medical negligence case . . .

Lord Ackner

To my mind, the first issue which the judge had to determine was an issue of causation: did the breach of duty cause the damage alleged? If it did not, as the judge so held, then no question of quantifying damage arises. The debate on the loss of a chance cannot arise where there has been a positive finding that before the duty arose the damage complained of had already been sustained or had become inevitable. . . .

In a sentence, the plaintiff was not entitled to any damages in respect of the deformed hip because the judge had decided that this was not caused by the admitted breach by the authority of their duty of care but was caused by the separation of the left femoral epiphysis when he fell some 12 feet from a rope on which he had been swinging.

On this simple basis I would allow this appeal. I have sought to stress that this case was a relatively simple case concerned with the proof of causation, on which the plaintiff failed, because he was unable to prove, on the balance of probabilities, that his deformed hip was caused by the authority's breach of duty in delaying over a period of five days a proper diagnosis and treatment. Where causation is in issue, the judge decides that issue on the balance of the probabilities. Unless there is some special situation, e.g. joint defendants where the apportionment of liability between them is required, there is no point or purpose in expressing in percentage terms the certainty or near certainty which the plaintiff has achieved in establishing his cause of action.

Once liability is established, on the balance of probabilities, the loss which the plaintiff has sustained is payable in full. It is not discounted by reducing his claim by the extent to which he has failed to prove his case with 100 per cent certainty. The decision by Simon Brown J in the subsequent case of *Bagley v North Herts Health Authority* (1986) 136 NLJ 1014, in which he discounted an award for a stillbirth because there was a 5 per cent risk that the plaintiff would have had a stillborn child even if the hospital had not been negligent, was clearly wrong. In that case, the plaintiff had established on a balance of probabilities, indeed with near certainty, that the hospital's negligence had caused the stillbirth. Causation was thus fully established. Such a finding does not permit any discounting: to do so would be to propound a wholly new doctrine which has no support in principle or authority and would give rise to many complications in the search for mathematical or statistical exactitude.

Of course, where the cause of action has been established, the assessment of that part of the plaintiff's loss where the future is uncertain, involves the evaluation of that uncertainty. In *Bagley*, if the child had, by reason of the hospital's breach of duty, been born with brain injury, which could lead in later life to epilepsy, then it would have been a classic case for the evaluation, *inter alia*, of the chance of epilepsy occurring and discounting, to the extent that the chance of that happening fell below 100 per cent, what would have been the sum of damages appropriate if epilepsy was a certain consequence. . . .

Lord Goff and **Lord Brandon** agreed with Lord Bridge, Lord Mackay and Lord Ackner.

Appeal allowed.

Gregg v Scott [2005] 2 AC 176

The defendant misdiagnosed a lump under the claimant's left arm as harmless; it was in fact a cancerous tumour, and the misdiagnosis led to delay in treatment of nine months, during which time the cancer had spread. The claimant sued in respect of his consequent loss of expectation of life. The trial judge ruled that the misdiagnosis was negligent, and went on to consider what would have happened if the claimant had been diagnosed with due care. For present purposes, it is enough to note the judge's finding that the claimant's prospects of recovery (taken to mean disease-free survival for ten years from the date of the negligence) would have been 45 per cent, i.e. less than even, even if a proper diagnosis had been made, and that the delay had reduced the likelihood of the claimant's survival for that period to 25 per cent as at the date of trial. The claim failed at first instance and, by a majority, before the Court of Appeal. On appeal to the House of Lords, two arguments were put forward on the claimant's behalf. The first was that the growth of the tumour caused by the delay amounted to a physical injury, so that damages for the lost chance of recovery were recoverable as a loss consequential upon physical injury. The second was that the lost chance of recovery was itself a compensatable head of damage. The first argument appealed only to Lord Hope (see commentary to the extracts) and the extract deals primarily with the second issue.

Lord Nicholls (dissenting)

[1] This appeal raises a question which has divided courts and commentators throughout the common law world. The division derives essentially from different perceptions of what

5 CAUSATION AND SCOPE OF LIABILITY

constitutes injustice in a common form type of medical negligence case. Some believe a remedy is essential and that a principled ground for providing an appropriate remedy can be found. Others are not persuaded. I am in the former camp.

[2] This is the type of case under consideration. A patient is suffering from cancer. His prospects are uncertain. He has a 45 per cent chance of recovery. Unfortunately his doctor negligently misdiagnoses his condition as benign. So the necessary treatment is delayed for months. As a result the patient's prospects of recovery become nil or almost nil. Has the patient a claim for damages against the doctor? No, the House was told. The patient could recover damages if his initial prospects of recovery had been more than 50 per cent. But because they were less than 50 per cent he can recover nothing.

[3] This surely cannot be the state of the law today. It would be irrational and indefensible. The loss of a 45 per cent prospect of recovery is just as much a real loss for a patient as the loss of a 55 per cent prospect of recovery. In both cases the doctor was in breach of his duty to his patient. In both cases the patient was worse off. He lost something of importance and value. But, it is said, in one case the patient has a remedy, in the other he does not.

[4] This would make no sort of sense. It would mean that in the 45 per cent case the doctor's duty would be hollow. The duty would be empty of content. For the reasons which follow I reject this suggested distinction. The common law does not compel courts to proceed in such an unreal fashion. I would hold that a patient has a right to a remedy as much where his prospects of recovery were less than 50–50 as where they exceeded 50–50. Perforce the reasoning is lengthy, in parts intricate, because this is a difficult area of the law . . .

Medical Negligence

[20] Against this background I turn to the primary question raised by this appeal: how should the loss suffered by a patient in Mr Gregg's position be identified? The Defendant says 'loss' is confined to an outcome which is shown, on balance of probability, to be worse than it otherwise would have been. Mr Gregg must prove that, on balance of probability, his medical condition after the negligence was worse than it would have been in the absence of the negligence. Mr Gregg says his 'loss' includes proved diminution in the prospects of a favourable outcome. Dr Scott's negligence deprived him of a worthwhile chance that his medical condition would not have deteriorated as it did . . .

[24] Given this uncertainty of outcome, the appropriate characterisation of a patient's loss in this type of case must surely be that it comprises the loss of the chance of a favourable outcome, rather than the loss of the outcome itself. Justice so requires, because this matches medical reality. This recognises what in practice a patient had before the doctor's negligence occurred. It recognises what in practice the patient lost by reason of that negligence. The doctor's negligence diminished the patient's prospects of recovery. And this analysis of a patient's loss accords with the purpose of the legal duty of which the doctor was in breach. In short, the purpose of the duty is to promote the patient's prospects of recovery by exercising due skill and care in diagnosing and treating the patient's condition.

[25] This approach also achieves a basic objective of the law of tort. The common law imposes duties and seeks to provide appropriate remedies in the event of a breach of duty. If negligent diagnosis or treatment diminishes a patient's prospects of recovery, a law which does not recognise this as a wrong calling for redress would be seriously deficient today. In respect of the doctors' breach of duty the law would not have provided an appropriate remedy. Of course, losing a chance of saving a leg is not the same as losing a leg: see Tony Weir, *Tort Law* (2002), p 76. But that is not a reason for declining to value the chance for whose loss the doctor was directly responsible. The law would rightly be open to reproach were it to provide a remedy if what is lost by a professional adviser's negligence is a financial opportunity or chance but refuse a remedy where what is lost by a doctor's negligence is the chance of health

or even life itself. Justice requires that in the latter case as much as the former the loss of a chance should constitute actionable damage . . .

Identifying a Lost Chance in Medical Negligence Cases

[34] I come next to a further twist in the story. It concerns an additional complication. It is a difficult part of this appeal. With 'loss of chance' cases such as *Chaplin v Hicks* [1911] 2 KB 786, identifying the 'chance' the claimant lost is straightforward enough. The position of the claimant in the *Chaplin* case, had there been no wrong, could not be decided satisfactorily because no one could know what would have been the outcome of the beauty contest if the claimant had appeared at the interview. It was this uncertainty which made it appropriate to treat her loss of a chance as itself actionable damage. Otherwise she would have had no remedy. The chance she lost was the opportunity to attend and be considered at the interview. Thus, in this type of case the claimant's actual position at the time of the negligence, proved on balance of probability if disputed, is not determinative of the crucial hypothetical fact: what would have been the claimant's position in the absence of the wrong?

[35] The position with medical negligence claims is different. The patient's actual condition at the time of the negligence will often be determinative of the answer to the crucially important hypothetical question of what would have been the claimant's position in the absence of the negligence. *Hotson v East Berkshire Heath Authority* [1987] AC 750 is an instance of this.

The relevant factual question concerning Stephen Hotson's condition immediately prior to the negligence was whether his fall from the tree had left sufficient blood vessels intact to keep his left femoral epiphysis alive. The answer to this question of actual fact ipso facto provided the answer to the vital hypothetical question: would avascular necrosis have been avoided if Stephen Hotson's leg had been treated promptly? The answer to the first question necessarily provided the answer to the second question, because the second question is no more than a mirror image of the first. Built into the formulation of the first question was the answer to the second question.

[36] This is not always so. Many cases are not so straightforward. Sometimes it is not possible to frame factual questions about a patient's condition which are (a) susceptible of sure answer and also (b) determinative of the outcome for the patient. As already noted, limitations on scientific and medical knowledge do not always permit this to be done. There are too many uncertainties involved in this field.

[37] The present case is a good example. Identifying the nature and extent of Mr Gregg's cancer at the time of the mistaken diagnosis (the first question), so far as this could be achieved with reasonable certainty, did not provide a simple answer to what would have been the outcome had he been treated promptly (the second question). There were several possible outcomes. Recourse to past experience in other cases, that is statistics, personalised so far as possible, was the best that could be done. These statistics expressed the various possible outcomes in percentage terms of likelihood.

[38] Thus, for present purposes medical negligence cases fall into one or other of two categories depending on whether a patient's condition at the time of the negligence does or does not give rise to significant medical uncertainty on what the outcome would have been in the absence of negligence. The *Hotson* case was in one category. There was no significant uncertainty about what would have happened to Stephen Hotson's leg if treated promptly, once his condition at the time of the negligence has been determined on the usual probability basis. The present case is in the other category. Identifying Mr Gregg's condition when he first visited Dr Scott did not provide an answer to the crucial question of what would have happened if there had been no negligence. There was considerable medical uncertainty about

what the outcome would have been had Mr Gregg received appropriate treatment nine months earlier . . .

[44] The way ahead must surely be to recognise that where a patient is suffering from illness or injury and his prospects of recovery are attended with a significant degree of medical uncertainty, and he suffers a significant diminution of his prospects of recovery by reason of medical negligence whether of diagnosis or treatment, that diminution constitutes actionable damage. This is so whether the patient's prospects immediately before the negligence exceeded or fell short of 50 per cent. 'Medical uncertainty' is uncertainty inherent in the patient's condition, uncertainty which medical opinion cannot resolve. This is to be contrasted with uncertainties arising solely from differences of view expressed by witnesses. Evidential uncertainties of this character should be resolved in the usual way . . .

Lord Hoffmann

Loss of a Chance

[72] The alternative submission was that reduction in the prospect of a favourable outcome ('loss of a chance') should be a recoverable head of damage. There are certainly cases in which it is. *Chaplin v Hicks* [1911] 2 KB 786 is a well-known example. The question is whether the principle of that case can apply to a case of clinical negligence such as this.

[73] The answer can be derived from three cases in the House of Lords: *Hotson v East Berkshire Area Health Authority* [1987] AC 750, *Wilsher v Essex Area Health Authority* [1988] AC 1074 and *Fairchild v Glenhaven Funeral Services Ltd* [2003] 1 AC 32 . . .

[79] What these cases show is that, as Helen Reece points out in an illuminating article ('Losses of Chances in the Law' (1996) 59 MLR 188) the law regards the world as in principle bound by laws of causality. Everything has a determinate cause, even if we do not know what it is. The blood-starved hip joint in *Hotson*, the blindness in *Wilsher*, the mesothelioma in *Fairchild*; each had its cause and it was for the plaintiff to prove that it was an act or omission for which the defendant was responsible. The narrow terms of the exception made to this principle in *Fairchild* only serves to emphasise the strength of the rule. The fact that proof is rendered difficult or impossible because no examination was made at the time, as in *Hotson*, or because medical science cannot provide the answer, as in *Wilsher*, makes no difference. There is no inherent uncertainty about what caused something to happen in the past or about whether something which happened in the past will cause something to happen in the future. Everything is determined by causality. What we lack is knowledge and the law deals with lack of knowledge by the concept of the burden of proof.

[80] Similarly in the present case, the progress of Mr Gregg's disease had a determinate cause. It may have been inherent in his genetic make-up at the time when he saw Mr Scott, as Hotson's fate was determined by what happened to his thigh when he fell out of the tree. Or it may, as Mance LJ suggests, have been affected by subsequent events and behaviour for which Dr Scott was not responsible. Medical science does not enable us to say. But the outcome was not random; it was governed by laws of causality and, in the absence of a special rule as in *Fairchild*, inability to establish that delay in diagnosis caused the reduction in expectation in life cannot be remedied by treating the outcome as having been somehow indeterminate . . .

[84] . . . In the present case it is urged that Mr Gregg has suffered a wrong and ought to have a remedy. Living for more than 10 years is something of great value to him and he should be compensated for the possibility that the delay in diagnosis may have reduced his chances of doing so. In effect, the Appellant submits that the exceptional rule in *Fairchild* should be generalised and damages awarded in all cases in which the defendant may have caused an

injury and has increased the likelihood of the injury being suffered. In the present case, it is alleged that Dr Scott may have caused a reduction in Mr Gregg's expectation of life and that he increased the likelihood that his life would be shortened by the disease....

Control Mechanisms

[86] The Appellant suggests that the expansion of liability could be held in reasonable bounds by confining it to cases in which the claimant had suffered an injury. In this case, the spread of the cancer before the eventual diagnosis was something which would not have happened if it had been promptly diagnosed and amounted to an injury caused by the Defendant. It is true that this is not the injury for which the Claimant is suing. His claim is for loss of the prospect of survival for more than 10 years. And the judge's finding was that he had not established that the spread of the cancer was causally connected with the reduction in his expectation of life. But the Appellant submits that his injury can be used as what Professor Jane Stapleton called a 'hook' on which to hang a claim for damage which it did not actually cause: see (2003) 119 LQR 388, 423.

[87] An artificial limitation of this kind seems to me to be lacking in principle. It resembles the 'control mechanisms' which disfigure the law of liability for psychiatric injury. And once one treats an 'injury' as a condition for imposing liability for some other kind of damage, one is involved in definitional problems about what counts as an injury. Presumably the internal bleeding suffered by the boy Hotson was an injury which would have qualified him to sue for the loss of a chance of saving his hip joint. What about baby Wilsher? The doctor's negligence resulted in his having excessively oxygenated blood, which is potentially toxic: see [1987] QB 730, 764–766. Was this an injury? The boundaries of the concept would be a fertile source of litigation.

[88] Similar comments may be made about another proposed control mechanism, which is to confine the principle to cases in which inability to prove causation is a result of lack of medical knowledge of the causal mechanism (as in *Wilsher*) rather than lack of knowledge of the facts (as in *Hotson's* case). Again, the distinction is not based upon principle or even expediency. Proof of causation was just as difficult for Hotson as it was for Wilsher. It could be said that the need to prove causation was more unfair on Hotson, since the reason why he could not prove whether he had enough blood vessels after the fall was because the hospital had negligently failed to examine him...

[I]n my opinion, the various control mechanisms proposed to confine liability for loss of a chance within artificial limits do not pass this test. But a wholesale adoption of possible rather than probable causation as the criterion of liability would be so radical a change in our law as to amount to a legislative act. It would have enormous consequences for insurance companies and the National Health Service. In company with my noble and learned friends Lord Phillips of Worth Matravers and Baroness Hale of Richmond, I think that any such change should be left to Parliament.

Baroness Hale

The Loss of a Chance Argument

[209] The second, and more radical, way of redefining the Claimant's damage is in terms of the loss of a chance. Put this way, his claim is not for the loss of an outcome, in this case the cure of his disease, which he would have enjoyed but for the negligence. His claim is for the reduced chance of achieving that outcome...

[210] In [*Hotson*], the claimant had actually suffered the adverse outcome, avascular necrosis. The risk of suffering that outcome as a result of falling from the tree was 75 per cent. The

defendant's negligent failure to detect the injury to his hip took away the remaining 25 per cent chance of avoiding it. Clearly he could not prove that the negligence had caused the outcome. It was more likely than not that it had made no difference. But might he have proved that it was more likely than not that the negligence had reduced his chance of avoiding that outcome?

[211] The House of Lords treated this as a case in which the die was already cast by the time the Claimant got to the hospital (or at least the Claimant could not prove otherwise). The Defendant had not even caused the loss of the chance of saving the situation, because by the time the Claimant got to them there was no chance. The coin had already been tossed, and had come down heads or tails. But there must be many cases in which that is not so. The coin is in the air. The Claimant does have a chance of a favourable outcome which chance is wiped out or significantly reduced by the negligence. The coin is whipped out of the air before it has been able to land.

[212] This is, therefore, a new case, not covered precisely by previous authority. The Appellant himself describes his argument as the 'policy approach'. He recognises that it is a question of legal policy whether the law should be developed as he argues it should be. The wide version of the argument would allow recovery for any reduction in the chance of a better physical outcome, or any increase in the chance of an adverse physical outcome, even if this cannot be linked to any physiological changes caused by the Defendant. A Defendant who has negligently increased the risk that the Claimant will suffer harm in future (for example from exposure to asbestos or cigarette smoke) would be liable even though no harm had yet been suffered. This would be difficult to reconcile with our once and for all approach to establishing liability and assessing damage. Unless damages were limited to a modest sum for anxiety and distress about the future, sensible quantification would have to 'wait and see'. The narrower version of the argument would require that there be some physiological change caused by the Defendant's negligence, bringing with it a reduced prospect of a favourable outcome . . .

[223] Until now, the gist of the action for personal injuries has been damage to the person. My negligence probably caused the loss of your leg: I pay you the full value of the loss of the leg (say £100,000). My negligence probably did not cause the loss of your leg: I do not pay you anything. Compare the loss of a chance approach: my negligence probably caused a reduction in the chance of your keeping that leg: I pay you the value of the loss of your leg, discounted by the chance that it would have happened anyway. If the chance of saving the leg was very good, say 90 per cent, the claimant still gets only 90 per cent of his damages, say £90,000. But if the chance of saving the leg was comparatively poor, say 20 per cent, the claimant still gets £20,000. So the claimant ends up with less than full compensation even though his chances of a more favourable outcome were good. And the defendant ends up paying substantial sums even though the outcome is one for which by definition he cannot be shown to be responsible.

[224] Almost any claim for loss of an outcome could be reformulated as a claim for loss of a chance of that outcome. The implications of retaining them both as alternatives would be substantial. That is, the claimant still has the prospect of 100 per cent recovery if he can show that it is more likely than not that the doctor's negligence caused the adverse outcome. But if he cannot show that, he also has the prospect of lesser recovery for loss of a chance. If (for the reasons given earlier) it would in practice always be tempting to conclude that the doctor's negligence had affected his chances to some extent, the claimant would almost always get something. It would be a 'heads you lose everything, tails I win something' situation. But why should the Defendant not also be able to redefine the gist of the action if it suits him better?

[225] The Appellant in this case accepts that the proportionate recovery effect must cut both ways. If the claim is characterised as loss of a chance, those with a better than evens chance would still only get a proportion of the full value of their claim. But I do not think that

he accepts that the same would apply in cases where the claim is characterised as loss of an outcome. In that case there is no basis for calculating the odds. If the two are alternatives available in every case, the defendant will almost always be liable for something. He will have lost the benefit of the 50 per cent chance that causation cannot be proved. But if the two approaches cannot sensibly live together, the claimants who currently obtain full recovery on an adverse outcome basis might in future only achieve a proportionate recovery. This would surely be a case of two steps forward, three steps back for the great majority of straightforward personal injury cases. In either event, the expert evidence would have to be far more complex than it is at present. Negotiations and trials would be a great deal more difficult. Recovery would be much less predictable both for claimants and for defendants' liability insurers. There is no reason in principle why the change in approach should be limited to medical negligence. Whether or not the policy choice is between retaining the present definition of personal injury in outcome terms and redefining it in loss of opportunity terms, introducing the latter would cause far more problems in the general run of personal injury claims than the policy benefits are worth.

[226] Much of the discussion in the cases and literature has centred round cases where the adverse outcome has already happened. The patient has lost his leg. Did the doctor's negligence cause him to lose the leg? If not, did it reduce the chances of saving the leg? But in this case the most serious of the adverse outcomes has not yet happened, and (it is to be hoped) may never happen. The approach to causation should be the same for both past and future events. What, if anything, has the doctor's negligence caused in this case? We certainly do not know whether it has caused this outcome, because happily Mr Gregg has survived each of the significant milestones along the way. Can we even say that it reduced the chances of a successful outcome, given that Mr Gregg has turned out to be one of the successful minority at each milestone? This is quite different from the situation in *Hotson*, where the avascular necrosis had already happened . . . Mr Gregg faced a risk of an adverse outcome which happily has not so far materialised, serious though the effects of his illness, treatment and prognosis have been. The complexities of attempting to introduce liability for the loss of a chance of a more favourable outcome in personal injury claims have driven me, not without regret, to conclude that it should not be done . . .

Lord Phillips gave a separate concurring opinion. **Lord Hope** concurred with Lord Nicholls' dissenting opinion, but added further grounds for dissenting from the majority.

Appeal dismissed.

COMMENTARY

The attraction of the but-for test is its simplicity: if the damage would have occurred even without the defendant's negligence that negligence can be ruled out as a factual cause of the injury. However, this assumes that a definitive answer can be given to the question. If the answer comes out as 'we don't know', or 'we don't know for certain', the test can give rise to difficulties. In deciding whether a past injury was caused by the defendant's negligence, the standard of proof used is the balance of probabilities. Hence if it is more likely than not that the negligence caused the damage, it is treated as if it did so. The probability is converted into a certainty. The extracts from *Barnett* and *Hotson* illustrate this proposition, as the plaintiffs failed because they could not show on the balance of probabilities that the damage for which they were claiming was caused by the defendant's negligence. (For what the author terms a 'limited defence' of the rule that the claimant must prove causation on the balance of probabilities, see S. Steel, *Proof of Causation in Tort Law* (Cambridge: CUP, 2015), ch. 3).

One way of avoiding this difficulty is to re-define the damage that the claimant suffers. What if the plaintiff's claim in *Hotson* was viewed as being not for the injury itself (the necrosis) but rather for the loss of the chance of avoiding that injury brought about by the defendant's negligence? In his speech in *Hotson*, Lord Mackay denied that the plaintiff had lost a chance of recovery because his fate had been sealed one way or the other when he arrived at the hospital (for criticism, see Stapleton, 'The Gist of Negligence, Part 2: The Relationship Between "Damage" and Causation' (1988) 104 LQR 389). However, the same could not necessarily be said of the claimant in *Gregg v Scott*, with the result that in that case the House of Lords had to meet this 'loss of a chance' argument head-on.

In contract law, it is well established that damages may be awarded for the loss of a chance (*Chaplin v Hicks* [1911] 2 KB 786, cited in *Hotson* and *Gregg*). And in tort, once the claimant has established on the balance of probabilities that some recognised damage was caused by the defendant's negligence, compensation may be awarded for the chance that loss consequential on that damage will occur in the future. Suppose, for example, that the claimant suffered a broken leg in a car accident and is estimated to have a 30 per cent chance of losing the movement in that leg in the future. The claimant is entitled to damages for that possibility, which will be calculated by assessing what the claimant would recover for loss of movement in the leg and then discounting that sum by 70 per cent to reflect the probability that that will not occur. In these cases, the recovery for the lost chance is conceived simply as a matter of quantifying the loss resulting from the breach of contract or the tort. However, as *Gregg* shows, when it comes to deciding whether the claimant has suffered damage for the purpose of *establishing liability* in tort, the courts have taken a more restrictive approach.

Loss of a Chance in *Gregg*

A majority of the House of Lords in *Gregg v Scott* rejected the claim for loss of a chance, but the reasoning of the majority Law Lords differed significantly. For Lord Hoffmann, the material issue in *Gregg* was no different from that in *Hotson*; in both cases the relationship between the negligence of the defendant and the beneficial outcome for which the claimant hoped was shrouded in uncertainty, and the law dealt with uncertainty through the burden of proof. Commenting on *Gregg* in the later case of *Barker v Corus*, extracted later in this section, Lord Hoffmann observed [at 38]:

Gregg v Scott [2005] 2 AC 176 was a case of uncertainty about the cause of a known event. Although this point was to some extent obscured by the fact that Mr Gregg was making a claim for loss of expectation of life and was still alive at the time when he brought his action, there was no finding of uncertainty about what the outcome would be. The judge found as a fact that his expectation of life was substantially less than it would have been if he had not contracted cancer. His loss of expectation of life was therefore damage which he was taken to have suffered at the time when he made his claim, exactly as if he had suffered a broken leg . . .

The uncertainty in the case was over what had been the cause of the reduced expectation of life. Was it the conditions that led him to contract cancer in the first place, or was it the negligent delay in his diagnosis and treatment? The judge found that the delay had increased the chances of a premature death but not enough to enable him to say on the balance of probabilities that it would not otherwise have happened.

According to Lord Hoffmann, it was not permissible to reframe the claim as one for loss of a chance so as to avoid these evidential difficulties. He therefore disagreed with Lord Nicholls, who drew a distinction between the evidential uncertainty in *Hotson* and the scientific uncertainty in *Gregg*. Not everyone thinks that this is a satisfactory way of distinguishing between the cases (see, e.g., Peel (2005) 121 LQR 364 at 367) but Lady Hale also thought that *Hotson* was a different kind of case, where their Lordships did not consider the loss of a chance argument because in their view there had been no chance to lose.

There was another complication in *Gregg*, however, because the adverse outcome to which the loss of the chance related (i.e. death by cancer) had not occurred at the time of the trial nor by the time of the appeal to the House of Lords. It was a case in which, to expand upon Lady Hale's metaphor, the tossed coin was still in the air, rather than (as in *Hotson*) covered on the back of the player's hand. This was a key consideration for the other member of the majority, Lord Phillips, who pointed out the difficulties of trying to assess the statistical chances in a case like *Gregg* where the adverse outcome had not yet occurred, and who expressly reserved (at [190]) his position in a case '[w]here medical treatment has resulted in an adverse outcome and negligence has increased the chance of that outcome'. On the facts of *Gregg*, Lord Phillips rejected the claim for loss of chance on the basis that the adverse outcome was still prospective, stating (at [190]): 'Awarding damages for the reduction of the prospect of a cure, when the long term result of treatment is still uncertain, is not a satisfactory exercise.' He was particularly influenced by the consideration that a patient's prognosis is liable to vary over time. In the circumstances of the case, the very fact that the claimant had survived until the date of the House of Lords' hearing demonstrated that his chances of surviving cancer-free for ten years from the date of his initial treatment were significantly higher than the 25 per cent figure settled upon by the trial judge.

The result, then, seems to be as follows. Lord Hoffmann could not distinguish the case from *Hotson* and saw no reason to take a different approach than was taken in that case. Lady Hale saw the case as distinguishable from *Hotson* but rejected the award of damages for loss of chance in the 'coin in the air' scenario as well. Lord Phillips agreed that the case was distinguishable from *Hotson*, kept his options open on the award of loss of chance damages in the *Hotson* scenario, but rejected the claim for the very reason that the coin was still in the air. For the minority, Lord Nicholls distinguished *Hotson* and would have allowed recovery where it was not clear that on the balance of probabilities the adverse outcome was already inevitable at the time of the defendant's breach of duty. Although he agreed with Lord Nicholls, the other member of the minority, Lord Hope, found an alternative ground for the decision: as the negligence was responsible for some physical injury—the growth of the tumour—this constituted 'damage' so as to complete the action in negligence, and the lost chance of avoiding the cancer could be claimed as loss consequential upon that damage. However, even if it was correct to characterise the enlargement of the tumour as a physical injury, this still did not solve the evidentiary difficulties, since (as Lord Phillips pointed out) there was no evidence that it had actually made any difference to the claimant's prospects of long-term survival.

Damages for Loss of a Chance after *Gregg*

So does *Gregg* preclude altogether the award of damages for the loss of a chance of avoiding personal injury? It is certainly not possible to succeed in such a claim where, as in *Gregg*, the personal injury has not yet occurred. Where the personal injury has occurred, it is suggested that *Gregg* itself does not prevent a claim for the loss of the chance of avoiding that outcome, even if the speeches of Lord Hoffmann and Lady Hale would appear to be distinctly unsympathetic to such a development, and—in some cases, at least—the decision in *Hotson* stands in the way of such a claim and would need to be overruled if damages are to be awarded (see Stapleton (2005) 68 MLR 996 at 1004). Whether such a claim should be allowed is another matter. The criticisms put forward by Lord Hoffmann and especially Lady Hale in *Gregg* are undoubtedly powerful, and the House of Lords is not the only apex court that has been wary of accepting loss of a chance of avoiding personal injury as actionable damage in negligence (see *Lawson v Laferriere* [1991] 1 SCR 541 (Supreme Court of Canada); *Tabet v Gett* (2010) 242 CLR 537 (High Court of Australia)).

Were such a development to be countenanced, then some important questions would need to be addressed. First, as *Gregg* indicates, there is no consensus on when a claimant might be said to have lost a chance. Lord Mackay in *Hotson* argued that, when the plaintiff arrived at the hospital, there was no chance to lose, the plaintiff either having sufficient blood cells alive such that with proper medical treatment he would have made a complete recovery, or not. This was also Lord Hoffmann's interpretation of *Hotson* in *Gregg* (at [75]): at the time of the negligence the claimant was either in the group who would improve with treatment or in the group that would not. Into which group he fell was a question of past fact to be determined on the balance of probabilities. As Reece has argued ('Losses of chances in the law' (1996) 59 MLR 188 at 196):

> [T]here was a time in the past when the cause of the necrosis could have been determined. If the blood vessels had been examined after the fall, then it would have been humanly possible to decide whether or not the plaintiff would develop necrosis even if he were treated. At the time of trial the cause was uncertain, but the uncertainty was epistemological not objective.

If, however, there was an 'objective' uncertainty, there being no time in the past at which the cause of the necrosis could have been determined (e.g. because the plaintiff's fate was still 'held in the balance'), then this might be regarded as a real 'loss of a chance' case meriting the award of compensation.

Another difficulty in accepting 'loss of a chance' as damage lies in fixing the value to be given to the chance. It is normally assumed that this should be arrived at by reference to the ultimate injury to which the chance relates, so that the loss of a 40 per cent chance of saving one's leg would be compensated by an award of 40 per cent of the damages that would be awarded for the loss of the leg. If the chance is so valued, however, is this not in effect an attempt to compensate for the underlying injury itself even though balance of probabilities causation has not been satisfied? As Voyiakis (2009) 72 MLR 909, 917 notes: 'Knowing how much risk I have imposed on you and how much compensation I would have to pay you if I had caused you actual physical harm does not by itself suggest how much I should pay for having exposed your physical health to danger.' But do you think that there is a plausible alternative to this way of valuing the chance?

However, perhaps the greatest difficulty with accepting loss of a chance of avoiding personal injury as actionable damage, identified by Lady Hale in *Gregg*, is its relationship with balance of probabilities causation. If the evidence suggests that the negligence caused the claimant to lose a 60 per cent of avoiding injury, then under the balance of probabilities approach the chance would be converted into a certainty and the claimant would recover 100 per cent of the damages. But if loss of a chance amounts to compensatable damage, then that would seem to entail that by framing their claim as one for loss of a chance a claimant with a 40 per cent lost chance would recover 40 per cent of the amount that would be awarded to compensate their injury, whilst by framing their claim as one for the injury itself a claimant with a 60 per cent lost chance would recover 100 per cent of that amount. Would that be fair? If not, would there be any way of avoiding that result?

The reluctance of courts to allow recovery for loss of a chance of avoiding personal injury has not been echoed where the loss to which the chance relates is financial in nature.

In *Allied Maples v Simmons & Simmons* [1995] 1 WLR 1602, the plaintiff sued its solicitors for its failure to advise against the deletion of a warranty in a sale of business agreement between the plaintiff and a third party which deprived the plaintiff of protection in respect of any contingent liabilities of the third party. The defendants argued that their negligence did not cause the plaintiff's loss because it could not be shown on the balance of probabilities that the third party would have accepted such a warranty. The Court of Appeal held that, while the plaintiff had to show on the balance of probabilities that it would have relied on the proper advice if given (see *McWilliams v Sir William Arrol* [1962] 1 WLR 295), it was not necessary to show that the third party would probably have given some protection to the plaintiff against these liabilities. Instead, it was enough to show that there was a 'substantial' chance that it would have done so, in which case compensation could be awarded for the loss of that chance (see also *Blue Circle Industries plc v Ministry of Defence* [1999] Ch 289, and the decision of the Australian High Court in *Sellars v Adelaide Petroleum NL* (1994) 179 CLR 332 allowing a claim for loss of a commercial opportunity). Although the differential treatment of loss of a chance claims in respect of personal injury and pure economic loss has been described as anomalous (see Stapleton (2003) 119 LQR 388 at 406–11), the distinction has been defended by Coote, 'Chance and the Burden of Proof in Contract and Tort' (1988) 62 ALJ 761 at 772:

> [T]he loss of a chance of financial gain goes to establishing the existence of the actionable tort only where the nature of the tort, or, as regards negligence, the category of case is such that economic loss is sufficient for the purpose. Loss of chance complies with the requirement because the chance itself has an economic value. No artificiality is involved. There would be such artificiality though, if the chance of physical injury or the loss of a chance of physical recovery were to be treated by the courts as amounting to a form of injury in itself.

Do you find this reasoning persuasive?

For criticism of awards of damages for loss of a chance in French law, see Khoury (2008) 124 LQR 103, 121–30, and for different approaches to this issue, see Stapleton (1988) LQR 389; Hill (1991) 54 MLR 511; Lunney (1995) 15 LS 1; Reece (1996) 59 MLR 188; Stauch (1997) 17 OJLS 205; Jansen (1999) 19 OJLS 271; Nolan, 'Causation and the Goals of Tort Law', in A. Robertson and H. Tang, *The Goals of Private Law* (Oxford: Hart, 2009), pp. 179–87; S. Green, *Causation in Negligence* (Oxford: Hart, 2015), ch. 7; S. Steel, *Proof of Causation in Tort Law* (Cambridge: CUP, 2015), ch. 6; G. Turton, *Evidential Uncertainty in Causation in Negligence* (Oxford: Hart, 2016), ch. 4; and Weinrib (2016) 36 OJLS 135, 157–63.

(b) Material Contribution to Injury

In *Hotson* and *Gregg* the House of Lords declined to depart from orthodox principles of tort law in response to the difficulty of proving causation in complex medical cases. But their Lordships have shown themselves more willing to innovate in a series of cases involving exposure to toxic substances in the workplace. The first stage was the recognition of a liability for the employer's 'material contribution' to the employee's injury in a situation where part of the toxic exposure causing the injury was 'innocent' and part of it was attributable to the employer's breach of duty. In such cases, it is not necessary for the claimant to demonstrate that he would not have suffered the injury 'but for' the employer's breach, though it appears that the breach must at least have made the injury worse than it would otherwise have been.

Bonnington Castings Ltd v Wardlaw [1956] AC 613

The pursuer complained that, after working in the defenders' workshop for eight years, he contracted pneumoconiosis as a result of inhaling silicone dust. The dust came from two sources. The first source was the operation of a pneumatic hammer. As there was no known protection against dust produced in this way, the defenders were not negligent with respect to this source. The second source was the working of swing grinders. The dust from this source was attributable to the defenders' failure properly to maintain the ducts of the dust-extraction plant for the grinders, which was found to have been both negligent and a breach of statutory duty. The issue for the House of Lords was whether the defenders' negligence and breach of duty had caused the pursuer's pneumoconiosis.

Lord Reid

. . . In my judgment, the employee must, in all cases, prove his case by the ordinary standard of proof in civil actions; he must make it appear at least that, on a balance of probabilities, the breach of duty caused, or materially contributed to, his injury.

The medical evidence was that pneumoconiosis is caused by a gradual accumulation in the lungs of minute particles of silica inhaled over a period of years. That means, I think, that the disease is caused by the whole of the noxious material inhaled and, if that material comes from two sources, it cannot be wholly attributed to material from one source or the other. I am in agreement with much of the Lord President's opinion in this case, but I cannot agree that the question is which was the more probable source of the respondent's disease, the dust from the pneumatic hammers or the dust from the swing grinders. It appears to me that the source of his disease was the dust from both sources, and the real question is whether the dust from the swing grinders materially contributed to the disease. What is a material contribution must be a question of degree. A contribution which comes within the exception *de minimis non curat lex* is not material, but I think that any contribution which does not fall within that exception must be material. I do not see how there can be something too large to come within the de minimis principle, but yet too small to be material. . . .

I think that the position can be shortly stated in this way. It may be that, of the noxious dust in the general atmosphere of the shop, more came from the pneumatic hammers than from the swing grinders, but I think it is sufficiently proved that the dust from the grinders made a substantial contribution. The respondent, however, did not only inhale the general atmosphere of the shop; when he was working his hammer, his face was directly over it, and it must often have happened that dust from his hammer substantially increased the concentration of noxious dust in the air which he inhaled. It is, therefore, probable that much the greater proportion of the noxious dust which he inhaled over the whole period came from the hammers. But, on the other hand, some certainly came from the swing grinders, and I cannot avoid the conclusion that the proportion which came from the swing grinders was not negligible. He was inhaling the general atmosphere all the time, and there is no evidence to show that his hammer gave off noxious dust so frequently, or that the concentration of noxious dust above it when it was producing dust was so much greater than the concentration in the general atmosphere, that the special concentration of dust could be said to be substantially the sole cause of his disease. . . .

In my opinion, it is proved not only that the swing grinders may well have contributed, but that they did, in fact, contribute, a quota of silica dust which was not negligible to the respondent's lungs and, therefore, did help to produce the disease. That is sufficient to establish liability against the appellants and I am, therefore, of opinion that this appeal should be dismissed. . . .

> **Lord Tucker** and **Lord Keith of Avonholme** delivered speeches in favour of dismissing the appeal, **Viscount Simonds** agreed with Lord Reid, and **Lord Somervell** simply concurred.
>
> Appeal dismissed.

COMMENTARY

There remains considerable debate over whether the 'material contribution' test is an exception to the but-for test or simply a specific application of it. Bailey, 'Causation In Negligence: What is a Material Contribution?' (2010) 30 LS 167 argues that it is a particular application of the but-for test to cases of cumulatively caused injury. In *Bonnington*, he argues, there was no doubt that at the time at which the accumulation of dust in the pursuer was sufficient to trigger the disease it had been caused *both* by the tortious and innocent dust (see also Stapleton (2013) 129 LQR 39). A different view is taken by Miller, 'Causation In Personal Injury After (and Before) *Sienkiewicz*' (2012) 32 LS 396, who comments (at 399):

> Regardless of the intentions of the House when determining *Bonnington*, the key to the judgment is that it covers various combinations of dust concentrations; it is not dependant on a knowledge of the magnitude, or even the existence, of a threshold in the relationship which links dust concentration with respiratory dysfunction.

Some of the difficulties in working out what *Bonnington* decided arise from the fact that the pursuer recovered full damages, i.e. damages for all the effects of the pneumoconiosis. It has since been decided, however, that where the defendant is responsible for only some of the injury suffered by the claimant, the latter is limited to proportionate damages reflecting the extent of the defendant's wrongful contribution to the disease. In *Holtby v Brigham & Cowan (Hull) Ltd* [2000] 3 All ER 421, the claimant developed asbestosis as a result of occupational exposure to asbestos dust over a period of several years, during which he had worked for several different employers. The Court of Appeal ruled that each employer could be held liable only for a part of the claimant's total disability and, in the absence of evidence pointing to any alternative basis of appointment, divided responsibility between them on a 'time-exposure' basis. (See also *Allen v British Rail Engineering* [2001] PIQR Q10: vibration white finger.) The explanation that the court gave for the award of full damages in *Bonnington* was that the question of apportionment had simply not been raised. (For some complications with *Holtby*, see Bailey, '"Material Contribution" After *Williams v The Bermuda Hospitals Board*' (2018) 38 LS 411, 416–17.) The *Holtby* approach can lead to the award of very limited damages against a defendant who is responsible for a minimal, but still 'material', exposure: see, for example, *Carder v Secretary of State for Health* [2017] ICR 392, where the defendant was held liable for contributing 2.3 per cent of the asbestos exposure that caused a former employee's asbestosis.

It is important to note that proportionate damages may be awarded only where the claimant's injury is 'divisible' (on the distinction between divisible and indivisible injury, see S. Green, *Causation in Negligence* (Oxford: Hart, 2015), ch. 5). The clearest examples are where there are two wholly different injuries, e.g., where D1 breaks C's arm and D2 breaks his leg. *Holtby* is a significant case because it awards proportionate damages in a case where cumulative exposure to a harmful substance causes a single condition which gets progressively worse the longer the exposure lasts. Its practical result is to throw the risk of the bankruptcy or untraceability of individual defendants onto the claimant, who must now sue, and recover against, all those who contributed to the injury if they are to get compensation for the whole of their loss. And where, as in *Bonnington*, an 'innocent' factor has contributed to the injury, it follows that the claimant's damages cannot exceed that proportion of their loss which is attributable to the guilty cause.

Gullifer (2001) 117 LQR 403 has questioned whether proportionate damages are to be awarded if the periods of 'guilty' and 'innocent' exposure are not consecutive (as in *Holtby*) but concurrent (as in *Bonnington*), citing the evidential difficulties of assessing the contribution of the defendant's wrongful act in the latter type of case (see also Green (2009) 125 LQR 44). But the evidential difficulties may be no less in cases of successive exposure, especially where, as in *Holtby*, the disease manifests itself only many years afterwards. In *Holtby*, Stuart-Smith LJ stated that 'the court only has to do the best it can using its common sense', adding that this was necessary in order 'to achieve justice, not only to the claimant but the defendant, and among defendants' (at 429).

Are awards of proportionate damages appropriate in cases of psychiatric injury attributable to multiple causes? In *Rahman v Arearose Ltd* [2001] QB 351, the claimant was beaten up in his workplace in a violent attack for which his employer was held responsible. He was taken to hospital where he received negligent treatment, leaving him blind in his right eye. Subsequently, he developed various psychiatric disorders, which his psychiatric report attributed, in different degrees, to the attack and the loss of his eye. The Court of Appeal accepted that the effects of the two incidents had 'a synergistic interaction' and apportioned responsibility for the resultant disorders between the employer and the hospital authority. (It should be noted that, unlike in the other cases considered here, each defendant was clearly liable for some harm and the question was how far the liability of each should extend.) This approach was approved in *Hatton v Sutherland* [2002] 2 All ER 1, where the Court of Appeal would have applied it in the context of claims for work-related stress had the issue arisen on the facts. According to Hale LJ (at [36]): 'Many stress-related illnesses are likely to have a complex aetiology with several different causes. In principle a wrongdoer should pay only for that proportion of the harm suffered for which he by his wrongdoing is responsible.' Similarly, in *BAE Systems (Operations) Ltd v Konczak* [2018] ICR 1, the Court of Appeal accepted that in principle psychiatric harm could be divisible, and Irwin LJ commented (at [92]) that to avoid giving the claimant a 'windfall', it was important to limit compensation 'to the consequences of identified injury attributable to the tort in question', even if this required employment of a 'rough and ready approach'. Nevertheless, the court in *BAE Systems* held that the Employment Tribunal had been entitled to hold that the claimant's psychiatric illness was indivisible, and it may be that in practice a finding that psychiatric injury is indivisible will ordinarily be made unless (as in *Rahman*) the claimant is suffering from several distinct psychiatric conditions. In *Simmons v British Steel plc* [2004] ICR 585, for example, the House of Lords showed no inclination to carve up the various causes of the pursuer's depression and applied the 'material contribution' test of *Bonnington* to hold the defender responsible for the totality of the injury. After surveying these authorities, Bailey (2018) 34 PN 42 at 45 observes:

> If *Rahman* is to be criticised it should simply be on the basis that the decision *on the facts* that the psychiatric injury suffered was divisible was unsound, particularly for its failure to attach weight (or sufficient weight) to the synergistic effect that different elements may have in generating a particular psychiatric symptom. Given the well-known difficulties in assembling medical evidence on these matters, it is certainly arguable that defendants should be discouraged from pursuing divisibility arguments unless really clear evidence of divisibility *of the injury* can be deployed.

Cf. the more robust response of Weir [2001] CLJ 237 at 238, who said of the claimant in *Rahman* that he 'is not half-mad because of what the first defendant did and half-mad because of what the second defendant did, he is as mad as he is because of what both of them did'.

Does the material contribution analysis extend to indivisible injuries, defined by Laws LJ in *Rahman* (at [19]) as cases 'where there is simply no rational basis for an objective apportionment of causative responsibility' for the injury? In principle, it is difficult to see how it can, since where the damage is indivisible either the defendant's negligence caused (the entirety of) the damage, or it did not cause the damage at all. Unlike in the case of divisible damage, there is no middle way, and hence the use of the language of 'material contribution' may serve merely to obscure the issue of whether the but-for test is satisfied. The limitation of the 'material contribution' analysis to divisible injury cases was accepted by the Court of Appeal in *AB v Ministry of Defence* (2011) 117 BMLR 101 at [150], and also in *Heneghan v Manchester Dry Docks Ltd* [2016] 1 WLR 2036, which concerned lung cancer, an indivisible condition. Responding to the argument of counsel for the claimant in *Heneghan* that the court should apply the *Bonnington* test, Lord Dyson MR said, at [46]:

> I do not agree. That test is to be applied where the court is satisfied on scientific evidence that the exposure for which the defendant is responsible has in fact contributed to the *injury*. This is readily demonstrated in the case of divisible injuries . . . whose severity is proportionate to the amount of exposure to the causative agent.

Nevertheless, in *Bailey v Ministry of Defence* [2009] 1 WLR 1052 the Court of Appeal employed a material contribution analysis to justify recovery in an indivisible injury case. The claimant in *Bailey* had choked on her own vomit, which she had been too weak to clear from her throat. The choking had then triggered a cardiac arrest, which in turn led her to suffer brain damage, an injury which the Court of Appeal correctly treated as indivisible. There were two causes of the weakness that stopped the claimant clearing the vomit from her throat (and which therefore also caused her brain damage): the fact that she was suffering from pancreatitis and the defendant's clinical negligence. In the Court of Appeal, Waller LJ reasoned that the defendant's negligence made a more than negligible and hence 'material' contribution to the claimant's weakened condition, and ruled that this was sufficient to establish causation of the brain damage, even though there was no finding that the brain damage itself would not have occurred but for the defendant's negligence. The defendant was held liable in full for the claimant's injury.

Some academic commentators have been critical of the use of the 'material contribution' test to justify recovery of damages in *Bailey*. In the opinion of Bailey, *op. cit.*, '[i]t would make the law more coherent if the term "material contribution" were confined to situations that satisfy the "but-for" test in the normal way' (at 184). And, although her analysis differs from that of Bailey, Stapleton, 'Unnecessary Causes' (2013) 129 LQR 39, agrees that a compensatory award of damages is not justified by the use of the material contribution test in cases of indivisible injury. Furthermore, Stapleton warns, awarding damages in such cases on the basis of a material contribution analysis could have an 'explosive impact on medical negligence' because 'it may often be the case that a breach by a medical provider increases the weakness of a patient, by some non-negligible but un-assessable degree, before the patient suffers an indivisible injury that would have been avoided had the patient been of adequate strength' (at 58).

In *Williams v Bermuda Hospitals Board* [2016] AC 888, the Privy Council was given an opportunity to consider whether the material contribution test had a role to play in cases of indivisible damage. The plaintiff in *Williams* presented at the emergency department of the defendant's hospital with acute appendicitis. It was decided to order a CT scan of his abdomen, but there was a considerable delay before the scan was performed. Following the scan, an operation was carried out to remove the plaintiff's appendix, and during the operation it became apparent that his appendix had ruptured and that this had caused an accumulation of pus in his pelvic region. This sepsis caused complications during the surgery, which resulted in damage to the plaintiff's heart and lungs. At the trial of the plaintiff's negligence action, the judge found that the delay in ordering the scan had been negligent, and had put back the start time of the operation by at least 140 minutes, but that the plaintiff had failed to establish that the delay had caused the complications. The Court of Appeal of Bermuda reversed the decision of the trial judge, holding that causation had been established on a material contribution analysis. On appeal to the Privy Council, the Board held that on the facts as found by the trial judge it was right to infer, on the balance of probabilities, that the defendant's negligence had materially contributed to the process whereby the sepsis had developed and affected the heart and lungs, and therefore that it had materially contributed to the damage suffered by those organs.

Lord Toulson, who gave the sole judgment in *Williams*, said that, although the Board took the view that the Court of Appeal had been right to hold the hospital liable in *Bailey*, this had not involved a departure from the 'but-for' test. However, the reason that his Lordship gave for this conclusion, that the claimant's pre-existing pancreatitis in *Bailey* fell within the so-called 'egg-shell skull' rule, is not convincing. The egg-shell skull rule (noted in III.1) is a remoteness of damage principle to the effect that, provided the initial injury suffered by the claimant was reasonably foreseeable, it does not matter that the consequences of that injury were not. It is of no relevance to the question of factual causation. In fact it seems to us that the Court of Appeal in *Bailey* was right to admit that their decision represented a departure from the 'but-for' rule, precisely because the claimant in the case did not establish on the balance of probabilities that the negligence led to the damage. Furthermore, the same seems to be true of the result in *Williams*. The key reasoning of the Privy Council on the facts of *Williams* was that, because the hospital's negligence had contributed to the sepsis, and the sepsis had caused the injuries to the heart and lungs, it followed that the hospital's negligence had 'contributed to' those injuries. However, assuming (as the Privy Council appears to have done) that those injuries were indivisible, the second use of 'contributed to' here cannot mean 'caused in a but-for sense', since the trial judge made a specific finding that the plaintiff had not established a but-for causal link between the delay and the plaintiff's injuries.

The reasoning in both *Bailey* and *Williams* is at times obscure, and the justifications for the outcomes in the two cases are not clear. One explanation would be to treat both decisions as based on factual inferences of but-for causation, and hence as not involving any departure from orthodox causation rules, or any extension of the material contribution concept to cases of indivisible harm (see Bailey, '"Material Contribution" After *Williams v The Bermuda Hospitals Board*' (2018) 38 LS 411). This interpretation would appear to be consistent with the judgment of Lord Toulson in *Williams*, but is open to the objection that the results of the cases cannot properly be explained by reference to inferences of this kind. An alternative interpretation is that the two cases represent a limited extension of the material contribution principle to cases where the defendant's negligence has contributed to a condition or state of affairs—in *Bailey*, the weakness; in *Williams*, the sepsis—that caused the damage complained of (see Plunkett (2016) 32 PN 158, 162). An interpretation along these lines is favoured by Stapleton and Steel (2016) 132 LQR 363, who say in their note on *Williams* that the Privy Council in the case had the opportunity to enunciate a clear principle that a 'claimant can establish that the defendant's breach was a cause of [indivisible damage] by demonstrating that the breach contributed to the process by which the [entire final] condition occurred'. However, although a principle along these lines does seem to be the best way of explaining the *results* in *Bailey* and *Williams*, it is difficult to discern such a principle from the *reasoning* in the cases. Nor is it clear what the limitations of such a departure from the usual but-for rule would be. For example, must it be certain that the condition or process in question caused the damage (as it seems to have been in these two cases), or would it be enough to establish on the balance of probabilities that it did so? And what, precisely, is meant by a 'condition' or 'process' for these purposes? For additional commentary on *Williams*, see Bailey (*op. cit.*); and Green (2016) 32 PN 169, who says (at 169) that the Privy Council 'missed a chance to arrest the expansion of the material contribution to injury approach into situations in which it does not fit, and in which it is not necessary'. For further consideration of the role of the material contribution test, see G. Turton, *Evidential Uncertainty in Causation in Negligence*, pp. 65–80; and on divisibility issues more generally see K. Oliphant (ed.), *Aggregation and Divisibility of Damage* (Vienna: Springer, 2009).

(c) Material Increase in Risk

McGhee v National Coal Board [1973] 1 WLR 1

The pursuer was sent by the defender, his employer, to clean brick kilns. This meant that he was exposed to abrasive brick dust, although this exposure was not negligent. However, in breach of duty the defender failed to provide adequate washing facilities, with the result that the pursuer had to cycle home before he could remove the dust. The pursuer contracted dermatitis, and sought damages from the defender. The medical evidence showed that the pursuer's dermatitis had been caused by the brick dust, and that the risk that he would contract the disease had been materially increased by the fact that he had to cycle home with the dust on his skin. However, it was not possible to say whether the additional exposure to the dust attributable to the negligence of the defenders had caused the dermatitis.

Lord Reid

In the present case the evidence does not show—perhaps no one knows—just how dermatitis of this type begins. It suggests to me that there are two possible ways. It may be that an accumulation of minor abrasions of the horny layer of skin is a necessary precondition for the onset of the disease. Or it may be that the disease starts at one particular abrasion and then spreads, so that multiplication of abrasions merely increases the number of places where the disease can start and in that way increases the risk of its occurrence . . . [I] think that in cases like this we must take a broader view of causation. The medical evidence is to the effect that the fact that the man had to cycle home caked with grime and sweat added materially to the risk that this disease might develop. It does not and could not explain just why that is so. But experience shows that it is so. Plainly that must be because what happens while the man remains unwashed can have a causative effect, although just how the cause operates is uncertain. I cannot accept the view expressed in the Inner House [of the Court of Session] that once the man left the brick kiln he left behind the causes which made him liable to develop dermatitis. That seems to me quite inconsistent with a proper interpretation of the medical evidence. Nor can I accept the distinction drawn by the Lord Ordinary between materially increasing the risk that the disease will occur and making a material contribution to its occurrence.

Lord Simon of Glaisdale, Lord Salmon, Lord Wilberforce and Lord Kilbrandon delivered speeches in favour of allowing the appeal.

Appeal allowed.

Fairchild v Glenhaven Funeral Services Ltd [2003] 1 AC 32

The three claimants had each worked for several employers for a substantial period during which time they were exposed, through their employers' negligence, to asbestos dust. Each contracted a mesothelioma, a form of cancer caused by exposure to asbestos. The precise manner in which asbestos caused mesothelioma was not known. It was accepted that, the greater the exposure to asbestos, the more likely it was that a mesothelioma would result, but there was no evidence to indicate whether the trigger was a single asbestos fibre or an accumulation of asbestos fibres. The Court of Appeal rejected all three claims, holding that mesothelioma was triggered on a single identifiable occasion and that none of the claimants could establish on the balance of probabilities which period of exposure had caused the disease. The claimants appealed to the House of Lords.

Lord Bingham of Cornhill

The essential question underlying the appeals may be accurately expressed in this way. If (1) C was employed at different times and for differing periods by both A and B, and (2) A and B were both subject to a duty to take reasonable care or to take all practicable measures to prevent C inhaling asbestos dust because of the known risk that asbestos dust (if inhaled) might cause a mesothelioma, and (3) both A and B were in breach of that duty in relation to C during the periods of C's employment by each of them with the result that during both periods C inhaled excessive quantities of asbestos dust, and (4) C is found to be suffering from a mesothelioma, and (5) any cause of C's mesothelioma other than the inhalation of asbestos dust at work can be effectively discounted, but (6) C cannot (because of the current limits of human science) prove, on the balance of probabilities, that his mesothelioma was the result of his inhaling asbestos dust during his employment by A or during his employment by B or during his employment by A and B taken together, is C entitled to recover damages against either A or B or against both A and B? . . .

It is common ground that in each of the three cases under appeal conditions numbered (1) to (5) above effectively obtained. . . .

. . . It is accepted that the risk of developing a mesothelioma increases in proportion to the quantity of asbestos dust and fibres inhaled: the greater the quantity of dust and fibre inhaled, the greater the risk. But the condition may be caused by a single fibre, or a few fibres, or many fibres: medical opinion holds none of these possibilities to be more probable than any other, and the condition once caused is not aggravated by further exposure. So if C is employed successively by A and B and is exposed to asbestos dust and fibres during each employment and develops a mesothelioma, the very strong probability is that this will have been caused by inhalation of asbestos dust containing fibres. But C could have inhaled a single fibre giving rise to his condition during employment by A, in which case his exposure by B will have had no effect on his condition; or he could have inhaled a single fibre giving rise to his condition during his employment by B, in which case his exposure by A will have had no effect on his condition; or he could have inhaled fibres during his employment by A and B which together gave rise to his condition; but medical science cannot support the suggestion that any of these possibilities is to be regarded as more probable than any other. There is no way of identifying, even on a balance of probabilities, the source of the fibre or fibres which initiated the genetic process which culminated in the malignant tumour. It is on this rock of uncertainty, reflecting the point to which medical science has so far advanced, that the three claims were rejected by the Court of Appeal . . .

Principle

. . . In the generality of personal injury actions, it is of course true that the claimant is required to discharge the burden of showing that the breach of which he complains caused the damage for which he claims and to do so by showing that but for the breach he would not have suffered the damage.

The issue in these appeals does not concern the general validity and applicability of that requirement . . . but is whether in special circumstances such as those in these cases there should be any variation or relaxation of it. The overall object of tort law is to define cases in which the law may justly hold one party liable to compensate another. Are these such cases? A and B owed C a duty to protect C against a risk of a particular and very serious kind. They failed to perform that duty. As a result the risk eventuated and C suffered the very harm against which it was the duty of A and B to protect him. Had there been only one tortfeasor, C would have been entitled to recover, but because the duty owed to him was broken by two tortfeasors and not only one, he is held to be entitled to recover against neither, because of his inability to prove what is scientifically unprovable. If the mechanical application of generally accepted rules leads to such a result, there must be room to question the appropriateness of such an approach in such a case. . . .

Policy

. . . The crux of cases such as the present, if the appellants' argument is upheld, is that an employer may be held liable for damage he has not caused. The risk is the greater where all the employers potentially liable are not before the court. This is so on the facts of each of the three appeals before the House, and is always likely to be so given the long latency of this condition and the likelihood that some employers potentially liable will have gone out of business or disappeared during that period. It can properly be said to be unjust to impose liability on a party who has not been shown, even on a balance of probabilities, to have caused the damage complained of. On the other hand, there is a strong policy argument in favour of compensating those who have suffered grave harm, at the expense of their employers who owed them a duty to protect them against that very harm and failed to do so, when the harm can only have been caused by breach of that duty and when science does not permit the victim accurately to attribute, as between several employers, the precise responsibility for the harm he has suffered. I am of opinion that such injustice as may be involved in imposing liability on a duty-breaking employer in these circumstances is heavily outweighed by the injustice of denying redress to a victim. Were the law otherwise, an employer exposing his employee to asbestos dust could obtain complete immunity against mesothelioma . . . claims by employing only those who had previously been exposed to excessive quantities of asbestos dust. Such a result would reflect no credit on the law . . .

Conclusion

To the question posed . . . [previously in] this opinion I would answer that where conditions (1)–(6) are satisfied C is entitled to recover against both A and B . . . It was not suggested in argument that C's entitlement against either A or B should be for any sum less than the full compensation to which C is entitled, although A and B could of course seek contribution against each other or any other employer liable in respect of the same damage in the ordinary way. No argument on apportionment was addressed to the House. I would in conclusion emphasise that my opinion is directed to cases in which each of the conditions specified in

(1)–(6) . . . above is satisfied and to no other case. It would be unrealistic to suppose that the principle here affirmed will not over time be the subject of incremental and analogical development. Cases seeking to develop the principle must be decided when and as they arise. For the present, I think it unwise to decide more than is necessary to resolve these three appeals which, for all the foregoing reasons, I concluded should be allowed. . . .

Lord Hoffmann, **Lord Rodger**, **Lord Nicholls** and **Lord Hutton** delivered separate concurring speeches.

Appeals allowed.

Barker v Corus UK Ltd [2006] 2 AC 572

This appeal concerned a number of cases where employees had died from mesothelioma as a result of exposure to asbestos dust in the workplace. In cases where all the exposure resulted from negligent sources, the actions were brought against the remaining solvent defendants, and these defendants had been held to be jointly and severally liable (i.e. liable for the full value of each claim) even though there were other parties who had also exposed the deceased to asbestos but who were now insolvent. In one case, the disease was contracted from exposure in three distinct periods: first, while the deceased was working for a company that was now insolvent; second, while he was working for the defendant; and, third, while he was self-employed. In this case it had been held that the defendant was jointly and severally liable but that the damages should be reduced by 20 per cent for the deceased's contributory negligence while self-employed. On appeal to the House of Lords, the defendants argued that their liability under the *Fairchild* principle should not be joint and several, but should instead be proportionate to the risk created by their negligence (in most cases, the amount of time spent working for the defendant, as contrasted with the deceased's total exposure).

Lord Hoffmann

The Limits of *Fairchild v Glenhaven Funeral Services Ltd* [2003] 1 AC 32

5. My Lords, the opinions of all of your Lordships who heard *Fairchild* expressed concern, in varying degrees, that the new exception should not be allowed to swallow up the rule. It is only natural that, the dyke having been breached, the pressure of a sea of claimants should try to enlarge the gap. Indeed, an attempt to extend the principle of liability for increasing the likelihood of an unfavourable outcome to the whole of medical negligence was narrowly rejected in *Gregg v Scott* [2005] 2 AC 176. But each member of the Committee in *Fairchild* stated the limits of what he thought the case was deciding in slightly different terms . . .

11. The assistance which can be derived from these various formulations is limited. No one expressly adverted to the case in which the claimant was himself responsible for a significant exposure. Lord Bingham's formulation requires that all possible sources of asbestos should have involved breaches of duty to the claimant; Lord Rodger allowed for a non-tortious exposure by a defendant who was also responsible for a tortious exposure but reserved his position on any other non-tortious exposure. The most that can be said of the others is that they did not formulate the issue in terms which excluded the possibility of liability when there had been non-tortious exposures . . .

17. It should not . . . matter whether the person who caused the non-tortious exposure happened also to have caused a tortious exposure. The purpose of the *Fairchild* exception is to provide a cause of action against a defendant who has materially increased the risk that the claimant will suffer damage and may have caused that damage, but cannot be proved to

have done so because it is impossible to show, on a balance of probability, that some other exposure to the same risk may not have caused it instead. For this purpose, it should be irrelevant whether the other exposure was tortious or non-tortious, by natural causes or human agency or by the claimant himself. These distinctions may be relevant to whether and to whom responsibility can also be attributed, but from the point of view of satisfying the requirement of a sufficient causal link between the defendant's conduct and the claimant's injury, they should not matter. . . .

Creating a Risk as Damage

35. Consistency of approach would suggest that if the basis of liability is the wrongful creation of a risk or chance of causing the disease, the damage which the defendant should be regarded as having caused is the creation of such a risk or chance. If that is the right way to characterise the damage, then it does not matter that the disease as such would be indivisible damage. Chances are infinitely divisible and different people can be separately responsible to a greater or lesser degree for the chances of an event happening, in the way that a person who buys a whole book of tickets in a raffle has a separate and larger chance of winning the prize than a person who has bought a single ticket.

36. Treating the creation of the risk as the damage caused by the defendant would involve having to quantify the likelihood that the damage (which is known to have materialised) was caused by that particular defendant. It will then be possible to determine the share of the damage which should be attributable to him. The quantification of chances is by no means unusual in the courts. . . .

Fairness

40. So far I have been concerned to demonstrate that characterising the damage as the risk of contracting mesothelioma would be in accordance with the basis upon which liability is imposed and would not be inconsistent with the concept of damage in the law of torts. In the end, however, the important question is whether such a characterisation would be fair. The *Fairchild* exception was created because the alternative of leaving the claimant with no remedy was thought to be unfair. But does fairness require that he should recover in full from any defendant liable under the exception? . . .

43. In my opinion, the attribution of liability according to the relative degree of contribution to the chance of the disease being contracted would smooth the roughness of the justice which a rule of joint and several liability creates. The defendant was a wrongdoer, it is true, and should not be allowed to escape liability altogether, but he should not be liable for more than the damage which he caused and, since this is a case in which science can deal only in probabilities, the law should accept that position and attribute liability according to probabilities. The justification for the joint and several liability rule is that if you caused harm, there is no reason why your liability should be reduced because someone else also caused the same harm. But when liability is exceptionally imposed because you may have caused harm, the same considerations do not apply and fairness suggests that if more than one person may have been responsible, liability should be divided according to the probability that one or other caused the harm . . .

Lord Scott, **Lord Walker** and **Baroness Hale** delivered concurring speeches. **Lord Rodger** dissented.

Appeals allowed in part.

Compensation Act 2006

3. Mesothelioma: damages

(1) This section applies where—
   (a) a person ('the responsible person') has negligently or in breach of statutory duty caused or permitted another person ('the victim') to be exposed to asbestos,
   (b) the victim has contracted mesothelioma as a result of exposure to asbestos,
   (c) because of the nature of mesothelioma and the state of medical science, it is not possible to determine with certainty whether it was the exposure mentioned in paragraph (a) or another exposure which caused the victim to become ill, and
   (d) the responsible person is liable in tort, by virtue of the exposure mentioned in paragraph (a), in connection with damage caused to the victim by the disease (whether by reason of having materially increased a risk or for any other reason).

(2) The responsible person shall be liable—
   (a) in respect of the whole of the damage caused to the victim by the disease (irrespective of whether the victim was also exposed to asbestos—
      (i) other than by the responsible person, whether or not in circumstances in which another person has liability in tort, or
      (ii) by the responsible person in circumstances in which he has no liability in tort), and
   (b) jointly and severally with any other responsible person.

(3) Subsection (2) does not prevent—
   (a) one responsible person from claiming a contribution from another, or
   (b) a finding of contributory negligence.

(4) In determining the extent of contributions of different responsible persons in accordance with subsection (3)(a), a court shall have regard to the relative lengths of the periods of exposure for which each was responsible; but this subsection shall not apply—
   (a) if or to the extent that responsible persons agree to apportion responsibility amongst themselves on some other basis, or
   (b) if or to the extent that the court thinks that another basis for determining contributions is more appropriate in the circumstances of a particular case . . .

Sienkiewicz v Greif (UK) Ltd [2011] 2 AC 229

In the lead appeal, the deceased, a mesothelioma victim, had been exposed to asbestos fibres from two sources: the defendant's negligence and environmental (non tortious) exposure. The defendant argued that, in these circumstances, *Fairchild* did not apply and the claimant needed to establish causation applying the usual balance of probabilities standard, which would require her to show that the defendant's negligence had 'doubled the risk' arising from non-tortious factors. On the facts, this was not established. The defendant also argued that, even if *Fairchild* did apply, the defendant's negligence still had to double the environmental risk to count as a 'material' increase in the risk. The Court of Appeal found for the claimant on the basis that the Compensation Act 2006, s. 3 (extracted earlier) mandated that a material increase in risk would satisfy causation.

Lord Phillips

The effect of section 3 of the Compensation Act 2006

70. The Court of Appeal treated section 3(1) as enacting that, in cases of mesothelioma, causation can be proved by demonstrating that the defendant wrongfully 'materially increased the risk' of a victim contracting mesothelioma. This was a misreading of the subsection. Section 3(1) does not state that the responsible person *will be* liable in tort if he has materially increased the risk of a victim of mesothelioma. It states that the section applies *where* the responsible person is liable in tort for materially increasing that risk. Whether and in what circumstances liability in tort attaches to one who has materially increased the risk of a victim contracting mesothelioma remains a question of common law. That law is presently contained in *Fairchild* and *Barker*. Those cases developed the common law by equating 'materially increasing the risk' with 'contributing to the cause' in specified and limited circumstances, which include ignorance of how causation in fact occurs. The common law is capable of further development. Thus section 3 does not preclude the common law from identifying exceptions to the 'material increase of risk' test, nor from holding, as more is learned about mesothelioma, that the material increase of risk test no longer applies. The *Fairchild/Barker* rule was adopted in order to cater for the ignorance that existed at the time of those decisions about the way in which mesothelioma is caused. Section 3 does not preclude the courts from reverting to the conventional approach of balance of probabilities in mesothelioma cases should advances in medical science in relation to this disease make such a step appropriate.

71. Greif contend that the Court should identify an exception to the *Fairchild/Barker* rule where there has been only one occupational exposure to risk and that, in those circumstances, the Court can and should apply the 'doubles the risk' test. Section 3 poses no bar to that contention; it must be considered on its merits.

Epidemiology and the nature of the 'doubles the risk' test

72. The 'doubles the risk' test is one that applies epidemiological data to determining causation on balance of probabilities in circumstances where medical science does not permit determination with certainty of how and when an injury was caused. The reasoning goes as follows. If statistical evidence indicates that the intervention of a wrongdoer more than doubled the risk that the victim would suffer the injury, then it follows that it is more likely than not that the wrongdoer caused the injury . . .

80. Epidemiology is the study of the occurrence and distribution of events (such as disease) over human populations. It seeks to determine whether statistical associations between these events and supposed determinants can be demonstrated. Whether those associations if proved demonstrate an underlying biological causal relationship is a further and different question from the question of statistical association on which the epidemiology is initially engaged.

81. Epidemiology may be used in an attempt to establish different matters in relation to a disease. It may help to establish what agents are capable of causing a disease, for instance that both cigarette smoke and asbestos dust are capable of causing lung cancer, it may help to establish which agent or which source of an agent, was the cause, or it may help to establish whether or not one agent combined with another in causing the disease.

82. Epidemiological data can be obtained by comparing the relevant experience (eg contraction of a disease) of a group or cohort that is subject to exposure to a particular agent with the experience of a group or cohort that is not. Where an agent is known to be capable of causing a disease, the comparison enables the epidemiologist to calculate the relevant risk (RR) that flows from the particular exposure. An RR of 1 indicates that there is no association between the particular exposure and the risk. An RR of 2 indicates that the particular exposure doubled

the chance that the victim would contract the disease. Statistically the likelihood that the victim would have contracted the disease without the particular exposure is then equal to the likelihood that the victim would not have contracted the disease but for that exposure. Where the RR exceeds 2 the statistical likelihood is that the particular exposure was the cause of the disease. The greater the RR the greater the statistical likelihood that the particular exposure caused the disease.

83. An RR of just over 2 is a tenuous basis for concluding that the statistical probable cause of a disease was also the probable biological cause, or cause in fact. The greater the RR the greater the likelihood that the statistical cause was also the biological cause. One reason why an RR of just over 2 is a tenuous basis for determining the biological cause is that the balance of that probability is a very fine one. Another is that the epidemiological data may not be reliable. One reason for this may be that the relevant survey or surveys have been insufficiently extensive to produce data that is truly representative. Epidemiologists conventionally seek to indicate the reliance that can be placed on an RR by determining 95 per cent confidence limits or intervals (CI) around it.

84. The approach that I have been describing focuses on one specific causal agent or a number of specific causal agents. There may well, however, be other causal factors that operate in conjunction with the agent exposure to which is the particular object of investigation, eg the age or genetic susceptibility of the victim. The identification of one probable cause of a disease does not preclude the possibility that there are other contributory causes . . .

Can the 'doubles the risk' test be applied in mesothelioma cases?

94. This question calls for consideration of the conundrum that I identified when considering the decisions in *Fairchild* and *Barker*. In the course of argument I put the conundrum to Mr Stuart-Smith [counsel for the appellants]. Why, if it was possible to equate increasing exposure to increasing risk, could one not postulate that, on balance of probabilities, where one employer had caused over 50 per cent of a victim's exposure, that employer had caused the victim's mesothelioma? Why could one not, by the same token, postulate that where over 50 per cent of the victim's exposure was not attributable to fault at all, on balance of probability, the victim's mesothelioma had not been caused tortiously? In short, why was there any need to apply the *Fairchild/Barker* rule where epidemiological evidence enabled one to use statistics to determine causation on balance of probability? . . .

97. [T]he first answer to the conundrum may be that, in the case of mesothelioma, epidemiological evidence alone has not been considered by the courts to be an adequate basis for making findings of causation: that so long as medical science is unable to demonstrate, as a matter of fact, the aetiology of mesothelioma, data relating incidence to exposure is not a satisfactory basis for making findings of causation.

98. Not only is the adequacy of epidemiological evidence relevant to the weight to be attached to it. So is its reliability . . .

103. The House of Lords was not, in *Fairchild* nor in *Barker* invited to consider the possibility that it might be possible in an appropriate case to demonstrate by epidemiological evidence that, on balance of probabilities, the mesothelioma had been caused by exposure that was not wrongful, or alternatively that such evidence might demonstrate that one particular employer had, on balance of probabilities, caused the disease. Had it been I do not believe that the House would have been persuaded that epidemiological evidence was sufficiently reliable to base findings as to causation upon it . . .

105. I would add that even if one could postulate with confidence that the extent of the contribution of a defendant to the victim's exposure to asbestos precisely reflected the likelihood that his breach of duty had caused the victim's disease, there would still be justification for the application of the *Fairchild* rule where all the exposure was wrongful. Imagine four

defendants each of whom had contributed 25 per cent to the victim's exposure so that there was a 25 per cent likelihood in the case of each defendant that he had caused the disease. The considerations of fairness that had moved the House in *Fairchild* would justify holding each of the defendants liable, notwithstanding the impossibility of proving causation on balance of probability.

106. Thus the conundrum is answered by saying that there are special features about mesothelioma, and the gaps in our knowledge in relation to it, that render it inappropriate to decide causation on epidemiological data as to exposure. . . .

What constitutes a material increase in risk?

107. Liability for mesothelioma falls on anyone who has materially increased the risk of the victim contracting the disease. What constitutes a *material* increase of risk? The parties were, I think, agreed that the insertion of the word 'material' is intended to exclude an increase of risk that is so insignificant that the court will properly disregard it on the *de minimis* principle. Mr Stuart-Smith submitted that there should be a test of what is *de minimis*, or immaterial, which can be applied in all cases. Exposure should be held immaterial if it did not at least double the environmental exposure to which the victim was subject. It does not seem to me that there is any justification for adopting the 'doubles the risk' test as the bench mark of what constitutes a material increase of risk. Indeed, if one were to accept Mr Stuart-Smith's argument that the 'doubles the risk' test establishes causation, his *de minimis* argument would amount to saying that no exposure is material for the purpose of the *Fairchild/Barker* test unless on balance of probability it was causative of the mesothelioma. This cannot be right.

108. I doubt whether it is ever possible to define, in quantitative terms, what for the purposes of the application of any principle of law, is *de minimis*. This must be a question for the judge on the facts of the particular case. In the case of mesothelioma, a stage must be reached at which, even allowing for the possibility that exposure to asbestos can have a cumulative effect, a particular exposure is too insignificant to be taken into account, having regard to the overall exposure that has taken place. The question is whether that is the position in this case . . .

Lord Brown

174. Mesothelioma claims are in a category all their own, so special indeed that Parliament in 2006 chose to legislate specifically for them: section 3 of the Compensation Act 2006. Whilst entertaining no doubt that the position now reached in respect of such claims is precisely as Lord Phillips and Lord Rodger have explained and that these appeals must accordingly fail, I think it only right to indicate just how unsatisfactory I for my part regard this position to be and how quixotic the path by which it has been arrived at . . .

184. In my judgment it could only be by reversing *Fairchild* and allowing no exception whatever to the normal rule of causation that this Court could now avoid what Lord Phillips . . . rightly describes as the 'draconian consequences' of coupling section 3 to the *Fairchild/Barker* principle: the liability in full even of someone 'responsible for only a small proportion of the overall exposure of a claimant to asbestos dust'. There is in my opinion simply no logical stopping place between the case of successive negligent employers dealt with in *Fairchild* itself (apparently circumscribed though that decision was) and the extreme ('draconian') position now arrived at, well exemplified as it seems to me by the facts of these very appeals. If, because of the 'rock of uncertainty', the law is to compensate by reference to negligence which merely increases the *risk* of such injury as then develops, why should not that relaxation of the normal rule of causation apply equally when, as here, there is but one negligent employer (or negligent occupier) as when there are several? As *Barker* recognised, there can

be no rational basis for confining the special rule within narrow bounds, whatever may have been contemplated by the House in *Fairchild*.

185. In short, the die was inexorably cast in *Fairchild*—although, as already suggested, it is doubtful if that was then recognised and it is noteworthy too that, even when in *Barker* it came to be recognised, it was then thought palatable only assuming that compensation was going to be assessed on an aliquot basis. Parliament, however, then chose—although, of course, only in mesothelioma cases—to go the whole hog.

186. The result must surely be this. As I began by saying, mesothelioma cases are in a category all their own. Whether, however, this special treatment is justified may be doubted. . . . The unfortunate fact is . . . that the courts are faced with comparable rocks of uncertainty in a wide variety of other situations too and that to circumvent these rocks on a routine basis—let alone if to do so would open the way, as here, to compensation on a full liability basis—would turn our law upside down and dramatically increase the scope for what hitherto have been rejected as purely speculative compensation claims. Although, therefore, mesothelioma claims must now be considered from the defendant's standpoint a lost cause, there is to my mind a lesson to be learned from losing it: the law tampers with the 'but-for' test of causation at its peril.

187. There is a rough justice about the law of personal injury liability as a whole. To compensate a claimant in full for a lost finger because there was a 60:40 chance that he would have worn protective gloves had they been made available to him may be regarded as rough justice for defendants. But it is balanced by the denial of compensation to a claimant who cannot establish that he would probably have worn the gloves—or whose finger the judge concludes was probably already doomed because of frostbite. Save only for mesothelioma cases, claimants should henceforth expect little flexibility from the courts in their approach to causation. . . . The same logic which requires that the claims of these respondents succeed to my mind requires also that the courts should in future be wary indeed before adding yet further anomalies in an area of law which benefits perhaps above all from clarity, consistency and certainty in its application.

Lord Rodger, **Lord Mance**, **Lord Kerr**, **Lord Dyson** and **Baroness Hale** delivered separate concurring judgments.

Appeals dismissed.

COMMENTARY

What if the best the claimant can do is to establish that the defendant's conduct increased the risk that they would suffer injury? Applying the usual rules for establishing causation, this would be insufficient: the defendant's negligence must have caused the injury or materially contributed to it, not merely increased the risk of it occurring. It is perhaps no surprise that in *McGhee*, the first case to suggest that an increase in risk could satisfy the causation requirement, 'material increase in risk' was equated with 'material contribution to injury', which made it appear as if the decision was little different from *Bonnington*. Indeed, the radical nature of *McGhee* was not recognised until well after it was decided. In *Wilsher v Essex Area Health Authority* [1988] AC 1074, for example, Lord Bridge declared (at 1090) that *McGhee* had not introduced any new principle of law and simply involved a 'robust and pragmatic' inference of factual causation from the evidence led in the case. In *Wilsher* the infant plaintiff suffered an illness that could have resulted from the defendant's negligence or from any of four other possible causes. On these facts the House of Lords held that as the plaintiff had failed to establish causation on the balance of probabilities his claim failed.

It was not until the twenty-first century that *McGhee* would be resurrected as the basis for a radical change in the law relating to factual causation. The trigger for that change was the increase in industrial disease caused by exposure to asbestos dust, and in particular mesothelioma. Mesothelioma claims have presented special difficulties for claimants because of the scientific uncertainties surrounding the aetiology of the disease. This led the House of Lords to accept that, in some circumstances, a defendant could be liable for merely increasing the risk that the claimant would contract mesothelioma. This step was initially taken in a case where all the sources of asbestos dust to which the claimant was exposed were tortious (*Fairchild*) but in *Barker* it was accepted that the *Fairchild* principle applied whenever the defendant increased the risk of the claimant contracting mesothelioma irrespective of whether the other possible sources were tortious, non-tortious or even due to the claimant's own contributory negligence. It was also held in *Barker* (Lord Rodger dissenting) that where the *Fairchild* principle applied, the defendant was liable to pay only proportionate damages to the claimant, fixed by reference to the extent to which the defendant's negligence had increased the risk of the claimant contracting the disease. (Would the court have been able to measure that on the facts of *McGhee*?) Although this limitation cast some doubt on the nature of the liability under the *Fairchild* principle (see the *Employers' Liability Insurance 'Trigger' Litigation*, discussed later in this section), in Lord Hoffmann's words it smoothed the 'rough justice' of *Fairchild*: if claimants were relieved from having to establish causation under the usual rules, defendants should not be liable as if they had been found to have caused the damage under those rules. However, almost immediately after *Barker* was decided, Parliament intervened to amend the Compensation Bill (which had not hitherto been concerned with this issue) to reinstate the joint and several liability created in *Fairchild*. The result is that, if the conditions for imposing liability set out in *Fairchild* are met (see s. 3(1)), the defendant is liable for the whole of the damage irrespective of the existence of other sources of exposure, whether from other 'responsible persons', non-tortious sources or the claimant's own actions (although a deduction for contributory negligence is possible: s. 3(3)(b)).

The scope of the *Fairchild* exception was subsequently considered in *Sienkiewicz*, where the Supreme Court adopted a somewhat Janus-faced approach to it. It is true that the exception was affirmed in circumstances where there were only two sources of exposure to asbestos fibres: environmental (non-tortious) exposure and the defendant's negligence. Furthermore, applying s. 3 of the 2006 Act, the Supreme Court held that, as long as the defendant's negligence resulted in a more than *de minimis* exposure, the defendant would be liable for all of the damage associated with the deceased's mesothelioma. However, in a case where the defendant contributed only about 15 per cent of the overall asbestos exposure, Lord Phillips described (at [56]) this result as 'draconian', and several of the Justices pointed out that, once the 'rock of uncertainty' had been removed because of increases in medical knowledge, the *Fairchild* exception would cease to exist. They also rejected the argument that s. 3 of the 2006 Act had enshrined in statute the rule that a material increase in risk was capable of satisfying the causation requirement. The section merely set out the position *if* a material increase in risk was held to establish the necessary causal link. Whether it actually did so remained a matter for the common law.

There were indications in *Sienkiewicz* that the *Fairchild* exception might henceforth be limited to mesothelioma cases (see Laleng (2011) 74 MLR 777, 778, arguing that it was 'implicit' in the judgments that it was so limited). However, in *International Energy Group Ltd v Zurich Insurance plc* [2016] AC 509 at [127] Lord Sumption said that in *Fairchild* the House had recognised 'that the legal issue was not necessarily peculiar to mesothelioma' and in *Heneghan v Manchester Dry Docks Ltd* [2016] 1 WLR 2036 the Court of Appeal applied the exception in a case involving lung cancer, thereby confirming its application beyond the mesothelioma context.

Nevertheless, for the *Fairchild* principle to apply outside of the mesothelioma context, it is clear that the claimant must establish a similar 'rock of uncertainty' in the medical evidence as in the case of mesothelioma. As Miller notes ((2012) 32 LS 396 at 410), in establishing this much will depend on the view taken of the available epidemiological evidence. Even though the defendant in *Sienkiewicz* had produced epidemiological evidence that the defendant's negligence had increased the risk by a specific percentage, the Supreme Court held that this did not detract from the uncertainty surrounding mesothelioma, which justified the existence of the rule.

Epidemiological Evidence

In the opinion of Lord Phillips in *Sienkiewicz*, the 'rock of uncertainty' could not be broken in mesothelioma cases because there were special features associated with mesothelioma that made it inappropriate to use epidemiological evidence to establish causation. But Lord Phillips (and Lord Dyson, at [222]) thought that in appropriate cases epidemiological evidence could be used to establish causation where multiple causes were involved. As Stapleton (2012) 128 LQR 221 argues, care must be taken when using epidemiological evidence as its reliability may depend on an understanding of the causal processes of the agent in question (hence her agreement with Lord Phillips that this lack of knowledge made any assessment of the risk from the defendant's negligence in *Sienkiewicz* statistically invalid). Assuming statistical validity, the approach of Lords Phillips and Dyson would seem to allow causation to be established under the 'doubling of the risk approach': if the epidemiological evidence is that the defendant's negligence doubled the risk then it can be held that on the balance of probabilities the negligence was a cause of the injury. However, other Justices were reluctant to go this far. Although some seemed doubtful as to the value of epidemiological evidence across the board (see, e.g., Lord Kerr's remark at [206] that there was a real danger that such evidence would carry a false air of authority), their primary concern related to the nature of such evidence and its focus on the general rather than the specific. An epidemiological study might find that out of 100 people, a certain disease was contracted by 30 people who were not exposed to an agent as a result of the defendant's negligence and by 70 who were. These figures would satisfy the 'doubling of the risk' test—the increased risk was 40 while the background risk was 30—but they would not of course show definitively whether the *individual* claimant was one of the 30 who contracted the illness from non-tortious causes or one of the 40 who contracted it as a result of the defendant's negligence. Although not excluding the possibility of causation being established solely on the basis of epidemiological evidence, Lords Rodger, Kerr and Mance, and Lady Hale, suggested that in most cases what was needed was evidence linking the disease in the individual claimant to the defendant's negligence. Similarly, while accepting that epidemiological evidence 'may sometimes be very helpful', Lord Toulson in *Williams v Bermuda Hospitals Board* [2016] AC 888 at [48] cautioned that 'inferring causation from proof of heightened risk is never an exercise to apply mechanistically'. (Cf. *Heneghan v Manchester Dry Docks Ltd* [2016] 1 WLR 2036 at [55], where Sales LJ appeared more receptive to the doubling of the risk test.)

For further discussion of the role of epidemiological evidence in establishing causation, see Dawid, 'The Role of Scientific and Statistical Evidence in Assessing Causality' in R. Goldberg (ed.), *Perspectives on Causation* (Oxford: Hart, 2011); McIvor, 'The "Doubles the Risk" Test for Causation and Other Related Judicial Misconceptions about Epidemiology', in *Challenging Orthodoxy*; McIvor, 'Debunking Some Judicial Myths about Epidemiology and Its Relevance to UK Tort Law' (2013) 21 Med L Rev 553; S. Steel, *Proof of Causation in Tort Law* (Cambridge: CUP, 2015), pp. 85–101; and G. Turton, *Evidential Uncertainty in Causation in Negligence*, pp. 93–121.

Increase in Risk as Injury and Proportionate Damages

In *Fairchild*, the House of Lords was not addressed on the question of proportionate damages, but the issue was raised squarely in *Barker*. A majority of their Lordships decided that, as causation was satisfied by the creation of a risk of injury rather than the causing of the injury itself on the balance of probabilities, it was appropriate that the extent of a defendant's liability should be limited by the extent of that risk. So in a *Fairchild*-type case, a defendant who was responsible for 40 per cent of the asbestos to which the claimant was exposed would be liable only for 40 per cent of the damages the claimant would have received had causation been proved on the ordinary rules. Lord Rodger disagreed, arguing that awarding proportionate damages would, in effect, be allowing recovery for the loss of a chance—something which had been rejected in *Gregg v Scott*—and that doing so would turn the *Fairchild* principle into an 'enclave' in which special rules applied.

The implications of the *Barker* proportionate recovery rule were considered by the Supreme Court in *Durham v BAI (Run Off) Ltd (Employers' Liability Insurance 'Trigger' Litigation)* [2012] 1 WLR 867, where the issue was the extent to which employers' liabilities to employees who had contracted mesothelioma were covered by their liability insurance policies. The case turned mainly on the wording of the policies in question, but Lord Phillips (dissenting) held that the policies did not cover the liabilities at all because under the *Fairchild* exception the liability was for the risk of contracting mesothelioma, not for the mesothelioma itself, and the policies did not cover liability for risk creation. This position was rejected by the other Justices. According to Lord Mance:

> 65. In reality, it is impossible, or at least inaccurate, to speak of the cause of action recognised in *Fairchild* and *Barker* as being simply 'for the risk created by exposing' someone to asbestos. If it were simply for that risk, then the risk would be the injury; damages would be recoverable for every exposure, without proof by the claimant of any (other) injury at all. That is emphatically not the law. . . . The cause of action exists because the defendant has previously exposed the victim to asbestos, because that exposure *may* have led to the mesothelioma, not because it did, and because mesothelioma has been suffered by the victim. As to the exposure, all that can be said (leaving aside the remote possibility that mesothelioma may develop idiopathically) is that *some* exposure to asbestos by someone, something or some event led to the mesothelioma. In the present state of scientific knowledge and understanding, there is nothing that enables one to know or suggest that the risk to which the defendant exposed the victim actually materialised. What materialised was at most a risk of the same kind to which someone, who may or may not have been the defendant, or something or some event had exposed the victim. The actual development of mesothelioma is an essential element of the cause of action. In ordinary language, the cause of action is 'for' or 'in respect of' the mesothelioma, and in ordinary language a defendant who exposes a victim of mesothelioma to asbestos is, under the rule in *Fairchild* and *Barker*, held responsible 'for' and 'in respect of' both that exposure and the mesothelioma.
>
> 66. This legal responsibility may be described in various ways. For reasons already indicated, it is over-simple to describe it as being for the risk. Another way is to view a defendant responsible under the rule as an 'insurer', but that too is hardly a natural description of a liability which is firmly based on traditional conceptions of tort liability as rooted in fault. A third way is to view it as responsibility for the mesothelioma, based on a 'weak' or 'broad' view of the 'causal requirements' or 'causal link' appropriate in the particular context to ground liability for the mesothelioma. This third

way is entirely natural. It was adopted by Lords Reid and Wilberforce in *McGhee*, by Lord Hoffmann, Lady Hale and (possibly) Lord Walker in *Barker* and by Lord Hoffmann in his extra-judicial commentary ['Causation', in *Perspectives on Causation*, ch. 1]. It seems to have received the perhaps instinctive endorsement of a number of members of this Court, including myself, in *Sienkiewicz*. Ultimately, there is no magic about concepts such as causation or causal requirements, wherever they appear. They have the meanings assigned to them and understood in ordinary usage in their context . . .

Similarly, in *International Energy Group Ltd v Zurich Insurance plc* [2016] AC 509 at [135], Lord Sumption said that the natural reading of the speeches of the majority in *Barker* was that the *Fairchild* principle was 'an exception to the ordinary rules of causation alone', and that by virtue of having contributed to the risk the defendant was 'liable for *the disease itself*' (emphasis added), in other words that the damage was the disease, rather than the increased risk of contracting it. For a powerful critique of the idea of risk as damage, see Turton, 'Risk and the Damage Requirement in Negligence Liability' (2015) 35 LS 75.

Although s. 3 of the Compensation Act 2006 has altered the law in respect of mesothelioma, the position at common law is that, in cases falling within the *Fairchild* exception, although the damage for which compensation is received may be indivisible, individual defendants are liable only for proportionate damages. In *International Energy Group Ltd v Zurich Insurance plc* [2016] AC 509, the Supreme Court firmly rejected an argument to the effect that the passing of s. 3 of the 2006 Act had altered the common law on this issue, as laid down in *Barker*. In the words of Lord Sumption, at [179], 'the Act left the common law intact, but carved an exception out of it for mesothelioma' (see also at [201], per Lord Neuberger and Lord Reed). Where proportionate damages are awarded, liability should be calculated 'according to each defendant's relative degree of contribution to the risk, usually measured by the duration and intensity of the exposure involved' (*Equitas Insurance Ltd v Municipal Mutual Insurance Ltd* [2020] 1 All ER 16 at [26], per Males LJ).

This exceptional use of proportionate liability is justified by the fact that the claimant is already receiving the benefit of a relaxation of the ordinary causation rules; to award full compensation to the claimant would balance the scales too far in their favour. It accords with a trend towards proportionate liability in cases of causal uncertainty in other European jurisdictions (see Oliphant, 'Uncertain Factual Causation in the Third Restatement: Some Comparative Notes' (2011) 37 Wm Mitchell L Rev 1599, 1624ff), and with the recommendations of the European Group on Tort Law in its *Principles of European Tort Law* (2005) Art 3:103–6. For a comparative overview of proportionate liability and causal uncertainty, see I. Gilead, M. Green and B. Koch (eds), *Proportional Liability: Analytical and Comparative Perspectives* (Berlin: de Gruyter, 2013).

A Single Agent?

In both *McGhee* and *Fairchild*, the agent that caused the disease (brick dust/asbestos dust) was undoubtedly the agent to which the defendant negligently exposed the claimant. This was not the case in *Wilsher*, where it was unknown which of five possible agents was the cause of the condition. Both Lord Rodger in *Fairchild* and Lord Hoffmann in *Barker* treated this as the distinguishing feature of *Wilsher*. It appears, however, that the *Fairchild* principle can apply even if the agents are not identical but operate in the same or substantially the same way, although no further guidance was given as to what a 'substantially similar' agency might be. Nor was any indication given as to why the usual rules of causation should be relaxed in 'similar agency' cases and not in others. In practice, the effect of the limit is to make it more likely that the *Fairchild* exception will apply in cases involving industrial diseases—such as *McGhee* and *Fairchild*—and less likely that it will apply in cases of medical negligence—such as *Wilsher*. Do you think that is justifiable? (For reasons why it might be, see Stauch [2009] CLJ 27.)

It is fair to say that the 'single agent' limitation on the scope of the *Fairchild* exception has not been well-received: for persuasive critiques of it, see G. Turton, *Evidential Uncertainty in Causation in Negligence*, pp. 212–15; and Wellington, 'Beyond Single Causative Agents: The *Fairchild* exception post-*Sienkiewicz*' (2013) 20 Torts LJ 1. Even Lord Hoffmann, writing extra-judicially, has described his own formulation of the restriction in *Barker* as 'absurd' ('Fairchild and After', in A. Burrows, D. Johnston and R. Zimmermann (eds), *Judge and Jurist: Essays in Memory of Lord Rodger of Earlsferry* (Oxford: OUP, 2013), p. 65). Furthermore, the limitation appears to have been misunderstood by the Court of Appeal in *Heneghan v Manchester Dry Docks Ltd* [2016] 1 WLR 2036, where the *Fairchild* principle was used in a lung cancer case despite the fact that there were two potential causal agents of the cancer, namely tobacco smoking and the asbestos fibres to which the deceased had negligently been exposed by the defendants, six former employers. In the leading judgment in *Heneghan*, Lord Dyson MR said that the facts of the case fell within the *Fairchild* principle because (inter alia) all the defendants 'exposed the deceased to the same agency that was implicated in causation (asbestos fibres)'. However, as Green points out in her note on the decision ((2017) 133 LQR 25, 27), this mis-states the single agent criterion, which in fact requires that it be clear that the damage *was caused by* a particular agent, or some other agent that operated in the same or substantially the same way. And while it could have been argued in *Heneghan* that tobacco and asbestos operate in the same or substantially the same way as regards the triggering of lung cancer, that was not the basis of the court's decision, and in any case such an argument would be somewhat tenuous, bearing in mind the current state of medical knowledge.

A Rock of Uncertainty?

In *Sienkiewicz* the Supreme Court made it clear that the *Fairchild* exception applied only where the claimant was faced with a 'rock of uncertainty', and that otherwise the ordinary causation rules would apply. This means that the exception can be relied on only where it is the state of scientific knowledge that makes it impossible to establish causation on the balance of probabilities, rather than, say, a gap in the factual matrix in the particular case. Hence the exception would not apply in a case like *Hotson*, discussed earlier, where it was known how the condition was caused and the plaintiff simply did not have the evidence to establish that on the facts it was attributable to the defendant's negligence. More controversially perhaps, the exception did not apply in *Gregg v Scott*, where Lord Nicholls' view that there was scientific uncertainty associated with the spread of the cancer was not accepted by the majority. (See the speech of Lord Hoffmann, extracted earlier.) The result is the creation of a special rule for cases of scientific uncertainty where the ordinary rules of causation will be relaxed. Do you think that the presence of 'scientific uncertainty' provides a particular justification for departing from the usual causation rules? Should uncertainty arising out of the limitations of science be treated differently from other kinds of uncertainty? (The Supreme Court of Canada thinks not: see *Clements v Clements* [2012] 2 SCR 181 at [38].)

Ibbetson and Steele, ([2011] CLJ 464, 468), claim that one justification for the *Fairchild* exception is that it seems 'unjust that negligent defendants as a group are privileged over the class of mesothelioma sufferers', which would be the consequence of applying the ordinary rules of causation. The case for relaxing those rules has long been considered especially strong where the claimant has undoubtedly been injured by the negligence of *someone* but is unable to prove which person in particular. (Remember this was the situation in *Fairchild*.) But it should be recognised that the same injustice can still occur in cases where the uncertainty is not scientific but factual, as in the 'two hunters' scenario discussed later. If the same privileging of defendants over claimants resulting from scientific uncertainty in mesothelioma cases is to be avoided, there is a case for applying the exception to cases of factual uncertainty, at least where all the possible causes of the damage are tortious. And although such a development is unlikely in the light of *Sienkiewicz* it will be seen in the next section ('The Problem of the Indeterminate Defendant'), that there are examples from other jurisdictions of the causation rules being relaxed in these circumstances.

The Problem of the Indeterminate Defendant

What Fleming called the problem of the 'indeterminate defendant' (*The American Tort Process* (Oxford: OUP, 1988), p. 261) arises where two or more defendants have acted negligently towards a claimant who has suffered injury as a result, but who is unable to establish whose negligent conduct was the cause. By this definition, *Fairchild* is an indeterminate defendant case but *McGhee* is not.

The classic example of the 'indeterminate defendant' problem is the 'two hunters' scenario which was discussed by several members of the House of Lords in *Fairchild*. In *Summers v Tice* 199 P 2d 1 (1948), the plaintiff was shot by one of two defendants, each of whom had fired negligently in the plaintiff's direction at roughly the same time. The Supreme Court of California rejected the defendants' argument that neither was liable because the plaintiff could not prove which of them had fired the bullet that struck him, and upheld the plaintiff's claim. Although only one of the defendants had actually caused the plaintiff's injury, they were equally culpable and the impossibility of anyone else determining who fired the fatal shot meant that it should rest with each of the defendants to absolve himself if he could. A comparable approach was taken by the Supreme Court of Canada in the factually similar case of *Cook v Lewis* [1951] SCR 830 (and note that in *Clements v Clements* [2012] 2 SCR 181, that court reiterated that liability should be imposed in indeterminate defendant cases, while rejecting the broader *Fairchild* exception). Furthermore, after reviewing decisions in both civil and common law systems, Lord Bingham in *Fairchild* came to the conclusion that most jurisdictions would afford a remedy to a claimant in these circumstances. And although the *Fairchild* exception is not limited to indeterminate defendant cases, the fact that it was itself such a case seems to have weighed heavily on their Lordships. According to Lord Hoffmann (*op. cit.*, p. 64):

The reasoning in *Fairchild* was simply that we thought it very unfair that an employer should be able to escape any liability for mesothelioma suffered by a worker whom he had negligently exposed to asbestos simply because the worker had also been (negligently or otherwise) exposed to asbestos by someone else.

The decision of the Court of Appeal in *Fitzgerald v Lane* [1987] QB 781 may rest on the same underlying considerations, although the factual circumstances were different. There, a pedestrian was hit successively by two cars whilst crossing the road and subsequently suffered tetraplegia. It could not be determined whether this resulted from the first or the second collision. A straightforward application of the but-for test would have left the plaintiff without a remedy, but the Court of Appeal, by a majority, followed *McGhee* and held both drivers liable. As Fleming has noted, since both defendants were negligent, '[i]t is arguable that the plaintiff's equities here overwhelmed the defendant's', as 'to deny recovery would let him—to coin a phrase—fall between two guilty tortfeasors' ('Probabilistic Causation in

Tort Law' (1989) 68 Can Bar Rev 661 at 671). (Note, however, that the issue in the case was whether the defendants *were* tortfeasors, as opposed to negligent persons who had not been proved to have committed a tort.)

The problem of the indeterminate defendant also arises in more complicated factual scenarios. In the American case of *Sindell v Abbott Laboratories* 607 P 2d 924 (1980), there were over 200 manufacturers of a generic drug which was prescribed to pregnant women. The drug was thought to be responsible for vaginal cancers in daughters of the women who had taken it, but because of the long latency period of the cancer it could not be determined which manufacturer had supplied the drug taken by the plaintiff's mother. The court held that the eleven manufacturers who were joined in the lawsuit were liable to compensate the plaintiff in proportion to their respective market shares in the drug, unless they could show that it could not possibly have been their product that caused her injuries. In his speech in *Fairchild*, Lord Hoffmann described the *Sindell* solution as 'imaginative', but declined to speculate as to whether it might be adopted in this jurisdiction. He noted, however, that it fell outside the scope of the *Fairchild* principle because the individual manufacturers did not materially increase the risk of injury to a given plaintiff: '[t]he risk from consuming a drug bought in one shop is not increased by the fact that it can also be bought in another shop' (at 130).

For analysis of the 'market-share' rule, see R. Goldberg, *Causation and Risk in the Law of Torts* (Oxford: Hart, 1999), ch. 2; L. Khoury, *Uncertain Causation in Medical Liability* (Oxford: Hart, 2006), pp. 114–17; and Weinrib, 'Causal Uncertainty' (2016) 36 OJLS 135, 148–52. And for a comparative analysis of the indeterminate defendant problem and a sophisticated argument for departing from the usual burden of proof in such cases, see S. Steel, *Proof of Causation in Tort Law* (Cambridge: CUP, 2015), ch. 4.

Fairchild in Retrospect

There is little doubt that the decision in *Fairchild*, coupled with later developments, has given rise to significant difficulties, not only in the law of tort, but also in the related fields of insurance and reinsurance (for a recent example, see *Equitas Insurance Ltd v Municipal Mutual Insurance Ltd* [2020] 1 All ER 16). These difficulties were highlighted by several members of the Supreme Court in the *International Energy Group* case, and led to the following observations on the part of Lord Neuberger and Lord Reed:

> 209. . . . . [I]n some types of case, it is better for the courts to accept that common law principle precludes a fair result, and to say so, on the basis that it is then up to Parliament . . . to sort the law out. In particular, the courts need to recognise that, unlike Parliament, they cannot legislate in the public interest for special cases, and they risk sowing confusion in the common law if they attempt to do so.
>
> 210. When the issue is potentially wide ranging with significant and unforeseeable (especially known unknown) implications, judges may be well advised to conclude that the legislature should be better able than the courts to deal with the matter in a comprehensive and coherent way . . . For the courts to develop the law on a case by case basis, pragmatically but without any clear basis in principle, as each decision leads to a new set of problems requiring resolution at the highest level, as has happened in relation to mesothelioma claims, is not satisfactory either in terms of legal certainty or in terms of public time and money.
>
> 211. In the case of mesothelioma claims, there can be no real doubt but if *Fairchild* [2003] 1 AC 32 had been decided the other way, in accordance with normal common law principles, Parliament would have intervened very promptly. That may very well have been a better solution, but it can fairly be said that that observation is made with the wisdom of hindsight.

Similar sentiments have been expressed by Lord Hoffmann, one of the judges who sat in the *Fairchild* case. Writing extra-judicially, he commented that in retrospect he believes that the House of Lords in *Fairchild* should have 'adhered to established principle, wrung their hands about the unfairness of the outcome in the particular case, and recommended to the Government that it pass appropriate legislation' (*op. cit.*, p. 68). The view that it might have been better for Parliament to resolve the issue in *Fairchild* rests on the different ways in which the common law and legislation operate. For as Lord Hoffmann also observed (at p. 65), while Parliament can 'simply enact a rule with arbitrary limitations'—such as an ad hoc exception to the but-for test in mesothelioma cases—this is not an option for the courts, since 'the common law develops by analogy, and rejects case-specific rationales from which no analogy can ever be drawn' (Morgan, 'Torts and Technology', in R. Brownsword, E. Scotford and K. Yeung (eds), *The Oxford Handbook of Law, Regulation and Technology* (Oxford: OUP, 2017), p. 527; for a fuller version of Morgan's argument as to why legislation should be used where exceptions to the usual causation rules are required, see 'Causation, Politics and Law: The English—and Scottish—Asbestos Saga', in *Perspectives on Causation*, ch. 4). Do you agree with Lord Hoffmann that in retrospect it would have been better if the House of Lords had decided against the claimants in *Fairchild*?

That Parliament would indeed have intervened had the House of Lords rejected the claims in *Fairchild* is suggested not only by the swift legislative response to the *Barker* decision, but also by the passage of the Mesothelioma Act 2014 and subsequent secondary legislation (SI 2014/916) setting up a compensation scheme for diffuse mesothelioma victims (and eligible dependants of those who have died from the disease) where the victim was wrongfully exposed to asbestos by an employer, but damages cannot be recovered because neither the employer nor their liability insurer can be traced. The scheme is funded by a levy on firms currently offering employers' liability insurance; for more on its background and operation, see Wikeley (2014) 21 J Soc Sec Law 65.

It is important to note, however, that some commentators have been more sanguine about the judicial development of exceptions to the orthodox rules on proof of causation. According to *Stapleton*, p. 87, for example, 'widespread doctrinal instability is unlikely to be threatened if the law were to adopt exceptions to the general rules of *proof* of the causal relation so long as: this happened only rarely; they were very clearly limited and specified; and they were supported by compelling justifications from the courts'. (See also Oliphant, 'Causation in Cases of Evidential Uncertainty: Juridical Techniques and Fundamental Issues' (2016) 91 Chi-Kent L Rev 587.) On this view, the problems generated by the *Fairchild* decision could have been avoided had the House of Lords been clearer as to the scope and the rationale of the exception their Lordships were recognising in that case.

3. Multiple Sufficient Causes

What happens when the claimant is injured by the defendant's negligence, but, before the trial, an unrelated event occurs which would have caused the claimant the same loss for which they are suing the defendant? Technically, the question is one that goes to damages rather than liability, since the defendant has clearly caused the claimant some damage, and so the issue is not whether the claimant has a cause of action but how much the defendant has to pay. (See Stiggelbout, 'The Case of "Losses In Any Event": A Question of Duty, Cause or Damages?' (2010) 30 LS 558.)

However, the issue has often been addressed in terms of causation, since whether the defendant should be required to pay damages in respect of the ongoing loss despite the supervening event might be thought to depend on whether their negligence is a cause of it. This difficult question is considered in the following extracts.

Baker v Willoughby [1970] AC 467

Following a car accident for which the defendant was responsible, the plaintiff suffered an injury to his left leg and stiffness in his right ankle. Before the case came to trial, the plaintiff was shot in a robbery, as a result of which his left leg had to be amputated. One issue for the House of Lords was whether the defendant's liability to pay damages in respect of the injury to that leg ended with the shooting. The facts are stated more fully in the speech of Lord Reid.

Lord Reid

The second question is more difficult. It relates to the proper measure of damages. The car accident occurred on 12 September 1964. The trial took place on 26 February 1968. But meanwhile, on 29 November 1967, the appellant had sustained a further injury and the question is whether or to what extent the damages which would otherwise have been awarded in respect of the car accident must be reduced by reason of the occurrence of this second injury.

There is no doubt that it is proper to lead evidence at the trial as to any events or developments between the date of the accident and the date of the trial which are relevant for the proper assessment of damages. The plaintiff may have died (*Williamson v John I Thornycroft & Co Ltd* [1940] 2 KB 658); or the needs of the widow (*Curwen v James* [1963] 1 WLR 748) or of the children (*Mead v Clarke Chapman & Co*, Ltd [1956] 1 WLR 76) may have become less because of her marriage. And it is always proper to take account of developments with regard to the injuries which were caused by the defendant's tort; those developments may show that any assessment of damages that might have been made shortly after the accident can now be seen to be either too small or too large. The question here is how far it is proper to take into account the effects of a second injury which was in no way connected with the first.

As a result of the car accident the appellant sustained fairly severe injury to his left leg and ankle, with the result that his ankle was stiff and his condition might get worse. So he suffered pain, loss of such amenities of life as depend on ability to move freely and a certain loss of earning capacity. The trial judge did not deal with these matters separately. He assessed the whole damage at £1,600 and making allowance for the appellant's contributory negligence awarded £1,200 with minor special damage. After the accident the appellant tried various kinds of work, finding some too heavy by reason of his partial incapacity. In November 1967 he was engaged in sorting scrap metal and while he was alone one day two men came in, demanded money, and, when they did not get it, one of them shot at him. The shot inflicted such serious injuries to his already damaged leg that it had to be amputated. Apparently he made a fairly good recovery but his disability is now rather greater than it would have been if he had not suffered this second injury. He now has an artificial limb whereas he would have had a stiff leg.

The appellant argues that the loss which he suffered from the car accident has not been diminished by his second injury. He still suffers from reduced capacity to earn although [these losses] may have been to some extent increased. And he will still suffer these losses for as long as he would have done because it is not said that the second injury curtailed his expectation of life. The respondent on the other hand argues that the second injury removed the very limb from which the earlier disability had stemmed, and that therefore no loss suffered thereafter can be attributed to the respondent's negligence. He says that the second injury submerged or obliterated the effect of the first and that all loss thereafter must be attributed to the second injury. The trial judge rejected this argument which he said was more ingenious than attractive. But it was accepted by the Court of Appeal.

The respondent's argument was succinctly put to your Lordships by his counsel. He could not run before the second injury; he cannot run now. But the cause is now quite different. The former cause was an injured leg but now he has no leg and the former cause can no longer operate. His counsel was inclined to agree that if the first injury had caused some neurosis or other mental disability, that disability might be regarded as still flowing from the first accident; even if it had been increased by the second accident the respondent might still have to pay for that part which he caused. I agree with that and I think that any distinction between a neurosis and a physical injury depends on a wrong view of what is the proper subject for compensation. A man is not compensated for the physical injury; he is compensated for the loss which he suffers as a result of that injury. His loss is not in having a stiff leg; it is in his inability to lead a full life, his inability to enjoy those amenities which depend on freedom of movement and his inability to earn as much as he used to earn or could have earned if there had been no accident. In this case the second injury did not diminish any of these. So why should it be regarded as having obliterated or superseded them?

If it were the case that in the eye of the law an effect could only have one cause then the respondent might be right. It is always necessary to prove that any loss for which damages can be given was caused by the defendant's negligent act. But it is commonplace that the law regards many events as having two causes; that happens whenever there is contributory negligence, for then the law says that the injury was caused both by the negligence of the defendant and by the negligence of the plaintiff. And generally it does not matter which negligence occurred first in point of time. . . .

[There is a] general rule that a wrongdoer must take the plaintiff (or his property) as he finds him; that may be to his advantage or disadvantage. In the present case the robber is not responsible or liable for the damage caused by the respondent; he would only have to pay for additional loss to the appellant by reason of his now having an artificial limb instead of a stiff leg. . . .

If the later injury suffered before the date of the trial either reduces the disabilities from the injury for which the defendant is liable, or shortens the period during which they will be suffered by the plaintiff then the defendant will have to pay less damages. But if the later injuries merely become a concurrent cause of the disabilities caused by the injury inflicted by the defendant, then in my view they cannot diminish the damages. Suppose that the plaintiff has to spend a month in bed before the trial because of some illness unconnected with the original injury, the defendant cannot say that he does not have to pay anything in respect of that month; during that month the original injuries and the new illness are concurrent causes of his inability to work and that does not reduce the damages. . . .

Lord Pearson

There is a plausible argument for the respondent on the following lines. The original accident, for which the respondent is liable, inflicted on the appellant a permanently injured left ankle, which caused pain from time to time, diminished his mobility and so reduced his earning capacity, and was likely to lead to severe arthritis. The proper figure of damages for those consequences of the accident, as assessed by the judge before making his apportionment, was £1,600. That was the proper figure for those consequences if they were likely to endure for a normal period and run a normal course. But the supervening event, when the robbers shot the appellant in his left leg, necessitated an amputation of the left leg above the knee.

The consequences of the original accident therefore have ceased. He no longer suffers pain in his left ankle, because there no longer is a left ankle. He will never have the arthritis. There is no longer any loss of mobility through stiffness or weakness of the left ankle, because it is no longer there. The injury to the left ankle, resulting from the original accident, is not still operating as one of two concurrent causes both producing discomfort and disability. It is not operating at all nor causing anything. The present state of disablement, with the stump and the artificial leg on the left side, was caused wholly by the supervening event and not at all by the original accident. Thus the consequences of the original accident have been submerged and obliterated by the greater consequences of the supervening event.

That is the argument, and it is formidable. But it must not be allowed to succeed, because it produces manifest injustice. The supervening event has not made the appellant less lame nor less disabled nor less deprived of amenities. It has not shortened the period over which he will be suffering. It has made him more lame, more disabled, more deprived of amenities. He should not have less damages through being worse off than might have been expected.

The nature of the injustice becomes apparent if the supervening event is treated as a tort (as indeed it was) and if one envisages the appellant suing the robbers who shot him. They would be entitled, as the saying is, to 'take the plaintiff as they find him' (*Performance Cars Ltd v Abraham* [1962] 1 QB 33). They have not injured and disabled a previously fit and able bodied man. They have only made an already lame and disabled man more lame and more disabled. Take, for example, the reduction of earnings. The original accident reduced his earnings from x per week to y per week, and the supervening event further reduced them from y per week to z per week. If the respondent's argument is correct, there is, as counsel for the appellant has pointed out, a gap. The appellant recovers from the respondent the x – y not for the whole period of the remainder of his working life, but only for the short period up to the date of the supervening event. The robbers are liable only for the y – z from the date of the supervening event onwards. In the Court of Appeal an ingenious attempt was made to fill the gap by holding that the damages recoverable from the later tortfeasors (the robbers) would include a novel head of damage, *viz*, the diminution of the appellant's damages recoverable from the original tortfeasor (the respondent). I doubt whether that would be an admissible head of damage; it looks too remote. In any case it would not help the appellant, if the later tortfeasors could not be found or were indigent and uninsured. These later tortfeasors cannot have been insured in respect of the robbery which they committed.

I think a solution of the theoretical problem can be found in cases such as this by taking a comprehensive and unitary view of the damage caused by the original accident. Itemisation of the damages by dividing them into heads and sub-heads is often convenient, but is not essential. In the end judgment is given for a single lump sum of damages and not for a total of items set out under heads and sub-heads. The original accident caused what may be called a 'devaluation' of the plaintiff, in the sense that it produced a general reduction of his capacity to do things, to earn money and to enjoy life. For that devaluation the original tortfeasor should be and remains responsible to the full extent, unless before the assessment of the damages something has happened which either diminishes the devaluation (e.g., if there is an unexpected recovery from some of the adverse effects of the accident) or by shortening the expectation of life diminishes the period over which the plaintiff will suffer from the devaluation. If the supervening event is a tort, the second tortfeasor should be responsible for the additional devaluation caused by him. . . .

Viscount Dilhorne, **Lord Guest** and **Lord Donovan** agreed with Lord Reid.

Appeal allowed.

COMMENTARY

If the defendant injures an already impaired claimant, then their liability is limited to putting the claimant back into the position they were in prior to the commission of the tort, in other words restoring them to the same impaired state. A good example is *Performance Cars v Abraham* [1962] 1 QB 33. The defendant negligently collided with the plaintiff's car, causing minor damage. Two weeks previously the car had been in another minor collision, which meant that one of its wings was in need of repainting. The cost of this work was irrecoverable from the defendant because he was required only to put the plaintiff's car back into the imperfect position it had been in before he collided with it. Applying this principle, had the plaintiff in *Baker v Willoughby* been able to find the robbers (and assuming they were worth suing), his claim against them would have been limited to the additional damage caused by the shooting. Hence, as Lord Pearson pointed out, if the first defendant was liable only up until the robbery, there would have been a gap in the damages, as neither tortfeasor would have been liable for the effects of the first injury after the date of the second tort. To avoid this, the House of Lords held that the damages for the first tort were not curtailed by the second tort. Is this a satisfactory solution?

Commenting on *Baker*, MacGregor (1970) 33 MLR 378 at 382–3 queried whether the same result would be reached where the supervening event was non-tortious. This situation is considered in the following extract.

Jobling v Associated Dairies Ltd [1982] AC 794

A back injury caused by the defendant's breach of statutory duty meant that the plaintiff could only take on light work. Before the action came to trial, he contracted an unrelated spinal disease (myelopathy) which rendered him unfit to work at all. The Court of Appeal held that the defendant was not liable to the plaintiff for his loss of earnings after he had contracted the disease. The plaintiff appealed to the House of Lords.

Lord Wilberforce

In an attempt to solve the present case, and similar cases of successive causes of incapacity according to some legal principle, a number of arguments have been invoked.

1. Causation arguments. The unsatisfactory character of these is demonstrated by the case of *Baker v Willoughby* [1970] AC 467. I think that it can now be seen that Lord Reid's theory of concurrent causes even if workable on the particular facts of *Baker v Willoughby* (where successive injuries were sustained by the same limb) is as a general solution not supported by the authority he invokes (*Harwood v Wyken Colliery Co* [1913] 2 KB 158) or workable in other cases. I shall not enlarge on this point in view of its more than sufficient treatment in other opinions.

2. The 'vicissitudes' argument. This is that since, according to accepted doctrine, allowance, and if necessary some discount, has to be made in assessing loss of future earnings for the normal contingencies of life, amongst which 'illness' is normally enumerated, so, if one of these contingencies becomes actual before the date of trial, this actuality must be taken into account. Reliance is here placed on the apophthegm 'the court should not speculate when it knows'. This argument has a good deal of attraction. But it has its difficulties: it raises at once the question whether a discount is to be made on account of all possible 'vicissitudes' or only on account of 'non-culpable' vicissitudes (i.e. such that if they occur there will be no

cause of action against anyone, the theory being that the prospect of being injured by a tort is not a normally foreseeable vicissitude) or only on account of 'culpable' vicissitudes (such as per contra). And if this distinction is to be made how is the court to act when a discounted vicissitude happens before trial? Must it attempt to decide whether there was culpability or not? And how is it to do this if, as is likely, the alleged culprit is not before it?

This actual distinction between 'culpable' and 'non-culpable' events was made, with supporting argument, in the Alberta case of *Penner v Mitchell* [1978] 5 WWR 328. One may add to it the rider that, as pointed out by Dickson J in the Supreme Court of Canada in *Andrews v Grand & Toy Alberta Ltd* (1978) 83 DLR (3d) 452 at 470, there are in modern society many public and private schemes which cushion the individual against adverse circumstances. One then has to ask whether a discount should be made in respect of (a) such cases or (b) cases where there is no such cushion. There is indeed in the 'vicissitude' argument some degree of circularity, since a discount in respect of possible events would only be fair if the actual event, discounted as possible, were to be taken into account when happening. But the whole question is whether it should be. One might just as well argue from what happens in 'actual' cases to what should happen in discountable cases.

In spite of these difficulties, the 'vicissitude' argument is capable in some, perhaps many, cases of providing a workable and reasonably just rule, and I would certainly not discountenance its use, either in the present case or in others.

The fact, however, is that to attempt a solution of these and similar problems, where there are successive causes of incapacity in some degree, on classical lines ('the object of damages for tort is to place the plaintiff in as good a position as if etc'; 'the defendant must compensate for the loss caused by his wrongful act, no more'; 'the defendant must take the plaintiff as he finds him' etc) is, in many cases, no longer possible. We do not live in a world governed by the pure common law and its logical rules. We live in a mixed world where a man is protected against injury and misfortune by a whole web of rules and dispositions, with a number of timid legislative interventions. To attempt to compensate him on the basis of selected rules without regard to the whole must lead either to logical inconsistencies or to over- or under-compensation. As my noble and learned friend Lord Edmund-Davies has pointed out, no account was taken in *Baker v Willoughby* of the very real possibility that the plaintiff might obtain compensation from the Criminal Injuries Compensation Board. If he did in fact obtain this compensation he would, on the ultimate decision, be over-compensated.

In the present case, and in other industrial injury cases, there seems to me no justification for disregarding the fact that the injured man's employer is insured (indeed since 1972 compulsorily insured) against liability to his employees. The state has decided, in other words, on a spreading of risk. There seems to me no more justification for disregarding the fact that the plaintiff (presumably; we have not been told otherwise) is entitled to sickness and invalidity benefit in respect of his myelopathy, the amount of which may depend on his contribution record, which in turn may have been affected by his accident. So we have no means of knowing whether the plaintiff would be over-compensated if he were, in addition, to receive the assessed damages from his employer, or whether he would be under-compensated if left to his benefit. It is not easy to accept a solution by which a partially incapacitated man becomes worse off in terms of damages and benefit through a greater degree of incapacity. Many other ingredients, of weight in either direction, may enter into individual cases. Without any satisfaction I draw from this the conclusion that no general, logical or universally fair rules can be stated which will cover, in a manner consistent with justice, cases of supervening events, whether due to tortious, partially tortious, non-culpable or wholly accidental events. The courts can only deal with each case as best they can in a manner so as to provide just and sufficient but not excessive compensation, taking all factors into account. I think that this is what *Baker v Willoughby* did, and indeed that Lord Pearson reached his decision in this way; the rationalisation of the decision, as to which I at least have doubts, need and should not be applied to other cases. In the present case the Court of Appeal reached the unanswerable conclusion that to apply *Baker v Willoughby* to the facts of the present case would produce an unjust result, and I am willing to accept the corollary that justice, so far as it can be perceived, lies the other way and that the supervening myelopathy should not be disregarded. If rationalisation is needed, I am willing to accept the 'vicissitudes' argument as the best available. I should be more firmly convinced of the merits of the conclusion if the whole pattern of benefits had been considered, in however general a way. The result of the present case may be lacking in precision and rational justification, but so long as we are content to live in a mansion of so many different architectures this is inevitable. . . .

Lord Russell of Killowen

There remains the question of the decision of this House in *Baker v Willoughby*. . . . I am not prepared to state disagreement with the decision. I am prepared to suggest that physical damage due to a subsequent tort is not to be regarded as a relevant vicissitude. Some of the reasons given in that case are susceptible of being taken as pointing in favour of the appellant in the instant appeal, but they do not persuade me that we are led by *Baker v Willoughby* to take a further step by allowing this appeal. . . .

Lord Keith of Kinkel

I am therefore of opinion that the majority in *Baker v Willoughby* were mistaken in approaching the problems common to the case of a supervening tortious act and to that of supervening illness wholly from the point of view of causation. While it is logically correct to say that in both cases the original tort and the supervening event may be concurrent causes of incapacity, that does not necessarily, in my view, provide the correct solution. In the case of supervening illness, it is appropriate to keep in view that this is one of the ordinary vicissitudes of life, and when one is comparing the situation resulting from the accident with the situation, had there been no accident, to recognise that the illness would have overtaken the plaintiff in any event, so that it cannot be disregarded in arriving at proper compensation, and no more than proper compensation.

Additional considerations come into play when dealing with the problems arising where the plaintiff has suffered injuries from two or more successive and independent tortious acts. In that situation it is necessary to secure that the plaintiff is fully compensated for the aggregate effects of all his injuries. As Lord Pearson noted in *Baker v Willoughby* [1970] AC 467 at 495 it would clearly be unjust to reduce the damages awarded for the first tort because of the occurrence of the second tort, damages for which are to be assessed on the basis that the plaintiff is already partially incapacitated. I do not consider it necessary to formulate any precise juristic basis for dealing with this situation differently from the case of supervening illness. It might be said that a supervening tort is not one of the ordinary vicissitudes of life, or that it is too remote a possibility to be taken into account, or that it can properly be disregarded because it carries its own remedy. None of these formulations, however, is entirely satisfactory. The fact remains that the principle of full compensation requires that a just and practical solution should be found. In the event that damages against two successive tortfeasors fall to be assessed at the same time, it would be highly unreasonable if the aggregate of both awards were less than the total loss suffered by the plaintiff. The computation should start from an assessment of that total loss. The award against the second tortfeasor cannot in fairness to him fail to recognise that the plantiff whom he injured was already to some extent incapacitated. In order that the plaintiff may be fully compensated, it becomes necessary to deduct the award so calculated from the assessment of the plaintiff's total loss and award the balance against the first tortfeasor. If that be a correct approach, it follows that, in proceedings against the first tortfeasor alone, the occurrence of the second tort cannot be successfully relied on by the defendant as reducing the damages which he must pay. That, in substance, was the result of the decision in *Baker v Willoughby*, where the supervening event was a tortious act, and to that extent the decision was, in my view, correct.

Before leaving the case, it is right to face up to the fact that, if a non-tortious supervening event is to have the effect of reducing damages but a subsequent tortious act is not, there may in some cases be difficulty in ascertaining whether the event in question is or is not of a tortious character, particularly in the absence of the alleged tortfeasor. Possible questions of contributory negligence may cause additional complications. Such difficulties are real, but are not sufficient, in my view, to warrant the conclusion that the distinction between tortious and non-tortious supervening events should not be accepted. The court must simply do its best to arrive at a just assessment of damages in a pragmatical way in the light of the whole circumstances of the case. . . .

Lord Bridge of Harwich

[His Lordship considered the decision in *Baker v Willoughby* and continued:]

Notwithstanding the course taken by the argument, in the speech of Lord Reid in this House (with which Lord Guest, Viscount Dilhorne and Lord Donovan agreed) there is no reference at all to the circumstance that the amputation of the plaintiff's leg was the result of a tort as a factor relevant to the decision. On the contrary, the reasoning in the speech applies equally to the effect of a supervening disability arising from illness or non-tortious accident. . . .

Having reached the conclusion that the ratio decidendi of *Baker's* case cannot be sustained, it remains to consider whether the case should still be regarded as authority, as a decision on its own facts, for the proposition that, when two successive injuries are both caused tortiously, the supervening disability caused by the second tort should, by way of exception to the general rule arising from the application of the vicissitudes principle, be disregarded when assessing the liability of the first tortfeasor for damages for loss of earnings caused by the first tort. I find it difficult to attribute such authority to the decision, when both the Court of Appeal and this House were expressly invited to adopt that proposition, and both, in different ways, declined the invitation. . . . In the instant appeal counsel for the respondents was content to accept the decision in *Baker's* case as correct on its facts, so your Lordships have not heard argument on the question. In these circumstances, the proper conclusion seems to me to be that the question should remain open for decision on another occasion, if and when it arises.

Lord Edmund-Davies delivered a speech in favour of dismissing the appeal.

Appeal dismissed.

COMMENTARY

What is the status of *Baker v Willoughby* after this decision? Is it authority (1) where there are multiple sufficient causes; (2) where the second sufficient cause is tortious; or (3) in neither case?

In *Baker*, Lord Reid attempted to deal with the problem by reference to a theory of concurrent causation: after the plaintiff had been shot there were two concurrent causes of what we might call the 'ongoing consequences' of the first tort. The House of Lords in *Jobling* took a different approach, which was based on the well-established principle that the ordinary vicissitudes of life (such as illness) are taken into account in assessing damages. When the court is assessing the damages payable in respect of post-trial losses, this is done globally by way of a percentage discount to reflect the fact that events unconnected with the tort might have caused the claimant some or all of the same loss. But where such a vicissitude has occurred pre-trial, it is taken into account, for there is then no need to speculate. How, then, could the decision in *Baker* be justified? Lord Bridge appeared to think that it could not be, whereas Lord Keith suggested that *Baker* was distinguishable because the 'vicissitude' was tortious (an explanation which Lord Wilberforce also considered to be 'the best available' *if* rationalisation were needed, albeit that he was not convinced that it was). In *Rahman v Arearose Ltd* [2001] QB 351, Laws LJ saw no inconsistency between the two cases: 'Once it is recognised that the first principle is that every tortfeasor should compensate the injured claimant in respect of that loss and damage for which he should justly be held responsible, the metaphysics of causation can be kept in their proper place . . .'. If pragmatism is the only way to achieve justice in this area, then it seems that both *Baker* and *Jobling* were correctly decided on their own facts.

Similar reasoning to that in *Jobling* has been relied upon in cases where there is an alternative hypothetical cause which would have resulted in the claimant suffering the same injury but for the defendant's negligence (see Stiggelbout, *op. cit.*). In the famous American case of *Dillon v Twin State Gas* 163 A 111 (1932), a child fell from a bridge towards almost certain death on the rocks below, but was in fact electrocuted by some electric wires which had been hung negligently by the defendant. It was accepted that the defendant's negligence was the cause of the child's death, but the damages were reduced to reflect his very short life-expectancy, namely, the period between the time when he hit the wires and when he would have hit the rocks (see also *Smith v Cawdle Fen Commissioners* [1938] 4 All ER 64). Although the practical results are similar (the defendant only pays damages for a limited time) the cases are different, as in *Jobling* the supervening event had actually happened, whilst in *Dillon* it had not. One reason why this might be significant is that in *Jobling* it was irrelevant that the onset of the disease occurred some time after the original injury; once it took place, the court had to take it into account. Conversely, in the case of hypothetical alternative causes, the temporal relationship between the defendant's negligence and the alternative cause might be more significant. For example, is it really likely that a court would reduce the damages of a claimant injured through a taxi-driver's negligence while on his way to the airport even if the plane he was due to catch had crashed, killing all those on board?

For comment on *Jobling*, see Evans (1982) 45 MLR 329 and Hervey (1981) 97 LQR 210 (the latter dealing with the decision of the Court of Appeal, which was affirmed by the House of Lords).

II. Intervening Acts

In this section we consider the circumstances in which a court will decide that an act which is a more immediate cause of the claimant's damage than the defendant's negligent conduct has the effect of relieving the defendant of liability for that damage. Traditionally, such an act has been described as a *novus actus interveniens*, which is said to 'break the chain of causation' between the defendant's negligence and the claimant's damage. This terminology reflects an assumption that the question of causation in negligence is not solely factual in nature, but also imports normative aspects. Hence the question of intervening acts is seen as one of 'legal causation'. According to a rival view, however, the use of the language of causation in this context—and the deployment of causal metaphors involving broken chains, etc—serves only to obscure the real issues in intervening act cases, which are instead conceived of as one component of a wider 'scope of liability' enquiry. This enquiry (which also encompasses the remoteness issue considered in the next section) is said to be quite distinct from the question of causation, which on this view is limited to the historical connection between the negligence and the damage. (For a recent statement of the latter view by its leading proponent, see *Stapleton*, pp. 89–101.) Although at times it will be convenient for us to employ the traditional causal language, we leave it to you to decide after reading the extracts and commentary that follow which of these two views you find more convincing as an explanation of the law.

Empress Car Co (Abertillery) Ltd v National Rivers Authority [1999] 2 AC 22

In a criminal prosecution, the issue for the House of Lords was whether the respondent had 'caused' polluting matter to enter controlled waters contrary to s. 85(1) of the Water Resources Act 1991. The House of Lords upheld the lower court's conviction. The result of the case is not important for present purposes, but Lord Hoffmann's comments on causation are of general relevance.

Lord Hoffmann

The courts have repeatedly said that the notion of 'causing' is one of common sense. So in *Alphacell Ltd v Woodward* [1972] AC 824 at 847 Lord Salmon said:

> . . . what or who has caused a certain event to occur is essentially a practical question of fact which can best be answered by ordinary common sense rather than by abstract metaphysical theory.

I doubt whether the use of abstract metaphysical theory has ever had much serious support and I certainly agree that the notion of causation should not be overcomplicated. Neither, however, should it be oversimplified. In the *Alphacell* case [1972] AC 824 at 834 Lord Wilberforce said in similar vein:

> In my opinion, 'causing' here must be given a common sense meaning and I deprecate the introduction of refinements, such as *causa causans*, effective cause or *novus actus*. There may be difficulties where acts of third persons or natural forces are concerned. . . .

The last concession was prudently made, because it is of course the causal significance of acts of third parties (as in this case) or natural forces that gives rise to almost all the problems about the notion of 'causing' and drives judges to take refuge in metaphor or Latin. I therefore propose to concentrate upon the way common sense notions of causation treat the intervention of third parties or natural forces. The principles involved are not complicated or difficult to understand, but they do in my opinion call for some explanation. . . .

The first point to emphasise is that common sense answers to questions of causation will differ according to the purpose for which the question is asked. Questions of causation often arise for the purpose of attributing responsibility to someone, for example, so as to blame him for something which has happened or to make him guilty of an offence or liable in damages. In such cases, the answer will depend upon the rule by which responsibility is being attributed. Take, for example, the case of the man who forgets to take the radio out of his car and during the night someone breaks the quarterlight, enters the car and steals it. What caused the damage? If the thief is on trial, so that the question is whether he is criminally responsible, then obviously the answer is that he caused the damage. It is no answer for him to say that it was caused by the owner carelessly leaving the radio inside. On the other hand, the owner's wife, irritated at the third such occurrence in a year, might well say that it was his fault. In the context of an inquiry into the owner's blameworthiness under a non-legal, common sense duty to take reasonable care of one's own possessions, one would say that his carelessness caused the loss of the radio. . . .

I turn next to the question of third parties and natural forces. In answering questions of causation for the purposes of holding someone responsible, both the law and common sense normally attach great significance to deliberate human acts and extraordinary natural events. A factory owner carelessly leaves a drum containing highly inflammable vapour in a place where it could easily be accidentally ignited. If a workman, thinking it is only an empty drum, throws in a cigarette butt and causes an explosion, one would have no difficulty in saying that the negligence of the owner caused the explosion. On the other hand, if the workman, knowing exactly what the drum contains, lights a match and ignites it, one would have equally little difficulty in saying that he had caused the explosion and that the carelessness of the owner had merely provided him with an occasion for what he did. One would probably say the same if the drum was struck by lightning. In both cases one would say that although the vapour-filled drum was a necessary condition for the explosion to happen, it was not caused by the owner's negligence. One might add by way of further explanation that the presence of an arsonist workman or lightning happening to strike at that time and place was a coincidence.

On the other hand, there are cases in which the duty imposed by the rule is to take precautions to prevent loss being caused by third parties or natural events. One example has already been given; the common sense rule (not legally enforceable, but neglect of which may expose one to blame from one's wife) which requires one to remove the car radio at night. A legal example is the well-known case of *Stansbie v Troman* [1948] 2 KB 48. A decorator working alone in a house went out to buy wallpaper and left the front door unlocked. He was held liable for the loss caused by a thief who entered while he was away. For the purpose of attributing liability to the thief (e.g. in a prosecution for theft) the loss was caused by his deliberate act and no one would have said that it was caused by the door being left open. But for the purpose of attributing liability to the decorator, the loss was caused by his negligence because his duty was to take reasonable care to guard against thieves entering.

These examples show that one cannot give a common sense answer to a question of causation for the purpose of attributing responsibility under some rule without knowing the purpose and scope of the rule. Does the rule impose a duty which requires one to guard against, or makes one responsible for, the deliberate acts of third persons? If so, it will be correct to say, when loss is caused by the act of such a third person, that it was caused by the breach of duty. In *Stansbie v Troman* [1948] 2 KB 48 at 51–52 Tucker LJ referred to a statement of Lord Sumner in *Weld-Blundell v Stephens* [1920] AC 956 at 986, in which he had said:

> In general . . . even though A is in fault, he is not responsible for injury to C which B, a stranger to him, deliberately chooses to do. Though A may have given the occasion for B's mischievous activity, B then becomes a new and independent cause. . . .

Tucker LJ went on to comment:

> I do not think that Lord Sumner would have intended that very general statement to apply to the facts of a case such as the present, where, as the learned judge points out, the act of negligence itself consisted in the failure to take reasonable care to guard against the very thing that in fact happened.

Before answering questions about causation, it is therefore first necessary to identify the scope of the relevant rule. This is not a question of common sense fact; it is a question of law. In *Stansbie v Troman* the law imposed a duty which included having to take precautions against burglars. Therefore breach of that duty caused the loss of the property stolen. In the example of the vapour-filled drum, the duty does not extend to taking precautions against arsonists. In other contexts there might be such a duty (compare *Mediterranean Freight Services Ltd v BP Oil International Ltd, The Fiona* [1994] 2 Lloyd's Rep 506 at 522) but the law of negligence would not impose one . . .

Knightley v Johns [1982] 1 WLR 349

The first defendant was to blame for a serious accident on the northbound carriageway of a road tunnel, the southbound carriageway of which was closed for repairs. A Mr Williams used an emergency telephone to report the accident to the police, but the message appeared to have been received and passed on in a somewhat confused form. The police inspector in charge at the scene forgot to close the entrance to the tunnel, and, in breach of police standing orders, commanded two officers on motorcycles, one of whom was the plaintiff, to ride down the northbound carriageway, against the traffic, to close it. The officers obeyed, even though this also constituted a breach of standing orders, and near the entrance to the tunnel the plaintiff was hit by an oncoming car, without negligence on the part of the driver. The trial judge absolved the inspector and the plaintiff of any negligence and imposed liability on the first defendant for the plaintiff's injuries. The first defendant appealed.

Stephenson LJ

On a Friday evening in October 1974 at about 8.20 in the twilight PC Knightley rode his motor bicycle the wrong way along a tunnel in Birmingham into collision with Mr Cotton's oncoming motor car. He sued Mr Cotton for negligence in causing him serious injuries. He also sued Police Inspector Sommerville and the Chief Constable of the West Midlands as the inspector's superior officer for the inspector's negligence in instructing or at the least permitting him to ride the wrong way. But the person he alleged to be first and foremost responsible for his accident and injuries was Mr Johns, because it was his negligence in overturning his motor car in the tunnel which was the cause of all the trouble. . . .

[After reaching the conclusion that the acts and omissions of the plaintiff and the inspector were causes of the plaintiff's accident and injuries for which the inspector was in law liable but the plaintiff was not, his Lordship continued:]

> Now comes the question the judge decided first: were they causes concurrent with the negligence of Mr Johns or were they new causes which broke the chain of causation?

[After considering the authorities, including cases involving the intervention of rescuers, his Lordship continued:]

At one end of the scale is wanton interference or disregard for the rescuer's own safety, which will break the chain; at the other, reasonable conduct which, according to what Lord Haldane said in *Canadian Pacific Rly Co v Kelvin Shipping Co Ltd* (1927) 138 LT 369 at 370 (and what Maugham LJ said in *Haynes v Harwood* [1935] 1 KB 146 at 162), will not. But there may be many intervening actions which cannot be characterised as either reasonable reaction or wanton intermeddling and recklessness. In this intermediate category come . . . tortious or criminal acts (wanton enough in one sense), the latter illustrated by [*Home Office v Dorset Yacht Co Ltd* [1970] AC 1004], the former by such cases of negligent driving into an obstruction negligently left on the highway as *Rouse v Squires* [1973] QB 889 at 898, where Cairns LJ regarded 'those who deliberately and recklessly drive into the obstruction' as disqualified by their own new act from recovering damages from those responsible for the obstruction. Of those who expose themselves to the danger of being injured by the negligence of others, rescuers are of course in a special category. For they will come to the rescue as often by deliberate and courageous choice as by instinctive reaction and they are unlikely to commit any crime or tort in so doing except the tort of failing to take reasonable care, which might be described as recklessness, for the safety of persons likely to be endangered by their actions, including of course themselves.

That brings me to the peculiarity of the present case, or rather to two peculiarities. One is that the action which injured the plaintiff might well have injured others such as Mr Cotton. The other is that between Mr Johns's negligent action and the plaintiff's own injury were interposed not merely his own decision to ride the wrong way along the tunnel hugging the wall of lane 1 when PC Easthope was riding ahead hugging the wall of lane 2 but a number of other acts and omissions for which he was not responsible, namely what was submitted to be 'a series of acts of ineptitude on the part of the police'. The judge, in his judgment, said:

> [Counsel for Mr Johns] submits that the first such act of ineptitude was failing to ascertain from Mr Williams precisely where the collision was. The next one was failing to close the tunnel before going into it in accordance with the standing orders. Having failed to close the tunnel he says it was inept to send the police officers back instead of using the telephone or sending them forward to radio for more assistance. There were, he says, clear breaches of the standing orders . . . and he says it is not foreseeable as likely to happen that police officers will ignore all those standing orders and all these things will happen.

. . .

[The judge] was, I think, rightly taking the law to be that, in considering the effects of carelessness, as in considering the duty to take care, the test is reasonable foreseeability, which I understand to mean foreseeability of something of the same sort being likely to happen, as against its being a mere possibility which would never occur to the mind of a reasonable man or, if it did, would be neglected as too remote to require precautions or to impose responsibility . . . The question to be asked is accordingly whether that whole sequence of events is a natural and probable consequence of Mr Johns's negligence and a reasonably foreseeable result of it. In answering the question it is helpful but not decisive to consider which of these events were deliberate choices to do positive acts and which were mere omissions or failures to act; which acts and omissions were innocent mistakes or miscalculations and which were negligent having regard to the pressures and the gravity of the emergency and the need to act quickly. Negligent conduct is more likely to break the chain of causation than conduct which is not; positive acts will more easily constitute new causes than inaction. Mistakes and mischances are to be expected when human beings, however well trained, have to cope with a crisis; what exactly they will do cannot be predicted, but if those which occur are natural the wrongdoer cannot, I think, escape responsibility for them and their consequences simply by calling them improbable or unforeseeable. He must accept the risk of some unexpected mischances . . . But what mischances?

The answer to this difficult question must be dictated by common sense rather than logic on the facts and circumstances of each case. In this case it must be answered in the light of the true view to be taken of the events leading up to Inspector Sommerville's acts, or rather his act and omission, and the plaintiff's, and PC Easthope's, acts. I have expressed my view of all these links in the chain leading from Mr Johns's negligence to the plaintiff's collision with Mr Cotton. I have decided, respectfully disagreeing with the judge, that the inspector was negligent in failing to close the tunnel and, respectfully agreeing with the judge, that the plaintiff was not negligent in riding the wrong way after being ordered to do so by the inspector or in deciding on the spur of the moment to ride his motor cycle close to the wall in lane 1.

I am also of the opinion that the inspector's negligence was not a concurrent cause running with Mr Johns's negligence, but a new cause disturbing the sequence of events leading from Mr Johns's overturning of his car to the plaintiff's accident and interrupting the effect of it. This would, I think, have been so had the inspector's negligence stood alone. Coming as it did on top of the muddle and misunderstanding of Mr Williams's telephone call and followed by the inspector's order to remedy his own negligence by a dangerous manoeuvre, it was the real cause of the plaintiff's injury and made that injury too remote from Mr Johns's wrongdoing to be a consequence of it.

In the long run the question is, as Lord Reid said in the *Dorset Yacht Co* case, one of remoteness of damage, to be answered, as has so often been stated, not by the logic of philosophers but by the common sense of plain men. . . . In my judgment, too much happened here, too much went wrong, the chapter of accidents and mistakes was too long and varied, to impose on Mr Johns liability for what happened to the plaintiff in discharging his duty as a police officer, although it would not have happened had not Mr Johns negligently overturned his car. The ordinary course of things took an extraordinary course. The length and the irregularities of the line leading from the first accident to the second have no parallel in the reported rescue cases, in all of which the plaintiff succeeded in establishing the original wrongdoer's liability. It was natural, it was probable, it was foreseeable, it was indeed certain, that the police would come to the overturned car and control the tunnel traffic. It was also natural and probable and foreseeable that some steps would be taken in controlling the traffic and clearing the tunnel and some things be done that might be more courageous than sensible. The reasonable hypothetical observer would anticipate some human errors, some forms of what might be called folly, perhaps even from trained police officers, and some unusual and unexpected accidents in the course of their rescue duties. But would he anticipate such a result as this from so many errors as these, so many departures from the common sense procedure prescribed by the standing orders for just such an emergency as this? I can see that it is a question on which the opinions of plain men and women in the jury box and judges who have now to perform their function may reasonably differ. I can only say that, in my opinion, the judge's decision carries Mr Johns's responsibility too far: in trying to be fair to the inspector the judge was unfair to Mr Johns. . . .

Dunn LJ agreed with Stephenson LJ. **Sir David Cairns** gave a short concurring judgment.

Appeal allowed.

COMMENTARY

As can be seen from this extract, the answer to the question of when an intervening act will be held to break the chain of causation is said to be a matter of common sense. Stephenson LJ emphasises that such decisions are highly fact-sensitive (see also *The Oropesa* [1943] P 32 at 36), although the guidelines his Lordship provides are useful pointers to what a court might hold. The tendency to express the principles applied in value-neutral terms should be noted—it also pervades the magisterial and influential treatise by H. Hart and T. Honoré, *Causation in the Law*, 2nd edn (Oxford: Clarendon Press, 1985)—but, as numerous commentators have observed, underlying such principles are often contentious notions of personal responsibility (see, e.g., *Conaghan & Mansell*, pp. 71–2, Stapleton (2006) 122 LQR 426 at 430–6). Nevertheless, it is still possible to offer some general observations as to how the courts approach different types of case.

Intervention by Deliberate Wrongful Act

In *Weld-Blundell v Stephens* [1920] AC 956 at 986, Lord Sumner stated: 'In general . . . even though A is in fault, he is not responsible for injury to C which B, a stranger to him, deliberately chooses to do. Though A may have given the occasion for B's mischievous activity, B then becomes a new and independent cause.' This principle is reflected in a line of cases denying liability where damage has been caused by deliberate acts of third parties (here conceived broadly to include all cases where they act voluntarily in order to exploit the situation created by the defendant: see Hart and Honoré, *op. cit.*, p. 136). As Lord Sumner's statement makes clear, traditionally the courts conceived of this as an issue going to (legal) causation, and where the intervening act occurs after a cause of action has already arisen, this remains the case. In *Lamb v Camden London Borough Council* [1981] QB 625, the plaintiff's property was damaged through the negligence of employees of the defendant council, and left unoccupied. When squatters gained entry to the property and caused further damage, the question of whether the council was liable for *that* damage had to be resolved through a legal causation analysis, since there was unquestionably *some* property damage for which the council was responsible, and hence recovery could not be denied on the ground that it had not owed the plaintiff a relevant duty of care.

Lamb was however an unusual case. More commonly, the entirety of the damage was brought about by the third party, and in this kind of case the issue of the defendant's responsibility for the consequences of the third party's deliberate and wrongful conduct is nowadays said to be whether the defendant owed the claimant a duty of care that encompassed such an intervention: see *Mitchell v Glasgow City Council* [2009] 1 AC 874. For the circumstances in which such a duty of care will be recognised, see Chapter 9.III.

Intervening Act of Claimant

Prior to the Law Reform (Contributory Negligence) Act 1945 (see Ch. 6.III.2), if the plaintiff was guilty of contributory negligence this generally operated as a complete defence to any claim as the plaintiff was regarded as the cause of their own damage. However, applying the 1945 Act a court which finds that the fault of both the defendant and the claimant caused the damage is required to apportion responsibility between the two, with the result that the claimant's damages are merely reduced, rather than the claim failing altogether. One result of this change is that nowadays in a case where the immediate cause of the claimant's damage is their own intervening act, the most appropriate solution will usually be to apportion responsibility between the parties and to make a suitable deduction from the damages for contributory negligence. Nevertheless, it is clear that the courts are still prepared to go further, and to decide that in a particular case the intervening conduct of the claimant broke the chain of causation between the defendant's prior negligence and the claimant's damage, with the result that the claim for that damage fails in its entirety.

An example of such a case is *McKew v Holland and Hannen and Cubitts (Scotland) Ltd* [1969] 3 All ER 1621. The pursuer suffered an injury at work which caused a stiffening and weakening of his leg. Shortly afterwards he went to inspect a flat, access to which was provided by a steep staircase with no handrail. As he was about to descend the stairs, his leg gave way, and, to avoid going down head-first, he threw himself forwards and landed on his right leg, breaking the ankle. The House of Lords held that the defender was not liable for the broken ankle. According to Lord Reid, the pursuer's attempt to descend the stairs without assistance was an unreasonable act, for the consequences of which the defender was not responsible. *McKew* can usefully be contrasted with *Spencer v Wincanton Holdings Ltd* [2010] PIQR P8 (noted by Hughes [2010] CLJ 228). Here, the defendant's negligence resulted in the claimant's leg being amputated. While filling his car with petrol, the claimant tripped over and suffered further injury. He had had available a prosthesis and walking sticks but did not use them. The Court of Appeal upheld the trial judge's finding that the defendant was liable for the additional injury caused by the fall subject to a reduction of one third of the damages for contributory negligence. Aikens LJ accepted that there was 'inevitably' a degree of tension between *McKew* unreasonableness (which broke the causal connection) and unreasonableness that merely went to contributory negligence. The difficulty, as Sedley LJ noted, is that the term 'unreasonable' covers a range of conduct from irrationality to simple incaution or unwisdom, and it is only where the degree of unreasonable conduct is very high that *McKew* will apply (see also *Emeh v Kensington & Chelsea Area Health Authority* [1984] 3 All ER 1044 at 1049 per Waller LJ).

In *McKew* and *Spencer* the question was not whether the defendant was liable at all—in both cases, they were clearly liable for the initial injuries—but rather the extent of their liability. However, it is also possible for a claimant's intervening act to defeat the claim altogether. In *Clay v TUI Ltd* [2018] 4 All ER 672 the claimant and members of his family had become trapped on the balcony of a hotel room in Tenerife in the early hours of the morning when the balcony door inadvertently locked. After about half an hour of rather desultory attempts to attract the attention of passers-by, the claimant tried to step across to the balcony of an adjacent room where his children were sleeping, but fell some twenty feet to the ground, sustaining serious injury. He brought a claim for damages against the defendant package holiday company on the ground that his injury had been caused by a defect in the lock of the door. A majority of the Court of Appeal upheld the decision of the trial judge that by trying to cross to the other balcony the claimant had broken the chain of causation. Since he and his relatives were in no danger, it was highly unreasonable of him to attempt a manoeuvre which posed an obvious risk of life-threatening injury. This case can be contrasted with *Sayers v Harlow UDC* [1958] 1 WLR 623, where the plaintiff was injured while attempting to climb out of a cubicle in a public lavatory where she was trapped due to the defendant's negligence. Despite the fact that her method of escape involved considerable risk, the Court of Appeal held that it had been reasonable of her to run this risk in the circumstances of the case. The fact-sensitivity of the intervening act doctrine is again demonstrated by these two decisions, and also by the disagreement in *Clay*, where Moylan LJ dissented on the ground that the claimant's conduct had not been unreasonable enough to eclipse the causative effect of the defective lock.

Although the unreasonableness of the claimant's act is the most important consideration when determining the limits of the defendant's responsibility, it is not the only one. In *Clay*, Hamblen LJ said (at [28]) that intervening conduct was more likely to constitute a *novus actus interveniens* the less foreseeable it was, the more unreasonable it was and the greater the extent to which it was 'voluntary and independent conduct'. The last of those considerations was of crucial importance in *Corr v IBC Vehicles Ltd* [2008] AC 884, where the deceased had killed himself after falling into a severe depression following a serious accident for which the defendant was responsible. The House of Lords rejected the argument that the deceased's suicide was a *novus actus interveniens* that prevented his widow claiming for loss of dependency under the Fatal Accidents Act. According to Lord Bingham, the rationale of the *novus actus* principle was that it was not fair to hold a defendant liable for damage caused not by the defendant's breach of duty but by some independent, supervening cause for which the defendant was not responsible, and an example of such a supervening cause was 'a voluntary, informed decision taken by the victim as an adult of sound mind'. On the facts, however, the deceased's suicide had not been a voluntary, informed decision of this kind, but the response of a man suffering from a severe mental illness which impaired his capacity to make reasoned and informed decisions about his future, an illness which was itself a consequence of the defendant's wrong.

The same result has been reached in other cases where the defendant has been responsible for creating the environment in which the deceased's suicidal tendencies developed. In *Kirkham v Chief Constable of Greater Manchester Police* [1990] 2 QB 283, where the police had failed to inform the prison authorities that the plaintiff was suffering from clinical depression and was suicidal, his suicide was held not to constitute a *novus actus*. The deceased in *Kirkham* had been suffering from mental illness, but in *Reeves v Commissioner of Police of the Metropolis* [2000] 1 AC 360, the House of Lords held that the suicide of a prisoner of sound mind in police custody did not negate the responsibility of the police for his death, since it had been conceded that the police had owed him a duty of care to prevent him killing himself. According to Lord Hoffmann (at 368): 'Once it is admitted that this is the rare case in which such a duty is owed, it seems to me self-contradictory to say that the breach could not have been a cause of the harm because the victim caused it to himself.' Lord Hobhouse dissented, holding that the voluntary, deliberate and informed act of a person precluded a causative link between the breach of duty and the consequences of that person's action.

Would the position be different if the prisoner is a suicide risk, not because he is mentally disturbed, but because he is a political prisoner attempting to gain publicity for a cause (see Lord Hobhouse in *Reeves* at 385)? For further discussion of *Reeves*, see Nolan (2000) 8 Tort L Rev 91.

Negligent Acts of Third Parties

Like the Law Reform (Contributory Negligence) Act 1945, the existence of legislation allowing for apportionment of responsibility between joint tortfeasors (by a process called contribution, now governed by the Civil Liability (Contribution) Act 1978) has implications for the question of whether the intervening negligent act of a third party negates the defendant's responsibility for any subsequent injury. Where the negligence of two parties is a factual cause of the same damage, it is possible for the court to hold that the conduct of only one of them is a legal cause, thereby absolving the other of liability. However, it is more likely that both parties will be held to be jointly and severally liability for the damage, meaning that the claimant is entitled to sue either for full damages, with the defendant who is sued then being free either to join the other party as a co-defendant, or alternatively to pay damages to the claimant and afterwards seek a partial indemnity from the other party in separate contribution proceedings. Either way, the court will have to apportion responsibility between the two tortfeasors, just as in cases of contributory negligence it must apportion responsibility between the claimant and the defendant. (Note that the effect of the doctrine of joint and several liability is to put the risk of the impecuniosity of one of two defendants on the other defendant, rather than the claimant; this is because the claimant can recover full damages from the pecunious defendant, but that defendant will then be unable to obtain contribution from the other defendant.)

A good example of contribution in practice is *Rouse v Squires* [1973] QB 889. A lorry driver, A, negligently drove his lorry so that it jack-knifed and blocked two lanes of a motorway. A car that was travelling behind the lorry then collided with it. A second lorry driver, F, parked his lorry just short of the accident scene, left its lights on to provide illumination and provided assistance. Finally, S, the driver of a third lorry, negligently failed to notice the accident until it was too late, and his lorry skidded into the back of F's vehicle, pushing it forwards so that it caused fatal injuries to F. In an action by F's widow, the trial judge held that S was wholly responsible for the second accident, but the Court of Appeal allowed an appeal, on the basis that the responsibility for that accident should be apportioned in the ratio 25/75 between A and S.

The result in *Rouse* should be compared with *Wright v Lodge* [1993] 4 All ER 299 (noted by Jones (1994) 2 Tort L Rev 133). A Mini car broke down on an unlit part of a dual carriageway, and, while the driver was attempting to restart it, it was hit by a speeding Scania lorry, with the result that one of the passengers in the Mini suffered injury. After hitting the Mini, the lorry crossed the central reservation and collided with other vehicles, killing one driver and injuring another. The lorry driver joined the driver of the Mini as a co-defendant. At the trial of the action the car driver was held to have been negligent in not pushing the Mini to the side of the road after it had broken down and ordered to pay 10 per cent of the passenger's damages. However, the judge held that the reckless driving of the lorry driver was the sole cause of the injuries to the drivers of the other vehicles with which the lorry had collided. This result was upheld by the Court of Appeal. According to Parker LJ (at 307):

[A]pproaching the matter as if he were a jury and taking a common sense view, [the judge] was, as we are, clearly entitled to conclude that the presence of the Scania in the westbound carriageway was wholly attributable to Mr Lodge's reckless driving. It was unwarranted and unreasonable. It was the violence of the swerve and braking which sent his lorry out of control. Such violence was due to the reckless manner in which he was driving and it was his reckless speed which resulted in the swerve, loss of control and headlong career onto, and overturn on, the westbound carriageway. It is true that it would not have been there had the Mini not obstructed the nearside lane of the eastbound carriageway but the passages which I have cited show clearly that this is not enough. It does not thereby necessarily become a legally operative cause.

(Cf. *Bland v Morris* [2006] RTR 31 where the driver who was partly responsible for the first accident was also held to have some responsibility for the second accident even though this involved the subsequent negligence of two other parties.)

Will the intervention of negligent medical treatment negate the defendant's responsibility for the subsequent injury? In the criminal law it does not necessarily do so (*R v Cheshire* [1991] 1 WLR 844) and a similar position applies in the civil law. Certainly later medical negligence does not *always* extinguish the original tortfeasor's liability, and it has been suggested that only where there has been gross negligence in relation to the intervening medical treatment will the causal link be broken (*Webb v Barclays Bank plc* [2001] EWCA Civ 1141). Where both the original and subsequent negligent parties are before the court it may be that apportionment of the damage is the fairest option (see *Prendergast v Sam & Dee Ltd, The Times*, 14 March 1989), but in *Rahman v Arearose Ltd* [2001] QB 351 it was conceded that the intervening medical negligence was the sole cause of some of the claimant's injuries. In *Wright v Cambridge Medical Group* [2013] QB 312, the claimant was suing the practice of a General Practitioner who had negligently failed to refer her to hospital timeously, but the case was complicated by the fact that, when the claimant had eventually been referred to hospital, the treatment she received there was also negligent. The combination of the delay and the negligent hospital treatment caused a permanent injury to the claimant's hip. A majority of the Court of Appeal (Elias LJ dissenting) held that the hospital's subsequent negligence did not absolve the defendant practice of legal responsibility for the hip injury. According to Lord Neuberger MR, at [37], the hospital's negligence was not 'such an egregious event, in terms of the degree or unusualness of the negligence . . . to defeat or destroy the causative link' between the GP's negligence and the claimant's injury. However, his Lordship also made it clear, at [32], that such decisions are highly fact-sensitive: 'where there are successive tortfeasors, the contention that the causative potency of the negligence of the first is destroyed by the subsequent negligence of the second depends very much on the facts of the particular case'.

Rescuers

An act of a rescuer attempting to perform a rescue necessitated by the defendant's negligence is very unlikely to amount to a *novus actus interveniens*. In *Baker v T. E. Hopkins* [1959] 1 WLR 966, the Court of Appeal allowed a Fatal Accidents Act claim that was brought following the death of a doctor who had been trying to rescue two workers trapped in a well as a result of the defendant's negligence. According to Morris LJ (at 975–6): 'Those who put men in peril can hardly be heard to say that they never thought that rescue might be attempted, or be heard to say that the rescue attempt was not caused by the creation of the peril.' See also *Tolley v Carr* [2011] RTR 7. Similarly, rescue attempts by third parties are unlikely to curtail the defendant's responsibility. In *The Oropesa* [1943] P 32, a collision took place off the coast of Nova Scotia between two steamships, *Oropesa* and *Manchester Regiment*, for which both were to blame. The damage to the *Manchester Regiment* was serious, and her master decided to take sixteen men to the *Oropesa* in a lifeboat to discuss salvage arrangements. The lifeboat capsized in heavy seas and nine men drowned. It was held by the Court of Appeal that the parents of one of the dead sailors could recover damages from the owners of the *Oropesa*. The master's decision to cross to the *Oropesa* in the lifeboat had not broken the chain of causation between the negligence that brought about the collision and the death of the plaintiffs' son because, even though he may have been guilty of an error of judgement, he was in a 'very perilous plight'.

III. Remoteness

Normally, as Lord Hoffmann pointed out in *South Australia Asset Management Corp v York Montague Ltd* [1997] AC 191 at 213, 'the law limits liability to those consequences which are attributable to that which made the act wrongful'. In negligence, what makes the defendant's conduct wrongful is the fact that it creates unreasonable risks, and it follows that in general negligence liability is imposed only where the consequence in question was the materialisation of one of the risks that made the defendant's conduct negligent in the first place (see US *Restatement of the Law of Torts: Liability for Physical and Emotional Harm*, 3d, 2010, § 29; *Wallace v Kam* (2013) 250 CLR 375 at [24]). This explains why a speeding motorist is not liable when a tree falls on his car and injures his passenger. Although the but-for test is satisfied here—if the motorist had not been speeding, the tree would not have hit the car—the risk of falling trees is not one of the risks that makes speeding negligent. This 'risk principle' (see Williams, 'The Risk Principle' (1961) 77 LQR 179) is bound up with foreseeability, since a risk that is not reasonably foreseeable to a person in the defendant's position cannot by definition be one of the risks that made the defendant's conduct negligent. Although the risk principle and its concomitant requirement that the damage must have been reasonably foreseeable now dominate the enquiry into 'remoteness of damage' in English negligence law, this was not always the case, as the following extract makes clear.

1. *Wagon Mound* and the Scope of Risk Approach

Overseas Tankship (UK) Ltd v Morts Dock & Engineering Co Ltd (The Wagon Mound (No. 1)) [1961] AC 388

The facts appear in the extract.

Viscount Simonds (giving the advice of the Privy Council)

The relevant facts can be comparatively shortly stated, inasmuch as not one of the findings of fact in the exhaustive judgment of the learned trial judge has been challenged. The respondents at the relevant time carried on the business of ship-building, ship-repairing and general engineering at Morts Bay, Balmain, in the Port of Sydney. They owned and used for their business the Sheerlegs Wharf, a timber wharf about four hundred feet in length and forty feet wide, where there was a quantity of tools and equipment. In October and November, 1951, a vessel known as the Corrimal was moored alongside the wharf and was being refitted by the respondents. Her mast was lying on the wharf and a number of the respondents' employees were working both on it and on the vessel itself, using for this purpose electric and oxy-acetylene welding equipment. At the same time, the appellants were charterers by demise of the SS Wagon Mound, an oil-burning vessel which was moored at the Caltex Wharf on the northern shore of the harbour at a distance of about six hundred feet from the Sheerlegs Wharf. She was there from about 9 am on 29 October until 11 am on 30 October 1951, for the purpose of discharging gasolene products and taking in bunkering oil. During the early hours of 30 October 1951, a large quantity of bunkering oil was, through the carelessness of the appellants' servants, allowed to spill into the bay, and, by 10.30 on the morning of that day, it had spread over a considerable part of the bay, being thickly concentrated in some places and particularly along the foreshore near the respondents' property. The appellants made no attempt to disperse the oil. The Wagon Mound unberthed and set sail very shortly after. When the respondents' works manager became aware of the condition of things in the vicinity of the wharf, he instructed their workmen that no welding or burning was to be carried on until further orders. He inquired of the manager of the Caltex Oil Co, at whose wharf the Wagon Mound was then still berthed, whether they could safely continue their operations on the wharf or on the Corrimal. The results of this inquiry, coupled with his own belief as to the inflammability of furnace oil in the open, led him to think that the respondents could safely carry on their operations. He gave instructions accordingly, but directed that all safety precautions should be taken to prevent inflammable material falling off the wharf into the oil. For the remainder of 30 October and until about 2 pm on 1 November, work was carried on as usual, the condition and congestion of the oil remaining substantially unaltered. But at about that time the oil under or near the wharf was ignited and a fire, fed initially by the oil, spread rapidly and burned with great intensity. The wharf and the Corrimal caught fire and considerable damage was done to the wharf and the equipment on it.

The outbreak of fire was due, as the learned judge found, to the fact that there was floating in the oil underneath the wharf a piece of debris on which lay some smouldering cotton waste or rag which had been set on fire by molten metal falling from the wharf; that the cotton waste or rag burst into flames; that the flames from the cotton waste set the floating oil afire either directly or by first setting fire to a wooden pile coated with oil and that, after the floating oil became ignited, the flames spread rapidly over the surface of the oil and quickly developed into a conflagration which severely damaged the wharf. He also made the all-important finding, which must be set out in his own words:

> The raison d'être of furnace oil is, of course, that it shall burn, but I find the [appellants] did not know and could not reasonably be expected to have known that it was capable of being set afire when spread on water.

It is on this footing that their Lordships will consider the question whether the appellants are liable for the fire damage . . .

It is inevitable that first consideration should be given to *Re Polemis and Furness, Withy & Co Ltd* [1921] 3 KB 560 which will henceforward be referred to as *Polemis*. For it was avowedly in deference to that decision and to decisions of the Court of Appeal that followed it that the full court was constrained to decide the present case in favour of the respondents . . .

What, then, did *Polemis* decide? . . . [It is clear that] the case proceeded as one in which, independently of contractual obligations, the claim was for damages for negligence. It was on this footing that the Court of Appeal held that the charterers were responsible for all the consequences of their negligent act, even though those consequences could not reasonably have been anticipated. The negligent act was nothing more than the carelessness of stevedores (for whom the charterers were assumed to be responsible) in allowing a sling or rope by which it was hoisted to come into contact with certain boards, causing one of them to fall into the hold. The falling board hit some substances in the hold and caused a spark; the spark ignited petrol vapour in the hold; there was a rush of flames and the ship was destroyed. The Special Case submitted by the arbitrators found that the causing of the spark could not reasonably have been anticipated from the falling of the board, though some damage to the ship might reasonably have been anticipated. They did not indicate what damage might have been so anticipated.

There can be no doubt that the decision of the Court of Appeal in *Polemis* plainly asserts that, if the defendant is guilty of negligence, he is responsible for all the consequences, whether reasonably foreseeable or not. The generality of the proposition is, perhaps, qualified by the fact that each of the lords justices refers to the outbreak of fire as the direct result of the negligent act. There is thus introduced the conception that the negligent actor is not responsible for consequences which are not 'direct', whatever that may mean. . . .

[After considering relevant authorities both before and after *Polemis*, his Lordship continued:]

Enough has been said to show that the authority of *Polemis* has been severely shaken, though lip-service has from time to time been paid to it. In their Lordships' opinion, it should no longer be regarded as good law. It is not probable that many cases will for that reason have a different result, though it is hoped that the law will be thereby simplified, and that, in some cases at least, palpable injustice will be avoided. For it does not seem consonant with current ideas of justice or morality that, for an act of negligence, however slight or venial, which results in some trivial foreseeable damage, the actor should be liable for all consequences, however unforeseeable and however grave, so long as they can be said to be 'direct'. It is a principle of civil liability, subject only to qualifications which have no present relevance, that a man must be considered to be responsible for the probable consequences of his act. To demand more of him is too harsh a rule, to demand less is to ignore that civilised order requires the observance of a minimum standard of behaviour. This concept, applied to the slowly developing law of negligence, has led to a great variety of expressions which can, as it appears to their Lordships, be harmonised with little difficulty with the single exception of the so-called rule in *Polemis*. For, if it is asked why a man should be responsible for the natural or necessary or probable consequences of his act (or any other similar description of them), the answer is that it is not because they are natural or necessary or probable, but because, since they have this quality, it is judged, by the standard of the reasonable man, that he ought to have foreseen them. Thus it is that, over and over again, it has happened that, in different judgments in the same case and sometimes in a single judgment, liability for a consequence has been imposed on the ground that it was reasonably foreseeable, or alternatively on the ground that it was natural or necessary or probable. The two grounds have been treated as conterminous, and so they largely are. But, where they are not, the question arises to which the wrong answer was given in *Polemis*. For, if some limitation must be imposed on the consequences for which the negligent actor is to be held responsible—and all are agreed that some limitation there must be—why should that test (reasonable foreseeability) be rejected which, since he is judged by what the reasonable man ought to foresee, corresponds with the common conscience of mankind, and a test (the 'direct' consequence) be substituted which leads to nowhere but the never ending and insoluble problems of causation . . .

At an early stage in this judgment, their Lordships intimated that they would deal with the proposition which can best be stated by reference to the well-known dictum of Lord Sumner [*Weld-Blundell v Stephens* [1920] AC 956 at p 984]: 'This, however, goes to culpability, not to compensation.' It is with the greatest respect to that very learned judge and to those who have echoed his words that their Lordships find themselves bound to state their view that this proposition is fundamentally false.

It is, no doubt, proper when considering tortious liability for negligence to analyse its elements and to say that the plaintiff must prove a duty owed to him by the defendant, a breach of that duty by the defendant, and consequent damage. But there can be no liability until the damage has been done. It is not the act but the consequences on which tortious liability is founded. Just as (as it has been said) there is no such thing as negligence in the air, so there is no such thing as liability in the air. Suppose an action brought by A for damage caused by the carelessness (a neutral word) of B, for example a fire caused by the careless spillage of oil. It may, of course, become relevant to know what duty B owed to A, but the only liability that is in question is the liability for damage by fire. It is vain to isolate the liability from its context and to say that B is or is not liable, and then to ask for what damage he is liable. For his liability is in respect of that damage and no other. If, as admittedly it is, B's liability (culpability) depends on the reasonable foreseeability of the consequent damage, how is that to be determined except by the foreseeability of the damage which in fact happened—the damage in suit? And, if that damage is unforeseeable so as to displace liability at large, how can the liability be restored so as to make compensation payable? But, it is said, a different position arises if B's careless act has been shown to be negligent and has caused some foreseeable damage to A. Their Lordships have already observed that to hold B liable for consequences, however unforeseeable, of a careless act, if, but only if, he is at the same time liable for some other damage, however trivial, appears to be neither logical nor just. This becomes more clear if it is supposed that similar unforeseeable damage is suffered by A and C, but other foreseeable damage, for which B is liable, by A only. A system of law which would hold B liable to A but not to C for the similar damage suffered by each of them could not easily be defended. Fortunately, the attempt is not necessary. For the same fallacy is at the root of the proposition. It is irrelevant to the question whether B is liable for unforeseeable damage that he is liable for foreseeable damage, as irrelevant as would the fact that he had trespassed on Whiteacre be to the question whether he had trespassed on Blackacre.

Again, suppose a claim by A for damage by fire by the careless act of B. Of what relevance is it to that claim that he has another claim arising out of the same careless act? It would surely not prejudice his claim if that other claim failed; it cannot assist it if it succeeds. Each of them rests on its own bottom and will fail if it can be established that the damage could not reasonably be foreseen. We have come back to the plain common sense stated by Lord Russell of Killowen in *Hay (or Bourhill) v Young* [1943] AC 92. As Denning LJ said in *King v Phillips* ([1953] 1 QB 429 at p 441) '... there can be no doubt since *Hay (or Bourhill) v Young* that the test of liability for shock is foreseeability of injury by shock.' Their Lordships substitute the word 'fire' for 'shock' and indorse this statement of the law.

Their Lordships conclude this part of the case with some general observations. They have been concerned primarily to displace the proposition that unforeseeability is irrelevant if damage is 'direct.' In doing so, they have inevitably insisted that the essential factor in determining liability is whether the damage is of such a kind as the reasonable man should have foreseen ...

Appeal allowed.

COMMENTARY

The extract sets out two approaches to remoteness of damage. The first, derived from the Court of Appeal decision in *Re Polemis and Furness, Withy & Co Ltd* [1921] 3 KB 560, is based on directness. The Privy Council in *The Wagon Mound* described this as meaning that if the defendant was guilty of negligence, he was responsible for all the consequences, whether reasonably foreseeable or not, as long as they were a 'direct' consequence of the negligence. However, it is probable that this was limited to situations where the plaintiff was foreseeably endangered by the negligence, as was the case in *Polemis*, where it was foreseeable that the falling plank would cause some damage to the plaintiff, albeit not fire damage (see Dias [1962] CLJ 178).

Whatever the precise nature of the directness approach, it was disapproved by the Privy Council in *The Wagon Mound* in favour of a test based upon reasonable foreseeability of damage. As duty and breach were based on the foresight of damage, it was only fair that remoteness was based on the same principle; hence the rejection of the split between culpability and compensation. Not everyone agrees that this necessarily follows; see, for example, J. Fleming, *The Law of Torts*, 9th edn (Sydney: LBC Information Services, 1998), p. 238.

But in truth, the premise does not compel the conclusion. It may be thought politic that the reason for creating liability should also delimit it, but it is just as tenable, and certainly as logical, to insist that there are good reasons within the framework of fault for holding a proven wrongdoer liable for injury he has caused even if it went beyond all ken. 'The judgment lies in the realm of values and what you choose depends upon what you want' (Gregory, 'Proximate Cause in Negligence—A Retreat from Rationalisation' (1938) 6 U Chi L Rev 36 at 47).

An obvious issue that arises if foreseeability is used as the basis of remoteness of damage is the relationship between foreseeability at the duty of care stage (see the 'foreseeable claimant' rule, discussed in Ch. 3.II.2) and foreseeability at the remoteness stage. The difference appears to be that at the duty of care stage, the question is whether the defendant could foresee that *the claimant* (or, perhaps more accurately, someone in the claimant's position) was a foreseeable victim of the defendant's negligence, whereas at the remoteness stage the question is whether the *particular damage suffered by the claimant* was reasonably foreseeable. Nevertheless, the two issues are clearly closely connected, and it has been argued that it would be preferable if they were to be considered alongside each other as part of an overarching 'scope of the risk' analysis (see, e.g., Nolan, 'Deconstructing the Duty of Care' (2013) 129 LQR 559 at 573).

Application of the *Wagon Mound* Principle

Whatever the merits or otherwise of the foreseeability requirement, it soon became apparent that the principle set out in *The Wagon Mound* would rarely be used to limit liability in cases of physical injury caused by negligence. The first concession came in *Smith v Leech Brain & Co* [1962] 2 QB 405, where the plaintiff suffered a burn to his lip as a result of the defendant's negligence. Because of a pre-malignant condition, the burn resulted in the plaintiff contracting cancer, from which he died. The Court of Appeal allowed his widow's action, holding that *The Wagon Mound* did not affect the longstanding thin, or 'egg-shell', skull rule. As long as the initial type of injury which he suffered (the burn) was foreseeable, the knock-on effects of that injury need not be. Shortly afterwards, the House of Lords decided *Hughes v Lord Advocate* [1963] AC 837, which showed that the courts might choose to limit the impact of the foreseeability requirement by adopting a broad definition of the type or kind of damage. The defender in *Hughes* had failed adequately to secure the entrance to a man-hole in the street. The 10-year-old pursuer and another boy took one of the warning paraffin lamps that had been left around the site and went into the man-hole, and when they came back out the pursuer accidentally knocked the lamp into the hole, which triggered an explosion and fire. The force of the explosion knocked the pursuer back into the hole and he was badly burned. It was argued for the defenders that applying *The Wagon Mound* the damage was too remote because although damage by paraffin burn had been foreseeable damage by explosion had not. This argument was rejected by the House of Lords. According to Lord Reid (at 847), '[t]his accident was caused by a known source of danger, but caused in a way which could not have been foreseen, and in my judgment that affords no defence'. Finally, it was always clear that, applying *The Wagon Mound* principle, provided that the type or kind of injury was foreseeable, its extent need not be. In *Vacwell Engineering Co Ltd v BDH Chemicals Ltd* [1971] 1 QB 88, the plaintiff was injured when chemicals supplied in glass ampoules reacted with water in which the ampoules were being washed and caused a large explosion. Because a small explosion had been foreseeable, all the damage that occurred was recoverable even though its extent could not have been anticipated.

Admittedly, in the first decade after *The Wagon Mound* there were a few cases in which recovery was denied on the ground that the plaintiff's physical injury was too remote. Two examples are *Doughty v Turner Manufacturing Co Ltd* [1964] 1 QB 518 and *Tremain v Pike* [1969] 1 WLR 1556. In *Doughty*, an asbestos lid fell into a vat of molten liquid, and shortly afterwards the plaintiff was burnt when some of the molten liquid erupted. His claim failed on the basis that, although burning by splashing had been foreseeable if the lid fell into the vat, the plaintiff's injury occurred because the temperature of the liquid changed the chemical composition of the lid and this had not been foreseeable and was therefore too remote. In *Tremain*, the plaintiff contracted Weil's disease as a result of exposure to rats' urine. The defendant had been negligent in allowing his farm to be overrun with rats, but the judge found that, while injuries such as rat bites were a foreseeable consequence of this negligence, the rare condition contracted by the plaintiff was not.

However, the clear trend in the more recent authorities is to define the type or kind of injury widely, and Lord Nicholls has doubted whether the distinction drawn in *Doughty* (described earlier) would commend itself to courts nowadays (*Attorney-General v Hartwell* [2004] 1 WLR 1273 at [29]). A good example of the modern approach is *Jolley v Sutton London Borough Council* [2000] 1 WLR 1082 (noted by Nolan (2001) 9 Tort L Rev 104). In this case the plaintiff 14-year-old boy and his friend were trying to repair a derelict boat that had been abandoned on the defendant's land when the jack which they were using to prop up the boat gave way and the boat collapsed on the plaintiff. Although the defendant conceded that it had been negligent not to remove the boat, the Court of Appeal held that the damage was too remote. While physical injury by, say, falling through rotten planks on the boat's deck was foreseeable, the injury the boy suffered when the boat collapsed on him was not. However, the House of Lords disagreed, preferring the trial judge's broader characterisation of the risk created by the council's negligence as that children would 'meddle with the boat at the risk of some physical injury'. (See also *Lear v Hickstead Ltd* [2016] 4 WLR 73.)

The earlier decision of the House of Lords in *Page v Smith* [1996] AC 155 seems to go even further, by suggesting that for remoteness purposes no distinction should be drawn between physical and psychiatric injury, which should instead be treated as a single type or kind of damage, namely 'personal injury'. This aspect of *Page v Smith* has however been severely criticised (see, e.g., Bailey and Nolan, 'The *Page v Smith* Saga' [2010] CLJ 495 at 519–26), and the courts seem reluctant to give full effect to it. In *Pratley v Surrey CC* [2004] ICR 159, for example, the Court of Appeal distinguished for remoteness purposes between psychiatric injury from over-work (which had been foreseeable) and a sudden collapse which occurred as a result of disappointment at the failure to implement ameliorative measures (which had not been). Simply characterising the risk as 'the risk of psychiatric illness' was considered overly broad. Nevertheless, generally the courts take a fairly broad-brush approach when defining the type or kind of damage. For example, when a viola player suffered 'acoustic shock' from being seated in close proximity to the brass section in the orchestra pit at the Royal Opera House Covent Garden, the Court of Appeal refused to distinguish for remoteness purposes between long-term and sudden hearing loss (*Royal Opera House Covent Garden Foundation v Goldscheider* [2019] PIQR P15). Do you think that holding is consistent with the decision in *Pratley*?

2. The *SAAMCO* decision

South Australia Asset Management Corp v York Montague Ltd [1997] AC 191

In three appeals, the House of Lords had to decide the extent of a valuer's liability in respect of a negligent valuation upon which a commercial lender had relied in making a loan. In each case it was conceded that the valuation had been negligent. As a result of the collapse of the property market at the end of the 1980s and early 1990s, the plaintiff lenders failed to recoup the amounts of the loans when the properties on which they were secured were sold. The Court of Appeal held that, in a case where the lender would not have made the loan if there had been a non-negligent valuation, the valuer was liable for the entire loss that the lender incurred on the transaction, including the proportion attributable to a fall in the market. The defendants appealed.

Lord Hoffmann

My Lords, the three appeals before the House raise a common question of principle. What is the extent of the liability of a valuer who has provided a lender with a negligent overvaluation of the property offered as security for the loan? The facts have two common features. The first is that if the lender had known the true value of the property, he would not have lent. The second is that a fall in the property market after the date of the valuation greatly increased the loss which the lender eventually suffered.

The Court of Appeal . . . decided that in a case in which the lender would not otherwise have lent (which they called a 'no-transaction' case), he is entitled to recover the difference between the sum which he lent, together with a reasonable rate of interest, and the net sum which he actually got back. The valuer bears the whole risk of a transaction which, but for his negligence, would not have happened. He is therefore liable for all the loss attributable to a fall in the market. They distinguished what they called a 'successful transaction' case, in which the evidence shows that if the lender had been correctly advised, he would still have lent a lesser sum on the same security. In such a case, the lender can recover only the difference between what he has actually lost and what he would have lost if he had lent the lesser amount. Since the fall in the property market is a common element in both the actual and the hypothetical calculations, it does not increase the valuer's liability.

The valuers appeal. They say that a valuer provides an estimate of the value of the property at the date of the valuation. He does not undertake the role of a prophet. It is unfair that merely because for one reason or other the lender would not otherwise have lent, the valuer should be saddled with the whole risk of the transaction, including a subsequent fall in the value of the property.

Much of the discussion, both in the judgment of the Court of Appeal and in argument at the Bar, has assumed that the case is about the correct measure of damages for the loss which the lender has suffered. . . .

I think that this was the wrong place to begin. Before one can consider the principle on which one should calculate the damages to which a plaintiff is entitled as compensation for loss, it is necessary to decide for what kind of loss he is entitled to compensation. A correct description of the loss for which the valuer is liable must precede any consideration of the measure of damages. For this purpose it is better to begin at the beginning and consider the lender's cause of action.

The lender sues on a contract under which the valuer, in return for a fee, undertakes to provide him with certain information. Precisely what information he has to provide depends, of course, upon the terms of the individual contract. There is some dispute on this point in respect of two of the appeals, to which I shall have to return. But there is one common element which everyone accepts. In each case the valuer was required to provide an estimate of the price which the property might reasonably be expected to fetch if sold in the open market at the date of the valuation.

There is again agreement on the purpose for which the information was provided. It was to form part of the material on which the lender was to decide whether, and if so how much, he would lend. The valuation tells the lender how much, at current values, he is likely to recover if he has to resort to his security. This enables him to decide what margin, if any, an advance of a given amount will allow for: a fall in the market; reasonably foreseeable variance from the figure put forward by the valuer (a valuation is an estimate of the most probable figure which the property will fetch, not a prediction that it will fetch precisely that figure); accidental damage to the property and any other of the contingencies which may happen. The valuer will know that if he overestimates the value of the property, the lender's margin for all these purposes will be correspondingly less.

On the other hand, the valuer will not ordinarily be privy to the other considerations which the lender may take into account, such as how much money he has available, how much the borrower needs to borrow, the strength of his covenant, the attraction of the rate of interest, or the other personal or commercial considerations which may induce the lender to lend.

Because the valuer will appreciate that his valuation, though not the only consideration which would influence the lender, is likely to be a very important one, the law implies into the contract a term that the valuer will exercise reasonable care and skill. The relationship between the parties also gives rise to a concurrent duty in tort (see *Henderson v Merrett Syndicates Ltd* [1995] 2 AC 145). But the scope of the duty in tort is the same as in contract.

A duty of care such as the valuer owes does not, however, exist in the abstract. A plaintiff who sues for breach of a duty imposed by the law (whether in contract or tort or under statute) must do more than prove that the defendant has failed to comply. He must show that the duty was owed to him and that it was a duty in respect of the kind of loss which he has suffered. Both of these requirements are illustrated by *Caparo Industries plc v Dickman* [1990] 2 AC 605. The auditors' failure to use reasonable care in auditing the company's statutory accounts was a breach of their duty of care. But they were not liable to an outside take-over bidder because the duty was not owed to him. Nor were they liable to shareholders who had bought more shares in reliance on the accounts because, although they were owed a duty of care, it was in their capacity as members of the company and not in the capacity (which they shared with everyone else) of potential buyers of its shares. Accordingly, the duty which they were owed was not in respect of loss which they might suffer by buying its shares. As Lord Bridge of Harwich said (at 627):

> It is never sufficient to ask simply whether A owes B a duty of care. It is always necessary to determine the scope of the duty by reference to the kind of damage from which A must take care to save B harmless.

In the present case, there is no dispute that the duty was owed to the lenders. The real question in this case is the kind of loss in respect of which the duty was owed.

How is the scope of the duty determined? In the case of a statutory duty, the question is answered by deducing the purpose of the duty from the language and context of the statute (see *Gorris v Scott* (1874) LR 9 Exch 125). In the case of tort, it will similarly depend upon the purpose of the rule imposing the duty. Most of the judgments in *Caparo* are occupied in examining the Companies Act 1985 to ascertain the purpose of the auditor's duty to take care that the statutory accounts comply with the Act. In the case of an implied contractual duty, the nature and extent of the liability is defined by the term which the law implies. As in the case of any implied term, the process is one of construction of the agreement as a whole in its commercial setting. The contractual duty to provide a valuation and the known purpose of that valuation compel the conclusion that the contract includes a duty of care. The scope of the duty, in the sense of the consequences for which the valuer is responsible, is that which the law regards as best giving effect to the express obligations assumed by the valuer: neither cutting them down so that the lender obtains less than he was reasonably entitled to expect, nor extending them so as to impose on the valuer a liability greater than he could reasonably have thought he was undertaking.

What therefore should be the extent of the valuer's liability? The Court of Appeal said that he should be liable for the loss which would not have occurred if he had given the correct advice. The lender having, in reliance on the valuation, embarked upon a transaction which he would not otherwise have undertaken, the valuer should bear all the risks of that transaction, subject only to the limitation that the damage should have been within the reasonable contemplation of the parties.

There is no reason in principle why the law should not penalise wrongful conduct by shifting on to the wrongdoer the whole risk of consequences which would not have happened but for the wrongful act. Hart and Honoré, *Causation in the Law* (2nd edn, 1985) p. 120 say that it would, for example, be perfectly intelligible to have a rule by which an unlicensed driver was responsible for all the consequences of his having driven, even if they were unconnected with his not having a licence. One might adopt such a rule in the interests of deterring unlicensed driving. But that is not the normal rule. One may compare, for example, *Western Steamship Co Ltd v NV Koninklijke Rotterdamsche Lloyd, The Empire Jamaica* [1955] P 259 at 264 per Evershed MR, in which a collision was caused by a 'blunder in seamanship of . . . a somewhat serious and startling character' by an uncertificated second mate. Although the owners knew that the mate was not certificated and it was certainly the case that the collision would not have happened if he had not been employed, it was held in limitation proceedings that the damage took place without the employers' 'actual fault or privity' because the mate was in fact experienced and (subject to this one aberration) competent (see [1955] P 259 at 271). The collision was not, therefore, attributable to his not having a certificate. The owners were not treated as responsible for all the consequences of having employed an uncertificated mate, but only for the consequences of his having been uncertificated.

Rules which make the wrongdoer liable for all the consequences of his wrongful conduct are exceptional and need to be justified by some special policy. Normally the law limits liability to those consequences which are attributable to that which made the act wrongful. In the case of liability in negligence for providing inaccurate information, this would mean liability for the consequences of the information being inaccurate.

I can illustrate the difference between the ordinary principle and that adopted by the Court of Appeal by an example. A mountaineer about to undertake a difficult climb is concerned about the fitness of his knee. He goes to a doctor who negligently makes a superficial examination and pronounces the knee fit. The climber goes on the expedition, which he would not have undertaken if the doctor had told him the true state of his knee. He suffers an injury which is an entirely foreseeable consequence of mountaineering, but has nothing to do with his knee.

On the Court of Appeal's principle, the doctor is responsible for the injury suffered by the mountaineer because it is damage which would not have occurred if he had been given correct information about his knee. He would not have gone on the expedition and would have suffered no injury. On what I have suggested is the more usual principle, the doctor is not liable. The injury has not been caused by the doctor's bad advice, because it would have occurred even if the advice had been correct. . . .

Your Lordships might, I would suggest, think that there was something wrong with a principle which, in the example which I have given, produced the result that the doctor was liable. What is the reason for this feeling? I think that the Court of Appeal's principle offends common sense because it makes the doctor responsible for consequences which, though in general terms foreseeable, do not appear to have a sufficient causal connection with the subject matter of the duty. The doctor was asked for information on only one of the considerations which might affect the safety of the mountaineer on the expedition. There seems no reason of policy which requires that the negligence of the doctor should require the transfer to him of all the foreseeable risks of the expedition.

I think that one can to some extent generalise the principle upon which this response depends. It is that a person under a duty to take reasonable care to provide information on which someone else will decide upon a course of action is, if negligent, not generally regarded as responsible for all the consequences of that course of action. He is responsible only for the consequences of the information being wrong. A duty of care which imposes upon the informant responsibility for losses which would have occurred even if the information which he gave had been correct is not in my view fair and reasonable as between the parties. It is therefore inappropriate either as an implied term of a contract or as a tortious duty arising from the relationship between them.

The principle thus stated distinguishes between a duty to provide information for the purpose of enabling someone else to decide upon a course of action and a duty to advise someone as to what course of action he should take. If the duty is to advise whether or not a course of action should be taken, the adviser must take reasonable care to consider all the potential consequences of that course of action. If he is negligent, he will therefore be responsible for all the foreseeable loss which is a consequence of that course of action having been taken. If his duty is only to supply information, he must take reasonable care to ensure that the information is correct and if he is negligent, will be responsible for all the foreseeable consequences of the information being wrong . . .

Lord Goff, **Lord Slynn**, **Lord Jauncey** and **Lord Nicholls** agreed with Lord Hoffmann.

Appeal allowed.

COMMENTARY

The analytical tool Lord Hoffmann used to limit liability was the 'scope of the duty' owed by the valuers to the lenders. The valuers undertook a duty to take reasonable care to provide an accurate valuation. Hence the liability of the valuers should be limited to the consequences of the valuation being inaccurate, and so any losses that would still have been suffered had it been accurate are excluded. For comment on *SAAMCO*, see Wightman (1998) 61 MLR 68, and the decision of the High Court of Australia in *Kenny & Good Pty Ltd v MGICA* (1999) 199 CLR 413, where Lord Hoffmann's general approach was rejected, although two members of the court agreed that the valuer's liability should be limited.

Although the *SAAMCO* decision has mostly been of relevance in cases of pure economic loss, Lord Hoffmann's mountaineer example concerned personal injury, and in *Meadows v Khan* [2022] AC 852 the Supreme Court applied *SAAMCO* in the medical negligence context. The claimant in *Meadows* was concerned about giving birth to a child with haemophilia and so consulted the defendant general practitioner to see if she was a carrier of the haemophilia gene. The defendant incorrectly and negligently advised her that she was not, when in fact she was. The claimant then fell pregnant and gave birth to a son, Adejuwon, who suffered from severe haemophilia. Had it not been for the defendant's negligence, this would have been tested for during the pregnancy, which (it was decided) would then have been terminated. Adejuwon was later diagnosed as also suffering from severe autism, this being entirely unrelated to the haemophilia. While it was accepted that the defendant was liable to compensate the claimant for the costs associated with Adejuwon's haemophilia, the Supreme Court held that she was not liable for the costs associated with his autism, since applying *SAAMCO* these fell outside the scope of the duty that she had owed to the claimant, which was limited to taking reasonable care when providing her with information relating to haemophilia. For comment on *Meadows*, see Nolan and Plunkett (2022) 138 LQR 175 and Turton (2022) 130 Med L Rev 724.

A challenge to Lord Hoffmann's approach in *SAAMCO* was rebuffed by the Supreme Court in *Hughes-Holland v BPE Solicitors* [2018] AC 599, where Lord Sumption said, at [34], that 'the decision in *SAAMCO* has often been misunderstood, not least by the writers who have criticised it'. His Lordship defended, at [38], the limitation of the valuer's liability in *SAAMCO* as, in effect, an application of the 'risk principle':

The question which [the *SAAMCO* principle] poses is . . . whether the loss flowed from the right thing, ie from the particular feature of the defendant's conduct which made it wrongful. That turns on an analysis of what did make it wrongful.

(See also *Manchester Building Society v Grant Thornton UK LLP* [2022] AC 783 at [17], per Lord Hodge and Lord Sales: 'in the case of negligent advice given by a professional adviser one looks to see what risk the duty was supposed to guard against and then looks to see whether the loss suffered represented the fruition of that risk'.) However, according to Stapleton (1997) 113 LQR 1 at 6:

. . . a formulaic 'sphere of risk' approach which relies simply on setting the scope of the duty in terms of the consequences which made the act wrongful is open to the same complaint and danger of manipulation; while Lord Hoffmann asserts that what makes the valuation wrongful is that it was inaccurate so that liability is limited to the results of this, someone else might assert that what makes it wrongful is that it was not a careful valuation, and liability should include the consequences of this such as the risk of the advisee locking himself into a transaction from which he cannot escape if the market begins to fall.

In contrast, both the language of remoteness of damage and a non-formulaic approach to duty have the advantage of signalling that there is no mechanical test which can be applied and that the court has to make a judgment about the extent of legal responsibility, a judgment which one hopes will evaluate the often complex concerns which go to produce the boundaries placed on civil obligations. . . .

Subsequently to *SAAMCO*, Lord Hoffmann accepted, extra-judicially, that 'scope of duty' terminology was inappropriate in this context, while nevertheless insisting upon the closeness of the link between the 'nature' of the duty and the extent of liability for breach of that duty ('Causation' (2005) 121 LQR 592 at 596). However, despite Lord Hoffmann's volte-face, the label seems to have stuck as far as the judiciary are concerned, and in *Meadows v Khan*, this terminology led a majority of the Supreme Court to seek to merge the *SAAMCO* principle with the duty of care concept itself (for criticism, see Nolan and Plunkett, *op. cit.*). By contrast, academic commentators tend to treat the *SAAMCO* principle as an aspect of remoteness. According to Stapleton ('Cause In Fact and the Scope of Liability For Consequences' (2003) 119 LQR 388), for example, cases like *SAAMCO* concern the circumstances in which a foreseeable type and kind of damage is nonetheless irrecoverable. An example of such a circumstance is where the consequences sought to be attributed to the defendant are 'coincidences', which is to say events the occurrence of which is not generally increased by the defendant's negligence. Thus in *SAAMCO*, the risk of a fall in the market was not generally increased by negligent valuations. Hence the loss caused by the fall was a coincidence and only exceptionally does the law attribute responsibility to the defendant for coincidental losses. (Note, however, that Stapleton's definition of a coincidence has been criticised by other writers, whose alternative definitions have the effect of subsuming the exclusion of coincidental losses into the 'scope of risk' approach: see Miller, 'Negligent Failure to Warn: Why is it so Difficult?' (2012) 28 PN 266 at 271–2; Clark and Nolan, 'A Critique of *Chester v Afshar*' (2014) 34 OJLS 659 at 670–3.)

A different approach to Stapleton's is adopted by Stauch (2001) 64 MLR 191, who argues that remoteness questions are much more a question of principle than their portrayal often suggests. He comments (at 199):

In particular, the concept has been too readily associated with outcome harm [i.e. the harm the claimant actually suffers] that results from negligent conduct. Instead, the question of whether the risk that made the defendant's conduct faulty subsequently materialised requires us to ask not so much 'what' that damage was, but 'how' it occurred.

In other words, instead of simply looking to the type of harm suffered, one should first ask what were the foreseeable risks associated with the defendant's negligence. As the notion of risk necessarily entails the potential causing of harm, Stauch argues there will be a foreseeable causal chain between the negligent conduct giving rise to the risk(s) and the causing of harm as a result of the risk materialising. Where the harm is caused in accordance with the foreseeable causal chain, such harm is not too remote; conversely, the greater the degree of diversion from the foreseeable causal chain the more likely it is that the harm will be held to be too remote to be recovered. Although Stauch does not claim that all questions of remoteness can be solved in this way, he argues it is more principled than the 'scope of duty' approach.

An example of this approach being used is *Clare v Perry* [2005] EWCA Civ 39. It was alleged that the defendant was careless by not taking steps to prevent persons from falling off a wall. The claimant was injured when she attempted to climb down the wall. The Court of Appeal rejected the claim; the risk to which the alleged negligence related was of someone accidentally falling off the wall, not deliberately trying to descend it. In Stauch's terms, the risk of injury by deliberately climbing down the wall diverted sufficiently from the foreseeable causal chain (an accidental fall) for recovery to be denied. One difficulty with this approach, however, may be defining the risks that made the defendant's conduct negligent. As Nolan observes ((2001) 9 Tort L Rev 101 at 104), 'when it comes to identifying the risk or risks that made the defendant's conduct negligent, consensus is often hard to come by'. Nevertheless, 'the scope of the risk' is in our view a useful concept when considering questions of remoteness, and in her most recent writing on this topic, Stapleton seems to accept as much, observing that a consequence will be too remote, inter alia, if it is not 'the materialisation of a risk that fell within the scope of the risks in relation to which the defendant owed a duty to exercise care' *(Stapleton, pp. 94–5).*

For discussion of some more specific remoteness principles that apply only in particular types of case—such as where there is concurrent liability in contract and tort for economic loss, or in cases of medical non-disclosure of risks—see *Winfield & Jolowicz,* paras 7-075–7-078.

6 DEFENCES TO NEGLIGENCE

I. Introduction

Even where a claimant satisfies the prima facie elements of a cause of action in negligence, there are four defences that a defendant can plead. Three of these (*volenti non fit injuria*, exclusion of liability and illegality) are complete defences. The fourth (contributory negligence) is a partial defence, which has the effect of reducing the damages awarded. The defence of *volenti non fit injuria* has been chipped away at over the years, both by judicial decision and statute, and nowadays it is rare for a claim to fail on this ground. Furthermore, the ability of the defendant to exclude liability for negligence has also been reduced, although not eliminated, by the Unfair Contract Terms Act 1977 and Consumer Rights Act 2015. By contrast, contributory negligence remains of great practical importance, and is routinely relied on by defendants in all sorts of negligence cases. Illegality also features regularly in the case law (perhaps in part because of the unavailability of *volenti* in many road accident cases) although the boundaries of this defence are unstable and have been the subject of much litigation in recent times.

For discussion of the concept of a tort defence, and a taxonomy of such defences, see J. Goudkamp, *Tort Law Defences* (Oxford: Hart, 2013).

II. *Volenti Non Fit Injuria*

1. Introduction

> **McTear v Imperial Tobacco Ltd** [2005] CSOH 69, 2005 2 SC 1
>
> The facts are not important for present purposes.
>
> **Lord Nimmo Smith**
>
> [7.204] The maxim volenti non fit injuria, literally translated, means . . . that a legal wrong is not done to one who is willing (or, perhaps preferably, one who consents). Invocation of the maxim is predicated on the assumption that negligence has otherwise been established and that if the defender's plea fails the pursuer must succeed. It is for this reason that the burden of proving it is on the defender who invokes it.

[7.205] The authorities do not seem to me to permit an entirely confident exposition of what must be proved in order for the plea to succeed. As can be seen from the cases referred to by counsel, it may be variously stated that the pursuer has voluntarily assumed the risk of the defender's negligence; or he has consented to a lack of reasonable care on the part of the defender that may produce the risk of injury; or he has agreed, expressly or impliedly, to waive any claim for any injury that may befall him due to the lack of reasonable care by the defender; or he has willingly accepted the risks arising from the want of reasonable care on the part of the defender, in awareness of the defender's negligence; or that he is consenting to lack of reasonable care on the part of the defender and to run the risk of the defender's negligence at his own expense; or that he has accepted the risk of the defender's negligence in the exercise of his legal duties and has absolved the defender from the consequences arising from that negligence. All of these ways of giving effect to the maxim may amount to the same thing, which is consent to the lack of reasonable care on the part of the defender and acceptance of the risk of harm arising therefrom. The consent may of course be inferred from the whole circumstances. I do not take it from the authorities that the pursuer need have expressly in mind the concept of negligence on the part of the defender, but he must knowingly consent to such conduct as may objectively be held to amount to negligence.

COMMENTARY

The defence of *volenti non fit injuria*, sometimes called voluntary assumption of risk, reflects the common sense notion that '[o]ne who has invited or assented to an act being done towards him cannot, when he suffers from it, complain of it as a wrong' (*Smith v Baker* [1891] AC 325 at 360, per Lord Herschell). The *volenti* defence is therefore the equivalent in negligence of the consent defence in the intentional torts (see Ch. 2.VI.3), but what exactly does it mean to say that a claimant has consented to the defendant's negligence?

In his judgment in the extracted case, Lord Nimmo Smith said that the *volenti* maxim 'may readily be applied in a situation where the pursuer's consent precedes the defender's negligent conduct', as in *Imperial Chemical Industries Ltd v Shatwell* [1965] AC 656 (extracted later), but that there is 'much greater difficulty where the conduct has taken place already before the pursuer becomes aware of it' (2005 2 SC 1 at [7.206]). Suppose, for example, that in *Donoghue v Stevenson* [1932] AC the pursuer had known that there was a snail in the ginger beer, but decided to drink it anyway. In this case, it is probably more appropriate to hold that the true cause of any harm that ensued was 'her own conscious volition in choosing to incur the risk or certainty of mischance' (*ibid.*), rather than the negligence of the defender, so that her claim would fail on grounds of legal causation rather than *volenti* (or, alternatively, that her damages should be reduced for contributory negligence).

If that is right, then might it make sense to limit the application of the *volenti* defence to situations where the claimant consented to the negligence of the defendant at or before the time of the breach of duty? In practice what this would mean is that the defendant would have to show that the claimant freely and voluntarily, with full knowledge of the nature and extent of the risk, consented to the unreasonable behaviour of the defendant of which the claimant now complains.

2. The Operation of the Defence

Woodley v Metropolitan District Railway Co (1877) 2 Ex D 384

The facts appear in the judgment of Cockburn CJ.

Cockburn CJ

The facts of the case were as follows: the plaintiff was a workman in the employ of a contractor engaged by the defendants to execute certain work on a side wall on their line of railway in a dark tunnel. Trains were passing the spot every ten minutes, and the line there being on a curve, the workmen would not be aware of the approach of the train till it was within twenty or thirty yards of them. The space between the rail and the wall, on which the workmen had to stand while at work, was just sufficient to enable them to keep clear of a train when sensible of its approach. The place in question was wholly without light. No one was stationed to give notice of an approaching train. The speed of the trains was not slackened when arriving near where the men were at work, nor was any signal given by sounding the steam whistle. It is unnecessary to say that the service on which the plaintiff was thus employed was one of extreme danger. While he was reaching across the rail to find a tool he had laid down a train came upon him suddenly, and struck and seriously injured him. . . .

That which would be negligence in a company, with reference to the state of their premises or the manner of conducting their business, so as to give a right to compensation for an injury resulting therefrom to a stranger lawfully resorting to their premises in ignorance of the existence of the danger, will give no such right to one, who being aware of the danger, voluntarily encounters it, and fails to take the necessary care for avoiding it. . . . He cannot, I think, make the company liable for injury arising from danger to which he voluntarily exposed himself. . . .

Judgment for the defendants.

COMMENTARY

Woodley is an extreme example of the scope of the *volenti* defence in the middle part of the nineteenth century in relation to negligence actions by employees against their employer. The case effectively equates knowledge of the risk with assent to the defendant's negligence. However, it was one of the last cases to take such a view. In 1891, the House of Lords in *Smith v Baker* [1891] AC 325 held that the defence did not apply where the defendant's negligence increased the risk to the plaintiff employee even though the employee knew the risk to which he was exposed. Lord Herschell stated:

[W]here . . . a risk to the employed, which may or may not result in injury, has been created or enhanced by the negligence of the employer, does the mere continuance in service, with knowledge of the risk, preclude the employed, if he suffers from such negligence, from recovering in respect of his employer's breach of duty? I cannot assent to the proposition that the maxim, 'Volenti non fit injuria' applies to such a case, and that the employer can invoke its aid to protect him from liability for his wrong.

An example of this more restrictive conception of the defence in the employment context is provided by *Bowater v Mayor, Aldermen and Burgesses of the Borough of Rowley Regis* [1944] KB 476, where Goddard LJ stated: 'For this maxim to apply it must be shown that a servant who is asked or required to use dangerous plant is a volunteer in the fullest sense; that, knowing of the danger, he expressly or impliedly said he would do the job at his own risk, and not that of his master. . . . ' As these conditions are rarely satisfied, the defence nowadays plays little role in actions between employers and employees (but note *Shatwell* extracted later).

For a discussion of *Woodley* in its historical context, see Banks, '*Woodley v Metropolitan District Railway Company* (1877)', in Mitchell & Mitchell, ch. 5.

It is in any case clear that mere knowledge of the risk is insufficient to establish the defence. The circumstances in which acting with knowledge of the risk will be deemed to amount to consent to the negligence are considered in the next extracted case.

Morris v Murray [1991] 2 QB 6

The plaintiff had been drinking with the deceased in a number of public houses over several hours. At the end of this period the deceased, who had a pilot's licence, suggested to the plaintiff that he go on a flight with him in his light aircraft. The plaintiff drove the deceased to the airfield, helped to fuel the plane and attempted to help start it. Flying conditions were poor and all regular club flying at the airfield had been cancelled. Further, the deceased took off down wind on an uphill runway that was wet and slippery. The flight was short and chaotic, as a witness account confirmed:

> He said in his statement that when he saw the plane his initial reaction was that he was looking at a model plane. He could not initially reconcile the flying attitude of the plane, that is to say its almost vertical climb and its close proximity to the ground, with anything other than a model aircraft. The plane was evidently recovering from a descent which brought it close to the ground. It climbed to about 300 feet, then stalled and dived into the ground.

The deceased was killed and the plaintiff severely injured. The autopsy on the deceased revealed, from the concentration of ethanol in his body and from his blood alcohol content, that he had consumed the equivalent of seventeen whiskies. At the trial of the plaintiff's action against the deceased's estate for negligence, the defences of *volenti* and contributory negligence were raised. The trial judge rejected the defence of *volenti* and reduced the plaintiff's damages by 20 per cent because of contributory negligence. The estate appealed.

Fox LJ

The reasoning of Asquith J [in *Dann v Hamilton* [1939] 1 KB 509, noted later] was that a person who voluntarily travels as a passenger with a driver who is known to the passenger to have driven negligently in the past cannot properly be regarded as volens to future acts of negligence by the driver. Should it then make any difference that the driver is likely to drive negligently on the material occasion, not because he is shown to have driven negligently in the past, but because he is known by the plaintiff to be under the influence of drink? Asquith J thought not and held that the plaintiff by embarking in the car, or re-entering it with the knowledge that through drink the driver had materially reduced his capacity for driving safely, did not implicitly consent to or absolve the driver from liability from any subsequent negligence on his part whereby she might suffer harm.

Having reached that conclusion, however, Asquith J continued (at 518) as follows:

> There may be cases in which the drunkenness of the driver at the material time is so extreme and so glaring that to accept a lift from him is like engaging in an intrinsically and

obviously dangerous occupation, inter-meddling with an unexploded bomb or walking on the edge of an unfenced cliff. It is not necessary to decide whether in such a case the maxim *volenti non fit injuria* would apply, for in the present case I find as a fact that the driver's degree of intoxication fell short of this degree.

The question before us, I think, is whether, as a matter of law, there are such cases as Asquith J refers to and, if so, whether this present case is one of them. . . .

[I]n general, I think that the *volenti* doctrine can apply to the tort of negligence, though it must depend on the extent of the risk, the passenger's knowledge of it and what can be inferred as to his acceptance of it. The passenger cannot be *volens* (in the absence of some form of express disclaimer) in respect of acts of negligence which he had no reason to anticipate and he must be free from compulsion. . . .

If the plaintiff had himself been sober on the afternoon of the flight it seems to me that, by agreeing to be flown by Mr Murray, he must be taken to have accepted fully the risk of serious injury. The danger was both obvious and great. He could not possibly have supposed that Mr Murray, who had been drinking all the afternoon, was capable of discharging a normal duty of care.

But as he himself had been drinking, can it be assumed that he was capable of appreciating the risks? The matter was not very deeply examined at the trial, but he was certainly not 'blind drunk'. In cross-examination, he agreed with the description 'merry'. He was capable of driving a car from the Blue Boar to the airfield and he did so for the purpose of going on a flight with Mr Murray. He helped to start the aircraft and fuel it. Immediately before take-off he asked Mr Murray whether he should not 'radio in' (a sensible inquiry). None of this suggests that his faculties were so muddled that he was incapable of appreciating obvious risks. Moreover, he gave no specific evidence to the effect 'I was really too drunk to know what I was doing'. Nor did anyone else give such evidence about him. . . .

In my opinion, on the evidence the plaintiff knew that he was going on a flight, he knew that he was going to be piloted by Mr Murray and he knew that Mr Murray had been drinking heavily that afternoon. The plaintiff's actions that afternoon, from leaving the Blue Boar to the take-off, suggest that he was capable of understanding what he was doing. There is no clear evidence to the contrary. I think that he knew what he was doing and was capable of appreciating the risks. I do not overlook that the plaintiff's evidence was that, if he had been sober, he would not have gone on the flight. That is no doubt so but it does not establish that he was in fact incapable of understanding what he was doing that afternoon.

If he was capable of understanding what he was doing, then the fact is that he knowingly and willingly embarked on a flight with a drunken pilot. The flight served no useful purpose at all: there was no need or compulsion to join it. It was just entertainment. The plaintiff cooperated fully in the joint activity and did what he could to assist it. He agreed in evidence that he was anxious to start the engine and to fly. A clearer source of great danger could hardly be imagined. The sort of errors of judgment which an intoxicated pilot may make are likely to have a disastrous result. The high probability was that Mr Murray was simply not fit to fly an aircraft. Nothing that happened on the flight itself suggests otherwise, from the take-off down wind to the violence of the manoeuvres of the plane in flight.

The situation seems to me to come exactly within Asquith J's example of the case where: the drunkenness of the driver at the material time is so extreme and so glaring that to accept a lift from him is like engaging in an intrinsically and obviously dangerous occupation . . . . I think that in embarking on the flight the plaintiff had implicitly waived his rights in the event of injury consequent on Mr Murray's failure to fly with reasonable care. . . .

Considerations of policy do not lead me to any different conclusion. *Volenti* as a defence has, perhaps, been in retreat during this century, certainly in relation to master and servant cases. It might be said that the merits could be adequately dealt with by the application of the contributory negligence rules. The judge held that the plaintiff was only 20 per cent to blame (which seems to me to be too low) but if that were increased to 50 per cent, so that the plaintiff's damages were reduced by half, both sides would be substantially penalised for their conduct. It seems to me, however, that the wild irresponsibility of the venture is such that the law should not intervene to award damages and should leave the loss where it falls. Flying is intrinsically dangerous and flying with a drunken pilot is great folly. The situation is very different from what has arisen in motoring cases.

I should mention that the defence of volenti has been abrogated in relation to passengers in motor vehicles covered by comprehensive insurance (see s. 148 of the Road Traffic Act 1972). It is not suggested, however, that there is any similar enactment relating to aircraft and applicable to this case. . . .

Stocker LJ

Where a plaintiff is aware that his driver is to some extent intoxicated his responsibility can be reflected by an apportionment on the basis of contributory negligence. Whether such a course is appropriate or whether the maxim *volenti* applies depends on the facts of each case. In particular it is relevant to consider the degree of intoxication and the nature of the act to be performed by the driver. In motoring cases it may well be that an apportionment on the basis of contributory negligence will usually be the appropriate course but in my view to pilot an aircraft requires a far higher standard of skill and care than driving a motor car and the effect of intoxication becomes all the more important. It seems to me from the authorities cited that this is the approach which the courts ought to apply to this problem: how intoxicated was the driver? How obvious was this to the plaintiff, and the extent of the potential risk to the plaintiff if he voluntarily accepts the offer of carriage?

In the light of these observations I turn next to the crucial issue in this case. Did the plaintiff voluntarily accept the risk of injury, and of the defendant's likely breach of duty in negligence with full knowledge of the facts?

I therefore first consider the position on the basis that the plaintiff himself was sober, or at least not so intoxicated as the result of alcohol as to be incapable of assessing the risk. I would unhesitatingly answer this question 'Yes'. The facts were: (1) the deceased pilot had consumed at least the equivalent of 17 whiskies and when absorption rate is considered over the period of time involved must, in fact, have consumed rather more. (2) The plaintiff was drinking with him over several hours and knew how much the deceased pilot had had to drink. (3) The risk of accident was manifest to any sober person when the activity to be carried out involves flying an aeroplane. The risk is far greater than driving a car in a similar condition of insobriety. The plaintiff had flown with the deceased pilot before; he co-operated and, indeed, encouraged the deceased pilot throughout; he drove the pilot to the airfield and filled the aeroplane with aviation spirit. The purpose of going to the airfield can only have been to fly in the aircraft. That the pilot was in fact incapable of flying the aircraft is demonstrated by a number of factors. Firstly he took off down wind and uphill, a highly dangerous manoeuvre itself, and in fact only just managed to get airborne shortly before the end of the runway. Evidence suggests that the aircraft was out of control virtually at all times thereafter. (4) The plaintiff not only accepted the offer of being taken for a joyride in the aircraft, but actively sought it. . . .

Thus on the basis that the plaintiff himself was capable of appreciating the full nature and extent of the risk and voluntarily accepted it, I would have no doubt whatever that this maxim would have applied to defeat his claim. If this was not a case of *volenti non fit injuria* I find it very difficult to envisage circumstances in which that can ever be the case.

[His Lordship went on to consider whether the intoxication of the plaintiff was such as to render him incapable of fully appreciating the nature and extent of the risk and of voluntarily accepting it, and concluded that it was not. He continued:]

To accept a flight in an aeroplane piloted by a pilot who has had any significant amount of drink, let alone the amount which manifestly this pilot had had, is to engage in an intrinsically and obviously dangerous occupation. For these reasons, in my judgment, the judge ought to have found that the plaintiff's claim should be rejected on the basis of the application of the maxim *volenti non fit injuria*. . . .

Sir George Waller delivered a short concurring judgment.

Appeal allowed.

COMMENTARY

In *Dann v Hamilton* [1939] 1 KB 509, the plaintiff, a passenger in a car whose driver had consumed some alcohol, was injured in an accident caused by negligent driving. Although she had the opportunity to leave the car when another person left it, she remained, and in response to the exiting passenger's comment that the two remaining passengers had 'more pluck than she had', the plaintiff remarked: 'You should be like me. If anything is going to happen it will happen.' It did, but she was still able to recover from the deceased driver's estate. What is the difference between this case and *Morris v Murray*? According to Fox LJ, the plaintiff in *Dann v Hamilton* was engaged in a quite ordinary social outing to London and back, with a driver who was not drunk until quite a late stage in the day, by which time it was not very easy for the plaintiff to extricate herself without giving offence and significant inconvenience. The whole situation bore little resemblance to the drunken escapade, heavily fraught with danger from the first, on which the plaintiff and deceased embarked in *Morris*. Do you agree? Note that contributory negligence, which would also then have operated as a complete defence, was not pleaded in *Dann v Hamilton*. If it had been, do you think a finding of contributory negligence would have been made? (Cf. *Allen v Chadwick* (2015) 256 CLR 148) Note also that *volenti* cannot now be relied upon by a driver as against a passenger in a road accident case: see s. 149 Road Traffic Act 1988.

If the plaintiff in *Morris* had been so drunk that he was incapable of appreciating the risk he was running, would the defence have applied? One can hardly accept a risk if one is incapable of appreciating it, but the contrary conclusion means, as Stocker LJ points out, that the more drunk the claimant is, the more likely his or her claim will succeed, which seems hard to justify.

Imperial Chemical Industries Ltd v Shatwell [1965] AC 656

The facts of this case are stated in the speech of Lord Reid.

Lord Reid

My Lords, this case arises out of the accidental explosion of a charge at a quarry belonging to the appellants which caused injuries to the respondent George Shatwell and his brother James, who were both qualified shotfirers. On 8 June 1960, these two men and another shotfirer, Beswick, had bored and filled fifty shot holes and had inserted electric detonators and connected them up in series. Before firing it was necessary to test the circuit for continuity. This should have been done by connecting long wires so that the men could go to a shelter some eighty yards away and test from there. They had not sufficient wire with them and Beswick went off to get more. The testing ought not to have been done until signals had been given, so that other men could take shelter, and these signals were not due to be given for at least another hour. Soon after Beswick had left George said to his brother 'Must we test them', meaning shall we test them, and James said 'yes'. The testing is done by passing a weak current through the circuit in which a small galvanometer is included and if the needle of the instrument moves when a connexion is made the circuit is in order. So George got a galvanometer and James handed two short wires to him. Then George applied the wires to the galvanometer and the needle did not move. This showed that the circuit was defective so the two men went round inspecting the connections. They saw nothing wrong and George said that that meant there was a dud detonator somewhere, and decided to apply the galvanometer to each individual detonator. James handed two other wires to him and George used them to apply the galvanometer to the first detonator. The result was an explosion which injured both men.

This method had been regularly used without mishap until the previous year. Then some research done by the appellants showed that it might be unsafe and in October 1959, the appellants gave orders that testing must in future be done from a shelter and a lecture was given to all the shotfirers, including the Shatwells, explaining the position. Then in December 1959, new statutory regulations were made (SI 1959 No. 2259) probably because the Ministry had been informed of the results of the appellants' research. These regulations came into operation in February 1960, and the Shatwells were aware of them. But some of the shotfirers appear to have gone on in the old way. An instance of this came to the notice of the management in May 1960, and the management took immediate action and revoked the shotfiring certificate of the disobedient man, and told the other shotfirers about this. George admitted in evidence that he knew all this. He admitted that they would only have had to wait ten minutes until Beswick returned with the long wires. When asked why he did not wait, his only excuse was that he could not be bothered to wait.

George now sues the appellants on the ground that he and his brother were equally to blame for this accident, and that the appellants are vicariously liable for his brother's conduct. He has been awarded £1,500, being half the agreed amount of his loss. There is no question of the appellants having been in breach of the regulation because the duty under the regulation is laid on the shotfirer personally. So counsel for George frankly and rightly admitted that if George had sued James personally instead of suing his employer the issue would have been the same. If this decision is right it means that if two men collaborate in doing what they know is dangerous and is forbidden and as a result both are injured, each has a cause of action against the other.

The appellants have two grounds of defence, first that James's conduct had no causal connexion with the accident the sole cause being George's own fault, and secondly *volenti non fit injuria*. . . .

[His Lordship held that the appellant could not succeed on the first ground, and then considered the early cases on *volenti non fit injuria* in actions between masters and servants, before continuing:]

More recently it appears to have been thought in some quarters that, at least as between master and servant, *volenti non fit injuria* is a dead or dying defence. That, I think, is because in most cases where the defence would now be available it has become usual to base the decision on contributory negligence. . . . I think that most people would say, without stopping to think of the reason, that there is a world of difference between two fellow servants collaborating carelessly, so that the acts of both contribute to cause injury to one of them, and two fellow servants combining to disobey an order deliberately, though they know the risk involved. It seems reasonable that the injured man should recover some compensation in the former case, but not in the latter. If the law treats both as merely cases of negligence, it cannot draw a distinction. In my view the law does and should draw a distinction. In the first case only the partial defence of contributory negligence is available. In the second *volenti non fit injuria* is a complete defence, if the employer is not himself at fault and is only liable vicariously for the acts of the fellow servant. If the plaintiff invited or freely aided and abetted his fellow servant's disobedience, then he was *volens* in the fullest sense. He cannot complain of the resulting injury either against the fellow servant or against the master on the ground of his vicarious responsibility for his fellow servant's conduct. I need not here consider the common case where the servant's disobedience puts the master in breach of a statutory obligation, and it would be wrong to decide in advance whether that would make any difference. There remain two other arguments for the respondent which I must deal with.

It was argued that in this case it has not been shown that George had a full appreciation of the risk. In my view it must be held that he had. He knew that those better qualified than he was took the risk seriously. He knew that his employers had forbidden this practice, and that it had then been prohibited by statutory regulation; and he knew that his employers were taking strong measures to see that the order was obeyed. If he did not choose to believe what he was told, I do not think that he could for that reason say that he did not fully appreciate the risk. He knew that the risk was that a charge would explode during testing, and no shotfirer could be in any doubt about the possible consequences of that. . . .

I can find no reason at all why the fact that these two brothers agreed to commit an offence by contravening a statutory prohibition imposed on them as well as agreeing to defy their employer's orders should affect the application of the principle *volenti non fit injuria* either to an action by one of them against the other or to an action by one against their employer based on his vicarious responsibility for the conduct of the other. I would therefore allow this appeal.

Lord Donovan

The duty to test from shelter is laid on the shotfirers themselves. George himself was well aware of his duty in this respect, and must have known of the reason for the rule, namely, the risk of premature explosion. When he asked James whether they should proceed to test, notwithstanding that they were both in the open, and obtained his agreement to that course, they were voluntarily accepting this known risk with their eyes open. Against this view of the matter it is argued for the respondent that, though he knew of the risk, he knew it also to be a remote one, and never dreamed that it would mature; and that to be affected by the plea of *volenti* he must be aware of the exact extent of the danger. I cannot accept this argument. George did know the extent of the risk, namely, that it was very remote. What he did not know, of course, was whether the risk would mature. But whoever does? The argument really is this: 'I didn't think it would happen to me.' This is not an answer, once the risk is known, and understood, and accepted. Next it is argued that for the defence based on the plea to succeed, it must be shown that there was no kind of pressure on George to accept the risk, but that it was his free and voluntary act. In the present case that was not so, it is said, because of the pressure represented by the willingness of James to help to carry out the test in the open; but what James did was to accept George's invitation so to test in the open and thereafter to cooperate. I cannot regard this as affecting George's complete freedom of choice in the matter. He remained perfectly free to change his mind. . . .

When George invited James to join him in testing the electrical circuit without taking shelter George knew the risk he was running and accepted it voluntarily. He did not, of course, in express language, waive such rights as he might have against James if the risk matured and he was injured; but in my opinion that must be taken to be the tacit effect of the agreement between the two of them to test the circuit in the open. The situation lacks nothing of the elements necessary to support the plea of *volenti non fit injuria*. Each knew the risk he ran: each accepted it quite voluntarily. . . .

Lord Hodson, **Lord Pearce** and **Viscount Radcliffe** delivered separate speeches in favour of allowing the appeal.

Appeal allowed.

COMMENTARY

This extract shows that the defence of *volenti* is not dead in the employment context, although the employer was only liable vicariously through the acts of another employee. As is suggested in D. Howarth et al., *Hepple & Matthews' Tort Law: Cases and Materials*, 7th edn (Oxford: Hart, 2016), p. 460, the position might have been different if James had been George's superior. In that situation, whilst there may have been knowledge of the risk, it would be more difficult to imply acceptance of the risk. For an analogous situation, see *Radclyffe v Ministry of Defence* [2009] EWCA Civ 635 (argued on duty of care) where the claimant soldier engaged in the dangerous conduct only because he felt pressured to do so by a superior officer.

In the Scottish case of *Hugh v National Coal Board* 1972 SC 252, the pursuer, an apprentice electrician employed by the defenders, was injured when his foot slipped under a train used to convey employees from the mine in which he worked to the lift cage. As the train approached the cage, many employees, including the pursuer, jumped off, a practice which was prohibited by both the defender and by statutory regulation. He was injured when, in the rush, several men fell causing him to lose his footing. Lord Keith, applying *Shatwell*, held that the defence of *volenti* barred the pursuer's claim. Do you agree that the two cases are indistinguishable?

3. Evaluation

A. Jaffey, 'Volenti Non Fit Injuria' [1985] CLJ 87

[W]here the plaintiff's relevant conduct occurred before the defendant's negligent act, the possibility of *volens* is confined to cases where (assuming there is no express agreement) there is some consensual relationship or transaction between the parties, which may carry with it an implied agreement under which the plaintiff forgoes any claim he might otherwise have. This is the point of Diplock LJ's well-known statement in *Wooldridge v Sumner*, 'In my view, the maxim, in the absence of express contract, has no application to negligence simpliciter where the duty of care is based solely on proximity or "neighbourship" in the Atkinian sense.' Where the defendant's duty of care stems merely from the fact of foreseeability of injury to the plaintiff, but there is no relationship or transaction between them, there is nothing from which an agreement can be inferred.

> Thus the desirable state of the law would be that put forward by Glanville Williams: the defence of consent or *volenti non fit injuria* (in the tort of negligence) requires an agreement—not necessarily a contract—between the parties under which the plaintiff agrees that identified possible future conduct of the defendant shall not be actionable. There should be no defence of voluntary assumption of risk covering cases where there is no such agreement between the parties made before the defendant's act. In other words the phrase 'voluntary assumption of risk' should be confined to cases where there is such an agreement, though it is more likely to be used in relation to an implied rather than an express agreement. Cases of a plaintiff merely freely encountering a risk of which he is aware should be dealt with under contributory negligence or in exceptional cases, under *nova causa interveniens*. Such a state of the law would not seem to be out of reach of the courts. . . .
>
> What are the circumstances in which an agreement will be implied in a less obvious case [sc. than *ICI v Shatwell*]? As we have seen, there must be a transaction or relationship between the parties. Then, if it is to be held that the parties tacitly agreed that if in the course of the transaction or relationship the defendant by his careless or unskilled conduct should injure the plaintiff the latter would forego any action, it is necessary that the plaintiff must have been fully aware, not merely of the possibility of negligence by the defendant (for that is always possible), but of facts making it highly likely that the defendant would commit some specific act of negligence—for instance the plaintiff knew that the defendant was incapable, or scarcely capable, of avoiding that act. Such knowledge on the plaintiff's part must exist, otherwise there would be no reason why he should have adverted to the possibility of liability on the defendant's part, let alone not agreeing to sue. . . . If the relationship or transaction exists, and also the requisite knowledge the question still remains whether the parties impliedly agreed that the defendant's conduct, if it occurred, should not be actionable. In effect the question is whether such a term should be implied in the relationship, and although the relationship itself may not be a contract, or even an agreement in the proper sense, the classic test of the 'officious bystander' will do very well. If the parties were asked what would be the position if the plaintiff were injured as a result of an act done by the defendant which the parties knew he was very likely to do in the course of the transaction or relationship, would they say, 'Of course there will be no liability if that happens' . . .

COMMENTARY

Is this approach consistent with the result in *Dann v Hamilton*? Or *Morris v Murray*? And to what extent is it consistent with the approach to *volenti* adopted by Lord Nimmo Smith in *McTear*? In particular, is it appropriate to treat an implied agreement to forego a claim you might have against another arising out of that other's negligence as giving rise to a defence of *volenti*, as opposed to a defence of exclusion of liability (discussed later)?

An alternative approach to Jaffey's has been put forward by Tan, '*Volenti Non Fit Injuria*: An Alternative Framework' (1995) 3 Tort L Rev 208. She suggests refashioning the defence as an assessment of the claimant's conduct. Accordingly, although the traditional elements of knowledge of the risk, agreement, voluntariness and the degree of danger of the defendant's activity would remain relevant, they would not be determinative. Rather, they would be considered along with other factors such as:

(i) whether the claimant was a rescuer;
(ii) whether the claimant was committing a crime or trespass;

(iii) the extent of the claimant's willing participation in the dangerous activity;
(iv) the claimant's mental capacity;
(v) whether the claimant was intoxicated;
(vi) whether the claimant was merely obeying her employer's instructions.

Tan argues that the flexibility inherent in this approach allows the defence to adapt to changes in social policy; for example the increasing recognition of the social evil of drink-driving. Do you agree? Are cases such as *Morris v Murray* better explained by Tan's approach than by attempting to find an implied agreement to accept the risk of injury due to the defendant's negligence?

III. Contributory Negligence

The claimant, without looking to check for traffic, steps out onto the road and is hit by the defendant's car, which is being driven too quickly. Should the defendant be held liable? Not much assistance is gained by looking at the issue solely as one of causation because the injury would not have been caused at all but for both the claimant's and the defendant's negligence. From the early part of the nineteenth century, however, the common law did attempt to solve the problem through the mechanism of causation. If the contributory negligence was the cause of the damage the claimant was barred from recovery, even though the defendant had also been negligent. This all-or-nothing approach—the plaintiff either received 100 per cent of the damages if the contributory negligence was not the cause of the damage or nothing if it was—offended against notions of justice, although the malleability of the causation concept and the benevolence of the juries that heard the cases allowed this unsatisfactory state of affairs to continue for longer than it might otherwise have done. The law was finally reformed in 1945 to allow the claimant's damages to be reduced, but not eliminated, as a result of his contributory negligence. The role of causation in contributory negligence was thus diminished, although not banished (see further J. Steele, 'Law Reform (Contributory Negligence) Act 1945: Collisions of a Different Sort', in *Tort Law and the Legislature*). A court can today concentrate on whether the claimant's conduct amounted to contributory negligence and, if it did, what the proper apportionment of damages should be between the negligent claimant and defendant.

1. Historical Background

Butterfield v Forrester (1809) 11 East 60, 103 ER 926

The plaintiff brought an action on the case against the defendant for obstructing a highway by placing a pole across part of a road. The plaintiff was injured when his horse crashed into the pole and he was thrown off. The pole was visible from a distance of about 100 yards and if the plaintiff had been riding normally 'he might have observed and avoided it'. However, the plaintiff, who had just left a public house, was 'riding violently' at the time of the accident. The action failed because of the plaintiff's contributory negligence.

> **Lord Ellenborough CJ**
>
> A party is not to cast himself upon an obstruction which has been made by the fault of another, and avail himself of it, if he do not use common and ordinary caution to be in the right. In cases of persons riding upon what is considered to be the wrong side of the road, that would not authorise another purposefully to ride up against them. One person being in fault will not dispense with another's using ordinary care for himself. Two things must occur to support this action, an obstruction in the road by the fault of the defendant, and no want of ordinary care to avoid it on the part of the plaintiff.
>
> *Rule refused.*

COMMENTARY

This case reflects the traditional dislike of the common law for attributing an injury to more than one legal cause. Either the defendant's negligence or the plaintiff's negligence was the cause. When civil cases were tried by juries this may not have mattered much, because a jury could find for the plaintiff on the basis that it was indeed the defendant's negligence that caused the damage but only award the plaintiff a fraction of the damages claimed in order to reflect the plaintiff's contributory fault. But the abrogation of jury trial from 1854 onwards required judges to deal with this issue. This was made no easier by the decision in *Davies v Mann* (1842) 10 M & W 547, 152 ER 588, which was regarded as the leading authority on the so-called 'last clear chance' doctrine: if the defendant had the last opportunity to avoid the damage then it was deemed to have been caused by their neglect, even if the plaintiff had been guilty of some prior contributory negligence. This became even more complicated with the development of a 'constructive last clear chance' doctrine: but for their own negligence, the defendant would have had the opportunity of avoiding the damage (see *British Columbia Electric Railway v Loach* [1916] 1 AC 719). The civil law jurisdiction of admiralty adopted the eminently more sensible practice of apportioning the loss equally where both parties' negligence was to blame for a collision at sea, an approach expanded by the Maritime Conventions Act 1911, which allowed damages to be apportioned in proportion to the degree to which each vessel was at fault. When the House of Lords applied the statute in *Admiralty Commissioners v Volute* [1922] 1 AC 129, their Lordships declined to apply the last opportunity rule, instead apportioning responsibility between the two negligent parties. In 1939, the Law Revision Committee, in its Eighth Report (Cmd. 6032), recommended legislative change to apply the admiralty rules to the common law and this was enacted in 1945. (See further on the work of the Law Revision Committee in this area, *Mitchell*, ch. 13.)

2. The 1945 Act

> **Law Reform (Contributory Negligence) Act 1945**
>
> **1. Apportionment of liability in case of contributory negligence**
>
> (1) Where any person suffers damage as the result partly of his own fault and partly of the fault of any other person or persons, a claim in respect of that damage shall not be

defeated by reason of the fault of the person suffering the damage, but the damages recoverable in respect thereof shall be reduced to such extent as the court thinks just and equitable having regard to the claimant's share in the responsibility for the damage: Provided that—

(a) this subsection shall not operate to defeat any defence arising under a contract;
(b) where any contract or enactment providing for the limitation of liability is applicable to the claim, the amount of damages recoverable by the claimant by virtue of this subsection shall not exceed the maximum limit so applicable.

(2) Where damages are recoverable by any person by virtue of the foregoing subsection subject to such reduction as is therein mentioned, the court shall find and record the total damages which would have been recoverable if the claimant had not been at fault.

...

(5) Where, in any case to which subsection (1) of this section applies, one of the persons at fault avoids liability to any other such person or his personal representative by pleading the Limitation Act 1939, or any other enactment limiting the time within which proceedings may be taken, he shall not be entitled to recover any damages . . . from that other person or representative by virtue of the said subsection.

(6) Where any case to which subsection (1) of this section applies is tried with a jury, the jury shall determine the total damages which would have been recoverable if the claimant had not been at fault and the extent to which those damages are to be reduced . . .

...

4. Interpretation

The following expressions have the meanings hereby respectively assigned to them, that is to say—

'court' means, in relation to any claim, the court or arbitrator by or before whom the claim falls to be determined;
'damage' includes loss of life and personal injury;
'fault' means negligence, breach of statutory duty or other act or omission which gives rise to a liability in tort or would, apart from this Act, give rise to the defence of contributory negligence.

COMMENTARY

'Fault' of both the claimant and the defendant is required for the Act to apply, but the s. 4 definition appears to suggest that the defendant's fault may consist of conduct that amounted to contributory negligence, and 'since contributory negligence did not at common law presuppose a duty of care, the result of this construction is to allow an action for damages for a fault that would not at common law have been a breach of a duty of care' (G. Williams, *Joint Torts and Contributory Negligence* (London: Stevens & Sons, 1951), p. 318). Williams' solution was to read s. 4 as having two parts: for the defendant fault is 'negligence, breach of statutory duty or other act or omission which gives rise to a liability in tort', whilst for the claimant fault is 'negligence, breach of statutory duty or other act or omission which . . . would, apart from this Act, give rise to, the defence of contributory negligence'. This interpretation has now been accepted as correct (see the decision of the Court of Appeal in *Forsikringsaktieselskapet Vesta v Butcher* [1988] 3 WLR 565, and of the House of Lords in *Standard Chartered Bank v Pakistan National Shipping (Nos 2 & 4)* [2003] 1 AC 959). As with defendant fault in negligence, the claimant's conduct is measured against an objective standard of care, so that, for example, the fact that they were heavily intoxicated at the time of the alleged contributory negligence does not lessen their responsibility (*Campbell v Advantage Insurance Co Ltd* [2021] EWCA Civ 1698). The 'fault' that may amount to contributory negligence has been construed widely but Lord Denning's view in *Murphy v Culhane* [1977] QB 94 that the defence might apply where the claimant initiated a criminal affray during the course of which they were injured has been doubted; in *Standard Chartered Bank v Pakistan National Shipping (Nos 2 & 4)* [2003] 1 AC 959 Lord Rodger noted that contributory negligence had never been available where the defendant intended to harm the claimant, and in *Pritchard v Co-Operative Group Ltd* [2012] QB 320 the Court of Appeal expressly disapproved Lord Denning's view, holding that the Act did not apply to trespass to the person torts. (For comment on *Pritchard* see Goudkamp (2011) 127 LQR 519; Pike, 'Contributory Negligence and Intentional Trespass to the Person' (2015) 4 Oxford University Undergraduate LJ 3.)

However, intentional acts of the *claimant* can constitute contributory negligence. In *Corr v IBC Vehicles Pty Ltd* [2008] AC 884, a majority of their Lordships thought that the suicide of the deceased (for which the defendant was held liable) could nonetheless be conduct justifying a reduction of the damages for contributory negligence. Even though the deceased had been suffering from a depressive illness—which was caused by the defendant's negligence and ultimately caused him to commit suicide—he retained some capacity and, in recognition of the value of personal autonomy, some responsibility had to be attributed to the deceased. O'Sullivan ([2008] CLJ 241, 244) comments:

Mr Corr's suicide was a fatal symptom of a ghastly illness, no more his 'fault' than if he had died of cancer triggered by the accident. To retort that he was not an 'automaton' shows no understanding of the effect of serious depression. The families of victims such as Mr Corr deserve better.

The majority in *Corr* were influenced by the decision in *Reeves v Commissioner of Police of the Metropolis* [2000] 1 AC 360, where the 'fault' in issue was the intentional and deliberate suicide of the deceased whilst in police custody. Although Lord Hoffmann considered that it would be unusual for such an act not to amount to a *novus actus interveniens*, where it did not (as in *Reeves*) it could nonetheless amount to fault and hence satisfy the requirement of s. 1(1) of the Act.

Jones v Livox Quarries [1952] 2 QB 608

The plaintiff, who worked in a quarry, rode on the back of a tracked vehicle (a 'traxcavator') on his way to the canteen for lunch. This action was contrary to the express instructions of the defendants, who were his employers. The plaintiff was injured when the back of the traxcavator was hit by another vehicle and the plaintiff was crushed. In the plaintiff's action against the defendants (who were vicariously liable for any negligence of the vehicle's driver), it was alleged that the plaintiff had been guilty of contributory negligence in riding on the back of the traxcavator. The trial judge found the defendants liable but reduced the award by 20 per cent for contributory negligence. However, he also held that the only risk to which the plaintiff exposed himself by his actions was falling off the vehicle. The plaintiff appealed against the reduction of the award for contributory negligence on the basis that that negligence had not caused the injury.

Denning LJ

Although contributory negligence does not depend on a duty of care, it does depend on foreseeability. Just as actionable negligence requires foreseeability of harm to others, so contributory negligence requires the foreseeability of harm to oneself. A person is guilty of contributory negligence if he ought reasonably to have foreseen that, if he did not act as a reasonable, prudent man, he might be hurt himself; and in his reckonings he must take into account the possibility of others being careless.

Once negligence is proved, then no matter whether it is actionable negligence or contributory negligence, the person who is guilty of it must bear his proper share of responsibility for the consequences. The consequences do not depend on foreseeability, but on causation. The question in every case is: What faults were there which caused the damage? Was his fault one of them? The necessity of causation is shown by the word 'result' in s. 1(1) of the Act of 1945, and it was accepted by this court in *Davies v Swan Motor Co (Swansea) Ltd* [1949] 2 KB 326.

There is no clear guidance to be found in the books about causation. All that can be said is that causes are different from the circumstances in which, or on which, they operate. The line between the two depends on the facts of each case. It is a matter of common sense more than anything else. In the present case, as the arguments of Mr Arthian Davies proceeded, it seemed to me that he sought to make foreseeability the decisive test of causation. He relied on the trial judge's statement that a man who rode on the towbar of the traxcavator 'ran the risk of being thrown off and no other risk'. That is, I think, equivalent to saying that such a man could reasonably foresee that he might be thrown off the traxcavator, but not that he might be crushed between it and another vehicle.

In my opinion, however, foreseeability is not the decisive test of causation. It is often a relevant factor, but it is not decisive. Even though the plaintiff did not foresee the possibility of being crushed, nevertheless in the ordinary plain common sense of this business the injury suffered by the plaintiff was due in part to the fact that he chose to ride on the towbar to lunch instead of walking down on his feet. If he had been thrown off in the collision, Mr Arthian Davies admits that his injury would be partly due to his own negligence in riding on the towbar; but he says that, because he was crushed, and not thrown off, his injury is in no way due to it. That is too fine a distinction for me. I cannot believe that that purely fortuitous circumstance can make all the difference to the case. . . .

In order to illustrate this question of causation, I may say that if the plaintiff whilst he was riding on the towbar, had been hit in the eye by a shot from a negligent sportsman, I should have thought that the plaintiff's negligence would in no way be a cause of his injury. It would only be part of the history. But I cannot say that in the present case. The man's negligence here was so much mixed up with his injury that it cannot be dismissed as mere history. His dangerous position on the vehicle was one of the causes of his damage. . . .

It all comes to this: If a man carelessly rides on a vehicle in a dangerous position, and subsequently there is a collision in which his injuries are made worse by reason of his position than they otherwise would have been, then his damage is partly the result of his own fault, and the damages recoverable by him fall to be reduced accordingly.

Singleton and **Hodson LJJ** delivered separate concurring judgments.

Appeal and cross-appeal dismissed.

COMMENTARY

Do you agree that the event which occurred was within the 'penumbra of danger' to which the precautions were directed, though of a slightly different kind from those which caused the precaution to be required? (See *Braverus Maritime Inc v Port Kembla Coal Terminal Ltd* [2005] FCAFC 25.) If, as the trial judge held, the only risk created by the plaintiff's contributory negligence was that of being thrown off the vehicle, did it make sense to reduce the plaintiff's damages when what actually occurred was not within that risk? Even if foreseeability may not be sufficient to establish contributory negligence, should it not be a necessary condition? If a defendant is not liable for a type or kind of damage which is unforeseeable, why should a claimant's damages be reduced when the injury results from an unforeseeable risk?

The issue of causation has been considered elsewhere, but it should be remembered that the 1945 Act only changed the *consequences* of a finding of contributory negligence. Whether there was, in fact, any causally relevant contributory negligence must still be determined, since the Act applies only where the damage was the result of the negligence of *both* the claimant *and* the defendant. And note that, as with the defendant's own liability, any negligence of the claimant must be both a factual *and a legal* cause of the damage. As Lord Reid said in *Stapley v Gypsum Mines Ltd* [1953] AC 663 at 681:

> One may find that, as a matter of history, several people have been at fault and that if any one of them had acted properly the accident would not have happened, but that does not mean that the accident must be regarded as having been caused by the fault of all of them. One must discriminate between those faults which must be discarded as being too remote and those which must not. Sometimes it is proper to discard all but one and to regard that one as the sole cause, but in other cases it is proper to regard two or more as having jointly caused the accident. . . .

See also the comments of Deane J in *March v E & MH Stramare Pty Ltd* (1991) 171 CLR 506.

Can the claimant's lifestyle choices be taken into account in assessing whether there is contributory negligence? If a claimant continues to smoke cigarettes in the knowledge that this is adverse to his health, there is authority that this can trigger the defence (*Badger v Ministry of Defence* [2006] 3 All ER 173). However, in two decisions—one involving a pathological gambler and one involving a claimant addicted to drugs and alcohol—the Court of Appeal has held that the lifestyle choices that created these conditions should not be considered as part of the contributory negligence enquiry where the defendant's negligence consisted of failing to treat or to take account of these conditions (*Calvert v William Hill Credit Ltd* [2009] Ch 330; *St George v Home Office* [2009] 1 WLR 1670). As the lifestyle choices were made well before the defendant's negligence, such events were generally 'too remote in time, place and circumstance' from the defendant's negligence and were, applying the words of Lord Denning in *Jones v Livox*, 'no more than part of the history' (*St George v Home Office* [2009] 1 WLR 1670 at [56], per Dyson LJ).

3. Apportionment

Stapley v Gypsum Mines Ltd [1953] AC 663

The facts are not relevant for present purposes.

Lord Reid

A court must deal broadly with the problem of apportionment, and, in considering what is just and equitable, must have regard to the blameworthiness of each party, but 'the claimant's share in the responsibility for the damage' cannot, I think, be assessed without considering the relative importance of his acts in causing the damage apart from his blameworthiness . . .

Froom v Butcher [1976] QB 286

The plaintiff, his wife and his daughter were injured when, without carelessness on his part, the car which he was driving was struck head-on by the defendant's car. Although the collision was the result of careless driving by the defendant, the injury to the plaintiff was exacerbated by the fact he had chosen not to wear a seat belt. Prior to the Court of Appeal decision there had been a number of first instance decisions reaching conflicting results as to whether failure to wear a seat belt constituted contributory negligence.

Lord Denning MR

The Cause of the Damage

In these seat belt cases, the injured plaintiff is in no way to blame for the accident itself. Sometimes he is an innocent passenger sitting beside a negligent driver who goes off the road. At other times he is an innocent driver of one car which is run into by the bad driving of another car which pulls out on to its wrong side of the road. It may well be asked: why should the injured plaintiff have his damages reduced? The accident was solely caused by the negligent driving by the defendant. Sometimes outrageously bad driving. It should not lie in his mouth to say: 'You ought to have been wearing a seat belt.' That point of view was strongly expressed in *Smith v Blackburn* [1974] RTR 533 at 536 by O'Connor J. He said:

> The idea that the insurers of a grossly negligent driver should be relieved in any degree from paying what is proper compensation for injuries is an idea that offends ordinary decency. Until I am forced to do so by higher authority, I will not so rule.

I do not think that is the correct approach. The question is not what was the cause of the accident. It is rather what was the cause of the damage. In most accidents on the road the bad driving, which causes the accident, also causes the ensuing damage. But in seat belt cases the cause of the accident is one thing. The cause of the damage is another. The accident is caused by the bad driving. The damage is caused in part by the bad driving of the defendant, and in part by the failure of the plaintiff to wear a seat belt. If the plaintiff was to blame in not wearing a seat belt, the damage is in part the result of his own fault. He must bear some share in the responsibility for the damage and his damages fall to be reduced to such extent as the court thinks just and equitable.

[His Lordship considered the arguments for and against wearing seat belts, holding that it was a sensible practice for them to be used, and continued:]

The Share of Responsibility

Whenever there is an accident, the negligent driver must bear by far the greater share of responsibility. It was his negligence which caused the accident. It also was a prime cause of the whole of the damage. But insofar as the damage might have been avoided or lessened by wearing a seat belt, the injured person must bear some share. But how much should this be? Is it proper to enquire whether the driver was grossly negligent or only slightly negligent? Or whether the failure to wear a seat belt was entirely inexcusable or almost forgivable? If such an enquiry could easily be undertaken, it might be as well to do it. In *Davies v Swan Motor Co* [1949] 2 KB 326 we said that consideration should be given not only to the causative potency of a particular factor, but also its blameworthiness. But we live in a practical world. In most of these cases the liability of the driver is admitted; the failure to wear a seat belt is admitted; the only question is: what damages should be payable? This question should not be prolonged by an expensive enquiry into the degree of blameworthiness on either side, which would be hotly disputed. Suffice it to assess a share of responsibility which will be just and equitable in the great majority of cases.

> Sometimes the evidence will show that the failure made no difference. The damage would have been the same, even if a seat belt had been worn. In such cases the damages should not be reduced at all. At other times the evidence will show that the failure made all the difference. The damage would have been prevented altogether if a seat belt had been worn. In such cases I would suggest that the damages should be reduced by 25 per cent. But often enough the evidence will only show that the failure made a considerable difference. Some injuries to the head, for instance, would have been a good deal less severe if a seat belt had been worn, but there would still have been some injury to the head. In such case I would suggest that the damages attributable to the failure to wear a seat belt should be reduced by 15 per cent.
>
> **Conclusion**
> . . . In the present case the injuries to the head and chest would have been prevented by the wearing of a seat belt and the damages on that account might be reduced by 25 per cent. The finger would have been broken anyway and the damages for it not reduced at all. Overall the judge suggested 20 per cent and Mr Froom has made no objection to it. So I would not interfere.
> I would allow the appeal and reduce the damages by £100.
>
> **Lawton LJ** and **Scarman LJ** agreed with Lord Denning.
>
> *Appeal allowed.*

COMMENTARY

Section 1 of the 1945 Act requires a court to apportion damages according to the claimant's share in the responsibility for the damage. Even though the word 'cause' is not used, Lord Reid makes clear in *Stapley* that the apportionment should be done on a causation plus fault basis. The court must therefore evaluate both the relative blameworthiness of each party's conduct and the extent to which that fault caused the damage, which is to say its 'causal potency' (on which, see Hamer, '"Factual Causation" and "Scope of Liability": What's the Difference?' (2014) 77 MLR 155, 181ff). The application of the contributory negligence doctrine to torts of strict liability shows that this must be the correct approach. In strict liability a defendant is liable even though he has not been at fault. Hence if fault were the sole basis of apportionment for contributory negligence, in a case of strict liability a claimant who had been at fault, however slightly, would recover nothing. This would make no sense. *Froom v Butcher* also affirms that the fault and causation inquiries are directed at the damage for which the claimant claims. Mr Froom's fault in not wearing a seatbelt did not have anything to do with causing the accident in the first place, but it did contribute to the damage he suffered.

In cases where the claimant's sole fault is failure to wear a seat belt—cf. *Owens v Brimmell* [1977] QB 859 and *Ashton v Turner* [1981] QB 137, where other considerations were in play—it has been said that 'the courts rarely depart from' the *Froom* guidelines (J. Goudkamp and D. Nolan, *Contributory Negligence: Principles and Practice* (Oxford: OUP, 2018), para. 3.28). Furthermore, the courts have rejected the argument that the guidelines should be reassessed because there is now greater awareness of the importance of wearing seat belts than there was when *Froom* was decided (*Gawler v Raettig* [2007] EWCA Civ 1560; *Stanton v Collinson* [2010] RTR 284). It seems, therefore, that the guidelines are here to say.

The failure to take other precautions against the risk of injury in traffic accidents has also been held to amount to contributory negligence to which the *Froom* guidelines apply, e.g. a motorcyclist's failure to wear a crash helmet (*O'Connell v Jackson* [1972] 1 QB 270; *Capps v Miller* [1989] 1 WLR 839) and failure to use an appropriate restraint for children being driven in a vehicle (*Hughes v Williams* [2012] EWHC 1078 (QB)). It has also been held that the failure of pedal cyclists to wear a helmet constitutes contributory negligence (*Smith v Finch* [2009] EWHC 53 (QB)), although it was not necessary for the judge to decide whether the *Froom* guidelines applied in such a case as on the facts the injury would have occurred even if a helmet had been worn. See further Fulbrook, 'Cycle helmets and contributory negligence' [2004] JPIL 171.

According to Goudkamp, 'Apportionment of damages for contributory negligence: a fixed or discretionary approach?' (2015) 35 LS 621, while guidelines like those given in *Froom* are desirable, for the courts to set figures for the appropriate reduction in particular types of contributory negligence case is incompatible with the broad discretion provided by the 1945 Act (see also R. Stevens, 'Contributory Fault: Analogue or Digital?', in *Defences in Tort*). Do you agree?

Jackson v Murray [2015] UKSC 5, [2015] 2 All ER 805

The facts are set out in the judgment of Lord Reed.

Lord Reed

1. A school minibus draws up on a country road on a winter's evening. Two children get off. One of the children tries to cross the road. She steps out from behind the minibus, into the path of an oncoming car. The driver is driving too fast: he has seen the bus, but has made no allowance for the possibility that a child might attempt to cross in front of him. He is not keeping a proper look-out, and does not see her, but he is going too fast to have stopped in time even if he had seen her. His car hits the child, causing her to sustain severe injuries. If he had been driving at a reasonable speed, and had been keeping a proper look-out, he would not have hit her.

2. The trial judge [[2012] CSOH 100, 2012 SCLR 605] finds that the accident was caused by the driver's negligence, but that the child was also contributorily negligent. He assesses her contributory negligence at 90 per cent, and reduces the award of damages accordingly. On appeal [[2012] CSIH 100, 2013 SCLR 429], the court reduces that assessment to 70 per cent. On a further appeal, this court is invited to reduce the assessment further.

3. How should responsibility be apportioned in a case of this kind? What principles should govern the review of an apportionment by an appellate court? These are the central questions posed by this appeal.

The facts of the case

4. The facts of the case, as found by the Lord Ordinary, Lord Tyre, are not in dispute. It should be said at the outset that he faced considerable difficulties in establishing the facts, and he exercised notable care in doing so.

5. The accident occurred on 12 January 2004 on the A98 road between Banff and Fraserburgh, near its junction with a private road leading to the farm where the pursuer lived with her parents and her twin sister. At that point, the A98 is 7.6 metres wide. Traffic is subject to a 60 mph speed limit. There is no street lighting.

6. The pursuer was then 13 years old. She and her sister travelled to and from school every day by school minibus. On the way home, the minibus dropped off the various children at or near their homes. In particular, it dropped off the pursuer and her sister on the opposite side of the road from the entrance to the farm road. They would then cross the road to the farm road.

7. On the day of the accident, the bus arrived at the farm road end at about 4.30 pm. It was then about 40 minutes after sunset, and the light was fading. Vehicles had their lights on. The bus stopped, with its headlights on, and signs to the front and rear indicating that it was a school bus. The driver put on the bus's hazard lights. A number of vehicles following the bus stopped behind it. The defender was driving home in the opposite direction. His lights were switched on. As he approached the scene, he saw the stationary bus on the other carriageway. He had a view of the stationary bus for at least 200 metres. He had seen the school bus on this road before. He was travelling at about 50 mph. He did not slow down. His position in evidence was that he could not remember whether he had thought at the time that the bus might have stopped to drop children off. He regarded the risk of children running out unexpectedly as irrelevant: such a risk was 'not his fault', as he put it.

8. Partly in view of the defender's evidence about the irrelevance, to his responsibilities as a driver, of the possibility that children might unexpectedly attempt to cross the road, the Lord Ordinary inferred that he did not address his mind to the risk that a person might emerge from behind the stationary bus and attempt to cross the road in front of his car.

9. The pursuer and her sister got off the bus on its nearside. The pursuer passed between the rear of the bus, which was still stationary, and the car behind it. She paused briefly at the offside rear of the bus and then took one or two steps into the road, before breaking into a run. She was struck by the defender's car, still travelling at about 50 mph. She was projected into the air by the force of the impact, and the car passed beneath her. She landed on the road surface. At the point of impact, she was running across the road. The defender was unaware of her presence until the moment of impact. Since she must have been within his line of vision for approximately 1.5 seconds between emerging from behind the bus and the moment of impact, the Lord Ordinary inferred that he was not keeping a look-out for the possibility of such an event occurring. If he had had in mind the possibility that someone might emerge, he would have seen her earlier than he did.

The negligence of the defender

10. The Lord Ordinary found that the defender had failed to drive with reasonable care. He ought in the first place to have kept a proper look-out. In the exercise of that duty, he ought to have identified the bus as being a school bus, or at least as a bus from which children were likely to alight. He ought then to have foreseen that there was a risk that a person might, however foolishly, attempt to cross the road. The defender had not done so. Either he did not identify the bus as a school bus, or he did not regard that as relevant to the manner in which he ought to drive towards it and past it. Secondly, the defender had failed to modify his driving. He did not reduce his speed from 50 mph as he approached the stationary bus. That was too high a speed at which to approach the hazard which it potentially presented. A reasonable speed in the circumstances would have been somewhere between 30 and 40 mph. He ought to have been travelling at no more than 40 mph for at least 100 metres before reaching the bus. Thirdly, the defender had failed to be vigilant for any child stepping out or running into the road. These findings are not now in dispute.

Causation

11. The Lord Ordinary found that the defender could not have reacted in the time available to him, after the pursuer emerged from behind the bus, so as to avoid hitting her. If, however, he had been travelling at a reasonable speed, the pursuer would have made it safely past the line of the car's travel before the car arrived at the point of impact, and the accident would not have occurred. . . .

Apportionment

...

20. Section 1(1) [of the Law Reform (Contributory Negligence) Act 1945] does not specify how responsibility is to be apportioned, beyond requiring the damages to be reduced to such extent as the court thinks just and equitable having regard to the claimant's share in the responsibility for the damage (not, it is to be noted, responsibility for the accident). Further guidance can however be found in the decided cases. . . .

[His Lordship reviewed the authorities and continued:]

Review of apportionment

27. It is not possible for a court to arrive at an apportionment which is demonstrably correct. The problem is not merely that the factors which the court is required to consider are incapable of precise measurement. More fundamentally, the blameworthiness of the pursuer and the defender are incommensurable. The defender has acted in breach of a duty (not necessarily a duty of care) which was owed to the pursuer; the pursuer, on the other hand, has acted with a want of regard for her own interests. The word 'fault' in section 1(1), as applied to 'the person suffering the damage' on the one hand, and the 'other person or persons' on the other hand, is therefore being used in two different senses. The court is not comparing like with like.

28. It follows that the apportionment of responsibility is inevitably a somewhat rough and ready exercise (a feature reflected in the judicial preference for round figures), and that a variety of possible answers can legitimately be given. That is consistent with the requirement under section 1(1) to arrive at a result which the court considers 'just and equitable'. Since different judges may legitimately take different views of what would be just and equitable in particular circumstances, it follows that those differing views should be respected, within the limits of reasonable disagreement. . . .

35. The question, therefore, is whether the court below went wrong. In the absence of an identifiable error, such as an error of law, or the taking into account of an irrelevant matter, or the failure to take account of a relevant matter, it is only a difference of view as to the apportionment of responsibility which exceeds the ambit of reasonable disagreement that warrants the conclusion that the court below has gone wrong. In other words, in the absence of an identifiable error, the appellate court must be satisfied that the apportionment made by the court below was not one which was reasonably open to it.

36. There may be cases of apportionment under the 1945 Act where the appellate court can identify an error on the part of the court below. . . .

37. Even in the absence of an identifiable error, a wide difference of view as to the apportionment which is just and equitable, going beyond what Lord Fraser described as the generous ambit within which a reasonable disagreement is possible, can in itself justify the conclusion that the court below has gone wrong. . . .

38. The need for the appellate court to be satisfied, in the absence of an identifiable error, that the apportionment made by the court below was outside the range of reasonable determinations is reflected in the fact that apportionments are not altered by appellate courts merely on the basis of a disagreement as to the precise figure. . . .

40. As the Extra Division recognised, it is necessary when applying section 1(1) of the 1945 Act to take account both of the blameworthiness of the parties and the causative potency of their acts . . . I would take the potentially dangerous nature of a car being driven at speed into account when assessing blameworthiness; but the overall assessment of responsibility should not be affected by the heading under which that factor is taken into account. Even leaving out of account the potentially dangerous nature of a car being driven at speed, I would not have assessed the causative potency of the conduct of the defender as being any less than that of the pursuer in the present case, the causation of the injury depended upon the combination of the pursuer's attempting to cross the road when she did,

and the defender's driving at an excessive speed and without keeping a proper look-out. If the pursuer had waited until the defender had passed, he would not have collided with her. Equally, if he had slowed to a reasonable speed in the circumstances and had kept a proper look-out, he would have avoided her.

41. Given the Extra Division's conclusion that the causative potency of the defender's conduct was greater than that of the pursuer's, their conclusion that 'the major share of the responsibility must be attributed to the pursuer', to the extent of 70 per cent, can only be explained on the basis that the pursuer was considered to be far more blameworthy than the defender. I find that difficult to understand, given the factors which their Lordships identified. As I have explained, they rightly considered that the pursuer did not take reasonable care for her own safety: either she did not look to her left within a reasonable time before stepping out, or she failed to make a reasonable judgment as to the risk posed by the defender's car. On the other hand, as the Extra Division recognised, regard has to be had to the circumstances of the pursuer. As they pointed out, she was only 13 at the time, and a 13 year old will not necessarily have the same level of judgment and self-control as an adult. As they also pointed out, she had to take account of the defender's car approaching at speed, in very poor light conditions, with its headlights on. As they recognised, the assessment of speed in those circumstances is far from easy, even for an adult, and even more so for a 13 year old. It is also necessary to bear in mind that the situation of a pedestrian attempting to cross a relatively major road with a 60 mph speed limit, after dusk and without street lighting, is not straightforward, even for an adult.

42. On the other hand, the Extra Division considered that the defender's behaviour was 'culpable to a substantial [degree]'. I would agree with that assessment. He had to observe the road ahead and keep a proper look-out, adjusting his speed in the event that a potential hazard presented itself. As the Extra Division noted, he was found to have been driving at an excessive speed and not to have modified his speed to take account of the potential danger presented by the minibus. The danger was obvious, because the minibus had its hazard lights on. Notwithstanding that danger, he continued driving at 50 mph. As the Lord Ordinary noted, the Highway Code advises drivers that 'at 40 mph your vehicle will probably kill any pedestrians it hits'. As in *Baker v Willoughby* [[1970] AC 467] and *McCluskey v Wallace* [1998 SC 711], that level of danger points to a very considerable degree of blameworthiness on the part of a driver who fails to take reasonable care while driving at speed.

43. In these circumstances, I cannot discern in the reasoning of the Extra Division any satisfactory explanation of their conclusion that the major share of the responsibility must be attributed to the pursuer: a conclusion which, as I have explained, appears to depend on the view that the pursuer's conduct was far more blameworthy than that of the defender. As it appears to me, the defender's conduct played at least an equal role to that of the pursuer in causing the damage and was at least equally blameworthy.

44. The view that parties are equally responsible for the damage suffered by the pursuer is substantially different from the view that one party is much more responsible than the other. Such a wide difference of view exceeds the ambit of reasonable disagreement, and warrants the conclusion that the court below has gone wrong. I would accordingly allow the appeal and award 50 per cent of the agreed damages to the pursuer.

Lady Hale and **Lord Carnwath** agreed with Lord Reed. **Lord Hodge** and **Lord Wilson** dissented.

Appeal allowed.

COMMENTARY

In most contributory negligence cases, there are no guidelines as to the appropriate discount, and applying s. 1(1) of the 1945 Act the judge has a broad discretion to determine the discount that is 'just and equitable' on the facts. As *Jackson v Murray* demonstrates, there is considerable scope for disagreement on this question: the first instance judge had imposed a discount of 90 per cent; on appeal the Inner House of the Court of Session reduced the discount to 70 per cent; and on further appeal a bare majority of the Supreme Court held that a reduction of 50 per cent was appropriate, with Lord Hodge and Lord Wilson taking the view that there was no basis for overturning the decision of the Inner House. In her note on the decision, Russell says ([2015] 9 SLT 39 at 47) that '[s]ome might consider the majority view ... to be somewhat harsh on the defender. He was after all driving well within the operative speed limit'. Do you agree? What discount would you have imposed on the facts of *Jackson*?

As Lord Reed emphasised in his judgment, at [28], judicial differences of opinion as to the appropriate discount in a particular case are legitimate, and 'should be respected, within the limits of reasonable disagreement'. It follows that an appellate court should be slow to disturb the apportionment decision of a trial judge, and that intervention is warranted only in the limited circumstances outlined by Lord Reed in *Jackson* (see also Lord Hodge, at [46]: an appellate court should overturn an apportionment decision only if the court below had 'manifestly and to a substantial degree gone wrong'). An empirical study found that appellate courts overturned determinations on apportionment in 33 per cent of cases in which they were asked to do so (J. Goudkamp and D. Nolan, *Contributory Negligence in the Twenty-First Century* (Oxford: OUP, 2019), para. 5.11). Does that figure indicate that appellate courts are in fact as reluctant to intervene on the apportionment question as they claim to be? And do you think that the test for appellate interference on apportionment was satisfied on the facts of *Jackson*?

Lord Reed also made the point in *Jackson*, at [28], that apportionment in contributory negligence cases was a 'rough and ready exercise', and that this was reflected in a 'judicial preference for round figures' (see similarly Stevens, *op. cit.*, p. 259, noting that when deciding on discounts for contributory negligence, 'judges seldom select finely tuned figures, 73/27 for example'). Lord Reed's observation is borne out by the same empirical study, in which it was found that the discounts most frequently imposed by trial judges were fractions used in everyday life, with the most popular being 50 per cent (one-half), followed by 25 per cent (one-quarter), 20 per cent (one-fifth) and then 33.3 per cent (one-third) (Goudkamp and Nolan, *op. cit.*, para. 4.20).

In the same study, it was also found that the lowest discount imposed by a trial judge for contributory negligence was 10 per cent, while the highest was 100 per cent, with the next highest being 90 per cent (*ibid.*). But is it correct for a court to order a reduction of 100 per cent for contributory negligence? The Court of Appeal has held that 100 per cent deductions are 'wrong in principle' (*Brumder v Motornet Service and Repairs Ltd* [2013] 1 WLR 2783 at [4], per Beatson LJ (citing two earlier authorities to the same effect, namely *Pitts v Hunt* [1991] 1 QB 24 and *Anderson v Newham College of Higher Education* [2003] ICR 212)). In our view, this is clearly right, as a finding of 100 per cent contributory negligence effectively absolves the defendant of any responsibility, so the condition of the application of the defence, that the fault of *both* parties contributed to the claimant's injury, is not met: see J. Goudkamp, 'Rethinking Contributory Negligence', in *Challenging Orthodoxy*, pp. 344–6.

In his assessment of the blameworthiness of the pursuer in *Jackson*, Lord Reed explicitly took into account, at [41], the fact that she was 13 years old at the time of the accident.

This accorded with principle: in *Gough v Thorne* [1966] 1 WLR 1387, which also involved a 13-year-old girl struck by a car while crossing a road, the Court of Appeal held that for the purposes of contributory negligence a child claimant's conduct should be judged against the standard of a reasonable child of the same age. According to Lord Denning MR, at 1390, a child 'has not the road sense or the experience of his or her elders'. Is there an age below which a child will not be found guilty of contributory negligence at all? In *Gough v Thorne*, Lord Denning MR said that 'a very young child cannot be guilty of contributory negligence', and in *Barnes v Flucker*, 1985 SLT 142, it was conceded by counsel that 5-year-old children were not capable of contributory negligence. However, in other Scottish decisions children aged between 4 and 6 have been found guilty of contributory negligence: see *Cass v Edinburgh & District Tramways Co Ltd* 1909 SC 1068 (aged 4); *McKinnell v White* 1971 SLT 61 (aged 5); *Harvey v Cairns* 1989 SLT 107 (aged 6). In the empirical study of the operation of the doctrine conducted by Goudkamp and Nolan (*op. cit.*), the youngest claimant found guilty of contributory negligence was aged 7 when he punched a pane of glass while at school (*N (A Child) v Newham LBC* [2007] CLY 2931), and a plea of contributory negligence also succeeded against a boy aged 8 who fell while climbing on a farm gate (*Anderson v Imrie* [2016] CSOH 171, 2017 Rep LR 21). Of the ten claimants under 12 in their sample found guilty of contributory negligence, six had been injured in road accidents. More generally, the authors found that pleas of contributory negligence were more likely to be successful where the claimant was a child than where the claimant was an adult (69 per cent versus 59 per cent), and that the average discount was also slightly higher where the claimant was a child (41 per cent, as against 39 per cent for adults: the average discount overall at first instance was 40 per cent). The authors (at para. 4.38) suggest that there are at least two possible explanations for these surprising findings. One of these is that 'in practice judges are not, contrary to authority, applying an age-relative standard of care to child claimants, but are holding them to an adult standard'. And the other is that 'children (or perhaps more specifically teenagers) are less risk-averse than people in other age groups, and so tend to take less care of their own safety', an explanation supported by medical evidence regarding adolescent behaviour. Do you think these are plausible explanations? Can you think of any others?

The apportionment between claimant and defendant that is triggered by a finding of contributory negligence is only one instance of the wider role played by principles of apportionment in private law. See further K. Barker and R. Grantham (eds), *Apportionment in Private Law* (Oxford: Hart, 2019).

IV. Exclusion of Liability

A defendant may seek to exclude or limit their potential liability to another person in negligence before exposing themselves to the risk of a possible claim. Although this is commonly done by means of a term in a contract between the parties—the student of the law of contract will be aware of the case and statute law on exemption clauses—it may also be done by an appropriately placed non-contractual notice or disclaimer. The typical scenario here is that an owner or occupier of land seeks by such a notice displayed at the entrance to the land to exclude or limit liability arising out of the state of the premises or some activity carried out on the land. At common law it is well established that such a notice may be effective to exclude or limit the owner or occupier's liability vis-à-vis a licensee on his land (*Ashdown v Samuel Williams & Sons Ltd* [1957] 1 QB 409), provided that (1) reasonable steps were taken to bring the notice to the licensee's attention; and (2) on the proper construction of the notice, it excluded or limited the liability in question. In *White v Blackmore* [1972] 2 QB 651, the deceased was a 'jalopy' racing driver who had been watching a race in which he was not competing when one of the cars left the track and collided with a safety rope near which he was standing. He was thrown into the air and later died from his injuries. When his widow brought a claim for damages against the organisers of the race, it was held that they had validly excluded their liability by means of notices posted at the entrance to the race venue and around the track. Although there was no evidence that the notices had been in position when the deceased had visited the track in the morning to enter his name for the races, it was sufficient that they were in place when he had returned to the track for the start of the races that afternoon. Furthermore, although the notices referred only to 'damage or personal injury (whether fatal or otherwise) howsoever caused to spectators and ticket-holders', a majority of the Court of Appeal held that at the time of the accident the deceased was acting as a spectator and was therefore within the class of persons caught by the notice. The use of the words 'howsoever caused' also made it clear that the exclusion of liability was intended to be comprehensive in scope. More detailed discussion of the common law rules governing exclusion and limitation clauses can be found in works on contract law: see, e.g., E. Peel, *Treitel's The Law of Contract*, 15th edn (London: Sweet & Maxwell, 2020), ch. 7.

It is important to remember that not all notices which attempt to protect the defendant from liability are exclusion notices. Suppose, for example, that A is about to use a bridge to cross a river and sees a notice stating: 'Warning. Bridge Dangerous—Use Bridge Further Upstream'. This is not an exclusion notice, but rather an attempt to discharge the duty owed to A (i.e., it goes to breach of duty). By contrast, a notice that says: 'The Occupier is Not Responsible for Any Loss or Damage Suffered by Users of the Bridge' will be regarded as an attempt to exclude liability. Such notices are now subject to the restrictions imposed by the Unfair Contract Terms Act 1977 (UCTA) and the Consumer Rights Act 2015 (CRA).

Unfair Contract Terms Act 1977

1. Scope of Part 1

(1) For the purposes of this Part of this Act, 'negligence' means the breach—

   (a) of any obligation, arising from the express or implied terms of a contract, to take reasonable care to exercise reasonable skill in the performance of the contract;

   (b) of any common law duty to take reasonable care or exercise reasonable skill (but not any stricter duty);

   (c) of the common duty of care imposed by the Occupiers' Liability Act 1957 or the Occupiers' Liability Act (Northern Ireland) 1957.

(3) In the case of both contract and tort, sections 2 to 7 apply (except where the contrary is stated in section 6(4)) only to business liability, that is liability for breach of obligations or duties arising—

   (a) from things done or to be done by a person in the course of a business (whether his own business or another's); or

(b) from the occupation of premises used for business purposes of the occupier; and references to liability are to be read accordingly but liability of an occupier of premises for breach of an obligation or duty towards a person obtaining access to the premises for recreational or educational purposes, being liability for loss or damage suffered by reason of the dangerous state of the premises, is not a business liability of the occupier unless granting that person such access for the purposes concerned falls within the business purposes of the occupier.

(4) In relation to any breach of duty or obligation, it is immaterial for any purpose of this Part of this Act whether the breach was inadvertent or intentional, or whether liability for it arises directly or vicariously.

2. Negligence liability

(1) A person cannot by reference to any contract term or to a notice given to persons generally or to particular persons exclude or restrict his liability for death or personal injury resulting from negligence.

(2) In the case of other loss or damage, a person cannot so exclude or restrict his liability for negligence except in so far as the term or notice satisfies the requirement of reasonableness.

(3) Where a contract term or notice purports to exclude or restrict liability for negligence a person's agreement to or awareness of it is not of itself to be taken as indicating his voluntary acceptance of any risk . . .

(4) This section does not apply to—

    (a) a term in a consumer contract, or

    (b) a notice to the extent that it is a consumer notice,

(but see the provision made about such contracts and notices in sections 62 and 65 of the Consumer Rights Act 2015) . . .

11. The 'reasonableness' test

(1) In relation to a contract term, the requirement of reasonableness for the purposes of this Part of this Act, section 3 of the Misrepresentation Act 1967 and section 3 of the Misrepresentation Act (Northern Ireland) 1967 is that the term shall have been a fair and reasonable one to be included having regard to the circumstances which were, or ought reasonably to have been, known to or in the contemplation of the parties when the contract was made.

(2) In determining for the purposes of section 6 or 7 above whether a contract term satisfies the requirement of reasonableness, regard shall be had in particular to the matters specified in Schedule 2 to this Act; but this subsection does not prevent the court or arbitrator from holding, in accordance with any rule of law, that a term which purports to exclude or restrict any relevant liability is not a term of the contract.

(3) In relation to a notice (not being a notice having contractual effect), the requirement of reasonableness under this Act is that it should be fair and reasonable to allow reliance on it, having regard to all the circumstances obtaining when the liability arose or (but for the notice) would have arisen.

(4) Where by reference to a contract term or notice a person seeks to restrict liability to a specified sum of money, and the question arises (under this or any other Act) whether the term or notice satisfies the requirement of reasonableness, regard shall be had in particular (but without prejudice to subsection (2) above in the case of contract terms) to—

(a) the resources which he could expect to be available to him for the purpose of meeting the liability should it arise; and
(b) how far it was open to him to cover himself by insurance.

(5) It is for those claiming that a contract term or notice satisfies the requirement of reasonableness to show that it does . . .

13. Varieties of exemption clause

(1) To the extent that this Part of this Act prevents the exclusion or restriction of any liability it also prevents—
   (a) making the liability or its enforcement subject to restrictive or onerous conditions;
   (b) excluding or restricting any right or remedy in respect of the liability, or subjecting a person to any prejudice in consequence of his pursuing any such right or remedy;
   (c) excluding or restricting rules of evidence or procedure;

and (to that extent) sections 2, 6 and 7 also prevent excluding or restricting liability by reference to terms and notices which exclude or restrict the relevant obligation or duty.

(2) But an agreement in writing to submit present or future differences to arbitration is not to be treated under this Part of this Act as excluding or restricting any liability.

14. Interpretation of Part 1

In this Part of this Act—
'business' includes a profession and the activities of any government department or local or public authority;
'consumer contract' has the same meaning as in the Consumer Rights Act 2015 (see section 61);
'consumer notice' has the same meaning as in the Consumer Rights Act 2015 (see section 61);
'goods' has the same meaning as in [the Sale of Goods Act 1979] . . .
'negligence' has the meaning given by section 1(1);
'notice' includes an announcement, whether or not in writing, and any other communication or pretended communication; and
'personal injury' includes any disease and any impairment of physical or mental condition.

Consumer Rights Act 2015

2. Key definitions

(2) 'Trader' means a person acting for purposes relating to that person's trade, business, craft or profession, whether acting personally or through another person acting in the trader's name or on the trader's behalf.

(3) 'Consumer' means an individual acting for purposes that are wholly or mainly outside that individual's trade, business, craft or profession.

(4) A trader claiming that an individual was not acting for purposes wholly or mainly outside the individual's trade, business, craft or profession must prove it . . .

(7) 'Business' includes the activities of any government department or local or public authority.

PART 2 - UNFAIR TERMS

61. Contracts and notices covered by this Part

(1) This Part applies to a contract between a trader and a consumer.

(2) This does not include a contract of employment or apprenticeship.

(3) A contract to which this Part applies is referred to in this Part as a 'consumer contract'.

(4) This Part applies to a notice to the extent that it—
   (a) relates to rights or obligations as between a trader and a consumer, or
   (b) purports to exclude or restrict a trader's liability to a consumer.

(5) This does not include a notice relating to rights, obligations or liabilities as between an employer and an employee.

(6) It does not matter for the purposes of subsection (4) whether the notice is expressed to apply to a consumer, as long as it is reasonable to assume it is intended to be seen or heard by a consumer.

(7) A notice to which this Part applies is referred to in this Part as a 'consumer notice'.

(8) In this section 'notice' includes an announcement, whether or not in writing, and any other communication or purported communication.

62. Requirement for contract terms and notices to be fair

(1) An unfair term of a consumer contract is not binding on the consumer.

(2) An unfair consumer notice is not binding on the consumer.

(3) This does not prevent the consumer from relying on the term or notice if the consumer chooses to do so.

(4) A term is unfair if, contrary to the requirement of good faith, it causes a significant imbalance in the parties' rights and obligations under the contract to the detriment of the consumer.

(5) Whether a term is fair is to be determined—
   (a) taking into account the nature of the subject matter of the contract, and
   (b) by reference to all the circumstances existing when the term was agreed and to all of the other terms of the contract or of any other contract on which it depends . . .

[Sub-sections (6) and (7) essentially replicate sub-sections (4) and (5) for notices.]

(8) This section does not affect the operation of—
   (d) section 65 (exclusion of negligence liability).

65. Bar on exclusion or restriction of negligence liability

(1) A trader cannot by a term of a consumer contract or by a consumer notice exclude or restrict liability for death or personal injury resulting from negligence.

(2) Where a term of a consumer contract, or a consumer notice, purports to exclude or restrict a trader's liability for negligence, a person is not to be taken to have voluntarily accepted any risk merely because the person agreed to or knew about the term or notice.

(3) In this section 'personal injury' includes any disease and any impairment of physical or mental condition.

(4) In this section 'negligence' means the breach of—

(b) a common law duty to take reasonable care or exercise reasonable skill,

(c) the common duty of care imposed by the Occupiers' Liability Act 1957 . . .

(5) It is immaterial for the purposes of subsection (4)—

(a) whether a breach of duty or obligation was inadvertent or intentional, or

(b) whether liability for it arises directly or vicariously.

(6) This section is subject to section 66 (which makes provision about the scope of this section).

66. Scope of section 65

(4) Section 65 does not apply to the liability of an occupier of premises to a person who obtains access to the premises for recreational purposes if—

(a) the person suffers loss or damage because of the dangerous state of the premises, and

(b) allowing the person access for those purposes is not within the purposes of the occupier's trade, business, craft or profession.

68. Requirement for transparency

(1) A trader must ensure that a written term of a consumer contract, or a consumer notice in writing, is transparent.

(2) A consumer notice is transparent for the purposes of subsection (1) if it is expressed in plain and intelligible language and it is legible.

69. Contract terms that may have different meanings

(1) If a term in a consumer contract, or a consumer notice, could have different meanings, the meaning that is most favourable to the consumer is to prevail.

COMMENTARY

Section 2(1) of UCTA and s. 65 of the CRA make any contract term or notice purporting to exclude liability for personal injury or death caused by negligence ineffective, and s. 2(2) of UCTA and s. 62 of the CRA subject any term or notice purporting to exclude liability for other forms of damage caused by negligence to a reasonableness test and a test of unfairness respectively.

UCTA limits only the exclusion or restriction of 'business liability' as defined in s. 1(3), and following the passage of the CRA s. 2 of UCTA no longer applies to 'consumer contracts' and 'consumer notices', which are now regulated by the later Act. Section 61 of the CRA defines consumer contracts and notices by reference to the relationship between a 'trader' and a 'consumer', terms themselves defined in s. 2 of that Act. Both Acts extend to liabilities arising in respect of the occupation of business premises. In considering the liability of a business occupier, it should be noted that under s. 1(3)(b) of UCTA excluding liability in respect of persons entering the premises for educational or recreational purposes will not amount to an exclusion of a business liability, unless granting them access for those purposes falls within the business purposes of the occupier. The equivalent provision of the CRA is s. 66(4), though this is limited to 'recreational purposes'. These provisions are designed to encourage business occupiers to allow visitors onto their land to see, for example, the ruins of a castle or a historic home, by enabling them to avoid liability for injuries caused by the state of their premises in cases where such visits do not fall within the occupier's business purposes. Hence a farmer who allows tourists free entry to their land to view a ruined monastery can freely exclude their liability towards them, whereas if the monastery were on land occupied by the National Trust (a conservation charity), the exclusion would be regulated by the legislation. Non-business occupiers, meanwhile, are totally free to exclude possible liabilities to their visitors (see Occupiers' Liability Act 1957, s. 2(1), extracted in Ch. 10.I.2).

Are UCTA and the CRA applicable in a case where the defendant relies on a contractual clause to show that the claimant voluntarily accepted the risk in question? In *Johnstone v Bloomsbury Health Authority* [1992] QB 333, an employment case, the Court of Appeal held that it was at least arguable that such a clause might fall foul of s. 2(1) of UCTA, as an effective *volenti* clause will by definition modify or restrict the duty owed to the claimant (see also the speech of Lord Hobhouse in *Reeves v Commissioner of Police of the Metropolis* [2000] 1 AC 360 at 395). However, the position remains unclear: *Johnstone* was settled before a final decision was reached, and the point has not been taken in other employment cases where it could have been raised (e.g. the occupational stress cases discussed in Ch. 7.IV).

UCTA and the CRA are not the only legislation regulating attempts to exclude and limit liability. Reference should also be made, in particular, to the Road Traffic Act 1988, s. 149; the Consumer Protection Act 1987, s. 7; and, in the context of employers' liability, the Law Reform (Personal Injuries) Act 1948, s. 1(3) and the Employers' Liability (Defective Equipment) Act 1969, s. 1(2).

v. Illegality (*Ex Turpi Causa Non Oritur Actio*)

Illegality is a defence that applies across private law, but its operation in tort has been fraught with difficulty and the precise basis on which a tort claim will fail on the ground of illegality is difficult to discern (see Law Commission, *The Illegality Defence in Tort* (Law Com. No. 160, 2001), Part IV, and Law Commission, *The Illegality Defence: A Consultative Report* (Consultation Paper No. 189, 2009), Parts 2 and 7). According to Virgo, 'Illegality's role in the law of torts' in M. Dyson (ed), *Unravelling Tort and Crime* (Cambridge: CUP, 2015), p. 174:

> Illegality in the law of tort has a bad reputation. The illegality doctrine is perceived to be complex, capricious and unjust. Fundamental questions relating to its role are under-examined and under-theorised. It is difficult even to identify an acceptable definition of illegality; to determine whether it should defeat tort claims in all, some or any cases, and, if it applies, what might be the basis for determining its application.

At its broadest the illegality defence is grounded in a general policy objection to awarding compensation to persons who suffer injury or loss while engaged in an illegal activity. This policy is often expressed in the Latin maxim *ex turpi causa non oritur actio* (no action can be founded upon a wicked act). Nonetheless it is clear that not every illegal act will bar the claimant from suing in negligence: driving with a broken headlight during daylight hours would not prevent the driver recovering damages if injured by another's negligence, even though they might be committing a criminal offence by breaching road traffic regulations. The difficulty lies in assessing the circumstances in which illegality will bar a tort claim.

Gray v Thames Trains Limited [2009] 1 AC 1339

The claimant was a victim of the Ladbroke Grove train crash in 1999. He suffered minor physical injuries as a result of the crash but subsequently developed a serious psychiatric condition. In August 2001 he stabbed to death someone with whom he had an altercation while driving. He was later convicted of manslaughter on the grounds of diminished responsibility and was ordered to be detained in hospital. He sued the defendants (whose employee's negligence had caused the crash) for, amongst other things, loss of earnings during the period in which he was and would be detained as a result of the killing, and general damages for his detention, conviction, feelings of guilt and remorse, and damage to reputation, as well as an indemnity against any claims which might be brought by dependants of the person he had killed. At first instance, Flaux J rejected these claims on illegality grounds. The Court of Appeal allowed an appeal in part, holding that whilst general damages were not recoverable, the claim for loss of earnings could be accepted. Both sides appealed to the House of Lords.

Lord Hoffmann

27. My Lords, the question in this case is in my opinion whether the intervention of Mr Gray's criminal act in the causal relationship between the defendants' breaches of duty and the damage of which he complains prevents him from recovering that part of his loss caused by the criminal act . . . On the one hand, but for the accident and the stress disorder which it caused, Mr Gray would not have killed and would therefore not have suffered the consequences for which he seeks compensation. On the other hand, the killing was a voluntary and deliberate act. The stress disorder diminished Mr Gray's responsibility but did not extinguish it. By reason of his own acknowledged responsibility, Mr Gray committed the serious crime of manslaughter and made himself liable to the sentence of the court. The question is whether these features of the causal relationship between the injury and the damage are such as to prevent Mr Gray from recovering.

29. . . . . [The appellants'] principal argument invokes a special rule of public policy. In its wider form, it is that you cannot recover compensation for loss which you have suffered in consequence of your own criminal act. In its narrower and more specific form, it is that you cannot recover for damage which flows from loss of liberty, a fine or other punishment lawfully imposed upon you in consequence of your own unlawful act. In such a case it is the law which, as a matter of penal policy, causes the damage and it would be inconsistent for the law to require you to be compensated for that damage.

30. . . . . The maxim *ex turpi causa* expresses not so much a principle as a policy. Furthermore, that policy is not based upon a single justification but on a group of reasons, which vary in different situations. . . .

32. The particular rule for which the appellants contend may, as I said, be stated in a wider or a narrow form. The wider and simpler version is that which was applied by Flaux J: you cannot recover for damage which is the consequence of your own criminal act. In its narrower form, it is that you cannot recover for damage which is the consequence of a sentence imposed upon you for a criminal act. I make this distinction between the wider and narrower version of the rule because there is a particular justification for the narrower rule which does not necessarily apply to the wider version.

33. I shall deal first with the narrower version . . .

[His Lordship considered a number of English and Commonwealth authorities and the decision of the Court of Appeal in the instant case and continued:]

44. . . . [T]he rule of public policy invoked in this case . . . may reflect more than one facet of public policy, but it is sufficient in the present case to say that the case against compensating Mr Gray for his loss of liberty is based upon the inconsistency of requiring someone to be compensated for a sentence imposed because of his own personal responsibility for a criminal act. . . .

50. My Lords, that is in my opinion sufficient to dispose of most of the claims which are the subject of this appeal. Mr Gray's claims for loss of earnings after his arrest and for general damages for his detention, conviction and damage to reputation are all claims for damage caused by the lawful sentence imposed upon him for manslaughter and therefore fall within the narrower version of the rule which I would invite your Lordships to affirm. But there are some additional claims which may be more difficult to bring within this rule, such as the claim for an indemnity against any claims which might be brought by dependants of the dead pedestrian and the claim for general damages for feelings of guilt and remorse consequent upon the killing. Neither of these was a consequence of the sentence of the criminal court.

51. I must therefore examine a wider version of the rule, which was applied by Flaux J. This has the support of the reasoning of the Court of Appeal in *Clunis v Camden & Islington Health Authority* [1998] QB 978 as well as other authorities. It differs from the narrower version in at least two respects: first, it cannot, as it seems to me, be justified on the grounds of inconsistency in the same way as the narrower rule. Instead, the wider rule has to be justified on the ground that it is offensive to public notions of the fair distribution of resources that a claimant should be compensated (usually out of public funds) for the consequences of his own criminal conduct. Secondly, the wider rule may raise problems of causation which cannot arise in connection with the narrower rule. The sentence of the court is plainly a consequence of the criminality for which the claimant was responsible. But other forms of damage may give rise to questions about whether they can properly be said to have been caused by his criminal conduct.

52. The wider principle was applied by the Court of Appeal in *Vellino v Chief Constable of the Greater Manchester Police* [2002] 1 WLR 218. The claimant was injured in consequence of jumping from a second-floor window to escape from the custody of the police. He sued the police for damages, claiming that they had not taken reasonable care to prevent him from escaping. Attempting to escape from lawful custody is a criminal offence. The Court of Appeal (Schiemann LJ and Sir Murray Stuart-Smith; Sedley LJ dissenting) held that, assuming the police to have been negligent, recovery was precluded because the injury was the consequence of the plaintiff's unlawful act.

53. This decision seems to me based upon sound common sense. The question, as suggested in the dissenting judgment of Sedley LJ, is how the case should be distinguished from one in which the injury is a consequence of the plaintiff's unlawful act only in the sense that it would not have happened if he had not been committing an unlawful act. An extreme example would be the car which is damaged while unlawfully parked. Sir Murray Stuart-Smith, at para 70, described the distinction:

> The operation of the principle arises where the claimant's claim is founded upon his own criminal or immoral act. The facts which give rise to the claim must be inextricably linked with the criminal activity. It is not sufficient if the criminal activity merely gives occasion for tortious conduct of the defendant.

54. This distinction, between causing something and merely providing the occasion for someone else to cause something, is one with which we are very familiar in the law of torts.

It is the same principle by which the law normally holds that even though damage would not have occurred but for a tortious act, the defendant is not liable if the immediate cause was the deliberate act of another individual . . . It might be better to avoid metaphors like 'inextricably linked' or 'integral part' and to treat the question as simply one of causation. Can one say that, although the damage would not have happened but for the tortious conduct of the defendant, it was caused by the criminal act of the claimant? . . . Or is the position that although the damage would not have happened without the criminal act of the claimant, it was caused by the tortious act of the defendant? . . .

55. However the test is expressed, the wider rule seems to me to cover the remaining heads of damage in this case. Mr Gray's liability to compensate the dependants of the dead pedestrian was an immediate 'inextricable' consequence of his having intentionally killed him. The same is true of his feelings of guilt and remorse. I therefore think that Flaux J was right and I would allow the appeal and restore his judgment.

Lord Phillips, Lord Rodger and **Lord Brown** delivered separate concurring speeches. **Lord Scott** agreed with Lord Hoffmann and Lord Rodger.

Appeal allowed.

COMMENTARY

Lord Hoffmann's speech in *Gray* divides the tort defence of illegality in two: there is a narrow version which applies to situations where the objection is that the claimant is attempting to avoid penalties imposed on them by the criminal law, and a wider version that one cannot recover for the consequences of one's own criminal act. We will consider the two versions of the tort defence in turn, before turning to recent developments in the law of illegality in private law more generally and the extent to which these affect how the defence operates in tort cases.

1. Claimants Seeking to Avoid the Consequences of Criminal Sanctions

As highlighted in Lord Rodger's speech in *Gray* (at [63]), the two different strands of the tort defence of illegality apply to two different kinds of case. The narrow version applies in cases where it is alleged that the defendant's negligence was responsible for the claimant committing a subsequent illegal act which resulted in the imposition of a criminal sanction. In these cases, it is not suggested that the cause of action as a whole is tainted by illegality. Hence in *Gray*, there was no doubt that the claimant could recover for any loss of earnings between the date of the tort and the date of the killing; that part of the claim was not connected with the criminal offence. However, in such cases the courts have generally refused to allow claims in respect of the legal consequences of a claimant's own criminal conduct, such as fines, imprisonment, or damages payable to the victim. A case of this kind that precedes *Gray* is *Clunis v Camden & Islington Health Authority* [1998] QB 978, where the claimant, who had a long history of mental illness, was convicted of manslaughter on the ground of diminished responsibility after stabbing a stranger to death in a tube station. He later sued the defendant health authority in negligence, alleging that its failure to care for him properly had caused him to commit the crime. The Court of Appeal held that his claim should be struck out, inter alia, on illegality grounds, as the claimant was founding his cause of action on the crime he had committed.

Gray and *Clunis* were cases where, as a matter of criminal law, the claimant was at least partly responsible for his conduct (this is the meaning of 'diminished responsibility'). If the claimant is not criminally responsible for their conduct at all—as where they are found not guilty of murder by reason of insanity—then the arguments for applying the illegality defence are considerably weaker, and in *Gray*, Lord Phillips suggested (at [15]) that in these circumstances the defence would not apply, which was also the opinion of Beldam LJ in *Clunis* and of the High Court of New Zealand in *Ellis v Counties Manukau District Health Board* [2007] 1 NZLR 196 at [172]–[173] (cf. *Hunter Area Health Service v Presland* (2005) 63 NSWLR 22, where a majority of the New South Wales Court of Appeal took a different view). His Lordship also left open the possibility that the defence would be inapplicable where the detention was the result of a criminal act of the claimant, but in the view of the sentencing judge in the criminal case, they did not bear significant personal responsibility for the crime. However, Lord Hoffmann was not persuaded, and in *Henderson v Dorset Healthcare University NHS Foundation Trust* [2021] AC 563 (extracted in the next section), Lord Hamblen—although not unsympathetic to the view that it would not be inconsistent with the criminal law to allow a tort claim in such a case—considered that there was insufficient cause to justify departing from what he considered to be the majority view in *Gray* on this matter (see at [97]–[111]). The result was that in *Henderson* the illegality defence barred a claim by a paranoid schizophrenic who was convicted of manslaughter on grounds of diminished responsibility after killing her mother, even though she was considered to have had no significant personal responsibility for her offence. Do you think that was a fair outcome?

Whatever the appropriate limits of the narrow version of the illegality defence, it would seem to command broad judicial and academic support, although such support is not universal. In an extended critical analysis of Lord Hoffmann's speech in *Gray*, Goudkamp has argued that it is doubtful whether either of the two consistency rationales that he believes might underlie the narrow version of the defence—which he labels 'goal consistency' and 'pronouncement consistency'—do in fact justify it ('A Long, Hard Look at *Gray v Thames Trains Ltd*', in *Hoffmann Festschrift*). He concludes, at p. 54, that, while the narrow rule 'might be justified', the justification must be sought not in a standalone consistency rationale, but in 'a consideration of all of the pros and cons' of the rule.

2. Claimants not Recovering for the Consequences of their Own Criminal Acts

(a) Joint Illegal Enterprise Cases

In *Gray*, Lord Hoffmann (at [51]) identified the wider strand of the illegality defence as being based 'on the ground that it is offensive to public notions of the fair distribution of resources that a claimant should be compensated (usually out of public funds) for the consequences of his own criminal conduct'. Most such cases are so-called 'joint illegal enterprise' cases where the claimant was injured by another participant in the course of a joint illegal activity. Take the example given by Lord Asquith in *National Coal Board v England* [1954] AC 403 at 428–9:

> If two burglars, A and B, agree to open a safe by means of explosives, and A so negligently handles the explosive charge as to injure B, B might find some difficulty in maintaining an action for negligence against A. But if A and B are proceeding to the premises which they intend burglariously to enter, and before they enter them B picks A's pocket and steals his watch, I cannot prevail on myself to believe that A could not sue in tort. . . . The theft is totally unconnected with the burglary.

An example of such a case is *Pitts v Hunt* [1991] 1 QB 24, where the plaintiff had suffered serious injury when the motorcycle on which he was a pillion passenger collided with another vehicle. The plaintiff had known that the driver of the motorcycle (who was killed in the accident) was both unlicensed and uninsured, and with the plaintiff's encouragement he had been driving in a dangerous and reckless manner. The plaintiff's action for damages against the personal representative of the deceased was barred on the ground of illegality. Another case of this kind is *McCracken v Smith* [2015] PIQR P19, where the Court of Appeal held that the illegality defence barred a claim by a pillion passenger on a stolen trials bike against the friend who was riding the bike dangerously when it collided with a minibus. Note, however, that in *McCracken* the illegality defence did not bar the claimant's action against the minibus driver—who was judged partly to blame for the accident—on the ground that he was not a party to the reckless and criminal conduct in which the claimant and his friend were engaged. At first blush, this seems rather odd, and it is important to understand that the analysis rested on a very particular take on the 'joint criminal enterprise' issue. According to this approach, it would produce incoherence if the claimant were allowed to recover in tort for damage caused by behaviour of the defendant for which the claimant was criminally responsible, applying the criminal law rules on accessory liability. This analysis was subsequently followed in two other cases involving dangerous driving, *Clark v Farley* [2018] PIQR P15 and *Wallett v Vickers* [2019] PIQR P6, in neither of which the criminal law test of intention 'to encourage or assist the perpetrator to do the prohibited act' (see *R v Jogee* [2017] AC 387) was judged to be satisfied, with the result that the illegality defence failed. According to Males LJ in *Wallett v Vickers* at [45]:

> Because the accessory or secondary party is equally responsible in law for the crime committed by the principal, an accessory who is injured by the principal's criminal conduct cannot sue the principal to recover compensation for his injuries. As an accessory he stands effectively in the shoes of the principal. If he were allowed to sue the principal, he would be claiming damages for conduct for which in law he is himself responsible. Accordingly, he can no more sue the principal than he could sue himself.

A similar analysis of the joint criminal enterprise issue can also be observed in the Australian case law (see, e.g., *Bevan v Coolahan* (2019) 101 NSWLR 86). Do you agree with this approach, or do you think that it rests on a confusion between criminal and civil responsibility? And can it be reconciled with the analysis of the Court of Appeal in *Beaumont v Ferrer* [2017] PIQR P1, noted later?

What is the justification for barring claims by reference to the wider strand of the illegality defence? In *Pitts v Hunt*, various different rationales were relied on. According to Balcombe LJ, the claim was denied because the illegality prevented a standard of care from being set. This approach has been criticised on the basis that it is usually *possible* to set a standard of care, so a court denying a claim on this basis is in fact making *a choice* not to set a standard of care (see *Miller v Miller* (2011) 242 CLR 446; Goudkamp [2012] CLJ 481 at 483). In contrast, Beldam LJ adopted a form of the 'public conscience' test: would it shock the public conscience if the claimant were allowed to recover? However, despite the fact that this rationale had been relied on previously, the majority in *Pitts* did not approve it and it was subsequently rejected by the House of Lords in a case involving resulting trusts, *Tinsley v Milligan* [1994] 1 AC 340 (and see also the tort case of *Stone & Rolls Ltd v Moore Stephens (a firm)* [2009] 1 AC 1391 at [97], per Lord Scott), though variants of it occasionally surface in the case law (see, e.g., *Gujra v Roath* [2018] 1 WLR 3208 at [30]).

The approach of the third judge in *Pitts*, Dillon LJ, is closest to the analysis of the defence adopted by Lord Hoffmann in *Gray*. This approach focuses on the causal connection between the illegality and the injury for which the claimant is seeking redress, and asks whether 'the real operative cause' (see *Flint v Tittensor* [2015] 1 WLR 4370 at [47], per Edis J) of the claimant's damage was the claimant's crime or the defendant's negligence. Exactly how this test can be applied to achieve consistent results remains open to question but it is useful to consider two joint illegal enterprise cases decided after *Gray* to see how it plays out in practice. In the first of the cases, *Delaney v Pickett* [2012] 1 WLR 2149 (noted by Goudkamp [2012] CLJ 481), the claimant was injured in an accident caused by the defendant, the driver of the vehicle in which he was travelling. At the time of the accident the parties were hiding a quantity of cannabis, a prohibited drug. Here it was held by the Court of Appeal that the claimant's personal injury action against the defendant was not barred by the illegality defence, because, applying *Gray*, the 'immediate cause' of the claimant's injury had been the defendant's negligent driving, and not the criminal activity in which the parties happened to be engaged at the relevant time. By contrast, in *Joyce v O'Brien* [2014] 1 WLR 70, the Court of Appeal held that a thief who fell out of the back of a van which was being used to transport a ladder that he and the driver had just stolen *was* barred by the illegality defence from recovering damages from the driver (who had been driving the van negligently). (For a similar case to *Joyce*, with a similar result, see *Smith v Stratton* [2015] EWCA Civ 1413, where the claimant and defendant were suspected drug dealers seeking to evade the police when their vehicle crashed at speed.) Although Lord Hoffmann in *Gray* was sceptical of tests that asked whether the claim was 'inextricably linked' to or an 'integral part' of the illegality, in our view it is hard to explain the differing results in these two cases without relying on language of this kind, and the causation test must ultimately boil down to the closeness of the connection between the illegality and the claim being made (for a helpful example of this kind of approach see the judgment of Lord Hughes in *Hounga v Allen* [2014] 1 WLR 2889, noted in V.3).

(b) Other Types of Case

The courts have also asked whether the claimant's criminal conduct was 'inextricably linked' with the alleged tort in a series of cases that did not involve a joint illegal enterprise between the parties. In *Cross v Kirkby* [2000] EWCA Civ 426, the claimant had attacked the defendant with a baseball bat and was then injured when the defendant used it to defend himself. His claim failed partly on illegality grounds, with Judge LJ justifying this outcome on the basis that the claim was inextricably linked with the illegality. A similar approach was taken in *Vellino v Chief Constable of Greater Manchester Police* [2002] 1 WLR 218. When the police went to arrest the claimant in his second floor flat, he broke away from them and jumped out of his bedroom window, causing himself severe injury. As he had been known to escape in this way previously, it was alleged that the police had been careless in not preventing him from doing so again, but a majority of the Court of Appeal (Sedley LJ dissenting) held that his claim was barred because of his illegal act of seeking to escape custody. According to Sir Murray Stuart-Smith, at [70], the illegality principle applied because '[t]he facts which gave rise to the claim' were 'inextricably linked with the [claimant's] criminal activity'. Finally, in *Beaumont v Ferrer* [2017] PIQR P1, the Court of Appeal held that two teenagers who tried to make off without paying a taxi fare could not recover damages from the taxi driver for serious injuries they suffered when they jumped out of his moving vehicle after he sought to thwart their criminal enterprise by driving away from their destination with the claimants still inside his cab. According to Longmore LJ, at [24], the claimants' criminal conduct was 'far from incidental (but integral) both to the claim itself and any negligence on the part of the [defendant]', and the fact that the defendant was not a party to their crime (as in the joint criminal enterprise cases discussed earlier) strengthened the case for applying the illegality defence.

(c) The Seriousness of the Criminal Conduct

In *Vellino*, Sir Murray Stuart-Smith also said, at [70], that criminal conduct had to be 'sufficiently serious' to merit the application of the illegality principle, albeit that '[g]enerally speaking a crime punishable with imprisonment could be expected to qualify'. Further guidance on this question was provided in *Les Laboratoires Servier v Apotex Inc* [2015] AC 430 (noted by Buckley (2015) 131 LQR 341; Fisher (2015) 78 MLR 854), where the Supreme Court held that the commission of a civil wrong not involving dishonesty (in this case infringement of a Canadian patent) would not amount to 'turpitude' for the purposes of the illegality defence. According to Lord Sumption, who gave the lead judgment (at [25]):

> The ex turpi causa principle is concerned with claims founded on acts which are contrary to the public law of the state and engage the public interest. The paradigm case is . . . a criminal act. In addition, it is concerned with a limited category of acts which, while not necessarily criminal, can conveniently be described as 'quasi-criminal' because they engage the public interest in the same way . . . [T]his additional category of non-criminal acts giving rise to the defence includes cases of dishonesty or corruption . . . some anomalous categories of misconduct, such as prostitution, which without itself being criminal are contrary to public policy and involve criminal liability on the part of secondary parties; and the infringement of statutory rules enacted for the protection of the public interest and attracting civil sanctions of a penal character . . .

Although Lord Sumption was anxious, at [19], to steer the courts away from making 'value judgments about the seriousness of the illegality', his Lordship accepted that there might be exceptional cases where even criminal or quasi-criminal acts would not constitute turpitude for the purposes of the illegality defence, instancing as examples 'trivial' offences (presumably routine traffic offences and the like) and strict liability offences where the claimant was not privy to the facts making his conduct unlawful. (Goudkamp, 'A Long, Hard Look at *Gray v Thames Trains Ltd*', op. cit., pp. 49–50 argues that these observations apply to the narrow version of the illegality defence as well as to the wide version. Do you think that they should?) The approach in *Les Laboratoires Servier* was followed by the Court of Appeal in *McCracken v Smith* [2015] PIQR P19, where the dangerous driving of a trials bike was held to amount to 'turpitude' for these purposes (cf. *Wallett v Vickers* [2019] PIQR P6 at [38], holding obiter that merely careless driving would not qualify), and seems also to have been endorsed by Lord Hamblen in *Henderson v Dorset Healthcare University NHS Foundation Trust* [2021] AC 563 at [112] (see the extract in the next section). Note, however, that Goudkamp (2021) 37 PN 171 at 179 argues that in the light of the developments discussed in the next section, and in particular the recognition of a 'disproportionality check' on the application of the illegality defence, what he calls the 'separate turpitude filter' has been rendered otiose.

Goudkamp, 'The Law of Illegality: Identifying the Issues', in S. Green and A. Bogg (eds), *Illegality after Patel v Mirza* (Oxford: Hart, 2018), p. 54 questions whether 'merely quasi-criminal conduct' should be capable of triggering the illegality defence, especially when not all criminal conduct does. He posits that perhaps such a potentially draconian doctrine 'should be reserved for situations that involve through and through criminal conduct'. Similarly, Virgo, *op. cit.*, p. 182 says that the 'denial of relief by reference to vague notions of immorality is very difficult to defend'. Do you agree?

3. *Patel* and *Henderson*

Patel v Mirza [2017] AC 467

The case concerned a claim in unjust enrichment for the repayment of money paid by the claimant to the defendant pursuant to an illegal contract between the parties.

Lord Toulson

The Way Forward

. . . 99. [T]here are two broad discernible policy reasons for the common law doctrine of illegality as a defence to a civil claim. One is that a person should not be allowed to profit from his own wrongdoing. The other, linked, consideration is that the law should be coherent and not self-defeating, condoning illegality by giving with the left hand what it takes with the right hand.

100. . . . In *Hall v Hebert* [1993] 2 SCR 159 McLachlin J favoured giving a narrow meaning to profit but, more fundamentally, she expressed the view, at pp 175–176, that, as a rationale, the statement that a plaintiff will not be allowed to profit from his or her own wrongdoing does not fully explain why particular claims have been rejected, and that it may have the undesirable effect of tempting judges to focus on whether the plaintiff is 'getting something' out of the wrongdoing, rather than on the question whether allowing recovery for something which was illegal would produce inconsistency and disharmony in the law, and so cause damage to the integrity of the legal system.

101. That is a valuable insight, with which I agree. I agree also with Professor Burrows' observation that this expression leaves open what is meant by inconsistency (or disharmony) in a particular case, but I do not see this as a weakness. It is not a matter which can be determined mechanistically. So how is the court to determine the matter if not by some mechanistic process? In answer to that question I would say that one cannot judge whether allowing a claim which is in some way tainted by illegality would be contrary to the public interest, because it would be harmful to the integrity of the legal system, without (a) considering the underlying purpose of the prohibition which has been transgressed, (b) considering conversely any other relevant public policies which may be rendered ineffective or less effective by denial of the claim, and (c) keeping in mind the possibility of overkill unless the law is applied with a due sense of proportionality. We are, after all, in the area of public policy. That trio of necessary considerations can be found in the case law . . .

[His Lordship discussed some relevant authorities and continued:]

107. In considering whether it would be disproportionate to refuse relief to which the claimant would otherwise be entitled, as a matter of public policy, various factors may be relevant . . . I would not attempt to lay down a prescriptive or definitive list because of the infinite possible variety of cases. Potentially relevant factors include the seriousness of the conduct, its centrality to the contract, whether it was intentional and whether there was marked disparity in the parties' respective culpability . . .

Summary and Disposal

120. The essential rationale of the illegality doctrine is that it would be contrary to the public interest to enforce a claim if to do so would be harmful to the integrity of the legal system (or, possibly, certain aspects of public morality, the boundaries of which have never been made entirely clear and which do not arise for consideration in this case). In assessing whether the public interest would be harmed in that way, it is necessary (a) to consider the underlying purpose of the prohibition which has been transgressed and whether that purpose will be enhanced by denial of the claim, (b) to consider any other relevant public policy on which the denial of the claim may have an impact and (c) to consider whether denial of the claim would be a proportionate response to the illegality, bearing in mind that punishment is a matter for the criminal courts. Within that framework, various factors may be relevant, but it would be a mistake to suggest that the court is free to decide a case in an undisciplined way. The public interest is best served by a principled and transparent assessment of the considerations identified, rather by than the application of a formal approach capable of producing results which may appear arbitrary, unjust or disproportionate . . .

COMMENTARY

In his note on *Patel v Mirza*, Goudkamp ((2017) 133 LQR 14) describes this decision as 'a pivotal moment in English private law', which replaced previous approaches to the illegality defence with a 'policy-based test pursuant to which various salient features are weighed'. *Patel* marked the culmination of a prolonged and sharp disagreement about the nature of the illegality defence in the Supreme Court. This disagreement had played out in three previous decisions of the court, none of which were negligence cases, namely *Hounga v Allen* [2014] 1 WLR 2889; *Les Laboratoires Servier v Apotex Inc* [2015] AC 430 (noted in V.2); and *Bilta (UK) Ltd v Nazir (No 2)* [2016] AC 1. In *Hounga* (noted by Goudkamp and Zou [2015] CLJ 13), where an illegal immigrant had sued her employer in the statutory tort of racial discrimination, Lord Wilson (with whom Lady Hale and Lord Kerr agreed) based his rejection of the illegality defence on public policy, and held that the policy of countering human trafficking and protecting its victims outweighed any considerations of public policy in favour of applying the defence on the facts. By contrast, Lord Hughes (with whom Lord Carnwath agreed) took the view that the illegality defence should fail for a different reason, namely that there was not a sufficiently close connection between the claimant's immigration offences and her discrimination claim. The decision in *Les Laboratoires Servier*, a case on patent law, turned on the 'turpitude' issue discussed earlier, but in his leading judgment Lord Sumption took issue with the majority position in *Hounga*, and made it clear that he preferred a rule-based approach to an open-ended discretionary one, which he thought would lead to inconsistency. Lord Toulson, by contrast, favoured a policy-based approach along the lines of that adopted by the majority in *Hounga*. In *Bilta (UK) Ltd v Nazir (No 2)*, the two opposing camps restated their positions, but no resolution was arrived at. It was clear that such a resolution was urgently required, and in *Patel* a panel of nine justices was assembled to provide it. In the end six of the justices (including Lord Toulson, who gave the leading judgment) opted for a discretionary approach, while the other three (Lord Mance, Lord Clarke and Lord Sumption) favoured a rule-based analysis. For evaluation of the discretionary approach adopted by the majority in *Patel*, see Green and Bogg, *op. cit.*

The significance of *Patel v Mirza* is most obvious in contract, trusts and unjust enrichment, not least because Lord Toulson specifically rejected the 'reliance test' laid down by the House of Lords in *Tinsley v Milligan* [1994] 1 AC 340, according to which the illegality defence applied where the claimant would have to rely on their illegal conduct in order to found their claim. This test had previously governed the operation of the illegality defence in those areas of private law, but was much less influential in the negligence context, perhaps because it was less well-suited to tort claims. As there was no explicit evaluation of *Gray v Thames Trains* in *Patel*, nor any extended discussion of the operation of the *ex turpi causa* principle in negligence cases, the impact of the decision (and of Lord Toulson's analysis) on negligence law was not immediately certain. The Supreme Court sought to clarify the position in the next extracted case.

Henderson v Dorset Healthcare University NHS Foundation Trust [2021] AC 563

The facts are set out in the judgment of Lord Hamblen.

Lord Hamblen (with whom Lord Reed, Lord Hodge, Lady Black, Lord Lloyd-Jones, Lady Arden and Lord Kitchin agreed)

I Introduction

1. The appellant, Ms Ecila Henderson, suffers from paranoid schizophrenia or schizoaffective disorder. On 25 August 2010 she stabbed her mother to death whilst experiencing a serious psychotic episode. She was charged with her mother's murder but, in view of the psychiatric evidence, the prosecution agreed to a plea of manslaughter by reason of diminished responsibility. That plea was accepted by the court and on 8 July 2011 Foskett J sentenced the appellant to a hospital order under section 37 of the Mental Health Act 1983 ('the 1983 Act') and an unlimited restriction order under section 41 of the 1983 Act. The appellant has remained subject to detention pursuant to the 1983 Act ever since and she is not expected to be released for some significant time.

2. The respondent, Dorset Healthcare University NHS Foundation Trust, has admitted liability in negligence in failing to return the appellant to hospital on the basis of her manifest psychotic state. The tragic killing of her mother would not have occurred had this been done.

3. The appellant advances various heads of damages against the respondent as a result of its admitted negligence. Liability for these heads of damages is denied on the grounds that the damages claimed by the appellant are the consequence of: (i) the sentence imposed on her by the criminal court; and/or (ii) her criminal act of manslaughter, and are therefore irrecoverable by reason of the doctrine of ex turpi causa non oritur actio/illegality.

4. Similar claims for damages to those made by the appellant were held to be irrecoverable by the House of Lords in *Gray v Thames Trains Ltd* [2009] AC 1339 ('*Gray*'), also a case of manslaughter on the grounds of diminished responsibility. The appeal raises the question of

whether *Gray* can be distinguished and, if not, whether it should be departed from, in particular in the light of the Supreme Court decision concerning illegality in *Patel v Mirza* [2017] AC 467 ('*Patel*'). . . .

IV The proceedings below

28. The appellant claimed damages under six heads of loss:

(1) General damages for personal injury (a depressive disorder and post-traumatic stress disorder ('PTSD')) consequent on her killing of her mother.
(2) General damages for her loss of liberty caused by her compulsory detention in hospital pursuant to sections 37 and 41 of the 1983 Act.
(3) General damages for loss of amenity arising from the consequences to her of having killed her mother.
(4) Past loss in the sum of £61,944 being the share in her mother's estate which she is unable to recover as a result of the operation of the provisions of the Forfeiture Act 1982.
(5) The cost of psychotherapy (by way of future loss).
(6) The cost of a care manager/support worker (by way of future loss).

29. In view of the respondent's position that the heads of loss were irrecoverable as a matter of law, on 17 February 2016 Master Cook ordered that there be a trial of a preliminary issue to determine that question.

30. The preliminary issue was heard over two days by Jay J who decided the issue in the respondent's favour [2017] 1 WLR 2673. Jay J held that the facts were materially identical to those in *Clunis v Camden and Islington Health Authority* [1998] QB 978 ('*Clunis*') and *Gray* and that those decisions were binding on him.

31. The Court of Appeal (Sir Terence Etherton MR, Ryder and Macur LJJ) dismissed the appellant's appeal against the order of Jay J. Like Jay J, the Court of Appeal held that the facts were materially identical to those in *Clunis* and *Gray* and that those decisions were binding on it.

V The issues

32. The principal issues to be determined on the appeal are:

(1) Whether *Gray* can be distinguished.
(2) If not, whether *Gray* should be departed from and *Clunis* overruled.
(3) If not, whether all heads of loss claimed are irrecoverable. . . .

(i) Gray

[His Lordship considered *Gray* and continued:]

58. So far as relevant to the present appeal, I would make the following observations on the judgments given in *Gray* [2009] AC 1339 in so far as they relate to public policy.

(1) Both the narrow claim and the wide claim failed on the grounds of public policy.
(2) All judges considered that the relevant policy in connection with the narrow claim was the need to avoid inconsistency so as to maintain the integrity of the legal system: 'the consistency principle'.
(3) Lord Hoffmann did not consider that this applied to the wide claim but held that a related policy did, namely that 'it is offensive to public notions of the fair distribution of resources that a claimant should be compensated (usually out of public funds) for the consequences of his own criminal conduct' (para 51). I understand this to mean that allowing a claimant to be compensated for the consequences of his own criminal conduct risks bringing the law

into disrepute and diminishing respect for it. It is an outcome of which public opinion would be likely to disapprove and would thereby undermine public confidence in the law: 'the public confidence principle'.

(4) The public confidence principle is also applicable to the narrow claim. It is related to the consistency principle since one of the reasons that the public would be likely to disapprove of the outcome is the inconsistency which it involves between the criminal law and the civil law.

(5) Although Lord Rodger appeared to consider that the consistency principle did not apply to the wide claim, the policy reasons he gives for rejecting the claim reflect that principle. The reason that a person cannot 'attribute . . . to others' acts for which he has been found criminally responsible, or 'seek rebate' of the consequences of those acts, is that it would be inconsistent with that finding of criminal responsibility. If a person has been found criminally responsible for certain acts it would be inconsistent for the civil courts to absolve that person of such responsibility and to attribute responsibility for those same acts to someone else.

(6) Whilst the consistency principle more obviously applies to the narrow claim, on analysis it applies to the wide claim as well. In relation to the narrow claim the inconsistency is with both the criminal court's finding of responsibility and the sentence it has imposed. In relation to the wide claim it is with the former only.

[His Lordship considered *Clunis* and *Patel* and continued:]

(iv) The application of Patel

73. An important issue which arises on this appeal concerns the width of the application of *Patel* [2017] AC 467 and how it applies in relation to existing case law.

74. First, it should be emphasised that *Patel* concerned common law illegality rather than statutory illegality. Where the effects of the illegality are dealt with by statute then the statute should be applied. . . .

76. Secondly, *Patel* concerned a claim in unjust enrichment, but there can be little doubt that it was intended to provide guidance as to the proper approach to the common law illegality defence across civil law more generally. . . . The approach set out in paras 101 and 120 is expressed in general and unqualified terms.

77. Thirdly, that does not mean that *Patel* represents 'year zero' and that in all future illegality cases it is *Patel* and only *Patel* that is to be considered and applied. That would be to disregard the value of precedent built up in various areas of the law to address particular factual situations giving rise to the illegality defence. Those decisions remain of precedential value unless it can be shown that they are not compatible with the approach set out in *Patel* in the sense that they cannot stand with the reasoning in *Patel* or were wrongly decided in the light of that reasoning. . . .

VII Issue (2)—whether Gray should be departed from and Clunis overruled

(i) Whether the reasoning in Gray cannot stand with the approach to illegality adopted by the Supreme Court in Patel

. . . 90. In my judgment, the essential reasoning in *Gray* is consistent with the approach adopted in *Patel*. *Gray* did not involve the reliance-based approach, nor did it follow or apply *Tinsley v Milligan* [1994] 1 AC 340. . . .

91. The court in *Gray* examined whether the narrower and the wider rules were, as was contended, 'a special rule of public policy'. As already explained, both Lord Hoffmann and Lord Rodger considered the policy reasons for the rules and concluded that they were justified

as a matter of public policy. Even though Lord Hoffmann endorsed a causation approach to the application of the wider rule, that involved a causal rule based on policy considerations. As the Court of Appeal said at para 64 of its judgment, it was a 'combination of public policy and causation'. . . .

93. *Gray* was correctly seen in *Patel* as being an example of a decision on illegality based on policy considerations rather than reliance. It was cited with apparent approval not only by Lord Toulson . . . but also by Lord Kerr . . . and Lord Neuberger . . .

94. In addition, the fundamental policy consideration relied upon in *Gray* was the need for consistency so as to maintain the integrity of the legal system, the very matter that was held in *Patel* to be the underlying policy question.

95. It is correct to observe that *Gray* involved no express consideration of proportionality. In *Patel* that did not, however, cause any doubt to be cast on the correctness of the decision and, for reasons explained below, the factual circumstances in *Gray* do not give rise to any issue of proportionality.

96. The approach adopted by the House of Lords in *Gray* therefore provides no reason why it should be departed from. If anything, it points to the contrary conclusion.

(ii) Whether it should be held that Gray does not apply where the claimant has no significant personal responsibility for the criminal act and/or there is no penal element in the sentence imposed

97. As already explained, the majority decided that the narrower and wider rules applied regardless of the degree of personal responsibility. The appellant contends that they were wrong so to do and that this part of the decision should be departed from. It is submitted that this case raises on the facts the second reservation expressed by Lord Phillips because the trial judge accepted that the appellant did not bear a significant degree of personal responsibility for her crime, and that this court should accept and apply that reservation.

98. The appellant's fundamental point is that there is no inconsistency or incoherence between the civil and the criminal law in a case in which the claimant has no significant personal responsibility for a criminal act.

[His Lordship summarised the argument of the appellant on this issue and continued:]

. . . 104. [There] are formidable arguments [in favour of this view] . . . I am, however, unable to accept that they meet the high hurdle of justifying departure from the House of Lords' relatively recent decision in *Gray* [2009] AC 1339.

105. As explained above, the key consideration as far as the majority in *Gray* were concerned was that the claimant had been found to be criminally responsible for his acts. That he had been convicted of manslaughter on the grounds of diminished responsibility meant that responsibility for his criminal acts was diminished, but it was not removed. It was not an insanity case and so, as Beldam LJ pointed out in *Clunis* [1998] QB 978, 989, 'he must be taken to have known what he was doing and that it was wrong'.

106. In such circumstances, the majority in *Gray* justifiably considered that inconsistency would arise not only if he was allowed to recover damages resulting from the sentence imposed, but also if they resulted from the intentional criminal act for which he had been held responsible. To allow recovery would be to attribute responsibility for that criminal act not, as determined by the criminal law, to the criminal but to someone else, namely the tortious defendant. There is a contradiction between the law's treatment of conduct as criminal and the acceptance that such conduct should give rise to a civil right of reimbursement. The criminal under the criminal law becomes the victim under tort law.

107. Whilst the wider rule may not involve, as the application of the narrower rule does, the law giving with one hand what it takes away with the other, it does involve, as Lord Hughes

JSC said in *Hounga v Allen* [2014] 1 WLR 2889, para 55, the law condoning 'when facing right what it condemns when facing left'.

108. If, as the appellant submits, the degree of personal responsibility is a matter for the trial judge to determine in the civil claim there is a clear risk of inconsistent decisions being reached in the criminal and the civil courts, both as to the degree of responsibility involved and as to how that is to be determined. If, as is further submitted, it is appropriate for the civil court to move away from the *M'Naghten* approach to insanity, and to develop its own approach to such issues, then the inconsistencies will be heightened.

109. Nor does the fact that there may be no penal element to the sentence imposed by the criminal court alter matters. As Lord Rodger observed at para 78 of *Gray*, even if the sentence is not regarded as being a punishment, 'this does not mean that the judge was treating the claimant as not being to blame for what he did'. A conviction for manslaughter by diminished responsibility still involves blame. The defendant would otherwise have been convicted of murder and some responsibility for the unlawful killing necessarily remains. Moreover, the fact of a criminal conviction for manslaughter is itself punitive.

110. A further difficulty with the appellant's argument is why significant personal responsibility is to be regarded as the threshold, precisely what that means and how it is to be determined. Whilst a sentencing judge will be concerned with the level of responsibility involved, he or she will not be specifically addressing the issue of significant personal responsibility. . . . In any event, any findings which may be made by the trial judge in the criminal proceedings will be solely for the purpose of sentencing.

111. It is not sufficient simply to say that this will be a matter of fact for the trial judge to determine in the civil claim. As the Law Commission's Discussion Paper illustrates, the issue of responsibility raises questions of great complexity and difficulty. . . . What the justification is for [the test proposed by the appellant of whether the claimant lacked capacity to conform their behaviour to the demands imposed by the criminal law] was not really explained, nor was its meaning. Not only is it a recipe for uncertainty, but it risks being tantamount to judicial legislation.

112. Finally, the appellant advances a related argument that the lack of significant personal responsibility means that there is insufficient turpitude to give rise to an illegality defence. This again ignores the seriousness of a criminal conviction for manslaughter . . . . As Lord Sumption JSC explained [in *Les Laboratoires Servier v Apotex Inc* [2015] AC 430] at para 29, there may be some exceptional cases where a criminal act will not constitute turpitude. The reservation made in *Gray* in relation to trivial offences may be an example of such a case, as may be strict liability offences where the claimant is not privy to the facts making his act unlawful. The serious criminal offence of manslaughter by reason of diminished responsibility does not come close to falling within such an exception and clearly engages the defence.

(iii) Whether the application of the trio of considerations approach set out in Patel leads to a different outcome

[His Lordship referred to the 'trio of considerations' set out by Lord Toulson in *Patel* at [120], and continued:]

114. The issues and the arguments in the present case have raised a number of questions as to the proper understanding and application of the trio of considerations.

115. . . . It is neither necessary nor desirable that consideration of the relevant policy considerations should give rise to a mini trial. They should usually be capable of being addressed as a matter of argument and at a level of generality that does not make evidence necessary, as is well illustrated by this court's decision in *Hounga v Allen* [2014] 1 WLR 2889.

116. Secondly, questions arise as to exactly how under the trio of considerations approach relevant policy considerations are to be weighed. It appears that this must involve a balancing between considerations arising at the first and second stages; the third stage relates to proportionality and factors specific to the case rather than general policy considerations. Stage (a) is directed at policy reasons which support denial of the claim and stage (b) is directed at policy reasons which support denial of the illegality defence. As Lord Toulson JSC makes clear at para 101, stage (b) is meant to operate 'conversely' to stage (a). . . .

119. It follows that stage (a) should not be interpreted as being confined to the specific purpose of the prohibition transgressed. Whilst that is of great importance, other general policy considerations that impact on the consistency of the law and the integrity of the legal system also fall to be taken into account. In the present case, for example, that would encompass the public policy considerations identified in *Gray* [2009] AC 1339, namely the consistency principle and the public confidence principle. Similarly, whilst preventing someone from profiting from his own wrong is not the rationale of the illegality defence, it is a relevant policy consideration, which is linked to the need for consistency and coherence in the law. For one branch of the law to enable a person to profit from behaviour which another branch of the law treats as being criminal or otherwise unlawful would tend to produce inconsistency and disharmony in the law, and so cause damage to the integrity of the legal system, as is recognised in *Patel* . . . In cases where it features, it too is a factor to be taken into account, even though it may not reflect the purpose of the prohibition transgressed.

120. In considering the issue of consistency and coherence in the law, the closeness of the connection between the claim and the illegal act may well be of relevance. The closer that connection is, the greater and more obvious may be the inconsistency and consequent risk of harm to the integrity of the legal system. The rejection by the majority in *Patel* of reliance as the test of illegality did not mean that reliance was thereby rendered irrelevant to the policy-based approach. It may not provide a satisfactory test of illegality, but it will often be a relevant factor.

121. Thirdly, questions arise as to the weight it may be appropriate to give to different policy considerations. At para 99 Lord Toulson JSC recognised the importance of the policy considerations that a person should not be allowed to profit from his own wrongdoing and that the law should be coherent. Where either or both of these considerations are engaged it would seem appropriate that they are given great weight. . . .

123. Fourthly, questions arise as to whether proportionality always has to be considered and as to how it is to be addressed. In some cases, of which *Hounga v Allen* [2014] 1 WLR 2889 is an example, it may be apparent that the balancing of policy considerations comes down firmly against denial of the claim. If so, it will not be necessary to go on to the third stage and the issue of proportionality. This is consistent with Lord Toulson JSC's statement at para 107 that these factors relate to 'whether it would be disproportionate to refuse relief to which the claimant would otherwise be entitled' and at para 101 that they fall to be considered to avoid 'the possibility of overkill'. In other words, they are a disproportionality check rather than a proportionality requirement.

124. In relation to proportionality, at para 107 Lord Toulson JSC identified four factors which were likely to be of particular relevance, namely: 'the seriousness of the conduct, its centrality [to the transaction], whether it was intentional and whether there was marked disparity in the parties' respective culpability.' Lord Toulson JSC refrained from saying anything about the potential weight of such factors, no doubt to avoid being prescriptive. I would, however, suggest that centrality will often be a factor of particular importance. When considering the circumstances relating to the illegality, whether there is a causal link between the illegality and the claim, and the closeness of that causal connection, will often be important considerations.

(a) Stage (a)—the underlying purpose of the prohibition which has been transgressed and whether that purpose will be enhanced by denial of the claim

125. As explained above, this stage involves identification of policy reasons which support denial of the claim. Considering first general policy considerations rather than the purpose of the prohibition, for the reasons explained in *Gray*, the consistency principle is engaged in this case. There is a need to avoid inconsistency so as to maintain the integrity of the legal system. Whilst that most obviously applies to the narrower rule, it also applies to the wider rule. As *Patel* makes clear, this is a central and very weighty public policy consideration.

126. For the reasons given by Lord Hoffmann in *Gray*, the public confidence principle is also engaged. Again, this applies to both the narrower and the wider rule.

127. In the present case, the gravity of the wrongdoing heightens the significance of the public confidence considerations, as does the issue of proper allocation of resources. NHS funding is an issue of significant public interest and importance and, if recovery is permitted, funds will be taken from the NHS budget to compensate the appellant for the consequences of her criminal conviction for unlawful killing.

128. This is also a case in which there is a very close connection between the claim and the illegality, thereby highlighting and emphasising the inconsistencies in the law which would be raised were the claim to succeed. The appellant's crime was the immediate and, on any view, an effective cause of all heads of loss claimed. Indeed, applying Lord Hoffmann's approach to causation in *Gray*, with which Lord Rodger and Lord Scott agreed, it was the sole effective cause of such loss.

129. In relation to the underlying purpose of the prohibition transgressed, an important purpose is to deter unlawful killing thereby providing protection to the public. As far as the public is concerned there could be no more important right to be protected than the right to life. It is clearly in the public interest that everything possible is done to enhance protection of that fundamental right. There is also a public interest in the public condemnation of unlawful killing and the punishment of those who behave in that way.

130. On behalf of the appellant it is submitted that it is absurd to suppose that a person suffering from diminished responsibility will be deterred from killing by the prospect of not being able to recover compensation for any loss suffered as a result of committing the offence. Indeed, more generally it is submitted that a person who is not deterred by a criminal sanction is unlikely to be deterred by being deprived of a right to compensation.

131. There is force in these points, but the question should not be considered solely at the granular level of diminished responsibility manslaughter cases. Looking at the matter more broadly there may well be some deterrent effect in a clear rule that unlawful killing never pays and any such effect is important given the fundamental importance of the right to life. To have such a rule also supports the public interest in public condemnation and due punishment.

(b) Stage (b)—any other relevant public policy on which the denial of the claim may have an impact

132. The appellant suggests four countervailing public policies.

133. The first is the policy of encouraging NHS bodies to care competently for the most vulnerable. It is said that it is recognised that imposing a duty of care can enhance standards. There is, however, no issue that a duty of care was owed. Indeed, liability for damages up to the date of the killing is admitted. It is unlikely that limiting the extent of the liability to the victim will affect the exercise of due care. In any event, there is a potential exposure in such cases to claims on behalf of victims as well as to regulatory sanctions. Focusing on the specific factual situation in the present case, there is no ready means of judging the likely consequences of removing the illegality defence from NHS bodies in claims by mental health patients who kill others. As the respondent submits, it does not seem likely that NHS staff or organisations need any encouragement to try to do their best to stop patients killing people.

134. The second is the policy of providing compensation to victims of torts where they are not significantly responsible for their conduct. It is not clear that there is any such general policy and the example of suicide cases which is relied upon raises different considerations, not least because suicide is not a crime.

135. The third is the policy of ensuring that public bodies pay compensation to those whom they have injured. This may be said to beg the question since it assumes that it was the respondent's negligence which injured the appellant rather than her own criminal act. Even if it was, this is not one of those cases where the injury was the very thing which the respondent was engaged to prevent and it is agreed that the killing by the appellant of her mother could not have been predicted.

136. The fourth is the policy of ensuring that defendants in criminal trials receive sentences proportionate to their offending. That is consistent with the purpose of the narrower rule which is to avoid giving back with one hand what has been taken by the other.

137. I recognise that there is force in at least some of the policy considerations relied upon by the appellant, but I do not consider that they begin to outweigh those which support denial of the claim. In particular, as *Gray* makes clear, the resulting inconsistency in the law is such as to affect the integrity of the legal system. The underlying policy question identified in *Patel* is accordingly engaged. . . .

(c) Stage (c)—whether denial of the claim would be a proportionate response to the illegality, bearing in mind that punishment is for the criminal courts

138. It is not suggested that there were factors relevant to proportionality aside from the four factors identified by Lord Toulson JSC at para 107 of his judgment in *Patel* . . .

139. As to the seriousness of the conduct, this was a very serious offence. It involved culpable homicide committed with murderous intent. As was acknowledged on behalf of the appellant, unlawful killing is the most serious conduct imaginable. The appellant knew what she was doing and that it was legally and morally wrong.

140. As to the centrality of the conduct to the transaction, the offending is central to all heads of loss claimed and, as held in *Gray*, is the effective cause of such loss.

141. As to whether the conduct was intentional, there was intent to kill or to do grievous bodily harm. Whilst there may have been no significant personal responsibility, there was nevertheless murderous intent.

142. As to whether there was a marked disparity in the parties' respective wrongdoing, the appellant was convicted of culpable homicide. Whilst she may not bear a significant degree of responsibility for what she did, she knew what she was doing and that it was morally and legally wrong. The respondent has admitted negligence in the appellant's treatment. It is not the case, however, that the respondent's staff did nothing in response to the appellant's mental health relapse.

143. In all the circumstances I do not consider that denial of the claim would be disproportionate. It would be a proportionate response to the illegality, bearing in mind that punishment is for the criminal court. The same would apply to the materially similar facts of *Gray*, even more clearly in so far as the offending in that case involved significant personal responsibility. The fact that proportionality was not specifically addressed in *Gray* does not therefore undermine the approach taken or the decision reached in that case.

144. For all these reasons, the application of the trio of considerations approach set out in *Patel* does not lead to a different outcome.

(iv) Conclusion on issue (2)

145. The appellant has not shown that *Gray* should be departed from and *Clunis* overruled. On the contrary, I consider that the decision in *Gray* should be affirmed as being

'*Patel*-compliant'—it is how *Patel* 'plays out in that particular type of case'. The clearly stated public policy based rules set out in *Gray* should be applied and followed in comparable cases.

VIII Issue (3)—whether all heads of loss claimed are irrecoverable

146. In the appellant's written case it was accepted that all heads of loss are irrecoverable pursuant to the ratio in *Gray*, save for (as was common ground) any losses for pain and suffering or loss of amenity that arose prior to the killing. The claim for general damages for loss of liberty was accepted as being barred by the narrower rule, the other heads by the wider rule. . . .

148. In my judgment, the appellant's concession was properly made. Damages for loss of liberty (head (ii)) and loss of amenity during her detention (part of head (iii)), are barred by the narrower rule. The other heads of loss are barred by the wider rule; indeed, two of them are expressly stated to be the consequence to the appellant of the killing of her mother (heads (i) and (iii)).

149. As to the Forfeiture Act claim, the reason that the appellant is unable to recover the full share of her mother's estate is because an order to that effect was made by the court pursuant to the provisions of the Forfeiture Act. In deciding what order to make the court has regard to the conduct of the offender and of the deceased, to such other circumstances as appear to the court to be material and to the justice of the case. It would be entirely inappropriate to subvert the operation of the specific and bespoke Forfeiture Act regime, and the court order made thereunder, by permitting the appellant to recover from the respondent what she was not permitted to recover under the Forfeiture Act.

IX Conclusion

150. For all the reasons outlined above, I consider that the appeal should be dismissed.

Appeal dismissed.

COMMENTARY

After reading this necessarily rather long extract, does it seem to you that *Patel* is having a positive effect on the operation of the illegality defence in the negligence context? For commentary on *Henderson*, see Fisher (2021) 84 MLR 1122; Goudkamp (2021) 37 PN 171.

The decision in *Henderson* clarifies the relationship between *Patel* and *Gray* by holding (1) that *Patel* applies across private law (including in negligence), but (2) that the courts still need to consider existing precedents on illegality in the area of law concerned unless they are incompatible with *Patel*, and (3) that *Gray* is not incompatible with *Patel* and so remains good law. Furthermore, *Henderson* confirms that both the narrow and the wide versions of the illegality defence have survived *Patel*. This seems like a sensible compromise position for the Supreme Court to have taken. Sidelining *Patel* completely in the negligence context was unrealistic, but it would also have been surprising if in effect *Patel* had been held to have overruled a House of Lords decision despite not having actually criticised it in any way.

Henderson appears to be consistent with the view of one commentator expressed in the aftermath of *Patel* that the causal approach adopted in *Gray* 'will probably continue to be employed in the negligence context', perhaps with the policy-based test from *Patel* 'being used as a cross-check' (Goudkamp (2017) 133 LQR 14 at 17). However it remains to be seen whether such a cross-check will actually make a difference, or will simply amount to 'window-dressing', with the judge manipulating the policy analysis to match the outcome arrived at by applying *Gray* and the other negligence cases. And it may even be that sometimes the cross-check is dispensed with altogether, and no express consideration given to *Patel* at all, at least 'when there is a directly applicable prior authority as to the effect of the illegality principle on claims of the relevant kind' (Fisher, *op. cit.*, at 1126). According to Fisher, *op. cit.*, at 1128:

> In essence, the *Henderson* court concluded that *Gray* and *Patel* were not in tension since their reasoning operates at different levels of abstraction: while *Patel* confirms a policy-balancing enquiry as the appropriate conceptual *model* for resolving private law claims arising out of illegal acts, *Gray* exemplifies the *application* of such a model to a particular species of claim (ie those in which the defendant's negligence induced the claimant's crime).

In the light of Lord Toulson's emphasis on the need to preserve the integrity of the legal system, *Patel* as interpreted in *Henderson* is in any case unlikely to make much of a difference in situations falling within the narrow version of the defence, especially now that the Supreme Court has authoritatively rejected Lord Phillips' suggested exception for cases where the claimant does not bear significant personal responsibility for the crime (see V.1) (this despite the apparent tension between ruling out consideration of the claimant's degree of responsibility and 'an instrumentalist enquiry holistically attentive to the moral implications of a successful or unsuccessful claim, which is what *Patel* expressly demands': Fisher, *op. cit.*, at 1130). As for the wide version of the defence, how will the courts approach the task of reconciling the *Patel* approach with the focus in *Gray* on the causal link between the illegality and the damage or loss for which the claimant is seeking compensation? In *Henderson* Lord Hamblen went out of his way to emphasise the significance of 'causal' analysis of the kind apparently endorsed in *Gray* when applying *Patel* in tort cases. According to his Lordship, when assessing the impact of Lord Toulson's first consideration the court should look at the closeness of the connection between the claim and the illegal act—which we have seen is the key to the *Gray* approach in 'wide version' cases—and when it comes to Lord Toulson's third consideration, the closeness of the connection between the illegality and the claim would again 'often be an important consideration' (at [124]). It can be argued, therefore, that while paying lip service to *Patel*, *Henderson* maintains the focus on the seriousness of the illegality and the closeness of the link between the illegality and the alleged tort which has characterised the operation of the illegality defence in negligence cases since *Gray*. As Fisher, *op. cit.*, notes, in this respect *Henderson* is but one example of decisions that have 'diluted the disruptive potential of *Patel*' by reasoning primarily on the basis of earlier cases on the type of claim in question, rather than by the 'direct first-order policy reasoning' that *Patel* appears to require. For other examples in the tort context, see *Gujra v Roath* [2018] 1 WLR 3208; *Clark v Farley* [2018] PIQR P15; and *Wallett v Vickers* [2019] PIQR P6 (where Males J remarked at [56] that it was common ground that the *Patel* policy analysis should not be employed where 'criminal joint enterprise is the decisive issue').

On the same day that it delivered its judgment in *Henderson* the Supreme Court also handed down *Grondona v Stoffel & Co* [2021] AC 540, a decision on the application of the illegality defence in the professional negligence context. The claimant was a party to a fraudulent mortgage arrangement whereby she used her good credit history to enable a third party ('M') indirectly to obtain finance from a high street lender which would not have lent to him directly. The claimant's solicitors had negligently failed to register the transfer of the property in question to the claimant, as a result of which M remained the registered owner. The solicitors argued that the claimant could not recover the losses she had suffered as a result of their negligence because of her involvement in the mortgage fraud. After going through the trio of considerations set out in *Patel*, Lord Lloyd-Jones (with whom the other Justices agreed) rejected that argument. As to the first consideration, mortgage fraud was a serious crime, but his Lordship doubted whether permitting the claim would significantly undermine the deterrence of such conduct, and nor would denying it assist the lender, whose position would probably be better protected were the claimant permitted to recover. On the second consideration, denying the claim would be inconsistent with the policy that victims of professional negligence should be compensated for their loss and 'would be a disincentive to the diligent performance by solicitors of their duties' (at [35]). Furthermore, since an equitable interest in the property had passed to the claimant despite the illegality, it would be incoherent for the law to then bar a claim against a third party in respect of its failure to protect that interest on the ground of that same illegality. (Note that the first two of these 'policies' amount to little more than general justifications for tort liability in this type of case, and that variations on them would therefore potentially apply in any tort claim.) Bearing in mind the analysis of the first two considerations, it was unnecessary to consider proportionality, but in any case the negligence claim was 'conceptually entirely separate' from the fraud, so that the link between the claim and the illegality was weak (at [43]). It followed that the claim would not produce 'an incoherent contradiction damaging to the integrity of the legal system' (at [46]), and so should be allowed to proceed. More generally, Lord Lloyd-Jones made it clear that the significance of the 'trio of considerations' lay simply in their 'bearing on determining whether to allow a claim would damage the integrity of the law by permitting incoherent contradictions' (at [26]). It followed: (1) that the evaluation of those considerations should not be a 'mechanistic process'; (2) that although the court should identify the policies to which the criminal law gave effect, this was simply to ascertain whether allowing the claim would be inconsistent with those policies or, where the policies were in tension, where the overall balance lay; and (3) that it might not be necessary in every case 'to complete an exhaustive examination of all stages of the trio of considerations', so that, for example, if it was clear from the policy assessment that the defence should not be applied then there would be no need to go on to consider proportionality (*ibid.*). His Lordship also observed that while the assessment of the first two considerations should be 'at a relatively high level of generality', when assessing proportionality the court would have to 'give close scrutiny to the detail of the case in hand' (*ibid.*).

The decision in *Grondona* suggests that it may be difficult to establish the illegality defence in a professional negligence case. It also shows, we would argue, how easy it is for a court to manipulate the policy analysis required by *Patel* to achieve the desired outcome. According to Lord Lloyd-Jones, allowing claims of this kind was unlikely to undermine the policy of deterring mortgage fraud, since the risk of a fraudster being left without a remedy should their solicitor be negligent was 'most unlikely to feature in their thinking' (at [29]). And yet apparently barring such claims on illegality grounds would disincentivise solicitors from taking care when instructed in mortgage transactions, even though (a) presumably any reputable solicitor would be unaware of the fraud and hence of the inability of the client to sue in the event of their negligence and (b) in a case like *Grondona*, where the solicitor was also acting for the lender, the lender might itself have a negligence claim against them (see at [31]). And why is it that—when it comes to the first consideration—denying tort claims is unlikely to deter mortgage fraud but may well have 'some deterrent effect' on those contemplating unlawful homicide (*Henderson* at [131])? Does the doctrine of illegality loom larger in the thinking of potential killers than in the thinking of potential fraudsters? (See O'Sullivan [2021] CLJ 215 at 219–20.)

In a scathing commentary on *Henderson* and *Grondona*, the barrister who acted for the defendant in *Grondona* is highly critical of what he sees as being the inconsistent application of public policy in the two cases, and questions how one would compare the personal culpability of someone who deliberately engaged in a substantial mortgage fraud with the claimant in *Henderson*, whose 'level of personal culpability, both criminal and moral, was at the lowest possible level' (Pooles (2021) 37 PN 165 at 169). He concludes his analysis of the current state of the law of illegality on a pessimistic note (at 170):

> I would suggest that the difficulty of predicting the outcome of public policy-based decision-making is likely to precipitate a new body of authority. In [*Bilta (UK) Ltd v Nazir* [2016] AC 1 at [61]] Lord Mance reflected that, 'by the end of the 20th century it [the defence of illegality] had become encrusted with an incoherent mass of inconsistent authority'. I would suggest that over the next few years it is probable that a new body of crust will develop.

4. The Rationale of the Illegality Defence

Much reliance was placed in the judgments in *Patel v Mirza* on the analysis of McLachlin J in *Hall v Hebert* [1993] 2 SCR 159, a case involving a road traffic accident where both the plaintiff and defendant had been drinking and driving the vehicle. The Supreme Court of Canada held that the illegality relating to the drink-driving did not bar the claim. In McLachlin J's view, the defence of illegality rested on the need to preserve the integrity of the legal system. Accordingly, a plaintiff should not obtain relief which would enable them to profit from a wrong or evade the criminal consequences of their action. However, compensatory damages arose from the *defendant*'s wrong, not the plaintiff's wrongful conduct, so to allow recovery would not permit a plaintiff to profit from their own turpitude (although some heads of damage might be irrecoverable, e.g. loss of future earnings as a burglar: see *Burns v Edman* [1970] 2 QB 541). (For academic endorsement of this approach, see Goudkamp, 'Can Tort Law be Used to Deflect the Impact of Criminal Sanctions? The Role of the Illegality Defence' (2006) 14 TLJ 20, and for an extra-judicial reaffirmation of it by McLachlin J (then McLachlin CJ) herself, see 'Weaving the Law's Seamless Web: Reflections on the Illegality Defence in Tort Law', in *Defences in Tort*.) The need for consistency in the law was also considered by the Law Commission in its 2001 consultation paper to be the best policy rationale for the illegality defence (*The Illegality Defence in Tort* (Law Com. No. 160, 2001) at para. 4.70):

> The policy of not allowing someone to profit or benefit from their own wrongdoing may also be seen as an example of the wider need for the law to maintain consistency. It can be argued that it would be inconsistent for the law to proscribe certain forms of conduct on the one hand but to allow someone who has committed such wrongdoing to benefit from it. This appears to us to be a parallel case to that of allowing a claimant to recover compensation for the consequences to himself or herself of his or her criminal act. Just as a person is not allowed to claim to recover the damage arising out of the criminal act that resulted in conviction and sentence, so he or she is not allowed to take any benefit from that wrongdoing. To hold otherwise would mean that in one case the law would be giving with one hand what it takes with another, in the other case it would be allowing crime to pay. Neither would promote 'consistency' in the law.

The widely divergent views received by the Law Commission in response to this consultation paper led ultimately to a second consultation paper on the application of the illegality defence in contract, trusts and tort actions (*The Illegality Defence: A Consultative Report*

(Law Com. No. 189, 2009)). In the later consultation paper, the Law Commission noted (at para. 2.15) that while there was a 'large degree of agreement' among the consultees to its original 2001 paper 'that the illegality defence helped to maintain internal consistency in the law, this was not seen to be the overriding rationale' of the defence, and that a large majority of those who responded to its earlier paper thought the defence should continue to be available to deny a claim for personal injury. Hence its final 2010 report (*The Illegality Defence*, Law Com. No. 320, 2010) did not comprehensively embrace the Canadian approach.

Instead, the Commission in its 2010 report recommended that the court should consider in each individual case whether the illegality defence could be justified on the basis of the policies underlying the defence. These included: (1) furthering the purpose of the rule which the illegal conduct has infringed; (2) consistency; (3) the claimant should not profit from their wrong; (4) deterrence; and (5) maintaining the integrity of the legal system. These were to be balanced in the circumstances of the individual case against the objective of achieving a just result, taking into account the relative merits of the parties and the proportionality of denying the claim. The Commission thought that the decision in *Gray v Thames Trains* indicated that the law was developing along these lines, such that no legislative reform was required, and the close parallels between Lord Toulson's analysis in *Patel v Mirza* and the Commission's recommended approach would appear to vindicate that conclusion.

For a comprehensive analysis of illegality in the negligence context, in which it is argued that from a corrective justice standpoint the only justification for applying the defence to deny a claim is the need to preserve the coherence of the legal system, see S. Erbacher, *Negligence and Illegality* (Oxford: Hart, 2017).

7 NEGLIGENCE: DUTY OF CARE PSYCHIATRIC ILLNESS

I. Introduction

In its Report on *Liability for Psychiatric Illness* (Law Com. No. 249, 1999), the Law Commission stated: 'The issue of liability for psychiatric illness provokes a range of strongly-held opinions' (para. 1.2). At one end of the spectrum is the view that psychiatric illness should be treated no differently from physical injury to the person, and that damages for the former should be no less extensive than the latter. At the other end is a deep scepticism about the reality of the conditions grouped together under the label of 'psychiatric illness', and about the need to provide compensation for them. Here one finds the view that 'liability for psychiatric illness should be abandoned altogether' (*ibid.*). Use of the outdated phrase 'nervous shock' to describe the injuries in question may contribute to a tendency to underestimate their gravity.

Despite initial doubts as to whether claims for harm caused by psychiatric means should be accepted at all, English law has steered a middle course between these two extreme views. An early example of judicial scepticism is *Victorian Railway Commissioners v Coultas* (1888) 13 App Cas 222, where Sir Richard Couch, delivering the judgment of the Judicial Committee of the Privy Council, pointed to the danger of admitting such claims (at 225–6):

> [I]n every case where an accident caused by negligence had given a person a serious nervous shock, there might be a claim for damages on account of mental injury. The difficulty which now often exists in cases of alleged physical injuries of determining whether they were caused by the negligent act would be greatly increased, and a wide field opened up for imaginary claims.

The Privy Council in *Coultas* held that psychiatric illness suffered by a woman when she was nearly hit by a train after being negligently allowed onto a level crossing by the gatekeeper was not a natural and reasonable result of the gatekeeper's negligence and so was too remote. This decision was, however, the subject of considerable criticism by contemporary commentators, and an Irish case from the same period took a less sceptical approach (*Bell v Great Northern Railway Co of Ireland* (1890) 26 LR Ir 428). In *Dulieu v White & Sons* [1901] 2 KB 669, another 'two-party' case in which the plaintiff was imperilled (or reasonably believed that she was) as a result of the defendant's negligence, the Divisional Court declined to follow *Coultas*. The right of such a 'primary victim' to recover damages for psychiatric illness was confirmed by the House of Lords in *Page v Smith* [1996] 1 AC 155 (extracted in II). On the *Coultas* decision, see Handford, '*Victorian Railways Commissioners v Coultas*: The Untold Story' (2021) 61 AJLH 416; and for a recent analysis of the early case law which challenges the view that it aracterised by scepticism about the reality of 'nervous shock' claims, see Goold and ly, 'Who's Afraid of Imaginary Claims? Common Misunderstandings of the Origin of the Action for Pure Psychiatric Injury in Negligence 1888-1943' (2022) 138 LQR 58.

To be contrasted with 'two-party' like *Coultas* and *Dulieu* cases are 'three-party' cases in which the claimant witnesses the injury (or threatened injury) of another person as a result of the defendant's negligence; here, the claimant may be described as a 'secondary' or 'ricochet' victim of the defendant's negligence. In these 'secondary victim' cases, concerns over floodgates and the more indirect nature of the relationship between the claimant and the defendant have caused the courts in decisions such as *Alcock v Chief Constable of South Yorkshire* [1992] 1 AC 310 to restrict liability by imposing a number of 'proximity requirements' which the claimant must satisfy in order to establish a duty of care. In the discussion that follows we look first at claims by primary victims (or 'participants'), then claims by secondary victims (or 'witnesses'), and then claims that do not fit into these two categories, before evaluating the current law and considering proposals for reform.

An important preliminary point about the law in this area is that to recover in negligence for mental harm, the claimant must establish that they are suffering from a recognised psychiatric illness, and not mere emotions such as grief, distress or anxiety (see, e.g., *Hinz v Berry* [1970] 2 QB 40 at 42–3, per Lord Denning MR). In recent decades, many of the psychiatric illness cases that have come before the courts have involved a condition known as post-traumatic stress disorder (PTSD), but the courts are prepared to allow claims in respect of any condition that is medically recognised. At least to a (non-medical) lay-person, the distinction between illness and emotion may sometimes seem rather fine, as perhaps with the distinction between pathological grief disorder and 'mere' grief (see *Vernon v Bosley* [1997] 1 All ER 577 at 610; Hedley, 'Nervous Shock: Wider Still and Wider?' [1997] CLJ 254). The difficulty of drawing such lines (along with other considerations) have led some commentators to question the law's current insistence on a recognised psychiatric condition. According to Rachel Mulheron, for example, a lower threshold of 'grievous mental harm' should be adopted ('Rewriting the requirement for a "recognized psychiatric injury" in negligence claims' (2012) 32 OJLS 77), while Orr ('Speaking with different voices: the problems with English law and psychiatric injury' (2016) 36 LS 547) is also critical of the extent to which the law in this area relies on medical tests of psychiatric illness, and argues that the courts should develop their own diagnostic guidelines. Nevertheless, the requirement of a recognised psychiatric illness applies in Australia, New Zealand (*van Soest v Residual Health Management Unit* [2000] 1 NZLR 179, though note the strong dissent of Thomas J) and Singapore (*Man Mohan Singh v Zurich Insurance (Singapore) Pte Ltd* [2008] 3 SLR(R) 735), although not in Canada, as confirmed by the Supreme Court in *Saadati v Moorhead* [2017] 1 SCR 543, where the plaintiff recovered damages for psychological injuries (including personality change and cognitive difficulties), even though it had not been demonstrated by expert evidence that he was suffering from a medically recognised psychiatric illness. For critical comment on *Saadati*, see Hafeez-Baig and English (2017) 25 Tort L Rev 92.

Where *physical* harm (e.g. a heart attack or miscarriage) is caused by psychiatric means, there is of course no need to show a recognised psychiatric illness. But such cases are still governed by the special duty of care rules that are discussed in this chapter; indeed, it is often overlooked that almost all of the early 'nervous shock' cases did not concern psychiatric illness, but rather the physical *sequelae* of trauma, such as miscarriages (see Goold and Kelly, *op. cit.*, 61–4.) An instructive modern case in this regard is *Donachie v Chief Constable of Greater Manchester* [2004] EWCA Civ 405. The claimant was a police officer who was required to fix a tagging device to the underside of a suspect's car in the course of a covert operation. Because the batteries were faulty, he had to make a total of nine trips to the vehicle before the device functioned, and he feared each time that he might be discovered and physically attacked. As a result of the extreme stress that this put him under, he suffered a stroke. Although his claim was for the physical disabilities caused by the stroke, the Court of Appeal applied the legal rules set down in the 'nervous shock' cases, holding that the claimant was entitled to recover as a primary victim because there had been a reasonable foreseeability of physical injury.

A second preliminary point is that psychiatric illness which is consequential on physical injury to the claimant's person is not subject to any special restrictions, so that if, for example, the claimant is badly hurt in a car accident which is the defendant's fault, and they suffer post-traumatic stress disorder as a result, then they can seek damages for that as part of their personal injury claim. It seems that this principle extends to psychiatric illness which is consequential on damage to the claimant's property, with the result that in such a case the claimant need not establish a standalone duty of care in respect of psychiatric injury, but can rely instead on the duty not negligently to damage the property. The relevant decision is *Attia v British Gas* [1988] QB 304, where the claimant suffered psychiatric illness after coming home to find that gas board employees, whilst attempting to install central heating, had caused an explosion and set the building on fire. According to the Court of Appeal, psychiatric injury caused by damage to the claimant's property was recoverable provided it was a reasonably foreseeable consequence of the property damage, and hence not too remote. (See also *Yearworth v North Bristol NHS Trust* [2010] QB 1, where, however, liability rested on bailment principles; and the Australian case of *Campbelltown City Council v Mackay* (1989) 15 NSWLR 501.) Note, however, that for this analysis to work, the property that is damaged must belong to the claimant, as the claim for damages for psychiatric harm is piggy-backing on the property damage claim, like a claim for consequential economic loss (see Ch. 8.I.1). It follows that where the claimant suffers post-traumatic stress disorder after seeing their *own* dog run over and killed, recovery is based on foreseeability alone, whereas if the dog belonged to the claimants' parents then the claimant would need to establish that the defendant owed them an independent duty of care in respect of psychiatric injury (which is extremely unlikely in the light of the restrictions discussed in this chapter).

The combination of the relatively generous treatment of consequential mental harm—and in particular the extension of the relevant principles to mental harm caused by damage to the claimant's property—and the relatively restrictive approach taken to claims by 'secondary victims' (see later) may lead to some odd results. Suppose, for example, that the claimant spent years restoring a vintage sports car, and that their aunt then went for a drive in it. Were another driver to cause a crash in which the vintage car was destroyed and the owner's aunt killed, it might be the case that the owner could recover damages for mental harm caused by the damage to their car but not for mental harm caused by the death of their aunt. Do you think that would be a justifiable outcome?

II. Primary Victims or Participants

In *Alcock v Chief Constable of South Yorkshire* [1992] 1 AC 310, Lord Oliver distinguished cases where the plaintiff merely witnessed the traumatic event from those where 'the injured plaintiff was involved, either mediately or immediately, as a participant' in the traumatic event (at 407).

While in the former case additional proximity requirements would need to be met for a duty of care to be established, in the case of a participant the duty of care owed to the plaintiff was often 'self-evident'. In subsequent case law, the language of 'participants' changed to 'primary victims', and although neither term is entirely clear in its meaning, they certainly include persons who are physically imperilled by the defendant's negligence and suffer psychiatric illness as a result. Liability in such circumstances was accepted as early as *Dulieu v White & Sons* [1901] 2 KB 669, and it was confirmed in *Page v Smith*, extracted shortly.

In *Alcock*, Lord Oliver identified two other types of participant, namely rescuers and innocent agents of traumatic events (at 408):

> It is well established that the defendant owes a duty of care not only to those who are directly threatened or injured by his careless acts but also to those who, as a result, are induced to go to their rescue and suffer injury in so doing. The fact that the injury suffered is psychiatric and is caused by the impact on the mind of becoming involved in personal danger or in scenes of horror and destruction makes no difference. 'Danger invites rescue. The cry of distress is the summons to relief . . . the act, whether impulsive or deliberate, is the child of the occasion' (see *Wagner v International Rly Co* (1921) 232 NY 176 at 180–181 per Cardozo J) . . .
>
> These are all cases where the plaintiff has, to a greater or lesser degree, been personally involved in the incident out of which the action arises, either through the direct threat of bodily injury to himself or in coming to the aid of others injured or threatened. Into the same category, I believe, fall those cases such as *Dooley v Cammell Laird & Co Ltd* [1951] 1 Lloyd's Rep 271, *Galt v British Railways Board* (1983) 133 NLJ 870 and *Wigg v British Railways Board* (1986) 136 NLJ 446 where the negligent act of the defendant has put the plaintiff in the position of being, or of thinking that he is about to be or has been, the involuntary cause of another's death or injury and the illness complained of stems from the shock to the plaintiff of the consciousness of this supposed fact. The fact that the defendant's negligent conduct has foreseeably put the plaintiff in the position of being an unwilling participant in the event establishes of itself a sufficiently proximate relationship between them and the principal question is whether, in the circumstances, injury of that type to that plaintiff was or was not reasonably foreseeable.

The position of rescuers was considered in the second case extracted here, *White v Chief Constable of South Yorkshire Police*, along with the question of whether those who, in the course of employment, attend a disaster caused by the negligence of their employer also fall within the special class of participants. The status of unwitting agents of another's death, injury or imperilment remains to be definitively resolved by the courts.

Page v Smith [1996] 1 AC 155

The case arose out of a car crash of moderate severity. The plaintiff was driving with due care when, suddenly and without warning, the defendant, coming in the opposite direction, turned into his path. The impact caused some physical damage to the cars but none to the occupants. Three hours later, however, the plaintiff felt exhausted and took to his bed. The exhaustion continued and the plaintiff never fully recovered. At the time of the appeal, despite the lapse of almost eight years, the plaintiff had not yet returned to work. The diagnosis was the recrudescence of a condition known as myalgic encephalomyelitis (ME), from a mild form of which the plaintiff had suffered sporadically in the past; this now became an illness of chronic intensity and permanency. At first instance, he was awarded damages of over £160,000, but the defendant's appeal to the Court of Appeal was allowed, primarily on the basis that it had not been reasonably foreseeable that a person of normal fortitude would have suffered psychiatric injury. The plaintiff appealed to the House of Lords.

Lord Lloyd

This is the fourth occasion on which the House has been called on to consider 'nervous shock'. On the three previous occasions, *Bourhill v Young* [1943] AC 92, *McLoughlin v O'Brian* [1983] 1 AC 410 and *Alcock v Chief Constable of the South Yorkshire Police* [1992] 1 AC 310, the plaintiffs were, in each case, outside the range of foreseeable physical injury. . . .

In all these cases the plaintiff was the secondary victim of the defendant's negligence. He or she was in the position of a spectator or bystander. In the present case, by contrast, the plaintiff was a participant. He was himself directly involved in the accident, and well within the range of foreseeable physical injury. He was the primary victim. This is thus the first occasion on which your Lordships have had to decide whether, in such a case, the foreseeability of physical injury is enough to enable the plaintiff to recover damages for nervous shock.

The factual distinction between primary and secondary victims of an accident is obvious and of long-standing. It was recognised by Lord Russell in *Bourhill v Young*, when he pointed out that Mrs Bourhill was not physically involved in the collision. In *Alcock* [1992] 1 AC 310 at 396 Lord Keith of Kinkel said that in the type of case which was then before the House, injury by psychiatric illness 'is a secondary sort of injury brought about by the infliction of physical injury, or the risk of physical injury, upon another person'. In the same case Lord Oliver of Aylmerton said of cases in which damages are claimed for nervous shock (at 407):

> Broadly they divide into two categories, that is to say those cases in which the injured plaintiff was involved, either mediately or immediately, as a participant, and those in which the plaintiff was no more than the passive and unwilling witness of injury caused to others.

Later in the same speech, he referred to those who are involved in an accident as the primary victims, and to those who are not directly involved, but who suffer from what they see or hear, as the secondary victims (see [1992] 1 AC 310 at 410–11). This is, in my opinion, the most convenient and appropriate terminology.

Though the distinction between primary and secondary victims is a factual one, it has, as will be seen, important legal consequences . . .

Foreseeability of psychiatric injury remains a crucial ingredient when the plaintiff is the secondary victim, for the very reason that the secondary victim is almost always outside the area of physical impact, and therefore outside the range of foreseeable physical injury. But where the plaintiff is the primary victim of the defendant's negligence, the nervous shock cases, by which I mean the cases following on from *Bourhill v Young*, are not in point. Since the defendant was admittedly under a duty of care not to cause the plaintiff foreseeable physical injury, it was unnecessary to ask whether he was under a separate duty of care not to cause foreseeable psychiatric injury. . . .

It may be said that . . . [this approach] would open the door too wide, and encourage bogus claims. As for opening the door, this is a very important consideration in claims by secondary victims. It is for this reason that the courts have, as a matter of policy, rightly insisted on a number of control mechanisms. Otherwise, a negligent defendant might find himself being made liable to all the world. Thus in the case of secondary victims, foreseeability of injury by shock is not enough. The law also requires a degree of proximity: see *Alcock* [1992] 1 AC 310 at 396 per Lord Keith, and the illuminating judgment of Stuart-Smith LJ in *McFarlane v E. E. Caledonia Ltd* [1994] 2 All ER 1 at 14. This means not only proximity to the event in time and space, but also proximity of relationship between the primary victim and the secondary victim. A further control mechanism is that the secondary victim will only recover damages for nervous shock if the defendant should have foreseen injury by shock to a person of normal fortitude or 'ordinary phlegm'.

None of these mechanisms are required in the case of a primary victim. Since liability depends on foreseeability of physical injury, there could be no question of the defendant finding himself liable to all the world. Proximity of relationship cannot arise, and proximity in time and space goes without saying.

Nor in the case of a primary victim is it appropriate to ask whether he is a person of 'ordinary phlegm'. In the case of physical injury there is no such requirement. The negligent defendant, or more usually his insurer, takes his victim as he finds him. The same should apply in the case of psychiatric injury. There is no difference in principle . . . between an eggshell skull and an eggshell personality. Since the number of potential claimants is limited by the nature of the case, there is no need to impose any further limit by reference to a person of ordinary phlegm. Nor can I see any justification for doing so.

As for bogus claims, it is sometimes said that if the law were such as I believe it to be, the plaintiff would be able to recover damages for a fright. This is not so. Shock by itself is not the subject of compensation, any more than fear or grief or any other human emotion occasioned by the defendant's negligent conduct. It is only when shock is followed by recognisable psychiatric illness that the defendant may be held liable.

There is another limiting factor. Before a defendant can be held liable for psychiatric injury suffered by a primary victim, he must at least have foreseen the risk of physical injury. So that if . . . the defendant bumped his neighbour's car while parking in the street, in circumstances in which he could not reasonably foresee that the occupant would suffer any physical injury at all, or suffer injury so trivial as not to found an action in tort, there could be no question of his being held liable for the onset of hysteria. Since he could not reasonably foresee any injury, physical or psychiatric, he would owe the plaintiff no duty of care. That example is, however, very far removed from the present.

So I do not foresee any great increase in unmeritorious claims. The court will, as ever, have to be vigilant to discern genuine shock resulting in recognised psychiatric illness. But there is nothing new in that. The floodgates argument has made regular appearances in this field, ever since it first appeared in *Victorian Railways Comrs v Coultas* (1888) 13 App Cas 222. I do not regard it as a serious obstacle here.

My provisional conclusion, therefore, is that . . . [t]he test in every case ought to be whether the defendant can reasonably foresee that his conduct will expose the plaintiff to risk of personal injury. . . .

In the case of a primary victim the question will almost always turn on whether the foreseeable injury is physical. But it is the same test in both cases, with different applications. There is no justification for regarding physical and psychiatric injury as different 'kinds' of injury. Once it is established that the defendant is under a duty of care to avoid causing personal injury to the plaintiff, it matters not whether the injury in fact sustained is physical, psychiatric or both. . . .

Applying that test in the present case, it was enough to ask whether the defendant should have reasonably foreseen that the plaintiff might suffer physical injury as a result of the defendant's negligence, so as to bring him within the range of the defendant's duty of care. It was unnecessary to ask, as a separate question, whether the defendant should reasonably have foreseen injury by shock; and it is irrelevant that the plaintiff did not, in fact, suffer any external physical injury . . . . It is no answer that the plaintiff was predisposed to psychiatric illness. Nor is it relevant that the illness takes a rare form or is of unusual severity. The defendant must take his victim as he finds him. . . .

Lord Ackner and **Lord Browne-Wilkinson** delivered separate speeches concurring with Lord Lloyd. **Lord Keith** and **Lord Jauncey** dissented.

Appeal allowed.

COMMENTARY

The House of Lords remitted the case to the Court of Appeal to determine the question of causation. The Court of Appeal found for the plaintiff on this issue in *Page v Smith (No. 2)* [1996] 3 All ER 272.

Primary and Secondary Victims

The distinction between primary and secondary victims was said by the Law Commission in its report on *Psychiatric Illness* to be 'more of a hindrance than a help' (para. 5.51). It noted that there was 'confusing inconsistency' as to how the line should be drawn (para. 5.45). In *W v Essex County Council* [2001] 2 AC 592 at 601, Lord Slynn commented: 'the categorisation of those claiming to be included as primary or secondary victims is not as I read the cases finally closed. It is a concept still to be developed in different factual situations.' In our view, such statements risk increasing the confusion. Furthermore, if the category of primary victims is enlarged, this may well undermine the proximity requirements currently applied in secondary victim cases. Even if one favours reforming the law on secondary victims, this is not the best way of going about it.

For the sake of clarity, we shall use the term 'primary victim' to denote persons who are physically harmed or imperilled by the defendant's negligence, but it should also be borne in mind that other types of 'participant' (i.e. rescuers and 'involuntary participants') may to some extent be relieved of the burden of satisfying the proximity requirements applicable to secondary victims.

How Wide is the Zone of Danger?

In *Page v Smith*, Lord Lloyd appeared confident that there was no problem of 'opening the door too wide' in respect of claims by primary victims. But it is possible to imagine incidents in which a very large number of people are traumatised by a fear of physical injury, for example where a disabled airplane limps over a city before finally crashing into a block of flats (see Trindade (1996) 112 LQR 22 at 24). Are all those who think even momentarily that the plane might come down on them to be regarded as primary victims? Unless the zone of danger is defined narrowly in such cases, there would seem to be the risk of a very large number of claims arising out of a single incident. It is therefore possible that in such a case the courts will use their hindsight as to what in fact happened—specifically, which building the plane actually hit—to limit the class of those who were foreseeably at risk. Note, however, that the test is one of foreseeability of physical injury as a result of the defendant's negligence, as opposed to foreseeability of injury as a result of an incident that that negligence brings about, so it is unclear how the use of hindsight can be justified. See further, Bailey and Nolan, 'The *Page v Smith* Saga: A Tale of Inauspicious Origins and Unintended Consequences' [2010] CLJ 495 at 514–15.

Reasonable Fear not Enough

In *McFarlane v E.E. Caledonia Ltd* [1994] 2 All ER 1, the Court of Appeal accepted that a plaintiff could recover for nervous shock caused by a reasonable fear of death or physical injury even if not in fact imperilled. According to Stuart-Smith LJ, the class of participant extended beyond the plaintiff who 'is in the actual area of danger created by the event, but escapes physical injury by chance or good fortune' and embraced 'the plaintiff [who] is not actually in danger, but because of the sudden and unexpected nature of the event . . . reasonably thinks that he is'. But it was still necessary, as in all primary victim cases, to show that the defendant ought reasonably to have foreseen that a person in the position of the plaintiff might be killed or suffer physical injury (or might fear such consequences).

McFarlane arose out of the Piper Alpha fire disaster. The plaintiff had been employed as a painter on an oil rig in the North Sea owned and operated by the defendants. One night when the plaintiff was off duty and lying on his bunk on a support vessel some 550 metres away, a series of massive explosions occurred on the rig. Over the next hour and three-quarters the plaintiff witnessed the explosions and consequent destruction of the rig before he was evacuated by helicopter. The explosions and fire caused the deaths of 164 men. The closest the plaintiff came to the fire was 100 metres when the support vessel moved in towards the rig in an attempt to fight the fire and render assistance. He claimed damages for psychiatric illness suffered as a result of the events he had witnessed. On the trial of a preliminary issue whether the defendants owed the plaintiff a duty to exercise reasonable care to avoid causing him psychiatric injury, the judge held, inter alia, that the plaintiff was owed such a duty, on the ground that he was a participant in the event who had been reasonably in fear for his life and safety and that his injury had resulted from the shock caused by his fear. The defendants' appeal was allowed on the basis that, even if the plaintiff had been reasonably albeit mistakenly in fear of his safety, this did not establish that this was something which the defendants ought reasonably to have foreseen. In any case, the court held that it was not established on the facts that the plaintiff had really been in fear for his own safety.

Primary Victims: Must the Harm be Caused by Fear?

It is natural to assume that the language of primary victims refers to cases where a claimant reasonably fears that they are going to be killed or injured and suffers psychiatric illness *as a result of that fear*—in *Dulieu v White & Sons* [1901] 2 KB 669 at 675, for example, Kennedy J referred to 'a shock which arises from a reasonable fear of personal injury to oneself'. However, in *Page* the focus appeared to be on whether the claimant was in fact foreseeably imperilled by the negligent conduct (as opposed to whether this triggered the psychiatric illness), and subsequent decisions have indeed proceeded on the basis that the claimant need only prove they were *actually* within the area of foreseeable physical risk, irrespective of whether the claimant was aware of this at the time or suffered psychiatric illness as a result of that awareness.

Young v Charles Church (1997) 39 BMLR 146 was a case arising out of the fatal electrocution of the plaintiff's workmate as a result of the defendant employer's negligence. While the plaintiff's back was turned, the deceased touched an overhead electric cable with a scaffolding pole and was electrocuted, dying instantly. On hearing a loud bang and hissing sound, the plaintiff immediately turned around and saw that his workmate had been killed and that the surrounding ground had burst into flames. He ran 600 yards to the security office to summon help and returned to the scene of the accident to wait for the arrival of an ambulance. As a result of what he saw and heard he suffered psychiatric injury and he claimed damages from the defendant as a primary victim. The Court of Appeal found the defendant liable for two alternative reasons: (1) the plaintiff was within the area of physical danger and (2) a special duty was owed to him by virtue of the employment context (no longer tenable: see the extract that follows). As regards the former basis for the decision, it is important to note that the plaintiff seems to have suffered psychiatric injury not as a result of any fear for his physical safety but as a result of witnessing the aftermath of a horrific accident in which his workmate was killed. In our opinion dispensing in this way with the requirement that the psychiatric illness should result from a fear for one's own physical safety appears to blur the distinction between primary and secondary victim cases and is likely to result in anomalies.

Criticism of *Page v Smith*

In *White v Chief Constable of South Yorkshire* [1999] 2 AC 455 at 477–80, Lord Goff (dissenting) stated that the decision in *Page v Smith* 'constituted a remarkable departure from ... generally accepted principles'. In particular, by dispensing with the requirement of foreseeability of psychiatric illness in primary victim cases, and requiring only that a primary victim establish the foreseeability of physical injury, the decision 'dethroned foreseeability of psychiatric injury from its central position as the unifying feature of this branch of the law'. Lord Goff noted academic criticism of *Page* (e.g. by Handford (1996) 4 Tort L Rev 5 and Trindade (1996) 112 LQR 22), and continued:

In summary the basic grounds of criticism appear to be threefold.

(a) There has been no previous support for any such approach, and there is authority in England and Australia to the contrary. In England, see Lord Oliver's opinion in the *Alcock* case [1992] 1 AC 310, 408 where he regarded the principle of foreseeability of psychiatric damage as applicable in cases concerned with participants, as in the case of secondary victims ...

(b) The approach favoured by Lord Lloyd appears to be inconsistent ... with ... *The Wagon Mound No. 1* [1961] AC 388 [extracted in Ch. 5.III.1] ... There a particular type of damage to property, *viz.* damage by fire, was differentiated from other types of damage to property for the purpose of deciding whether the defendant could reasonably have foreseen damage of that particular type, so as to render him liable in damages in tort for such damage. That differentiation was made on purely common sense grounds, as a matter of practical justice. On exactly the same grounds, a particular type of personal injury, *viz.* psychiatric injury, may, for the like purpose, properly be differentiated from other types of personal injury. It appears to be in no way inconsistent with the making of that common sense judgment, as a matter of practical justice, that scientific advances are revealing that psychiatric illnesses may have a physical base, or that psychiatric injury should be regarded as another form of personal injury ...

(c) The majority in *Page v Smith* [1996] AC 155 may have misunderstood the so-called eggshell skull rule ... The maxim only applies where liability has been established. The criticism is therefore that Lord Lloyd appears to have taken an exceptional rule relating to compensation and treated it as being of general application, thereby creating a wider principle of liability.

(For further criticism of *Page v Smith*, see Bailey and Nolan, *op. cit.*)

In *Rothwell v Chemical & Insulating Co Ltd* [2008] 1 AC 281 the House of Lords referred to Lord Goff's criticisms of *Page v Smith*, but declined to rule that it was wrongly decided. Lord Hoffmann stated (at [32]):

I do not think that it would be right to depart from *Page v Smith*. It does not appear to have caused any practical difficulties and is not, I think, likely to do so if confined to the kind of situation which the majority in that case had in mind. That was a foreseeable event (a collision) which, viewed in prospect, was such as might cause physical injury or psychiatric injury or both. Where such an event has in fact happened and caused psychiatric injury, the House decided that it is unnecessary to ask whether it was foreseeable that what actually happened would have that consequence. Either form of injury is recoverable.

By contrast, Lord Hope (at [52]) and Lord Mance (at [104]) expressly reserved their opinion on the correctness of the decision in *Page v Smith*, the latter seeing some force in the argument that it caused uncertainty, argument and artificiality. On the facts, however, it was not necessarily to decide on the matter because the present case was considered distinguishable. One of the claimants in *Rothwell* had suffered clinical depression in consequence of his becoming aware that he was at future risk of suffering mesothelioma or some other asbestos-related illness as a result of his negligent exposure to asbestos dust in the workplace in the 1960s. In 2000, an X-ray showed that he had developed pleural plaques around his lungs. Pleural plaques do not themselves constitute actionable damage (as the Law Lords ruled in the other appeals heard in *Rothwell*), nor do they lead to any asbestos-related conditions, but they do signal the presence in the lungs of asbestos fibres which may independently cause life-threatening or fatal diseases, and it was this knowledge that had triggered the claimant's psychiatric illness. His claim against his former employers failed, despite the fact that physical harm (asbestos-related disease) had been a foreseeable consequence of the negligence, with the result that he appeared to be a 'primary victim' applying *Page*. Various reasons were put forward by their Lordships for this conclusion, some of which are hard to fathom, but the most readily comprehensible of which was Lord Hope's assertion (at [54]) that the primary victim category 'should be confined to persons who suffer psychiatric injury caused by fear or distress resulting from involvement in an accident caused by the defendant's negligence or its immediate aftermath'. For comment and analysis see Jones (2008) 24 PN 13; Leczykiewicz (2008) 124 LQR 548; Steele [2008] CLJ 28 and Turton (2008) 71 MLR 1009.

White v Chief Constable of South Yorkshire [1999] 2 AC 455

A number of police officers sued the chief constable of their force (their de facto employer), in respect of post-traumatic stress disorder suffered in the aftermath of the Hillsborough football stadium disaster. Three of the officers had been on duty at the stadium at the time. One of these had attempted to help free spectators who were trapped in the overcrowded pens and two of them had attended a makeshift morgue set up at the ground. Two other officers had been drafted in to help in the aftermath at the ground. All five officers had witnessed chaotic and gruesome scenes. A sixth officer had not been on duty at the ground and had acted as liaison officer between the hospital staff and the casualty bureau; she had also dealt with relatives and later went to the temporary morgue at the ground with personal effects. The chief constable admitted that the disaster had been caused by negligence for which he was vicariously responsible and had accepted liability towards other officers more directly concerned in the events of the disaster, but denied that he owed any duty of care to the officers bringing the claim. Having failed at first instance, five of the officers appealed to the Court of Appeal which held that four of them were entitled to succeed either on the basis that they had encountered exceptionally horrific scenes in the course of their employment or that they were rescuers, but that no duty had been owed to the liaison officer. The court considered that the fact that police officers might be described as professional rescuers was not relevant to the outcome of the appeal. The chief constable appealed to the House of Lords.

Lord Hoffmann

[T]he plaintiffs draw two distinctions between their position and that of spectators or bystanders. The first is that they had a relationship analogous to employment with the Chief Constable. Although constitutionally a constable holds an office rather than being employed, there is no dispute that his Chief Constable owes him the same duty of care which he would to an employee. The plaintiffs say that they were therefore owed a special duty which required the Chief Constable and those for whom he was vicariously liable to take reasonable care not to expose them to unnecessary risk of injury, whether physical or psychiatric. Secondly, the plaintiffs (and in this respect there is no difference between the police and many others in the crowd that day) did more than stand by and look. They actively rendered assistance and should be equated to 'rescuers', who, it was said, always qualify as primary victims.

[His Lordship considered the first point of distinction and rejected it as irrelevant. He continued:]

The second way in which the plaintiffs put their case is that they were not 'bystanders or spectators' but participants in the sense that they actually did things to help. They submit that there is an analogy between their position and that of a 'rescuer', who, on the basis of the decision of Waller J in *Chadwick v British Railways Board* [1967] 1 WLR 912, is said to be treated as a primary victim, exempt from the control mechanisms [applicable to secondary victims] . . .

There is no authority which decides that a rescuer is in any special position in relation to liability for psychiatric injury. And it is no criticism of the excellent judgment of Waller J in *Chadwick v British Railways Board* [1967] 1 WLR 912 to say that such a question obviously never entered his head. Questions of such nicety did not arise until the *Alcock* control mechanisms had been enunciated.

There does not seem to me to be any logical reason why the normal treatment of rescuers on the issues of foreseeability and causation should lead to the conclusion that, for the purpose of liability for psychiatric injury, they should be given special treatment as primary victims when they were not within the range of foreseeable physical injury and their psychiatric injury was caused by witnessing or participating in the aftermath of accidents which caused death or injury to others . . .

Should then your Lordships take the incremental step of extending liability for psychiatric injury to 'rescuers' (a class which would now require definition) who give assistance at or after some disaster without coming within the range of foreseeable physical injury? It may be said that this would encourage people to offer assistance. The category of secondary victims would be confined to 'spectators and bystanders' who take no part in dealing with the incident or its aftermath. On the authorities, as it seems to me, your Lordships are free to take such a step.

In my opinion there are two reasons why your Lordships should not do so. The less important reason is the definitional problem to which I have alluded. The concept of a rescuer as someone who puts himself in danger of physical injury is easy to understand. But once this notion is extended to include others who give assistance, the line between them and bystanders becomes difficult to draw with any precision. For example, one of the plaintiffs in *Alcock*, a Mr O'Dell, went to look for his nephew. 'He searched among the bodies . . . and assisted those who staggered out from the terraces.' (See [1992] 1 AC 310 at 354.) He did not contend that his case was different from those of the other relatives and it was also dismissed. Should he have put himself forward as a rescuer?

But the more important reason for not extending the law is that in my opinion the result would be quite unacceptable. I have used this word on a number of occasions and the time has come to explain what I mean. I do not mean that the burden of claims would be too great for the insurance market or the public funds, the two main sources for the payment of damages in tort. The Law Commission may have had this in mind when they said that removal of all the control mechanism would lead to an 'unacceptable' increase in claims, since they described it as a 'floodgates' argument. These are questions on which it is difficult to offer any concrete evidence and I am simply not in a position to form a view one way or the other. I am therefore willing to accept that, viewed against the total sums paid as damages for personal injury the increase resulting from an extension of liability to helpers would be modest. But I think that such an extension would be unacceptable to the ordinary person because (though he might not put it this way) it would offend against his notions of distributive justice. He would think it unfair between one class of claimants and another, at best not treating like cases alike and, at worst, favouring the less deserving against the more deserving. He would think it wrong that policemen, even as part of a general class of persons who rendered assistance, should have the right to compensation for psychiatric injury out of public funds while the bereaved relatives are sent away with nothing . . .

It may be said that the common law should not pay attention to these feelings about the relative merits of different classes of claimants. It should stick to principle and not concern itself with distributive justice. An extension of liability to rescuers and helpers would be a modest incremental development in the common law tradition and, as between these plaintiffs and these defendants, produce a just result. My Lords, I disagree. It seems to me that in this area of the law, the search for principle was called off in *Alcock v Chief Constable of South Yorkshire* [1992] 1 AC 310. No one can pretend that the existing law, which your Lordships have to accept, is founded upon principle. I agree with Jane Stapleton's remark (see P. Birks (ed.), *The Frontiers of Liability*, OUP, 1994, vol. 2, p. 87) that:

> once the law has taken a wrong turning or otherwise fallen into an unsatisfactory internal state in relation to a particular cause of action, incrementalism cannot provide the answer.

Consequently your Lordships are now engaged, not in the bold development of principle, but in a practical attempt, under adverse conditions, to preserve the general perception of the law as a system of rules which is fair between one citizen and another . . .

Naturally I feel great sympathy for the plaintiffs' claims, as I do for all those whose lives were blighted by that day at Hillsborough. But I think that fairness demands that your Lordships should reject them. . . . I would therefore allow these appeals and dismiss the actions.

Lord Griffiths (dissenting on the 'rescuer' question)

What rescuer ever thinks of his own safety? It seems to me that it would be a very artificial and unnecessary control, to say a rescuer can only recover if he was in fact in physical danger. A danger to which he probably never gave thought, and which in the event might not cause physical injury. . . . I do not share the view that the public would find it in some way offensive that those who suffered disabling psychiatric illness as a result of their efforts to rescue the victims should receive compensation, but that those who suffered the grief of bereavement should not. Bereavement and grief are a part of the common condition of mankind which we will all endure at some time in our lives. It can be an appalling experience but it is different in kind from psychiatric illness and the law has never recognized it as a head of damage. We are human and we must accept as a part of the price of our humanity the suffering of bereavement for which no sum of money can provide solace or comfort. I think better of my fellow men than to believe that they would, although bereaved, look like dogs in the manger upon those who went to the rescue at Hillsborough.

Lord Steyn gave a separate speech concurring with Lord Hoffmann. **Lord Browne-Wilkinson** agreed with Lord Steyn and Lord Hoffmann. **Lord Goff** dissented (on both the 'employee' and the 'rescuer' questions).

Appeal allowed.

COMMENTARY

A majority of the House of Lords held that as regards liability for psychiatric illness no distinctive duty is owed to a person simply by virtue of their employment relationship with the defendant or their status as a rescuer. As the plaintiffs in this case were not themselves physically endangered by the events at Hillsborough, it followed that their claims had to fail. Do you think that the decision leaves the law in a satisfactory state?

On the employment issue, all except Lord Goff were agreed that it was irrelevant that the defendant happened to be (in effect) the officers' employer. According to Lord Steyn (at 497):

> It is a non sequitur to say that because an employee is under a duty of care to an employee not to cause him physical injury, the employee should as a necessary consequence of that duty . . . be under a duty not to cause the employee psychiatric injury.

Lord Hoffmann agreed. The liability of an employer to his employees for negligence was not a separate tort with separate rules, but merely 'an aspect of the general law of negligence' (at 505). It followed that the restrictions on recovery for psychiatric illness could not be bypassed simply because there was an employment relationship between the parties. In our view, this aspect of the decision in *White* is to be welcomed. The employment argument was contrary to principle, and its acceptance would have produced anomalies. Why should the mere fact that their colleagues happened to be responsible for the disaster have meant that traumatised police officers could recover, while others similarly involved, such as paramedics or firefighters, could not?

Rescuers

In *Chadwick v British Railways Board* [1967] 1 WLR 912, an action was brought by the plaintiff as personal representative of her late husband in respect of injuries to him which she alleged were caused by the Lewisham train disaster in 1957. Two trains collided in foggy conditions as a result of the admitted negligence of the defendants. Ninety people were killed. The accident happened at 6 pm, some 200 yards from the Chadwicks' house. Mr Chadwick immediately ran out of the house to help. Mrs Chadwick did not see him again until 3 am, when he came in, covered with mud, with blood on his hands. He went out again and did not return until 6 am. He would not go to bed and he was upset and shaking. It was alleged that, whereas before the accident he was a cheerful busy man carrying on a window-cleaning business and with many spare-time activities, the shock of his experiences that night made him psychoneurotic, and he no longer took the interest in life which he had taken and was unable to work for a considerable time. He required hospital treatment for approximately six months. Waller J held that the defendants owed the deceased a duty of care as a foreseeable victim of their negligence and awarded damages for lost wages and for misery and discomfort arising from his diminished enjoyment of life and for his periods of treatment in hospital. In *White*, Lord Steyn distinguished *Chadwick* (at 499) on the basis of an observation by the judge that there had been 'an element of personal danger' in the rescue work performed by Mr Chadwick. His Lordship therefore interpreted the case as authority for recovery by rescuers only when they were in danger during the course of the rescue or reasonably believed that they were (albeit that, as with other 'primary victims', the shock need not be caused by the perception of danger).

White was applied in *Cullin v London Fire & Civil Defence Authority* [1999] PIQR P314, where the claimants were firefighters who suffered psychiatric injury after attending fires at which colleagues of theirs had been killed. The defendant's argument that their claims should be struck out on the ground that their trauma did not result from fear for their own safety was rejected by the Court of Appeal. It was enough that the claimants had been at physical risk while fighting the fires, even if it was not this that had caused their trauma.

An alternative way of arriving at the same result in *White* would have been to hold that *professional* rescuers cannot recover for nervous shock, as Waller J had done at first instance. Admittedly, the House had rejected this so-called 'fireman's rule' (which applies in many American states) in *Ogwo v Taylor* [1988] AC 431, but the injury there was physical and, in the light of the more restrictive approach taken to recovery for psychiatric illness generally, the application of the rule in this context could be justified. Nevertheless, Lord Hoffmann considered that barring claims because the claimant's occupation required them to run the risk of such injury 'would be too great an affront to the idealised model of the law of torts as a system of corrective justice between equals' (at 511). Do you agree?

Unwitting Agents of Misfortune

Another category of possible 'participants' was identified by Lord Oliver in *Alcock* (at 408) as follows:

> The negligent act of the defendant has put the plaintiff in the position of being, or of thinking that he is about to be or has been, the involuntary cause of another's death or injury and the illness complained of stems from the shock to the plaintiff of the consciousness of this supposed fact.

The leading authority on this 'involuntary participant' or 'unwitting agent' category is *Dooley v Cammell Laird & Co Ltd* [1951] 1 Lloyd's Rep 271. The plaintiff, a crane operator in a dockyard, suffered an aggravation of his pre-existing neurasthenia when the rope carrying his load suddenly broke as a result of the defendants' negligence and the load fell into the hold of the ship which he was loading. Although he could not see if the load had hit anybody—and nobody was in fact injured—he felt so wretched afterwards that he was unable to return to work as a crane operator. Donovan J ruled that he was entitled to damages. (Cf. *Monk v PC Harrington Ltd* [2009] PIQR P3, where it was held that there was no reasonable basis for the claimant's belief that he was responsible for the accident that triggered his psychiatric illness and so it was not reasonably foreseeable that someone in his position would suffer psychiatric injury as a result of such a belief.)

Dooley was distinguished in *Hunter v British Coal* [1999] QB 140, where it was held that in this category of case the secondary victim requirement of proximity in time and space (see III) still applies. As a result of the defendants' negligence in failing to maintain the prescribed minimum vehicle clearances, the plaintiff struck a water hydrant whilst manoeuvring his vehicle in a coal mine, causing water to flow out. Having been unable to close up the hydrant valve, he went off in search of a hosepipe to channel the escaping water safely away, leaving a fellow employee, C, at the scene. When he was 30 metres away from the scene, the hydrant burst and he rushed to find a stop valve to shut the water off, which he managed to do after about ten minutes. While doing this, he heard a message over the tannoy that a man had been injured and, on his way back to the scene of the accident, he met a workmate who told him that it looked as if C was dead. The plaintiff immediately felt that he was responsible and as a result he suffered clinical depression, for which he sought damages. The Court of Appeal (Hobhouse LJ dissenting) held that he was not entitled to damages as he had not been present at the scene of the second accident or come upon its aftermath; he had reacted only to what he was told. The fact that he had been involved in the circumstances leading up to that accident and that his illness had been triggered by guilt about what had happened did not entitle him to bypass the requirement of proximity in time and space applicable in secondary victim cases.

As a result of the *Hunter* decision it is difficult to know how an 'unwitting agent' should be classified, as, like rescuers, this type of claimant does not fall neatly into either the 'primary victim' or 'secondary victim' categories. Indeed, the restrictive approach taken towards rescuers in *White* and the limiting effect of *Hunter* cast doubt on whether the 'unwitting agent' category would survive at all. Nevertheless, the special status of such claimants was upheld in *W v Essex County Council* [2001] 2 AC 592, where the claimants had fostered a 15-year-old boy placed with them by the defendant local authority. After the boy had arrived at their home, he sexually abused the claimant's own children, with the result that the claimants suffered psychiatric illness, and they sued the defendant on the ground that it had known that the boy was an abuser. Refusing to strike out the claim, Lord Slynn said that it was arguable that the parents were 'involuntary participants' because they had brought the boy into their home, and blamed themselves for not detecting the abuse earlier.

III. Secondary Victims or Witnesses

In *Dulieu v White*, Kennedy J stated in an obiter dictum that liability for psychiatric illness was limited by a requirement that there 'must be a shock which arises from a reasonable fear of personal injury to oneself' (at 675). If accepted, this would have altogether precluded liability to someone who merely witnessed, or reasonably feared, the death or injury of another person. However, Kennedy J's dictum was rejected by a majority of the Court of Appeal in *Hambrook v Stokes Bros* [1925] 1 KB 141. In that case, the defendants were held liable for a fatal 'nervous shock' suffered by a woman who watched as a runaway lorry careered down a hill towards the spot—just out of her view—where she knew her children to be, and who was almost immediately informed that a child answering the description of one of hers had been injured. Atkin LJ dismissed the supposed limitation on liability established in the earlier case in the following terms (at 157; see also Bankes LJ at 151):

> It would result in a state of the law in which a mother, shocked by fright for herself, would recover, while a mother shocked by her child being killed before her eyes, could not, and in which a mother traversing the highway with a child in her arms could recover if shocked by fright for herself, while if she could be cross-examined into an admission that the fright was really for her child, she could not. In my opinion such distinctions would be discreditable to any system of jurisprudence in which they formed part.

Although the possibility of a duty of care to a mere witness was established in *Hambrook*, the precise circumstances in which it would arise were not fully specified. A number of questions remained unanswered. Would the duty arise when the witness had no relationship with the person injured or imperilled? If not, what sort of relationship was required? Did it make any difference if the psychiatric illness arose not from the direct perception of a traumatic event, but from being told about it later? Initially, these and other questions were subsumed under an all-embracing test of foreseeability. In *Bourhill v Young* (extracted in Ch. 3.II.2), the House of Lords rejected a claim by a woman who suffered nervous shock (allegedly causing her to miscarry) as a result of an accident in which the defendant motorcyclist was killed. Although she heard the accident occur, and came immediately to the scene, she was not related to the deceased. On those facts, it was held that it had not been reasonably foreseeable that a person of normal fortitude would suffer nervous shock. Following *Bourhill*, claims by witnesses for nervous shock were determined by reference to whether such injury had been foreseeable on the facts. In theory, this was a relatively liberal approach, which mirrored the position in physical injury cases, although in practice recovery was still quite limited, owing to the tendency of the courts to apply the test quite strictly on the facts (as in *Bourhill* itself), and because of the assumption of 'ordinary fortitude', which meant that a claimant who suffered psychiatric illness only because they were particularly susceptible to it could not recover unless the defendant was aware of the susceptibility (which was of course unlikely in an accident case).

More recently, however, the courts have adopted an explicitly more restrictive approach and sought to limit liability for psychiatric illness suffered by witnesses by making the existence of a duty of care depend not only on the foreseeability of psychiatric illness (proof of which remains a precondition of liability) but also on the satisfaction of various additional requirements of proximity.

McLoughlin v O'Brian [1983] 1 AC 410

The plaintiff, Mrs McLoughlin, suffered nervous shock after a car crash in which her husband and three of her children were seriously injured, the injuries to one of her children proving fatal. The plaintiff was at home some two miles away at the time the accident happened, but news of the accident was communicated to her by a friend an hour or so afterwards. She was driven to the hospital to which her loved ones had been taken and arrived there approximately two hours after the accident. At the hospital she witnessed scenes which the House of Lords accepted were 'distressing in the extreme' (at 417, per Lord Wilberforce): she saw her children cut and bruised, and begrimed with dirt and oil, and she heard their sobs and screams; while she was with them, her son lapsed into unconsciousness. For the purposes of determining the question of legal liability, it was assumed that she had suffered what was described as severe shock, organic depression and a change of personality as a consequence of these experiences. Her claim for damages against the defendant, who was to blame for the accident, was rejected at trial and by the Court of Appeal. She appealed to the House of Lords.

Lord Wilberforce stated that the foreseeability of nervous shock was not enough to establish liability and went on to consider the policy arguments against the extension of liability to meet the facts of the present case:

First, it may be said that such extension may lead to a proliferation of claims, and possibly fraudulent claims, to the establishment of an industry of lawyers and psychiatrists who will formulate a claim for nervous shock damages, including what in America is called the customary miscarriage, for all, or many, road accidents and industrial accidents. Second, it may be claimed that an extension of liability would be unfair to defendants, as imposing damages out of proportion to the negligent conduct complained of. In so far as such defendants are insured, a large additional burden will be placed on insurers, and ultimately on the class of persons insured: road users or employers. Third, to extend liability beyond the most direct and plain cases would greatly increase evidentiary difficulties and tend to lengthen litigation. Fourth, it may be said (and the Court of Appeal agreed with this) that an extension of the scope of liability ought only to be made by the legislature, after careful research. . . .

[S]ome of the arguments are susceptible of answer. Fraudulent claims can be contained by the courts, which, also, can cope with evidentiary difficulties. The scarcity of cases which have occurred in the past, and the modest sums recovered, give some indication that fears of a flood of litigation may be exaggerated: experience in other fields suggests that such fears usually are. If some increase does occur, that may only reveal the existence of a genuine social need . . .

But, these discounts accepted, there remains, in my opinion, just because 'shock' in its nature is capable of affecting so wide a range of people, a real need for the law to place some limitation on the extent of admissible claims. It is necessary to consider three elements inherent in any claim: the class of persons whose claims should be recognised; the proximity of such persons to the accident; and the means by which the shock is caused. As regards the class of persons, the possible range is between the closest of family ties, of parent and child, or husband and wife, and the ordinary bystander. Existing law recognises the claims of the first; it denies that of the second, either on the basis that such persons must be assumed to be possessed of fortitude sufficient to enable them to endure the calamities of modern life or that defendants cannot be expected to compensate the world at large. In my opinion, these positions are justifiable, and since the present case falls within the first class it is strictly unnecessary to say more.

I think, however, that it should follow that other cases involving less close relationships must be very carefully scrutinised. I cannot say that they should never be admitted. The closer the tie (not merely in relationship, but in care) the greater the claim for consideration. The claim, in any case, has to be judged in the light of the other factors, such as proximity to the scene in time and place, and the nature of the accident.

As regards proximity to the accident, it is obvious that this must be close in both time and space. It is after all, the fact and consequence of the defendant's negligence that must be proved to have caused the 'nervous shock'. Experience has shown that to insist on direct and immediate sight or hearing would be impractical and unjust and that under what may be called the 'aftermath' doctrine, one who, from close proximity comes very soon on the scene, should not be excluded. . . . The High Court of Australia's majority decision in *Chester v Waverley Municipal Council* (1939) 62 CLR 1, where a child's body was found floating in a trench after a prolonged search, may perhaps be placed on the other side of a recognisable line (Evatt J in a powerful dissent placed it on the same side). . . .

Finally, and by way of reinforcement of 'aftermath' cases, I would accept, by analogy with 'rescue' situations, that a person of whom it could be said that one could expect nothing else than that he or she would come immediately to the scene (normally a parent or a spouse) could be regarded as being within the scope of foresight and duty. Where there is not immediate presence, account must be taken of the possibility of alterations in the circumstances, for which the defendant should not be responsible.

Subject only to these qualifications, I think that a strict test of proximity by sight or hearing should be applied by the courts.

Lastly, as regards communication, there is no case in which the law has compensated shock brought about by communication by a third party. In *Hambrook v Stokes Bros* [1925] 1 KB 141, indeed, it was said that liability would not arise in such a case, and this is surely right. . . . The shock must come through sight or hearing of the event or of its immediate aftermath. Whether some equivalent of sight or hearing, e.g. through simultaneous television, would suffice may have to be considered.

My Lords, I believe that these indications, imperfectly sketched, and certainly to be applied with common sense to individual situations in their entirety, represent either the existing law, or the existing law with only such circumstantial extension as the common law process may legitimately make. They do not introduce a new principle. Nor do I see any reason why the law should retreat behind the lines already drawn. I find on this appeal that the appellant's case falls within the boundaries of the law so drawn. I would allow her appeal.

Lord Bridge

In approaching the question whether the law should, as a matter of policy, define the criterion of liability in negligence for causing psychiatric illness by reference to some test other than that of reasonable foreseeability it is well to remember that we are concerned only with the question of liability of a defendant who is, *ex hypothesi*, guilty of fault in causing the death, injury or danger which has in turn triggered the psychiatric illness. A policy which is to be relied on to narrow the scope of the negligent tortfeasor's duty must be justified by cogent and readily intelligible considerations, and must be capable of defining the appropriate limits of liability by reference to factors which are not purely arbitrary. A number of policy considerations which have been suggested as satisfying these requirements appear to me, with respect, to be wholly insufficient. I can see no grounds whatever for suggesting that to make the defendant liable for reasonably foreseeable psychiatric illness caused by his negligence would be to impose a crushing burden on him out of proportion to his moral responsibility. However liberally the criterion of reasonable foreseeability is interpreted, both the number of successful claims in this field and the quantum of damages they will attract are likely to be moderate.

I cannot accept as relevant the well-known phenomenon that litigation may delay recovery from a psychiatric illness. If this were a valid policy consideration, it would lead to the conclusion that psychiatric illness should be excluded altogether from the heads of damage which the law will recognise. It cannot justify limiting the cases in which damages will be awarded for psychiatric illness by reference to the circumstances of its causation. To attempt to draw a line at the furthest point which any of the decided cases happen to have reached, and to say that it is for the legislature, not the courts, to extend the limits of liability any further, would be, to my mind, an unwarranted abdication of the court's function of developing and adapting principles of the common law to changing conditions, in a particular corner of the common law which exemplifies, par excellence, the important and indeed necessary part which that function has to play. In the end I believe that the policy question depends on weighing against each other two conflicting considerations. On the one hand, if the criterion of liability is to be reasonable foreseeability simpliciter, this must, precisely because questions of causation in psychiatric medicine give rise to difficulty and uncertainty, introduce an element of uncertainty into the law and open the way to a number of arguable claims which a more precisely fixed criterion of liability would exclude. I accept that the element of uncertainty is an important factor. I believe that the 'floodgates' argument, however, is, as it always has been, greatly exaggerated. On the other hand, it seems to me inescapable that any attempt to define the limit of liability by requiring, in addition to reasonable foreseeability, that the plaintiff claiming damages for psychiatric illness should have witnessed the relevant accident, should have been present at or near the place where it happened, should have come upon its aftermath and thus have had some direct perception of it, as opposed to merely learning of it after the event, should be related in some particular degree to the accident victim—to draw a line by reference to any of these criteria must impose a largely arbitrary limit of liability. . . .

My Lords, I have no doubt that this is an area of the law of negligence where we should resist the temptation to try yet once more to freeze the law in a rigid posture which would deny justice to some who, in the application of the classic principles of negligence derived from *Donoghue v Stevenson* [1932] AC 562, ought to succeed, in the interests of certainty, where the very subject matter is uncertain and continuously developing, or in the interests of saving defendants and their insurers from the burden of having sometimes to resist doubtful claims.

Lord Edmund-Davies, **Lord Russell of Killowen** and **Lord Scarman** delivered separate concurring speeches.

Appeal allowed.

COMMENTARY

This was the first of four decisions in which the House of Lords developed the modern approach to nervous shock claims (see also *Page* and *White*, discussed earlier, and *Alcock*, extracted next). Perhaps inevitably, *McLoughlin* left certain issues unresolved. Amongst these was the fundamental question of whether the courts should adopt a restrictive or expansive approach to liability for psychiatric illness. Although Lord Wilberforce was circumspect in setting out the precise criteria that had to be satisfied before a claim would be allowed, other members of the House of Lords (notably Lord Bridge and Lord Scarman) seemed to adopt a broader approach, following Lord Wilberforce's own 'two-stage' test for the existence of a duty of care set out in *Anns v Merton London Borough* [1978] AC 728, under which the reasonable foreseeability of psychiatric injury was on its own sufficient to give rise to a prima facie duty of care. (Ironically, this was clearly not Lord Wilberforce's own approach in *McLoughlin*, perhaps indicating that his two-stage test in *Anns* had been misinterpreted by other members of the House: see further Ch. 3.II.3). The ambiguities arising out of the competing approaches in *McLoughlin* were resolved in the next extracted case.

Alcock v Chief Constable of South Yorkshire [1992] 1 AC 310

This was a test case brought by friends and relatives of some of the victims of the Hillsborough football stadium disaster, in which ninety-seven people were killed and hundreds injured in a crush at the Leppings Lane end of the ground during the 1989 FA Cup semi-final match between Liverpool and Nottingham Forest. The case brought together a number of claims identified as representative of the various legal issues raised by the group of claims as a whole. For the purposes of the test case, it was presumed that the plaintiffs had suffered post-traumatic stress disorder as a result of their experiences. Various relationships with the victims were represented, including parent/child, brothers and fiancés. The selected plaintiffs were also situated in different locations at the time of the accident (some in the ground itself, some outside, some at home in Liverpool) and the experiences they had undergone also varied (some had witnessed the events unfold from elsewhere in the stadium, some had seen live or recorded television coverage, some had identified bodies in the makeshift mortuary erected at the ground). The defendant chief constable admitted that the disaster had been caused by the negligence of his officers, but argued that no duty of care had been owed to the plaintiffs. The case eventually reached the House of Lords, where the plaintiffs appealed against the Court of Appeal's ruling in favour of the defendant.

Lord Keith

It was argued for the appellants in the present case that reasonable foreseeability of the risk of injury to them in the particular form of psychiatric illness was all that was required to bring home liability to the respondent. In the ordinary case of direct physical injury suffered in an accident at work or elsewhere, reasonable foreseeability of the risk is indeed the only test that need be applied to determine liability. But injury by psychiatric illness is more subtle, as Lord Macmillan observed in *Bourhill v Young* [1943] AC 92 at 103. In the present type of case it is a secondary sort of injury brought about by the infliction of physical injury, or the risk of physical injury, upon another person. That can affect those closely connected with that person in various ways. One way is by subjecting a close relative to the stress and strain of caring for the injured person over a prolonged period, but psychiatric illness due to such stress and strain has not so far been treated as founding a claim in damages. So I am of the opinion that in addition to reasonable foreseeability liability for injury in the particular form of psychiatric illness must depend in addition upon a requisite relationship of proximity between the claimant and the party said to owe the duty. Lord Atkin in *M'Alister (or Donoghue) v Stevenson* [1932] AC 562 at 580, described those to whom a duty of care is owed as being—

> persons who are so closely and directly affected by my act that I ought reasonably to have them in contemplation as being so affected when I am directing my mind to the acts or omissions which are called in question.

The concept of a person being closely and directly affected has been conveniently labelled 'proximity', and this concept has been applied in certain categories of cases, particularly those concerned with pure economic loss, to limit and control the consequences as regards liability which would follow if reasonable foreseeability were the sole criterion.

As regards the class of persons to whom a duty may be owed to take reasonable care to avoid inflicting psychiatric illness through nervous shock sustained by reason of physical injury or peril to another, I think it sufficient that reasonable foreseeability should be the guide. I would not seek to limit the class by reference to particular relationships such as husband and wife or parent and child. The kinds of relationship which may involve close ties of love and affection are numerous, and it is the existence of such ties which leads to mental disturbance when the loved one suffers a catastrophe. They may be present in family relationships or those of close friendship, and may be stronger in the case of engaged couples than in that of persons who have been married to each other for many years. It is common knowledge that such ties exist, and reasonably foreseeable that those bound by them may in certain circumstances be at real risk of psychiatric illness if the loved one is injured or put in peril. The closeness of the tie would, however, require to be proved by a plaintiff, though no doubt being capable of being presumed in appropriate cases. The case of a bystander unconnected with the victims of an accident is difficult. Psychiatric injury to him would not ordinarily, in my view, be within the range of reasonable foreseeability, but could not perhaps be entirely excluded from it if the circumstances of a catastrophe occurring very close to him were particularly horrific.

In the case of those within the sphere of reasonable foreseeability the proximity factors mentioned by Lord Wilberforce in *McLoughlin v O'Brian* [1983] 1 AC 410 at 422, must, however, be taken into account in judging whether a duty of care exists. The first of these is proximity of the plaintiff to the accident in time and space. For this purpose the accident is to be taken to include its immediate aftermath, which in *McLoughlin*'s case was held to cover the scene at the hospital which was experienced by the plaintiff some two hours after the accident. . . .

As regards the means by which the shock is suffered, Lord Wilberforce said in *McLoughlin*'s case [1983] 1 AC 410 at 423 that it must come through sight or hearing of the event or of its immediate aftermath. He also said that it was surely right that the law should not compensate shock brought about by communication by a third party. . . .

Of the present appellants two, Brian Harrison and Robert Alcock, were present at the Hillsborough ground, both of them in the West Stand, from which they witnessed the scenes in [Leppings Lane] pens 3 and 4. Brian Harrison lost two brothers, while Robert Alcock lost a brother-in-law and identified the body at the mortuary at midnight. In neither of these cases was there any evidence of particularly close ties of love or affection with the brothers or brother-in-law. In my opinion the mere fact of the particular relationship was insufficient to place the plaintiff within the class of persons to whom a duty of care could be owed by the defendant as being foreseeably at risk of psychiatric illness by reason of injury or peril to the individuals concerned.

The same is true of other plaintiffs who were not present at the ground and who lost brothers, in one case a grandson. I would, however, place in the category of members to which risk of psychiatric illness was reasonably foreseeable Mr and Mrs Copoc, whose son was killed, and Alexandra Penk, who lost her fiancé. In each of these cases the closest ties of love and affection fall to be presumed from the fact of the particular relationship, and there is no suggestion of anything which might tend to rebut that presumption. These three all watched scenes from Hillsborough on television, but none of these depicted suffering of recognisable individuals, such being excluded by the broadcasting code of ethics, a position known to the defendant. In my opinion the viewing of these scenes cannot be equiparated with the viewer being within 'sight or hearing of the event or of its immediate aftermath', to use the words of Lord Wilberforce in *McLoughlin v O'Brian* [1983] 1 AC 410 at 423, nor can the scenes reasonably be regarded as giving rise to shock, in the sense of a sudden assault on the nervous system. They were capable of giving rise to anxiety for the safety of relatives known or believed to be present in the area affected by the crush, and undoubtedly did so, but that is very different from seeing the fate of the relative or his condition shortly after the event. The viewing of the television scenes did not create the necessary degree of proximity.

My Lords, for these reasons I would dismiss each of these appeals.

Lord Ackner

[W]hile it may be very difficult to envisage a case of a stranger, who is not actively and foreseeably involved in a disaster or its aftermath, other than in the role of rescuer, suffering shock-induced psychiatric injury by the mere observation of apprehended or actual injury of a third person in circumstances that could be considered reasonably foreseeable, I see no reason in principle why he should not, if in the circumstances, a reasonably strong-nerved person would have been so shocked. In the course of argument your Lordships were given, by way of an example, that of a petrol tanker careering out of control into a school in session and bursting into flames. I would not be prepared to rule out a potential claim by a passer-by so shocked by the scene as to suffer psychiatric illness. . . .

Although the television pictures certainly gave rise to feelings of the deepest anxiety and distress, in the circumstances of this case the simultaneous television broadcasts of what occurred cannot be equated with the 'sight or hearing of the event or its immediate aftermath'. Accordingly shocks sustained by reason of these broadcasts cannot found a claim. I agree, however, with Nolan LJ [in the Court of Appeal] that simultaneous broadcasts of a disaster cannot in all cases be ruled out as providing the equivalent of the actual sight or hearing of the event or its immediate aftermath. Nolan LJ gave an example of a situation where it was reasonable to anticipate that the television cameras, whilst filming and transmitting pictures of a special event of children travelling in a balloon, in which there was media interest, particularly amongst the parents, showed the balloon suddenly bursting into flames (see [1991] 3 All ER 88 at 122). Many other such situations could be imagined where the impact of the simultaneous television pictures would be as great, if not greater, than the actual sight of the accident. . . .

[His Lordship proceeded to consider the case of Brian Harrison, who witnessed the tragedy, in which his two brothers were killed, from his seat in the West Stand:]

The quality of brotherly love is well known to differ widely—from Cain and Abel to David and Jonathan. I assume that Mr Harrison's relationship with his brothers was not an abnormal one. His claim was not presented upon the basis that there was such a close and intimate relationship between them as gave rise to that very special bond of affection which would make his shock-induced psychiatric illness reasonably foreseeable by the chief constable.

> Accordingly, the learned judge did not carry out the requisite close scrutiny of their relationship. Thus there was no evidence to establish the necessary proximity which would make his claim reasonably foreseeable. . . .
>
> **Lord Jauncey**
>
> My Lords, what constitutes the immediate aftermath of an accident must necessarily depend upon the surrounding circumstances. To essay any comprehensive definition would be a fruitless exercise. In *McLoughlin v O'Brian* the immediate aftermath extended to a time somewhat over an hour after the accident and to the hospital in which the victims were waiting to be attended to. It appears that they were in very much the same condition as they would have been had the mother found them at the scene of the accident. In these appeals the visits to the mortuary were made no earlier than nine hours after the disaster and were made not for the purpose of rescuing or giving comfort to the victim but purely for the purpose of identification. This seems to me to be a very different situation from that in which a relative goes within a short time after an accident to rescue or comfort a victim. I consider that not only the purpose of the visits to the mortuary but also the times at which they were made take them outside the immediate aftermath of this disaster.
>
> **Lord Oliver** and **Lord Lowry** concurred.
>
> *Appeal dismissed.*

COMMENTARY

The House of Lords made it clear that it was following the approach of Lord Wilberforce in *McLoughlin*, notwithstanding hints of a broader approach in the earlier decision, especially in the speech of Lord Scarman; in *Alcock*, however, their Lordships did not accept that Lord Bridge had differed from Lord Wilberforce in any material respect. Do you agree? See further D. Nolan, '*Alcock v Chief Constable of South Yorkshire Police* (1991)' in Mitchell & Mitchell.

It is in any case evident from *Alcock* that (at least in secondary victim cases) psychiatric illness is to be dealt with more restrictively than physical injury. The House of Lords laid down a number of specific proximity requirements that must be satisfied in cases where psychiatric illness results from the experience of witnessing a traumatic event. These may be termed the requirements of proximity of relationship, proximity in time and space, and proximity of perception (described by some as the requirements of dearness, nearness and hear-ness).

Proximity of Relationship

It is first necessary for the claimant to establish 'a close tie of love and affection' with the person injured or endangered. Such a tie can in some cases be rebuttably presumed from the nature of the relationship: parent/child relationships, spousal relationships and relationships between those engaged to be married are all of this character. In the case of other relationships, the claimant must rebut the presumption that there is no close tie of love and affection similar to that generally observable in parental and spousal relationships. (Cf. the more liberal approach of the Law Commission to the relationship issue as set out in V.2.)

At first instance in *Alcock*, Hidden J had ruled that all relationships within the nuclear family, including sibling relationships, involved close ties of love and affection (see [1992] 1 AC 310 at 337–8). However, this approach was rejected by House of Lords, which took a narrower view. The quality of sibling relationships was so varied that the presumption of a close tie was not applicable in such cases. Hence no duty was owed, for instance, to Brian Harrison, who witnessed the events from inside the stadium in the knowledge that his brothers were at the Leppings Lane end. And while it had indeed been open to him to plead that his relationship with his brothers went beyond that which is normal between siblings, before the decision of the House of Lords no-one would have realised that this was a precondition of liability in such a case. It must be said that it seems rather harsh to disallow a claim for not being pleaded in a way that had not previously been suggested was necessary. In a subsequent action also arising out of the Hillsborough tragedy, when the plaintiff had the benefit of knowing what he had to prove, the court did in fact accept that he had enjoyed a close tie of love and affection with his deceased half-brother (*McCarthy v Chief Constable of South Yorkshire Police*, noted in the *Daily Telegraph*, 12 December 1996), the judge finding that their family was 'very close-knit'. Similarly, in *Shorter v Surrey and Sussex Healthcare NHS Trust* (2015) 144 BMLR 136 a relationship between sisters who were described as especially close qualified, while in *RE (A Minor) v Calderdale and Huddersfield NHS Foundation Trust* (2017) 156 BMLR 204 a claim by a grandmother was allowed. Such decisions seem to suggest that this requirement is being applied rather more generously than the speeches in *Alcock* might suggest.

This first proximity requirement does however appear to close the door on claims by mere 'bystanders' (i.e. those with no prior relationship with the person injured or imperilled), although Lord Ackner and Lord Keith were prepared to accept that there might be liability where the accident witnessed by a bystander was particularly horrific. (One wonders why the terrible scenes at Hillsborough were not considered horrific enough.) In any case, it is not clear how any 'scale of horrors' could be devised, especially given the subjective nature of reactions to such events. This practical difficulty, coupled with a fear that the resultant liability would in effect be based on nothing more than reasonable foreseeability, led the Court of Appeal to rule out bystander recovery in *McFarlane v E.E. Caledonia Ltd* [1994] 2 All ER 1 (the case arising out of the Piper Alpha fire tragedy noted in II). It has subsequently been held that a secondary victim is a 'bystander' for these purposes where they in fact had a close tie with an immediate victim but were unaware of this at the time of the traumatic event (*Young v Downey* [2020] EWHC 3457 (QB); cf. the facts of *King v Philcox* (2015) 255 CLR 304, a case decided under the South Australian Civil Liability Act 1936). For an argument in favour of the extension of liability to bystanders, see Oughton and Lowry, 'Liability to Bystanders for Negligently Inflicted Psychiatric Harm' (1995) 46 NILQ 18.

Proximity in Time and Space

In *Alcock*, Lord Oliver said that (at 416):

The necessary element of proximity between plaintiff and defendant is furnished, at least in part, by both physical and temporal propinquity and also by the sudden and direct visual impression on the plaintiff's mind of actually witnessing the event or its immediate aftermath.

In practice, this means that even if the secondary victim succeeds in establishing that they had a close tie of love and affection with the person injured or imperilled, they must also establish that they were sufficiently proximate in time and space to the event which caused the shock. This requirement will be straightforwardly satisfied where the claimant saw or heard the event with their own unaided senses, but it is clear that the claimant need not actually be at the scene of the accident at the time it occurs as long as they arrive within the 'immediate aftermath'. This was first accepted in a number of Commonwealth decisions, for example where a mother ran 100 yards from her home to see the unconscious body of her son (*Benson v Lee* [1972] VR 879) and where a man arrived home minutes after a gas explosion had killed his three children (*Fenn v City of Peterborough* (1976) 73 DLR (3d) 177). Subsequently, in *McLoughlin v O'Brian*, extracted earlier, the House of Lords held that the aftermath of an accident extended not only *temporally* forward from the accident, but also *spatially* away from the accident scene to the hospital to which the victims were taken. This development was followed by the High Court of Australia in *Jaensch v Coffey* (1984) 155 CLR 549, where Deane J observed that 'the aftermath . . . extends to the ambulance taking an injured person to hospital for treatment and to the hospital itself during the period of immediate post-accident treatment' (at 608). Query therefore whether Mrs McLoughlin would have recovered if she had arrived at the hospital after her injured husband and children had been cleaned up, operated upon and bandaged.

In *Galli-Atkinson v Seghal* [2003] Lloyd's Rep Med 285, the claimant's 16-year-old daughter was killed by a car which mounted the pavement. The claimant went looking for her, came across the police cordon at the accident scene about an hour after the accident had happened and was told that her daughter was dead. About an hour later, she and her husband went to the mortuary and saw the girl's body, which had devastating and disfiguring injuries. The court ruled that this constituted an uninterrupted sequence of events and that the accident's immediate aftermath extended to the mortuary visit, which had not been just for the purpose of identifying the body, but to 'complete the story' for the claimant, who until that point had refused to accept that the girl in the accident was her daughter. Can this decision be reconciled with the ruling in *Alcock* that the relatives who travelled to Hillsborough to search for their loved ones and subsequently identified their bodies in the temporary mortuary at the stadium were not entitled to invoke the aftermath doctrine? (Cf. *Walters v North Glamorgan NHS Trust* [2003] PIQR P16, noted later.)

In *Taylor v Novo* [2014] QB 150 (noted by Nolan (2014) 30 PN 176), the claimant was present when her mother suddenly collapsed and died due to a hidden deep vein thrombosis caused by an accident at work three weeks previously. The Court of Appeal ruled that the 'event' to which the claimant had to be proximate in time and space was the original accident, at which she had not been present, and not its consequences three weeks later. Lord Dyson MR pointed out that extending liability to such a case would mean that the claimant would potentially have been able to recover even if her mother's death had occurred months or even years after the original accident, which would stretch the concept of 'legal proximity' between the parties that Lord Oliver had emphasised in *Alcock* too far. In *Paul v Royal Wolverhampton NHS Trust* [2022] PIQR P8, the Court of Appeal considered three conjoined appeals where the claimants had suffered psychiatric injury after witnessing (or coming upon the immediate aftermath of) the sudden death of a close relative as a result of earlier clinical negligence. In the title appeal, for example, the claimants were two young sisters who had suffered mental injury after seeing their father die of a heart attack which was caused by the failure to carry out a coronary angiography when he had attended the defendant's hospital some fourteen months earlier. Sir Geoffrey Vos MR, who gave the leading judgment, considered that the proximity requirements set out in *Alcock* applied with the same force in clinical negligence cases as in traumatic accident cases. And while he accepted that, applying those requirements, the relevant 'event' in the cases under appeal could be conceptualised as the consequence of the defendant's negligence to which the secondary victim *had* been proximate in time and space (e.g. in *Paul* the father's heart attack), his Lordship considered that the court was unable to adopt this analysis in the light of its earlier decision in *Taylor v Novo*. Although he admitted to reservations about the interpretation of the *Alcock* limits in *Taylor*, that was a matter for the Supreme Court. In a separate judgment, Underhill LJ said that if the matter had been free of authority, he would have been minded to hold that the claimants should be entitled to recover. At the time of writing, an appeal of the *Paul* decision to the Supreme Court was pending.

Bearing in mind the facts of the appeals in *Paul* (and also of the childbirth cases discussed in IV), do you think that—regardless of their merits in accident cases—the *Alcock* limits are well-suited to the medical negligence context?

Proximity of Perception

Lord Oliver's observation also makes clear that the claimant must suffer psychiatric injury as a result of directly seeing (or hearing) the accident or its immediate aftermath. There can be no liability where they are merely told about the accident by a third party (*Ravenscroft v Rederiaktiebolaget Transatlantic* [1992] 2 All ER 470n). In *Palmer v Tees Health Authority* [2000] PIQR P1, the claimant sought damages for psychiatric conditions triggered by the abduction and murder of her 4-year-old daughter by a psychiatric patient whom the defendant health authority had discharged from its care. The child's body was discovered four days after her abduction, during which period the claimant had suffered from visions and nightmares; she did not see the body until some two or three days later. The Court of Appeal struck out her claim, partly on the basis that—whatever her fears and whatever she had imagined, and regardless of the fact that these fears and imaginings were subsequently shown to be justified—the claimant had not suddenly appreciated by sight or sound a horrifying event. But in *W v Essex County Council* [2001] 2 AC 592 (noted in II), a more flexible approach was taken. In that case the House of Lords declined to strike out a claim for psychiatric illness by parents whose children had been sexually abused by a foster child placed with them by the defendant local authority, even though they had not actually witnessed the abuse, but only been told of it afterwards. According to Lord Slynn (at 601):

[T]he concept of 'the immediate aftermath' of the incident has to be assessed in the particular factual situation. I am not persuaded that in a situation like the present the parents must come across the abuser or the abused 'immediately' after the sexual incident has terminated. All the incidents here happened in the period of four weeks before the parents learned of them. It might well be that if the matter were investigated in depth a judge would think that the temporal and spatial limitations were not satisfied. On the other hand he might find that the flexibility to which Lord Scarman referred [in *McLoughlin v O'Brian*] indicated that they were.

On the facts of *Alcock*, the House of Lords denied that the experience of watching the events on television was equivalent to direct perception of those events. However, Lord Ackner was prepared to accept that there might be circumstances in which the proximity requirement would be satisfied by the viewing of live television pictures, and he drew in this regard on an example that was given by Nolan LJ in the Court of Appeal ([1992] 1 AC 310 at 386–7):

I would not seek to exclude the possibility in principle of a duty of care extending to the watchers of a television programme. For example, if a publicity seeking organisation made arrangements for a party of children to go up in a balloon, and for the event to be televised so that their parents could watch, it would be hard to deny that the organisers were under a duty to avoid mental injury to the parents as well as physical injury to the children, and that there would be a breach of that duty if through some careless act or omission the balloon crashed.

What do you think distinguishes the images transmitted in this example from those transmitted from Hillsborough? And do you think it would have made any difference to the result in *Alcock* if one of the plaintiffs, while watching live television coverage of the tragic events, had been able to identify a close relative being crushed against the fencing at the Leppings Lane end, for example because the relative was wearing distinctive clothes?

A difficult and unresolved question is *how much* perception of the accident the claimant must have. In *Alcock*, would it have been enough that a man had witnessed only generalised chaos from the far end of the ground, knowing that his children were standing in the Leppings Lane pens but unaware whether they were in fact injured or imperilled? (See Mullis [1991] All ER Rev 371 at 376.) The Court of Appeal's decision in *Hambrook v Stokes Bros* [1925] 1 KB 141, where the accident occurred out of sight round a corner, suggests that a reasonable fear for the safety of a loved one is sufficient in such a case. But even if this reasoning is accepted in principle, it might be difficult to disentangle the effects of witnessing the shocking scenes from those of the grief and distress consequent upon being told subsequently that the children had in fact been injured or killed. The rule here appears to be that the 'shock' need only be *a* cause, and not necessarily the *sole* cause, of the claimant's psychiatric condition (*Vernon v Bosley* [1997] 1 All ER 577), although arguably in awarding damages the court should endeavour, where possible, to disentangle the effect of the shock from that of the other causes of the claimant's illness (see analogously *Hatton v Sutherland* [2002] 2 All ER 1, as discussed in Ch. 5.I.2(b)).

For an argument that the *Alcock* approach to broadcast images is not suited to our contemporary world of unregulated transmission of extreme events via social media, see Chatterjee, 'Rethinking *Alcock* in the New Media Age' (2016) 7 JETL 272.

The 'Shock' Requirement

In *Alcock*, the House of Lords emphasised the requirement that psychiatric illness should be induced by shock, which Lord Ackner described as 'the sudden appreciation by sight or sound of a horrifying event, which violently agitates the mind' ([1992] 1 AC 310 at 400). Psychiatric illness 'caused in other ways . . . attracts no damages' (*ibid.*). His Lordship gave as examples of claims that would be barred by this requirement depression arising from the experience of living without a loved one and stress-related illness arising from the wayward conduct of a brain-damaged child or the strain of caring for an injured spouse (citing Brennan J in *Jaensch v Coffey* (1984) 155 CLR 549 at 569).

In *Sion v Hampstead Health Authority* [1994] 5 Med LR 170, the Court of Appeal entertained an allegation of stress-related illness suffered by a father who had mounted a two-week-long vigil at the hospital bedside of his dying son. The court declined to hold that the defendant health authority had owed the father a duty of care as on the facts pleaded his illness had not been caused by a single shocking event (see also *Taylorson v Shieldness Produce Ltd* [1994] PIQR P329). *Sion* can be contrasted with *Walters v North Glamorgan NHS Trust* [2003] PIQR P16, where the Court of Appeal ruled that a thirty-six-hour period beginning when the claimant's son suffered an epileptic fit and ending when he died in her arms was a single horrifying event. *Walters* was itself distinguished in *Ronayne v Liverpool Women's Hospital NHS Foundation Trust* [2015] PIQR P20, where the claimant was distressed by seeing his extremely ill wife twice in a period of twenty-four hours, before and after emergency surgery necessitated by a negligently performed hysterectomy some ten days earlier. The Court of Appeal ruled that this was not a single event as the two hospital visits were part of a much longer sequence and were in any case interrupted by the claimant's return home between them. The court also ruled that the scenes the claimant witnessed were not 'horrifying' by objective standards: his wife's appearance was as would ordinarily be expected of a person in hospital in her circumstances and was not 'exceptional'. (See also *Shorter v Surrey and Sussex Healthcare NHS Trust* (2015) 144 BMLR 136.)

The shock requirement is a particularly controversial limit on recovery for psychiatric harm, and has been widely criticised. The principal argument in favour of the requirement—though not one clearly articulated by the courts—seems to be that it provides the necessary demonstration of a clear causal connection between the negligence of the defendant and the psychiatric injury (since, e.g., in a long-term care case, there could be other things that cause or contribute to the depression). However, most commentators are not convinced, and in its report the Law Commission recommended that the limit be abolished: *Liability for Psychiatric Illness* (Law Com. No. 249, 1999), paras 5.31–33. In *Tame v New South Wales* (2002) 211 CLR 317, that step was taken by the High Court of Australia. According to Gummow and Kirby JJ, the shock requirement had no root in principle, and so was arbitrary and inconsistent in its application, and the difficulties of causation and remoteness raised by protracted suffering cases should be dealt with by the relevant principles and not by denial of a duty of care. Their Honours also highlighted the difficulty of drawing a line between sudden shock and more protracted suffering, a point that would seem to be borne out by the recent English case law on the requirement, and the increasingly contrived search for a triggering 'event'. The requirement was nevertheless defended by the government in its response to the Law Commission's report, on the basis (1) that it ensured that the causal link between negligence and illness was satisfied, and that without it cases would become more complex and more costly; and (2) that without it there would be no finality for the defendant, as there would always be the possibility of claims arising a long time after the accident (Department for Constitutional Affairs, *The Law on Damages* (2007), ch. 3). Do you find these arguments convincing?

In any case, claims by primary victims need not satisfy the shock requirement (a point confirmed in *YAH v Medway NHS Foundation Trust* [2019] 1 WLR 1413) and nor does it apply in stress cases of the kind discussed in IV. See further on the requirement, Teff, 'The Requirement of "Sudden Shock" in Liability for Negligently Inflicted Psychiatric Damage' (1996) 4 Tort L Rev 44; and Burrows and Burrows, 'A Shocking Requirement in the Law of Negligence Liability for Psychiatric Illness' (2016) 24 Med L Rev 278.

Claims Against the Immediate Victim

In *Greatorex v Greatorex* [2000] 1 WLR 1970, the defendant was injured in a road accident caused by his own careless driving. It just so happened that his father was one of the fire officers who attended the scene, and who helped extricate him from the car in which he was trapped. He then sued his son for damages for the post-traumatic stress disorder he sustained as a result (knowing, of course, that any award would be covered by his son's insurance). Although the claimant satisfied the *Alcock* control mechanisms for secondary victims because he had a close tie of love and affection with his son and had arrived at the scene in the immediate aftermath of the accident, his claim failed. Adopting a view that had provisionally appealed to Lord Oliver in *Alcock* (at 418), Cazelet J ruled that a defendant who imperilled or injured themselves owed no duty of care to a person who suffered psychiatric injury as a result. In his view, the policy arguments in favour of a duty of care were outweighed by those that ran against it. He identified the two main considerations leading him to that conclusion in the following passage (at 1984–6):

> [T]he issue which I have to resolve raises, as it seems to me, a question which impinges upon a person's right of self-determination. . . . Both counsel maintain that self-harming, whether by

negligence or deliberately, would not be expected to give rise to any criminal liability. . . . There is, of course, a duty not to cause foreseeable physical injury to another in such circumstances, but in my judgment to extend that duty so as to bring within its compass purely psychiatric injury would indeed be to create a significant further limitation upon an individual's freedom of action. That seems to me to be a powerful objection to the imposition of such a duty. . . .

Home life may involve many instances of a family member causing himself injury through his own fault. Should the law allow one family member, B, to sue another family member, A, or his estate in respect of psychiatric illness suffered as a result of B either having been present when the injury was sustained or having come upon A in his injured state? . . . To allow a cause of action in this type of situation is to open up the possibility of a particularly undesirable type of litigation within the family, involving questions of relative fault as between its members. . . . I appreciate, of course, that one member of the family may already sue another family member in respect of physical injury caused by that other, so that in cases of physical injury there is already the potential for personal injury litigation within the family; but the fact that family members have the same right as others to make a claim for physical injury does not necessarily mean that they should have the right to make a claim for a different kind of harm in respect of which, because of the first *Alcock* control mechanism, others have no such right. Further, where a family member suffers psychiatric harm as a result of the self-inflicted injuries of another family member, the psychiatric illness in itself may well have an adverse effect upon family relationships which the law should be astute not to exacerbate by allowing litigation between those family members. In my judgment, to permit a cause of action for purely psychiatric injury in these circumstances would be potentially productive of acute family strife.

Do you find these arguments convincing? Note that Cazalet J's second argument seems to assume that in a case of this kind the person bringing the claim will necessarily be in a close relationship with the immediate victim, but that this is not true: such a claim could be brought by an 'involuntary participant' (see, e.g., *FAI General Insurance Co Ltd v Lucre* (2000) 50 NSWLR 261, where the plaintiff suffered PTSD after his truck was involved in an accident caused by the negligence of a car driver, who was killed), or by a rescuer endangered in the course of the rescue. The decision to bar claims against the immediate victim may also give rise to difficulties where both the immediate victim and a third party are to blame for the accident, since if the claimant sues the third party, they can recover in full applying the principle of joint and several liability, but the third party will be unable to recover a contribution from the immediate victim, since following *Greatorex* their conduct was not tortious (see *Alcock* at 418, per Lord Oliver). The New South Wales Court of Appeal rejected the bar in the *FAI General Insurance* case (but cf. *Homsi v Homsi* (2016) 51 VR 694), and the Scottish Law Commission recommended that it be overturned by legislation: *Damages for Psychiatric Injury* (Scot Law Com. No. 196, 2004), paras 3.64–3.65. (Cf. Law Commission, *Liability for Psychiatric Illness* (Law Com. No. 249, 1999), para. 5.42, where it was suggested that in the light of the self-determination concern any bar on claims against immediate victims should be limited to instances of deliberate self-harm.)

Liability for Communicating Distressing News

Suppose the live television broadcasts coming from the Hillsborough stadium had included—in breach of the broadcasters' code of practice—close-up pictures of individuals caught in the crush and close to death. Could relatives claim that the television company was at fault in showing the pictures and liable for PTSD suffered as a consequence of seeing them? It is far from obvious that the courts would recognise a duty of care in such a case. The public interest in the dissemination of information might well be taken to preclude the imposition of liability on the negligent communicator of distressing news (*aliter*, perhaps, if there was intent to harm the recipient). What appears to have been the first claim of this nature in the English courts was brought in *AB v Tameside & Glossop Health Authority* [1997] 8 Med LR 91, where a number of patients of the defendant health authority complained of the way they had been informed that a health worker had been found to be HIV-positive and that they had thereby been exposed to a very remote risk of infection; the patients alleged, inter alia, that they should have been informed face to face rather than by letter. The case provides no authority on the matter under consideration, however, as the existence of a duty was conceded by the defendants; in any case, the claim failed because the Court of Appeal held that the defendants had not been negligent in breaking the news in the way they did. It is nonetheless noteworthy that Brooke LJ intimated that any duty that arose was but a particular incident of the pre-existing relationship between health authority and patient, a view that accords with the judgments of Gummow, Kirby and Callinan JJ in *Tame v New South Wales* (2002) 211 CLR 317 that no general duty of care is owed by a bearer of bad tidings to their recipient.

For comment on *AB*, see Mullany (1998) 114 LQR 380 (defending the duty concession, and emphasising the effect that bad news may have on the health of the patient) and Dziobon and Tettenborn (1997) 13 PN 70 (arguing against the imposition of a duty in view of its restricting effect on speech and news reporting).

Another type of case in which the liability of the communicator of shocking news might arise is where *erroneous* information is passed on. In an early Australian case, *Barnes v Commonwealth* (1937) SR (NSW) 511, liability was imposed on state authorities who falsely told the plaintiff that her husband had been admitted to an asylum. The issue arose in *Allin v City & Hackney Health Authority* [1996] 7 Med LR 167, where the plaintiff recovered damages for PTSD suffered as a result of being told after a difficult birth that her baby had died; six hours later, she learned that the baby had in fact survived. As in *AB*, however, the defendants had conceded that they owed a duty of care, so *Allin* cannot be regarded as authority on the duty issue. Noting the contrast with *Ravenscroft*, Jones has argued that the imposition of liability in such circumstances would be 'bizarre': 'which event is worse', he asks, 'being told (correctly) that someone has negligently killed your child or negligently being told (incorrectly) that your child has died?' ((1997) 13 PN 111 at 113). Mullany is again more sympathetic, arguing that '[i]t would be offensive if liability could lie under *Hedley Byrne* for economic loss caused by a negligent misstatement but not for psychiatric injury caused by the same wrong' ((1998) 114 LQR 380 at 385).

IV. Other Types of Case

Although historically most of the 'nervous shock' claims that came before the courts involved accidents, in recent decades the courts have increasingly been faced with psychiatric illness cases that do not fit this paradigm. In the words of Brooke LJ in *Leach v Chief Constable of Gloucestershire Constabulary* [1999] 1 WLR 1421 at 1434:

> Most of the cases in the books are concerned with situations in which a plaintiff suffers psychiatric illness as a result of his own imperilment . . . or reasonable fear of danger to himself, or as a result of the physical injury or imperilment of a third party . . . which has been caused by the defendant . . . There is, however, a less familiar line of cases in which . . . a defendant has neither imperilled nor caused physical injury to anyone.

A good illustration of such a case is *McLoughlin v Jones* [2002] QB 1312, where a claimant who had suffered psychiatric illness after being imprisoned for a crime he did not commit recovered damages from the solicitors whose negligence had caused him to be convicted in the first place. And another example is *Home Office v Butchart* [2006] 1 WLR 1155, where a prisoner sued the prison authorities for the trauma he suffered after he was placed in a cell with another prisoner who was known to be a suicide risk and who did in fact commit suicide. The Court of Appeal held that the duty of care that the prison authorities owed prisoners encompassed psychiatric injury, and refused to strike out the claim.

In cases of this kind, the special duty of care limits that we have been discussing do not apply, although there may be difficult issues concerning breach, causation and remoteness. The explanation for the lack of duty limits in such cases is unclear. One possibility is that they are not secondary victim cases, and that the special limits apply only to those (though the claimant in *Butchart*, for example, *does* seem to have been a secondary victim, since it was the suicide of his fellow prisoner that caused his illness). Another possible explanation is that in these cases the defendant has assumed a responsibility towards the claimant that puts the defendant under a duty to take reasonable care of the claimant's mental health.

In practice, by far the most important category of these non-accident cases concerns the widespread phenomenon of occupational stress. The first case of this kind to reach the English courts was *Walker v Northumberland County Council* [1995] 1 All ER 737 (noted by Nolan (1995) 24 ILJ 280), where the plaintiff was a social worker who sued his employer in respect of two breakdowns which he suffered as a result of overwork and stress brought on by the nature of the tasks on which he was engaged. Colman J held that the defendant was not to blame for the first breakdown, but was liable for the consequences of the second, since by then the risk was obvious and it should have reduced the claimant's workload. Following a spate of similar cases in the wake of *Walker*, the Court of Appeal considered a number of such claims in the next extracted case.

Hatton v Sutherland [2002] EWCA Civ 76, [2002] All ER 1

This was in effect a test case to determine the nature of the legal duty imposed on employers in respect of psychiatric illness through stress at work, and the circumstances in which a court might find that an employer was in breach of this duty. The Court of Appeal was faced with four conjoined appeals. The extract deals only with the general principles governing such claims and not with the individual cases.

Hale LJ

18. Several times while hearing these appeals we were invited to go back to first principles. Liability in negligence depends upon three inter-related requirements: the existence of a duty to take care; a failure to take the care which can reasonably be expected in the circumstances; and damage suffered as a result of that failure. These elements do not exist in separate compartments: the existence of the duty, for example, depends upon the type of harm suffered. Foreseeability of what might happen if care is not taken is relevant at each stage of the enquiry. Nevertheless, the traditional elements are always a useful tool of analysis, both in general and in particular cases.

Duty

19. The existence of a duty of care can be taken for granted. All employers have a duty to take reasonable care for the safety of their employees: to see that reasonable care is taken

to provide them with a safe place of work, safe tools and equipment, and a safe system of working: see *Wilsons & Clyde Coal Co Ltd v English* [1938] AC 57. However, where psychiatric harm is suffered, the law distinguishes between 'primary' and 'secondary' victims. A primary victim is usually someone within the zone of foreseeable physical harm should the defendant fail to take reasonable care: see *Page v Smith* [1996] AC 155. A secondary victim is usually someone outside that zone: typically such a victim foreseeably suffers psychiatric harm through seeing, hearing or learning of physical harm tortiously inflicted upon others. There are additional control mechanisms to keep liability towards such people strictly within bounds: see *Alcock v Chief Constable of South Yorkshire Police* [1992] 1 AC 310. . . .

20. In *Petch v Commissioners of Customs and Excise* [1993] ICR 789, CA, it was accepted that the ordinary principles of employers' liability applied to a claim for psychiatric illness arising from employment, although the claim failed. In the landmark case of *Walker v Northumberland County Council* [1995] 1 All ER 737, Colman J applied those same principles in upholding the claim. Both have recently been cited with approval in this Court in *Garrett v London Borough of Camden* [2001] EWCA Civ 395. Also in [*White v Chief Constable of South Yorkshire Police* [1999] 2 AC 455], Lord Hoffmann stated, at p 504F, that

> The control mechanisms were plainly never intended to apply to all cases of psychiatric injury. They contemplate that the injury has been caused in consequence of death or injury suffered (or apprehended to have been suffered or as likely to be suffered) by someone else.

As to *Walker*, he commented, at p 506A, that:

> the employee . . . was in no sense a secondary victim. His mental breakdown was caused by the strain of doing the work which his employer had required him to do.

21. In summary, therefore, claims for psychiatric injury fall into four different categories:

(1) tortious claims by primary victims: usually those within the foreseeable scope of physical injury, for example, the road accident victim in *Page v Smith* [1996] AC 155; some primary victims may not be at risk of physical harm, but at risk of foreseeable psychiatric harm because the circumstances are akin to those of primary victims in contract (see (3) below);

(2) tortious claims by secondary victims: those outside that zone who suffer as a result of harm to others, for example, the witnesses of the Hillsborough disaster in *Alcock v Chief Constable of South Yorkshire Police* [1992] 1 AC 310;

(3) contractual claims by primary victims: where the harm is the reasonably foreseeable product of specific breaches of a contractual duty of care towards a victim whose identity is known in advance, for example, the solicitors' clients in *Cook v Swinfen* [1967] 1 WLR 457, CA, [*McLoughlin v Jones* [2002] QB 1312], or the employees in *Petch v Commissioners of Customs and Excise* [1993] ICR 789, *Walker v Northumberland County Council* [1995] 1 All ER 737, *Garrett v London Borough of Camden* [2001] EWCA Civ 395, and in all the cases before us;

(4) contractual claims by secondary victims: where the harm is suffered as a result of harm to others, in the same way as secondary victims in tort, but there is also a contractual relationship with the defendant, as with the police officers in [*White*] *v Chief Constable of South Yorkshire Police* [1999] 2 AC 455.

22. There are, therefore, no special control mechanisms applying to claims for psychiatric (or physical) injury or illness arising from the stress of doing the work which the employee is required to do. But these claims do require particular care in determination, because they give

rise to some difficult issues of foreseeability and causation and, we would add, identifying a relevant breach of duty.

Foreseeability

23. *[T]he threshold question is whether this kind of harm to this particular employee was reasonably foreseeable*. The question is not whether psychiatric injury is foreseeable in a person of 'ordinary fortitude'. The employer's duty is owed to each individual employee, not to some as yet unidentified outsider: see *Paris v Stepney Borough Council* [1951] AC 367. The employer knows who his employee is. It may be that he knows, as in *Paris*, or ought to know, of a particular vulnerability; but he may not. *Because of the very nature of psychiatric disorder, as a sufficiently serious departure from normal or average psychological functioning to be labelled a disorder, it is bound to be harder to foresee than is physical injury*. Shylock could not say of a mental disorder, 'If you prick us, do we not bleed?' *But it may be easier to foresee in a known individual than it is in the population at large* . . .

24. However, are there some occupations which are so intrinsically stressful that resulting physical or psychological harm is always foreseeable? Mr Lewis [counsel for one of the defendants] appeared to accept that this was so: he gave the examples of traffic police officers who regularly deal with gruesome accidents or child protection officers who regularly investigate unthinkable allegations of child abuse . . .

The notion that some occupations are in themselves dangerous to mental health is not borne out by the literature . . . : it is not the job but the interaction between the individual and the job which causes the harm. Stress is a subjective concept: the individual's perception that the pressures placed upon him are greater than he may be able to meet. Adverse reactions to stress are equally individual, ranging from minor physical symptoms to major mental illness.

25. All of this points to there being a single test: *whether a harmful reaction to the pressures of the workplace is reasonably foreseeable in the individual employee concerned. Such a reaction will have two components: (1) an injury to health; which (2) is attributable to stress at work*. The answer to the foreseeability question will therefore depend upon the interrelationship between the particular characteristics of the employee concerned and the particular demands which the employer casts upon him. As was said in [*McLoughlin v Jones* [2002] QB 1312], expert evidence may be helpful although it can never be determinative of what a reasonable employer should have foreseen. A number of factors are likely to be relevant.

26. These include the *nature and extent of the work being done by the employee*. Employers should be more alert to picking up signs from an employee who is being over-worked in an intellectually or emotionally demanding job than from an employee whose workload is no more than normal for the job or whose job is not particularly demanding for him or her. It will be easier to conclude that harm is foreseeable if the employer is putting pressure upon the individual employee which is in all the circumstances of the case unreasonable. Also relevant is whether there are signs that others doing the same work are under harmful levels of stress. There may be others who have already suffered injury to their health arising from their work. Or there may be an abnormal level of sickness and absence amongst others at the same grade or in the same department. But if there is no evidence of this, then the focus must turn to the individual.

27. More important are the *signs from the employee himself*. Here again, it is important to distinguish between signs of stress and signs of impending harm to health. Stress is merely the mechanism which may but usually does not lead to damage to health. *Walker* is an obvious illustration: Mr Walker was a highly conscientious and seriously overworked manager of a social work area office with a heavy and emotionally demanding case load of child abuse cases. Yet although he complained and asked for help and for extra leave, the judge held

that his first mental breakdown was not foreseeable. There was, however, liability when he returned to work with a promise of extra help which did not materialise and experienced a second breakdown only a few months later. If the employee or his doctor makes it plain that unless something is done to help there is a clear risk of a breakdown in mental or physical health, then the employer will have to think what can be done about it.

28. Harm to health may sometimes be foreseeable without such an express warning. Factors to take into account would be frequent or prolonged absences from work which are uncharacteristic for the person concerned; these could be for physical or psychological complaints; but there must also be good reason to think that the underlying cause is occupational stress rather than other factors; this could arise from the nature of the employee's work or from complaints made about it by the employee or from warnings given by the employee or others around him.

29. But when considering what the reasonable employer should make of the information which is available to him, from whatever source, what assumptions is he entitled to make about his employee and to what extent is he bound to probe further into what he is told? *Unless he knows of some particular problem or vulnerability, an employer is usually entitled to assume that his employee is up to the normal pressures of the job.* It is only if there is something specific about the job or the employee or the combination of the two that he has to think harder. But thinking harder does not necessarily mean that he has to make searching or intrusive enquiries. *Generally he is entitled to take what he is told by or on behalf of the employee at face value.* . . .

31. These then are the questions and the possible indications that harm was foreseeable in a particular case. But how strong should those indications be before the employer has a duty to act? Mr Hogarth argued [for one of the defendants] that only 'clear and unequivocal' signs of an impending breakdown should suffice. That may be putting it too high. But *in view of the many difficulties of knowing when and why a particular person will go over the edge from pressure to stress and from stress to injury to health, the indications must be plain enough for any reasonable employer to realise that he should do something about it.*

COMMENTARY

One of the claimants in *Hatton* successfully appealed to the House of Lords (*Barber v Somerset County Council* [2004] 1 WLR 1089), but the Law Lords unanimously approved the statements of legal principle and practical guidance in Hale LJ's judgment. A note of caution was struck by Lord Walker, however. He said (at [65]) that the judgment should not be read 'as having anything like statutory force', and that '[e]very case will depend on its own facts'. The point is further made out by *Daw v Intel Corp (UK) Ltd* [2007] 2 All ER 126, where the defendant employer sought to rely on their provision of a counselling service and medical assistance as discharging their duty of care, relying on Hale LJ's statement ([2002] 2 All ER 1 at [43]) that '[a]n employer who offers a confidential advice service, with referral to appropriate counselling or treatment services, is unlikely to be found in breach of duty'. The Court of Appeal reached a different conclusion on the facts, noting that the indications of impending breakdown made it plain that immediate management action was required. Pill LJ commented (at [45]) that '[t]he reference to counselling services in *Hatton* does not make such services a panacea by which employers can discharge their duty of care in all cases'. (See also *Dickins v O2 plc* [2009] IRLR 58, where *Daw* was applied.) Moreover, an argument that Hale LJ specifically rejected—that some jobs are so inherently stressful that psychiatric injury is necessarily foreseeable—was recently accepted by the High Court of Australia in

Kozarov v Victoria (2022) 273 CLR 115, where the plaintiff had worked in a specialist unit that prosecuted serious sexual offences involving adults and children. According to Kiefel CJ and Keane J (at [6]):

[T]he circumstances of a particular type of employment may be such that the work to be performed by the employee is inherently and obviously dangerous to the psychiatric health of the employee (just as other kinds of work are inherently and obviously dangerous to the physical health of the employee). In any such case, the employer is duty-bound to be proactive in the provision of measures to enable the work to be performed safely by the employee. The present was such a case.

Hale LJ's 'threshold question' (at [23]) of whether harm to the particular employee was reasonably foreseeable means that in general an employer need take no special steps to fulfil their duty of care unless they know of a risk to a particular employee. This foreseeability hurdle effectively insulates the employer from liability in the common scenario where the employee will not admit to experiencing stress for fear of appearing unable to cope (*Pratley v Surrey County Council* [2004] ICR 159). Nevertheless, if stress-induced illness is foreseeable—for example, because of a previous breakdown—it is not necessarily contributory negligence for the employee not to voice their concerns that the job may again be becoming too much for them (*Young v Post Office* [2002] IRLR 660).

The causation enquiry may be very complex in cases of work stress, because many different psychological and sociological factors determine whether a person is prone to psychiatric illness, including genetic predisposition, childhood experiences and social support. As Hale LJ said in *Hatton* (at [5]):

While some of the major mental illnesses have a known or strongly suspected organic origin, this is not the case with many of the most common disorders. Their causes will often be complex and depend upon the interaction between the patient's personality and a number of factors in the patient's life.

The complex aetiology of psychiatric illness may also give rise to difficulties when it comes to apportioning responsibility in cases of this kind: see Chapter 5.I.2(b).

Although Hale LJ was at pains to distinguish the work-stress cases from the line of authority concerning secondary victims, the dividing line is not always clear. In *Hartman v South Essex Mental Health NHS Trust* [2005] ICR 782, the claimant was a healthcare officer at the defendant's prison, who was required as part of his duties to recover the bodies of prisoners who had committed suicide. In seventeen years, he attended eight suicides. After the last of these—when he had helped cut down the body, remove a ligature and attempt a revival—he developed a stress-related illness. The trial judge found that psychiatric injury was reasonably foreseeable in the circumstances, and the Court of Appeal ruled that this was sufficient to establish a duty of care. It was immaterial that the stress was caused by a traumatic episode or episodes rather than day-to-day work. In effect, the Court of Appeal seems to have treated the case as one of work stress and so relieved the claimant of the need to satisfy the *Alcock* limits on secondary victim claims. At first blush, this analysis is difficult to square with the holding in *White* that the fact that the parties are in an employment relationship does not entitle a secondary victim to circumvent those restrictions, but the difference is that whereas in *White* the employer (through other employees) was to blame for the incident that triggered the trauma, in *Hartman* the alleged breach of duty related not to the suicides themselves but rather to the failure to provide the claimant with counselling and other support after they had occurred. (Cf. *Leach v Chief Constable of Gloucestershire* [1999] 1 WLR 1421; *The Age Co Ltd v YZ* [2019] VR 189.)

It has been held that an employer owes no duty of care in respect of mental harm caused by the way in which an employee is dismissed from employment, as the jurisdiction of the employment tribunals in such matters is intended to be exclusive (*Johnson v Unisys Ltd* [2003] 1 AC 518; *Edwards v Chesterfield Royal Hospital NHS Foundation Trust* [2012] 2 AC 22). The duty may, however, arise in respect of disciplinary action short of dismissal (e.g. suspension: *Gogay v Hertfordshire County Council* [2000] IRLR 703), even where it leads ultimately to dismissal (*Eastwood v Magnox Electric plc* [2005] 1 AC 503). In the last-mentioned case, at [33], Lord Nicholls described the resulting distinctions as 'awkward and unfortunate' and recommended legislative attention.

Relevance of Obligations under the Contract of Employment

If the employee has, under their contract of employment, undertaken an agreed amount of work, can the employer nonetheless breach the duty of care owed to them in tort by requiring the employee to perform that work? The issue did not arise directly in *Barber v Somerset County Council* [2004] 1 WLR 1089, but Lord Rodger observed, at [34]:

> The contract of employment will usually regulate what is to happen if an employee becomes unable, due to illness or injury, to carry out his duties. There may be provision for a defined period on full pay, followed by a further defined period on reduced pay, followed by termination of the contract. At the end of the process the employer is free to make new arrangements . . . Whatever the position, however, the introduction of a tortious duty of reasonable care on the employer to provide assistance so that the employee can return to work and draw his normal pay, but do less than his full duties for an indefinite period, does not sit easily with such contractual arrangements. Nor does it seem likely to promote efficiency within the enterprise or department.

See also *Koehler v Cerebos (Australia) Ltd* (2005) 222 CLR 44, another case of occupational stress, where a majority of the High Court of Australia held that an employer could not be liable for psychiatric injury brought about by an employee's performance of the duties originally stipulated in the contract of employment, since 'insistence upon performance of a contract cannot be in breach of a duty of care' (at [29]) and the law of negligence should not inhibit freedom of contract. The Court did however add the caveat that the performance of the employee's contractual duties might be subject to some implied limitation, which would be a question of construction of the contract. (Do you think that such a limit on work-stress claims is best understood as going to breach, or is there another explanation for it?) For comment on *Koehler*, see Lunney (2005) 2 UNELJ 75 and Handford, 'Liability for Work Stress: *Koehler* Ten Years On' (2015) 39 UWALR 150.

A Wider Principle of Assumption of Responsibility?

A number of commentators have proposed a principle of assumed responsibility as a means of rationalising the occupational stress cases and other cases falling outside the established categories of primary and secondary victims (see, e.g., S. Deakin and Z. Adams, *Markesinis and Deakin's Tort Law*, 8th edn (Oxford: OUP, 2019), pp. 119–23; cf. *Kozarov v Victoria* (2022) 273 CLR 115 at [100]–[104], per Edelman J). Such a principle would apply not only in the employment sphere, but also to other contractual relationships (e.g. solicitor/client, as in *McLoughlin v Jones*) and even to non-contractual assumptions of responsibility (e.g. by the prison authorities to a prisoner, as in *Home Office v Butchart*). On this view, the assumption of responsibility relieves the claimant of establishing either that he was physically imperilled (and so a 'primary victim' in the classic sense) or that he satisfied the secondary victim limits laid down in *Alcock*. Many of the relevant cases concern the doctor/patient relationship.

A typical scenario is where a mother gives birth to a disabled baby as a consequence of negligence in her ante-natal care, and suffers psychiatric illness when she finds out about the child's condition. The hospital's relationship with the mother clearly gives rise to a duty of care that encompasses both her physical and her mental health, so that, for example, it is not necessary to show that the mother directly perceived her child's disability at the time of its delivery (*Farrell v Merton, Sutton and Wandsworth Health Authority* (2001) 57 BMLR 158), though note that in cases of stillbirth caused by clinical negligence, the mother has been classified as a primary victim on the footing that the mother and the unborn child are a single legal entity (*Wild v Southend University Hospital NHS Foundation Trust* [2016] PIQR P3; *Zeromska-Smith v United Lincolnshire Hospitals NHS Trust* [2019] EWHC 980 (QB)), and that this analysis has been extended to any childbirth case where the negligence occurred while the baby was *in utero*: see *RE (A Minor) v Calderdale and Huddersfield NHS Foundation Trust* (2017) 156 BMLR 204 (birth of an apparently lifeless baby) and *YAH v Medway NHS Foundation Trust* [2019] 1 WLR 1413 (birth of a disabled baby). On the current authorities it seems unlikely that a duty is also owed to the father of the child in such a case, and in this instance the primary victim analysis is clearly not available (in *Wild* the father sued as a secondary victim). In *YAH* it seems in any case to have been assumed that the duty to the mother and (perhaps) father extends only to the immediate consequences of the negligent treatment, and does not allow recovery for psychiatric illness suffered through the stress of caring for a disabled child. Query whether the recognition of a duty in the circumstances of *AB v Tameside & Glossop Health Authority* [1997] 8 Med LR 91 and *Allin v City & Hackney Health Authority* (both noted in III) might be warranted on the basis of the defendant's assumption of responsibility for its patient's mental health. (But is it right that a mother should be able to claim damages from a doctor who negligently and inaccurately reports the death of her baby during childbirth, but not from a police officer guilty of the same error in reporting the baby's death in a car accident? See Jones (1997) 13 PN 111 at 113; Mullany (1998) 114 LQR 380 at 383.)

The assumption of responsibility concept may also account for the duty owed by a school to protect its pupils from bullying (*Bradford-Smart v West Sussex County Council* [2002] 1 FCR 425: no breach on the facts) and the analogous duty owed by employers to their employees (*Waters v Commissioner of Police of the Metropolis* [2000] 1 WLR 1607). Another possible application of the principle is *Al-Kandari v J. R. Brown & Co* [1988] QB 665, where the defendant solicitors were held liable for the plaintiff's psychiatric illness resulting from (inter alia) the abduction of her children to Kuwait by her husband, the defendants' client. The defendants, who were representing the husband in custody proceedings, assumed responsibility to the plaintiff by agreeing to safeguard the husband's passport with a view to preventing precisely the events that occurred, but they negligently failed to do so. (This aspect of the case is brought out more clearly in the report of the first instance judgment: see [1987] QB 514.) The duty of care in respect of psychiatric illness arguably owed by a local authority social services department to the foster family with whom it places a child may also best be regarded as flowing from the former's assumption of responsibility to the latter (*W v Essex County Council* [2001] 2 AC 592, noted in II).

Stress-Related Illness Caused by the Fear of Developing Physical Illness

A separate category of cases—or perhaps a sub-category of those considered under the preceding heading—is where the claimant suffers a stress-related illness as a result of the fear of developing a physical illness, having been placed at risk of the latter by the defendant's negligence. In *Aston v Imperial Chemical Industries Group* (unreported, QBD, 21 May 1992;

noted by Law Commission, *Liability for Psychiatric Illness*, p. 27n), Rose J awarded damages in respect of a depressive illness suffered by the plaintiff as a result of anxiety that exposure to carcinogenic fumes in his workplace might cause angiosarcoma of the liver, a usually fatal condition with a latency period of about fifteen years.

In *Re Creutzfeldt-Jakob Disease Litigation* [1998] 41 BMLR 157, Morland J held that a group of plaintiffs who had been treated for dwarfism with the growth hormone HGH were owed a duty of care by the Department of Health in respect of psychiatric illness caused by their becoming aware that their treatment was capable of infecting them with Creutzfeldt-Jacob Disease and hence that an unknown number of them might be incubating the disease. In a preliminary hearing on various points of law, the judge ruled that the plaintiffs could not be treated as primary victims in the *Page v Smith* sense. This was because (1) they did not fear immediate physical injury but rather that at some time in the future they would be struck down by a ghastly, untreatable, terminal illness, and (2) because treating them as such would in any case be contrary to public policy as it would open up the possibility of a huge number of claims arising out of the exposure of individuals to toxic substances such as asbestos or radioactive materials, which would in turn make insurance difficult or impossible for the producers, prescribers and suppliers of such products and could inhibit them from warning members of the public of dangers of which they became aware. Morland J was however able to find a duty of care on the alternative, and narrower, basis that the relationship between the defendant and the recipients of HGH was one of close proximity, akin to that of doctor and patient. Subsequently, six members of the plaintiff group succeeded in recovering damages from the Health Department (*Andrews v Secretary of State for Health*, unreported, QBD, 19 June 1998).

In *Rothwell v Chemical & Insulating Co Ltd* [2008] 1 AC 281 (noted in II), the House of Lords agreed with Morland J's view that *Page v Smith* did not apply to cases of anxiety at possible future injury. One of the appeals in *Rothwell* (*Grieves*) concerned a case of clinical depression resulting from the claimant's fear, on discovering that he had asbestos fibres in his lungs, that he might in future develop a life-threatening or fatal disease. He brought an action for damages against his previous employers, who had negligently exposed him to the asbestos. The House of Lords explicitly followed the approach to employers' liability established by Hale LJ in *Hatton v Sutherland* [2002] 2 All ER 1, extracted earlier. Though that judgment was concerned with occupational stress, it applied to any psychiatric injury caused by the employer's breach of duty. The threshold question was whether psychiatric injury was reasonably foreseeable in the particular employee. On the facts, the defendant employers were unlikely to have had specific knowledge of how the claimant might react to his discovery, long after he had left their employment, that he was at risk from asbestos-related disease. They were therefore entitled to assume that he was a person of ordinary fortitude, and there was no evidence from which it could be concluded that such a person might reasonably foreseeably suffer psychiatric injury in consequence of their negligence. The action therefore failed.

In *Rothwell* the House of Lords distinguished the *Creutzfeldt-Jakob Disease* case as Morland J had there made a factual finding that the claimant's psychiatric injury was reasonably foreseeable in the circumstances. *Rothwell* should not therefore be understood as ruling out liability altogether in 'fear of the future' cases, but rather as an application on particular facts of the ordinary requirement of reasonable foreseeability of psychiatric injury. Nevertheless, it seems likely that the considerations that made the psychiatric injury unforeseeable in *Grieves* will also be present in the majority of cases, and that successful claims will therefore be rare.

For a comprehensive discussion of this type of psychiatric injury claim, see P. Handford, *Tort Liability for Mental Harm*, 3rd edn (Ryde, NSW: Law Book Co, 2017), ch. 29.

v. Evaluation and Reform

1. Criticisms of the Current Law

It is apparent from the earlier parts of this chapter that the English law of liability for psychiatric illness has attracted severe criticism. Almost everyone is agreed that the current state of the law is unsatisfactory. This, according to Stapleton, is the area of the law of tort where the 'silliest' rules now prevail (*op. cit.*, p. 95). Todd too finds that the law is 'in a dreadful mess' ((1999) 115 LQR 345 at 349). And for Jones, the result in practice is 'a long list of anomalies' ((1997) 13 PN 111 at 113). Even the judiciary has conceded that—as Lord Hoffmann put it in *White*—'the search for principle' in this area of the law has been 'called off'. The House of Lords in that case viewed the law as so far beyond judicial repair that the only sensible maxim to adopt was—in Lord Steyn's words—'thus far and no further' (at 500):

> My Lords, the law on the recovery of compensation for pure psychiatric harm is a patchwork quilt of distinctions which are difficult to justify. There are two theoretical solutions. The first is to wipe out recovery in tort for pure psychiatric injury. . . . But that would be contrary to precedent and, in any event, highly controversial. Only Parliament could take such a step. The second solution is to abolish all the special limiting rules applicable to psychiatric harm. . . . Precedent rules out this course and, in any event, there are cogent policy considerations against such a bold innovation. In my view the only sensible general strategy for the courts is to say thus far and no further. The only prudent course is to treat the pragmatic categories as reflected in authoritative decisions such as *Alcock* and *Page v Smith* as settled for the time being but by and large to leave any expansion or development in this corner of the law to Parliament. In reality there are no refined analytical tools which will enable the courts to draw lines by way of compromise solution in a way which is coherent and morally defensible. It must be left to Parliament to undertake the task of radical law reform.

Many of the criticisms of the current law are directed at the practicality and consistency of the legal principles in question, but there is also a significant debate as to whether the law should continue to attempt a balance between a limited right to recover damages in respect of psychiatric illness and the fear of opening the floodgates of liability. This effectively was the approach advocated by the Law Commission, whose reform proposals are extracted later in this section, albeit the Commission would have struck that balance in a way that was more generous to claimants than the current law. The Law Commission's approach should be contrasted with that of Handford, on the one hand, and Stapleton, on the other, who take more extreme and opposing approaches to liability for psychiatric illness (see the following extracts). All these analyses can be fruitfully read in the light of the more fundamental critique advanced by two feminist commentators, also extracted in this section.

P. Handford, *Tort Liability for Mental Harm*, 3rd edn (Ryde, NSW: Law Book Co, 2017), paras 1.190 and 1.220

[T]he fact that an injury cannot always be seen by the naked eye does not mean that it is any less of a 'real' injury than those which involve the breaking of bones, the spilling of blood, the scarring of tissue or physical pain. Indeed, it can be argued that the mental repercussions of trauma are more serious, more deserving of the law's attention than those of a physical nature. Mental conditions frequently persist long after organic injuries have disappeared. Broken bones knit, wounds heal often without scarring or permanent disability and those that do scar, although unsightly, leave less of a mark than scars on the mind. Physical pain usually subsides, often long before the psychological impact of distressing events disappears. The after-effects of trauma may never fully dissipate. . . . [A]s a general observation, an injured mind is far more difficult to nurse back to health than an injured body and is arguably more debilitating and disruptive of a greater number of aspects of human existence . . .

Liberalisation [of the law governing liability for mental harm] will not see a deluge of psychiatric damage claims because most claimants will be unable to clear the still significant hurdles to relief. To date litigation in this area has been relatively limited, especially outside the United States, and even in jurisdictions where the law has developed [along more liberal lines] the increase in claims has not been major. The difference is that the claims of those who do sue will be adjudicated according to more sensible doctrine and bearing the relevant literature and observations in mind. Denial will be based on sound legal and scientific reasoning rather than the perceived need to prevent trespass beyond artificially constructed boundaries.

COMMENTARY

The author contends that liability for psychiatric harm should be treated in the same way as physical injury, and that proximity requirements used to limit liability in this area should be abandoned. In most cases, the reasonable foreseeability of psychiatric illness should be enough to give rise to a duty of care, a position which the author maintains would not lead to a flood of litigation because the requirement that the illness be reasonably foreseeable is 'a considerable hurdle to surmount in itself' (para. 1.200). In the first edition of the book (1993) and in a number of subsequent commentaries, Handford and his original co-author Mullany have subjected decisions in this area to strenuous and sustained criticism from this perspective (see, e.g., (1997) 113 LQR 410; (1998) 114 LQR 380; (1999) 115 LQR 30).

A similar approach is to be found in H. Teff, *Causing Psychiatric and Emotional Harm: Reshaping the Boundaries of Legal Liability* (Oxford: Hart, 2009). Amongst judicial approaches, the most similar to that of Handford is to be found in Lord Bridge's speech in *McLoughlin v O'Brian*, extracted in II.

J. Stapleton, 'In Restraint of Tort', in P. Birks (ed.), *The Frontiers of Liability*, vol. 2 (Oxford: OUP, 1994)

[A]ppellate courts suspect, and with reason it seems to me, that once a general duty to avoid nervous shock was recognised, many more individuals would be recognised as presenting the relevant symptoms to their GPs. Recovery from grief is a complex and mysterious process. May it not be a major concern of judges that while the prospect of compensation for, say, a broken leg may inhibit recuperation to a minor degree, the prospect of compensation for grief would have a much more powerful disincentive to rehabilitation and one which medical evidence would find extremely difficult to unravel from the original condition? If a central factor in grief and depression is anger, might not the adversarial nature of legal process be especially counter-productive? Associated with this concern is the very real one of characterising the relevant actionable damage. We are told that pathological grief is compensatable . . . but not normal grief. Leaving aside the perplexing question of why this is so, we are still confronted by the possibility that with hindsight and in the context of a civil claim, medical opinion may define 'pathological' grief much more loosely than the law would find tolerable. After all, the boundary between normal and pathological grief is of virtually no significance for medical treatment.

So the concerns about recovery for nervous shock are real, but the available techniques for controlling it are not only artificial but bring the law into disrepute. That at present claims can turn on the requirement of 'close ties of love and affection' is guaranteed to produce outrage. Is it not a disreputable sight to see brothers of Hillsborough victims turned away because they had no more than brotherly love towards the victims? . . .

Some US jurisdictions who had once recognised a tort relating to privacy have now abolished it because it was felt that no reasonable boundaries for the cause of action could be found, and this was an embarrassment to the law. Should not our courts wipe out recovery for pure nervous shock on the same basis?

COMMENTARY

Stapleton's approach is an extreme one, and perhaps deliberately provocative. It is not easy to find commentators prepared to go quite as far as she does. But similar concerns that liability for psychiatric illness may have been treated too expansively are evident, for example in P. S. Atiyah, *The Damages Lottery* (Oxford: Hart, 1997), pp. 56–62.

The Law Commission noted in its report on *Liability for Psychiatric Illness* (extracted in V.2) that 'medical and legal experts in the field . . . have impressed upon us how life-shattering psychiatric illness can be and how, in many instances, it can be more debilitating than physical injuries' (para. 1.9). Do you think Stapleton's approach gives adequate consideration to such evidence? And do you think it acceptable that on her approach a claimant who suffered minor physical injury would be able to recover for consequential mental harm, while all claims for 'pure' (i.e. non-consequential) mental harm would be barred, regardless of the circumstances?

M. Chamallas with L. K. Kerber, 'Women, Mothers and the Law of Fright: A History' (1990) 88 Mich L Rev 814 at 814

The law of torts values physical security and property more highly than emotional security and human relationships. This apparently gender-neutral hierarchy of values has privileged men, as the traditional owners and managers of property, and has burdened women, to whom the emotional work of maintaining human relationship has commonly been assigned. The law has often failed to compensate women for recurring harms—serious though they may be in the lives of women—for which there is no precise masculine analogue. This phenomenon is evident in the history of tort law's treatment of fright-based physical injuries, a type of claim historically brought more often by female plaintiffs. There are two paradigm cases of fright-based physical injury: the pregnant plaintiff who suffers a miscarriage or stillbirth as a result of being frightened and the mother who suffers nervous shock when she witnesses her child's injury or death. These claims were classified in the law as emotional harms and a number of special doctrinal obstacles were created to contain recovery in such cases.

COMMENTARY

The cases considered in this chapter show that emotional harm—at least in the modern law—cannot be regarded as a condition which affects women alone. But there is a strong argument that considerations of gender do indeed, as Chamallas and Kerber suggest, provide a historical explanation for the slow and reluctant recognition of psychiatric illness as worthy of compensation. The way such gender considerations operate is a complex matter, and a number of different views are possible, but one plausible account is that the typical domestic situation of women once made them especially prone to psychiatric illness, which was therefore regarded as a 'feminine' condition in contrast with the 'masculine' virtues of courage and fortitude which it was thought to undermine. Hence arose a tendency to regard psychiatric illness as arising from the victim's pre-existing susceptibility (see e.g. *Bourhill v Young*, extracted in Ch. 3.II.2). Other traces of stereotypical attitudes towards women may also be evident in fears that those claiming in respect of psychiatric illness might be prone to exaggerate or to lie about their condition. (Though note that the widespread assumption that such fears were a hallmark of the early English case law on 'nervous shock' has been challenged: Goold and Kelly, 'Who's Afraid of Imaginary Claims? Common Misunderstandings of the Origin of the Action for Pure Psychiatric Injury in Negligence 1888-1943' (2022) 138 LQR 58.) And even the requirements for a successful psychiatric illness claim may be analysed in gender terms, for example the general requirement of a 'shock' which, by focusing upon a single causative event outside normal human experience, precludes consideration of the stresses and frustrations that are common to many women's experience of workplace and domestic environments. For a wider discussion of such issues see N. Priaulx, 'Endgame: On Negligence and Reparation for Harm' in J. Richardson and E. Rackley (eds), *Feminist Perspectives on Tort Law* (Abingdon: Routledge, 2012), ch. 3.

2. Proposals for Reform

Liability for psychiatric illness arises in England exclusively as a matter of common law, but—as has been noted—there are growing calls for legislative reform. Whether the English law in this area should be the subject of such reform was considered by the Law Commission in a report published in 1998.

Law Commission, *Liability for Psychiatric Illness*
(Law Com. No. 249, 1998)

[After a lengthy consultation process and a thorough consideration of the question of liability for psychiatric illness, the Law Commission confined its proposals to the secondary victim scenario, as it was prepared to leave the law relating to other categories of claimant—including rescuers and 'involuntary participants'—to be further developed by the courts as and when deemed necessary. It summarised its basic recommendations as follows:]

We recommend that, where it is reasonably foreseeable that such a plaintiff might suffer psychiatric illness, the plaintiff's proximity to the scene of the 'accident', and the manner by which he or she learns of it, should not be used as criteria to restrict the claim. In addition, we make two recommendations that are of general application to psychiatric illness claims. First, the requirement that the psychiatric illness be induced by a shock should be abandoned. And secondly, where the plaintiff's psychiatric illness is suffered as a result of another person's death, injury or imperilment, it should not be an absolute bar to recovery that that person is the defendant him or herself.

[The Commission then addressed the factors that it felt justified this approach to liability for psychiatric illness:]

After much deliberation, we . . . remain persuaded that at this point in time . . . the 'floodgates argument' . . . requires special policy limitations to be imposed over and above the test of reasonable foreseeability. In particular, we are concerned that the dividing line between what level of mental disturbance does and does not amount to a psychiatric illness is a matter of degree not kind and that the concept of psychiatric illness has widened significantly over the past few years. Our review of the relevant medical literature has led us to believe that the adoption of a simple foreseeability test would or could result in a significant increase in the number of claims which, at least at this point in time, would be unacceptable. This in turn might lead the courts to make use of policy considerations, concealed beneath the foreseeability test, in an attempt to restrict the number of successful claims. Such confusion could only result in an increased volume of litigation. While we accept that it is difficult to be sure that a move to a pure reasonable foreseeability test would open the floodgates of litigation, we believe that there is at least a significant risk of that consequence. It would be imprudent to take that risk when we can leave the courts free to develop the common law in the light of the effects of our more limited reforms. . . . Accordingly, we recommend that . . . special limitations over and above reasonable foreseeability should continue to be applied to claims for psychiatric illness where the defendant has injured or imperilled someone other than the plaintiff, and the plaintiff, as a result, has suffered psychiatric illness.

Having reached the conclusion that there should be special limitations over and above reasonable foreseeability, we need to consider whether all three *Alcock* proximity requirements need be maintained, and if not, whether the restrictions should focus on the relationship between the immediate victim and the plaintiff, or on the plaintiff's closeness to and means of perception of the accident. We believe that the imposition of all three proximity requirements is unduly restrictive, and that it is the last two limitations that have resulted in the most arbitrary decisions. How many hours after the accident the mother of an injured child manages to reach the hospital should not be the decisive factor in deciding whether the defendant may be liable for the mother's consequential psychiatric illness. We consider that so long as special control mechanisms over and above foreseeability are required in order to limit the potential number of claimants, the most acceptable method of achieving this is to restrict the claimants by reference to their connection with the immediate victim. Provided that the requirement for a close tie of love and affection between the plaintiff and the immediate victim is retained, the main floodgates objection of the possibility of many claims arising from a single event is limited. Furthermore, the advice we received from medical consultees supports the view that where there is a close tie of love and affection between the plaintiff and the immediate victim, the plaintiff's proximity to the accident or its aftermath is not always a relevant factor in determining his or her reaction to it.

COMMENTARY

The Commission explained its understanding of the 'floodgates' argument, which it regarded as the most convincing justification for a restrictive approach to liability for psychiatric illness as follows (pp. 83–4, fn. 9):

> The 'floodgates' argument may itself be subdivided into two distinct concerns: (i) the fear of a proliferation of claims from a single event (probably the argument's central force) and (ii) the possibility of a mass of claims from a mass of separate events. Both possibilities give rise to the concern that such a proliferation of claims would clog the court system and divert too many of society's resources into compensating the victims of psychiatric illness at the expense of other equally or more deserving plaintiffs. If the system fails to cope, the law will fall into disrepute and this would be a disservice to those few who most deserve legal support. In addition, the first possibility raises objections that to allow a mass of claims from a single event would place an undue burden on the defendant disproportionate to the negligent conduct.

Notwithstanding the fears expressed in this paragraph, the Law Commission was content to recommend a limited expansion in liability for psychiatric illness (as indicated in the extract) even while accepting that this would lead to an increase in the number and total burden of personal injury claims. It speculated that, in relation to road traffic accidents, 'a reasonable assumption seems to be that our proposals would give rise to a 10 per cent increase in the number of personal injury claims' (para. 1.12), and that 'it is reasonable to estimate that our proposals would give rise to an increase in motor insurance premiums in the range of two to five per cent' (para. 1.13). Furthermore, the Commission conceded that the rise in other sectors of the insurance market, for example employers' liability, was likely to be higher (para. 1.13n). Do you think that the public is willing to pay extra for its motor vehicle insurance, and extra also for products which are increased in price as a result of higher employers' liability insurance premiums, in order to finance an increase in the scope of tort liability for psychiatric illness? (Would *you* be willing to pay extra?)

A few of the more specific recommendations made by the Law Commission should also be briefly considered.

(i) The Commission proposed that legislation should initially draw the line at cases where the loved one has in fact been killed, injured or imperilled by the defendant, and should not extend it to a case where the plaintiff reasonably believes that the loved one has been imperilled, etc. (para. 6.18). Would such a case give rise to liability at common law?

(ii) The Commission endorsed the idea of laying down by statute a fixed list of relationships of love and affection (encompassing spouses, parents, children, siblings and cohabitants), though without prejudice to the courts' ability to recognise that other relationships satisfied this requirement on the facts of individual cases (para. 6.26). What would be the advantages of a statutory list of this nature?

(iii) Although the Commission did not feel able to extend liability under its proposed legislation to include bystanders, it did not wish 'to be construed as impeding the judicial development of liability to bystanders' (para. 7.15). However, it is not easy to see how liability could be extended to bystanders without adopting the rejected criterion of reasonable foreseeability of psychiatric illness.

(iv) The Commission recommended that the requirement that the psychiatric illness be shock-induced be abandoned (para. 5.33). This would mean that a relative who suffers a psychiatric illness as a result of nursing the victim of an accident would be able to claim against the negligent tortfeasor.

Do you think that these changes would result in (1) a more coherent, and (2) a fairer approach to the recovery of damages for negligently inflicted psychiatric damage? And do you agree with *Stapleton*, p. 20, that this area of tort law 'is better suited to legislative consideration given the artificial and controversial line-drawing required'?

Similar proposals to those of the Law Commission were made by the Scottish Law Commission, *Damages for Psychiatric Injury* (Scot Law Com. No. 196, 2004), although that body also recommended that *White v Chief Constable of South Yorkshire* be overturned, so that rescuers would not have to be exposed to danger in order to claim, and that (contrary to the decision in *Page v Smith*) even primary victims would be required to establish that psychiatric illness to a person in their position had been reasonably foreseeable.

In May 2007, the UK government provisionally rejected the Law Commission's reform proposals in a Department of Constitutional Affairs (DCA) consultation paper, *The Law on Damages* (CP 9/07), considering it preferable to allow the courts to continue to develop the law in this area. In the government's view, the courts had interpreted the *Alcock* requirements 'in a flexible and sensitive way' (para. 89). Noting that medical knowledge of psychiatric illness was still developing, the consultation paper stated (*ibid.*):

It is difficult at this stage to see how legislation could successfully assimilate the differing perspectives and arguments in this complex area into a simple and coherent system which would improve upon the current principles established by the courts, without running the risk of imposing rigid requirements which are not readily able to accommodate developments in medical knowledge and jurisprudence, and without opening the way to speculative and inappropriate claims.

The consultation paper dismissed the Law Commission's idea of a statutory list of close relationships, which might allow undesirable claims by long-separated spouses or brothers and sisters who have lost touch. By implication, it also rejected the Law Commission's recommendation that proximity in time and space and proximity of perception should be abandoned as preconditions of liability to secondary victims. Relying exclusively on a test of close relationship would expand the class of potential claimants and lead to a significant increase in insurance premiums. For similar reasons, the consultation paper affirmed the law's existing requirement of shock, finding also that this serves a useful purpose in ensuring the causation test is met: 'Without shock the evidential complexities of the case increase and investigating it becomes more costly. It would be more difficult to establish whether the claimant's illness was directly caused by the act or omission in question, and not by some other intervening event' (para. 90). Another advantage of the shock requirement was that it offered closure to the negligent party by guarding against claims arising long after the event. Following a consultation process, the proposals of the Scottish Law Commission were also rejected by the Scottish government (*Civil Law of Damages: Issues in Personal Injury, Scottish Government Response to the Consultation*, 2013), which observed (*ibid.*, p. 18):

While analysis of the responses revealed overall agreement that the current system relating to damages for psychiatric injury has defects, there was no general consensus that what was proposed by the SLC would be an improvement on the current situation.

For commentary on the Law Commission and Scottish Law Commission reports, see respectively Teff (1998) 61 MLR 849 and Nolan (2005) 68 MLR 983.

By contrast, in *Tame v New South Wales* (2002) 211 CLR 317, a majority of the High Court of Australia rejected the *Alcock* 'control mechanisms', and the distinction between primary and secondary victims, and adopted instead a simple test of reasonable foreseeability: ought the defendant to have foreseen that his conduct might result in psychiatric harm to the plaintiff? Whether *physical* injury was reasonably foreseeable was a quite separate matter, of no relevance to a claim for psychiatric injury. Applying the test of reasonable foreseeability might involve consideration of factors to which English law attached significance, like the plaintiff's abnormal sensitivity and their closeness in time and space to an immediately traumatic event. But neither normal fortitude nor direct perception of a shocking event, or its immediate aftermath, was to be regarded as critical to the recognition of a duty of care under Australian law. In responding to the policy concerns in this area, Gummow and Kirby JJ argued that these could be dealt with by the application of the ordinary principles of causation, remoteness, etc., that many of these concerns also applied in physical injury cases, and that they would recede if full force were given to the distinction between mere distress and a recognised psychiatric illness. Rigid restrictions of the kind set out in *Alcock* 'operated in an arbitrary and capricious manner' and brought the law into disrepute (at [190]).

For comment on *Tame* see Trindade (2003) 119 LQR 204. Note, however, that recovery for negligently inflicted psychiatric injury in most Australian jurisdictions is now governed by legislation which is much more restrictive than the common law as set out in *Tame*, and in some instances even more restrictive than the *Alcock* controls (see, e.g., Civil Liability Act 2002 (NSW) Part 3). For comparison see *van Soest v Residual Health Management Unit* [2000] 1 NZLR 179, where a majority of the New Zealand Court of Appeal adopted the English approach, although Thomas J (dissenting) favoured the more liberal approach later taken by the Australian High Court in *Tame*.

Compare the government's general satisfaction with the approach taken by the English courts with the views expressed by the courts themselves (e.g. in *White*, extracted earlier). Do *you* think that the approach taken has been satisfactory? If not, whose responsibility do you think it should be to develop the law? (Cf. Lord Steyn's 'thus far and no further approach' in *White*, expressly endorsed in *Rothwell v Chemical & Insulating Co Ltd* [2008] 1 AC 281 at [54], per Lord Hope and [95], per Lord Rodger.)

8 NEGLIGENCE: DUTY OF CARE—ECONOMIC LOSS

I. The Basic Exclusionary Rule

1. Introduction

As a general rule, recovery of pure economic loss is not possible in the English law of negligence, though this general exclusionary rule is qualified by the principle accepted in *Hedley Byrne & Co Ltd v Heller & Partners Ltd* [1964] AC 465 (extracted in III) that a duty to take care in relation to pure economic loss may arise if the defendant assumes responsibility for the claimant's economic welfare. Instead, '[e]conomic interests are protected by the law of contract and by those torts that are usually described as the economic torts, such as deceit, duress, intimidation, conspiracy, and inducing breach of contract' (*Brookfield Multiplex Ltd v Owners–Strata Plan No 61288* (2014) 254 CLR 185 at [121] per Crennan, Bell and Keane JJ; on the economic torts, see *Winfield & Jolowicz*, ch. 19). English law is not unique in taking this rather restrictive approach. German law also limits the scope of liability for the negligent infringement of purely economic interests. The *Bürgerliches Gesetzbuch* (BGB) does not list economic interests amongst the protected rights (*Rechtsgüter*) specified in its general negligence liability section (Article 823 I BGB), although the German courts might have interpreted the words 'some other right' (*ein sonstiges Recht*) in that section so as to encompass them. In fact, the courts interpreted that phrase narrowly, by and large excluding economic interests, although the 'right to an established and active business' (*Recht am eingerichteten und ausgeübten Gewerbebetrieb*) has been held to fall within the concept of 'other right'. Interesting questions arise as to the extent to which recognition of this right allows recovery in cases where English law excludes liability on the basis that the loss is purely economic (e.g. in the 'cable case' scenario, considered later). French law by contrast takes a more relaxed view, and all sorts of economic losses are recoverable in tort provided that they satisfy the tests of certainty and directness.

It is important to note that the general exclusionary rule applies only to losses that are purely economic, with 'economic' here meaning 'financial' or 'pecuniary' in nature. Of course, many actions in negligence are 'economic' in this sense. In a routine personal injury claim, for example, the claimant can recover for the financial consequences of the injury, such as lost earnings and medical expenses (see Ch. 15.IV). However, such losses are not *purely* economic, because they stem from physical damage (i.e. personal injury or property damage) suffered by the claimant. Pure economic loss is defined as financial loss that does not arise out of physical damage suffered by the claimant at the hands of the defendant. The distinction between pure economic loss and loss which is consequential upon physical damage is considered further later (see especially the *Spartan Steel* case).

2. Case Law

The classic early authority for the rule that pure economic loss cannot generally be recovered in negligence is *Cattle v Stockton Waterworks Co* (1875) LR 10 QB 453. The plaintiff was engaged by K on a lump sum basis to make a tunnel under a road which passed through K's land on an embankment. The defendant's water main ran under the road, and a leak in the main led to the plaintiff's workings being flooded, which resulted in delays and additional costs. Blackburn J held that the fact that the leak made the plaintiff's contract with K less profitable gave him no right of action against the defendant. Shortly afterwards, the decision was approved by the House of Lords in its decision in *Simpson v Thompson* (1877) 3 App Cas 279.

With the rapid expansion of liability for negligence occasioned by *Donoghue v Stevenson*, it became possible to question the continuing authority of the decision in *Cattle*, as the following extract shows.

Spartan Steel and Alloys Ltd v Martin & Co Ltd [1973] QB 27

The plaintiffs manufactured stainless steel alloys at a factory which was supplied with electricity by a cable directly from a power station. The factory worked twenty-four hours a day, and continuous power was required to maintain the temperature in a furnace in which metal was melted. The defendants' employees, who were working on a nearby road, damaged the cable while using an excavating shovel. The electricity board shut off the power supply to the factory for over fourteen hours until the cable was fixed. There was a danger that a 'melt' in the furnace might solidify and damage the furnace's lining, so the plaintiffs poured oxygen onto the melt and removed it. They claimed damages from the defendants in respect of: (1) a reduction in the value of the melt which had been removed from the furnace; (2) the loss of a profit that they would have made from that melt had the electricity not been cut off; and (3) the loss of a profit on another four melts which they would have put into the furnace during the time that the electricity was interrupted. The defendants accepted that their employees had been negligent, but disputed the amount of their liability.

Lord Denning MR

At bottom I think the question of recovering economic loss is one of policy. Whenever the courts draw a line to mark out the bounds of duty, they do it as a matter of policy so as to limit the responsibility of the defendant. Whenever the courts set bounds to the damages recoverable—saying that they are, or are not, too remote—they do it as matter of policy so as to limit the liability of the defendant.

In many of the cases where economic loss has been held not to be recoverable, it has been put on the ground that the defendant was under no duty to the plaintiff. Thus where a person is injured in a road accident by the negligence of another, the negligent driver owes a duty to the injured man himself, but he owes no duty to the servant of the injured man: see *Best v Samuel Fox & Co Ltd* [1952] AC 716 at 731; nor to the master of the injured man: *Inland Revenue Comrs v Hambrook* [1956] 2 QB 656 at 660; nor to anyone else who suffers loss because he had a contract with the injured man: see *Simpson & Co v Thomson* (1877) 3 App Cas 279 at 289; nor indeed to anyone who only suffers economic loss on account of the accident: see *Kirkham v Boughey* [1958] 2 QB 338 at 341. Likewise, when property is damaged by the negligence of another, the negligent tortfeasor owes a duty to the owner or possessor of the chattel, but not to one who suffers loss only because he had a contract entitling him to use the chattel or giving him a right to receive it at some later date: see *Elliott Steam Tug Co v Shipping Controller* [1922] 1 KB 127 at 139 and *Margarine Union GmbH v Cambay Prince Steamship Co Ltd* [1969] 1 QB 219 at 251, 252.

In other cases, however, the defendant seems clearly to have been under a duty to the plaintiff, but the economic loss has not been recovered because it is too remote. Take the illustration given by Blackburn J in *Cattle v Stockton Waterworks Co* (1875) LR 10 QB 453 at 457: when water escapes from a reservoir and floods a coalmine where many men are working; those who had their tools or clothes destroyed could recover, but those who only lost their wages could not. Similarly, when the defendants' ship negligently sank a ship which was being towed by a tug, the owner of the tug lost his remuneration, but he could not recover it from the negligent ship although the same duty (of navigation with reasonable care) was owed to both tug and tow: see *Société Remorquage à Hélice v Bennetts* [1911] 1 KB 243 at 248. In such cases if the plaintiff or his property had been physically injured, he would have recovered; but, as he suffered only economic loss, he is held not entitled to recover. This is, I should think, because the loss is regarded by the law as too remote: see *King v Phillips* [1953] 1 QB 429 at 439, 440.

On the other hand, in the cases where economic loss by itself has been held to be recoverable, it is plain that there was a duty to the plaintiff and the loss was not too remote. Such as when one ship negligently runs down another ship, and damages it, with the result that the cargo has to be discharged and reloaded. The negligent ship was already under a duty to the cargo-owners; and they can recover the cost of discharging and reloading it, as it is not too remote: see *Morrison Steamship Co Ltd v Greystoke Castle* (cargo owners) [1947] AC 265. Likewise, when a banker negligently gives a reference to one who acts on it, the duty is plain and the damage is not too remote: see *Hedley Byrne & Co Ltd v Heller & Partners Ltd* [1964] AC 465.

The more I think about these cases, the more difficult I find it to put each into its proper pigeon-hole. Sometimes I say: 'There was no duty.' In others I say: 'The damage was too remote.' So much so that I think the time has come to discard those tests which have proved so elusive. It seems to me better to consider the particular relationship in hand, and see whether or not, as a matter of policy, economic loss should be recoverable . . .

So I turn to the relationship in the present case. It is of common occurrence. The parties concerned are the electricity board who are under a statutory duty to maintain supplies of electricity in their district; the inhabitants of the district, including this factory, who are entitled by statute to a continuous supply of electricity for their use; and the contractors who dig up the road. Similar relationships occur with other statutory bodies, such as gas and water undertakings. The cable may be damaged by the negligence of the statutory undertaker, or by the negligence of the contractor, or by accident without any negligence by anyone; and the power may have to be cut off whilst the cable is repaired. Or the power may be cut off owing to a short-circuit in the power house; and so forth. If the cutting off of the supply causes economic loss to the consumers, should it as matter of policy be recoverable? And against whom?

The first consideration is the position of the statutory undertakers. If the board do not keep up the voltage or pressure of electricity, gas or water—or, likewise, if they shut it off for repairs—and thereby cause economic loss to their consumers, they are not liable in damages, not even if the cause of it is due to their own negligence. The only remedy (which is hardly ever pursued) is to prosecute the board before the justices. Such is the result of many cases . . . If such be the policy of the legislature in regard to electricity boards, it would seem right for the common law to adopt a similar policy in regard to contractors. If the electricity boards are not liable for economic loss due to negligence which results in the cutting off of the supply, nor should a contractor be liable.

The second consideration is the nature of the hazard, namely, the cutting of the supply of electricity. This is a hazard which we all run. It may be due to a short circuit, to a flash of lightning, to a tree falling on the wires, to an accidental cutting of the cable, or even to the negligence of someone or other. And when it does happen, it affects a multitude of persons; not as a rule by way of physical damage to them or their property, but by putting them to inconvenience, and sometimes to economic loss. The supply is usually restored in a few hours, so the economic loss is not very large. Such a hazard is regarded by most people as a thing they must put up with—without seeking compensation from anyone. Some there are who install a stand-by system. Others seek refuge by taking out an insurance policy against breakdown in the supply. But most people are content to take the risk on themselves. When the supply is cut off, they do not go running round to their solicitor. They do not try to find out whether it was anyone's fault. They just put up with it. They try to make up the economic loss by doing more work next day. This is a healthy attitude which the law should encourage.

The third consideration is this. If claims for economic loss were permitted for this particular hazard, there would be no end of claims. Some might be genuine, but many might be inflated, or even false. A machine might not have been in use anyway, but it would be easy to put it down to the cut in supply. It would be well-nigh impossible to check the claims. If there was economic loss on one day, did the applicant do his best to mitigate it by working harder next day? And so forth. Rather than expose claimants to such temptation and defendants to such hard labour—on comparatively small claims—it is better to disallow economic loss altogether, at any rate when it stands alone, independent of any physical damage.

The fourth consideration is that, in such a hazard as this, the risk of economic loss should be suffered by the whole community who suffer the losses—usually many but comparatively small losses—rather than on the one pair of shoulders, that is, on the contractor on whom the total of them, all added together, might be very heavy.

The fifth consideration is that the law provides for deserving cases. If the defendant is guilty of negligence which cuts off the electricity supply and causes actual physical damage to person or property, that physical damage can be recovered: see *Baker v Crow Carrying Co Ltd*, unreported, CA 1960, referred to by Buckley LJ in *S.C.M. (UK) Ltd v W. J. Whittall & Son Ltd* [1971] 1 QB 337 at 356, and also any economic loss truly consequential on the material damage: see *British Celanese Ltd v A.H. Hunt (Capacitors) Ltd* [1969] 1 WLR 959 and *S.C.M. (UK) Ltd v W. J. Whittall & Son Ltd* [1971] 1 QB 337. Such cases will be comparatively few. They will be readily capable of proof and will be easily checked. They should be and are admitted.

These considerations lead me to the conclusion that the plaintiffs should recover for the physical damage to the one melt (£368), and the loss of profit on that melt consequent thereon (£400); but not for the loss of profit on the four melts (£1,767), because that was economic loss independent of the physical damage. I would, therefore, allow the appeal and reduce the damages to £768.

Lawton LJ gave a separate judgment in which he concurred with Lord Denning MR. **Edmund-Davies LJ** dissented, holding that all foreseeable loss, including economic loss, that was directly attributable to the negligence ought to be recoverable.

Appeal allowed.

COMMENTARY

In *Spartan Steel*, the plaintiffs had suffered physical damage to property (the melt that was removed from the furnace), consequential economic loss (the loss of profit on that melt) and pure economic loss (the loss of profit on the four melts that would have been processed had the electricity not been cut off). The Court of Appeal allowed the plaintiffs to recover for the first two heads of damage, but not for the third. Further guidance on the recoverability of *consequential* economic loss was given by the Court of Appeal in *Conarken Group Ltd v Network Rail Infrastructure Ltd* [2011] 2 CLC 1. Employees of the defendants negligently damaged railway infrastructure owned by the claimant, Network Rail. The defendants agreed that they were liable for the cost of repairing the infrastructure and for associated costs related to the damage (such as train crew overtime, additional fuel and buses and taxis for passengers). However, they disputed their liability to pay the amounts the claimant became contractually liable to pay third parties—train operating companies (TOCs) that ran trains over the tracks owned by the claimant—as a result of the damage, largely because the formula for calculating these losses relied on the effect the damage would have on the future profits of the train operating companies. The trial judge allowed the claimant to recover for these consequential economic losses and the Court of Appeal upheld this decision. According to Jackson LJ (at [145]), the following four principles could be discerned from the authorities:

(i) Economic loss which flows directly and foreseeably from physical damage to property may be recoverable. The threshold test of foreseeability does not require the tortfeasor to have any detailed knowledge of the claimant's business affairs or financial circumstances, so long as the general nature of the claimant's loss is foreseeable.

(ii) One of the recognised categories of recoverable economic loss is loss of income following damage to revenue generating property.

(iii) Loss of future business as a result of damage to property is a head of damage which lies on the outer fringe of recoverability. Whether the claimant can recover for such economic loss depends upon the circumstances of the case and the relationship between the parties.

(iv) In choosing the appropriate measure of damages for the purposes of assessing recoverable economic loss, the court seeks to arrive at an assessment which is fair and reasonable as between the claimant and the defendant.

Liability in the 'cable case' scenario exemplified by *Spartan Steel* has been confirmed by the French courts on a number of occasions (see the cases extracted in *van Gerven*, pp. 198–9), whereas in German law, where liability for pure economic loss is generally excluded, the same result has been reached as in *Spartan Steel* (BGHZ 29, 65, NJW, 479, extracted in *van Gerven*, pp. 187–8).

Although *Spartan Steel* concerned economic loss arising out of damage to property owned by another, a similarly restrictive approach is taken where the economic loss arises out of a personal injury suffered by a third party. For example, in *Islington LBC v University College London Hospital* [2006] PIQR P3, the Court of Appeal held that the defendant hospital was not liable to a local council that was required to provide residential care to a patient injured due to the hospital's negligence; Ouseley J noted that the case was similar to a business being deprived of the services of a negligently treated patient or of a negligently injured road user, where no claim would lie. However, some jurisdictions have taken a different approach. In *Barclay v Penberthy* (2012) 246 CLR 258, a plane chartered by a marine technology company crashed shortly after take-off, and several employees of the company were killed or injured. The High Court of Australia held that the pilot and his employer owed a tortious duty of care to the company in respect of the pure economic loss it had suffered as a result of the crash, since they had known how important the employees were to the success of the project in which the company was then engaged. And in Italy, the Corte di Cassazione in its famous *Meroni* decision (*Torino Calcio SpA v Romero*, Cass. civ., SU, 26.1.1971, no. 174) ruled that a football club could recover damages after its star player (Meroni) was killed in a car accident caused by the defendant's negligence. A similar claim had previously succeeded in France (*Football Club de Metz v Wiroth*, Colmar, Ch. dét. à Metz, 20.1.1955). However, a majority of European jurisdictions would reject such a claim. See further M. Bussani and V. V. Palmer (eds), *Pure Economic Loss in Europe* (Cambridge: CUP, 2003), pp. 134–5 and 241–54.

The loss suffered by the claimant in such cases is sometimes referred to as 'relational economic loss', in that it results from damage to the property or person of a third party, and the claimant suffers the loss because of his or her relationship with that third party, which is typically a contractual one. Where the contractual arrangements are such that the consequences of the physical harm fall substantially on the claimant, a case may be put for allowing an action to the claimant, even though the loss is purely economic. After all, the other party to the contract (who has the right to sue) has not suffered the substantial loss, and cannot under orthodox contractual principles recover for a loss suffered by someone else (cf. *The Albazero* [1977] AC 774; *Linden Gardens Trust Ltd v Lenesta Sludge Disposals Ltd* [1994] 1 AC 85; *Alfred McAlpine Construction Ltd v Panatown Ltd* [2001] 1 AC 518). The paradoxical position may arise that the person who has suffered the loss has no claim, while the person who has the claim has suffered no loss (cf. *White v Jones*, extracted in IV). Conversely, it can be argued that the claimant could have protected themselves against the loss by changing the terms of the contract with the third party, who would then be able to recover from the defendant in their tort claim for the property damage or personal injury the additional costs of compensating the claimant under the contract (provided these were not too remote).

Courts in other Commonwealth jurisdictions have shown a willingness to expand the frontiers of liability for relational economic loss, albeit only cautiously, since (as Lord Denning pointed out in *Spartan Steel*) this type of claim raises 'floodgates' concerns. In *Canadian National Railway Co v Norsk Pacific Steamship Co* [1992] 1 SCR 1021, the Supreme Court of Canada recognised a claim for relational economic loss where the plaintiff railway company was deprived of the use of a railway bridge—which belonged to a third party with whom the plaintiff had negotiated a contractual licence—as the result of damage to the bridge caused when the defendant's boat was negligently driven into it. The majority of the court held that liability arose because the plaintiff was engaged in a joint venture with the owner of the bridge:

> [W]here the plaintiff's operations are so closely allied to the operations of the party suffering physical damage and to its property (which—as damaged—causes the plaintiff's loss) that it can be considered a joint venturer with the owner of the property, the plaintiff can recover its economic loss even though the plaintiff has suffered no physical damage to its own property. To deny recovery in such circumstances would be to deny it to a person who for practical purposes is in the same position as if he or she owned the property physically damaged.

For relaxation of the exclusionary rule in this context in Australia, see *Caltex Oil (Australia) v The Dredge 'Willemstad'* (1976) 136 CLR 529; *Perre v Apand Pty Ltd* (1999) 198 CLR 180; and *Barclay v Penberthy* (discussed earlier).

Suppose a variant of the facts of *Spartan Steel*, in which the operator of a frozen food facility is forced to incur expenses to prevent the food from thawing out after the defendant carelessly cuts the power supply. Would these expenses be pure economic loss? And should economic loss be recoverable when it is incurred to prevent physical damage being suffered as a result of another's negligence? (For discussion of these issues, see Fleming, 'Preventive Damages', in N. Mullany (ed.), *Torts in the Nineties* (Sydney: Law Book Co, 1997); Nolan, 'Preventive Damages' (2016) 132 LQR 68). More generally, do you think that English law should be more flexible in departing from the exclusionary rule?

3. Justifications for the Exclusionary Rule

Canadian National Railway Co v Norsk Pacific Steamship Co [1992] 1 SCR 1021 (Supreme Court of Canada)

The facts of this case are given in the commentary preceding this extract.

McLachlin J

Are there practical reasons why the recovery of economic loss should be confined to cases where the plaintiff has sustained physical damage or injury or relied on a negligent misrepresentation? Will extension of recovery of economic loss to other situations open the floodgates of liability, prove so uncertain as to be unworkable, or have an adverse economic impact? Such questions are difficult to answer, but some assistance may be gained from looking at what has happened where the rule has been broadened and from examining the merits of the economic arguments urged in support of restricting recovery.

(1) The Comparative Evidence

The comparative historical perspective provides little support for the need for a rule which confines recovery of economic loss to cases where the plaintiff has suffered physical loss or has relied on a negligent misstatement. The civil law in Canada and abroad appears to function adequately without recourse to such a rule. In the common law jurisdictions of Canada, where the availability of damages for pure economic loss has been accepted for a decade and a half, the twin spectres of unlimited recovery and unworkable uncertainty have not materialised. And to the extent that recovery for pure economic loss has been allowed in the United States, it seems not to have provoked adverse consequences but rather to have satisfied the public demand for justice so essential to maintaining the vitality of the law of negligence.

(2) Economic Theory

The arguments advanced under this head proceed from the premise that a certain type of loss should not be seen in terms of fault but seen rather as the more or less inevitable by-product of desirable but inherently dangerous (or 'risky') activity. Viewing the activity thus, it is argued that it may well be just to distribute its costs among all who benefit from that activity, and conversely unfair to impose it upon individuals who (assuming human error to be the inevitable by-product of human activity) are viewed as the 'faultless' instruments causing the loss. This basis for administering losses has been variously described as 'collectivisation of losses' or 'loss distribution' . . . It arguably amounts to a rejection or diminution of the concept of personal fault on which our law of tort (and the civil law of delict) is based.

Three arguments are put forward: (1) the insurance argument; (2) the loss spreading argument; and (3) the 'contractual allocation of risk' argument. None of them, in my view, establishes that the extension of recovery granted by the courts in this case is unfair or inefficient.

The insurance argument says that the plaintiff is in a better position to predict economic loss consequent on an accident, and hence better able to obtain cheap insurance against the contingency. From a macro-economic point of view, this will result in an overall saving. The argument, however, depends on a number of questionable assumptions. As Bishop, 'Economic Loss in Tort' (1982) 2 OJLS 1 at p. 2, puts it:

> It is said that the victim, even when he sustains large losses, is the least cost insurer where financial loss is concerned. This argument must overcome two difficulties. First, the common law restriction of financial loss recovery reduces incentives to tortfeasors to take care. For example it is cheaper for a builder to dig without checking for the presence of gas mains or electricity cables. Such reduced care will, in the long run, result in more accidents. So, if the insurance argument is to be sustained, the victim must be not only the better insurer, but better by some margin so great that it justifies the losses from more frequent and more severe injury. Second, it seems doubtful that either victim or tortfeasor could in fact insure at reasonable cost in the insurance markets of the real world. There does exist 'key man' or business interruption insurance, but no general insurance against lost profit—a type of insurance that would suffer from extreme moral hazard problems. The price of market insurance will always include some cost for administration. Most firms will find the price too high to justify purchase. Usually the only insurance available will be self-insurance. Why should we assume that victims do that better than tortfeasors?

The loss spreading justification asserts that it is better for the economic well-being of society to spread the risk among many parties rather than place it on the shoulders of the tortfeasor.

Again, this argument is based on questionable assumptions. To quote Bishop, *supra*, at p. 2, once more:

> [This argument] is a variant of the insurance argument. The tortfeasor, for example a small construction firm, easily could be bankrupted by the claims, for example those arising from interrupted power supply. In such cases it is said that numerous small losses to victims are to be preferred to one large loss to the tortfeasor. The victims as a class are natural self-insurers of the loss. The tortfeasor would have to engage in expensive market transactions to insure. Perhaps this is so, but there are two points against it. First not only the question of justice or of efficient risk distribution are involved. Where losses are spread by relieving the tortfeasor of liability we can expect more accidents, and so more losses, to occur. Second, some of the victims may sustain large losses not small ones. In any case, the loss spreading rationale cannot justify the numerous cases where *there is only one victim*. [Emphasis in original.]

A third argument focuses on the ability of persons who stand to suffer economic loss due to the damage to the property of another, to allocate the risk within their contracts effectively with property owners. The law of negligence has no business compensating such persons, it is argued, because it makes better economic sense for them to provide for the possibility of damage to the bridge by negotiating a term that in the event of failure the owner of the bridge would compensate them . . .

The 'contractual allocation of risk' argument rests on a number of important, but questionable assumptions. First, the argument assumes that all persons or business entities organise their affairs in accordance with the laws of economic efficiency, assigning liability to the 'least-cost risk avoider.' Second, it assumes that all parties to a transaction share an equality of bargaining power which will result in the effective allocation of risk. It is not considered that certain parties who control the situation (e.g. the owners of an indispensable bridge) may refuse to indemnify against the negligence of those over whom they have no control, or may demand such an exorbitant premium for this indemnification that it would be more cost-effective for the innocent victim to insure itself. Thirdly, it overlooks the historical centrality of personal fault to our concept of negligence or 'delict' and the role this may have in curbing negligent conduct and thus limiting the harm done to innocent parties, not all of whom are large enterprises capable of maximising their economic situation. Given the uncertainty of these premises, it is far from clear that the Court should deny recovery of pure economic loss on the basis of arguments based on allocation of risk.

(3) Summary of Pragmatic Considerations

I conclude that it has not been shown that the approach enunciated by this Court in [*City of Kamloops v Nielsen* [1984] 2 SCR 2] threatens to open the floodgates of indeterminate liability, leads to undue uncertainty, or causes unfair or inefficient economic allocation of resources. On the contrary, the *Kamloops* approach is arguably sensitive to these concerns. Moreover, should the courts in following this approach extend liability too far, it is open to the legislatures of this country to impose limits. There is no practical reason evident at this stage for the courts to retreat to the inflexibility of a rule that never countenances recovery of economic loss except where the plaintiff has suffered physical damage or injury or has relied on a negligent misrepresentation.

COMMENTARY

McLachlin J refers to the earlier decision of the Supreme Court of Canada in *City of Kamloops v Nielsen* [1984] 2 SCR 2. This case adopted as the law of Canada the two-stage approach to establishing the duty of care set out by Lord Wilberforce in *Anns v Merton London Borough* [1978] AC 728. Relying on this approach the Canadian Supreme Court for a time exhibited a willingness to go beyond the English authorities in allowing claims for pure economic loss (see in particular *Winnipeg Condominium Corporation No 36 v Bird Construction Co* [1995] 1 SCR 85, extracted in II). However, in recent years the Court has taken a more conservative approach, and in its most recent decision a majority held that, to recover for pure economic loss in negligence, a plaintiff must establish both that the loss was the result of an interference with a legally recognised right and that there was sufficient proximity between the plaintiff and the defendant (*1688782 Ontario Inc v Maple Leaf Foods Inc* (2020) 450 DLR (4th) 181).

Is a court in a position to answer questions relating to insurance and loss spreading? In dissent, La Forest J considered the same factors but came to a different result on the facts, arguing that lawyers 'should inform themselves about fundamental matters of insurability'. Within the confines of private litigation is this a realistic expectation? Even if judges were prepared to undertake such analysis, doubts have been expressed over the availability of the necessary empirical data (Markesinis (1993) 109 LQR 5 at 10). As regards the utility of courts' attempts at comparative research and economic analysis, Weir offers the following, rather uncharitable view ('Errare Humanum Est', in P. Birks (ed.), *The Frontiers of Liability*, vol. 2 (Oxford: OUP, 1994), p. 107):

It is fortunate that there are, or were, so many trees in that ex-dominion, for otherwise one might wonder at spending over 100 pages on futile exercises in comparative law and juvenile law and economics . . . What is quite clear is that no practitioner is aided in the slightest by the contrary disquisitions, more suitable to a law review—if one could get them published—than to the law reports.

Do you think Canadian practitioners were given much guidance by the decision in *Norsk* as to how future cases might be decided?

II. Defective Product Economic Loss

Pure economic loss claims involving the manufacture of defective goods and the construction of defective buildings have caused the courts particular problems. The duty of care formulated by Lord Atkin in *Donoghue v Stevenson* referred to foresight of physical injury or damage to property as a consequence of negligent behaviour. But if goods simply fail to work, there is no physical 'damage' on which to base a duty of care; the appropriate claim would seem to be in contract. The claimant's argument is that the goods are not of an acceptable quality, and quality is protected, if at all, through contractual warranties. A similar analysis would apply where a building was uninhabitable because of defective design or construction. Where is the damage on which to base a *Donoghue v Stevenson* duty of care? What if the goods or the building cause physical harm to themselves, for example the electrical appliance blows up or cracks start to appear in the walls of the building? On one view, there is little to distinguish such cases from those of pure unfitness for use. The basic complaint is that the owner's expectations in acquiring the goods or the building have been frustrated because they received something of lesser quality than they were expecting, and as a result paid more than the thing that they bought was worth. Accordingly, the loss suffered is purely economic. Of course, in such a case it may be easier to tell that the good or building is of a lesser quality, and that the producer or builder has been negligent, but this does not change the nature of the complaint. If the protection of expectations is properly seen as the preserve of the law of contract, why should the owner be allowed to look beyond this for a remedy in the law of tort?

In two cases in the 1970s, the Court of Appeal and the House of Lords recognised negligence claims for economic losses arising out of the defective construction of a building (see *Dutton v Bognor Regis Urban District Council* [1972] 1 QB 373; *Anns v Merton London Borough* [1978] AC 728). In *Anns*, a defect in the building's foundations caused subsidence, leading to the appearance of cracks in the building's walls. The House of Lords allowed a claim for the recovery of repair costs, on the basis that such repair was necessary in order to avoid a 'present or imminent danger to the health or safety of the persons occupying it'. In Lord Wilberforce's view, the plaintiff had suffered 'material physical damage'. A complicating feature of the case was that the plaintiff had brought proceedings not against the builder but against the local authority, which had the power under statute to supervise the building work. The precise principle on which the House of Lords based its decision was notoriously unclear. Was it necessary to show an imminent danger to health or safety? If so, was this because the claim was against a public body exercising powers under a statute designed to protect health and safety? Or did this requirement have to be satisfied in every claim in respect of a defective building (even against the builder)? And on what basis did Lord Wilberforce conclude that there was 'material physical damage'? These issues, and more generally the appropriateness of the liability recognised in *Anns*, were considered in the two decisions of the House of Lords extracted next.

D & F Estates Ltd v Church Comrs for England [1989] AC 177

The plaintiffs were, respectively, the lessee and the occupiers of a flat in a building called Chelwood House which was owned by the first defendants. The building had been erected in the 1960s by the third defendants (the builders) who had engaged a sub-contractor to carry out the necessary plastering work. The builders reasonably believed the sub-contractor to be skilled and competent but in fact the sub-contractor carried out the work negligently. In 1980, the plaintiffs found that the plaster in their flat was loose and brought an action against, inter alia, the builders claiming the cost of remedial work. The judge awarded the plaintiffs damages against the builders but the Court of Appeal reversed this decision on the ground that the builders had discharged the duty of care that they owed to the plaintiffs as future occupiers. The plaintiffs appealed to the House of Lords, where their Lordships considered a submission that the cost of repairing the defective plaster was not damage which the plaintiffs could recover in tort since it represented pure economic loss.

Lord Bridge of Harwich

[T]he liability of the builder of a permanent structure which is dangerously defective . . . can only arise if the defect remains hidden until the defective structure causes personal injury or damage to property other than the structure itself. If the defect is discovered before any damage is done, the loss sustained by the owner of the structure, who has to repair or demolish it to avoid a potential source of danger to third parties, would seem to be purely economic. Thus, if I acquire a property with a dangerously defective garden wall which is attributable to the bad workmanship of the original builder, it is difficult to see any basis in principle on which I can sustain an action in tort against the builder for the cost of either repairing or demolishing the wall. No physical damage has been caused. All that has happened is that the defect in the wall has been discovered in time to prevent damage occurring. I do not find it necessary for the purpose of deciding the present appeal to express any concluded view as to how far, if at all, the ratio decidendi of *Anns v Merton London Borough* [1978] AC 728 involves a departure from this principle establishing a new cause of action in negligence against a builder when the only damage alleged to have been suffered by the plaintiff is the discovery of a defect in the very structure which the builder erected.

My example of the garden wall, however, is that of a very simple structure. I can see that more difficult questions may arise in relation to a more complex structure like a dwelling house. One view would be that such a structure should be treated in law as a single indivisible unit. On this basis, if the unit becomes a potential source of danger when a hitherto hidden defect in construction manifests itself, the builder, as in the case of the garden wall, should not in principle be liable for the cost of remedying the defect . . .

However, I can see that it may well be arguable that in the case of complex structures, as indeed possibly in the case of complex chattels, one element of the structure should be regarded for the purpose of the application of the principles under discussion as distinct from another element, so that damage to one part of the structure caused by a hidden defect in another part may qualify to be treated as damage to 'other property', and whether the argument should prevail may depend on the circumstances of the case. It would be unwise and it is unnecessary for the purpose of deciding the present appeal to attempt to offer authoritative solutions to these difficult problems in the abstract . . .

In the instant case the only hidden defect was in the plaster. The only item pleaded as damage to other property was 'cost of cleaning carpets and other possessions damaged or dirtied by falling plaster; £50'. Once it appeared that the plaster was loose, any danger of personal injury or of further injury to other property could have been simply avoided by the timely removal of the defective plaster. The only function of plaster on walls and ceilings, unless it is itself elaborately decorative, is to serve as a smooth surface on which to place decorative paper or paint. Whatever case there may be for treating a defect in some part of the structure of a building as causing damage to 'other property' when some other part of the building is injuriously affected, as for example cracking in walls caused by defective foundations, it would seem to me entirely artificial to treat the plaster as distinct from the decorative surface placed on it . . .

It seems to me clear that the cost of replacing the defective plaster itself, either as carried out in 1980 or as intended to be carried out in future, was not an item of damage for which the builder of Chelwood House could possibly be made liable in negligence under the principle of *Donoghue v Stevenson* [1932] AC 562 or any legitimate development of that principle. To make him so liable would be to impose on him for the benefit of those with whom he had no contractual relationship the obligation of one who warranted the quality of the plaster as regards materials, workmanship and fitness for purpose. I am glad to reach the conclusion that this is not the law, if only for the reason that a conclusion to the opposite effect would mean that the courts, in developing the common law, had gone much farther than the legislature were prepared to go in 1972, after comprehensive examination of the subject by the Law Commission, in making builders liable for defects in the quality of their work to all who subsequently acquire interests in buildings they have erected. The statutory duty imposed by the [Defective Premises Act 1972] was confined to dwelling houses and limited to defects appearing within six years. The common law duty, if it existed, could not be so confined or so limited. I cannot help feeling that consumer protection is an area of law where legislation is much better left to the legislators.

Lord Oliver of Aylmerton

My Lords, I have had the advantage of reading in draft the speech prepared by my noble and learned friend Lord Bridge, and I agree that the appeal should be dismissed for the reasons which he has given. In particular, I agree with his conclusion that, quite apart from the question of [the builder's] liability for the negligent performance by their sub-contractors of the duties under the plastering sub-contract, the cost of replacing the defective plaster would, in any event, be irrecoverable.

It is, I think, clear that the decision of this House in *Anns v Merton London Borough* [1978] AC 728 introduced, in relation to the construction of buildings, an entirely new type of product liability, if not, indeed, an entirely novel concept of the tort of negligence . . . In the first place, in no other context has it previously been suggested that a cause of action in tort arises in English law for the defective manufacture of an article which causes no injury other than injury to the defective article itself. If I buy a secondhand car to which there has been fitted a pneumatic tyre which, as a result of carelessness in manufacture, is dangerously defective and which bursts, causing injury to me or to the car, no doubt the negligent manufacturer is liable in tort on the ordinary application of *Donoghue v Stevenson*. But if the tyre bursts without causing any injury other than to itself or if I discover the defect before a burst occurs, I know of no principle on which I can claim to recover from the manufacturer in tort the cost of making good the defect which, in practice, could only be the cost of supplying and fitting a new tyre. That would be, in effect, to attach to goods a non-contractual warranty of fitness which would follow the goods into whosoever hands they came. Such a concept was suggested, obiter, by Lord Denning MR in *Dutton's* case [1972] 1 QB 373 at 396, but it was entirely unsupported by any authority and is, in my opinion, contrary to principle. . . .

My Lords, I have to confess that the underlying logical basis for and the boundaries of the doctrine emerging from *Anns v Merton London Borough* are not entirely clear to me and it is in any event unnecessary for the purposes of the instant appeal to attempt a definitive exposition. This much at least seems clear: that in so far as the case is authority for the proposition that a builder responsible for the construction of the building is liable in tort at common law for damage occurring through his negligence to the very thing which he has constructed, such liability is limited directly to cases where the defect is one which threatens the health or safety of occupants or of third parties and (possibly) other property. In such a case, however, the damages recoverable are limited to expenses necessarily incurred in averting that danger. The case cannot, in my opinion, properly be adapted to support the recovery of damages for pure economic loss going beyond that, and for the reasons given by my noble and learned friend Lord Bridge, with whose analysis I respectfully agree, such loss is not in principle recoverable in tort unless the case can be brought within the principle of reliance established by *Hedley Byrne v Heller* [1964] AC 465. In the instant case the defective plaster caused no damage to the remainder of the building and in so far as it presented a risk of damage to other property or to the person of any occupant that was remediable simply by the process of removal. I agree, accordingly, for the reasons which my noble and learned friend Lord Bridge has given, that the cost of replacing the defective plaster is not an item for which the builder can be held liable in negligence. I too would dismiss the appeal.

Lord Ackner, **Lord Templeman** and **Lord Jauncey** concurred.

Appeal dismissed.

COMMENTARY

Perhaps one should not shed many tears for the plaintiffs in this case. As Weir, 'Errare Humanum Est', in P. Birks (ed.), *The Frontiers of Liability*, vol. 2 (Oxford: OUP, 1994), p. 106 comments:

In *D & F Estates* . . . the plaintiffs, who, as it appeared, had got their London flat gratuitously from a property company in which they were interested, and were now living in the south of France, were complaining that the plaster was starting to fall off the walls to the risk of their persons(!) only fifteen years after the flat was completed. The trial judge awarded them a sum of over £89,000 plus interest. The principle which led to this was surely ripe for lopping.

The lopping began in the decision of the House of Lords, which affirmed that damage to a building attributable to its defective construction generally constitutes pure economic loss. As the action was brought against the builder, it was not strictly speaking necessary to consider whether *Anns* was still good law, although following this decision its position could well be described as perilous. The opportunity directly to consider the correctness of *Anns* came soon after, in the next extracted case.

Murphy v Brentwood District Council [1991] 1 AC 398

The plaintiff had bought one of a pair of semi-detached houses in Brentwood, which had been built and sold by ABC Homes. The foundations of the house took the form of a concrete raft, whose design had been approved by the council in the performance of its statutory powers under the Public Health Act 1936, on the recommendation of independent consulting engineers. After ten or more years had passed, serious cracks began to appear in the walls of the house, which an investigation showed were caused by the concrete raft having subsided differentially. The plaintiff was unable to afford remedial work, which in any case would have been uneconomical, and so sold the house for some £35,000 less than its estimated worth without the defects—to a builder who was aware of them. The plaintiff (or his insurers) sued the council, whom the trial judge found had been negligent in considering the suitability of the design: their duty of care had not been discharged by acting on the advice of competent independent engineers.

Lord Keith of Kinkel

My Lords, this appeal raises directly the question whether *Anns v Merton London Borough* [1978] AC 728 was in all respects correctly decided . . .

In my opinion it must now be recognised that, although the damage in *Anns* was characterised as physical damage by Lord Wilberforce, it was purely economic loss. . . .

[T]he next point for examination is whether the avoidance of [pure economic loss] fell within the scope of any duty of care owed to the plaintiffs by the local authority. On the basis of the law as it stood at the time of the decision the answer to that question must be in the negative. The right to recover for pure economic loss, not flowing from physical injury, did not then extend beyond the situation where the loss had been sustained through reliance on negligent misstatements, as in *Hedley Byrne v Heller* [1964] AC 465. Further, though the purposes of the 1936 Act as regards securing compliance with building byelaws covered the avoidance of injury to the safety or health of inhabitants of houses and of members of the public generally, these purposes did not cover the avoidance of pure economic loss to owners of buildings (see *Governors of the Peabody Donation Fund v Sir Lindsay Parkinson & Co Ltd* [1985] AC 210 at 241). On analysis, the nature of the duty held by *Anns* to be incumbent on the local authority went very much further than a duty to take reasonable care to prevent injury to safety or health. The duty held to exist may be formulated as one to take reasonable care to avoid putting a future inhabitant owner of a house in a position in which he is threatened, by reason of a defect in the house, with avoidable physical injury to person or health and is obliged, in order to continue to occupy the house without suffering such injury, to expend money for the purpose of rectifying the defect.

The existence of a duty of that nature should not, in my opinion, be affirmed without a careful examination of the implications of such affirmation. To start with, if such a duty is incumbent on the local authority, a similar duty must necessarily be incumbent also on the builder of the house. If the builder of the house is to be so subject, there can be no grounds in logic or in principle for not extending liability on like grounds to the manufacturer of a chattel. That would open up an exceedingly wide field of claims, involving the introduction of something in the nature of a transmissible warranty of quality. The purchaser of an article who discovered that it suffered from a dangerous defect before that defect had caused any damage would be entitled to recover from the manufacturer the cost of rectifying the defect, and, presumably, if the article was not capable of economic repair, the amount of loss sustained through discarding it. Then it would be open to question whether there should not also be a right to recovery where the defect renders the article not dangerous but merely useless. The economic loss in either case would be the same. There would also be a problem where the defect causes the destruction of the article itself, without causing any personal injury or damage to other property. A similar problem could arise, if the *Anns* principle is to be treated as confined to real property, where a building collapses when unoccupied . . .

In *D & F Estates Ltd v Church Comrs for England* [1989] AC 177 both Lord Bridge and Lord Oliver expressed themselves as having difficulty in reconciling the decision in *Anns* with pre-existing principle and as being uncertain as to the nature and scope of such new principle as it introduced. Lord Bridge suggested that in the case of a complex structure such as a building one element of the structure might be regarded for *Donoghue v Stevenson* purposes as distinct from another element, so that damage to one part of the structure caused by a hidden defect in another part might qualify to be treated as damage to 'other property' (see [1989] AC 177 at 206). I think that it would be unrealistic to take this view as regards a building the whole of which had been erected and equipped by the same contractor. In that situation the whole package provided by the contractor would, in my opinion, fall to be regarded as one unit rendered unsound as such by a defect in the particular part. On the other hand, where, for example, the electric wiring had been installed by a sub-contractor and due to a defect caused by lack of care a fire occurred which destroyed the building, it might not be stretching ordinary principles too far to hold the electrical sub-contractor liable for the damage . . . But, even if Lord Bridge's theory were to be held acceptable, it would not seem to extend to the founding of liability on a local authority, considering that the purposes of the 1936 Act are concerned with averting danger to health and safety, not danger or damage to property. Further, it would not cover the situation which might arise through discovery, before any damage had occurred, of a defect likely to give rise to damage in the future.

Liability under the *Anns* decision is postulated on the existence of a present or imminent danger to health or safety. But, considering that the loss involved in incurring expenditure to avert the danger is pure economic loss, there would seem to be no logic in confining the remedy to cases where such danger exists. There is likewise no logic in confining it to cases where some damage (perhaps comparatively slight) has been caused to the building, but refusing it where the existence of the danger has come to light in some other way, for example through a structural survey which happens to have been carried out, or where the danger inherent in some particular component or material has been revealed through failure in some other building. Then there is the question whether the remedy is available where the defect is rectified, not in order to avert danger to an inhabitant occupier himself, but in order to enable an occupier, who may be a corporation, to continue to occupy the building through its employees without putting those employees at risk.

In my opinion it is clear that *Anns* did not proceed on any basis of established principle, but introduced a new species of liability governed by a principle indeterminate in character but having the potentiality of covering a wide range of situations, involving chattels as well as real property, in which it had never hitherto been thought that the law of negligence had any proper place . . .

In my opinion there can be no doubt that *Anns* has for long been widely regarded as an unsatisfactory decision. In relation to the scope of the duty owed by a local authority it proceeded on what must, with due respect to its source, be regarded as a somewhat superficial examination of principle and there has been extreme difficulty, highlighted most recently by the speeches in the *D & F Estates* case, in ascertaining on exactly what basis of principle it did proceed. I think it must now be recognised that it did not proceed on any basis of principle at all, but constituted a remarkable example of judicial legislation. It has engendered a vast spate of litigation, and each of the cases in the field which have reached this House has been distinguished. Others have been distinguished in the Court of Appeal. The result has been to keep the effect of the decision within reasonable bounds, but that has been achieved only by applying strictly the words of Lord Wilberforce and by refusing to accept the logical implications of the decision itself. These logical implications show that the case properly considered has potentiality for collision with long-established principles regarding liability in the tort of negligence for economic loss. There can be no doubt that to depart from the decision would re-establish a degree of certainty in this field of law which it has done a remarkable amount to upset.

So far as policy considerations are concerned, it is no doubt the case that extending the scope of the tort of negligence may tend to inhibit carelessness and improve standards of manufacture and construction. On the other hand, overkill may present its own disadvantages, as was remarked in *Rowling v Takaro Properties Ltd* [1988] AC 473 at 502. There may be room for the view that *Anns*-type liability will tend to encourage owners of buildings found to be dangerous to repair rather than run the risk of injury. The owner may, however, and perhaps quite often does, prefer to sell the building at its diminished value, as happened in the present case.

It must, of course, be kept in mind that the decision has stood for some 13 years. On the other hand, it is not a decision of the type that is to a significant extent taken into account by citizens or indeed local authorities in ordering their affairs. No doubt its existence results in local authorities having to pay increased insurance premiums, but to be relieved of that necessity would be to their advantage, not to their detriment. To overrule it is unlikely to result in significantly increased insurance premiums for householders. It is perhaps of some significance that most litigation involving the decision consists in contests between insurance companies, as is largely the position in the present case. The decision is capable of being regarded as affording a measure of justice, but as against that the impossibility of finding any coherent and logically based doctrine behind it is calculated to put the law of negligence into a state of confusion defying rational analysis. It is also material that *Anns* has the effect of imposing on builders generally a liability going far beyond that which Parliament thought fit to impose on house builders alone by the Defective Premises Act 1972, a statute very material to the policy of the decision but not adverted to in it. There is much to be said for the view that in what is essentially a consumer protection field, as was observed by Lord Bridge in *D & F Estates Ltd v Church Comrs for England* [1989] AC 177 at 207, the precise extent and limits of the liabilities which in the public interest should be imposed on builders and local authorities are best left to the legislature.

My Lords, I would hold that *Anns* was wrongly decided as regards the scope of any private law duty of care resting on local authorities in relation to their function of taking steps to secure compliance with building byelaws or regulations and should be departed from . . .

My Lords, for these reasons I would allow the appeal.

Lord Bridge of Harwich

Dangerous Defects and Defects of Quality

If a manufacturer negligently puts into circulation a chattel containing a latent defect which renders it dangerous to persons or property, the manufacturer, on the well-known principles established by *Donoghue v Stevenson* [1932] AC 562 will be liable in tort for injury to persons or damage to property which the chattel causes. But if a manufacturer produces and sells a chattel which is merely defective in quality, even to the extent that it is valueless for the purpose for which it is intended, the manufacturer's liability at common law arises only under and by reference to the terms of any contract to which he is a party in relation to the chattel; the common law does not impose on him any liability in tort to persons to whom he owes no duty in contract but who, having acquired the chattel, suffer economic loss because the chattel is defective in quality. If a dangerous defect in a chattel is discovered before it causes any personal injury or damage to property, because the danger is now known and the chattel cannot be safely used unless the defect is repaired, the defect becomes merely a defect in quality. The chattel is either capable of repair at economic cost or it is worthless and must be scrapped. In either case the loss sustained by the owner or hirer of the chattel is purely economic. It is recoverable against any party who owes the user a relevant contractual duty. But it is not recoverable in tort in the absence of a special relationship of proximity imposing on the tortfeasor a duty of care to safeguard the plaintiff from economic loss. There is no such special relationship between the manufacturer of a chattel and a remote owner or hirer.

I believe that these principles are equally applicable to buildings. If a builder erects a structure containing a latent defect which renders it dangerous to persons or property, he will be liable in tort for injury to persons or damage to property resulting from that dangerous defect. But, if the defect becomes apparent before any injury or damage has been caused, the loss sustained by the building owner is purely economic. If the defect can be repaired at economic cost, that is the measure of the loss. If the building cannot be repaired, it may have to be abandoned as unfit for occupation and therefore valueless. These economic losses are recoverable if they flow from breach of a relevant contractual duty, but, here again, in the absence of a special relationship of proximity they are not recoverable in tort. The only qualification I would make to this is that, if a building stands so close to the boundary of the building owner's land that after discovery of the dangerous defect it remains a potential source of injury to persons or property on neighbouring land or on the highway, the building owner ought, in principle, to be entitled to recover in tort from the negligent builder the cost of obviating the danger, whether by repair or by demolition, so far as that cost is necessarily incurred in order to protect himself from potential liability to third parties . . .

The Complex Structure Theory

In my speech in the *D v F Estates* case [1989] AC 177 at 206–207 I mooted the possibility that in complex structures or complex chattels one part of a structure or chattel might, when it caused damage to another part of the same structure or chattel, be regarded in the law of tort as having caused damage to 'other property' for the purpose of the application of *Donoghue v Stevenson* principles. I expressed no opinion as to the validity of this theory, but put it forward for consideration as a possible ground on which the facts considered in *Anns* might be distinguishable from the facts which had to be considered in *D & F Estates* itself. I shall call this for convenience 'the complex structure theory' and it is, so far as I can see, only if and to the extent that this theory can be affirmed and applied that there can be any escape from the conclusions I have indicated above under the rubric 'Dangerous defects and defects of quality'.

The complex structure theory has, so far as I know, never been subjected to express and detailed examination in any English authority.

[His Lordship considered the 'extreme application of the complex structure theory treating each part of the entire structure as a separate item of property', and continued:]

[S]uch an application of the theory seems to me quite unrealistic. The reality is that the structural elements in any building form a single indivisible unit of which the different parts are essentially interdependent. To the extent that there is any defect in one part of the structure it must to a greater or lesser degree necessarily affect all other parts of the structure. Therefore any defect in the structure is a defect in the quality of the whole and it is quite artificial, in order to impose a legal liability which the law would not otherwise impose, to treat a defect in an integral structure, so far as it weakens the structure, as a dangerous defect liable to cause damage to 'other property'.

A critical distinction must be drawn here between some part of a complex structure which is said to be a 'danger' only because it does not perform its proper function in sustaining the other parts and some distinct item incorporated in the structure which positively malfunctions so as to inflict positive damage on the structure in which it is incorporated. Thus, if a defective central heating boiler explodes and damages a house or defective electrical installation malfunctions and sets the house on fire, I see no reason to doubt that the owner of the house, if he can prove that the damage was due to the negligence of the boiler manufacturer in the one case or the electrical contractor in the other, can recover damages in tort on *Donoghue v Stevenson* principles. But the position in law is entirely different where, by reason of the inadequacy of the foundations of the building to support the weight of the superstructure, differential settlement and consequent cracking occurs. Here, once the first cracks appear, the structure as a whole is seen to be defective and the nature of the defect is known. Even if, contrary to my view, the initial damage could be regarded as damage to other property caused by a latent defect, once the defect is known the situation of the building owner is analogous to that of the car owner who discovers that the car has faulty brakes. He may have a house which, until repairs are effected, is unfit for habitation, but, subject to the reservation I have expressed with respect to ruinous buildings at or near the boundary of the owner's property, the building no longer represents a source of danger and as it deteriorates will only damage itself.

For these reasons the complex structure theory offers no escape from the conclusion that damage to a house itself which is attributable to a defect in the structure of the house is not recoverable in tort on *Donoghue v Stevenson* principles, but represents purely economic loss which is only recoverable in contract or in tort by reason of some special relationship of proximity which imposes on the tortfeasor a duty of care to protect against economic loss . . .

Imminent Danger to Health or Safety

A necessary element in the building owner's cause of action against the negligent local authority, which does not appear to have been contemplated in *Dutton* but which, it is said in *Anns*, must be present before the cause of action accrues, is that the state of the building is such that there is present or imminent danger to the health or safety of persons occupying it. Correspondingly the damages recoverable are said to include the amount of expenditure necessary to restore the building to a condition in which it is no longer such a danger, but presumably not any further expenditure incurred in any merely qualitative restoration. I find these features of the *Anns* doctrine very difficult to understand. The theoretical difficulty of reconciling this aspect of the doctrine with previously accepted legal principle was pointed out by Lord Oliver in *D & F Estates* [1989] AC 177 at 212–13. But apart from this there are, as it appears to me, two insuperable difficulties arising from the requirement of imminent danger to health or safety as an ingredient of the cause of action which lead to quite irrational and capricious consequences in the application of the *Anns* doctrine. The first difficulty will arise where the relevant defect in the building, when it is first discovered, is not a present or imminent danger to health or safety. What is the owner to do if he is advised that the building will gradually deteriorate, if not repaired, and will in due course become a danger to health and safety, but that the longer he waits to effect repairs the greater the cost will be? Must he spend £1,000 now on the necessary repairs with no redress against the local authority? Or is he entitled to wait until the building has so far deteriorated that he has a cause of action and then to recover from the local authority the £5,000 which the necessary repairs are now going to cost? I can find no answer to this conundrum. A second difficulty will arise where the latent defect is not discovered until it causes the sudden and total collapse of the building, which occurs when the building is temporarily unoccupied and causes no damage to property except to the building itself. The building is now no longer capable of occupation and hence cannot be a danger to health or safety. It seems a very strange result that the building owner should be without remedy in this situation if he would have been able to recover from the local authority the full cost of repairing the building if only the defect had been discovered before the building fell down.

Liability for Economic Loss

All these considerations lead inevitably to the conclusion that a building owner can only recover the cost of repairing a defective building on the ground of the authority's negligence in performing its statutory function of approving plans or inspecting buildings in the course of construction if the scope of the authority's duty of care is wide enough to embrace purely economic loss. The House has already held in *D & F Estates* that a builder, in the absence of any contractual duty or of a special relationship of proximity introducing the *Hedley Byrne* principle of reliance, owes no duty of care in tort in respect of the quality of his work. As I pointed out in *D & F Estates*, to hold that the builder owed such a duty of care to any person acquiring an interest in the product of the builder's work would be to impose on him the obligations of an indefinitely transmissible warranty of quality.

By s. 1 of the Defective Premises Act 1972 Parliament has in fact imposed on builders and others undertaking work in the provision of dwellings the obligations of a transmissible warranty of the quality of their work and of the fitness for habitation of the completed dwelling. But, besides being limited to dwellings, liability under that Act is subject to a limitation period of six years from the completion of the work and to the exclusion provided for by s. 2. It would be remarkable to find that similar obligations in the nature of a transmissible warranty of quality, applicable to buildings of every kind and subject to no such limitations or exclusions as are imposed by the 1972 Act, could be derived from the builder's common law duty of care or from the duty imposed by building byelaws or regulations. In *Anns* Lord Wilberforce expressed the opinion that a builder could be held liable for a breach of statutory duty in respect of buildings which do not comply with the byelaws. But he cannot, I think, have meant that the statutory obligation to build in conformity with the byelaws by itself gives rise to obligations in the nature of transmissible warranties of quality. If he did mean that, I must respectfully disagree. I find it impossible to suppose that anything less than clear express language such as is used in s. 1 of the 1972 Act would suffice to impose such a statutory obligation . . .

In *Dutton* [1972] 1 QB 373 at 397–8 Lord Denning MR said:

> [M]rs Dutton has suffered a grievous loss. The house fell down without any fault of hers. She is in no position herself to bear the loss. Who ought in justice to bear it? I should think those who were responsible. Who are they? In the first place, the builder was responsible. It was he who laid the foundations so badly that the house fell down. In the second place, the council's inspector was responsible. It was his job to examine the foundations to see if they would take the load of the house. He failed to do it properly. In the third place, the council should answer for his failure. They were entrusted by Parliament with the task of seeing that houses were properly built. They received public funds for the purpose. The very object was to protect purchasers and occupiers of houses. Yet, they failed to protect them. Their shoulders are broad enough to bear the loss.

These may be cogent reasons of social policy for imposing liability on the authority. But the shoulders of a public authority are only 'broad enough to bear the loss' because they are financed by the public at large. It is pre-eminently for the legislature to decide whether these policy reasons should be accepted as sufficient for imposing on the public the burden of providing compensation for private financial losses. If they do so decide, it is not difficult for them to say so.

I would allow the appeal.

Lord Oliver of Aylmerton

In the 13 years which have elapsed since the decision of this House in *Anns v Merton London Borough* [1978] AC 728 the anomalies which arise from its literal application and the logical difficulty in relating it to the previously established principles of the tort of negligence have become more and more apparent. This appeal and the appeal in *Dept of the Environment v Thomas Bates & Son Ltd* [1991] 1 AC 499 which was heard shortly before it, have highlighted some of the problems which *Anns* has created and underline the urgent need for it now to be re-examined . . .

[D]espite the categorisation of the damage as 'material, physical damage' (see *Anns* [1978] AC 728 at 759 per Lord Wilberforce), it is, I think, incontestable on analysis that what the plaintiffs suffered was pure pecuniary loss and nothing more. If one asks, 'What were the damages to be awarded for?' clearly they were not to be awarded for injury to the health or person of the plaintiffs, for they had suffered none. But equally clearly, although the 'damage' was described, both in the Court of Appeal in *Dutton* and in this House in *Anns*, as physical or material damage, this simply does not withstand analysis. To begin with, it makes no sort of sense to accord a remedy where the defective nature of the structure has manifested itself by some physical symptom, such as a crack or a fractured pipe, but to deny it where the defect has been brought to light by, for instance, a structural survey in connection with a proposed sale. Moreover, the imminent danger to health or safety which was said to be the essential ground of the action was not the result of the physical manifestations which had appeared but of the inherently defective nature of the structure which they revealed. They were merely the outward signs of a deterioration resulting from the inherently defective condition with which the building had been brought into being from its inception and cannot properly be described as damage caused to the building in any accepted use of the word 'damage'.

In the speech of Lord Bridge and in my own speech in *D & F Estates Ltd v Church Comrs for England* [1989] AC 167 there was canvassed what has been called 'the complex structure theory'. This has been rightly criticised by academic writers, although I confess that I thought that both Lord Bridge and I had made it clear that it was a theory which was not embraced with any enthusiasm but was advanced as the only logically possible explanation of the categorisation of the damage in *Anns* as 'material, physical damage'. Lord Bridge has, in the course of his speech in the present case, amply demonstrated the artificiality of the theory and, for the reasons which he has given, it must be rejected as a viable explanation of the underlying basis for the decision in *Anns*. However that decision is analysed, therefore, it is in the end inescapable that the only damage for which compensation was to be awarded and which formed the essential foundation of the action was pecuniary loss and nothing more. The injury which the plaintiff suffers in such a case is that his consciousness of the possible injury to his own health or safety or that of others puts him in a position in which, in order to enable him either to go on living in the property or to exploit its financial potentiality without that risk, whether substantial or insubstantial, he has to expend money in making good the defects which have now become patent . . .

The fact is that the categorisation of the damage in *Anns* as 'material, physical damage', whilst, at first sight, lending to the decision some colour of consistency with the principle of *Donoghue v Stevenson*, has served to obscure not only the true nature of the claim but, as a result, the nature and scope of the duty on the breach of which the plaintiffs in that case were compelled to rely . . .

I frankly doubt whether, in searching for such limits [on the duty of care], the categorisation of the damage as 'material', 'physical', 'pecuniary', or 'economic' provides a particular useful contribution. Where it does, I think, serve a useful purpose is in identifying those cases in which it is necessary to search for and find something more than the mere reasonable foreseeability of damage which has occurred as providing the degree of 'proximity' necessary to support the action . . . The infliction of physical injury to the person or property of another universally requires to be justified. The causing of economic loss does not. If it is to be categorised as wrongful it is necessary to find some factor beyond the mere occurrence of the loss and the fact that its occurrence could be foreseen. Thus the categorisation of damage as economic serves at least the useful purpose of indicating that something more is required and it is one of the unfortunate features of *Anns* that it resulted initially in this essential distinction being lost sight of . . .

Lord Mackay, Lord Brandon, Lord Ackner and **Lord Jauncey of Tullichettle** concurred.

Appeal allowed.

COMMENTARY

The action in *Murphy* was against the local authority for failing to ensure that the builder constructed the house in accordance with local authority by-laws. The liability of the builder was not in issue, although it was accepted that the liability of the local authority could not be any more extensive than that of the builder. However, in a case heard together with *Murphy* (*Department of the Environment v Thomas Bates and Son Ltd* [1991] 1 AC 499), the House of Lords affirmed that a builder did not owe a duty of care to a remote purchaser in respect of pure economic loss suffered through the defective construction of a building, an unsurprising result given the decision in *D & F Estates*.

Lord Bridge suggested in *Murphy* that recovery might be permitted for the cost of obviating the danger a defective building posed to neighbouring property or those on the highway, although Lord Oliver was 'not at the moment convinced of the basis for making such a distinction' (at 489). A claim based on 'Lord Bridge's exception' was allowed in *Morse v Barratt (Leeds) Ltd* (1992) 9 Constr LJ 158, but in *Thomas v Taylor Wimpey Developments Ltd* [2019] PNLR 26, HHJ Keyser KC held that the exception did not represent the law, even though he conceded that a distinction could be made between risks of injury to those on the defective premises and those on adjacent property (at [27]):

> If the condition of a property presents a danger to those on it, the owner of that property is in a position to obviate that danger by steps including, ultimately, vacating the property and excluding others from it. (That is a graphic indication of the potential extent of the owner's economic loss.) But if the condition of the property presents a risk of injury to those on adjacent land, the owner has no right to control the use of that adjacent land and thereby obviate the risk to those upon it. He can only remove the risk of injury to those on adjacent land by remedying the defect.

Commenting on this decision, Carrington (2019) 35 PN 260 at 263–4, argues that because in these circumstances the owner is under a positive duty to remove the danger, there 'does seem to be a good reason in principle for [Lord Bridge's] qualification'. Do you agree? Suppose that a manufacturer of hydrochloric acid packages the acid in unsuitable drums, and that a consignment of the drums begins to leak while on board the claimant's ship. If the drums remain on the vessel, the leaking acid will damage the fabric of the vessel, and yet they cannot simply be abandoned at sea or on land. Instead, the claimant is legally required as the custodian of the drums to put the vessel into a special decontamination dock and to pay for the drums to be removed and disposed of in compliance with environmental regulations. In *Losinjska Plovidba v Transco Overseas (The Orjula)* [1995] 2 Lloyd's Rep 395 at 403, Mance J said that it was arguable that in these circumstances the claimant should be entitled to recover the resultant costs from the manufacturer of the acid:

> [I]f property is put into circulation which remains positively dangerous unless preventive measures are taken to neutralize the danger, a person who is obliged to take such steps and does not have the option simply to abandon the property may have a claim in tort against a person who negligently put the article into circulation.

But if that is right, then how can the position of a property owner whose property poses a threat to third parties beyond its boundaries be distinguished? See further, Benson, 'Economic Loss in Tort Law', in D. Owen (ed), *Philosophical Foundations of Tort Law* (Oxford: Clarendon Press, 1995) at pp. 440–4, and the majority judgment in *1688782 Ontario Inc v Maple Leaf Foods Inc* (2020) 450 DLR (4th) 181, which demonstrates the potential significance of this kind of analysis when it comes to recovery of economic losses caused by the supply of dangerous buildings and products.

The New Zealand courts, in contrast with *Murphy*, subsequently imposed liability on the local authority in a defective premises case without finding it necessary to consider the liability of the builder, on the basis that potential home buyers relied on councils (in the sense that they expected the council to carry out its functions carefully) to inspect building work in order to ensure it complied with building by-laws (*Invercargill CC v Hamlin* [1994] 3 NZLR 513). This decision was affirmed by the Privy Council ([1996] AC 624) on the basis that it was for the New Zealand courts to decide whether, as a matter of policy, it was appropriate to hold councils under a duty of care in respect of the inspection of building work. The Supreme Court of New Zealand, by a majority, subsequently held that *Hamlin* applies to non-residential buildings (*Body Corporate No 207624 v North Shore City Council* [2013] 2 NZLR 297). Where it applies, the *Hamlin* liability extends not just to situations where the defect threatens injury to person or property but also to departures from minimum standards of workmanship required under applicable building codes (i.e. to defectiveness, not just dangerousness). However, as reiterated in *Body Corporate No 207624*, the duty is one of reasonable care, not a requirement to ensure that there is compliance with the building codes. For comment on the New Zealand cases leading up to *Body Corporate No 207624*, see Todd, 'Difficulties with Leaky Building Litigation' (2012) 20 Tort L Rev 19.

Complex Structures

The line between property damage and pure economic loss is not always easy to draw. In *Aswan Engineering v Lupdine* [1987] 1 WLR 1, the claim was against a manufacturer of pails in which a waterproofing compound, Lupguard, had been stored. The pails, left out in the sun on a Kuwaiti dockside, melted and the Lupguard was lost. If the pails and the Lupguard were treated as one item of property, any defective manufacture had not caused damage to anything else; hence the only loss was purely economic (i.e. the value of the melted pails and the lost Lupguard). However, if the pails could be regarded as separate from the Lupguard, it could be said that their defective manufacture had damaged other property (the Lupguard contained in them) and hence the owner could bring a claim for property damage. Although it was not necessary to decide the issue, the Court of Appeal seem to have thought that, strictly speaking, it was a claim for property damage, even though, as Lloyd LJ remarked (at 21), the product the claimants had been sold was Lupguard *in* pails, not Lupguard *and* pails. The issue is of great practical importance given the differing conditions for establishing a duty of care between property damage and pure economic loss. How would the complex structures argument recognised by members of the House of Lords in *D & F Estates* and *Murphy* apply to such a case? Would the purchaser of a bottle of wine whose contents were ruined by a defective cork suffer property damage (because one item of property, the cork, had damaged another, the wine) or pure economic loss (because one single composite item of property, the bottle of wine, had damaged itself)? Note that in the defective premises context, there was held to be no damage to 'other property', but only pure economic loss, where part of a building burnt down due to deficiencies in a firewall (*Bellefield Computer Services Ltd v E Turner & Sons* [2000] BLR 97), and where chilled water pipework corroded because its insulation was inadequate (*Linklaters Business Services v Sir Robert McAlpine Ltd (No. 2)* (2010) 133 Con LR 211). For further discussion see Tettenborn, 'Components and Product Liability: Damage to "Other Property"' [2000] LMCLQ 338.

Legislation on Defective Premises

Mr Murphy bought his newly built home in 1970. If the house had been built a few years later, he might have benefited from the statutory tort action introduced by the Defective

Premises Act 1972. Section 1(1) of the Act provides that a person taking on work for or in connection with the provision of a dwelling owes a duty, inter alia, to every person who acquires an interest (whether legal or equitable) in the dwelling that the work be done in a workmanlike or professional manner, such that when finished it is 'fit for habitation' (see *Rendlesham Estates plc v Barr Ltd* [2015] 1 WLR 3663 on the meaning of this phrase). The duty extends to the failure to carry out necessary work as well as carrying it out badly (see *Andrews v Schooling* [1991] 1 WLR 783 at 792). The fact that liability is based on a failure to carry out the work in a workmanlike or professional manner means that the duty may be stricter in some ways than the negligence standard. On whom is the duty imposed? Those 'taking on work' in connection with the provision of a dwelling include the builder, subcontractors and any professional advisers involved in the provision of the dwelling, such as architects or surveyors (see, e.g., *Bole v Huntsbuild Ltd* (2009) 127 Con LR 154), but not an inspector tasked with the statutory function of ensuring compliance with building regulations (*Lessees and Management Co of Herons Court v Heronslea Ltd* [2019] 1 WLR 5849). A person who, in the course of a business which consists of or includes 'providing or arranging' for the provision of dwellings or installations in dwellings, arranges for another to take on relevant work is treated as having taken on the work (s. 1(4)), although the owner of a dwelling does not 'take on work' for these purposes merely by giving instructions for work to be done, or employing someone to work (*Mirza v Bhandal*, unreported, QBD, 27 April 1999).

The number of reported cases dealing with s. 1 of the 1972 Act is small. This is partly because the liability under s. 1(1) is excluded in cases where an 'approved' scheme confers rights in respect of defects in the dwelling (s. 2), and in the years following the passage of the Act most newly built houses were covered by such a scheme, operated by the National House Building Council (NHBC). However, the NHBC no longer submits its scheme for approval, with the result that it has been postulated that 'the Act now has a much wider field of operation' (*Winfield & Jolowicz*, para. 10–054). Another reason for the dearth of case law is that the limitation period under the Act was until recently very short: six years from the date of completion of the dwelling (s. 1(5)). By contrast, where a negligence claim is brought in respect of latent damage, the claimant can initiate proceedings up to three years after the date at which the existence of a cause of action was reasonably discoverable, subject to a 'longstop' of fifteen years from the date of the defendant's negligent conduct (Limitation Act 1980, ss. 14A and 14B; these provisions, which were inserted by the Latent Damage Act 1986, were primarily designed to facilitate negligence claims in defective building cases, and lost much of their significance following the *Murphy* decision).

In the aftermath of the 2017 Grenfell Tower disaster, and the resultant crisis relating to flammable cladding and other dangerous features of high-rise residential buildings, Parliament passed the Building Safety Act 2022, which significantly strengthens the position of persons seeking redress for damage or loss caused by defective premises. One way in which it does this is by enhancing the ambit and effectiveness of the Defective Premises Act 1972. Section 134 of the 2022 Act inserts a new provision into the earlier Act (s. 2A) which extends the duty to carry out work in a workmanlike or professional manner to include work undertaken on an existing dwelling—i.e. refurbishment work—provided this is done in the course of a business. (By contrast, the only modifications that come within the terms of s. 1 are those that are 'substantial', and which result in something 'wholly different' from what was there before: *Jensen v Faux* [2011] 1 WLR 3038.) Even more significantly, s. 135 of the 2022 Act extends the limitation period for claims under the 1972 Act to fifteen years for work done after the 2022 Act comes into force and a whopping thirty years for work done before that date, with a one year 'buffer' period for claims that would become time-barred shortly after the coming into force of these new limitation provisions. The 2022 Act also makes two other significant changes to the liability landscape in this context. First, it brings into force s. 38 of the Building Act 1984, which gives a claim for damage (meaning personal injury or property damage) caused by a breach of building regulations, as well as extending the limitation period for such a claim to fifteen years. And, secondly, s. 148 of the 2022 Act creates a new cause of action for personal injury, damage to property or economic loss caused by a defective construction product which is used in the construction or refurbishment of a dwelling (or a building containing a dwelling) and which causes it to be unfit for habitation. Claims under s. 148 can be brought by those with a legal or equitable interest in the relevant building against a construction product manufacturer. This cause of action again comes with a fifteen-year limitation period from the completion of the relevant work, with a retrospective thirty-year period for defective cladding products (s. 149).

The House of Lords in *Murphy* considered that the passing of the Defective Premises Act 1972 militated against the imposition of a more extensive common law duty of care. Do you agree? More generally, were their Lordships right to hold that pure economic loss was not recoverable in negligence in the defective premises context? This question is explored in the following extracts.

E. Quill, 'Consumer Protection in Respect of Defective Buildings' (2006) 14 Tort L Rev 105

There are two problems with [the reasoning in *Murphy*]. First of all, to say that a building is just a big product fails to recognise the greater practical and economic significance that building purchases entail, particularly in the case of the purchase of one's home. Second, and more importantly, the analogy overlooks the fact that tort law's protection against economic loss in the case of manufactured goods is not necessary, as the buyer's vulnerability has been largely addressed by consumer protection legislation. Manufactured goods are generally bought from retailers, with the built in protections for the consumer [provided by the legislation governing sale of goods] . . . [Conversely,] [b]uildings are not generally distributed through a commercial chain in the way that goods are; apart from the initial transaction with the builder, they are usually bought directly from the previous owner. Except perhaps for large commercial entities, buyers cannot generally in practice obtain contractual protection against such loss. If the average house buyer asked the seller to give an undertaking to accept responsibility for the economic cost of latent defects, the seller would simply refuse to sell and wait for another buyer . . .

The result in *Murphy* may be justified in England, as many persons are not vulnerable; the fact that an individual may be more vulnerable than the rest does not necessarily require an exception, though one may be desirable. The combination of statutory provisions and insurance arrangements may be considered to provide a sufficient, if imperfect, level of protection. Despite the fact that such an interpretation is plausible, it is submitted that the degree of vulnerability of homeowners and small business in England does still warrant the imposition of a duty and that the position adopted in *Murphy* is unsatisfactory.

Winnipeg Condominium Corporation No. 36 v Bird Construction Co [1995] 1 SCR 85 (Supreme Court of Canada)

The issue in this case was whether a contractor responsible for the construction of a building could be liable in negligence to a subsequent purchaser of the building, who was not in contractual privity with the contractor, for the cost of repairing defects in the building resulting from negligence in its construction. The Supreme Court of Canada was asked to determine whether Canadian law should continue to follow the *Anns* approach, adopted by the court in *City of Kamloops v Nielsen* [1984] 2 SCR 2, in the light of the departure from that approach by the House of Lords in *D & F Estates* and *Murphy*. The judgment of the court was delivered by La Forest J.

La Forest J

In my view, the reasonable likelihood that a defect in a building will cause injury to its inhabitants is . . . sufficient to ground a contractor's duty in tort to subsequent purchasers of the building for the cost of repairing the defect if that defect is discovered prior to any injury and if it poses a real and substantial danger to the inhabitants of the building . . . If a contractor can be held liable in tort where he or she constructs a building negligently and, as a result of that negligence, the building causes damage to persons or property, it follows that the contractor should also be held liable in cases where the dangerous defect is discovered and the owner of the building wishes to mitigate the danger by fixing the defect and putting the building back into a non-dangerous state. In both cases, the duty in tort serves to protect the bodily integrity and property interests of the inhabitants of the building . . .

Apart from the logical force of holding contractors liable for the cost of repair of dangerous defects, there is also a strong underlying policy justification for imposing liability in these cases. Under the law as developed in *D & F Estates* and *Murphy*, the plaintiff who moves quickly and responsibly to fix a defect before it causes injury to persons or damage to property must do so at his or her own expense. By contrast, the plaintiff who, either intentionally or through neglect, allows a defect to develop into an accident may benefit at law from the costly and potentially tragic consequences. In my view, this legal doctrine is difficult to justify because it serves to encourage, rather than discourage, reckless and hazardous behaviour. Maintaining a bar against recoverability for the cost of repair of dangerous defects provides no incentive for plaintiffs to mitigate potential losses and tends to encourage economically inefficient behaviour. . . .

Allowing recovery against contractors in tort for the cost of repair of dangerous defects thus serves an important preventative function by encouraging socially responsible behaviour . . .

[N]o serious risk of indeterminate liability arises with respect to this tort duty. In the first place, there is no risk of liability to an indeterminate class because the potential class of claimants is limited to the very persons for whom the building is constructed: the inhabitants of the building. The fact that the class of claimants may include successors in title who have no contractual relationship with the contractors does not, in my view, render the class of potential claimants indeterminate. . . .

Secondly, there is no risk of liability in an indeterminate amount because the amount of liability will always be limited by the reasonable cost of repairing the dangerous defect in the building and restoring that building to a non-dangerous state. Counsel for [the defendant] advanced the argument that the cost of repairs claimed for averting a danger caused by a defect in construction could, in some cases, be disproportionate to the actual damage to persons or property that might be caused if that defect were not repaired. For example, he expressed concern that a given plaintiff could claim thousands of dollars in damage for a defect which, if left unrepaired, would cause only a few dollars damage to that plaintiff's other property. However, in my view, any danger of indeterminacy in damages is averted by the requirement that the defect for which the costs of repair are claimed must constitute a real and substantial danger to the inhabitants of the building, and the fact that the inhabitants of the building can only claim the reasonable cost of repairing the defect and mitigating the danger. The burden of proof will always fall on the plaintiff to demonstrate that there is a serious risk to safety, that the risk was caused by the contractor's negligence, and that the repairs are required to alleviate the risk.

Finally, there is little risk of liability for an indeterminate time because the contractor will only be liable for the cost of repair of dangerous defects during the useful life of the building. Practically speaking, I believe that the period in which the contractor may be exposed to liability for negligence will be much shorter than the full useful life of the building. With the passage of time, it will become increasingly difficult for owners of a building to prove at trial that any deterioration in the building is attributable to the initial negligence of the contractor and not simply to the inevitable wear and tear suffered by every building . . .

Appeal allowed.

COMMENTARY

The Supreme Court of Canada limited the duty of care owed by a builder to dangerous defects, and this enabled La Forest J to justify the duty as protective of 'the bodily integrity and property interests' of the building's inhabitants. This limitation was seized upon by the majority in *1688782 Ontario Inc v Maple Leaf Foods Inc* (2020) 450 DLR (4th) 181 as a means of reconciling the *Winnipeg Condominium* decision with their holding that economic loss is recoverable in negligence only when it flows from an interference with a right recognised by tort law. According to their Honours (at [46]):

[R]ecovery for the economic loss sustained in *Winnipeg Condominium* was founded upon the idea that, in the eyes of the law, the defendant negligently interfered with rights in person or property . . . In our view, this normative basis for the [recognition of the duty of care in that case]—that it protects a right to be free from injury to one's person or property—also delimits its scope. This is because this basis vanishes where the defect presents no imminent threat.

The majority therefore refused to extend the liability rule in *Winnipeg Condominium* to encompass the cost of repairing non-dangerous defects in buildings or products, which raised 'different questions pertaining to issues such as implied conditions and warranties as to quality and fitness for purpose, and not of real and substantial threats to person or property'. Defects of this kind, which did not 'implicate a right protected under tort law', were 'better channelled through the law of contract, which is the typical vehicle for allocating risks where the only complaint is of defective quality' (at [47]).

By contrast, the High Court of Australia has held that builders may owe a duty of care to downstream purchasers in respect of non-dangerous defects as well as dangerous ones (*Bryan v Maloney* (1995) 182 CLR 609), although the duty does not generally extend to commercial or investment property (*Woolcock Street Investments Pty Ltd v CDG Pty Ltd* (2004) 216 CLR 515; *Brookfield Multiplex Ltd v Owners–Strata Plan No 61288* (2014) 254 CLR 185). The justification given for this latter limitation is that, compared to a buyer of an ordinary dwelling, a buyer of commercial or investment property is presumed to be better able to protect themselves against loss caused by the negligence of the builder or architect (in *Brookfield Multiplex*, for example, the contracts of sale to the subsequent purchasers contained detailed provisions governing the quality of the building work). However, S. Todd, 'Policy Issues in Defective Property Cases', in J. Neyers, E. Chamberlain and S. Pitel (eds), *Emerging Issues in Tort Law* (Oxford: Hart, 2007), argues that commercial purchasers cannot sensibly be treated differently and that all remote purchasers 'are vulnerable to suffering loss through acquiring structures for long term use but with hidden defects' (p. 231), a view that has been adopted in New Zealand, where the duty of care is not limited to residential purchasers (*Body Corporate No 207624 v North Shore City Council* [2013] 2 NZLR 297, noted earlier).

The position has therefore been reached where the apex courts of the Commonwealth have adopted at least four different approaches to the liability of a builder to a downstream purchaser for economic loss caused by defects in a building. *D & F Estates* and *Murphy* (House of Lords) refuse to recognise a duty in any case; *Winnipeg Condominium* (Supreme Court of Canada) imposes a duty only in respect of dangerous defects; *Brookfield Mutiplex* (High Court of Australia) imposes a duty in respect of both dangerous and non-dangerous defects, but generally only to residential purchasers; and *Body Corporate No 207624* (New Zealand Supreme Court) imposes a duty in respect of dangerous and non-dangerous defects, to both residential and commercial/investment purchasers. Which of these approaches do you consider preferable, and why? Do you think that the decisions in the other Commonwealth jurisdictions successfully meet the practical objections to the *Anns* approach raised in *D & F Estates* and *Murphy*?

One particular aspect of the reasoning in *Murphy* that has proved unpalatable to other Commonwealth courts is the use of reasoning applicable to products by way of analogy to premises. In *Winnipeg Condominium*, La Forest J thought that the idea that one could discard a house instead of repairing it smacked of unreality. Similarly, in *Bryan v Maloney* Mason CJ, Gaudron and Deane JJ noted (at 625) that the purchase of a house was likely to represent 'one of the most significant, and possibly the most significant, investment the subsequent owner will make during his or her lifetime'. And in *RSP Architects Planners & Engineers v Management Corporation Strata Title Plan No 1075* [1999] 2 SLR(R) 134, where the Singapore Court of Appeal refused to follow *Murphy*, it was observed (at [43]) that 'to treat houses and consumer goods alike would be to ignore simple realities'. If the 'simple reality' is that the owner cannot discard the house and must live in it, what happens if/when the defect ultimately results in physical injury or property damage? La Forest J in *Winnipeg Condominium* seemed to assume that such an owner could recover damages, but this is contrary to Lord Keith's view in *Murphy* that, although the ordinary *Donoghue v Stevenson* duty is owed in respect of physical injury or property damage, 'that principle is not apt to bring home liability towards an occupier who knows the full extent of the defect yet continues to occupy the building', presumably on the basis that the continued occupation of the premises would break the chain of causation between the builder's negligence and the later injury or damage. However, in *Targett v Torfaen Borough Council* [1992] 3 All ER 27 the Court of Appeal did not adopt this analysis. The defendant in the case had designed and built council flats, one of which was occupied by the plaintiff as a weekly tenant. Access to the flat was provided by two flights of stairs. The lower flight had no handrail nor was there any artificial light provided in the vicinity. The plaintiff was injured whilst descending the lower flight of stairs in darkness. The Court of Appeal rejected an argument, derived from *Murphy*, that because the plaintiff knew of the dangerous state of the stairs but continued to occupy the premises, this barred his claim. Nicholls LJ said:

[K]nowledge of the existence of a danger does not always enable a person to avoid the danger. In simple cases it does. In other cases, especially where buildings are concerned, it would be absurdly unrealistic to suggest that a person can always take steps to avoid a danger once he knows of its existence, and that if he does not do so he is the author of his own misfortune. Here, as elsewhere, the law seeks to be realistic. Hence the established principle . . . that knowledge or opportunity for inspection *per se*, and without regard to any consequences they may have in the circumstances, cannot be conclusive against the plaintiff. Knowledge, or opportunity for inspection, does not by itself always negative the duty of care or break the chain of causation. Whether it does so depends on all the circumstances. It will only do so when it is reasonable to expect the plaintiff to remove or avoid the danger, and unreasonable for him to run the risk of being injured by the danger.

III. The *Hedley Byrne* Exception

1. The *Hedley Byrne* Decision

The most significant exception to English law's general exclusion of liability in negligence for pure economic loss is that a duty of care may arise in respect of such loss where the defendant assumes a relevant responsibility towards the claimant. This exception, which was first recognised by the House of Lords in the seminal case of *Hedley Byrne & Co Ltd v Heller & Partners Ltd* [1964] AC 465, is in many respects more similar to liability in contract (which is also based on an undertaking by the defendant) than it is to tortious liability for physical damage under *Donoghue v Stevenson*.

The assumption of responsibility doctrine has been the subject of significant development since it was first identified in *Hedley Byrne* in 1963 as a basis on which negligence liability could be imposed for pure economic loss. We first consider the *Hedley Byrne* decision itself, before proceeding to consider its application in cases of negligent misstatement (see III.2), and then its extension in the 1990s to the negligent provision of services (see III.3).

It is important to emphasise at the outset that while the *Hedley Byrne* exception is no longer limited to negligent misrepresentation, the case itself was centrally concerned with that issue. At the time of the *Hedley Byrne* decision there was a developed set of rules governing misrepresentations which had induced a contract, but the only remedy afforded by the law of contract was the rescission of the contract in question. Damages were available for economic loss caused by a negligent misstatement only where there was fraud or the parties were in a fiduciary relationship. The exception for fraud traced its history to *Pasley v Freeman* (1789) 3 TR 51, but the modern law was set out in *Derry v Peek* (1889) 14 App Cas 337, which concerned the liability of company directors for false statements in a prospectus. The claim was in deceit, rather than negligence, and the House of Lords held that, in an action for deceit, the claimant must prove that the misstatement had been made with knowledge of its falsity or at least recklessness as to whether it was true or false (which remains the law today). In the aftermath of *Derry v Peek* it was thought that the case had not only clarified the elements of the tort of deceit, but had also established that, in the absence of contract, an innocent but negligent misrepresentation could not give rise to liability in damages. However, in *Nocton v Lord Ashburton* [1914] AC 932, a solicitor was held liable for a non-fraudulent statement made to a client, with the duty of care being founded on the fiduciary relationship between the parties. Lord Haldane argued that this was not inconsistent with *Derry*, a view which he reiterated in *Robinson v National Bank of Scotland* 1916 SC (HL) 154 at 157:

I think, as I said in *Nocton*'s case, that an exaggerated view was taken by a good many people of the scope of the decision in *Derry v Peek*. The whole of the doctrine as to fiduciary relationships, as to the duty of care arising from implied as well as express contracts, as to the duty of care arising from other special relationships which the courts may find to exist in particular cases, still remains, and I should be very sorry if any word fell from me which should suggest that the courts are in any way hampered in recognising that the duty of care may be established when such cases really occur.

Nevertheless, by the time of *Hedley Byrne* the only special relationship that was recognised as giving rise to a duty to take care in respect of a statement was a fiduciary relationship. An example of this restrictive approach is *Candler v Crane, Christmas & Co* [1951] 2 KB 164. The plaintiff was a potential investor in a company for which the defendants were the auditors. The plaintiff asked to see the company accounts before making his decision, and the managing director of the company asked the defendants to prepare the accounts and to show them to and discuss them with the plaintiff. After showing the accounts to his own accountant the plaintiff decided to invest in the company. In fact, the accounts were carelessly prepared, contained numerous false statements and gave a wholly misleading picture of the state of the company, which was wound up within a year, the plaintiff losing the whole of his investment. By a majority of 2:1 the Court of Appeal held that, in the absence of fraud or of any contractual or fiduciary relationship between the parties, a false but careless statement gave rise to no liability. Denning LJ dissented, holding that the accountants owed a limited duty to any third person to whom they showed their accounts or to whom they knew that their clients were going to show them, when, to the knowledge of the accountants, that person would consider their accounts with a view to the investment of money or taking other action to his potential benefit or detriment.

The restrictive approach represented by the majority's decision in *Candler* was challenged before the House of Lords in *Hedley Byrne*.

Hedley Byrne & Co Ltd v Heller & Partners Ltd [1964] AC 465

The appellants, a firm of advertising agents, placed substantial orders for advertising time on television and advertising space in newspapers on behalf of a client, Easipower Ltd, on terms by which they became personally liable to the television and newspaper companies. After becoming concerned as to Easipower's creditworthiness, the appellants asked their bank (the National Provincial Bank) to contact the respondents (Easipower's bankers) to seek a credit reference. The reply came back that Easipower was '[b]elieved to be respectably constituted and considered good for its normal business engagements' and that they 'would not undertake any commitments they are unable to fulfil'. The appellants subsequently asked in writing whether the respondents considered Easipower 'trustworthy, in the way of business, to the extent of £100,000 per annum', to which the respondents replied—in a letter marked 'CONFIDENTIAL. For your private use and without responsibility on the part of the bank or its officials'—that Easipower was a 'respectably constituted company, considered good for its ordinary business engagements', while adding that 'Your figures are larger than we are accustomed to see'. The appellants relied on these statements by extending further credit to Easipower, as a result of which they lost over £17,000 when Easipower went into liquidation. The appellants sought to recover this loss from the respondents on the ground that the replies to their inquiries had been negligent. McNair J held that the respondents had owed no duty of care to the appellants, a decision affirmed by the Court of Appeal, which was bound by the authority of *Candler* but which held in any case that it would be unreasonable to impose on a banker the obligation suggested.

Lord Reid

My Lords, this case raises the important question whether and in what circumstances a person can recover damages for loss suffered by reason of his having relied on an innocent but negligent misrepresentation . . .

Before coming to the main question of law it may be well to dispose of an argument that there was no sufficiently close relationship between these parties to give rise to any duty. It is said that the respondents did not know the precise purpose of the inquiries and did not even know whether National Provincial Bank Ltd wanted the information for its own use or for the use of a customer: they knew nothing of the appellants. I would reject that argument. They knew that the inquiry was in connection with an advertising contract, and it was at least probable that the information was wanted by the advertising contractors. It seems to me quite immaterial that they did not know who these contractors were: there is no suggestion of any speciality which could have influenced them in deciding whether to give information or in what form to give it. I shall therefore treat this as if it were a case where a negligent misrepresentation is made directly to the person seeking information, opinion or advice, and I shall not attempt to decide what kind or degree of proximity is necessary before there can be a duty owed by the defendant to the plaintiff.

The appellants' first argument was based on *Donoghue (or McAlister) v Stevenson*. That is a very important decision, but I do not think that it has any direct bearing on this case. That decision may encourage us to develop existing lines of authority, but it cannot entitle us to disregard them. Apart altogether from authority I would think that the law must treat negligent words differently from negligent acts. The law ought so far as possible to reflect the standards of the reasonable man, and that is what *Donoghue (or McAlister) v Stevenson* sets out to do. The most obvious difference between negligent words and negligent acts is this. Quite careful people often express definite opinions on social or informal occasions, even when they see that others are likely to be influenced by them; and they often do that without taking that care which they would take if asked for their opinion professionally, or in a business connection. The appellants agree that there can be no duty of care on such occasions, and we were referred to American and South African authorities where that is recognised, although their law appears to have gone much further than ours has yet done. But it is at least unusual casually to put into circulation negligently-made articles which are dangerous. A man might give a friend a negligently-prepared bottle of home-made wine and his friend's guests might drink it with dire results, but it is by no means clear that those guests would have no action against the negligent manufacturer. Another obvious difference is that a negligently-made article will only cause one accident, and so it is not very difficult to find the necessary degree of proximity or neighbourhood between the negligent manufacturer and the person injured. But words can be broadcast with or without the consent or the foresight of the speaker or writer. It would be one thing to say that the speaker owes a duty to a limited class, but it would be going very far to say that he owes a duty to every ultimate 'consumer' who acts on those words to his detriment. It would be no use to say that a speaker or writer owes a duty, but can disclaim responsibility if he wants to. He, like the manufacturer, could make it part of a contract that he is not to be liable for his negligence: but that contract would not protect him in a question with a third party at least if the third party was unaware of it.

So it seems to me that there is good sense behind our present law that in general an innocent but negligent misrepresentation gives no cause of action. There must be something more than the mere misstatement. I therefore turn to the authorities to see what more is required. The most natural requirement would be that expressly or by implication from the circumstances the speaker or writer has undertaken some responsibility, and that appears to me not to conflict with any authority which is binding on this House. Where there is a contract there is no difficulty as regards the contracting parties: the question is whether there is a warranty. The refusal of English law to recognise any *jus quaesitum tertio* causes some difficulties, but they are not relevant here. Then there are cases where a person does not merely make a statement, but performs a gratuitous service. I do not intend to examine the cases about that, but at least they show that in some cases that person owes a duty of care apart from any contract, and to that extent they pave the way to holding that there can be a duty of care in making a statement of fact or opinion which is independent of contract . . .

[His Lordship considered *Derry v Peek*, *Nocton v Lord Ashburton* and *Robinson v National Bank of Scotland*, and, after referring to the extract from the latter set out in the text above, continued:]

This passage makes it clear that Lord Haldane did not think that a duty to take care must be limited to cases of fiduciary relationship in the narrow sense of relationships which had been recognised by the Court of Chancery as being of a fiduciary character. He speaks of other special relationships, and I can see no logical stopping place short of all those relationships where it is plain that the party seeking information or advice was trusting the other to exercise such a degree of care as the circumstances required, where it was reasonable for him to do that, and where the other gave the information or advice when he knew or ought to have known that the inquirer was relying on him. I say 'ought to have known' because in questions of negligence we now apply the objective standard of what the reasonable man would have done.

A reasonable man, knowing that he was being trusted or that his skill and judgment were being relied on, would, I think, have three courses open to him. He could keep silent or decline to give the information or advice sought: or he could give an answer with a clear qualification that he accepted no responsibility for it or that it was given without that reflection or inquiry which a careful answer would require: or he could simply answer without any such qualification. If he chooses to adopt the last course he must, I think, be held to have accepted some responsibility for his answer being given carefully, or to have accepted a relationship with the inquirer which requires him to exercise such care as the circumstances require.

If that is right then it must follow that *Candler v Crane, Christmas & Co* was wrongly decided . . .

[His Lordship held that, on the facts, it would be difficult to decide what duty, beyond a duty of honesty, a banker would owe to the recipient of a credit reference relating to one of its customers, but found for the respondents on the basis that their disclaimers of responsibility showed that they never undertook any duty to exercise care in giving their replies.]

Lord Morris of Borth-y-Gest

Leaving aside cases where there is some contractual or fiduciary relationship there may be many situations in which one person voluntarily or gratuitously undertakes to do something for another person and becomes under a duty to exercise reasonable care . . . Apart from cases where there is some direct dealing, there may be cases where one person issues a document which should be the result of an exercise of the skill and judgment required by him in his calling and where he knows and intends that its accuracy will be relied on by another . . .

[His Lordship proceeded to discuss *Derry v Peek*, *Nocton v Ashburton* and other authorities, and continued:]

The guidance which Lord Haldane gave in *Nocton v Ashburton* was repeated by him in his speech in *Robinson v National Bank of Scotland*. He clearly pointed out that *Derry v Peek* did not affect (a) the whole doctrine as to fiduciary relationships (b) the duty of care arising from implied as well as express contracts and (c) the duty of care arising from other special relationships which the courts may find to exist in particular cases.

My Lords, I consider that it follows and that it should now be regarded as settled that if someone possessed of a special skill undertakes, quite irrespective of contract, to apply that skill for the assistance of another person who relies on such skill, a duty of care will arise. The fact that the service is to be given by means of, or by the instrumentality of, words can make no difference. Furthermore if, in a sphere in which a person is so placed that others could reasonably rely on his judgment or his skill or on his ability to make careful inquiry, a person takes it on himself to give information or advice to, or allows his information or advice to be passed on to, another person who, as he knows or should know, will place reliance on it, then a duty of care will arise . . .

[I]n my judgment the bank in the present case, by the words which they employed, effectively disclaimed any assumption of a duty of care. They stated that they only responded to the inquiry on the basis that their reply was without responsibility. If the inquirers chose to receive and act upon the reply they cannot disregard the definite terms upon which it was given . . .

I would therefore dismiss the appeal.

Lord Devlin

Counsel for the respondents has given your Lordships three reasons why the appellants should not recover. The first is founded on a general statement of the law which, if true, is of immense effect. Its hypothesis is that there is no general duty not to make careless statements. No one challenges that hypothesis. There is no duty to be careful in speech, as there is a duty to be honest in speech. Nor indeed is there any general duty to be careful in action. The duty is limited to those who can establish some relationship of proximity such as was found to exist in *Donoghue v Stevenson*. A plaintiff cannot therefore recover for financial loss caused by a careless statement unless he can show that the maker of the statement was under a special duty to him to be careful. Counsel submits that this special duty must be brought under one of three categories. It must be contractual; or it must be fiduciary; or it must arise from the relationship of proximity, and the financial loss must flow from physical damage done to the person or the property of the plaintiff. The law is now settled, counsel submits, and these three categories are exhaustive. It was so decided in *Candler v Crane, Christmas & Co* [1951] 2 KB 164 and that decision, counsel submits, is right in principle and in accordance with earlier authorities . . .

[The distinction between negligence in word and negligence in deed] is . . . said to depend on whether financial loss is caused through physical injury or whether it is caused directly. The interposition of the physical injury is said to make a difference of principle. I can find neither logic nor common sense in this. If irrespective of contract, a doctor negligently advises a patient that he can safely pursue his occupation and he cannot and the patient's health suffers and he loses his livelihood, the patient has a remedy. But if the doctor negligently advises him that he cannot safely pursue his occupation when in fact he can and he loses his livelihood, there is said to be no remedy. Unless, of course, the patient was a private patient and the doctor accepted half a guinea for his trouble: then the patient can recover all [in contract]. I am bound to say, my Lords, that I think this to be nonsense. It is not the sort of nonsense that can arise even in the best system of law out of the need to draw nice distinctions between borderline cases. It arises, if it is the law, simply out of a refusal to make sense. The line is not drawn on any intelligible principle. It just happens to be the line which those who have been driven from the extreme assertion that negligent statements in the absence of contractual or fiduciary duty give no cause of action have in the course of their retreat so far reached . . .

It would be surprising if the sort of problem that is created by the facts of this case had never until recently arisen in English law. As a problem it is a by-product of the doctrine of consideration. If the respondents had made a nominal charge for the reference, the problem would not exist. If it were possible in English law to construct a contract without consideration, the problem would move at once out of the first and general phase into the particular; and the question would be, not whether on the facts of the case there was a special relationship, but whether on the facts of the case there was a contract.

The respondents in this case cannot deny that they were performing a service. Their sheet anchor is that they were performing it gratuitously and therefore no liability for its performance can arise. My Lords, in my opinion this is not the law. A promise given without consideration to perform a service cannot be enforced as a contract by the promisee; but if the service is in fact performed and done negligently, the promisee can recover in an action in tort . . .

[After considering cases where liability had been imposed for the performance of a voluntary act, and noting that there were examples of the liability extending to purely financial loss, his Lordship continued:]

My Lords, it is true that this principle of law has not yet been clearly applied to a case where the service which the defendant undertakes to perform is or includes the obtaining and imparting of information. But I cannot see why it should not be: and if it had not been thought erroneously that *Derry v Peek* (1889) 14 App Cas 337 negatived any liability for negligent statements, I think that by now it probably would have been. It cannot matter whether the information consists of fact or of opinion or is a mixture of both, nor whether it was obtained as a result of special inquiries or comes direct from facts already in the defendant's possession or from his general store of professional knowledge. One cannot, as I have already endeavoured to show, distinguish in this respect between a duty to inquire and a duty to state.

I think, therefore, that there is ample authority to justify your Lordships in saying now that the categories of special relationships, which may give rise to a duty to take care in word as well as in deed, are not limited to contractual relationships or to relationships of fiduciary duty, but include also relationships which in the words of Lord Shaw in *Nocton v Lord Ashburton* ([1914] AC 932 at 972) are 'equivalent to contract', that is, where there is an assumption of responsibility in circumstances in which, but for the absence of consideration, there would be a contract. Where there is an express undertaking, an express warranty as distinct from mere representation, there can be little difficulty. The difficulty arises in discerning those cases in which the undertaking is to be implied. In this respect the absence of consideration is not irrelevant. Payment for information or advice is very good evidence that it is being relied on and that the informer or adviser knows that it is. Where there is no consideration, it will be necessary to exercise greater care in distinguishing between social and professional relationships and between those which are of a contractual character and those which are not. It may often be material to consider whether the adviser is acting purely out of good nature or whether he is getting his reward in some indirect form. The service that a bank performs in giving a reference is not done simply out of a desire to assist commerce. It would discourage the customers of the bank if their deals fell through because the bank had refused to testify to their credit when it was good.

I have had the advantage of reading all the opinions prepared by your Lordships and of studying the terms which your Lordships have framed by way of definition of the sort of relationship which gives rise to a responsibility towards those who act on information or advice and so creates a duty of care towards them. I do not understand any of your Lordships to hold that it is a responsibility imposed by law on certain types of persons or in certain sorts of situations. It is a responsibility that is voluntarily accepted or undertaken either generally where a general relationship, such as that of solicitor and client or banker and customer, is created, or specifically in relation to a particular transaction. In the present case the appellants were not . . . the customers or potential customers of the bank. Responsibility can attach only to the single act, i.e., the giving of the reference, and only if the doing of that act implied a voluntary undertaking to assume responsibility. This is a point of great importance because it is, as I understand it, the foundation for the ground on which in the end the House dismisses the appeal. I do not think it possible to formulate with exactitude all the conditions under which the law will in a specific case imply a voluntary undertaking, any more than it is possible to formulate those in which the law will imply a contract. But in so far as your Lordships describe the circumstances in which an implication will ordinarily be drawn, I am prepared to adopt any one of your Lordships' statements as showing the general rule . . .

I shall . . . content myself with the proposition that wherever there is a relationship equivalent to contract there is a duty of care. Such a relationship may be either general or particular. Examples of a general relationship are those of solicitor and client and of banker and customer . . . There may well be others yet to be established. Where there is a general relationship of this sort it is unnecessary to do more than prove its existence and the duty follows. Where, as in the present case, what is relied on is a particular relationship created ad hoc, it will be necessary to examine the particular facts to see whether there is an express or implied undertaking of responsibility. . . .

Lord Pearce

The reason for some divergence between the law of negligence in word and that of negligence in act is clear. Negligence in word creates problems different from those of negligence in act. Words are more volatile than deeds. They travel fast and far afield. They are used without being expended and take effect in combination with innumerable facts and other words. Yet they are dangerous and can cause vast financial damage. How far they are relied on unchecked . . . must in many cases be a matter of doubt and difficulty. If the mere hearing or reading of words were held to create proximity, there might be no limit to the persons to whom the speaker or writer could be liable. Damage by negligent acts to persons or property on the other hand is more visible and obvious; its limits are more easily defined . . .

How wide the sphere of the duty of care in negligence is to be laid depends ultimately on the courts' assessment of the demands of society for protection from the carelessness of others. Economic protection has lagged behind protection in physical matters where there is injury to person and property. It may be that the size and the width of the range of possible claims has acted as a deterrent to extension of economic protection . . .

The true rule is that innocent misrepresentation *per se* gives no right to damages. If the misrepresentation was intended by the parties to form a warranty between two contracting parties, it gives on that ground a right to damages (*Heilbut, Symons & Co v Buckleton* [1913] AC 30). If an innocent misrepresentation is made between parties in a fiduciary relationship it may, on that ground, give a right to claim damages for negligence. There is also in my opinion a duty of care created by special relationships which, though not fiduciary, give rise to an assumption that care as well as honesty is demanded.

Was there such a special relationship in the present case as to impose on the respondents a duty of care to the appellants as the undisclosed principals for whom National Provincial Bank Ltd was making the inquiry? The answer to that question depends on the circumstances of the transaction. If, for instance, they disclosed a casual social approach to the inquiry no such special relationship or duty of care would be assumed (see *Fish v Kelly* (1864) 17 CBNS 194). To import such a duty the representation must normally, I think, concern a business or professional transaction whose nature makes clear the gravity of the inquiry and the importance and influence attached to the answer . . . A most important circumstance is the form of the inquiry and of the answer. Both were here plainly stated to be without liability. . . . If both parties say expressly (in a case where neither is deliberately taking advantage of the other) that there shall be no liability, I do not find it possible to say that a liability was assumed . . .

    I would, therefore, dismiss the appeal.

Lord Hodson delivered a concurring speech.

Appeal dismissed.

COMMENTARY

Introducing an edited collection produced to commemorate the 50th anniversary of *Hedley Byrne*, Barker commented that although the importance of the case was clear, 'determining exactly what it stood for at the time—or indeed what it stands for now—is rather more difficult and remains a matter of persistent controversy' ('*Hedley Byrne v Heller*: Issues at the Beginning of the Twenty-First Century', in K. Barker, R. Grantham and W. Swain (eds), *The Law of Misstatements: 50 Years on from* Hedley Byrne v Heller (Oxford: Hart, 2015), p. 3). Nor is that the full extent of the controversy that surrounds the case, for as Paul Mitchell writes in an important historical study of the decision ('*Hedley Byrne & Co Ltd v Heller & Partners Ltd* (1963)', in *Mitchell and Mitchell*, p. 173), despite the fact that the *Hedley Byrne* principle has been shaping the development of the law of negligence since 1963, it 'has still somehow not been fully accepted'.

    Part of the problem is that the different speeches emphasise different considerations, while generally the language of the speeches is very expansive and open-ended. Mitchell, *op. cit.*, argues that this was no accident, and that at the time the House of Lords was developing a more creative judicial mindset, and a more assertive approach to earlier authority, with Lord Devlin in particular anxious to use the opportunity provided by the *Hedley Byrne* appeal to develop the law of negligence along more rational lines. Weir, 'Errare Humanum Est', in P. Birks (ed.), *Frontiers of Liability*, vol. 2 (Oxford: OUP, 1994), p. 105n, was less charitable, commenting:

Never has there been such a judicial jamboree as *Hedley Byrne* where one almost has the feeling that their lordships had been on a trip to Mount Olympus and perhaps smoked a joint on the bus. Something certainly went to their heads, presumably not the merits of the claim, which they dismissed.

But then, three decades before he wrote those words, Weir had penned a disapproving case note on *Hedley Byrne* [1963] CLJ 216, questioning why A should be held to owe B a duty of care in respect of B's economic interests where B had provided no consideration to A in return (see also D. Campbell, 'The Curious Incident of the Dog that did Bark in the Night-Time: What Mischief does *Hedley Byrne v Heller* Correct?', in Barker et al., *op. cit.*). Can you think of an answer to that question?

    Whether or not their Lordships were right to recognise that a duty of care could arise in such circumstances, the connection between liability under *Hedley Byrne* and liability in contract is a strong one. It was only because of the absence of consideration that there was no contractual duty of care in the case, and Lord Devlin said that it was in situations that were 'equivalent to contract' that a duty of care would arise. There are also some features of *Hedley Byrne* liability that are reminiscent of contract, including the fact that the duty of care is owed only to a particular person or persons to whom responsibility has been assumed, and that liability can be limited or excluded by an appropriate disclaimer, which indeed was what happened in *Hedley Byrne* itself. The contractual flavour of *Hedley Byrne* liability is such that in an essay in the anniversary collection, Beever ('The Basis of the *Hedley Byrne* Action') maintains that it is best understood as contractual in nature. But that is a controversial view, and in the same book Robertson and Wang ('The Assumption of Responsibility') express strong disagreement with it, arguing instead that there is no fundamental difference between *Hedley Byrne* liability and liability based on *Donoghue v Stevenson*. Assumption of responsibility, they say, 'is not a distinctive category of obligation, but simply a particular manifestation of' Lord Atkin's neighbour principle' (Barker et al., *op. cit.*, p. 82). According to a third view, *Hedley Byrne* liability is *sui generis*, and falls somewhere between contract and core tort (see, e.g., Nolan, 'Assumption of Responsibility: Four Questions' (2019) 72 CLP 123). This view is endorsed by Mitchell (*op. cit.*), who argues that the central concept of assumption of responsibility predates contract and tort as categories, and does not really fit neatly into either. In a careful historical analysis of its origins, Mitchell traces the principle back to the old form of the action on the case that relied on an undertaking by the defendant (known as 'assumpsit', meaning 'he undertook'). Hence his conclusion (at p. 197) that:

Seen with the benefit of the historical background, the House of Lords' use of assumption of responsibility in *Hedley Byrne* was not a radical departure at all. On the contrary, it was a return to first principle.

Stapleton, 'Duty of Care and Economic Loss: A Wider Agenda' (1991) 107 LQR 249 at 260 notes that the plaintiff in *Hedley Byrne* had to overcome two hurdles: that against recovery for negligent words as opposed to negligent acts, and that against recovery of pure economic loss as opposed to loss connected with physical damage. She comments: 'With hindsight it is surprising how far the attention of the House of Lords was absorbed by the first question.' Lord Devlin could find 'neither logic nor common sense' (at 517) in any distinction between pure economic loss and loss connected with physical damage, while Lord Hodson thought it was 'difficult to see why liability as such should depend on the nature of the damage' (at 509). Only in the speech of Lord Pearce is there any analysis of the reasons why liability for pure economic loss might be restricted, and even that is very brief. Perhaps one should not be too critical of their Lordships. It is clear that any duty owed by a statement maker—whatever the nature of the loss—needs well-defined limits, a point illustrated by *Sutradhar (FC) v National Environment Research Council* [2006] 4 All ER 490, where the House of Lords unanimously rejected the proposition that the authors of a report on water quality in Bangladesh had owed a duty of care in respect of physical injury caused by alleged errors in the report to a large section of the population of that country (see further Lunney (2006) 14 Tort L Rev 129, and Ch. 9.I).

Their Lordships were agreed in *Hedley Byrne* that there were circumstances in which liability might arise in respect of pure economic loss suffered through reliance upon the negligent provision of information or advice. It is not clear, however, that they considered that a banker giving a reference in the form of a brief expression of opinion as to the creditworthiness of a customer thereby assumed a duty of care to the person requesting the reference, and hence that a duty of care would have been owed in the case but for the disclaimer.

Subsequently, however, it has generally been assumed that a banker does indeed owe a duty of care in such circumstances (see *Mutual Life & Citizens Assurance Co Ltd v Evatt* [1971] AC 793), not least because it is part of the business of a bank to give advice on the creditworthiness of its customers. But would a duty also be owed where the defendant chose to provide information in a commercial setting even though the giving of such advice did not form part of its core business? In the *Mutual Life* case the plaintiff suffered economic loss after relying on advice requested from the defendant assurance company about the financial stability of one of its subsidiary companies. The majority of the Privy Council held that no duty of care was owed, the *Hedley Byrne* duty being limited to advisers who carry on the business or profession of giving advice of the kind sought and to advice given by them in the course of that business. Lords Reid and Morris (both of whom delivered speeches in *Hedley Byrne* itself) dissented, holding that all that was required was that the advice was given on a business occasion or in the course of business activities. The minority approach was favoured in *Esso Petroleum v Mardon* [1976] QB 801, and in *Spring v Guardian Assurance plc* [1995] 2 AC 296 at 320 Lord Goff noted that the decision in *Mutual Life* had attracted serious criticism in the 'light of the formidable dissenting opinion' in that case. Applying that approach, it was held, for example, that an auctioneer could owe a duty of care to a potential bidder in respect of advice it proffered to that bidder about a lot coming up for auction, even if this was not seen as its core business (see *Thomson v Christie, Manson & Woods Ltd* [2005] EWCA Civ 555).

Lord Reid indicated in *Hedley Byrne* that it was unlikely that a duty of care would arise when information or advice was provided in a social context, but it does not follow that such a duty cannot arise between friends. In *Chaudhry v Prabhaker* [1989] 1 WLR 29, the plaintiff had asked the defendant—a friend 'who had had a lot to do with motor cars'—to find her a used car, stipulating that it should not have been in an accident. The defendant negligently recommended a car that had been in an accident and was unroadworthy and worthless. When the plaintiff sought damages from him, he conceded that he owed her a duty of care, and a majority of the Court of Appeal thought the concession had been rightly made, because the agency arrangement held to exist between the parties indicated that the occasion was not a social one (cf. May LJ, who thought that to impose a *Hedley Byrne* duty in this and similar situations would make social relations and responsibilities between friends unnecessarily hazardous). Similarly, in *Burgess v Lejonvarn* [2017] BLR 277, it was held that an architect owed a duty of care to some friends she was helping with the initial stages of a garden landscaping project, since although she was working for free, the context was relatively formal and it was expected that the arrangement would lead to her later being engaged for further work for which she would be paid. By contrast, a duty of care would be unlikely to arise in respect of 'a piece of brief ad hoc advice of the type occasionally proffered by professional people in a less formal context' (see the decision at first instance: *Burgess v Lejonvarn* [2016] EWHC 40 (TCC) at [186], per Alexander Nissen KC).

Apart from the traditional list of persons who give professional advice (e.g. solicitors, accountants, surveyors, engineers), the wide language of *Hedley Byrne* has been used to impose a duty on a range of other defendants, including public authorities. In *Welton v North Cornwall District Council* [1997] 1 WLR 570 an environmental health officer of the defendant told the plaintiffs that unless certain alterations were made to their guest house (so as to meet statutory requirements) he would close the business down. In fact, the alterations were not required and the plaintiffs successfully sued to recover their wasted costs, the Court of Appeal holding that the statement fell within the *Hedley Byrne* principle. However, in cases of this kind the status of the defendant as a public authority exercising statutory functions should not be disregarded. In *Harris v Evans* [1998] 1 WLR 1285, the plaintiff, who was the owner of a bungee jumping business, suffered economic loss when local authorities took enforcement action against his business in reliance on allegedly negligent advice given by the defendant health and safety inspector. The Court of Appeal held that it would be seriously detrimental to the proper discharge by enforcement authorities of their duties if they were exposed to potential liability to the owners of businesses adversely affected by their decisions. The defendant had therefore not owed a duty of care to the plaintiff, whose only redress was via the relevant statutory scheme. In *Harris*, Sir Richard Scott V-C confessed (at 1301) to having some difficulty with the decision in *Welton*, because in his view it was a precondition of public authority liability under the *Hedley Byrne* principle that the duty of care contended for was consistent with the relevant statutory framework, and no consideration had been given to that issue in the earlier case.

Can *Hedley Byrne* liability attach to representations made on a website? In *Patchett v Swimming Pool & Allied Trades Association Ltd* [2010] 2 All ER (Comm) 138, the claimants relied on information provided on the defendant's website to choose a contractor to build their swimming pool. The Court of Appeal rejected an argument that 'special considerations' applied to representations made on a website but also made it clear that *Hedley Byrne* liability could arise in respect of such representations on the application of the usual principles. On the facts, however, the majority held that the website made it clear that the statements it contained were not to be relied upon without further enquiry, so no duty of care was owed. (See also *Taberna Europe v Selskabet AF 1 September 2008* [2017] QB 633, where the posting of an 'investor presentation' on the defendant's website gave rise to a duty of care towards a potential investor whom the defendant intended to rely upon it.)

Do you think their Lordships in *Hedley Byrne* envisaged the decision applying to these types of case?

2. *Hedley Byrne* and the Supply of Information

The paradigm example of *Hedley Byrne* liability involves a two-party situation: A gives information or advice to B which B relies upon to his detriment. But what if A gives information to B, who passes it to C, and it is C who relies on it to his detriment? If A is liable to anyone who receives and relies on the information this may create a potential 'floodgates' problem. As Lord Reid pointed out in *Hedley Byrne*, 'words can be broadcast with or without the consent or the foresight of the speaker or writer. It would be one thing to say that the speaker owes a duty to a limited class, but it would be going very far to say that he owes a duty to every ultimate "consumer" who acts on those words to his detriment.' Nevertheless, *Hedley Byrne* has been extended to impose a duty on the maker of a statement in favour of a third-party recipient of that information. The extension and its limits are considered in the following extracts.

Smith v Eric S Bush (A Firm); Harris v Wyre Forest District Council [1990] 1 AC 831

The issue for the House of Lords in these appeals was whether a valuer owed a duty of care to the purchaser of a house in circumstances where the valuer had been instructed to carry out the valuation, not by the purchaser, but by the purchaser's mortgagee. In both cases the purchaser paid a fee to the mortgagee to have the valuation carried out. In *Smith* the valuation was carried out by a third party, whilst in *Harris* it was undertaken by an employee of the mortgagee council, a Mr Lee. In *Smith* the valuation was passed onto and read by the purchaser; in *Harris* the purchaser did not see the valuation but assumed that, because the council was prepared to lend the money, the house must have been valued at the proposed purchase price. In both cases the purchasers were aware of disclaimers of liability by the surveyors in relation to the surveys. In *Smith* the disclaimer was to the effect that neither the society nor its surveyor warranted that the report and valuation would be accurate and that the report and valuation would be supplied without any acceptance of responsibility; in *Harris* it said that the valuation was confidential and was intended solely for the information of the local authority and that no responsibility whatsoever was implied or accepted by the local authority for the value or condition of the property by reason of the inspection and report. In both cases the purchasers bought the house without having an independent survey carried out, and in both cases the survey was carried out negligently, resulting in economic loss to the purchasers. In *Smith* the plaintiff was successful at first instance and on appeal, whilst in *Harris* the plaintiff won at first instance but the decision was overturned by the Court of Appeal on the basis that the disclaimer prevented the council from owing a duty of care. The House of Lords dismissed the appeal in *Smith* and allowed the appeal in *Harris*. The extracts concern the question whether, quite apart from the disclaimers, the valuers owed a duty of care to the purchasers. However, it should also be noted that their Lordships held that the disclaimers fell foul of the Unfair Contract Terms Act 1977 (see further Ch. 6.IV), and so did not prevent any duty of care that might otherwise have been owed from arising.

Lord Templeman

These two appeals are based on allegations of negligence in circumstances which are akin to contract. Mr and Mrs Harris paid £22 to the council for a valuation. The council employed, and therefore paid, Mr Lee, for whose services as a valuer the council are vicariously liable. Mrs Smith paid £36.89 to the Abbey National for a report and valuation and the Abbey National paid the surveyors for the report and valuation. In each case the valuer knew or ought to have known that the purchaser would only contract to purchase the house if the valuation was satisfactory and that the purchaser might suffer injury or damage or both if the valuer did not exercise reasonable skill and care. In these circumstances I would expect the law to impose on the valuer a duty owed to the purchaser to exercise reasonable skill and care in carrying out the valuation. . . .

In the present appeals the relationship between the valuer and the purchaser is 'akin to contract'. The valuer knows that the consideration which he receives derives from the purchaser and is passed on by the mortgagee, and the valuer also knows that the valuation will determine whether or not the purchaser buys the house . . .

In general, I am of the opinion that in the absence of a disclaimer of liability the valuer who values a house for the purpose of a mortgage, knowing that the mortgagee will rely and the mortgagor will probably rely on the valuation, knowing that the purchaser mortgagor has in effect paid for the valuation, is under a duty to exercise reasonable skill and care and that duty is owed to both parties to the mortgage for which the valuation is made. Indeed, in both the appeals now under consideration the existence of such a dual duty is tacitly accepted and acknowledged because notices excluding liability for breach of the duty owed to the purchaser were drafted by the mortgagee and imposed on the purchaser . . .

Lord Griffiths

Counsel for the council [in the *Harris* case] and Mr Lee . . . submitted, on the authority of *Hedley Byrne & Co Ltd v Heller & Partners Ltd* [1964] AC 465, that it was essential to found liability for a negligent misstatement that there had been 'a voluntary assumption of responsibility' on the part of the person giving the advice. I do not accept this submission and I do not think that voluntary assumption of responsibility is a helpful or realistic test for liability. It is true that reference is made in a number of the speeches in the *Hedley Byrne* case to the assumption of responsibility as a test of liability but it must be remembered that those speeches were made in the context of a case in which the central issue was whether a duty of care could arise when there had been an express disclaimer of responsibility for the accuracy of the advice. Obviously, if an adviser expressly assumes responsibility for his advice, a duty of care will arise, but such is extremely unlikely in the ordinary course of events. The House of Lords approved a duty of care being imposed on the facts in *Cann v Wilson* (1888) 39 Ch D 39 and in *Candler v Crane, Christmas & Co* [1951] 2 KB 164. But, if the surveyor in *Cann v Wilson* or the accountant in *Candler v Crane, Christmas & Co* had actually been asked if he was voluntarily assuming responsibility for his advice to the mortgagee or the purchaser of the shares, I have little doubt he would have replied: 'Certainly not. My responsibility is limited to the person who employs me.' The phrase 'assumption of responsibility' can only have any real meaning if it is understood as referring to the circumstances in which the law will deem the maker of the statement to have assumed responsibility to the person who acts on the advice . . .

The essential distinction between the present case and the situation being considered in the *Hedley Byrne* case and in the two earlier cases is that in those cases the advice was being given with the intention of persuading the recipient to act on it. In the present case the purpose of providing the report is to advise the mortgagee but it is given in circumstances in which it is highly probable that the purchaser will in fact act on its contents, although that was not the primary purpose of the report. I have had considerable doubts whether it is wise to increase the scope of the duty for negligent advice beyond the person directly intended by the giver of the advice to act on it to those whom he knows may do so . . .

I have already given my view that the voluntary assumption of responsibility is unlikely to be a helpful or realistic test in most cases. I therefore return to the question in what circumstances should the law deem those who give advice to have assumed responsibility to the person who acts on the advice or, in other words, in what circumstances should a duty of care be owed by the adviser to those who act on his advice? I would answer: only if it is foreseeable that if the advice is negligent the recipient is likely to suffer damage, that there is a sufficiently proximate relationship between the parties and that it is just and reasonable to impose the liability. In the case of a surveyor valuing a small house for a building society or local authority, the application of these three criteria leads to the conclusion that he owes a duty of care to the purchaser. If the valuation is negligent and is relied on damage in the form of economic loss to the purchaser is obviously foreseeable. The necessary proximity arises from the surveyor's knowledge that the overwhelming probability is that the purchaser will rely on his valuation, the evidence was that surveyors knew that approximately 90 per cent of purchasers did so, and the fact that the surveyor only obtains the work because the purchaser is willing to pay his fee. It is just and reasonable that the duty should be imposed for the advice is given in a professional as opposed to a social context and liability for breach of the duty will be limited both as to its extent and amount. The extent of the liability is limited to the purchaser of the house: I would not extend it to subsequent purchasers. The amount of the liability cannot be very great because it relates to a modest house. There is no question here of creating a liability of indeterminate amount to an indeterminate class. I would certainly wish to stress, that in cases where the advice has not been given for the specific purpose of the recipient acting on it, it should only be in cases when the adviser knows that there is a high degree of probability that some other identifiable person will act on the advice that a duty of care should be imposed. It would impose an intolerable burden on those who give advice in a professional or commercial context if they were to owe a duty not only to those to whom they give the advice but to any other person who might choose to act on it . . .

The essence of the case against [Mr Lee] is that he as a professional man realised that the purchaser was relying on him to exercise proper skill and judgment in his profession and that it was reasonable and fair that the purchaser should do so. Mr Lee was in breach of his duty of care to the Harris's and the local authority, as his employers, are vicariously liable for that negligence.

Lord Jauncey of Tullichettle

It is tempting to say that in this case the relationship between Mrs Smith and the surveyors was, in the words of Lord Shaw in *Nocton v Lord Ashburton* [1914] AC 932 at 972, quoted by Lord Devlin in *Hedley Byrne & Co Ltd v Heller & Partners Ltd* [1964] AC 465 at 528–529, 'equivalent to contract' inasmuch as she paid for the surveyors' report. However, I do not think that Lord Devlin, when he used those words, had in mind the sort of tripartite situation which obtained here, but rather was he considering a situation where the provider and receiver of information were in contact with one another either directly or through their agents, and where, but for the lack of payment, a contract would have existed between them. In the present case a contract existed between the building society and the surveyors who carried out their inspection and produced their report in pursuance of that contract. There was accordingly no room for a contract between Mrs Smith and the surveyors. I prefer to approach the matter by asking whether the facts disclose that the surveyors in inspecting and reporting must, but for the disclaimers, by reason of the proximate relationship between them, be deemed to have assumed responsibility towards Mrs Smith as well as to the building society who instructed them.

There can be only an affirmative answer to this question. The four critical facts are that the surveyors knew from the outset (1) that the report would be shown to Mrs Smith, (2) that Mrs Smith would probably rely on the valuation contained therein in deciding whether to buy the house without obtaining an independent valuation, (3) that if, in these circumstances, the valuation was, having regard to the actual condition of the house, excessive Mrs Smith would be likely to suffer loss and (4) that she had paid to the building society a sum to defray the surveyors' fee.

In the light of this knowledge the surveyors could have declined to act for the building society, but they chose to proceed. In these circumstances they must be taken not only to have assumed contractual obligations towards the building society but delictual [tortious] obligations towards Mrs Smith, whereby they became under a duty towards her to carry out their work with reasonable care and skill. It is critical to this conclusion that the surveyors knew that Mrs Smith would be likely to rely on the valuation without obtaining independent advice. In both *Candler v Crane, Christmas & Co* [1951] 2 KB 164 and *Hedley Byrne & Co Ltd v Heller & Partners Ltd* [1964] AC 465 the provider of the information was the obvious and most easily available, if not the only available, source of that information. It would not be difficult therefore to conclude that the person who sought such information was likely to rely on it. In the case of an intending mortgagor the position is very different since, financial considerations apart, there is likely to be available to him a wide choice of sources of information, to wit independent valuers to whom he can resort, in addition to the valuer acting for the mortgagee. I would not therefore conclude that the mere fact that a mortgagee's valuer knows that his valuation will be shown to an intending mortgagor of itself imposes on him a duty of care to the mortgagor. Knowledge, actual or implied, of the mortgagor's likely reliance on the valuation must be brought home to him. Such knowledge may be fairly readily implied in relation to a potential mortgagor seeking to enter the lower end of the housing market but [it is doubtful] that such ready implication would arise in the case of a purchase of an expensive property whether residential or commercial . . .

I would only add three further matters in relation to this part of the case. In the first place the duty of care owed by the surveyors to Mrs Smith resulted from the proximate relationship between them arising in the circumstances hereinbefore described. Such duty of care was accordingly limited to Mrs Smith and would not extend to 'strangers' (to use the words of Denning LJ in *Candler v Crane, Christmas & Co* [1951] 2 KB 164 at 181) who might subsequently derive a real interest in the house from her. In the second place the fact that A is prepared to lend money to B on the security of property owned by or to be acquired by him cannot *per se* impose on A any duty of care to B. Much more is required. Were it otherwise a loan by A to B on the security of property, real or personal, would ipso facto amount to a warranty by A that the property was worth at least the sum lent. In the third place the sum sought by Mrs Smith as a mortgage was relatively small and represented only a small proportion of the purchase price. The house with all its defects was worth substantially more than that sum, and had the report merely stated that the house was adequate security for that sum Mrs Smith would have had no complaint. However, the report contained a 'mortgage valuation' of the house, which valuation wholly failed to reflect the structural defect. It is that valuation of which Mrs Smith is entitled to complain . . .

[His Lordship found it more difficult to hold that in *Harris v Wyre Forest DC* the surveyor knew his report would be relied upon by the plaintiff, but was not prepared to dissent on this point and allowed the appeal in that case.]

Lord Keith and **Lord Brandon** concurred.

Appeal in Smith v Eric S Bush *dismissed*. Appeal in Harris v Wyre Forest District Council *allowed*.

COMMENTARY

The difficulty in applying the *Hedley Byrne* principle to the facts of these cases is clear: the defendants did not make any representation to the plaintiffs directly. The surveys were prepared for the building society and local authority respectively. For the plaintiffs in the *Smith* appeal to succeed the principle had to be extended to situations where information was prepared for one party, passed on to another and then relied upon by that other to his detriment, but even that extension did not cover the facts of the *Harris* appeal, as in that case the information was not passed on to the plaintiff, who never saw the survey.

For Lord Templeman, a duty was established because the relationship between the plaintiffs and defendants was 'akin' to contract. However, as Lord Jauncey points out, it is unlikely this was the type of situation envisaged by Lord Devlin when he used this term in *Hedley Byrne*, because in that case the defendant supplied the information directly to the plaintiffs (through their agents) in circumstances where there was no contractual obligation to provide the information to anyone else, whereas in *Smith* and *Harris* the defendant supplied the information to a third party, and in *Smith* this was pursuant to a contractual duty owed to that third party to do so. Hence Lord Griffiths and Lord Jauncey held that the duty of care was established through a sufficiently proximate relationship based upon payment by the plaintiffs for the survey and knowledge by the defendants of the high likelihood that the plaintiffs would rely on the survey without obtaining any independent advice. Is this reasoning materially different from Lord Templeman's? (See further *Customs and Excise*

Commissioners v Barclays Bank plc, extracted in IV.) By contrast, both Lord Griffiths and Lord Jauncey indicated that a duty would not necessarily arise in respect of higher value properties, presumably because in such cases a purchaser would be expected to look after their own interests by commissioning their own survey. Similar reasoning underpins the decision of the Court of Appeal in *Scullion v Bank of Scotland* [2011] 1 WLR 3212 that a valuer of property acting for a mortgagee did not owe a duty to a buy-to-let purchaser (i.e. someone buying the property as an investment). Here it was not the value of the property that was relevant but the purpose of buying it: as Lord Neuberger MR put it (at [49]), 'commercial purchasers of low to middle value residential properties, such as those buying to let, can properly be regarded as less deserving of protection of the common law against the risk of negligence than those buying to occupy as their residence'. (See also *Seddon v Driver and Vehicle Licensing Agency* [2019] 1 WLR 4593, where one of the reasons why the Court of Appeal held that the DVLA did not owe a duty of care to the purchaser of a classic car for £250,000 as to the accuracy of the information in the registration document was that it would not have expected him to rely on the document as sole evidence of the vehicle's provenance.)

A more fundamental problem with extending the valuer's duty to the purchaser is that in some cases the interests of the purchaser and lender are not the same. The purchaser is interested in the valuation of the property *vis-à-vis* the purchase price. Conversely, the lender is interested in its value for the purpose of ensuring that, if the borrower (purchaser) cannot repay the loan, the property is of sufficient value to cover the outstanding debt. When the loan represents the bulk of the purchase price, these interests may converge, but where the loan represents a smaller proportion of the purchase price, the divergence in the interests of the lender and the purchaser means that it may not be appropriate to impose a duty of care towards the latter on a valuer instructed by the former. (See also *Scullion v Bank of Scotland* [2011] 1 WLR 3212 at [52].)

Valuers have been held liable to third parties in contexts other than the purchase of real property. In *Killick v PricewaterhouseCoopers* [2001] 1 Lloyd's Rep PN 18 the defendant was appointed by directors of a company to value the company's shares for the purpose of determining the amount to be paid to the estate of a deceased shareholder who was required by the articles of association to sell his shares in the company. Neuberger J held that the defendant owed a duty of care to the shareholder's executor, one reason being that the defendant knew the specific purpose of its appointment. As the House of Lords was anxious to point out in *Smith v Bush*, however, that decision is not to be taken as imposing a general liability on information providers to third parties. This was made explicit in the following case.

Caparo Industries plc v Dickman [1990] 2 AC 605

The respondent company, Caparo, owned shares in another company, Fidelity. Shortly before the publication of Fidelity's audited accounts for the tax year ending 31 March 1984, Caparo started to buy more shares in the company, and it proceeded to make a successful takeover bid after the accounts (which showed a £1.2 million pre-tax profit) were made public. It was later discovered that Fidelity had not made a profit during that tax year; in fact it had made a loss of £400,000. Caparo brought an action against Fidelity's auditors for the loss it suffered as a result of paying an excessive price for Fidelity's shares, alleging that the auditors owed it a duty of care because they could foresee that a potential takeover bidder, or alternatively an existing shareholder, would rely on the accounts in order to make investment decisions about the level of its shareholdings in Fidelity. An application to strike out the claim as disclosing no cause of action was upheld by the trial judge, but the Court of Appeal allowed the appeal in so far as it related to Caparo's claim in its capacity as an existing shareholder. The auditors appealed to the House of Lords.

Lord Bridge

The salient feature of all these cases [sc. where *Hedley Byrne* liability was imposed] is that the defendant giving advice or information was fully aware of the nature of the transaction which the plaintiff had in contemplation, knew that the advice or information would be communicated to him directly or indirectly and knew that it was very likely that the plaintiff would rely on that advice or information in deciding whether or not to engage in the transaction in contemplation. In these circumstances the defendant could clearly be expected, subject always to the effect of any disclaimer of responsibility, specifically to anticipate that the plaintiff would rely on the advice or information given by the defendant for the very purpose for which he did in the event rely on it. So also the plaintiff, subject again to the effect of any disclaimer, would in that situation reasonably suppose that he was entitled to rely on the advice or information communicated to him for the very purpose for which he required it. The situation is entirely different where a statement is put into more or less general circulation and may foreseeably be relied on by strangers to the maker of the statement for any one of a variety of different purposes which the maker of the statement has no specific reason to anticipate. To hold the maker of the statement to be under a duty of care in respect of the accuracy of the statement to all and sundry for any purpose for which they may choose to rely on it is not only to subject him, in the classic words of Cardozo CJ, to 'liability in an indeterminate amount for an indeterminate time to an indeterminate class' (see *Ultramares Corp v Touche* (1931) 255 NY 170 at 179), it is also to confer on the world at large a quite unwarranted entitlement to appropriate for their own purposes the benefit of the expert knowledge or professional expertise attributed to the maker of the statement. Hence, looking only at the circumstances of these decided cases where a duty of care in respect of negligent statements has been held to exist, I should expect to find that the 'limit or control mechanism . . . imposed on the liability of a wrongdoer towards those who have suffered economic damage in consequence of his negligence' (see the *Candlewood* case [1986] AC 1 at 25) rested on the necessity to prove, in this category of the tort of negligence, as an essential ingredient of the 'proximity' between the plaintiff and the defendant, that the defendant knew that his statement would be communicated to the plaintiff, either as an individual or as a member of an identifiable class, specifically in connection with a particular transaction or transactions of a particular kind (e.g. in a prospectus inviting investment) and that the plaintiff would be very likely to rely on it for the purpose of deciding whether or not to enter on that transaction or on a transaction of that kind . . .

These considerations amply justify the conclusion that auditors of a public company's accounts owe no duty of care to members of the public at large who rely on the accounts in deciding to buy shares in the company. If a duty of care were owed so widely, it is difficult to see any reason why it should not equally extend to all who rely on the accounts in relation to other dealings with a company such as lenders or merchants extending credit to the company. A claim that such a duty was owed by auditors to a bank lending to a company was emphatically and convincingly rejected by Millett J in *Al Saudi Banque v Clark Pixley (a firm)* [1990] Ch 313. The only support for an unlimited duty of care owed by auditors for the accuracy of their accounts to all who may foreseeably rely on them is to be found in some jurisdictions in the United States of America, where there are striking differences in the law in different states. In this jurisdiction I have no doubt that the creation of such an unlimited duty would be a legislative step which it would be for Parliament, not the courts, to take.

The main submissions for Caparo are that the necessary nexus of proximity between it and the auditors giving rise to a duty of care stems from (1) the pleaded circumstances indicating the vulnerability of Fidelity to a take-over bid and from the consequent probability that another company, such as Caparo, would rely on the audited accounts in deciding to launch a take-over bid or (2) the circumstance that Caparo was already a shareholder in Fidelity when it decided to launch its take-over bid in reliance on the accounts. . . .

[His Lordship then considered the position of auditors in relation to the shareholders of a public limited liability company arising from the relevant provisions of the Companies Act 1985, and continued:]

No doubt these provisions establish a relationship between the auditors and the shareholders of a company on which the shareholder is entitled to rely for the protection of his interest. But the crucial question concerns the extent of the shareholder's interest which the auditor has a duty to protect. The shareholders of a company have a collective interest in the company's proper management and in so far as a negligent failure of the auditor to report accurately on the state of the company's finances deprives the shareholders of the opportunity to exercise their powers in general meeting to call the directors to book and to ensure that errors in management are corrected, the shareholders ought to be entitled to a remedy. But in practice no problem arises in this regard since the interest of the shareholders in the proper management of the company's affairs is indistinguishable from the interest of the company itself and any loss suffered by the shareholders, e.g. by the negligent failure of the auditor to discover and expose a misappropriation of funds by a director of the company, will be recouped by a claim against the auditor in the name of the company, not by individual shareholders.

I find it difficult to visualise a situation arising in the real world in which the individual shareholder could claim to have sustained a loss in respect of his existing shareholding referable to the negligence of the auditor which could not be recouped by the company. But on this part of the case your Lordships were much pressed with the argument that such a loss might occur by a negligent undervaluation of the company's assets in the auditor's report relied on by the individual shareholder in deciding to sell his shares at an undervalue. The argument then runs thus. The shareholder, *qua* shareholder, is entitled to rely on the auditor's report as the basis of his investment decision to sell his existing shareholding. If he sells at an undervalue he is entitled to recover the loss from the auditor. There can be no distinction in law between the shareholder's investment decision to sell the shares he has or to buy additional shares. It follows, therefore, that the scope of the duty of care owed to him by the auditor extends to cover any loss sustained consequent on the purchase of additional shares in reliance on the auditor's negligent report.

I believe this argument to be fallacious. Assuming without deciding that a claim by a shareholder to recover a loss suffered by selling his shares at an undervalue attributable to an undervaluation of the company's assets in the auditor's report could be sustained at all, it would not be by reason of any reliance by the shareholder on the auditor's report in deciding to sell: the loss would be referable to the depreciatory effect of the report on the market value of the shares before ever the decision of the shareholder to sell was taken. A claim to recoup a loss alleged to flow from the purchase of overvalued shares, on the other hand, can only be sustained on the basis of the purchaser's reliance on the report. The specious equation of 'investment decisions' to sell or to buy as giving rise to parallel claims thus appears to me to be untenable. Moreover, the loss in the case of the sale would be of a loss of part of the value of the shareholder's existing holding, which, assuming a duty of care owed to individual shareholders, might sensibly lie within the scope of the auditor's duty to protect. A loss, on the other hand, resulting from the purchase of additional shares would result from a wholly independent transaction having no connection with the existing shareholding.

I believe it is this last distinction which is of critical importance and which demonstrates the unsoundness of the conclusion reached by the majority of the Court of Appeal. It is never sufficient to ask simply whether A owes B a duty of care. It is always necessary to determine the scope of the duty by reference to the kind of damage from which A must take care to save B harmless:

> The question is always whether the defendant was under a duty to avoid or prevent that damage, but the actual nature of the damage suffered is relevant to the existence and extent of any duty to avoid or prevent it.

(See *Sutherland Shire Council v Heyman* (1985) 60 ALR 1 at 48, per Brennan J.)

Assuming for the purpose of the argument that the relationship between the auditor of a company and individual shareholders is of sufficient proximity to give rise to a duty of care, I do not understand how the scope of that duty can possibly extend beyond the protection of any individual shareholder from losses in the value of the shares which he holds. As a purchaser of additional shares in reliance on the auditor's report, he stands in no different position from any other investing member of the public to whom the auditor owes no duty.

Lord Oliver considered the purpose behind the statutory requirement for an audit, and continued:

[T]he history of the legislation is one of an increasing availability of information regarding the financial affairs of the company to those having an interest in its progress and stability. It cannot fairly be said that the purpose of making such information available is solely to assist those interested in attending general meetings of the company to an informed supervision and appraisal of the stewardship of the company's directors, for the requirement to supply audited accounts to, for instance, preference shareholders having no right to vote at general meetings and to debenture holders, cannot easily be attributed to any such purpose. Nevertheless, I do not, for my part, discern in the legislation any departure from what appears to me to be the original, central and primary purpose of these provisions, that is to say the informed exercise by those interested in the property of the company, whether as proprietors of shares in the company or as the holders of rights secured by a debenture trust deed, of such powers as are vested in them by virtue of their respective proprietary interests.

It is argued on behalf of the respondents (Caparo) that there is to be discerned in the legislation an additional or wider commercial purpose, namely that of enabling those to whom the accounts are addressed and circulated to make informed investment decisions, for instance by determining whether to dispose of their shares in the market or whether to apply any funds which they are individually able to command in seeking to purchase the shares of other shareholders. Of course, the provision of any information about the business and affairs of a trading company, whether it be contained in annual accounts or obtained from other sources, is capable of serving such a purpose just as it is capable of serving as the basis for the giving of financial advice to others, for arriving at a market price, for determining whether to extend credit to the company, or for the writing of financial articles in the press. Indeed, it is readily foreseeable by anyone who gives the matter any thought that it might well be relied on to a greater or lesser extent for all or any of such purposes. It is, of course, equally foreseeable that potential investors having no proprietary interest in the company, might well avail themselves of the information contained in a company's accounts published in the newspapers or culled from an inspection of the documents to be filed annually with the registrar of companies (which includes the audited accounts) in determining whether or not to acquire shares in the company. I find it difficult to believe, however, that the legislature, in enacting provisions clearly aimed primarily at the protection of the company and its informed control by the body of its proprietors, can have been inspired also by consideration for the public at large and investors in the market in particular . . .

The extension of the concept of negligence since the decision of this House in *Hedley Byrne & Co Ltd v Heller & Partners Ltd* [1964] AC 465 to cover cases of pure economic loss not resulting from physical damage has given rise to a considerable and as yet unsolved difficulty of definition. The opportunities for the infliction of pecuniary loss from the imperfect performance of everyday tasks on the proper performance of which people rely for regulating their affairs are illimitable and the effects are far reaching. A defective bottle of ginger beer may injure a single consumer but the damage stops there. A single statement may be repeated endlessly with or without the permission of its author and may be relied on in a different way by many different people. Thus the postulate of a simple duty to avoid any harm that is, with hindsight, reasonably capable of being foreseen becomes untenable without the imposition of some intelligible limits to keep the law of negligence within the bounds of common sense and practicality. . . .

Leaving this on one side, however, it is not easy to cull from the speeches in the *Hedley Byrne* case any clear attempt to define or classify the circumstances which give rise to the relationship of proximity on which the action depends and, indeed, Lord Hodson expressly stated (and I respectfully agree) that he did not think it possible to catalogue the special features which must be found to exist before the duty of care will arise in the given case (see [1964] AC 465 at 514). Lord Devlin is to the same effect (at 530). The nearest that one gets to the establishment of a criterion for the creation of a duty in the case of a negligent statement is the emphasis to be found in all the speeches on 'the voluntary assumption of responsibility' by the defendant. This is a convenient phrase but it is clear that it was not intended to be a test for the existence of the duty for, on analysis, it means no more than that the act of the defendant in making the statement or tendering the advice was voluntary and that the law attributes to it an assumption of responsibility if the statement or advice is inaccurate and is acted on. It tells us nothing about the circumstances from which such attribution arises . . .

[After considering the decision of the House of Lords in *Smith v Eric S Bush (A Firm); Harris v Wyre Forest DC*, his Lordship continued:]

Thus *Smith v Eric S Bush*, although establishing beyond doubt that the law may attribute an assumption of responsibility quite regardless of the expressed intentions of the adviser, provides no support for the proposition that the relationship of proximity is to be extended beyond circumstances in which advice is tendered for the purpose of the particular transaction or type of transaction and the adviser knows or ought to know that it will be relied on by a particular person or class of persons in connection with that transaction. The judgment of Millett J in the recent case of *Al Saudi Banque v Clark Pixley (a firm)* [1990] Ch 313 (decided after the decision of the Court of Appeal in the instant case) contains an analysis of the decision of this House in *Smith v Eric S Bush* and concludes (and I agree) that it established a more stringent test of the requirements for proximity than that which had been applied by the Court of Appeal in the instant case . . .

My Lords, no decision of this House has gone further than *Smith v Eric S Bush* but your Lordships are asked by Caparo to widen the area of responsibility even beyond the limits to which it was extended by the Court of Appeal in this case and to find a relationship of proximity between the adviser and third parties to whose attention the advice may come in circumstances in which the reliance said to have given rise to the loss is strictly unrelated either to the intended recipient or to the purpose for which the advice was required. My Lords, I discern no pressing reason of policy which would require such an extension and there seems to me to be powerful reasons against it . . .

As I have already mentioned, it is almost always foreseeable that someone, somewhere and in some circumstances, may choose to alter his position on the faith of the accuracy of a statement or report which comes to his attention and it is always foreseeable that a report, even a confidential report, may come to be communicated to persons other than the original or intended recipient. To apply as a test of liability only the foreseeability of possible damage without some further control would be to create a liability wholly indefinite in area, duration and amount and would open up a limitless vista of uninsurable risk for the professional man . . .

In my judgment, accordingly, the purpose for which the auditors' certificate is made and published is that of providing those entitled to receive the report with information to enable them to exercise in conjunction those powers which their respective proprietary interests confer on them and not for the purposes of individual speculation with a view to profit. The same considerations as limit the existence of a duty of care also, in my judgment, limit the scope of the duty and I agree with O'Connor LJ that the duty of care is one owed to the shareholders as a body and not to individual shareholders.

To widen the scope of the duty to include loss caused to an individual by reliance on the accounts for a purpose for which they were not supplied and were not intended would be to extend it beyond the limits which are so far deducible from the decisions of this House. It is not, as I think, an extension which either logic requires or policy dictates and I, for my part, am not prepared to follow the majority of the Court of Appeal in making it. In relation to the purchase of shares of other shareholders in a company, whether in the open market or as a result of an offer made to all or a majority of the existing shareholders, I can see no sensible distinction, so far as a duty of care is concerned, between a potential purchaser who is, vis-à-vis the company, a total outsider and one who is already the holder of one or more shares.

Lord Roskill, **Lord Ackner** and **Lord Jauncey** delivered concurring speeches.

Appeal allowed.

COMMENTARY

Why did the plaintiffs win in *Smith* and *Harris* but lose in *Caparo*? The short answer is the significance attached by the House of Lords to the purpose of the statement. In *Caparo* the auditors did not carry out the audit merely because the company felt it needed its accounts audited; rather, there was a statutory duty under the companies legislation for the company to appoint an auditor and produce audited accounts. The reason for this requirement was held to be the need to provide shareholders with information about the company's performance so that, if the shareholders thought it necessary, action could be taken at a general meeting of the company against those responsible for its management, the board of directors. Hence the audited accounts were (their Lordships reasoned) provided to allow shareholders, as a body, to exercise this supervisory jurisdiction over the company, and not to give potential investors information on which to make investment decisions, nor to assist existing shareholders, as individuals, to make decisions about levels of shareholding in the company. And as Moore-Bick LJ pointed out in *Taberna Europe v Selskabet AF 1 September 2008* [2017] QB 633 at [7]:

The courts have long recognised the danger of allowing third parties to rely on documents produced for a purpose other than that to which they had been put or directed at an audience of which they are not themselves members.

What was different about *Smith* and *Harris*? Although the statement was made *to* the building society and council it was made *for* the specific transaction that the plaintiffs were negotiating. In contrast, the purpose for which the audit was made in *Caparo* (as found by their Lordships: cf. Mullis and Oliphant (1991) 7 PN 22 at 26) had nothing to do with the transaction in respect of which it was relied upon. Note that the Companies Act 2006, Part 16, which introduced new statutory provisions for the audit of companies, does not appear to change this view as the primary duty of the auditor remains one that is linked to the proper performance of the company rather than the provision of financial information about the company to the general public.

It should not be thought that a financial investigation carried out by accountants under statute is incapable of giving rise to a duty of care to anyone other than the subject of the audit. The key question remains the purpose behind the statutory requirement. In *Law Society v KPMG Peat Marwick* [2000] 1 WLR 1921 the Court of Appeal held that the defendant accountants owed a duty of care to the claimant in respect of a report on the activities of a certain firm of solicitors. Even though the solicitors paid for the report, it was prepared for the purpose of providing the Law Society with information enabling it to decide whether to exercise its regulatory powers, and of thereby protecting the contents of the Solicitors' Compensation Fund which the Law Society maintains to provide redress to the victims of solicitors' fraud. The duty was owed to the Law Society as trustee of the compensation fund, and extended to losses incurred by the fund as a result of pay-outs to the firm's defrauded clients.

Although *Smith v Bush* and *Caparo* can be distinguished on the 'purpose' basis, it is not an entirely satisfactory way of reconciling the results. No doubt the surveyors in *Smith and Harris*, if asked what was the purpose of the surveys they carried out, would have said that they were intended to enable the building society and the council to decide whether to lend the plaintiffs the funds to purchase the houses. In effect, the House of Lords deemed the surveys to have an additional purpose, namely to provide information to the prospective purchasers which would help them to decide whether to buy the properties in question. But note that, although it was highly likely that the purchasers would rely on the surveys in that manner, subsequent cases suggest that the mere fact that information or advice will foreseeably be relied upon in a certain way is not enough to make that one of the purposes of providing the information. For example, in *Seddon v Driver and Vehicle Licensing Agency* [2019] 1 WLR 4593 at [66], where it was denied that the DVLA owed a duty of care to a purchaser of a classic car who relied on the information in the registration document, Hamblen LJ held that such documents were provided for the 'statutory purpose of collecting tax . . . and ensuring vehicles operating on the roads in the UK are registered' and not 'for the private purpose of informing the commercial decisions of those who may choose to purchase registered vehicles', despite the fact that anyone who buys a used car in the United Kingdom knows full well the importance of the registration document as evidence of the true ownership of the vehicle and other matters. (Cf. Witting (2000) 20 OJLS 615, who argues that it is the statement maker's actual knowledge that the claimant will rely on the statement that requires him to act with reasonable care; and see *Taberna Europe v Selskabet AF 1 September 2008* [2017] QB 633 at [11], where it was suggested that what matters is that the statement maker *intended* the recipient to rely on the statement in a particular way.)

Can the results in *Smith v Bush* and *Caparo* be reconciled in other ways? In a very perceptive analysis at first instance in *Morgan Crucible Co plc v Hill Samuel Bank Ltd* [1990] 3 All ER 330, a case that followed hot on the heels of *Caparo*, and which also concerned a company takeover, the then Hoffmann J argued that they could. (It is worth noting that the Court of Appeal were less impressed than we are with Hoffmann J's judgment, and reversed his decision: [1991] 1 All ER 148.) According to Hoffmann J, when it came to the determination of the duty of care issue in a negligent misstatement case, the knowledge, intentions and purposes of the parties were 'an impoverished set of concepts', and 'by no means the only relevant factors' ([1990] 3 All ER 330 at 333–4). He drew several distinctions between *Smith* and *Caparo* which related to 'the different economic relationships between the parties and the nature of the markets in which they were operating' (at 334).

One of those distinctions was that the plaintiff in *Smith* had paid for the survey, whereas Caparo, at least in its capacity as a potential investor, had paid nothing for the audit. This is important, because it means that in *Smith* there was no 'free-rider' problem: the plaintiff had, in effect, bought the right to rely on the survey to the surveyor's knowledge.

Another distinction was that whereas the typical plaintiff in a case like *Smith* was 'a person of modest means . . . making the most expensive purchase of his or her life', Caparo was an 'entrepreneur taking his risks for high rewards'. As Weir [1990] CLJ 212 noted:

> [Caparo] was not investing in Fidelity plc, it was buying it, taking it over. Caparo was a predator. Nor was Caparo exactly wet behind the ears. With a turnover of over £150m it is among the top 500 manufacturing companies in Britain. Its chairman, Mr Swarj Paul, chairs over twenty other companies. Allegedly the directors of Fidelity were fraudulent. Greed foiled by fraud is not quite maiden virtue rudely strumpeted, but it is hurtful all the same, and none the less so when the fraud is facilitated by negligence. But if Caparo were conned out of their booty, let them go against the vendors for fraud or breach of contract. Let not the predator turn and rend those who failed to catch the fraudster who succeeded in catching him. Caveat praedator is a sound and moral rule.

Then again, the vast majority of Fidelity's shareholders were not interested in taking over the company but simply wanted to make a sound investment. As they were unlikely to have the resources to undertake an independent assessment of Fidelity's financial position, did they have any real choice but to rely on the audited accounts?

Finally, Hoffmann J also distinguished between the position of the defendants in the two types of case. While surveyors could protect themselves relatively easily through insurance, some accountants might not be able to secure sufficient insurance cover. (This is because the amount of money involved when auditing large company accounts may be huge, and so the potential liability is enormous if things go wrong: for example, in *Deloitte & Touche v Livent Inc* [2017] 2 SCR 855, a company sued its auditors for over 450 million Canadian dollars—roughly £270 million at the time of writing.) Moreover, at the time of *Caparo*, many firms of accountants were partnerships, in which each partner was personally liable for the debts of the partnership. When combined with potentially uninsurable liabilities, this could potentially have had a chilling effect on the work of auditors, and in particular discouraged all but a few very large accountancy firms from taking on the work of auditing the accounts of large public companies.

A decade after *Caparo* was decided, Parliament passed the Limited Liability Partnerships Act 2000, which created a new kind of business entity, the limited liability partnership ('LLP'). The LLP has a separate legal identity from that of its members, and it is that entity which is responsible for the debts of the partnership rather than the individual partners. Accordingly, it is now possible for the individual partners of firms of accountants and solicitors to limit their personal liability to investors and shareholders in a way that was not possible at the time of *Caparo*. Moreover, the Companies Act 2006, ss. 534–8 now allows auditors to limit their liability to companies they audit, and s. 1157 of the Act allows a court in proceedings for negligence against an auditor to relieve him, either wholly or in part, from his liability on such terms as it thinks fit if the court hearing the case considers that the auditor may be liable but that he acted honestly and reasonably, and that having regard to all the circumstances of the case (including those connected with his appointment) he ought fairly to be excused. In the light of these changes to the statutory framework governing the liability of auditors, do you think that the decision in *Caparo* should be reconsidered? More generally, was Hoffmann J right to argue that it was a mistake to base the existence of a duty of care in cases such as *Smith* and *Caparo* 'on subtle distinctions of knowledge and purpose rather than the realities of the economic relationships between the parties and the market in which they are operating' ([1990] 3 All ER 330 at 337)? Are judges well equipped to assess those 'realities'?

The principles set out in the *Caparo* decision as to the scope of the assumed duty of care, and the persons to whom it is owed, are of general application and not limited to auditors. A recent decision of the Supreme Court applying these principles is *Banca Nazionale del Lavoro SPA v Playboy Club London Ltd* [2018] 1 WLR 4041. In this case the claimant casino wanted a credit reference for one of its customers from the customer's bank, the defendant. However, it was the casino's practice not to request such a reference itself, but to use a more discreet procedure whereby the request was made by an associated company (Burlington Street Services), which did not reveal the purpose of the enquiry or the fact that it was making it on behalf of a third party. The bank provided the reference to Burlington, who passed it on to the casino, which relied on it by extending credit to the customer. The customer defaulted and the casino sought the money it had lost from the bank, on the basis that the reference had been woefully misleading. The Court held that since the bank had not known that Burlington was acting on behalf of the casino it had assumed no responsibility towards the casino and so owed it no duty of care in respect of the contents of the reference. According to Lord Sumption (at [7]) it was 'fundamental' to liability under the *Hedley Byrne* principle that 'the defendant is assuming a responsibility to an identifiable (although not necessarily identified) person or group of persons, and not to the world at large or to a wholly indeterminate group'. His Lordship also reiterated the central message of the *Caparo* decision that in a case where the claim is brought by a third party, rather than the person to whom the statement is made, the fact that the defendant knew that it was likely to be communicated to and relied on by the third party is not enough: that must be part of the statement's known purpose. Again, however, *Banca Nazionale* shows the difficulty of identifying the precise purpose or purposes for which a statement is made, with Lord Mance taking a broader view of the purpose of the bank's reference than Lord Sumption, while agreeing that no duty was owed to the casino as an undisclosed third party. For comment on the decision, see Grower and Sherman (2019) 135 LQR 177, and O'Sullivan, 'The Contract/Tort Borderline', in W. Day and S. Worthington (eds), *Challenging Private Law: Lord Sumption on the Supreme Court* (Oxford: Hart, 2020), pp. 130–9.

Other common law courts have reached decisions in line with *Caparo*: see in particular *Esanda Finance Corporation Ltd v Peat Marwick Hungerfords* (1997) 188 CLR 241; and *Hercules Management Ltd v Ernst & Young* [1997] 2 SCR 165. In *Hercules Management*, La Forest J agreed with the reasoning in *Caparo* as to the purpose of the statutory audit, and held that it did not matter whether the reports prepared by the auditor were relied upon in assessing the prospect of further investments or in evaluating existing investments, as in both cases the accounts were being used to guide individual or personal investment decisions, and this was not the purpose for which they had been prepared. In *Caparo* Lord Bridge had suggested that there might be a distinction between a decision to sell existing shares for too little as a result of an audit which negligently undervalued a company and a decision to pay too much for shares as a result of an audit which negligently overvalued one. However, as La Forest J pointed out, the logic of this distinction is not obvious: if it is not the purpose of an audit to guide investment decisions, then the nature of the particular investment decision (i.e. whether to buy or sell) is irrelevant. For comment on *Esanda* and *Hercules*, see Phegan (1997) 5 TLJ 4, and for a later Supreme Court of Canada decision where the scope of the auditor's possible liability was determined by closely scrutinising the purpose of its report, see *Deloitte & Touche v Livent Inc* [2017] 2 SCR 855.

It might be thought that the decision in *Caparo* heralded an era of limiting liability for professionals. The next subsection, however, indicates how an expanded view of *Hedley Byrne* has in fact opened up new possibilities for using negligence law to hold professionals to account.

3. *Hedley Byrne* and the Provision of Services

Hedley Byrne was a case which concerned the provision of information or advice, and the basic fact pattern involved—that the claimant relied to their detriment on a representation made by the defendant—was relatively simple. Nonetheless, it is clear that *Hedley Byrne* liability can extend beyond the provision of information to the performance of services. It is difficult to quibble with such an extension, particularly when it comes to the liability of professionals. It would be an odd result if a solicitor could be liable under *Hedley Byrne* for careless advice but not for carelessly drafting a document. Of course, the solicitor would also be liable in contract, so the practical effect of imposing liability in tort is to provide the claimant with a different limitation period (six years from the date of damage rather than six years from the date on which the contract was breached), and perhaps different rules as to damages. As has been seen in relation to information and advice, however, more difficulties arise when it comes to extending a tort remedy to persons who are adversely affected by the provision of a service performed by the defendant under a contract with another party. The next extracted case is a good example, as it involves both contractual counterparties of the defendant and third parties. It is also the decision which confirmed beyond any doubt that *Hedley Byrne* liability can attach to the performance of professional services, and is not limited to the provision of information and advice.

Henderson v Merrett Syndicates Ltd [1995] 2 AC 145

The litigation in this case arose out of the substantial losses suffered by many Lloyds insurance syndicates in the early 1990s. Members of certain syndicates ('Names') brought actions against those responsible for the management of the syndicates in both contract and tort, and the House of Lords was faced with applications to have some of these claims struck out as disclosing no cause of action. Two of the many issues that were before the House were (1) whether the existence of a contract between the parties precluded recognition of a concurrent duty of care in tort between those parties, and (2) whether the syndicate managers owed a tortious duty of care to the Names (some of whom had contracts with the managers and some of whom did not). As regards (1) their Lordships accepted that there could be concurrent liability in contract and tort, although the content of the tort duty might be affected by the terms of the contract between the parties. The extract focuses on the second issue.

Lord Goff of Chieveley

My Lords, every person who wishes to become a Name at Lloyd's and who is not himself or herself an underwriting agent must appoint an underwriting agent to act on his or her behalf, pursuant to an underwriting agency agreement. Underwriting agents may act in one of three different capacities. (1) They may be members' agents, who (broadly speaking) advise Names on their choice of syndicates, place Names on the syndicates chosen by them, and give general advice to them. (2) They may be managing agents, who underwrite contracts of insurance at Lloyd's on behalf of the Names who are members of the syndicates under their management, and who reinsure contracts of insurance and pay claims. (3) They may be combined agents, who perform both the role of members' agents, and the role of managing agents in respect of the syndicates under their management.

Until 1990, the practical position was as follows. Each Name entered into one or more underwriting agency agreements with an underwriting agent, which was either a members' agent or a combined agent. Each underwriting agency agreement governed the relationship between the Name and the members' agent, or between the Name and the combined agent in so far as it acted as a members' agent. If however the Name became a member of a syndicate which was managed by the combined agent, the agreement also governed the relationship between the Name and the combined agent acting in its capacity of managing agent. In such a case the Name was known as a direct Name. If however the Name became a member of a syndicate which was managed by some other managing agent, the Name's underwriting agent (whether or not it was a combined agent) entered into a sub-agency agreement under which it appointed the managing agent its sub-agent to act as such in relation to the Name. In such a case the Name was known as an indirect Name . . .

The main argument advanced by the managing agents against the existence of a duty of care in tort was that the imposition of such a duty upon them was inconsistent with the contractual relationship between the parties. In the case of direct Names, where there was a direct contract between the Names and the managing agents, the argument was that the contract legislated exclusively for the relationship between the parties, and that a parallel duty of care in tort was therefore excluded by the contract. In the case of indirect Names, reliance was placed on the fact that there had been brought into existence a contractual chain, between Name and members' agent, and between members' agent and managing agent; and it was said that, by structuring their contractual relationship in this way, the indirect Names and the managing agents had deliberately excluded any direct responsibility, including any tortious duty of care, to the indirect Names by the managing agents. In particular, the argument ran, it was as a result not permissible for the Names to pray in aid, for limitation purposes, the more favourable time for accrual of a cause of action in tort. To do so, submitted the managing agents, would deprive them of their contractual expectations, and would avoid the policy of Parliament that there are different limitation regimes for contract and tort.

Such was the main argument advanced on behalf of the managing agents. Moreover, as appears from my summary of it, the argument is not precisely the same in the case of direct Names and indirect Names respectively. However, in any event, I think it desirable first to consider the principle upon which a duty of care in tort may in the present context be imposed upon the managing agents, assuming that to impose such a duty would not be inconsistent with the relevant contractual relationship. In considering this principle, I bear in mind in particular the separate submission of the managing agents that no such duty should be imposed, because the loss claimed by the Names is purely economic loss. However the identification of the principle is, in my opinion, relevant to the broader question of the impact of the relevant contract or contracts.

The Governing Principle

Even so, I can take this fairly shortly. I turn immediately to the decision of this House in *Hedley Byrne & Co Ltd v Heller & Partners Ltd*. There, as is of course well known, the question arose whether bankers could be held liable in tort in respect of the gratuitous provision of a negligently favourable reference for one of their customers, when they knew or ought to have known that the plaintiff would rely on their skill and judgment in furnishing the reference, and the plaintiff in fact relied upon it and in consequence suffered financial loss. Your Lordships' House held that, in principle, an action would lie in such circumstances in tort; but that, in the particular case, a duty of care was negatived by a disclaimer of responsibility under cover of which the reference was supplied.

The case has always been regarded as important in that it established that, in certain circumstances, a duty of care may exist in respect of words as well as deeds, and further that liability may arise in negligence in respect of pure economic loss which is not parasitic upon physical damage. But, perhaps more important for the future development of the law, and certainly more relevant for the purposes of the present case, is the principle upon which the decision was founded. The governing principles are perhaps now perceived to be most clearly stated in the speeches of Lord Morris of Borth-y-Gest (with whom Lord Hodson agreed) and of Lord Devlin . . .

[His Lordship quoted from these speeches and continued:]

From these statements, and from their application in *Hedley Byrne*, we can derive some understanding of the breadth of the principle underlying the case. We can see that it rests upon a relationship between the parties, which may be general or specific to the particular transaction, and which may or may not be contractual in nature. All of their Lordships spoke in terms of one party having assumed or undertaken a responsibility towards the other. On this point, Lord Devlin spoke in particularly clear terms . . . Further, Lord Morris spoke of that party being possessed of a 'special skill' which he undertakes to 'apply for the assistance of another who relies upon such skill.' But the facts of *Hedley Byrne* itself, which was concerned with the liability of a banker to the recipient for negligence in the provision of a reference gratuitously supplied, show that the concept of a 'special skill' must be understood broadly, certainly broadly enough to include special knowledge. Again, though *Hedley Byrne* was concerned with the provision of information and advice, the example given by Lord Devlin of the relationship between solicitor and client, and his and Lord Morris's statements of principle, show that the principle extends beyond the provision of information and advice to include the performance of other services. It follows, of course, that although, in the case of the provision of information and advice, reliance upon it by the other party will be necessary to establish a cause of action (because otherwise the negligence will have no causative effect), nevertheless there may be other circumstances in which there will be the necessary reliance to give rise to the application of the principle. In particular, as cases concerned with solicitor and client demonstrate, where the plaintiff entrusts the defendant with the conduct of his affairs, in general or in particular, he may be held to have relied on the defendant to exercise due skill and care in such conduct.

In subsequent cases concerned with liability under the *Hedley Byrne* principle in respect of negligent misstatements, the question has frequently arisen whether the plaintiff falls within the category of persons to whom the maker of the statement owes a duty of care. In seeking to contain that category of persons within reasonable bounds, there has been some tendency on the part of the courts to criticise the concept of 'assumption of responsibility' as being 'unlikely to be a helpful or realistic test in most cases' (see *Smith v Eric S Bush* [1990] 1 AC 831, 864–865, per Lord Griffiths; and see also *Caparo Industries Plc v Dickman* [1990] 2 AC 605, 628, per Lord Roskill). However, at least in cases such as the present, in which the same problem does not arise, there seems to be no reason why recourse should not be had to the concept, which appears after all to have been adopted, in one form or another, by all of their Lordships in *Hedley Byrne*.

. . . Furthermore, especially in a context concerned with a liability which may arise under a contract or in a situation 'equivalent to contract' it must be expected that an objective test will be applied when asking the question whether, in a particular case, responsibility should be held to have been assumed by the defendant to the plaintiff: see *Caparo Industries Plc v Dickman* [1990] 2 AC 605, 637, per Lord Oliver of Aylmerton. In addition, the concept provides its own explanation why there is no problem in cases of this kind about liability for pure economic loss; for if a person assumes responsibility to another in respect of certain services, there is no reason why he should not be liable in damages to that other in respect of economic loss which flows from the negligent performance of those services. It follows that, once the case is identified as falling within the *Hedley Byrne* principle, there should be no need to embark upon any further enquiry whether it is 'fair, just and reasonable' to impose liability for economic loss—a point which is, I consider, of some importance in the present case. The concept indicates too that in some circumstances, for example where the undertaking to furnish the relevant service is given on an informal occasion, there may be no assumption of responsibility; and likewise that an assumption of responsibility may be negatived by an appropriate disclaimer. I wish to add in parenthesis that, as Oliver J recognised in *Midland Bank Trust Co Ltd v Hett, Stubbs & Kemp* [1979] Ch 384, 416 . . . an assumption of responsibility by, for example, a professional man may give rise to liability in respect of negligent omissions as much as negligent acts of commission, as for example when a solicitor assumes responsibility for business on behalf of his client and omits to take a certain step, such as the service of a document, which falls within the responsibility so assumed by him. . . .

Lord Keith, **Lord Mustill** and **Lord Nolan** agreed with Lord Goff. **Lord Browne-Wilkinson** delivered a concurring speech.

Appeals dismissed.

COMMENTARY

The genesis of Lord Goff's analysis can be found in the earlier House of Lords decision in *Spring v Guardian Assurance plc* [1995] 2 AC 296. The plaintiff sued his former employer with respect to a reference it had prepared about him, which negligently stated that he was a person 'of little or no integrity'. The result was that the plaintiff was unable to obtain further employment in the industry. Two objections were made to the plaintiff's claim: first, that the plaintiff had suffered only pure economic loss, which was not generally recoverable; and, secondly, that the imposition of a duty of care would be inconsistent with the defence of qualified privilege available to referees in the tort of defamation (which limited the referee's liability to circumstances where he acted maliciously: see Ch. 12.IV.3(d)). By a 4:1 majority the House of Lords allowed the claim. Leaving aside the qualified privilege argument (which was rejected by the House of Lords), on what basis was the duty of care owed? Two of their Lordships applied general duty of care principles, and found that the tripartite duty test from *Caparo Industries plc v Dickman* had been satisfied. However, Lord Goff, with whom Lord Lowry agreed on this issue, argued that a duty of care was owed according to the principles laid out in *Hedley Byrne*. It should be noted that *Spring* did not fall within the narrow *Hedley Byrne* fact pattern adverted to above. The defendant provided the plaintiff employee with no advice, nor did it make a representation to him. Rather, the reference was given to a third party, the prospective employer. Further, the plaintiff did not rely on the reference, at least not in the sense of using it to decide how he should act. Again, it was the future employer who relied on the reference in that sense. And the employer had no special skill or expertise in writing references nor did it hold itself out as possessing such skill. How then could Lord Goff find a duty based on *Hedley Byrne*?

In a judgment unaided by argument from counsel, Lord Goff redefined the scope of the *Hedley Byrne* exception. The basis of *Hedley Byrne* was an assumption of responsibility by the defendant to the plaintiff. As to when such an assumption of responsibility would be considered to have occurred, Lord Goff said that (at 318):

> where the plaintiff entrusts the defendant with the conduct of his affairs, in general or in particular, the defendant may be held to have assumed responsibility to the plaintiff, and the plaintiff to have relied on the defendant to exercise due care and skill, in respect of such conduct.

His Lordship questioned whether any special skill was required, noting the powerful arguments in the minority speeches in *Mutual Life v Evatt* requiring only that the defendant was acting in a professional capacity, but ultimately he reserved his opinion on this issue. He was content to point out that the defendant in *Spring*, possessing special information about the plaintiff (his employment history), had been entrusted with the task of writing the plaintiff's reference, and was therefore under a duty to take care in performing that task. Furthermore, the fact that the defendant was obliged to write the reference under the rules of its regulator did not prevent an assumption of responsibly from arising. As can be seen, this line of reasoning was taken up and expanded in *Henderson*, where it was endorsed by all the other members of the House (see also *Williams v Natural Life Health Foods Ltd* [1998] 1 WLR 830), and where, expanding on *Spring*, Lord Goff made it clear that the liability under *Hedley Byrne* could attach to the performance of services.

The notion of entrusting the conduct of one's affairs to another sounds like something from the law of fiduciaries. However, in his speech in *Henderson*, Lord Browne-Wilkinson said that a fiduciary's requirement to act carefully to avoid causing economic loss to the person in whose interest he is acting was merely an example of the wider responsibility placed on those who have agreed to act in the interests of others. But in what sense had the managing agents agreed to act in the best interests of the indirect Names? (cf. *Customs and Excise Commissioners v Barclays Bank plc*, extracted in IV, where several members of the House of Lords found some difficulty in seeing an assumption of responsibility in *Henderson*).

On the facts of *Henderson*, the indirect Names were not the only party to whom the managing agents had assumed responsibility. They had expressly assumed responsibility to the member's agents for the management of the syndicates under a contract. What if the indirect Names claimed that the managing agents owed them a duty in tort which went beyond that which was expressly assumed under the contract with the member's agents? Both Lord Goff and Lord Browne-Wilkinson accepted that the existence of a contract might affect the scope of any assumption of responsibility in tort by a party to that contract to a third party. However, that presented no problem on the facts of *Henderson*, as the responsibilities assumed by the managing agents in contract to the member's agents and in tort to the indirect Names were of the same nature and extent. But would an assumption of responsibility analysis hold if that were not the case? In *Dean v Allin & Watts* [2001] 2 Lloyd's Rep 249 the Court of Appeal held that a solicitor had assumed responsibility in tort to the lender even though his client (the person to whom the solicitor was under a contractual obligation) was the borrower, since both parties wanted the lender to have an effective security. However, such situations are likely to be rare, as the general rule is that a solicitor acting for one party to an arm's length transaction will not owe a duty of care to the other party (see *Gran Gelato v Richcliff (Group) Ltd* [1992] Ch 560 and *NRAM Ltd v Steel* [2018] 1 WLR 1190, where the Supreme Court held that the solicitor acting for a borrower in a loan transaction was not liable to the lender for losses it suffered as a result of a mistake the solicitor made in the documentation relating to the loan).

Hedley Byrne and Contract

An issue considered in *Henderson* was whether the presence of a contract between the parties excludes the possibility of a concurrent duty in tort, based on *Hedley Byrne*. There was earlier authority that a solicitor owed a concurrent duty in contract and tort to his client (*Midland Bank Trust Co Ltd v Hett, Stubbs & Kemp* [1979] Ch 384), but a later Privy Council decision (*Tai Hing Cotton Mill Ltd v Liu Chong Hing Bank Ltd* [1986] AC 80 at 193) doubted that 'there was anything to the advantage of the law's development in searching for a liability in tort where the parties are in a contractual relationship'. Further, the Privy Council were not prepared to accept that the parties' mutual obligations in tort could be any greater than those assumed expressly or by necessary implication in their contract. The reasoning behind this is clear: where the parties have expressly set out the rights and obligations to be assumed under the contract, the law of tort has no business re-writing the bargain. But this does not answer the question whether a concurrent tortious duty, no more extensive than the contractual duty, may be owed between parties to a contract. This question was answered in the affirmative in *Henderson*, Lord Goff holding that (at 194):

> an assumption of responsibility coupled with the concomitant reliance may give rise to a tortious duty of care irrespective of whether there is a contractual relationship between the parties, and in consequence, unless his contract precludes him from doing so, the plaintiff, who has available to him concurrent remedies in contract and tort, may choose that remedy which appears to him to be the most advantageous.

However, in *Robinson v PE Jones (Contractors) Ltd* [2012] QB 44, the Court of Appeal, while affirming that any tortious duty was limited by the obligations assumed under the contract, stressed that Lord Goff's speech did not mean that a tortious duty was *always* assumed by parties in a contractual relationship. While the employment of persons to provide professional advice and services—as in *Henderson*—commonly gave rise to an assumption of responsibility, there was nothing on the facts of *Robinson*—which involved an ordinary house building contract—to suggest the defendant had assumed a responsibility to the claimant to prevent the claimant suffering pure economic loss. More generally, the Court of Appeal affirmed the primacy of contract over tort in situations where the parties are in a contractual relationship: as Jackson LJ put it (at [79]), 'there is no reason why the law of tort should impose duties which are identical to the obligations negotiated by the parties'. Furthermore, Jackson LJ was, in the absence of authority, inclined to the view that in such cases any tort duty was limited to personal injury and damage to property, and did not extend to pure economic loss. Indeed, Stanley Burnton LJ appears to have held that this was in fact the law, at least in construction cases: 'the builder/vendor of a building does not by reason of his contract to construct or to complete the building assume any liability in the tort of negligence in relation to defects in the building giving rise to purely economic loss' (at [92]). It remains to be seen whether this analysis will be generally accepted.

The existence of a contract may also have an effect on any tort duty owed even where the contract is between the claimant or defendant and a third party. If the parties to a complicated transaction have arranged it through a network of contracts setting out the rights and responsibilities of the parties, should the law of tort intervene by holding that parties in the network who owe each other no contractual duty nonetheless owe a tort duty? In *Simaan General Contracting Co v Pilkington Glass Ltd (No. 2)* [1988] QB 758 the plaintiff was the main contractor responsible for constructing a building in Abu Dhabi. The plaintiff sub-contracted part of the construction of the building (curtain-walling), one of the conditions being that a particular type of the defendant's glass was used. The defendant supplied glass which was the wrong colour, and it was ultimately rejected by the plaintiff with the result that neither it nor its sub-contractor were paid by the building owner. As Bingham LJ noted, the problem arose because the plaintiff, instead of suing its sub-contractor in contract, chose to sue the defendant, with whom it had no contract, in tort. But according to his Lordship, there was no basis on which the defendant could be said to have assumed a direct responsibility for the quality of the goods to the plaintiff. This was because (at 781) 'such a responsibility is, I think, inconsistent with the structure of the contract the parties have chosen to make' (see also *Rolls Royce New Zealand Ltd v Carter Holt Harvey Ltd* [2005] 1 NZLR 324).

It is not therefore surprising that one of the arguments in *Henderson* against a duty of care being owed by the defendant managing agents to the indirect Names was that the contractual structure chosen by the parties militated against any such duty. The managing agents only assumed responsibility to the member's agents under their contracts. This was rejected by Lord Goff, who held that the assumption of responsibility to one party under a contract did not prevent a similar assumption to a non-party in respect of the services to be performed under that contract. However, his Lordship was quick to point out that such a case would be rare: 'in many cases in which a contractual chain comparable to that in the present case is constructed it may well prove to be inconsistent with an assumption of responsibility which has the effect of, so to speak, short circuiting the contractual structure so put in place by the parties'. As an example of a contractual structure which would prevent a duty of care from being owed, Lord Goff used the following example:

> Let me take the analogy of the common case of an ordinary building contract, under which main contractors contract with the building owner for the construction of the relevant building, and the main contractor sub-contracts with sub-contractors or suppliers (often nominated by the building owner) for the performance of work or the supply of materials in accordance with standards and subject to terms established in the sub-contract   if the sub-contracted work or materials do not in the result conform to the required standard, it will not ordinarily be open to the building owner to sue the sub-contractor or supplier direct under the *Hedley Byrne* principle, claiming damages from him on the basis that he has been negligent in relation to the performance of his functions. For there is generally no assumption of responsibility by the sub-contractor or supplier direct to the building owner, the parties having so structured their relationship that it is inconsistent with any such assumption of responsibility.

The problem, as Hedley [1995] CLJ 27 points out, is 'how, precisely, do we tell when the parties' contracts are a definitive statement of all the rights their arrangements create?'. Sometimes the answer to this question may be obvious enough: in *Riyad Bank v Ahli United Bank plc* [2006] 2 Lloyd's Rep 292, for example, the contractual structure that was adopted reflected the desire of a Saudi Arabian bank not to be directly linked to a Kuwait investment fund for fear that that would deter Saudi investors, so that it said nothing as to the obligations the parties assumed to each other in tort. It is possible that one reason why Lord Goff used a building contract as an example of a situation where a tortious duty of care would not normally arise as between parties in a contractual network was that in most such contracts the parties are free (within commercial constraints) to negotiate their own contracts, whereas in *Henderson* for at least some of the indirect Names it may not have been possible for them to negotiate any kind of contractual structure other than the one that was offered to them when they signed up. But is this really a satisfactory ground on which to distinguish the two scenarios? *Stapleton*, pp. 54–5, is not convinced. Why, she asks, were the indirect Names (whom she describes as 'high stakes investors') not 'left to rely either on whatever contractual protection they had secured from the [managing agents] or their ability to walk away'?

IV. Economic Loss Recovery Beyond *Hedley Byrne*

As we have seen, recovery of pure economic loss in negligence was first countenanced in *Hedley Byrne v Heller*, and the analytical tool which was used for this purpose was the doctrine of assumption of responsibility. When later courts looked to expand liability for pure economic loss, some judges felt that this concept had its limitations and preferred to employ a more general test for the existence of a duty of care, such as the three-stage approach associated with the speech of Lord Bridge in *Caparo Industries plc v Dickman*, discussed in Chapter 3.II.3. However, at around the same time, other judges—most notably Lord Goff—sought to expand the scope of the doctrine of assumption of responsibility, with the result that the vast majority of cases in which a duty of care for pure economic loss had been imposed could be justified on this basis. This posed some challenges for the lower courts, who were left unclear as to whether and when liability for pure economic loss could arise in the absence of an assumption of responsibility by the defendant towards the claimant. The issue was considered by the House of Lords in the next extracted case.

Customs and Excise Commissioners v Barclays Bank plc [2007] 1 AC 181

Customs and Excise (the claimant) was in the process of recovering debts owed to it by two companies and it obtained 'freezing' injunctions over the assets of the companies, including bank accounts they held with the defendant bank. (A freezing injunction prevents the assets which are the subject of the injunction from being dealt with so as to avoid them being dissipated by their owners in anticipation of judgment being entered against the owners.) Barclays was notified of the injunction but in breach of it carelessly failed to prevent payments out of the two companies' accounts with the result that Customs and Excise was unable to recover all of the debts it was owed. Customs and Excise brought an action in negligence against the defendant but the House of Lords held that the defendant had not owed Customs and Excise a duty of care. In the course of reaching this decision their Lordships discussed the question of what approach should be taken when deciding whether to recognise a duty of care in respect of pure economic loss.

Lord Hoffmann

31. How does one determine whether a duty of care is owed? In cases of pure economic loss such as this, it is not sufficient that the bank ought reasonably to have foreseen that unless they had proper systems in place and their employees took reasonable care to give effect to any freezing orders which came along, the beneficiaries of those orders might suffer loss. In the case of personal or physical injury, reasonable foreseeability of harm is usually enough, in accordance with the principle in *Donoghue v Stevenson* [1932] AC 562, to generate a duty of care. In the case of economic loss, something more is needed.

32. The Court of Appeal applied what it called the 'threefold test' proposed by Lord Bridge of Harwich in *Caparo Industries plc v Dickman* [1990] 2 AC 605, 617–618 . . .

33. Longmore LJ held that this test was satisfied. Foreseeability was conceded; service of the order created proximity (even though the bank 'may not be particularly willing to have a relationship to the commissioners': see para 30) and it was 'eminently fair, reasonable and just' that a bank should take care not to allow a defendant to flout the order. The order placed a burden on the bank but provided for the bank to be paid its reasonable charges for compliance. Peter Gibson LJ agreed: 'practical justice requires the recognition of such a duty': para 63. So did Lindsay J.

34. Mr Brindle, who appeared for the bank, said that this was the wrong approach. One should ask whether the bank had assumed responsibility for monitoring the account. As authority for applying this test, he relied upon Lord Goff of Chieveley's analysis in *Henderson v Merrett Syndicates Ltd* [1995] 2 AC 145, 180–181. In this case, he said, the bank never assumed responsibility. If anything, it had responsibility thrust upon it.

35. There is a tendency, which has been remarked upon by many judges, for phrases like 'proximate', 'fair, just and reasonable' and 'assumption of responsibility' to be used as slogans rather than practical guides to whether a duty should exist or not. These phrases are often illuminating but discrimination is needed to identify the factual situations in which they provide useful guidance. For example, in a case in which A provides information to C which he knows will be relied upon by D, it is useful to ask whether A assumed responsibility to D: *Hedley Byrne & Co Ltd v Heller & Partners Ltd* [1964] AC 465: *Smith v Eric S Bush* [1990] 1 AC 831. Likewise, in a case in which A provides information on behalf of B to C for the purpose of being relied upon by C, it is useful to ask whether A assumed responsibility to C for the information or was only discharging his duty to B: *Williams v Natural Life Health Foods Ltd* [1998] 1 WLR 830. Or in a case in which A provided information to B for the purpose of enabling him to make one kind of decision, it may be useful to ask whether he assumed responsibility for its use for a different kind of decision: *Caparo Industries plc v Dickman* [1990] 2 AC 605. In these cases in which the loss has been caused by the claimant's reliance on information provided by the defendant, it is critical to decide whether the defendant (rather than someone else) assumed responsibility for the accuracy of the information to the claimant (rather than to someone else) or for its use by the claimant for one purpose (rather than another). The answer does not depend upon what the defendant intended but, as in the case of contractual liability, upon what would reasonably be inferred from his conduct against the background of all the circumstances of the case. The purpose of the inquiry is to establish whether there was, in relation to the loss in question, the necessary relationship (or 'proximity') between the parties . . .

36. It is equally true to say that a sufficient relationship will be held to exist when it is fair, just and reasonable to do so. Because the question of whether a defendant has assumed responsibility is a legal inference to be drawn from his conduct against the background of all the circumstances of the case, it is by no means a simple question of fact. Questions of fairness and policy will enter into the decision and it may be more useful to try to identify these questions than simply to bandy terms like 'assumption of responsibility' and 'fair, just and reasonable' . . .

Lord Rodger of Earlsferry

48. Mr Brindle . . . argued that no one owed a duty of care to avoid causing financial harm to another unless he had voluntarily undertaken responsibility towards that other person. Here Barclays had not undertaken any responsibility to the commissioners for the way in which they would freeze the companies' accounts. They had just been required to act due to the notification of the order. Mr Sales argued in reply that assumption of responsibility was not the only criterion for holding that someone owed a duty of care. It was just one factor to be taken into account. The correct approach was to adopt the so-called 'threefold test' and to ask whether the loss was reasonably foreseeable, whether the parties were in a relationship of proximity and whether it would be fair, just and reasonable that the defendant should owe a duty of care to the claimant. It is common ground that in this case the loss was reasonably foreseeable.

49. There is no doubt that some passages in speeches in your Lordships' House provide support for the view that voluntary assumption of responsibility is the touchstone of liability for pure economic loss.

[His Lordship considered a number of cases discussing voluntary assumption of responsibility and continued:]

51. Part of the function of appeal courts is to try to assist judges and practitioners by boiling down a mass of case law and distilling some shorter statement of the applicable law. The temptation to try to identify some compact underlying rule which can then be applied to solve all future cases is obvious. Mr Brindle submitted that in this area the House had identified such a rule in the need to find that the defendant had voluntarily assumed responsibility. But the unhappy experience with the rule so elegantly formulated by Lord Wilberforce in *Anns v Merton London Borough Council* [1978] AC 728, 751–2, suggests that appellate judges should follow the philosopher's advice to 'Seek simplicity, and distrust it'.

52. Therefore it is not surprising that there are cases in the books—notably *Ministry of Housing and Local Government v Sharp* [1970] 2 QB 223, approved by Lord Slynn of Hadley in *Spring v Guardian Assurance plc* [1995] 2 AC 296, 332f–g—which do not readily yield to analysis in terms of a voluntary assumption of responsibility, but where liability has none the less been held to exist. I see no reason to treat these cases as exceptions to some over-arching rule that there must be a voluntary assumption of responsibility before the law recognises a duty of care. Such a rule would inevitably lead to the concept of voluntary assumption of responsibility being stretched beyond its natural limits—which would in the long run undermine the very real value of the concept as a criterion of liability in the many cases where it is an appropriate guide. In any event, as the words which I have quoted from his speech in *Merrett Syndicates* make clear, Lord Goff himself recognised that, although it may be decisive in many situations, the presence or absence of a voluntary assumption of responsibility does not necessarily provide the answer in all cases . . .

53. In the absence of any single touchstone, the House finds itself in the familiar position, envisaged by Lord Bridge of Harwich in *Caparo Industries plc v Dickman* [1990] 2 AC 605, 618, where a court faced with a novel situation must apply the threefold test . . .

COMMENTARY

In *Customs and Excise*, the House of Lords denied that assumption of responsibility was the sole determinant of recovery for pure economic loss in negligence. Whilst it was accepted that answering the duty of care question by reference to this test might be suitable in some, perhaps even most, cases, it could not be regarded as *the* test for a duty of care in cases of pure economic loss. According to Lord Mance, for example (at [87]), 'it has been said on a number of occasions that it is artificial or unhelpful to insist on fitting all claims for breach of a duty of care to avoid economic loss within the conception of assumption of responsibility'. Their Lordships' analysis is supported by a number of decisions—of which *Ministry of Housing and Local Government v Sharp* [1970] 2 QB 223 and the similar case of *Sebry v Companies House* [2016] 1 WLR 2499 perhaps provide the best examples—where a duty of care was recognised in respect of pure economic loss even though it could not plausibly be argued that the defendant had assumed any responsibility to the claimant. In addition, there are some post-*Customs and Excise* cases where the courts have taken it as read that a duty of care in respect of economic loss can be derived from the application of a general duty test, and need not be based on an assumption of responsibility (see, e.g., *Rowley v Secretary of State for Work and Pensions* [2007] 1 WLR 2861; *Smeaton v Equifax plc* [2013] 2 All ER 959; *Sebry v Companies House*; *CGL Group Ltd v Royal Bank of Scotland plc* [2018] 1 WLR 2137).

Having said all that, recent developments may have reduced the influence of *Customs and Excise* as an authority in the economic loss context. In particular, the principal alternative to assumption of responsibility that their Lordships countenanced in such cases, the *Caparo* three-stage test, has lost much (if not all) of its significance following *Robinson v Chief Constable of West Yorkshire Police* [2018] AC 736 (extracted in Ch.3.II.4), while the emphasis in that decision on the importance of precedent and principle in duty of care analysis suggests that assumption of responsibility is likely to play a central role in future economic loss cases. Furthermore, in recent Supreme Court economic loss decisions that doctrine has been treated as determinative of the duty issue (see *NRAM Ltd v Steel* [2018] 1 WLR 1190; *Banca Nazionale del Lavoro SPA v Playboy Club London Ltd* [2018] 1 WLR 4041) and described as 'the foundation of this area of law' (*Banca Nazionale* at [7]), though admittedly these were both cases involving negligent misstatements, where *Hedley Byrne* has always been regarded as foundational (even in other jurisdictions: see, e.g., *Deloitte & Touche v Livent Inc* [2017] 2 SCR 855). Finally, it must be borne in mind when evaluating the importance of the *Customs and Excise* decision that their Lordships fell somewhat short when it came to providing the lower courts with clear guidance as to the resolution of economic loss cases. All in all, it is therefore somewhat uncertain whether those courts will in the future feel obliged to limit recovery for economic loss to situations which fit the assumption of responsibility paradigm, or whether they will continue to follow the lead given in *Customs and Excise* and adopt a more flexible approach. It may of course be asked whether it really matters what approach is employed to determine whether a duty of care is owed in such cases, especially when one bears in mind how flexible the assumption of responsibility concept has proven to be. Indeed, Lord Bingham expressed the view in *Customs and Excise* that it was very unlikely that earlier pure economic loss cases would have been decided differently if different tests had been applied. Do you agree? And more generally, do you think that it matters what concepts the courts use to determine whether or not there is a duty of care in respect of pure economic loss?

Arguably the most important instance of negligence liability for pure economic loss which cannot be explained on an assumption of responsibility basis is the liability of a solicitor who is instructed to draw up or modify a will, and whose negligent performance of the task deprives a beneficiary of the legacy that the testator intended them to have. This scenario was the subject of the next extracted case.

White v Jones [1995] 2 AC 207

A solicitor was instructed to draw up a new will for a testator. Unlike the old will, the new will contained legacies of £9,000 for the testator's two daughters. Due to the solicitor's negligence the new will had not been drafted by the time the testator died, with the result that the daughters did not receive the intended legacies. The daughters brought a claim against the solicitor in negligence. The trial judge held that the solicitor owed no duty of care to the beneficiaries, distinguishing the earlier decision in *Ross v Caunters* [1980] Ch 297 on the ground that in that case there had been a defect in the form of execution of the will, rather than a failure to draw it up. The Court of Appeal allowed an appeal, and awarded the plaintiffs the value of their lost legacies. The defendant appealed to the House of Lords.

Lord Goff

The Conceptual Difficulties

. . . It is right however that I should immediately summarise [the conceptual difficulties arising from the claim]. They are as follows.

(1) First, the general rule is well established that a solicitor acting on behalf of a client owes a duty of care only to his client . . .

(2) A further reason is given which is said to reinforce the conclusion that no duty of care is owed by the solicitor to the beneficiary in tort. Here, it is suggested, is one of those situations in which a plaintiff is entitled to damages if, and only if, he can establish a breach of contract by the defendant. First, the plaintiff's claim is one for purely financial loss; and as a general rule, apart from cases of assumption of responsibility arising under the principle in *Hedley Byrne & Co Ltd v Heller & Partners Ltd* [1964] AC 465, no action will lie in respect of such loss in the tort of negligence. Furthermore, in particular, no claim will lie in tort for damages in respect of a mere loss of an expectation, as opposed to damages in respect of damage to an existing right or interest of the plaintiff. Such a claim falls within the exclusive zone of contractual liability; and it is contrary to principle that the law of tort should be allowed to invade that zone . . . The present case, it is suggested, falls within that exclusive zone. Here, it is impossible to frame the suggested duty except by reference to the contract between the solicitor and the testator—a contract to which the disappointed beneficiary is not a party, and from which, therefore, he can derive no rights. Second, the loss suffered by the disappointed beneficiary is not in reality a loss at all; it is, more accurately, a failure to obtain a benefit. All that has happened is that what is sometimes called a *spes succesionis* has failed to come to fruition. As a result, he has not become better off; but he is not made worse off. A claim in respect of such a loss of expectation falls, it is said, clearly within the exclusive zone of contractual liability.

(3) A third, and distinct, objection is that, if liability in tort was recognised in cases [of this kind] it would be impossible to place any sensible bounds to cases in which such recovery was allowed. In particular, the same liability should logically be imposed in cases where an *inter vivos* transaction was ineffective, and the defect was not discovered until the donor was no longer able to repair it . . .

[His Lordship noted a number of other conceptual problems, and continued:]

The Impulse to do Practical Justice

Before addressing the legal questions which lie at the heart of the present case, it is, I consider, desirable to identify the reasons of justice which prompt judges and academic writers to conclude, like Megarry V-C in *Ross v Caunters*, that a duty should be owed by the testator's solicitor to a disappointed beneficiary. The principal reasons are, I believe, as follows.

(1) In the forefront stands the extraordinary fact that, if such a duty is not recognised, the only persons who might have a valid claim (i.e. the testator and his estate) have suffered no loss, and the only person who has suffered a loss (i.e. the disappointed beneficiary) has no claim: see *Ross v Caunters* [1980] Ch 297 at 303 per Megarry V-C. It can therefore be said that, if the solicitor owes no duty to the intended beneficiaries, there is a lacuna in the law which needs to be filled. This I regard as being a point of cardinal importance in the present case.

(2) The injustice of denying such a remedy is reinforced if one considers the importance of legacies in a society which recognises (subject only to the incidence of inheritance tax, and statutory requirements for provision for near relatives) the right of citizens to leave their assets to whom they please, and in which, as a result, legacies can be of great importance to individual citizens, providing very often the only opportunity for a citizen to acquire a significant capital sum; or to inherit a house, so providing a secure roof over the heads of himself and his family; or to make special provision for his or her old age. In the course of the hearing before the Appellate Committee Mr Matheson (who was instructed by the Law Society to represent the appellant solicitors) placed before the Committee a schedule of claims of the character of that in the present case notified to the Solicitors' Indemnity Fund following the judgment of the Court of Appeal below. It is striking that, where the amount of the claim was known, it was, by today's standards, of a comparatively modest size. This perhaps indicates that it is where a testator instructs a small firm of solicitors that mistakes of this kind are most likely to occur, with the result that it tends to be people of modest means, who need the money so badly, who suffer.

(3) There is a sense in which the solicitors' profession cannot complain if such a liability may be imposed upon their members. If one of them has been negligent in such a way as to defeat his client's testamentary intentions, he must regard himself as very lucky indeed if the effect of the law is that he is not liable to pay damages in the ordinary way. It can involve no injustice to render him subject to such a liability, even if the damages are payable not to his client's estate for distribution to the disappointed beneficiary (which might have been the preferred solution) but direct to the disappointed beneficiary.

(4) That such a conclusion is required as a matter of justice is reinforced by consideration of the role played by solicitors in society. The point was well made by Cooke J in *Gartside v Sheffield Young & Ellis* [1983] NZLR 37 at 43, when he observed:

> To deny an effective remedy in a plain case would seem to imply a refusal to acknowledge the solicitor's professional role in the community. In practice the public relies on solicitors (or statutory officers with similar functions) to prepare effective wills.

The question therefore arises whether it is possible to give effect in law to the strong impulse for practical justice which is the fruit of the foregoing considerations. For this to be achieved, I respectfully agree with Nicholls V-C [in the Court of Appeal in *White*] when he said that the court will have to fashion 'an effective remedy for the solicitor's breach of his professional duty to his client' in such a way as to repair the injustice to the disappointed beneficiary (see [1993] 3 WLR 730 at 739).

The Tortious Solution

I therefore return to the law of tort for a solution to the problem. For the reasons I have already given, an ordinary action in tortious negligence on the lines proposed by Megarry V-C in *Ross v Caunters* must, with the greatest respect, be regarded as inappropriate, because it does not meet any of the conceptual problems which have been raised. Furthermore, for the reasons I have previously given, the *Hedley Byrne* principle cannot, in the absence of special circumstances, give rise on ordinary principles to an assumption of responsibility by the testator's solicitor towards an intended beneficiary. Even so, it seems to me that it is open to your Lordships' House, as in *Linden Gardens Trust Ltd v Lenesta Sludge Disposals Ltd* [1994] 1 AC 85, to fashion a remedy to fill a lacuna in the law and so prevent the injustice which would otherwise occur on the facts of cases such as the present. In the *Lenesta Sludge* case, as I have said, the House made available a remedy as a matter of law to solve the problem of transferred loss in the case before them. The present case is, if anything, *a fortiori*, since the nature of the transaction was such that, if the solicitors were negligent and their negligence did not come to light until after the death of the testator, there would be no remedy for the ensuing loss unless the intended beneficiary could claim. In my opinion, therefore, your Lordships' House should in cases such as these extend to the intended beneficiary a remedy under the *Hedley Byrne* principle by holding that the assumption of responsibility by the solicitor towards his client should be held in law to extend to the intended beneficiary who (as the solicitor can reasonably foresee) may, as a result of the solicitor's negligence, be deprived of his intended legacy in circumstances in which neither the testator nor his estate will have a remedy against the solicitor. Such liability will not of course arise in cases in which the defect in the will comes to light before the death of the testator, and the testator either leaves the will as it is or otherwise continues to exclude the previously intended beneficiary from the relevant benefit . . . That is therefore the solution which I would recommend to your Lordships.

Lord Browne-Wilkinson

My Lords, I have read the speech of my noble and learned friend, Lord Goff of Chieveley, and agree with him that this appeal should be dismissed. In particular, I agree that your Lordships should hold that the defendant solicitors were under a duty of care to the plaintiffs arising from an extension of the principle of assumption of responsibility explored in *Hedley Byrne & Co Ltd v Heller & Partners Ltd* [1964] AC 465. In my view, although the present case is not directly covered by the decided cases, it is legitimate to extend the law to the limited extent proposed using the incremental approach by way of analogy advocated in *Caparo Industries plc v Dickman* [1990] 2 AC 605 . . .

The law of England does not impose any general duty of care to avoid negligent misstatements or to avoid causing pure economic loss even if economic damage to the plaintiff was foreseeable. However, such a duty of care will arise if there is a special relationship between the parties. Although the categories of cases in which such a special relationship can be held to exist are not closed, as yet only two categories have been identified, *viz.* (1) where there is a fiduciary relationship and (2) where the defendant has voluntarily answered a question or tenders skilled advice or services in circumstances where he knows or ought to know that an identified plaintiff will rely on his answers or advice. In both these categories the special relationship is created by the defendant voluntarily assuming to act in the matter by involving himself in the plaintiff's affairs or by choosing to speak. If he does so assume to act or speak he is said to have assumed responsibility for carrying through the matter he has entered upon. In the words of Lord Reid in *Hedley Byrne v Heller* [1964] AC 465 at 486, he has 'accepted a relationship . . . which requires him to exercise such care as the circumstances require', i.e. although the extent of the duty will vary from category to category, some duty of care arises from the special relationship. Such relationship can arise even though the defendant has acted in the plaintiff's affairs pursuant to a contract with a third party.

I turn then to apply those considerations to the case of a solicitor retained by a testator to draw a will in favour of an intended beneficiary. As a matter of contract, a solicitor owes a duty to the testator to use proper skill in the preparation and execution of the will and to act with due speed. But as the speech of Lord Goff demonstrates, that contractual obligation is of little utility. Breach by the solicitor of such contractual duty gives rise to no damage suffered by the testator or his estate; under our existing law of contract, the intended beneficiary, who has suffered the damage, has no cause of action on the contract.

Has the intended beneficiary a cause of action based on breach of a duty of care owed by the solicitor to the beneficiary? The answer to that question is dependent upon whether there is a special relationship between the solicitor and the intended beneficiary to which the law attaches a duty of care. In my judgment the case does not fall within either of the two categories of special relationships so far recognised. There is no fiduciary duty owed by the solicitor to the intended beneficiary. Although the solicitor has assumed to act in a matter closely touching the economic well-being of the intended beneficiary, the intended beneficiary will often be ignorant of that fact and cannot therefore have relied upon the solicitor.

However, it is clear that the law in this area has not ossified. Both Viscount Haldane LC [in *Nocton v Lord Ashburton* [1914] AC 932] and Lord Devlin [in *Hedley Byrne v Heller* [1964] AC 465] envisage that there might be other sets of circumstances in which it would be appropriate to find a special relationship giving rise to a duty of care. In *Caparo Industries plc v Dickman* [1990] 2 AC 605 at 618 Lord Bridge . . . recognised that the law will develop novel categories of negligence 'incrementally and by analogy with established categories'. In my judgment, this is a case where such development should take place since there is a close analogy with existing categories of special relationship giving rise to a duty of care to prevent economic loss.

The solicitor who accepts instructions to draw a will knows that the future economic welfare of the intended beneficiary is dependent upon his careful execution of the task. It is true that the intended beneficiary (being ignorant of the instructions) may not rely on the particular solicitor's actions. But . . . in the case of a duty of care flowing from a fiduciary relationship liability is not dependent upon actual reliance by the plaintiff on the defendant's actions but on the fact that, as the fiduciary is well aware, the plaintiff's economic well-being is dependent upon the proper discharge by the fiduciary of his duty. Second, the solicitor by accepting the instructions has entered upon, and therefore assumed responsibility for, the task of procuring the execution of a skilfully drawn will knowing that the beneficiary is wholly dependent upon his carefully carrying out his function. That assumption of responsibility for the task is a feature of both the two categories of special relationship so far identified in the authorities. It is not to the point that the solicitor only entered on the task pursuant to a contract with the third party (i.e. the testator). There are therefore present many of the features which in the other categories of special relationship have been treated as sufficient to create a special relationship to which the law attaches a duty of care. In my judgment the analogy is close.

Moreover, there are more general factors which indicate that it is fair, just and reasonable to impose liability on the solicitor. Save in the case of those rash testators who make their own wills, the proper transmission of property from one generation to the next is dependent upon the due discharge by solicitors of their duties. Although in any particular case it may not be possible to demonstrate that the intended beneficiary relied upon the solicitor, society as a whole does rely on solicitors to carry out their will-making functions carefully. To my mind it would be unacceptable if, because of some technical rules of law, the wishes and expectations of testators and beneficiaries generally could be defeated by the negligent actions of solicitors without there being any redress. It is only just that the intended beneficiary should be able to recover the benefits which he would otherwise have received.

Further, negligence in the preparation and execution of a will has certain unique features. First, there can be no conflict of interest between the solicitor and client (the testator) and the intended beneficiary. There is therefore no objection to imposing on a solicitor a duty towards a third party there being no possible conflict of interest. Second, in transactions *inter vivos* the transaction takes immediate effect and the consequences of solicitors' negligence are immediately apparent. When discovered, they can either be rectified (by the parties) or damages recovered by the client. But in the case of a negligently drawn will, the will has no effect at all until the death. It will have been put away in the deed box not to surface again until the testator either wishes to vary it or dies. In the majority of cases the negligence will lie hidden until it takes effect on the death of the testator, i.e. at the very point in time when normally the error will become incapable of remedy.

In all these circumstances, I would hold that by accepting instructions to draw a will, a solicitor does come into a special relationship with those intended to benefit under it in consequence of which the law imposes a duty to the intended beneficiary to act with due expedition and care in relation to the task on which he has entered . . .

Lord Nolan delivered a separate speech in favour of dismissing the appeal. **Lord Mustill** and **Lord Keith** delivered dissenting speeches.

Appeal dismissed.

COMMENTARY

Lord Mustill's dissenting speech is worthy of serious attention (although space could not be found to accommodate it here). The speech begins by questioning the assumptions which, he argues, underlie the plaintiffs' claims. One assumption was that there must be something wrong with the law if the plaintiffs did not succeed, which, in the circumstances, would require that the plaintiffs' disappointment should be relieved by an award of money and that the money should, if the law permits, come from the solicitor. Another assumption was that some form of action should be granted simply because the solicitor had been negligent. His Lordship (at 278) found little to commend this view:

The purpose of the courts when recognising tortious acts and their consequences is to compensate those plaintiffs who suffer actionable breaches of duty, not to act as second-line disciplinary tribunals imposing punishment in the shape of damages.

Accordingly, the question of law was this: if A promises B to perform a service for B which B intends, and A knows, will confer a benefit on C if it is performed, does A owe C a duty in tort to perform that service carefully? After considering the authorities (including *Hedley Byrne* and *Henderson*), his Lordship held that an essential element of the special relationship necessary for a *Hedley Byrne* duty to arise was 'mutuality'. This term seems to mean some kind of reciprocal dealings between the parties—satisfied, in *Hedley Byrne*, by the request of the credit reference by Hedley Byrne's bankers and the response by Heller & Partners. But on the facts of *White* there were no such dealings. Indeed, there was no relationship at all, in any ordinary sense, between parties who were linked only by the fact that if the solicitor did their job (and if the testator executed the will and did not revoke it) the intended beneficiary might be better off. Nor could the problem be solved by trying to find an assumption of responsibility by the solicitor to the beneficiary (at 289): 'The solicitor does of course undertake the task of preparing the will, in the sense of agreeing to take it on. But this is between himself and his client.' The solicitor undertook the task of drawing up a will which would in fact benefit the beneficiaries but he prepared it *for* the testator, not for the beneficiaries, and the 'cardinal feature' of the *Hedley Byrne* case was that 'the defendants undertook the job for the plaintiffs' (at 290).

Equally important is Lord Mustill's unwillingness to acquiesce in the creation of a special pocket of tort liability for the particular situation in *White*. His Lordship (at 291) accepted that a 'broad new type of claim may properly be met by a broad new type of rationalisation' but 'rationalisation there must be, and it does not conduce to the orderly development of the law, or to the certainty which practical convenience demands, if duties are simply conjured up as a matter of positive law, to answer the apparent justice of an individual case'. In his Lordship's view, there was nothing to distinguish a solicitor from a much wider category of persons, so that the reasoning which allowed the beneficiary to recover must also apply 'where A promises B for reward to perform a service for B, in circumstances where it is foreseeable that performance of the service with care will cause C to receive a benefit, and that failure to perform it may cause C not to receive that benefit'. This would involve a very considerable expansion of the tort of negligence beyond its existing boundaries, and Lord Mustill could not discern reasons of principle which would justify recognition of such an extensive new area of potential liability.

The Different Approaches of Lord Goff and Lord Browne-Wilkinson

For Lord Goff, *White v Jones* could not be decided in favour of the plaintiff by applying *Hedley Byrne*, for the work had not been carried out for the beneficiary and in most such cases (although perhaps not on the facts of *White*) there was no reliance by the beneficiary. To establish liability through a deemed assumption of responsibility is simply to impose liability 'according to the justice of the case', a course of action Lord Mustill found unacceptable. Not everyone agrees with Lord Goff's view that the adoption of this approach causes the conceptual difficulties 'to fade innocuously away' (Haydon [1995] CLJ 238, 240). Nonetheless, Lord Goff and Lord Mustill would appear to have been in broad agreement over the core requirements of *Hedley Byrne*.

Lord Browne-Wilkinson's approach is more complicated. For his Lordship, the case could be decided by the assumption of responsibility principle discussed in *Hedley Byrne*. But *Hedley Byrne* was not the seminal case; rather, as the speeches in *Hedley Byrne* indicated, it was *Nocton v Lord Ashburton* [1914] AC 932—the case where Viscount Haldane had found a solicitor liable to his client on the basis of the 'special relationship' between them (in that case a fiduciary relationship). Given that a fiduciary relationship could be a 'special relationship' for the purpose of imposing a duty of care in respect of pure economic loss, this meant that neither mutuality nor reliance were required, for a negligent trustee was liable for economic loss even if the beneficiary had never dealt with the trustee or relied on them in any way.

Conversely, we have seen that neither Lord Goff nor Lord Mustill envisaged the *Hedley Byrne* special relationship arising in the absence of some form of reciprocal dealings. And the difficulty with dispensing with this requirement is that it becomes difficult to limit those to whom one assumes responsibility (the hallmark of the special relationship). Lord Browne-Wilkinson held that it is the assumption of responsibility for the task that creates the special relationship, but as Lord Mustill emphasised, in *White* the task was taken on for the testator, and not for the beneficiaries (see also Nolan, 'Assumption of Responsibility: Four Questions' (2019) 72 CLP 123 at 130–1). The problem with Lord Browne-Wilkinson's approach to assumption of responsibility is that it robs the concept of any real utility, since voluntary action by the defendant is a prerequisite of liability in negligence in any case (see further Barker, 'Unreliable Assumptions in the Law of Negligence' (1993) 109 LQR 461 at 474). It is therefore unsurprising that Lord Browne-Wilkinson's approach did not find favour with Gummow J in the High Court of Australia in *Hill v Van Erp* (1997) 188 CLR 159 (a case which also concerned the liability of a solicitor to a disappointed beneficiary) and unfortunate that it was endorsed and employed in *Sebry v Companies House* [2016] 1 WLR 2499, where Edis J held that, when the Registrar of Companies undertook to record a winding-up order against a company on the companies register, he assumed a responsibility to the company to take reasonable care to ensure that the order was registered against the right company.

Apart from 'assumption of responsibility for the task', on what other grounds did Lord Browne-Wilkinson find a special relationship in *White*? His Lordship held that, as in the case of a fiduciary, the solicitor is aware that the plaintiff's economic wellbeing is dependent upon the proper discharge of his duty. But this means no more than that it was foreseeable that the beneficiary would suffer loss if the solicitor was negligent (see also *Sebry v Companies House* at [111]: 'the special relationship between the Registrar and the company arises because it is foreseeable that if a company is wrongly said . . . to be in liquidation it will suffer serious harm'), and it has never been the case that a duty of care arises in respect of pure economic loss just because such loss was foreseeable. Besides, the analogy with fiduciaries in this context is unhelpful because, although a fiduciary may be liable for negligently caused foreseeable pure economic loss, the reason for this is not merely that the loss was foreseeable, but that there was a fiduciary relationship between the parties. Apart from the foresight of loss, Lord Browne-Wilkinson's other reasons for imposing a duty of care were policy considerations, the most significant being the importance of wills to the passing of property from one generation to the next. As Blake (1995–6) 6 KCLJ 101 at 104 points out, it follows that his Lordship's approach amounted to a test of foreseeability of harm coupled with a policy analysis, and was therefore reminiscent of the long abandoned 'two-stage' test for the existence of a duty of care put forward by Lord Wilberforce in *Anns v Merton London Borough Council* [1978] AC 728.

The Limits of *White v Jones*

In a series of cases in the 1990s, claimants probed the limits of the decision in *White*, but attempts to expand the scope of the liability that was recognised in that case met with a cautious response. Lord Goff said in *White* that if an *inter vivos* gift did not take effect because of negligence of the defendant, and the mistake came to light while the donor was still alive, but the donor chose not to rectify situation, then the intended donee would not have a remedy against the defendant. This was confirmed in *Hemmens v Wilson Browne* [1995] Ch 223, where A instructed B to draft a document giving C an enforceable right to call on A to pay C £110,000. The document that B drafted did not in fact confer enforceable rights on C, and when A refused to pay the money to C, C's tort claim against B was dismissed because A was able to rectify the situation. However, Judge Moseley QC accepted that the position might have been different if that had not been the case, because for example A had died or lost mental capacity before the mistake came to light.

Lord Goff also limited the ratio of *White* to cases where 'neither the testator nor his estate will have a remedy against the solicitor', which seemed to suggest that if the estate *did* have a remedy, then the beneficiary would not. The point arose in *Carr-Glynn v Frearsons (a firm)* [1999] Ch 326, where A had left C her half-share in a property called 'Homelands', the will having been drawn up by B. B had warned A that it was unclear whether she held her share in 'Homelands' as a joint tenant or a tenant in common, and that if it was the former, then she would have to sever the joint tenancy for the gift to C to take effect. A said that she would obtain the title deeds to clarify the position, but she did not do so, and when she died four years later, it transpired that the property *was* held on a joint tenancy, with the result that her share passed to the surviving joint tenant rather than to C. C sued B for the value of the lost share, arguing that B should have made sure that the position was clarified, and the joint tenancy severed, before A's death. At first instance ([1997] 2 All ER 614), Lloyd J held that B was not liable, on the ground that, since B's alleged negligence had resulted in a loss to A's estate (which had not been enhanced by the half share of 'Homelands'), the case did not fall within the ratio of *White v Jones*, which was limited to 'the straightforward case of the distribution in one way rather than another of the same gross estate' (at 628). However, the Court of Appeal disagreed. Chadwick LJ felt strongly that C should have a claim regardless, since the recovery of damages by the estate of A would not benefit C, as they would form part of the residue, and the plaintiff was not the residuary beneficiary under the will. While agreeing with Lloyd J that the facts did not come within the ratio of *White*, his Lordship nevertheless considered that it was consistent with the reasoning of the majority in that case to extend the principle laid down there to 'cases in which the estate does have a remedy but where the estate's remedy will be of no advantage to the disappointed beneficiary' ([1999] Ch 326 at 333). Do you agree?

Perhaps the most ambitious invocation of *White* was in *Goodwill v British Pregnancy Advisory Service* [1996] 1 WLR 1397, where it was argued that it applied when C became pregnant in the course of a sexual relationship with A, three years after B carried out a vasectomy on A. C's argument that B had been employed by A to confer a benefit on A's future sexual partners was rejected as unrealistic by Peter Gibson LJ, who emphasised that the decision in *White* had been in response to a very particular situation of perceived injustice and should not readily be extended beyond that. *Goodwill* reflects the fact that *White* has rarely been relied upon successfully outside the wills context, but an exception is *Gorham v British Telecommunications plc* [2000] 1 WLR 2129, where the Court of Appeal held that, if an insurance company advises A on insurance provision for pension and life cover, it owes A's dependants a duty not to give A negligent advice which will adversely affect the interests of the dependants as A had intended them to be. The court reasoned that, as in *White*, practical justice required that the dependants have a remedy against the insurance company, since by the time its negligence came to light, it was too late for the position to be rectified in any other way.

Concluding Reflections

Tony Weir's typically acerbic response to *White* was the comment that 'while Lord Goff opted for a pocket of liability, regardless of principle, Lord Browne-Wilkinson produced a principle out of his pocket and Lord Mustill found the pocket irreconcilable with any principle' (*Weir*, p. 71). In any case, whatever one makes of the details of their reasoning, it is clear that the majority were determined to fashion a remedy in order to avoid an outcome which they considered would be unjust. As Lord Steyn commented in a later case, '[c]oherence must sometimes yield to practical justice' (*Williams v Natural Life Health Foods Ltd* [1998] 1 WLR 830 at 837). Courts elsewhere have also struggled to find any kind of principled reasoning in the case of the disappointed beneficiary. In *Hill v Van Erp* (1997) 188 CLR 159, the High Court of Australia held by a 4:1 majority that a solicitor owed a duty of care to an intended beneficiary of a will. None of the majority considered that this outcome could be based on *Hedley Byrne*, and instead the result was justified by reference to policy arguments similar to those relied upon by the majority in *White*, as well as the fact that recognising a duty of care in these circumstances presents no problems of indeterminate liability. McHugh J dissented, agreeing with Lord Mustill that positive duties could not be conjured up to meet the justice of a case. Further, his Honour argued (at 213):

If the rule of law is to have any meaning, if judicial decisions are to be based on more than a judge's sense of justice, like cases must be decided alike and in accordance with a principle that transcends the immediate facts of the case.

There is clearly much force in this observation, and in Lord Mustill's comment in *White* (at 291) that the approach adopted by the majority in that case 'does not conduce to the orderly development of the law, or to the certainty which practical convenience demands'. It might be thought that the solution to this conundrum is to fashion a remedy for the beneficiary in contract, by creating an exception to the privity doctrine (see Lorenz and Markesinis (1993) 56 MLR 558). However, when Parliament reformed that doctrine a few years after *White*, by passing the Contracts (Rights of Third Parties) Act 1999, the new exceptions it thereby created to the 'third party rule' (i.e. the rule that a person cannot sue on a contract to which they are not a party) did not encompass the *White* scenario. In particular, s. 1(1)(b) of the Act, which laid down that (if certain conditions were satisfied) a third party could enforce a term of a contract where the term 'purported to confer a benefit' on them, would not avail a disappointed beneficiary. For while the due performance of the contract between the testator and the solicitor should (if the will remains in force) *result in* the beneficiary receiving a legacy, it is the will itself that *purports to confer* the benefit on the beneficiary, and not the contract to draw it up (see Barker, 'Are We Up to Expectations? Solicitors, Beneficiaries and the Contract/Tort Divide' (1994) 14 OJLS 137; Law Commission, *Privity of Contract: Contracts for the Benefit of Third Parties* (Law Com. No. 242, 1996), paras 7.19–7.27). Another possible answer to the disappointed beneficiary problem, suggested by Weir (1995) 111 LQR 357, might be to reform the law of testamentary dispositions, so that the legacy intended for the beneficiary in fact reaches them, but the formalities surrounding wills are there for good reason, and watering them down is likely to give rise to other problems (see Cretney's response to Weir at (1996) 112 LQR 54).

When one bears in mind the complications attendant upon other solutions to the problem of the disappointed beneficiary, and the strength on the facts of *White* of what Lord Goff called 'the impulse to do practical justice', it must be said that it is hard to criticise the majority for reaching the conclusion that they did, even if their reasoning was not always consistent or persuasive. Nor, it must be said, has the decision given rise to many difficulties in the nearly three decades since it was handed down.

v. The Duty of Care and Pure Economic Loss—Evaluation

As has already been demonstrated, the current approach to the recovery of pure economic loss in negligence has its difficulties. Can the balance struck by the courts between pro-and anti-liability cases be justified? In this final section, we first consider an economic analysis of the liability rules in this area which provides some support for the current approach, before introducing the debate between rights-based and policy-based analyses of the current law.

1. Economic Analysis and Negligent Misrepresentation

W. Bishop, 'Negligent Misrepresentation through Economists' Eyes' (1980) 96 LQR 360

One peculiarity of information, considered as an economic good, is that the person who produces it may not, and usually will not, be able to appropriate all the social benefit that flows from its production. The meaning and significance of this are best considered by means of an example. Suppose someone discovers air currents in the upper atmosphere which can be predicted easily. This information will be valuable to anyone flying an aircraft, as this knowledge will enable him to chart his flight path so as to minimise fuel costs. It is unlikely that the discoverer will be able to become rich through his discovery even though the discovery saves many millions of dollars in resources that would otherwise be wasted. First, he may not be able to convince the purchaser of its value without giving him the very information he is trying to sell. Second, even if he sells the information to one airline, then that airline can easily pass the information onto others, perhaps at some financial gain to itself. If it seeks to guard the information it will have to control closely its employees, see that they never change jobs, and so on. In general, information, once produced, can be reproduced to others at small cost. Even though the social benefit of the information is large the private benefit to the producer is small . . .

The typical market in economic theory is the market for goods. The producer of a good sells it to the user, appropriating to himself all, or substantially all, of the benefit of the good that his efforts brought into existence. Or as is said in economics, private benefit equals social benefit. If the producer must pay all of the social cost of producing the good, then he will produce it only so long as the (marginal) social cost of doing so equals the (marginal) social benefit.

Much of tort law is concerned with ensuring that the producer is faced with the full social costs of production. When these diverge from private cost they are called external costs of production, or externalities. Nuisance and negligence law is typically concerned to internalise to the producer these external costs. When this is done production will be optimal in quantity and price, in the sense that all those goods, and only those goods, will be produced whose marginal social benefit equals their marginal social costs of production.

The contrast with the information market is sharp. Here the market will fail to achieve the social optimum. This happens not because of an external cost but because of an external benefit; the market failure is not on the supply side but on the demand side. The information producer may be faced with the full social cost, but because he cannot cover those costs through the sale of the product to those who benefit he does not produce as much of the good as is socially optimal; indeed he may produce none at all.

The application of this analysis to liability for negligent misrepresentation is the following. Such a liability rule is an attempt to make the information provider confront the total social cost of his action. But if he cannot reap the total social benefit he will not produce enough, if any, information. If there were no liability rule and if the private costs of information production were small, the optimal amount might be produced—though the quality of the information would probably be lower than ideal. But if we augment the costs through liability we risk inducing producers to curtail production, leaving us worse off than before.

Economic analysis suggests the following approach to cases of negligent misrepresentation. Courts should in general apply ordinary rules of negligence. However, where the misrepresentation in question results from the production of valuable information there is prima facie case for more restricted liability. Liability should be restricted when (a) the information is of a type that is valuable to many potential users, (b) the producer of the information cannot capture in his prices the benefits flowing to all users of the information, and (c) the imposition of liability to all persons harmed would raise potential costs significantly enough to discourage information production altogether. When these three conditions are met the court should impose liability on the defendant in relation to a limited class only. This class should include all information users with whom the producer has a trading relationship, whether direct or indirect. The class can be extended beyond this, but such extension should be limited by the principle expressed in (c), that is it should not be extended so widely that potential defendants would be discouraged from engaging in the activity that generates the information.

COMMENTARY

Whether one is a disciple of the law and economics movement or not, this rationalisation for the present liability rules in relation to the recovery of pure economic loss goes some way towards explaining the results in the cases discussed earlier in the chapter. Bishop's analysis provides an account of why the floodgates concern—the fear of 'liability to an indeterminate class for an indeterminate time in an indeterminate amount' (*Ultramares Corporation v Touche* (1931) 174 NE 441 at 444, per Cardozo J)—is particularly weighty in this context. Lord Oliver, rejecting the existence of a duty of care in *Caparo*, argued:

> To apply as a test of liability only the foreseeability of possible damage without some further control would be to create a liability wholly indefinite in area, duration and amount and would open up a limitless vista of uninsurable risk for the professional man.

It appears that his fear was that, if this new kind of uninsurable risk was opened, professionals would simply cease to provide the information in question, to the detriment of society as a whole.

In cases where liability has been found, economic analysis suggests that such concerns should not be present. Do the cases reflect this? Bishop argues that in *Hedley Byrne*, although the information provided by Heller & Partners may have been of interest to others, it was primarily given for a specific purpose in a non-public document; hence in reality it was not likely to be of benefit to a wide class. Conversely, Heller & Partners also received a benefit, but not in monetary terms. Rather, it retained the business of its customers who expected their bank to provide references as to their creditworthiness and who, if they valued this service sufficiently, would be prepared to have the cost of misinformation spread equally amongst them (through higher bank charges). The cost of a liability rule (the award of damages if the reference was negligent) could be offset against the benefit to the bank of retaining or gaining customers. Thus social cost would roughly equate with social benefit. What about *Smith v Bush* and *Caparo*? Although Bishop's article appeared before these cases were decided, his analysis also provides an explanation of their differing results. In *Smith*, the information (the survey) was effectively paid for by the plaintiff. It was of benefit to a very small class of persons—those interested in buying the house within a short period of the survey. Thus it was likely that the social benefit of the survey was recouped through the surveyor's fees (although there may have been a volume discount offered to the bank but in any event the possibility of regular work from the bank is itself of value to the surveyor). The situation was vastly different in *Caparo*. The information provided by the auditors was public and was of benefit to a wide variety of investors and shareholders. It was not possible for the total social benefit provided by the auditors to be recouped in fees; hence, according to Bishop's analysis, the House of Lords correctly limited the class to whom the auditors could be liable for financial loss (cf. *Esanda Finance Corporation Limited v Peat Marwick Hungerfords* (1997) 188 CLR 241, where McHugh J expressly considered the economic consequences of imposing a wide liability on auditors).

The same analysis may also be instructive when considering the disagreement between the majority and minority in *White v Jones*. The primary social benefit of making a will is to the beneficiaries and testator. For those who favoured allowing the beneficiaries' claim, the benefit provided to those parties could be adequately recouped by the solicitor's fees. For those against, there were two issues with that. First, the solicitor cannot be said to recoup the benefit through the fees charged because, at the date the will is made, it may not be known what benefit the beneficiary will be receiving. As McHugh J stated in *Hill v Van Erp* (1997) 188 CLR 159 at 216, 'It does not seem reasonable that the solicitor who has received a small fee from a testator should be liable years after the event for many hundreds of thousands of dollars because a person with whom the solicitor has had no dealings has failed to secure a benefit.' The second, related point is that because of this potential liability to the beneficiaries the solicitor will have to take out insurance (if possible), and as a result the cost of providing the service to testators will increase. Ultimately, therefore, it is those who make wills (and not those who benefit from them) who have to meet the cost, and this is likely to mean that the optimum level of service provision is not achieved.

Of course, not everyone buys into the law and economics argument; almost nobody agrees on what level and cost of services is economically desirable and, as P. Cane (*Tort Law and Economic Interests*, 2nd edn (Oxford: OUP, 1996), p. 178) points out: 'At the end of the day, courts have to choose to favour one party or the other: to be "pro-plaintiff" or "pro-defendant".' However, there is little doubt that, at least on a subconscious level, considerations of this kind have influenced the law's view as to recovery for pure economic loss, at least in some types of case. Depending on one's wider view as to the influence that economic considerations should have on the law, this will be seen as either enlightened or regressive.

2. Rights-Based and Policy-Based Analyses of the Current Law

A. Beever, *Rediscovering the Law of Negligence* (Oxford: Hart, 2007)

The Principled Approach

[I]n *Spartan Steel*, Edmund Davies LJ argued that the principled approach would allow for recovery of consequential loss and relational economic loss. In fact, however, that is not the case. The view involves a very fundamental error that arises because of what David Stevens and Jason Neyers regard as the greatest weakness of the common law: its remedial mentality ((1999) 37 Alberta Law Review 221, 227) . . . The focus of analysis is invariably on the question 'should the claimant recover?', with various policies being offered for different views. The prior question, 'does the claimant have a right that could ground recovery?', has gone largely unasked. The problem with economic loss will be solved if we balance the copious prudence (ie policy) that the topic of economic loss has engendered with a little *juris* (ie strict legal analysis). When we do so, we will see that we need not agree with David Ibbetson's lament that there is nothing in the law of negligence 'to restrain the urge to move from the proposition that a person has suffered loss from the negligence of another to the conception that the loss ought to be compensated' ((2003) 26 NSWLJ 475, 488). This formulation overlooks the distinction between factual losses that flow from the violation of a primary right and those that do not.

COMMENTARY

The rights-based approach advocated by Beever is defined in contradistinction to a loss-based model, according to which negligently inflicted loss (including purely economic loss) should be recoverable unless there are policy reasons to restrict recovery. According to *Stevens*, pp. 20–1:

> Economic loss whether deliberately or carelessly inflicted, is not, without more, actionable. On the 'loss-based' model this exclusionary rule is difficult to explain . . . The common law could start with the assumption that we each have a right not to have loss inflicted upon us. It would then be necessary to carve out wide-ranging exceptions where this would be objectionable as a matter of policy. This is not the common law's starting point. There is no 'exclusionary rule' for economic loss. The common law's starting position is that the infliction of economic loss does not *per se* infringe any right of the claimant. This is true of both intentionally and negligently inflicted economic loss. On a rights-based model it is not the ocean of no-liability which requires mapping, but the isolated islands of rights.

Although in this passage Stevens appears to countenance a right not to suffer pure economic loss—while denying that English law recognises such a right—in a later essay he denied that such a right was even possible (see Stevens, 'Rights and Other Things', in *Rights and Private Law*, p. 119). Nolan ('Rights, Damage and Loss' (2017) 37 OJLS 255) agrees with Stevens that a right not to suffer pure economic loss is 'conceptually impossible', assuming that suffering 'loss' is defined as 'being worse off' in some sense (in this context, financially worse off). According to Nolan, the structure of his argument 'could not be simpler' (p. 262):

> It rests on two independent claims, from the truth of which the conclusion follows as a matter of logic. The claims are: (1) that a wrong (in other words, the violation of a right) occurs in a moment of time; and (2) that whether or not a person has suffered loss as a result of another's conduct cannot be determined at any given moment in time. It follows that the causing of loss cannot be a wrong, and hence that a right not to suffer loss is impossible.

Whether a right not to suffer pure economic loss is impossible, or simply not recognised by the law, on the rights-based view there is no inherent right of a claimant which can form the basis of a claim for recovery of pure economic loss in negligence. Admittedly, rights-based accounts of negligence law do generally allow for recovery of pure economic loss where, as in *Hedley Byrne v Heller*, the defendant has assumed responsibility to the claimant, thereby creating the necessary right, in much the same as a binding contractual undertaking creates rights. However, in the absence of an assumption of responsibility (or another event which generates a primary right in the claimant to be protected against the infliction of pure economic loss), there should be no liability. One result of this analysis is to bypass reliance on policy arguments as a justification for the general no-recovery rule (assuming, that is, that the identification of the relevant rights does not involve any 'policy' concerns), which is of course consistent with the scepticism with which rights theorists view such arguments in the first place.

Not everyone is convinced by the rights-based analysis. Barker ('Relational Economic Loss and Indeterminacy: The Search for Rational Limits' in S. Degeling, J. Edelman and J. Goudkamp (eds), *Torts in Commercial Law* (Sydney: Lawbook Co, 2011)) argues that, if the no 'prior right' thesis is correct, there seems little room for development of the law. In his view (p. 172), '[t]here may be no such existing right precisely because courts are engaged in the process of determining whether to bring it into being'. Barker also observes that the arguments of rights theorists by and large do not correspond to the way judges understand the problem when they are dealing with economic loss cases. Unless we ignore what the judges say and treat their reasoning as a sham, the rights thesis 'does not provide a viable internal explanation of the law—that is, an explanation which takes seriously judges' own stated reasons for deciding cases the way they do' (p. 173). The need to take seriously what the judges say is also a theme of *Stapleton*. But is this a valid criticism of the rights theorists? After all, Barker and Stapleton have consistently criticised the doctrine of assumption of responsibility as (in effect) a 'sham', and yet the judges seem to take that concept seriously. Furthermore, if, as many commentators believe, the results of the English cases on economic loss are more consistent with a rights analysis than a policy analysis, then—at least as far as English law is concerned—is it not the rights theorists who are providing an 'internal' explanation of the law, and the policy theorists who are providing an external critique of it (assuming, which seems reasonable, that ultimately what the judges *do* is more important than what they *say*)? Finally, in an important recent decision on economic loss, *1688782 Ontario Inc v Maple Leaf Foods Inc* (2020) 450 DLR (4th) 181, a majority of the Supreme Court of Canada expressly adopted a rights analysis, holding (at [18]–[19]) that in negligence 'the loss sought to be recovered must be the result of an interference with a legally cognizable right' and that there was 'no general right, in tort, protecting against the negligent or intentional infliction of pure economic loss'. (It should be noted, however, that the majority went on to engage in a detailed policy analysis, thereby demonstrating that the rights and policy approaches to the economic loss problem are not necessarily mutually exclusive.)

On the other side of the debate, some scholars accept that policy concerns are relevant to determining the duty of care question in pure economic loss cases but want to see consistency in the way such concerns are treated. In an influential article to this effect, Stapleton, 'Duty of Care and Economic Loss: A Wider Agenda' (1991) 107 LQR 249, argued that the decisions of the House of Lords in economic loss cases (at the time she was writing) depended not on a reasoned application of policy arguments to the facts of the individual case but upon a 'pockets' approach to liability. She identified three pockets—negligent misstatement (as in *Hedley Byrne*), dependence on property of a third party (as in *Spartan Steel*) and defective property (as in *Murphy v Brentwood*). According to Stapleton, the success or otherwise of a claim depended upon the pocket to which it was allocated, but this produced undesirable results because, although there may be similar policy issues in cases allocated to different pockets, the law in each pocket developed separately; consequently, the treatment of these policy concerns unjustifiably varied between pockets. An example of this type of 'tail wagging the dog' scenario can be seen, Stapleton contended, by comparing *D & F Estates Ltd v Church Commissioners* [1989] AC 177 and *Smith v Eric S Bush* [1990] 1 AC 831, both extracted earlier. Both cases dealt with a defect in property. In both cases there were no concerns over multiple or indeterminate claims, nor was there any problem with the claims being of an indeterminate amount. However, different results were reached because the cases were decided in different pockets, one under the more favourable (for the claimant) *Hedley Byrne* pocket and one under the no-recovery 'defective premises' pocket. This produces illogical results, argued Stapleton, in that one may sue a surveyor in tort for negligently failing to detect a defect in a house which results in pure economic loss but not the builder responsible for creating it, even if the same type of loss is suffered. Accordingly, to avoid this situation, Stapleton suggested that the 'pockets' approach should be replaced with the following agenda of policy concerns:

(1) the absence or controllability of the threat of indeterminate liability;

(2) the inadequacy of alternative means of protection;

(3) that the area is not one more appropriate to Parliamentary action; and

(4) that a duty would not allow a circumvention of a positive arrangement regarding allocation of risk which had been accepted by the plaintiff.

A slightly more structured, but similar, approach has been advocated by Giliker, 'Revisiting Pure Economic Loss: Lessons to Be Learnt From the Supreme Court of Canada'

(2005) 25 LS 49. Drawing on the approach of the Canadian Supreme Court, Giliker suggests that claims for pure economic loss should be divided into a number of categories—including negligent misstatements, negligent performance of services and defective products—for the purposes of identifying the policy factors relevant to each type of claim. This differs from the 'pockets' approach criticised by Stapleton because the choice of category does not determine the outcome; rather it is the first stage of a process for determining whether a duty will be owed, and the role of categories is to focus the courts' attention on why recovery should be limited by reference to the policy factors that are relevant to the category in question. (Cf. Witting, 'Duty of Care: An Analytical Approach' (2005) 25 OJLS 33.)

In *Customs and Excise* Lord Walker (at [71]) thought that there had been 'some modest progress' in the direction recommended by Stapleton; in fact the most tangible example of this is Lord Mance's speech in the same case. His Lordship recognised that the answer to the 'fair, just and reasonable' limb of the *Caparo* test required the court to consider 'relevant factors' which he identified as including indeterminate liability, the availability of adequate alternative protection for the claimant, the availability of insurance and whether any duty imposed on the defendant in tort would be inconsistent with other duties it owed (in contract or under the general law). His Lordship's approach to policy concerns is much more comprehensive than some earlier decisions of the House of Lords: for instance, although policy factor (4) was considered in *Henderson*, factors (1) and (2) were equally relevant but received scant if any attention. Although the number of potential claimants was determinate, the value of the claims was not because the defendants were liable for the Names' losses and (which was a key feature of the arrangement) each Name had unlimited liability. Similarly, the Names all had contracts with member's agents which provided an alternative means of protecting themselves, and the only reason the Names were suing in tort was to secure a more favourable limitation period. Do these factors suggest that a duty should not have been owed on the policy-based approach? And could the rights-based approach have produced the same result without the policy analysis recommended by Stapleton? (See *Stevens*, p. 184.)

While there is some evidence of Stapleton's approach being used in the English courts (see Stanton, 'Decision-making in the Tort of Negligence in the House of Lords' (2007) Tort L Rev 93), it has proven more influential in Commonwealth jurisdictions with a more expansive approach to liability in this area, particularly Australia, where the 'salient features' test for the existence of a duty of care puts policy considerations front and centre in the analysis (on this test, see *Plunkett*, pp. 65–9, and for an example of its application to economic loss claims, see *Johnson Tiles v Esso Australia* [2003] VSC 27). By contrast with more liberal liability regimes, the basic structure of the English law on pure economic loss—a general no-recovery rule, with the most important exception being based on a doctrine of assumption of responsibility—is largely consistent with a rights-based analysis. What is more, it is possible that the renewed emphasis on principle and precedent in duty of care reasoning (and the concomitant downplaying of policy) ushered in by Lord Reed's judgment in *Robinson v Chief Constable of West Yorkshire* may mean that the role of policy-based analysis in economic loss cases diminishes in the future. Stapleton's approach has also been subject to criticism, and not only from rights theorists, for whom it is of course anathema (see, e.g., *Stevens*, ch. 3). After all, the adoption of the criteria she identifies would not relieve the court from the task of making difficult value judgements, and because of this one commentator—who is certainly no rights theorist—has doubted their value: 'there is a world of difference between being able to select relevant policy factors for discussion in economic loss cases and finding within them appropriate guidance' (Witting, 'Duty of Care: An Analytical Approach'

(2005) 25 OJLS 33 at 44). In any case, if the kinds of policy concerns Stapleton highlights are to be considered, it is clearly desirable that this be done explicitly, so that the policy factors considered determinative by the court can be identified and a discussion at the policy level on the proper limits (if any) of the tort of negligence in the recovery of pure economic loss can take place. (The need for transparency in this respect is a central theme of the writings on pure economic loss of Kit Barker, who shares Stapleton's preference for multifactorial policy analysis: see, e.g., Barker, 'Economic Loss and the Duty of Care: A Study in the Exercise of Legal Justification', in C. Rickett (ed.), *Justifying Private Law Remedies* (Oxford: Hart, 2008).) Whether such an approach—especially in the absence of some form of categorisation—provides the necessary degree of guidance to legal practitioners is a different matter: it is hardly reassuring that in the *Johnson Tiles* case, where a multifactorial policy analysis was employed to resolve multiple relational loss claims, the judgment ran to some 145 pages. Arguing that the law is in fact developing new pockets, which provide some guidance, Stanton comments ((2007) Tort L Rev 93 at 106):

> Overt use of policy lays the House [of Lords] open to the charge that results are being driven by factors that are difficult to predict. However, the foundations of the law that is being developed would seem to be strong because the pockets are being built on the basis of policies suited to the particular function rather than being driven by principles set at a level of generality which pay no attention to the particular situation at issue.

For further work by Stapleton on the policy factors said to be relevant in negligence actions for pure economic loss (including some of those discussed in this chapter), see 'Duty of Care Factors: A Selection from the Judicial Menus', in P. Cane and J. Stapleton (eds), *The Law of Obligations* (Oxford: OUP, 1998) and Stapleton, 'Comparative Economic Loss: Lessons from Case-Law-Focused "Middle Theory"' (2002) 50 UCLA L Rev 531.

9 NEGLIGENCE: DUTY OF CARE—OMISSIONS AND ACTS OF THIRD PARTIES

I. Acts and Omissions

The law has historically been reluctant to impose liability for omissions as opposed to positive acts. The duty to intervene to assist another person who is at risk of injury is of limited scope. A doctor coming across an accident victim lying injured on the road has no obligation to render assistance; a strong swimmer can with impunity ignore the cries for help of someone who is drowning at sea; and it is evidently quite unthinkable that there should be 'liability in negligence on the part of one who sees another about to walk over a cliff with his head in the air and forbears to shout a warning' (*Yuen Kun Yeu v Attorney General of Hong Kong* [1988] AC 175 at 192, per Lord Keith). In short, there is no duty to be a good Samaritan. A number of reasons have been put forward to account for this reluctance to impose liability for omissions, notable amongst them being the over-burdensome nature of duties of affirmative action and the unfairness of singling out one of countless people who 'did nothing' to help the claimant. The issue was fully considered by Lord Hoffmann and Lord Nicholls in the course of their speeches in *Stovin v Wise*, extracted as follows.

Stovin v Wise [1996] AC 923

The facts of this case are not material for present purposes.

Lord Hoffmann

There are sound reasons why omissions require different treatment from positive conduct. It is one thing for the law to say that a person who undertakes some activity shall take reasonable care not to cause damage to others. It is another thing for the law to require that a person who is doing nothing in particular shall take steps to prevent another from suffering harm from the acts of third parties . . . or natural causes. One can put the matter in political, moral or economic terms. In political terms it is less of an invasion of an individual's freedom for the law to require him to consider the safety of others in his actions than to impose upon him a duty to rescue or protect. A moral version of this point may be called the 'Why pick on me?' argument. A duty to prevent harm to others or to render assistance to a person in danger or distress may apply to a large and indeterminate class of people who happen to be able to do something. Why should one be held liable rather than another? In economic terms, the efficient allocation of resources usually requires an activity should bear its own costs. If it benefits from being able to impose some of its costs on other people (what economists call 'externalities') the market is distorted because the activity appears cheaper than it really is. So liability to pay compensation for loss caused by negligent conduct acts as a deterrent against increasing the cost of the activity to the community and reduces externalities. But there is no similar justification for requiring a person who is not doing anything to spend money on behalf of someone else. Except in special cases (such as marine salvage) English law does not reward someone who voluntarily confers a benefit on another. So there must be some special reason why he should have to put his hand in his pocket.

Lord Nicholls (dissenting)

The distinction between liability for acts and liability for omissions is well known. It is not free from controversy. In some cases the distinction is not clear cut. The categorisation may depend upon how broadly one looks when deciding whether the omission is a 'pure' omission or is part of a larger course of activity set in motion by the defendant. Failure to apply the handbrake when parking a vehicle is the classic illustration of the latter. Then the omission is the element which makes the activity negligent . . .

Despite the difficulties, the distinction is fundamentally sound in this area of the law. The distinction is based on a recognition that it is one matter to require a person to take care if he embarks on a course of conduct which may harm others. He must take care not to create a risk of danger. It is another matter to require a person, who is doing nothing, to take positive action to protect others from harm for which he was not responsible, and to hold him liable in damages if he fails to do so. The law has long recognised that liability can arise more readily in the first situation than the second. This is reasonable. In the second situation a person is being compelled to act, and to act for the benefit of another. There must be some special justification for imposing an obligation of this character. Compulsory altruism needs more justification than an obligation not to create dangers to others when acting for one's own purposes . . .

The classic example of the absence of a legal duty to take positive action is where a grown person stands by while a young child drowns in a shallow pool. Another instance is where a person watches a nearby pedestrian stroll into the path of an oncoming vehicle. In both instances the callous bystander can foresee serious injury if he does nothing. He does not control the source of the danger, but he has control of the means to avert a dreadful accident. The child or pedestrian is dependent on the bystander: the child is unable to save himself, and the pedestrian is unaware of his danger. The prospective injury is out of all proportion to the burden imposed by having to take preventive steps. All that would be called for is the simplest exertion or a warning shout.

Despite this, the recognised legal position is that the bystander does not owe the drowning child or the heedless pedestrian a duty to take steps to save him. Something more is required than being a bystander. There must be some additional reason why it is fair and reasonable that one person should be regarded as his brother's keeper and have legal obligations in that regard. When this additional reason exists, there is said to be sufficient proximity. That is the customary label.

COMMENTARY

Although Lord Nicholls was dissenting, his views on the correct general approach to the imposition of liability for omissions largely coincided with those of Lord Hoffmann. For an elegant and persuasive critique of Lord Hoffmann's justifications for the standard no-liability rule see J. Kortmann, *Altruism in Private Law: Liability for Nonfeasance and Negotiorum Gestio* (Oxford: OUP, 2005), ch. 3, and, for further discussion, Quill, 'Affirmative Duties of Care in the Common Law' (2011) 2 JETL 151 at 164–82; Tofaris and Steel, 'Negligence Liability for Omissions and the Police' [2016] CLJ 128 at 129–33; Steel, 'Rationalising Omissions Liability in Negligence' (2019) 135 LQR 484 at 493–5.

In *Sutradhar v National Environment Research Council* [2006] 4 All ER 490 the House of Lords restated the general rule in forcible terms. As part of its overseas aid programme, the British government commissioned the British Geological Survey (BGS) to test the performance of deep irrigation wells in Bangladesh. The tests could identify the presence of a number of toxins in the water, but not the presence of arsenic, which the defendant did not consider at the time to be a potential problem. In fact, arsenic contamination of drinking water precipitated a major environmental disaster in Bangladesh, with between 35 million and 77 million of the country's 125 million inhabitants at risk. The claimant developed symptoms associated with arsenical poisoning after he began drinking from an irrigation well in an area in which the BGS had tested. He claimed damages on the basis that the BGS had breached its positive duty to test for arsenic. The House of Lords struck out the claim, which Lord Hoffmann described, at [2], as 'hopeless'. He elaborated, at [27]:

> [T]he fact that one has expert knowledge does not in itself create a duty to the whole world to apply that knowledge in solving its problems . . . BGS therefore owed no positive duties to the government or people of Bangladesh to do anything. They can be liable only for the things they did . . . not for what they did not do.

The House of Lords also struck out the claimant's alternative claim of negligent misrepresentation (considered in Ch. 8.III.1). See further Lunney (2006) 14 Tort L Rev 129.

Cf. *R v Imperial Tobacco Canada Ltd* [2011] 3 SCR 45, rejecting the argument that the State of Canada had negligently failed to warn its citizens of the risks of smoking low-tar cigarettes (in the context of the defendant tobacco company's attempts to recover compensation from Canada in the event of its own liability to consumers of its cigarettes); the defendant had indicated no basis on which it could be found that Canada had a positive duty to act.

The Distinction between Acts and Omissions

In the extract from *Stovin v Wise*, Lord Nicholls raises the question of the differentiation of positive acts from omissions, commenting that '[i]n some cases the distinction is not clear cut'. In fact, the terms 'act' and 'omission' are at a purely linguistic level no more than labels that can be applied interchangeably to every instance of human conduct; the distinction does not reflect any deep, philosophical subdivision of human conduct into two essentially different types. The point is further elaborated by *Hart & Honoré*, pp. 138–9:

> Human conduct can be described alternatively in terms of acts or omissions. 'A medical man who diagnoses a case of measles as a case of scarlet fever may be said to have omitted to make a correct diagnosis; he may equally well be said to have made an incorrect diagnosis' (*Harnett v Bond* [1924] 2 KB 517 at 541, per Bankes LJ). Sometimes it is more appropriate to describe the conduct as an omission; if there is a legal duty to do an act, and the subject has not done it, the legally relevant description will be in terms of an omission to perform the act in question. But the description of conduct as an omission may not imply any bodily movements by the person whose conduct is in question: e.g. if the description is: 'The defendant failed to inspect the electrical wiring.' Consequently those courts and writers who are impressed by 'setting in motion' as a prime instance of causation, and who further conclude that we can only set things in motion by ourselves making movements, find it difficult to understand how an omission to act can negative causal connection.

It is now thought, at least in England, that there is no special difficulty about omissions . . . In truth, no rational distinction can be drawn between the causal status of acts and omissions.

By this analysis the authors are able to undermine the claim which is occasionally made that it is only positive acts—'making things happen'—that can operate as causes, and hence give rise to liability, because 'doing nothing' can bring nothing about. In fact, omissions can be legally causative, at least where there is a duty to act.

It would be wrong to conclude, however, that no rational distinction can be drawn between acts and omissions in determining whether they give rise to liability. In the tort context, the terms 'act' and 'omission' are applied to reflect a common-sense distinction between 'making things worse' and 'not making things better' (*N v Poole Borough Council* [2020] AC 780 at [28], per Lord Reed; see further Steel, 'Rationalising Omissions Liability in Negligence' (2019) 135 LQR 484 at 486–91). Liability for the latter results in significantly greater restrictions on liberty of action than does liability for the former, for it requires the defendant, who must already ensure that his activities do not expose others to unreasonable risks, to sacrifice his pursuit of those activities—possibly, in some cases, to drop everything else—in the interests of another person. But even here it must be admitted that the distinction is only one of degree, and that different duties of affirmative action restrict liberty of action to different extents. In which case, it is fair to ask why liability for a failure to act should not be imposed where the action required entails very little on the defendant's part but prevents the claimant suffering serious injury. (See further *Atiyah*, pp. 70–5; cf. Logie [1989] CLJ 115.)

Duties of Rescue: A Comparative Overview

English law recognises no duty of rescue in the absence of special circumstances (e.g. an undertaking to safeguard the person imperilled), though someone who actually undertakes a rescue is potentially liable if the rescue exposes the person at risk to a new or increased danger which materialises (see *Horsley v Maclaren* (1972) 22 DLR (3d) 545, applied in England in *Day v High Performance Sports Ltd* [2003] EWHC 197 (QB)). It is pertinent to note here that, in the United States, concern lest potential tort liabilities should deter would-be rescuers has led all states to pass so-called 'Good Samaritan' statutes which recognise an immunity from suit in at least some categories of such cases (see *Dobbs, Heyden & Bublick*, § 409). Comparable statutory immunities have been introduced in Australia, but the legislative response in the United Kingdom has so far been limited to specifying that the fact that a person was acting heroically by intervening in an emergency to assist an individual in danger is to be taken into account in determining the steps that the person was required to take to meet the standard of care (Social Action, Responsibility and Heroism Act 2015, ss. 1 and 4, extracted in Ch 4.II.3).

A number of other jurisdictions *do* recognise affirmative duties of rescue. By Article 222-6 of the French *Code pénal*, criminal liability is imposed on 'anyone who wilfully refrains from helping and assisting a person in danger, when he could have done so or caused others to do so without risk to himself or third parties' (*van Gerven*, p. 281); where the danger materialises and injury results, breach of this duty is actionable in damages under the *Code civil*, which makes no explicit distinction between acts and omissions in its provisions on tortious liability. A handful of United States jurisdictions have also made failure to perform so-called 'easy' rescues punishable in criminal law, though there has been as yet very little case-law discussion of whether an injured person can bring a civil action for damages in such a case (see Franklin, 'Vermont Requires Rescue: A Comment' (1972) 25 Stan L Rev 51; *Dobbs, Heyden & Bublick*, § 405). However, the American Law Institute's *Restatement Third, Torts: Liability for Physical and Emotional Harm* (2010), in a striking departure from previous Restatements, now provides (§ 38): 'When a statute requires an actor to act for the protection of another, the court may rely on the statute to decide that an affirmative duty exists and to determine the scope of the duty.' It is contemplated that this might form the basis for a liability in tort for breach of a criminal law statute imposing a duty of easy rescue.

For comparative analysis, see Kortmann, *op. cit.*, ch. 4; *van Dam*, para. 808; Schiff, 'Samaritans: Good, Bad and Ugly: A Comparative Law Analysis' (2005) 11 Roger Williams U L Rev 77.

Evaluation

The common law's failure to recognise a duty of rescue has been criticised by a number of commentators. Finding the decisions which uphold this rule 'revolting to any moral sense', W. Keeton et al., *Prosser & Keeton on the Law of Torts*, 5th edn (St Paul, Minn.: West Publishing Co, 1984) comment: 'The remedy in such cases is left to the "higher law" and the "voice of conscience", which, in a wicked world, would seem to be singularly ineffective either to prevent the harm or to compensate the victim' (pp. 376, 375). A similar position is taken by Bender, 'A Feminist's Primer on Feminist Theory and Tort' (1988) 38 J Leg Ed 3, who works it (passim) into her feminist critique of the law:

> Tort law needs to be more of a system of response and caring than it is now. Its focus should be on interdependence and collective responsibility rather than on individuality, and on safety and help for the injured rather than on 'reasonableness' and economic efficiency . . . [I]mplicit male norms have been used to skew legal analysis . . . Not only does 'reasonable person' still mean 'reasonable man'—'reason' and 'reasonableness' are gendered concepts as well. Gender distinctions have often been reinforced by dualistic attributions of reason and rationality to men, emotion and intuition (or instinct) to women . . . The 'no duty [to rescue]' rule is a consequence of a legal system devoid of care and responsiveness to the safety of others.

However, not all advocates of a duty of rescue would go so far as to endorse the degree of mutual obligation envisaged by Bender. See, e.g., Weinrib, 'The Case for a Duty to Rescue' (1981) 90 Yale LJ 247, supporting the imposition of a duty to rescue in cases of emergency when the rescuer can act without prejudice to themselves, but rejecting any more widely applicable duty of beneficence.

In fact, Weinrib subsequently retracted his support for even a limited affirmative duty restricted to emergencies as he now considers such a duty inconsistent with the fundamental distinction between misfeasance and nonfeasance that is inherent in the correlative structure of tort law: tort law corrects the injustice effected by the defendant doing something that is incompatible with a right of the claimant, and there is no general duty of affirmative action because a person imperilled ordinarily has no right to expect another person to come to his aid (see 'Correlativity, Personality, and the Emerging Consensus on Corrective Justice' (2001) 2 Theoretical Inq L 107 at 139). For further development of this basic idea in the context of English law, see *Beever*, chs 6 and 9; *Stevens*, 9ff.

Do you think that the common law is justified in refusing to recognise any general duty to rescue, even if easy? Do you agree with Steel (*op. cit.*, p. 494) that '[s]ometimes considerations of extreme need trump considerations of freedom'?

II. Liability for Omissions

Despite the general principle excluding liability for omissions, liability may arise in certain exceptional circumstances. But no precise categorisation is possible of the various situations in which a duty of affirmative action is recognised. As Tony Honoré has written, the cases 'do not fall into any neat pattern ... They seem not to derive from or be reducible to a single principle' ('Are Omissions Less Culpable?', in P. Cane and J. Stapleton (eds), *Essays for Patrick Atiyah* (Oxford: OUP, 1991), p. 47).

It is nevertheless helpful to identify a number of loosely defined circumstances that may give rise to duties of affirmative action. Amongst these are:

- the defendant's creation of a source of danger, even if entirely without fault;
- the defendant's assumption of responsibility for the claimant's welfare; and
- the defendant's status as holding an office or position of responsibility (e.g. as a parent or employer, or as the owner or occupier of land).

The extracted cases that follow illustrate these broad general categories, though it should be noted that not infrequently the categories overlap and it is a combination of factors, not one individual factor, that accounts for the decision reached on the facts.

The factors serve to create duties of affirmative action on both private persons and public bodies but it should be noted at the outset that the latter may also have wider duties of affirmative action under the Human Rights Act 1998. The Act's impact and other considerations that are particular to public bodies are considered later in IV.

Capital & Counties plc v Hampshire County Council [1997] QB 1004

This was a consolidated appeal involving three separate actions.

In the *Hampshire* case, the defendant fire brigade attended a fire on the plaintiffs' premises, its cause apparently unknown, and the fire officer, Station Officer Mitchell, ordered the plaintiffs' sprinkler system to be turned off. That was held to have been a negligent mistake that had an adverse effect on restraining the fire, which spread rapidly and eventually destroyed the whole building.

In the *London* case, the plaintiffs' industrial premises were showered with flaming debris following an explosion on nearby waste land; the explosion was set off deliberately by the second defendants, who were a company specialising in special effects for film and television. When the fire brigade rung by the first defendants arrived at the scene of the explosion they satisfied themselves that all the fires there had been extinguished and left the scene without inspecting the plaintiffs' premises which were severely damaged when a fire broke out there later on.

In the *West Yorkshire* case, the plaintiffs' chapel was destroyed by a fire (cause unknown) which the defendant fire authority had failed to extinguish. The plaintiffs alleged that this was attributable to the defendants' negligence, and breach of statutory duty, in failing to ensure that its fire hydrants were in working order and capable of providing an adequate water supply. Of the seven fire hydrants surrounding the chapel, four failed to work for one reason or another, and three were either never found, or found so late as to be of little use, as a result of inadequate signing.

The Court of Appeal, in a judgment delivered by Stuart-Smith LJ, first considered the question: 'Is there a common law duty on the fire brigade to answer calls to fires or to take reasonable care to so do?' His conclusion was that there were no considerations sufficient to give rise to such a duty of affirmative action (at 1030):

> In our judgment the fire brigade are not under a common law duty to answer the call for help and are not under a duty to take care to do so. If therefore they fail to turn up or fail to turn up in time because they have carelessly misunderstood the message, got lost on the way or run into a tree, they are not liable ...

His Lordship then considered whether a duty of care might arise once the fire brigade had arrived on the scene and started to fight the fire.

Stuart-Smith LJ (delivering the judgment of the Court)

Does the fire brigade owe a duty of care to the owner of property on fire, or anyone else to whom the fire may spread, once they have arrived at the fire ground and started to fight the fire?

. . . Counsel for the plaintiffs in the *Hampshire* case submit that there are two approaches in principle which lead to the conclusion of liability in their case.

First it is . . . argued that Station Officer Mitchell's act of switching off the sprinklers was a positive act of misfeasance which foreseeably caused the fire to get out of control and spread and cause the loss of blocks B and C and part of block A which would not otherwise have been affected . . . By reason of the differing circumstances in each appeal this line of argument is only of direct assistance to the plaintiffs in the *Hampshire* case. The alternative ground upon which it is said that proximity will arise is where someone possessed of a special skill undertakes, quite irrespective of contract, to apply that skill for the assistance of another person who relies upon such skill, and there is direct and substantial reliance by the plaintiffs on the defendant's skill . . .

We turn to consider the first of these submissions. The peculiarity of fire brigades, together with other rescue services, such as ambulance or coastal rescue and protective services such as the police, is that they do not as a rule create the danger which causes injury to the plaintiff or loss to his property. For the most part they act in the context of a danger already created and damage already caused, whether by the forces of nature, or the acts of some third party or even of the plaintiff himself, and whether those acts are criminal, negligent or non-culpable.

But where the rescue/protective service itself by negligence creates the danger which caused the plaintiff's injury there is no doubt in our judgment the plaintiff can recover . . . The judge [in the *Hampshire* case] held that at the time the sprinkler systems were turned off, the fire was being contained, but that once they were turned off it rapidly went out of control, spreading to blocks B and C which had been deprived of their own sprinkler protection . . . [T]he defendants by their positive act exacerbated the fire so that it rapidly spread . . .

We now turn to consider the second submission made on behalf of all the plaintiffs that the requisite proximity exists. It involves the concept of assumption of responsibility by the fire brigade and particular reliance by the owner. As a general rule a sufficient relationship of proximity will exist when someone possessed of special skill undertakes to apply that skill for the assistance of another person who relies upon such skill and there is direct and substantial reliance by the plaintiff on the defendant's skill (see *Hedley Byrne & Co Ltd v Heller & Partners* [1964] AC 465 and *Henderson v Merrett Syndicates Ltd* [1995] 2 AC 145). There are many instances of this. The plaintiffs submit that that which is most closely analogous is that of doctor and patient or health authority and patient. There is no doubt that once the relationship of doctor and patient or hospital authority and admitted patient exists, the doctor or the hospital owe a duty to take reasonable care to effect a cure, not merely to prevent further harm. The undertaking is to use the special skills which the doctor and hospital authorities have to treat the patient . . . In *Cassidy v Ministry of Health* [1951] 2 KB 343 at 360 Denning LJ said:

> In my opinion, authorities who run a hospital, be they local authorities, government boards, or any other corporation, are in law under the self-same duty as the humblest doctor. Whenever they accept a patient for treatment, they must use reasonable care and skill to cure him of his ailment.

9 NEGLIGENCE: DUTY OF CARE—OMISSIONS AND ACTS OF THIRD PARTIES

... [I]t is clear that no such duty of care exists, even though there may be close physical proximity, simply because one party is a doctor and the other has a medical problem which may be of interest to both . . . [W]e consider that [counsel for the defendants in the *Hampshire* case] is right when he submitted that the fire brigade's duty is owed [to] the public at large to prevent the spread of fire and that this may involve a conflict between the interests of various owners of premises. It may be necessary to enter and cause damage to A's premises in order to tackle a fire which has started in B's. During the Great Fire of London the Duke of York had to blow up a number of houses not yet affected by fire, in order to make a fire break . . .

Plaintiffs' counsel argue that the provisions of sub-ss. (3) and (2) of s. 30 [of the Fire Services Act 1947] which confer on the senior fire brigade officer present sole charge and control of fire fighting operations and make it a criminal offence wilfully to obstruct or interfere with any member of a fire brigade engaged in fire fighting, establish a proximate relationship, once responsibility for fighting the fire is taken over by the brigade.

This argument has its attraction, particularly on the somewhat extreme facts of the *Hampshire* case . . . [T]he plaintiffs had two systems of fire fighting, one very effective in the form of automatic sprinklers, the other the manual fire-fighting capability of their employees. Station Officer Mitchell rendered the first ineffectual and ordered out of the building the plaintiffs' employees who were attempting to attack the fire.

But it seems to us that the statute imposes control of operations on the senior officer for the benefit of the public generally where there may be conflicting interests. By taking such control that officer is not to be seen as undertaking a voluntary assumption of responsibility to the owner of the premises on fire, whether or not the latter is in fact reliant upon it . . .

In our judgment, a fire brigade does not enter into a sufficiently proximate relationship with the owner or occupier of premises to come under a duty of care merely by attending at the fire ground and fighting the fire; this is so, even though the senior officer actually assumes control of the fire-fighting operation.

COMMENTARY

The plaintiffs failed in their argument that a fire brigade which took control of fire-fighting operations, and ordered others to stop their independent efforts to put out the blaze, thereby assumed responsibility to the owners of the premises to which they had been called. But, in the *Hampshire* case, the court was able to impose liability on the basis that there was a positive act of misfeasance which foreseeably caused the fire to get out of control. It was assumed in this case that it was the act of the defendant's fire officer which was negligent. What if the officer had acted reasonably at the time he had the sprinklers switched off, but subsequently realised the risk that the fire might spread and then did nothing about it? And why could the act of ordering others to stop fighting a fire independently not constitute a 'positive act of misfeasance' sufficient to give rise to liability?

The Court of Appeal's approach is very reminiscent of that taken by the House of Lords in *East Suffolk Rivers Catchment Board v Kent* [1941] AC 74. There, a breach in a sea wall caused by a very high tide led to the flooding of the plaintiff-respondents' land. The defendant-appellants in the exercise of their statutory powers undertook the repair of the wall, but carried out the work so inefficiently that the repairs of the breach, which the evidence suggested should have taken only 14 days, continued for 178 days, prolonging the period during which the respondents' land was under water. The House of Lords (Lord Atkin dissenting) held that the catchment board had not assumed any responsibility to the landowner beyond its undoubted duty not to cause additional damage. Lord Porter explained (at 105):

where, as here, the damage was not caused by any positive act on the part of the appellants but was caused and would have occurred to the like extent if they had taken no steps at all, I cannot see that the loss which the respondents suffered was due to any breach of a duty owed by the appellants. Their duty was to avoid causing damage, not either to prevent future damage due to causes for which they were not responsible or to shorten its incidence. The loss which the respondents suffered was due to the original breach, and the appellants' failure to close it merely allowed the damage to continue during the time which they took in mending the broken bank.

Capital & Counties was applied in *OLL Ltd v Secretary of State for Transport* [1997] 3 All ER 897, a tortfeasor's action for contribution, where May J struck out a claim against the coastguard which alleged that it was negligent in misleading independent rescuers as to the likely location of a group of children on a canoeing expedition who were adrift at sea. According to the judge, the situation was not the same as in the *Hampshire* case, where the defendant had caused direct physical harm by his positive conduct actually at the scene. Could it not be argued, however, that the defendants had nevertheless made the children worse off by depriving them of the assistance of the independent rescuers?

Much the same principles as are applied to the fire service and coastguard also govern the duty of the police to take positive steps to protect persons from crime: see *Michael v Chief Constable of South Wales Police* [2015] AC 1732, extracted later.

Kent v Griffiths [2001] QB 36

The claimant suffered an asthma attack and her doctor, attending at her home, telephoned the London Ambulance Service (LAS) for an ambulance to take the claimant immediately to hospital. The call was accepted but, for reasons which were never explained, the ambulance took some forty minutes to travel the 6½ miles to the claimant's home. While in the ambulance on the way to the hospital, the claimant suffered a respiratory arrest which resulted in permanent brain damage. In her subsequent action for damages against (amongst others) the ambulance service, the judge found that the ambulance could and should have arrived at the claimant's home some fourteen minutes earlier and that, if it had done so, there was a high probability that the respiratory arrest would have been averted. He found that the ambulance service had breached its duty of care to the claimant and allowed her claim for damages. The ambulance service appealed.

Lord Woolf

There are obvious similarities between the facts of this case and . . . the *Capital & Counties* type of situation. The activities of the fire services are subject to a statutory framework, so are the functions of ambulance services. Section 3(1) of the National Health Service Act 1977 imposes on the Secretary of State a duty to provide, throughout England and Wales, to such extent as he considers necessary to meet all reasonable requirements, 'medical, dental, nursing and ambulance services': sections 1 and 3(1) of the National Health Service Act 1977. This duty is an exhortatory or target duty which does not create a statutory right, the breach of which can give rise to a private law right to damages. As the police and the fire services can be summoned by 999 calls so can the ambulance service, as in this case . . .

Here what was being provided was a health service. In the case of health services under the 1977 Act the conventional situation is that there is a duty of care. Why should the position of the ambulance staff be different from that of doctors or nurses? In addition the arguments based on public policy are much weaker in the case of the ambulance service than they are in the case of the police or the fire service. The police and fire services' primary obligation

9 NEGLIGENCE: DUTY OF CARE—OMISSIONS AND ACTS OF THIRD PARTIES

is to the public at large. In protecting a particular victim of crime, the police are performing their more general role of maintaining public order and reducing crime. In the case of fire the fire service will normally be concerned not only to protect a particular property where a fire breaks out but also to prevent fire spreading. In the case of both services, there is therefore a concern to protect the public generally. The emergency services that can be summoned by a 999 call do, in the majority of situations, broadly carry out a similar function. But in reality they can be very different. The ambulance service is part of the health service. Its care function includes transporting patients to and from hospital when the use of an ambulance for this purpose is desirable. It is therefore appropriate to regard the LAS as providing services of the category provided by hospitals and not as providing services equivalent to those rendered by the police or the fire service. Situations could arise where there is a conflict between the interests of a particular individual and the public at large. But, in the case of the ambulance service in this particular case, the only member of the public who could be adversely affected was the claimant. It was the claimant alone for whom the ambulance had been called.

Cases could arise where an ambulance is required to attend a scene of an accident in which a number of people need transporting to hospital. That could be said to be a different situation, but, as the numbers involved would be limited, I would not regard this as necessarily leading to a different result. The result would depend on the facts. I would be resistant to a suggestion that the ambulance service could be regarded as negligent because by an error of judgment a less seriously injured patient was transported to hospital leaving a more seriously injured patient at the scene who, as a result, suffered further injuries. In such a situation, on the facts, it is most unlikely that there would be conduct which could be properly regarded as negligent. The requirement to establish that there has been a lack of care provides the LAS with the necessary protection.

An important feature of this case is that there is no question of an ambulance not being available or of a conflict in priorities. Again I recognise that where what is being attacked is the allocation of resources, whether in the provision of sufficient ambulances or sufficient drivers or attendants, different considerations could apply. There then could be issues which are not suited for resolution by the courts. However, once there are available, both in the form of an ambulance and in the form of manpower, the resources to provide an ambulance on which there are no alternative demands, the ambulance service would be acting perversely 'in circumstances such as the present', if it did not make those resources available. Having decided to provide an ambulance an explanation is required to justify a failure to attend within reasonable time . . .

[T]here is no reason why there should not be liability if the arrival of the ambulance was delayed for no good reason. The acceptance of the call in this case established the duty of care.

Aldous and **Laws LJJ** agreed.

Appeal dismissed.

COMMENTARY

Do you agree with Lord Woolf that the fire and ambulance service scenarios are properly distinguished on the basis that the fire service, when responding to a call, is acting in pursuance of a public duty, whilst the ambulance service typically is not? This may have been true in *Kent*, where the ambulance was called for a particular individual, but cases will arise where the ambulance service has competing calls on its resources, for example a serious accident with a large number of casualties, not all of whom can be taken to hospital at once.

Lord Woolf apparently thought that there would still be a duty in such a case, and that the conflicting pressures on the ambulance service would be relevant only to the question of breach. If the need to prove a lack of care would really provide the ambulance service with enough protection (against what?), why not adopt the same analysis with respect to the fire service?

In *Kent*, Lord Woolf noted that ambulance services were provided under statutory provisions the breach of which did not give rise to a private law right to damages, yet found that the ambulance service might be liable for common law negligence. It is now clear that no positive duty to act can be founded merely on the presence of statutory powers which, if exercised, might have prevented the damage to the claimant, but the outcome in *Kent* can still be defended on the basis that the ambulance service assumed responsibility for the claimant when it accepted the 999 call. What if, after receiving the call, the operator had replied: 'Sorry, all our ambulances are busy today'? In such a case, there would arguably be no assumption of responsibility at all. Or does the ambulance service assume responsibility when the operator picks up the phone, or even by virtue of its well-publicised participation in the emergency calls system? Consider how the different analyses might affect the ambulance service's liability in a case where the emergency calls system has broken down and callers are unable to get though. See also the discussion of assumption of responsibility in the context of emergency calls to the police in *Michael v Chief Constable of South Wales Police* [2015] AC 1732 and a local authority's social work team in *N v Poole Borough Council* [2020] AC 780, both extracted later in this chapter.

Is Reliance Necessary?

In *Kent*, the Court of Appeal found that the duty was established by the ambulance service's 'acceptance' of the 999 call (cf. the trial judge who thought the duty arose only on the allocation of an ambulance to the claimant). The judgment contains nothing to suggest that there had to be detrimental reliance upon this by the claimant or another person. In fact, the claimant's doctor gave evidence that, if she had been told that it would be forty minutes before the ambulance arrived, she would probably have asked the claimant's husband to drive them to the hospital. But the Court of Appeal appears not to have attached any significance to this evidence and thus treated detrimental reliance on the assumption of responsibility as irrelevant. Do you think that the result would have been the same even if the claimant had been in a remote place with no alternative means of transport?

Barrett v Ministry of Defence [1995] 1 WLR 1217

The deceased, a serving naval airman, got himself exceedingly drunk while celebrating a promotion on his remote Norwegian base, where drink prices were according to the judge 'astonishingly cheap'. Over the course of the evening, he had been served drinks at bars on the base, and been brought drinks by friends. He was found unconscious and a duty officer organised for him to be taken by stretcher to his room, but no one kept watch over the deceased to ensure that he was lying in a safe position. While unconscious, the deceased choked on his own vomit and died. A disciplinary inquiry subsequently revealed that outbreaks of drunkenness were common at the base, and the senior naval officer at the base admitted he had not fulfilled his responsibility, imposed by navy regulations, of discouraging drunkenness. The deceased's widow brought an action for damages on behalf of his estate and dependants.

9 NEGLIGENCE: DUTY OF CARE—OMISSIONS AND ACTS OF THIRD PARTIES

At trial, the judge found the defendant to have been negligent in tolerating excessive drinking at the base, but reduced the award of damages by one-quarter because of the deceased's contributory negligence. The defendant appealed.

Beldam LJ

The judge said that the deceased was a heavy drinker introduced to a potentially dangerous situation. In these circumstances the judge held that it was foreseeable in this particular environment that the deceased would succumb to heavy intoxication. Although it was only in exceptional circumstances that a defendant could be fixed with a duty to take positive steps to protect a person of full age and capacity from his own weakness, he considered in the exceptional circumstances that arose in this case it was just and reasonable to impose a duty to take care on the defendant. He also held that the defendant was in breach of that duty because it failed to enforce the standards it itself set in matters of discipline . . .

The judge also held that once the deceased had collapsed, the defendant had assumed responsibility for him and had taken inadequate steps to care for him. No medical officer or medical attendant was informed and supervision of the deceased was wholly inadequate by the standards which the defendant's own officers accepted were necessary. The defendant does not challenge the judge's findings that it was in breach of duty to take care of the deceased once he had collapsed and it had assumed responsibility for him. The defendant's principal ground of appeal is that the judge was wrong to hold that it was under any duty to take care to see that the deceased, a mature man 30 years of age, did not consume so much alcohol that he became unconscious. If the deceased himself was to be treated as a responsible adult, he alone was to blame for his collapse. On this basis the judge's apportionment of liability was plainly wrong. Even if the judge's finding of this duty were to stand, the deceased ought to have been regarded as equally responsible for his own death . . .

In the present case the judge posed the question whether there was a duty at law to take reasonable steps to prevent the deceased becoming unconscious through alcohol abuse. He said his conclusion that there was such a duty was founded on the fact that: 'It was foreseeable in the environment in which the defendant grossly failed to enforce their regulations and standing orders that the deceased would succumb to heavy intoxication.' And in these circumstances it was just and reasonable to impose a duty.

The plaintiff argued for the extension of a duty to take care for the safety of the deceased from analogous categories of relationship in which an obligation to use reasonable care already existed. For example, employer and employee, pupil and schoolmaster, and occupier and visitor. It was said that the defendant's control over the environment in which the deceased was serving and the provision of duty-free liquor, coupled with the failure to enforce disciplinary rules and orders, were sufficient factors to render it fair, just and reasonable to extend the duty to take reasonable care found in the analogous circumstances. The characteristic which distinguishes those relationships is reliance expressed or implied in the relationship which the party to whom the duty is owed is entitled to place on the other party to make provision for his safety. I can see no reason why it should not be fair, just and reasonable for the law to leave a responsible adult to assume responsibility for his own actions in consuming alcoholic drink. No one is better placed to judge the amount that he can safely consume or to exercise control in his own interest as well as in the interest of others. To dilute self-responsibility and to blame one adult for another's lack of self-control is neither just nor reasonable and in the development of the law of negligence an increment too far.

Should the individual members of the senior rates' mess who bought rounds of drinks for a group of mess mates and the deceased each be held to have had a share in the responsibility for his death? Or should responsibility only devolve on two or three of them who bought the last rounds? In the course of argument Mr Nice for the plaintiff experienced great difficulty in articulating the nature of the duty. Eventually he settled on two expositions. It was a duty owed by the defendant to any serviceman at this base in this environment to take into account group behaviour and arising from a duty to provide for the servicemen's accommodation and welfare there was a duty to take reasonable care to prevent drunkenness/drinking '(a) to a level which endangered his safety or (b) such as to render him unconscious.' The impracticality of the duty so defined is obvious. The level of drinking which endangers safety depends upon the behaviour of the person affected. The disinhibiting effects of even two or three drinks may on occasions cause normally sober and steady individuals to behave with nonchalant disregard for their own and others' welfare and safety.

The plaintiff placed reliance on *Crocker v Sundance Northwest Resorts Ltd* (1988) 51 DLR (4th) 321, a decision of the Supreme Court of Canada, and on another Canadian case, *Jordan House Ltd v Menow* (1973) 38 DLR (3d) 105. In the first case the defendant was held liable to an intoxicated plaintiff for permitting him to take part in a dangerous ski hill race which caused him to be injured. The defendant had taken the positive step of providing him with the equipment needed for the race knowing that he was in no fit state to take part. The plaintiff had consumed alcohol in the defendant's bars. Liability was based not on permitting him to drink in the bars but in permitting him to take part in the race. In the *Jordan House* case the plaintiff was a habitual customer of the defendant. He became intoxicated from drinking heavily. The defendant proprietor evicted him knowing he was unsteady and incapable in spite of the fact that he would have to cross a busy thoroughfare. The court held that these circumstances, including the fact that at the time he was evicted the plaintiff's relationship with the defendant was that of invitee/invitor, were sufficient to justify the imposition of a duty to take care for the safety of the customer. In each of these cases the court founded the imposition of a duty on factors additional to the mere provision of alcohol and the failure strictly to enforce provisions against drunkenness.

In the present case I would reverse the judge's finding that the defendant was under a duty to take reasonable care to prevent the deceased from abusing alcohol to the extent he did. Until he collapsed, I would hold that the deceased was in law alone responsible for his condition. Thereafter, when the defendant assumed responsibility for him, it accepts that the measures taken fell short of the standard reasonably to be expected. It did not summon medical assistance and its supervision of him was inadequate.

The final question is how far the deceased should be regarded as responsible for his death. The amount of alcohol he had consumed not only caused him to vomit, it deprived him of the spontaneous ability to protect his air passages after he had vomited. His fault was therefore a continuing and direct cause of his death. Moreover his lack of self-control in his own interest caused the defendant to have to assume responsibility for him. But for his fault, it would not have had to do so. How far in such circumstances is it just and equitable to regard the deceased as the author of his misfortune? The deceased involved the defendant in a situation in which it had to assume responsibility for his care and I would not regard it as just and equitable in such circumstances to be unduly critical of the defendant's fault. I consider a greater share of blame should rest upon the deceased than on the defendant and I would reduce the amount of the damages recoverable by the plaintiff by two-thirds, holding the defendant one-third to blame.

Saville and **Neill LJJ** agreed.

Appeal allowed.

COMMENTARY

The basis of the court's decision was the defendant's assumption of responsibility for the deceased's health and safety, and not its supply to him of dangerous quantities of drink. The result, it seems, would have been the same even if the drink had come from some other source. The duty presumably arose at the moment when the senior officer ordered that the deceased be taken to his room, though the Court of Appeal did not rule on this because the defendant did not challenge the judge's finding that responsibility had been assumed.

Barrett may be compared with *Jebson v Ministry of Defence* [2000] 1 WLR 2055, where the plaintiff soldier was injured whilst engaged in drunken frolicking. The injury was sustained after a night out on the town arranged by the plaintiff's camp commander, who had laid on transport to take the troops back to barracks. On the way, the plaintiff tried to climb onto the canvas roof of the lorry in which he was travelling but lost his footing and fell onto the road. The Court of Appeal found that the commander had impliedly undertaken responsibility for the safety of soldiers who he should have foreseen would be drunk and rowdy. It was therefore his duty to ensure they were properly supervised on their way back to their base. On the facts, there had been a breach of this duty as the commander had neglected even to put anyone formally in charge of the troops, though the plaintiff's damages were reduced by 75 per cent for contributory negligence. In contrast with *Barrett*, the plaintiff's injury was caused by his behaviour whilst drunk, and not simply by the effects of alcohol on his body. But it is doubtful that the result would have been any different if (say) he had drunk himself comatose whilst out on the town, got inadvertently left behind and choked on his own vomit, for the commander appears to have assumed responsibility for the soldiers' wellbeing over the course of the entire evening.

The risks associated with alcohol are well-known and willingly confronted by imbibers. The Court of Appeal was obviously very concerned that imposing liability purely on the basis of the defendant's supply of the alcohol would undesirably dilute individual responsibility, a position which led the High Court of Australia to deny that a licensed club owed a duty of care to its patrons to take care to prevent them from drinking to excess (*Cole v South Tweed Heads Rugby League Football Club* (2004) 217 CLR 469; see also *CAL No 14 Pty Ltd v Scott* (2009) 239 CLR 390). In Canada, however, a contrary decision was reached in *Jordan House Ltd v Menow* (1973) 38 DLR (3rd) 105. The plaintiff was ejected from the defendant's hotel in a state of extreme inebriation and was struck by a vehicle as he made his way home on foot along the main highway. The Supreme Court found that the defendant had breached its duty of care towards him by continuing to serve him when he was intoxicated and turning him out onto the road when there was a probable risk of personal injury. (Cf *Childs v Desormeaux* [2006] 1 SCR 641, distinguishing between commercial and social hosts in the context of liability to third parties: see later in III.)

English law's reluctance to recognise a duty on the purveyors of alcohol may be contrasted with its approach to the supply of products which present dangers that are not obvious to ordinary people. It is well established, for example, that manufacturers must supply appropriate instructions and warnings with their products (*Vacwell v BDH* [1971] 1 QB 88). The liability for failure to warn can often be regarded as one for misfeasance rather than pure nonfeasance, as the supply of the product and the failure to warn may be two aspects of a single course of conduct that makes the claimant worse off. But a liability for nonfeasance proper may arise where a latent defect is discovered in a product after it has reached the consumer, for the discovery of the defect may create a new duty to take reasonable steps to warn past customers (*Hobbs (Farms) v Baxenden* [1992] 1 Lloyd's Rep 54 at 65, per Sir Michael

Ogden QC; see also *Rivtow Marine Ltd v Washington Iron Works* [1974] SCR 1189). It has been argued that the approach of the courts in such cases in fact reflects a broader principle by which the *innocent* doing of harm or creation of a risk gives rise to a positive duty. The classic example is the motorist who without fault runs into another person: it is suggested in such a case that the motorist has a duty to summon help, even though they were not to blame for the accident (see Honoré, *op. cit.*, p. 47).

Assumption of Responsibility: Further Analysis

Most frequently, duties of affirmative action are undertaken by contract, in which case liability may be concurrent in contract and tort (see *Henderson v Merrett Syndicates Ltd*, extracted in Ch. 8.III.3). But a contractual undertaking may be sufficient to generate a duty of affirmative action towards a third party, as where a testator engages a solicitor to write a will in favour of certain beneficiaries (see *White v Jones*, extracted in Ch. 8.IV). Or the undertaking of responsibility may arise wholly independently of contract, as where school authorities assume responsibility for the welfare of young children (see *Barnes v Hants County Council* [1969] 1 WLR 1563). In many cases, the undertaking will be made by non-verbal conventions which 'are often unclear in their implications' (Honoré, *op. cit.*, p. 47) and the court will be left with the difficult task of determining precisely what the duty is. Honoré elaborates:

> A good example, important in practice, is that of a householder who allows someone, family, friend, or stranger, into his home for a cup of tea, or as a guest at a party, or for a short or longer visit. Opening the door and inviting in is significant, but what duty does it import if the visitor wants to stay on, or falls ill, or is reluctant to leave because of the weather, or has no alternative accommodation?

Honoré suggests that liability is likely to be restricted to those cases where the guest is rendered dependent upon the host, for example because of sudden and incapacitating illness.

It will usually be possible to infer an assumption of responsibility only in cases where there is an intention to benefit a small and clearly defined class. In *Sutradhar v National Environment Research Council*, noted earlier, the Court of Appeal found it 'absurd' to suggest that the British Geological Survey, by undertaking testing of the wells, had assumed responsibility to a large part of the Bangladeshi population in relation to the safety of its water: see [2004] PNLR 30 at [24], per Kennedy LJ (affirmed without reference to this point by the House of Lords). Cf. *Watson v British Boxing Board of Control* [2001] QB 1134: boxing regulator assuming responsibility for the adequacy of emergency medical facilities for fighters in an approved title bout.

As noted earlier, there has been a tendency in English law to require proof of an undertaking by the defendant on a particular occasion, rather than resting a duty of affirmative action on some wider basis, such as the defendant's office or position of responsibility. On the facts of *Barrett*, there was nothing to be gained by investigating the possibility that the officer's mere occupation of a position of responsibility *vis-à-vis* the deceased might have been enough to give rise to a duty to take care of him. But what if the commanding officer, having come across the deceased in a comatose state, had simply ignored him? It may be that on these facts the officer would have been bound to assume responsibility for the deceased, in accordance with the established principle that employers owe a duty to take reasonable care of employees who are taken sick or injured while at work (*Kasapis v Laimos* [1959] 2 Lloyd's Rep 378 at 381, per Salmon J).

Another clear example of affirmative duties arising by virtue of the defendant's position of responsibility is in the case of hazards which arise on the defendant's land and pose danger to their neighbours.

Goldman v Hargrave [1967] 1 AC 645 (Privy Council)

The appellant was the owner and occupier of land adjacent to that of the respondents. On 25 February 1961, lightning struck a tall redgum tree on the appellant's land and it began to burn. Early the next morning the appellant telephoned the district fire officer and asked for a tree-feller to be sent. The tree was cut down about midday the same day. Up to this time the appellant's conduct in relation to the fire was not open to criticism. But he then decided to let the tree burn itself out and took no further steps to prevent the fire spreading. It was found that he could have extinguished the fire by spraying it with water either that same evening or the following morning; this would have been the prudent way of proceeding. On 1 March the weather changed and strong gusts of wind caused the fire to revive and spread on to the respondents' adjoining property, causing extensive damage. The respondents failed at first instance in their actions for damages, but succeeded before the High Court of Australia. The appellant appealed to the Privy Council.

Lord Wilberforce (delivering the opinion of the Privy Council)

[T]he case is not one where a person has brought a source of danger on to his land, nor one where an occupier has so used his property as to cause a danger to his neighbour. It is one where an occupier, faced with a hazard accidentally arising on his land, fails to act with reasonable prudence so as to remove the hazard. The issue is therefore whether in such a case the occupier is guilty of legal negligence, which involves the issue whether he is under a duty of care, and if so, what is the scope of that duty . . .

What then is the scope of an occupier's duty, with regard to his neighbour, as to hazards arising on his land? With the possible exception of hazard of fire, to which their Lordships will shortly revert, it is only in comparatively recent times that the law has recognised an occupier's duty as one of a more positive character than merely to abstain from creating, or adding to, a source of danger or annoyance. It was for long satisfied with the conception of separate or autonomous proprietors, each of which was entitled to exploit his territory in a 'natural' manner and none of whom was obliged to restrain or direct the operations of nature in the interest of avoiding harm to his neighbours . . .

A decision which, it can now be seen, marked a turning point in the law was that of *Job Edwards Ltd v Birmingham Navigations* [1924] 1 KB 341. The hazard in that case was a fire which originated in a refuse dump placed on land by the act of a third party. When the fire threatened to invade the neighbouring land, the owners of the latter, by agreement, entered and extinguished the fire at a cost of some £1,000. The issue in the action was whether the owners of the land, where the fire was, were liable to bear part of the cost. The Court of Appeal by a majority answered this question negatively, but Scrutton LJ's dissenting judgment contained the following passage (at pp. 357–8):

> There is a great deal to be said for the view that if a man finds a dangerous and artificial thing on his land, which he and those for whom he is responsible did not put there; if he knows that if left alone it will damage other persons; if by reasonable care he can render it harmless, as if by stamping on a fire just beginning from a trespasser's match he can extinguish it; that then if he does nothing, he has 'permitted it to continue', and becomes responsible for it. This would base the liability on negligence, and not on the duty of insuring damage from a dangerous thing under *Rylands v Fletcher*. I appreciate that to get negligence you must have a duty to be careful, but I think on principle that a landowner has a duty to take reasonable care not to allow his land to remain a receptacle for a thing which may, if not rendered harmless, cause damage to his neighbours.

... In 1940 the dictum of Scrutton LJ passed into the law of England when it was approved by the House of Lords in *Sedleigh-Denfield v O'Callaghan* [1940] AC 880. Their Lordships need not cite from this case in any detail since it is now familiar law. It establishes the occupier's liability with regard to a hazard created on his land by a trespasser, of which he has knowledge, when he fails to take reasonable steps to remove it . . .

The appellant, inevitably, accepts the development, or statement, of the law which the *Sedleigh-Denfield* case contains—as it was accepted by the High Court of Australia. He seeks to establish, however, a distinction between the type of hazard which was there involved, namely one brought about by human agency such as the act of a trespasser, and one arising from natural causes, or Act of God. In relation to hazards of this kind it was submitted that an [occupier is under no duty to abate] it, and that his liability only commences if [he does some act which] causes the risk or danger to his neighbour's [property...]

[Their Lordships reject] the suggested distinction, that it is well [established that] regards many hazardous conditions arising [from natural causes]—particularly is this the case as regards [fire, which] unless detected in flagrante delicto, is [...] when faced with the initial stages of a [fire, whether natural or] man-made before he can decide on his [...] bound to prove the human origin of the [...] so, however irresponsibly the occupier [...] inconvenient, but also it lacks, in their [...]

> **Held — In favour of C, D liable in nuisance. (Allowing fire to burn out instead of using water to diminish it was an unforeseeable risk and unreasonable (Privy Council)**

Within the class of situations in which the occupier is himself without responsibility for the origin of the fire, one may ask in vain what relevant difference there is between a fire caused by a human agency such as a trespasser and one caused by Act of God or nature. A difference in degree—as to the potency of the agency—one can see but none that is in principle relevant to the occupier's duty to act. It was suggested as a logical basis for the distinction that in the case of a hazard originating in an act of man, an occupier who fails to deal with it can be said to be using his land in a manner detrimental to his neighbour and so to be within the classical field of responsibility in nuisance, whereas this cannot be said when the hazard originates without human action so long at least as the occupier merely abstains. The fallacy of this argument is that, as already explained, the basis of the occupier's liability lies not in the use of his land: in the absence of 'adoption' there is no such use: but in the neglect of action in the face of something which may damage his neighbour. To this, the suggested distinction is irrelevant.

Their Lordships advised that the appeal should be dismissed.

COMMENTARY

This is a very interesting case to contrast with *Capital & Counties v Hampshire CC* (see earlier). Although the latter case decides that the fire service owes no duty of care to the owner or occupier of burning property simply by virtue of its attendance at the fire scene, *Goldman* makes it clear that the owner/occupier owes a duty to neighbours who are threatened by the fire. If the owner/occupier is prevented from fighting the fire by the attendance of the fire brigade, and the fire brigade fights the fire so negligently that it escapes onto neighbouring land, whom (if anyone) can the neighbour sue for damages?

For the historical background to the case and further discussion see Lunney, '*Goldman v Hargrave* (1967)', *Mitchell & Mitchell*, ch. 8.

In such cases, the owner/occupier's liability seems to arise by virtue of the responsibility he assumes as an incident of his ownership or occupation of the land, which should be regarded as a privilege, of benefit to the owner/occupier but carrying with it certain obligations, including that of ensuring that the land does not become an unreasonable source of danger to neighbours. See *Robinson v Chief Constable of West Yorkshire* [2018] AC at [69], per Lord Reed, explaining that these are 'responsibilities which can be understood as arising from [the occupier's] exclusive right of possession'. The same obligations often arise concurrently in the separate tort of private nuisance (see Ch. 11). But note that negligence may be the only possible claim where the claimant is not the owner of the land affected, or where the complaint is of personal injury or interference with some other interest which is not an interest in land. (These restrictions on the scope of liability in nuisance were recognised by the House of Lords in *Hunter v Canary Wharf* [1997] AC 655 (HL): considered in Ch. 11.II.3.) Comparable considerations underlie the occupier's affirmative duty to ensure that their land is reasonably safe for those coming onto it, whether as visitors or trespassers. This duty, recognised initially by the common law, is now governed by the Occupiers' Liability Acts of 1957 and 1984 (see Ch. 10).

The negligence liability of a landowner in respect of dangers created by trespassers, as opposed to natural hazards, is considered later in this chapter.

It is now worth considering what other positions of responsibility besides that of the owner/occupier of land give rise to duties of affirmative action.

Other Offices and Positions of Responsibility

In general, English law has tended to base liability on an assumption of responsibility on a specific occasion, rather than on a general responsibility attaching to particular offices or positions. In the case of a doctor, for instance, it is clear that responsibility is generally limited to the doctor–patient relationship and does not arise simply because the doctor is in the best position to help an injured person. A doctor coming upon someone injured in the street is not obliged to act as a good Samaritan (see *Capital & Counties v Hampshire CC*, extracted earlier; but it may make a difference if a GP were requested to give immediately necessary treatment to an accident or emergency victim in their practice area, as this would be required by their statutory terms of service: see J. Laing and J. McHale (eds), *Principles of Medical Law*, 4th edn (Oxford: OUP, 2017), para. 3.37). However, staff in a hospital casualty department may assume a duty of care by helping or advising a person who is seeking attention (*Barnett v Chelsea & Kensington Hospital Management Committee* [1969] 1 QB 428), and it may yet be held that, as a casualty ward is presented as a service to those requiring treatment in an emergency, there would be a duty to treat a person who collapses in the ward even if they have not yet seen a doctor or nurse. See further Williams, 'Medical Samaritans: Is there a Duty to Treat?' (2001) 21 OJLS 393.

Notwithstanding this reluctance to recognise general responsibilities arising out of offices or positions, there are perhaps some cases which can be classified under this heading. The position of occupiers *vis-à-vis* entrants on their premises and of employers *vis-à-vis* their employees has already been considered. It may also be mentioned in this context that institutions that take in and provide accommodation or other services for vulnerable persons will often owe a duty of care that extends to the prevention of even self-inflicted injury: see, e.g., *Reeves v Commissioner of Police of the Metropolis* [2000] 1 AC 360 (suicide by prisoner remanded in custody; Lord Hoffmann noted, at 369, that amongst such prisoners there is a particularly high risk of suicide even if they are of sound mind) and *Savage v South Essex Partnership NHS Foundation Trust* [2009] 1 AC 681 (suicide by psychiatric patient after absconding from hospital; as to the common law duty of care, see [3] per Lord Scott).

In *Secretary of State for the Home Department v Robb* [1995] Fam 127, it was held that prison authorities have no right to stop a prisoner from committing suicide by starving themselves to death. How is this consistent with the recognition of a duty to prevent a prisoner taking their own life? Perhaps it is because such a duty is only to deprive the prisoner, so far as possible, of the means of taking their own life, rather than actually to use force against them. If so, what if a guard were to go into a cell while the prisoner was attempting to asphyxiate himself: would they have the duty (or the right) to use force to stop them?

The Parent–Child Relationship

One situation in which we might expect to find a general responsibility for the welfare of another is where there is a parent–child relationship. However, there is no clear English authority on the point, and courts in other common law jurisdictions have tended to limit the parent's responsibility to those particular occasions on which they have undertaken to care for the child (see further McIvor, 'Expelling the Myth of the Parental Duty to Rescue' (2000) 12 CFLQ 229). Hence, Barwick CJ has stated in the High Court of Australia (*Hahn v Conley* (1971) 126 CLR 276 (HC) at 283–4):

whilst in particular situations and because of their nature or elements, there will be a duty on the person into whose care the child has been placed and accepted to take reasonable care to protect the child against foreseeable danger, there is no general duty of care in that respect imposed by the law upon a parent simply because of the blood relationship.

A critical concern in such cases has been that families might be threatened with financial ruin if a third party sued by an infant plaintiff were to seek contribution from the infant's parents as joint tortfeasors (see *McCallion v Dodd* [1966] NZLR 710 at 727, per Turner J). In the United States, such considerations resulted in the even more extreme response of the judicial recognition of a parental immunity against suits brought by their children (see, e.g., *Hewellette v George*, 68 Miss 703, 9 So 885 (1891)). However, in more recent times many courts have resiled from that position by refusing to recognise the immunity, abolishing it or developing exceptions to it (see *Rousey v Rousey*, 528 A 2d 416 (1987) and, generally, Dobbs, Heyden & Bublick, § 358).

One thing that does seem clear in English law is that there is no general duty of 'good parenting': see *Barrett v Enfield London Borough Council* [2001] 2 AC 550 at 587, per Lord Hutton. In *XA v YA* [2011] PIQR P1, Thirlwall J cited Lord Hutton's dictum in the context of a claim by a man who had been repeatedly and severely beaten by his father as a child, and alleged that his mother was negligent in failing to stop the beatings. The judge found that this claim was time-barred, but proceeded to make some observations about the existence of a duty of care (at [139]ff). She accepted that a duty of care would arise where a parent was looking after the child on a particular occasion, but inclined to the view that it would not be fair, just and reasonable to recognise a duty of care in respect of the family's ongoing life in general, which on the facts could only have been discharged by the mother leaving the father and taking the children with her or by the children being taken into care. Is this tantamount to saying that the mother has no legal obligation to do anything at all to protect the child so long as she is not actually present when an assault occurs?

On the liability of parents to their children generally, see C. McIvor, *Third Party Liability in Tort* (Oxford: Hart, 2006), pp. 21–4 and, for a comparative European analysis, M. Martín-Casals (ed.), *Children in Tort Law, Part II: Children as Victims* (Vienna: Springer, 2006).

* The Claimant's claim failed, the court said D (Mother) did not owe a duty of care to her son under common law + claim was statute barred s 11 of the Limitation Act.

III. Liability for the Acts of a Third Party

The question of liability for the acts of a third party raises similar considerations to those examined in the previous section. Indeed, often the complaint is actually of an omission, for example a failure to control a third party, or to prevent a dangerous situation from being sparked off by a third party. But not all third-party cases involve omissions. Sometimes the complaint is simply that the defendant provided the third party with the opportunity or the means to injure the claimant, and it is that conduct which is alleged to be negligent, regardless of whether the defendant unreasonably failed at some subsequent point of time to intervene to prevent the injury.

Third-party act cases often raise the same objections to the imposition of liability as do 'pure' omissions cases (i.e. those not involving third-party action). But there is also an additional difficulty: in some circumstances, the intervention of a third party 'breaks the chain of causation' or, as many modern authorities prefer to see things, falls outside the scope of the defendant's liability (see Ch. 5.II). This is generally the case with deliberate third-party interventions, and may also be the case with grossly negligent interventions. For this reason, considerations which may be sufficient to ground a duty of affirmative action in the pure omissions cases (e.g. the fact that the defendant's conduct, taken as a whole, has exposed the claimant to increased danger) may not warrant the imposition of liability in respect of injury caused by a third party. If a motorist without fault injures a pedestrian in a collision, there may be a duty to stop and render assistance, and the motorist may be held liable if they neglect the duty and the pedestrian suffers from exposure as a consequence. But it seems unlikely that the motorist could be held liable for theft of the pedestrian's wallet by an opportunistic pickpocket, even though this would not have occurred but for the failure to render assistance and even though the motorist had left the pedestrian exposed to a danger against which they were unable to defend themselves.

Nevertheless, the law does impose liability for the acts of third parties in certain exceptional situations which are broadly similar to those where there is liability for pure omissions. Those who see it as problematic to trace causation through the intervening act resolve this difficulty by recognising a special type of duty—a duty to control a third party, a duty to safeguard a dangerous thing, etc.—which allows for the compensation of injuries where there is a weaker form of causal connection than is usually required, for example where the defendant provides the means or opportunity for a third party to bring about the harm. The defendant's liability is not, on this analysis, for causing the harm, but for occasioning it (see Hart & Honoré, pp. 194–204).

> **Home Office v Dorset Yacht Co** [1970] AC 1004
>
> A party of borstal trainees was working on Brownsea Island in Poole Harbour under the supervision and control of three borstal officers. During the night seven of the trainees escaped. It was alleged that at the time of the escape the officers had retired to bed, in breach of their instructions, leaving the trainees to their own devices. The escapees went aboard a yacht which they found nearby, set it in motion and caused it to collide with the plaintiffs' yacht which was moored in the vicinity. The yacht was damaged by the collision and subsequently

by the conduct of the trainees when they boarded the vessel. The plaintiffs sued the Home Office for damages. Preliminary proceedings were initiated in order to determine whether the Home Office or the borstal officers owed a duty of care to the plaintiffs. It was admitted that the Home Office would be vicariously liable if an action lay against any of the officers. The Court of Appeal having found in favour of the plaintiffs, the Home Office appealed to the House of Lords.

Lord Reid

[I]t is said that the respondents must fail because there is a general principle that no person can be responsible for the acts of another who is not his servant or acting on his behalf. But here the ground of liability is not responsibility for the acts of the escaping trainees; it is liability for damage caused by the carelessness of these officers in the knowledge that their carelessness would probably result in the trainees causing damage of this kind. So the question is really one of remoteness of damage. And I must consider to what extent the law regards the acts of another person as breaking the chain of causation between the defendants' carelessness and the damage to the plaintiff.

There is an obvious difference between a case where all the links between the carelessness and the damage are inanimate so that, looking back after the event, it can be seen that the damage was in fact the inevitable result of the careless act or omission, and a case where one of the links is some human action. In the former case the damage was in fact caused by the careless conduct, however unforeseeable it may have been at the time that anything like this would happen. At one time the law was that unforeseeability was no defence (*Re Polemis and Furness, Whithy & Co Ltd* [1921] 3 KB 560). But the law now is that there is no liability unless the damage was of a kind which was foreseeable (*Overseas Tankship (UK) Ltd v Morts Dock & Engineering Co Ltd (The Wagon Mound)* [1961] AC 388).

On the other hand, if human action (other than an instinctive reaction) is one of the links in the chain, it cannot be said that, looking back, the damage was the inevitable result of the careless conduct. No one in practice accepts the possible philosophic view that everything that happens was predetermined. Yet it has never been the law that the intervention of human action always prevents the ultimate damage from being regarded as having been caused by the original carelessness. The convenient phrase *novus actus interveniens* denotes those cases where such action is regarded as breaking the chain and preventing the damage from being held to be caused by the careless conduct. But every day there are many cases where, although one of the connecting links is deliberate human action, the law has no difficulty in holding that the defendant's conduct caused the plaintiff loss.

> There are some propositions that . . . are . . . beyond question in connection with this class of case. One is that human action does not *per se* sever the connected sequence of acts. The mere fact that human action intervenes does not prevent the sufferer from saying that damages for injury due to that human action, as one of the elements in the sequence, is recoverable from the original wrongdoer.

(per Lord Wright in *Lord v Pacific Steam Navigation Co Ltd, The Oropesa* [1943] P 32 at 37).

What then is the dividing line? Is it foreseeability or is it such a degree of probability as warrants the conclusion that the intervening human conduct was the natural and probable result of what preceded it? There is a world of difference between the two. If I buy a ticket in a lottery or enter a football pool it is foreseeable that I may win a very large prize—some competitor must win it. But, whatever hopes gamblers may entertain, no one could say that winning such a prize is a natural and probable result of entering such a competition . . .

[W]here human action forms one of the links between the original wrongdoing of the defendant and the loss suffered by the plaintiff, that action must at least have been something very likely to happen if it is not to be regarded as *novus actus interveniens* breaking the chain of causation. I do not think that a mere foreseeable possibility is or should be sufficient, for then the intervening human action can more properly be regarded as a new cause than as a consequence of the original wrongdoing. But if the intervening action was likely to happen I do not think it can matter whether that action was innocent or tortious or criminal. Unfortunately tortious or criminal action by a third party is often the 'very kind of thing' which is likely to happen as a result of the wrongful or careless act of the defendant. And in the present case, on the facts which we must assume at this stage, I think that the taking of a boat by the escaping trainees and their unskilful navigation leading to damage to another vessel were the very kind of thing that these borstal officers ought to have seen to be likely.

There was an attempt to draw a distinction between loss caused to the plaintiff by failure to control an adult of full capacity and loss caused by failure to control a child or mental defective. As regards causation, no doubt it is easier to infer *novus actus interveniens* in the case of an adult but that seems to me to be the only distinction. In the present case on the assumed facts there would in my view be no *novus actus* when the trainees damaged the respondents' property and I would therefore hold that damage to have been caused by the borstal officers' negligence.

Lord Morris of Borth-y-Gest

[A] normal or even modest measure of prescience and prevision must have led any ordinary person, but rather specially an officer in charge, to realise that the boys might wish to escape and might use a yacht if one was near at hand to help them to do so. That is exactly what it is said that seven boys did. In my view, the officers must have appreciated that either in an escape attempt or by reason of some other prompting the boys might interfere with one of the yachts with consequent likelihood of doing some injury to it. The risk of such a happening was glaringly obvious. The possibilities of damage being done to one of the nearby yachts (assuming that they were nearby) were many and apparent. In that situation and in those circumstances I consider that a duty of care was owed by the officers to the owners of the nearby yachts. The principle expressed in Lord Atkin's classic words in his speech in *Donoghue v Stevenson* [1932] AC 562 at 580 would seem to be directly applicable.

Lord Pearson

It seems to me that this case ought to, and does, come within the *Donoghue v Stevenson* principle unless there is some sufficient reason for not applying the principle to this case. Therefore, one has to consider the suggested reasons for not applying the principle here.

Proximity or remoteness. As there is no evidence, one can only judge from the allegations in the statement of claim. It seems clear that there was sufficient proximity; there was geographical proximity and it was foreseeable that the damage was likely to occur unless some care was taken to prevent it. In other cases a difficult problem may arise as to how widely the 'neighbourhood' extends, but no such problem faces the respondents in this case.

Act of third party. In *Weld-Blundell v Stephens* [1920] AC 956 at 986 Lord Sumner said:

> In general (apart from special contracts and relations and the maxim respondeat superior), even though A is in fault, he is not responsible for injury to C which B, a stranger to him, deliberately chooses to do.

In *Smith v Leurs* (1945) 70 CLR 256 at 261–2 Dixon J said:

> apart from vicarious responsibility, one man may be responsible to another for the harm done to the latter by a third person; he may be responsible on the ground that the act of the third person could not have taken place but for his own fault or breach of duty. There is more than one description of duty the breach of which may produce this consequence.

> For instance, it may be a duty of care in reference to things involving special danger. It may even be a duty of care with reference to the control of actions or conduct of the third person. It is, however, exceptional to find in the law a duty to control another's actions to prevent harm to strangers. The general rule is that one man is under no duty of controlling another to prevent his doing damage to a third. There are, however, special relations which are the source of a duty of this nature. It appears now to be recognised that it is incumbent upon a parent who maintains control over a young child to take reasonable care so to exercise that control as to avoid conduct on his part exposing the person or property of others to unreasonable danger. Parental control, where it exists, must be exercised with due care to prevent the child inflicting intentional damage on others or causing damage by conduct involving unreasonable risk of injury to others.

In my opinion, this case falls under the exception and not the rule, because there was a special relation. The borstal boys were under the control of the Home Office's officers, and control imports responsibility. The boys' interference with the boats appears to have been a direct result of the Home Office's officers' failure to exercise proper control and supervision. Problems may arise in other cases as to the responsibility of the Home Office's officers for acts done by borstal boys when they have completed their escape from control and are fully at large and acting independently. No such problem faces the respondents in this case.

Lord Diplock

The branch of English law which deals with civil wrongs abounds with instances of acts and, more particularly, of omissions which give rise to no legal liability in the doer or omitter for loss or damage sustained by others as a consequence of the act or omission, however reasonably or probably that loss or damage might have been anticipated. The very parable of the good Samaritan (Luke x, verse 30) which was evoked by Lord Atkin in *Donoghue v Stevenson* illustrates, in the conduct of the priest and of the Levite who passed by on the other side, an omission which was likely to have as its reasonable and probable consequence damage to the health of the victim of the thieves, but for which the priest and Levite would have incurred no civil liability in English law. Examples could be multiplied. One may cause loss to a tradesman by withdrawing one's custom although the goods which he supplies are entirely satisfactory . . . [O]ne need not warn . . . [one's neighbour] of a risk of physical danger to which he is about to expose himself unless there is some special relationship between one and him such as that of occupier of land and visitor; one may watch one's neighbour's goods being ruined by a thunderstorm although the slightest effort on one's part could protect them from the rain and one may do so with impunity unless there is some special relationship between one and him such as that of bailor and bailee . . .

In the present appeal, too, the conduct of the Home Office which is called in question differs from the kind of conduct discussed in *Donoghue v Stevenson* in at least two special characteristics. First, the actual damage sustained by the respondents was the direct consequence of a tortious act done with conscious volition by a third party responsible in law for his own acts and this act was interposed between the act of the Home Office complained of and the sustension of damage by the respondents. Secondly, there are two separate 'neighbour relationships' of the Home Office involved, a relationship with the respondents and a relationship with the third party. These are capable of giving rise to conflicting duties of care. This appeal, therefore, also raises the lawyer's question 'Am I my brother's keeper'? A question which may also receive a restricted reply . . .

It is common knowledge, of which judicial notice may be taken, that borstal training often fails to achieve its purpose of reformation, and that trainees when they have ceased to be detained in custody revert to crime and commit tortious damage to the person and property of others. But so do criminals who have never been apprehended and criminals who have been released from custody on completion of their sentences or earlier pursuant to a statutory power to do so. The risk of sustaining damage from the tortious acts of criminals is shared by the public at large. It has never been recognised at common law as giving rise to any cause of action against anyone but the criminal himself. It would seem arbitrary and therefore unjust to single out for the special privilege of being able to recover compensation from the authorities responsible for the prevention of crime a person whose property was damaged by the tortious act of a criminal, merely because the damage to him happened to be caused by a criminal who had escaped from custody before completion of his sentence instead of by one who had been lawfully released or who had been put on probation or given a suspended sentence or who had never been previously apprehended at all. To give rise to a duty on the part of the custodian owed to a member of the public to take reasonable care to prevent a borstal trainee from escaping from his custody before completion of the trainee's sentence there should be some relationship between the custodian and the person to whom the duty is owed which exposes that person to a particular risk of damage in consequence of that escape which is different in its incidence from the general risk of damage from criminal acts of others which he shares with all members of the public.

What distinguishes a borstal trainee who has escaped from one who has been duly released from custody, is his liability to recapture, and the distinctive added risk which is a reasonably foreseeable consequence of a failure to exercise due care in preventing him from escaping is the likelihood that in order to elude pursuit immediately on the discovery of his absence the escaping trainee may steal or appropriate and damage property which is situated in the vicinity of the place of detention from which he has escaped.

So long as Parliament is content to leave the general risk of damage from criminal acts to lie where it falls without any remedy except against the criminal himself, the courts would be exceeding their limited function in developing the common law to meet changing conditions if they were to recognise a duty of care to prevent criminals escaping from penal custody owed to a wider category of members of the public than those whose property was exposed to an exceptional added risk by the adoption of a custodial system for young offenders which increased the likelihood of their escape unless due care was taken by those responsible for their custody.

I should therefore hold that any duty of a borstal officer to use reasonable care to prevent a borstal trainee from escaping from his custody was owed only to persons whom he could reasonably foresee had property situate in the vicinity of the place of detention of the detainee which the detainee was likely to steal or to appropriate and damage in the course of eluding immediate pursuit and recapture. Whether or not any person fell within this category would depend on the facts of the particular case including the previous criminal and escaping record of the individual trainee concerned and the nature of the place from which he escaped.

[On the facts of the present case, Lord Diplock agreed that the borstal officers did owe a duty of care to the plaintiff yacht club.]

Viscount Dilhorne (dissenting) stated that the absence of any authority for the duty alleged showed that no such duty in fact existed. He added: 'If there should be one, that is, in my view, a matter for the legislature and not for the courts.'

Appeal dismissed.

COMMENTARY

This case provides an excellent example of the way in which different judicial approaches can lead to the same result. Lord Reid conceived the legal issue arising in respect of intervening acts as one of causation, and relied upon considerations of foreseeability or probability as the key to determining whether the causal chain could be traced through the deliberate conduct of the boys; it was the degree of foreseeability or probability present on the facts that served to distinguish those cases where liability should be imposed from those where it should not. The other Law Lords, however, focused on the existence and scope of the defendant's duty of care, Lord Morris addressing these questions in terms of the foreseeability of the risk, Lord Pearson (explicitly) and Lord Diplock (implicitly) relying on considerations of proximity; for them, this provided a mechanism for limiting the scope of the defendant's liability in an appropriate case. Tension between the different approaches still exists in the current law, though they are unlikely to lead to different outcomes on the facts of individual cases.

Would the Home Office be liable for the loss occasioned by a burglary committed by a trainee on parole or a prisoner permitted to go out to attend a funeral? Lord Reid thought that, in the vast majority of such cases, there would be no liability, emphasising that 'it would have to be shown that the commission of the offence was the natural and probable, as distinct from merely a foreseeable, result of the release—that there was no *novus actus interveniens*' (at 1032). A comparable scenario arose in *K v Secretary of State for the Home Department* [2002] EWCA Civ 775. The claimant was raped by a foreign citizen, who had a criminal record in the United Kingdom and had been detained by the Home Office pending deportation, but was then released for unexplained reasons. She sued the Home Office for damages, but the Court of Appeal struck out her claim for lack of any relationship of proximity between her and the Home Office such as would create a duty of care. The defendant's mere knowledge that another person posed an especially grave risk of harm to the public at large was not enough to create the necessary proximity: 'A defendant does not become the world's insurer against the grave danger (where the danger is general) posed by a third agency, which he might control but does not, by virtue only of the fact that he appreciates that the danger exists' (at [29], per Laws LJ). The result is in accord with the view of C. McIvor, *Third Party Liability in Tort* (Oxford: Hart, 2006), who argues that the duty to control is limited to situations in which there is a very strong relationship of control between the 'responsible' defendant and the 'irresponsible' third party, the claimant comes within a narrowly defined class of potential victims and the harm-causing conduct of the third party was highly foreseeable in the circumstances (p. 19).

Cf. *Kalma v African Minerals Ltd* [2020] EWCA Civ 144, where the defendants, owners of a large iron ore mine in Sierra Leone, were found to have had no control over police they called to deal with fuel thefts and other attempts by local residents to disrupt the mine's operation, nor to be in a relationship of proximity with residents injured or in one case killed when the police violently overreacted to the situation. For those reasons, and because the victims fell within a large and indeterminate class of local inhabitants who might foreseeably have suffered harm, the defendant company owed no duty of care.

'Control Imports Responsibility'

It had been established prior to the *Dorset Yacht* case that a school may be held liable to a third party injured by the foreseeable negligence of a pupil under its control. In *Carmarthenshire County Council v Lewis* [1955] AC 549, the deceased lorry driver lost his life when he was forced to swerve his vehicle in an effort to avoid a small boy and drove into a lamp post. The boy, aged about four, had strayed onto the busy main road from the grounds of a nursery school maintained by the appellants, the local education authority, after being left unattended in the classroom for around ten minutes; during his teacher's absence he got out of the classroom and made his way out of the school playground through an unlocked gate. The deceased's widow successfully brought an action against the education authority in negligence but it was only in the House of Lords that the authority was held liable for its own negligence in failing to prevent the child escaping (rather than vicariously liable for the negligence of the teacher). Although the leading speech of Lord Reid focused on the foreseeability of the chain of events that occurred, consistently with his approach in the *Dorset Yacht* case some years later, the modern approach is to limit the scope of any duty of care quite restrictively, and, viewed from this perspective, it is probably best to regard the case as resting on the school authority's assumption of responsibility for control of the child, which created a relationship of proximity with those who were foreseeably endangered by him. This responsibility can be seen as a counterpart to that which the authority assumes to the children themselves. The latter entails, amongst other things, a duty to provide assistance to any child who falls ill while at school and to protect pupils from accidental injury at the hands of third parties (e.g. if allowed to stray onto a busy main road: see *Barnes v Hants County Council* [1969] 1 WLR 1563). The duty no doubt extends to protecting schoolchildren from deliberate acts (e.g. of a known paedophile who is seen wandering in school grounds). See further McIvor, *op. cit.*, pp. 24–35.

The *Dorset Yacht* case goes beyond *Carmarthenshire County Council v Lewis* by recognising a liability for negligent failure to prevent intentional misconduct by a minor for whom the defendant has assumed responsibility, even though the minor is old enough to be held responsible for his actions himself. Since then, efforts have been made to extend the case's authority from the context of a custodial relationship to other categories of relationship, as considered in the following sections of this commentary.

Psychiatric Patients

In *Tarasoff v University of California*, 551 P 2d 334 (1976), the Supreme Court of California held that a psychologist, whose patient confided to him his intention to kill a particular woman, might have a duty to warn the woman of the risk to her life and could be held liable if his breach of that duty was a contributory cause of her death at the patient's hands. A comparison may be made with the English case of *Palmer v Tees Health Authority* [2000] PIQR P1, where it was alleged that the defendant health authority was responsible for the abduction and murder of the claimant's 4-year-old daughter by a psychiatric patient who had been discharged from the defendant's hospital the previous year; he remained an out-patient but had failed to attend his most recent appointment. The claimant contended that the defendant had been negligent in failing to recognise the risk that the man might commit serious offences against children, and consequently to take steps to reduce the risk, for example by keeping him in hospital. The Court of Appeal struck out the action on the basis of a lack of proximity. The defendant had not assumed any responsibility towards the victim, who had been just an unidentifiable member of the large class of those at risk. The court reserved its opinion as to whether there might be sufficient proximity where the victim was identified or identifiable in advance, but Pill LJ commented (at 19):

> I see force in the submission that the question whether the identity of a victim is known ought not to determine whether the proximity test is passed. It is forcefully argued that the difference between the threat 'I will kill X' and the threat 'I will kill the first bald-headed man I meet' ought not to determine whether a duty is placed upon a defendant, though it would obviously go to the extent of the duty and the measures necessary to discharge it.

The issue subsequently came before the Court of Appeal in *Selwood v Durham County Council* [2012] PIQR P20 in an appeal from a striking-out order. The claimant was the designated social worker for one of the children of a mentally disturbed and violent man. In the course of family court proceedings relating to his children, which aggravated his mental health problems, the man was admitted to hospital as a voluntary patient. It was alleged that, while there, he repeatedly talked of wanting to harm the claimant and, in the course of a review of his situation, had said that he would 'kill her on the spot' if he saw her. At the end of the review, the man's doctor said that he could go home on a week's leave. The claimant was not told of the threat or the leave. Two days later, she was attacked and stabbed by the man at a scheduled case conference, suffering serious injuries. The man subsequently pleaded guilty to attempted murder. Ruling that the health authority treating him had arguably owed the claimant a duty of care, the Court of Appeal emphasised that this was not a case of a duty being owed to the world at large but one in which the claimant was a member of a small group of social workers who worked in close proximity and cooperation with the health authority's own employees. Do you think that a pre-existing relationship with the claimant ought to be regarded as necessary for the recognition of a duty of care in such a case? Cf. the alternative claim available under the Human Rights Act (considered later in IV) where, as here, the defendant is a public hospital.

Landlords and Tenants

In *Mitchell v Glasgow City Council* [2009] 1 AC 874, the deceased was attacked and killed by his next-door neighbour in council accommodation following a prolonged period of hostile, aggressive and antisocial behaviour on the neighbour's part. The council had known of the matter for some considerable time, and had issued the neighbour with warnings over his conduct. After further antisocial behaviour, it summoned the neighbour to a meeting, where he was told he could face eviction. He lost his temper and became abusive. On leaving the meeting, he returned home and committed the fatal assault. The deceased's family brought an action for damages against the council, alleging that it should have informed the deceased of its meeting with the neighbour, warned him he was at risk and alerted the police—none of which it had done. Rejecting the claim on the basis that the council owed the deceased no duty of care, the House of Lords affirmed that (at [29], per Lord Hope):

> as a general rule . . . a duty to warn another person that he is at risk of loss, injury or damage as the result of the criminal act of a third party will arise only where the person who is said to be under that duty has by his words or conduct assumed responsibility for the safety of the person who is at risk.

On the facts, there was no basis for saying that the council had assumed a responsibility to advise the deceased of the steps that it was taking, or in some other way had induced him to rely on its doing so. As the council knew of its tenant's history of aggression towards the deceased, and was responsible (culpably or not) for his outburst of anger on the occasion in question, was it justifiable for the House of Lords to conclude that the council owed the deceased no duty of care?

Mitchell governs the common law liability of both public and private landlords, but it should be noted that, under the Human Rights Act, a landlord that is a 'public authority' under the Act may have a duty to intervene where it knows or ought to know of a real and immediate risk to the tenant's life and may be required to compensate if it fails to do so. The Law Lords found that this demanding test was not satisfied on the facts of the case. For further analysis of the 'real and immediate risk' test see later in this chapter.

Parent Company Liability for Subsidiaries

One of the rapidly developing areas of negligence litigation in recent years has been parent company liability for the harmful activities of its subsidiary in another country. These cases raise a variety of factual and legal issues—for example, relating to jurisdiction and applicable law—but for present purposes what is significant is the attempt to establish that the parent company in the United Kingdom owed a duty of care to those suffering damage overseas, premised on its control of the subsidiary's activities. The liability has now been accepted in principle in two decisions of the Supreme Court, although in both of them the question for decision was only whether the existence of the duty of care was sufficiently arguable to be a triable issue, so one must be cautious not to read too much into the two judgments.

In *Lungowe v Vedanta Resources plc* [2020] AC 1045, a UK company was the parent of a subsidiary in Zambia that owned and operated a large copper mine there. The claimants were a group of 1,826 Zambian citizens living in the area. They were very poor members of rural farming communities served by watercourses which provided their only source of drinking water for themselves and their livestock, and irrigation for their crops. They claimed that their health and their farming activities had been damaged by repeated discharges of toxic matter from the mine into those watercourses over several years. They sought damages in the English courts, alleging (amongst other things) negligence on the part of the UK parent company in exercising its control over the Zambian subsidiary. The case came to the Supreme Court on the preliminary issue of whether the UK parent owed the local residents an arguable duty of care. Lord Briggs, giving the judgment of the Court, stated the relevant principles:

> 49. . . . [T]he liability of parent companies in relation to the activities of their subsidiaries is not, of itself, a distinct category of liability in common law negligence. Direct or indirect ownership by one company of all or a majority of the shares of another company (which is the irreducible essence of a parent/subsidiary relationship) may enable the parent to take control of the management of the operations of the business or of land owned by the subsidiary, but it does not impose any duty upon the parent to do so, whether owed to the subsidiary or, a fortiori, to anyone else. Everything depends on the extent to which, and the way in which, the parent availed itself of the opportunity to take over, intervene in, control, supervise or advise the management of the relevant operations (including land use) of the subsidiary. All that the existence of a parent-subsidiary relationship demonstrates is that the parent had such an opportunity.

On the pleaded facts, the Court ruled that it was indeed arguable that the UK parent had sufficient control of the Zambian subsidiary to give rise to a duty of care. It held itself out in its own published materials as exercising supervision and control over the subsidiary, and as having responsibility for the latter's environmental standards, and had taken active steps to implement those standards by training, monitoring and enforcement. That provided a sufficient basis for finding that further investigation of the facts at trial, with full disclosure of relevant documents, might disclose the requisite supervision and control for the alleged duty of care (see [53] and [61]). Lord Briggs underlined that indicia provided in earlier cases (*Chandler v Cape plc* [2012] 1 WLR 3111 and *AAA v Unilever plc* [2018] EWCA Civ 1532) as to the situations in which a parent company might be found to owe a duty of care to its subsidiary's employees or others affected by its activities ought not to be treated as a straitjacket as ultimately the issue turns on the application of basic principle.

A year after the *Vedanta* judgment, the same issue returned to the Supreme Court in *Okpabi v Royal Dutch Shell plc* [2021] 1 WLR 1294—to the apparent surprise of Lord Hamblen, delivering the judgment of the Court, who thought it might reasonably have been expected that the guidance provided by the *Vedanta* decision would have resolved the case before him without the need for a hearing (at [2]). That not being the case, Lord Hamblen reiterated the key parts of what Lord Briggs had said in *Vedanta*, underlining that the liability of parent companies in relation to the activities of their subsidiaries is not of itself a distinct category of negligence liability but to be determined on ordinary, general principles of the law of tort regarding the imposition of a duty of care, with a particular focus on the extent to which, and the way in which, the parent took over, intervened in, controlled, supervised or advised the management of the subsidiary's operations (at [25] and [146]). Lord Hamblen explained further:

> 147. In considering that question, control is just a starting point. The issue is the extent to which the parent did take over or share with the subsidiary the management of the relevant activity (here the pipeline operation). That may or may not be demonstrated by the parent controlling the subsidiary. In a sense, all parents control their subsidiaries. That control gives the parent the opportunity to get involved in management. But control of a company and de facto management of part of its activities are two different things. A subsidiary may maintain de jure control of its activities, but nonetheless delegate de facto management of part of them to emissaries of its parent.

The case involved environmental damage caused by oil spills in the Niger Delta affecting two local communities, who complained their water sources could no longer be safely used. The Nigerian company operating the pipelines that were alleged to have discharged the oil was a subsidiary of Royal Dutch Shell plc, domiciled in the United Kingdom. It was alleged that the latter owed the members of the two communities a duty of care on the basis that it exercised significant control over material aspects of the subsidiary's operations and/or assumed responsibility for those operations, including by the promulgation and imposition of mandatory health, safety and environmental policies, standards and manuals which failed to protect the claimants against the risk of foreseeable harm from the operations (at [7]). The Supreme Court ruled that this pleaded case raised a real issue to be tried, overturning the decision of the Court of Appeal, which had fallen into error in taking the view that the promulgation by a parent company of group-wide policies or standards could never in itself give rise to a duty of care (at [143]). That was clearly inconsistent with *Vedanta*.

It seems difficult to reconcile the court's insistence that, in Lord Hamblen's words, 'control is just a starting point', and that everything depends on how and to what extent the parent took over, intervened in, controlled, supervised or advised the management of the subsidiary's operations, with the clear statements in both cases that parent company liability is not a category of liability with its own special rules, but turns on the application of ordinary general principles of negligence. The court was evidently concerned to avoid the formulaic listing of specific situations in which the parent company would owe a duty of care in respect of its subsidiary's activities, and to encourage a more fact-sensitive inquiry into how and to what extent the parent actually exercised control over the subsidiary, but that is not inconsistent with a recognition that parent-subsidiary cases form a distinct pocket of case law whose development will likely be relatively autonomous from that of other instances of affirmative duties of control in negligence.

Another interesting issue left by the two judgments relates to assumption of responsibility as a factor militating in favour of a duty of care. In *Vedanta*, Lord Briggs said, at [53]: 'the parent may incur the relevant responsibility to third parties if, in published materials, it holds itself out as exercising that degree of supervision and control of its subsidiaries, even if it does not in fact do so. In such circumstances its very omission may constitute the abdication of a responsibility which it has publicly undertaken.' In *Okpabi*, at [148], Lord Hamblen cited this this as '[a] specific example of a case in which a duty of care may arise regardless of the exercise of control'. This would seem to suggest a more liberal approach to the assumption of responsibility concept than has been apparent in other recent cases (see later in IV in particular), though it is not necessarily to be disapproved for that reason alone. We shall only truly know how these principles are to be developed when they come to be applied in cases that go to full trial on the facts (noting again that *Vedanta* and *Okpabi* were both hearings of preliminary issues on the basis of the facts stated in the pleadings). That may not be for some time, as van Dam suggests that one consequence of the two decisions may be to give claimants a stronger hand to reach a settlement out of court, as indeed occurred in *Vedanta* following the Supreme Court decision ('Breakthrough in Parent Company Liability: Three Shell Defeats, the End of an Era and New Paradigms' (2021) 18 ECFR 714 at 732, 720). For further discussion, see also Witting, 'The Corporate Group: System, Design and Responsibility' [2021] CLJ 581.

Smith v Littlewoods Organisation Ltd [1987] AC 241

The respondents purchased a cinema with a view to demolishing it and replacing it with a supermarket. Having taken possession of the cinema, they employed contractors to make site investigations and do some preliminary work on foundations, but thereafter the cinema was left empty and unattended by the respondents or any of their employees. Within a period of two or three weeks, it appeared that the main building was no longer lockfast and was being regularly entered by unauthorised persons. Debris began to accumulate outside the cinema and on two occasions attempts to start fires inside and adjacent to the cinema were observed by a passer-by but neither the respondents nor the police were informed. A short time afterwards, a fire was started in the cinema which seriously damaged two adjoining properties, one of which had to be demolished. The appellants, the owners of the affected properties, claimed damages against the respondents on the ground that the damage to their properties had been caused by the respondents' negligence. The judge found the claims established and awarded the appellants damages, but this decision was reversed by the Inner House of the Court of Session in Scotland. The appellants appealed to the House of Lords.

Lord Brandon

The particular facts of the present case appear to me to raise two, and only two, questions, on the answers to which the determination of the appeals depends.

The first question is: what was the general duty owed by Littlewoods, as owners and occupiers of the disused cinema, to the appellants, as owners or occupiers of other buildings near to the cinema? The answer to that question is, in my view, that Littlewoods owed to the appellants a duty to exercise reasonable care to ensure that the cinema was not, and did not become, a source of danger to neighbouring buildings owned or occupied by the appellants.

The second question is whether that general duty encompassed a specific duty to exercise reasonable care to prevent young persons obtaining unlawful access to the cinema and, having done so, unlawfully setting it on fire. The answer to that question, in accordance with general principles governing alike the law of delict in Scotland and the law of negligence in England, must depend on whether the occurrence of such behaviour was reasonably foreseeable by Littlewoods. It should have been reasonably foreseeable by Littlewoods if they had known of the activities of young persons observed by certain individuals in the locality. But they did not know of such activities because the individuals concerned did not inform either

Littlewoods or the police of them, nor did the police themselves observe them. In the absence of information about such activities, either from the individuals referred to or from the police, I am of opinion that the occurrence of the behaviour in question was not reasonably foreseeable by Littlewoods. I conclude, therefore, that the general duty of care owed by Littlewoods to the appellants did not encompass the specific duty referred to above.

For these reasons I would dismiss the appeals.

Lord Griffiths

The fire in this case was caused by the criminal activity of third parties on Littlewoods' premises. I do not say that there will never be circumstances in which the law will require an occupier of premises to take special precautions against such a contingency but they would surely have to be extreme indeed. It is common ground that only a 24-hour guard on these premises would have been likely to prevent this fire, and even that cannot be certain, such is the determination and ingenuity of young vandals.

There was nothing of an inherently dangerous nature stored in the premises, nor can I regard an empty cinema stripped of its equipment as likely to be any more alluring to vandals than any other recently vacated premises in the centre of a town. No message was received by Littlewoods from the local police, fire brigade or any neighbour that vandals were creating any danger on the premises. In short, so far as Littlewoods knew, there was nothing significantly different about these empty premises from the tens of thousands of such premises up and down the country. People do not mount 24-hour guards on empty properties and the law would impose an intolerable burden if it required them to do so save in the most exceptional circumstances. I find no such exceptional circumstances in this case and I would accordingly dismiss the appeals.

Lord Mackay of Clashfern

It is plain from the authorities that the fact that the damage, on which a claim is founded, was caused by a human agent quite independent of the person against whom a claim in negligence is made does not, of itself, preclude success of the claim, since breach of duty on the part of the person against whom the claim is made may also have played a part in causing the damage.

[His Lordship referred with approval to the speech of Lord Reid in the *Dorset Yacht* case, and held that the mere possibility of the third party's intervention was insufficient to establish a liability. He continued:]

It is true, as has been pointed out by Oliver LJ in *Lamb v Camden London Borough* [1981] QB 625 at 642, that human conduct is particularly unpredictable and that every society will have a sprinkling of people who behave most abnormally. The result of this consideration, in my opinion, is that, where the only possible source of the type of damage or injury which is in question is agency of a human being for whom the person against whom the claim is made has no responsibility, it may not be easy to find that as a reasonable person he was bound to anticipate that type of damage as a consequence of his act or omission. The more unpredictable the conduct in question, the less easy to affirm that any particular result from it is probable and in many circumstances the only way in which a judge could properly be persuaded to come to the conclusion that the result was not only possible but reasonably foreseeable as probable would be to convince him that, in the circumstances, it was highly likely. In this type of case a finding that the reasonable man should have anticipated the consequence of human action as just probable may not be a very frequent option. Unless the judge can be satisfied that the result of the human action is highly probable or very likely he may have to conclude that all that the reasonable man could say was that it was a mere possibility. Unless the needle that measures the probability of a particular result flowing from the conduct of a human agent is near the top of the scale it may be hard to conclude that it has risen sufficiently from the bottom to create the duty reasonably to foresee it.

In summary I conclude, in agreement with both counsel, that what the reasonable man is bound to foresee in a case involving injury or damage by independent human agency, just as in cases where such agency plays no part, is the probable consequences of his own act or omission, but that, in such a case, a clear basis will be required on which to assert that the injury or damage is more than a mere possibility.

[His Lordship dismissed the appeal on the basis that the appellants had not established a probability that the vacant property would be set on fire with consequent risk of damage to neighbouring premises.]

Lord Goff of Chieveley

There is no general duty of care to prevent others from suffering loss or damage caused by the deliberate wrongdoing of third parties . . .

That there are special circumstances in which a defender may be held responsible in law for injuries suffered by the pursuer through a third party's deliberate wrongdoing is not in doubt. For example, a duty of care may arise from a relationship between the parties which gives rise to an imposition or assumption of responsibility on or by the defender, as in *Stansbie v Troman* [1948] 2 KB 48, where such responsibility was held to arise from a contract. In that case a decorator, left alone on the premises by the householder's wife, was held liable when he went out leaving the door on the latch and a thief entered the house and stole property. Such responsibility might well be held to exist in other cases where there is no contract, as for example where a person left alone in a house has entered as a licensee of the occupier. Again, the defender may be vicariously liable for the third party's act; or he may be held liable as an occupier to a visitor on his land. Again, as appears from the dictum of Dixon J in *Smith v Leurs* (1945) 70 CLR 256 at 262, a duty may arise from a special relationship between the defender and the third party, by virtue of which the defender is responsible for controlling the third party: see, for example, *Home Office v Dorset Yacht Co Ltd*. More pertinently, in a case between adjoining occupiers of land, there may be liability in nuisance if one occupier causes or permits persons to gather on his land, and they impair his neighbour's enjoyment of his land. Indeed, even if such persons come onto his land as trespassers, the occupiers may, if they constitute a nuisance, be under an affirmative duty to abate the nuisance. As I pointed out in *P Perl (Exporters) Ltd v Camden London BC* [1984] QB 342 at 359, there may well be other cases.

These are all special cases. But there is a more general circumstance in which a defender may be held liable in negligence to the pursuer, although the immediate cause of the damage suffered by the pursuer is the deliberate wrongdoing of another. This may occur where the defender negligently causes or permits to be created a source of danger, and it is reasonably foreseeable that third parties may interfere with it and, sparking off the danger, thereby cause damage to persons in the position of the pursuer. The classic example of such a case is, perhaps, *Haynes v Harwood* [1935] 1 KB 146, where the defendant's carter left a horse-drawn van unattended in a crowded street and the horses bolted when a boy threw a stone at them. A police officer who suffered injury in stopping the horses before they injured a woman and children was held to be entitled to recover damages from the defendant . . .

Haynes v Harwood was a case concerned with the creation of a source of danger in a public place. We are concerned in the present case with an allegation that the defenders should be held liable for the consequences of deliberate wrongdoing by others who were trespassers on the defenders' property . . . Liability might well be imposed in such a case . . . where the defender has negligently caused or permitted the creation of a source of danger on his land,

and where it is foreseeable that third parties may trespass on his land and spark it off, thereby damaging the pursuer or his property . . .

Turning to the facts of the present case, I cannot see that the defenders should be held liable . . . First, I do not consider that the empty cinema could properly be described as an unusual danger in the nature of a fire hazard. . . . Nor can I see that the defenders should be held liable for having failed to take reasonable steps to abate a fire risk created by third parties on their property without their fault. If there was any such fire risk, they had no means of knowing that it existed. . . .

[T]o impose a general duty on occupiers to take reasonable care to prevent others from entering their property would impose an unreasonable burden on ordinary householders and an unreasonable curb on the ordinary enjoyment of their property.

Lord Keith agreed with both Lord Mackay and Lord Goff.

Appeal dismissed.

B. S. Markesinis, 'Negligence, Nuisance and Affirmative Duties of Action' (1989) 105 LQR 104

Five Law Lords delivered opinions of varying lengths in *Smith's* case. In Lord Brandon's view the case raised two and only two questions: (a) whether a general duty was owed by the defenders to the plaintiff to ensure that their premises did not become a source of danger and (b) whether 'the general duty encompassed a specific duty to exercise reasonable care to prevent young persons obtaining unlawful access to the cinema [the defenders' premises], and, having done so, unlawfully setting it on fire.' The terminology of 'general' and 'specific' duty may not be entirely recognisable in the academic discussions of the elements of the tort of negligence . . . However, it is arguable that when referring to a 'specific duty', Lord Brandon had in mind what is more commonly referred to as the element of 'careless breach of the duty', not least since it appears clear from his short opinion that the answer to this second question will vary from case to case and should thus not receive a blanket negative answer. Whatever interpretation one adopts, one thing seems reasonably clear: Lord Brandon was not opting for a blanket exclusion of liability through the denial of a notional duty of care . . .

[Markesinis considers the opinion of Lord Griffiths, whose reasoning he found substantially the same as Lord Brandon's, and then turns to the opinion of Lord Mackay LC.]

[T]he non-liability rule, based on what was reasonably foreseeable, could, in text-book terms, be translated to suggest that the damage was remote . . . Nevertheless, I suspect that the Lord Chancellor's insistence in *Smith's* case on what is reasonable on the facts of each case seems to point more towards the expected standard that must be attained by each defendant in the light of the likelihood of the occurrence of the harm. To put it differently, though the vague concept of foreseeability was frequently used in all these judgments [including those in *Lamb* and *Perl*], what I think the Lord Chancellor was saying is that, in view of all the surrounding circumstances, the more likely it is that the harm will occur the more likely that an obligation will be imposed on the defendant to do something about it. In fact, at the end of his judgment, the Lord Chancellor summarises his views by saying that

> in my opinion *various factors* will be taken into account by the reasonable man in considering cases involving fire on the one hand and theft on the other but since this is the principle

the precise weight to be given to these factors in any particular case will depend upon the circumstances . . . I consider that much must depend on what the evidence shows is done by ordinary people in like circumstances to those in which the claim of breach of duty arises. [Italics added by Markesinis.]

This, it is submitted, is not remoteness language but standard of care language in which the foreseeability of harm is just one of many factors that have to be weighed by the judge before determining the expected standard of care . . .

Be that as it may, what I think is important in this opinion is not whether the Lord Chancellor's terminology should, in text-book terms, be placed under the heading of careless breach of duty or remote damage but rather on the fact that recovery is denied to this plaintiff rather than to all plaintiffs in similar situations . . . [L]iability was *not denied generally* and in all cases through the use of the device of duty of care. Professor Fleming put it succinctly when he wrote that 'if the policy against recovery is *quite categorical, too insistent to be confided every time to the chance arbitrament of each individual trial judge or jury's speculations about "risk" or "cause"*, the rule in question is nowadays generally formulated as one of "no duty"' (*Law of Torts*, 7th edn, 1987, p. 126) [italics added by Markesinis] . . .

[T]he Lord Chancellor (and, at least, two of his colleagues) felt it was inappropriate to resort to the blunderbuss weapon of duty of care . . .

COMMENTARY

A landowner's liability to a neighbour for damage caused by trespassers had already been addressed by the House of Lords in the tort of private nuisance, where liability can be established if the defendant 'adopted' or 'continued' the nuisance (see *Sedleigh-Denfield v O'Callaghan* [1940] AC 880). In negligence, it had also been established that a landowner owes a duty to protect neighbours from natural hazards arising on the land (see *Goldman v Hargrave*, extracted earlier). But the issue of liability in negligence for harm to neighbours resulting from the entry of trespassers onto the defendant's land was not raised before the House of Lords until the extracted case.

In *Smith v Littlewoods*, all the members of the House of Lords were keen to restrict the liability of owners and occupiers for harm caused to neighbouring property by trespassers on their land. But they sought to do so in different ways (see Markesinis, *op. cit.*). Lord Brandon, Lord Griffiths and Lord Mackay seem to have conceded the existence of a duty of care, but to have ruled that there was no breach of that duty. Lord Goff, by way of contrast, clearly ruled that no duty of care ever arose on the facts. Lord Keith expressed his concurrence with the opinions of both Lord Mackay and Lord Goff, but did not advert at all to the significant differences in approach between them.

Later cases show a distinct preference for Lord Goff's reasoning. In *Mitchell v Glasgow City Council* [2009] 1 AC 874 at [15], Lord Hope expressly cited Lord Goff's opinion in *Smith v Littlewoods* as authority for the proposition that 'the law does not impose a duty to prevent a person from being harmed by the criminal act of a third party based simply upon foreseeability'. See also *Michael v Chief Constable of South Wales Police* [2015] AC 1732 at [97], per Lord Toulson (extracted in IV). It now seems clear that Lord Goff's approach—starting with a general rule of no duty in respect of harm caused by the act of a third party, but then admitting limited exceptions to it—is the right way to approach such cases.

Lord Goff expressed particular concern that imposing a general duty of care on owners and occupiers of land would result in an unreasonable burden upon ordinary householders.

In his view, it was 'less objectionable' that occupiers should themselves take steps to guard against theft and vandalism wherever this was possible, and should be left to bear such losses as did occur. He noted that, in the vast majority of cases, these losses would be covered by insurance.

Lord Goff accepted, however, that a duty of care might arise where an occupier knows or has the means of knowing that trespassers are entering the land and in doing so constitute a danger to neighbouring property, for example by wrongfully lighting fires. Following Lord Goff's dictum, the Court of Appeal imposed liability for breach of duty in another case involving trespass to land, *Clark Fixing Ltd v Dudley Metropolitan Borough Council* [2001] EWCA Civ 1898. The defendant council acquired property, the roof of which was shared with adjoining premises. Trespassers entered the defendant's premises, starting a fire which spread via the roof to the claimants' premises next door and caused considerable damage. Unlike *Smith*, the council was well aware that there had been previous intrusions and fires, the claimants having complained of such events on a number of occasions. The council was therefore under a duty to take reasonable precautions against the spread of fire, for example by removing all readily moveable combustible material, which could have been achieved at trifling expense. The council had failed to do this and was therefore liable for its negligence.

What of the occupier's duty to prevent those who enter their premises as their visitors from injuring others? One context in which this issue has arisen in other jurisdictions is the serving of alcoholic drinks. The owner of a bar or some similar establishment clearly owes a duty to act to prevent a patron from causing injury to other persons on the premises (see, e.g., *Adeels Palace Pty Ltd v Moubarak* (2009) 239 CLR 420). But it is less certain that the duty extends to persons who might be injured when the patron leaves the premises (e.g. in a collision caused while driving home under the influence). The Supreme Court of Canada has indicated that a duty of care is in fact owed in such circumstances by the occupier of commercial premises serving alcohol (*Stewart v Pettie* [1995] 1 SCR 131), but not by a 'social host' (*Childs v Desormeaux* [2006] 1 SCR 641), at least where they do not enhance the risk by (e.g.) serving an obviously drunk guest whom they know is going to drive home. Although both commercial and social hosts have some control over the patron/guest, respect for the latter's rights of autonomy militated against a duty being found: 'A person who accepts an invitation to attend a private party does not park his autonomy at the door. The guest remains responsible for his or her conduct' (*Childs*, at [45] per McLachlin CJ).

Do you think the distinction between commercial and social occupiers justifies the difference in result in the two contexts?

Regarding another exception to the general 'no duty' rule recognised by Lord Goff—namely, where the defendant assumes responsibility for the safety of the claimant's property, as exemplified by *Stansbie v Troman* [1948] 2 KB 48—see now *Rushbond Plc v JS Design Partnership LLP* [2021] EWCA Civ 1889.

IV. Nonfeasance by Public Bodies

As the role of a public authority is in many cases supervisory or regulatory, complaints made against them frequently relate to nonfeasance rather than misfeasance. Notwithstanding the general reluctance of the courts to recognise duties of affirmative action, suits of this nature have long been successful in circumstances where a private organisation or individual might equally have been liable (see, e.g., *Welton v North Cornwall District Council* [1997] 1 WLR 570). But until recently it was a controversial question whether the mere existence of a statutory duty or power could be sufficient to give rise to a common law duty to act, even in circumstances in which a private individual would not be held legally responsible.

In *East Suffolk Rivers Catchment Board v Kent* [1941] AC 74, a majority of the House of Lords apparently answered this question in the negative, holding that a rivers authority repairing a breach in the sea wall could not be held liable for unnecessary delays in the work which prolonged the period during which the plaintiff's pasture land was flooded. The reason given was that it could not be said that the delay had caused the plaintiff any damage he would not have sustained had the authority done nothing. Lord Romer stated the principle to be applied in such cases in the following terms (at 102):

> Where a statutory authority is entrusted with a mere power it cannot be made liable for any damage sustained by a member of the public by reason of a failure to exercise that power. If in the exercise of their discretion they embark upon an execution of the power, the only duty they owe to any member of the public is not thereby to add to the damages that he would have suffered had they done nothing. So long as they exercise their discretion honestly, it is for them to determine the method by which and the time within which and the time during which the power shall be exercised; and they cannot be made liable, except to the extent that I have just mentioned, for any damage that would have been avoided had they exercised their discretion in a more reasonable way.

The question for the courts subsequently, metaphorically speaking, has been whether to make a breach in the *East Suffolk* wall (cf. Harris (1997) 113 LQR 398).

The common law's principal challenge to the authority of the *East Suffolk* case was made by Lord Wilberforce in *Anns v Merton LBC* [1978] AC 728. His Lordship held that the *East Suffolk* ruling could not be taken to preclude a finding that the statutory scheme under which a public body operated gave rise to a duty of care. In his opinion, the decision predated the development of a generalised liability in respect of negligent conduct, which was only accepted some years after Lord Atkin's formulation of the neighbour principle in *Donoghue v Stevenson*. On the facts of *Anns*, this analysis allowed the House of Lords to decide that a local authority with statutory responsibility for inspecting building works in the interests of public health and safety was liable to lessees of a new block of flats who suffered loss as a result of the authority's negligent failure properly to inspect the property's foundations; it was necessary to repair the defective foundations, and cracks in the walls that they had caused, in order to protect the plaintiffs' health and safety. This result was especially controversial because the plaintiff's loss was purely economic—it arose from an inherent defect in the property—and *Anns* has since been overruled on this point (see *Murphy v Brentwood District Council* [1991] 1 AC 398, discussed in Ch. 8.II). The separate issue of whether a statutory power can give rise to a common law duty of care was raised again in the case of *Stovin v Wise* [1996] AC 923, where Lord Hoffmann noted that there was no authority in support of that proposition before the decision in *Anns*. He was doubtful of Lord Wilberforce's explanation of *East Suffolk*, but was content to leave open the question of whether *Anns* had been wrong to create an exception to Lord Romer's statement of principle (at 953).

The issue came before the House of Lords again in *Gorringe v Calderdale Metropolitan Borough Council* [2004] 1 WLR 1057, concerning the defendant highway authority's claimed liability for a motor vehicle collision that was alleged to have been attributable to its failure to paint the word 'Slow' on the road surface to warn motorists of a hazardous section of road. Rejecting the claim, the House of Lords accepted that highway authorities owe a common law duty of care not to cause accidents by their positive acts—for example, creating a one-way street but failing to put up a 'No Entry' sign at its end—but found no basis on which liability could arise for nonfeasance. Though highway authorities have a statutory obligation to maintain the highway (Highways Act 1980, s. 41), and can be held liable in the tort of breach of statutory duty for damage resulting from their failure to perform this obligation, *Gorringe* was not a case of a highway maintenance failure. Further, the defendant authority's more general statutory duty to promote road safety and prevent accidents (Road Traffic Act 1988, s. 39—breach of which is not actionable in damages) did not give rise to a common law duty of care.

Lord Hoffmann, at [32], reiterated what he had said previously in *Stovin v Wise*, stating that he found it 'difficult to imagine a case in which a common law duty can be founded simply upon the failure (however irrational) to provide some benefit which a public authority has power (or a public law duty) to provide.' Lord Scott, at [71], expressed his agreement but added:

> I would be inclined to go further. In my opinion, if a statutory duty does not give rise to a private right to sue for breach, the duty cannot create a duty of care that would not have been owed at common law if the statute were not there.

In *Customs and Excise Comrs v Barclays Bank plc* [2007] 1 AC 181, Lord Hoffmann (at [39]) seems to have accepted Lord Scott's unequivocal approach, stating that a statutory duty 'cannot' generate a common law duty of care.

This approach may be seen as a consequence of the 'equality principle' discussed in Chapter 3.III.1(a). It entails that public authorities have a duty of affirmative action in negligence only in circumstances where a private person would owe such a duty. Confirmation that this is indeed the correct approach in the modern law is to be found in the following extracted cases.

Michael v Chief Constable of South Wales Police [2015] AC 1732

The case concerned the tragic murder of a young woman by her former partner. This might have been prevented if the police had responded promptly to a 999 call the deceased made shortly before the fatal attack upon her. The claimants, the victim's estate and her dependants, commenced proceedings against the two police forces involved, claiming damages for negligence and under the Human Rights Act 1998. The police forces applied to strike out the claims and/or for summary judgment. The application was dismissed by the judge but the Court of Appeal reversed that decision in part, granting summary judgment in the negligence claim but allowing the Human Rights Act claim to continue. The claimants appealed and the defendants cross-appealed. The extract addresses only the claim in negligence. The Human Rights Act aspect is considered later in this chapter.

Lord Toulson JSC (with whom Lord Neuburger, Lord Mance, Lord Reed and Lord Hodge agreed)

5. Ms Michael lived in Cardiff with her two children who were aged seven years and ten months at the date of her death. On 5 August 2009 at 2.29 am Ms Michael dialled 999 from her mobile phone. She lived in the area of the South Wales Police, but the call was picked up by a telephone mast in Gwent and was routed to the Gwent Police call centre. It was received by a civilian call handler. The conversation was recorded and it has been transcribed. Ms Michael

9 NEGLIGENCE: DUTY OF CARE—OMISSIONS AND ACTS OF THIRD PARTIES

said that her ex-boyfriend was aggressive, had just turned up at her house in the middle of the night and had hit her. He had found her with another man. He had taken her car to drive the other man home and had said that when he came back he was going to hit her. She said that he was going to be back 'any minute literally'.

6. She was asked by the call handler if she could lock the doors to keep him out. She replied that she could lock the doors, but she did not know what he would do. She did not know if he had a key or how he got into her house.

7. The next part of the transcript reads:
'he come back and . . . he told the guy to get out of the room, and then he bit my ear really hard and its like all swollen and all bruised at the moment, and he just said "I'm going to drop him home and (inaudible) [fucking kill you]".'

8. There is no explanation on the face of the transcript why the last three words are preceded by '(inaudible)' and appear in square brackets . . .

9. The call ended with the call handler telling Ms Michael that her call had come through to Gwent Police and that she would pass the call on to the police in Cardiff. She added 'they will want to call you back so please keep your phone free'.

10. The call was graded by Gwent Police as a 'G1' call. This meant that it required an immediate response by police officers. Ms Michael's home was no more than five or six minutes' drive from the nearest police station.

11. The Gwent call handler immediately called South Wales Police and gave an abbreviated version of what Ms Michael had said. No mention was made of a threat to kill. South Wales Police graded the priority of the call as 'G2'. This meant that officers assigned to the case should respond to the call within 60 minutes.

12. At 2.43 am Ms Michael again called 999. The call was again received by Gwent Police. Ms Michael was heard to scream and the line went dead.

13. South Wales Police were immediately informed. Police officers arrived at Ms Michael's address at 2.51 am. They found that she had been brutally attacked. She had been stabbed many times and was dead. Her attacker was soon found and arrested. He subsequently pleaded guilty to murder and was sentenced to life imprisonment.

14. Data held by South Wales Police recorded a history of abuse or suspected domestic abuse towards Ms Michael by the same man. On four occasions between September 2007 and April 2009 incidents had been reported to the police and entries had been made on a public protection referral for domestic abuse form, but in two instances the risk indications section of the form was not completed.

15. The consequences are stark and tragic. Ms Michael has lost her life in the most violent fashion. Her children have lost their mother and breadwinner. Her parents have lost their daughter and have taken on the responsibility and work of bringing up their grandchildren.

16. An investigation by the Independent Police Complaints commission led to a lengthy report. It contained serious criticisms of both police forces for individual and organisational failures. . . .

[D]id the police owe a duty of care to Ms Michael on receiving her 999 call?

97. English law does not as a general rule impose liability on a defendant (D) for injury or damage to the person or property of a claimant (C) caused by the conduct of a third party (T): *Smith v Littlewoods Organisation Ltd* [1987] AC 241, 270 (a Scottish appeal in which a large number of English and Scottish cases were reviewed). The fundamental reason, as Lord Goff explained, is that the common law does not generally impose liability for pure omissions. It is one thing to require a person who embarks on action which may harm others to exercise care. It is another matter to hold a person liable in damages for failing to prevent harm caused by someone else.

98. The rule is not absolute. Apart from statutory exceptions, there are two well recognised types of situation in which the common law may impose liability for a careless omission.

99. The first is where D was in a position of control over T and should have foreseen the likelihood of T causing damage to somebody in close proximity if D failed to take reasonable care in the exercise of that control. The *Dorset Yacht* case [1970] AC 1004 is the classic example, and in that case Lord Diplock set close limits to the scope of the liability . . . Ms Michael's murderer was not under the control of the police, and therefore there is no question of liability under this exception.

100. The second general exception applies where D assumes a positive responsibility to safeguard C under the *Hedley Byrne* principle, as explained by Lord Goff in *Spring v Guardian Assurance plc* [1995] 2 AC 296. It is not a new principle. It embraces the relationships in which a duty to take positive action typically arises: contract, fiduciary relationships, employer and employee, school and pupil, health professional and patient. The list is not exhaustive. This principle is the basis for the claimants' main submission . . . There has sometimes been a tendency for courts to use the expression 'assumption of responsibility' when in truth the responsibility has been imposed by the court rather than assumed by D. It should not be expanded artificially.

101. These general principles have been worked out for the most part in cases involving private litigants, but they are equally applicable where D is a public body. *Mitchell v Glasgow City Council* [2009] AC 874 is a good example . . .

102. It is true that the categories of negligence are never closed (*Heaven v Pender* (trading as *West India Graving Dock Co*) (1883) 11 QBD 503), and it would be open to the court to create a new exception to the general rule about omissions . . .

113. . . . It is a feature of our system of government that many areas of life are subject to forms of state controlled licensing, regulation, inspection, intervention and assistance aimed at protecting the general public from physical or economic harm caused by the activities of other members of society (or sometimes from natural disasters). Licensing of firearms, regulation of financial services, inspections of restaurants, factories and children's nurseries, and enforcement of building regulations are random examples. To compile a comprehensive list would be virtually impossible, because the systems designed to protect the public from harm of one kind or another are so extensive.

114. It does not follow from the setting up of a protective system from public resources that if it fails to achieve its purpose, through organisational defects or fault on the part of an individual, the public at large should bear the additional burden of compensating a victim for harm caused by the actions of a third party for whose behaviour the state is not responsible. To impose such a burden would be contrary to the ordinary principles of the common law.

115. The refusal of the courts to impose a private law duty on the police to exercise reasonable care to safeguard victims or potential victims of crime, except in cases where there has been a representation and reliance, does not involve giving special treatment to the police. It is consistent with the way in which the common law has been applied to other authorities vested with powers or duties as a matter of public law for the protection of the public . . .

116. The question is therefore not whether the police should have a special immunity, but whether an exception should be made to the ordinary application of common law principles which would cover the facts of the present case.

[Lord Toulson proceeded to consider a possible new exception to the general rule about omissions where the police are aware or ought reasonably to be aware of a threat to the life or physical safety of an identifiable person or member of an identifiable small group. In doing so, he addressed the argument that such an exception ought to be recognised in view of the need to protect victims of domestic violence:]

118. I recognise fully that the statistics about the incidence of domestic violence and the facts of individual cases such as the present are shocking. I recognise also that the court has been presented with fresh material on the subject. However, I am not persuaded that they should cause the court to create a new category of duty of care for several reasons.

119. If the foundation of a duty of care is the public law duty of the police for the preservation of the Queen's peace, it is hard to see why the duty should be confined to potential victims of a particular kind of breach of the peace. Would a duty of care be owed to a person who reported a credible threat to burn down his house? Would it be owed to a company which reported a credible threat by animal rights extremists to its premises? If not, why not?

120. It is also hard to see why it should be limited to particular potential victims. If the police fail through lack of care to catch a criminal before he shoots and injures his intended victim and also a bystander (or if he misses his intended target and hits someone else), is it right that one should be entitled to compensation but not the other, when the duty of the police is a general duty for the preservation of the Queen's peace? Similarly if the intelligence service fails to respond appropriately to intelligence that a terrorist group is intending to bring down an airliner, is it right that the service should be liable to the dependants of the victims on the plane but not the victims on the ground? . . . These questions underline the fact that the duty of the police for the preservation of the peace is owed to members of the public at large, and does not involve the kind of close or special relationship ('proximity' or 'neighbourhood') necessary for the imposition of a private law duty of care. . . .

Should the police be held to have assumed responsibility to take reasonable care for Ms Michael's safety?

138. Mr Bowen [for the claimants] submitted that what was said by the Gwent call handler who received Ms Michael's 999 call was arguably sufficient to give rise to an assumption of responsibility on the *Hedley Byrne* principle as amplified in *Spring v Guardian Assurance plc* [1995] 2 AC 296. I agree with the Court of Appeal that the argument is not tenable. The only assurance which the call handler gave to Ms Michael was that she would pass on the call to the South Wales Police. She gave no promise how quickly they would respond. She told Ms Michael that they would want to call her back and asked her to keep her phone free, but this did not amount to advising or instructing her to remain in her house, as was suggested. Ms Michael's call was made on her mobile phone. Nor did the call handler's inquiry whether Ms Michael could lock the house amount to advising or instructing her to remain there. The case is very different from *Kent v Griffiths* [2001] QB 36 where the call handler gave misleading assurances that an ambulance would be arriving shortly.

[Lord Toulson proceeded to uphold the Court of Appeal's decision granting summary judgment to the two police forces on the negligence claim.]

Lord Kerr JSC (dissenting on the question of the common law duty of care)

164. It has been recognised that proximity of relationship can exist where there is a voluntary assumption of responsibility by the police but in cases where this issue has arisen, rules have been applied to strictly restrict its ambit. Relying on those cases (*Alexandrou v Oxford* [1993] 4 All ER 328; *Capital & Counties plc v Hampshire County Council* [1997] QB 1004 and Lord Brown's observations in the *Van Colle* and *Smith* cases [2009] AC 225, para 135) the defendants argue that unless there was an explicit promise by the police that they would attend immediately and that Ms Michael had expressly relied on this, the conditions for voluntary assumption of responsibility would not be in place . . .

165. One must, I believe, question the logic of this position. Should someone in a vulnerable state, fearing imminent attack, who believes that an assurance of timeous assistance

has been made when, through negligence on the part of the police, that impression has been wrongly created, be treated differently from another who has in fact received an explicit assurance of immediate help, if both have relied on what they believed to be a clear promise that police would attend and avert the apprehended danger? The fact that an easily imagined example such as this can demonstrate the anomaly of the current state of the law in relation to voluntary assumption of responsibility indicates that a more expansive (or, at least, a more nuanced) approach is warranted. But it does more than that. It also illustrates the undesirability of creating a set of rules that may at first sight appear reasonable but which bring about incongruous results when applied to cases even slightly different from those in contemplation at the time of their conception.

166. One is driven therefore to the conclusion that the question whether there is a sufficient relationship of proximity must be primarily dependent on the particular facts of an individual case . . .

167. Proximity in this context means, as I have already said, a closeness of association. In the case of the police it must transcend the ordinary contact that a member of the public has with the police force in general. But the notion that it can only arise where there has been an express assumption of responsibility by unambiguous undertakings on the part of the police and explicit reliance on those by the claimant or victim is not only arbitrary, it fails to reflect the practical realities of life. When someone such as Ms Michael telephones the police she is in a highly vulnerable, agitated and frightened state. Is it to be supposed that there must pass between her and the police representative to whom she speaks a form of words which can be said to amount to an express assumption of responsibility before liability can arise? That the incidence of liability should depend on the happenstance of the telephonist uttering words that can be construed as conveying an unmistakable undertaking that the police will prevent the feared attack is surely unacceptable.

168. Whether a relationship of proximity can be said to exist should be determined by a close examination of all the circumstances with a view to discovering whether sufficient information has been conveyed to or is otherwise available to the police to alert them to the urgent need to take action which it is within their power to take. That the information be specific and the threat imminent are prerequisites of the proximity relationship . . . Imprecise information or indefinite timing as to the materialising of any threat cannot be enough to stimulate the police to urgent action and, as I see it, this is an essential dimension of the proximity relationship. In essence that relationship entails the engagement of the police to a response which is out of the ordinary and which is a direct reaction to the plight of the individual under threat. It does not matter if the information is received from a source other than the intended victim. What is critical is that the police know of an imminent threat to a particular individual and that they have the means of preventing that threat and protecting the individual concerned. This is personalised to the intended victim and arises because of the quality of the information which the police have and because they have the capacity to stop the attack. . . .

175. In my view, the time has come to recognise the legal duty of the police force to take action to protect a particular individual whose life or safety is, to the knowledge of the police, threatened by someone whose actions the police are able to restrain. I am not convinced that this requires a development of the common law but, if it does, I am sanguine about that prospect. Certainly, I do not believe that rules relating to liability for omissions should inhibit the law's development to this point.

Baroness Hale supported the dissenting analysis of Lord Kerr on the common law duty of care.

Appeal and cross-appeal dismissed.

COMMENTARY

Michael was far from the first case to address the possible liability of the police to victims of crime for their failure to prevent its occurrence. *Hill v Chief Constable of West Yorkshire* [1989] AC 53 arose out of the murder of a young woman by the notorious serial killer, Peter Sutcliffe, known as the Yorkshire Ripper. She was his last victim, more than five years after the first. The victim's mother sued the police as her daughter's personal representative, alleging that the police had sufficient information pointing to Sutcliffe as the likely perpetrator that they should have apprehended him before this final attack. The House of Lords rejected the claim for want of the necessary relationship of proximity (as well as for other reasons not material here). Distinguishing the case from *Dorset Yacht* on the basis that there was no special relationship between either the police and the killer or between the police and the victim, Lord Keith explained (at 62):

> It is plain that vital characteristics which were present in the *Dorset Yacht* case and which led to the imposition of liability are here lacking. Sutcliffe was never in the custody of the police force. Miss Hill was one of a vast number of the female general public who might be at risk from his activities but was at no special distinctive risk in relation to them, unlike the owners of yachts moored off Brownsea Island in relation to the foreseeable conduct of the borstal boys . . . In the case of an escaped criminal his identity and description are known. In the instant case the identity of the wanted criminal was at the material time unknown and it is not averred that any full or clear description of him was ever available.

The *Hill* decision did not address the situation where a victim of crime had requested the assistance of the police, but they had not responded adequately. The Supreme Court subsequently ruled in *Smith v Chief Constable of Sussex Police* [2009] 1 AC 225 that the police owed no duty of care even in such circumstances, mainly for the policy reasons that had prevailed in *Hill* (see further in Ch. 3.II.4). The issue returned to the Supreme Court in *Michael*, where the claimants' main contention was that the police had assumed responsibility towards Ms Michael and so came under a duty of care towards her. This would have brought her within one of the established exceptions to the general rule of no liability for careless omissions (the other mentioned by Lord Toulson is where the defendant is in a position of control over a third party who causes the damage). An alternative argument for the claimants was that a new exception to that general rule should now be recognised.

Assumption of Responsibility

Given it was the claimants' main argument, it is surprising that Lord Toulson, at [138], rejected with such brevity their contention that the police had assumed responsibility towards Ms Michael, and that he did so without addressing several important questions. First, as Goudkamp observes ((2016) 131 LQR 519 at 523):

> it is hard to see why, as Lord Toulson seemed to think, an explicit statement should have been required in order for responsibility to be assumed. Surely Ms Michael implicitly understood, justifiably, that police officers would arrive expeditiously.

As Lord Kerr points out in his dissent, at [165], the majority's approach entails an invidious distinction between a caller who receives and relies upon an explicit assurance of immediate help and one who—vulnerable and fearing imminent attack—mistakenly construes what the call-handler has said. Another potential anomaly arises from the possible need for reliance upon any assurance given: Ms Michael may well have been in such a desperate situation that the police were her only possible source of assistance, so there was no question of her foregoing alternative means of help that might be available to persons whose plight is not so serious (see McBride, *'Michael* and the Future of Tort Law' (2016) 32 PN 14 at 25). Lastly, the focus on what precisely the caller is told creates the risk that call-handlers will be pressured to resort to pre-scripted responses and even obfuscation, and so fail to meet the real needs of callers (Cf. Broman (2015) 31 PN 195 at 197f).

Lord Toulson, at [69], cited *An Informer v A Chief Constable* [2013] QB 579 as an example of a duty of care arising from an assumption of responsibility by the police, coupled with reliance by the claimant. There the Court of Appeal accepted that the police assumed responsibility to the claimant as someone they had recruited as a covert human intelligence source, having given them express assurances about their security, but the responsibility they assumed was limited to their physical safety and wellbeing and did not extend to safeguarding them against pure economic loss resulting from ongoing investigations. See also *Swinney v Chief Constable of the Northumbria Police* [1997] QB 464, where the Court of Appeal declined to strike out an action for damages for personal injury attributed to the police's failure to keep an informant's identity confidential, but note that the subsequent trial found on the facts that there was no breach of the duty of care the police had assumed towards the claimant (*Swinney v Chief Constable of Northumbria (No. 2)* (1999) 11 Admin LR 811). Another illustration of the application of the assumption of responsibility concept to the police is provided by *Costello v Chief Constable of Northumbria Police* [1999] ICR 752, ruling that a police officer owed a duty to give assistance to a fellow officer who was attacked by a suspect in police custody. The officer had been in close attendance for the specific purpose of coming to the aid of the plaintiff if she needed help and to that extent he had assumed a responsibility for her safety. These cases are some distance removed from the facts of *Michael*, but they demonstrate that there is certainly scope for a duty of care to arise on the basis of an assumption of responsibility by the police to a particular person.

Do you think it would have made a difference on the facts of the extracted case if the call-handler had told Ms Michael 'Don't leave your house. The police will be with you shortly'? *Should* it make a difference?

Looking more broadly at the position of the emergency services, we can see a contrasting approach as between the police and the fire service, on the one hand, and the ambulance service on the other. The majority analysis in *Michael* echoes that of the Court of Appeal in *Capital & Counties plc v Hampshire County Council* [1997] QB 1004 (extracted earlier in II), rejecting the contention that fire officers assumed responsibility to the owner of a burning property when they took control at the scene. Conversely, it was established in *Kent v Griffiths* [2001] QB 36 (also extracted in II) that the ambulance service owes a duty of care to an ill or injured person whom it undertakes to attend when it accepts the 999 call made by them or on their behalf. Lord Woolf MR justified this difference in outcome on the basis that the ambulance service provides a health service for the benefit of a particular individual for whom the ambulance is called, whereas the primary obligation of the police and fire service is to the public at large. If the existence of an assumption of responsibility turns on precisely what the defendant said to the claimant (or their representative), why should it matter which of the emergency services is involved?

A New Exception to the General Rule About Omissions?

The claimants also argued that a new exception should be made to the general rule of no liability for omissions and that a duty of care was owed under a narrower liability principle which applies where the police are aware of a serious and special risk of physical harm to an identifiable person. A principle of that nature had been proposed by Lord Bingham in his dissenting opinion in *Smith v Chief Constable of Sussex Police* [2009] 1 AC 225, but rejected by the majority of the House of Lords in that case, and the same general idea—formulated in a number of slightly different ways—was resuscitated here, finding favour with Lord Kerr and Lady Hale. But the majority of the Supreme Court was again opposed. As Lord Toulson's judgment indicates, at [119]f, one concern was that the scope of the suggested principle could not be kept in check without arbitrary restrictions on its range of application. Lord Toulson, at [121]f (not included in the extract), also considered that there was no way of knowing whether the recognition of a duty of care in such cases would have a positive or negative effect on the performance of the police in dealing with domestic violence, but that it was sure to have potentially significant financial implications. These seem likely to materialise anyway, given the alternative claim that remains possible under the Human Rights Act, and actions brought on that basis will provide empirical evidence as to the impact of civil liability on the investigation and response to what Lord Toulson conceded was the 'shocking' issue of domestic violence. See further Conaghan, 'Investigating Rape: Human Rights and Police Accountability' (2015) 37 LS 54, broadening the focus to violence against women generally, with reference to the decision in *D v Commissioner of Police for the Metropolis* [2016] QB 161 (subsequently upheld on appeal: [2019] AC 196).

The anomalous outcomes that Lord Toulson predicted would follow if a narrow liability principle were adopted might be avoided, according to Tofaris and Steel ('Negligence Liability for Omissions and the Police' [2016] CLJ 128 at 151), if its formulation were to refer to a person at special risk of injury, rather than a person who is threatened by another. This would be sufficient to deal with the case of the injured bystander, considered to be problematic by Lord Toulson at [120], as people in the vicinity generally—not just the person threatened—might satisfy this requirement. The authors argue in favour of a duty resting on the police to all persons at special risk of harm that the police know or should have known about, and have the power to protect against, in circumstances where the person at risk is in a position of dependence on the police. In the authors' view, the law restricts the liberty of ordinary citizens to arm themselves and otherwise to protect themselves against criminal attack, obliging them to entrust their safety to the police, and this provides a good reason—along with the moral responsibility of the police for the victim's harm and the need for accountability—for recognising this 'status-based' exception to the general rule about omissions. In *Michael*, both dissenting justices (Lord Kerr and Lady Hale) acknowledged the strength of the arguments advanced by Tofaris and Steel, referring to a pre-publication version of their article, and would have found the police owed a duty of care on the facts. Do *you* find those arguments convincing? More generally, should the omissions principle apply with the same force in cases involving public defendants as it does in cases involving private defendants? (For contrasting views on this question, see Cornford, 'The Negligence Liability of Public Authorities for Omissions' [2019] CLJ 545; Nolan, 'The Liability of Public Authorities for Failing to Confer Benefits' (2011) 127 LQR 260 at 284–6; and Tofaris and Steel, *op. cit.*, 129–33.)

The Liability of Local Authorities

Cases involving local authorities (county and borough councils, and the like) have also served to focus attention on many of the issues we have been addressing, but the case-law development has followed a somewhat muddled course, with greater clarity of approach emerging only recently.

In its seminal but problematic decision in *X and Others (Minors) v Bedfordshire County Council* [1995] 2 AC 633, the House of Lords was faced with five separate appeals raising the issue of the liability of a local authority for the careless performance of its statutory functions with regard to the protection of children who are at risk of child abuse and the provision of suitable education to children with special needs. The two child abuse cases formed a contrasting pair. In one (the *Bedfordshire* case) the allegation was that the local authority had failed to act expeditiously to put five children from the same family onto the child protection register and to take them into care. The children sought damages for their consequent ill-treatment and illness, neglect of their proper development and impairment of their health. In the other (the *Newham* case), the allegation was that the local authority had acted negligently in taking the decision to remove the first plaintiff, a girl, from the second plaintiff, her mother, and her cohabiting partner, on the basis of a misunderstanding of an allegation the girl was making against another relative. The mistake was subsequently discovered and the child returned to her mother. Both child and mother claimed that their enforced separation had caused them to suffer a psychiatric disorder diagnosed as anxiety neurosis, for which they sought damages.

It will be apparent that the alleged negligence in the *Bedfordshire* case was an omission to act, whereas in the *Newham* case it was the positive act of taking the girl into care. But the House of Lords made nothing of the act-omission distinction, relying instead on policy considerations—in particular, the negative effect the recognition of a duty of care would have on the work of social services—in ruling that both claims should be denied. This now seems out of step with the approach that has emerged—or, perhaps more accurately, been reinstated—in *Michael* and other later decisions, where the act-omission distinction is identified as fundamental. Conversely, the policy reasoning in *X v Bedfordshire* has not survived the implementation of the Human Rights Act 1998, or so the Court of Appeal ruled in *D v East Berkshire Community Health NHS Trust* [2004] QB 558, finding that the Act's creation of a claim against a public authority for violation of a Convention right meant that the policy concerns militating against the recognition of a duty of care had lost their force. This point was not at issue in the subsequent appeal to the House of Lords, but the Law Lords seem to have conceded its correctness (see, e.g., Lord Nicholls at [82]).

If the facts of the *Bedfordshire* case were to be repeated now, it seems likely that the crucial question for the court would be whether the local authority, directly or through its staff, had assumed responsibility for the children who were at risk in their family home. In fact, the concept of assumption of responsibility was employed in *X v Bedfordshire* itself in the three special educational needs cases heard alongside the two child abuse appeals. These were all striking-out applications, but the concept was subsequently applied in *Phelps v Hillingdon LBC* [2001] 2 AC 619 after a full hearing on the facts.

Further consideration of how the concept of assumption of responsibility plays out in the context of claims against local authorities is to be found in the following extract.

N v Poole Borough Council [2020] AC 780

The claimants sought damages for personal injuries they alleged they had suffered while they were children living in the area of the respondent council. According to the pleadings, in 2006 they were placed with their mother in a council house on an estate in the town of Poole, adjacent to another family who to the council's knowledge had persistently engaged in anti-social behaviour. The elder boy, then aged nine, was severely disabled both mentally and physically, and required constant care. The council made extensive adaptations to the house in order to meet his needs and provided him with a care package through its child health and disability team; he had an allocated social worker. Following an altercation, the mother reported the neighbouring family to the council, resulting in the police attending and issuing a warning to them. They consequently targeted the mother and the children for harassment and abuse which persisted over several years, involving physical assaults, threats of violence, verbal abuse and criminal damage. This was reported to the council, and various measures were taken against the neighbours, including eviction, the obtaining of injunctions, proceedings for contempt of court, anti-social behaviour orders and sentences of imprisonment. The harassment nevertheless continued. In 2008, the younger boy, two years his brother's junior, expressed suicidal ideas and in 2009 he ran away from home leaving a suicide note. He consequently received psychotherapy and was allocated the same social worker as his brother and made subject to a child protection plan. The claimants and their mother were eventually rehoused away from the estate in December 2011.

The claimants brought legal proceedings alleging that the abuse and harassment they suffered between 2006 and 2011 had caused them physical and psychological harm for which the council was liable by reason of its own negligence or the negligence of its social workers or other employees. The council applied unsuccessfully to have the claim struck out at first instance for want of a duty of care but appealed successfully to the Court of Appeal. The claimants appealed to the Supreme Court.

Lord Reed (with whom Lady Hale, Lord Wilson, Lord Hodge and Lady Black agreed)

1. This appeal is concerned with the liability of a local authority for what is alleged to have been a negligent failure to exercise its social services functions so as to protect children from harm caused by third parties. The principal question of law which it raises is whether a local authority or its employees may owe a common law duty of care to children affected by the manner in which it exercises or fails to exercise those functions, and if so, in what circumstances. . . .

25. It is accepted that the provisions of the 1989 [Children] Act which impose duties on local authorities do not create a statutory cause of action. The question is whether local authorities may instead be liable at common law for breach of a duty of care in relation to the performance of their functions under the Act . . .

64. *Robinson* [*Robinson v Chief Constable of West Yorkshire Police* [2018] AC 736] did not lay down any new principle of law, but . . . the decision confirmed, following *Michael* [*Michael v Chief Constable of South Wales* [2015] AC 1732] and numerous older authorities, that public authorities are generally subject to the same general principles of the law of negligence as private individuals and bodies, except to the extent that legislation requires a departure from those principles. That is the basic premise of the consequent framework for determining the existence or non-existence of a duty of care on the part of a public authority.

65. It follows (1) that public authorities may owe a duty of care in circumstances where the principles applicable to private individuals would impose such a duty, unless such a duty would be inconsistent with, and is therefore excluded by, the legislation from which their powers or duties are derived; (2) that public authorities do not owe a duty of care at common law merely because they have statutory powers or duties, even if, by exercising their statutory functions, they could prevent a person from suffering harm; and (3) that public authorities can come under a common law duty to protect from harm in circumstances where the principles applicable to private individuals or bodies would impose such a duty, as for example where the authority has created the source of danger or has assumed a responsibility to protect the claimant from harm, unless the imposition of such a duty would be inconsistent with the relevant legislation.

The present case

74. . . . Whether a local authority or its employees owe a duty of care to a child in particular circumstances depends on the application in that setting of the general principles most recently clarified in the case of *Robinson*. Following that approach, it is helpful to consider in the first place whether the case is one in which the defendant is alleged to have harmed the claimant, or one in which the defendant is alleged to have failed to provide a benefit to the claimant, for example by protecting him from harm. The present case falls into the latter category.

75. Understandably, the reasoning of Irwin LJ in the Court of Appeal in the present case did not follow the approach set out in *Robinson*, which was decided after the Court of Appeal had given its decision . . . [I]n cases such as *Gorringe, Michael* and *Robinson* both the House of Lords and this court adopted a different approach (or rather, reverted to an earlier approach) to the question whether a public authority is under a duty of care. That approach is based on the premise that public authorities are prima facie subject to the same general principles of the common law of negligence as private individuals and organisations, and may therefore be liable for negligently causing individuals to suffer actionable harm but not, in the absence of some particular reason justifying such liability, for negligently failing to protect individuals from harm caused by others. Rather than justifying decisions that public authorities owe no duty of care by relying on public policy, it has been held that even if a duty of care would ordinarily arise on the application of common law principles, it may nevertheless be excluded or restricted by statute where it would be inconsistent with the scheme of the legislation under which the public authority is operating. In that way, the courts can continue to take into account, for example, the difficult choices which may be involved in the exercise of discretionary powers . . .

78. The claim against the council is based . . . on an assumption of responsibility or 'special relationship'. The particulars of claim state:

> In purporting to investigate the risk that the claimants' neighbours posed to the claimants and subsequently in attempting to monitor the claimants' plight as set out in the sequence of events above, the defendant had accepted a responsibility for the claimants' particular difficulties and/or there was a special nexus or special relationship between the claimants and the defendant. The defendant purported to protect the claimants by such investigation and in as far as such investigation is shown to have been carried out negligently and/or negligently acted on the defendant is liable for breach of duty.

The 'sequence of events' referred to is a chronology of events. In relation to investigation and monitoring by the council's social services department, it refers to the assignment of social workers to the claimants, to the various assessments of their needs, and to meetings at which the appropriate response to . . . [the younger brother's] behaviour was discussed.

79. Irwin LJ rejected the contention that there was an assumption of responsibility by the council . . . I have also come to the conclusion that the particulars of claim do not provide a basis on which an assumption of responsibility might be established, for the following reasons.

80. As Lord Browne-Wilkinson explained in relation to the educational cases in *X (Minors) v Bedfordshire* . . . a public body which offers a service to the public often assumes a responsibility to those using the service. The assumption of responsibility is an undertaking that reasonable care will be taken, either express or more commonly implied, usually from the reasonable foreseeability of reliance on the exercise of such care. Thus, whether operated privately or under statutory powers, a hospital undertakes to exercise reasonable care in the medical treatment of its patients. The same is true, mutatis mutandis, of an education authority accepting pupils into its schools.

81. In the present case, on the other hand, the council's investigating and monitoring the claimants' position did not involve the provision of a service to them on which they or their mother could be expected to rely. It may have been reasonably foreseeable that their mother would be anxious that the council should act so as to protect the family from their neighbours, in particular by re-housing them, but anxiety does not amount to reliance. Nor could it be said that the claimants and their mother had entrusted their safety to the council, or that the council had accepted that responsibility. Nor had the council taken the claimants into its care, and thereby assumed responsibility for their welfare. The position is not, therefore, the same as in *Barrett v Enfield* [[2001] 2 AC 550]. In short, the nature of the statutory functions relied on in the particulars of claim did not in itself entail that the council assumed or undertook a responsibility towards the claimants to perform those functions with reasonable care.

82. It is of course possible, even where no such assumption can be inferred from the nature of the function itself, that it can nevertheless be inferred from the manner in which the public authority has behaved towards the claimant in a particular case. Since such an inference depends on the facts of the individual case, there may well be cases in which the existence or absence of an assumption of responsibility cannot be determined on a strike out application. Nevertheless, the particulars of claim must provide some basis for the leading of evidence at trial from which an assumption of responsibility could be inferred. In the present case, however, the particulars of claim do not provide a basis for leading evidence about any particular behaviour by the council towards the claimants or their mother, besides the performance of its statutory functions, from which an assumption of responsibility might be inferred. . . .

83. I would therefore conclude . . . that the particulars of claim do not set out an arguable claim that the council owed the claimants a duty of care. Although *X (Minors) v Bedfordshire* cannot now be understood as laying down a rule that local authorities do not under any circumstances owe a duty of care to children in relation to the performance of their social services functions, as the Court of Appeal rightly held in *D v East Berkshire*, the particulars of claim in this case do not lay a foundation for establishing circumstances in which such a duty might exist.

84. The council is also sought to be held liable on the basis of vicarious liability for the negligence of its employees. . . .

85. . . . It appears from the particulars of claim that social workers carried out assessments of the claimants' needs on the council's instructions, and provided the council (and others who may have been involved in decision-making) with information and professional advice about the children for the purpose of enabling the council to perform its statutory functions.

86. There is no doubt that, in carrying out those functions, the social workers were under a contractual duty to the council to exercise proper professional skill and care. The question is whether, in addition, they also owed a similar duty to the claimants under the law of tort. That depends on whether the social workers assumed a responsibility towards the claimants to perform their functions with reasonable care. In considering that question, it may be helpful to compare the position of the social workers with the positions of the educational psychologists and the advisory teacher in *X (Minors) v Bedfordshire*, and the educational psychologists in *Phelps v Hillingdon*.

87. In the former case, Lord Browne-Wilkinson accepted in relation to the *Dorset* proceedings that the local authority could be vicariously liable for negligence on the part of its educational psychologists because they were providing professional advice to parents on which the parents had foreseeably relied. In the *Hampshire* proceedings, he accepted that an advisory teacher, brought in to advise on a pupil's educational needs, owed a duty to the child to exercise reasonable skill and care provided he knew that his advice would be communicated to the pupil's parents, and could therefore reasonably foresee that they would rely on such advice.

In *Phelps v Hillingdon*, the duty of care of the educational psychologist towards the child was again based on the fact that it was reasonably foreseeable that the child's parents would rely on the advice provided. Those were all cases where the duty of care arose on the basis of the *Hedley Byrne* principle. In the present case, on the other hand, there is no suggestion that the social workers provided advice on which the claimants' mother would foreseeably rely.

88. As has been explained, however, the concept of an assumption of responsibility is not confined to the provision of information or advice. It can also apply where, as Lord Goff put it in *Spring v Guardian Assurance plc*, the claimant entrusts the defendant with the conduct of his affairs, in general or in particular. Such situations can arise where the defendant undertakes the performance of some task or the provision of some service for the claimant with an undertaking that reasonable care will be taken. Such an undertaking may be express, but is more commonly implied, usually by reason of the foreseeability of reliance by the claimant on the exercise of such care. In the present case, however, there is nothing in the particulars of claim to suggest that a situation of that kind came into being.

89. The existence of an assumption of responsibility can be highly dependent on the facts of a particular case, and where there appears to be a real possibility that such a case might be made out, a court will not decide otherwise on a strike out application. In the circumstances which I have described, however, the particulars of claim do not in my opinion set out any basis on which an assumption of responsibility might be established at trial . . .

Conclusion

91. The particulars of claim in these proceedings do not disclose any recognisable basis for a cause of action. The complaint is that the council or its employees failed to fulfil a common law duty to protect the claimants from harm inflicted by their neighbours by exercising certain statutory powers. The relevant provisions do not themselves create a cause of action. Reliance is placed on an assumption of responsibility arising from the relationship between the claimants and the council or its employees, but there is nothing to suggest that those relationships possessed the necessary characteristics for an assumption of responsibility to arise. . . . Although the court does not have before it all the evidence which might emerge at a trial, there is no reason to believe that the claimants could overcome these fundamental problems as to the legal basis of their claim. That being so, it is to the advantage of all concerned that the claim should not proceed to what would be a costly but inevitably fruitless trial . . .

Appeal dismissed.

COMMENTARY

After *Michael* and *N v Poole* it is clear that the liability of a public authority in negligence must now be based on the application of ordinary private law principles, which means that either the public authority must have caused damage by its positive conduct, or that the circumstances fall within a category of case in which the principles applicable to private persons would impose an affirmative duty of care. In both the extracted cases, the relevant category was where the public authority assumes responsibility towards the claimant or victim.

Lord Reed's analysis in *N v Poole* contains a helpful typology of the situations in which an assumption of responsibility by a public authority might be found. At [82], he distinguishes between situations where an assumption of responsibility can be inferred from the nature of the function the public authority was performing, and those where it can otherwise be inferred from the manner in which the public authority has behaved towards the claimant or victim in a particular case. Examples of the former are the provision of a service on which the claimant or victim reasonably foreseeably relies (e.g. the provision of medical treatment or accepting a pupil into a school) and the acceptance of a responsibility for a person's safety (e.g. where a council takes a vulnerable child into protective care). This analysis suggests a two-stage inquiry: first, a court should address whether an assumption of responsibility can be inferred from the function the public authority was performing; secondly, if it cannot do that, it should consider whether an assumption of responsibility can be otherwise inferred from the words or conduct of the public authority on the specific facts. Over time, the courts may be expected to address whether public authority functions other than healthcare and educational provision are such as to raise such an inference, and this will tend to promote consistency and predictability in the law. But a lot will still fall to be assessed at the second stage of the inquiry, in light of the particular facts of the individual case.

If *Kent v Griffiths* were to be repeated today, would the assumption of responsibility found there arise at the first or second stage of the inquiry outlined above?

Creation of a Source of Danger

Though it was not relevant to the decision, Lord Reed accepted in *N v Poole*, at [65], that a public authority can come under a common law duty to protect from harm where it created the source of danger from which the harm arose. By way of example, in *Yetkin v Mahmood* [2011] QB 827, a pedestrian was injured at a designated crossing over a dual carriageway when, her view seriously obscured by shrubs the council had planted in the central reservation and failed to trim back, she stepped out in front of an oncoming vehicle and was hit by it. Finding the council partly liable for the accident, the Court of Appeal justified the imposition of an affirmative duty of care on the basis that this was a case where the council was itself responsible for creating the hazard. The court distinguished the House of Lords' decision in *Gorringe*, where the Law Lords had taken the view that on the facts of the case the highway authority's *failure* to paint a 'Slow' marking on the road had not amounted to the creation of a danger. In that earlier decision, at [92], Lord Brown conceded that there might be other circumstances in which a highway authority might be found to have created a source of danger, giving as examples a 'crass mistake' in the painting of road markings indicating it was safe to overtake, and the signalling of a one-way street with no 'No Entry' signs at the other end; such mistakes might 'induce . . . a perfectly careful motorist into the path of danger'. However, the House of Lords in *Gorringe* was notably unenthusiastic about *Bird v Pearce* [1979] RTR 369, where the Court of Appeal held that by painting white lines indicating priority at a series of junctions along a road, and then failing to repaint lines that had been obliterated at one junction, a highway authority had itself created a source of danger that would not have existed had no lines been painted at all. That decision must now be treated as dubious.

By contrast, in *Sandhar v Department of Transport, Environment and the Regions* [2005] 1 WLR 1632, where the claimant argued that the defendant government department had created a trap by fostering a public expectation that major roads would be salted in frosty conditions, and then failing to salt one, the Court of Appeal dismissed the argument on the ground that there was no evidence that the driver involved had relied on any such expectation. And in *Sumner v Colborne* [2019] QB 430, where the claimant cyclist was injured in a collision with the defendant's car when it emerged into his path from a minor road, the defendant sought unsuccessfully to bring contribution proceedings against the highway authorities responsible for the two roads, alleging that the junction was dangerous because visibility was obstructed by vegetation that had been allowed to grow on land owned by the authority responsible for the major road. The Court of Appeal dismissed the contribution proceedings against both authorities. Regarding the authority responsible for the minor road, the alleged negligence was a simple failure to act—namely, to cut back the vegetation—and the case was therefore indistinguishable from *Stovin v Wise* [1996] AC 923 (visibility at junction obstructed by raised bank on land that the authority had the power to require to be removed). Regarding the authority responsible for the major road, its only positive act was to fence the area where the vegetation grew, meaning that livestock could no longer graze there, and it would not be fair, just and reasonable to impose a duty on landowners to ensure that vegetation on their property did not affect sightlines on neighbouring highways. The court distinguished *Yetkin v Mahmood* on the basis that the overgrown vegetation there was on the highway—specifically, in the central reservation—and was therefore the highway authority's responsibility.

These creation of danger cases blur the line between omissions and positive acts, as the initial creation of the danger and subsequent failure to remedy it can be seen as part of a single sequence, even if the defendant's negligence only relates to the failure to remedy. In cases like *Yetkin*, the defendant's conduct taken as a whole demonstrably made the claimant worse off, which clearly distinguishes them from cases of failure to confer a benefit like *N v Poole*.

If the police attend an accident caused by a slippery road surface, take charge of the situation then leave without neutralising the danger, can they be said to have performed positive acts that made the situation worse inasmuch as, if they had not attended, the fire service would have taken control and neutralised the danger itself? Cf. *Tindall v Chief Constable of Thames Valley Police* [2022] EWCA Civ 25, where the Court of Appeal was not persuaded by an argument to that effect. Compare *Transport Arendonk v Chief Constable of Essex Police* [2020] RTR 22, where the High Court declined to strike out a claim in respect of the theft of goods from the claimant's lorry, which they alleged had been exposed to precisely that risk by the police's action in arresting the driver after he failed a breath test, thereby leaving the lorry unattended in a layby, and refusing his request to telephone the claimant. A positive act making the claimant worse off?

The Distinct Claim under the Human Rights Act

A background presence in all the recent decisions about the affirmative duties owed by public authorities has been the positive obligations imposed on such authorities by the HRA. Loss suffered as the result of the violation of those obligations (which are extensive) may be compensated by an award of damages under the remedial mechanism established by the Act (ss. 7, 8, extracted in Ch. 1.III.2).

In *Van Colle v Chief Constable of Hertfordshire* [2009] 1 AC 225, the House of Lords affirmed that the police, as a public authority under the Act, may have a positive obligation to take reasonable preventive measures to protect the Article 2, ECHR rights of an individual whose life they know or ought to know is at real and immediate risk as a result of the criminal acts of a third party. In this respect, the Law Lords adopted the approach taken by the European Court of Human Rights in *Osman v United Kingdom* [1999] 1 FLR 193. They emphasised that the test of real and immediate risk is not easily satisfied, the threshold being high (see also *In re Officer L* [2007] 1 WLR 2135 at [20], per Lord Carswell). The *Van Colle* case itself illustrates the height of the hurdle. The deceased was murdered after reporting to the police that he had received telephone threats while scheduled to act as a prosecution witness at the trial of a minor criminal. A disciplinary tribunal found that the officer in charge of the case was guilty of not performing his duties conscientiously and diligently in respect of witness intimidation. But the House of Lords concluded unanimously that the warning signs in the case were very much less clear and obvious than those in *Osman* (itself a case where the risk was found not to have been real and immediate) and concluded that no liability under the HRA arose on the facts.

By contrast, in *Michael v Chief Constable of South Wales* (extracted earlier), the Supreme Court considered that there was enough evidence of a real and immediate risk to life to warrant a full trial in circumstances where a woman made an emergency call to the police after being threatened by her former partner, who stabbed her to death later the same night.

The real and immediate risk test has also been applied in the context of suicides by psychiatric patients undergoing treatment in public hospitals: *Savage v South Essex Partnership NHS Foundation Trust* [2009] 1 AC 681 (preliminary proceedings) and *Rabone v Pennine Care NHS Trust* [2012] 2 AC 72 (compensation awarded). Though this is a situation in which it is clear that a common law duty of care is owed to the patient, the HRA claim has the practical advantage of outflanking restrictions on the class of other persons entitled to compensation in the event of the patient's unlawful death: see further in Chapter 16.III.3.

See also *Mitchell v Glasgow City Council* [2009] 1 AC 874, noted in III (real and immediate risk test not satisfied in case of fatal attack on tenant of defendant council by his neighbour).

Do you think it desirable that two separate claims—one at common law and one under the HRA—should potentially exist side-by-side in actions against public authorities? For discussion of how the separate claims might pursue different ends, and how they should best be coordinated, see Steele, 'Damages in tort and under the Human Rights Act: remedial or functional separation?' [2008] CLJ 606; du Bois, 'Human Rights and the Tort Liability of Public Authorities' (2011) 127 LQR 589; and Nolan, 'Negligence and Human Rights Law: The Case for Separate Development' (2013) 76 MLR 286.

10 STATUTORY LIABILITY REGIMES

As the authors of a book on statutory torts point out, 'statutes play a significant role in the modern law of tort' (*Stanton*, para. 1.001; see also *Tort Law and the Legislature*). And while it is undoubtedly true that most of the English law of tort is still based upon common law principles, there are a number of situations where statutory liability regimes have been created.

Two of the most important of these statutory regimes concern the liability of occupiers to those coming onto their land (governed by the Occupiers' Liability Acts of 1957 and 1984) and liability in respect of defective products (governed by the Consumer Protection Act 1987). In both these areas Parliament has intervened to remedy perceived failings in the common law. The Occupiers' Liability Acts replaced the previous common law liability of occupiers, which was generally thought to need rationalisation. A different catalyst prompted the passing of the Consumer Protection Act 1987: a Directive from the European Community requiring uniformity in the product liability laws of member states forced the United Kingdom to legislate and to create a form of strict liability in the 1987 Act. The 1987 Act has not, however, replaced the common law, and in particular it remains open to a claimant in a product liability case to sue in negligence if the elements of that cause of action are satisfied. Although in general it will be easier to establish liability under the Act than in negligence, there are some limitations on the statutory action (e.g. in respect of damage to commercial property) which do not apply to a common law claim, with the result that the common law remains significant.

The final part of this chapter considers the action for breach of statutory duty. This differs from the action for negligence in that liability is based not on a common law duty of care but on a duty imposed on the defendant by Parliament. The claimant is thus able to invoke an alternative cause of action to negligence, perhaps so as to benefit from a strict rather than a fault-based liability (depending upon the precise terms of the legislation in question) or to bypass restrictions on the scope of the duty of care in negligence (although the claimant must still establish causation and damage). A major impetus for the development of breach of statutory duty as an independent tort was the restrictions placed on the liability of employers to their employees at common law, and many of the early claims arose out of statutory duties imposed on employers. The actionability of the regulations governing health and safety at work has recently been severely circumscribed by legislation, with the result that the practical significance of the breach of statutory duty tort is now much diminished. However, breach of statutory duty claims can still be brought in a wide variety of circumstances, against public as well as private defendants, while the relationship between statutory regulation and tort law remains of much theoretical interest.

I. Occupiers' Liability

Occupiers' liability is the 'liability of an occupier of premises for injuries to persons who come on to those premises' (*North*, para. 1.05). Although in essence a form of negligence liability, occupiers' liability is the subject of separate treatment for a number of reasons. One is that this area of law is now governed by legislation, namely the Occupiers' Liability Act 1957 and the Occupiers' Liability Act 1984. A second is that the old common law of occupiers' liability relied on distinct concepts not employed elsewhere in the law of negligence, and some of these concepts (e.g. 'occupier') are also used in the statutory liability regime. And the final reason is that occupiers' liability routinely arises out of omissions by occupiers, rather than positive conduct on their part. In general negligence law, liability for omissions is the exception rather than the rule (see Ch. 9), but the opposite is true in the case of occupiers' liability, and the extensive positive obligations that occupiers owe to their visitors (and sometimes even to non-visitors) explain—at least to some extent—both why the old common law in this area was so complex, and why the current law is governed by statute.

1. The Law pre-1957

Although occupiers' liability has largely been regulated by statute since 1957, reference to the earlier law is required as the legislation incorporates some common law concepts. The common law of occupiers' liability was complicated and unsatisfactory and depended upon the classification of entrants onto the occupier's land into one of three, or possibly four, categories: the contractual entrant, the invitee, the licensee and the trespasser. This was necessary because the precise duty owed by the occupier varied depending on the status of the entrant (see Dixon J in the Australian case of *Lipman v Clendinnen* (1932) 46 CLR 550).

In *Robert Addie and Sons (Collieries) Ltd v Dumbreck* [1929] AC 358, Lord Hailsham LC described the duties owed to the various categories of entrant as follows. The highest duty was owed to persons who were present at the invitation of the occupier, that duty being to take reasonable care that the premises were safe. In the case of licensees (express or implied) the obligation was less stringent: the occupier had no general duty of care with regard to the safety of the premises, but was bound not to create a trap or to allow to exist upon the premises any concealed danger that was not apparent to the visitor, but which was known—or ought to have been known—to the occupier. Finally, when it came to trespassers the occupier had no duty to take reasonable care for their protection or even to protect them from concealed danger. The trespasser came onto the premises at their own risk, and the occupier was liable only where the trespasser's injury was due to an act of the occupier done with the intention of harming the trespasser, or with reckless disregard to their presence.

Although Lord Hailsham described three types of entrant, his first category is probably an amalgam of two categories, the contractual entrant (e.g. a hotel guest) and the invitee (e.g. a customer in a shop), with the duty of reasonable care in respect of the safety of the premises being limited to the contractual entrant. As for the status of an invitee, such as a customer, this was discussed in *Indermaur v Dames* (1866) LR 1 CP 274, where Willes J (at 287) noted that 'his protection does not depend upon the fact of a contract being entered into in the way of the shopkeeper's business during the stay of the customer, but upon the fact that the customer has come into the shop in pursuance of a tacit invitation given by the shopkeeper, with a view to business which concerns himself.' Such an entrant was entitled to the exercise of reasonable care by the occupier to prevent damage from unusual danger, of which the occupier knew or ought to have known. The duty arose even though the invitee was aware of the danger and was not necessarily fulfilled by warning him of it. It should be noted that 'invitee' was a legal term of art: the entrant had to be on the occupier's premises for 'a purpose in which the occupier himself has some concern, a pecuniary, material or business interest' (per Dixon J in *Lipman* at 556). Hence, even though the occupier might invite a friend over for a social dinner, such a person would be a licensee, not an invitee, and so would be owed only a lesser duty of care. But it was far better to be a licensee than a trespasser, for as the previous paragraph shows, the trespasser received minimal protection: they could not be treated as an outlaw and deliberately or recklessly harmed, but beyond that no duty was owed.

One consequence of the lack of protection given to trespassers by the old common law of occupiers' liability was that plaintiffs who appeared to be trespassers sometimes argued that they had an implied licence to be on the premises, so that they were owed a duty of care as a licensee. While judges may not have been very sympathetic towards adult trespassers using this argument, the position was different for children who, as Lord Buckmaster put it in *Addie* (at 379), 'could know nothing of the law of trespass or licence' (although his Lordship's sympathy did not extend to actually allowing the plaintiff to recover in that case). A leading example of the more lenient line taken towards children is *Cooke v Midland Great Western Railway of Ireland* [1909] AC 229, where the plaintiff was a young child who had been seriously injured while playing on an unlocked railway turntable on the defendant's land. The defendant's employees were aware that children were in the habit of playing with the turntable, which they could easily access though a gap in a fence separating the defendant's land from a public road. An appeal from a jury finding for the plaintiff was dismissed by the House of Lords, Lord Macnaghten noting (at 236) that it did not seem unreasonable to hold that:

> [I]f [the defendants] allow their property to be open to all comers, infants as well as children of maturer age, and place upon it a machine attractive to children and dangerous as a plaything, they may be responsible in damages to those who resort to it with their tacit permission, and who are unable, in consequence of their tender age, to take care of themselves.

The result of this kind of analysis, which became known as the doctrine of 'allurement', was to promote the child to the status of a licensee, with the result that the child was granted the more extensive protection accorded to that status, and the chances of them recovering damages were increased. (See further on *Cooke* and other early twentieth-century occupiers' liability cases involving children, *Mitchell*, pp. 111–27; and for an illuminating discussion of the equivalent American doctrine, see Atkinson, 'Creating the Responsible Child: Risk, Responsibility, and the Attractive Nuisance Doctrine' (2017) 42 *Law & Social Inquiry* 1122, who attributes a hardening of judicial attitudes towards child trespassers over time to changing visions of childhood, with a romantic nineteenth-century conception of the child as innocent, irrational and impulsive giving way in the early twentieth century to a perception of children as rational individuals capable of weighing risks and bearing responsibility, as embodied in the development of the standard of the 'reasonable child'.)

2. The 1957 Act

The subtleties that were required to draw distinctions between the various classes of entrants, particularly licensees and invitees, provoked criticism of this branch of the common law. As a result, the question of occupiers' liability was referred to the Law Reform Committee, which published a report on the issue in 1954 (*Third Report: Occupiers' Liability to Invitees, Licensees and Trespassers*). The main recommendations of the report were that the distinction between invitees and licensees be abolished and that the occupier owe the same duty to everyone on the premises with their permission, namely a duty to take reasonable care to ensure that the premises were reasonably safe for use by the visitor for the purpose to which the permission related. The Committee argued that the distinction between invitees and licensees (together with the different duty the occupier owed to each) was artificial:

> A reasonable occupier of premises surely does not say to himself (for instance) 'These steps are dangerously slippery with frozen snow but they don't amount to a trap. I am expecting no visitors except Jones, who is coming to dinner. He is a mere licensee, and I need not do anything about the steps so far as he is concerned' . . . Nor, on the other hand, does he say to himself 'I must clear the snow off the steps because Brown is coming to see me on business. He will be an invitee, and if he slips on the steps I may find myself liable to him in damages'. Surely the reasonable occupier's thought is more likely to be 'These steps are dangerous. I must clear the snow off them. Otherwise someone coming to my house may slip and get hurt.'

As a result of the Committee's report, Parliament passed the Occupiers' Liability Act 1957, which embodied the main recommendations made by the Committee. See further on the background to the Act, S. Bailey, 'Occupiers' Liability: the Enactment of "Common Law" Principles', in *Tort Law and the Legislature*.

Occupiers' Liability Act 1957

An Act to amend the law of England and Wales as to the liability of occupiers and others for injury or damage resulting to persons or goods lawfully on any land or other property from dangers due to the state of the property or to things done or omitted to be done there . . .

1. Preliminary

(1) The rules enacted by the two next following sections shall have effect, in place of the rules of the common law, to regulate the duty which an occupier of premises owes to his visitors in respect of dangers due to the state of the premises or to things done or omitted to be done on them.

(2) The rules so enacted shall regulate the nature of the duty imposed by law in consequence of a person's occupation or control of premises and of any invitation or permission he gives (or is to be treated as giving) to another to enter or use the premises, but they shall not alter the rules of the common law as to the persons on whom a duty is so imposed or to whom it is owed; and accordingly for the purpose of the rules so enacted the persons who are to be treated as an occupier and as his visitors are the same (subject to subsection (4) of this section) as the persons who would at common law be treated as an occupier and as his invitees or licensees.

(3) The rules so enacted in relation to an occupier of premises and his visitors shall also apply, in like manner and to the like extent as the principles applicable at common law to an occupier of premises and his invitees or licensees would apply, to regulate—
   (a) the obligations of a person occupying or having control over any fixed or moveable structure, including any vessel, vehicle or aircraft; and
   (b) the obligations of a person occupying or having control over any premises or structure in respect of damage to property, including the property of persons who are not themselves his visitors.

(4) A person entering any premises in exercise of rights conferred by virtue of—
   (a) section 2(1) of the Countryside and Rights of Way Act 2000, or
   (b) an access agreement or order under the National Parks and Access to the Countryside Act 1949, is not, for the purposes of this Act, a visitor of the occupier of the premises.

2. Extent of occupiers' ordinary duty

(1) An occupier of premises owes the same duty, the 'common duty of care', to all his visitors, except in so far as he is free to and does extend, restrict, modify or exclude his duty to any visitor or visitors by agreement or otherwise.

(2) The common duty of care is a duty to take such care as in all the circumstances of the case is reasonable to see that the visitor will be reasonably safe in using the premises for the purposes for which he is invited or permitted by the occupier to be there.

(3) The circumstances relevant for the present purpose include the degree of care, and of want of care, which would ordinarily be looked for in such a visitor, so that (for example) in proper cases—
   (a) an occupier must be prepared for children to be less careful than adults; and
   (b) an occupier may expect that a person, in the exercise of his calling, will appreciate and guard against any special risks ordinarily incident to it, so far as the occupier leaves him free to do so.

(4) In determining whether the occupier of premises has discharged the common duty of care to a visitor, regard is to be had to all the circumstances, so that (for example)—
   (a) where damage is caused to a visitor by a danger of which he had been warned by the occupier, the warning is not to be treated without more as absolving the occupier from liability, unless in all the circumstances it was enough to enable the visitor to be reasonably safe; and
   (b) where damage is caused to a visitor by a danger due to the faulty execution of any work of construction, maintenance or repair by an independent contractor employed by the occupier, the occupier is not to be treated without more as answerable for the danger if in all the circumstances he had acted reasonably in entrusting the work to an independent contractor and had taken such steps (if any) as he reasonably ought in order to satisfy himself that the contractor was competent and that the work had been properly done.

(5) The common duty of care does not impose on an occupier any obligation to a visitor in respect of risks willingly accepted as his by the visitor (the question whether a risk was so accepted to be decided on the same principles as in other cases in which one person owes a duty of care to another).

(6) For the purposes of this section, persons who enter premises for any purpose in the exercise of a right conferred by law are to be treated as permitted by the occupier to be there for that purpose, whether they in fact have his permission or not.

3. Effect of contract on occupier's liability to third party

(1) Where an occupier of premises is bound by contract to permit persons who are strangers to the contract to enter or use the premises, the duty of care which he owes to them as his visitors cannot be restricted or excluded by that contract, but (subject to any provision of the contract to the contrary) shall include the duty to perform his obligations under the contract, whether undertaken for their protection or not, in so far as those obligations go beyond the obligations otherwise involved in that duty.

(2) A contract shall not by virtue of this section have the effect, unless it expressly so provides, of making an occupier who has taken all reasonable care answerable to strangers to the contract for dangers due to the faulty execution of any work of construction, maintenance or repair or other like operation by persons other than himself, his servants and persons acting under his direction and control.

(3) In this section 'stranger to the contract' means a person not for the time being entitled to the benefit of the contract as a party to it or as the successor by assignment or otherwise of a party to it, and accordingly includes a party to the contract who has ceased to be so entitled.

(4) Where by the terms or conditions governing any tenancy (including a statutory tenancy which does not in law amount to a tenancy) either the landlord or the tenant is bound, though not by contract, to permit persons to enter or use premises of which he is the occupier, this section shall apply as if the tenancy were a contract between the landlord and the tenant.

(5) This section, in so far as it prevents the common duty of care from being restricted or excluded, applies to contracts entered into and tenancies created before the commencement of this Act, as well as to those entered into or created after its commencement; but, in so far as it enlarges the duty owed by an occupier beyond the common duty of care, it shall have effect only in relation to obligations which are undertaken after that commencement or which are renewed by agreement (whether express or implied) after that commencement . . .

5. Implied term in contracts

(1) Where persons enter or use, or bring or send goods to, any premises in exercise of a right conferred by contract with a person occupying or having control of the premises, the duty he owes them in respect of dangers due to the state of the premises or to things done or omitted to be done on them, in so far as the duty depends on a term to be implied in the contract by reason of its conferring that right, shall be the common duty of care.

(2) The fore going subsection shall apply to fixed and moveable structures as it applies to premises.

(3) This section does not affect the obligations imposed on a person by or by virtue of any contract for the hire of, or for the carriage for reward of persons or goods in, any vehicle, vessel, aircraft or other means of transport, or by virtue of any contract of bailment.

(4) This section does not apply to contracts entered into before the commencement of this Act.

COMMENTARY

As is made clear in s. 1, the Act replaces the common law rules as to an occupier's liability, but only to the extent set out in the section. Classification as an 'occupier' or a 'visitor' is determined by applying the existing common law rules, a visitor being an entrant who would have been classified as an invitee or licensee. Thus a shop customer and a dinner guest are both visitors and are owed the common duty of care set out in s. 2, as (by virtue of s. 5) is the contractual entrant (unless the standard of care is dealt with by an express term of the contract). Visitors also include those who enter with the implied permission of the occupier, such as a person who walks up the occupier's drive to put a leaflet through the front door (see further on implied permission, *Winfield & Jolowicz*, para. 10–009), while s. 2(6) expressly extends the protection of the Act to those who enter premises in the exercise of a right conferred by law, such as firefighters trying to extinguish a fire or police officers with a warrant to enter.

What if the permission to enter comes not from the occupier themselves, but from an employee or contractor of the occupier? In *Ferguson v Welsh* [1987] 1 WLR 1553, the defendant council had awarded a demolition contract to a Mr Spence, who—it was alleged—had then arranged for subcontractors (the Welsh brothers) to do the work, in breach of Mr Spence's contract with the council. An employee of the Welsh brothers was injured after a wall collapsed during the course of the demolition, and one of the issues that arose was the status of the employee *vis-à-vis* the council. The House of Lords held that where an independent contractor of the occupier invited someone onto the premises in breach of an express prohibition of the occupier, that person should be classified as a visitor if they honestly believed that the contractor was entitled to invite them in (a principle that would apply *a fortiori* in a case where the invitation came from an employee of the occupier). This conclusion rested on agency principles, as this passage from the speech of Lord Keith shows (at 1559):

> It was maintained . . . that by putting Mr Spence into occupation of the building for purposes of demolition the council had clothed him with apparent or ostensible authority to invite other persons onto the premises, including sub-contractors and their employees. Such persons would know nothing of the limitation on Mr Spence's actual authority, and were not reasonably to be treated as trespassers in a question with the council. In my opinion, there is evidence capable of establishing that Mr Spence had ostensible authority from the council to invite the Welsh brothers and their employees onto the site. Mr Spence was placed in control of the site for demolition purposes, and to one who had no knowledge of the council's policy of prohibiting sub-contracts this would indicate that he was entitled to invite whomsoever he pleased onto the site for the purpose of carrying out demolition.

The employee was therefore a visitor of the council, although on the facts there was no liability under the 1957 Act.

The position of entrants who are not visitors (such as trespassers) is governed not by the 1957 Act, but by the Occupiers' Liability Act 1984 (extracted I.3). A visitor who exceeds the scope of their permission becomes a trespasser, so that any claim which might then arise would be governed by the 1984 Act (see *Harvey v Plymouth City Council* [2010] PIQR P18). In this respect the old cases dealing with the doctrine of allurement remain worthy of attention as they provide examples of situations where apparently trespassing children may be regarded as visitors and hence be owed the common duty of care.

Would the position of children be better dealt with by a special rule? As Bailey notes (*op. cit.*, p. 196), when the 1957 Act was before Parliament an amendment that would have treated a child under the age of 11 as a lawful visitor unless the occupier had taken reasonably sufficient steps to prevent the child entering or using the premises was rejected.

(a) Occupier

Wheat v E. Lacon & Co Ltd [1966] AC 552

The first defendant was a brewery (Lacons), which owned a public house. Under a contract with the brewery, Mr and Mrs Richardson were responsible for the management of the public house. The contract allowed the brewery to enter the premises to view the state of repair. It also allowed the Richardsons to occupy the public house (including the first floor) although the agreement stated that this occupation did not create any tenancy nor give the manager any estate or interest in the land. The brewery allowed Mrs Richardson to take paid lodgers in the residential part of the public house. One of the methods of access from the ground floor to the first was a back staircase. The plaintiff's husband (a paying guest of Mrs Richardson) was found dead at the bottom of the back stairs. It appeared that he had fallen while attempting to get to the bar on the ground floor to buy some drinks. There was a light at the top of the staircase but there was no bulb in it at the time of the accident. There was also a handrail down one side of the staircase terminating directly above the third step. The plaintiff brought an action under the Fatal Accidents Acts 1846–1908 and the Law Reform (Miscellaneous Provisions) Act 1934, against the brewery, Mr Richardson and Mrs Richardson for damages in respect of her husband's death, alleging negligence and breach of duty under the Occupiers' Liability Act 1957. The plaintiff's claim against all three defendants was dismissed at first instance and an appeal as regards the brewery was dismissed by the Court of Appeal, a majority holding that the brewery were not occupiers of the public house. The plaintiff appealed to the House of Lords.

Lord Denning

In the Occupiers' Liability Act, 1957, the word 'occupier' is used in the same sense as was used in the common law cases on occupiers' liability for dangerous premises. It was simply a convenient word to denote a person who had a sufficient degree of control over premises to put him under a duty of care towards those who came lawfully on to the premises. Those persons were divided into two categories, invitees and licensees: and a higher duty was owed to invitees than to licensees. But by the year 1956 the distinction between invitees and licensees had been reduced to vanishing point. The duty of the occupier had become simply a duty to take reasonable care to see that the premises were reasonably safe for people coming lawfully on to them: and it made no difference whether they were invitees or licensees: see *Slater v Clay Cross Co Ltd* [1956] 2 QB 264. The Act of 1957 confirmed the process. It did away, once and for all, with invitees and licensees and classed them all as 'visitors'; and it put upon the occupier the same duty to all of them, namely, the common duty of care. This duty is simply a particular instance of the general duty of care which each man owes to his 'neighbour.' . . . Translating this general principle into its particular application to dangerous premises, it becomes simply this: wherever a person has a sufficient degree of control over premises that he ought to realise that any failure on his part to use care may result in injury to a person coming lawfully there, then he is an 'occupier' and the person coming lawfully there is his 'visitor': and the 'occupier' is under a duty to his 'visitor' to use reasonable care. In order to be an 'occupier' it is not necessary for a person to have entire control over the premises. He need not have exclusive occupation. Suffice it that he has some degree of control. He may share the control with others. Two or more may be 'occupiers.' And whenever this happens, each is under a duty to use care towards persons coming lawfully on to the premises, dependent on his degree of control. If each fails in his duty, each is liable to a visitor who is injured in consequence of his failure, but each may have a claim to contribution from the other.

In *Salmond on Torts*, 14th ed. (1965), p. 372, it is said that an 'occupier' is 'he who has the immediate supervision and control and the power of permitting or prohibiting the entry of other persons.' This definition was adopted by Roxburgh J in *Hartwell v Grayson, Rollo and Clover Docks Ltd* [1947] KB 901 and by Diplock LJ in the present case. There is no doubt that a person who fulfils that test is an 'occupier.' He is the person who says 'come in.' But I think that test is too narrow by far. There are other people who are 'occupiers,' even though they do not say 'come in.' If a person has any degree of control over the state of the premises it is enough. The position is best shown by examining the cases in four groups.

First, where a landlord let premises by demise to a tenant, he was regarded as parting with all control over them. He did not retain any degree of control, even though he had undertaken to repair the structure. Accordingly, he was held to be under no duty to any person coming lawfully on to the premises, save only to the tenant under the agreement to repair. In *Cavalier v Pope* [1906] AC 428 it was argued that the premises were under the control of the landlord because of his agreement to repair: but the House of Lords rejected that argument. That case has now been overruled by section 4 of the Act of 1957 to the extent therein mentioned.

Secondly, where an owner let floors or flats in a building to tenants, but did not demise the common staircase or the roof or some other parts, he was regarded as having retained control of all parts not demised by him. Accordingly, he was held to be under a duty in respect of those retained parts to all persons coming lawfully on to the premises. So he was held liable for a defective staircase in *Miller v Hancock* [1893] 2 QB 177; for the gutters in the roof of *Hargroves, Aronson & Co v Hartopp* [1905] 1 KB 472 and for the private balcony in *Sutcliffe v Clients Investment Co Ltd* [1924] 2 KB 746. The extent of the duty was held to be that owed to a licensee, and not to an invitee: see *Fairman v Perpetual Investment Building Society* [1923] AC 74; *Jacobs v London County Council* [1950] AC 361. Since the Act of 1957 the distinction between invitees and licensees has been abolished, and the extent of the duty is now simply the common duty of care. But the old cases still apply so as to show that the landlord is responsible for all parts not demised by him, on the ground that he is regarded as being sufficiently in control of them to impose on him a duty of care to all persons coming lawfully on to the premises.

Thirdly, where an owner did not let premises to a tenant but only licensed a person to occupy them on terms which did not amount to a demise, the owner still having the right to do repairs, he was regarded as being sufficiently in control of the structure to impose on him a duty towards all persons coming lawfully on to the premises. So he was held liable for a visitor who fell on the defective step to the front door in *Hawkins v Coulsdon and Purley UDC* [1954] 1 QB 319; and to the occupier's wife for the defective ceiling which fell on her in *Greene v Chelsea Borough Council* [1954] 2 QB 127. The extent of the duty was that owed to a licensee, but since the Act of 1957 the duty is the common duty of care to see that the structure is reasonably safe.

Fourthly, where an owner employed an independent contractor to do work on premises or a structure, the owner was usually still regarded as sufficiently in control of the place as to be under a duty towards all those who might lawfully come there. In some cases he might fulfil that duty by entrusting the work to the independent contractor: see *Haseldine v CA Daw & Son* [1941] 2 KB 343 and section 2(4) of the Act of 1957. In other cases he might only be able to fulfil it by exercising proper supervision himself over the contractor's work, using due diligence himself to prevent damage from unusual danger: see *Thomson v Cremin* [1956] 1 WLR 103n as explained by Lord Reid in *Davie v New Merton Board Mills Ltd* [1959] AC 604. But in addition to the owner, the courts regarded the independent contractor as himself being sufficiently in control of the place where he worked as to owe a duty of care towards all persons coming lawfully there. He was said to be an 'occupier' also: see *Hartwell's* case; but this is only a particular instance of his general duty of care: see *Billings (AC) & Sons Ltd v Riden* [1958] AC 240 per Lord Reid.

In the light of these cases, I ask myself whether the brewery company had a sufficient degree of control over the premises to put them under a duty to a visitor. Obviously they had complete control over the ground floor and were 'occupiers' of it. But I think that they had also sufficient control over the private portion. They had not let it out to Mr Richardson by a demise. They had only granted him a licence to occupy it, having a right themselves to do repairs. That left them with a residuary degree of control which was equivalent to that retained by the Chelsea Corporation in *Greene's* case. They were in my opinion 'an occupier' within the Act of 1957. Mr Richardson, who had a licence to occupy, had also a considerable degree of control. So had Mrs Richardson, who catered for summer guests. All three of them were, in my opinion, 'occupiers' of the private portion of the 'Golfer's Arms.' There is no difficulty in having more than one occupier at one and the same time, each of whom is under a duty of care to visitors . . .

Lord Morris

The conclusion I reach is that as regards the premises as a whole both Lacons and the manager were occupiers, but that by mutual arrangement Lacons would not (subject to certain overriding considerations) exercise control over some parts. They gave freedom to their manager to live in his home in privacy. They gave him freedom to furnish it as and how he chose. They gave him freedom to receive personal guests, and also to receive guests for reward. I think it follows that both Lacons and the Richardsons were 'occupiers' *vis-à-vis* Mr Wheat and his party. Both Lacons and the Richardsons owed Mr Wheat and his party a duty. The duty was the common duty of care. The measure and the content of that duty were not, however, necessarily the same in the case of Lacons and in the case of the Richardsons. The duty was to take such care as in all the circumstances of the case was reasonable to see that Mr Wheat and his party would be reasonably safe in using the premises as guests for reward. Lacons did not know that Mr Wheat and his party were to arrive but they had given permission to their manager to take guests, and the result was that Mr Wheat and his party were on the premises with Lacons' permission. The 'circumstances of the case' would, however, vary as between Lacons and the Richardsons. Thus, if after Mr Wheat and his party had arrived they had been ascending the main staircase and if it had collapsed and caused them injury a question would have arisen whether either Lacons or the Richardsons or any or all of them had been lacking in their duty. 'The circumstances of the case' in such a situation would have, or might have, been quite different so far as Lacons were concerned from what they would have been so far as the Richardsons were concerned. If, to take another possibility, the Wheats had entered a living-room of the Richardsons which had been fitted and equipped and furnished by the Richardsons and had suffered some mishap which arose from the state or condition of the equipment or furnishings 'the circumstances of the case' would have been, or might have been, quite different so far as the Richardsons were concerned from the circumstances so far as Lacons were concerned.

In the illustrations to which I have referred it might be or could be that there would be some failure on the part of Lacons to take care in regard to the staircase and no failure on the part of the Richardsons: so it might be or could be that there would be some failure on the part of the Richardsons in regard to some equipment or furnishing in a living-room and no failure on the part of Lacons.

It may, therefore, often be that the extent of the particular control which is exercised within the sphere of joint occupation will become a pointer as to the nature and extent of the duty which reasonably devolves upon a particular occupier . . .

[The House of Lords went on to hold that the claim against the brewery failed because it was not in breach of the common duty of care.]

Appeal dismissed.

COMMENTARY

It has been said that the terms 'occupied', 'occupier' and 'occupation' are not legal terms of art, with 'one single and precise legal meaning applicable in all circumstances' (*Graysim Holdings Ltd v P & O Property Holdings Ltd* [1996] AC 329 at 334, per Lord Nicholls). On the contrary, Lord Nicholls noted, the meaning of 'occupier' varies with context: its meaning 'in the context of the Rent Acts, for instance, is not in all respects the same as in the context of the Occupiers' Liability Act 1957'. Accordingly, care should be taken in using cases from areas other than occupiers' liability for the purpose of deciding who is an occupier under the Act.

However, it does not follow that terms such as 'occupier' bear the meaning they would in common parlance, for it could hardly be said in ordinary speech that the brewery in *Wheat* 'occupied' the residential accommodation of its manager. Although the Richardsons were occupiers for the purposes of the Act, there may, as Lord Denning points out, be more than one occupier if each exhibits sufficient control. In this context, however, it is worth noting Lord Morris's comment that the extent of control may be relevant to the 'nature and extent' of the particular occupier's duty. Even though the level of control of the brewery was sufficient to make it an occupier under the Act, the nature of the control did not make it responsible for the failure to ensure a light bulb was fitted. Such day-to-day maintenance of the property was the job of the occupier in residence, namely the Richardsons (albeit that on the facts they were found not to have neglected this responsibility). (See also *Shtern v Cummings* [2014] UKPC 18, where the defendant's ownership of the land on which a hotel was situated might have entailed some responsibility for the building's structural condition, but not for the state of a refrigerator used in the ordinary running of the hotel business.)

If the brewery had granted the pub manager a tenancy, not merely a contractual licence, then it would no longer have been an occupier. As Lord Denning noted, at common law, the landlord was deemed to relinquish control by leasing the property and thus owed no duty of care to anyone (other than the tenant under the terms of the lease), and this was regardless of whether the lease imposed an obligation to maintain or repair (*Cavalier v Pope* [1906] AC 428). The immunity that this decision gave to landlords was partly abrogated by s. 4 of the 1957 Act (referred to by Lord Denning), a provision later repealed and replaced with s. 4 of the Defective Premises Act 1972, which provides (in s. 4(1)) that:

Where premises are let under a tenancy which puts on the landlord an obligation to the tenant for the maintenance or repair of the premises the landlord owes to all persons who might reasonably be expected to be affected by defects in the state of the premises a duty to take such care as is reasonable in all the circumstance to see that they are reasonably safe from personal injury or from damage to their property caused by a relevant defect.

For a discussion of the effect of this section see *Winfield & Jolowicz*, para. 10–058.

(b) The Scope of the 1957 Act

At common law, a distinction was drawn between an occupier's 'occupancy' duties and an occupier's 'activity' duties. Applying this distinction, the specific rules relating to occupiers' liability were limited to dangers arising out of the 'static condition of the premises', with dangers caused by 'what was being done on the premises' being governed by ordinary negligence law (see *Dunster v Abbott* [1954] 1 WLR 58 at 62, per Denning LJ). The fact that s. 1(1) of the 1957 Act says that it regulates 'the duty which an occupier of premises owes to his visitors in respect of dangers due to the state of the premises *or to things done or omitted to be done on them*' (our italics) might be understood to mean that the scope of the Act extends to at least some activities carried out on the land, but some courts have held that the distinction between 'occupancy' and 'activity' duties survives the Act. For example, the Court of Appeal in *Fairchild v Glenhaven Funeral Services* [2002] 1 WLR 1052 (approving the speech of Lord Goff in *Ferguson v Welsh* [1987] 1 WLR 1553) held that, as the common duty of care imposed by s. 2(2) of the Act was limited to the safety of the visitor in *using the premises*, it did not apply to an activity carried out on the premises by a third party who was there with the consent of the occupier, although in such a case the occupier could be made liable by the application of ordinary common law principles of negligence if the appropriate conditions were satisfied. Similarly, in *Revill v Newbery* [1996] QB 567, the Court of Appeal held that the Occupiers' Liability Act 1984 does not govern the liability of the occupier for his activities on the land. (See also *Ogwo v Taylor* [1988] AC 431.)

On the other hand, in *Tomlinson v Congleton Borough Council* [2004] 1 AC 46 the phrase 'things done or omitted to be done' on the premises was interpreted by Lord Hoffmann and Lord Hobhouse as meaning that liability under the Act could extend to some activity conducted by the occupier, or by others with their consent, that creates a risk to persons on the premises (e.g. if shooting is taking place on the premises, or speedboats are allowed to go into an area where swimmers are present). Admittedly, this interpretation was obiter, and their Lordships did not discuss the line of authority to the contrary, but in an earlier case, *Cunningham v Reading Football Club Ltd* [1992] PIQR P141, a duty under both the Act and the common law was held to extend to taking care to ensure that the state of the premises was not such as to enable third parties, including other lawful entrants, to cause harm to visitors by ripping up lumps of concrete and using them as projectiles. Was this imposing liability for an activity of a third party who was on the land with the consent of the occupier (consistently with *Tomlinson*), or was it imposing liability for a static feature of the premises which was dangerous because it could be exploited by third parties (consistently with *Ferguson*)?

This lack of clarity is less important than it might seem at first glance. After all, there are 'many occasions when an occupier may be legally liable in negligence in respect of the activities which he permits or encourages on his land' (*Bottomley v Todmorden Cricket Club* [2004] PIQR P18 at [42], per Brooke LJ), so that, even if the Act does not apply, the occupier may owe a duty at common law with respect to activities carried out on the land. Furthermore, as Brooke LJ noted in the same paragraph, it is rarely necessary to draw a distinction between occupancy and activity duties as the common duty of care under the Act is practically indistinguishable from a common law duty of care. The result is that even cases post-*Fairchild* do not always draw the distinction between occupancy and activity duties (see, e.g., *Maguire v Sefton Metropolitan Borough Council* [2006] 1 WLR 2550). When assessing the merits of the distinction, it is important to recall that one reason for separating out occupiers' liability cases from the ordinary law of negligence in the first place is that they tend to involve duties of positive conduct, so that this is an area where omissions liability—otherwise a rare phenomenon in the law of tort—is commonplace. Drawing on this observation, Bailey, *op. cit.*, pp. 207–8, argues that 'it is the nature of the occupier's responsibility' that should determine the applicability of the Act, which should be limited to cases where (1) the risk arises from a natural deterioration in the state of the premises; (2) the risk arises from conduct of the occupier that was not careless when carried out; and (3) the negligent act of a third party (not being the occupier's employee) creates a risk on the premises, whether by changing the physical state of the premises or otherwise, such as by careless driving. These are situations where the gist of the complaint against the occupier is a failure to act to protect the safety of the visitor, the core concern of occupiers' liability. (For further discussion of the occupancy/activity duty distinction, see *North*, ch. 6, who accepts that the distinction 'remains relevant in determining the scope of the 1957 Act', even if he does not necessarily agree with Bailey as to precisely how it should be drawn.)

Another strand of relatively recent case law has emphasised the words 'dangers due to the state of the premises or to things done or omitted to be done on them' in s. 1(1) of the 1957 Act (substantially repeated in s. 1(1)(a) of the Occupiers' Liability Act 1984). At a basic level, this can be useful, since requiring the claimant to identify what precisely the alleged 'danger' is can help to clarify some of the issues that the court must consider (e.g., when asking whether a duty arises applying s. 1(3) of the 1984 Act). However, the courts have also emphasised that the relevant 'danger' must be one that is associated with the land, rather than the use that the entrant makes of the land (cf. Bailey, *op. cit.*), and this can give rise to difficulties. Hence it has been argued, for example, that the risk of diving into water of unknown depth is not a risk associated with the state of the premises, but arises from the visitor's obviously dangerous activity (*Donoghue v Folkstone Properties Ltd* [2003] QB 1008; *Tomlinson v Congleton Borough Council* [2004] 1 AC 46). Likewise the risk of falling from an external fire escape if one choses to use it as a climbing frame (*Keown v Coventry Healthcare NHS Trust* [2006] 1 WLR 953; see also *Kolasa v Ealing Hospital NHS Trust* [2015] EWHC 289 (QB), where the claimant fell after drunkenly clambering over the perimeter wall of a hospital); or the risk of overbalancing while trying to slide down the banister of some stairs (*Geary v JD Wetherspoon Plc* [2011] EWHC 1506 (QB)). This approach gives rise to a number of questions. First, in the diving scenario, should it make any difference if, instead of hitting their head on the bottom of the lake, the claimant hits their head on an object that is protruding from the bottom? (See *Rhind v Astbury Water Park Ltd* [2004] EWCA Civ 756, where the relevant danger was found to be attributable to the state of the premises but the claim failed because the claimant was a trespasser and the defendant had no reason to know that the object was there.) Secondly, should this approach apply where the very purpose for which the occupier allows the visitor onto the land is to engage in the activity which is allegedly dangerous? For example, can the occupier of a ski resort argue that the Act does not apply if a skier is injured by crashing into a tree because this is not a danger due to the state of the premises or to things done or omitted to be done on them, even if the risk could have been avoided by placing the ski-piste on a different (tree-less) part of the land? (See, generally, Buckley, 'Occupiers' Liability in England and Canada' (2006) 35 Comm L World Rev 197.)

Two final points to note about the scope of the 1957 Act arise from s. 1(3). According to s. 1(3)(a), the provisions in the legislation apply not only to premises (i.e. land and buildings), but also to 'any fixed or moveable structure, including any vessel, vehicle or aircraft'. This phrase has been held to encompass an inflatable sculpture (*Furmedge v Chester-Le-Street DC* [2011] EWHC 1226 (QB) and even a ladder (see *Wheeler v Copas* [1981] 3 All ER 405). And secondly, s. 1(3)(b) makes clear that the Act extends to property damage, including damage to the property of persons who are not themselves visitors (so that if, for example, a visitor brings on to the premises property belonging to a third party, which is damaged as a result of a breach of the common duty of care, the property's owner can recover damages from the occupier under the Act). See further on these two issues, *North*, ch. 4 and paras 7.16–7.32, respectively.

(c) The Common Duty of Care

In cases that do fall within the scope of the 1957 Act, an occupier owes a visitor the common duty of care set out in s. 2(2), namely a duty to take reasonable care to ensure that the visitor will be reasonably safe in using the premises for the purposes for which they are invited or permitted to be there. Given the similarity between the duty of care at common law and the common duty of care under the Act (see *North*, para. 5.15), it is unsurprising that the factors relevant to breach of duty at common law are also relevant to breach under the Act—for example, the gravity of the potential harm to the visitor, the cost of preventing that harm, the likelihood of the harm occurring and the utility of the defendant's activity. (See, e.g., *G4S Care and Justice Services (UK) v Manley* [2016] EWHC 2355 (QB), which turned on the heightened foreseeability of harm to a particularly vulnerable claimant—a prisoner with mobility problems who fell in his darkened cell during a power cut.) Note, however, that the common duty of care relates to the visitor's use of the premises *for the purposes for which they are invited or permitted by the occupier to be there*. Thus a warning that the floor of an ensuite bathroom is slippery might exonerate the occupier *vis-à-vis* a dinner guest who would not be expected to use it but not *vis-à-vis* a hotel guest. Furthermore, in determining whether there has been a breach of the common duty of care, s. 2(3) and (4) of the Act set out a number of specific factors that must be considered, where applicable.

(i) Children

According to s. 2(3)(a) of the 1957 Act, an occupier must be prepared for children to be less careful than adults. (As with the remainder of s. 2(3) and s. 2(4), this provision merely expresses what is already implicit in the reasonable care standard, as clearly a reasonable occupier would be prepared for this anyway.) A precaution sufficient for an adult visitor may be inadequate for a child. For example, a written warning might place an adult on guard against a potential danger, but would be of little use in warning a toddler who cannot yet read. Nonetheless, the occupier's duty is one of reasonable care, and it must be remembered that it is almost impossible to make premises completely safe for children. This is especially so where a child escapes momentarily from its parents; although such a scenario may be foreseeable by the occupier, there may be nothing that can reasonably be done in such circumstances to protect the child (see, e.g., *Bourne Leisure Ltd v Marsden* [2009] EWCA Civ 671).

A key authority on child claimants is *Phipps v Rochester Corporation* [1955] 1 QB 450. The plaintiff, aged 5, and his 7-year-old sister were walking across a large open space of grass, which was part of a building site being developed by the defendant. While crossing the open space the plaintiff fell into a deep trench which had been dug in the grassland by the defendant as part of the development and broke his leg. Although the trench would have been obvious to an adult, the trial judge, Devlin J, accepted that it constituted a danger to a small child. In determining what steps the occupier should have taken, Devlin J commented (at 471):

> I think that it would be an unjustifiable restriction of the principle [that a licensor must give warning of any known danger which would not be perceived by a licensee using reasonable care for his own safety] if one were to say that although the licensor may in determining the extent of his duty have regard to the fact that it is the habit, and also the duty, of prudent people to look after themselves, he may not in that determination have a similar regard to the

fact that it is the habit, and also the duty, of prudent people to look after their little children. If he is entitled, in the absence of evidence to the contrary, to assume that parents will not normally allow their little children to go out unaccompanied, he can decide what he should do and consider what warnings are necessary on that basis.

It followed that the defendant occupier was not in breach. The risk was obvious and the occupier could assume that parents would not expose their children to this risk; it was not necessary, in Devlin J's words, for the occupier to 'assume parental responsibility'. Similarly, in an earlier House of Lords case, Lord Shaw said that occupiers were 'entitled to take into account that reasonable parents will not permit their children to be sent into the midst of familiar and obvious dangers except under protection or guardianship' (*Glasgow Corpn v Taylor* [1922] 1 AC 44 at 61). Although *Phipps* was pre-1957, Devlin J's reasoning has been followed in cases on the common duty of care (see, e.g., *Simkiss v Rhondda Borough Council* (1983) 81 LGR 460) and as in all such cases, the outcomes where young children suffer injury are very fact sensitive. Hence in *Moloney v Lambeth Borough Council* (1966) 64 LGR 440, liability was imposed when a 4-year-old child fell through the balustrade of a staircase in a block of flats, since the occupier should have anticipated that children might be unaccompanied in that place, whereas in *Marsden v Bourne Leisure Ltd* [2009] EWCA Civ 671, where a 2-year-old child wandered off and drowned in a holiday park pond, the danger was considered to be too obvious for the occupier to be under a duty to warn parents of it.

Phipps creates something of a dilemma for the child claimant. To succeed it must be argued that the state of the premises was dangerous, for if it is not there is no breach of the common duty of care. But in cases like *Phipps*, where the parents allowed their children onto the land unaccompanied, the defendant can respond in two ways. First, it can be said that, if the parents thought it safe for their children to enter the land, the occupier is also entitled to think that it was safe and hence the common duty of care has not been breached. Conversely, if the parents did not think it safe to let the children onto the land unaccompanied, why were the children in fact let onto the land?

However, the dilemma should not be overstated. If the danger is latent, even a prudent parent will not discover it, so the *Phipps* reasoning no longer applies. In addition, the dilemma facing the child claimant faces any claimant where the danger is patent (i.e. obvious), for the obviousness of the danger tends to reduce the risk it poses and if the entrant knew of the danger but nonetheless entered any consequent injury might be deemed to be caused by the entrant's own action, or the defence of contributory negligence might apply. Of course, in cases like *Phipps* the argument is not that the claimant child was negligent, but that his parents were. But then, in theory at least, there might be an action against the parent in this scenario (assuming, as seems plausible, that somebody exercising parental control owes a duty to the child to take reasonable care not to expose the child to the risk of physical injury).

(ii) Special Risks Associated with Particular Callings

Occupiers need not warn a person of special risks ordinarily incident to the person's job as they can reasonably expect that the person will appreciate and guard against those risks (s. 2(3)(b)). In *Roles v Nathan* [1963] 1 WLR 1117 the plaintiffs were the widows of two chimney sweeps who had been overcome by carbon monoxide fumes while cleaning boiler flues. The deceased men had been warned a number of times of the dangers of poisoning from carbon monoxide gas and had been told to take precautions, but had ignored the advice given to them. The Court of Appeal rejected the widows' claims against the occupier, and Lord Denning MR said:

> The householder can reasonably expect the sweep to take care of himself so far as any dangers from the flues are concerned. These chimney sweeps ought to have known that there might be dangerous fumes about and ought to have taken steps to guard against them . . . When a householder calls in a specialist to deal with a defective installation on the premises, he can reasonably expect the specialists to appreciate and guard against the dangers arising from the defect.

What constitutes a special risk associated with a particular job is a question of fact. For example, in *Neame v Johnson*, unreported, CA, 24 November 1992, it was held that the risk of falling over books or other material left on the floor of residential accommodation was one associated with being an ambulance paramedic. However, it does not necessarily follow from the fact that the state of the premises is a risk only to a person exercising a particular calling that it is ordinarily incidental to their work within the meaning of s. 2(3)(b). In *Williams v Department of the Environment*, unreported, QBD, 30 November 1981, Tudor Evans J held that the risk of injury from an exposed spindle in a boiler was not incidental to the calling of an industrial heating engineer employed to service the boiler, even though the spindle was unlikely to pose a risk to anyone else entering the area. The exposed spindle was 'simply part of the plaintiff's place of work which made it unsafe and with which he was not involved' (see also *Woollins v British Celanese Ltd* [1966] 1 KIR 438). However, if the visitor's calling involves the use of the premises in a way in which they would not normally be used, the risk associated with the special use is one associated with that calling. In *West v T Clarke Ltd*, unreported, QBD, 20 May 1982, which concerned an electrician, Jupp J commented:

> Now, what of the occupiers? They are responsible for the safety of the premises, and when they invite people in they must take care that the premises are safe if used within the scope of the invitation. When an electrician is invited in, the same applies. It is for the occupiers to see that he can go about his business in safety so far as the premises are concerned, but there must come a time when the electrician ceases to be using the premises in an ordinary kind of way and begins to make use of them in a way which is ordinarily incident to his calling. At that point he ceases to rely on the occupier to keep him safe and free from risk. He has to rely on himself. When and where that point is reached is in my judgment a matter of fact and degree. I am quite clear that the point is not governed in the case of an electrician by being confined to dangers from electrical wirings and electrical circuits. It must include when going into a loft or roof space, making sure that the precise place from which he is going to work is safe. Just where that is will depend on the facts of each particular case.

(iii) Warnings

One way of discharging the common duty of care may be for the occupier to warn visitors of risks associated with the premises. However, according to s. 2(4)(a), for such a warning to be effective in this regard, it must, in all the circumstances, have enabled the visitor to be reasonably safe. The genesis of this sub-section lies in the pre-Act decision of the House of Lords in *London Graving Dock Co Ltd v Horton* [1951] AC 151. The plaintiff welder was injured when some staging on the ship on which he was working failed. He had complained about the dangerous state of the staging throughout the previous month but the defendant occupier had done nothing to remedy the problem. It was accepted that as an invitee the plaintiff was owed a duty to warn of unusual dangers and that the staging was an unusual danger, but a majority of the House of Lords held that the defendant was not in breach as the plaintiff had had full knowledge of that danger, irrespective of whether he could be said to have accepted the risk. The practical effect of this reasoning, as Lord Reid pointed out in a powerful dissent, was to equate knowledge of a risk with acceptance of the risk, a proposition which the majority accepted would have been incorrect if the plaintiff had been an employee of the defendant (see Ch. 6.II and *Smith v Austin Lifts Ltd* [1959] 1 WLR 100 at 117, per Lord Denning).

The Act makes clear that whether a warning is sufficient to discharge the common duty of care imposed by s. 2(2) is a question of fact requiring a weighing of the relevant circumstances, including the reason for the visitor's presence on the premises, the nature of the danger, the knowledge of the visitor and the practicability of the possible means of removing or reducing the risk. An example of the change made by the Act is given by Lord Denning in *Roles v Nathan* [1963] 1 WLR 1117 at 1124:

> Suppose for instance, that there was only one way of getting into and out of premises, and it was by a footbridge over a stream which was rotten and dangerous. According to *Horton's* case, the occupier could escape all liability to any visitor by putting up a notice: 'This bridge is dangerous,' even though there was no other way by which the visitor could get in or out, and he had no option but to go over the bridge. In such a case, section 2(4) makes it clear that the occupier would nowadays be liable. But if there were two footbridges, one of which was rotten, and the other safe a hundred yards away, the occupier could still escape liability, even today, by putting up a notice: 'Do not use this footbridge. It is dangerous. There is a safe one further upstream.' Such a warning is sufficient because it does enable the visitor to be reasonably safe.

Need an occupier warn of risks that are obvious? In *Darby v National Trust* [2001] PIQR P27, the claimant's husband had drowned while swimming in a pond on the defendant's property. The Court of Appeal held that the defendant's failure to warn of the danger of swimming in the pond was not negligent: the risks of doing so were 'perfectly obvious', and any general notice advising visitors not to swim 'would have told [him] no more than he already knew'. In particular, the Court of Appeal was not prepared to accept that there was a different risk associated with swimming in the pond than with swimming in the sea or any other open water. If a warning notice was required in one case, it was required in all, and, in the opinion of May LJ: 'it cannot be the duty of the owner of every stretch of coastline to have notices warning of the dangers of swimming in the sea'.

(iv) Occupier's Use of Independent Contractors

Section 2(4)(b) of the 1957 Act provides that an occupier discharges the common duty of care in circumstances where:

(i) The breach was caused by the faulty execution of an act of construction, maintenance, or repair of an independent contractor;

(ii) It was reasonable for the occupier to employ the contractor to undertake the task in question; and

(iii) The occupier took reasonable steps to ensure the contractor was competent and the work was properly done.

Where the independent contractor has been engaged to perform a task requiring the exercise of special skill, courts have normally found that the occupier can avail himself of s. 2(4)(b) even if the contractor has carried out the task negligently (assuming reasonable care has been taken in choosing the contractor in the first place). And note that, although limited to works of 'construction, maintenance and repair', the logic of s. 2(4)(b) would seem to extend to all situations in which an occupier employs an independent contractor, and the courts have relied on it by analogy in cases that do not fall strictly within its terms (see, e.g., *Gwilliam v West Hertfordshire Hospital NHS Trust* [2003] QB 443 at [11], per Lord Woolf CJ; see also *North*, para. 9.22).

Haseldine v Daw [1941] 2 KB 343

The plaintiff was injured when the lift in which he was riding malfunctioned and crashed to the ground. The plaintiff sued, among others, the landlord of the property where the accident happened, as occupier of that part of the premises. The landlord had entered into a service contract for the lift with a competent firm of engineers and the lift had recently been serviced.

Scott LJ

The invitor is bound to take that kind of care which a reasonably prudent man in his place would take—neither more nor less. The landlord of a block of flats, as occupier of the lifts, does not profess as such to be either an electrical or, as in this case, a hydraulic engineer. Having no technical skill he cannot rely on his own judgment, and the duty of care towards his invitees requires him to obtain and follow good technical advice. If he did not do so, he would, indeed, be guilty of negligence. To hold him responsible for the misdeeds of his independent contractor would be to make him insure the safety of his lift.

Goddard LJ

Towards an invitee the occupier has the duty of taking care that the premises are reasonably safe. I need not quote the classic passage from the judgment of Willes J in *Indermaur v Dames* [see earlier], but he there points out that whether reasonable care has been taken is to be determined as a matter of fact. It seems to me that, by employing a first class firm of lift engineers to make periodical inspections of the lift, to adjust it and to furnish reports upon it, the landlord did all that a reasonable man could do towards seeing that it was safe, especially when it is remembered that he also had the advantage of quarterly inspections by the insurance company's engineer. But it is argued that, if the engineers were negligent, it cannot be said that the occupier has discharged his duty. With this, I cannot agree. An occupier or any other person may have, either by contract or by law, such a degree of duty imposed on him that he cannot discharge it by employing a contractor to do work for him, but where the duty is to take care that the premises are safe I cannot see how it can be discharged better than by the employment of competent contractors. Indeed, one may well ask how otherwise could the duty be discharged?

Landlord's appeal allowed.

COMMENTARY

In principle it is hard to fault this reasoning, but it appears that the landlord had known that the lift had never been completely overhauled during its thirty-five years of operation, that the engineers had reported that some of its workings were badly worn and scoured and that the engineers' preferred options were to replace the worn parts or to electrify the lift. Although the engineers did not suggest that the lift was unsafe, could it have been argued that it was negligent not to have carried out these repairs and improvements (see *Dimitrelos v 14 Martin Place Pty Ltd* [2007] NSWCA 85 at [16] per Young CJ in Eq)? (One of the reasons they were not carried out was that the landlord was 'disinclined to incur the expenditure'.) On the other hand it might seem harsh to require the occupier to 'second guess' an expert. As Salmon J said in a case involving negligence by an independent electrical contractor, 'I cannot think it incumbent upon [the occupiers] to send one of their directors or servants to a polytechnic to take a course in electrical engineering and then attempt the rewiring themselves' (*Green v Fibreglass Ltd* [1958] 2 QB 245). The reasoning in *Haseldine* has been applied following the 1957 Act to relieve occupiers from liability in relation to electrical work carried out by an independent contractor (*Cook v Broderip* [1968] EG 128) and in respect of the negligence of a contractor responsible for the choice and installation of glass in a shop front-door (*Smith v Storey*, unreported, CA, 26 June 1980).

It may have been difficult for the landlord in *Haseldine* to check whether the lift had been properly serviced, but where the work is less skilled there may be an obligation on the occupier to ascertain if the work has been properly done. In *Woodward v Mayor of Hastings* [1945] KB 174 the plaintiff was injured when he fell off an icy step on school premises. The step had been negligently left in an icy state by a cleaner. The Court of Appeal held that the cleaner was the agent of the defendant occupier and was liable on this basis, but that, even if she was not, the defendant was liable from the mere fact of the occupation of the premises. The defendant argued that as the task had been delegated to some competent person the reasoning in *Haseldine* absolved him from liability, but this was rejected, Du Parcq LJ commenting that 'the craft of the charwoman may have its mysteries, but there is no esoteric quality in the nature of the work which the cleaning of a snow-covered step demands'. The obvious distinction between *Haseldine* and *Woodward* is the complexity of the delegated task: the more complex the task, the more likely it is that the occupier will satisfy the common duty of care by employing a competent contractor, although the occupier might remain liable if the contractor's negligence was apparent even to a layperson. Not everyone has found this distinction satisfactory (see *Riverstone Meat Co Pty Ltd v Lancashire Shipping Co Ltd* [1961] AC 807 at 879, per Lord Hodson), but subsequent cases have implicitly adopted it. In *Ferguson v Welsh* [1987] 1 WLR 1553 a majority of the House of Lords held that an occupier, whether under the Act or at common law, was not normally required to inspect work done by an independent demolition contractor to check whether a safe system of work was in place. However, if the occupier knew that an unsafe system was in place it might be required to take action. Lord Goff differed from the majority on this latter point, arguing that mere knowledge was insufficient to make the occupier liable as the occupier was not required to supervise activities on its land which did not relate to the safety of the premises, a view approved by the Court of Appeal in *Fairchild v Glenhaven Funeral Services* [2002] 1 WLR 1052. However, the better view is that the approach of the majority in *Ferguson* still applies to the 'occupancy' duty of the occupier. Thus in the case of specialist independent contractors if, but only if, the occupier has reason to believe that work carried out by an independent contractor has left the premises in a dangerous state, further action may be required on their part.

In *Gwilliam v West Hertfordshire Hospital NHS Trust* [2003] QB 443, the 63-year-old claimant was injured while using a 'splat-wall', a form of entertainment which involved leaping from a trampoline onto a Velcro wall. The splat-wall was provided by an independent contractor as part of a charity fair organised by the defendant occupier to raise funds, and it was due to the independent contractor's negligence that the claimant was injured. As the liability insurance of the independent contractor had expired, the claimant was unable to recover her full damages from him, and she sued the occupier for negligently failing to ensure that the independent contractor had adequate liability insurance. The majority (Lord Woolf CJ and Waller LJ) held that the defendant had been under a duty to inquire as to the insurance position of the independent contractor, although on the facts the occupier had taken all reasonable steps in this regard, so that there was no breach of the duty. Sedley LJ dissented on the question of whether the occupier's duty of care extended to checking the contractor's insurance position: in such a case any negligence of the occupier caused a visitor only a purely economic loss, and in Sedley LJ's view such losses were not recoverable under the Act (recall that the common duty of care is limited to taking reasonable care with regard to the *safety* of the visitor). Unsurprisingly, in *Naylor v Payling* [2004] PIQR P615 the Court of Appeal held that there is no *general* requirement that an occupier check on the insurance position of an independent contractor; and subsequently the Court of Appeal in *Glaister v Appleby-in-Westmorland Town Council* [2010] PIQR P6 expressed a preference for the reasoning of Sedley LJ in *Gwilliam*.

(v) Exclusion of Liability and Volenti

Section 2(1) of the Act allows an occupier—'in so far as he is free' to do so—to extend, restrict, modify or exclude his duty to a visitor by agreement or otherwise. The main restriction on an occupier's ability to exclude or limit liability is provided by the Unfair Contract Terms Act 1977 (UCTA), or, in the case of a consumer relationship, the Consumer Rights Act 2015 (CRA) (for the definition of a consumer notice or contract governed by the CRA, see s. 61 of the Act). The result is that the restrictions in s. 2 of UCTA and Part 2 of the CRA apply, so that, in respect of business liability (or, in the case of the CRA, the liability of a 'trader' towards a 'consumer'), the occupier cannot exclude liability for death or personal injury (UCTA, s. 2(1); CRA, s. 65), and attempts to limit such liability for other types of damage are either subject to a reasonableness requirement (UCTA, s. 2(2)), or will not bind the visitor if held to be 'unfair' (CRA, s. 62). Because of the changes made by UCTA and the CRA, care must be taken when looking at earlier cases which were necessarily decided on different principles (see, e.g., *Ashdown v Samuel Williams & Sons Ltd* [1957] 1 QB 409 and *White v Blackmore* [1972] 2 QB 651). Attention should also be drawn to UCTA, s. 1(3)(b), which states that, in certain circumstances, access to premises for recreational or educational purposes may fall outside the business purposes of the occupier and therefore beyond the scope of the Act, and the equivalent provision in the CRA, s. 66(4) (which however is limited to 'recreational purposes').

Whether the attempt to exclude or restrict liability is effective (i.e. whether it forms part of the agreement between the parties, or, if a notice, whether reasonable steps have been taken to bring the notice to the attention of the claimant) depends upon the application of the normal rules relating to these issues and raises no problems specific to occupiers' liability. See further on the law relating to exclusion of liability, Chapter 6.IV.

Section 2(5) allows the occupier the defence of *volenti non fit injuria*. As the sub-section states that whether a risk has been accepted is to be decided on the same principles applicable to the ordinary law of negligence it will not be discussed further here.

3. The 1984 Act

As noted earlier, at common law the trespasser received the least protection of any entrant on the occupier's premises. The minimal duty set out in *R. Addie & Sons (Collieries) Ltd v Dumbreck* [1929] AC 358 reflected a wider view that trespassers were wrongdoers and in one sense deserved what they got. Furthermore, taking precautions against uninvited guests was considered too onerous a burden to place on landowners. However, although the term 'trespasser' covered people whose claims might be regarded as of little merit—such as burglars— it also included those whose claims might be regarded as much stronger—such as children. Dissatisfaction with the law, especially as it affected child entrants, encouraged the courts to find implied licences so that children became lawful visitors. Furthermore, where the injury was caused by the occupier's activities (rather than the state of the premises) a trespasser might recover on ordinary *Donoghue v Stevenson* principles. In *Videan v British Transport Commission* [1963] 2 QB 650, the Court of Appeal divided over whether the occupier also owed a duty to a trespasser with respect to the state of the premises (the 'occupation' duty). Lord Denning accepted that with regard to an occupier's activities, a duty of care was owed at common law based simply on the foreseeability of the presence of a trespasser. However, the same principle did not apply where the occupier's liability 'is as occupier and nothing else'. By contrast, Pearson LJ considered that a duty of 'common humanity' was owed to the trespasser in respect of both activities and occupation *per se*, a position that appears to have been adopted by the House of Lords in *British Railways Board v Herrington* [1972] AC 877, where Lord Diplock said (at 939–40):

> My Lords, I conclude therefore that there is no duty owed by an occupier to any trespasser unless he actually knows of the physical facts in relation to the state of his land or some activity carried out on it, which constitute a serious danger to persons on the land who are unaware of those facts. He is under no duty to any trespasser to make inspections or enquiries to ascertain whether there is any such danger. Where he does know of physical facts which a reasonable man would appreciate involved danger of serious injury to the trespasser his duty is to take reasonable steps to enable the trespasser to avoid the danger. What constitute reasonable steps will depend on the kind of trespasser to whom the duty is owed . . .

The duty recognised in *Herrington* was a lesser duty than that under the 1957 Act, being owed only when a reasonable person, knowing the physical facts actually known to the occupier, would appreciate that a trespasser's presence at the point and time of the danger was so likely that in all the circumstances it would be inhumane not to take appropriate steps to eliminate, reduce or warn of the danger. Whether it was inhumane not to offer some protection would be judged objectively and depended on all the circumstances of the case, including (per Lord Diplock) the permanent or intermittent character of the danger; the severity of the injuries which it was likely to cause; in the case of children, the attractiveness to them of that which constituted the dangerous object or condition of the land; and the expense involved in giving effective warning of the danger to the kind of trespasser likely to be injured, in relation to the occupier's resources.

Subsequently, the issue of liability to trespassers was referred to the Law Commission, which published its *Report on Liability for Damage or Injury to Trespassers and Related Questions of Occupiers' Liability* (Law Com. No. 75) in 1976. The Commission considered that no clear principle emerged from *Herrington* because of the divergence between the speeches, and recommended legislation. This report formed the basis for the Occupiers' Liability Act 1984 (see further Bailey, *op. cit.*, pp. 201–7).

Occupiers' Liability Act 1984

An Act to amend the law of England and Wales as to the liability of persons as occupiers of premises for injury suffered by persons other than their visitors . . .

1. Duty of occupier to persons other than his visitors

(1) The rules enacted by this section shall have effect, in place of the rules of the common law, to determine—
   (a) whether any duty is owed by a person as occupier of premises to persons other than his visitors in respect of any risk of their suffering injury on the premises by reason of any danger due to the state of the premises or to things done or omitted to be done on them; and
   (b) if so, what that duty is.

(2) For the purposes of this section, the persons who are to be treated respectively as an occupier of any premises (which, for those purposes, include any fixed or movable structure) and as his visitors are—
   (a) any person who owes in relation to the premises the duty referred to in section 2 of the Occupiers' Liability Act 1957 (the common duty of care), and
   (b) those who are his visitors for the purposes of that duty.

(3) An occupier of premises owes a duty to another (not being his visitor) in respect of any such risk as is referred to in subsection (1) above if—
   (a) he is aware of the danger or has reasonable grounds to believe that it exists;
   (b) he knows or has reasonable grounds to believe that the other is in the vicinity of the danger concerned or that he may come into the vicinity of the danger (in either case, whether the other has lawful authority for being in that vicinity or not); and
   (c) the risk is one against which, in all the circumstances of the case, he may reasonably be expected to offer the other some protection.

(4) Where, by virtue of this section, an occupier of premises owes a duty to another in respect of such a risk, the duty is to take such care as is reasonable in all the circumstances of the case to see that he does not suffer injury on the premises by reason of the danger concerned.

(5) Any duty owed by virtue of this section in respect of a risk may, in an appropriate case, be discharged by taking such steps as are reasonable in all the circumstances of the case to give warning of the danger concerned or to discourage persons from incurring the risk.

(6) No duty is owed by virtue of this section to any person in respect of risks willingly accepted as his by that person (the question whether a risk was so accepted to be decided on the same principles as in other cases in which one person owes a duty of care to another).

(6A) At any time when the right conferred by section 2(1) of the Countryside and Rights of Way Act 2000 is exercisable in relation to land which is access land for the purposes of Part I of that Act, an occupier of the land owes (subject to subsection (6C) below) no duty by virtue of this section to any person in respect of—
   (a) a risk resulting from the existence of any natural feature of the landscape, or any river, stream, ditch or pond whether or not a natural feature, or
   (b) a risk of that person suffering injury when passing over, under or through any wall, fence or gate, except by proper use of the gate or of a stile.

(6AA) Where the land is coastal margin for the purposes of Part 1 of that Act (including any land treated as coastal margin by virtue of s 16 of that Act) subsection (6A) has effect as if for paragraphs (a) and (b) of that subsection there were substituted 'a risk resulting from the existence of any physical feature (whether of the landscape or otherwise)'.

(6B) For the purposes of subsection (6A) above, any plant, shrub or tree, of whatever origin, is to be regarded as a natural feature of the landscape.

(6C) Subsection (6A) does not prevent an occupier from owing a duty by virtue of this section in respect of any risk where the danger concerned is due to anything done by the occupier—

(a) with the intention of creating that risk, or
(b) being reckless as to whether that risk is created.

(7) No duty is owed by virtue of this section to persons using the highway, and this section does not affect any duty owed to such persons.

(8) Where a person owes a duty by virtue of this section, he does not, by reason of any breach of the duty, incur any liability in respect of any loss of or damage to property.

(9) In this section—

'highway' means any part of a highway other than a ferry or waterway;
'injury' means anything resulting in death or personal injury, including any disease and any impairment of physical or mental condition; and
'movable structure' includes any vessel, vehicle or aircraft.

1A. Special considerations relating to access land

In determining whether any, and if so what, duty is owed by virtue of section 1 by an occupier of land at any time when the right conferred by section 2(1) of the Countryside and Rights of Way Act 2000 is exercisable in relation to the land, regard is to be had, in particular, to—

(a) the fact that the existence of that right ought not to place an undue burden (whether financial or otherwise) on the occupier,

(b) the importance of maintaining the character of the countryside, including features of historic, traditional or archaeological interest, and

(c) any relevant guidance given under section 20 of that Act.

COMMENTARY

Section 1(1) provides that any common law duty owed by the occupier to persons other than visitors is superseded by the provisions of the Act. The terms 'occupier' and 'visitor' have the same meaning as in the 1957 Act. In *Revill v Newbery* [1996] QB 567, Neill LJ held that the 1984 Act imposed a duty on the occupier as an occupier, so that where the claim related to an activity of the occupier the ordinary common law of negligence applied and the fact that the defendant was also an occupier was 'irrelevant'. The result is that the Act's main role, analogous to that of the 1957 Act, is to impose in limited circumstances a positive duty to act reasonably to ensure that the state of the premises is not a danger to trespassers and other non-visitors.

The Existence of the Duty

Whether a duty arises is determined by s. 1(3), which roughly equates to the elements set out in Lord Diplock's speech in *Herrington*. Section 1(3)(a) and (b) contain a partly objective, partly subjective test, and, as in *Herrington*, there seems to be no requirement to carry out inspections of one's premises. In *Swain v Puri* [1996] PIQR P442, the argument that the words 'reasonable grounds to believe' in s. 1(3)(b) encompassed a situation where the occupiers ought to have known that the trespasser might come into the vicinity of the danger was rejected by the Court of Appeal. According to Evans LJ, what was required was 'actual knowledge including "shut-eye" knowledge either of the actual risk or of primary facts' from which the court might draw the necessary inference. By 'shut-eye' knowledge was meant knowledge which was 'equivalent to actual knowledge as a matter of law, and it may be equated... with an element of wilfulness though not with negligence alone'. Thus the occupier cannot close their eyes to the obvious, knowing that, if they did look, they would discover facts which would indicate the presence of trespassers. However, mere negligence in ascertaining the facts from which it could be inferred that trespassers were in the vicinity of the danger was not enough.

Does the fact that an occupier took precautions to prevent trespassers from entering the premises and hence coming into the vicinity of the danger assist the claimant in establishing that the s. 1(3)(b) requirement is satisfied? Not according to *White v City of St Albans*, unreported, CA, 2 March 1990, where it was denied that this was evidence that the occupier had known that trespassers were in the vicinity of the danger. Section 1(3)(b) also requires that the presence of the trespasser in the vicinity must be known to the occupier *at the time* when the trespass takes place. This was graphically illustrated in *Donoghue v Folkestone Properties Ltd* [2003] QB 1008, where the claimant dived into a harbour in the early hours of a midwinter day and hit his head on an underwater obstruction. Although the occupier knew that others trespassed by diving into the harbour, that was in the summer. The Court of Appeal held that the section required the occupier to know or have reasonable grounds to know of the presence of the trespasser, either individually or as a member of a class, in the vicinity of the danger at the relevant time. This was not the case for the claimant, as the occupier had no reason to know of the presence of trespassers diving into the water late at night in midwinter, even if it knew that other people trespassed at different times of the year. It followed that s. 1(3)(b) was not satisfied and no duty was owed under the 1984 Act. The result, as Lord Phillips MR noted (at [55]), is that the existence of a duty may vary as between summer and winter, and even as between different times of the day.

Satisfaction of the requirement in s. 1(3)(c) is necessary for a duty to arise under the 1984 Act, but there is undoubtedly an overlap between the considerations relevant to this issue and those relevant to breach of duty under s. 1(4). One way of distinguishing the two provisions is to use s. 1(3)(c) to take account of the claimant's attributes: it may be, for example, that an innocent trespasser can reasonably expect some protection against a risk, but a burglar cannot, or that a child can reasonably expect some protection but not an adult (see further *Donoghue v Folkestone Properties* [2003] QB 1008). It seems clear, however, that the courts have given s. 1(3)(c) a broader meaning than this, and have used it to resolve the question of whether the occupier owed a duty by reference to whether the occupier was at fault (even though the fault enquiry ought surely to be governed by s. 1(4)). This phenomenon is illustrated by the following extracted case.

Tomlinson v Congleton Borough Council [2004] 1 AC 46

The defendant was the occupier of a country park with an artificial lake that had been created by flooding an old sand quarry. The lake was used for various water sports, while the surrounding beach was used for picnicking and sunbathing. Swimming in the lake was prohibited for safety reasons, and the defendant put up warning signs to this effect, but many people ignored the signs and continued to swim in the water. The claimant (Mr Tomlinson) was a visitor to the park who had waded into the lake and then thrown himself forward in a dive. Unfortunately he had misjudged the depth of the water and hit his head on the sandy lake bottom, suffering catastrophic injury. Prior to the accident, the defendant had decided to take further steps to discourage swimming in the lake, but the work—which would have included bulldozing the beach at the edge of the lake and planting bull rushes in its place— had not been carried out when the accident happened. The claimant's action failed at first instance, but a majority of the Court of Appeal found the defendant liable. The House of Lords unanimously allowed the defendant's appeal. One ground of their Lordships' decision—that there was no danger relating to the state of the premises—has been discussed earlier (see I.2(b)). The extract deals with the question of whether the other conditions for liability were satisfied. Although their Lordships (by a majority) thought the claimant was correctly classified as a trespasser, they also considered the position had he been a lawful visitor under the 1957 Act.

Lord Hoffmann

The 1957 and 1984 acts contrasted

[38] In the case of the 1984 Act, there is the additional consideration that unless in all the circumstances it is reasonable to expect the occupier to do something, that is to say, to 'offer the other some protection', there is no duty at all. One may ask what difference there is between the case in which the claimant is a lawful visitor and there is in principle a duty under the 1957 Act but on the particular facts no duty to do anything, and the case in which he is a trespasser and there is on the particular facts no duty under the 1984 Act. Of course in such a case the result is the same. But Parliament has made it clear that in the case of a lawful visitor, one starts from the assumption that there is a duty whereas in the case of a trespasser one starts from the assumption that there is none.

The balance under the 1957 Act

[39] My Lords, it will in the circumstances be convenient to consider first the question of what the position would have been if Mr Tomlinson had been a lawful visitor owed a duty under s 2(2) of the 1957 Act. Assume, therefore, that there had been no prohibition on swimming. What was the risk of serious injury? To some extent this depends upon what one regards as the relevant risk. As I have mentioned, the judge thought it was the risk of injury through diving while the Court of Appeal thought it was any kind of injury which could happen to people in the water. Although, as I have said, I am inclined to agree with the judge, I do not want to put the basis of my decision too narrowly. So I accept that we are concerned with the steps, if any, which should have been taken to prevent any kind of water accident. According to the Royal Society for the Prevention of Accidents, about 450 people drown while swimming in the United Kingdom every year (see *Darby v National Trust* [2001] PIQR P372 at 374). About 25–35 break their necks diving and no doubt others sustain less serious injuries. So there is obviously some degree of risk in swimming and diving, as there is in climbing, cycling, fell walking and many other such activities.

[40] I turn then to the cost of taking preventative measures. Ward LJ described it (£5,000) as 'not excessive'. Perhaps it was not, although the outlay has to be seen in the context of the

other items (rated 'essential' and 'highly desirable') in the borough council budget which had taken precedence over the destruction of the beaches for the previous two years.

[41] I do not however regard the financial cost as a significant item in the balancing exercise which the court has to undertake. There are two other related considerations which are far more important. The first is the social value of the activities which would have to be prohibited in order to reduce or eliminate the risk from swimming. And the second is the question of whether the council should be entitled to allow people of full capacity to decide for themselves whether to take the risk.

[42] The Court of Appeal made no reference at all to the social value of the activities which were to be prohibited. The majority of people who went to the beaches to sunbathe, paddle and play with their children were enjoying themselves in a way which gave them pleasure and caused no risk to themselves or anyone else. This must be something to be taken into account in deciding whether it was reasonable to expect the council to destroy the beaches.

[43] I have the impression that the Court of Appeal felt able to brush these matters aside because the council had already decided to do the work. But they were held liable for having failed to do so before Mr Tomlinson's accident and the question is therefore whether they were under a legal duty to do so. Ward LJ placed much emphasis upon the fact that the council had decided to destroy the beaches and that its officers thought that this was necessary to avoid being held liable for an accident to a swimmer. But the fact that the council's safety officers thought that the work was necessary does not show that there was a legal duty to do it. In *Darby's* case the claimant's husband was tragically drowned while swimming in a pond on the National Trust estate at Hardwick Hall. Miss Rebecca Kirkwood, the water and leisure safety consultant to the Royal Society for the Prevention of Accidents, gave uncontradicted evidence, which the judge accepted, that the pond was unsuitable for swimming because it was deep in the middle and the edges were uneven. The National Trust should have made it clear that swimming in the pond was not allowed and taken steps to enforce the prohibition. But May LJ said robustly that it was for the court, not Miss Kirkwood, to decide whether the Trust was under a legal duty to take such steps. There was no duty because the risks from swimming in the pond were perfectly obvious.

Free will

[44] The second consideration, namely the question of whether people should accept responsibility for the risks they choose to run, is the point made by Lord Phillips MR in *Donoghue v Folkestone Properties Ltd* [2003] 3 All ER 1101 at [53] and which I said was central to this appeal. Mr Tomlinson was freely and voluntarily undertaking an activity which inherently involved some risk. By contrast, Miss Bessie Stone, to whom the House of Lords held that no duty was owed, was innocently standing on the pavement outside her garden gate at 10 Beckenham Road, Cheetham when she was struck by a ball hit for six out of the Cheetham Cricket Club ground. She was certainly not engaging in any activity which involved an inherent risk of such injury. So compared with *Bolton v Stone* [extracted in Ch. 4.I], this is an *a fortiori* case.

[45] I think it will be extremely rare for an occupier of land to be under a duty to prevent people from taking risks which are inherent in the activities they freely choose to undertake upon the land. If people want to climb mountains, go hang gliding or swim or dive in ponds or lakes, that is their affair. Of course the landowner may for his own reasons wish to prohibit such activities. He may think that they are a danger or inconvenience to himself or others. Or he may take a paternalist view and prefer people not to undertake risky activities on his land. He is entitled to impose such conditions, as the council did by prohibiting swimming. But the law does not require him to do so.

[46] My Lords, as will be clear from what I have just said, I think that there is an important question of freedom at stake. It is unjust that the harmless recreation of responsible parents and children with buckets and spades on the beaches should be prohibited in order to comply with what is thought to be a legal duty to safeguard irresponsible visitors against dangers which are perfectly obvious. The fact that such people take no notice of warnings cannot create a duty to take other steps to protect them. I find it difficult to express with appropriate moderation my disagreement with the proposition of Sedley LJ ([2003] 3 All ER 1122 at [45]) that it is 'only where the risk is so obvious that the occupier can safely assume that nobody will take it that there will be no liability'. A duty to protect against obvious risks or self-inflicted harm exists only in cases in which there is no genuine and informed choice, or in the case of employees, or some lack of capacity, such as the inability of children to recognise danger (see *British Railways Board v Herrington* [1972] AC 877) or the despair of prisoners which may lead them to inflict injury on themselves (see *Reeves v Metropolitan Police Comr* [2000] 1 AC 360) . . .

[50] My Lords, for these reasons I consider that even if swimming had not been prohibited and the council had owed a duty under s 2(2) of the 1957 Act, that duty would not have required them to take any steps to prevent Mr Tomlinson from diving or warning him against dangers which were perfectly obvious. If that is the case, then plainly there can have been no duty under the 1984 Act. The risk was not one against which he was entitled under s 1(3)(c) to protection. I would therefore allow the appeal and restore the decision of Jack J. It follows that the cross-appeal against the apportionment of damages must be dismissed.

Lord Hobhouse of Woodborough

[73] . . . The key is in the circumstances and what it is reasonable to expect of the occupier. The reference to warnings and discouragements in sub-s (5) and the use of the words 'some protection' in sub-s (3)(c) both demonstrate that the duty is not as onerous as Mr Tomlinson argues. Warnings can be disregarded (as was the case here); discouragements can be evaded; the trespasser may still be injured (or injure himself) while on the premises. There is no guarantee of safety any more than there is under the 1957 Act. The question remains what is it reasonable to expect the occupier to do for unauthorised trespassers on his land. The trespasser by avoiding getting the consent of the occupier, avoids having conditions or restrictions imposed upon his entry or behaviour once on the premises. By definition, the occupier cannot control the trespasser in the same way as he can control a visitor. The Acts both lay stress upon what is reasonable in all the circumstances. Such circumstances must be relevant to the relative duties owed under the two Acts.

[74] Returning to the facts of this case, what more was it reasonable to expect of the council beyond putting up the notices and issuing warnings and prohibitions? . . . [t]his is a case where, as held by the judge, all the relevant characteristics of this mere were already obvious to Mr Tomlinson. In these circumstances, no purpose was in fact served by the warning. It told Mr Tomlinson nothing he did not already know . . . The location was not one from which one could dive into water from a height. There was a shallow gradually sloping sandy beach. The bather had to wade in and Mr Tomlinson knew exactly how deep the water was where he was standing with the water coming up to a little above his knees. Mr Tomlinson's case is so far from giving a cause of action under the statute that it is hard to discuss coherently the hypotheses upon which it depends. There was no danger; any danger did not arise from the state of the premises; any risk of striking the bottom from diving in such shallow water was obvious; Mr Tomlinson did not need to be warned against running that risk; it was not reasonable to expect the occupier to offer the claimant (or any other trespasser) any protection against that obvious risk . . .

COMMENTARY

According to s. 1(3)(c) of the 1984 Act, for a duty to arise the risk must be one against which, in all the circumstances of the case, the occupier may reasonably be expected to offer the non-visitor some protection. In *Tomlinson*, given the social utility of the permitted enjoyment of the lake and the fact that the claimant had chosen to engage in an activity with an obvious risk, this requirement was not satisfied. Both Lord Hoffmann and Lord Hobhouse were influenced by concerns that the law should not intervene so as to limit the autonomous right of an individual to engage in activities that carried an obvious degree of risk, especially where this would result in the elimination of a recreational facility which was used safely by the vast majority of visitors. Their Lordships also made it clear that the result would have been the same had the claimant been a visitor: the common duty of care did not require steps to be taken to prevent the claimant from undertaking an activity with obvious risks (see also *Edwards v Sutton London Borough Council* [2017] PIQR P2: fall from footbridge with low parapets). This reasoning, however, comes perilously close to 'concretising' the breach enquiry, which must always depend on the precise circumstances of the case (see Ch. 4.I). In *James v White Lion Hotel* [2021] QB 1153, the argument that *Tomlinson* established an absolute principle that a visitor of full age and capacity who chooses to run an obvious risk cannot recover damages on the basis that an occupier has not prevented them from doing so was quite rightly rejected, the Court of Appeal holding that no such principle could displace the normal fact-sensitive analysis required by s. 2 of the 1957 Act. Further extracts from the *Tomlinson* decision may be found in Chapter 1.III.3 and Chapter 4.II.3, and note *Siddorn v Patel* [2007] EWHC 1248 (QB) where the risk of falling through a skylight as a result of dancing on a roof was held not to fall within s. 1(1)(a) of the 1984 Act, a result consistent with *Tomlinson*. See also *Vairy v Wyong Shire Council* (2005) 223 CLR 422 and *Mulligan v Coffs Harbour City Council* (2005) 223 CLR 486, where the High Court of Australia held that the obviousness of the risk was only one factor to consider in assessing whether it was unreasonable not to take a precaution against it, while accepting that this factor might be decisive in particular cases.

The influence of *Tomlinson* has been felt beyond occupier's liability; the decision is also relevant to the breach of duty enquiry in common law negligence, though that did not prevent Parliament from reiterating its core message in s. 1 of the Compensation Act 2006 (see Ch. 4.II.3). Should the reasoning in *Tomlinson* apply to risks that arise other than in respect of the claimant's activity on the land? If an adult is trespassing on land on which there is a large, obvious but unfenced pit into which he falls, could the claim be met by arguing that the risk was obvious and that therefore it would not be reasonable to expect the occupier to offer protection against it, as required by s. 1(3)(c)? Finally, note that s. 1(3)(c) must be interpreted by reference to the individual claimant: depending on the circumstances, for example, it may be reasonable not to offer protection to adult trespassers but unreasonable not to do so in the case of children.

For comment on *Tomlinson* see Lunney (2003) 11 Tort L Rev 140.

The Standard of Care

Once the three conditions in s. 1(3) are satisfied, a duty of care arises, with the standard of care being based on reasonableness in the circumstances of the case (s. 1(4)). The standard of care under the 1984 Act may be different from that at common law, as under the *Herrington* approach the resources of the occupier were relevant in deciding what was reasonable, whereas the statutory standard seems wholly objective (see Jones (1984) 47 MLR 713 at 719, and *North*, para. 11.33; though compare the statement by Stuart-Smith LJ in *Ratcliff v McConnell* [1999] 1 WLR 670 at 680 that 'the considerations enunciated' by Lord Diplock in *Herrington* are 'still apposite'). The standard is, however, one of reasonableness, and while child trespassers evoke greater sympathy than most the occupier is not an insurer of their safety. In *Platt v Liverpool City Council* [1997] CLY 4864, a child trespasser was killed and his friend injured when the house in which they were playing collapsed. It was accepted that s. 1(3) of the 1984 Act was satisfied but the Court of Appeal found no breach of the duty that arose. Unoccupied council houses had their doors and windows covered with metal sheets and were inspected once a day to check the sheeting had not been removed. In addition, the property in question was surrounded by 'a corrugated metal 22-gauge fence, 8 feet high, secured on a timber frame and secured to wooden posts embedded in concrete. The corrugated metal sheeting was attached to the frame by 2-inch-long nails with a screw thread which could not be removed without special tools.' Rejecting a suggestion that the council should have hired security guards, Kennedy LJ thought it 'simply absurd' to argue that the council had failed to exercise reasonable care.

Warnings

Section 1(5) of the 1984 Act provides that any duty that arises may be discharged by an appropriate warning. In theory, warnings should be more effective in the case of trespassers, since they have no business being on the land in the first place. Hence a suitable warning notice may satisfy the occupier's obligations under the 1984 Act on the basis that telling a trespasser of the risk and 'leaving the ball in his court' was all that the occupier could reasonably be expected to do (cf. the position under s. 2 of the 1957 Act, where a warning will not absolve the occupier from liability unless in all the circumstances it was enough to enable the visitor to be reasonably safe in using the premises). However, much will depend on the circumstances, and it will be harder to show that a notice is, of itself, sufficient where the trespassers anticipated by the occupier are children.

It may also be necessary to draw a distinction between notices which merely delimit the scope of an entrant's permission to be on the premises, and those which affirm the existence of a danger and warn of it. In *Westwood v Post Office* [1974] 1 AC 1 a notice outside a door stated: 'Only the authorised attendant is permitted to enter.' The notice related to lift machinery stored in the room, but the plaintiff's husband, who had no licence to enter the room, fell through a defective trapdoor and was killed. When the case reached the House of Lords, Lord Kilbrandon noted:

The notice said nothing about danger. On the contrary, its terms insinuated that the room was safe enough for the authorised attendant. It is perfectly possible, if not probable, that the notice was put up because the lift motor room was the place in which were kept those tools and spares for the safety of which the authorised attendant alone would be responsible to his employers; the notice may well have been so understood.

Although these comments related to whether the deceased had been guilty of any contributory negligence by entering the room with knowledge of the notice, they are equally relevant to the question of breach of the occupier's duty of care. The notice did not draw attention to the particular danger which killed the deceased, and a notice that does no more than to instruct people to keep out will not in general be sufficient to discharge a duty owed to a trespasser.

A warning notice may also have the effect of triggering the defence of *volenti*, which is expressly preserved by s. 1(6) of the 1984 Act. In *Ratcliff v McConnell* [1999] 1 WLR 670 a warning at the shallow end of a pool stating 'Deep end shallow dive' was one factor that led the Court of Appeal to reject a trespasser's claim for damages for injury caused by diving in at the shallow end of the pool. The defendants took steps to keep the pool locked after hours, and the plaintiff knew that after-hours access was prohibited. He also admitted that he had paid 'no regard' to the prohibition on access and was going to do what he wanted anyway. On these facts Stuart-Smith LJ (at 684) thought it 'quite plain' that the plaintiff was aware of the risk and willingly accepted it. In the light of the decision of the House of Lords in *Tomlinson*, however, it is unlikely that the defence of *volenti* would now be needed in such a case: the obvious nature of the risk is such that it would not be reasonable for the occupier to be expected to offer protection against it (s. 1(3)(c)).

Exclusion of Liability

Unlike the 1957 Act, there is no reference to excluding the duty under the 1984 Act. Furthermore, it seems that neither UCTA nor the CRA would defeat any attempt to exclude the duty, as these statutes apply only to common law negligence and the 1957 Act. The Law Commission Report on which the 1984 Act was based (*Report on Liability for Damage or Injury to Trespassers and Related Questions of Occupiers' Liability* (Law Com. No. 75, 1976)) expressly provided for exclusion of the duty by contract term or notice to the extent that this was reasonable or fair, but no such provision was included in the Act itself (as to why this was so, see Bailey, *op. cit.*, pp. 204–5).

The rationale for the ability of the occupier to exclude the duty in the case of a non-contractual visitor is that the occupier is free to impose conditions on their permission for the visitor to enter (e.g. 'You may enter my land, but only if you do not stray from the path'), and that a condition of the licence to enter can be the visitor's agreement to an exclusion of liability. However, this conditional licence analysis does not work with non-visitors, such as trespassers, since they do not enter the occupier's land pursuant to a licence in the first place, so that there is nothing on which the exclusion of liability can 'bite'. Therefore, it can be argued that it is simply not possible for the occupier to exclude the duty that may be owed to a non-visitor under the 1984 Act. On the other hand, if this is right, then an apparent paradox arises, since it would seem that a lawful visitor could be in a weaker position than a trespasser, since the duty owed to the visitor can be completely excluded by a non-business occupier. Can this be what was intended? (*North*, para. 11.48, thinks not, and argues that the better view is that the duty under the 1984 Act *can* be excluded, though he fails to explain how such an exclusion would take effect in the absence of a licence.)

Damage to Property

The duty that may arise under the 1984 Act does not extend to property damage (s. 1(8)), so a claim by a non-visitor for property damage would presumably be governed by the common law. It is difficult to see how the duty of common humanity could encompass property damage, although in *Tutton v Walter* [1986] QB 61 it was argued that the plaintiff's bees, which foraged across land sprayed by the defendant with a poisonous chemical, were 'trespassing' and hence were owed that duty. The trial judge decided that the categories of visitor and trespasser were inapt to be applied to the bees and that the ordinary law of negligence was applicable, although it was also held that the same result would have been reached if the duty of common humanity was the relevant standard. Could an occupier be liable at common law if they knew their neighbour's dog frequently strayed onto their property and omitted to take reasonable precautions to ensure the dog's safety? Does the duty of common humanity extend beyond humans? (See further *North*, paras 11.52–11.53.)

Non-Visitors Other than Trespassers

It should be remembered that not all non-visitors are trespassers. Those entering upon land pursuant to a public right of way are not trespassers but neither are they visitors, as they have no licence from the occupier to be on the land. Where a public right of way is maintainable at public expense as defined in the Highways Act 1980, a statutory duty similar to that of common law negligence is imposed on the local highway authority (Highways Act 1980, ss. 41, 58). Where this is not the case, s. 1(7) makes it clear that the 1984 Act creates no new duty on the occupier to users of public rights of way. This can lead to unfortunate results. In *McGeown v Northern Ireland Housing Executive* [1995] 1 AC 233, the plaintiff failed in her claim for injuries she sustained when she tripped over a hole in a public footpath. As the footpath was not a highway maintainable at public expense, and neither the 1957 nor the 1984 Act applied, the occupier was not liable. The result of the case is that, apparently, no-one is responsible as a matter of private law for the upkeep of public rights of way not maintainable at public expense. If the occupier of land subject to a public right of way which they know is constantly used by children discovers a bomb just below the surface, are they able to sit back and do nothing? Should the occupier not at least owe the *Herrington* duty of common humanity? See Buckley [1984] Conv 413 at 415.

While agreeing with the result, Lord Browne-Wilkinson in *McGeown* suggested that not all persons exercising a public right of way fell outside the 1957 Act. For example, persons using some parts of a shopping centre might be classified as invitees even though entering the shopping centre in the exercise of a public right of way. According to his Lordship such a person would be owed the common duty of care under the 1957 Act, for if this was not the position, '[w]ho, other than the occupier, is to maintain these structures which are used for the occupier's own business reasons?'. However, Lord Browne-Wilkinson's suggestion is difficult to square with the approach of the rest of the House of Lords, and the Northern Ireland Court of Appeal subsequently rejected the argument that an invitee using a right of way on the defendant's land could be owed a duty under the 1957 Act, which in the Court's view had completely abolished any distinction between invitees and licensees (*Campbell v Northern Ireland Housing Executive* [1995] NI 167).

In *Barlow v Wigan Metropolitan Borough Council* [2021] 3 All ER 223, the claimant had been injured after tripping over an exposed tree root on a path in a public park occupied by the defendant council. In correspondence before action the council's lawyers argued that the path was a public right of way, so that applying *McGeown* they had owed the claimant no duty of care under the 1957 Act in respect of her use of the path, though they would have owed her such a duty if she was using other parts of the park, such as the grass next to the path. This was enough to dissuade the claimant from relying on the 1957 Act, and her claim was brought under s. 41 of the Highways Act alone. But Bean LJ was not convinced that the council's lawyers were right. His Lordship suspected that the true ratio of *McGeown* was that no duty of care was owed '*if a person is only lawfully on a defendant's land* because of the existence of a public right of way which he or she is using' (at [13], emphasis added). If that is right, then it would follow that if I tripped over an obstacle on a public footpath on your property while walking to your house for lunch, you could be liable to me under the 1957 Act, but not if I was a rambler using the path to cross your land.

Countryside and Rights of Way Act 2000

A new class of non-visitors who are nonetheless not trespassers was created by the Countryside and Rights of Way Act 2000. The Act provides for general rights of access to 'access land' subject to compliance with the conditions set out in s. 2. Amendments to the 1984 Act make it clear that it is this Act, and not the 1957 legislation, which applies to persons entering upon access land. However, the extent of an occupier's liability to persons entering access land was a contentious issue when the Countryside and Rights of Way Bill was before Parliament. The resulting compromise can be found in ss. 1(6A) and 1A of the 1984 Act. First, in such cases no duty is owed under the 1984 Act in respect of natural features of the land, certain other features whether natural or not, and certain injuries resulting from walls, fences or gates. An exception is provided where the risk was created intentionally or recklessly. Secondly, where a duty may be owed in such cases, s. 1A states that the need not to place an undue burden on the occupier and the importance of maintaining the character of the countryside should be considered when determining what the discharge of any such duty requires. A paradox of the 2000 Act is that those who abuse the privilege of access granted by s. 2 become trespassers, and this may make them better off, under the terms of the 1984 Act, than they would be as an entrant on access land under the 2000 Act. This is because while the trespasser has the general protection of the 1984 Act, in the circumstances set out in s. 1(6A) the entrant under the 2000 Act is protected only against intentionally or recklessly inflicted harm. It is in any case doubtful whether these protective provisions are really necessary, for as the editors of *Winfield & Jolowicz* note (para. 10–043), liability in respect of natural hazards encountered by people exercising their 'right to roam' would in any case be unlikely after *Tomlinson v Congleton Borough Council* (see earlier).

11. Product Liability

The law of tort has long provided a remedy where physical injury has been caused by a defective product. Although in the nineteenth century, the courts were reluctant to impose a general tort duty on manufacturers in respect of defective products, liability in negligence has regularly been imposed on product manufacturers since the landmark decision of the House of Lords in *Donoghue v Stevenson* [1932] AC 562 (see Ch. 3.I.2). Across the Atlantic, however, courts in the United States were from the middle of the twentieth century imposing a more exacting standard on product manufacturers—that of strict liability, that is, liability without fault. Admittedly, there were also English law cases where the negligence standard imposed on manufacturers was almost indistinguishable from strict liability in practice (see *Grant v Australian Knitting Mills*, extracted in Ch. 3.I.3) but nonetheless as a matter of principle the manufacturer's liability remained rooted in negligence. The failure of the tort system to provide compensation to those who suffered birth defects after their mothers had used the drug thalidomide to combat morning sickness during pregnancy brought calls for a stricter liability in English law, and the *Pearson Commission* recommended (para. 317) that strict liability be imposed on producers of defective products. However, it was not until the Council of the European Communities issued Directive 85/374/EEC requiring the member states to harmonise their product liability laws that the United Kingdom passed the Consumer Protection Act 1987, which imposed strict tort liability for defective products (and which remains in force notwithstanding the UK's withdrawal from the European Union). We look first at the possible rationales for strict product liability, before turning to consider the 1987 Act.

1. Rationales for Strict Liability for Defective Products

> **Escola v Coca-Cola Bottling Co of Fresno** (1944) 150 P 2d 436
>
> The plaintiff was injured when a bottle of Coca-Cola exploded as she was putting it into a refrigerator. The manufacturer's potential negligence liability to a consumer had already been established in *MacPherson v Buick Motor Co*, 217 NY 382 (1916), the US equivalent of *Donoghue v Stevenson*, but the question remained whether the manufacturer faced any stricter liability. The extract is concerned with the appropriate basis of such a liability.
>
> **Traynor J**
>
> I concur in the judgment, but I believe the manufacturer's negligence should no longer be singled out as the basis of a plaintiff's right to recover in cases like the present one. In my opinion it should now be recognised that a manufacturer incurs an absolute liability when an article that he has placed on the market, knowing that it is to be used without inspection, proves to have a defect that causes injury to human beings. *MacPherson v Buick Motor Co* established the principle, recognised by this court, that irrespective of privity of contract, the manufacturer is responsible for an injury caused by such an article to any person who comes in lawful contact with it. In these cases the source of the manufacturer's liability was his negligence in the manufacturing process or in the inspection of component parts supplied by others. Even if there is no negligence, however, public policy demands that responsibility be fixed wherever it will most effectively reduce the hazards to life and health inherent in defective products that reach the market. It is evident that the manufacturer can anticipate some hazards and guard against the recurrence of others, as the public cannot. Those who suffer injury from defective products are unprepared to meet its consequences. The cost of injury and the loss of time or health may be an overwhelming misfortune to the person injured and a needless one, for the risk of injury can be insured by the manufacturer and distributed among the public as a cost of doing business. It is to the public interest to discourage the marketing of products having defects that are a menace to the public. If such products nevertheless find their way into the market it is to the public interest to place the responsibility for whatever injury they may cause upon the manufacturer, who, even if he is not negligent in the manufacture of the product, is responsible for its reaching the market.

COMMENTARY

The judgment in *Escola* reflects the view that the cost to the manufacturer of producing a product should include the cost of any damage caused by a defect in the product, so that the losses caused by such defects can be spread among all consumers of the products in question by means of higher prices (the 'loss-spreading' basis for strict liability). It can also be argued that strict liability reduces the flow of defective products to the market and increases overall economic efficiency (the 'deterrence' basis of strict liability). These arguments, and other possible justifications for strict product liability are considered in the next extract, from an influential article by William Prosser that was published some sixteen years after *Escola*, around the time many US jurisdictions were adopting strict liability in this context.

W. L. Prosser, 'The Assault upon the Citadel (Strict Liability to the Consumer)' (1960) 69 Yale LJ 1099, 1114–24

The Arguments

One may well ask at the outset, why is not liability for negligence enough? Why do the plaintiffs want strict liability; and have they any valid claim to it?

Where the action is against the manufacturer of the product, an honest estimate might very well be that there is not one case in a hundred in which strict liability would result in recovery where negligence does not. When a negligence action is brought against a manufacturer, the plaintiff is faced with two initial tasks. One is to prove that his injury has been caused by a defect in the product. The other is to prove that the defect existed when the product left the hands of the defendant. For neither of these is strict liability of any aid to him whatever. It cannot prove the causation; and it cannot trace that cause to the defendant. Once over these two hurdles, the plaintiff has a third task, to prove that the defect was there because of the defendant's negligence. This is by far the easiest of the three, and it is one in which the plaintiff almost never fails.

It is true that he has the burden of proof on the issue of negligence. It is true also that he seldom, if ever, has any direct evidence of what went on in the defendant's plant. But in every jurisdiction, he is aided by the doctrine of *res ipsa loquitur*, or by its practical equivalent. In all jurisdictions this at least gives rise to a permissible inference of the defendant's negligence, which gets the plaintiff to the jury. And in cases against manufacturers, once the cause of the harm is laid at their doorstep, a jury verdict for the defendant on the negligence issue is virtually unknown.

It is true that there have been occasional cases in which the defect has been of such a character that it could not have been prevented by any ordinary care, and the application of *res ipsa* has been denied. But such cases are so extremely rare as to be almost negligible, and over many years very few of them have appeared in the books. It is also true that it is open to the defendant to rebut the inference of negligence by proof of his own due care. But, again with very rare exceptions, the courts are agreed that such evidence does not entitle the defendant to a directed verdict, and raises only an issue for the jury. And again it must be repeated, once the cause of the injury is proved to lie with the defendant, once it is brought home to his plant, the jury finds for the plaintiff. Why, then, do the plaintiffs and their cohorts clamor so loudly for strict liability of the manufacturer, and why are the defendants equally vociferous in their opposition?

No writer seems to have suggested that the answer lies in the preparation for trial, the negotiations for settlement, and the amount of the verdict. So long as the negligence issue remains the case, it must be litigated, and plaintiff's counsel must be prepared to examine and to cross-examine witnesses, including even experts. He may even be forced to look up a little law, which is a thing from which some personal injury lawyers notoriously shrink. So long as there is the possibility that negligence may not be found, the defendant is encouraged by vain hopes, and the plaintiff gnawed by lingering doubts; and a case which *can* be decided for the defendant is worth less, in terms of settlement, than one which can not. And so long as the defendant can introduce evidence of his own due care, the possibility remains that it may influence the size of the verdict, as jurymen impressed with it stubbornly hold out for no liability, or a smaller sum.

All this, however, is but half of the picture. There are other sellers than the manufacturer of the product. It will pass through the hands of a whole line of other dealers, and the plaintiff may have good reason to sue any or all of them. The manufacturer is often beyond the jurisdiction. He may even, in some cases, be unknown. If he is identified and can be sued, it is very often impossible to pin the liability upon him. Even where there is a proved defect which speaks of obvious negligence on the part of someone, it may still not be possible to prove that it was on the part of the maker. The cracked Coca Cola bottle may have been cracked long after it left his plant. And even when the cause can be fixed upon the manufacturer, he may turn out, in these days of chain stores and large supply houses, to be a small concern, operating on a shoestring, and financially the least responsible person in the whole chain of distribution. If the plaintiff is to recover at all, he must often look to the wholesaler, the jobber, and the retailer.

It is here that negligence liability breaks down. The wholesaler, the jobber, and the retailer normally are simply not negligent. They are under no duty to test or inspect the chattel, and they do not do so; and when, as is usually the case today, it comes to them in a sealed container, examination becomes impossible without destroying marketability. No inference of negligence can arise against these sellers, and *res ipsa loquitur* is of no use at all.

It is true that against the retailer, the consumer who buys for himself and is injured can rely, in all but a few states, upon the old sales warranties of merchantable quality and fitness for the purpose. But so long as the privity wall stands firm, these warranties are of no avail against the wholesaler; nor do they protect the buyer's wife or child, his employee, his guest, his donee, or his sub-purchaser. The result has been utterly preposterous decisions as those holding that the wife who buys the sausage, handles it, cooks it, eats it, and is poisoned by it, cannot recover because she was merely buying as the agent of her husband, who was to pay the bill and so is regarded as the contracting party; whereas the husband, who never saw the food, can recover on a warranty for the loss of her services. The arrant folly of this has led to some remarkable legal gymnastics, in the form of contradictory presumptions or holdings as to agency, and to specific provisions in the new Uniform Commercial Code and in a Connecticut statute, which extend the retailer's warranty to all members of the buyer's household.

Such are the plaintiff's grievances, and such his claim to redress. When we come to the arguments adduced in support of his claim, we are confronted with more than a few which have a specious and unconvincing sound, and would appear to have been concocted in the heads of professors rather than based upon any realities of the situation. It is said, for example, that strict liability will provide a healthy and highly desirable incentive for producers to make their products safe. A skeptic may well question whether the callous manufacturer, who is unmoved by the prospect of negligence liability, plus *res ipsa loquitur*, and by the effect of any injury whatever upon the reputation of his goods, will really be stimulated by the relatively slight increase in possible liability to take additional precautions against defects which cannot be prevented by only reasonable care.

... It is said, again, that the doctrine of *res ipsa loquitur* is applied, in many cases, to impose liability upon defendants who in reality have not been negligent at all; and that the strict liability merely formulates, as a general rule, what goes on all the time in fact. The hypothesis is very likely true, although it is not capable of proof, and the number of instances in which it has [occurred] is probably far smaller than the proponents would have us believe; but the conclusion does not follow. One might as well say that because circumstantial evidence sometimes results in the conviction of the innocent, all criminal defendants should be found guilty . . .

Entitled to more respect is the 'risk-spreading' argument, which maintains that the manufacturers, as a group and an industry, should absorb the inevitable losses which must result in a complex civilization from the use of their products, because they are in the better position to do so, and through their prices to pass such losses on to the community at large. This contention has become identified with the concurring opinion of Justice Traynor of California in *Escola v. Coca Cola Bottling Co.*. . . .

[Prosser quoted from the opinion of Traynor J in *Escola* (see previous extract) and continued:]

Dean Pound once denounced this as a piece of 'authoritarian law', and a major step in the direction of socialism. Assuming that we are not nowadays disposed to flee shrieking in terror from the prospect of a spot of socialism in our law when the public interest demands it, the question remains whether our courts, our legislators, and public sentiment in general, are yet ready to adopt so sweeping a legal philosophy, and to impose so heavy a burden abruptly and all at once upon all producers. Thus far there has been relatively little indication that the time is yet ripe for what may very possibly be the law of fifty years ahead. As in the case of the related agitation for strict liability on the part of all automobile drivers, there are too many vested interests in the way, and the sudden change is likely to be regarded as too radical and disruptive; and progress in the direction of any such broad general rule cannot be expected to be rapid.

Dedicated writers have laid great stress upon liability insurance as the controlling and decisive factor in this situation. It seems very significant that, except for the casual reference in the lone opinion of Justice Traynor in the passage quoted above, no court, so far as can be discovered, ever has so much as mentioned insurance in a products-liability case. What insurance can do, of course, is to distribute losses proportionately among a group who are to bear them. What it cannot and should not do is to determine whether the group shall bear them in the first instance—and whether, for example, consumers shall be compelled to accept substantial price increases on everything they buy in order to compensate others for their misfortunes. Even the distribution of the losses through insurance may be a process that has its flaws. Until we develop, by analogy to workmen's compensation, a comprehensive system of compulsory insurance with rigidly limited damages—which no one as yet seems to have proposed specifically in this particular field—there will always be uninsured defendants, there will always be liability in excess of coverage, and there will be members of the group whose competitive situation does not permit them to pass on the cost of the insurance to their customers. Liability insurance is obviously not to be ignored; but it is a makeweight, and not the heart and soul of the problem. . . .

All this aside, the arguments which have proved convincing to the courts which have accepted the strict liability are three:

1. The public interest in human life, health and safety demands the maximum possible protection that the law can give against dangerous defects in products which consumers must buy, and against which they are helpless to protect themselves; and it justifies the imposition upon all suppliers of such products, of full responsibility for the harm they cause, even though the supplier has not been negligent. This argument, which in the last analysis rests upon public sentiment, has had its greatest force in the cases of food, where there was once popular outcry against an evil industry, and injuries and actions have multiplied, and public feeling is most obvious. It is now being advanced as to other products for bodily use, such as cosmetics. It suggests that as to still other products, distinctions may yet be drawn according to the probable danger, the frequency of injury, and what the public reasonably and rightfully expects.

2. The supplier, by placing the goods upon the market, represents to the public that they are suitable and safe for use; and by packaging, advertising or otherwise, he does everything that he can to induce that belief. He intends and expects that the product will be purchased and used in reliance upon his assurance of safety; and it is in fact so purchased and used.

> The middleman is no more than conduit, a mere mechanical device, through whom the thing sold is to reach the ultimate user. The supplier has invited and solicited the use; and when it leads to disaster, he should not be permitted to avoid the responsibility by saying that he has made no contract with the consumer.
>
> 3. It is already possible to enforce strict liability by resort to a series of actions, in which the retailer is first held liable on a warranty to his purchaser, and indemnity on a warranty is then sought successively from other suppliers, until the manufacturer finally pays the damages, with the added costs of repeated litigation. This is an expensive, time-consuming, and wasteful process, and it may be interrupted by insolvency, lack of jurisdiction, disclaimers, or the statute of limitations, anywhere along the line. What is needed is a blanket rule which makes any supplier in the chain liable directly to the ultimate user, and so short-circuits the whole unwieldy process. This is in the interest, not only of the consumer, but of the courts, and even on occasion of the suppliers themselves.

COMMENTARY

When considering this extract, it must be borne in mind that product liability claims in the United Kingdom are not determined by juries, and that Prosser's observations about the likely outcome once a case gets to a jury are therefore irrelevant in the domestic context.

The title of Prosser's article is instructive. The 'citadel' to which it refers is privity of contract, which was very much seen as the problem in the early American literature on product liability. The difficulty was that the purchaser of a defective product already benefitted from strict liability as against the retailer, by virtue of the implied terms as to quality in the contract of sale (in the United Kingdom, see now Sale of Goods Act 1979, ss. 13–15; Consumer Rights Act 2015, ss. 9–11). However, 'vertical privity' meant that the buyer could not avail themselves of this contractual strict liability as against the manufacturer—so that instead a series of claims had to be brought up the entire chain of contracts—and, even more problematically, 'horizontal privity' meant that an injured non-buyer could not avail themselves of the contractual strict liability at all, but must instead claim in negligence under *Donoghue v Stevenson*, and prove fault (see Whittaker, 'The EEC Directive on Product Liability' (1985) 5 Yearbook Eur Law 233 at 239). Hence, when a woman was injured after drinking lemonade containing grains of carbolic acid, she was unable to sue the retailer in contract because her husband had bought the lemonade (*Daniels v R. White & Sons Ltd* [1938] 4 All ER 258). As Prosser says, this was a difficult position to defend, and the desire to extend contract-type protections to third parties was a key impetus of the move to strict tort liability in the United States. Indeed, the first steps in that direction employed contractual reasoning, beginning with an express contractual warranty to the third party based on the advertising of the product (*Baxter v Ford Motor Co* (1932) 12 P 2d 409), and later an implied warranty of safety (*Henningsen v Bloomfield Motors* (1960) 161 A 2d 69). It was only in the early 1960s that the courts abandoned these contractual techniques and openly embraced the idea of strict liability in tort (*Greenman v Yuba Power Products Inc* (1963) 377 P 2d 897; *Restatement of the Law (Second), Torts* (1977), § 402A(1)). When considering the operation of strict product liability regimes such as the Consumer Protection Act 1987, it is worth remembering the origins of this kind of liability in attempts to circumvent privity of contract, as some of the key concepts that are employed (e.g. 'defectiveness') possess a somewhat contractual flavour.

At the same time, it was not immediately obvious why strict tort liability should be imposed where damage was caused by a defective product, rather than in some other way. In that connection, it is noteworthy that Prosser is somewhat dismissive of the arguments from deterrence and loss-spreading put forward by Traynor J in *Escola*. Was he right to be? And are his arguments for strict product liability more convincing?

For a critical evaluation of the arguments that have been put forward for strict product liability, see H. Koziol, 'Introductory Lecture', in H. Koziol et al. (eds), *Product Liability: Fundamental Questions in a Comparative Perspective* (Berlin: De Gruyter, 2017).

Council Directive 85/374/EEC

Whereas approximation of the laws of the Member States concerning the liability of the producer for damage caused by the defectiveness of his products is necessary because the existing divergences may distort competition and affect the movement of goods within the common market and entail a differing degree of protection of the consumer against damage caused by a defective product to his health or property;

Whereas liability without fault on the part of the producer is the sole means of adequately solving the problem, peculiar to our age of increasing technicality, of a fair apportionment of the risks inherent in modern technological production . . .

COMMENTARY

The rationale of the European Directive is complicated by the need to justify imposing a strict product liability regime at the European level. Hence while the second of the extracted recitals arguably reveals a moral basis for liability without fault, perhaps based (tacitly) on something like the Traynor J's 'enterprise' theory, the first recital shows how the Directive was shaped by the requirements of the European single market. Whittaker, *op. cit.*, at 234 explains the thinking, but is sceptical:

The first reason given [for the Directive] is, not surprisingly, economic. The burden of product liability itself, or more likely insurance against it, is one of the costs borne by manufacturers. If the rules of liability differ, then manufacturers' costs will differ according to the legal system in question. Harmonisation of the rules of liability will thus smooth out this distortion of the market. However, this argument is not entirely convincing and to the extent it does convince, the amount of time spent on the Directive appears something of an over-reaction by comparison with other more serious distortions in the market. The Commission had itself maintained that the increased costs of imposing strict liability on manufacturers would not be over-burdensome. According to one commentator . . . [t]he change from fault to strict liability would . . . have a 'minimal effect' on product prices.

Although, as Whittaker points out, the single market rationale is an economic one, it is a rather different economic rationale from that of deterrence theory in tort. The Court of Justice of the European Union (CJEU) clearly regards economic harmonisation as the primary objective of the Directive, and has consistently held that member states cannot impose a more stringent form of product liability than that allowed by the Directive (Case C–52/00, *Commission v France* [2002] ECR I–3827; Case C–154/00, *Commission v Greece* [2002] ECR I–3879; Case C–402/03, *Skov AEG v Bilka Lavprisvarehus A/S* [2006] ECR I–199), even if the more stringent law preceded the Directive (Case C–183/00, *Sanchez v Medicina Asturiana SA* [2002] ECR I–3901). According to the Court, if member states were allowed to have such laws then the different level of consumer protection this would produce might distort competition between traders and impede the free movement of goods. Although this reasoning suggests that *any* variation between the member states would potentially distort competition, the Directive expressly allowed for a number of derogations whereby individual member states when implementing the Directive were permitted to exercise a choice with regard to certain aspects of the strict liability regime (e.g., whether to include agricultural products, whether to allow a 'development risks' defence, and the level of damages). At first glance such variations would seem to be in conflict with the harmonisation rationale for the Directive favoured by the CJEU. However, according to the European Commission, the balance between the competing interests struck by the Directive included, amongst others, the presence of the development risks defence, and at the time the Directive was adopted it intended to provide for limited harmonisation only (*Fourth Report on the Application of Directive 85/374 on Liability for Defective Products* COM(2011) 547 final, p. 10). Seen in this light, the decisions of the CJEU can be interpreted, not as requiring complete harmonisation, but as ensuring that the compromise between the interests of claimants, manufacturers and their insurers represented by the Directive is enforced in all member states. This balance, of course, may change over time; hence the amendment to remove the derogation for agricultural products: see II.2. For further analysis, see S. Whittaker, *Liability for Products: English Law, French Law, and European Harmonization* (Oxford: OUP, 2005), pp. 440–4 and 659–61.

The rationales of the Directive have not found universal support (see, e.g., Stapleton (1986) 6 OJLS 392, arguing that difficulties with proving a causal link between a defect and the claimant's injury may prevent the true cost of the defect being borne by the producer). Nonetheless, decisions in cases such as *A v National Blood Authority* [2001] 3 All ER 289 and *Abouzaid v Mothercare (UK) Ltd*, CA, *The Times*, 20 February 2001 demonstrate that, while the Directive may not have solved all of the difficulties for a claimant in recovering damages for harm caused by a defective product, the strict liability regime that it established is qualitatively different from negligence liability.

2. The Consumer Protection Act 1987

The Directive was implemented in the United Kingdom by the passage of the Consumer Protection Act 1987. The relevant provisions of the Act are extracted first. However, since s.1(1) of the Act states that it is to be interpreted in the light of the Directive, the text of the latter is of considerable importance, and so the extract from the Act is followed by some key articles of the Directive, the wording of which may prove significant when interpreting the equivalent provisions of the Act. It should be noted that the interpretation provision is not affected by the UK's withdrawal from the European Union, and although it is true that when applying the Act the UK courts are no longer bound by future decisions of the CJEU on the correct interpretation of the Directive (European Union (Withdrawal) Act 2018, s. 6), these decisions will no doubt still prove influential. (On the continuing effect of EU case law after Brexit, see Whittaker, 'Retaining European Union law in the United Kingdom' (2021) 137 LQR 477 at 483–8.)

Consumer Protection Act 1987

An Act to make provision with respect to the liability of persons for damage caused by defective products . . .

PART I

1. Purpose and construction of Part 1

(1) This Part was enacted for the purpose of making such provision as was necessary in order to comply with the product liability Directive and shall be construed accordingly.

(2) In this Part, except in so far as the context otherwise requires—

'dependant' and 'relative' have the same meanings as they have in, respectively, the Fatal Accidents Act 1976 and the Damages (Scotland) Act 2011 (ASP);
'producer', in relation to a product, means—
  (a) the person who manufactured it;
  (b) in the case of a substance which has not been manufactured but has been won or abstracted, the person who won or abstracted it;
  (c) in the case of a product which has not been manufactured, won or abstracted but essential characteristics of which are attributable to an industrial or other process having been carried out (for example, in relation to agricultural produce), the person who carried out that process;

'product' means any goods or electricity and (subject to subsection (3) below) includes a product which is comprised in another product, whether by virtue of being a component part or raw material or otherwise; and

'the product liability Directive' means the Directive of the Council of the European Communities, dated 25th July 1985, (No 85/374/EEC) on the approximation of the laws, regulations and administrative provisions of the member States concerning liability for defective products.

(3) For the purposes of this Part a person who supplies any product in which products are comprised, whether by virtue of being component parts or raw materials or otherwise, shall not be treated by reason only of his supply of that product as supplying any of the products so comprised.

2. Liability for defective products

(1) Subject to the following provisions of this Part, where any damage is caused wholly or partly by a defect in a product, every person to whom subsection (2) below applies shall be liable for the damage.

(2) This subsection applies to—
  (a) the producer of the product;
  (b) any person who, by putting his name on the product or using a trade mark or other distinguishing mark in relation to the product, has held himself out to be the producer of the product;
  (c) any person who has imported the product into the United Kingdom in order, in the course of any business of his, to supply it to another.

(3) Subject as aforesaid, where any damage is caused wholly or partly by a defect in a product, any person who supplied the product (whether to the person who suffered the damage, to

the producer of any product in which the product in question is comprised or to any other person) shall be liable for the damage if—

(a) the person who suffered the damage requests the supplier to identify one or more of the persons (whether still in existence or not) to whom subsection (2) above applies in relation to the product;

(b) that request is made within a reasonable period after the damage occurs and at a time when it is not reasonably practicable for the person making the request to identify all those persons; and

(c) the supplier fails, within a reasonable period after receiving the request, either to comply with the request or to identify the person who supplied the product to him . . .

(5) Where two or more persons are liable by virtue of this Part for the same damage, their liability shall be joint and several.

(6) This section shall be without prejudice to any liability arising otherwise than by virtue of this Part.

3. Meaning of 'defect'

(1) Subject to the following provisions of this section, there is a defect in a product for the purposes of this Part if the safety of the product is not such as persons generally are entitled to expect; and for those purposes 'safety', in relation to a product, shall include safety with respect to products comprised in that product and safety in the context of risks of damage to property, as well as in the context of risks of death or personal injury.

(2) In determining for the purposes of subsection (1) above what persons generally are entitled to expect in relation to a product all the circumstances shall be taken into account, including—

(a) the manner in which, and purposes for which, the product has been marketed, its get-up, the use of any mark in relation to the product and any instructions for, or warnings with respect to, doing or refraining from doing anything with or in relation to the product;

(b) what might reasonably be expected to be done with or in relation to the product; and

(c) the time when the product was supplied by its producer to another;

and nothing in this section shall require a defect to be inferred from the fact alone that the safety of a product which is supplied after that time is greater than the safety of the product in question.

4. Defences

(1) In any civil proceedings by virtue of this Part against any person ('the person proceeded against') in respect of a defect in a product it shall be a defence for him to show—

(a) that the defect is attributable to compliance with any requirement imposed by or under any enactment or with any retained obligation; or

(b) that the person proceeded against did not at any time supply the product to another; or

(c) that the following conditions are satisfied, that is to say—

(i) that the only supply of the product to another by the person proceeded against was otherwise than in the course of a business of that person's; and

(ii) that section 2(2) above does not apply to that person or applies to him by virtue only of things done otherwise than with a view to profit; or

(d) that the defect did not exist in the product at the relevant time; or

(e) that the state of scientific and technical knowledge at the relevant time was not such that a producer of products of the same description as the product in question might be expected to have discovered the defect if it had existed in his products while they were under his control; or
(f) that the defect—
   (i) constituted a defect in a product ('the subsequent product') in which the product in question had been comprised; and
   (ii) was wholly attributable to the design of the subsequent product or to compliance by the producer of the product in question with instructions given by the producer of the subsequent product.

(2) In this section 'the relevant time', in relation to electricity, means the time at which it was generated, being a time before it was transmitted or distributed, and in relation to any other product, means—

   (a) if the person proceeded against is a person to whom subsection (2) of section 2 above applies in relation to the product, the time when he supplied the product to another;
   (b) if that subsection does not apply to that person in relation to the product, the time when the product was last supplied by a person to whom that subsection does apply in relation to the product.

5. Damage giving rise to liability

(1) Subject to the following provisions of this section, in this Part 'damage' means death or personal injury or any loss of or damage to any property (including land).

(2) A person shall not be liable under section 2 above in respect of any defect in a product for the loss of or any damage to the product itself or for the loss of or any damage to the whole or any part of any product which has been supplied with the product in question comprised in it.

(3) A person shall not be liable under section 2 above for any loss of or damage to any property which, at the time it is lost or damaged, is not—

   (a) of a description of property ordinarily intended for private use, occupation or consumption; and
   (b) intended by the person suffering the loss or damage mainly for his own private use, occupation or consumption.

(4) No damages shall be awarded to any person by virtue of this Part in respect of any loss of or damage to any property if the amount which would fall to be so awarded to that person, apart from this subsection and any liability for interest, does not exceed £275.

(5) In determining for the purposes of this Part who has suffered any loss of or damage to property and when any such loss or damage occurred, the loss or damage shall be regarded as having occurred at the earliest time at which a person with an interest in the property had knowledge of the material facts about the loss or damage.

(6) For the purposes of subsection (5) above the material facts about any loss of or damage to any property are such facts about the loss or damage as would lead a reasonable person with an interest in the property to consider the loss or damage sufficiently serious to justify his instituting proceedings for damages against a defendant who did not dispute liability and was able to satisfy a judgment.

(7) For the purposes of subsection (5) above a person's knowledge includes knowledge which he might reasonably have been expected to acquire—

  (a) from facts observable or ascertainable by him; or
  (b) from facts ascertainable by him with the help of appropriate expert advice which it is reasonable for him to seek;

but a person shall not be taken by virtue of this subsection to have knowledge of a fact ascertainable by him only with the help of expert advice unless he has failed to take all reasonable steps to obtain (and, where appropriate, to act on) that advice . . .

6. Application of certain enactments

(1) Any damage for which a person is liable under section 2 above shall be deemed to have been caused—

  (a) for the purposes of the Fatal Accidents Act 1976, by that person's wrongful act, neglect or default . . .

(2) Where—

  (a) a person's death is caused wholly or partly by a defect in a product, or a person dies after suffering damage which has been so caused;
  (b) a request such as mentioned in paragraph (a) of subsection (3) of section 2 above is made to a supplier of the product by that person's personal representatives or, in the case of a person whose death is caused wholly or partly by the defect, by any dependant or relative of that person; and
  (c) the conditions specified in paragraphs (b) and (c) of that subsection are satisfied in relation to that request,

this Part shall have effect for the purposes of the Law Reform (Miscellaneous Provisions) Act 1934, [and] the Fatal Accidents Act 1976 . . . as if liability of the supplier to that person under that subsection did not depend on that person having requested the supplier to identify certain persons or on the said conditions having been satisfied in relation to a request made by that person.

(3) Section 1 of the Congenital Disabilities (Civil Liability) Act 1976 shall have effect for the purposes of this Part as if—

  (a) a person were answerable to a child in respect of an occurrence caused wholly or partly by a defect in a product if he is or has been liable under section 2 above in respect of any effect of the occurrence on a parent of the child, or would be so liable if the occurrence caused a parent of the child to suffer damage;
  (b) the provisions of this Part relating to liability under section 2 above applied in relation to liability by virtue of paragraph (a) above under the said section 1; and
  (c) subsection (6) of the said section 1 (exclusion of liability) were omitted.

(4) Where any damage is caused partly by a defect in a product and partly by the fault of the person suffering the damage, the Law Reform (Contributory Negligence) Act 1945 and section 5 of the Fatal Accidents Act 1976 (contributory negligence) shall have effect as if the defect were the fault of every person liable by virtue of this Part for the damage caused by the defect.

(5) In subsection (4) above 'fault' has the same meaning as in the said Act of 1945 . . .

7. Prohibition on exclusions from liability

The liability of a person by virtue of this Part to a person who has suffered damage caused wholly or partly by a defect in a product, or to a dependant or relative of such a person, shall not be limited or excluded by any contract term, by any notice or by any other provision . . .

45. Interpretation

(1) In this Act, except in so far as the context otherwise requires . . .

'business' includes a trade or profession and the activities of a professional or trade association or of a local authority or other public authority;

'goods' includes substances, growing crops and things comprised in land by virtue of being attached to it and any ship, aircraft or vehicle . . .

'modifications' includes additions, alterations and omissions, and cognate expressions shall be construed accordingly . . .

'personal injury' includes any disease and any other impairment of a person's physical or mental condition;

'premises' includes any place and any ship, aircraft or vehicle . . .

'substance' means any natural or artificial substance, whether in solid, liquid or gaseous form or in the form of a vapour, and includes substances that are comprised in or mixed with other goods;

'supply' and cognate expressions shall be construed in accordance with section 46 below; . . .

46. Meaning of 'supply'

(1) Subject to the following provisions of this section, references in this Act to supplying goods shall be construed as references to doing any of the following, whether as principal or agent, that is to say—

   (a) selling, hiring out or lending the goods;
   (b) entering into a hire-purchase agreement to furnish the goods;
   (c) the performance of any contract for work and materials to furnish the goods;
   (d) providing the goods in exchange for any consideration other than money;
   (e) providing the goods in or in connection with the performance of any statutory function; or
   (f) giving the goods as a prize or otherwise making a gift of the goods;

and, in relation to gas or water, those references shall be construed as including references to providing the service by which the gas or water is made available for use . . .

(3) Subject to subsection (4) below, the performance of any contract by the erection of any building or structure on any land or by the carrying out of any other building works shall be treated for the purposes of this Act as a supply of goods in so far as, but only in so far as, it involves the provision of any goods to any person by means of their incorporation into the building, structure or works.

(4) Except for the purposes of, and in relation to, notices to warn, references in this Act to supplying goods shall not include references to supplying goods comprised in land where the supply is effected by the creation or disposal of an interest in the land . . .

(8) Where any goods have at any time been supplied by being hired out or lent to any person, neither a continuation or renewal of the hire or loan (whether on the same or different terms) nor any transaction for the transfer after that time of any interest in the goods to the person to whom they were hired or lent shall be treated for the purposes of this Act as a further supply of the goods to that person.

(9) A ship, aircraft or motor vehicle shall not be treated for the purposes of this Act as supplied to any person by reason only that services consisting in the carriage of goods or passengers in that ship, aircraft or vehicle, or in its use for any other purpose, are provided to that person in pursuance of an agreement relating to the use of the ship, aircraft or vehicle for a particular period or for particular voyages, flights or journeys.

Council Directive 85/374/EEC

Article 1

The producer shall be liable for damage caused by a defect in his product.

Article 2

For the purpose of this Directive, 'product' means all movables even if incorporated into another movable or into an immovable. . . .

Article 4

The injured person shall be required to prove the damage, the defect and the causal relationship between defect and damage. . . .

Article 6

1. A product is defective when it does not provide the safety which a person is entitled to expect, taking all circumstances into account . . .

Article 7

The producer shall not be liable as a result of this Directive if he proves:

. . .

(c) that the product was neither manufactured by him for sale or any form of distribution for economic purpose nor manufactured or distributed by him in the course of his business; or . . .

(e) that the state of scientific and technical knowledge at the time when he put the product into circulation was not such as to enable the existence of the defect to be discovered . . .

Article 8

1. Without prejudice to the provisions of national law concerning the right of contribution or recourse, the liability of the producer shall not be reduced when the damage is caused both by a defect in product and by the act or omission of a third party.

2. The liability of the producer may be reduced or disallowed when, having regard to all the circumstances, the damage is caused both by a defect in the product and by the fault of the injured person or any person for whom the injured person is responsible.

COMMENTARY

In *A v National Blood Authority* [2001] 3 All ER 289 at 297, Burton J declined (with the agreement of counsel) to apply the text of the Consumer Protection Act 1987, stating that 'the practical course was to go straight to the fount, the Directive itself'. Arnull [2001] EL Rev 213 at 214 comments:

That approach goes further than required by the case law of the Court of Justice. It could be taken to imply that, whatever the national implementing legislation may say, an English court will always give effect to the requirements of a directive. Such an outcome would be hard to reconcile with both the nature of directives and the approach of the Court of Justice, which has been careful to emphasise that it is only in cases of ambiguity that an interpretation consistent with Community law must be preferred.

Nor was Burton J's unorthodox approach followed in *Wilkes v DePuy International Ltd* [2018] QB 627, where Hickinbottom J said (at [53]) that the claimant's action was derived from the Act, not the Directive, so that the 'focus is therefore on the Act, not the Directive'.

In *Gee v DePuy International Ltd* [2018] Med LR 347 at [73] Andrews J said that while the effective protection of consumers is a key objective of the Directive, it is not 'the main or overriding objective' and that it was important to bear this in mind when applying the Act. It followed, according to Lord Tyre in *Hastings v (First) Finsbury Orthopaedics Ltd* 2019 SLT 1411 at [96] that there was 'no justification for construing either the Directive or the Act in a manner more favourable to the consumer than to the producer'.

The basic structure of the liability established by both the Directive and the Act is the same. In the Act, the central provisions are in s. 2, and these impose liability on the producer, own brander or importer for damage caused wholly or partly by a defect in a product. The onus is on the claimant to establish the damage, the defect and the causal link between the two. The claimant must also establish that the defendant is liable for the damage under the terms of the Act. The burden of proof then shifts to the defendant, for whom several defences are available.

While the Occupiers' Liability Acts extracted in the previous section of this chapter impose duties (of care) on occupiers towards entrants on their land in certain circumstances, the word 'duty' does not appear once in the extract from the 1987 Act. This is because what the Act creates is a liability rule, whereby if certain conditions are satisfied, X is liable to Y, despite X not having breached a duty owed to Y. It can be easier to impose strict liability via such a rule than by means of a right/duty relationship of the kind characteristic of other areas of tort law, such as negligence and nuisance, and strict liability under the rule in *Rylands v Fletcher* (discussed in Ch. 11) also seems to arise without the breach of any duty on the defendant's part. See further on liability rules, Jaffey, 'Duties and Liabilities in Private Law' (2006) 12 *Legal Theory* 137.

Who May be Liable?

One advantage of liability rules is the flexibility that they give when it comes to determining who bears the liability in question, and full use is made of this flexibility in the relevant provisions of the 1987 Act. Section 2(2) of the Act identifies a number of possible defendants. The first and most important of these is the producer of the product (as defined in s. 1(2)). The second is the own brander or apparent producer, that is, someone who by putting his name on the product or using trade or other distinguishing marks holds himself out to be the producer of the product. An example might be a fast-food chain in respect of an item produced by a franchisee. Much will however depend on the circumstances. Could one of the big supermarket chains qualify under this provision in respect of products marketed under their own name? Does anyone really think Tesco Strawberry Jam is produced by Tesco? And would it be significant that it said on the jar that it was 'Made *for* Tesco' (emphasis added)? On the last point, see Whittaker (1985) 5 Yearbook Eur Law 233 at 267, arguing that a 'robust view' should be taken of attempts to escape liability under this heading, and that 'the standpoint of the reasonable consumer' should be adopted when deciding on its application, so that if a defendant's name or trademark is likely to be relied on by a consumer, then 'small print on the product should not be allowed to avoid the liability which this reliance invites'. (See further on 'own branders', Simões, 'Private Labels and Products Liability: Hypermarkets as Apparent Producers' [2013] JR 469.) A third category of defendant is the importer of the product into the United Kingdom—before the UK's withdrawal from the EU, it was *into the EU*—where this was done in the course of business and for the purpose of 'supply' to another as defined in s. 46. This ensures that there will be a defendant within the United Kingdom.

The mere supply of goods does not attract primary liability under the Act, but s. 2(3) lays down that a supplier who is asked by an injured person to identify one or more of the persons who are primarily liable (i.e. the producer, the own brander or the importer) is themselves liable if they do not within a reasonable time either comply with the request or identify the person who supplied the product to them. It is therefore essential for their own sakes that suppliers keep adequate records. Of course, suppliers may still be subject to strict liability under the terms of the supply contract (which will include any terms implied into the contract by the Sale of Goods Act 1979 or Consumer Rights Act 2015).

For further detail on persons subject to liability under the Act, see *Fairgrieve and Goldberg*, ch. 8.

Meaning of Product

Liability under the 1987 Act attaches only to damage caused by products. 'Product' is defined in s. 1(2) as goods, a term which is itself defined in s. 45 to include 'substances, growing crops and things comprised in land by virtue of being attached to it and any ship, aircraft, or vehicle'. It also includes a product which is comprised in another product. A building is not a 'good' (see also Article 2 of the Directive, which defines 'product' as 'all movables'), although a component incorporated into a building (such as piece of timber or a window pane) is a 'product' and so may give rise to liability. Hence while a builder cannot be liable as a producer, the producers of defective components of a building may be, and a builder may potentially be liable as a supplier of such components.

The Directive allowed member states to exclude agricultural products from the scheme of strict liability, and the United Kingdom did so unless such products had undergone an 'industrial process'. However, Council Directive 99/34 extended the Products Liability Directive to primary agricultural products by amending Article 2, and in 2000 the terms of the Act were amended accordingly. (See further, Hodges, 'Reform of the Product Liability Directive 1998–9' [1999] Consumer LJ 35 at 35–7.) In the view of the Commission, the different rules as to liability for agricultural produce across the member states distorted competition for such produce in the single market, and consumers were entitled to expect high levels of safety in agricultural produce. It was also hoped that the amendment would increase consumer confidence in the safety of agricultural products, following food safety scandals such as the supply of beef infected with BSE.

Does the strict liability under the Act apply to dangerously misleading information, such as an inaccurate guide to edible mushrooms? If the information is not contained in a physical thing (such as a book or map) then the answer is surely no, on the ground that there is no 'product' to which the liability can attach. But where there is an information product, does the concept of defectiveness extend beyond its physical characteristics (such as a razor-sharp edge on the spine of a book) to encompass the dangerous information it conveys? In Case C-65/20, *VI v KRONE—Verlag Gesellschaft mbH & Co KG* the CJEU suggested not, holding that no action lay under the 1985 Directive for injury caused by inaccurate health advice published in a newspaper (an article on the use of a grated horseradish poultice as a rheumatism treatment said that it should be held against the affected area for between two to five hours instead of two to five minutes!). According to the Court, services fell outside the scope of the Directive, and health advice by its nature constituted a service. Moreover, the service in question was 'not part of the inherent characteristics of the printed newspaper which alone permit an assessment as to whether the product is defective' (at [36]). A commentator on *Krone* questions the characterisation of a newspaper's health advice column as a 'service', but nevertheless supports the decision on the basis that strict liability for information provision would have a 'chilling effect' on the communication of information and freedom of expression (Machnikowski [2022] Eur Rev Priv Law 191 at 199). Do you agree? If so, do you think that limiting strict liability to the 'inherent characteristics' of a product provides a workable test for excluding information from the ambit of the Directive?

It remains to be seen whether the English courts will follow the lead of the CJEU on this issue. On the one hand, it would admittedly be very strange if there was strict liability for the hardcopy version of the edible mushroom guide but only negligence liability for the e-book. Nor is it clear who the 'producer' of the book would be (in *Krone* the defendant was the publisher of the newspaper, but is not the 'manufacturer' of a newspaper the printer?). On the other hand, it is not at all easy to see the basis in the Act for excluding information conveyed by a product from an assessment of its 'safety', and it is also hard to see how this could be done without also excluding warnings and instructions, which s. 3(2)(a) of the Act makes clear are highly pertinent to the defectiveness enquiry (discussed later). See further on this issue, Whittaker (1989) 105 LQR 125 and Stapleton (1989) 9 Tel Aviv Univ Stud in Law 147.

Meaning of Defect

A product has a defect if its safety 'is not such as persons generally are entitled to expect' (s. 3), regardless of whether the producer took reasonable care to ensure the product's safety. Unlike in negligence, therefore, the focus is on the safety of the product, and not the conduct of the producer or other defendant. But, although liability is not fault-based, doubts have been expressed as to the strictness of the liability for defects on the basis that the risk/utility comparison that underpins negligence may resurface in the assessment of a product's defectiveness. Where there are allegations about the safety of a particular pharmaceutical drug, for example, it has been argued that one can only assess defectiveness by engaging in a balancing exercise in which the drug's generally beneficial properties are weighed against its rare, harmful side-effects, having regard to how frequently they occur and how serious they are if they occur (see Newdick [1985] 101 LQR 405). The strictness of the liability, and the meaning of defect, received judicial consideration in the following two cases.

A v National Blood Authority [2001] EWHC 446 (QB), [2001] 3 All ER 289

The claimants were infected with the Hepatitis C virus from blood transfusions organised by the defendant. The blood was collected from donors, and although it was known that there was a risk that such blood might be infected with the virus, it was impossible to avoid the risk because the virus had not yet been identified or because no tests available at the time could detect the presence of the virus. The claimants sued under the Consumer Protection Act 1987, arguing that the supply of blood to them was the supply of a defective product, and that this had caused them damage. The defendant alleged that the unavoidability of the risk was a factor to be considered in determining whether the product was defective.

Burton J considered the specific circumstances listed in Article 6, and accepted that the list was not exhaustive, and then continued:

35. The dispute therefore is as to what further, if anything, falls to be considered within '*all circumstances*'. There is no dispute between the parties . . . that consideration of the fault of the producer is excluded; but does consideration of '*all circumstances*' include consideration of the conduct to be expected from the producer, the level of safety to be expected from a producer of that product? The parties agree that the starting point is the particular product with the harmful characteristic, and if its inherent nature and intended use (e.g., poison) are dangerous, then there may not need to be any further consideration, provided that the injury resulted from that known danger. However, if the product was not intended to be dangerous, that is the harmful characteristic was not intended, by virtue of the intended use of the product, then there must be consideration of whether it was safe and the level of safety to be legitimately expected. At this stage, the Defendants assert that part of the investigation consists of what steps could have been taken by a producer to avoid that harmful characteristic. The Defendants assert that conduct is to be considered not by reference to identifying the individual producer's negligence, but by identifying and specifying the safety precautions that the public would or could reasonably expect from a producer of the product. The exercise is referred to as a balancing act; the more difficult it is to make safe, and the more beneficial the product, the less is expected and vice versa, an issue being whether a producer has complied with the safety precautions reasonably to be expected . . .

The Claimants however assert that, given that it is common ground that the Article imposes liability irrespective of fault, the exercise of considering what could or should have been done by the producer is an impermissible and irrelevant exercise, which lets questions of fault back in by the back door . . .

Non-Standard Products

36. In any event, however, the Claimants make a separate case in relation to the blood products here in issue: namely that they are what is called in the United States 'rogue products' or 'lemons', and in Germany '*Ausreisser*'—escapees or 'off the road' products. These are products which are isolated or rare specimens which are different from the other products of a similar series, different from the products as intended or desired by the producer . . .

[Burton J stated that he preferred to call such products 'non-standard', explaining:]

Thus a *standard* product is one which is and performs as the producer intends. A *non-standard* product is one which is different, obviously because it is deficient or inferior in terms of safety, from the standard product: and where it is the harmful characteristic or characteristics present in the non-standard product, but not in the standard product, which has or have caused the material injury or damage. Some Community jurisdictions in implementing the Directive have specifically provided that there will be liability for 'non-standard' products, i.e., that such will automatically be defective within Article 6: Italy and Spain have done so by express legislation . . .

Conclusions on Article 6

55. I do not consider it to be arguable that the consumer had an actual expectation that blood being supplied to him was not 100 per cent clean, nor do I conclude that he had knowledge that it was, or was likely to be, infected with Hepatitis C. It is not seriously argued by the Defendants . . . that there was any public understanding or acceptance of the infection of transfused blood by Hepatitis C. Doctors and surgeons knew, but did not tell their patients unless asked, and were very rarely asked. It was certainly, in my judgment, not known and accepted by society that there was such a risk . . .

56. I do not consider that the legitimate expectation of the public at large is that legitimately expectable tests will have been carried out or precautions adopted. Their legitimate expectation is as to the safeness of the product (or not). The Court will act as . . . the *appointed representative of the public at large*, but in my judgment it is impossible to inject into the consumer's legitimate expectation matters which would not by any stretch of the imagination be in his actual expectation. He will assume perhaps that there are tests, but his expectations will be as to the safeness of the blood. In my judgment it is as inappropriate to propose that the public should not 'expect the unattainable'—in the sense of tests or precautions which are impossible—at least unless it is informed as to what is unattainable or impossible, as it is to reformulate the expectation as one that the producer will not have been negligent or will have taken all reasonable steps.

57. In this context I turn to consider what is intended to be included within '*all circumstances*' in Article 6. I am satisfied that this means all relevant circumstances. It is quite plain to me that . . . the Directive was intended to eliminate proof of fault or negligence. I am satisfied that this was not simply a legal consequence, but that it was also intended to make it easier for claimants to prove their case, such that not only would a consumer not have to prove that the producer did not take reasonable steps, or all reasonable steps, to comply with his duty of care, but also that the producer did not take all legitimately expectable steps either . . .

63. I conclude therefore that *avoidability* is not one of the *circumstances* to be taken into account within Article 6 . . .

65. [I]n my judgment, the infected bags of blood were non-standard products. I have already recorded that it does not seem to me to matter whether they would be categorised in US tort law as manufacturing or design defects. They were in any event different from the norm which the producer intended for use by the public . . .

I do not accept that all the blood products were equally defective because all of them carried the risk. That is a very philosophical approach. It is one which would . . . be equally apt to a situation in which one tyre in one million was defective because of an inherent occasional blip in the strength of the rubber's raw material. The answer is that the test relates to the use of the blood bag. For, and as a result of, the intended use, 99 out of 100 bags would cause no injury and would not be infected, unlike the one hundredth.

Even in the case of standard products such as drugs, side-effects are to my mind only capable of being 'socially acceptable' if they are made known . . .

But I am satisfied, as I have stated above, that the problem was not known to the consumer. However, in any event, I do not accept that the consumer expected, or was entitled to expect, that his bag of blood was defective even if (which I have concluded was not the case) he had any knowledge of any problem. I do not consider . . . that he was expecting or entitled to expect a form of Russian roulette. That would only arise if, contrary to my conclusion, the public took that as socially acceptable . . . For such knowledge and acceptance there would need to be at the very least publicity and probably express warnings, and even that might not . . . be sufficient . . .

66. . . . Where, as here, there is a harmful characteristic in a non-standard product, a decision that it is defective is likely to be straightforward, and I can make my decision accordingly. However the consequence of my conclusion is that '*avoidability*' is also not in the basket of *circumstances*, even in respect of a harmful characteristic in a standard product. So I shall set out what I consider to be the structure for consideration under Article 6. It must be emphasised that safety and intended, or foreseeable, use are the lynchpins: and, leading on from these, what legitimate expectations there are of safety in relation to foreseeable use . . .

67. The first step must be to identify the harmful characteristic which caused the injury (Article 4). In order to establish that there is a defect in Article 6, the next step will be to conclude whether the product is standard or non-standard. This will be done (in the absence

of admission by the producer) most easily by comparing the offending product with other products of the same type or series produced by that producer. If the respect in which it differs from the series includes the harmful characteristic, then it is, for the purpose of Article 6, non-standard. If it does not differ, or if the respect in which it differs does not include the harmful characteristic, but all the other products, albeit different, share the harmful characteristic, then it is to be treated as a standard product.

Non-standard Products

68. The *circumstances* specified in Article 6 may obviously be relevant—the product may be a second—as well as the circumstances of the supply. But it seems to me that the primary issue in relation to a non-standard product may be whether the public at large accepted the non-standard nature of the product—i.e., they accept that a proportion of the products is defective (as I have concluded they do not in this case). That, as discussed, is not of course the end of it, because the question is of *legitimate* expectation, and the Court may conclude that the expectation of the public is too high or too low. But manifestly questions such as warnings and presentations will be in the forefront. However I conclude that the following are not relevant:

i. Avoidability of the harmful characteristic—i.e. impossibility or unavoidability in relation to precautionary measures.

ii. The impracticality, cost or difficulty of taking such measures.

iii. The benefit to society or utility of the product: (except in the context of whether—with full information and proper knowledge—the public does and ought to accept the risk) . . .

Standard Products

71. If a standard product is unsafe, it is likely to be so as a result of alleged error in design, or at any rate as a result of an allegedly flawed system. The harmful characteristic must be identified, if necessary with the assistance of experts. The question of presentation/time/circumstances of supply/social acceptability etc. will arise as above. The sole question will be safety for the foreseeable use. If there are any comparable products on the market, then it will obviously be relevant to compare the offending product with those other products, so as to identify, compare and contrast the relevant features. There will obviously need to be a full understanding of how the product works—particularly if it is a new product . . . so as to assess its safety for such use. Price is obviously a significant factor in legitimate expectation, and may well be material in the comparative process. But again it seems to me there is no room in the basket for:

i. what the producer could have done differently:

ii. whether the producer could or could not have done the same as the others did . . .

Wilkes v DePuy International Ltd [2016] EWHC 3096 (QB), [2018] QB 627

In January 2007 the claimant underwent a surgical procedure to insert an artificial left hip joint made up of metal components manufactured by the defendant. One of these components was a steel femoral shaft called a 'C-Stem', the neck of which featured a fine groove at the point where it was connected to the metal femoral head. Three years later, a fatigue fracture occurred in the grooved area of the C-Stem's neck. The claimant sued the defendant in negligence and under the Consumer Protection Act 1987, alleging that the C-Stem was defective because the groove created an excessive concentration of stress at its neck. The defendant denied this, arguing that the groove was a beneficial feature, because (inter alia) it enabled the C-Stem to be used with both metal and ceramic femoral heads. The issue before the judge was whether the C-Stem was defective for the purposes of the Act.

Hickinbottom J

13. [W]hether a product has an acceptable level of safety . . . necessarily involves some balancing of risks and potential benefits including, of course, potential utility. Given that no medicinal product is free from risk, and thus 'safety' in this field is inherently and necessarily a relative concept, a medical device will only be allowed onto the market if the product is assessed as having a positive risk-benefit ratio, in this sense. In this judgment, [unless] otherwise required, I shall use the term 'risk-benefit' rather than 'risk-utility', on the basis that, for these purposes, 'benefit' includes 'utility' . . .

59. Clearing the decks can be done very briefly. Section 2(1) of the Act provides that 'subject to the following provisions of this Part, where any damage is caused wholly or partly by a defect in a product, every person to whom section 2(2) below applies shall be liable for the damage'. It is common ground that, for the purposes of the Act, the C-Stem is a 'product': and the Defendant comes within section 2(2) as a producer of the C-Stem.

60. And so to 'defect' . . .

[Hickinbottom J referred to the definition of defect in s. 3 of the Act and continued:]

62. . . . With regard to 'defect' in this context, some clear and uncontroversial propositions can be made.

63. First, whilst, in relation to a product, negligence focuses upon the acts and omissions of those involved in production etc, the Directive and the Act focus rather upon the condition or state of the product itself. This is fundamental to the move away from fault-based liability, heralded by the Directive.

64. Second, the condition of the product required by the Directive and Act is not put in terms of (e.g.) fitness for purpose or efficacy, but rather in terms of safety and only in terms of safety, the required hallmark of defect being a lack of safety.

65. Third . . . safety is inherently and necessarily a relative concept. Certainly . . . no medicinal product, if effective, can be absolutely safe . . . [H]owever consumer expectations are defined and gauged, there cannot be a sensible expectation that any medicine or medicinal product is entirely risk-free. As I have described, the potential benefits (including potential utility) of such a product have to be balanced against its risks.

66. Of course, that is not done (or not only done), with the benefit of hindsight, by considering the benefits actually obtained by a specific patient, and the adverse effects actually suffered by him: for a patient who suffers a severe adverse reaction or failure of a product, then of course that may overwhelm any therapeutic benefit he personally gains from it. Medicinal products are prescribed and used to alleviate symptoms and/or improve the patient's condition and functionality. The potential benefits of a medicinal product for a particular patient are often very substantial. Properly informed patients will often wish to accept risks posed by such a product, rather than continue to bear the symptoms and/or lack of functionality that attaches to the conditions for which the product is prescribed and from which they suffer . . . What have to be balanced are, or at least include, the potential benefits of the medicinal product for the specific patient against the risks for that patient, at the time the product is used. I say 'include' because a particular medicinal product (such as a vaccine) may require consideration of a wider range of risks and benefits, including the public interest . . .

68. The Directive and Act set a standard of safety for virtually all products supplied to consumers . . . The standard of safety which people are entitled to expect across the whole range of these products is incapable of precise definition in a framework document such as the Directive; but, of course, more assistance and guidance could have been given than is found in that document. As Professor Stapleton has said, as it is left, the definition of 'defect' used is at best circular, and at worst empty, because 'what a person is entitled to expect is the very question a definition of defect should be answering' (J Stapleton, 'Product Liability' at page 234: quoted in Miller & Goldberg at paragraph 10.18). However, those responsible for the Directive clearly, and deliberately, declined to give better particulars . . .

69. The reference to judges being able to deal with matters on a case-by-case basis reflects the fact that—as is rightly common ground before me—the test for safety in this context requires an objective approach. Therefore, the relevant level of safety is not that which a particular patient considers the product should provide; nor even the level of safety which members of the public generally may consider it ought to provide. The level of safety is not assessed by reference to actual expectations of an actual or even a notional individual or group of individuals. Section 3(1), reflecting article 6 of the Directive (which refers to 'the safety which a person is *entitled* to expect'), defines 'defect' in terms of 'the safety of the product is not such as persons generally are *entitled* to expect . . . ' (emphases added). That can only be a reference to an entitlement as a matter of law, not actual individual or even general expectation . . .

70. The fact that 'expectation' in this context is objective in that sense is vitally important; because 'expectation' can be (and, in common parlance, is often) used in a different way. Mr Myhill [counsel for the defendant] gave an example. A person undergoing spinal surgery with a 1 per cent chance of being rendered paraplegic as a result of his operation due to a non-negligent complication, of which he is appropriately warned, if asked, would not say that he 'expected' that complication to occur. It could be said that he does not expect it to occur. However, the patient is not *entitled* to expect that it will not do so, or that paraplegia will not happen to him, because there is a known (if very small) risk that it will, about which he was properly informed. The surgeon does not guarantee the aspired outcome. It is a risk that the patient bears.

71. In [*A v National Blood Authority* [2001] 3 All ER 289], the parties had agreed that the question raised by the definition of 'defect' under the Directive and Act concerned the 'legitimate expectation' of persons generally; a formulation to which Burton J assented (at [31(vi)]). However, Mr Myhill submitted that the use of the phrase 'legitimate expectation' in this context was an unnecessary and unhelpful gloss on the Act, particularly as it is used as term of art elsewhere, e.g. in public law. I agree. If by 'legitimate expectation' here is meant simply 'expectation as a matter of law', it would be unobjectionable; but, in my respectful view, a test of what persons generally are 'entitled to expect' requires no gloss, and does not benefit from being re-described.

72. Therefore, in considering whether a product suffered from a defect, the court must assess the appropriate level of safety, exercising its judgment, and taking into account the information and the circumstances before it, whether or not an actual or notional patient or patients, or indeed other members of the public, would in fact have considered each of those factors and all of that information . . .

75. Having dealt with the uncontentious, we must now consider the potentially controversial, namely the circumstances which should (and any which cannot properly) be taken into account in making this assessment of safety. It is uncontroversial that the weight to be given to a relevant circumstance will, of course, be a matter for the court.

76. In determining the level of safety which the public is entitled to expect in this sense, section 3 of the Act, directly reflecting article 6 of the Directive, requires 'all circumstances' to be taken into account, 'including' three specific matters. 'All circumstances' must mean

'all relevant circumstances': there can be no place for a requirement to consider the irrelevant, nor any basis for demanding less than all relevant circumstance[s] be taken into account.

77. The circumstances which are relevant in a particular case is itself a matter of law; but it is to be noted that neither the Directive nor the Act imposes any restriction on the considerations that may be taken into account. The three specific matters set out in section 3(1)(a) are circumstances which must be considered ('... shall be taken into account...'); but they are clearly not intended to be an exhaustive list of relevant circumstances, nor are they such that any other circumstance, to be relevant, must be shown to be *eiusdem generis*.

78. There has been a great deal of consideration, before me and in the cases and the academic texts, as to the circumstances which are or are not relevant, and therefore can or cannot be taken into account. However, by whatever criteria 'acceptability' is gauged, assessment of whether the safety of a product is at an acceptable level requires a holistic approach... involving the application of judgment to the exercise of balancing all relevant considerations. Given the wide range of products (and their intended use) to which the Directive and Act apply, the court must maintain a flexible approach to the assessment of the appropriate level of safety, including which circumstances are relevant and the weight to be given to each, those factors being quintessentially dependent upon the particular facts of any case. That was the intention—and, certainly, the effect—of the Directive...

79. Accordingly, whilst over time cases may indicate which characteristics may be relevant in particular sets of circumstances (e.g. where the product is a prescription-only medicine), in my view, any attempt at formal rigid categorisation of products for these purposes is in conflict with the inherent flexibility of the Directive, and is likely to be both difficult and unwise. The issue raised by the Act in terms of defect is necessarily one of open-textured judgment, untrammelled by any rigid rules outside the few that appear in the Act itself... The Act, reflecting the Directive, simply requires consideration of whether, at the time the producer first put the product into circulation, that product did or did not have the level of safety that persons generally are entitled to expect (in the sense that I have described), taking into account all relevant circumstances including those set out in section 3(2). Like other such questions raised in the law, on the particular facts of a specific case, the assessment may be difficult in practice; but it is conceptually simple. In my view, the courts should guard against either over-complicating, or over-analysing, the exercise.

80. Before me, the following circumstances came under particular scrutiny: (i) risk-benefit; (ii) the 'avoidability' (or 'non-avoidability') of the defect; (iii) whether the product is 'standard' or 'non-standard', in accordance with the distinction drawn by Burton J in *A v NBA* ...; (iv) the compliance (or non-compliance) with appropriate standards; (v) the compliance (or non-compliance) with any relevant regime under which the product is regulated... I will deal with those in turn.

Risk-benefit and Avoidability

81. These two matters can conveniently be taken together.

82. Section 3(2)(a) requires 'the purposes for which the product has been marketed' to be taken into account. Primary amongst the purposes for which a medicinal product is marketed is the relief of a patient's symptoms and/or betterment of his condition and/or increase in his ability to function. Given that such a product will inevitably have some risks attached, as I have explained, any assessment of its safety will necessarily require the risks involved in use of that product to be balanced against its potential benefits including its potential utility. As such a product will almost always involve design compromises, the effect of eliminating or reducing a particular risk can only be seen in the context of any adverse consequences of doing so, in the form of increased risks of a different sort or reduced benefit and utility. Consequently, the practicability of producing a product of risk-benefit equivalence must

therefore potentially be a relevant circumstance in the assessment of a product's safety. It is inherent in the relative nature of 'safety'.

83. Although not relevant in this case—because the Defendant does not suggest that cost was a factor in its design decision-making—in my view, without inappropriately moving the focus from the product to the acts and omissions of the producer and/or others, cost too must be potentially relevant. This is illustrated by an example given in Miller & Goldberg at paragraph 10.82(c):

> ... [N]o doubt it is the case that a car would be safer for its occupants if the strength of its shell were such that it would not buckle in a high speed crash and even safer if it were built with bullet-proof glass lest it should be driven through areas with a drug-fuelled gun culture. However, it would never be seriously suggested that an ordinary passenger car would be regarded as defective by virtue of the fact that it lacked such characteristics.

84. With regard to 'avoidability' ... Mr Trotman [counsel for the claimant] submitted that the avoidability or non-avoidability of the defect was not a circumstance that was relevant to the issue of defect.

85. I accept that, in considering avoidability, there is a danger of unduly focusing upon the acts and omissions of the designer/producer of the product, rather than the product itself. However, I consider that whether, and the ease with which and extent to which, a risk might be avoided, may, in appropriate cases, be a circumstance that is relevant to the question of level of safety and therefore defect under the Act ...

87. On this issue, the cases are not of any great assistance. In *A v NBA*, although there are ambivalent passages, Burton J appears to have closed the issue of 'avoidability' in the case of what he termed 'non-standard' products (see [68]), but probably left it open for 'standard' products (see [73]) ...

88. The nuanced nature of the issue was apparent in *Bogle v McDonald's Restaurants Limited* [2002] EWHC 490 (QB), a case concerning injuries caused by the spillage of hot drinks served by the defendant in fast food outlets. Field J purported to adopt Burton J's approach to avoidability; although, expressly, he adopted the proposition that 'the avoidability of risk of harm is not a relevant circumstance' in respect of even 'standard' products (see [73(d)]). However, he proceeded to consider the issue of safety, as the Directive required, in the context of the purposes for which the product had been sold. Clearly, the risk of scalding could be avoided by serving drinks cold; but he noted that the public want to be able to buy tea and coffee served hot. That is indisputable. Although phrased in terms of expectations, in substance, Field J appears to have considered avoidability as a soft-edged concept in the context of (effectively) a risk-benefit analysis, albeit, because of the facts of that case, very different factors bore upon the analysis in that case compared with this ... In other words, although the risk of scalding was avoidable in absolute terms, the cost of avoiding it in terms of utility was unacceptably high. Thus, avoidability as seen in the broader context of the risk-benefit balance was, in substance, taken into account.

89. In my judgment, that is the correct approach. Whether a particular risk is 'avoidable' is not an issue that will often be capable of being considered discretely, in a vacuum. In any event, it will not in itself be determinative of the issue of defect. However, in my view, in an appropriate case and without inappropriately moving the focus of the exercise, the ease and extent to which a risk can be eliminated or mitigated may be a circumstance that bears upon the issue of the level of safety that the public generally is entitled to expect.

Standard/Non-standard

... 94. In my respectful view, the categorisation of defects into 'standard'/'non-standard', as a classification, is unnecessary and undesirable. It is not, of course, a classification deriving from the Directive or Act. In my judgment, whether a particular product is within the producer's specification, and is compliant with relevant standards . . . may be relevant circumstances in relation to whether the level of safety is that to which persons generally are entitled to expect; but to raise the distinction to a rigid categorisation is positively unhelpful and potentially dangerous . . .

96. . . . I appreciate that, where a particular specimen of a product is out of specification (or otherwise 'non-standard'), then risk-benefit of an in-specification product is unlikely to have much, if any, weight: but I would not advocate a rule of law that it must have none. In assessing the safety of a product, the court should consider the relevant circumstances, in a suitably flexible way: no more and no less.

Standards

97. It was, rightly, common ground that non-compliance with any appropriate mandatory standards will provide evidence of defect; and that compliance with such standards, whilst not providing a complete defence, will provide evidence that, in respect of the matters to which those standards go, the level of safety required by the Act has been satisfied and the product, in those respects, is therefore not defective . . .

98. In an appropriate case, compliance with such standards will have considerable weight; because they have been set at a level which the appropriate regulatory authority has determined is appropriate for safety purposes.

Regulatory regime

99. The same is true, as is again common ground before me, with regard to compliance or non-compliance with regulations which apply to a product.

100. As such regulations are made by Parliament—or those to whom Parliament has delegated the function, because of their particular expertise and experience in the field—it has been said that '[s]uch evidence [of compliance] will be regarded as particularly cogent, and indeed often effectively dispositive of the matter, where the regulations are updated and detailed' (Miller & Goldberg at paragraph 10.77). Certainly, where every aspect of the product's design, manufacture and marketing has been the subject of the substantial scrutiny, by a regulatory body comprised of individuals selected for their experience and expertise in the product including its safety, on the basis of full information, and that body has assessed that the level of safety is acceptable, then it may be challenging for a claimant to prove that the level of safety that persons generally are entitled to expect is at a higher level . . .

101. Of course, the simple fact of regulatory approval is not an automatic defence under the Act—nor even a prima facie defence, as in the United States. However, in my view, such approval may be evidence (and, in an appropriate case, powerful evidence) that the level of safety of the product was that which persons generally were entitled to expect . . .

The Alleged Defects

114. In the Particulars of Claim . . . it was alleged that the C-Stem implanted into the Claimant suffered from manufacturing defects and/or design defects.

115. I can deal with the former shortly. Paragraphs 6 and 7 of the Particulars of Claim set out various defects that were alleged to arise from the manufacture, as opposed to the design, of the product. One—that the thread at the neck was formed by machining rather than rolling—was in fact a design feature, and can best be dealt with as such. With regard to the rest . . . There is no evidence of any manufacturing defect, or other defect in the sense of the C-Stem implanted into the Claimant being outside the design specification . . .

[Hickinbottom J went on to reject the claimant's argument that the C-Stem was defective in design, inasmuch as persons generally would not have expected it to suffer from early fracture arising out of a known stress concentration factor, when simple design measures could have removed the same. In rejecting this argument, Hickinbottom J was influenced by various considerations, including the fact that (1) there were possible disadvantages of the alternative design proposed by the claimant, which included increased costs to hospitals; (2) other manufacturers made the same design choice as the defendant; (3) the C-Stem complied with all relevant mandatory standards and regulatory requirements; (4) the risk of stem fracture was small; (5) the information provided with the C-Stem expressly warned of that risk, and identified factors—such as patient obesity, and high levels of patient activity—that would increase it; and (6) the consequences of such a fracture were relatively limited, in that the artificial hip would simply have to be replaced.]

Defect: Conclusion

... 134. The failure of the C-Stem—earlier than was predicted—was unfortunate, and one can only have sympathy for the Claimant who was required to have a revision procedure, certainly earlier than he had hoped. However, the Defendant is only liable under the Act if the C-Stem had a defect, as defined in the Act, at the time it was put onto the market. For the reasons I have given, the Claimant has failed to satisfy me that the C-Stem supplied to him suffered from such a defect, i.e. that its safety was not such as persons generally were entitled to expect . . .

[Hickinbottom J therefore concluded that, having regard to the failure of the C-Stem by fracture, the defendant was not liable to the claimant under the provisions of the Act.]

COMMENTARY

Three preliminary points should be made about the test of defectiveness under the Consumer Protection Act. The first is that (as Hickinbottom J points out in *Wilkes* at [64]) defectiveness is assessed solely in terms of *safety*. If, therefore, a product is 'safe but shoddy', the Act does not apply. The second point is that the test of defectiveness is objective. The standpoint is that of the 'public at large' (in the words of Burton J in the *National Blood Authority* case), but the issue is what persons are *entitled* to expect—their 'entitlement as a matter of law' (*Wilkes* at [69])—not what they actually *do* expect, a point that it seems Burton J lost sight of at times. The third and final point, which follows from the second, is that, once it is appreciated that the test of defectiveness in the Act is not a subjective 'consumer expectation' test, it becomes apparent that it is a very open-textured standard (described in *Wilkes* at [68] as an 'empty vessel'), which can only be elucidated by decisions made in cases brought under the Act. In the words of Andrews J in *Gee v DePuy International Ltd* [2018] Med LR 347 at [73], '[t]he concept of "defect" introduced by the Directive is an autonomous one, defined in terms of failure to meet an objective standard of safety that the Court must evaluate'.

The Distinction between Standard and Non-Standard Products

One of the preliminary questions Burton J said in the *National Blood Authority* case should be asked in approaching a claim under the Act was whether the product in question was standard or non-standard. The distinction between standard and non-standard products serves broadly the same purpose as that which is often made between design defects and manufacturing defects (see *Winfield & Jolowicz*, para. 11–029). It appears that Burton J preferred his terminology so as to side-step the question whether it could truly be said that a bag of infected blood had been defectively manufactured, or merely that it had been produced from defective material. In *Wilkes*, Hickinbottom J was sceptical about the standard/non-standard distinction *as a classification*, although he accepted that it was a relevant circumstance, and himself employed the distinction between manufacturing and design defects when applying the test of defectiveness on the facts. In our opinion, experience in the United States demonstrates that the use of such a classification is essential if a regime of strict product is to function effectively, and we find it difficult to see how one can meaningfully consider the defectiveness question in this context without it. In any case, Hickinbottom J's scepticism seems not to have been shared by Andrews J in *Gee v DePuy International Ltd* [2018] Med LR 347 at [158]–[159], who described the distinction as a 'useful starting point in the analysis', and said that it might 'have a significant bearing on the circumstances that are relevant to the evaluation of its safety' (see also *Hastings v (First) Finsbury Orthopaedics Ltd* 2019 SLT 1411 at [105]).

Non-Standard Products

A product is non-standard for present purposes if it is less safe than it was intended to be by its producer, and this will clearly be a very powerful consideration in favour of a finding of defectiveness, with the result that generally speaking it should not be difficult for a claimant to establish that a non-standard product is defective. Hence, as Whittaker (1985) 5 Yearbook Eur Law 233 at 246 observes:

> Here the plaintiff's position would appear to have been enhanced, as it can simply be asserted that, for example, a consumer of ginger beer is entitled to expect it to contain no foreign bodies, a wearer of underwear to expect no excess deposit of chemicals in its composition. He would not need to adduce evidence that the producer's system of checking or manufacture were in some way negligently inadequate.

Furthermore, Burton J was clearly right to hold in the *National Blood Authority* case that the avoidability of the defect is not usually relevant in non-standard product cases, as otherwise 'defectiveness' would become too close to a negligence standard. However, while Burton J conceded (at [66]) that where there was a harmful characteristic in a non-standard product a decision that it was defective was 'likely to be straightforward', he refused to accept that non-standard products were *automatically* defective, as he notes is the case in Italy and Spain, where this is expressly laid down in the legislation implementing the Directive. In particular, Burton J took the view that a particular non-standard product might be held not to be defective under the Act on the basis that the public at large accepted that a proportion of products of the same type would be flawed, although he went on to hold that the blood at issue in the case was not such a product, since the risk of infection was not generally known and therefore could not be regarded as socially acceptable.

The upshot of Burton J's analysis seems to be, then, that a non-standard product will be defective under the Act, unless there is social acceptance of the possibility of the product being flawed. This exception is problematic, however, since it seems to look to what the public *actually* expect, rather than what the public are *entitled to* expect, and in our view it would therefore be preferable if the courts were to adopt a simpler approach, under which a manufacturing defect would *always* render a product defective for the purposes of the legislation. This approach would also seem to be consistent with the CJEU's characterisation of a product as defective where it has an 'abnormal potential for damage' (Cases C-503–504/13, *Boston Scientific Medizintechnik GmbH v AOK Sachsen-Anhalt–Die Gesundheitskasse* [2015] 3 CMLR 173 at [40]), since by definition a manufacturing defect is 'abnormal' (though whether a test of 'abnormality' is much help to the judge in a standard product case is questionable).

Would you accept the proposition that persons generally are entitled to expect, as a barest minimum, that products will attain the level of safety intended by the producer?

Standard Products

In contrast to cases involving non-standard products, it will seldom be straightforward to establish that a standard product is defective because the claimant must attack the design or make-up of the product line as a whole, which complicates the defectiveness enquiry. Unlike in a non-standard product case—where the court can simply compare the product in question with the standard product line from which it deviates—in a standard product case there is no objective benchmark against which to assess the product, and so the court must second-guess conscious choices by the producer. Furthermore, as Hickinbottom J points out in *Wilkes* (at [13]), safety is relative, not absolute. No product is perfectly safe, because safety must be traded off against cost and convenience. It follows that (as the analysis in *Wilkes* illustrates) standard product cases require a balancing of risks and gains, costs and benefits. A similar approach was adopted in a second case involving artificial hips, *Gee v DePuy International Ltd* [2018] Med LR 347, where it was held that the propensity of the prostheses in question to shed metal debris through normal use did not render them defective, even though this sometimes triggered an immune reaction in the wearer. The recognition in these two cases that 'the risk-benefit ratio of a medicinal product will be relevant' to the determination of defectiveness has been described by the authors of a leading work on product liability as a 'welcome clarification of English law' (*Fairgrieve and Goldberg*, para. 11.42).

Since a risk/benefit analysis may well require consideration of the avoidability of the defect, that becomes a potentially relevant factor in standard product cases, as was recognised in both *Wilkes* and *Gee*. In particular, when assessing whether a standard product has a defect it may be helpful to consider whether the risks it poses could have been mitigated or eliminated by the use of a feasible alternative design. An illustrative case is *Abouzaid v Mothercare (UK) Ltd*, CA, *The Times*, 20 February 2001, where the defendants were held liable under the Act when a 12-year-old boy was injured by the plastic buckle on an elastic strap used to fasten a pushchair accessory to the pushchair. The boy let the strap slip from his fingers when the elastic was taut and the recoil caused the buckle to strike him in the eye. When holding that the product was defective, the Court of Appeal highlighted the fact that the product could easily have been made safer had the producer, for example, used a non-elasticated method of fastening. However, where the alternative design would significantly diminish the product's utility (or increase its cost) then the court may conclude that there is no defect. In *Bogle v McDonald's Restaurants Ltd* [2002] EWHC 490 (QB), discussed in *Wilkes* at [88], claims under the Act by customers allegedly scalded by hot drinks served in McDonald's restaurants were dismissed. According to Field J, 'the basic utility of being able to buy hot drinks to be consumed on the premises from a cup with the lid off' justified the risks involved in serving coffee at a high temperature with lids that did not prevent the coffee from spilling if the cup was knocked over. When considering alternative designs, the court can compare the product alleged to be defective with similar products on the market, but for a finding of defectiveness to be made it will need to be shown that there is a material difference between them in terms of safety. Hence in *Gee*, it was held that the mere fact that a hip prosthesis had a marginally worse safety record than competitor products did not make it defective.

The risk/benefit test used in standard product cases is, of course, reminiscent of the breach of duty inquiry in negligence, but as Andrews J pointed out in *Gee* the court is entitled when weighing the risks and benefits to take into account everything that is now known about the product, 'irrespective of whether that information was available at the time it was put on the market or has come to light subsequently' ([2018] Med LR 347 at [84]; see also *Hastings v (First) Finsbury Orthopaedics Ltd* 2019 SLT 1411 at [124]). Needless to say, this is not the case in negligence, where the question is always considered from the perspective of the reasonable producer at the time of marketing, and for this and other reasons there is clear blue water between fault liability and strict liability, even in standard product cases (see further *Winfield & Jolowicz*, para. 11–034). That this is so is illustrated by *Abouzaid*, where the claim under the Act succeeded but a parallel claim in common law negligence failed on the ground that a reasonable producer at the time the product was marketed would not have foreseen the risk posed by the plastic buckle.

In *Wilkes*, Hickinbottom J made it clear that compliance or non-compliance with applicable mandatory standards and regulatory requirements would be a potentially important consideration in assessing defectiveness (see also *Gee* at [170]–[178]). However, that this consideration is not necessarily decisive is shown by *Tesco Stores Ltd v Pollard* [2006] EWCA Civ 393, where it was alleged that a bottle of dishwasher powder was defective because its child-resistant cap did not conform to the relevant British Design Standard. Dismissing the claim, Laws LJ held that the relevant expectation was merely that a child-resistant cap would be more difficult to open than an ordinary screwtop, and that since this was true of the cap in the case the product was not defective.

When it became apparent that a brand of pacemaker implanted in patients with heart problems was susceptible to failure, so that all such pacemakers had to be replaced, the CJEU held (Cases C-503–504/13, *Boston Scientific Medizintechnik GmbH v AOK Sachsen-Anhalt–Die Gesundheitskasse* [2015] 3 CMLR 173) (1) that the existence of a potential defect in *some* products in a particular product line could amount to a defect in *all* products in that line; and (2) that the surgical intervention necessary to replace the pacemakers constituted 'personal injury' for the purposes of the Directive. The result was that the producer of the pacemakers was potentially liable to all the patients who were affected. For commentary on this decision, see Fairgrieve and Pilgerstorfer [2017] EBLR 879.

A difficult issue in this context is how to justify the conclusion that 'inherently dangerous products' like cigarettes are not defective, even when it seems clear that their global risks outweigh their global benefits. Perhaps if the cigarette were a new invention, a court would feel able to label its carcinogenic properties a 'defect' for the purposes of the Act. However, where a product like this has been used and enjoyed for many years, and Parliament has not seen fit to make it illegal, a finding of defectiveness would surely be regarded as the court overstepping the boundary of its institutional competence and treading on ground best left to the elected representatives of the people (see *McTear v Imperial Tobacco Ltd* 2005 2 SC 1, a negligence case concerning cigarettes). After all, what in effect would amount to a judicial ban on a particular type of product has obvious implications for consumer autonomy, as a German court pointed out in the so-called 'chocolate bar' case when dismissing a product liability claim by a diabetic chocoholic against a confectionary manufacturer (OLG Düsseldorf, 20 December 2002, 14 U 99/02). So the most that a court can realistically do in such a case is to ensure that the product's users are given adequate warning of its dangers, though even a warning may not be required if the risks are notorious, as the health risks of excessive sugar consumption were held to be in the 'chocolate bar' case. See further on product liability and cigarettes, *Fairgrieve and Goldberg*, paras 9.125–9.132.

Warnings, Instructions and Misuse

If the risk is not obvious, the absence of a warning may render a product defective, and conversely such a warning may be enough to protect the producer from liability (see, e.g., *Worsley v Tambrands Ltd* [2000] PIQR P95, where the warnings provided in respect of the risk of toxic shock syndrome from the use of a tampon prevented a finding that the tampons were defective). Similarly, a product may be defective because the instructions accompanying it are inadequate or confusing (see *Palmer v Palmer*, discussed below). See further on 'marketing defects' of this kind, *Fairgrieve and Goldberg*, ch. 12.

Can a product be defective if it only becomes dangerous if misused? According to s. 3(2)(b) of the Act, when determining defectiveness account should be taken of 'what might reasonably be expected to be done with or in relation to the product', which would suggest an affirmative answer to that question in the case of foreseeable misuse (as Whittaker, *op. cit.*, 244 says, the question is not 'the *reasonable use* to which the product could be expected to be put'). However, a risk arising out of *any* kind of foreseeable misuse is not enough to make a product defective: in *Chadwick v Continental Tyres* [2008] CSOH 24 at [29], Lord Uist said that such a conclusion would be 'patently irrational in the context of applying the public expectation test'. Nevertheless in some cases a failure to warn of or otherwise ameliorate risks associated with misuse might render a product defective. Hence a toy that contains toxic paint is likely to be deemed defective if marketed to young children, as it is well known that they often put toys in their mouths (Wuyts, 'The Product Liability Directive–More than Two Decades of Defective Products in Europe' (2014) 5 JETL 1 at 20), and in *Palmer v Palmer* [2006] EWHC 1284 (QBD), a device that enabled slack to be introduced into seatbelts was held to be defective because its poor design and inadequate instructions meant that users tended to introduce excessive slack into the belt, thereby making it less effective in preventing injury. Finally, note that misuse by the claimant may amount to contributory negligence and thus go to reduce the damages awarded (s. 6(4)).

Damage

For a claim to lie under the Act the defect in the product must have caused damage actionable under the legislation. Damage is defined in s. 5 as death or personal injury or any loss of or damage to property. Pure economic loss is not actionable, and accordingly diminution in the value of the product caused by a defect cannot be recovered. However, difficulty is created by the wording of s. 5(2), which bars recovery 'for the loss of or any damage to the product itself or for the loss of or any damage to the whole or any part of any product which has been supplied with the product in question comprised in it'. This provision is the (somewhat clumsy) legislative solution to the 'complex product' issue, which is analogous to the 'complex structure' problem discussed in Chapter 8.II. Suppose, for example, that a defective tyre is supplied with a new car, and that when it explodes the car is damaged. Applying s. 5(2) this damage is irrecoverable. However, if the tyre is a substitute that was added to the car after the owner bought the vehicle, then the damage to the car can be recovered, as there was no supply of the car with the tyre 'comprised in it' (though strangely the position would be otherwise if the car was owned by a car hire company which had hired the car to a customer after the tyre had been fitted, as the hire would count as a 'supply' applying s. 46, as indeed would the lending of the car by a private individual to a friend). Is this distinction justifiable? And is it consistent with the Directive, Article 9 of which refers to 'damage to, or destruction of, any item of property other than the defective product itself'?

Note also that s. 5(3) limits claims for property damage to types of property ordinarily intended for private use, occupation or consumption and that the property damaged must also have been intended by the person suffering the loss or damage mainly for their own private use, occupation or consumption. The effect of this provision is to exclude claims for damage to commercial property, which must therefore be brought in negligence instead. In addition, no action lies for property damage where the amount of the award would be less than £275 (s. 5(4)), which was a considerably more valuable sum in 1987 than it is today.

Causation

The defect in the product must cause the damage, and the normal causation rules apply, so that the action will fail if the defect cannot be shown, on the balance of probabilities, to have caused the damage (*McGlinchey v General Motors (UK) Ltd* [2012] CSIH 91). Note that the damage must be caused by the *defect*, rather than the *product*. Suppose, for example, that you stand on a heater which is defective because of a wiring fault, and it collapses, causing you injury. There is no recovery under the Act, because although the defective product was a factual cause of the damage, the damage was not caused by the defect itself. Similarly, if the defect is the absence of a warning, the claimant must show that it would probably have been heeded. However, once the claimant has proved that the defect caused the damage, that is sufficient for recovery, and it is not necessary also to establish what caused the defect (as would be required in a negligence action): see *Ide v ATB Sales Ltd* [2008] PIQR P13. Hence, 'if an electrical appliance bursts into flames if it is left plugged in, or a fridge explodes' it is clearly defective, and the claimant need not establish why this happened, though naturally the position may be otherwise if the damage could have arisen even if the product was not defective, for example 'in consequence of the manifestation of a known risk that could arise in normal use' (*Gee* at [99]–[100]). As a result, in product liability cases concerned with one-off *accidents*, proving causation should not be overly burdensome for claimants, but in *disease* cases—as where it is alleged that a drug causes cancer—the same evidential difficulties that claimants frequently face in negligence litigation (discussed in Ch. 5) can arise, and this may explain why, according to the European Commission, consumer organisations 'are critical of the fact that that it is difficult for injured persons to prove the link between damage and defect', particularly because they must bear the cost of doing so, and are at a disadvantage when it comes to obtaining technical information about the product (*Fifth Report on the Application of Directive 85/374 on Liability for Defective Products*, COM(2018) 246 final, p. 6).

As well as being a *factual* cause of the damage, the defect must also have been the *legal* cause, and it seems likely that reckless or deliberate conduct by the claimant—such as a deliberate and unreasonable decision to use a product known to be dangerously defective—may constitute a *novus actus* which relieves the producer of liability under the Act. Whether the same principle extends to intervening conduct of third parties is less clear, however; the statement in Article 8(1) of the Directive that 'the liability of the producer shall not be reduced when the damage is caused both by a defect in the product and by the act or omission of a third party' suggests not.

As to remoteness of damage, whether the negligence test of foreseeability applies is unclear: see further, *Winfield & Jolowicz*, para. 11–051; Newdick (1987) 103 LQR 288 at 297–300.

Limitation

A claimant has three years to bring a claim, from either the date on which the action accrued (which is when the damage occurs) or, if later, the date of their knowledge of the material facts giving rise to the cause of action (Limitation Act 1980, s. 11A(4)). In addition, however, there is a 'long-stop' limitation period of ten years from the date that the product was supplied by the defendant (*ibid.*, s.11A(4)). (The equivalent provision of the Directive refers to the time when the product was put into circulation, which the CJEU held in Case C-127/04, *O'Byrne v Sanofi* [2006] ECR I-1313 occurs when it is taken out of the manufacturing process operated by the producer and enters a marketing process in a form in which it is offered to the public in order to be used or consumed.) In personal injury claims, s. 33 of the 1980 Act gives the court a discretion to override the usual statutory limitation period, but no such discretion exists in the case of the ten-year long-stop. The purpose of the long-stop is to enable potential defendants to 'close their books' once ten years has elapsed from their supply of a product, but it means that where, for example, a claimant contracts cancer because they used a defective drug more than a decade ago, they will be unable to rely on the Act and will have to sue in negligence instead.

Defences

Once a claimant can show damage attributable to a defect in a product for which the defendant is responsible under the Act, liability is strict. However, s. 4 provides a number of defences: liability is strict, not absolute. Most of the defences set out in the section are self-explanatory, but some require comment. Section 4(1)(a) provides a defence where the defect is attributable to compliance with any requirement imposed by law. Note that it is not enough that the product complies with such a requirement; rather, the defendant must establish that the defect was the *inevitable result* of that compliance—in other words, that it was not possible to comply with the provision without rendering the productive defective. This is unlikely to be a frequent occurrence.

The s. 4(1)(c) defence of non-commercial production or supply is somewhat complex, but the upshot is as follows. If the *supplier* of the product is sued, it is a defence for them to show that the supply by them was not in the course of their business. An example would be a sale of a used car by a private individual. Where the action is brought against a producer, own-brander or importer, the defendant must establish *both* that the supply by them was not in the course of their business *and* that they produced the product (etc.) other than with a view to profit. Hence the home baker who donates a cake to a charity jumble sale is not liable, but the home brewer who sells damson wine to their neighbours could be. The CJEU has held that strict liability may arise under the Directive where the defendant's activity has no economic or business purpose and the product is used in the course of a specific medical service which is financed entirely from public funds and for which the patient is not required to pay any consideration (see Case C-203/99, *Veedfald v Arhus Amtskommune* [2001] ECR I–3569). In *A v National Blood Authority* [2001] 3 All ER 289 (decided before the *Veedfald* case) Burton J agreed (at 318) with the opinion of the Advocate General in *Veedfald*—subsequently adopted by the CJEU—that there was no necessary reason why a public authority or non-profit-making organisation should be in a different position from a commercial producer if the product is unsafe.

Section 4(1)(d), which gives a defence where the defect did not exist in the product at the time of the defendant's supply, may be more important than was originally thought. In *Piper v JRI (Manufacturing) Ltd* (2006) 92 BMLR 141, the defendant argued that, because of the steps it took in its manufacturing processes, the defect could not have existed in the product in question at the time of supply, and this was accepted as establishing the defence. This is an interesting decision. The defendant did not rely on evidence that the *specific* product had no defect; rather, it relied on its general quality control as well as suggesting an alternative possible cause of the defect. It does not follow, however, that a manufacturer can satisfy the defence solely by pleading the infallibility of its manufacturing process; it is imperative that the producer identify a possible source of the defect after the product left its hands. For example, if the defendant in *Grant v Australian Knitting Mills* (extracted in Ch. 3.I.3) had been sued under the Act, it is unlikely that it could have successfully relied on this defence even though its manufacturing process produced proportionally fewer defects than that in *Piper*; there was simply no credible explanation for the excess sulphites in the undergarments other than that process.

The most controversial defence to strict liability is the 'development risks' defence in s. 4(1)(e), which deals with what Advocate General Tesauro describes in the next extracted case as 'risks present in production sectors in which an advance in technological and scientific knowledge may make a product appear defective *ex post*, whereas it was not regarded as such at the time when it was manufactured'. The Directive made the inclusion of this defence optional, although most member states chose to adopt it, with only two (Finland and Luxembourg) not using it at all, and most adopting it for all types of products. Where the defence is adopted, the wording in the implementing legislation must accord with the equivalent wording in the Directive. The following case extract considers whether the terms of s. 4(1)(e) in fact accord with Article 7 of the Directive, according to which the defence arises where 'the state of scientific and technical knowledge at the time when the producer put the product into circulation was not such as to enable the existence of the defect to be discovered'.

Case C–300/95 *Commission v United Kingdom* [1997] ECR I-2649

The European Commission brought infringement proceedings against the United Kingdom for not properly implementing Directive 85/374/EEC, on the basis that while Article 7 of the Directive required an objective assessment of the state of scientific and technical knowledge, s. 4(1)(e) of the 1987 Act appeared to call for a more subjective assessment by focusing on the conduct of the reasonable producer. It was argued that this had the effect of substantially weakening the strict liability introduced by the Directive.

Opinion of Advocate General Tesauro

It should first be observed that, since [Article 7(e) of the Directive] refers solely to the 'scientific and technical knowledge' at the time when the product was marketed, it is not concerned with the practices and safety standards in use in the industrial sector in which the producer is operating. In other words, it has no bearing on the exclusion of the manufacturer from liability that no one in that particular class of manufacturer takes the measures necessary to eliminate the defect or prevent it from arising if such measures are capable of being adopted on the basis of the available knowledge.

Other matters which likewise are to be regarded as falling outside the scope of Article 7(e) are aspects relating to the practicability and expense of measures suitable for eliminating the defect from the product. Neither, from this point of view, can the fact that the producer did not appraise himself of the state of scientific and technical knowledge or does not keep up to date with developments in this area as disclosed in the specialist literature, be posited as having any relevance for the purposes of excluding liability on his part. I consider, in fact, that the producer's conduct should be assessed using the yardstick of the knowledge of an expert in the sector (eg if a chemist or a pharmacologist has to keep up to date with the characteristics of a given substance, similar knowledge will be required for present purposes of an industrialist producing pharmaceuticals containing the same substance).

Some additional considerations need to be explored, however, in order to tie down the concept 'state of knowledge'.

The progress of scientific culture does not develop linearly in so far as new studies and new discoveries may initially be criticised and regarded as unreliable by most of the scientific community, yet subsequently after the passage of time undergo an opposite process of 'beatification' whereby they are virtually unanimously endorsed. It is therefore quite possible that at the time when a given product is marketed, there will be isolated opinions to the effect that it is defective, whilst most academics do not take that view. The problem at this juncture is to determine whether in such a situation, that is to say, where there is a risk that is not certain and will be agreed to exist by all only ex post, the producer may still rely on the defence provided for in Article 7(e) of the Directive.

In my view, the answer to this question must be in the negative. In other words, the state of scientific knowledge cannot be identified with the views expressed by the majority of learned opinion, but with the most advanced level of research which has been carried out at a given time . . .

Where in the whole gamut of scientific opinion at a particular time there is also one isolated opinion (which, as the history of science shows, might become with the passage of time *opinio communis*) as to the potentially defective and/or hazardous nature of the product, the manufacturer is no longer faced with an unforeseeable risk, since, as such, it is outside the scope of the rules imposed by the directive.

The aspect which I have just been discussing is closely linked with the question of the availability of scientific and technical knowledge in the sense of the accessibility of the sum of knowledge at a given time to interested persons. It is undeniable that the circulation of information is affected by objective factors, such as, for example, its place or origin, the language in which it is given and the circulation of the journals in which it is published.

To be plain, there exist quite major differences in point of the speed in which it gets into circulation and the scale of its dissemination between a study of a researcher in a university in the United States published in an international English-language international journal and, to take an example given by the Commission, similar research carried out by an academic in Manchuria published in a local scientific journal in Chinese, which does not go outside the boundaries of the region.

In such a situation, it would be unrealistic and, I would say, unreasonable to take the view that the study published in Chinese has the same chances as the other of being known to a European product manufacturer. So, I do not consider that in such a case a producer could be held liable on the ground that at the time at which he put the product into circulation the brilliant Asian researcher had discovered the defect in it.

More generally, the 'state of knowledge' must be construed so as to include all data in the information circuit of the scientific community as a whole, bearing in mind, however, on the basis of a reasonableness test the actual opportunities for the information to circulate.

Having thus identified the scope of the Community provision, I consider that I am unable to share the Commission's proposition that there is an irremediable conflict between it and the national provision at issue. Indeed, there is no denying that the wording of s. 4(1)(e) of the Act contains an element of potential ambiguity: in so far as it refers to what might be expected of the producer, it could be interpreted more broadly that it should.

Notwithstanding this, I do not consider that the reference to the 'ability of the producer', despite its general nature, may or even must (necessarily) authorise interpretations contrary to the rationale and the aims of the directive.

In the first place, consideration of the producer is central not only to the rules of the directive taken as whole, but also to Article 7(e), which, although it does not mention him, is aimed at the producer himself, as the person having to discharge the burden of proof in order to avoid incurring liability. From this angle, the provision of the Act merely expresses in a clear way a concept which is implicit in the Community provision.

Secondly, the reference contained in the Act to the producer's ability to discover the defect is not sufficient to make the test which it lays down a subjective one. That reference can certainly be regarded, as the United Kingdom has argued, as an objectively verifiable and assessable parameter, which is in no way influenced by consideration of the actual subjective knowledge of the producer or by his organisational and economic requirements. By virtue of that parameter, it must therefore be proved, in order to exclude liability on the part of the producer, that it was impossible, in the light of the most advanced scientific and technical knowledge objectively and reasonably obtainable and available, to consider that the product was defective.

Judgment

Certain general observations can be made as to the wording of Article 7(e) of the directive.

First, as the Advocate General rightly observes . . . since that provision refers to 'scientific and technical knowledge at the time when [the producer] put the product into circulation', Article 7(e) is not specifically directed at the practices and safety standards in use in the industrial sector in which the producer is operating, but, unreservedly, at the state of scientific and technical knowledge, including the most advanced level of such knowledge, at the time when the product in question was put into circulation.

Second, the clause providing for the defence in question does not contemplate the state of knowledge of which the producer in question actually or subjectively was or could have been apprised, but the objective state of scientific and technical knowledge of which the producer is presumed to have been informed.

However, it is implicit in the wording of Article 7(e) that the relevant scientific and technical knowledge must have been accessible at the time when the product in question was put into circulation.

It follows that, in order to have a defence under Article 7(e) of the directive, the producer of a defective product must prove that the objective state of scientific and technical knowledge, including the most advanced level of such knowledge, at the time when the product in question was put into circulation was not such as to enable the existence of the defect to be discovered. Further, in order for the relevant scientific and technical knowledge to be successfully pleaded against the producer, that knowledge must have been accessible at the time when the product in question was put into circulation . . .

[T]he Commission has failed to make out its claim that the result intended by Article 7(e) of the directive would clearly not be achieved in the domestic legal order. First, s. 4(1)(e) of the Act places the burden of proof on the producer wishing to rely on the defence, as Art. 7 of the directive requires. Second, s. 4(1)(e) places no restriction on the state and degree of scientific and technical knowledge at the material time which is to be taken into account. Third, its wording as such does not suggest, as the Commission alleges, that the availability of the defence depends on the subjective knowledge of a producer taking reasonable care in the light of the standard precautions taken in the industrial sector in question . . . Lastly, there is nothing in the material produced to the court to suggest that the courts in the United Kingdom, if called upon to interpret s. 4(1)(e), would not do so in the light of the wording and the purpose of the directive so as to achieve the result which it has in view.

COMMENTARY

The CJEU decision seems to entail (1) that the test when applying the development risks defence is whether the relevant information was 'accessible' to the producer at the time the product was supplied (or at least to an expert in the sector, to use the Advocate General's terminology), but (2) that the information that is treated as relevant is not limited to that which is currently employed in the sector in question but includes the most advanced level of scientific and technical knowledge that is accessible (even if other experts disagree). This is because, in these circumstances, the risk has become foreseeable. A question remains as to what constitutes 'accessible' information. The Advocate General suggested that work published in a regional Chinese scientific journal might not be accessible, but in *A v National Blood Authority* [2001] 3 All ER 289 at 326 Burton J said that the 'Manchurian exception' should be limited to an unpublished document or unpublished research.

The CJEU decision has attracted criticism, both for the burden it imposes on producers in satisfying the defence (Hodges (1998) 61 MLR 560), and, conversely, for requiring that the risk information be 'accessible' (a requirement described as 'perplexing' and 'gratuitous and illogical': Mildred and Howells (1998) 61 MLR 570 at 572). Stapleton, 'The Conceptual Imprecision of "Strict" Product Liability' (1998) 6 Torts LJ 260 is particularly critical of the Court's take on the phrase 'the state of scientific and technical knowledge', commenting (at 271) that:

[S]uch an interpretation . . . does not accord with the ordinary meaning we give to that term, generates very strange results and does not address the question of what qualifies as 'scientific knowledge' and when. For example, would we really say that where an obscure Siberian mystic tells her mother, say in 1980, of her guess that scrapie might jump genus barriers, then the idea that meat might be rendered defective by Creutzfeldt-Jakob disease was (a) 'scientific knowledge' and (b) an idea which had entered the state of scientific knowledge at that time? Surely we understand by the term 'the state of scientific and technical knowledge' something far more discriminating? Before we 'count' an idea as forming part of 'scientific knowledge', do we not implicitly expect the idea to have come from or be backed by someone of appropriate training?

It is undoubtedly true that the decision places formidable hurdles in the path of a producer seeking to rely on the defence, but can this be said to be inconsistent with the Directive's purpose?

Another point that has been clarified is that the defence relates to risks that could not have been foreseen, not to known risks about which nothing can be done. In *A v National Blood Authority* [2001] 3 All ER 289 Burton J held that a known but unavoidable risk in a product did not qualify for the s. 4(1)(e) defence, with the caveat that if the risk was one that affected the legitimate expectations of consumers in relation to the product it might influence the decision as to whether the product was defective. The refusal to extend the defence to known but unavoidable risks is contrary to decisions in two other jurisdictions—one from the Netherlands (*Scholten v Sanquin Bloedvoorziening*, Rb Amsterdam, 3 February 1999, NJ 1999, 621) and one from Australia (*Graham Barclay Oysters Pty Ltd v Ryan* (2001) 211 CLR 540, a case under Australian legislation virtually identical to the 1987 Act), but Burtons J's approach seems correct, since the purpose of the defence is to protect producers from liability for the materialisation of development risks—which is to say risks that are unknowable at the time of production—precisely because it is said to be difficult (or at least very expensive) to insure against such risks. By contrast, it should be possible to insure against a known but unavoidable product risk (and if it is not, this is probably an indication that continued production is not justified).

On the importance of the development risks defence, see the European Commission's *Third Report on the Application of Directive 85/374 on Liability for Defective Products*, COM(2006) 496 final, para. 3.3, and, more generally, R. Goldberg, *Medicinal Product Liability and Regulation* (Oxford: Hart, 2013), ch. 8, and Marie-Ève Arbour, 'Portrait of Development Risk as a Young Defence' (2014) 59 McGill LJ 913. Arbour is sceptical about the need for the defence, pointing out (at 940–1) that there is little in the way of empirical research to back up the claim that without it strict product liability would stifle innovation. A recent study by the European Commission of the operation of the Directive across the EU did not reveal noticeable differences between member states that included the defence in their national legislation and those that did not (*Evaluation of Directive 85/374 on Liability for Defective Products*, SWD(2018) 157 final, p. 26).

The Effectiveness of the Act

Relatively few cases have been decided under Part I of the Consumer Protection Act 1987, a factor that may be attributable to the general cost of litigating in the United Kingdom (see generally *Fourth Report on the Application of Directive 85/374, op. cit.*, p. 4). However, in recent years there has been something of an upsurge in claims under the Act, including high-profile class actions against the manufacturers of artificial hips and other medical devices. Furthermore, the Act may play a role in encouraging producers to settle claims, especially in multi-party claims alleging a defect in a product's basic design, where it had previously proved very difficult to establish negligence (see, e.g., Glaxo's £7 million settlement of claims relating to the drug Myodil in 1995, and more generally *Fourth Report on the Application of Directive 85/374, op. cit.*, p. 4). In addition, consumers may prefer to seek redress from producers through non-legal avenues (e.g. informal mediation through customer services departments), and where a legal remedy is sought, a simple contractual claim against the retailer may be seen as preferable, especially where the amount involved is small.

The European Commission undertakes periodic reviews of the effectiveness of the Directive. In its fourth such review, in 2011 (*Fourth Report on the Application of Directive 85/374, op. cit.*), the Commission considered some of the issues raised in the 1999 Commission Green Paper on possible improvements to the Directive (*Liability for Defective Products*, COM(99) 396 final) including the burden of proof, development risks and the threshold for property damage claims, and concluded that these were not in need of reform. For critical analysis of the 2011 report, see Fairgrieve, Howells and Pilgerstorfer, 'The Product Liability Directive: Time to get Soft?' (2013) 4 JETL 1. In 2018 the Commission published its fifth review, in which it concluded that the Directive continued to be 'an adequate tool', although clarification was required as to the legal understanding of certain key concepts (such as product, producer, defect, damage and the burden of proof) and that further consideration needed to be given to 'certain products, such as pharmaceuticals, which may pose a challenge to the performance of the Directive' (*Fifth Report on the Application of Directive 85/374 on Liability for Defective Products*, COM(2018) 246 final, p. 2). The fifth report was accompanied by a more comprehensive evaluation of the functioning and performance of the Directive in the period 2000–2016 (*Evaluation of Directive 85/374 on Liability for Defective Products, op. cit.*). According to the evaluation study, the number of claims under the Directive that were brought to national courts across the EU doubled in that period, with over half of those cases involving raw materials, pharmaceutical products and vehicles. Issues regarding the Directive's operation in the pharmaceutical context were again highlighted, with representatives of victims of medicines complaining of the difficulty of establishing defectiveness and causation, especially within the timeframe set by the three- and ten-year limitation periods. This was exacerbated by the problem of gaining access to technical information held by producers in respect of drugs and other complex products. For commentary on the 2018 report, see Fairgrieve, 'Reforming the European Product Liability Directive: Plus ça Change, Plus c'est la Même Chose?' [2019] JPIL 35.

3. The Future of Product Liability

Technological change threatens to undermine the strict product liability regime established by the Consumer Protection Act 1987, but also raises difficult questions for fault-based liability systems such as common law negligence. In its fifth review of the 1985 Directive, the European Commission questioned whether 'the existing product liability framework is appropriate to ensure effective redress for consumers and investment stability for businesses' in the light of certain characteristics of new technologies (*Fifth Report on the Application of Directive 85/374, op. cit.*, p. 6). The following year the New Technologies 'formation' of the Commission's Expert Group on Liability and New Technologies published its report on *Liability for Artificial Intelligence and Other Emerging Digital Technologies* (2019), in which it said that some of the key concepts underpinning the Directive regime, as adopted in 1985, were now 'an inadequate match for the potential risks of emerging digital technologies' (p. 27) and that those technologies were blurring the distinction between products and services on which that regime was founded. Conversely, producer interests have defended the Directive as 'technology-neutral', and warned against premature reform 'without concrete evidence of real life problems' (*Evaluation of Directive 85/374 on Liability for Defective Products, op. cit.*, p. 34). In the report that is extracted next, the Commission considers the challenges that technological change may pose for product liability law, in particular developments in artificial intelligence, the 'Internet of Things' and robotics.

> **European Commission, *Report on the Safety and Liability Implications of Artificial Intelligence, the Internet of Things and Robotics***
>
> COM(2020) 64 final
>
> **1. Introduction**
>
> Artificial Intelligence (AI), the Internet of Things (IoT) and robotics will create new opportunities and benefits for our society. The Commission has recognised the importance and potential of these technologies and the need for significant investment in these areas. It is committed to making Europe a world-leader in AI, IoT and robotics. In order to achieve this goal, a clear and predictable legal framework addressing the technological challenges is required. . . .
>
> **1.2 Characteristics of AI, IoT and robotics technologies**
>
> AI, IoT and robotics share many characteristics. They can combine **connectivity**, **autonomy** and **data dependency** to perform tasks with little or no human control or supervision. AI equipped systems can also improve their own performance by learning from experience. Their **complexity** is reflected in both the plurality of economic operators involved in the **supply chain**

and the multiplicity of components, parts, software, systems or services, which together form the new technological ecosystems. Added to this is the **openness** to updates and upgrades after their placement on the market. The vast amounts of data involved, the reliance on algorithms and the **opacity** of AI decision-making, make it more difficult to predict the behaviour of an AI-enabled product and to understand the potential causes of a damage. Finally, connectivity and openness can also expose AI and IoT products to **cyber-threats**. . . .

3. Liability

. . . Taking out proper insurance can mitigate the negative consequences of accidents by providing for a smooth compensation for the victim. Clear liability rules help insurance companies to calculate their risks and to claim reimbursement from the party ultimately liable for the damage. For example, if an accident is caused by a defect, the motor insurer can claim reimbursement from the manufacturer after compensating the victim.

However, the characteristics of emerging digital technologies like AI, the IoT and robotics challenge aspects of Union and national liability frameworks and could reduce their effectiveness. Some of these characteristics could make it hard to trace the damage back to a human behaviour, which could give grounds for a fault-based claim in accordance with national rules. This means that liability claims based on national tort laws may be difficult or overly costly to prove and consequently victims may not be adequately compensated. It is important that victims of accidents of products and services including emerging digital technologies like AI do not enjoy a lower level of protection compared to similar other products and services, for which they would get compensation under national tort law. This could reduce societal acceptance of those emerging technologies and lead to hesitance to use them.

It will need to be assessed whether challenges of the new technologies to the existing frameworks could also cause legal uncertainty as to how existing laws would apply (e.g. how the concept of fault would apply to damage caused by AI). These could in turn discourage investment as well as increase information and insurance costs for producers and other businesses in the supply chain, especially European SMEs [small and medium size enterprises]. . . .

This chapter explains how new technologies challenge the existing frameworks and in what way these challenges could be addressed. Furthermore, specificities of some sectors, for example health care, may deserve additional considerations.

Complexity of products, services and the value-chain: Technology and industry have evolved drastically over the last decades. Especially the dividing line between products and services may no longer be as clear-cut as it was. Products and the provision of services are increasingly intertwined. While complex products and value chains are not new to European industry or its regulatory model, software and also AI merit specific attention in respect of product liability. Software is essential to the functioning of a large number of products and may affect their safety. It is integrated into products but it may also be supplied separately to enable the use of the product as intended. Neither a computer nor a smartphone would be of particular use without software. This means that software can make a tangible product defective and lead to physical damage . . . This could eventually result in the liability of the producer of the product under the Product Liability Directive.

However, as software comes in many types and forms, answers related to the classification of software as a service or as a product may not always be straightforward. Thus while software steering the operations of a tangible product could be considered part or component of that product, some forms of stand-alone software could be more difficult to classify.

Although the Product Liability Directive's definition of product is broad, its scope could be further clarified to better reflect the complexity of emerging technologies and ensure that compensation is always available for damage caused by products that are defective because of software or other digital features. This would better enable economic actors, such as software developers, to assess whether they could be considered producers according to the Product Liability Directive.

AI applications are often integrated in **complex IoT environments** where many different connected devices and services interact. Combining different digital components in a complex ecosystem and the plurality of actors involved can make it difficult to assess where a potential damage originates and which person is liable for it. Due to the complexity of these technologies, it can be very difficult for victims to identify the liable person and prove all necessary conditions for a successful claim, as required under national law. The costs for this expertise may be economically prohibitive and discourage victims from claiming compensation.

In addition, products and services relying on AI will interact with traditional technologies, leading to added complexity also when it comes to liability. For example, autonomous cars will share the road with traditional ones for a certain time. Similar complexity of interacting actors will arise in some services sectors (such as traffic management and healthcare) where partially automated AI systems will support human decision-making.

According to the Report from the New Technologies formation of the Expert Group on Liability and New Technologies, adaptations of national laws to facilitate the burden of proof for the victims of AI-related damage could be considered. For example, the burden of proof could be linked to the compliance (by a relevant operator) with specific cyber-security or other safety obligations set by law: if one does not comply with these rules, a change to the burden of proof as regards fault and causation could apply.

The Commission is seeking views whether and to what extent it may be needed to mitigate the consequences of complexity by alleviating/reversing the burden of proof required by national liability rules for damage caused by the operation of AI applications, through an appropriate EU initiative.

As regards Union legislation, according to the Product Liability Directive, a product that does not meet mandatory safety rules would be considered defective, regardless of the producers' fault. There may, however, also be reasons to contemplate ways on how to facilitate the burden of proof for victims under the Directive: the Directive relies on national rules on the evidence and the establishment of causation.

Connectivity and openness: It is currently not entirely clear what safety expectations may be with regard to damage that results from cybersecurity breaches in the product and whether such damage would be adequately compensated under the Product Liability Directive.

Cybersecurity weaknesses may exist from the outset, when a product is put into circulation, but they may also appear at a later stage, well after the product was put into circulation.

In fault-based liability frameworks, establishing clear cyber-security obligations allows the operators to determine what they have to do in order to avoid the consequences of liability.

Under the Product Liability Directive, the question if a producer could have foreseen certain changes taking account of the product's reasonably foreseeable use may become more prominent. For example, one might see an increase in the use of the 'later defect defence' according to which a producer is not liable if the defect did not exist at the time the product was put into circulation or in the 'development risk defence' (that the state of the art knowledge at the time could not have foreseen the defect). In addition, liability could be reduced where the injured party does not perform safety relevant updates. This could potentially be regarded as contributory negligence by the injured person and therefore reduce a producer's liability. As the notion of foreseeable reasonable use and questions of contributory negligence, such as the failure to download a safety update, may become more prevalent, injured persons might find it more difficult to get compensation for damage caused by a defect in a product.

Autonomy and opacity: Where AI applications are able to act autonomously, they perform a task without every step being pre-defined and with less or eventually entirely without immediate human control or supervision. Algorithms based on machine-learning can be difficult, if not impossible, to understand (the so-called 'black-box effect').

In addition to complexity discussed above, due to the black-box effect in some AI, getting compensation could become difficult for damage caused by autonomous AI-applications. The need to understand the algorithm and the data used by the AI requires analytical capacity and technical expertise that victims could find prohibitively costly. In addition, access to the algorithm and the data could be impossible without the cooperation of the potentially liable party. In practice, victims may thus not be able to make a liability claim. In addition, it would be unclear, how to demonstrate the fault of an AI acting autonomously, or what would be considered the fault of a person relying on the use of AI.

National laws have already developed a number of solutions to reduce the burden of proof for victims in similar situations.

A guiding principle for Union product safety and product liability remains that it is for producers to ensure that all products put on the market should be safe, throughout their life-cycle as well as for the use of the product that can reasonably be expected. This means that a manufacturer would have to make sure that a product using AI respects certain safety parameters. The features of AI do not preclude that there is an entitlement to safety expectations for products, whether they are automatic lawnmowers or surgery robots.

Autonomy can affect the safety of the product, because it may alter a product's characteristics substantially, including its safety features. It is a question under what conditions self-learning features prolong liability of the producer and to what extent should the producer have foreseen certain changes.

In close coordination with corresponding changes in the Union safety framework, the notion of 'putting into circulation' that is currently used by the Product Liability Directive could be revisited to take into account that products may change and be altered. This could also help to clarify who is liable for any changes that are made to the product.

According to the Report from the New Technologies formation of the Expert Group on Liability and New Technologies, the operation of some autonomous AI devices and services could have a specific risk profile in terms of liability, because they may cause significant harm to important legal interests like life, health and property, and expose the public at large to risks. This could mainly concern AI devices that move in public spaces (e.g. fully autonomous vehicles, drones and package delivery robots) or AI-based services with similar risks (e.g. traffic management services guiding or controlling vehicles or management of power distribution). The challenges of autonomy and opacity to national tort laws could be addressed following a risk-based approach. Strict liability schemes could ensure that whenever that risk materialises, the victim is compensated regardless of fault. The impact of choosing who should be strictly liable for such operations on the development and uptake of AI would need to be carefully assessed and a risk-based approach be considered.

For the operation of AI applications with a specific risk profile, the Commission is seeking views on whether and to what extent strict liability, as it exists in national laws for similar risks to which the public is exposed (for instance for operating motor vehicles, airplanes or nuclear power plants), may be needed in order to achieve effective compensation of possible victims. The Commission is also seeking views on coupling strict liability with a possible obligation to conclude available insurance, following the example of the Motor Insurance Directive, in order to ensure compensation irrespective of the liable person's solvency and to help reducing the costs of damage.

For the operation of all other AI applications, which would constitute the large majority of AI applications, the Commission is reflecting whether the burden of proof concerning causation and fault needs to be adapted. In this respect, one of the issues flagged by the Report from the New Technologies formation of the Expert Group on Liability and New Technologies is the situation when the potentially liable party has not logged the data relevant for assessing liability or is not willing to share them with the victim.

4. Conclusion

The emergence of new digital technologies like AI, the IoT and robotics raise new challenges in terms of product safety and liability like connectivity, autonomy, data dependency, opacity, complexity of products and systems, software updates and more complex safety management and value chains. . . .

The new challenges in terms of safety create also new challenges in terms of liability. Those liability related challenges need to be addressed to ensure the same level of protection compared to victims of traditional technologies, while maintaining the balance with the needs of technological innovation. This will help create trust in these new emerging digital technologies and create investment stability.

While in principle the existing Union and national liability laws are able to cope with emerging technologies, the dimension and combined effect of the challenges of AI could make it more difficult to offer victims compensation in all cases where this would be justified. Thus, the allocation of the cost when damage occurs may be unfair or inefficient under the current rules. To rectify this and address potential uncertainties in the existing framework, certain adjustments to the Product Liability Directive and national liability regimes through appropriate EU initiatives could be considered on a targeted, risk-based approach, i.e. taking into account that different AI applications pose different risks.

COMMENTARY

The Commission identifies several features of the new technologies under discussion that pose challenges for existing product liability regimes. These include 'complexity' (including the involvement of multiple parties in production, the technological sophistication of the product itself and the interplay of software and hardware); 'openness' (the fact that the product is constantly updating and/or upgrading); and 'opacity' (the reliance of the product on algorithms, and the difficulty of tracking decision-making by artificial intelligence systems). The result is that it may be increasingly difficult to identify the cause of a product malfunction or accident and also the party responsible for it. The difficulties this will cause for fault-based systems of product liability are obvious, but they extend to strict liability systems as well. Furthermore, the liability regime established by the 1985 Directive rests on a distinction between goods and services (with strict liability limited to the former) which technological developments threaten to make obsolete, as we move from 'smart' televisions and phones to smart fridges, dishwashers and cars, not to mention increasingly complex commercial products, robots and the like. With products of this kind, it is increasingly likely that any 'defect' will be attributable to a software error, and yet this may place additional hurdles in the path of a consumer seeking redress for damage the product has caused. In particular, the producer of the product itself may not be responsible for the software that has caused the malfunction; the problem may have arisen as a result of a software update after the product was put into circulation, so that the producer may have a defence under s. 4(1)(d) of the 1987 Act; the malfunction may have been caused by a cyber-security breach, raising questions of legal causation; and the defect may have arisen because of user error or failure to update the software, again raising questions of legal causation, and also contributory negligence. This issue is complicated by the fact that it is unclear whether software that is supplied without a physical medium is a 'product' for the purposes of the 1987 Act (see further, *Fairgrieve and Goldberg*, paras 9.98–9.105).

The Commission identifies various ways in which product liability law might develop in order to meet these challenges, including extending the definitions of 'product' and 'producer', and reversing the burden of proof so as to counter the 'opacity' concern (or 'black box' problem). Reversal of the burden of proof is a particularly interesting solution to consider, since this technique can be used in both fault-based and strict liability systems, and because it may incentivise producers to make their systems as transparent as possible in the hope that if things do wrong, they will stand some chance of establishing that it was not their fault, or (in strict liability) their responsibility. Furthermore, as the Commission points out, the threat of a reversal of the burden of proof could be used to encourage producers to comply with safety and cyber-security regulations, which might even extend to the transparency of the processes controlling the product. However, this technique works only if there is ultimately a single entity to which the consumer can look for redress when a product malfunctions, no matter how complex the product is.

An alternative solution to these challenges may be to adopt a simpler strict liability regime, shorn of complications such as defectiveness and the sorts of defences that limit liability under the 1987 Act. Under this approach, legislation simply lays down that if damage is caused by a certain kind of product (such as a robot or drone) then a stipulated person or entity is liable, subject to a limited range of defences which are ideally kept as simple and straightforward as possible. An example of a liability regime of this kind is the one established by the Automated and Electric Vehicles Act 2018 for driverless cars.

Automated and Electric Vehicles Act 2018

An Act to make provision about automated vehicles and electric vehicles . . .

2. Liability of insurers etc where accident caused by automated vehicle

(1) Where—
    (a) an accident is caused by an automated vehicle when driving itself on a road or other public place in Great Britain,
    (b) the vehicle is insured at the time of the accident, and
    (c) an insured person or any other person suffers damage as a result of the accident,
the insurer is liable for that damage.

(2) Where—
    (a) an accident is caused by an automated car when driving itself on a road or other public place in Great Britain,
    (b) the vehicle is not insured at the time of the accident,
    (c) section 143 of the Road Traffic Act 1988 (users of motor vehicles to be insured or secured against third-party risks) does not apply to the vehicle at that time . . . and
    (d) a person suffers damage as a result of the accident,
the owner of the vehicle is liable for that damage.

(3) In this Part 'damage' means death or personal injury, and any damage to property other than—
    (a) the automated vehicle,
    (b) goods carried for hire or reward in or on that vehicle . . . or

(c) property in the custody, or under the control, of—
  (i) the insured person (where subsection (1) applies), or
  (ii) the person in charge of the automated vehicle at the time of the accident (where subsection (2) applies). . . .

(5) This section has effect subject to section 3.

(6) Except as provided by section 4, liability under this section may not be limited or excluded by a term of an insurance policy or in any other way.

(7) The imposition by this section of liability on the insurer or vehicle owner does not affect any other person's liability in respect of the accident.

3. Contributory negligence etc

(1) Where—
  (a) an insurer or vehicle owner is liable under section 2 to a person ('the injured party') in respect of an accident, and
  (b) the accident, or the damage resulting from it, was to any extent caused by the injured party,

  the amount of the liability is subject to whatever reduction under the Law Reform (Contributory Negligence) Act 1945 would apply to a claim in respect of the accident brought by the injured party against a person other than the insurer or vehicle owner.

(2) The insurer or owner of an automated vehicle is not liable under section 2 to the person in charge of the vehicle where the accident that it caused was wholly due to the person's negligence in allowing the vehicle to begin driving itself when it was not appropriate to do so.

4. Accident resulting from unauthorised software alterations or failure to update software

(1) An insurance policy in respect of an automated vehicle may exclude or limit the insurer's liability under section 2(1) for damage suffered by an insured person arising from an accident occurring as a direct result of—
  (a) software alterations made by the insured person, or with the insured person's knowledge, that are prohibited under the policy, or
  (b) a failure to install safety-critical software updates that the insured person knows, or ought reasonably to know, are safety-critical.

(2) But as regards liability for damage suffered by an insured person who is not the holder of the policy, subsection (1)(a) applies only in relation to software alterations which, at the time of the accident, the person knows are prohibited under the policy.

(3) Subsection (4) applies where an amount is paid by an insurer under section 2(1) in respect of damage suffered, as a result of an accident, by someone who is not insured under the policy in question.

(4) If the accident occurred as a direct result of—
  (a) software alterations made by an insured person, or with an insured person's knowledge, that were prohibited under the policy, or
  (b) a failure to install safety-critical software updates that an insured person knew, or ought reasonably to have known, were safety-critical,

  the amount paid by the insurer is recoverable from that person to the extent provided for by the policy.

(5) But as regards recovery from an insured person who is not the holder of the policy, subsection (4)(a) applies only in relation to software alterations which, at the time of the accident, the person knew were prohibited under the policy.

(6) For the purposes of this section—
   (a) 'software alterations' and 'software updates', in relation to an automated vehicle, mean (respectively) alterations and updates to the vehicle's software;
   (b) software updates are 'safety-critical' if it would be unsafe to use the vehicle in question without the updates being installed.

5. Right of insurer etc to claim against person responsible for accident

(1) Where—
   (a) section 2 imposes on an insurer, or the owner of a vehicle, liability to a person who has suffered damage as a result of an accident ('the injured party'), and
   (b) the amount of the insurer's or vehicle owner's liability to the injured party in respect of the accident (including any liability not imposed by section 2) is settled,

any other person liable to the injured party in respect of the accident is under the same liability to the insurer or vehicle owner.

(2) For the purposes of this section, the amount of the insurer's or vehicle owner's liability is settled when it is established—
   (a) by a judgment or decree,
   (b) by an award in arbitral proceedings or by an arbitration, or
   (c) by an enforceable agreement.

(3) If the amount recovered under this section by the insurer or vehicle owner exceeds the amount which that person has agreed or been ordered to pay to the injured party (ignoring so much of either amount as represents interest), the insurer or vehicle owner is liable to the injured party for the difference.

(4) Nothing in this section allows the insurer or vehicle owner and the injured party, between them, to recover from any person more than the amount of that person's liability to the injured party. . . .

6. Application of enactments

. . .

(3) For the purposes of section 3(1), the Law Reform (Contributory Negligence) Act 1945 and section 5 of the Fatal Accidents Act 1976 (contributory negligence) have effect as if the behaviour of the automated vehicle were the fault of the person made liable for the damage by section 2 of this Act.

. . .

8. Interpretation

(1) For the purposes of this Part—
   (a) a vehicle is 'driving itself' if it is operating in a mode in which it is not being controlled, and does not need to be monitored, by an individual; . . .

(3) In this Part—
   . . . (b) a reference to an accident caused by an automated vehicle includes a reference to an accident that is partly caused by an automated vehicle.

COMMENTARY

It is hoped that by removing driver error automated vehicles will herald a new era of much safer roads, with far fewer traffic accidents. And since such a high proportion of personal injury claims arise out of such accidents, over the longer term the advent of the driverless car is likely to have a transformative effect on the law of tort, at least in practice. At the same time, however, a driverless car is an immensely complex product and there is still plenty of scope for accidents caused by malfunctioning hardware or software, particularly in the early years of their use. It is therefore not surprising that the prospect of automated vehicles being used on public roads brought forth a legislative response. The basic liability system established by the Act is simple. The insurer of a driverless car—or its owner where the vehicle is not subject to compulsory insurance—is strictly liable for any damage that results from an accident caused by the vehicle when it is driving itself (s. 2), while the liability of other persons (such as other road users, or the vehicle's producer) in respect of the damage is preserved (s. 2(7)), and the insurer enabled to seek an indemnity from such other person (s. 5). The insurer's liability is reduced where the claimant was guilty of contributory negligence (s. 3(1)) and eliminated altogether where the accident was 'wholly due' to the fault of the person in charge of the vehicle in allowing it to begin driving itself when this was not appropriate (s. 3(2)).

The overall aim and effect of the 2018 Act is to ensure that the injured party gets compensation quickly and easily, while allowing for secondary claims by the insurer to channel 'the loss to any person bearing responsibility for it under existing principles of tortious liability' (Oliphant, 'Liability for Road Accidents Caused by Driverless Cars' [2019] Sing Comp L Rev 190 at 194). This is achieved by means of what has been described as a 'radical new approach to motor insurance', whereby the insurer no longer indemnifies the road user against their own liability but instead bears the liability itself (*Automated Vehicles: A Joint Preliminary Consultation Paper* (Law Com. Consultation Paper No. 240, 2018) para. 6.15). The appeal of this solution is obvious. The difficult concepts that determine liability under the Consumer Protection Act 1987 ('defect', 'development risk', etc.), are nowhere to be seen, while the fixing of strict liability on the insurer means that the injured party is freed from the burden of engaging with the new technology and what caused it to malfunction (though the problems of complexity, openness and opacity identified above may still bedevil secondary claims by the insurer against other parties: see Law Com. Consultation Paper No. 240, paras 6.61ff). As for the issue of the owner not installing safety-critical software updates, etc., this meets with a robust response in s. 4, which entitles insurers to exclude their liability to the insured where such a failure is to blame for the accident. Then again, the Act is not free from difficulty. Like many strict liability regimes, it puts a lot of weight on causation—what does it mean to say that an automated vehicle has 'caused' an accident (s. 2(1)), and when will that accident nevertheless be 'wholly due' to the negligence of the person in charge of the vehicle at the time (s. 3(2))?—and the strictness of the liability may also cause difficulties when it comes to applying the rules on contributory negligence in s. 3(1) (see further on these issues, Law Com. Consultation Paper No. 240, paras 6.31–6.51). It should also be remembered that a regime of insurer liability is dependent on an underlying system of compulsory insurance of the kind that has been in place for motor vehicles for almost a century (see now the Road Traffic Act 1988, ss. 143ff). Were it considered appropriate to extend the 2018 Act's approach to other new technologies it would therefore be necessary either to establish compulsory insurance regimes for these as well (as was suggested by the European Commission in its report extracted earlier for AI applications 'with a specific risk profile', such as drones) or alternatively to attach the strict liability to a different person, such as the keeper or owner of the relevant thing (cf. the Animals Act 1971, which imposes strict liability on the 'keeper' of an animal for damage it causes).

It can of course be argued that burdening new technologies with wide-ranging strict liabilities shorn of the kind of protections afforded to producers by the Consumer Protection Act 1987 will stifle innovation and increase entry costs so as to exclude smaller enterprises from entering the relevant product markets. However, there is little in the way of empirical evidence to back up this concern, and in most cases it seems likely that the associated costs will be relatively easily absorbed by insurance (and then passed on to consumers in the form of higher prices). Indeed, it is possible that the introduction of comprehensive strict liability systems for new technologies may actually foster innovation by smoothing the way to social acceptance of the attendant risks and giving consumers the confidence to adopt them at an early stage.

The Law Commission and the Scottish Law Commission recently completed a review of the legal framework governing automated vehicles and concluded that the 2018 Act was 'good enough for now', although they recommended that equivalent measures be put in place to provide compensation in respect of damage caused by uninsured driverless cars. The Commissions accepted that certain aspects of the legislation—in particular, the provisions on causation and contributory negligence—would need to be reviewed and perhaps clarified, but in their view this should be done in the light of practical experience, once driverless cars were on the roads (*Automated Vehicles: A Joint Report* (Law Com. No. 404, 2022), para. 13.18):

No-one can foresee the full effect of AVs, or the many different possible circumstances surrounding the incidents that might result. Moreover, it is difficult to predict how the courts will apply legal tests to factual situations which have not yet occurred.

III. Breach of Statutory Duty

The fact that the defendant has breached a statutory duty of a criminal or regulatory kind may well be relevant in a negligence case as evidence of breach of the common law duty of care. In some common law jurisdictions (e.g. Canada) this is the sole significance of such a breach for tort law purposes, while in others (including most US states) the breach of a statutory duty of this kind is not merely evidence of negligence, but conclusive of the issue (see further on this 'statutory negligence', III.4). By contrast, in English law breach of statutory duty is a standalone tort, so that where the breach of such a duty leads to damage, this may itself give rise to a cause of action wholly independent of negligence. As Lord Wright stated in *London Passenger Transport Board v Upson* [1949] AC 155 at 168, 'a claim for damages for breach of a statutory duty . . . is a specific common law right which is not to be confused with a claim for negligence'.

The action for breach of statutory duty is distinguishable from the other statutory liabilities discussed in this chapter because—unlike the Occupiers' Liability Acts and the Consumer Protection Act 1987—the statutory duties in question are not solely tortious in nature and significance; rather, their primary significance lies in public law, whether administrative law, criminal law or regulatory law. Straightforward examples include breaches of industrial safety regulations or environmental standards legally prescribed for certain activities. Hence the tort has been defined as 'a common law liability inferred by the courts in order to allow an individual to claim compensation for damages suffered as a result of [a breach of statutory provisions] which do not expressly provide a remedy in tort' (*Stanton*, para. 1.009).

As we shall see, most of the case law on this tort revolves around the question of whether the breach of a given statutory duty is actionable in damages at common law (see IV.2). If the answer to that question is affirmative, then the claimant need establish only that the duty was breached and that as a result he or she suffered damage that was within the scope of protection of the duty (on this last requirement, see III.3). Although the elements of the tort are therefore straightforward, one difficult issue that can arise is whether the relevant duty is strict or incorporates a fault standard (see Stanton, 'New Forms of the Tort of Breach of Statutory Duty' (2004) 120 LQR 324 at 331–3). This is ultimately a question of statutory interpretation and need not be pursued further here, but it should be noted that many statutory duties have a strict or absolute character, with the result that the availability of a claim for breach of statutory duty can offer a claimant significant advantages when compared to a negligence claim. (For analysis of the terms 'absolute' and 'strict' liability see *Allison v London Underground* [2008] ICR 719 at [31], per Smith LJ.) It should also be noted that many statutory duties incorporate standards that are not easily classified as 'fault' or 'strict', such as the requirement that an employer do what is 'practicable' or 'reasonably practicable' to ensure a result. The case law on these sorts of provisions is complex and need not concern us here (for an overview, see *Winfield & Jolowicz*, para. 9–012), but it is important to emphasise that they are not to be conflated with the standard of reasonable care used in negligence.

1. The Development of the Tort

It was not until the second half of the nineteenth century that tort liability for breach of statutory duty received proper attention from the courts. Admittedly, there had prior to that time been occasional references to the issue by judges and treatise writers. In a famous passage in *Comyn's Digest*, for instance, there appears the bold and unqualified pronouncement that '[i]n every case where a statute enacts or prohibits a thing for the benefit of a person, he shall have a remedy upon the same statute for the thing enacted for his advantage, or for the recompense of a wrong done to him contrary to the said law' (*Com. Dig.*, 'Action upon Statute', F). But it was not until the proliferation of regulatory legislation in the Victorian era that the question of civil liability for breach of statutory duty became a matter urgently requiring judicial attention. Some of the early cases took an expansive view of the liability (but cf. *Doe d. Murray, Bishop of Rochester v Bridges* (1831) B & Ad 847). In *Couch v Steel* (1854) 3 E & B 402, a sailor had fallen ill at sea, and because the ship, contrary to the statutory requirement, was not carrying appropriate medication, he suffered avoidable injury to his health. His claim for damages succeeded before Lord Campbell CJ who, adverting to the passage in *Comyn's Digest* just cited, held that there was a right to sue for 'breach of a public duty', notwithstanding the existence of a criminal penalty for the statutory violation in question.

But such liability was quickly reined in, no doubt as a result of fears that the bounds of civil liability would expand in parallel with new legislative regulation, and hence extend far beyond the scope of the negligence liabilities of the time (see *Winfield & Jolowicz*, para. 8–005). A key decision in this respect was *Atkinson v Newcastle Waterworks Co* (1877)

2 Ex D 441, where the plaintiff's premises had been destroyed by fire because the pressure in the defendant waterworks company's pipes was inadequate. The plaintiff brought an action for damages against the defendant for not keeping its pipes charged in breach of s. 42 of the Waterworks Clauses Act 1847, which provided that:

> The undertakers shall at all times keep charged with water, under such pressure as aforesaid [which by s. 35 was such pressure as would make the water reach the top storey of the highest houses within the area in question], all their pipes to which fire-plugs shall be fixed, unless prevented by frost, unusual drought, or other unavoidable cause or accident, or during necessary repairs, and shall allow all persons at all times to take and use such water for extinguishing fire, without making compensation for the same.

Breach of this duty was punishable by a fine of £10. The Court of Appeal held that the provision did not give rise to a private right of action. According to Lord Cairns LC (at 446), if the law were otherwise the defendants 'would virtually become gratuitous insurers of the safety from fire, so far as water is capable of producing that safety, of all the houses within the district over which their powers were to extend' (though in fact, of course, they would only be liable if they breached their duty and this breach was causative of the fire damage). The decision in *Atkinson* marked the demise of the view advanced by Lord Campbell in *Couch v Steel* that those protected by a penal statute could prima facie bring a civil action upon it. In its place, the Court of Appeal adopted a narrow 'construction' approach which required consideration of whether the statute was intended to give rise to private rights. Lord Cairns distinguished *Couch* on the ground that it concerned a public general Act of Parliament, rather than a private Act of the kind which authorised the operations of the defendants in *Atkinson*, which would have been understood at the time as analogous to a bargain between the defendants as a private enterprise and the state, the balance of which might be upset by the implication of an obligation to make compensation in these circumstances. Nevertheless, it became apparent that Lord Campbell's view could not be sustained even in relation to public Acts (see, e.g., *Phillips v Britannia Hygienic Laundry Co Ltd* [1923] 2 KB 832, extracted in the next section). In the end, therefore, the *Atkinson* decision 'consigned the tort [of breach of statutory duty] to a history of haphazard applications' (*Stanton*, para. 2.002).

Despite the narrower approach ushered in by *Atkinson*, breach of statutory duty nevertheless succeeded in establishing itself as a significant cause of action in one context, namely the workplace. By the middle of the nineteenth century, the negligence liability of employers to their employees had been radically curtailed by an 'unholy trinity' of defences, namely *volenti*, contributory negligence (then a total defence) and common employment (the doctrine according to which an employer was not generally liable for damage caused to one employee by the negligence of another: see further, the 6th edition of this work, at pp. 559–60). However, in the decades that followed, there was a widespread perception that the courts had gone too far in restricting employers' liability, as was evident in the passage through Parliament of the Employers' Liability Act 1880 (although it allowed employees only very limited claims) and the Workmen's Compensation Act 1897, which foreshadowed the social security legislation of the twentieth century. It was against this background that increasingly the tort of breach of statutory duty came to be used to circumvent the limitations of the action in negligence in the employment context. In *Baddeley v Earl Granville* (1887) 19 QBD 423, the defence of *volenti* was ruled inapplicable to breach of statutory duty (see further *Wheeler v New Merton Board Mills* [1933] 2 KB 669; exceptionally, the defence may be raised where the employer is only placed in breach by the actions of the claimant or of another employee acting in tandem with the claimant: *ICI v Shatwell* [1965] AC 656). Then, in the next extracted case, the Court of Appeal accepted, first, that industrial safety legislation could give rise to private rights of action and, secondly, that it was not possible to raise the common employment defence in an action brought to enforce those rights.

Groves v Lord Wimborne [1898] 2 QB 402

The plaintiff was employed at the defendant's iron works in which he worked a steam winch with revolving cog-wheels. The cog-wheels were dangerous to a person working the winch unless fenced. There was evidence that there had originally been a guard or fence to the cog-wheels, but it had for some reason been removed, and there had been no fence to the wheels while the plaintiff was employed at the winch, a period of about six months. While working the winch, the plaintiff's right arm was caught by the cog-wheels, and was so badly injured that the forearm had to be amputated. He alleged that the defendant had been in breach of the statutory duty imposed upon him by the Factory and Workshop Act 1878, s. 5(3), a breach which (if proved) would be punishable under the terms of the same statute by fine (s. 82). The trial judge held that an action would not lie for breach of the statutory duty imposed by the Act but he asked the jury to assess the damages provisionally, which they did at the sum of £150. The judge entered judgment for the defendant. The plaintiff appealed.

A. L. Smith LJ

The Act in question, which followed numerous other Acts in pari materia, is not in the nature of a private legislative bargain between employers and workmen, as the learned judge seemed to think, but is a public Act passed in favour of the workers in factories and workshops to compel their employers to do certain things for their protection and benefit. The first question is what duty is imposed by that Act upon the occupiers of factories and workshops with regard to the fencing of machinery. By s. 5 it is enacted that 'with respect to the fencing of machinery the following provisions shall have effect.' Then by sub-s. 3 of the section, as amended by the Factory and Workshop Act, 1891, s. 6, sub-s. 2, 'All dangerous parts of the machinery, and every part of the mill gearing shall either be securely fenced, or be in such position or of such construction as to be equally safe to every person employed in the factory as it would be if it were securely fenced'; and by sub-s. 4, 'All fencing shall be constantly maintained in an efficient state while the parts required to be fenced are in motion or use for the purpose of any manufacturing process'; and 'a factory in which there is a contravention of this section shall be deemed not to be kept in conformity with this Act.'

In the present case it is admitted that machinery on the defendant's premises which came within these provisions was not fenced as required by the Act, and that injury was thereby occasioned to the plaintiff, a boy employed on the works. On proof of a breach of this statutory duty imposed on the defendant, and injury resulting to the plaintiff therefrom, prima facie the plaintiff has a good cause of action . . . Could it be doubted that, if s. 5 stood alone, and no fine were provided by the Act for contravention of its provisions, a person injured by a breach of the absolute and unqualified duty imposed by that section would have a cause of action in respect of that breach? Clearly it could not be doubted. That being so, unless it appears from the whole 'purview' of the Act, to use the language of Lord Cairns in the case of *Atkinson v Newcastle Waterworks Co* (1877) 2 Ex D 441, that it was the intention of the Legislature that the only remedy for breach of the statutory duty should be by proceeding for the fine imposed by s. 82, it follows that, upon proof of a breach of that duty by the employer and injury thereby occasioned to the workman, a cause of action is established.

The question therefore is whether the cause of action which prima facie is given by s. 5 is taken away by any provisions to be found in the remainder of the Act. It is said that the provisions of ss. 81, 82, and 86 have that effect, and that it appears thereby that the purview of the Act is that the only remedy, where a workman has been injured by a breach of the duty imposed by s. 5, shall be by proceeding before a court of summary jurisdiction for a fine under s. 82, which fine is not to exceed £100. In dealing with the question whether this was the intention of the Legislature, it is material, as Kelly CB pointed out in giving judgment in the case of *Gorris v Scott* (1874) LR 9 Ex 125, to consider for whose benefit the Act was passed, whether it was passed in the interests of the public at large or in those of a particular class of persons. The Act now in question, as I have said, was clearly passed in favour of workers employed in factories and workshops, and to compel their employers to perform certain statutory duties for their protection and benefit. It is to be observed in the first place that under the provisions of s. 82 not a penny of the fine necessarily goes to the person injured or his family. The provision is only that the whole or any part of it may be applied for the benefit of the injured person or his family, or otherwise, as a secretary of state determines. Again, if proceedings for the fine are taken before magistrates, upon what considerations are they to act in determining the amount of the fine? One matter to be considered clearly would be the character of the neglect to fence. This neglect might be either of a serious or of a venial character. Suppose that it was of the latter character, but a person was unfortunately killed or injured in consequence of it. What fine are the magistrates to impose? Are they to impose a fine of the same amount as if it were a flagrant case of neglect to fence? The first thing one would say that they would have to consider would be whether the offence was of a grave character or otherwise. It may be said that in determining the amount of the fine the character of the injury sustained by the workman would be considered, but I am not sure that that is the meaning of the section. It seems to me that the fine is inflicted by way of punishment of the employer for neglect of the duty imposed by the Act, and must be proportionate to the character of the offence. This consideration and the fact that whatever penalty the magistrates inflict does not necessarily go to the injured workman or his family lead me to the conclusion that it cannot have been the intention of the Legislature that the provision which imposes upon the employer a fine as a punishment for neglect of his statutory duty should take away the prima facie right of the workman to be fully compensated for injury occasioned to him by that neglect. Another observation which makes the matter still clearer arises from the fact that, having regard to the provisions of s. 87, it may not be the employer, presumably a person of means and capable of paying a substantial fine, who would have to pay the fine. Under that section the employer may be exempted from the penalty, and the fine may be imposed upon the actual offender, who may be a workman employed at weekly wages; and yet it is said that a fine payable by such a person is the only remedy given by the statute to the injured workman for breach by the occupier of the imperative statutory duty. I cannot read this statute in the manner in which it is sought to be read by the defendant. I think that s. 5 does give to the workman a right of action upon the statute for injury caused by a breach of the statutory duty thereby imposed, and that he is not relegated to the provisions for the imposition of a fine on the employer, or it may be a workman, as his sole remedy.

[His Lordship proceeded to rule also that the defence of common employment (subsequently abolished by Law Reform (Personal Injuries) Act 1948) did not apply to a claim for breach of statutory duty.]

Rigby and **Vaughan Williams LJJ** delivered separate concurring judgments.

Appeal allowed.

COMMENTARY

A. L. Smith LJ was concerned to emphasise that the existence of a fine of up to a £100 for a breach of the obligation in question did not preclude the conclusion that it was privately actionable, even though it was possible that the whole or part of any such fine might be used (at the discretion of the Secretary of State) to benefit those injured as a result of the breach. According to *Winfield & Jolowicz*, para. 8–011, the result in *Groves* was 'rather surprising', since the fact that Parliament had expressly adverted to the matter of compensation gave some force to the argument that no civil claim for breach of the provision was intended.

The circumvention of the doctrine of common employment in this decision was linked to the non-delegable nature of the statutory duty imposed on the employer. Stanton, *op. cit.*, 338, says:

> The non-delegable nature of all species of statutory duties is well established. In origin it probably derives from the nineteenth century theory which regarded public authority duties owed to a locality as essentially contractual. However, since *Groves v Lord Wimborne* established breach of statutory duty as a tortious remedy for breach of industrial safety legislation and, in doing so, created a tort free from the defence of common employment, a more general theory has dominated. If Parliament has chosen to impose a duty upon a person by statute, it is impossible for that person to avoid the Parliamentary allocation of responsibility by delegating the performance of that duty to another person. The performance may be delegated, but not the responsibility.

The decision in *Groves* signalled the start of the rapid development of civil liability for breach of industrial safety legislation. Indeed, Glanville Williams highlighted health and safety at work as 'well nigh the only area in which penal legislation has been held to create statutory torts' (see 'The Effect of Penal Legislation in the Law of Tort' (1960) 23 MLR 233 at 244), and had it not been for the rather unusual historical context of workplace safety claims in the late nineteenth century, it may well be that English law would have developed a doctrine of statutory negligence along American lines rather than a separate and distinct tort of breach of statutory duty. The timing of the decision is no coincidence in this regard. Only the year before Parliament had passed the Workmen's Compensation Act 1897, which provided for compensation to be paid to those injured at work on a no-fault basis. As the authors of *Stanton* observe (para. 2.002), '[t]here was clearly something of a consensus at this time that the human victims of the industrial revolution should be granted more protection than had previously been obtained through the concept of fault liability'.

However, despite being a fixture of the English legal landscape for more than a century, the presumption of actionability applying to workplace health and safety obligations was reversed by s. 69 of the Enterprise and Regulatory Reform Act 2013, amending s. 47(2) of the Health and Safety at Work Act 1974. The reform implemented a recommendation of an independent review of health and safety legislation (R. E. Löfstedt, *Reclaiming Health and Safety for All* (2011)), which questioned the reasonableness of making employers compensate for injuries even where they had taken all practicable precautions, the obligations imposed on them being strict rather than framed in terms of reasonable care or practicability. As regulations issued under that Act have almost entirely superseded previous legislation, and as only very few of the regulations contain express liability provisions (see, e.g., Management of Health and Safety at Work Regulations SI 1999/3242, reg 22), there is now practically no scope for civil claims for breach of occupational health and safety laws. Injured workers must instead bring their claims on the basis of common law negligence, where they bear the evidential burden of proving the employer's fault. Health and safety standards remain relevant, however, in determining the precautions against injury that a reasonable employer would take and, because what is required evolves with the passage of time, precautions that were first made compulsory by statute may now also be required so as to discharge the employer's common law duty of care (see, e.g., *Kennedy v Cordia (Services) LLP* [2016] 1 WLR 597: risk assessment). Undoubtedly, though, the 2013 reforms dealt a hammer blow to the practical significance of breach of statutory duty as a cause of action. Nevertheless, breach of statutory duty in its traditional form 'is not completely dead' (see Stanton, *op. cit.*, 325, where the author gives recent examples of its operation outside the industrial safety context), and Parliament sometimes creates bespoke statutory torts which operate in a manner analogous to a claim for breach of statutory duty (e.g., s. 150 of the Financial Services and Markets Act 2000; see further on this phenomenon, Stanton, *op. cit.*, 326–8). It is also conceivable that future legislative changes might bring about a revival in the fortunes of the tort.

2. The Indicators of Parliamentary Intent

Once it was recognised that not all statutory breaches could give rise to a private right of action, it became apparent that some 'screening mechanism' was required to separate those that did from those that did not (see *The Queen in the Right of Canada v Saskatchewan Wheat Pool* [1983] 1 SCR 205 at 217). And the end result of the fluctuating nineteenth-century case law was that the courts settled on the intention of Parliament as the determinant of whether the breach of a given legislative provision was privately actionable. In the next extracted passage, Lord Browne-Wilkinson sets out the essence of this approach.

X (Minors) v Bedfordshire County Council [1995] 2 AC 633

The facts are not relevant for the purpose of the extract.

Lord Browne-Wilkinson

The basic proposition is that in the ordinary case a breach of statutory duty does not, by itself, give rise to any private law cause of action. However, a private law cause of action will arise if it can be shown, as a matter of construction of the statute, that the statutory duty was imposed for the protection of a limited class of the public and that Parliament intended to confer on members of that class a private right of action for breach of the duty. There is no general rule by reference to which it can be decided whether a statute does create such a right of action but there are a number of indicators. If the statute provides no other remedy for its breach and the Parliamentary intention to protect a limited class is shown, that indicates that there may be a private right of action since otherwise there is no method of securing the protection the statute was intended to confer. If the statute does provide some other means of enforcing the duty that will normally indicate that the statutory right was intended to be enforceable by those means and not by private right of action: *Cutler* v. *Wandsworth Stadium Ltd* [1949] A.C. 398; *Lonrho Ltd* v. *Shell Petroleum Co. Ltd (No. 2)* [1982] A.C. 173. However, the mere existence of some other statutory remedy is not necessarily decisive. It is still possible to show that on the true construction of the statute the protected class was intended by Parliament to have a private remedy. Thus the specific duties imposed on employers in relation to factory premises are enforceable by an action for damages, notwithstanding the imposition by the statutes of criminal penalties for any breach: see *Groves v. Wimborne (Lord)* [1898] 2 Q.B. 402.

Although the question is one of statutory construction and therefore each case turns on the provisions in the relevant statute, it is significant that your Lordships were not referred to any case where it had been held that statutory provisions establishing a regulatory system or a scheme of social welfare for the benefit of the public at large had been held to give rise to a private right of action for damages for breach of statutory duty. Although regulatory or welfare legislation affecting a particular area of activity does in fact provide protection to those individuals particularly affected by that activity, the legislation is not to be treated as being passed for the benefit of those individuals but for the benefit of society in general. Thus legislation regulating the conduct of betting or prisons did not give rise to a statutory right of action vested in those adversely affected by the breach of the statutory provisions, i.e. bookmakers and prisoners: see *Cutler's* case [1949] A.C. 398; *Reg. v. Deputy Governor of Parkhurst Prison, Ex parte Hague* [1992] 1 A.C. 58. The cases where a private right of action for breach of statutory duty have been held to arise are all cases in which the statutory duty has been very limited and specific as opposed to general administrative functions imposed on public bodies and involving the exercise of administrative discretions.

COMMENTARY

As Lord Browne-Wilkinson points out in this passage, when determining Parliament's intention the courts make use of a number of 'indicators'. In the past, the classic point of departure was a dictum of Lord Tenterden in *Doe d. Murray, Bishop of Rochester v Bridges* (1831) B & Ad 847 at 859:

[W]here an Act creates an obligation, and enforces the performance in a specified manner, we take it as a general rule that performance cannot be enforced in any other manner. If the obligation is created, but no mode of enforcing its performance is ordained, the common law may, in general, find a mode suited to the particular nature of the case.

In other words, the presence of an alternative means of enforcing the statutory duty gave rise to a presumption against the recognition of a private right of action, while its absence raised a presumption in favour. This basic starting point was confirmed by the House of Lords in *Lonhro Ltd v Shell Petroleum Co Ltd* [1982] AC 173, although Lord Diplock also made clear that there were exceptions to the presumption against the actionability of penal legislation, most notably where the statute was passed to benefit a particular class of the public (as to which, see the next extracted case). Subsequently, however, the courts—perhaps motivated by a concern not to outflank the tort of negligence—moved towards a less schematised and more flexible approach, under which greater importance was attached to other considerations, such as whether the duty is merely regulatory in character and whether it expresses only a vague political aspiration, with both these factors weighing heavily against the imposition of liability (see respectively *R v Deputy Governor of Parkhurst Prison, ex p. Hague* [1992] 1 AC 58 and *O'Rourke v Camden London Borough Council* [1998] AC 188, both extracted later in this section).

In *Campbell v Peter Gordon Joiners Ltd* [2016] AC 1513, however, the Supreme Court was content to assume that the presumptions enshrined in Lord Diplock's *Lonhro* judgment remained a reliable guide, although disagreeing on how they should be applied to the facts. As Lord Toulson highlighted in his dissent at [27], in applying the relevant principles, 'the court has a choice whether to adopt a formalistic approach or to look through the artificiality and consider the function, substance and effect of the provision in real terms'. A lack of consistency in how judges approach this choice has created a situation in which the cases defy easy categorisation, and perhaps all that is possible is to give examples of cases where a private law remedy is recognised and those where it is not. Indeed, such is the difficulty of identifying any intelligible principles in this area that Lord Denning has remarked—perhaps not entirely in jest—that '[t]he dividing line between the pro-cases and the contra-cases is so blurred and so ill-defined that you might as well toss a coin to decide it' (*Ex parte Island Records Ltd* [1978] 1 Ch 122 at 135). Having said that, it is also possible to discern in the more recent case law a general tendency on the part of the courts not to recognise a private law claim, and as a result it has been argued that 'the process of detailed construction of particular legislative provisions can be generalised as based on a general presumption against the inference of the tort' (*Stanton*, para. 2.009).

Phillips v Britannia Hygienic Laundry Co Ltd [1923] 2 KB 832

By s. 6(1) of the Locomotives on Highways Act 1896, the Local Government Board was empowered to make regulations with respect to the use of light locomotives on highways, and their construction, and the conditions under which they could be used. Breach of any such regulation was punishable by fine (s. 7). Article II, cl. 6, of the Motor Cars (Use and Construction) Order 1904, made under s. 6, provided: 'The motor car and all the fittings thereof shall be in such a condition as not to cause, or to be likely to cause, danger to any person on the motor car or on any highway.'

A lorry (considered to be both a 'light locomotive' and a 'motor car' within the statutory scheme) was involved in an accident on the highway when one of its axles broke and a wheel came off, damaging the plaintiff's vehicle. It was discovered that the axle had been in a dangerously defective condition but that this was not attributable to any fault on the part of the owners of the lorry, who had recently sent it to a competent firm of mechanics to be overhauled and repaired. The plaintiff brought an action against the lorry's owners for a breach of Article II, cl. 6, of the Order. The county court's decision in favour of the plaintiff was reversed by the Divisional Court. The plaintiff appealed to the Court of Appeal.

Bankes LJ

In the case we are considering the statute creates an obligation and provides a remedy for its non-observance, and the question is whether the scope and language of the statute indicate that the general rule is to prevail so that the remedy provided is the only remedy, or whether an exception to that general rule is to be admitted . . .

The injury here was done to the appellant's van; and the appellant, a member of the public, claims a right of action as one of a class for whose benefit cl. 6 was introduced. He contends that the public using the highway is the class so favoured. I do not agree. In my view the public using the highway is not a class; it is itself the public and not a class of the public. The clause therefore was not passed for the benefit of a class or section of the public. It applies to the public generally, and it is one among many regulations for breach of which it cannot have been intended that a person aggrieved should have a civil remedy by way of action in addition to the more appropriate remedy provided, namely a fine. In my opinion therefore this case is not an exception to the general rule; that rule applies, and the appeal must be dismissed.

Atkin LJ

I am of the same opinion. This is an important question, and I have felt some doubt upon it, because it is clear that these regulations are in part designed to promote the safety of the public using highways. The question is whether they were intended to be enforced only by the special penalty attached to them in the Act. In my opinion, when an Act imposes a duty of commission or omission, the question whether a person aggrieved by a breach of the duty has a right of action depends on the intention of the Act. Was it intended to make the duty one which was owed to the party aggrieved as well as to the State, or was it a public duty only? That depends on the construction of the Act and the circumstances in which it was made and to which it relates. One question to be considered is, Does the Act contain reference to a remedy for breach of it? Prima facie if it does that is the only remedy. But that is not conclusive. The intention as disclosed by its scope and wording must still be regarded, and it may still be that, though the statute creates the duty and provides a penalty, the duty is nevertheless owed to individuals. Instances of this are *Groves v Lord Wimborne* [1898] 2 QB 402 and *Britannic Merthyr Coal Co v David* [1910] AC 74. To my mind . . . the question is not to be solved by considering whether or not the person aggrieved can bring himself within some special class of the community or whether he is some designated individual. The duty may be of such paramount importance that it is owed to all the public. It would be strange if a less important duty, which is owed to a section of the public, may be enforced by an action, while a more important duty owed to the public at large cannot. The right of action does not depend on whether a statutory commandment or prohibition is pronounced for the benefit of the public or for the benefit of a class. It may be conferred on any one who can bring himself within the benefit of the Act, including one who cannot be otherwise specified than as a person using the highway . . . Therefore the question is whether these regulations, viewed in the circumstances in which they were made and to which they relate, were intended to impose a duty which is a public duty only or whether they were intended, in addition to the public duty, to impose a duty enforceable by an individual aggrieved. I have come to the conclusion that the duty they were intended to impose was not a duty enforceable by individuals injured, but a public duty only, the sole remedy for which is the remedy provided by way of a fine. They impose obligations of various kinds, some are concerned more with the maintenance of the highway than with the safety of passengers; and they are of varying degrees of importance; yet for breach of any regulation a fine not exceeding £10 is the penalty. It is not likely that the Legislature, in empowering a department to make regulations for the use and construction of motor cars, permitted the department to impose new duties in favour of individuals and new causes of action for breach of them in addition to the obligations already well provided for and regulated by the common law of those who bring vehicles upon highways. In particular it is not likely that the Legislature intended by these means to impose on the owners of vehicles an absolute obligation to have them roadworthy in all events even in the absence of negligence. For these reasons I think the appeal should be dismissed.

Younger LJ also agreed.

Appeal dismissed.

COMMENTARY

The reasoning of Bankes LJ in particular is premised upon the classic approach whereby penal legislation gives rise to no private rights unless passed for the benefit of a particular class of the public. By insisting that road users were not a class of the public but the public itself, Bankes LJ was able to find that the basic presumption of non-actionability applied. For further discussion of the decision and its context, see *Mitchell*, pp. 196–201.

This decision may usefully be contrasted with *Groves v Lord Wimborne*. Why should industrial safety legislation give rise to a potential liability in damages while road safety legislation does not? *Atiyah* comments (p. 95):

Perhaps the court was influenced—consciously or unconsciously—by the fact that in 1923 it was still not compulsory to insure against third-party liability, and it may have shrunk from imposing a form of liability without fault on individual motorists, who might not have had the resources to meet a judgment for damages. Had this issue arisen after compulsory insurance was introduced in 1930, the result might have been different.

London Passenger Transport Board v Upson [1949] AC 155 is a rare example of a case in which road safety regulations have been held to create a cause of action in tort. The duty in question was the obligation to approach a pedestrian crossing at such a speed as to enable the vehicle to stop. Although the obligation was strict in nature, breach would in the ordinary course of events give rise to a strong inference of negligence on the part of the driver, and it is perhaps this factor which distinguishes the case from *Phillips*; the presence of a latent defect in the vehicle does not give rise to the same inference of negligence. (As the claim in breach of statutory duty succeeded in *Upson*, it was not necessary to determine whether—for the purposes of the plaintiff's alternative claim in negligence—the driver had in fact been careless. The fact that he had the lights in his favour and that his view was obstructed by the presence of a taxi unlawfully parked on the crossing produced at least some doubt on this issue.)

Another noteworthy decision is *Monk v Warbey* [1935] 1 KB 75. The plaintiff claimed damages for personal injuries sustained as the result of a collision with a car owned by the defendant. The car had been lent by the defendant to a third party without the benefit of a policy of insurance in respect of third-party risks. This was an offence under s. 35(1) of the Road Traffic Act 1930, but the Court of Appeal held that it was also actionable in tort. The duty of motor vehicle owners not to allow their vehicle to be driven by an uninsured person was introduced for the very purpose of making provision for third parties who suffered injury through negligent driving in such circumstances. And yet, according to Greer LJ, s. 35 would 'be no protection . . . if no civil remedy were available for a breach of the section' and the existence of a criminal liability would be 'a poor consolation to the injured person' (at 80–1). Nevertheless, the imposition of liability on a party who, not having personally caused any physical damage, owed no common law duty of care was later described by Williams as 'an improper type of judicial invention' ((1960) 23 MLR 233 at 259). Whatever the truth of this claim, the felt need to protect those injured by uninsured drivers led in 1946 to the insurance industry setting up a fund administered by a Motor Insurers' Bureau to provide compensation in such cases. This rendered largely obsolete the remedy recognised in *Monk v Warbey*, which in any event is of no use if the defendant lacks the means to satisfy the damages award.

The Court of Appeal declined to apply *Monk v Warbey* in the related context of legislation requiring that employers take out insurance against liabilities to their employees. In *Richardson v Pitt-Stanley* [1995] QB 123, the plaintiff had been injured in a work accident for which his employer was liable; the employer went into liquidation and was unable to satisfy the judgment. What was more, the employer had failed to comply with its obligation to insure against liability imposed by the Employers' Liability (Compulsory Insurance) Act 1969. This Act made it a criminal offence to fail to insure; the criminal liability extended to any director of the company who consented to, connived at or by neglect facilitated the company's breach of the obligation. The plaintiff brought an action against the directors for breach of the statutory duty, but the Court of Appeal held that no civil remedy arose. In the view of Stuart-Smith LJ, protection of the plaintiff's economic interests was not the sole purpose of the Act, which might equally be viewed as designed to protect the insured employer against the potentially disastrous consequences to its business of a heavy claim or loss. This reasoning was powerfully criticised in the dissenting judgment of Sir John Megaw (at 135):

> The purpose was to give protection to a particular class of individuals, the employees, to eliminate, or, at least reduce, the risk to an injured employee of finding that he was deprived of his lawful compensation because of the financial position of the employer. I am confident that it was no part of the purpose or intention of Parliament in enacting this legislation to confer a benefit or protection on the employer.

That criticism was accepted by the Supreme Court in *Campbell v Peter Gordon Joiners Ltd* [2016] AC 1513, but the majority reached the same outcome as the Court of Appeal in *Richardson* by a different route: as the obligation to insure was imposed on the company, not its directors, the latter could not be civilly liable for its breach. The Supreme Court minority found this difficult to reconcile with the provision made in the 1969 Act for the imposition of criminal penalties on directors. To Lord Toulson and Lady Hale, dissenting, the majority's approach was overly formalistic as (per Lady Hale at [48]) '[t]here can be no difference in substance between imposing criminal liability for failing to do something and imposing a duty to do it.' For them, the criminal penalties on both the company and its directors were part of an overall legislative scheme plainly intended for the protection of employees. (This final point suggests reliance on the 'spirit' of the statute when construing the scope of its private actionability, but for trenchant criticism of that idea, see Geistfeld, 'Tort Law in the Age of Statutes' (2014) 99 Iowa L Rev 957 at 979.)

For another example of a breach of statutory duty action that failed on the ground that the statute was not intended for the protection of the class of persons of which the claimant was a member, see *Cutler v Wandsworth Stadium Ltd* [1949] AC 398 (purpose of statutory provision requiring operators of dog tracks to provide space for the use of bookmakers was the regulation of dog racing and not to benefit bookmakers). And on the difficulty of reconciling the authorities on the issue, see *Winfield & Jolowicz*, para. 8–007.

R v Deputy Governor of Parkhurst Prison, ex p. Hague [1992] 1 AC 58

The plaintiff claimed that he was unlawfully segregated from other prisoners without the appropriate authorisations and, as a result, in breach of rule 43(2) of the Prison Rules 1964, and brought an action for damages relying on, inter alia, the tort of breach of statutory duty. For further extracts, see Chapter 2.VI.2.

Lord Bridge

Mr Sedley [for the plaintiff] has constructed an elaborate argument resting on a premise which he describes as 'the ground rule' for ascertaining whether a plaintiff has a cause of action for breach of statutory duty. It all depends, he submits, on whether he belongs to a class which the statutory provision was intended to protect and has suffered a detriment in consequence of a breach of the duty of a kind from which the provision was intended to protect him. If so, then in the absence of any other specific provision in the statute, such as a criminal penalty, to enforce performance of the statutory duty, it necessarily follows, Mr Sedley submits, that the law affords a remedy in damages for its breach. Hence the question of statutory construction is not the broad question whether an intention to give a cause of action can be inferred from the provision in question read in its context, but the narrower question whether the provision is intended to protect the interests of a class of which the plaintiff is a member. This then leads on to the conclusion that certain provisions of the Prison Rules 1964, which were intended to protect the interests of prisoners, and in particular rule 43(2) which was intended to protect prisoners from unlawful segregation, must give rise to a cause of action in favour of any prisoner who suffers a detriment from a breach of the duty imposed.

I believe the fallacy in this argument is that it relies on authorities relating to statutory duties imposed for no other purpose than to protect various classes of person from the risk of personal injury to which they are exposed and seeks to apply certain dicta in those authorities to a totally different statutory context. Thus *Groves v Lord Wimborne* [1898] 2 QB 402 was concerned with the question whether a breach of the duty to fence dangerous machinery imposed by section 5(4) of the Factory and Workshop Act 1878 gave a cause of action to a workman thereby injured notwithstanding the criminal sanctions also imposed by the statute for breach of the duty . . .

[L]ike any other question of statutory construction, the question whether an enactment gives rise to a cause of action for breach of statutory duty is a question of ascertaining the intention of the legislature . . . I can find nothing in rule 43 or in any context that is relevant to the construction of rule 43 which would support the conclusion that it was intended to confer a right of action on an individual prisoner. The purpose of the rule, apart from the case of prisoners who need to be segregated in their own interests, is to give an obviously necessary power to segregate prisoners who are liable for any reason to disturb the orderly conduct of the prison generally. The rule is a purely preventive measure. The power is to be exercised only in accordance with the procedure prescribed by sub-rule (2). But where the power has been exercised in good faith, albeit that the procedure followed in authorising its exercise was not in conformity with rule 43(2), it is inconceivable that the legislature intended to confer a cause of action on the segregated prisoner.

Lord Jauncey

[I]t must always be a matter for consideration whether the legislature intended that private law rights of action should be conferred upon individuals in respect of breaches of the relevant statutory provision. The fact that a particular provision was intended to protect certain individuals is not of itself sufficient to confer private law rights of action upon them, something more is required to show that the legislature intended such conferment . . .

The [Prison] rules are wide-ranging in their scope covering a mass of matters relevant to the administration and good government of a prison. Many of these do not directly relate to prisoners and I do not consider that those which do were ever intended to confer private law rights in the event of a breach. The rules are regulatory in character, they provide a framework within which the prison regime operates but they are not intended to protect prisoners against loss, injury and damage nor to give them a right of action in respect thereof. I would only add that if a prisoner suffered in health as a result of segregation contrary to the rules he would in all probability have a right of action in negligence against the prison authorities. If, as in the case of Hague, he suffered no damage to health then a breach of the rules would not result in loss or injury of the kind which normally flows from a breach of statutory duty and which the statute is designed to prevent . . .

Finally, I should emphasise that the conclusion which I have reached on this part of the appeal does not leave a prisoner without a remedy if the rules are broken to his detriment. He may complain to the governor or board of visitors under rule 8(1) and in the event of a complaint to the latter a report may be made to the Secretary of State under section 6(3) of the Act. He may also challenge any administrative decision of the Secretary of State or the governor which he considers to contravene the provisions of the Act or the rules by judicial review proceedings. In the case of a continuing wrong done to him a prisoner could expect that a hearing in judicial review proceedings could be obtained with little delay. These public law remedies are additional to any private law remedies which would be available to him such as damages for misfeasance in public office, assault or negligence.

COMMENTARY

In this case, and the next extracted case, the House of Lords was faced with statutory duties that were not reinforced by any penal sanction. Yet they declined to treat that fact as giving rise to a presumption of civil liability. These decisions therefore mark an important departure from the classic approach of Lord Tenterden in *Doe d. Murray, Bishop of Rochester v Bridges* (1831) B & Ad 847, and replace it with a more open-textured enquiry, in which significance is attached when determining Parliament's intention to a range of considerations (e.g. the regulatory character of the statute and the availability of alternative remedies). The existence of alternative public law remedies was also a decisive factor against recognition of a private right of action in *Cullen v Chief Constable of the Royal Ulster Constabulary* [2003] 1 WLR 1763, which concerned a failure to explain to a person in custody why they were being denied access to a lawyer, in breach of s. 15 of the Northern Ireland (Emergency Provisions) Act 1987.

Lord Jauncey made it clear in this case that it was not sufficient for a finding of actionability that a particular provision was intended to protect certain individuals, despite the focus on this issue in earlier case law concerning penal legislation (see especially *Phillips v Britannia Hygienic Laundry Co Ltd*, extracted earlier). Instead the focus in this case and the next extracted case is on whether there can be discerned in the legislation 'a Parliamentary intention, not merely to confer a benefit on the members of a defined class of persons, but . . . to confer enforceable private law rights . . . on such persons' (*Stanton*, para. 2.019). On this reasoning, while the fact that the provision in question is designed to benefit the public as a whole excludes the possibility of it being actionable, the converse does not hold.

O'Rourke v Camden London Borough Council [1998] AC 188

Following his release from prison, the plaintiff had nowhere to live and he applied to the defendant council for accommodation. Under s. 62 of the Housing Act 1985, local authorities were obliged, where they had reason to believe that an applicant for housing might be homeless, to make such inquiries as were necessary to satisfy themselves as to whether this was in fact the case. Pending such a determination, the authority was obliged under s. 63(1) to provide temporary accommodation if it had 'reason to believe that an applicant may be homeless and have a priority need'. The plaintiff alleged that although the defendant had agreed to make inquiries under s. 62 and had placed him in temporary hotel accommodation pending the outcome of these inquiries, it had wrongfully evicted him from the hotel after less than two weeks without offering him anywhere else to stay. He claimed damages for breach of statutory duty. The judge in the county court struck out the particulars of the claim as disclosing no reasonable cause of action. On the plaintiff's appeal, the Court of Appeal held that s. 63(1) created a private law duty sounding in damages and reinstated the claim for breach of statutory duty. The defendant appealed to the House of Lords.

Lord Hoffmann

The question is whether section 63(1) creates a duty to Mr O'Rourke which is actionable in tort. There is no doubt that, like several other provisions in Part III [sc. of the Act], it creates a duty which is enforceable by proceedings for judicial review. But whether it gives rise to a cause of action sounding in damages depends upon whether the Act shows a legislative intention to create such a remedy. In *X (Minors) v Bedfordshire County Council* [1995] 2 AC 633, 731, the principles were analysed by Lord Browne-Wilkinson in a speech with which the other members of the House agreed. He said that although there was no general rule by reference to which it could be decided that a statute created a private right of action, there were a number of 'indicators.' The indicator upon which Mr Drabble, who appeared for Mr O'Rourke, placed most reliance was the common sense proposition that a statute which appears intended for the protection of a limited class of people but provides no other remedy for breach should ordinarily be construed as intended to create a private right of action. Otherwise, as Lord Simonds said in *Cutler v Wandsworth Stadium Ltd* [1949] AC 398 at 407, 'the statute would be but a pious aspiration.'

Camden, on the other hand, says that although Part III does not expressly enact any remedy for breach, that does not mean that it would be toothless without an action for damages or an injunction in private law. It is enforceable in public law by individual homeless persons who have *locus standi* to bring proceedings for judicial review. Furthermore, there are certain contra-indications which make it unlikely that Parliament intended to create private law rights of action.

The first is that the Act is a scheme of social welfare, intended to confer benefits at the public expense on grounds of public policy. Public money is spent on housing the homeless not merely for the private benefit of people who find themselves homeless but on grounds of general public interest: because, for example, proper housing means that people will be less likely to suffer illness, turn to crime or require the attention of other social services. The expenditure interacts with expenditure on other public services such as education, the National Health Service and even the police. It is not simply a private matter between the claimant and the housing authority. Accordingly, the fact that Parliament has provided for the expenditure of public money on benefits in kind such as housing the homeless does not necessarily mean that it intended cash payments to be made by way of damages to persons who, in breach of the housing authority's statutory duty, have unfortunately not received the benefits which they should have done . . .

A second contra-indication is that Part III of the Act of 1985 makes the existence of the duty to provide accommodation dependent upon a good deal of judgment on the part of the housing authority. The duty to inquire under section 62(1) arises if the housing authority 'have reason to believe' that the applicant may be homeless and the inquiries must be such as are 'necessary to satisfy themselves' as to whether he is homeless, whether he has a priority need and whether he became homeless intentionally. When the investigations are complete, the various duties under section 65 of the Act arise only if the authority are 'satisfied' that the applicant is homeless and the extent of those duties depends upon whether or not they are 'satisfied' as to two other matters, namely that he has a priority need and that he became homeless intentionally. If a duty does arise, the authority has a wide discretion in deciding how to provide accommodation and what kind of accommodation it will provide. The existence of all these discretions makes it unlikely that Parliament intended errors of judgment to give rise to an obligation to make financial reparation. Control by public law remedies would appear much more appropriate . . .

[While reserving his position on whether subsequent developments in judicial review procedure could be taken into account in this regard, Lord Hoffmann proceeded to consider the adequacy of public law remedies available for breach of the Housing (Homeless Persons) Act 1977 at the time it was enacted and concluded that:]

[T]he existing procedure was in most cases adequate to provide a swift remedy for a homeless person complaining of breach of duty. Lord Diplock said in *O'Reilly v Mackman* [1983] 2 AC 237 at 281 that:

> as [the old] Order 53 was applied in practice, as soon as the application for leave had been made it provided a very speedy means, available in urgent cases within a matter of days rather than months, for determining whether a disputed decision was valid in law or not.

Accordingly there is in my view no reason to construe the Act of 1977 on the assumption that in the absence of a remedy in damages, it would at the time it was enacted have been no more than 'a pious aspiration.' The machinery for enforcing it was in place . . .

I would therefore hold that the breach of statutory duty of which the plaintiff complains gives rise to no cause of action in private law and I would allow the appeal . . .

Lord Goff, **Lord Mustill**, **Lord Nicholls** and **Lord Steyn** concurred.

Appeal allowed.

COMMENTARY

In *O'Rourke*, the House of Lords overruled *Thornton v Kirklees Metropolitan Borough Council* [1979] QB 626, in which the Court of Appeal had held that the forerunners of the provisions considered in the present case, contained in the Housing (Homeless Persons) Act 1977, *did* give rise to a private law remedy.

Lord Hoffmann cited with approval the statement of Lord Browne-Wilkinson in *X (Minors) v Bedfordshire County Council* [1995] 2 AC 633 (extracted earlier) that even where regulatory or welfare legislation provides protection to certain individuals, it is not to be treated as being passed for their benefit but for the benefit of society in general. In both *X v Bedfordshire CC* and *O'Rourke*, the question of whether the statute in question was passed for the benefit of a section of the public was apparently posed as a preliminary to *any* successful action for breach of statutory duty, rather than being used to warrant an exception to the general non-actionability of penal legislation (as was assumed to be its role in, e.g., *Groves v Lord Wimborne* and *Phillips v Britannia Laundry*, extracted earlier). More recently, this approach has been applied in the context of legislation relating to the court service (*St John Poulton's Trustee in Bankruptcy v Ministry of Justice* [2011] Ch 1: failure to send notice of bankruptcy petition to land registry) and utility providers (*Morrison Sports Ltd v Scottish Power UK plc* [2010] 1 WLR 1934: fire caused by faulty electricity meter). The latter case is especially notable because the statute expressly contemplated that regulations issued under it might be designed to reduce the risk of personal injury and property damage, but the Supreme Court nevertheless ruled that the duties in question were of a general public character, and not intended to benefit a particular class of person.

Another noteworthy feature of both *X v Bedfordshire CC* and *O'Rourke* is the reluctance of the courts to attach private law liability to breach of a statutory duty which is imposed on a public authority but at the same time attended by considerable discretion as to the manner of its exercise. In *X v Bedfordshire CC*, for example, the duties of local authorities to protect children in their area from abuse were held not to be actionable in private law, with one of the reasons for this conclusion being that the decisions pursuant to these duties were highly sensitive and might have to be made as a matter of urgency in the absence of all the evidence. In these circumstances the House of Lords considered that it was unlikely that Parliament had intended that such decisions could give rise to tort liability, even if it were established in a particular case that an improper exercise of the discretion amounted to a breach of the relevant duty.

The restrictive approach taken in cases like *X v Bedfordshire CC* and *O'Rourke* greatly curtails the scope for breach of statutory duty claims relating to the exercise by public authorities of their statutory obligations. (See also *Phelps v Hillingdon London Borough Council* [2001] 2 AC 619, concerning provision of education.) Drawing a parallel with the liability of public authorities for common law negligence, the authors of *Stanton*, para. 14.004, comment:

> It has been argued that the use of the construction approach in this way has the underlying purpose of protecting discretionary decisions of public bodies from attack by way of a claim for damages. It certainly has this effect and, although it operates on a different set of criteria, is closely related to the controls which limit the use of negligence as a damages remedy against bodies which exercise statutory functions. The effective result in relation to both torts is that decisions as to the appropriate allocation of resources made in the exercise of a discretion conferred by statute rarely, if ever, give rise to claims for damages in private law proceedings.

3. The Scope of Protection

Even if it is concluded that Parliament did intend the statute to be privately actionable, it must also be shown that the claim in question falls within the scope of the statute's protection, that is, that the claimant is a member of the class that the legislation was intended to benefit, and that they suffered an injury of the type that it was intended to guard against.

Gorris v Scott (1874) LR 9 Exch 125

The defendant shipowner agreed to transport the claimant's sheep from Hamburg to Newcastle. The sheep were carried on the deck of the ship and during a storm many of them were washed overboard and lost. The claimant sued the defendant, relying on the breach of an order made by the Privy Council in pursuance of the Contagious Diseases (Animals) Act 1869. This order required that when sheep or cattle were brought to Britain by sea the place on the ship occupied by the animals must be divided into pens of certain dimensions and the floors of these pens furnished with battens or footholds. The purpose of the Act was to prevent animals with an infectious disease from passing it to other animals, and the purpose of the order was to avoid overcrowding which might hasten the spread of disease. It was assumed, for the purposes of a demurrer (an application to strike out the claim) that if the defendant had complied with the order, the sheep would not have been lost.

Kelly CB

[I]f we could see that it was the object, or among the objects of this Act, that the owners of sheep and cattle coming from a foreign port should be protected by the means described against the danger of their property being washed overboard, or lost by the perils of the sea, the present action would be within the principle. But, looking at the Act, it is perfectly clear that its provisions were all enacted with a totally different view; there was no purpose, direct or indirect, to protect against such damage; but, as is recited in the preamble, the Act is directed against the possibility of sheep or cattle being exposed to disease on their way to this country. The preamble recites that 'it is expedient to confer on Her Majesty's most honourable Privy Council power to take such measures as may appear from time to time necessary to prevent the introduction into Great Britain of contagious or infectious diseases among cattle, sheep, or other animals, by prohibiting or regulating the importation of foreign animals,' and also to provide against the 'spreading' of such diseases in Great Britain. Then follow numerous sections directed entirely to this object. Then comes s. 75, which enacts that 'the Privy Council may from time to time make such orders as they think expedient for all or any of the following purposes.' What, then, are these purposes? They are 'for securing for animals brought by sea to ports in Great Britain a proper supply of food and water during the passage and on landing,' 'for protecting such animals from unnecessary suffering during the passage and on landing,' and so forth; all the purposes enumerated being calculated and directed to the prevention of disease, and none of them having any relation whatever to the danger of loss by the perils of the sea. That being so, if by reason of the default in question the plaintiffs' sheep had been overcrowded, or had been caused unnecessary suffering, and so had arrived in this country in a state of disease, I do not say that they might not have maintained this action. But the damage complained of here is something totally apart from the object of the Act of Parliament, and it is in accordance with all the authorities to say that the action is not maintainable.

Pigott, **Pollock** and **Amphlett BB** concurred.

COMMENTARY

This decision establishes that a breach of statutory duty action will fail unless one of the purposes of the legislative provision that has been violated was to protect against the kind of damage or loss for which the action is brought. The operation of this principle is also illustrated by *Fytche v Wincanton Logistics plc* [2004] ICR 975, where an employee who suffered frostbite in his toes as a result of his employer's failure to comply with a statutory duty to provide him with steel-capped boots was denied damages on the ground that the duty was aimed at the risk of damage by crushing, not cold. (The same principle also applies in US 'statutory negligence' law: see, e.g., *Boronkay v Robinson & Carpenter* (1928) 160 NE 400, where it was held that the parking of a coal truck on the left hand side of the road in violation of a traffic law did not give rise to liability for the death of a child thrown under the truck's wheels by a hook and chain on its side as the purpose of the law was simply to facilitate the safe passage of others along the highway.)

In *Donaghey v Boulton & Paul Ltd* [1968] AC 1, the House of Lords held that a breach of regulations requiring the use of crawling boards on 'roofs ... covered with fragile materials through which a person is liable to fall a distance of more than 10 feet' was actionable in damages despite the fact that the plaintiff had fallen, not through the fragile material, but a hole in the roof. *Gorris* was distinguished on the basis that the plaintiff had been injured in the kind of accident, namely a fall from the roof, at which the regulation in question was directed. Lord Reid explained (at 26):

> It is one thing to say that if the damage suffered is of a kind totally different from that which it is the object of the regulation to prevent, there is no civil liability. But it is quite a different thing to say that civil liability is excluded because the damage, though precisely of the kind which the regulation was designed to prevent, happened in a way not contemplated by the maker of the regulation.

His Lordship thought that the principles were analogous to those of remoteness of damage in the tort of negligence where it is accepted that, provided that harm of the type that occurred was foreseeable, it is immaterial that the precise way in which the harm came about was not (see Ch. 5.III.1).

The parallel requirement that the claimant must be a member of the class that the statute was intended to benefit has proved significant in a number of industrial injury cases. In *Hartley v Mayoh & Co* [1954] 1 QB 383, for example, the Court of Appeal ruled that a fire officer attending a fire in factory premises, and who was fatally electrocuted because of a wiring fault, was not a 'person employed' intended to be protected by the applicable regulations. Conversely, the same term (in other regulations) has been held to extend to a driver visiting the defendant's factory to collect material bought by his employer (*McDonald v National Grid Electricity Transmission Plc* [2015] AC 1128) and indeed any person working in a factory, no matter who the employer (*Massey-Harris-Ferguson v Piper* [1956] 2 QB 396). Another case that illustrates this requirement is *Knapp v Railway Executive* [1949] 2 All ER 508, where it was held that the duty to keep the gates of a railway level-crossing in the proper position was for the protection of those using the crossing, and not the drivers of trains.

4. Evaluation and Reform

We saw at the outset of this section that the practical importance of the tort of breach of statutory duty has been significantly reduced by the 2013 reforms that have emasculated it in the one context where it had previously made a real difference, namely workplace health and safety. In other areas, the clear tendency of the courts over the course of the last forty years or so has been to limit the scope of the tort's operation, partly, one suspects, out of concern that it might serve to outflank the restrictions placed on negligence liability over the same period, but perhaps also reflecting a more general trend away from strict liability, as shown, for example, by the post-war demise of the rule in *Rylands v Fletcher* as a cause of action of more than theoretical significance (see Ch. 11.III).

Matters are not helped by the fact that the governing test of legislative intention is thoroughly discredited. According to the Supreme Court of Canada in *The Queen in the Right of Canada v Saskatchewan Wheat Pool* [1983] 1 SCR 205 at 211:

> The uncertainty and confusion in the relation between breach of statute and a civil cause of action for damages arising from the breach is of long standing. The commentators have little but harsh words for the unhappy state of affairs, but arriving at a solution, from the disarray of cases, is extraordinarily difficult. It is doubtful that any general principle or rationale can be found in the authorities to resolve all of the issues or even those which are transcendent.

These criticisms apply with equal force to the tort of breach of statutory duty in English law. The judicial method of looking for indicators of Parliament's presumed intent has produced results that are arbitrary and inconsistent, and is premised upon the fiction that Parliament has really turned its mind to the civil actionability of all the statutes it passes. If Parliament had actually done so, would it not have been easy for it also to have stated clearly what its intention was? In the next extract some of the difficulties with the Parliamentary intention test are exposed.

E. Alexander, 'Legislation and the Standard of Care in Negligence' (1964) 42 Can Bar Rev 243

The main objection to courts manufacturing nonexistent legislative intentions is the difficulty of discovering the bases on which they either find or refuse to find these fictional intentions. The courts would like to blame the legislatures for this difficulty . . .

The search for a fictional legislative intention to confer civil causes of action impels the courts to pretend that the legislatures control the effect of legislation on civil liability. In reality of course, the courts control the effect of legislation on civil liability, where the legislature is silent on the civil consequences of a breach of statute. The pretence is taken for reality, however, and a number of consequences usually follow a court's discovery of the fictional legislative intention to confer civil causes of action: the plaintiff is considered to have an action on the statute; the persons who can complain of a breach of the statute, and the kind of harm against which they can claim protection, are considered to depend on the intention of the legislature; whether the statute imposes strict liability is also considered to depend on the intention of the legislature.

COMMENTARY

Alexander concludes that the courts should discard their search for an elusive legislative intention, a view that is widely shared (a 'barefaced fiction': *Fleming*, p. 205). For example, in an influential early article on the topic (extracted next), Thayer, 'Public Wrong and Private Action' (1914) 27 Harv L Rev 317 at 320, argued that the courts should ascertain the legislature's expressed intent but 'refrain from conjecture as to its unexpressed intent', with the tendency to such speculation being 'responsible for much of the confusion in the law'. And the authors of a contemporary English work on legislative torts state that the techniques used by the courts to determine the actionability of statutory breaches 'are generally viewed as inadequate and as liable to lead to arbitrary results' (*Stanton*, para. 1.009; see also *Winfield & Jolowicz*, para. 8–015). Perhaps the only possible defence for the approach adopted is that over time the presumptions used by the courts should make whether a legislative intent will be inferred predictable, in which case Parliament can then anticipate outcomes it dislikes and forestall them by express provision (Fricke, 'The Action upon the Statute' (1960) 76 LQR 240 at 264), but this arguably over-estimates both the predictive qualities of the presumptions employed and Parliament's appetite for such second-guessing of the courts.

A solution to the problem of the fictional search for legislative intent which was suggested by the Law Commission in the late 1960s was a statutory presumption of actionability, the effect of which would have been that a breach of a statutory duty would sound in damages unless the statute said otherwise (*The Interpretation of Statutes* (Law Com. No. 21, 1969), para. 38). However, this proposal garnered little support in Parliament and has been described as 'a briefly argued recommendation which paid little attention to the areas in which the presumption might operate' (*Stanton*, para. 2–041). Other objections which have been made to this kind of statutory presumption are that it might lead to liability being imposed in circumstances that were simply unforeseen by Parliament and that it would not have any bearing on the private actionability of earlier legislation, which would still have to be addressed by the application of common law principles (see further Buckley, 'Liability in Tort for Breach of Statutory Duty' (1984) 100 LQR 204 at 231–2). An alternative solution would be to generalise the approach that now applies in the workplace health and safety context, so that breach of a given duty would be non-actionable unless the statute in question expressly said otherwise. A statutory presumption to this effect would surely be the final nail in the coffin of the tort as a cause of action of practical significance. (For other possible ways of modifying the current approach to give more coherence and predictability to the law, see *Stanton*, paras 2.040–2.041.)

That raises the question of whether, given that the tort of negligence already imposes a generalised liability for damage caused by fault, it is really necessary to have a separate cause of action for breach of statutory duty. An alternative favoured by some commentators is to treat a breach of a statutory duty as 'statutory negligence', giving rise to liability only where there is a common law duty of care but providing in such cases that the statutory breach is conclusive as to fault (or 'negligence *per se*'). This is the dominant approach in the United States, and in the following extracts two American commentators respectively defend and critique this doctrine, by comparison with the rival view according to which statutory breaches are merely evidence of negligence.

E. Thayer, 'Public Wrong and Private Action' (1914) 27 Harv L Rev 317

The doctrine that a breach of the law is 'evidence of negligence' is in truth perplexing and difficult of comprehension . . . [T]o invite the jury [in modern English law, the judge] to consider when and to what extent it is reasonable to break the law is a strange thing. The prudent man, it seems, is a law-abiding person within limits, but he does not carry his respect for law to extremes. What tests or considerations are to guide the jury in determining when he may reasonably become lawless? The proposition that his breach of law is 'prima facie evidence' of negligence helps but little, for the very statement implies that the prima facie impropriety may be rebutted. If so, what will rebut it? The doctrine in any form puts the court in an unsuitable attitude toward the legislature . . .

[Thayer proceeds to argue in favour of the negligence *per se* approach, illustrating his argument by reference to a hypothetical ordinance making it a criminal offence to leave a horse unhitched on the highway:]

The ordinance has foreclosed the question whether an unhitched horse is a dangerous thing, not because it was passed with any specific reference to civil suits, but because the state, through its legislative organs, has condemned the act of leaving him unhitched by reason of its tendency to bring about just such harm as this. This can only mean that the act is labelled 'dangerous'. It is an unjust reproach to our old friend the ordinary prudent man to suppose that he would do such a thing in the teeth of the ordinance. It would mean changing his nature, and giving over the very traits which brought him into existence. And when by so doing he caused the very harm which the ordinance aimed to prevent, he would be the first to admit that he should break the ordinance at his peril.

C. Morris, 'The Role of Criminal Statutes in Negligence Actions' (1949) 49 Col L Rev 21

The Doctrine of Negligence Per Se

In most jurisdictions the courts, once they find a duty of due care, follow the doctrine of negligence per se and hold that violation of a criminal statute is conclusive of breach of that duty.

Thayer viewed this as merely substituting a 'new and exacter standard' for looser methods of trial—a minor variation in procedure. But in some cases if the law is changed so that the issue of breach of duty is measured by the criminal proscription instead of by the reasonably-prudent-man formula the new practice will result in novel civil liability—that may or may not be wise.

[Morris then gives a hypothetical example involving a car owner who leaves their vehicle unlocked in a public place. The vehicle is stolen and the thief runs over a pedestrian. Although he concedes that liability is possible here in negligence, he says it is unlikely 'without proof of special risk of theft'. He continues:]

A case like our hypothetical one was litigated recently—with one significant additional factor: leaving an unlocked car in a public place had been made a [criminal offence]. The pedestrian was awarded damages. This liability is novel; it is not only a minor procedural change from an indefinite to a more exact standard. The test for criminal responsibility is calculated to require more care than the reasonably prudent man would exercise before the enactment of the ordinance in at least some circumstances.

When criminal legislation imposes punishment in the absence of fault, use of the statutory proscription as a new and more exact standard for judging negligence transforms liability-only-for-fault into liability-without-fault. . . .

Often, of course, the violator of a criminal statute is guilty of sufficient fault for liability. In many instances Thayer's analysis is the correct one—the substitution of the criminal proscription for the reasonably-prudent-man formula is the use of a more exact standard to accomplish with greater smoothness the results that the common law had always tried to reach. But even though the criminal proscription normally is a good test of negligence, if it is used inflexibly in all cases it may produce some untoward results. The doctrine of negligence per se purports to rob the judge of judicial functions. It places responsibilities on a legislature that could not possibly conceive of all cases to which its proscription might apply and that has not provided for civil liability, and that, therefore, surely has not considered proper limitations and excuses. At times violation of the criminal law is not unreasonable. If the doctrine of negligence per se is applied obdurately to reasonable violators their liability can be justified only on some basis other than fault—if at all.

COMMENTARY

The statutory negligence approach can result in the imposition of liability only where the common law recognises a duty of care. Familiar limitations on the scope of the duty of care, for example, in respect of omissions or pure economic loss, may therefore preclude the imposition of liability for statutory negligence in appropriate cases. An example given by Thayer was of a statute requiring occupiers to remove snow and ice from the pavement outside their premises: if a pedestrian injured as a result of the occupier's failure to perform his duty should sue, 'he will make no headway by the aid of common-law principles' (at 329).

One perceived advantage of the statutory negligence approach is that it reduces complexity by relying upon a single principle of liability, namely, negligence. Treating breach of statutory duty as a separate tort arguably superimposes a second principle of liability for which there is no demonstrated need, and, worse, invites claimants to seek to side-step limitations on liability in negligence on the basis not of properly weighed policy arguments but of a fictitious Parliamentary intent. Recent experience suggests that such claims are likely to meet with little success (see especially *X v Bedfordshire CC*, discussed earlier) but it might be thought that the law should not even hold out the possibility of succeeding and thereby encourage claimants to waste their time, money and effort. Of course, this is not to say that the boundaries of liability in negligence ought not themselves to be extended; only that they should not be circumvented by a spurious appeal to the legislative will. Conversely, Stanton ((2004) 120 LQR 324 at 333) has defended the continued existence of an independent tort, arguing that:

The imperialistic nature of the tort of negligence has swamped and distorted too many areas of tort and, in doing so, has threatened to deprive tort of important techniques. To place breach of statutory duty in a negligence framework would impose a range of characteristics upon it.

The most obvious problem would be that the general irrecoverability of pure economic loss would come into play . . . A significant number of the most important traditional breach of statutory duty cases deal with this form of loss and it is notable that nothing is made of this fact in the judgments.

(It should be noted that while there is no doubt that recovery of pure economic loss is easier in claims for breach of statutory duty than it is in negligence, the courts have sometimes taken into account the nature of the damage when determining whether Parliament intended breach of a given statutory provision to be actionable: see *Winfield & Jolowicz*, para. 8–012.)

If cases involving a breach of statutory duty are to be dealt with as a species of negligence, then should the violation of the legislative norm be treated as conclusive of negligence or merely as possible evidence of it? The former solution (the doctrine of 'negligence *per se*') is open to several objections, some of which are put by Morris in his article. First, it may result in the imposition of a very large liability in damages in respect of a very minor infringement of a statute, for which the penalty might only be a small fine. Secondly, it makes no distinction between criminal prohibitions aimed at dangerous conduct and those which deal not with health and safety but, for example, with questions of public order or good government. For this reason (amongst others) it may be necessary to fall back upon an investigation of Parliament's intent, with all the problems that entails, in order to determine the mischief at which the statute was aimed. (More generally, the sheer volume of regulatory instruments in the modern era might be thought to pose problems for the negligence *per se* doctrine.) Lastly, the doctrine will frequently result in strict liability, depending upon the construction of the statute in question, and yet it provides no principled justification for the imposition of liability without proof of fault; in any case, it seems likely that the specification of statutory duties in strict or absolute terms owes less to principle or policy than to legislative happenstance.

The perceived defects in the negligence *per se* approach have led a number of US jurisdictions to treat breach of statutory duty as merely evidence of negligence, and this is also the approach adopted in Canada, where the Supreme Court rejected both negligence *per se* and a freestanding tort of breach of statutory duty in *The Queen in the Right of Canada v Saskatchewan Wheat Pool* [1983] 1 SCR 205. This approach has the benefit of greater flexibility, and does not entail the imposition of liability in the absence of fault (as in the unavoidable accident cases considered earlier). As breach of a statutory norm is already evidence of negligence (see *Winfield & Jolowicz*, para. 6–030) it involves abolishing the tort of breach of statutory duty and instead simply applying ordinary negligence principles, as is now done in workplace health and safety cases following the 2013 reforms. Amongst proponents of this approach on this side of the Atlantic stands the notable figure of Glanville Williams ('The Effect of Penal Legislation in the Law of Tort' (1960) 23 MLR 233); more recently, it has been endorsed by Davis, 'Farewell to the Action for 'Breach of Statutory Duty' in N. J. Mullany and A. M. Linden (eds), *Torts Tomorrow: A Tribute to John Fleming* (Sydney: LBC Information Services, 1998); and Nolan, 'Tort and Regulation', in J. Goudkamp, M. Lunney and L. McDonald (eds), *Taking Law Seriously: Essays in Honour of Peter Cane* (Oxford: Hart, 2022).

Which do *you* think is the best approach to determining the relevance of the breach of a statutory duty to the imposition of liability in tort?

11 NUISANCE AND THE RULE IN *RYLANDS V FLETCHER*

One of the oldest actions known to the common law is the action for nuisance. Its foundation can be traced to the twelfth century, to the establishment of the Assize of Nuisance. The origins of the modern tort of private nuisance are, however, found in the development of the action on the case for nuisance. As has been noted previously, this form of action required the claimant to show some damage before the cause of action was complete. The damage in the action on the case for nuisance was primarily damage to land, which included not only damage to the land itself and any buildings on it, but also damage to other things affixed to the land (e.g. trees or crops) as well as damage to the amenity value of the land (e.g. interference with the enjoyment of the land through sound, smell, vibrations, etc.). These various aspects of the interests protected by the tort of nuisance are explained in *St Helens Smelting Co v Tipping* (extracted later); however, the protection of amenity interests should not confuse one into thinking that nuisance protects personal as opposed to proprietary or possessory interests in land, a point made clear by a majority of the House of Lords in *Hunter v Canary Wharf* [1997] AC 655 (extracted in II.4).

The nuisance action takes two forms in modern law: public and private nuisance. Most of this chapter is concerned with the tort of private nuisance. Public nuisance is a crime, the prosecution of which is usually left to public bodies acting under statutory powers. Nonetheless, a private individual may sue for a public nuisance where they have suffered special damage, that is, damage over and above the damage suffered by the public at large.

To succeed in an action for private nuisance, the claimant must establish both that the interference with their use and enjoyment of their land is of a kind that is actionable in nuisance, and that the particular interference is unreasonable. In practice, most nuisance cases are concerned with the latter issue. What constitutes an unreasonable interference in this context is a question of fact, and is determined in the light of various factors which will be considered later in the chapter. Another question that arises is the question of fault. Does the finding that the defendant is liable for an unreasonable interference with the claimant's use and enjoyment of land mean that they are at fault? If so, what is the difference between negligence and nuisance? This question of fault is connected to another issue, which is when a person who has not themselves created a nuisance can nevertheless be liable for it.

A claimant in an action for nuisance can claim one of two remedies: damages or an injunction. In deciding whether to accede to the claimant's request for an injunction, can, or should, a court take into account the public benefit of the defendant's conduct? This question raises some fundamental issues about the interplay between public policy and private rights, for if the activity benefits the public it is poor policy to stop it, but if an activity which amounts to a nuisance is allowed to continue for this reason the claimant's private right has been expropriated in the public interest. The interplay, and possible tension, between private rights and the public interest is also observable when it comes to the relationship between tort law and planning and regulatory law, which is an important feature of the modern law of nuisance. Additional complexities arise out of the relationship between the principles of common law nuisance and the right to respect for private and family life in Article 8 of the ECHR, as incorporated into domestic law by the Human Rights Act 1998.

It is important to note at the outset that many public and private nuisances can today be remedied by a local authority issuing an abatement notice under the Environmental Protection Act 1990. Such a notice may be issued where a 'statutory nuisance' exists. Section 79(1) of the Act sets out a number of matters that may be deemed to be statutory nuisances provided they are in such a state or condition as to be prejudicial to health or a nuisance (with 'nuisance' here meaning a private or public nuisance at common law). The matters include the state of the premises, smoke, fumes/gases from private dwellings, industrial dust or pollution, accumulations and deposits, animals and noise. Failure to comply with an abatement notice without reasonable excuse is an offence, although there is provision for an appeal. For more detail on statutory nuisances, see R. Malcolm and J. Pointing, *Statutory Nuisance: Law and Practice*, 2nd edn (Oxford: OUP, 2011). There are also a number of environmental statutes (e.g. the Clean Air Act 1993) which regulate conduct that might amount to a nuisance. For further discussion, see J. Murphy, *The Law of Nuisance* (Oxford: OUP, 2010), ch. 8.

1. Public and Private Nuisance

At the outset of any discussion of nuisance, it is important to distinguish between private and public nuisance. Private nuisance, which is a tort, protects an occupier's right to use and enjoy their land free from unreasonable interferences. Public nuisance is a broad principle of criminal liability. A public nuisance can be defined as an act or omission that endangers the life, health, property or comfort of the public, or obstructs the public in the exercise or enjoyment of rights common to all Her Majesty's subjects (see *Archbold: Criminal Pleading, Evidence and Practice* (2021 edn, paras 31–40)). As the Court of Appeal pointed out in *In re Corby Group Litigation* [2009] QB 335, the two forms of nuisance are quite different; in particular, public nuisance is not limited to conduct interfering with the enjoyment of land, but encompasses a broad range of conduct endangering the life, safety and health of the public, which gives it a potentially greater scope of application (e.g. in the protection of the environment: see Parpworth, 'Public Nuisance in the environmental context' (2009) 11 *Journal of Planning and Environmental Law* 1526).

Because public nuisance is a crime, primary responsibility for enforcement lies with public officers or bodies, such as the Attorney General or local councils. The primary penalty for the offence is a fine, although where the public nuisance is ongoing the Attorney General can bring an action for an injunction to put a stop to it, either on his own initiative or at the request of a member of the public (this latter is called a 'relator action'), as can a local authority which considers it 'expedient for the promotion or protection of the interests of the inhabitants of their area' (Local Government Act 1972, s. 222).

Whilst the criminal aspects of public nuisance are beyond the scope of this book (for more detail see *Simplification of Criminal Law: Public Nuisance and Outraging Public*

Decency (Law Com. No. 358, 2015), which recommends wholesale reform of the crime), public nuisance is significant for our purposes because it may also give rise to civil liability in specified circumstances. In particular, a private individual who has suffered special damage over and above that suffered by the public generally as a result of a public nuisance may recover damages for this loss. Although the precise meaning of 'special damage' is difficult to pin down, it includes personal injury, property damage and interference with a private right, and more generally encompasses cases where the claimant suffers a kind of damage different from that suffered by the public in general (see *Oliphant*, paras 22.81–3). It follows that where the public nuisance takes the form of an obstruction of the highway, an owner of premises fronting onto the highway would have standing to sue if, for example, the obstruction interfered with their private right of access to their premises, or if it diminished the value of their property.

The differences between private and public nuisance are considered further in the following extract.

Attorney General v PYA Quarries Ltd [1957] 2 QB 169

An injunction was granted against the defendant in respect of its quarrying operations. It made improvements to the system of blasting, and then appealed against the original order on the basis that the remaining dust and vibrations caused as a result of its operations did not warrant the continuance of the injunction. It was argued that the trial judge had not distinguished between private and public nuisance and that the dust and vibration only amounted to a private nuisance remediable in damages and not a public nuisance for which the Attorney General could seek an injunction. In the course of his judgment, Denning LJ considered the difference between public and private nuisance.

Denning LJ

The classic statement of the difference [between private and public nuisance] is that a public nuisance affects Her Majesty's subjects generally, whereas a private nuisance only affects particular individuals. But this does not help much. The question, 'When do a number of individuals become Her Majesty's subjects generally?' is as difficult to answer as the question 'When does a group of people become a crowd?' Everyone has his own views. Even the answer 'Two's company, three's a crowd' will not command the assent of those present unless they first agree on 'which two'. So here I decline to answer the question how many people are necessary to make up Her Majesty's subjects generally. I prefer to look to the reason of the thing and to say that a public nuisance is a nuisance which is so widespread in its range or so indiscriminate in its effect that it would not be reasonable to expect one person to take proceedings on his own responsibility to put a stop to it, but that it should be taken on the responsibility of the community at large.

Take the blocking up of a public highway or the non-repair of it. It may be a footpath very little used except by one or two householders. Nevertheless, the obstruction affects everyone indiscriminately who may wish to walk along it. Take next a landowner who collects pestilential rubbish near a village . . . The householders nearest to it suffer the most, but everyone in the neighbourhood suffers too. In such cases the Attorney-General can take proceedings for an injunction to restrain the nuisance: and when he does so he acts in defence of the public right, not for any sectional interest. . . . But when the nuisance is so concentrated that only two or three property owners are affected by it . . . then they ought to take proceedings on their own account to stop it and not expect the community to do it for them. . . .

> Applying this test, I am clearly of opinion that the nuisance by stones, vibration and dust in this case was at the date of the writ so widespread in its range and so indiscriminate in its effect that it was a public nuisance.
>
> *Appeal dismissed.*

COMMENTARY

In *R v Rimmington; R v Goldstein* [2006] 1 AC 459 Lord Rodger doubted, at least in the criminal context, whether it was satisfactory to seek to identify a public nuisance by asking whether the nuisance was so widespread that it would not be reasonable to expect one person to take proceedings to put a stop to it. In his opinion (at [44]), 'it has remained an essential characteristic of a public nuisance that it affects the community, members of the public as a whole, rather than merely individuals' (see further Pointing, 'Public Nuisance: Beyond Highway 61 Revisited?' (2011) 13 Env L Rev 25). As the 'community' is not a legal entity, however, it is hard to see how damage to the community can be established independently of the number of people in that community who are affected. So how many members of the community must be affected to constitute a nuisance to the public as a whole? In *Gillingham Borough Council v Medway (Chatham) Dock Co Ltd* [1993] QB 343 the defendants had been granted planning permission by the plaintiff to operate a commercial port in the area formerly used as naval dockyards. As a consequence, the access road to the dock was used twenty-four hours a day, with the result that the residents of two nearby roads were adversely affected. It was conceded by the defendant's counsel that the conduct, if it was a nuisance, affected a sufficient number of people to be classed as a public nuisance. See also *East Dorset District Council v Eaglebeam Ltd* [2006] EWHC 2378 (QB) where a nuisance affecting a 'substantial' number of houses was held to be a public nuisance.

A public nuisance is established when 'the reasonable comfort and convenience of life of a class of Her Majesty's subjects' are affected by the activity in question. It should be noted, however, that the same activity may give rise to a claim in private nuisance as interfering with each individual's use and enjoyment of their land. This is so even where a separate claim in public nuisance for special damage is available. In *Halsey v Esso Petroleum* [1961] 1 WLR 683 the plaintiff complained of, amongst other things, the noise that resulted from lorries entering and exiting the defendant's refinery. Veale J held that the plaintiff had a claim for private nuisance, as he was not complaining of interference with his right to use the highway (a public right) but of interference with the use and enjoyment of his property. Such interference may also amount to a public nuisance for which the claimant can sue—see not only *Halsey* but also *Attorney General v Gastonia Coaches* [1977] RTR 219 and *Vanderpant v Mayfair Hotels* [1930] 1 Ch 138—so in practice it may not matter which cause of action the claimant uses, although public nuisance may offer some advantages. In particular, whereas standing to sue in private nuisance is limited to those with an interest in the land affected, and claims for personal injury are not permitted (see *Hunter v Canary Wharf Ltd*, extracted in II.4), neither of these limitations applies to claims in public nuisance (see *In re Corby Group Litigation*).

The differences between claims for damages in public and private nuisance are illustrated by *Tate & Lyle Industries v GLC* [1983] 2 AC 509. The defendants erected ferry terminals in the River Thames, as a result of which parts of the river bed silted up. The plaintiffs had built a jetty into the river, but the silting meant that large vessels were unable to access the jetty, and the plaintiffs were put to the expense of carrying out dredging operations to resolve this. The plaintiffs' claims in negligence and private nuisance failed because the alteration to the depth of the water had not threatened to cause damage to their property or interfered with their riparian rights. However, they succeeded in public nuisance because the defendant's activities had interfered with the public right of navigation enjoyed by all users of the river and the cost of the dredging work amounted to special damage (see also *Jan de Nul (UK) Ltd v Axa Royale Belge* [2002] 1 Lloyd's Rep 583).

The private action for public nuisance is a strange beast, and may be best thought of as a historical accident, perhaps even born of the shared language of the crime of public nuisance and the tort of private nuisance. Neyers ('Reconceptualising the Tort of Public Nuisance' [2017] CLJ 87) maintains otherwise, arguing that what he calls 'the tort of public nuisance' is a mechanism for recognising privately actionable rights to pass and repass along public highways and to fish in public waters. This analysis of the tort claim for public nuisance is consistent with the origins of the action, which lie in interferences with public rights of way, or 'purprestures' (see Spencer, 'Public Nuisance—A Critical Examination' [1989] CLJ 55), but whether it serves to explain the modern tort, which goes well beyond interferences with such public rights, is another matter.

II. Private Nuisance

1. The Nature of Private Nuisance

Williams v Network Rail Infrastructure Ltd [2019] QB 601

The claimants' bungalows backed onto a railway embankment owned by the defendant ('NR'), on which there was a large stand of Japanese knotweed, an invasive weed that can cause structural damage and which is very hard to eliminate. There was evidence that underground stems of the weed ('rhizomes') had infiltrated the foundations of the claimants' properties, and although as yet no damage had occurred to the bungalows, this had significantly diminished their market value. The claimants sought damages from NR in nuisance on the grounds (1) that the encroachment of the knotweed onto their properties amounted to a nuisance even if it had not yet caused any physical damage, or alternatively (2) that the presence of the knotweed on the defendant's land amounted to a nuisance because of its effect on the value of their properties. The recorder rejected the claim on the first ground because the encroachment had not caused any physical damage, but gave judgment for the claimants on the second ground, holding that the amenity value of land could include the ability to dispose of it at a proper market value. The defendant appealed.

Sir Terence Etherton MR

1. . . . This appeal raises a range of issues, most of which can be grouped under the overarching question of what kinds of damage give rise to an actionable claim in the tort of private nuisance. . . .

General principles

38. In recent times a number of decisions at the highest level have introduced greater coherence and consistency to the legal principles governing the cause of action for private nuisance. The consequence is that it is neither necessary nor profitable to focus on historic cases of nuisance and the early development of the cause of action. In particular, in view of the clarification of the principles in more modern times, the resolution of the present appeal will not be found simply in an examination of the old forms of action, including the historic distinction between the form of action of trespass, on the one hand, and the action on the case, on the other hand, or in considering the distinction between the three ways in which it was formerly recognised that a person might suffer interference with their rights over land: disseisina, nocumentum and transgressio. . . .

39. I would summarise as follows the present principles of the cause of action of nuisance.

40. First, a private nuisance is a violation of real property rights. That means that it involves either an interference with the legal rights of an owner of land, including a legal interest in land such as an easement and a profit à prendre, or interference with the amenity of the land, that is to say the right to use and enjoy it, which is an inherent facet of a right of exclusive possession . . . It has been described as a property tort. . . .

41. Secondly, although nuisance is sometimes broken down into different categories, these are merely examples of a violation of property rights as I have described them. In [*Hunter v Canary Wharf Ltd* [1997] AC 655] at p 695C, for example, Lord Lloyd said that nuisances are of three kinds:

> (1) nuisance by encroachment on a neighbour's land, (2) nuisance by direct physical injury to a neighbour's land; and (3) nuisance by interference with a neighbour's quiet enjoyment of his land.

The difficulty with any rigid categorisation is that it may not easily accommodate possible examples of nuisance in new social conditions or may undermine a proper analysis of factual situations which have aspects of more than one category but do not fall squarely within any one category, having regard to existing case law.

42. Thirdly, the frequently stated proposition that damage is always an essential requirement of the cause of action for nuisance because nuisance is derived from the old form of action on the case must be treated with considerable caution. . . . It is clear both that this proposition is not entirely correct and also that the concept of damage in this context is a highly elastic one. In particular, interference with an easement or a profit à prendre is actionable as a nuisance without the need to prove specific damage . . . Furthermore, in the case of an artificial object protruding into a claimant's property from the neighbouring land, Mr David Hart QC, for NR, accepted that the claimant has a cause of action in nuisance without proof of damage. Although McNair J said in *Kelsen v Imperial Tobacco Co (of Great Britain and Ireland) Ltd* [1957] 2 QB 334 that an advertising sign erected by the defendant which projected into the airspace above the plaintiff's shop was a trespass and was not capable of constituting a nuisance, he so held without any reference to the previous authority to the contrary in *Baten's Case* (1610) 9 Co Rep 53b and *Fay v Prentice* (1845) 1 CB 828 and so *Kelsen's* case must be considered per incuriam in relation to that issue. So far as concerns such nuisance from encroachment by an artificial object, the better view may actually be that damage is formally required but damage is always presumed: *Baten's Case*; *Fay v Prentice* at p 841. That, in itself, shows both the artificiality and elasticity of any requirement of damage for the purpose of establishing nuisance.

43. It is also well established that, in the case of nuisance through interference with the amenity of the claimant's land, physical damage is not necessary to complete the cause of

action. To paraphrase Lord Lloyd's observations in *Hunter's* case [1997] AC 655, 696C, in relation to his third category, loss of amenity, such as results from noise, smoke, smell or dust or other emanations, may not cause any diminution in the market value of the land, such as may directly follow from, and reflect, loss caused by tangible physical damage to the land, but damages may nevertheless be awarded for loss of the land's intangible amenity value. Reflecting the fact that the cause of action is one for interference with property rights, loss of amenity value and the right to claim damages for it does not turn on any exceptional sensitivity or insensitivity of the person entitled to exclusive possession: *Barr v Biffa Waste Services Ltd* [2013] QB 455, para 36. What is relevant is the objective effect on the amenity value of the land itself, and it is that effect which satisfies any requirement there may be to show damage. Provided, by reference to all the circumstances of the case and the character of the locality, and according to the objective standards of the average person, the interference with amenity is sufficiently serious, there will be an actionable private nuisance.

44. Fourthly, nuisance may be caused by inaction or omission as well as by some positive activity. An occupier will be liable for continuing a nuisance created by another person if, with knowledge or presumed knowledge of its existence, he or she fails to take reasonable means to bring it to an end when they had ample time to do so: *Sedleigh-Denfield v O'Callaghan* [1940] AC 880, 894. An occupier will also be liable if he or she fails to act with reasonable prudence to remove a hazard, whether natural or man-made, on their land of which he or she was aware and where it was foreseeable that it would risk damaging their neighbour's land and goes on to do so: *Goldman v Hargrave* [1967] 1 AC 645; *Leakey v National Trust for Places of Historic Interest or Natural Beauty* [1980] QB 485.

45. Finally, the broad unifying principle in this area of the law is reasonableness between neighbours (real or figurative): the *Delaware Mansions* case [2002] 1 AC 321, paras 29, 34.

Appeal Ground (I)

46. The recorder's conclusion that the presence of knotweed on NR's land within seven metres of the claimants' properties was an actionable nuisance simply because it diminished the market value of the claimants' respective properties, because of lender caution in such situations, was wrong in principle.

48. The purpose of the tort of nuisance is not to protect the value of property as an investment or a financial asset. Its purpose is to protect the owner of land (or a person entitled to exclusive possession) in their use and enjoyment of the land as such as a facet of the right of ownership or right to exclusive possession. The decision of the recorder in the present case extends the tort of nuisance to a claim for pure economic loss. Counsel for the claimants did not identify any case in which a similar decision was reached or, more generally, where the amenity of a property has been held, for the purposes of actionable private nuisance, to include the right to realise or otherwise deploy the value of the property in the financial interests of the owner. Contrary to the view of the recorder, that would not be an incremental development of the common law by way of analogy but a radical reformulation of the purpose and scope of the tort. . . .

54. I do not agree with the analysis and decision of the recorder rejecting the claim in nuisance based on the spread of the knotweed rhizomes on to the claimants' respective properties from NR's land.

55. Japanese knotweed was rightly described by the recorder, at para 5, as 'a pernicious weed'. It does not only carry the risk of future physical damage to buildings, structures and installations on the land. Its presence, and indeed the mere presence of its rhizomes, imposes an immediate burden on the owner of the land in terms of an increased difficulty in the ability to develop, and in the cost of developing, the land, should the owner wish to do so. . . . For all those reasons, Japanese knotweed and its rhizomes can fairly be described, in the sense of

the decided cases, as a 'natural hazard'. They affect the owner's ability fully to use and enjoy the land. They are a classic example of an interference with the amenity value of the land.

56. The recorder found that: (1) NR had actual knowledge of the presence of Japanese knotweed on its land behind the claimants' respective bungalows in 2013; (2) NR was, or ought to have been, aware of the risk of damage and loss of amenity to adjoining properties caused by the close proximity of knotweed no later than some time in 2012 with the publication of the EA code of practice and the RICS paper; and (3) NR failed reasonably to prevent the interference with the claimants' enjoyment of their properties. That is sufficient, on the well-established principles I have outlined earlier, to give rise to a cause of action in nuisance: *Goldman v Hargrave* [1967] 1 AC 645; *Leakey v National Trust for Places of Historic Interest or Natural Beauty* [1980] QB 485. If, and in so far as, damage is required to complete that cause of action, it is constituted by the diminished ability of the claimants to use and enjoy the amenity of their properties. . . .

Conclusion

83. For all those reasons, I would uphold the decision of the recorder but for different reasons to those which he gave.

Appeal dismissed.

COMMENTARY

For commentary on *Williams*, see Steel (2019) 135 LQR 192 and Wilde (2019) 31 JEL 343.

Etherton MR's description of private nuisance as a 'property tort' echoed Lord Hoffmann's seminal analysis of the cause of action in *Hunter v Canary Wharf Ltd* (extracted later). According to D. Nolan, '"A Tort Against Land": Private Nuisance as a Property Tort', in D. Nolan and A. Robertson (eds), *Rights and Private Law* (Oxford: Hart, 2011), p. 459, once understood as 'a tort which protects rights in land', private nuisance is 'a thoroughly coherent cause of action'. You might ask yourself whether or not you agree with that assessment after reading the remainder of this chapter, but in any case it is undeniable that the implications of viewing private nuisance as a property tort are profound.

Nuisance is not the only tort that protects real property interests. Where the interference with those interests is more direct—as where, for example, someone enters your land without your permission—then an action will lie for trespass to land. The origins of the bifurcation between nuisance and trespass lie in the ancient distinction between the action in trespass and the action on the case (see Ch. 1.I.2), which explains why in theory nuisance requires 'damage', even if—as Etherton MR makes clear—in practice this does not operate as a separate element of liability, additional to the basic requirement of an unreasonable interference with the use and enjoyment of the claimant's land. The precise dividing line between trespass and nuisance is a bit blurry, though the traditional view (again reflective of the trespass/case distinction) is that trespass deals with direct interferences with land and nuisance with indirect ones. The direct/indirect distinction is itself elusive, but in this context it seems clear that an interference is always indirect—and hence at most a nuisance—where no person or physical object enters the claimant's land. Where there is a 'boundary crossing' of this kind, trespass lies if the relevant act of the defendant is initially unlawful (e.g. *Kelsen v Imperial Tobacco Co* [1957] 2 QB 334, where the defendant erected a sign that projected over the claimant's land) and nuisance where it is not (e.g. the encroachment of the knotweed in the extracted case). See further, Keeton, 'Trespass, Nuisance and Strict Liability' (1959) 59 Col L Rev 457 at 464–70 and Nolan, *op. cit.*, pp. 481–4; and on trespass to land, see *Winfield & Jolowicz*, ch. 14.

The orthodox definition of private nuisance is 'an unlawful interference with a person's use and enjoyment of land, or some right over, or in connection with it' (*Winfield & Jolowicz*, para. 15–010). This definition is drawn broadly, and encompasses the three categories of case that Etherton MR mentions, namely encroachment, physical damage to the land and interference with the enjoyment of the land. However, as he made clear, there must be some actual harm to the land or its amenity: 'merely diminishing the economic value of the land' is not a nuisance (Steel, *op. cit.*, 194), and the same is true of conduct that affects only the profitability of a business being conducted on the land (see the great Australian case of *Victoria Park Racing and Recreation Grounds Ltd v Taylor* (1937) 58 CLR 479, discussed in M. Lunney, *A History of Australian Tort Law 1901–1945* (Cambridge: CUP, 2018), pp. 266–76). In *Laws v Florinplace* [1981] 1 All ER 659, it was held that there was a triable issue as to whether the mere presence of a sex shop in the vicinity of the plaintiffs' houses in Pimlico could potentially amount to a nuisance (see also *Thompson-Schwab v Costaki* [1956] 1 WLR 335, which concerned a brothel that had opened in the street where the plaintiff lived). Vinelott J referred (at 662) to evidence from one of the claimants 'that the continuance of the defendants' business would severely injure the value of his property', and to evidence from estate agents as to the effect of the establishment on local property prices. Is *Laws* compatible with the reasoning in *Williams* (see the latter case, at [51])? And more generally, should the mere presence of an unpleasant or distressing activity in the vicinity of a property be capable of amounting to a nuisance? (See Coletta, 'The Case for Aesthetic Nuisance: Rethinking Traditional Judicial Attitudes' (1987) 48 Ohio State LJ 141; and for an extreme example involving a 'glass morgue', see J. E. Penner, *Property Rights: A Re-Examination* (Oxford: OUP, 2020), pp. 153–4.) The precise parameters of the notion of an interference with use and enjoyment of land are explored by D. Nolan, 'The Essence of Private Nuisance', in B. McFarlane and S. Agnew (eds), *Modern Studies in Property Law: Volume 10* (Oxford: Hart, 2019), who argues that the traditional definition needs tweaking, and that the defining characteristic of the tort is an interference with the abstract usability of land, so that strictly speaking private nuisance is not concerned with whether the claimant can use or enjoy their land, but with 'whether (and to what extent) their land is capable of being used and enjoyed'. For an alternative view, which conceives of nuisance as a form of indirect, or constructive, dispossession, see Penner, *op. cit.*, ch. 7.

Etherton MR reminds us in *Williams* that private nuisance protects rights that one owner has over the land of another, such as a right of way or a right to light (forms of easement) or a right to take wood or turf from another property (forms of profit à prendre). Indeed, the early history of the tort is dominated by cases of this kind: see *Baker*, ch. 23. In this sort of case, the same basic requirements of liability apply, so that, for example, the interference with a right of way or a right to light must be substantial to constitute a nuisance (in the light context, see *Colls v Home and Colonial Stores Ltd* [1904] AC 179). The law of acquired rights, or 'servitudes', also intersects with private nuisance in another way, since a potential defendant can acquire a right to create a nuisance *vis-à-vis* a neighbouring property, usually by long user or 'prescription' (see II.5(a)). Although tort lawyers style this a 'defence' of prescription, in property law terms it is simply an easement which one property (the defendant's) has acquired over another (the claimant's).

Conversely, there are certain types of interference with the use and enjoyment of land which are not actionable in nuisance in any circumstances, and regardless of how severe the interference is on the facts. The list of these 'no rights' is short. The oldest example is the rule that one cannot claim in nuisance for the obstruction of the view from one's property. This rule goes back to an obiter dictum of Wray CJ in the unreported sixteenth-century case of *Bland v Moseley* (see *Aldred's Case* (1610) 9 Co Rep 57b at 58b), and seems to be well-established, although Pontin, 'A Room with a View in English Nuisance Law: Exploring Modernisation Hidden Within the "Textbook Tradition"' (2018) 38 LS 627 questions whether the authorities cited for it are as definitive as they are generally considered to be. A connected rule is that there is no right to the free and uninterrupted passage of air over neighbouring land (*Webb v Bird* (1862) 13 CBNS 841), while another well-established rule of this kind is that an occupier has no right to receive percolating water from a neighbour's property (*Bradford Corporation v Pickles* [1895] AC 587; see II.2(c)). Although most of the cases on these 'no rights' date back to the nineteenth century or earlier, there are also two important modern authorities. In *Hunter v Canary Wharf Ltd* [1997] AC 655, the House of Lords held that no action lies in private nuisance for interference with television reception caused by a nearby building (the position was left open where the interference is caused by an activity of the defendant—as where electronic equipment interferes with the signal). And in *Fearn v Board of Trustees of the Tate Gallery* [2020] Ch 621, the Court of Appeal confirmed the previous understanding that nuisance does not protect privacy, so that an owner of property has no right not to be overlooked. (On privacy protection through other causes of action, see Ch. 13.)

The facts of *Fearn* illustrate the significance of the holding that in a particular type of case no possibility of a nuisance claim lies at all. The defendant art gallery had opened an external viewing platform on the tenth floor of one of its buildings, from which it was possible to see directly into the living areas of the claimants' flats in a luxury residential development some 35 metres away. Many of those using the platform stared into the flats, or photographed and filmed their interiors, and some even posted the images on social media, all of which caused much distress to the occupants. The claimants' action for an injunction requiring closure of part of the platform failed both at first instance ([2019] Ch 369) and on appeal, but for very different reasons. At first instance, Mann J held that an interference with privacy was capable of amounting to a nuisance, but that the interference in the case was not unreasonable, because (inter alia) the locality was an inner city urban environment, the floor-to-ceiling windows of the flats made them particularly sensitive to this kind of intrusion, and the residents could protect themselves by means of blinds and the like. By contrast, the Court of Appeal held that it did not matter whether the interference was material or not because as a matter of authority and principle an invasion of privacy by overlooking was simply not capable of grounding a claim in private nuisance. In a joint judgment, the court gave various reasons for this rule, including the fact that a right not to be overlooked would unduly constrain building in towns and cities, and that if the law were otherwise it would be difficult to draw a line between cases of acceptable and unacceptable overlooking. It followed that inappropriate overlooking was better dealt with by planning law. Nolan (2021) 137 LQR 1 welcomes the ruling in *Fearn*, arguing (at 4) that extending nuisance to protect privacy threatened to generate much litigation, even though the first instance decision 'suggested that it would be very difficult to win an action of this kind'. However, Howarth [2020] CLJ 394 is less enthusiastic: in his view, nuisance is needed as a back-up in this type of case, in case mistakes are made in the planning process, as (he argues) must have happened on the facts of *Fearn*. Economu (2021) 52 VUWLR 1 is also critical of the Court of Appeal in *Fearn*, arguing that the decision of Mann J was a step in the right direction insofar as it would have helped to fill a gap in the protection of physical privacy in English law. At the time of writing, an appeal in *Fearn* had been heard by the Supreme Court.

Various attempts have been made to explain the 'no rights' cases by reference to some overarching general principle, but none of these are entirely convincing. Perhaps the most influential such explanation is that put forward in a book focused on *Bradford Corporation v Pickles* by M. Taggart, *Private Property and Abuse of Rights in Victorian England* (Oxford: OUP, 2002), p. 189:

Historically, nuisance cases, almost without exception, concern the spread of something—be it odours, noise, water, gunshots, or whatever—from one property to another so as to interfere unreasonably with the use and enjoyment of the latter property. What happened in *Pickles* was the prevention of something (there percolating water) which the neighbour had no right to receive escaping from one property to another. *Pickles* stands for the proposition that it is not tortious in such circumstances to deprive someone of emanations from your property, even if maliciously motivated.

Taggart's explanation contains a kernel of truth, for it is undoubtedly the case that, as Lord Goff noted in the *Hunter* case, actions for private nuisance generally lie in respect of emanations from the defendant's land, not for the erection of something on the defendant's land which interferes with the ability of the claimant to receive something on their land. However, his explanation of the 'no rights' cases is flawed, because it is equally clear that an emanation is not a *prerequisite* of a claim in private nuisance, so that, for example, an occupier who substantially interferes with the flow of surface water in a stream or river to a neighbour's land can be liable in nuisance (see *Orr-Ewing v Colquhoun* (1877) 2 App Cas 839), as can a person who blocks the access to another's land (*J Lyons & Sons v Wilkins* [1899] 1 Ch 255; for other examples, see *Oliphant*, para. 22.12). A more prosaic explanation for these rules is that—for pragmatic reasons of the kind put forward in *Fearn*—it is simply considered preferable to exclude certain categories of interference with the use and enjoyment of land from the ambit of the law of nuisance altogether, 'rather than relying on a fact-sensitive enquiry into whether a particular instance of interference is substantial or unreasonable' (Nolan (2021) 137 LQR 1 at 4).

2. Unreasonable Interference

Although negligence involves liability to one's legal neighbours, it is the tort of private nuisance that deals with liability to one's physical neighbours. Part of being a good neighbour involves tolerance, and the fact that one party uses land to the annoyance of another does not create civil liability. Liability in private nuisance arises only when the conduct of the defendant amounts to an unreasonable user of land in that it causes an unreasonable interference with the claimant's use of land. Whether or not there has been a nuisance is a question of fact, the court weighing several factors in the particular circumstances of the case and asking if the conduct interferes with the claimant's use of his land 'not merely according to the elegant and dainty habits of living but according to plain and sober notions among our people' (*Walter v Selfe* (1851) 4 De G & Sm 315 at 322, per Knight Bruce V-C). Ultimately, the question is whether an ordinary person could reasonably be expected to put up with the interference (see *Barr v Biffa Waste Services Ltd* [2013] QB 455 at [74], per Carnwath LJ;

Lawrence v Fen Tigers Ltd [2014] AC 822 at [5], per Lord Neuberger, and at [193], per Lord Carnwath).

Whether conduct amounts to an unreasonable interference (or, as it sometimes called, an 'unreasonable user') is assessed objectively, and depends upon a number of factors, the most important of which are the nature and extent of the interference, the locality where the alleged nuisance is committed and the reasonableness of the defendant's conduct. However, courts have generally rejected the utilitarian argument that where the defendant's conduct is for the public benefit it cannot amount to a nuisance, the common law being slow to extinguish private rights in the public interest. In the rest of this section, we consider these factors in more detail.

(a) Objective Assessment of the Gravity of the Interference

Robinson v Kilvert (1889) 41 Ch D 88

The plaintiff was the tenant of premises, let to him by the defendant landlords, which were used as a paper warehouse. The defendants retained the use of the cellar of the premises, and after the lease commenced they began a manufacturing process that required the air in the cellar to be hot and dry. To achieve this the cellar was heated, with the result that the temperature of the floor above was raised to 80°F (about 26°C). The heat had the effect of drying out the brown paper that the plaintiff stored in the warehouse, which made it less valuable. One issue for the Court of Appeal was whether the raising of the temperature was a nuisance.

Cotton LJ

Now the heat is not excessive, it does not rise above 80° at the floor, and in the room itself it is not nearly so great. If a person does what in itself is noxious, or which interferes with the ordinary use and enjoyment of a neighbour's property, it is a nuisance. But no case has been cited where the doing of something not in itself noxious has been held a nuisance, unless it interferes with the ordinary enjoyment of life, or the ordinary use of property for the purposes of residence or business. It would, in my opinion, be wrong to say that the doing of something not in itself noxious is a nuisance because it does harm to some particular trade in the adjoining property, although it would not prejudicially affect any ordinary trade carried on there, and does not interfere with the ordinary enjoyment of life. Here it is shewn that ordinary paper would not be damaged by what the Defendants are doing, but only a particular kind of paper, and it is not shewn that there is heat such as to incommode the workpeople on the Plaintiff's premises. I am of opinion, therefore, that the Plaintiff is not entitled to relief on the ground that what the Defendants are doing is a nuisance.

Lopes LJ

I think the Plaintiff cannot complain of what is being done as a nuisance. A man who carries on an exceptionally delicate trade cannot complain because it is injured by his neighbour doing something lawful on his property, if it is something which would not injure anything but an exceptionally delicate trade. . . . In the present case the Defendants are not shewn to have done anything which would injure an ordinary trade, and cannot, in my opinion, be held liable on the ground of nuisance. . . .

Appeal dismissed.

COMMENTARY

'A man cannot increase the liabilities of his neighbour by applying his own property to special uses, whether for business or pleasure' (*Eastern and South African Telegraph Company Ltd v Cape Town Tramways Companies Ltd* [1902] AC 381 at 393). Where the injury to the claimant is a result of their especially sensitive activity, no claim will lie. Although this principle is entrenched in the law of nuisance, examples of it being used to defeat a claim are rare. In *Heath v Mayor of Brighton* (1908) 98 LT 718 the vicar and trustees of a church sought an injunction to stop the noise emanating from the defendant's power station, which it was alleged disturbed the vicar's deliberations over his sermons, but as no-one else appeared to have been bothered the injunction was refused. Another example is *Bridlington Relay v Yorkshire Electricity Board* [1965] Ch 436 where the plaintiffs, whose business was providing a relay service for sound and television broadcasts, sought an injunction to prevent the defendants from operating a new power line they had erected because it interfered with the relay service. One of the grounds on which Buckley J refused the injunction was the 'exceptionally sensitive' nature of the plaintiff's business. More recently, in *Network Rail Infrastructure Ltd v Morris* [2004] Env LR 41 the Court of Appeal considered whether electro-magnetic interference with the sound of electric guitars in the claimant's recording studio, caused by the defendant's nearby signalling system, constituted a nuisance. One of the defendant's arguments was that the claimant's use of land was extra-sensitive. The Court of Appeal divided over whether the claimant's use of land was extra-sensitive, although the claim failed in any case on the ground that the interference had not been foreseeable.

In *Morris* Buxton LJ cast doubt on the need for a separate 'abnormal sensitivity' principle, arguing that the issue should instead be subsumed into the open-ended test of reasonableness as between neighbours which he considered governed liability in nuisance. But in *Fearn v Board of Trustees of the Tate Gallery* [2020] Ch 621 (noted earlier), Etherton MR robustly defended the principle, observing that it follows from the fact that private nuisance is a property tort concerned with the impact of the defendant's interference on the utility of the claimant's land that the gravity of that interference is assessed objectively, so that any particular sensitivity—or indeed *in*sensitivity—of the claimant or their chosen use of the land is generally disregarded (see also *Williams v Network Rail*, extracted earlier, at [43]: '[w]hat is relevant is the objective effect on the amenity value of the land itself'). At the same time, however, the Court of Appeal in *Fearn* disagreed with Mann J's holding at first instance that the principle was relevant in that case, apparently on the basis that the principle did not encompass the physical state of the claimant's land. One of us has criticised that limitation, however, arguing that (Nolan (2021) 137 LQR 1 at 5):

[T]he fact that the design, layout etc. of the claimant's property makes it unusually sensitive to a particular form of interference should be a relevant consideration when assessing whether a given instance of such interference is actionable in nuisance. Suppose, for example, that in the 'Three Little Pigs' fairy tale the threat to the houses of the little pigs had come from vibrations generated by a nearby factory, rather than the Big Bad Wolf. Would not their choice of construction materials (respectively, straw, sticks and bricks) have been highly pertinent in subsequent nuisance litigation?

In *Marsh v Baxter* (2015) 49 WAR 1, the claimant was a farmer in Western Australia who used his land to produce organic cereal crops. He sued a neighbour in nuisance because genetically modified (GM) canola seed strayed from his neighbour's land onto his property, with the result that his produce lost its organic certification. The Supreme Court of Western Australia held that since incursions of GM material would not significantly affect the usual farming activities in the area in question, and since organic farming was only an isolated practice there, the stray seed was not a nuisance. Do you agree with the implication that organic farming is an abnormally sensitive activity?

(b) The Locality

St Helen's Smelting Co v Tipping (1865) 11 HL Cas 642

The plaintiff bought a large country estate on the outskirts of St Helen's in June 1860, and several months later the defendant began extensive smelting works on its premises nearby. The plaintiff alleged that gas emissions from the defendant's works had caused damage to trees and shrubs on his land. The jury found for the plaintiff, and the defendant challenged the direction given by the trial judge, Mellor J. Appeals to the Court of Exchequer Chamber and the House of Lords were dismissed. One issue for decision was whether an instruction to the jury that there was no liability in nuisance if the defendant's activity was carried on in a 'convenient' or 'suitable' place was correct in law.

Lord Westbury

My Lords, in matters of this description it appears to me that it is a very desirable thing to mark the difference between an action brought for a nuisance upon the ground that the alleged nuisance produces material injury to the property, and an action brought for a nuisance on the ground that the thing alleged to be a nuisance is productive of sensible personal discomfort. With regard to the latter, namely, the personal inconvenience and interference with one's enjoyment, one's quiet, one's personal freedom, anything that discomposes or injuriously affects the senses or the nerves, whether that may or may not be denominated a nuisance, must undoubtedly depend greatly on the circumstances of the place where the thing complained of actually occurs. If a man lives in a town, it is necessary that he should subject himself to the consequences of those operations of trade which may be carried on in his immediate locality, which are actually necessary for trade and commerce, and also for the enjoyment of property, and for the benefit of the inhabitants of the town and the public at large. If a man lives in a street where there are numerous shops, and a shop is opened next door to him, which is carried on in a fair and reasonable way, he has no ground for complaint, because to himself individually there may arise much discomfort from the trade carried on in that shop. But when an occupation is carried on by one person in the neighbourhood of another, and the result of that trade, or occupation, or business, is a material injury to property, then there unquestionably arises a very different consideration. I think, my Lords, that in a case of that description, the submission which is required from persons living in society to that amount of discomfort which may be necessary for the legitimate and free exercise of the trade of their neighbours, would not apply to circumstances the immediate result of which is sensible injury to the value of the property. . . .

My Lords . . . the only ground upon which your Lordships are asked to set aside [the] verdict, and to direct a new trial, is this, that the whole neighbourhood where these copper smelting works were carried on, is a neighbourhood more or less devoted to manufacturing purposes of a similar kind. . . . My Lords, I apprehend that that is not the meaning of the word 'suitable', or the meaning of the word 'convenient', which has been used as applicable to the subject. The word 'suitable' unquestionably cannot carry with it this consequence, that a trade may be carried on in a particular locality, the consequences of which trade may be injury and destruction to the neighbouring property . . .

Lord Cranworth and **Lord Wensleydale** agreed with Lord Westbury.

Judgment of the Exchequer Chamber affirmed.

COMMENTARY

The contemporary significance of this case can be gauged from the fact that the House of Lords exercised their right to request the judges from the superior courts (Queens Bench, Common Pleas and Exchequer) to attend the hearing and to offer an opinion. This was only done for cases of public importance (for a related example, see *McNaghten*'s case (1843) 10 C & F 200). Six of them were able to attend (including two of the most eminent nineteenth-century judges, Willes and Blackburn) and, before Lord Westbury gave his speech, they advised that the direction given by Mellor J was good in law. For a historical analysis of the case and its context, see B. Pontin, *Nuisance Law and Environmental Protection: A Study of Nuisance Injunctions in Practice* (Witney: Lawtext, 2013), ch. 3.

St Helen's sets out the important distinction between activities of a neighbour which cause 'material injury to property' (where the locality in which the activity is pursued is irrelevant) and those which cause 'sensible personal discomfort' (where the locality is relevant). But what is material damage to property, and why should locality be less important in such a case? The phrase is generally understood to mean physical damage to property (see, e.g., *Weir*, p. 428), but Lord Westbury's attempt to justify drawing the distinction is unhelpful—both interference with amenity and damage to property cause 'sensible injury to the value of the property'. Moreover, in *Hunter v Canary Wharf Ltd* [1997] AC 655 it was affirmed that both material physical damage and loss of amenity amount to interference with property interests, and this would suggest that, in deciding whether conduct amounts to a nuisance, the same factors should be considered. If both are property interests, why should a lengthy exposure to obnoxious smells be treated differently from a similar length of exposure that causes material damage to property? Nevertheless, it seems clear that the distinction continues to play an important role in the law of nuisance. Where the claimant suffers physical property damage, the court will readily conclude that the interference is unreasonable. Conversely, where the interference is solely with amenity, the court must conduct a more complex enquiry, in which account will be taken of the nature of the locality and the extent to which the defendant's activity is well suited to it.

Taking the locality into account in amenity nuisance cases seems intuitively fair, though it is surprisingly hard to pin down quite why that is (for a thorough, but somewhat inconclusive, exploration of the possible rationales, see Steel, 'The Locality Principle in Private Nuisance' [2017] CLJ 145). Perhaps the best explanation is that the social rules of 'give and take' vary between different localities, with the result that what a claimant can reasonably be expected to tolerate must be assessed by reference to the nature of the area in which they choose to live (*McBride & Bagshaw*, p. 406; see also *Shoreham-by-Sea UDC v Dolphin Canadian Proteins Ltd* (1972) 71 LGR 261 at 266, per May J: '[T]his is an industrial area. The local inhabitants are not entitled to expect to sit in a sweet-smelling orchard').

What precisely is meant by 'the nature of the locality' in this context, though, and can the defendant's own activity be taken into account when assessing it? The answer to the first question seems to be what is the dominant land use (e.g. residential, commercial, industrial or agricultural), or, where such an approach is overly monolithic, what is the 'established *pattern* of uses' (see Lawrence v Fen Tigers Ltd [2014] AC 822 at [60], per Lord Neuberger). Until recently there was no clear judicial pronouncement on the second question, presumably because it was assumed that the courts would simply ignore the defendant's activity when assessing the nature of a particular neighbourhood for the purposes of applying the locality principle. Unfortunately, however, the Supreme Court rather muddied the waters on the issue in Lawrence v Fen Tigers Ltd [2014] AC 822 (extracted later). According to Lord Neuberger in Lawrence, prima facie the defendant's activities *are* to be taken into account when assessing the character of the locality, but this conclusion is based on a statement in the *St Helen's* case which reads as no more than an expression of the locality principle itself. Furthermore, the qualification which his Lordship then adds (at [65]) that 'to the extent that [the defendant's] activities are a nuisance to the claimant, they should be left out of account when assessing the character of the locality' is (with respect) difficult to understand, since the character of the neighbourhood is being assessed precisely because it may determine whether or not the defendant's activity *is* a nuisance to the claimant. Hence, as Elspeth Reid points out ([2015] Edin LR 383 at 386), 'it is difficult to see how this perplexing procedure can be followed without the first part of the enquiry rendering the second redundant'. (Perhaps a more persuasive analysis would have been to say that the defendant's activity should be taken into account except to the extent that it is *alleged to be* a nuisance?) Lord Neuberger accepts that the circularity involved in his reasoning is problematic, but dismisses the possibility that the defendant's activity should simply be ignored on the grounds that, while it might 'often be the simplest and fairest way of dealing with the issue', in some cases it could be unfair on the defendant (at [72]). Quite why it could be unfair was not, however, made clear. Lord Carnwath was also of the view (at [187]) that the defendant's activity 'can clearly be taken into account if it is part of the established pattern of use'. Lord Carnwath's approach was preferred in *Jones v Ministry of Defence* [2021] EWHC (QB) 2276, where the locality in a case of alleged noise nuisance from an RAF training base was described as 'largely agricultural, but one in which very loud noise from aircraft using RAF Mona is heard on frequent occasions', with the result that the noise inevitably generated by the base was held not to be a nuisance. This suggests to us that the discussion in *Lawrence* of the relevance of the defendant's activity to the characterisation of the locality may give rise to significant problems, and hence we hope that Reid (*op. cit.*, 386) is right when she says that *Lawrence* is unlikely to be the final word on the subject.

Where locality is to be taken into account, it is in any case important to recognise that a defendant's use of land may amount to a nuisance even if it is a type of activity suitable for the area. The locality principle does not provide an immunity; it must be weighed up against other relevant factors, such as the ease with which the interference could be eliminated or reduced (see Steel, *op. cit.*, 149). A good example of this balancing exercise is *Halsey v Esso Petroleum* [1961] 1 WLR 683, where Veale J said (at 691–2):

> So far as the present case is concerned, liability for nuisance by harmful deposits could be established by proving damage by the deposits to the property in question, provided of course that the injury was not merely trivial. Negligence is not an ingredient of the cause of action, and the character of the neighbourhood is not a matter to be taken into consideration. On the other hand, nuisance by smell or noise is something to which no absolute standard can be applied. It is always a question of degree whether the interference with comfort or convenience is sufficiently serious

to constitute a nuisance. The character of the neighbourhood is very relevant and all the relevant circumstances have to be taken into account. What might be a nuisance in one area is by no means necessarily so in another. In an urban area, everyone must put up with a certain amount of discomfort and annoyance from the activities of neighbours, and the law must strike a fair and reasonable balance between the right of the plaintiff on the one hand to the undisturbed enjoyment of his property, and the right of the defendant on the other hand to use his property for his own lawful enjoyment.

Similar sentiments were expressed by Thesiger LJ in *Sturges v Bridgman* (1879) 11 Ch D 852 at 865: 'what would be a nuisance in Belgrave Square would not necessarily be so in Bermondsey'. A more modern example is provided by *Baxter v Camden London Borough Council (No. 2)* [2001] 1 AC 1 where the plaintiff complained of noise created by her upstairs neighbours, both being tenants of the defendant in a converted house. The action in nuisance failed because the noise was part of the ordinary use of premises and '[o]ccupiers of low cost, high density housing must be expected to tolerate higher levels of noise from their neighbours than others in more substantial and spacious premises' (as Tuckey LJ had put it in the Court of Appeal: [2001] QB 1 at 10; cf. *Sampson v Hodson-Pressinger* [1981] 3 All ER 710).

Of course, the character of a neighbourhood can change over time; conduct that might not have amounted to a nuisance in nineteenth-century Bermondsey might well amount to one in Bermondsey today. Generally, this kind of change is unplanned and incremental, but it may also be brought about by a single planning decision of a local authority. If a claimant is complaining of conduct that has been authorised by a planning consent, one question that arises is whether the locality of the neighbourhood should be judged by reference to the locality before or after the development to which consent was given. In *Gillingham Borough Council v Medway (Chatham) Dock Co Ltd* [1993] QB 343 it was alleged that the lorries accessing the defendants' port complex through a residential area made the port a public nuisance. Buckley J accepted that the grant of planning permission for the port was not itself a defence to the action (see II.5(b)), but said (at 359) that where planning consent had been given for a development or change of use, the question of nuisance 'will thereafter fall to be decided by reference to a neighbourhood with that development or use and not as it was previously'. Since the noise from the lorries was not excessive in an area containing a commercial port, the action failed. The *Gillingham* principle proved controversial, and its significance was downplayed by the Court of Appeal in *Wheeler v JJ Saunders Ltd* [1996] Ch 19, where it was held that planning permission allowing an intensification of the defendant's pig farming activities had not altered the character of an area, and *Gillingham* was distinguished on the ground that it concerned a strategic planning decision affected by considerations of public interest (see also *Watson v Croft Promosport Ltd* [2009] 3 All ER 249, where the 'essentially rural' character of the locality was not changed by planning permission for use of land as a motor circuit). The Supreme Court was asked to consider the validity of the *Gillingham* principle in the next extracted case.

Lawrence v Fen Tigers Ltd [2014] AC 822

The claimants had bought a bungalow in a rural location in Suffolk a few hundred metres from a complex consisting of a stadium used for various motor sports and a track used for motocross racing. The bungalow (which had been built in the 1950s) was surrounded by fields and there were no other residential properties within a half-mile radius. Permanent planning permission had been granted for speedway racing at the stadium some twenty years previously, and stock car and banger racing were covered by a certificate of lawful use. Permanent planning permission had also been granted four years earlier for motocross events at the track, albeit with detailed conditions as to the frequency and timing of these events, and the level of noise they generated. The claimants were upset by the noise from the motorsports events held at the stadium and track, and brought proceedings in private nuisance against a number of defendants associated with the facilities. The judge held ([2011] 4 All ER 1314n) that the noise amounted to a nuisance for which some of the defendants were liable in varying extents, and awarded damages for past interference and injunctive relief imposing decibel limits and operating restrictions. This decision was reversed by the Court of Appeal ([2012] 1 WLR 2127). The claimants appealed to the Supreme Court.

Lord Neuberger

The issues raised by this appeal

1. This appeal raises a number of points in connection with the law of private nuisance, a common law tort . . . It should also be mentioned at the outset that the type of nuisance alleged in this case is nuisance in the sense of personal discomfort, in particular nuisance by noise, as opposed to actual injury to the claimant's property (such as discharge of noxious material or removal of support).

3. A nuisance can be defined, albeit in general terms, as an action (or sometimes a failure to act) on the part of a defendant, which is not otherwise authorised, and which causes an interference with the claimant's reasonable enjoyment of his land, or to use a slightly different formulation, which unduly interferes with the claimant's enjoyment of his land . . .

The effect of planning permission on an allegation of nuisance

77. The interrelationship of planning permission and nuisance has been considered in a number of cases, and has been discussed in a number of articles and books. The grant of planning permission for a particular use is potentially relevant to a nuisance claim in two ways. First, the grant, or terms and conditions, of a planning permission may permit the very noise (or other disturbance) which is alleged by the claimant to constitute a nuisance. In such a case, the question is the extent, if any, to which the planning permission can be relied on as a defence to the nuisance claim. Secondly, the grant, or terms and conditions, of a planning permission may permit the defendant's property or another property in the locality to be used for a certain purpose, so that the question is how far that planning permission can be relied on by the defendant as changing the character of the locality.

81. However, that leaves open the question as to what weight, if any, should be given to the fact that planning permission has been granted for the very activities which a claimant contends give rise to a nuisance by noise. More particularly, what weight, if any, should be given to the fact that there is a planning permission for a use which will inevitably give rise to the noise which is said to constitute a nuisance, and/or which contains terms or conditions which specifically allow the emission of the noise which is said by a claimant to constitute a nuisance?

82. The implementation of a planning permission can give rise to a change in the character of the locality, but, subject to one possible point, it is no different from any other building work or change of use which does not require planning permission. Thus, if the implementation of a planning permission results in the creation of a nuisance to a claimant, then, subject to one possible point, it cannot be said that the implementation has led to a change in the character of the locality—save, as explained above, (i) to the extent that the implementation could have been effected in a way which would not have created a nuisance, or (ii) if the defendant can show a prescriptive right to create the nuisance, or (iii) the court has decided to award the claimant damages rather than an injunction in respect of the nuisance.

83. I have described the conclusions in the preceding paragraph as being 'subject to one possible point'. That point is the extent, if any, to which a defendant, in seeking to rebut a claim in nuisance, can rely on the fact that the grant, or terms and conditions, of a planning permission permit the very noise (or other disturbance) which is alleged by the claimant to constitute the nuisance (or which is relied on by the defendant as forming part of the character of the locality).

86. It seems to me that the effect of Jackson LJ's analysis is that, where the planning permission is granted for a use of the defendant's property which inevitably results in, or specifically permits, what would otherwise be a nuisance to the claimant, that use is to be treated as part of the character of the locality, if the permission relates to a large area, but not if it relates to a small area. Further, as is apparent from the contrasting outcomes in *Gillingham* and *Hirose*, as against *Wheeler* and *Watson*, where the planning permission for the nuisance-making activity is 'strategic' in nature or relates to a 'major development', it would defeat the claim for nuisance, whereas where it is for a small area, it would have no effect on the nuisance claim. As mentioned in para 73 above, that is scarcely surprising, as once one accepts that the noise complained of forms part of the character of the locality for the purpose of considering what constitutes a nuisance, it is hard to see how that very noise could be held to be a nuisance.

87. In my judgment, the conclusion reached by the Court of Appeal on this issue is unsatisfactory, both in principle and in practice, although it is only fair to add that they may understandably have considered that their hands were tied by the decisions mentioned in paras 84–86 above [including *Hirose Electrical UK Ltd v Peak Ingredients Ltd* [2011] Env LR 34 and *Watson v Croft Promosport Ltd* [2009] 3 All ER 249]. Logically, the fact that the alleged nuisance arising from the defendant's property is permitted by the planning authority should be a decisive factor, a relevant factor, or an irrelevant factor when assessing whether it is a nuisance. Which of those three possibilities applies should not depend on whether the permission relates to a large or small area of land. Furthermore, while Jackson LJ was at pains to emphasise that the grant of planning permission would not defeat a nuisance claim, it seems to me that that was precisely the effect of a planning permission for a large area, according to the reasoning of Buckley J in *Gillingham*, of the Court of Appeal in *Watson*, and of Jackson LJ in this case.

88. It also would be somewhat paradoxical if the greater the likely disagreeable impact of a change of use permitted by the planning authorities, the harder it would be for a claimant to establish a claim in nuisance. Yet that seems to be the effect of Jackson LJ's analysis, as the greater the area covered by the planning permission (i) the more likely it is to provide a defence to a claim in nuisance, and (ii) the more intrusive any noise or other intrusion is likely to be. Quite apart from this, it is hard to know what is meant by a large area.

89. The grant of planning permission for a particular development does not mean that that development is lawful. All it means is that a bar to the use imposed by planning law, in the public interest, has been removed. Logically, it might be argued, the grant of planning permission for a particular activity in 1985 or 2002 should have no more bearing on a claim that that activity causes a nuisance than the fact that the same activity could have occurred in the 19th century without any permission would have had on a nuisance claim in those days.

90. Quite apart from this, it seems wrong in principle that, through the grant of a planning permission, a planning authority should be able to deprive a property owner of a right to object to what would otherwise be a nuisance, without providing her with compensation, when there is no provision in the planning legislation which suggests such a possibility . . .

91. As for practical considerations, I am not impressed by the suggested difference between 'a strategic planning decision affected by considerations of public interest' (or a planning decision relating to a 'major development') and other planning decisions. No doubt

all planning applications take into account the public interest, and the difference between a 'strategic' planning permission (or a planning permission for a 'major development'), and other planning permissions seems to me to be a recipe for uncertainty.

94. Accordingly, I consider that the mere fact that the activity which is said to give rise to the nuisance has the benefit of a planning permission is normally of no assistance to the defendant in a claim brought by a neighbour who contends that the activity cause a nuisance to her land in the form of noise or other loss of amenity.

95. A planning authority has to consider the effect of a proposed development on occupiers of neighbouring land, but that is merely one of the factors which has to be taken into account. The planning authority can be expected to balance various competing interests, which will often be multifarious in nature, as best it can in the overall public interest, bearing in mind relevant planning guidelines. Some of those factors, such as many political and economic considerations which properly may play a part in the thinking of the members of a planning authority, would play no part in the assessment of whether a particular activity constitutes a nuisance—unless the law of nuisance is to be changed fairly radically. Quite apart from this, when granting planning permission for a change of use, a planning authority would be entitled to assume that a neighbour whose private rights might be infringed by that use could enforce those rights in a nuisance action; it could not be expected to take on itself the role of deciding a neighbour's common law rights.

96. However, there will be occasions when the terms of a planning permission could be of some relevance in a nuisance case. Thus, the fact that the planning authority takes the view that noisy activity is acceptable after 8.30 am, or if it is limited to a certain decibel level, in a particular locality, may be of real value, at least as a starting point as Lord Carnwath JSC says in para 218 below, in a case where the claimant is contending that the activity gives rise to a nuisance if it starts before 9.30 am, or is at or below the permitted decibel level. While the decision whether the activity causes a nuisance to the claimant is not for the planning authority but for the court, the existence and terms of the permission are not irrelevant as a matter of law, but in many cases they will be of little, or even no, evidential value, and in other cases rather more.

Lord Sumption, **Lord Mance** and **Lord Clarke of Stone-cum-Ebony** gave concurring judgments broadly agreeing with Lord Neuberger. **Lord Carnwath** also gave a judgment allowing the appeal.

Appeal allowed.

COMMENTARY

When applying his conclusions on the law to the facts of the case, Lord Neuberger commented (at [138]) that 'as already explained, the fact that a particular use has been granted planning permission is not normally a matter of much weight' in determining whether the use is a nuisance. Lord Sumption agreed (at [156]) that the existence of planning permission was 'of very limited relevance' to this question; planning powers did not exist to 'enforce or override private rights in respect of land use'. By contrast, Lord Carnwath expressed support (at [223]) for a narrow version of the *Gillingham* principle, on the basis that in 'exceptional cases' a grant of planning permission that was the result of a considered assessment of the appropriate balance between public and private interests and which led to a 'fundamental change in the pattern of uses' could not sensibly be ignored in assessing the character of the relevant locality.

The rejection of the *Gillingham* principle by a majority of the judges in *Lawrence* marked the end of a period of considerable uncertainty, and to that extent should be welcomed. Furthermore, as Lord Neuberger pointed out (at [87]) in the cases in which the principle applied it effectively operated as a defence, thereby contradicting the orthodoxy that direct legislative authority is required to override private rights in this context (see later, II.5(b)). Nevertheless, the relationship between private nuisance and administrative action is a complex one, and a faint echo of the *Gillingham* principle lives on in the idea that the grant of planning permission will at least militate against the issuing of an injunction (see II.6). In addition, their Lordships made it clear that planning permission may continue to influence the unreasonable interference enquiry, albeit more indirectly than under the *Gillingham* principle. Hence the fact that the planning authorities were prepared to grant permission for a use in a particular location may itself be indicative of the nature of the locality in question. Furthermore, it is noteworthy that in the extract Lord Neuberger expressed his agreement with Lord Carnwath's suggestion (at [218]) that where the planning permission for the defendant's activity established a detailed and carefully considered framework of (say) noise levels and time limits, this might serve as a benchmark or starting point for the court's consideration of the acceptability of the interference, with proof by the defendant of compliance with the framework militating against a finding of unreasonable interference, and proof to the contrary militating in favour of such a finding. For further analysis of *Lawrence*, see Howarth [2014] CLJ 247; Lees [2014] Conv 449; Dixon [2014] Conv 79; Lee [2014] JPL 705; and Pontin (2015) 27 JEL 119.

(c) The Reasonableness of the Defendant's Conduct

Christie v Davey [1893] 1 Ch 316

The plaintiffs were the occupiers of one half of a semi-detached property. They were a musical family, and used the house for playing, practising and teaching music. This annoyed the defendant, their next-door neighbour, who wrote to them in the following terms:

> During this week we have been much disturbed by what I at first thought were the howlings of your dog, and, knowing from experience that this sort of thing could not be helped, I put up with the annoyance. But, the noise recurring at a comparatively early hour this morning, I find I have been quite mistaken, and that it is the frantic effort of some one trying to sing with piano accompaniment, and during the day we are treated by way of variety to dreadful scrapings on a violin, with accompaniments. If the accompaniments are intended to drown the vocal shrieks or teased catgut vibrations, I can assure you it is a failure, for they do not. I am at last compelled to complain, for I cannot carry on my profession with this constant thump, thump, scrape, scrape, and shriek, shriek, constantly in my ears. It may be a pleasure or source of profit to you, but to me and mine it is a confounded nuisance and pecuniary loss, and, if allowed to continue, it must most seriously affect our health and comfort.

As the letter was ignored, the defendant commenced a series of noises in his house whenever the playing of music was going on in the plaintiffs' house—such as knocking on the party-wall, beating on trays, whistling, shrieking and imitating what was being played in the plaintiffs' house. The plaintiffs sought an injunction against the defendant in respect of this conduct, and the defendant counter-claimed for an injunction against the plaintiffs. North J rejected the counter-claim but granted the plaintiffs their injunction.

North J

The result is that I think I am bound to interfere for the protection of the Plaintiffs. In my opinion the noises which were made in the Defendant's house were not of a legitimate kind. They were what, to use the language of Lord Selborne in *Gaunt v Fynney* (1873) LR 8 Ch App 8, 'ought to be regarded as excessive and unreasonable.' I am satisfied that they were made deliberately and maliciously for the purpose of annoying the Plaintiffs. If what has taken place had occurred between two sets of persons both perfectly innocent, I should have taken an entirely different view of the case. But I am persuaded that what was done by the Defendant was done only for the purpose of annoyance, and in my opinion it was not a legitimate use of the Defendant's house to use it for the purpose of vexing and annoying his neighbours. I am not satisfied with the Defendant's attempts to explain away the Plaintiffs' statements. This being so, I am bound to give the Plaintiffs the relief which they ask.

COMMENTARY

Since the question of whether an interference is unreasonable boils down to whether the claimant can reasonably be expected to put up with it—what is called in Scots law the principle of 'reasonable tolerability'—it is not surprising that the reasonableness of the defendant's conduct is a key consideration. We must all put up with a degree of interference which is an inevitable consequence of the reasonable conduct of our neighbours, as Goddard LJ explained in *Metropolitan Properties Ltd v Jones* [1939] 2 All ER 202 at 205:

If my neighbour is going to put up some bookcases in his house, or put in a new fireplace, for a day or two I shall be exposed, no doubt, to a considerable disturbance . . . but the law does not regard that as a nuisance. A man may be doing that which is necessary for his house, or his own comfort, just as I may do the same thing in my own house the following month. It is one of those things which one has to put up with.

Conversely, where the defendant's activity has no legitimate purpose, but is motivated solely by a desire to injure the claimant, the interference that it causes is more likely to be unreasonable, as was the case in *Christie*. Another example is *Hollywood Silver Fox Farm v Emmett* [1936] 1 All ER 825, where, because of a dispute between the plaintiff and defendant, the defendant instructed his son to fire bird-scaring cartridges as near as possible to the breeding pens of the plaintiff's silver foxes whilst remaining on the defendant's land. As a result, one vixen would not breed and another ate her cubs. Applying *Christie*, Macnaghten J held that the plaintiff was entitled to damages and an injunction, as the malice rendered the discharge of the firearm a nuisance.

These two decisions can be contrasted with *Bradford Corporation v Pickles* [1895] AC 587, where the defendant owned land which contained a spring that supplied water to one of the plaintiff corporation's reservoirs. As a consequence of some drainage work proposed by Pickles, the water feeding the spring was to be diverted, which would have dried up the reservoir. Although the trial judge dismissed the defendant's explanation for the work, and found that his real motive was to force the corporation to pay him not to do it, the House of Lords held that the corporation was not entitled to an injunction to prevent the work from being carried out. Lord Halsbury LC said (at 594):

If it was a lawful act, however ill the motive might be, he had a right to do it. If it was an unlawful act, however good his motive might be, he would have no right to do it. Motives and intentions in such a question as is now before your Lordships seem to me to be absolutely irrelevant.

Several attempts have been made to reconcile the decisions in *Christie v Davey* and *Bradford v Pickles*. Perhaps the best explanation, suggested in *Winfield & Jolowicz*, para. 15–025, is that in *Bradford v Pickles* no legally protected interest of the plaintiff was affected by the defendant's conduct, since previous cases had established that no interest in percolating waters exists until appropriation, and it therefore followed that the motive of the defendant was irrelevant. By contrast, in *Christie v Davey* a legally protected interest of the plaintiff was affected (namely the right to be free from unreasonable noise interference), and so it was appropriate to take into account the defendant's motive.

Whatever the explanation, the reproachable (or, if you prefer, admirable) motives of Edward Pickles did not cause him to prosper. According to the researches of Brian Simpson, Pickles emigrated to Canada at the turn of the twentieth century, having spent his money in vain on elaborate underground workings (*Victorian Law and the Industrial Spirit*, Selden Society Lecture, 1995). For a more generous view of Pickles (and a more critical view of the corporation), see Campbell, 'Gathering the Water: Abuse of Rights after the Recognition of Government Failure' (2010) 7 J Juris 487.

(d) Public Benefit

Bamford v Turnley (1862) 3 B & S 66, 122 ER 27

The plaintiff complained that the smoke and smell generated by the defendant's use of his land (burning bricks) amounted to a nuisance. The defendant succeeded at trial, and the plaintiff sought a rule for the defendant to show cause why judgment should not be entered for the plaintiff (in modern parlance, appealed against the decision). The Court of Queen's Bench refused the rule, but it was granted in the Court of Exchequer Chamber. One argument before the court was that the defendant's activity was for the public benefit.

Bramwell B

[I]t is said that, temporary or permanent, it is lawful because it for the public benefit. Now, in the first place, that law to my mind is a bad one which, for the public benefit, inflicts loss on an individual without compensation. But further, with great respect, I think this consideration misapplied in this and in many other cases. The public consists of all the individuals of it, and a thing is only for the public benefit when it is productive of good to those individuals on the balance of loss and gain to all. So that if all the loss and all the gain were borne and received by one individual, he on the whole would be a gainer. But whenever this is the case—whenever a thing is for the public benefit, properly understood—the loss to the individuals of the public who lose will bear compensation out of the gains of those who gain. It is for the public benefit that there should be railways, but it would not be unless the gain of having the railway was sufficient to compensate the loss occasioned by the use of the land required for its site; and accordingly no one thinks it would be right to take an individual's land without compensation to make a railway. It is for the public benefit that trains should run, but not unless they pay their expenses. If one of those expenses is the burning down of a wood of such value that the railway owners would not run the train and burn down the wood if it were their own, neither is it for the public benefit they should if the wood is not their own. If, though the wood were their own, they still would find it compensated them to run trains at the cost of burning the wood, then they obviously ought to compensate the owner of such wood, not being themselves, if

> they burn it down in making their gains. So in like way in this case a money value indeed cannot easily be put on the plaintiff's loss, but it is equal to some number of pounds or pence, £10, £50, or what not: unless the defendant's profits are enough to compensate this, I deny that it is for the public benefit he should do what he has done; if they are, he ought to compensate.

COMMENTARY

Modern law-and-economics scholars could not have put the argument better than Bramwell B: to gauge the proper cost of an activity the injury caused to outsiders must be taken into account (see Coase, 'The Problem of Social Cost' (1960) 3 JLE 1). In economic terms, if net utility (social benefit) after the activity is undertaken is greater than that before it, the activity is economically desirable and should be undertaken; in Bramwellian terms, the activity is for the public benefit only if it is profitable after paying compensation to those injured by it.

Although the authorities are clear that 'it is generally no defence to a claim of nuisance that the [defendant's activity] is of benefit to the public' (*Lawrence v Fen Tigers Ltd* [2014] AC 822 at [193], per Lord Carnwath), public benefit is nevertheless a consideration that is taken into account when considering whether the interference with the claimant's use and enjoyment is unreasonable (see, e.g., *Jones v Ministry of Defence* [2021] EWHC (QB) 2276 at [63]). The overall position, then, is as stated by *Fleming*, p. 504:

> Likewise, some consideration will be given to the fact that the offensive enterprise is essential and unavoidable in the particular locality, like a coal mine, quarry, or some public utility or service such as early morning milk delivery. This argument, however, must not be pushed too far. In particular, it should be remembered that we are here concerned with reciprocal rights and duties of private individuals, and a defendant cannot simply justify his infliction of great harm upon the plaintiff by urging that a greater benefit to the public at large has accrued from his conduct.

If it is necessary to go further than this, and extinguish private rights for public interest reasons, then this has generally been thought to be a matter for Parliament (see Lindley LJ in *Shelfer v City of London Electric Lighting Company* [1895] 1 Ch 287 at 316), and much of the development of the railways, mentioned by Bramwell B, took place through private Acts of Parliament allowing for compulsory land acquisition with payment of compensation to those affected (R. Kostal, *Law and English Railway Capitalism 1825–1875* (Oxford: OUP, 1994), ch. 4; A. W. B. Simpson, *Victorian Law and the Industrial Spirit*, Selden Society Lecture, 1995). On the history of the role of nuisance in mediating between public and private interests, see Brenner, 'Nuisance Law and the Industrial Revolution' (1974) 3 J Leg St 403; McLaren, 'Nuisance Law and the Industrial Revolution—Some Lessons from Social History' (1983) 3 OJLS 155; Pontin, 'Tort Law and Victorian Government Growth: The Historiographical Significance of Tort in the Shadow of Chemical Pollution and Factory Safety Regulation' (1998) 18 OJLS 661; and Pontin, 'Nuisance Law and the Industrial Revolution: A Reinterpretation of Doctrine and Institutional Competence' (2012) 75 MLR 1010. In more recent times, the issue has returned to the courts in the form of decisions on the effect of planning and regulatory consents to carry out conduct which might otherwise amount to a nuisance (see further II.2(b) and II.5(b)).

If public benefit is not a defence to a nuisance action, might it nevertheless be taken into account when deciding what remedy is to be awarded to the claimant? (See II.6.)

Finally, what exactly do courts and commentators mean when they refer to the 'public interest' or 'public benefit' in this context? See further Lee, 'Public Interest in Private Nuisance' [2015] CLJ 329, who points out that little attention has been given to this question, and suggests that a defensible vision of the public interest for these purposes would be one that focused on administrative and regulatory decisions that purport to promote collective interests, provided proper scrutiny is given to the quality of the processes by which these decisions are reached. This would avoid the need for the courts themselves 'to assess diverse and competing claims of public interest in substantive terms', which she doubts they generally have the capacity to do (at 347).

3. Nuisance, Negligence and Fault

The question of whether nuisance is a fault-based tort or a strict liability tort does not admit of a simple answer. In cases of ongoing interference where the defendant is the creator of the nuisance, fault is not required (so the taking of reasonable care is not a defence: see, e.g., *Rapier v London Tramways Co* [1893] 2 Ch 588), but foreseeability of the type of damage done is a prerequisite of recovery of damages for past harm, and whether or not the defendant acted reasonably may be relevant in determining whether the interference is unreasonable. (In particular, the defendant's failure to take reasonable care will weigh heavily against them, since 'the claimant cannot reasonably be expected to put up with interference which could be reduced by the adoption of reasonable ameliorative measures': *Winfield & Jolowicz*, para. 15–017.) Furthermore, the defence of statutory authority (see II.5(b)) is available only if the defendant has taken reasonable steps to minimise the interference. However, where the defendant is not the creator of the nuisance, but only the occupier of the land on which it originates, liability is generally dependent on a finding of lack of reasonable care. It follows that in such cases there is the potential for overlap between nuisance and negligence, and indeed similar fact patterns have been treated more or less indifferently as giving rise to liability in the two torts.

(a) Foreseeability

Cambridge Water Co Ltd v Eastern Counties Leather plc [1994] 2 AC 264

The facts are not relevant for present purposes, but are set out with a further extract in III.2.

Lord Goff

Foreseeability of Damage in Nuisance

It is, of course, axiomatic that in this field we must be on our guard, when considering liability for damages in nuisance, not to draw inapposite conclusions from cases concerned only with a claim for an injunction. This is because, where an injunction is claimed, its purpose is to restrain further action by the defendant which may interfere with the plaintiff's enjoyment of his land, and *ex hypothesi* the defendant must be aware, if and when an injunction is granted, that such interference may be caused by the act which he is restrained from committing. It follows that these cases provide no guidance on the question whether foreseeability of harm of the relevant type is a prerequisite of the recovery of damages for causing such harm to the plaintiff. In the present case, we are not concerned with liability in damages in respect of a nuisance which has arisen through natural causes, or by the act of a person for whose actions the defendant is not responsible, in which cases the applicable principles in nuisance have become closely associated with those applicable in negligence: see *Sedleigh-Denfield v O'Callagan* [1940] AC 880 and *Goldman v Hargrave* [1967] 1 AC 645. We are concerned with the liability of a person where a nuisance has been created by one for whose actions he is responsible. Here, as I have said, it is still the law that the fact that the defendant has taken all reasonable care will not of itself exonerate him from liability, the relevant control mechanism being found within the principle of reasonable user. But it by no means follows that the defendant should be held liable for damage of a type which he could not reasonably foresee; and the development of the law of negligence in the past sixty years points strongly towards a requirement that such foreseeability should be a prerequisite of liability in damages for nuisance, as it is of liability in negligence. For if a plaintiff is in ordinary circumstances only able to claim damages in respect of personal injuries where he can prove such foreseeability on the part of the defendant, it is difficult to see why, in common justice, he should be in a stronger position to claim damages for interference with the enjoyment of his land where the defendant was unable to foresee such damage. Moreover, this appears to have been the conclusion of the Privy Council in *The Wagon Mound (No. 2), Overseas Tankship (UK) Ltd v Miller Steamship Co Pty Ltd* [1967] 1 AC 617. The facts of the case are too well known to require repetition, but they gave rise to a claim for damages arising from a public nuisance caused by a spillage of oil in Sydney Harbour. Lord Reid, who delivered the advice of the Privy Council, considered that, in the class of nuisance which included the case before the Board, foreseeability is an essential element in determining liability. He then continued at 640:

> It could not be right to discriminate between different cases of nuisance so as to make foreseeability a necessary element in determining damages in those cases where it is a necessary element in determining liability, but not in others. So the choice is between it being a necessary element in all cases of nuisance or in none. In their Lordships' judgment the similarities between nuisance and other forms of tort to which *The Wagon Mound (No. 1)* applies far outweigh any differences, and they must therefore hold that the judgment appealed from is wrong on this branch of the case. It is not sufficient that the injury suffered by the respondents' vessels was the direct result of the nuisance if that injury was in the relevant sense unforeseeable.

It is widely accepted that this conclusion, although not essential to the decision of the particular case, has nevertheless settled the law to the effect that foreseeability of harm is indeed a prerequisite of the recovery of damages in private nuisance, as in the case of public nuisance . . . It is unnecessary in the present case to consider the precise nature of this principle; but it appears from Lord Reid's statement of the law that he regarded it essentially as one relating to remoteness of damage.

COMMENTARY

Lord Goff confirms in his speech that liability in nuisance is not dependent on the defendant having failed to take reasonable care in carrying out the activity that caused the interference. However, his Lordship also makes clear that a defendant will be liable in damages only for the reasonably foreseeable consequences of their conduct. In most nuisance cases, this requirement is easily satisfied, as the defendant will have known full well what effect their conduct was having, as where, for example they engaged in a noisy activity that was obviously audible to their neighbours. However, foreseeability may become an issue where the harm in respect of which the claimant seeks damages resulted from a one-off event (such as a flood) or an ongoing interference which was hidden from the defendant's view (see, e.g., *Ilford UDC v Beal* [1925] 1 KB 671).

(b) Fault and Nuisances Created by Third Parties

Thus far we have focused on nuisances created by the defendant. But a defendant can also be held liable in respect of a nuisance created by a third party on land which they either occupy or own. Where the defendant is an occupier, the liability that may arise in nuisance is largely fault-based, with the result that if the claimant has suffered harm actionable in negligence—which in this context means physical damage to property—the liability that attaches in nuisance closely mirrors that in negligence. In the words of Lord Walker in *Transco plc v Stockport Metropolitan Borough Council* [2004] 2 AC 1 at [96], in such cases the territory of private nuisance 'overlaps with (indeed, is a sort of condominium with) that of negligence'. The circumstances in which an occupier can be held liable for a nuisance created by a third party were discussed in the next extracted case.

Sedleigh-Denfield v O'Callaghan [1940] AC 880

A pipe had been built on the defendants' land to drain water from a ditch. The pipe was constructed by the local authority without the defendants' knowledge, and insofar as it extended onto the defendants' land it amounted to a trespass to land and the workers who built it were trespassers. No grate had been placed at the entrance of the pipe to prevent debris from entering it, and when the pipe became blocked by debris after a heavy storm, it overflowed, flooding the plaintiff's neighbouring land. It was held by the House of Lords that since a member of the defendant religious order had known of the pipe's existence, it had to be assumed that the order had knowledge of it as well.

Lord Atkin

In this state of the facts, the legal position is not, I think, difficult to discover. For the purpose of ascertaining whether, as here, the plaintiff can establish a private nuisance, I think that nuisance is sufficiently defined as a wrongful interference with another's enjoyment of his land or premises by the use of land or premises either occupied—or, in some cases, owned—by oneself. The occupier or owner is not an insurer. There must be something more than the mere harm done to the neighbour's property to make the party responsible. Deliberate act or negligence is not an essential ingredient, but some degree of personal responsibility is required, which is connoted in my definition by the word 'use'. This conception is implicit in all the decisions which impose liability only where the defendant has 'caused or continued' the nuisance. We may eliminate, in this case, 'caused'. What is the meaning of 'continued'? In the context in which it is used, 'continued' must indicate mere passive continuance. If a man uses on premises something which he finds there, and which itself causes a nuisance by noise, vibration, smell or fumes, he is himself, in continuing to bring into existence the noise, vibration, smell or fumes, causing a nuisance. Continuing, in this sense, and causing are the same thing. It seems to me clear that, if a man permits an offensive thing on his premises to continue to offend—that is, if he knows that it is operating offensively, is able to prevent it, and omits to prevent it—he is permitting the nuisance to continue. In other words, he is continuing it. The liability of an occupier has been carried so far that it appears to have been decided that, if he comes to occupy, say, as tenant, premises upon which there exists a nuisance caused by a previous occupier, he is responsible, even though he does not know that either the cause or the result is in existence. . . .

In the present case, however, there is, as I have said, sufficient proof of the knowledge of the defendants both of the cause and of its probable effect. What is the legal result of the original cause being due to the act of a trespasser? In my opinion, the defendants clearly continued the nuisance, for they come clearly within the terms I have mentioned above. They knew the danger, they were able to prevent it, and they omitted to prevent it.

Lord Wright

In my opinion, for reasons which I shall briefly explain, I think that the appeal should succeed. If it were merely a question of the physical conditions, no one would question that a case of private nuisance was established. The interposition of the pipe as the means of carrying the water from the ditch in place of the former open watercourse was not in itself objectionable. The trouble was that no protecting grid was put in place, and there was nothing to prevent the pipe from getting choked. There was thus the risk of a flood, which might spread, as in fact happened, to the appellant's premises, causing damage which in the actual result was considerable. . . .

[W]here, as here, a plaintiff is damaged by his land being flooded, the facts bring it well within the sphere of nuisance. Such a case has a certain similarity with those to which the rule of *Rylands v Fletcher* applies, but there are obvious differences in substance. There are, indeed, well-marked differences between the two juristic concepts. This case has, therefore, properly been treated as a case of nuisance. It has affinity also with a claim for negligence, because the trouble arose from the negligent fitting of the grid. But the gist of the present action is the unreasonable and unjustified intervention by the defendant in the use of his land with the plaintiff's right to enjoy his property. Negligence, moreover, is not a necessary condition of a claim for nuisance. What is done may be done deliberately, and in good faith and in a genuine belief that it is justified. Negligence here is not an independent cause of action but is ancillary to the actual cause of action, which is nuisance. . . .

[His Lordship considered some authorities where liability had not been imposed in public nuisance, and continued:]

In these modern cases, the plaintiff failed because he did not establish that the defendant either knew or ought to have known [of the nuisance]. In the present case, it is, in my opinion, clear on the facts . . . that the respondents, by their servant, knew, or at least ought to have known, of the nuisance. On the law, as I have accepted it, the respondents' responsibility would seem to follow.

Lord Romer

The question to be decided is whether the respondents can be held liable for the damage caused to the appellant by the floods that took place in April 1937, and in November 1937, which were without question due to the accumulation in the culvert of rubbish which would not have been there had a proper grid been provided in the respondents' ditch. My Lords, I should have thought that, consistently with well-established principles of law, this question only permitted of an answer in the affirmative. An owner or occupier of land must so use it that he does not thereby substantially interfere with the comfortable enjoyment of their land by his neighbours. The user of the ditch by the construction of the culvert was not, indeed, a user of their land by the respondents at all. It was the act of a trespasser. Nevertheless, the respondents continued thereafter to use the ditch for the purpose of draining their adjoining fields, without taking steps to ensure that the water did not accumulate therein, and, as a consequence, flood the appellant's premises. Such steps were well within their power. All that it was necessary to do was to provide a grid which would prevent the rubbish which fell into the ditch from passing into the culvert. In these circumstances, it seems to me that they committed a nuisance upon their land, for which they must be held responsible.

Lord Porter

It is clear that an occupier may be liable though (i) he is wholly blameless (ii) he is not only ignorant of the existence of the nuisance but also without means of detecting it, and (iii) he entered into occupation after the nuisance had come into existence . . . Such a liability is, I think, inconsistent with the contention that the occupier is not liable for the acts of a trespasser of which he has knowledge, though possibly it might be contended that he is responsible for the acts of his predecessor in title, but not for those of a trespasser. Such a contention, however, is, I think, unsound, and the true view is that the occupier of land is liable for a nuisance existing on his property to the extent that he can reasonably abate it, even though he neither created it nor received any benefit from it. It is enough if he permitted it to continue after he knew, or ought to have known, of its existence. To this extent, but to no greater extent, he must be proved to have adopted the act of the creator of the nuisance. . . .

Viscount Maugham delivered a separate concurring speech.

Appeal allowed.

COMMENTARY

The House of Lords held the defendants liable because they had continued or adopted the nuisance. A nuisance was continued if the defendant had (or should have had) knowledge of the existence of a threat which a state of affairs on their land posed to their neighbour and failed to take reasonable steps to bring the nuisance to an end, and adopted if the defendant made use of the state of affairs for their own purposes.

Some of the issues arising out of *Sedleigh-Denfield*, and out of the relationship between nuisance and negligence in this context, are considered in the following extract.

C. Gearty, 'The Place of Private Nuisance in a Modern Law of Torts' [1989] CLJ 214, 235-7

An occupier of land 'continued' a nuisance if 'with knowledge or presumed knowledge of its existence he failed to take any reasonable means to bring it to an end though with ample time to do so.' Lord Wright and Lord Romer expressly approved this analysis of the law. It is easy to apply where the nuisance is one which interferes with personal comfort: a trespasser sneaking onto D's land and building something from which noxious gases are emitted; an intruder dumping an old electronic device which causes a noise nuisance and so on. It also works fairly well where the trespasser creates a state of affairs which causes damage to neighbouring land—though here we have preferred to speak of negligence. In all of these situations, the idea of D continuing something that is an ongoing nuisance has meaning. Difficulty arises where physical damage to property is caused by a single isolated event. How can such an occurrence be regarded as a nuisance capable of being known before it happens?

The facts of *Sedleigh-Denfield* make this crystal clear. The pipe lying in the ditch without its grid was not a nuisance. It interfered with nobody's comfort. It caused no damage to anyone. It may have had the potential to be a nuisance, but then so does any radio before it is turned on or any leaking lake-side tank before it is filled with oil. Neither Viscount Maugham nor Lord Wright addressed this point. They simply assumed that there was a nuisance which, applying an objective test, the occupiers ought to have seen and ought to have done something about. Neither pinpointed what the nuisance actually was. Lord Romer attempted to draw a distinction between a potential and an actual nuisance:

> The respondents did not themselves create this potential nuisance [ie the pipe without the grid], and cannot therefore be held liable for its creation. But an occupier of land upon which a nuisance has been created by another person is liable if he 'continues' the nuisance . . . I agree with my noble and learned friend upon the woolsack, whose opinion I have had the privilege of reading, that the occupier 'continues' a nuisance if with knowledge or presumed knowledge of its existence he fails to take any reasonable means to bring it to an end though with ample time to do so. Judging them by this criteria, the respondents clearly continued the potential nuisance created by [the trespasser].

The response to this last point could well be, so what? Occupiers are not liable in nuisance simply because they own empty factories which would be noisy if they were working.

The two remaining law lords were aware of the problem. Lord Porter observed that 'the nuisance [was] not the existence of the pipe unprotected by a grid but the flooding of the appellant's garden.' Lord Atkin agreed that it was not a nuisance though it could 'threaten to become' one. This reasoning forced their Lordships even further away from nuisance. Liability attached because the defendants 'ought . . . as reasonable persons to have recognised the probability, or at least the possibility of a flood occurring.' Lord Atkin noted that the facts were such that 'when the ditch was flowing in full stream an obstruction might reasonably be expected in the pipe, from which obstruction flooding of the plaintiff's ground might reasonably be expected to result.'

We may note a distinction here. Three of their Lordships attached the label 'nuisance' to whatever could be said, in retrospect, to have been the cause of the damage. The remaining two defined nuisance as the damage-causing event. Both approaches made liability dependent upon what D, as a reasonable landowner, ought to have seen and how he ought to have behaved. The extent of the harm to P—the traditional concern of nuisance—hardly mattered at all and, indeed, is very difficult to discern from the judgments in *Sedleigh-Denfield*. This was negligence pure and simple, confused by an ill-fitting and woolly disguise of nuisance. It seems that the only people who were not your neighbours in the *Donoghue v Stevenson* sense were those who actually were.

COMMENTARY

Sedleigh-Denfield raised two important issues—first, whether an occupier can be liable for a nuisance created on their land by a third party (considered by the House of Lords); and secondly, whether an isolated event can amount to a nuisance (not discussed in any detail). Gearty argues that in both situations any liability imposed in nuisance mirrors the liability that would be imposed in negligence, at least where property damage is the result.

An example of this in the context of acts of third parties is *Smith v Littlewoods Corporation* (extracted in Ch. 9.III) where the liability of the cinema owner was discussed entirely in terms of negligence. Would anything have been gained by arguing the case in nuisance?

One reason for the reliance on nuisance in *Sedleigh-Denfield* may have been the traditional reluctance of the common law of negligence to impose a duty of positive action. However, it has since been recognised that the occupier of land may owe a duty in negligence to act positively to prevent harm to their neighbour (see *Goldman v Hargrave*, noted later). Hence, as Lord Cooke said in *Delaware Mansions Ltd v Westminster City Council* [2002] 1 AC 321 at 333: 'The label nuisance or negligence is treated as of no real significance. In this field, I think, the concern of the common law lies in working out the fair and just content and incidents of a neighbour's duty rather than affixing a label and inferring the extent of the duty from it.'

Given these developments, what benefits might there be in arguing the case in nuisance rather than negligence if a similar case arose today? (See Lee, 'What is Private Nuisance?' (2003) 119 LQR 298.)

The reasoning in *Sedleigh-Denfield* has been used to impose liability on occupiers for nuisances caused by the actions of their predecessors in title (*Bybrook Barn Centre Ltd v Kent County Council* [2001] BLR 55), and of third parties who used the defendant's land as a base from which to engage in activities off the defendant's land which interfered with the claimant's use and enjoyment of their land. In *Lippiatt v South Gloucestershire Council* [2000] QB 51, the plaintiffs alleged that travellers camped on the defendant's land had trespassed on their farms and caused a nuisance. The Court of Appeal refused to strike out the plaintiff's claim (see also *Winch v Mid-Bedfordshire District Council* [2002] All ER (D) 380, where *Lippiatt* was applied to hold the defendant council liable). But is this type of case really on all fours with *Sedleigh-Denfield*, where the third party's conduct created a dangerous state of affairs on the defendant's property? And what if the travellers had driven to a nearby town and caused a nuisance there? Would the defendant still have been liable? (For criticism of the *Lippiatt* decision, and a suggested alternative approach to third-party cases, see Bright, 'Liability for the Bad Behaviour of Others' (2001) 21 OJLS 311.)

Another basis on which one person can be held liable for a nuisance created by a third party is authorisation. If, for example, an occupier hires their premises out for a purpose which involves a special danger of nuisance, then they will be liable for any nuisance which results, as this amounts to authorisation (see, e.g., *De Jager v Payneham and Magill Lodges Hall Inc* (1984) 36 SASR 498). Most of the case law on authorisation concerns landlords who have been sued for a nuisance caused by a tenant in the demised property, where it must be shown either that the landlord expressly authorised the nuisance (which is obviously unlikely) or that the nuisance was virtually certain to result from the purposes for which the property was let. This latter test was satisfied in *Tetley v Chitty* [1986] 1 All ER 663, where a council which leased land for use as a go-kart track was held liable for the noise the go-karts generated, but not in *Smith v Scott* [1973] Ch 314, where a council which let a house to a 'problem' family was not liable when they caused a nuisance to their neighbours (see also *Lawrence v Fen Tigers Ltd (No. 2)* [2015] AC 106). It should also be noted that a landlord is not deemed to have authorised their tenant's nuisance because they knew about but did not exercise their right to end the tenancy (see, e.g., *Hussain v Lancaster City Council* [2000] QB 1; for a failed attempt to get round this rule by relying on the Human Rights Act 1998 as against a local authority landlord, see *Mowan v Wandsworth London Borough Council* (2001) 33 HLR 56). See further on landlord liability in nuisance, Bright, *op. cit.*; and Morgan, 'Nuisance and the Unruly Tenant' [2001] CLJ 382.

Finally, it seems that even if no third party is involved, a fault-based liability similar to that applicable to occupiers is imposed where the alleged nuisance is constituted by an isolated escape, or by an ongoing interference which would not have been apparent to the defendant as a consequence of their activity (because, for example, it was the result of a hidden process of the kind operating in *Cambridge Water*). In *Northumbrian Water Ltd v Sir Robert McAlpine Ltd* [2014] BLR 605, the Court of Appeal made it clear that in cases of this kind a claim for damages was unlikely to succeed without either fault or a non-natural use that brought the case within the ambit of the rule in *Rylands v Fletcher*, an analysis consistent with earlier case law involving isolated escapes (see, e.g., *British Celanese Ltd v A.H. Hunt* [1969] 1 WLR 959; *S.C.M. (UK) Ltd v W.J. Whittal & Son Ltd* [1971] 1 QB 337). It follows that there is little to be gained by framing such a claim in nuisance, the cause of action for which is in effect limited to cases where there is a degree of continuity in the interference (as has long been argued by some commentators to be desirable: see Newark, 'The Boundaries of Nuisance' (1949) 65 LQR 480; Gearty, *op. cit.*; J. Murphy, *The Law of Nuisance* (Oxford: OUP, 2010), paras 1.19–1.24.). However, it has been suggested that the position may be different if the claimant is alleging interference only with their amenity. In *Anglian Water Services Ltd v Crawshaw Robbins & Co Ltd* [2001] BLR 173, Stanley Burnton J said: 'A single act which caused a stench to come onto a neighbour's land, for example by damaging a pipe carrying noxious gas, would constitute actionable nuisance . . . I doubt if a bad smell would support a claim in negligence; it would in nuisance.' In these situations, the claimant will still need to show an absence of reasonable care, but it seems that, in the absence of physical damage of the kind that would ground a negligence claim, the cause of action must be classified as nuisance.

(c) Nuisance and Acts of Nature

If an occupier could be liable in respect of a nuisance created by a third party, was this also the case where it arose from an act of nature or the natural condition of the land? The attitude of the courts to this issue has not always been consistent. In *Lemmon v Webb* [1894] 3 Ch 1 and *Smith v Giddy* [1904] 2 KB 448 an occupier of land was assumed to be liable where the overhanging branches of trees growing on his land caused damage to his neighbour's property. However, an occupier who allowed thistles to grow on his land was not liable when the seeds blew onto his neighbour's land, causing a proliferation of thistles, Lord Coleridge CJ commenting that '[t]here can be no duty as between adjoining occupiers to cut the thistles, which are the natural growth of the soil' (*Giles v Walker* (1890) 24 QBD 656).

The issue of an occupier's liability for damage caused by an act of nature came before the Privy Council in *Goldman v Hargrave* [1967] 1 AC 645. The plaintiff and defendant were neighbours in the Western Australian bush, and, due to a lightning strike on the defendant's property a redgum tree caught fire. Although the defendant took some steps to alleviate the risk that this posed, these were inadequate and the fire spread to the plaintiff's property and caused damage. The Privy Council held that the occupier of land owed a duty to their neighbour to take reasonable steps to remove any hazards arising on their property, whether natural or man-made. The duty arose where the occupier knew or should have known of the hazard and the risk it posed to neighbouring property. The standard was one of reasonable care, but because the duty to act was imposed on the occupier, their individual circumstances and resources were to be taken into account when applying this standard. The Privy Council (at 656–7) clearly considered that the liability, if it arose, was in negligence:

> Their Lordships propose to deal with these issues as stated, without attempting to answer the disputable question whether if responsibility is established it should be brought under the heading of nuisance or placed in a separate category. . . . The present case is one where liability, if it exists, rests upon negligence and nothing else; whether it falls within or overlaps the boundaries of nuisance is a question of classification which need not here be resolved.

(See further on this case, M. Lunney, 'Goldman v Hargrave (1967)', in *Mitchell & Mitchell*.)

The leading English case on natural nuisance is *Leakey v National Trust* [1980] QB 485. The plaintiffs owned two houses which had been built at the base of a large mound ('Burrow Mump') on the defendants' land. As a consequence of natural weathering parts of the mound had broken off and fallen onto the plaintiffs' land, and it was established that, by 1968 at the latest, the defendants were aware of this occurrence. In the summer of 1976 a large crack opened in the mound, but the defendants refused to take any remedial action on the basis that they were not responsible for any damage caused by a natural movement of land. A few weeks later a significant quantity of debris from the mound fell onto the plaintiffs' land and the plaintiffs sought an injunction requiring the defendants to abate the nuisance as well as damages. Both the trial judge and the Court of Appeal held that the defendants were liable to the plaintiffs in nuisance. Megaw LJ (at 514) responded to the argument that the proper cause of action was negligence and not nuisance as follows:

> The plaintiffs' claim is expressed in the pleadings to be founded in nuisance. There is no express reference to negligence in the statement of claim. But there is an allegation of a breach of duty, and the duty asserted is, in effect, a duty to take reasonable care to prevent part of the defendants' land from falling on to the plaintiffs' property. I should, for myself, regard that as being properly described as a claim in nuisance. But even if that were, technically, wrong, I do not think that the point could or should avail the defendants in this case. If it were to do so, it would be a regrettable modern instance of the forms of action successfully clanking their spectral chains; for there would be no conceivable prejudice to the defendants in this case that the word 'negligence' had not been expressly set out in the statement of claim.

The result of these cases is that where the alleged nuisance is caused by a natural occurrence an action may be commenced in either nuisance or negligence, but that liability will be determined according to principles applicable to the law of negligence, slightly modified in that the defendant's circumstances are considered in determining what is a reasonable response to the risk posed by the natural occurrence. Two other concessions in favour of occupiers were made in *Holbeck Hall Hotel Ltd v Scarborough Borough Council* [2000] QB 836, where the defendant council was accused of failing to take reasonable steps to prevent erosion of a coastal cliff area that it owned, with the result that part of the claimant's hotel fell into the sea. Although the Court of Appeal held that, applying *Leakey*, the council had a duty to take reasonable steps to reduce or remove any threat to the claimant's property from the failure of the support provided by its land, it concluded that the damage to the hotel fell outside the scope of that duty. That conclusion followed from two separate holdings favourable to occupiers sued in nuisance for an omission. The first was that, in such cases, both the type *and the extent* of the harm must have been foreseeable. And the second was that liability for continuing a nuisance could arise only if the occupier either saw or should have seen the problem on the face of their land, and not where the threat to neighbouring property was discoverable only by further investigation. On the facts, the risk of damage to the hotel itself (as opposed to its grounds) would have been revealed only by geological investigation, and so the council was not liable for it.

4. Who Can Sue

In *Malone v Laskey* [1907] 2 KB 141 the Court of Appeal held that only a person with a possessory or proprietary interest in the land affected by the nuisance could bring a claim in respect of it. This view was challenged in *Khorasandjian v Bush* [1993] QB 727, where a majority of the Court of Appeal (Peter Gibson J dissenting) held that the plaintiff, who was seeking an injunction against a former boyfriend plaguing her with phone calls, could rely on private nuisance in respect of calls to the landline in her mother's house, where she lived. This development was considered in the next extracted case.

Hunter v Canary Wharf Ltd [1997] AC 655

Two appeals were heard by the House of Lords relating to alleged nuisances caused by the development of Canary Wharf in east London. The appeals raised two issues: first, whether interference with television reception caused by the erection of a tall building (the Canary Wharf Tower) was capable of amounting to an actionable nuisance; and secondly, who had standing in private nuisance. The House of Lords held unanimously that no claim could arise in respect of interference with television reception caused by a building, and by a 4–1 majority (Lord Cooke dissenting) that only those with a proprietary interest in the property affected could sue. The extracts deal with the second issue.

Lord Goff

The question therefore arises whether your Lordships should be persuaded to depart from established principle, and recognise [a right to sue in nuisance] in others who are no more than mere licensees on the land. . . . [I]t is right for present purposes to regard the typical cases of private nuisance as being those concerned with interference with the enjoyment of land and, as such, generally actionable only by a person with a right in the land. Characteristic examples of cases of this kind are those concerned with noise, vibrations, noxious smells and the like. The two appeals with which your Lordships are here concerned arise from actions of this character.

For private nuisances of this kind, the primary remedy is in most cases an injunction, which is sought to bring the nuisance to an end, and in most cases should swiftly achieve that objective. The right to bring such proceedings is, as the law stands, ordinarily vested in the person who has exclusive possession of the land. He or she is the person who will sue, if it is necessary to do so. Moreover he or she can, if thought appropriate, reach an agreement with the person creating the nuisance, either that it may continue for a certain period of time, possibly on the payment of a sum of money, or that it shall cease, again perhaps on certain terms including the time within which the cessation will take place. The former may well occur when an agreement is reached between neighbours about the circumstances in which one of them may carry out major repairs to his house which may affect the other's enjoyment of his property. An agreement of this kind was expressly contemplated by Fletcher Moulton LJ in his judgment in *Malone v Laskey* [1907] 2 KB 141 at 153. But the efficacy of arrangements such as these depends upon the existence of an identifiable person with whom the creator of the nuisance can deal for this purpose. If anybody who lived in the relevant property as a home had the right to sue, sensible arrangements such as these might in some cases no longer be practicable.

Moreover, any such departure from the established law on this subject, such as that adopted by the Court of Appeal in the present case, faces the problem of defining the category of persons who would have the right to sue. The Court of Appeal adopted the not easily identifiable category of those who have a 'substantial link' with the land, regarding a person who occupied the premises 'as a home' as having a sufficient link for this purpose. But who is to be included in this category? It was plainly intended to include husbands and wives, or partners, and their children, and even other relatives living with them. But is the category also to include the lodger upstairs, or the au pair girl or resident nurse caring for an invalid who makes her home in the house while she works there? If the latter, it seems strange that the category should not extend to include places where people work as well as places where they live, where nuisances such as noise can be just as unpleasant or distracting. In any event, the extension of the tort in this way would transform it from a tort to land into a tort to the person, in which damages could be recovered in respect of something less serious than personal injury and the criteria for liability were founded not upon negligence but upon striking a balance between the interests of neighbours in the use of their land. This is, in my opinion, not an acceptable way in which to develop the law.

It was suggested in the course of argument that at least the spouse of a husband or wife who, for example as freeholder or tenant, had exclusive possession of the matrimonial home should be entitled to sue in private nuisance. For the purposes of this submission, your Lordships were referred to the relevant legislation, notably the Matrimonial Homes Act 1983 and the Family Law Act 1996. I do not, however, consider it necessary to go through the statutory provisions. As I understand the position, it is as follows. If under the relevant legislation a spouse becomes entitled to possession of the matrimonial home or part of it, there is no reason why he or she should not be able to sue in private nuisance in the ordinary way. But I do not see how a spouse who has no interest in the matrimonial home has, simply by virtue of his or her cohabiting in the matrimonial home with his or her wife or husband whose freehold or leasehold property it is, a right to sue. No distinction can sensibly be drawn between such spouses and other cohabitees in the home, such as children, or grandparents. Nor do I see any great disadvantage flowing from this state of affairs. If a nuisance should occur, then the spouse who has an interest in the property can bring the necessary proceedings to bring the nuisance to an end, and can recover any damages in respect of the discomfort or inconvenience caused by the nuisance. Even if he or she is away from home, nowadays the necessary authority to commence proceedings for an injunction can usually be obtained by telephone. Moreover, if the other spouse suffers personal injury, including injury to health, he or she may, like anybody else, be able to recover damages in negligence. The only disadvantage is that the other spouse cannot bring an independent action in private nuisance for damages for discomfort or inconvenience. . . .

Lord Lloyd of Berwick

If the occupier of land suffers personal injury as a result of inhaling [smoke coming from a neighbouring property], he may have a cause of action in negligence. But he does not have a cause of action in nuisance for his personal injury, nor for interference with his personal enjoyment. It follows that the quantum of damages in private nuisance does not depend on the number of those enjoying the land in question. It also follows that the only persons entitled to sue for loss in amenity value of the land are the owner or the occupier with the right to exclusive possession. . . .

Lord Hoffmann

Up to about 20 years ago, no one would have had the slightest doubt about who could sue. Nuisance is a tort against land, including interests in land such as easements and profits. A plaintiff must therefore have an interest in the land affected by the nuisance. . . .

But the concept of nuisance as a tort against land has recently been questioned by the decision of the Court of Appeal in *Khorasandjian v Bush* [1993] QB 727. . . .

[His Lordship considered this case, and continued:]

This reasoning, which is echoed in some academic writing and the Canadian case of *Motherwell v Motherwell* (1976) 73 DLR (3d) 62, which the Court of Appeal followed, is based upon a fundamental mistake about the remedy which the tort of nuisance provides. It arises, I think, out of a misapplication of an important distinction drawn by Lord Westbury LC in *St Helen's Smelting Co v Tipping* (1865) 11 HL Cas 642 at 650, 11 ER 1483 at 1486. In that case, the plaintiff bought a 1,300 acre estate in Lancashire. He complained that his hedges, trees and shrubs were being damaged by pollution from the defendants' copper smelting works a mile and a half away. The defendants said that the area was full of factories and chemical works and that if the plaintiff was entitled to complain, industry would be brought to a halt.

St Helen's Smelting Co v Tipping was a landmark case. It drew the line beyond which rural and landed England did not have to accept external costs imposed upon it by industrial pollution. But there has been, I think, some inclination to treat it as having divided nuisance into two torts, one of causing 'material injury to the property', such as flooding or depositing poisonous substances on crops, and the other of causing 'sensible personal discomfort', such as excessive noise or smells. In cases in the first category, there has never been any doubt that the remedy, whether by way of injunction or damages, is for causing damage to the land. It is plain that in such a case only a person with an interest in the land can sue. But there has been a tendency to regard cases in the second category as actions in respect of the discomfort or even personal injury which the plaintiff has suffered or is likely to suffer. On this view, the plaintiff's interest in the land becomes no more than a qualifying condition or springboard which entitles him to sue for injury to himself.

If this were the case, the need for the plaintiff to have an interest in land would indeed be hard to justify. . . . But the premise is quite mistaken. In the case of nuisances 'productive of sensible personal discomfort', the action is not for causing discomfort to the person but, as in the case of the first category, for causing injury to the land. True it is that the land has not suffered 'sensible' injury, but its utility has been diminished by the existence of the nuisance. It is for an unlawful threat to the utility of his land that the possessor or occupier is entitled to an injunction and it is for the diminution in such utility that he is entitled to compensation. . . .

There may of course be cases in which, in addition to damages for injury to his land, the owner or occupier is able to recover damages for consequential loss. He will, for example, be entitled to loss of profits which are the result of inability to use the land for the purposes of his business. Or if the land is flooded, he may also be able to recover damages for chattels or livestock lost as a result. But inconvenience, annoyance or even illness suffered by persons on land as a result of smells or dust are not damage consequential upon the injury to the land. It is rather the other way about: the injury to the amenity of the land consists in the fact that the persons on it are liable to suffer inconvenience, annoyance or illness.

It follows that damages for nuisance recoverable by the possessor or occupier may be affected by the size, commodiousness and value of his property but cannot be increased merely because more people are in occupation and therefore suffer greater collective discomfort. If more than one person has an interest in the property, the damages will have to be divided among them. If there are joint owners, they will be jointly entitled to the damages.

If there is a reversioner and the nuisance has caused damage of a permanent character which affects the reversion, he will be entitled to damages according to his interest. But the damages cannot be increased by the fact that the interests in the land are divided; still less according to the number of persons residing on the premises. . . .

Once it is understood that nuisances 'productive of sensible personal discomfort' do not constitute a separate tort of causing discomfort to people but are merely part of a single tort of causing injury to land, the rule that the plaintiff must have an interest in the land falls into place as logical and, indeed, inevitable (see *St Helen's Smelting Co v Tipping* (1865) 11 HL Cas 642 at 650, 11 ER 1483 at 1486).

Is there any reason of policy why the rule should be abandoned? Once nuisance has escaped the bounds of being a tort against land, there seems no logic in compromise limitations, such as that proposed by the Court of Appeal in this case, requiring the plaintiff to have been residing on land as his or her home. This was recognised by the Court of Appeal in *Khorasandjian's* case, where the injunction applied whether the plaintiff was at home or not. There is a good deal in this case and other writings about the need for the law to adapt to modern social conditions. But the development of the common law should be rational and coherent. It should not distort its principles and create anomalies merely as an expedient to fill a gap. . . .

So far as the claim is for personal injury, it seems to me that the only appropriate cause of action is negligence. It would be anomalous if the rules for recovery of damages under this head were different according as to whether, for example, the plaintiff was at home or at work. It is true, as I have said, that the law of negligence gives no remedy for discomfort or distress which does not result in bodily or psychiatric illness. But this is a matter of general policy and I can see no logic in making an exception for cases in which the discomfort or distress was suffered at home rather than somewhere else.

Finally, there is the position of spouses. It is said to be contrary to modern ways of thinking that a wife should not be able to sue for interference with the enjoyment of the matrimonial home merely because she has no proprietary right in the property. To some extent, this argument is based upon the fallacy which I have already discussed, namely that the action in nuisance lies for inconvenience or annoyance caused to people who happen to be in possession or occupation of land. But so far as it is thought desirable that the wife should be able to sue for injury to a proprietary or possessory interest in the home, the answer, in my view, lies in the law of property, not the law of tort. The courts today will readily assume that a wife has acquired a beneficial interest in the matrimonial home. If so, she will be entitled to sue for damage to that interest. On the other hand, if she has no such interest, I think it would be wrong to create a quasi-proprietary interest only for the purposes of giving her *locus standi* to sue for nuisance. What would she be suing for? Mr Brennan QC, who appeared for the plaintiffs, drew our attention to the rights conferred on a wife with no proprietary interest by the Matrimonial Homes Act 1983. The effect of these provisions is that a spouse may, by virtue of an order of the court upon a break-up of the marriage, become entitled to exclusive possession of the home. If so, she will become entitled to sue for nuisance. Until then, her interest is analogous to a contingent reversion. It cannot be affected by a nuisance which merely damages the amenity of the property while she has no right to possession.

Lord Cooke of Thorndon

Private nuisance is commonly said to be an interference with the enjoyment of land and to be actionable by an occupier. But 'occupier' is an expression of varying meanings, as a perusal of legal dictionaries shows. . . . Where interference with an amenity of a home is in issue there is no a priori reason why the expression should not include, and it appears natural that it should include, anyone living there who has been exercising a continuing right to enjoyment of that amenity. . . . A temporary visitor, however, someone who is 'merely present in the house' (a phrase used by Fletcher Moulton LJ in *Malone v Laskey* [1907] 2 KB 141 at 154), would not enjoy occupancy of sufficiently substantial nature. . . .

Malone's case, a case of personal injury from a falling bracket rather than an interference with amenities, is not directly in point, but it is to be noted that the wife of the subtenant's manager, who had been permitted by the subtenant to live in the premises with her husband, was dismissed by Gorell Barnes P as a person who had 'no right of occupation in the proper sense of the term' and by Fletcher Moulton LJ as being 'merely present' (see [1907] 2 KB 141 at 151). My Lords, whatever the acceptability of those descriptions 90 years ago, I can only agree with the Appellate Division of the Alberta Supreme Court in *Motherwell v Motherwell* (1976) 73 DLR (3d) 62 at 77, that they are 'rather light treatment of a wife, at least in today's society where she is no longer considered subservient to her husband'. Current statutes give effect to current perceptions by according spouses a special status in respect of the matrimonial home, as by enabling the court to make orders regarding occupation (see in England the Family Law Act 1996, ss 30 and 31). Although such provisions and orders thereunder do not of themselves confer proprietary rights, they support in relation to amenities the force and common sense of the words of Clement JA in *Motherwell v Motherwell* (at 78):

> Here we have a wife harassed in the matrimonial home. She has a status, a right to live there with her husband and children. I find it absurd to say that her occupancy of the matrimonial home is insufficient to found an action in nuisance.

As between spouses and de facto partners the question whether contributions in money or services give a proprietary equitable interest in a matrimonial home is a notoriously difficult one today, wrestled with throughout the common law world. Nuisance actions would seem better left free of the complication of this side issue.

The status of children living at home is different and perhaps more problematical but, on consideration, I am persuaded by the majority of the Court of Appeal in *Khorasandjian v Bush* [1993] QB 727 and the weight of North American jurisprudence to the view that they, too, should be entitled to relief for substantial and unlawful interference with the amenities of their home . . .

[His Lordship considered the position in other common law jurisdictions, and the views of academic writers, and continued:]

My Lords, there is a maxim *communis error facit jus*. I have collected the foregoing references not to invoke it, however, but to suggest respectfully that on this hitherto unsettled issue the general trend of leading scholarly opinion need not be condemned as erroneous. Although hitherto the law of England on the point has not been settled by your Lordships' House, it is agreed on all hands that some link with the land is necessary for standing to sue in private nuisance. The precise nature of that link remains to be defined, partly because of the ambiguity of 'occupy' and its derivatives. In ordinary usage the verb can certainly include 'reside in', which is indeed the first meaning given in the *Concise Oxford Dictionary*.

In logic more than one answer can be given. Logically it is possible to say that the right to sue for interference with the amenities of a home should be confined to those with proprietary interests and licensees with exclusive possession. No less logically, the right can be accorded to all who live in the home. Which test should be adopted, that is to say which should be the governing principle, is a question of the policy of the law. It is a question not capable of being answered by analysis alone. All that analysis can do is expose the alternatives. Decisions such as *Malone*'s case do not attempt that kind of analysis, and in refraining from recognising that value judgements are involved they compare less than favourably with the approach of the present-day Court of Appeal in *Khorasandjian*'s case and this case. The reason why I prefer the alternative advocated with unwonted vigour of expression by the doyen of living tort writers [this was a reference to John Fleming] is that it gives better effect to widespread conceptions concerning the home and family.

Of course in this field, as in most others, there will be borderline cases and anomalies wherever the lines are drawn. Thus there are, for instance, the lodger and, as some of your Lordships note, the aupair girl (although she may not figure among the present plaintiffs). It would seem weak, though, to refrain from laying down a just rule for spouses and children on the ground that it is not easy to know where to draw the lines regarding other persons. Without being wedded to this solution, I am not persuaded that there is sufficient justification for disturbing the conclusion adopted by [the Court of Appeal in the present case]. Occupation of the property as a home is, to me, an acceptable criterion, consistent with the traditional concern for the sanctity of family life and the Englishman's home—which need not in this context include his workplace. As already mentioned, it is consistent also with international standards.

Other resident members of the family, including such de facto partners and lodgers as may on the particular facts fairly be considered as having a home in the premises, could therefore be allowed standing to complain of truly serious interference with the domestic amenities lawfully enjoyed by them. By contrast, the policy of the law need not extend to giving a remedy in nuisance to non-resident employees in commercial premises. The employer is responsible for their welfare. On this part of the case I have only to add that normally there should not be any difficulty about sensible compromises with the author of the nuisance. Members of a household impliedly authorise the householder to represent them in such matters . . .

D. Nolan, '"A Tort Against Land": Private Nuisance as a Property Tort', in D. Nolan and A. Robertson (eds), *Rights and Private Law* (Oxford: Hart, 2012)

It seems to me, however, that the standing issue demonstrates the desirability of the property tort analysis, as becomes clear if we consider the implications of abandoning the requirement that the claimant have an interest in the affected land. First, courts would have to fashion an entirely new standing rule, and it is difficult to see what it would be. Some link with the land would obviously be required, but the test formulated in the Court of Appeal in *Hunter*—that the claimant must have a 'substantial link' with the property—was so vague as to be almost useless. Secondly, since presumably even the critics of the interest in land requirement would retain it for cases of encroachment or physical damage to the land, abandoning the requirement in cases with interference with comfort and convenience would effectively split the tort [of private nuisance] down the middle, with two different versions of the cause of action emerging, each with its own standing rule. Quite apart from anything else, this would clearly complicate matters in cases straddling the divide. Thirdly, it is difficult to see how the objective approach to the assessment of damages for private nuisance (which focuses on the impact of the interference on the utility of the land) could survive a relaxation of the standing rules, and unclear what principles would emerge to take its place. And finally, it is hard to see how the line could be held at private nuisance. A trespasser may well cause distress or inconvenience to licensees such as children living in the family home, so there would be little logic in jettisoning the interest in land requirement in private nuisance but maintaining it in the tort of trespass to land.

COMMENTARY

The decision in *Hunter* did not meet with universal approval (see Cane (1997) 113 LQR 515; O'Sullivan [1997] CLJ 483; Oliphant (1998) 6 Tort L Rev 21). However, as the extract from Nolan illustrates, it also has its supporters. Writing from a rights perspective, Nolan defends the standing requirement set out in *Hunter* because private nuisance is a property tort (see II.1). It should not protect personal interests as it would create incoherence in the law if persons with no interest in the land could sue in private nuisance. Viewed from this perspective, the decision in *Hunter* is to be welcomed because it explains the tort of private nuisance in a coherent and principled way.

There is little doubt that, historically, the forbears of the modern tort of nuisance (the assize of nuisance and the action on the case) were concerned with the protection of interests in land (see Loengard, 'The Assize of Nuisance' [1978] CLJ 144; and more generally *Baker*, ch. 24). But should the historical tie to land law be retained? While coherence in the law was no doubt a central factor in their Lordships' decision, it did not prevent them from considering whether there were reasons for modifying the standing rules. But after considering the policy grounds for expanding the scope of private nuisance, the majority in *Hunter* found no pressing case for doing so. In particular, the concern which underlay the decision in *Khorasandjian*, the need to provide a remedy for the defendant's harassing behaviour, has been mitigated by the passage of the Protection from Harassment Act 1997 (see Ch. 2.V), and in any event Lord Hoffmann felt that the legal basis for prohibiting such conduct should lie in the law relating to intentional torts rather than nuisance.

Even accepting that private nuisance is a tort against land, the full ramifications of this analysis remain somewhat unclear. Lord Hoffmann accepted that some forms of damage consequential on the nuisance (such as loss of profits, or damage to or destruction of chattels) were recoverable, but he denied that 'inconvenience, annoyance or even illness' suffered by persons on the land was damage consequential upon the injury to the land; rather 'the injury to the amenity of the land consists in the fact that the persons on it are liable to suffer inconvenience, annoyance or illness'. The Court of Appeal subsequently held that a claimant can expect to receive only nominal damages for interference with the amenity of land that is unoccupied (*Dobson v Thames Water Utilities* [2009] 3 All ER 319; see later). Is that consistent with Lord Hoffmann's analysis? Nor is it obvious why their Lordships were prepared to countenance compensation for damage caused to the claimant's chattels by the nuisance, but not for personal injury that occurs in the same way (see Oliphant (1998) 6 Tort L Rev 21). Nevertheless, the House of Lords subsequently affirmed that damages for death or personal injury are not recoverable in private nuisance (*Transco plc v Stockport Metropolitan Borough Council* [2004] 2 AC 1) and in such a case the claimant must rely on negligence instead.

Whatever the limitations of the common law, the passage of the Human Rights Act 1998 provides a possible alternative route to redress for those without a proprietary interest in the affected land but who nonetheless reside there. Under s. 7 of the 1998 Act, a public authority may be liable in damages if it interferes with a person's right to respect for his 'private and family life, his home and his correspondence' as laid down by Article 8 of the ECHR. And since the right to respect for one's home encompasses peaceful enjoyment of it, where a public authority causes a serious nuisance this can amount to a violation of the Article 8 right of those affected. A key advantage of the human rights route in this context is that the protection afforded by Article 8 extends to all those for whom the affected premises is their home (see, e.g., *Khatun v United Kingdom* (1998) 26 EHRR CD212). However, damages are awarded under the 1998 Act only where this is necessary to afford just satisfaction to the claimant (s. 8), and in *Dobson v Thames Water Utilities* [2009] 3 All ER 319, the Court of Appeal held that in a case of this kind one factor to be considered in determining whether this test is satisfied is whether those with a proprietary interest in the affected land have recovered damages for the interference in private nuisance. The court in *Dobson* did not decide that, for example, an award of nuisance damages to the parents of a child would *necessarily* prevent the child from recovering damages under the 1998 Act, instead holding that each case would need to be determined on its own facts. However, it was suggested that such an award might well have this effect, as indeed it did when the case later came to trial: see *Dobson v Thames Water Utilities Ltd (No. 2)* (2011) 140 Con LR 135. It follows that for a person without standing in nuisance the 1998 Act is far from a panacea. For comment on *Dobson*, see Tofaris [2009] CLJ 273; D. Nolan, 'Nuisance', in D. Hoffman (ed.), *The Impact of the UK Human Rights Act on Private Law* (Cambridge: CUP, 2011), pp. 181–6.

In addition to giving a possible cause of action to those without a property interest where the interference is caused by a public authority, it was thought that the Human Rights Act 1998 might also affect the standing rules of nuisance itself, by virtue of its supposed 'horizontal effect' on disputes between private parties. In *McKenna v British Aluminium Ltd* [2002] Env LR 30, Neuberger J held that it was at least arguable that, in the light of the 1998 Act, the standing requirement in nuisance should be relaxed to allow persons whose enjoyment of their home had been interfered with, but who did not have a proprietary interest, to sue in nuisance. However, the standing rule as laid down in *Hunter* was not questioned in the later case of *Dobson*, while in *Fearn v Board of Trustees of the Tate Gallery* [2020] Ch 621 (noted in II.1), the Court of Appeal was somewhat dismissive of the 'horizontal effect' idea in this context, commenting (at [91]) that 'overlaying the common law tort of private nuisance with Article 8 would significantly distort the tort in some important respects', and citing the standing rules as an example of the differences between the two forms of liability. It follows that it is now rather unlikely that the courts will water down the requirement of a proprietary interest so as to align the common law more closely with the position under the ECHR. See further on the relationship between nuisance and human rights, Nolan, *op. cit.*; and *Giliker*, pp. 156–61.

5. Defences

(a) Claimant Coming to the Nuisance and Prescription

Miller v Jackson [1977] QB 966

The plaintiffs purchased a house which was next to a small cricket ground. Cricket had been played at the ground since 1905, and the plaintiffs' house had been built in 1972. As a consequence of the proximity of the house to the ground cricket balls were hit into the plaintiffs' garden during the cricket season, some of which caused damage to the plaintiffs' property. Despite the erection of a chain fence to a height of just under 15 feet, cricket balls continued to land on the plaintiffs' property. The cricket club offered to supply and fit a safety net over the garden, to pay for any damage or expenses and to install unbreakable glass in the windows of the plaintiffs' house. The plaintiffs rejected these offers and commenced proceedings in negligence and nuisance, seeking damages and an injunction. It was conceded by the club that, as long as cricket was played on the ground, there was no way in which it could stop balls going into the plaintiffs' premises. The trial judge upheld the plaintiffs' claim and granted an injunction.

Lord Denning MR

It is the very essence of a private nuisance that it is the unreasonable use by a man of his land to the detriment of his neighbour . . .

I would, therefore, adopt this test: is the use by the cricket club of this ground for playing cricket a reasonable use of it? To my mind it is a most reasonable use. Just consider the circumstances. For over 70 years the game of cricket has been played on this ground to the great benefit of the community as a whole, and to the injury of none. No one could suggest that it was a nuisance to the neighbouring owners simply because an enthusiastic batsman occasionally hit a ball out of the ground for six to the approval of the admiring onlookers. Then I would ask: does it suddenly become a nuisance because one of the neighbours chooses to build a house on the very edge of the ground, in such a position that it may well be struck by the ball on the rare occasion when there is a hit for six? To my mind the answer is plainly No. The building of the house does not convert the playing of cricket into a nuisance when it was not so before. If and insofar as any damage is caused to the house or anyone in it, it is because of the position in which it was built. Suppose that the house had not been built by a developer, but by a private owner. He would be in much the same position as the farmer who previously put his cows in the field. He could not complain if a batsman hit a six out of the ground and, by a million to one chance, it struck a cow or even the farmer himself. He would be in no better position than a spectator at Lord's or the Oval or at a motor rally. At any rate, even if he could claim damages for the loss of the cow or the injury, he could not get an injunction to stop the cricket. If the private owner could not get an injunction, neither should a developer or a purchaser from him . . .

In this case it is our task to balance the right of the cricket club to continue playing cricket on their cricket ground, as against the right of the householder not to be interfered with. On taking the balance, I would give priority to the right of the cricket club to continue playing cricket on the ground, as they have done for the last 70 years. It takes precedence over the right of the newcomer to sit in his garden undisturbed. After all he bought the house four years ago in mid-summer when the cricket season was at its height. He might have guessed that there was a risk that a hit for six might possibly land on his property. If he finds that he does not like it, he ought, when cricket is played, to sit in the other side of the house or in the front garden, or go out; or take advantage of the offers the club have made to him of fitting unbreakable glass, and so forth. Or, if he does not like that, he ought to sell his house and move elsewhere. I expect there are many who would gladly buy it in order to be near the cricket field and open space. At any rate he ought not to be allowed to stop cricket being played on this ground.

Geoffrey Lane LJ

Was there here a use by the defendants of their land involving an unreasonable interference with the plaintiffs' enjoyment of their land? There is here in effect no dispute that there has been and is likely to be in the future an interference with the plaintiffs' enjoyment of No. 20 Brackenridge. The only question is whether it is unreasonable. It is a truism to say that this is a matter of degree. What that means is this. A balance has to be maintained between on the one hand the rights of the individual to enjoy his house and garden without the threat of damage and on the other hand the rights of the public in general or a neighbour to engage in lawful pastimes. Difficult questions may sometimes arise when the defendants' activities are offensive to the senses, for example by way of noise. Where, as here, the damage or potential damage is physical the answer is more simple. There is, subject to what appears hereafter, no excuse I can see which exonerates the defendants from liability in nuisance for what they have done or from what they threaten to do. It is true no one has yet been physically injured. That is probably due to a great extent to the fact that the householders in Brackenridge desert their gardens whilst cricket is in progress. The danger of injury is obvious and is not slight enough to be disregarded. There is here a real risk of serious injury.

There is, however, one obviously strong point in the defendants' favour. They or their predecessors have been playing cricket on this ground (and no doubt hitting sixes out of it) for 70 years or so. Can someone by building a house on the edge of the field in circumstances where it must have been obvious that balls might be hit over the fence, effectively stop cricket being played? Precedent apart, justice would seem to demand that the plaintiffs should be left to make the most of the site they have elected to occupy with all its obvious advantages and all its equally obvious disadvantages. It is pleasant to have an open space over which to look from your bedroom and sitting room windows, so far as it is possible to see over the concrete wall. Why should you complain of the obvious disadvantages which arise from the particular purpose to which the open space is being put? Put briefly, can the defendants take advantage of the fact that the plaintiffs have put themselves in such a position by coming to occupy a house on the edge of a small cricket field, with the result that what was not a nuisance in the past now becomes a nuisance? If the matter were *res integra*, I confess I should be inclined to find for the defendants. It does not seem just that a long-established activity, in itself innocuous, should be brought to an end because someone chooses to build a house nearby and so turn an innocent pastime into an actionable nuisance. Unfortunately, however, the question is not open. In *Sturges v Bridgman* this very problem arose. The defendant had carried on a confectionary shop with a noisy pestle and mortar for more than 20 years. Although it was noisy, it was far enough away from neighbouring premises not to cause trouble to anyone, until the plaintiff, who was a physician, built a consulting-room on his own land but immediately adjoining the confectionary shop. The noise and vibrations seriously interfered with the consulting-room and became a nuisance to the physician. The defendant contended that he had acquired the right either at common law or under the Prescription Act 1832 by uninterrupted use for more than 20 years to impose the inconvenience. It was held by the Court of Appeal, affirming the judgement of Jessel MR, that use such as this which was, prior to the construction of the consulting room, neither preventable nor actionable, could not found a prescriptive right. That decision involved the assumption, which so far as one can discover has never been questioned, that it is no answer to a claim in nuisance for the defendant to show that the plaintiff brought the trouble on his own head by building or coming to live in a house so close to the defendant's premises that he would inevitably be affected by the defendant's activities, where no one had been affected previously. See also *Bliss v Hall* (1838) 4 Bing NC 183. It may be that this rule works injustice, it may be that one would decide the matter differently in the absence of authority. But we are bound by the decision in *Sturges v Bridgman* and it is not for this court as I see it to alter a rule which has stood for so long.

Cumming-Bruce LJ agreed with Geoffrey Lane LJ that the cricket club's activities amounted to a nuisance but thought an injunction was an inappropriate remedy. **Lord Denning MR** agreed that, if, contrary to his judgment, the conduct did amount to a nuisance, an injunction should not be granted.

Appeal allowed.

COMMENTARY

One issue for the court in *Miller* was whether it was a defence to a nuisance action to argue that the plaintiff 'came to the nuisance'. The majority of the Court of Appeal (Lord Denning MR dissenting) held that it was not, and that the playing of cricket amounted to a nuisance despite the fact that it had been going on long before the plaintiffs had arrived on the scene. In doing so, the majority followed a clear line of authority to the effect that, in the words of Lord Halsbury in *Fleming v Hislop* (1886) 11 App Cas 686 at 697, 'whether the man went to the nuisance or the nuisance came to the man, the rights are the same'.

The import of the basic 'coming to the nuisance' rule is clear: where the claimant moves into a property which is already affected by a nuisance, they do not lose the right to sue for that nuisance, even if they are aware of the nuisance when they move in. Despite Lord Denning's opinion to the contrary in *Miller*, in our view this must be right. After all, as one of us has pointed out (Nolan, 'A Tort Against Land', *op. cit.*, pp. 483–4), using the tort of trespass to land as an analogy:

[I]t would surely be very odd to argue that if a person moved into a property knowing that someone else regularly trespassed on it, then for that reason he or she should be barred from seeking an injunction to prevent further trespassing by that person, thereby short-circuiting (as would a coming to the nuisance defence) established principles governing the acquisition of land rights by prescription.

(See also A. Beever, *The Law of Private Nuisance* (Oxford: Hart, 2013), ch. 6.) Furthermore, any harshness that this rule may be thought to cause defendants is mitigated by two considerations. One is that the locality principle (discussed in II.2(b)) means that the claimant is entitled to only the amenities consistent with the locality in which they choose to live. And the other is that a finding as to the claimant's knowledge of the defendant's pre-existing activity when they moved into their property may well be relevant when a court decides whether to grant them an injunction, as held by Cumming-Bruce LJ in *Miller* (see also *Lawrence v Fen Tigers Ltd* [2012] 1 WLR 2127 at [37]; and see generally on remedies, II.6).

It is important to note, however, that there is a second rule which is closely related to the 'coming to the nuisance rule', namely that the claimant can still maintain an action where the defendant's activity only becomes a nuisance because of a change in the use or configuration of neighbouring property brought about by the claimant. In *Sturges v Bridgman* (1879) 11 Ch D 852, for example, the Court of Appeal held that a confectioner's noisy equipment was causing a nuisance to a physician in a neighbouring property, even though it only began to cause problems after the doctor built a consulting-room in his garden, right next to the confectioner's kitchen. This second rule is more controversial than the first, and appears not always to have been the law (see, e.g., *Lawrence v Obee* (1814) 3 Camp 514, 170 ER 1465, where it was held that the plaintiff had brought the nuisance upon herself by creating a new window near her neighbour's privy). The second rule was recently questioned by Lord Neuberger in the next extracted case.

Lawrence v Fen Tigers Ltd [2014] AC 822

The facts of this case, and additional extracts, are given in II.2(b).

Lord Neuberger

'Coming to the nuisance'

47. For some time now, it has been generally accepted that it is not a defence to a claim in nuisance to show that the claimant acquired, or started to occupy, her property after the nuisance had started—ie that it is no defence that the claimant has come to the nuisance . . .

51. In my view, the law is clear, at least in a case such as the present, where the claimant in nuisance uses her property for essentially the same purpose as that for which it has been used by her predecessors since before the alleged nuisance started: in such a case, the defence of coming to the nuisance must fail . . .

52. Furthermore, the notion that coming to the nuisance is no defence is consistent with the fact that nuisance is a property-based tort, so that the right to allege a nuisance should, as it were, run with the land. It would also seem odd if a defendant was no longer liable for nuisance owing to the fact that the identity of his neighbour had changed, even though the use of his neighbour's property remained unchanged. . . .

53. There is much more room for argument that a claimant who builds on, or changes the use of, her property, after the defendant has started the activity alleged to cause a nuisance by noise, or any other emission offensive to the senses, should not have the same rights to complain about that activity as she would have had if her building work or change of use had occurred before the defendant's activity had started. That raises a rather different point from the issue of coming to the nuisance, namely whether an alteration in the claimant's property after the activity in question has started can give rise to a claim in nuisance if the activity would not have been a nuisance had the alteration not occurred.

55. It is unnecessary to decide this point on this appeal, but it may well be that it could and should normally be resolved by treating any pre-existing activity on the defendant's land, which was originally not a nuisance to the claimant's land, as part of the character of the neighbourhood at least if it was otherwise lawful. After all, until the claimant built on her land or changed its use, the activity in question will, ex hypothesi, not have been a nuisance . . .

56. On this basis, where a claimant builds on, or changes the use of, her land, I would suggest that it may well be wrong to hold that a defendant's pre-existing activity gives rise to a nuisance provided that (i) it can only be said to be a nuisance because it affects the senses of those on the claimant's land, (ii) it was not a nuisance before the building or change of use of the claimant's land, (iii) it is and has been, a reasonable and otherwise lawful use of the defendant's land, (iv) it is carried out in a reasonable way, and (v) it causes no greater nuisance than when the claimant first carried out the building or changed the use. (This is not intended to imply that in any case where one or more of these requirements is not satisfied, a claim in nuisance would be bound to succeed.)

58. Accordingly, it appears clear to me that it is no defence for a defendant who is sued in nuisance to contend that the claimant came to the nuisance, although it may well be a defence, at least in some circumstances, for a defendant to contend that, as it is only because the claimant has changed the use of, or built on, her land that the defendant's pre-existing activity is claimed to have become a nuisance, the claim should fail.

COMMENTARY

Lord Neuberger's forceful reiteration of the basic 'coming to the nuisance' rule is to be welcomed, as it had been implicitly challenged in the Court of Appeal in *Lawrence*, where Jackson LJ had commented ([2012] 1 WLR 2127 at [86]) that the claimants' predicament was 'a consequence of their decision to purchase a house in an area where motor sports were an established activity', and that this fact 'was or should have been apparent' to them and their professional advisers when they had bought their property. However, Lord Neuberger casts doubt on the second rule, and although these remarks were obiter—since the claimants in *Lawrence* had not altered the use of their property—they may prove influential, albeit that any lower court remains bound by *Sturges v Bridgman*, a decision difficult to reconcile with this aspect of Lord Neuberger's reasoning. (A point that seems to have been missed in *Jones v Ministry of Defence* [2021] EWHC (QB) 2276 at [67]–[71], where the judge applied Lord Neuberger's analysis, albeit obiter as it had already been determined that there was no nuisance anyway.) If the second rule were to be departed from, then the result would be that those arriving first in a place would effectively be able to dictate, at least to some extent, the uses to which later arrivals could put their properties. Does that seem reasonable to you? (Note that, as with the basic coming to the nuisance rule, the locality principle has a softening effect here, since it 'provides some protection to existing uses from novel uses': Steel, 'The Locality Principle in Private Nuisance' [2017] CLJ 145 at 163–4.)

When evaluating the principle that it is no defence that the claimant came to the nuisance, it is important to note that where the defendant's conduct has amounted to a nuisance for twenty years a defence of prescription may be available (i.e. the defendant may have acquired a right to cause the interference free from any liability in nuisance). However, it is not enough that the conduct is carried on for in excess of twenty years; it must cause a nuisance for twenty years. In *Sturges v Bridgman* the defendant had carried out his operations as a confectioner for over twenty years, but as the nuisance arose only because of a recent alteration to the doctor's premises the defence failed. In addition, because the prescriptive right is based on acquiescence, the claimant must have knowledge of the interference for such a right to arise (see *Liverpool Corporation v Coghill & Son Ltd* [1918] 1 Ch 307—no acquired right in respect of hidden pollution). Finally, it is important to note that for a right to commit a nuisance to arise, the level of the interference with the claimant's property must be uniform for the entire prescriptive period of twenty years. (This is because the prescriptive right is a form of easement—i.e., a right which the owner of one property has over another property—and like any easement the scope of the right that has been acquired must be certain.) In practice, this last requirement severely limits the significance of the prescription defence, and as a result there are very few examples of it succeeding (for an exception, see *Thomas v Thomas* (1835) 2 Cr M&R 34, where the defendant acquired the right to discharge rainwater onto neighbouring land). It also means that the chances of an acquired right to cause noise or smell are virtually nil, since the level of such interference is almost certain to vary over the course of two decades, although in *Lawrence* it was held that in theory a prescriptive right to commit a noise nuisance can be acquired.

A powerful objection to a coming to a nuisance defence is that it would effectively bypass the limitations that apply to the defence of prescription, as the defendant would instantly acquire the right to commit a nuisance as soon as the property affected by it either changed hands (the basic rule) or was reconfigured by the claimant (the second rule). See further on the relationship between a coming to the nuisance defence and acquired rights (or 'servitudes'), C. Kennefick, 'Nuisance and Coming to the Nuisance: The Porous Boundary between Torts and Servitudes in England and France', in J.-S. Borghetti and S. Whittaker (eds), *French Civil Liability in Comparative Perspective* (Oxford: Hart, 2019), who says (at p. 231) that Lord Neuberger's analysis of the coming to the nuisance issue in *Lawrence* was 'seriously weakened by his failure to consider fully the perspective of property law', and that his partial questioning of the orthodox rejection of the defence should not be followed.

(b) Statutory Authority and Regulatory Compliance

'It has long been the case that no action lies for doing that which the legislature has authorised, if it be done without negligence, although it occasions damage; but an action does lie for doing that which the legislature has authorised, if it be done negligently' (*Geddis v*

Proprietors of Bann Reservoirs (1878) 3 App Cas 430 at 455, per Lord Blackburn). In *Allen v Gulf Oil Refining Ltd* [1981] AC 1001 the defendant built and operated an oil refinery under the authority of a private Act of Parliament, the Gulf Oil Refining Act 1965. The plaintiff was one of a number of residents of the surrounding area who had been adversely affected by noxious odours, vibrations and offensive noise levels emanating from the refinery, as well as alleging that she and members of her family lived in fear of explosion at the refinery. The defendant pleaded statutory authority, and a majority of the House of Lords held that the 1965 Act expressly or by necessary implication gave authority to both construct and operate the refinery, and that this authority conferred on the defendant immunity from proceedings for any nuisance which was the inevitable result of constructing and operating a refinery on the land, however carefully it was sited, constructed and operated. (See further on *Allen*, M. Wilde, 'Nuisance Law in Industrial Wales (Part 2)', in P. Bishop and M. Stallworthy (eds), *Environmental Law and Policy in Wales* (Cardiff: University of Wales Press, 2013).) The question is thus essentially one of statutory construction—was the activity causing the nuisance authorised by Parliament—although the defendant also bears the burden of establishing that the activity could not have been carried on without a nuisance resulting (see further on this requirement, *Winfield & Jolowicz*, para. 15-058).

It should be noted that the statutory authority defence is potentially subject to review for compliance with human rights law. If the authorised activity interferes with a person's right to respect for their home under Article 8 of the ECHR, or with their right to peaceful enjoyment of their possessions under Article 1 of the First Protocol, then provision for compensation in the relevant legislation (as is common) might well be enough to satisfy the requirements of the Convention. However, in the absence of compensation, or where the compensation provided is manifestly inadequate, it has been suggested that a court might refuse to recognise the defence of statutory authority on the ground that its application would be incompatible with the claimant's Convention rights (see D. Nolan, 'Nuisance', in D. Hoffman (ed.), *The Impact of the UK Human Rights Act on Private Law* (Cambridge: CUP, 2011), pp. 188–91). The most straightforward route to such a conclusion would be for the courts in such cases to use s. 3 of the Human Rights Act 1998 (which requires that, so far as is possible, a court interpret legislation in such a way as to comply with the Convention) to 'read down' the relevant statute so as to ensure that it provides authorisation only where this would not amount to a violation of the claimant's rights.

The defence of statutory authority does not extend to decisions of administrative authorities acting under statutory powers, such as regulatory agencies and planning authorities. In Weir's words, 'administrators cannot authorise torts' (T. Weir, *An Introduction to Tort Law*, 2nd edn (Oxford: OUP, 2006), p. 163). Hence it is a well-established rule that the grant of planning permission in respect of the defendant's activity does not provide a defence to a nuisance action (for recent confirmation of this, see *Lawrence v Fen Tigers Ltd* [2014] AC 822, extracted in II.2(b)). While statutory authority can plausibly be interpreted as a Parliamentary endorsement of the defendant's activity, the obtaining of planning permission simply makes lawful what would otherwise be a criminal offence, and there is 'neither necessity nor justification for regarding such a licence as negativing established principles of civil liability' (Tromans [1995] CLJ 494 at 495). Furthermore, as Peter Gibson LJ pointed out in *Wheeler v JJ Saunders Ltd* [1996] Ch 19 (at 35) if the grant of planning permission were a licence to commit nuisance, then private rights would be extinguished 'without compensation as a result of administrative decisions which cannot be appealed and are difficult to challenge' (see also *Lawrence v Fen Tigers Ltd* [2014] AC 822 at [90], per Lord Neuberger, describing this outcome as 'wrong in principle'). Note, however, that s. 158 of the Planning

Act 2008 confers statutory authority on all 'nationally significant infrastructure projects' granted planning permission under the special procedures laid down in that legislation. Those whose land has been injuriously affected and who are prevented from bringing a nuisance action by the statutory authority defence in s. 158 can claim compensation from those carrying out the authorised works. In these situations, private interests are expropriated in the public interest but with some right to compensation. (For commentary on this aspect of the 2008 Act, see Bishop and Jenkins, 'Planning and Nuisance' (2011) 23 JEL 285 at 295–301.)

Turning to the effect of regulatory compliance on nuisance law, Lee points out ('Public Interest in Private Nuisance' [2015] CLJ 329 at 348) that 'a regulatory process of some sort will almost always have been applied to any activity' claimed to be a private nuisance. But what is the relationship between such a process and nuisance liability? The leading case is *Barr v Biffa Waste Services Ltd* [2013] QB 455, where nuisance actions were brought by residents living near the defendant's landfill site in respect of the smell caused by the waste deposited there. The deposit of waste was at all times assumed to have been in compliance with the conditions attached to a waste management permit issued by the Environment Agency, and the defendant argued that it followed that the nuisance actions must fail. This argument was firmly rejected by the Court of Appeal. According to Carnwath LJ, there was no principle that the common law should 'march in step' with a statutory scheme covering similar subject-matter, and in his Lordship's view it would be quite wrong for the terms of a waste permit issued under regulatory legislation to be treated as 'cutting down the common law rights of local residents' (at [102]), when they had neither agreed to, nor even been consulted on, its terms. He concluded (at [76]):

> An activity which is conducted in contravention of planning or environmental controls is unlikely to be reasonable. But the converse does not follow. Sticking to the rules is an aspect of good neighbourliness, but it is far from the whole story—in law as in life.

(In *Lawrence v Fen Tigers Ltd* [2014] AC 822 at [91], Lord Neuberger agreed with this statement, although Lord Carnwath himself seemed to be having second thoughts: see [198].)

The historical interplay between private nuisance law and regulation has been the subject of valuable work by Ben Pontin, who concludes that the relationship is an 'essentially pluralist' one, in which each is 'equally important in complementary ways' ('Nuisance Law and the Industrial Revolution: A Reinterpretation of Doctrine and Institutional Competence' (2012) 75 MLR 1010 at 1034). The suggestion that nuisance law should play a lesser role in environmental protection would, he argues, represent a departure from past practice, where the regulatory frameworks assumed the continuing significance of common law controls (see his 'Tort Law and Victorian Government Growth: The Historiographical Significance of Tort in the Shadow of Chemical Pollution and Factory Safety Regulation' (1998) 18 OJLS 661). By contrast, in her work on this relationship, Maria Lee has argued that 'private law (and the protections it provides) will find itself increasingly circumscribed in a world dominated by collective determinations of the public interest' unless it engages in what she terms 'a realistic analysis' of those determinations ('*Hunter v Canary Wharf Ltd* (1997)', in *Mitchell & Mitchell*, p. 333; see also 'Tort Law and Regulation: Planning and Nuisance' [2011] JPL 986; 'Nuisance and Regulation in the Court of Appeal' [2013] JPL 277; 'Public Interest in Private Nuisance' [2015] CLJ 329). Whilst acknowledging the potential inadequacies of planning and regulatory mechanisms, Lee contends that the solution to this lies in close scrutiny in nuisance litigation of the processes by which public interest considerations were taken into account as part of the regulatory or planning approval for the defendant's activity. (See also A. Beever, *The Law of Nuisance* (Oxford: Hart, 2013), pp. 140–1, arguing that planning permission should be capable of operating as a defence to a nuisance claim, but only if the planning authority took the claimant's private rights into account when making its decision.) In response, Nolan has argued that it is a 'well-established principle that decisions taken in the public interest curtail private law rights only if they amount to a direct expression of legislative will' and that the decisions of both planners and regulators fall 'well short of that benchmark' (D. Nolan, 'Nuisance, Regulation and Planning: The Limits of Statutory Authority', in *Defences in Tort*, p. 202). Nolan also questions how realistic it is for a judge to be expected to evaluate public law planning and regulatory processes in the course of determining a private law nuisance claim, while Pontin, *Nuisance Law and Environmental Protection* (*op. cit.*), p. 185 comments that 'the commentary (and case law) has not yet gone as far as to provide a clear idea of the specific quality (or qualities) of the administrative process which can justify changing the common law'. Finally, it is important to remember that regulators can get things wrong, so that 'the ability of private law to re-open regulatory judgments can make a positive contribution to the collective, as well as to the individual, interest' (Lee [2015] CLJ 329, 349). On the relationship between regulation and tort law more generally, see D. Nolan, 'Tort and Regulation', in J. Goudkamp, M. Lunney and L. McDonald (eds), *Taking Law Seriously: Essays in Honour of Peter Cane* (Oxford: Hart, 2022).

6. Remedies

A claimant in nuisance may seek an injunction to prevent the nuisance from continuing, or damages for any loss already caused by the nuisance, or both. Where the nuisance has caused damage to property, damages are assessed according to the normal principles relating to this type of damage (generally the cost of either replacing or repairing the property, whichever is less). More difficult is the assessment of damages for loss of amenity. In *Bone v Seale* [1975] 1 WLR 797 the plaintiffs could not show that the foul smell from the defendant's pig farm had caused a reduction in the capital value of their properties, even though it did constitute a nuisance. In considering what damages the plaintiffs were entitled to Stephenson LJ thought that there was 'some parallel' between damages for loss of amenity in personal injury claims and the loss of amenity as a result of a nuisance. However, this analogy was rejected by Lord Hoffmann in *Hunter v Canary Wharf* [1997] AC 855 on the ground that the focus in nuisance is not on the claimant's personal discomfort or distress, but on the diminished utility of the property caused by the interference, which should therefore be the measure of damages in an amenity nuisance case. While accepting this analysis, the Court of Appeal in *Dobson v Thames Water Utilities* [2009] 3 All ER 319 nevertheless held that when assessing the diminution in utility value account should be taken of 'the actual impact' and the 'actual experiences' of those in occupation of the property, albeit that on Lord Hoffmann's approach these are relevant only insofar as they provide evidence of the impact of the interference on the land itself. There is in any case a degree of tension between *Hunter* and *Dobson* on this issue, which is illustrated by the fact that while in *Hunter* their Lordships made it clear that the damages in nuisance are not to be affected by the number of household members inconvenienced by a particular interference, but rather the objective qualities of the affected property, in *Dobson* Waller LJ suggested (at [34]) that only nominal damages should be awarded where the property was unoccupied at the relevant time, and the claimant suffered no actual pecuniary loss. As that qualification suggests, in addition to compensation for the injury to their land, the claimant is also entitled to damages for any consequential loss caused by the nuisance, such as rental income lost due to the flooding of their tenants' houses (see *Rust v Victoria Graving Dock Co* (1887) 36 Ch D 113, where on the facts the loss was too remote) or a reduction in hotel takings attributable to the noise and dust from nearby building works (*Andreae v Selfridge & Co Ltd* [1938] Ch 1).

Where a nuisance is ongoing, the claimant is prima facie entitled to an injunction requiring the defendant to put a stop to it. As injunctions are an equitable remedy, before the Judicature Acts they were the preserve of the Court of Chancery, which in 1858 was given the power to award damages in a case where an injunction was sought, 'either in addition to or in substitution for' an injunction (Chancery Amendment Act 1858 ('Lord Cairns' Act'), s. 2). The power survived the merging of law and equity in the Judicature Acts, when it became exercisable by the common law courts (today the power is to be found in the Senior Courts Act 1981, s. 50). The following extract deals with the circumstances in which a court will exercise its discretion to award damages in lieu of an injunction.

Shelfer v City of London Electric Lighting Company [1895] 1 Ch 287

An electric lighting company erected powerful engines and other works on land near to a house which was subject to a lease. Owing to excavations for the foundations of the engines, and to vibration and noise from the working of them, structural injury was caused to the house, and annoyance and discomfort to the tenant. The tenant and the reversioners brought separate actions against the company for an injunction and damages in respect of the nuisance. The Court of Appeal allowed an appeal against the trial judge's refusal to grant an injunction, and considered the circumstances in which the power to award damages in lieu of an injunction should be used.

A. L. Smith LJ

Many Judges have stated, and I emphatically agree with them, that a person by committing a wrongful act (whether it be a public company for public purposes or a private individual) is not thereby entitled to ask the Court to sanction his doing so by purchasing his neighbour's rights, by assessing damages in that behalf, leaving his neighbour with the nuisance, or his lights dimmed, as the case may be.

In such cases the well-known rule is not to accede to the application, but to grant the injunction sought, for the plaintiff's legal right has been invaded, and he is prima facie entitled to an injunction.

There are, however, cases in which this rule may be relaxed, and in which damages may be awarded in substitution for an injunction as authorised by this section.

In any instance in which a case for an injunction has been made out, if the plaintiff by his acts or laches has disentitled himself to an injunction the Court may award damages in its place. So again, whether the case be for a mandatory injunction or to restrain a continuing nuisance, the appropriate remedy may be damages in lieu of an injunction, assuming a case for an injunction to be made out.

In my opinion, it may be stated as a good working rule that—

(1) If the injury to the plaintiff's legal rights is small,

(2) And is one which is capable of being estimated in money,

(3) And is one which can be adequately compensated by a small money payment,

(4) And the case is one in which it would be oppressive to the defendant to grant an injunction:—then damages in substitution for an injunction may be given.

> There may also be cases in which, though the four above-mentioned requirements exist, the defendant by his conduct, as, for instance, hurrying up his buildings so as if possible to avoid an injunction, or otherwise acting with a reckless disregard to the plaintiff's rights, has disentitled himself from asking that damages may be assessed in substitution for an injunction.
>
> It is impossible to lay down any rule as to what, under the differing circumstances of each case, constitutes either a small injury, or one that can be estimated in money, or what is a small money payment, or an adequate compensation, or what would be oppressive to the defendant. This must be left to the good sense of the tribunal which deals with each case as it comes up for adjudication. . . . Each case must be decided upon its own facts; but to escape the rule it must be brought within the exception.

COMMENTARY

Shelfer made it clear that the powers given to the courts under Lord Cairns' Act did not alter the position as it was understood before the Act's passage, namely that 'unless there be something special in the case' a claimant subject to an ongoing violation of their legal rights was 'entitled as of course to an injunction' (*Imperial Gas Light and Coke Company v Broadbent* (1859) 7 HLC 600 at 612, per Lord Kingsdown). Of course, this did not mean that damages could never be awarded in lieu of an injunction, but rather that it would be rare in nuisance cases, since for the interference to amount to a nuisance in the first place, it had to be shown that it was unreasonable, in which case it would be difficult to characterise the injury to the claimant's legal rights as small, as required by A. L. Smith LJ's 'working rule'. Having said that, his Lordship also referred to the need for the court to consider whether it would be oppressive to the defendant to grant the claimant an injunction, and—even though his criteria were cumulative—by emphasising this consideration the courts in later cases were sometimes able to take a broader approach to the circumstances in which damages in lieu could be awarded (see, e.g., *Jaggard v Sawyer* [1995] 1 WLR 269 at 288). If the plaintiffs in *Hunter v Canary Wharf* [1997] AC 855 had been able to establish that the interference with television reception caused by the Canary Wharf Tower amounted to a nuisance, could they have sought an injunction ordering it to be taken down? (Note though that an injunction granted in those circumstances would be a mandatory injunction, where the cost to the defendant of complying with the injunction is a relevant factor—see *Redland Bricks v Morris* [1970] AC 652.)

Nevertheless, *Shelfer* undoubtedly signalled a strict approach to the remedial discretion, as epitomised by the comment by Lindley LJ in his judgment that where there was a continuing actionable nuisance the jurisdiction to award damages instead of an injunction should not be exercised 'except under very exceptional circumstances' ([1895] 1 Ch 287 at 316). It is therefore not surprising that subsequently the decision came to stand for the proposition that a claimant should be denied a prohibitory injunction against a continuing nuisance only if all four of Smith LJ's criteria were met (see, e.g., *Pride of Derby and Derbyshire Angling Associations Ltd v British Celanese Ltd* [1953] 1 Ch 149). Otherwise, Lord Morris commented in *Redland Bricks* (at 664), the plaintiff was entitled to an injunction 'as of course'.

Although this might seem to have been a very harsh rule for defendants, it is worth noting that injunctive relief is not quite as blunt an instrument as might appear to be the case at first blush. In the first place, the court should limit the terms of the injunction so that it only catches the interference that is wrongful. In *Kennaway v Thompson* [1981] QB 88, for example, although the overall level of noise generated by power-boat races organised by the defendant was unreasonable, some noise from the activity was lawful, and so the injunction that was issued merely put limits on the frequency and duration of the races, rather than banning them altogether. Secondly, a technique frequently used by judges, particularly in the nineteenth century, is to grant an injunction but then to suspend its operation for a period to enable the defendant to modify their activity in such a way as to avoid it causing a nuisance (see, e.g., *Pennington v Brinsop Hall Coal Co* (1877) 5 Ch D 769). Another technique which has the effect of softening the blow is to issue a contingent injunction, which is only triggered if the defendant fails to take measures to reduce or eliminate the interference. A long series of these were issued in various nineteenth-century river pollution cases, with the result that the courts were required to take on a long-term managerial or supervisory function: see L. Rosenthal, *The River Pollution Dilemma in Victorian England: Nuisance Law versus Economic Efficiency* (Farnham: Ashgate, 2014), pp. 52–5. Finally, even where the court's order does require the defendant to cease their activity immediately, it is always open to the parties to reach a negotiated settlement, whereby the claimant agrees not to enforce the injunction in return for monetary compensation. (This outcome is functionally equivalent to an award of damages in lieu of an injunction, with the difference being that it is the parties who set the price for the continuation of the nuisance, rather than the court.)

The upshot of this flexibility is that any assumption that a grant of injunctive relief against a corporate defendant will necessarily result in the closing down of the defendant's operations is false. Indeed, in an in-depth and engaging study of the previously neglected question of what actually happens after injunctions are awarded in nuisance cases, Pontin found that 'no "socially useful" enterprise . . . ceased to do business as a result of the injunction awarded against it' (B. Pontin, *Nuisance Law and Environmental Protection: A Study of Nuisance Injunctions in Practice* (Witney: Lawtext, 2013), p. 166). Instead:

> [I]n the time afforded by the court suspending the injunction as a matter of course in each instance, the defendant enterprise discovered alternatives to outright closure, including, variously, inventing a clean mode of operation . . . ; relocating to a less 'sensitive' location . . . ; and seeking to acquire the right to pollute in a private transaction in which entitlements were exchanged . . .

It should, however, be noted that aspects of Pontin's analysis are controversial, and for a different historical perspective on these issues, see Rosenthal, *op. cit.*

A particularly contentious question to which the courts have not given a consistent answer is whether an injunction can be refused on the ground that there is a strong public interest in the continuation of the defendant's activity. The traditional view on this question was expressed by Lindley LJ in *Shelfer*, when he said (at 316) that:

> Expropriation, even for a money consideration, is only justifiable when Parliament has sanctioned it. Courts of Justice are not like Parliament, which considers whether proposed works will be so beneficial to the public as to justify exceptional legislation, and the deprivation of people of their rights with or without compensation.

However, in *Miller v Jackson* (extracted earlier), a majority of the Court of Appeal departed from this rule and held that in all the circumstances, including the contribution that the cricket club made to village life, it was not appropriate to grant an injunction that would have stopped cricket being played. *Miller* can be contrasted in this respect with subsequent decisions of the Court of Appeal which took a harder line. In the *Kennaway* case—which was decided shortly after *Miller*—an injunction was granted even though the powerboat races attracted large numbers of spectators, while in *Watson v Croft Promosport Ltd* [2009] 3 All ER 249, where an injunction was issued to restrain activities at a motorsports venue, Sir Andrew Morritt CVO made it clear the public interest in the defendant's activity was relevant only in marginal cases where the damage to the claimant was minimal (which was not the case in *Watson*). (Cf. *Dennis v Ministry of Defence* [2003] EWHC 793 (QB), where Buckley J refused to issue a declaration in respect of a noise nuisance caused by the training of Harrier Jump Jet pilots at an RAF base, since it was the only venue where such training was being carried out.) In *Lawrence v Fen Tigers Ltd*, the Supreme Court considered these authorities, and signalled a departure from the traditional approach to the public interest issue, as well as *Shelfer* more generally, as the following extract reveals.

Lawrence v Fen Tigers Ltd [2014] AC 822

The facts of this case, and additional extracts, are given in II.2(b).

Lord Neuberger

The award of damages instead of an injunction

101. Where a claimant has established that the defendant's activities constitute a nuisance, prima facie the remedy to which she is entitled (in addition to damages for past nuisance) is an injunction to restrain the defendant from committing such nuisance in the future . . .

102. The question which arises is what, if any, principles govern the exercise of the court's jurisdiction to award damages instead of an injunction . . .

[His Lordship considered the relevant authorities and continued:]

116. It seems to me that there are two problems about the current state of the authorities on this question of the proper approach for a court to adopt on the question whether to award damages instead of an injunction.

117. The first is what at best might be described as a tension, and at worst as an inconsistency, between two sets of judicial dicta since *Shelfer* [1895] 1 Ch 475 . . .

118. The second problem is the unsatisfactory way in which it seems that the public interest is to be taken into account when considering the issue whether to grant an injunction or award damages . . . As part of this second problem, there is a question as to the extent to which it is relevant that the activity giving rise to the nuisance has the benefit of a planning permission.

119. So far as the first problem is concerned, the approach to be adopted by a judge when being asked to award damages instead of an injunction should, in my view, be much more flexible than that suggested in the recent cases of *Regan* [v *Paul Properties Ltd*] [2007] Ch 135 and *Watson* [v *Croft Promosport Ltd*] [2009] 3 All ER 249. It seems to me that (i) an almost mechanical application of AL Smith LJ's four tests, and (ii) an approach which involves damages being awarded only in 'very exceptional circumstances', are each simply wrong in principle, and give rise to a serious risk of going wrong in practice . . .

120. The court's power to award damages in lieu of an injunction involves a classic exercise of discretion, which should not, as a matter of principle, be fettered, particularly in the very constrained way in which the Court of Appeal has suggested in *Regan* and *Watson*. And, as a matter of practical fairness, each case is likely to be so fact-sensitive that any firm guidance is likely to do more harm than good . . .

121. . . . [I]t is only right to acknowledge that this does not prevent the courts from laying down rules as to what factors can, and cannot, be taken into account by a judge when deciding whether to exercise his discretion to award damages in lieu. Indeed, it is appropriate to give as much guidance as possible so as to ensure that, while the discretion is not fettered, its manner of exercise is as predictable as possible. I would accept that the prima facie position is that an injunction should be granted, so the legal burden is on the defendant to show why it should not . . .

123. Where does that leave AL Smith LJ's four tests? While the application of any such series of tests cannot be mechanical, I would adopt a modified version of the view expressed by Romer LJ in *Fishenden* [v *Higgs & Hill Ltd* (1935)] 153 LT 128, 141. First, the application of the four tests must not be such as 'to be a fetter on the exercise of the court's discretion'. Secondly, it would, in the absence of additional relevant circumstances pointing the other way, normally be right to refuse an injunction if those four tests were satisfied. Thirdly, the fact that those tests are not all satisfied does not mean that an injunction should be granted.

124. As for the second problem, that of [the relevance of the] public interest, I find it hard to see how there could be any circumstances in which it arose and could not, as a matter of law, be a relevant factor . . . The fact that a defendant's business may have to shut down if an injunction is granted should, it seems to me, obviously be a relevant fact, and it is hard to see why relevance should not extend to the fact that a number of the defendant's employees would lose their livelihood, although in many cases that may well not be sufficient to justify the refusal of an injunction. Equally, I do not see why the court should not be entitled to have regard to the fact that many other neighbours in addition to the claimant are badly affected by the nuisance as a factor in favour of granting an injunction.

125. It is also right to mention planning permission in this context. In some cases, the grant of planning permission for a particular activity (whether carried on at the claimant's, or the defendant's, premises) may provide strong support for the contention that the activity is of benefit to the public, which would be relevant to the question of whether or not to grant an injunction. Accordingly, the existence of a planning permission which expressly or inherently authorises carrying on an activity in such a way as to cause a nuisance by noise or the like, can be a factor in favour of refusing an injunction and compensating the claimant in damages. This factor would have real force in cases where it was clear that the planning authority had been reasonably and fairly influenced by the public benefit of the activity, and where the activity cannot be carried out without causing the nuisance complained of. However, even in such cases, the court would have to weigh up all the competing factors.

126. In some such cases, the court may well be impressed by a defendant's argument that an injunction would involve a loss to the public or a waste of resources on account of what may be a single claimant, or that the financial implications of an injunction for the defendant would be disproportionate to the damage done to the claimant if she was left to her claim in damages. In many such cases, particularly where an injunction would in practice stop the defendant from pursuing the activities, an injunction may well not be the appropriate remedy

. . .

Lord Sumption

157. . . . An injunction is a remedy with significant side-effects beyond the parties and the issues in the proceedings. Most uses of land said to be objectionable cannot be restrained by injunction simply as between the owner of that land and his neighbour. If the use of a site for (say) motocross is restrained by injunction, that prevents the activity as between the defendant and the whole world. Yet it may be a use which is in the interest of very many other people who derive enjoyment or economic benefits from it of precisely the kind with which the planning system is concerned. An injunction prohibiting the activity entirely will operate in practice in exactly the same way as a refusal of planning permission, but without regard to the factors which a planning authority would be bound to take into account. The obvious solution to this problem is to allow the activity to continue but to compensate the claimant financially for the loss of amenity and the diminished value of his property. In a case where planning permission has actually been granted for the use in question, there are particularly strong reasons for adopting this solution. It is what the law normally provides for when a public interest conflicts with a proprietary right . . .

159. The ordinary principle is that the court does not grant an injunction in a case where there is an adequate legal remedy. In particular, it does not do so where damages would be an adequate remedy . . . However, this principle has never been consistently followed in cases of nuisance.

[His Lordship referred to the relevant authorities and continued:]

160. . . . [T]he *Shelfer* principle was based mainly on the court's objection to sanctioning a wrong by allowing the defendant to pay for the right to go on doing it. This seems an unduly moralistic approach to disputes, and if taken at face value would justify the grant of an injunction in all cases, which is plainly not the law . . .

161. In my view, the decision in *Shelfer* [1895] 1 Ch 287 is out of date, and it is unfortunate that it has been followed so recently and so slavishly. It was devised for a time in which England was much less crowded, when comparatively few people owned property, when conservation was only beginning to be a public issue, and when there was no general system of statutory development control. The whole jurisprudence in this area will need one day to be reviewed in this court. There is much to be said for the view that damages are ordinarily an adequate remedy for nuisance and that an injunction should not usually be granted in a case where it is likely that conflicting interests are engaged other than the parties' interests. In particular, it may well be that an injunction should as a matter of principle not be granted in a case where a use of land to which objection is taken requires and has received planning permission. However, at this stage, in the absence of argument on these points, I can do no more than identify them as calling for consideration in a case in which they arise . . .

Lord Mance

167. With regard to remedy, I am broadly in agreement with Lord Neuberger PSC. However, I would adopt the qualifications made by Lord Carnwath JSC in paras 246 and 247. I do not think that a grant of planning permission can give rise to any presumption that there should be no injunction . . .

168. I would only add in relation to remedy that the right to enjoy one's home without disturbance is one which I would believe that many, indeed most, people value for reasons largely if not entirely independent of money. With reference to Lord Sumption JSC's concluding paragraph (para 161 above), I would not therefore presently be persuaded by a view that 'damages are ordinarily an adequate remedy for nuisance' and that 'an injunction should not usually be granted in a case where it is likely that conflicting interests are engaged other than the parties' interests' – a suggested example of the latter being given as a case where a use of land has received planning permission. I would see this as putting the significance of planning permission and public benefit too high, in the context of the remedy to be afforded for a private nuisance. As already indicated, I agree with Lord Neuberger PSC's nuanced approach.

COMMENTARY

Since the defendants had not argued against injunctive relief as a remedy in the lower courts, Lord Carnwath considered (at [238]) that the Supreme Court should approach the issue with caution, 'conscious that anything we say can be no more than guidance'. With that caveat, his Lordship agreed (at [239]) that 'the opportunity should be taken to signal a move away from' the *Shelfer* criteria, and that this was particularly relevant in cases where an injunction would have serious consequences for third parties, 'such as employees of the defendant's business, or, in this case, members of the public using or enjoying the stadium'. Since the point had not been argued below, and their Lordships considered it inappropriate for them to decide such a fact-sensitive issue *ab initio*, the order for injunctive relief given at first instance was restored, with the proviso that the defendants could apply to have it discharged, and damages awarded in lieu.

The upshot would seem to be that all the judges in *Lawrence* agreed that a more flexible approach to the question of injunctive relief should be adopted; that the courts should not adhere slavishly to the *Shelfer* criteria; and that considerable weight could if appropriate be given to public interest considerations, and to the granting of planning permission for the defendant's activity. Lord Sumption went further, and favoured a presumption against injunctive relief (and note that Lord Clarke left this issue open, at [170]), but his approach was sharply criticised by Lord Mance, and the dominant view, as expressed by Lord Neuberger, was that the burden of proof remained with the defendant, who must therefore persuade the court not to issue an injunction where liability was imposed. Lord Carnwath and Lord Mance also made it clear that in their opinion the burden of proof should not switch to the claimant simply because planning permission had been granted for the defendant's activity.

While the precise ramifications of the discussion of remedies in *Lawrence* will only become apparent with time, the degree to which the decision changes the law on injunctions should not be overstated. After all, the *Shelfer* principles were not completely disavowed, only reduced in importance, and a majority of their Lordships accepted that there should still be a presumption in favour of a prohibitory injunction in the case of a continuing nuisance. Furthermore, the indications are that the lower courts are following the relatively conservative guidance given by Lord Neuberger, in preference to Lord Sumption's more radical approach (see, e.g., *Beaumont Business Centres Ltd v Florala Properties Ltd* [2020] EWHC 550 (Ch) at [330]).

Whether the downgrading of the *Shelfer* criteria and the acceptance of the relevance of public interest arguments are welcome developments in the law of nuisance remedies is a question on which opinions sharply differ. Some commentators have been pushing for greater flexibility and a move away from *Shelfer* for some time (see, e.g., Jolowicz, 'Damages in Equity—A Study of Lord Cairns' Act' [1975] CLJ 224; Tromans, 'Nuisance: Prevention or Payment?' [1982] CLJ 87; M. Wilde, 'Nuisance Law and Damages in Lieu of an Injunction: Challenging the Orthodoxy of the *Shelfer* Criteria', in *Challenging Orthodoxy*), while Lee, 'Tort Law and Regulation: Planning and Nuisance' [2011] JPL 986, 990 has argued that greater remedial flexibility may represent an appropriate private law response to the growth of the regulatory state. And according to Wilde (*op. cit.*, p. 384), 'there is no historic or doctrinal reason' for a rule excluding public interest arguments from the remedial analysis. Conversely, some property lawyers have objected strongly to what they see as a forced sale of the claimant's proprietary rights (see, e.g., Dixon [2014] Conv 79), and take the view that only Parliament has the authority to expropriate private rights in this way (see P. Davies, 'Injunctions in Tort and Contract', in S. Worthington and G. Virgo (eds), *Commercial Remedies: Resolving Controversies* (Cambridge: CUP, 2017)). Furthermore, any approach that attaches considerable weight to public interest considerations is open to the objection that it may be difficult for a judge to determine where the public interest lies (see Davies, *op. cit.*), while there may of course also be a countervailing public interest in shutting down activities that are damaging the environment.

There was undoubtedly a strong case for saying that the *Shelfer* criteria were sometimes applied in an overly rigid way, and to that extent the more open and sophisticated approach ushered in by *Lawrence* is to be welcomed. However, we have seen that the injunction is itself a flexible instrument, and historical research suggests that when the full range of available judicial techniques are employed the threat of injunctive relief can 'provide an effective means of persuading the parties to reach agreement or to encourage the adoption of alternative production methods' (Wilde, *op. cit.*, p. 388). Moreover, the *Shelfer* criteria made the exercise of the remedial discretion in nuisance cases relatively predictable, and the courts now face the difficult task of replacing them with a new approach which strikes an appropriate balance between certainty and flexibility.

For a detailed commentary on the approach to this issue in *Lawrence*, see D. Nolan, 'Injunctions', in W. Day and S. Worthington (eds), *Challenging Private Law: Lord Sumption on the Supreme Court* (Oxford: Hart, 2020), who argues that, in addition to the well-established factors emphasised in the case law—such as the gravity of the injury to the claimant and any high-handedness of the defendant—the courts should take account when exercising their broader remedial discretion of (1) whether injunctive relief is likely to incentivise the defendant to seek out new ways of reducing or eliminating the interference; (2) whether in the court's view the claimant's motivation in litigating is primarily financial; and (3) the ease of assessing damages in lieu of an injunction on the facts. (As to the principles governing the assessment of such damages, there was some discussion of this in *Lawrence* (e.g., at [128]–[132], per Lord Neuberger) and see now *One Step (Support) Ltd v Morris-Garner* [2019] AC 649.)

III. The Rule in *Rylands v Fletcher*

We have seen in the preceding sections that the law of nuisance has occasionally been applied to isolated events causing damage to a neighbour's property. It was argued earlier that in such cases liability is more properly to be founded on the law of negligence rather than nuisance; however, an exception must be made for cases falling within the ambit of the rule in *Rylands v Fletcher*. Where there has been an escape of a dangerous thing in the course of a non-natural use of land, the occupier is liable for damage to another as a result of the escape. This is so irrespective of whether the occupier has been at fault (i.e. it is a tort of strict liability). However, liability is not absolute; there are defences, and the defendant is only liable for the foreseeable consequences of the escape. Because of its strict liability nature, the rule in *Rylands v Fletcher* is of great historical and theoretical interest, even if, for reasons which will become apparent, it is now of limited practical significance.

1. The *Rylands v Fletcher* Case

Fletcher v Rylands (1866) LR 1 Exch 265

The defendants were mill owners who employed independent contractors to build a reservoir to supply water to their mill. Unbeknownst to them, the reservoir was constructed over five disused mine shafts, which led into the disused underground workings of an old mine. There was a connection between these workings and the workings of the plaintiff's mines. When the reservoir was filled the water burst into the shafts and then flowed through the workings into the plaintiff's mines. The plaintiff sought damages for the flooding of its mines from the defendants.

Blackburn J

We think that the true rule of law is, that the person who for his own purposes brings on his lands and collects and keeps there anything likely to do mischief if it escapes, must keep it in at his peril, and, if he does not do so, is prima facie answerable for all the damage which is the natural consequence of its escape. He can excuse himself by shewing that the escape was owing to the plaintiff's default; or perhaps that the escape was the consequence of vis major, or the act of God; but as nothing of this sort exists here, it is unnecessary to inquire what excuse would be sufficient. The general rule, as above stated, seems on principle just. The person whose grass or corn is eaten down by the escaping cattle of his neighbour, or whose mine is flooded by the water from his neighbour's reservoir, or whose cellar is invaded by the filth of his neighbour's privy, or whose habitation is made unhealthy by the fumes and noisome vapours of his neighbour's alkali works, is damnified without any fault of his own; and it seems but reasonable and just that the neighbour, who has brought something on his own property which was not naturally there, harmless to others so long as it is confined to his own property, but which he knows to be mischievous if it gets on his neighbour's, should be obliged to make good the damage which ensues if he does not succeed in confining it to his own property. But for his act in bringing it there no mischief could have accrued, and it seems but just that he should at his peril keep it there so that no mischief may accrue, or answer for the natural and anticipated consequences. And upon authority, this we think is established to be the law whether the things so brought be beasts, or water, or filth, or stenches.

COMMENTARY

When the case went on appeal to the House of Lords (*Rylands v Fletcher* (1868) LR 3 HL 330), the decision of the Court of Exchequer Chamber was upheld. Lord Cairns drew a distinction between flooding which arose as a result of a natural use of the land and was caused by the forces of nature (which would not be actionable) and flooding as a result of a non-natural use of land (which would be). Whether there is a difference between something 'not naturally' on the land (the expression used by Blackburn J) and 'non-natural user' is doubtful, as Lord Cairns explained non-natural user as meaning 'that which in its natural condition was not in or upon it'. Nonetheless, subsequent cases adopted the term 'non-natural use of land' and applied it in a way which was more restrictive than Blackburn J's original formulation.

The subject of damage caused by the failure of dams was very topical at the time of the litigation in *Rylands*. In March 1864 the Bradfield Reservoir of the Sheffield Waterworks Company failed, inundating the Loxley valley and flooding parts of Sheffield to a depth of nine feet. At least 238 people were killed. On the relationship between contemporaneous dam disasters and the decision in *Rylands*, see A. W. B. Simpson, 'Bursting Reservoirs and Victorian Tort Law: *Rylands and Horrocks v Fletcher* (1868)', in his *Leading Cases in the Common Law* (Oxford: OUP, 1995). Another historical aside of interest is the identity of the third law lord who decided the case alongside Lord Cairns and Lord Cranworth, who appears to have been the Bishop of Armagh, the practice of the time being to call on lay peers to make up a quorum where necessary—see Heuston (1970) 86 LQR 160; Yale (1970) 86 LQR 311.

2. Nuisance and *Rylands v Fletcher*

Cambridge Water Co v Eastern Counties Leather plc [1994] 2 AC 264

In the course of operating its tannery the defendant used a chemical (PCE), some of which was spilt onto the floor of its factory. Over a period of time the PCE which had been spilt seeped through the ground and was carried (and was still being carried at the date of trial) by way of an underground water-flow to the plaintiff's borehole several miles away. This resulted in the water from the borehole becoming polluted with the chemical to an extent that it failed to satisfy the minimum health requirements for drinking water, and the plaintiff was forced to find an alternative supply of water. The plaintiff sued the defendant in negligence, nuisance and under *Rylands v Fletcher* for the cost of developing the alternative source of water. The claims were dismissed at first instance, the trial judge holding that the negligence and nuisance claims failed because the type or kind of harm suffered by the plaintiff was not foreseeable, and that the use of land was not 'non-natural' for the purposes of *Rylands v Fletcher*. The Court of Appeal rejected the plaintiff's appeal against the decision on *Rylands v Fletcher* but allowed its appeal in respect of the tort of nuisance (for reasons we need not consider further here). The House of Lords reversed the decision on nuisance and also rejected the claim based on *Rylands*, holding that, as in negligence and nuisance, the type or kind of harm suffered as a result of the escape must be reasonably foreseeable.

Lord Goff

Nuisance and the Rule in *Rylands v Fletcher*

In order to consider the question in the present case in its proper legal context, it is desirable to look at the nature of liability in a case such as the present in relation both to the law of nuisance and the rule in *Rylands v Fletcher*, and for that purpose to consider the relationship between the two heads of liability.

I begin with the law of nuisance. Our modern understanding of the nature and scope of the law of nuisance was much enhanced by Professor Newark's seminal article on 'The Boundaries of Nuisance' (1949) 65 LQR 480. The article is avowedly a historical analysis, in that it traces the nature of the tort of nuisance to its origins, and demonstrates how the original view of nuisance as a tort to land (or more accurately, to accommodate interference with servitudes, a tort directed against the plaintiff's enjoyment of rights over land) became distorted as the tort was extended to embrace claims for personal injuries, even where the plaintiff's injury did not occur while using land in his occupation. In Professor Newark's opinion (p. 487), this development produced adverse effects, *viz.*, that liability which should have arisen only under the law of negligence was allowed under the law of nuisance which historically was a tort of strict liability; and that there was a tendency for 'cross-infection to take place, and notions of negligence began to make an appearance in the realm of nuisance proper.' But in addition, Professor Newark considered, at pp. 487–8, it contributed to a mis-appreciation of the decision in *Rylands v Fletcher*:

> This case is generally regarded as an important landmark—indeed, a turning point—in the law of tort; but an examination of the judgments shows that those who decided it were quite unconscious of any revolutionary or reactionary principles implicit in the decision. They thought of it as calling for no more than a restatement of settled principles, and Lord Cairns went so far as to describe those principles as 'extremely simple.' And in fact the main principle involved was extremely simple, being no more than the principle that negligence is not an element in the tort of nuisance. It is true that Blackburn J. in his great judgment in the Exchequer Chamber never once used the word 'nuisance,' but three times

he cited the case of fumes escaping from an alkali works—a clear case of nuisance—as an instance of liability under the rule which he was laying down. Equally it is true that in 1866 there were a number of cases in the reports suggesting that persons who controlled dangerous things were under a strict duty to take care, but as none of these cases had anything to do with nuisance Blackburn J. did not refer to them.

But the profession as a whole, whose conceptions of the boundaries of nuisance were now becoming fogged, failed to see in *Rylands v Fletcher* a simple case of nuisance. They regarded it as an exceptional case—and the Rule in *Rylands v Fletcher* as a generalisation of exceptional cases, where liability was to be strict on account of 'the magnitude of danger, coupled with the difficulty of proving negligence' [Pollock, *Law of Torts*, (14th edn, 1939), p. 386] rather than on account of the nature of the plaintiff's interest which was invaded. They therefore jumped rashly to two conclusions: firstly, that the Rule in *Rylands v Fletcher* could be extended beyond the case of neighbouring occupiers; and secondly, that the Rule could be used to afford a remedy in cases of personal injury. Both these conclusions were stoutly denied by Lord Macmillan in *Read v Lyons* [1947] AC 156, but it remains to be seen whether the House of Lords will support his opinion when the precise point comes up for decision.

We are not concerned in the present case with the problem of personal injuries, but we are concerned with the scope of liability in nuisance and in *Rylands v Fletcher*. In my opinion it is right to take as our starting point the fact that, as Professor Newark considered, *Rylands v Fletcher* was indeed not regarded by Blackburn J as a revolutionary decision: see, e.g., his observations in *Ross v Fedden* (1872) 26 LT 966, 968. He believed himself not to be creating new law, but to be stating existing law, on the basis of existing authority; and, as is apparent from his judgment, he was concerned in particular with the situation where the defendant collects things upon his land which are likely to do mischief if they escape, in which event the defendant will be strictly liable for damage resulting from any such escape. It follows that the essential basis of liability was the collection by the defendant of such things upon his land; and the consequence was a strict liability in the event of damage caused by their escape, even if the escape was an isolated event. Seen in its context, there is no reason to suppose that Blackburn J intended to create a liability any more strict than that created by the law of nuisance; but even so he must have intended that, in the circumstances specified by him, there should be liability for damage resulting from an isolated escape.

Of course, although liability for nuisance has generally been regarded as strict, at least in the case of a defendant who has been responsible for the creation of a nuisance, even so that liability has been kept under control by the principle of reasonable user—the principle of give and take as between neighbouring occupiers of land, under which 'those acts necessary for the common and ordinary use and occupation of land and houses may be done, if conveniently done, without subjecting those who do them to an action:' see *Bamford v Turnley* (1862) 3 B & S 62, 83, per Bramwell B. The effect is that, if the user is reasonable, the defendant will not be liable for consequent harm to his neighbour's enjoyment of his land; but if the user is not reasonable, the defendant will be liable, even though he may have exercised reasonable care and skill to avoid it. Strikingly, a comparable principle has developed which limits liability under the rule in *Rylands v Fletcher*. This is the principle of natural use of the land. I shall have to consider the principle at a later stage in this judgment. The most authoritative statement of the principle is now to be found in the advice of the Privy Council delivered by Lord Moulton in *Rickards v Lothian* [1913] AC 263, 280, when he said of the rule in *Rylands v Fletcher*:

> It is not every use to which land is put that brings into play that principle. It must be some special use bringing with it increased danger to others, and must not merely be the ordinary use of the land or such a use as is proper for the general benefit of the community.

> It is not necessary for me to identify precise differences which may be drawn between this principle, and the principle of reasonable user as applied in the law of nuisance. It is enough for present purposes that I should draw attention to a similarity of function. The effect of this principle is that, where it applies, there will be no liability under the rule in *Rylands v Fletcher*; but that where it does not apply, i.e. where there is a non-natural use, the defendant will be liable for harm caused to the plaintiff by the escape, notwithstanding that he has exercised all reasonable care and skill to prevent the escape from occurring.

COMMENTARY

According to Lord Goff, the historical genesis of the rule in *Rylands v Fletcher* was in the tort of nuisance, with *Rylands* being a particular application of that tort to isolated escapes. This view has subsequently been accepted by the House of Lords (*Transco plc v Stockport Metropolitan Borough Council* [2004] 2 AC 1). However, academic commentators have been less convinced that *Rylands* can be explained in this way, arguing that *Rylands* derives from a general (if vague) principle of the medieval legal system of strict liability for causing harm. This was quite different from private nuisance which was intimately connected to the protection of rights in land (see *Hunter v Canary Wharf*, extracted earlier). Murphy, 'The Merits of *Rylands v Fletcher*' (2004) 24 OJLS 643 and Nolan, 'The Distinctiveness of *Rylands v Fletcher*' (2005) 121 LQR 421 argue that the different derivations of the two causes of action are reflected in the fact that the conditions for liability differ. Nuisance requires an unreasonable interference with land, whilst *Rylands v Fletcher* requires a non-natural use of land. And as Nolan (2005) 121 LQR 421 at 434–5 comments:

> The unreasonable user issue is ultimately concerned with whether or not the interference with the claimant's land is tolerable, so the focus is not so much on the nature of the defendant's activity—though this is a factor to be considered—but on whether the resulting discomfort or inconvenience is something which the claimant can, in all the circumstances, be expected to put up with. The non-natural use concept is quite different, for here the focus is not on the harm to the claimant, or even a balancing of the two parties' interests, but simply on the nature of the defendant's activity.

Given, however, that *Rylands* is now seen as a subset of nuisance, this distinction does not explain why the *Rylands* subset should have a separate, and more restrictive, condition of liability than for an ordinary nuisance action. A possible explanation is that the courts wish to confine the stricter liability under *Rylands* within narrower bounds than apply to nuisance proper, so that there must be some exceptional feature of the defendant's use of land that justifies the liability, amounting to a 'non-natural user'. As Lord Hoffmann pointed out in *Transco*, it is tempting to see in this idea the beginnings of a theory of 'enterprise liability'—a policy of requiring the 'costs' of an unusually dangerous enterprise on land to be internalised (by making the party responsible for the enterprise liable for damage caused to others by the materialisation of the risks created by that enterprise). It seems unlikely, however, that this was the motivation for the decision in *Rylands* itself (see Oliphant, '*Rylands v Fletcher* and the Emergence of Enterprise Liability in the Common Law', in *European Tort Law 2004*), and, in contrast to many jurisdictions in the United States, it has not developed into a general theory of strict liability for extra-hazardous activities. An attempt to extend *Rylands* in this way was rejected by Lord Goff in *Cambridge Water* on a number of grounds, perhaps the most telling being the failure of the Law Commission to recommend any proposals to implement strict liability for ultra-hazardous or especially dangerous activities (see Law Commission, *Civil Liability for Dangerous Things and Activities* (Law Com. No. 32, 1970)). In the later case of *Transco*, Lord Bingham found Lord Goff's reason for refusing to extend the *Rylands* rule 'compelling', and argued that any such development was a matter for Parliament rather than the courts.

As the orthodoxy is now that nuisance and *Rylands* are linked, it was not surprising that the House of Lords in *Cambridge Water* held that liability under *Rylands v Fletcher*, as in nuisance, only arises where the damage suffered by the claimant was foreseeable. But this does not mean that the manner of the escape must be foreseeable. The only requirement is that, in the event of an escape—whether foreseeable or not—the damage suffered by the claimant is of a type or kind that was a reasonably foreseeable consequence of such an escape (see Cross, 'Does Only the Careless Polluter Pay? A Fresh Examination of the Tort of Nuisance' (1991) 111 LQR 445). This requirement was the reason why the claim failed in *Cambridge Water*: although some damage from the spillage of PCE might be imagined, pollution of the plaintiff's water supply could not.

Again, if *Rylands v Fletcher* is simply a subset of the tort of nuisance, rules as to standing and damages should be the same for both, and in *Transco* it was therefore accepted that only a person with a proprietary interest in the affected land can rely on the *Rylands* rule. The link with nuisance also suggests that an action lies only for damage to real property interests (although, as in nuisance, damages might also be recoverable for consequential damage to chattels: see II.4). Hence in *Transco* their Lordships approved the obiter view of Lord Macmillan in *Read v J Lyons & Co Ltd* [1947] AC 156 that liability under *Rylands v Fletcher* did not extend to personal injury, recovery for which therefore required proof of negligence. There were in fact cases before *Read v Lyons* in which damages were recovered for personal injury under the rule (see, e.g., *Miles v Forest Rock Granite Co* (1918) 34 TLR 500; *Hale v Jennings Bros* [1938] 1 All ER 579), but after *Transco* these must be regarded as having been wrongly decided. Whether this privileging of property interests over bodily integrity is a satisfactory outcome is another matter. The restriction in question has not been favoured in other jurisdictions (see, e.g., *Brooks v Canadian Pacific Railway Ltd* (2007) 283 DLR (4th) 540 at [103], per Dawson J), nor by the majority of commentators, one of whom (Tylor, 'The Restriction of Strict Liability' (1947) 10 MLR 396 at 400) pointed out that:

> The suggestion that I can recover for an explosion wrecking my conservatory or a horse trespassing on my rose bed, but not for an explosion blowing me out of my deck chair in my own garden, or a horse treading on my face as I sleep on my lawn, has little to commend it.

3. The Elements of a *Rylands v Fletcher* Claim

(a) Escape

In *Read v Lyons* [1947] AC 156 the plaintiff munitions inspector had been injured when a shell exploded at the defendant's munitions factory. As no negligence was alleged against the defendant, the plaintiff relied on *Rylands v Fletcher*, but the House of Lords rejected the claim because there had been no 'escape'. According to Viscount Simon (at 168), 'escape', for the purpose of applying the *Rylands* rule meant 'escape from a place where the defendant has occupation of or control over to a place which is outside his occupation or control'. It followed that if the plaintiff had been injured by the explosion when leaving the factory, her ability to recover damages would depend on whether she had passed through the factory gates. Lord Porter admitted that there was force in the criticism that the requirement could lead to arbitrary results, but said that the limitation was justified as the liability under *Rylands* was an exception to the general rule of fault-based liability and hence should be restricted. In any case, as Lord Bingham pointed out in *Transco* (at [9]), the requirement is consistent with the view of the rule as an offshoot of nuisance, as in a *Rylands*-type scenario there can be no interference with the claimant's land (the defining feature of private nuisance) unless something escapes from the defendant's.

It had been thought that in cases involving fire, it was not the flammable material collected by the defendant that must escape, but the fire it caused. However, in *Gore v Stannard (t/a Wyvern Tyres)* [2014] QB 1, the Court of Appeal held that the thing that escaped and caused the damage must also be the dangerous thing accumulated by the defendant, thereby emasculating the rule in the fire context (see later). Does it follow that if A accumulates volatile chemicals on their land and these cause an explosion that damages B's house, then B can recover only for damage (if any) caused by the impact of the chemicals themselves, and not by the force of the blast? (Cf. *Miles v Forest Rock Granite Co* (1918) 34 TLR 500—recovery under the rule for damage done by a rock thrown out of a quarry during blasting.)

(b) Dangerousness

In the early twentieth-century heyday of the rule, almost anything could count as a dangerous thing escape of which was capable of giving rise to liability under *Rylands v Fletcher*. *Winfield & Jolowicz* (para. 16–009) lists the following examples from the cases: fire, gas, explosions, electricity, oil, noxious fumes, colliery spoil, rusty wire from a decayed fence, vibrations, poisonous vegetation, a flag pole and a fairground 'chair-o-plane'. Perhaps the most remarkable case is *Attorney General v Corke* [1933] Ch 89, where the accumulation of a group of itinerant travellers satisfied the requirement, Bennett J (at 94–5) holding that persons whose homes were in caravans moving about from place to place 'have habits of life many of which are offensive to those who have fixed homes, and when collected together in large numbers, on a comparatively small parcel of land, such persons would be expected by reasonable people to do the kind of things which have been complained of in this action and of which proof has been given'. Setting aside the—themselves rather offensive—assumptions that underlie this analysis, it is questionable whether the judges who decided *Rylands v Fletcher* had noxious persons in mind, and subsequent cases involving alleged failures to exercise control over persons on the defendant's land have founded liability on nuisance rather than *Rylands v Fletcher* (see *Lippiatt v South Gloucestershire Council* [2000] QB 51, discussed in II.3(b)).

Despite the expansive approach taken in the case law to the requirement that the defendant must have accumulated a dangerous thing on his land, Lord Bingham made it clear in *Transco* (see the next extract) that the requirement should have real bite, and 'should not be at all easily satisfied'. However, he also acknowledged that this requirement could not be considered in complete isolation from the requirement of non-natural use, and there is much to be said for Lord Walker's view in *Transco* that the two questions should be considered together, so that the more dangerous the thing is the more likely it is to amount to a non-natural use, etc.

(c) Non-Natural Use of Land

The most important limitation on liability under *Rylands v Fletcher* is the requirement that the damage must be caused by a 'non-natural use' of the defendant's land. The meaning of this requirement has fluctuated over time, but the most recent authority on it is the next extracted case.

Transco plc v Stockport Metropolitan Borough Council [2004] 2 AC 1

The defendant council was responsible for laying a water pipe to supply water to a residential tower block that it owned. Without fault on the part of the defendant, the pipe broke and a considerable volume of water was released, one consequence of which was that the embankment through which the claimant's gas pipe ran collapsed and the claimant was required to undertake urgent repairs to ensure the pipe did not crack. At first instance, the claimant recovered the cost of the repairs under the rule in *Rylands v Fletcher* but the defendant's appeal was allowed by the Court of Appeal. The House of Lords dismissed a further appeal, holding that the water pipe was not a non-natural use.

Lord Bingham

10 It has from the beginning been a necessary condition of liability under the rule in *Rylands v Fletcher* that the thing which the defendant has brought on his land should be 'something which . . . will naturally do mischief if it escape out of his land' (LR 1 Ex 265, 279 per Blackburn J), 'something dangerous . . .', 'anything likely to do mischief if it escapes', 'something . . . harmless to others so long as it is confined to his own property, but which he knows to be mischievous if it gets on his neighbour's' (p 280), 'anything which, if it should escape, may cause damage to his neighbour' (LR 3 HL 330, 340, per Lord Cranworth). The practical problem is of course to decide whether in any given case the thing which has escaped satisfies this mischief or danger test, a problem exacerbated by the fact that many things not ordinarily regarded as sources of mischief or danger may none the less be capable of proving to be such if they escape. I do not think this condition can be viewed in complete isolation from the non-natural user condition to which I shall shortly turn, but I think the cases decided by the House give a valuable pointer. In *Rylands v Fletcher* itself the courts were dealing with what Lord Cranworth (LR 3 HL 330, 342) called 'a large accumulated mass of water' stored up in a reservoir, and I have touched on the historical context of the decision in paragraph 3(3) above. *Rainham Chemical Works* [1921] 2 AC 465, 471, involved the storage of chemicals, for the purpose of making munitions, which 'exploded with terrific violence'. In *Attorney General v Cory Bros & Co Ltd* [1921] 1 AC 521, 525, 530, 534, 536, the landslide in question was of what counsel described as an 'enormous mass of rubbish', some 500,000 tons of mineral waste tipped on a steep hillside. In *Cambridge Water* [1994] 2 AC 264 the industrial solvents being used by the tannery were bound to cause mischief in the event, unforeseen on the facts that they percolated down to the water table. These cases are in sharp contrast with those arising out of escape from a domestic water supply (such as *Carstairs v Taylor* (1871) LR 6 Ex 217, *Ross v Fedden* (1872) 26 LT 966 or *Anderson v Oppenheimer* (1880) 5 QBD 602) which, although decided on other grounds, would seem to me to fail the mischief or danger test. Bearing in mind the historical origin of the rule, and also that its effect is to impose liability in the absence of negligence for an isolated occurrence, I do not think the mischief or danger test should be at all easily satisfied. It must be shown that the defendant has done something which he recognised, or judged by the standards appropriate at

the relevant place and time, he ought reasonably to have recognised, as giving rise to an exceptionally high risk of danger or mischief if there should be an escape, however unlikely an escape may have been thought to be.

11 No ingredient of *Rylands v Fletcher* liability has provoked more discussion than the requirement of Blackburn J (LR 1 Ex 265, 280) that the thing brought on to the defendant's land should be something 'not naturally there', an expression elaborated by Lord Cairns (LR 3 HL 330, 339) when he referred to the putting of land to a 'non-natural use': see Stallybrass, 'Dangerous Things and the Non-Natural User of Land' (1929) 3 CLJ 376–397; Goodhart, 'Liability for Things Naturally on the Land' (1932) 4 CLJ 13–33; Newark, 'Non-Natural User and *Rylands v Fletcher*' (1961) 24 MLR 557–71; Williams, 'Non-Natural Use of Land' [1973] CLJ 310–22; Weir, '*Rylands v Fletcher* Reconsidered' [1994] CLJ 216. Read literally, the expressions used by Blackburn J and Lord Cairns might be thought to exclude nothing which has reached the land otherwise than through operation of the laws of nature. But such an interpretation has been fairly described as 'redolent of a different age' (*Cambridge Water* [1994] 2 AC 264, 308), and in *Read v J Lyons & Co Ltd* [1947] AC 156, 169, 176, 187 and *Cambridge Water*, at p. 308, the House gave its imprimatur to Lord Moulton's statement, giving the advice of the Privy Council in *Rickards v Lothian* [1913] AC 263, 280:

> It is not every use to which land is put that brings into play that principle. It must be some special use bringing with it increased danger to others, and must not merely be the ordinary use of the land or such a use as is proper for the general benefit of the community.

I think it clear that ordinary user is a preferable test to natural user, making it clear that the rule in *Rylands v Fletcher* is engaged only where the defendant's use is shown to be extraordinary and unusual. This is not a test to be inflexibly applied: a use may be extraordinary and unusual at one time or in one place but not so at another time or in another place (although I would question whether, even in wartime, the manufacture of explosives could ever be regarded as an ordinary user of land, as contemplated by Viscount Simon, Lord Macmillan, Lord Porter and Lord Uthwatt in *Read v J Lyons & Co Ltd* [1947] AC 156, 169–170, 174, 176–177, 186–187). I also doubt whether a test of reasonable user is helpful, since a user may well be quite out of the ordinary but not unreasonable, as was that of *Rylands*, Rainham Chemical Works or the tannery in *Cambridge Water*. Again, as it seems to me, the question is whether the defendant has done something which he recognises, or ought to recognise, as being quite out of the ordinary in the place and at the time when he does it. In answering that question, I respectfully think that little help is gained (and unnecessary confusion perhaps caused) by considering whether the use is proper for the general benefit of the community. In *Rickards v Lothian* itself, the claim arose because the outflow from a wash-basin on the top floor of premises was maliciously blocked and the tap left running, with the result that damage was caused to stock on a floor below: not surprisingly, the provision of a domestic water supply to the premises was held to be a wholly ordinary use of the land. An occupier of land who can show that another occupier of land has brought or kept on his land an exceptionally dangerous or mischievous thing in extraordinary or unusual circumstances is in my opinion entitled to recover compensation from that occupier for any damage caused to his property interest by the escape of that thing, subject to defences of Act of God or of a stranger, without the need to prove negligence.

Lord Hoffmann

44 It remains, however, if not to rationalise the law of England, at least to introduce greater certainty into the concept of natural user which is in issue in this case. In order to do so, I think it must be frankly acknowledged that little assistance can be obtained from the kinds of user which Lord Cairns must be assumed to have regarded as 'non-natural' in *Rylands v Fletcher*

itself. They are, as Lord Goff of Chieveley said in the *Cambridge Water* case [1994] 2 AC 264, 308, 'redolent of a different age'. So nothing can be made of the anomaly that one of the illustrations of the rule given by Blackburn J is cattle trespass. Whatever Blackburn J and Lord Cairns may have meant by 'natural', the law was set on a different course by the opinion of Lord Moulton in *Rickards v Lothian* [1913] AC 263 and the question of what is a natural use of land or, (the converse) a use creating an increased risk, must be judged by contemporary standards.

45 Two features of contemporary society seem to me to be relevant. First, the extension of statutory regulation to a number of activities, such as discharge of water (section 209 of the Water Industry Act 1991) pollution by the escape of waste (section 73(6) of the Environmental Protection Act 1990) and radioactive matter (section 7 of the Nuclear Installations Act 1965). It may have to be considered whether these and similar provisions create an exhaustive code of liability for a particular form of escape which excludes the rule in *Rylands v Fletcher*.

46 Secondly, so far as the rule does have a residuary role to play, it must be borne in mind that it is concerned only with damage to property and that insurance against various forms of damage to property is extremely common. A useful guide in deciding whether the risk has been created by a 'non-natural' user of land is therefore to ask whether the damage which eventuated was something against which the occupier could reasonably be expected to have insured himself. Property insurance is relatively cheap and accessible; in my opinion people should be encouraged to insure their own property rather than seek to transfer the risk to others by means of litigation, with the heavy transactional costs which that involves. The present substantial litigation over £100,000 should be a warning to anyone seeking to rely on an esoteric cause of action to shift a commonplace insured risk.

47 In the present case, I am willing to assume that if the risk arose from a 'non-natural user' of the council's land, all the other elements of the tort were satisfied. . . .

48 The damage which eventuated was subsidence beneath a gas main: a form of risk against which no rational owner of a gas main would fail to insure. The casualty was caused by the escape of water from the council's land. But the source was a perfectly normal item of plumbing. The pipe was, it is true, considerably larger than the ordinary domestic size. But it was smaller than a water main. It was installed to serve the occupiers of the council's high rise flats; not strictly speaking a commercial purpose, but not a private one either.

49 In my opinion the Court of Appeal was right to say that it was not a 'non-natural' user of land. I am influenced by two matters. First, there is no evidence that it created a greater risk than is normally associated with domestic or commercial plumbing. True, the pipe was larger. But whether that involved greater risk depends upon its specification. One cannot simply assume that the larger the pipe, the greater the risk of fracture or the greater the quantity of water likely to be discharged. I agree with my noble and learned friend, Lord Bingham of Cornhill, that the criterion of exceptional risk must be taken seriously and creates a high threshold for a claimant to surmount. Secondly, I think that the risk of damage to property caused by leaking water is one against which most people can and do commonly insure. This is, as I have said, particularly true of Transco, which can be expected to have insured against any form of damage to its pipe. It would be a very strange result if Transco were entitled to recover against the council when it would not have been entitled to recover against the water authority for similar damage emanating from its high-pressure main [because the authority had a specific statutory immunity].

Lord Hobhouse, **Lord Scott** and **Lord Walker** gave separate concurring speeches.

Appeal dismissed.

COMMENTARY

Their Lordships were agreed that the question of non-natural use boiled down to whether the use was ordinary, and that this was linked to the risks it created. They also agreed that the requirement imposed a high threshold: Lord Bingham said the use must be extraordinary and unusual; Lord Hoffmann that the risk created must be exceptional; and Lord Walker that it was the extraordinary risk to neighbouring property if an escape occurred which made the use non-natural. On the facts of *Transco*, even though the water pipe was considerably larger than an ordinary domestic water pipe (because it was supplying a tower block), as a supply of water to domestic property it was still an ordinary use of land. Conversely, in *Cambridge Water* Lord Goff said (at 309) that the 'storage of substantial quantities of chemicals on industrial premises should be regarded as an almost classic case of non-natural use'. It would seem to follow that the manufacture of explosives would clearly also count as a non-natural use, and although this was questioned in *Read v Lyons*—at least in wartime—the rejection of a 'general community benefit' component in the test of ordinary use led Lord Bingham and Lord Walker in *Transco* to doubt that analysis, and the latter (at [105]) considered that a munitions factory was another classic example of non-natural use.

Lord Hoffmann said in *Transco* that a useful guide in deciding whether a particular risk was created by a non-natural use was to ask whether the resultant damage was something against which the occupier could reasonably be expected to have insured themselves. Property insurance was cheap and accessible, and people should be encouraged to insure their property rather than to seek to transfer the risk to others by expensive litigation. However, this reasoning was criticised by Lord Hobhouse (at [60]), who pointed out that some risks might be insurable only at prohibitive rates, that the allocation of the risk determines who bears the economic burden of insuring against the risk, and that the same argument could be used to justify abolishing negligence actions in road traffic cases, since all drivers could take out comprehensive car insurance. In our view Lord Hobhouse's reasoning is to be preferred; after all, it would surely seem strange that if an escape of water flooded both domestic premises (often insured) and a council-owned adventure playground (often not insured), there might be recovery for the latter, but not for the former (see Bagshaw (2004) 120 LQR 388 at 390). This was also the opinion of Judge Peter Coulson QC in *LMS International Ltd v Styrene Packaging and Insulation Ltd* [2006] Build LR 50, who refused to attach any significance to the insurance position of a claimant who had brought an action under the rule.

The equation of non-natural with non-ordinary use significantly limits the range of activities to which strict liability attaches, and the narrow approach to the concept adopted in *Transco* means that the scope of operation of the rule is now very restricted. In *Burnie Port Authority v General Jones Pty Ltd* (1994) 179 CLR 520, a majority of the High Court of Australia held that the game was no longer worth the candle, and that in that jurisdiction the rule in *Rylands v Fletcher* should henceforth be subsumed into the law of negligence. The majority (at 541) felt that the use of terms such as 'special' or 'not ordinary' use 'goes a long way to depriving the requirement of "non-natural" use of objective content'. But in his dissenting judgment in *Burnie* (at 589), McHugh J defended the concept and distinguished it from negligence:

[I]n determining the issue of non-natural use, factors that would be decisive on an issue of negligence will frequently be of only marginal relevance on the issue of non-natural use. Often, they will be irrelevant to the latter issue. In determining whether a use of land is natural, the court does not look at all the particular circumstances of the individual occupier but whether, in the time, place, and circumstances of the particular community, the character of the use of the land by that occupier constitutes a non-natural use. Thus, in the classic *Rylands v Fletcher* situation, land is used for a non-natural purpose even though the particular amount of water stored is small and the walls of the reservoir are thick and high. Similarly, burning a domestic fire to warm a room does not constitute a non-natural use of the premises because the fire has no guard and is left unattended. Non-natural use of land is a different concept from the negligent use of the land.

For discussion of the *Burnie Port* decision, see Heuston and Buckley (1994) 110 LQR 506; Lunney (1994–5) 5 KCLJ 133 and Nolan (2005) 121 LQR 421 at 440–6, and for a valuable comparative discussion of *Transco* (in the context of European civil law jurisdictions) see van Boom, 'Some Remarks on the Decline of *Rylands v Fletcher* and the Disparity of European Strict Liability Regimes' [2005] ZEuP 618–37.

4. Defences

Rickards v Lothian [1913] AC 263

The plaintiff was the lessee of part of the second floor of a building owned by the defendant. As a result of a tap being left on in the top floor lavatory water overflowed and damaged some of the plaintiff's stock on the second floor. The jury at the trial found that the act of turning on the tap was the 'malicious act of some person'. One issue for the Privy Council was the effect of this finding on a *Rylands v Fletcher* action.

Lord Moulton (delivering the opinion of the Privy Council)

It will be seen that Blackburn J, with characteristic carefulness, indicates that exceptions to the general rule may arise where the escape is in consequence of *vis major*, or the act of God, but declines to deal further with that question because it was unnecessary for the decision of the case then before him. A few years later the question of law thus left undecided in *Fletcher v Rylands* came up for decision in a case arising out of somewhat similar circumstances. The defendant in *Nichols v Marsland* (1876) 2 Ex D 1 had formed on her land certain ornamental pools which contained large quantities of water. A sudden and unprecedented rainfall occurred, giving rise to a flood of such magnitude that the jury found that it could not reasonably have been anticipated. This flood caused the lakes to burst their dams, and the plaintiff's adjoining lands were flooded. The jury found that there was no negligence in the construction or maintenance of the lakes. But they also found that if such a flood could have been anticipated the dams might have been so constructed that the flooding would have been prevented. Upon these findings the judge at the trial directed a verdict for the plaintiff, but gave leave to move to enter a verdict for the defendant. On the argument of the rule the Court of Exchequer directed the verdict to be entered for the defendant, and on appeal to the Exchequer Chamber that judgment was unanimously affirmed.

The judgment of the Court of Exchequer Chamber (Cockburn CJ, James and Mellish LJJ, and Baggallay JA) was read by Mellish LJ. After pointing out that the facts of the case rendered it necessary to decide the point left undecided in *Fletcher v Rylands*, he proceeds to lay down the law thereupon in the following language:

> If, indeed, the damages were occasioned by the act of the party without more—as where a man accumulates water on his own land, but, owing to the peculiar nature or condition of the

> soil, the water escapes and does damage to his neighbour—the case of *Rylands v Fletcher* establishes that he must be held liable. The accumulation of water in a reservoir is not in itself wrongful; but the making it and suffering the water to escape, if damage ensue, constitutes a wrong. But the present case is distinguished from that of *Rylands v Fletcher* in this, that it is not the act of the defendant in keeping this reservoir, an act in itself lawful, which alone leads to the escape of the water, and so renders wrongful that which but for such escape would have been lawful. It is the supervening vis major of the water caused by the flood, which, superadded to the water in the reservoir (which of itself would have been innocuous), caused the disaster. A defendant cannot, in our opinion, be properly said to have caused or allowed the water to escape, if the act of God or the Queen's enemies was the real cause of its escaping without any fault on the part of the defendant. If a reservoir was destroyed by an earthquake, or the Queen's enemies destroyed it in conducting some warlike operation, it would be contrary to all reason and justice to hold the owner of the reservoir liable for any damage that might be done by the escape of the water. We are of opinion therefore that the defendant was entitled to excuse herself by proving that the water escaped through the act of God.
>
> Their Lordships are of opinion that all that is there laid down as to a case where the escape is due to 'vis major or the King's enemies' applies equally to a case where it is due to the malicious act of a third person, if indeed that case is not actually included in the above phrase. To follow the language of the judgment just recited—a defendant cannot in their Lordships' opinion be properly said to have caused or allowed the water to escape if the malicious act of a third person was the real cause of its escaping without any fault on the part of the defendant . . .
>
> *Appeal allowed.*

COMMENTARY

As indicated in the extract, Blackburn J suggested in *Rylands v Fletcher* itself that a number of defences could be relied upon. Nolan (2005) 121 LQR 421 at 430 notes that those defences go to establishing that the true cause of the claimant's damage was not the accumulation of the defendant, thereby reinforcing the view that liability under *Rylands* derives from older notions of strict liability where the defendant could avoid liability only by showing that the damage was not caused by him (see also *Ibbetson*, pp. 57–63). One defence specifically mentioned by Blackburn J was act of God, described in *Tennent v Earl of Glasgow* (1864) 2 M (HL) 22 at 26–7 as an escape caused directly by natural causes without human intervention in circumstances which no human foresight can provide against and of which human prudence is not bound to recognise the possibility. However, although the defence was applied in *Nichols v Marsland*—a case mentioned in the extract—it has not been relied upon successfully since, and in *Greenock Corporation v Caledonian Railway* [1917] AC 556 the House of Lords interpreted the defence very narrowly, even doubting its application in *Nichols*.

If the escape is caused by the deliberate act of a stranger, then a defence may be available, as was the case in *Rickards*. But who is a 'stranger' for these purposes? In *Perry v Kendricks Transport Ltd* [1956] 1 WLR 85 the plaintiff, a boy of 10, was injured when the petrol tank of a disused coach parked on the defendants' land exploded. The petrol tank had been drained and the cap secured. As the plaintiff approached the coach he saw two other boys near the coach and as he drew alongside the vehicle these boys jumped away and there was an explosion. The trial judge found that the cap of the tank had been removed that day by persons unknown and that one of the two boys had thrown a lighted match into the tank, causing the fumes to ignite. The trial judge dismissed a claim in negligence, and the plaintiff appealed, relying on *Rylands v Fletcher*, but the Court of Appeal held that the defence of act of a stranger applied. According to Jenkins LJ (at 91), a stranger was someone over whom the occupier had no control, and in such cases it would be wrong to see the accumulation of the dangerous thing or the conduct of the occupier or persons on the land with his consent as the cause of the damage, although if 'it was a reasonable and probable consequence of [the occupiers'] action, which they ought to have foreseen, that children might meddle with the dangerous thing and cause it to escape' then a negligence claim would lie.

A trespasser is clearly a stranger, but what about licensees or guests of the occupier? *Winfield & Jolowicz*, para. 16-026 suggests that the defence is not available in respect of the conduct of such persons unless the act in question is 'wholly alien to the licence or invitation'.

There are also three other possible defences to an action under *Rylands v Fletcher*, namely statutory authority, consent and default of the claimant; see further *Winfield & Jolowicz*, paras 16-026–16-035.

5. *Rylands v Fletcher* and Liability for Fire

At various times throughout the history of the common law it has been posited that an occupier is strictly liable for the spread of fire from their land, at least where it was lit by themselves or by someone on the land with their permission (see, e.g., *Beaulieu v Finglam* (1401) in J. H. Baker and S. Milsom, *Sources of English Legal History*, 2nd edn (Oxford: OUP, 2010), pp. 610–11). It is doubtful whether this was ever really the law, however, as in most cases the issue presented for decision was whether there had been negligence in tending the fire (Arnold, 'Introduction', in *id* (ed.), *Select Cases of Trespass in the King's Courts, 1307–1399*, vol. 1 (Selden Society vol. 100, 1984), pp. lxviii–lxx). And by the end of the seventeenth century it was clear that the liability of an occupier was not strict where the fire was started or was spread by the act of a stranger or through an act of nature (*Turberville v Stamp* (1697) 1 Ld Raym 264, 91 ER 1072).

The current position is that an occupier is liable for damage caused by the spread of a fire that started on their land where there is negligence, either by the occupier or by someone on the land with their leave and licence (see Lord Denning in *H. & N. Emanuel v Greater London Council* [1971] 2 All ER 835; *Ribee v Norrie* [2001] PIQR P128). The effect is to impose on occupiers a non-delegable duty of care in respect of fires lit on their land, so that negligence is the touchstone of liability, albeit not necessarily the negligence of the occupier. The view that there is no special rule of strict liability for the spread of fire was confirmed by the Court of Appeal in *Gore v Stannard (t/a Wyvern Tyres)* [2014] QB 1.

However, even if there is no special rule of strict liability relating to damage caused by fire, can the general strict liability rule in *Rylands v Fletcher* apply in such a case? In *Musgrove v Pandelis* [1919] 2 KB 43, the Court of Appeal held that it could. The defendant occupied a garage in which he parked his car, the plaintiff owning the remainder of the building. The defendant employed a chauffeur, and on one occasion when he was attempting to start the car it caught fire. The fire could have been controlled by turning off the petrol tap immediately, but negligently the chauffeur first went to find a cloth with which to turn it off, and by the time he returned the fire was too intense for him to perform this operation. The defendant was held to be subject not only to vicarious liability for the negligence of his employee, but also to primary liability under *Rylands v Fletcher*. It is important to note that some adaptation of the *Rylands* rule was required for it encompass the facts of *Musgrove*. Liability seems to have been based on the fact that *the car* was a dangerous thing, even though it was not the car but the fire which started in the car that caused the damage (compare the facts of *Rylands*, where it was the water in the reservoir that was dangerous and which escaped and caused the damage). The fire-variant of *Rylands* recognised in *Musgrove* was applied in a number of later cases, albeit with differing degrees of enthusiasm (see, e.g., *Mason v Levy Auto Parts* [1967] 2 QB 530; *Johnson (t/a Johnson Butchers) v BJW Property Developments Ltd* [2002] 3 All ER 574). However, the Court of Appeal in *Gore v Stannard (t/a Wyvern Tyres)* [2014] QB 1 rejected the notion that there was *any* fire-variant of *Rylands*. In this case the defendant stored large numbers of tyres on its business premises for commercial purposes. A fire started due to an electrical fault for which the defendant was not responsible, which intensified because of the presence of the tyres. It spread to the claimant's neighbouring premises, causing severe damage. Despite the earlier authorities applying *Rylands* in situations where the dangerous thing had been the thing that had caught fire (but it had been the fire itself which had then escaped), the Court of Appeal held that the fire itself was the dangerous thing, with the result that the rule could apply only where the defendant had deliberately (or perhaps negligently in the view of Ward LJ at [48]) started the fire on their premises. In the light of the limited role that the House of Lords had envisaged for *Rylands* in *Transco*, it was not appropriate to recognise a special pocket of *Rylands* liability in fire cases. It follows that the 'lingering sense that fire may be different' when it comes to the operation of the *Rylands* rule has now been 'snuffed out' (Steele and Merkin, 'Insurance between Neighbours: *Stannard v Gore* and Common Law Liability for Fire' (2013) 25 JEL 305 at 310).

While it is true that the House of Lords in *Transco* did not discuss the issue of *Rylands* and fire, the decision of the Court of Appeal in *Gore v Stannard* is consistent with Lord Bingham's aim in *Transco* of restating the rule in such a way as to achieve maximum certainty and clarity. The problem with the fire-variant of *Rylands* is that it equates the dangerous thing brought onto the land with the fire that escapes. Conventional liability under *Rylands* is for things which would be dangerous if they escaped, not for things which are liable to catch fire. Furthermore, if the rule does extend to things that are particularly dangerous if they catch fire, then the potential scope of liability is expanded significantly, as that is true of many things. Liability could of course have been limited by the non-natural use requirement, but in the fire-variant cases whether a use was non-natural or not seemed to be determined by the likelihood that the thing in question would catch fire and that the fire would spread to adjoining premises (see *LMS International Ltd v Styrene Packaging and Insulation Ltd* [2006] Build LR 50). This bore little relationship to the meaning of non-natural use in ordinary *Rylands* cases, where the focus is on the extraordinary nature of the defendant's activity, and meant that the requirement was less of a hurdle for claimants in fire cases. Arguably, therefore, the Court of Appeal in *Gore v Stannard* adopted the best solution by simply rejecting the fire variant of *Rylands*, leaving claimants to any remedy they might have in negligence, where they can rely on the non-delegable duty discussed earlier.

In an in-depth analysis of *Gore v Stannard*, Steele and Merkin, *op. cit.*, argue that the decision cannot properly be assessed without considering the prevalence of first-party insurance for fire damage, particularly since the strict liability imposed under the *Rylands* rule itself has frequently been understood as a form of 'insurance'. As they say ((2013) 25 JEL 305 at 317):

> Whilst arguments that insurance is irrelevant to tort reasoning or at least 'fraught with difficulty' are, as we have seen, still encountered, where the principle in question is recognised to be one of insurance and loss bearing it is highly relevant to consider familiar insurance

patterns against which that principle must operate. This does not threaten to demolish the common law principles but calls attention to their purpose. What is needed for *Rylands* liability to be appropriate is a sufficient reason for placing the loss with the creator of a risk.

Not everyone will agree with the characterisation of the *Rylands* rule as a principle of insurance, but it is hard to argue with the claim that in cases of property damage caused by fire the insurance context should be borne in mind; indeed, in the case itself, Ward LJ commented that the 'moral of the story' was 'make sure you have insurance cover for losses occasioned by fire on your premises' (at [50]). For other commentary on *Gore v Stannard*, see Tofaris [2013] CLJ 11, and for an excellent historical discussion of liability for fire, see Ogus, 'Vagaries in Liability for the Escape of Fire' [1969] CLJ 104.

6. The Future of *Rylands v Fletcher*

In *Transco*, one question for the House of Lords was whether there remained any point in continuing to recognise whatever cause of action *Rylands* had established. As noted earlier, in *Burnie Port Authority v General Jones Pty Ltd* (1994) 179 CLR 520 a majority of the High Court of Australia incorporated the rule within the tort of negligence. However, all five members of the House of Lords in *Transco* rejected arguments that the rule should no longer have a separate existence, albeit with different degrees of enthusiasm. Thus for Lord Hoffmann the primary reason for retaining the rule was that, given its longevity and Lord Goff's apparent acceptance of it in *Cambridge Water*, it would go beyond the judicial function now to abolish it. Other of their Lordships were more positive. Lord Walker noted (at [99]) that, although its scope for operation had been restricted (and perhaps severely restricted) by the growth of statutory regulation of hazardous activities and the continuing development of the law of negligence, it would be premature to conclude that the principle was for practical purposes obsolete. And Lord Bingham said (at [6]) that 'there is in my opinion a category of case, however small it may be, in which it seems just to impose liability even in the absence of fault'. He considered that the *Cambridge Water* case, had there been foreseeability of damage, fell within that category.

The question remains, however, as to why strict liability should be imposed in the narrow band of cases in which the *Rylands* rule still applies. As Lord Hoffmann said in *Transco* (at [41]): 'It is hard to find any rational principle which explains the rule and its exceptions.' (See also Steele and Merkin, *op. cit.*, 307, observing that '[t]he technical limitations initially applying to the rule . . . have progressively taken priority over any underlying principle.') Academic commentators have divided over whether the rule in its current form should be retained. Nolan, 'The Distinctiveness of *Rylands v Fletcher*' (2005) 121 LQR 421 argues it should be abolished whilst Murphy, 'The Merits of *Rylands v Fletcher*' (2004) 24 OJLS 643 at 669 maintains that the rule serves as a 'useful residual mechanism for securing environmental protection by individuals affected by harmful escapes from polluting heavyweight industrialists'. The matter, however, may be somewhat moot; as several of their Lordships noted in *Transco*, there have been no reported cases successfully relying on the rule since the Second World War and, although there have been examples of the fire variant of *Rylands* (see the previous subsection), the decision of the Court of Appeal in *Gore v Stannard* has now emasculated the rule in the fire context. Furthermore, the restrictive approach taken in *Transco* means that successful actions are even less likely in the future. (But note that in

Color Quest Ltd v Total Downstream UK plc [2009] EWHC 540 (Comm), which concerned massive explosions at an oil storage depot, liability to some claimants under the rule in *Rylands v Fletcher* was admitted by the defendants; the issue was not considered on appeal: [2011] QB 86.) All told, therefore, it is difficult to quibble with Jefford J's recent dismissal of *Rylands v Fletcher* as 'a rule of limited utility' (*Lindsay v Berkeley Homes (Capital) plc* [2018] EWHC 2042 (TCC) at [38]), or with Bagshaw's claim ((2004) 120 LQR 388 at 392) that going forward the main effect of the imperfections of the rule 'will probably be to challenge law students and textbook writers'.

12 DEFAMATION

1. Introduction

No areas of the law excite more interest, or controversy, than the law of defamation, considered here, and privacy, considered in Chapter 13. The combination of celebrity litigants, gossipy tittle-tattle and frequently salacious allegations often results in lurid coverage in the popular press and wider media. Though many of the cases may appear frivolous, they raise issues of real importance relating to the appropriate balance to be struck between freedom of expression (guaranteed by Article 10 of the European Convention on Human Rights) and individual interests in reputation and private information (encompassed by the right to respect for private and family life under Article 8 of the Convention). Recent legislation (the Defamation Act 2013) has sought to improve this balance by limiting the 'chilling effect' that potential liabilities in defamation may have on freedom of expression. But the public debate has also been shaped by widespread concern about unethical and illegal practices by some sections of the press, which led to the setting up of a public inquiry under Lord Justice Leveson, whose recommendations are addressed at appropriate points of this chapter and the next.

As the legal principles are rather complicated, a preliminary overview may be useful. A defamatory statement is one which has caused or is likely to cause serious harm to another person's reputation. Defamation takes two forms: *libel*, referring to publications that are in permanent form or that are broadcast on stage or screen or by electronic means; and *slander*, referring to publications in transient form (e.g. casual conversations). As a general rule, slander, unlike libel, only gives rise to liability if it results in consequential loss ('special damage'). A defamatory statement is actionable without proof of its falsity, but the defendant has a complete defence if they succeed in demonstrating its *truth*; the publication of true statements, whether or not it is in the public interest, cannot generally amount to defamation. Other defences are also available to the defendant in a defamation action, for example that the statement was the expression of an *honest opinion* or that it was made to an interested party on a *matter of public interest* or in performance of a duty or protection of an interest (on which occasions, a defence of *privilege* may arise). As for remedies, a claimant who learns of the prospective publication of defamatory material may seek an *interim injunction* (sometimes known as a 'gagging order') to prevent the publisher from going ahead; the interim injunction, if awarded, will last until such time as there is a full trial of the case. If the publication has already taken place, the claimant will at trial inevitably seek, in addition to a *permanent injunction*, *damages* for injury to reputation and for any consequential economic loss; in some cases, *exemplary damages* may be awarded.

II. Libel and Slander

1. The Distinction between Libel and Slander

Lachaux v Independent Print Ltd [2020] AC 612

The facts of this case are summarised with the further extract in III.1(b).

Lord Sumption (with whom Lord Kerr, Lord Wilson, Lord Hodge and Lord Briggs agreed)

4. The law distinguishes between defamation actionable per se and defamation actionable only on proof of special damage. But although sharing a common label, these are very different torts with distinct historical origins. Libel, which is always actionable per se, originated in the disciplinary jurisdiction of the ecclesiastical courts and the criminal jurisdiction of the Court of Star Chamber. The gist of the tort is injury to the claimant's reputation and the associated injury to his or her feelings. Defamation actionable per se comprised, in addition to all libels, four categories of slander which were assimilated to libel on account of their particular propensity to injure the reputation of the claimant. These categories were (i) words imputing criminal offences, (ii) words imputing certain contagious or infectious diseases, and (iii) words tending to injure a person in his or her office, calling, trade or profession. The Slander of Women Act 1891 added (iv) words imputing unchastity to a woman. In these cases, the law presumes injury to the claimant's reputation and awards general damages in respect of it. These are not merely compensatory, but serve to vindicate the claimant's reputation . . . Special damage, ie pecuniary loss caused by the publication, may be recovered in addition, but must be proved.

5. By comparison, slander which is not actionable per se originated as a common law action on the case, and is governed by principles much closer to those of the law of tort generally. The law does not presume injury to reputation by mere oral statements and treats injury to feelings as insufficient to found a cause of action. Special damage, representing pecuniary loss rather than injury to reputation, must be proved . . . The interest which the law protects in cases where a defamatory statement is actionable per se differs from that which it protects in other cases. The gist of the tort where the statement is not actionable per se is not injury to reputation but, as Bowen LJ observed in *Ratcliffe v Evans* [1892] 2 QB 524, 532, wrongfully inflicted pecuniary loss: cf. *Jones v Jones* [1916] 2 AC 481, 490 (Viscount Haldane). Indeed, it is an open question, which has given rise to conflicting dicta, whether general damage is recoverable at all in such cases.

. . .

19. Section 14 [of the Defamation Act 2013] . . . abolishes two of the four categories of slander actionable per se, by repealing the Slander of Women Act 1891 which made the imputation of unchastity to a woman actionable per se, and by providing that an imputation that a person has a contagious or infectious disease is not to be actionable without proof of special damage.

COMMENTARY

As Lord Sumption explains, English law divides defamatory statements into two classes—libels and slanders—and requires, with certain exceptions, that 'special damage' be proved in relation to the latter. The distinction has historical origins, stretching back to the early days of the tort in the sixteenth and seventeenth centuries. (See W. S. Holdsworth, *History* of *English Law*, vol. VIII, 2nd edn (1937), p. 361f; Kaye, 'Libel and Slander—Two Torts or One?' (1975) 91 LQR 524; P. Mitchell, *The Making of the Modern Law of Defamation* (Oxford: Hart, 2005), ch. 1.) Since the seventeenth century, written statements have been actionable without proof of special damage, the reasoning being that the fact of writing demonstrated particular malice (*King v Lake* (1667) 1 Hardres 470). Although this may suggest a distinction between libel and slander based on the difference between written and oral statements, defamation need not take the form of words and it has become necessary to determine whether visual images and gestures constitute libel or slander. The development of modern methods of communication (e.g. in the areas of film, television, telephone and the internet) further complicated the matter. In some areas, statute has come to the common law's aid. Defamatory words, pictures, visual images and gestures on radio or television or any other 'programme service' are to be treated as libels by s. 166 of the Broadcasting Act 1990. In addition, 'the publication of [defamatory] words in the course of a performance of a play' is, by s. 4(1) of the Theatres Act 1968, also treated as libel.

Other ways of communicating meaning have also been considered by the courts. The test applied is one that looks to the permanence or transience of the 'statement'. In *Monson v Tussauds Ltd* [1894] 1 QB 671 at 692, Lopes LJ stated:

Libels are generally in writing or printing, but this is not necessary; the defamatory matter may be conveyed in some other permanent form. For instance, a statue, a caricature, an effigy, chalk-marks on a wall, signs or pictures may constitute a libel.

This definition of libel covered the facts of the case before the Court of Appeal, in which a waxworks model of the plaintiff was placed in an exhibition in the same room as a number of actual or alleged murderers and next to the Chamber of Horrors; the plaintiff had recently been tried for murder but the case against him had been 'not proven' (a special Scottish verdict implying neither guilt nor innocence).

A number of statutes also apply the test of whether the communication was 'in permanent form' (see, e.g., Theatres Act 1968, s. 4(1): 'the publication of words in the course of a performance of a play shall . . . be treated as publication in permanent form'; see also Broadcasting Act 1990, s. 166). No doubt the test will lead to distinctions of degree: while Lopes LJ considered that chalk-marks on a wall might constitute a libel, what about sky-writing by an aeroplane or a Snapchat photo message that disappears after ten seconds?

By way of exception to the general approach to spoken words, reading a libellous statement aloud amounts to libel, not slander. See *Forrester v Tyrrell* (1893) 9 TLR 257, where the Court of Appeal found that a person reading aloud from a defamatory letter was liable in libel; it was immaterial that they had not handed the letter around. It seems the rule will not apply when the libel is merely repeated rather than read out.

2. Slander: General Requirement of Special Damage

Libel is actionable *per se*, whereas slander generally requires proof of actual injury ('special damage'). For slander, the cause of action therefore accrues only when the actual injury is suffered, rather than (as for libel) on the publication itself. What amounts to actual injury? Mere loss of reputation is insufficient. So too is the loss of the society of friends. However, if the claimant has lost out on the hospitality of friends, that would amount to material loss (see *Moore v Meagher* (1807) 1 Taunt 39; *Davies v Solomon* (1871) LR 7 QB 112). More obvious examples are where the claimant loses their job or suffers diminished trading profits as a result of the slander.

Why liability for slander should be restricted in a way that libel is not has never been wholly convincingly explained. In the seventeenth century, Hale CB suggested that words written and published contained 'more malice'—perhaps we should say 'deliberation'—than words spoken (*King v Lake* (1667) Hardres 470 at 471; but cf. Kaye (1975) 91 LQR 524 at 531–2, and Mitchell, *op. cit.*, pp. 4–6), and another judge, speaking of the 'diffusive' effect of a libel in a public newspaper (*Harman v Delany* (1731) 2 Strange 898, Fitzgibbon 253), apparently had it in mind that libels were more easily communicated to the public at large. Subsequent judges and commentators have treated such reasoning with scepticism, but there is no doubt that the distinction is firmly entrenched in the law.

Thorley v Lord Kerry (1812) 4 Taunton 355, 128 ER 367

The facts are not material for present purposes.

Barnewall for the Plaintiff . . . denied that there was any solid ground, either in authority or principle, for the distinction supposed to have prevailed in some cases, that certain words are actionable when written, which are not actionable when spoken . . . The reason assigned, that the printing or writing indicates a greater degree of malice than mere speaking, is a bad one; for it is not the object of an action at law to punish moral turpitude, but to compensate a civil injury: the compensation must be proportionate to the measure of the damage sustained; but it cannot be said that publication of written slander is in all cases attended with a greater damage than spoken slander, for if a Defendant speaks words to an hundred persons assembled, he disseminates the slander and increases the damage an hundred-fold as much as if he only wrote it in a letter to one.

Mansfield CJ

[F]or myself, after having heard it extremely well argued, and especially, in this case, by Mr Barnewall, I cannot, upon principle, make any difference between words written and words spoken, as to the right which arises on them of bringing an action. For the Plaintiff . . . it has been truly urged, that in the old books and abridgments no distinction is taken between words written and spoken. But the distinction has been made between written and spoken slander as far back as Charles the Second's time, and the difference has been recognised by the Courts for at least a century back, . . . [T]he law gives a very ample field for retribution by action for words spoken in the cases of special damage, of words spoken of a man in his trade or profession, of a man in office, of a magistrate or officer; for all these an action lies. But for mere general abuse spoken, no action lies.

In the arguments both of the judges and counsel, in almost all the cases in which the question has been, whether what is contained in a writing is the subject of an action or not, it has been considered, whether the words, if spoken, would maintain an action. It is curious that they have also adverted to the question, whether it tends to produce a breach of the peace: but that is wholly irrelevant, and is no ground for recovering damages. So it has been argued that writing shews more deliberate malignity; but the same answer suffices, that the action is not maintainable upon the ground of the malignity, but for the damage sustained. So, it is argued that written scandal is more generally diffused than words spoken, and is therefore actionable; but an assertion made in a public place, as upon the Royal Exchange, concerning

> a merchant in London, may be much more extensively diffused than a few printed papers dispersed, or a private letter: it is true that a newspaper may be very generally read, but that is all casual. . . .
>
> The tendency of the libel to provoke a breach of the peace, or the degree of malignity which actuates the writer has nothing to do with the question. If the matter were for the first time to be decided at this day, I should have no hesitation in saying, that no action could be maintained for written scandal which could not be maintained for the words if they had been spoken.

COMMENTARY

Mansfield CJ found no principled justification for the distinction between libel and slander but felt compelled to accept it by weight of precedent. Judicial reconsideration now seems unlikely, and legislative reform is not currently on the agenda. However, the question whether libel should be differentiated from slander has twice been raised in official reports. The Porter Committee (*Report of the Committee on the Law of Defamation*, 1948, Cmd. 7536, paras 38, 40) favoured retention of the distinction:

> Slander is often trivial, not infrequently good-tempered and harmless, and in that form commonly enough a topic of conversation. If all slander were actionable *per se*, the scope for trivial but costly litigation might be enormously increased. So far as slander in ordinary conversation is concerned, it is not normally taken seriously by speaker or listener, and, in the great majority of cases, does little or no harm . . . [A] change in the law in England and Wales at the present date would, we think, be likely to encourage frivolous actions.

By contrast, the Faulks Committee (*Report of the Committee on Defamation*, 1975, Cmnd. 5909) considered this last fear to be 'unfounded', partly because words spoken by way of vulgar abuse or merely as a joke would remain non-actionable, while the expense of litigation was a powerful disincentive to would-be litigants who, even if successful, might find their irrecoverable costs burdensome (paras 87–9). In Faulks's view (para. 86):

> The distinction between libel and slander is entirely attributable to historical accident, but for which it would never have come into being. It represents one of the few spheres (if not the only one) in which the forms of action continue to rule us from the grave. It renders this part of the law unreasonable and unnecessarily complicated and refined, carrying a host of rules and exceptions, derived partly from precedent and partly from statute, which are illogical, difficult to learn, and in certain applications, it must be added, unjust.

The committee recommended that the distinction between libel and slander be abolished and that slander be assimilated to libel (para. 91). As will already be apparent, the recommendation was never implemented.

Slanders Actionable *Per Se*

Until 2013, there were four exceptions to the rule that slander requires actual injury to be proved, and hence four types of case in which slander could be said to be actionable *per se*. But the Defamation Act 2013 abolishes two of the previous categories, meaning that just two survive.

(i) Imputation of Criminal Conduct

Where the defendant imputes to the claimant criminal conduct punishable with imprisonment, the slander is actionable without proof of damage. The leading case is *Gray v Jones* [1939] 1 All ER 795 in which the defendant said to the plaintiff, 'you are a convicted person.

I will not have you here'. It was irrelevant in this case that the plaintiff, against whom the allegation was that he *had been* convicted, was not put in jeopardy of any further prosecution as (according to Atkinson J) the reason for the rule was that the misconduct alleged was so serious that other people were likely to shun the plaintiff and exclude him from their society. However, spoken words which convey a mere suspicion that the claimant has committed a crime punishable by imprisonment will not support an action without proof of special damage (*Simmons v Mitchell* (1880) 6 App Cas 156, PC).

(ii) Imputation of Unfitness in Business

By s. 2 of the Defamation Act 1952, 'words calculated to disparage the plaintiff in any office, profession, calling, trade or business' are actionable without proof of actual injury. At common law it appeared to be the case that this exception only applied where the words were directed against the plaintiff 'in the way of' their profession or calling, etc. Thus, accusations of sexual misconduct by a schoolmaster with the caretaker's wife were not actionable, at least where there was no allegation that this would lower his professional reputation (*Jones v Jones* [1916] 2 AC 481; *aliter*, presumably, if the misconduct was alleged to have been with a pupil). This requirement was abolished by the 1952 legislation, which makes it clear that such statements are actionable *per se* 'whether or not the words are spoken of the plaintiff in the way of his office, profession, calling, trade or business'.

(iii) Imputation of Certain Contagious Diseases (Abolished)

Words which impute that the claimant is suffering from a serious contagious or infectious disease were actionable *per se* at common law but this was changed by statute in 2013. In the leading case, the allegation '[h]e has got that damned pox from going to that woman on the Derby road' was held to warrant the award of £50 without proof of special damage, a sexually transmitted venereal disease falling within the exception (*Bloodworth v Gray* (1844) 7 Man & G 334). The rule entailed that orally accusing a person of having AIDS would also be actionable without proof of damage, but an oral accusation of insanity would not (not infectious), and neither would an oral accusation that the claimant had a cold (not serious). However, in a general review of the law of defamation, the Ministry of Justice found that the rule was 'outdated in the modern context' and recommended its abolition (*Draft Defamation Bill Consultation*, Cm. 8020, 2011, para. 6). This was effected by the Defamation Act 2013, which states that '[t]he publication of a statement that conveys the imputation that a person has a contagious or infectious disease does not give rise to a cause of action for slander unless the publication causes the person special damage' (s. 14(2)).

(iv) Imputation of Unchastity (Abolished)

The Slander of Women Act 1891 previously provided that 'words spoken or published ... which impute unchastity or adultery to any woman or girl shall not require special damage to render them actionable' (s. 1). A woman having sex out of marriage was once considered unchaste, and falsely calling a woman unchaste, according to Asquith LJ (*Kerr v Kennedy* [1942] 1 KB 409 at 411), 'is calculated both to bring her into social disfavour and, as the phrase runs, to damage her prospects in the marriage market and thereby her finances'. However, there was never any equivalent legislative provision or common law rule for men. Finding the law here not only 'outdated' but also 'potentially discriminatory', the Ministry of Justice recommended the repeal of the 1891 Act (*Draft Defamation Bill Consultation*, Cm. 8020, 2011, para. 6) and this was effected by s. 14(1) of the Defamation Act 2013.

For discussion of how ideas about female 'sexual purity' have been reflected in defamation case law see *Mitchell*, pp. 87–93.

III. Defamation: Elements of the Cause of Action

1. The Statement must be Defamatory

(a) Introduction

A defamatory statement is one which has a tendency to lower a person's standing amongst right-thinking people (the requirement of a tendency to defame) and which has caused or is likely to cause serious harm to that person's reputation (the serious harm requirement). The first of these requirements was established by common law; the second by statute (Defamation Act 2013, s. 1). The relationship between the two requirements was recently addressed by the Supreme Court in *Lachaux v Independent Print Ltd* [2020] AC 612.

Lachaux v Independent Print Ltd [2020] AC 612

Lord Sumption (with whom Lord Kerr, Lord Wilson, Lord Hodge and Lord Briggs agreed)

Introduction

1. The tort of defamation is an ancient construct of the common law. It has accumulated, over the centuries, a number of formal rules with no analogue in other branches of the law of tort. Most of them originated well before freedom of expression acquired the prominent place in our jurisprudence that it enjoys today. Its coherence has not been improved by attempts at statutory reform. Statutes to amend the law of defamation were enacted in 1888, 1952, 1996 and 2013, each of which sought to modify existing common law rules piecemeal, without always attending to the impact of the changes on the rest of the law. The Defamation Act 2013 is the latest chapter in this history. Broadly speaking, it seeks to modify some of the common law rules which were seen unduly to favour the protection of reputation at the expense of freedom of expression . . . One of the principal provisions of the new Act was section 1, which provided that a statement was not to be regarded as defamatory unless it had caused or was likely to cause 'serious harm' to the claimant's reputation. . . .

The common law background . . .

6. For present purposes a working definition of what makes a statement defamatory, derived from the speech of Lord Atkin in *Sim v Stretch* [1936] 2 All ER 1237, 1240, is that 'the words tend to lower the plaintiff in the estimation of right-thinking members of society generally.' Like other formulations in the authorities, this turns on the supposed impact of the statement on those to whom it is communicated. But that impact falls to be ascertained in accordance with a number of more or less artificial rules. First, the meaning is not that which other people may actually have attached to it, but that which is derived from an objective assessment of the defamatory meaning that the notional ordinary reasonable reader would attach to it. Secondly, in an action for defamation actionable per se, damage to the claimant's reputation is presumed rather than proved. It depends on the inherently injurious character (or 'tendency', in the time-honoured phrase) of a statement bearing that meaning. Thirdly, the presumption is one of law, and irrebuttable.

7. In two important cases decided in the decade before the Defamation Act 2013, the courts added a further requirement, namely that the damage to reputation in a case actionable per se must pass a minimum threshold of seriousness. . . .

[Lord Sumption referred to *Jameel (Yousef) v Dow Jones & Co Inc* [2005] QB 946 and *Thornton v Telegraph Media Group Ltd* [2011] 1 WLR 1985, then turned to the question of the correct interpretation of s. 1(1) of the Act, establishing the statutory requirement of serious harm:]

11. . . . The case on behalf of Mr Lachaux [the claimant] is that the Act leaves unaffected the common law presumption of general damage and the associated rule that the cause of action is made out if the statement complained of is inherently injurious or, as Lord Phillips put it in *Jameel* and Tugendhat J in *Thornton*, it has a 'tendency' to injure the claimant's reputation. The effect of the provision on this view of the matter is simply that the inherent tendency of the words must be to cause not just some damage to reputation but serious harm to it. The defendant publishers dispute this. Their case is that the provision introduces an additional condition to be satisfied before the statement can be regarded as defamatory, on top of the requirement that the words must be inherently injurious. It must also be shown to produce serious harm in fact. They submit that unless it was self-evident that such a statement must produce serious harm to reputation, this would have to be established by extraneous evidence. Warby J, after a careful analysis of the Act and the antecedent common law, substantially accepted the defendant publishers' case on the law. But he found, on the facts, that the relevant newspaper articles did cause serious harm to Mr Lachaux. The Court of Appeal (McFarlane, Davis and Sharp LJJ) [2018] QB 594, preferred Mr Lachaux's construction of section 1, but they upheld the judge's finding of serious harm.

12. Although the Act must be construed as a whole, the issue must turn primarily on the language of section 1. This shows, very clearly to my mind, that it not only raises the threshold of seriousness . . . but requires its application to be determined by reference to the actual facts about its impact and not just to the meaning of the words.

COMMENTARY

An early common law test as to whether or not a statement has a tendency to defame was to ask whether the words complained of were 'calculated to injure the reputation of another by exposing him to hatred, contempt, or ridicule' (*Parmiter v Coupland* (1840) 6 M & W 105 at 108, per Parke B). But Lord Atkin in *Sim v Stretch* (1936) 52 TLR 669 at 671 suggested a broader approach:

[T]he conventional phrase exposing the plaintiff to 'hatred, ridicule or contempt' is probably too narrow . . . I do not intend to ask your Lordships to lay down a formal definition, but after collating the opinions of many authorities I propose in the present case the test: would the words tend to lower the plaintiff in the estimation of right-thinking members of society generally?

This 'working definition' (per Lord Sumption in *Lachaux*) is not to be regarded as exhaustive. In a number of cases, a statement which adversely affects a person's standing in the community may be defamatory even though it does not lower the general estimation of that person's worth (e.g. imputations of disease or insolvency). A number of verbal formulations have been suggested, for example that the words tend to make right-thinking people shun or avoid the claimant (*Villers v Monsley* (1769) 2 Wils 403; 95 ER 886) or tend to exclude them from society.

The common law test looks only to the *tendency* of the defendant's words, not how people actually interpreted or reacted to them. However, the words must always be considered in the precise circumstances and context of their publication, and what may be defamatory of one person is not necessarily defamatory of another (cf. *Palmer v Boyer* (1594) Cro Eliz 342: barrister alleged to know 'as much law as a jackanapes'; surely not defamatory of a lay person—but what of a first-year law student?). The additional statutory requirement of serious harm, by contrast, is not concerned with the tendency of the words but requires reference to the actual facts about their impact, as Lord Sumption in *Lachaux* makes clear (see further in (b)).

Whether particular words are defamatory is a question of fact, not law; hence previous decisions are not binding authority and cannot act as anything more than a guide to the case at hand, all the more so given possible variations in the circumstances and context of publication. As the question of defamatory meaning is one of fact, it was traditionally for the jury to decide, although only after the court had addressed the threshold question of whether the words were *capable* of bearing a defamatory meaning, which is a question of law. Where there is no jury, as is now usually the case (see Defamation Act 2013, s. 11, amending Senior Courts Act 1981, s. 69), the judge has only to determine the *actual* meaning of the statement and whether it was in fact defamatory.

A statement need not be verbal. A picture, as the saying goes, is worth a thousand words. A visual image acquires its meaning from its context, and in particular from its juxtaposition with other images or with verbal expressions. In *Monson v Tussauds Ltd* [1894] 1 QB 671 it was held that a waxworks model of the plaintiff carried a defamatory meaning arising out of its placement in the defendants' exhibition in the same room as a number of actual or alleged murderers and next to the Chamber of Horrors. The plaintiff had been tried for murder but the case against him had been 'not proven'. This was held to be an actionable libel.

Jokes and Insults

A defamatory allegation must strike at the claimant's reputation; insults and jokes may merely bruise the ego rather than lower a person's estimation in the eyes of others. (Insults of a racial or sexual nature, or directed at some other 'protected characteristic', may give rise to a claim under the Equality Act 2010 in prescribed circumstances.) It has been observed that 'exhibitions of bad manners or discourtesy' ought not to be 'placed on the same level as attacks on character'; they are not actionable wrongs (*Sim v Stretch* (1936) 52 TLR 669 at 672, per Lord Atkin). In the past, it was nevertheless possible to say that '[t]he writing and publishing of anything which renders a man ridiculous is actionable' (*Villers v Monsley* (1769) 1 Bos & P 331, per Lord Wilmot CJ), and that 'no one can cast about firebrands and death, and then escape from being responsible by saying he was in sport' (*Capital and Counties Bank v Henty* (1882) 7 App Cas 741 at 772, per Lord Blackburn).

In *Berkoff v Burchill* [1996] 4 All ER 1008, the question was whether the journalist Julie Burchill had defamed the actor and film-director Stephen Berkoff by describing him as hideously ugly. A majority of the Court of Appeal found that the description was *capable* of being defamatory (i.e. might properly be found defamatory by a jury) inasmuch as it conveyed its meaning by way of ridicule. Following the implementation of the Defamation Act 2013, it will generally be for the judge—not the jury—to determine both whether the words *actually* have a tendency to defame and whether they have caused or are likely to cause serious harm. If the *Berkoff* case were to be replayed today, it is quite possible that it would fail in respect of both requirements.

It is in any case clear that a joke will not lower a person's reputation if it is apparent that it was not meant to be treated seriously (e.g. as indicating a truly held view). In *Charleston v News Group Newspapers Ltd* [1995] 2 AC 65, the House of Lords considered a mock exposé on the front page of the *News of the World* in which the plaintiffs—Harold and Madge in the popular soap opera *Neighbours*—were pictured naked but for bondage gear and apparently engaged in sexual intercourse; the headline read 'Strewth! What's Harold up to with our Madge? Porn Shocker for Neighbours Stars'. However, the captions on the pictures and the text of the article made it clear that the images were computer-generated: the actors were 'the unwitting stars of a sordid computer game' in which their faces were superimposed without their knowledge or consent on the bodies of porn models. 'The remainder of the article', Lord Bridge noted (at 69), 'castigate[d] the makers of the "sordid computer game" in a tone of self-righteous indignation which contrast[ed] oddly with the prominence given to the main photograph'. His Lordship accepted that the publication must have been 'deeply offensive and insulting' to the plaintiffs, but held that it was not defamatory. The publication had to be read as a whole, and the headline and pictures considered in isolation could not give rise to liability; it was necessary always to consider whether the text of the article was sufficient to 'neutralise' the libellous implication of the headline, even though many readers might take note only of the latter.

A Tendency to Defame: Other Examples

Numerous other examples may be given of statements having a tendency to defame. Imputations of criminal conduct will generally satisfy the requirement, albeit that to say that someone has committed a parking offence or a minor speeding violation is unlikely to be regarded as doing so. An allegation that the claimant has committed a civil wrong may also have a tendency to defame, at least if the civil liability entails fault on the part of the wrongdoer (*Groom v Crocker* [1939] 1 KB 194: negligence relating to road traffic accident); likewise accusations of morally disreputable behaviour (*Austin v Culpepper* (1684) 2 Show 313: 'dishonesty'; *MacLaren v Robertson* (1859) 21 D 183: 'liar'). Matters pertaining to sexual behaviour may be more problematic, especially as social attitudes here have changed very significantly with the passage of time. At the beginning of the twentieth century it was held that an allegation that a woman had had a child out of wedlock could be defamatory (*Chattell v Daily Mail* (1901) 18 TLR 165), but it is unthinkable that to say the same now would be an actionable defamation. Imputations of homosexuality have on several occasions been found to be defamatory (see *Gatley*, para. 2.29), and, even if opinion about homosexuality has changed considerably over the years, it was accepted as recently as *Cruise v Express Newspapers plc* [1999] QB 931 that calling a man married to a woman 'gay' was capable of being defamatory. (Should saying the same of a single man, or woman, be treated differently?)

Turning to matters financial, to say that someone is insolvent may well have a tendency to defame, because it will stop others trading with him, but merely to say that someone owes money is not defamatory, as that 'is true of every house-holder . . . on most days of the month' (*Wolfenden v Giles* (1892) 2 Br Col R 284 at 284, per Begbie CJ). Remarks made about a person's race or national origins give rise to issues of particular sensitivity. At various times, it has been held defamatory to describe an individual as German or as an 'international Jew financier', but special factors probably account for the result of these cases (see respectively *Slazenger Ltd v Gibbs* (1916) 33 TLR 35: 'German'—during World War I; *Camrose v Action Press, The Times*, 14–16 October 1937: 'international Jew financier'—*Gatley*, para. 2.25n suggests that the case turned on an imputation of disloyalty). Even in the middle of the twentieth century, courts in the American South held it defamatory to state that a white person was black (see, e.g., *Natchez Times v Dunigan*, 72 So 2d 681 (1954)), but this was probably never the law in England (see *Hoare v Silverlock* (1848) 12 QB 630 at 632). In any case, here as elsewhere standards of (supposed) right-thinking opinion have been subject to considerable changes over the course of time; indeed, it has more recently been held in the United States that it was defamatory of a corporation to state, at the time of apartheid, that it had had dealings with the government of South Africa (*Southern Air Transport Inc v American Broadcasting Co*, 877 F 2d 1010 (US App DC, 1989)).

'Shun or avoid'

A separate category of statements that can be defamatory is where the words cause the claimant to be shunned or avoided even though they impute something to them that is not their fault—for example, an illness (*Warnes v Forge* [2020] 4 WLR 91 at [71], per Elisabeth Laing J). In the past, an allegation that someone has been raped or otherwise assaulted has been treated as falling into this category. In *Youssopoff v Metro-Goldwyn-Mayer Pictures Ltd* (1934) 50 TLR 581 the Court of Appeal so held in respect of an allegation that the plaintiff had been seduced or raped by Rasputin, 'the Mad Monk'. The court felt that the reality of the situation was that the words tended 'to make the plaintiff be shunned and avoided and that without any moral discredit on her part' (at 587, per Slesser LJ). The 'shun and avoid' category was again considered in *Warnes v Forge*, where the judge rejected the proposition that an allegation of mental illness could never be defamatory, and proceeded on the basis that the context in which such a statement is made might be determinative. The words in question alleged that the claimant was mentally ill and should be ignored for that reason, and thus were precisely designed to persuade a reasonable reader to shun and avoid him. In that context, they were indeed defamatory.

(b) The Serious Harm Requirement

Defamation Act 2013

1 Serious harm

(1) A statement is not defamatory unless its publication has caused or is likely to cause serious harm to the reputation of the claimant.

(2) For the purposes of this section, harm to the reputation of a body that trades for profit is not 'serious harm' unless it has caused or is likely to cause the body serious financial loss.

Lachaux v Independent Print Ltd [2020] AC 612

The claimant, Lachaux, was a French aerospace engineer who at the relevant time lived with his British wife Afsana and their son Louis in the United Arab Emirates (UAE). The marriage broke down and acrimonious divorce and custody proceedings ensued in the UAE courts, resulting in Lachaux taking custody of the boy. A number of British newspapers published articles making allegations about Lachaux's conduct towards Afsana and he commenced libel actions in the English High Court against the defendant newspaper publishers. At a hearing to determine the meaning of the words of which Lachaux complained, Eady J ruled that the articles bore the meanings (inter alia) that Lachaux had been violent and abusive towards his wife during their marriage, made use of the UAE courts to deprive her of custody and contact with her son, had callously and without justification taken Louis out of her possession and then falsely accused her of abducting him. At trial, the newspapers maintained that the statements in the articles were not defamatory because they did not meet the threshold of seriousness in s. 1(1) of the Defamation Act 2013.

Lord Sumption (with whom Lord Kerr, Lord Wilson, Lord Hodge and Lord Briggs agreed)

12. Although the Act must be construed as a whole, the issue must turn primarily on the language of section 1. This shows, very clearly to my mind, that it not only raises the threshold of seriousness above that envisaged in *Jameel (Yousef)* and *Thornton*, but requires its application to be determined by reference to the actual facts about its impact and not just to the meaning of the words.

13. In the first place, the relevant background to section 1 is the common law position, as I have summarised it. Parliament is taken to have known what the law was prior to the enactment. It must therefore be taken to have known about the decisions in *Jameel (Yousef)* and *Thornton* and the basic principles on which general damages were awarded for defamation actionable per se. There is a presumption that a statute does not alter the common law unless it so provides, either expressly or by necessary implication. But this is not an authority to give an enactment a strained interpretation. It means only that the common law should not be taken to have been altered casually, or as a side-effect of provisions directed to something else. The Defamation Act 2013 unquestionably does amend the common law to some degree. Its preamble proclaims the fact ('an act to amend the law of defamation'). It is not disputed that there is a common law presumption of damage to reputation, but no presumption that it is 'serious'. So the least that section 1 achieved was to introduce a new threshold of serious harm which did not previously exist . . .

14. Secondly, section 1 necessarily means that a statement which would previously have been regarded as defamatory, because of its inherent tendency to cause some harm to reputation, is not to be so regarded unless it 'has caused or is likely to cause' harm which is 'serious'. The reference to a situation where the statement 'has caused' serious harm is to the consequences of the publication, and not the publication itself. It points to some historic harm, which is shown to have actually occurred. This is a proposition of fact which can be established only by reference to the impact which the statement is shown actually to have had. It depends on a combination of the inherent tendency of the words and their actual impact on those to whom they were communicated. The same must be true of the reference to harm which is 'likely' to be caused. In this context, the phrase naturally refers to probable future harm. Ms Page QC, who argued Mr Lachaux's case with conspicuous skill and learning, challenged this. She submitted that 'likely to cause' was a synonym for the inherent tendency which gives rise to the presumption of damage at common law. It meant, she said, harm which was *liable* to be caused given the tendency of the words. That argument was accepted in the Court of Appeal . . . [T]hese suggestions seem to me to be rather artificial in a context which indicates that both past and future harm are being treated on the same footing, as functional equivalents. If past harm may be established as a fact, the legislator must have assumed that 'likely' harm could be also . . .

15. Thirdly it is necessary to read section 1(1) with section 1(2). Section 1(2) is concerned with the way in which section 1(1) is to be applied to statements said to be defamatory of a body trading for profit. It refers to the same concept of 'serious harm' as section 1(1), but provides that in the case of such a body it must have caused or be likely to cause 'serious financial loss'. The financial loss envisaged here is not the same as special damage, in the sense in which that term is used in the law of defamation. Section 1 is concerned with harm

to reputation, whereas (as I have pointed out) special damage represents pecuniary loss to interests other than reputation. What is clear, however, is that section 1(2) must refer not to the harm done to the claimant's reputation, but to the loss which that harm has caused or is likely to cause. The financial loss is the measure of the harm and must exceed the threshold of seriousness. As applied to harm which the defamatory statement 'has caused', this necessarily calls for an investigation of the actual impact of the statement. A given statement said to be defamatory may cause greater or lesser financial loss to the claimant, depending on his or her particular circumstances and the reaction of those to whom it is published. Whether that financial loss has occurred and whether it is 'serious' are questions which cannot be answered by reference only to the inherent tendency of the words. The draftsman must have intended that the question what harm it was 'likely to cause' should be decided on the same basis.

16. Finally, if serious harm can be demonstrated only by reference to the inherent tendency of the words, it is difficult to see that any substantial change to the law of defamation has been achieved by what was evidently intended as a significant amendment. The main reason why harm which was less than 'serious' had given rise to liability before the Act was that damage to reputation was presumed from the words alone and might therefore be very different from any damage which could be established in fact. If, as Ms Page submits, the presumption still works in that way, then this anomaly has been carried through into the Act. Suppose that the words amount to a grave allegation against the claimant, but they are published to a small number of people, or to people none of whom believe it, or possibly to people among whom the claimant had no reputation to be harmed. The law's traditional answer is that these matters may mitigate damages but do not affect the defamatory character of the words. Yet it is plain that section 1 was intended to make them part of the test of the defamatory character of the statement.

17. I agree, as the judge did, that this analysis is inconsistent with the previous common law governing statements actionable per se. But it is inconsistent with it only to this extent: that the defamatory character of the statement no longer depends only on the meaning of the words and their inherent tendency to damage the claimant's reputation. To that extent Parliament intended to change the common law. But I do not accept that the result is a revolution in the law of defamation, any more than the lower thresholds of seriousness introduced by the decisions in *Jameel* and *Thornton* effected such a revolution . . .

Application to this case

21. On the footing that (as I would hold) Mr Lachaux must demonstrate as a fact that the harm caused by the publications complained of was serious, Warby J held that it was. He heard evidence from Mr Lachaux himself and three other witnesses of fact, and received written evidence from his solicitor. He also received agreed figures, some of them estimates, of the print runs and estimated readership of the publications complained of and the user numbers for online publications. He based his finding of serious harm on (i) the scale of the publications; (ii) the fact that the statements complained of had come to the attention of at least one identifiable person in the United Kingdom who knew Mr Lachaux and (iii) that they were likely to have come to the attention of others who either knew him or would come to know him in future; and (iv) the gravity of the statements themselves, according to the meaning attributed to them by Sir David Eady. Mr Lachaux would have been entitled to produce evidence from those who had read the statements about its impact on them. But I do not accept, any more than the judge did, that his case must necessarily fail for want of such evidence. The judge's finding was based on a combination of the meaning of the words, the situation of Mr Lachaux, the circumstances of publication and the inherent probabilities. There is no reason why inferences of fact as to the seriousness of the harm done to Mr Lachaux's reputation should not

be drawn from considerations of this kind. Warby J's task was to evaluate the material before him, and arrive at a conclusion on an issue on which precision will rarely be possible. A concurrent assessment of the facts was made by the Court of Appeal. Findings of this kind would only rarely be disturbed by this court, in the absence of some error of principle potentially critical to the outcome. . . .

Disposal

26. For these reasons, while I would state the law differently from the Court of Appeal, I would dismiss these appeals on the facts.

Appeal dismissed.

COMMENTARY

Following the Supreme Court's resolution of the issue of 'serious harm' in the claimant's favour, he was successful in claiming damages totalling £160,000 from the newspaper publisher defendants (*Lachaux v Independent Print Ltd* [2021] EWHC 1797 (QB)).

As Lord Sumption explains in the extract, the statutory reform came on the back of two judicial developments of the common law. In *Jameel v Dow Jones & Co* [2005] QB 946, the Court of Appeal had introduced a procedural threshold of seriousness to be applied to the damage to the claimant's reputation in defamation claims; a claim not meeting that threshold could be struck out as an abuse of process. And in *Thornton v Telegraph Media Group* [2011] 1 WLR 1985 Tugendhat J held that, in addition to this procedural threshold, there was also a substantive threshold of seriousness that had to be met before a statement could satisfy the legal definition of 'defamatory'. These judicial developments of the law paved the way for the enactment in statutory form of the serious harm requirement, which was presented as a desirable reform removing the scope for trivial and unfounded actions succeeding (*Draft Defamation Bill Consultation*, para. 4). As Lord Sumption makes clear in the extract, the 2013 Act both raises the threshold of seriousness above that envisaged in *Jameel* and *Thornton*, and also requires its application to be determined by reference to the actual facts about its impact and not just to the meaning of the words (para. 12).

In *Sobrinho v Impresa Publishing SA* [2016] EWHC 66 (QB), [2016] EMLR 12, Dingemans J identified 'a number of uncontroversial propositions that can be stated about s. 1 of the 2013 Act', which remain pertinent even after *Lachaux*:

46. . . . [F]irst, a claimant must now establish in addition to the requirements of the common law relating to defamatory statements, that the statement complained of has in fact caused or is likely to cause serious harm to his reputation. 'Serious' is an ordinary word in common usage. Section 1 requires the claimant to prove as a fact, on the balance of probabilities, that the statement complained of has caused or will probably cause serious harm to the claimant's reputation. It should be noted that unless serious harm to reputation can be established an injury to feelings alone, however grave, will not be sufficient.

47. Secondly it is open to the claimant to call evidence in support of his case on serious harm and it is open to the defendant to call evidence to demonstrate that no serious harm has occurred or is likely to do so. However a Court determining the issue of serious harm is, as in all cases, entitled to draw inferences based on the admitted evidence. Mass media publications of very serious defamatory allegations are likely to render the need for evidence of serious harm unnecessary. This does not mean that the issue of serious harm is a 'numbers game'. Reported cases have

shown that very serious harm to a reputation can be caused by the publication of a defamatory statement to one person.

48. Thirdly there are obvious difficulties in getting witnesses to say that they read the words and thought badly of the claimant . . . This is because the claimant will have an understandable desire not to spread the contents of the article complained of by asking persons if they have read it and what they think of the claimant, and because persons who think badly of the claimant are not likely to co-operate in providing evidence.

49. Fourthly, where there are publications about the same subject matter which are not the subject of complaint (because of limitation issues or because of jurisdictional issues) there can be difficult points of causation which arise . . .

50. Fifthly, as Bingham LJ stated in *Slipper v BBC* [1991] 1 QB 283 at 300, the law would part company with the realities of life if it held that the damage caused by publication of a libel began and ended with publication to the original publishee. Defamatory statements are objectionable not least because of their propensity 'to percolate through underground channels and contaminate hidden springs' through what has sometimes been called 'the grapevine effect'. However it must also be noted that Bingham LJ continued and said 'Usually, in fairness to a defendant, such effects must be discounted or ignored for lack of proof' before going on to deal with further publications which had been proved to be natural, provable and perhaps even intentional results of the publication sued upon.

What may be termed the 'time dimension' of the s. 1 requirement should also be noted. In *Cooke v Mirror Group Newspapers* [2015] 1 WLR 895, Bean J explained:

31. The words 'has caused' involve looking backwards in time, the words 'or is likely to cause' involve looking forwards. The Act does not make clear the moment which marks the dividing line between past and future. It cannot be the moment of publication, since at that moment no harm 'has been caused'. The two logical possibilities seem to be the date of issue of the claim and the date of the trial (or of the trial of the preliminary issue of serious harm). Either of these has the curious effect that whether a statement is held to have been defamatory on the day it was published might depend respectively on the timing of the issue of proceedings, or the timing of the trial.

32. I prefer Mr Tomlinson's submission [for the claimants] that the date from which one looks backwards (to see whether substantial harm has been caused) or forwards (to see whether substantial harm is likely to be caused) is the date on which the claim is issued. This would also correspond, in so far as past harm is concerned, with the common law rule that, subject to certain exceptions, slander is not actionable unless by the date on which the writ was issued, special damage had already occurred.

The effect of shifting the focus from the common law test of whether the words, as published, had a 'tendency to defame', to the question of whether serious harm has or is likely to be caused, is that events *after* the publication become relevant to determining actionability. But how do they become relevant? One view is that the cause of action lies inchoate until serious harm is caused or its future occurrence becomes probable, while conversely a publication may change from defamatory to non-defamatory by reason of a prompt and full retraction and apology (*Lachaux v Independent Print Ltd* [2016] QB 402 at [66] and [68], per Warby J). The other view, expressed by Lord Sumption in *Lachaux* at [18] is that the cause of action accrues on publication and later events are only of evidential significance:

The impact of the publication on the claimant's reputation will in practice occur at that moment in almost all cases, and the cause of action is then complete. If for some reason it does not occur at that moment, the subsequent events will be evidence of the likelihood of its occurring. In either case, subsequent events may serve to demonstrate the seriousness of the statement's impact including, in the case of a body trading for profit, its financial implications. It does not follow that those events must have occurred before the claimant's cause of action can be said to have accrued. Their relevance is purely evidential.

The point was not fully argued in the Supreme Court so Lord Sumption's analysis, though obviously deserving of considerable respect, cannot be regarded as resolving the issue definitively.

Whichever view prevails, the outcome is still surprising, because the partly forwards-looking formulation in terms of the likelihood of future occurrence means that 'a claimant might be able to sue successfully, hence recover compensatory damages, for a loss that has not yet occurred—and of course might never occur at all' (Descheemaeker, 'Three Errors in the Defamation Act 2013' (2015) 6 JETL 24 at 32).

As regards the 'serious harm' requirement generally, see Sewell, 'More serious harm than good? An empirical observation and analysis of the effects of the serious harm requirement in section 1(1) of the Defamation Act 2013' (2020) 12 J Media L 47. As regards s. 1(2) see further in VI.

(c) The Standard of Right-Thinking Opinion

'To write or say of a man something that will disparage him in the eyes of a particular section of the community but will not affect his reputation in the eyes of the average right-thinking man is not actionable within the law of defamation' (*Tolley v Fry* [1930] 1 KB 467 at 479, per Greer LJ). In a defamation action, the court must inquire into the beliefs of 'right-thinking' members of society: the question asked is whether the right-thinking person would construe the words in their ordinary meaning as lowering the reputation of the claimant. The courts accordingly inquire as to what people *should* think, not as to what they actually think. No doubt this varies over the course of time (as previously noted), but there are certain constants, for example in relation to allegations that the claimant has given information about the commission of a crime to the police.

Byrne v Deane [1937] 1 KB 818

Automatic gambling machines ('diddler machines'), which were kept illegally on the premises of a golf club of which the defendants were proprietors, were removed by the police after someone had informed them of the machines' presence. A verse appeared soon afterwards on some sheets of paper which were put up on the walls of the club. In a punning reference to the plaintiff, the last two lines of the verse read: 'But he who gave the game away, may he byrnn in hell and rue the day'. The issue for the Court of Appeal was whether the trial judge had been correct to leave to the jury the question whether the words were defamatory, in the sense that they meant that the plaintiff was 'guilty of underhand disloyalty' to his fellow members and should be ostracised by them. The defendants admitted that they had seen the notice on the wall, but denied having written it or put it there.

Slesser LJ

Now, in my view, to say or to allege of a man—and for this purpose . . . it does not matter whether the allegation is true or is not true—that he has reported certain acts, wrongful in law, to the police, cannot possibly be said to be defamatory of him in the minds of the general public.

We have to consider in this connection the *arbitrium boni*, the view which would be taken by the ordinary good and worthy subject of the King, and I have assigned to myself no other criterion than what a good and worthy subject of the King would think of some person of whom it had been said that he had put the law into motion against wrongdoers, in considering that such a good and worthy subject would not consider such an allegation in itself to be defamatory. . . .

[I]t has been argued here that these words in the present case cannot really be said to be defamatory because in substance the crime which it is suggested in the libel that this gentleman is endeavouring to prevent is really of so trivial a character, and one which is so popular with the mass of the people, that to prevent an innocent indulgence in the use of these machines, which have been described as 'diddlers' and also as 'fruit' machines, is not preventing a crime, the whole thing is so trivial, and that the real substance of the case is the dislike and animosity which must be created in the minds of his fellow members of the club against the plaintiff. I find it quite impossible, speaking for myself, to draw a distinction between one crime and another in this particular. In no case as it seems to me can it be said that merely to say of a man that he has given information which will result in the ending of a criminal act is in itself defamatory where he is doing no more than reporting to the police that which if known by the police might well end in the discovery of an illegal act and its suppression.

Greene LJ

If the allegation that he reported the matter to the police is not defamatory, in my judgment the allegation that in reporting the matter to the police he was guilty of disloyalty cannot be defamatory.

If that be right, the matter resolves itself into this: Are words capable of a defamatory meaning which say of the plaintiff that he reported to the police that on the club premises of which he was a member a criminal offence was being habitually committed? Now, it is said that the ordinary sense of society would say of a man who had done that in the case of this particular criminal offence that he had behaved in a disloyal and underhand fashion. It is said that this particular offence is one which can be looked at with an indulgent eye, and that there is something dishonourable in setting in motion the constitutional machinery provided in this country for the suppression of crime. I myself find it embarrassing to take into consideration questions of the way in which members of clubs might regard such an action. It seems to me that no distinction can be drawn between various categories of crime. I suggested in the course of the argument the case where members of a club were habitually engaged in having cock-fights conducted on the club premises, and I asked the question whether to say of a man that he had reported that to the police would be defamatory, and the answer that I got was not to my mind a satisfactory one. But to take the matter further: supposing in the club the members were engaged in habitually defrauding guests at cards, could it be said to be defamatory if a member of the club reported that to the police? and so on. It seems to me that if the argument is to be accepted it would involve the Court in this position: that it would have to differentiate between different kinds of crime and put in one category crimes which are of so bad a character as to call for universal reprobation even among the more easy-minded, and in another category crimes which many people think are stupid and ought never to have been made crimes at all.

It seems to me that, whatever may be the view of individuals on matters of that kind, this Court cannot draw a distinction of that description. In point of fact it may very well be that the

> Legislature in its wisdom has made into a crime something which the public conscience of many persons in this country does not consider involves any sort of moral reprobation; but this Court it seems to me cannot be concerned with considerations of that kind, and in my judgment to say of a man that he has put in motion the proper machinery for suppressing crime is a thing which cannot on the face of it be defamatory.
>
> **Greer LJ** dissented.
>
> *Appeal allowed.*

COMMENTARY

In *Mawe v Pigott* (1869) Ir R 4 CL 54 at 62, Lawson J stated: 'The very circumstances which will make a person be regarded with disfavour by the criminal classes will raise his character in the estimation of right-thinking men. We can only regard the estimation in which a man is held by society generally.' A contrasting (non-criminal) case is *Myroft v Sleight* (1921) 90 LJKB 883: McCardie J accepted that 'it would not be defamatory merely to say of an ordinary trade unionist ... that he had openly continued at work in spite of the orders of his union', but on the facts of the case it was possible to find a separate imputation of disloyalty or hypocrisy which was in fact defamatory. (The plaintiff, who had voted in favour of strike action, was alleged to have asked his employer to let him continue working.) For another example of an implied imputation of hypocrisy see *Shah v Akram* (1981) 79 LS Gaz 814 (allegation that a Muslim had insulted the Prophet).

Is the true rule of law from such cases that the courts cannot have regard to the opinion of a limited class of people like the members of a club or a union, or that it can only have regard to the opinions of 'right-thinking people'? Or is it a mixture of both? Compare the American approach: do the words hurt the plaintiff's standing with 'a considerable and respectable class in her community' (*Peck v Tribune Clo*, 214 US 185 (1909); supported by *Gatley*, para. 2.21 on the basis that 'the English test is arguably based upon the assumption of a consensus of moral opinion in society which, if it ever existed, has now passed away').

Reputation in an Illegal Calling or Activity

'The law does not regard a reputation illegally attained as proper to be protected' (*Wilkinson v Sporting Life* (1933) 49 CLR 365 at 379, per Evatt J). The cited case concerned an allegation that the plaintiff intended to cheat the public in the course of his undeniably illegal betting business. Despite the general rule just quoted, this allegation was found to be defamatory because the imputation of dishonesty tended to lower the plaintiff's estimation *as a person*, not merely as the practitioner of illegal activities.

(d) Meaning and the Question of Innuendo

In deciding whether or not the words used are in fact defamatory the jury is asked first to consider the meaning of the words in their 'natural and ordinary' sense. Though the jury may be invited to consider a number of possible meanings, it is assumed that only one 'natural and ordinary' meaning is 'correct' (*Slim v Daily Telegraph* [1968] 2 QB 157 at 171ff, per Diplock LJ, admitting that the assumption is 'artificial'). In some cases, however, the claimant may allege an additional or alternative 'innuendo' meaning. A *false or popular innuendo* is where the words bear a meaning that is not their literal meaning but instead constitutes an inference or implication from the words themselves. The question is whether a reasonable reader might 'read between the lines' (see *Lewis v Daily Telegraph* [1964] AC 234, extracted later in this section). In such cases, the natural and ordinary meaning of the words is not their literal but their inferential meaning. A *true or legal innuendo*, by contrast, involves something more than reading between the lines. There is a true innuendo wherever the claimant argues that facts or circumstances which are not apparent from the words themselves ('extrinsic evidence') give those words a meaning they would not ordinarily have. A good illustration of a true innuendo can be seen in the case of *Cassidy v Daily Mirror Newspapers Ltd* [1929] 2 KB 331, also extracted later in this section.

Stocker v Stocker [2020] AC 593

The facts are stated in the opinion of Lord Kerr.

Lord Kerr (with whom Lord Reed, Lady Black, Lord Briggs and Lord Kitchin agreed)

1. 'He tried to strangle me.' What would those words convey to the 'ordinary reasonable reader' of a Facebook post?

Background

2. The respondent to this appeal, Ronald Stocker, is the former husband of the appellant, Nicola Stocker. Their marriage ended in acrimony in 2012. Mr Stocker subsequently formed a relationship with Ms Deborah Bligh. On 23 December 2012 an exchange took place between Mrs Stocker and Ms Bligh on the Facebook website. In the course of that exchange, Mrs Stocker informed Ms Bligh that her former husband (now Ms Bligh's partner) had tried to strangle her. It is now clear that the date on which this is alleged to have occurred is 23 March 2003.

3. Mrs Stocker also said that her husband had been removed from the house following a number of threats that he had made; that there were some 'gun issues'; and that the police felt that he had broken the terms of a non-molestation order. These statements and the allegation that Mr Stocker had tried to strangle her were the basis on which he took proceedings against her for defamation.

4. The allegations about threats, gun issues and the breach of a non-molestation order are relevant to provide context to the statement that Mr Stocker had tried to strangle Mrs Stocker. They paint a picture of acute marital conflict and on that account set the scene for any reader of the Facebook post. That reader would know that Mrs Stocker's statement that her former husband had tried to strangle her was made against the background that this had been, towards the end of its life, a most disharmonious marriage.

The proceedings in the High Court

5. Mr Stocker issued proceedings against his former wife, claiming that the statement that he had tried to strangle her was defamatory of him. He claimed that the meaning to be given to the words 'tried to strangle me' was that he had tried to kill her. Mrs Stocker denied that the words bore that meaning. She claimed that, in the context of domestic violence, the words do not impute an intention to kill. What they would be understood to mean, she said, was that her husband had violently gripped her neck, inhibiting her breathing so as to put her in fear of being killed.

6. Mr Stocker also claimed that the statement that he had uttered threats and breached a non-molestation order was defamatory and was to be taken as implying that he was a dangerous and thoroughly disreputable man. Mrs Stocker refuted this. She said that it was not reasonable to infer that she had suggested that her husband was dangerous on account of his having been arrested a number of times. It is to be observed, however, that in the defence filed on her behalf, Mrs Stocker averred that the statement that her husband was dangerous and disreputable was justified. It seems likely that this was by way of alternative plea. In any event, for reasons that will later appear, this is immaterial because of the rule concerning the substantial truth of the statements made by the alleged defamer.

7. At the start of the defamation proceedings, Mitting J, the trial judge, suggested that the parties should refer to the Oxford English Dictionary's definition of the verb, 'strangle'. This provided two possible meanings: (a) to kill by external compression of the throat; and (b) to constrict the neck or throat painfully . . .

8. Mr Stocker gave evidence that, on the occasion when the altercation which led to his wife accusing him of trying to strangle her took place, he had been standing on a stool or a chair while she was adjusting the length of a pair of his trousers. She had pricked him with a pin. He had sworn at her. She swore back at him and he placed his hand over her mouth to prevent her raised voice from waking their sleeping son. The judge rejected this account, saying, at para 43:

> I do not accept [Mr Stocker's] account that he merely put one hand over [Mrs Stocker's] mouth while he was standing on the stool or chair. His hand would have been at his thigh level. He could not have exerted more than momentary pressure on her mouth, from which she could instantly have escaped. Nor could he have left the reddening marks on her neck or throat which I am satisfied were seen by the police. I do not, however, believe that he threatened to kill her or did anything with his hands with that intention. I do not believe that he was capable even in temper of attempted murder. The most likely explanation about what happened is that he did in temper attempt to silence her forcibly by placing one hand on her mouth and the other on her upper neck under her chin to hold her head still. His intention was to silence, not to kill.

. . .

14. . . . [Mitting J] referred to the two dictionary definitions which I have set out at para 7 above and continued at para 36:

> If the defendant had said 'he strangled me', the ordinary reader would have understood her to have used the word in the second sense for the obvious reason that she was still alive. But the two Facebook comments cannot have been understood to refer to 'trying' to strangle her in that sense because, as she said, the police had found handprints on her neck. These could only have been caused by the painful constriction of her neck or throat. If understood in that sense, she could not have been taken to have said that the defendant had tried to strangle her because he had succeeded. The ordinary reader would have understood that the defendant had attempted to kill her by external compression of her throat or neck with his hands and/or fingers.

. . .

24. . . . [I]t seems to me plain that . . . what the judge did was to regard the two definitions as the only possible meanings which he could consider or, at the very least, the starting point for his analysis, rather than a cross-check or confirmation of the correct approach.

25. Therein lies the danger of the use of dictionary definitions to provide a guide to the meaning of an alleged defamatory statement. That meaning is to be determined according to how it would be understood by the ordinary reasonable reader. It is not fixed by technical, linguistically precise dictionary definitions, divorced from the context in which the statement was made.

26. Moreover, once the verb, 'strangle' is removed from its context and given only two possible meanings before it is reconnected to the word, 'tried' the chances of a strained meaning are increased. The words must be taken together so as to determine what the ordinary reasonable reader would understand them to mean. Mitting J examined the word 'strangle' in conspicuous detail before considering it in conjunction with the word, 'tried'. Having determined that 'strangle' admitted of only two possible meanings, he then decided that 'tried' could be applied to only one of these. Underpinning his reasoning is the unarticulated premise that 'to try' is necessarily 'to try and fail'. Since Mr Stocker had not failed to constrict his wife's throat, the judge concluded that the only feasible meaning of the words was that he had tried (and failed) to kill her. But that is not how the words are used in common language. If I say, 'I tried to regain my breath', I would not be understood to have tried but failed to recover respiratory function.

The single meaning rule

32. Section 11 of the Defamation Act 2013 abolished the statutory right to trial by jury (in section 69(1) of the Senior Courts Act 1981). Under the previous dispensation, the judge would determine which meanings the allegedly defamatory words were capable of bearing and exclude those which she or he considered they were not capable of bearing. The judge would then put to the jury the various possible meanings and, with appropriate directions, invite the jury to decide which of those adumbrated meanings was the one to be attributed to the words said to be defamatory.

33. The almost complete abolition of jury trial meant that the task of choosing a single meaning fell to the judge alone. The exercise of choosing a single immutable meaning from a series of words which are capable of bearing more than one has been described as artificial–see, in particular, Diplock LJ in *Slim v Daily Telegraph Ltd* [1968] 2 QB 157, 172C. But the single meaning rule has had its robust defenders. In *Oriental Daily Publisher Ltd v Ming Pao Holdings Ltd* [2013] EMLR 7, Lord Neuberger of Abbotsbury, sitting as a judge of the Hong Kong Court of Final Appeal, said at para 138 that the criticism of the rule's artificiality and (implicitly) its irrationality was misplaced. He suggested that the identification of a single meaning to be accorded a statement arose 'in many areas of law, most notably . . . the interpretation of statutes, contracts and notices' - para 140.

34. Whether the analogy between a single defamatory meaning and a sole meaning to be given to a contractual term, statutory provision or notice is apt (which I take leave to doubt), it is clear that the single meaning approach is well entrenched in the law of defamation and neither party in the present appeal sought to impeach it. And, whatever else may be said of it, it provides a practical, workable solution. Where a statement has more than one plausible meaning, the question of whether defamation has occurred can only be answered by deciding that one particular meaning should be ascribed to the statement.

35. It is then for the judge to decide which meaning to plump for. Guidance as to how she or he should set about that mission was provided in *Jeynes* [*Jeynes v News Magazines Ltd* [2008] EWCA Civ 130] . . . At para 14, Sir Anthony Clarke MR set out the essential criteria:

> (1) The governing principle is reasonableness. (2) The hypothetical reasonable reader is not naïve, but he is not unduly suspicious. He can read between the lines. He can

read in an implication more readily than a lawyer and may indulge in a certain amount of loose thinking, but he must be treated as being a man who is not avid for scandal and someone who does not, and should not, select one bad meaning where other non-defamatory meanings are available. (3) Over-elaborate analysis is best avoided. (4) The intention of the publisher is irrelevant. (5) The article must be read as a whole, and any "bane and antidote" taken together. (6) The hypothetical reader is taken to be representative of those who would read the publication in question. (7) In delimiting the range of permissible defamatory meanings, the court should rule out any meaning which, 'can only emerge as the produce of some strained, or forced, or utterly unreasonable' interpretation . . . ' (see Eady J in *Gillick v Brook Advisory Centres* approved by this court [2001] EWCA Civ 1263 at para 7 and Gatley on Libel and Slander (10th ed), para 30.6). (8) It follows that 'it is not enough to say that by some person or another the words *might* be understood in a defamatory sense.' *Neville v Fine Arts Co* [1897] AC 68 per Lord Halsbury LC at 73.

36. Sharp LJ added a rider to the second of these criteria in *Rufus v Elliott* [2015] EWCA Civ 121 when she said at para 11:

To this I would only add that the words 'should not select one bad meaning where other non-defamatory meanings are available' are apt to be misleading without fuller explanation. They obviously do not mean in a case such as this one, where it is open to a defendant to contend either on a capability application or indeed at trial that the words complained of are not defamatory of the claimant, that the tribunal adjudicating on the question must then select the non-defamatory meaning for which the defendant contends. Instead, those words are 'part of the description of the hypothetical reasonable reader, rather than (as) a prescription of how such a reader should attribute meanings to words complained of as defamatory': see *McAlpine v Bercow* [2013] EWHC 1342 (QB), paras 63 to 66.

37. Clearly, therefore, where a range of meanings is available and where it is possible to light on one meaning which is not defamatory among a series of meanings which are, the court is not obliged to select the non-defamatory meaning. The touchstone remains what would the ordinary reasonable reader consider the words to mean. Simply because it is theoretically possible to come up with a meaning which is not defamatory, the court is not impelled to select that meaning.

38. All of this, of course, emphasises that the primary role of the court is to focus on how the ordinary reasonable reader would construe the words. And this highlights the court's duty to step aside from a lawyerly analysis and to inhabit the world of the typical reader of a Facebook post. To fulfil that obligation, the court should be particularly conscious of the context in which the statement was made, and it is to that subject that I now turn.

Context

39. The starting point is the sixth proposition in *Jeynes*—that the hypothetical reader should be considered to be a person who would read the publication—and, I would add, react to it in a way that reflected the circumstances in which it was made . . .

41. The fact that this was a Facebook post is critical. The advent of the 21st century has brought with it a new class of reader: the social media user. The judge tasked with deciding how a Facebook post or a tweet on Twitter would be interpreted by a social media user must keep in mind the way in which such postings and tweets are made and read.

42. In *Monroe v Hopkins* [2017] EWHC 433 (QB); [2017] 4 WLR 68, Warby J at para 35 said this about tweets posted on Twitter:

> The most significant lessons to be drawn from the authorities as applied to a case of this kind seem to be the rather obvious ones, that this is a conversational medium; so it would be wrong to engage in elaborate analysis of a 140 character tweet; that an impressionistic approach is much more fitting and appropriate to the medium; but that this impressionistic approach must take account of the whole tweet and the context in which the ordinary reasonable reader would read that tweet. That context includes (a) matters of ordinary general knowledge; and (b) matters that were put before that reader via Twitter.

43. I agree with that, particularly the observation that it is wrong to engage in elaborate analysis of a tweet; it is likewise unwise to parse a Facebook posting for its theoretically or logically deducible meaning. The imperative is to ascertain how a typical (ie an ordinary reasonable) reader would interpret the message. That search should reflect the circumstance that this is a casual medium; it is in the nature of conversation rather than carefully chosen expression; and that it is pre-eminently one in which the reader reads and passes on. . . .

Further discussion

47. It will be clear from what I have said already that, in my view, Mitting J fell into legal error by relying upon the dictionary definition of the verb 'to strangle' as dictating the meaning of Mrs Stocker's Facebook post, rather than as (as Sharp LJ suggested) a check. In consequence, he failed to conduct a realistic exploration of how the ordinary reader of the post would have understood it. Readers of Facebook posts do not subject them to close analysis. They do not have someone by their side pointing out the possible meanings that might, theoretically, be given to the post. Anyone reading this post would not break it down in the way that Mitting J did by saying, well, strangle means either killing someone by choking them to death or grasping them by the throat and since Mrs Stocker is not dead, she *must* have meant that her husband tried to kill her—no other meaning is conceivable.

48. In view of the judge's error of law, his decision as to the meaning of the Facebook post cannot stand, and this court must either determine the meaning for itself, or if that is not possible, remit the case for a rehearing. It is entirely appropriate in this case for us to take the former course, determining the meaning ourselves.

49. I return to the ordinary reader of the Facebook post. Such a reader does not splice the post into separate clauses, much less isolate individual words and contemplate their possible significance. Knowing that the author was alive, he or she would unquestionably have interpreted the post as meaning that Mr Stocker had grasped his wife by the throat and applied force to her neck rather than that he had tried deliberately to kill her.

50. Ironically, perhaps, this conclusion is reinforced by the consideration that only one meaning is to be attributed to the statement. Taking a broad, overarching view, and keeping in mind that only one meaning could be chosen, the choice to be made between the meaning of the words being that Mr Stocker grasped his wife by the neck or that he tried to kill her is, in my opinion, a clear one. If Mrs Stocker had meant to convey that her husband had attempted to kill her, why would she not say so explicitly? And, given that she made no such allegation, what would the ordinary reasonable reader, the casual viewer of this Facebook post, think that it meant? In my view, giving due consideration to the context in which the message was posted, the interpretation that Mr Stocker had grasped his wife by the neck is the obvious, indeed the inescapable, choice of meaning.

Appeal allowed.

COMMENTARY

Disputes as to what meanings an allegedly defamatory statement can bear often form a major part of the pre-trial 'jockeying for position' between the parties which has been a feature of many of the cases in this area. As Lord Kerr observes, trial of defamation actions was traditionally by jury, in contrast with most other actions in tort, including all actions for personal injury, which have long only been heard by a judge sitting alone. It became necessary, therefore, to develop rules to divide responsibility for the decision of different issues as between judge and jury, and this led to a great deal of technicality. Because the determination of what allegations and evidence could be put in front of the jury was crucial, a whole succession of preliminary points might be taken as each side attempted to define the legal and factual issues in the way most favourable to itself. Defamation Act 2013, s. 11 now prescribes that trial of defamation claims should ordinarily be without a jury, so the technicality should be reduced to some extent. It will no longer be necessary for the judge to rule, first, whether published material was *capable* of bearing the meaning contended for by the claimant, and then to ask the jury whether it *in fact* bore that meaning. The meaning of the published material will normally just be for the judge. But as *Stocker* makes clear, the judge must be wary of relying on dictionary definitions and alive to the context in which the publication occurred, bearing in mind in particular that posts on social media are typically understood impressionistically and should not be over-analysed to ascertain their meaning. As regards social media and the law of defamation generally, see Mangan, 'Regulating for Responsibility: Reputation and Social Media' (2015) 29 Int'l Rev L, Computers & Tech 16.

It will already be apparent that there is an intrinsic link between questions of meaning and the defence of truth (see further in IV.1). A defendant pleading truth must prove that each of the meanings the claimant is able to attribute to the words is true, or at least that that the harm from any unproven charges is not serious, having regard to what has in fact been shown to be true. In *Stocker*, the Supreme Court found that the defendant was entitled to the defence both regarding the specified imputation ('tried to strangle me') and the wider allegation that the claimant was dangerous and disreputable. The Court highlighted in particular the undisputed evidence that the claimant had grasped his wife by the throat so tightly as to leave red marks on her neck visible to police officers two hours after the attack on her took place.

Lewis v Daily Telegraph [1964] AC 234

Details of a police investigation into the affairs of a large public company, Rubber Improvements Ltd, were leaked to the *Daily Telegraph*, which put a piece on the story on its front pages:

INQUIRY ON FIRM BY CITY POLICE

Officers of the City of London Fraud Squad are inquiring into the affairs of Rubber Improvement Ltd and its subsidiary companies. The investigation was requested after criticisms of the chairman's statement and the accounts by a shareholder at the recent company meeting. The chairman of the company . . . is Mr John Lewis, former Socialist MP for Bolton.

A similar piece appeared in the *Daily Mail*. Lewis and his companies were subsequently absolved of all allegations of impropriety, and they issued writs against the proprietors of the two newspapers alleging that '[b]y the said words the defendants meant and were understood to mean that the affairs of the plaintiffs and/or its subsidiaries were conducted fraudulently or dishonestly or in such a way that the police suspected that their affairs were so conducted'. The defendants denied this, arguing that there were no grounds for imagining that reasonable readers would treat it as doing anything more than convey (accurate) information about the inquiry. The plaintiffs succeeded against both newspapers in separate trials, but, in a consolidated appeal, the Court of Appeal ruled that the judges had erred in leaving the cases to the jury. The plaintiffs appealed to the House of Lords.

Lord Reid

The essence of the controversy between the parties is that the appellants maintain that these passages are capable of meaning that they were guilty of fraud. The respondents deny this: they admit that the paragraphs are libellous but maintain that the juries ought to have been directed that they are not capable of the meaning which the appellants attribute to them. The learned judge directed the juries in such a way as to leave it open to them to accept the appellants' contention, and it is obvious from the amounts of damages awarded that the juries must have done this.

The gist of the two paragraphs is that the police, the City Fraud Squad, were inquiring into the appellants' affairs. There is no doubt that in actions for libel the question is what the words would convey to the ordinary man: it is not one of construction in the legal sense. The ordinary man does not live in an ivory tower and he is not inhibited by a knowledge of the rules of construction. So he can and does read between the lines in the light of his general knowledge and experience of worldly affairs. I leave aside questions of innuendo where the reader has some special knowledge which might lead him to attribute a meaning to the words not apparent to those who do not have that knowledge. That only arises indirectly in this case . . .

What the ordinary man would infer without special knowledge has generally been called the natural and ordinary meaning of the words. But that expression is rather misleading in that it conceals the fact that there are two elements in it. Sometimes it is not necessary to go beyond the words themselves, as where the plaintiff has been called a thief or a murderer. But more often the sting is not so much in the words themselves as in what the ordinary man will infer from them, and that is also regarded as part of their natural and ordinary meaning. Here there would be nothing libellous in saying that an inquiry into the appellants' affairs was proceeding: the inquiry might be by a statistician or other expert. The sting is in inferences drawn from the fact that it is the fraud squad which is making the inquiry. What those inferences should be is ultimately a question for the jury, but the trial judge has an important duty to perform . . .

In this case it is, I think, sufficient to put the test in this way. Ordinary men and women have different temperaments and outlooks. Some are unusually suspicious and some are unusually naive. One must try to envisage people between these two extremes and see what is the most damaging meaning they would put on the words in question. So let me suppose a number of ordinary people discussing one of these paragraphs which they had read in the newspaper. No doubt one of them might say—'Oh, if the fraud squad are after these people you can take it they are guilty.' But I would expect the others to turn on him, if he did say that, with such remarks as—'Be fair. This is not a police state. No doubt their affairs are in a mess or the police would not be interested. But that could be because Lewis or the cashier has been very stupid or careless. We really must not jump to conclusions. The police are fair and know their job and we shall know soon enough if there is anything in it. Wait till we see if they charge him. I wouldn't trust him until this is cleared up, but it is another thing to condemn him unheard.'

What the ordinary man, not avid for scandal, would read into the words complained of must be a matter of impression. I can only say that I do not think that he would infer guilt of fraud merely because an inquiry is on foot. And, if that is so, then it is the duty of the trial judge to direct the jury that it is for them to determine the meaning of the paragraph but that they must not hold it to impute guilt of fraud because as a matter of law the paragraph is not capable of having that meaning. So there was here, in my opinion, misdirection of the two juries sufficiently serious to require that there must be new trials.

Lord Hodson

It is in conjunction with secondary meanings that much of the difficulty surrounding the law of libel exists. These secondary meanings are covered by the word 'innuendo', which signifies pointing out what and who is meant by the words complained of. . . . The first subdivision of the innuendo has lately been called the false innuendo as it is no more than an elaboration or embroidering of the words used without proof of extraneous facts. The true innuendo is that which depends on extraneous facts which the plaintiff has to prove in order to give the words the secondary meaning of which he complains. . . .

There is one cause of action based on the words in their natural and ordinary meaning and another based on the words in such meaning as may be alleged in a true innuendo, but not a third cause of action based on the false innuendo . . .

Lord Morris of Borth-y-Gest (dissenting)

My Lords, a reasonable reader will probably be a fair-minded reader. The fair-minded reader would assume that a responsible newspaper would also be fair. If there was some private police inquiry in progress, the purpose of which was to ascertain whether or not there had been fraud or dishonesty, what possible justification could there be for proclaiming this far and wide to all the readers of a newspaper? If confidential information was received to the effect that there was a police inquiry, on what basis could the publishing of such information be warranted? . . . If there was a police inquiry by a 'Fraud Squad' which might result in the conclusion that any suspicion of fraud or dishonesty was wholly unwarranted, how manifestly unfair it would be to make public mention of the inquiry. What purpose could there be in doing so? With these thoughts and questions in his mind, a reasonable reader might well consider that no responsible newspaper would dare to publish, or would be so cruel as to publish, the words in question unless the confidential information, which in some manner they had obtained, was not information merely to the effect that there was some kind of inquiry in progress but was information to the effect that there was fraud or dishonesty. Some reasonable readers might therefore think that the words conveyed the meaning that there must have been fraud or dishonesty.

Lord Devlin delivered a separate conourring speech. **Lord Tucker** concurred with the speech of **Lord Reid**.

Appeal dismissed. Retrial ordered.

COMMENTARY

As noted earlier, there is an intrinsic link between the meaning or meanings given to the words in question, and the onus on a defendant who seeks to rely on the defence of truth. In *Lewis*, it seems the defendants were aggrieved that their defence of truth was undermined because the jury might have construed the allegation to be that the plaintiffs were guilty of fraud, and not merely that they were suspected of it, even on reasonable grounds. Naturally, this might also have inflated the damages awarded. The defendants won before the Lords, and so were entitled to another trial, before a different jury, in which they could raise their defence again.

In the later case of *Chase v News Group Newspapers Ltd* [2003] EMLR 11 at [45], Brooke LJ identified three different levels of gravity of defamatory allegations of this nature: (1) the claimant has in fact committed the offence; (2) there are reasonable grounds to suspect that the claimant has committed the offence; and (3) there are grounds for investigating whether the claimant was responsible for the offence. These are now conventionally referred to as *Chase* levels 1, 2 and 3. In *Lewis*, the burden for the defendant at the retrial would have been to prove that the plaintiff had been reasonably suspected of guilt (*Chase* level 2) but not that he was in fact guilty (*Chase* level 1), as that was not what the defendant had alleged. In order to do so, he would now have to identify particular conduct on the part of the claimant giving rise to such a suspicion (see *Shah v Standard Chartered Bank* [1999] QB 241).

Innuendoes

In the course of his concurring speech in *Lewis*, Lord Devlin (at 278) gave the following explanation of a true innuendo:

> a derogatory implication . . . might not be detected at all, except by a person who was already in possession of some specific information. Thus, to say of a man that he was seen to enter a named house would contain a derogatory implication for anyone who knew that that house was a brothel but not for anyone who did not . . .

Where the claimant alleges a true innuendo, they must particularise in their statement of case the facts and matters which they rely upon in support of the extended meaning. As a general matter of pleading, claimants must specify in their particulars of claim the defamatory meaning or meanings which they allege that the words complained of conveyed. They should detail both the natural and ordinary meaning for which they contend and, where appropriate, any true innuendo meaning. In the latter case, they must also identify the extraneous facts which they allege gave the words a defamatory meaning. See CPR, Practice Direction 53, para. 2.3.

As the extract from Lord Hodson's speech makes clear, a single publication may give rise to more than one cause of action: one in respect of the ordinary meaning of the words; another in respect of each true innuendo arising from the words. What significance does this have in practice? Why does a false innuendo not give rise to a separate cause of action?

Defamatory Meaning Unknown to the Defendant

The intention of the defendant in making the statement is wholly irrelevant, so the lack of any intention to defame is no defence if the words would be understood as defamatory by those to whom they were communicated. As the following extract shows, this applies even in the case of a true innuendo where the defendant does not know the facts which made an apparently innocent statement defamatory.

Cassidy v Daily Mirror Newspapers Ltd [1929] 2 KB 331

The defendants published a photograph taken of Kettering Cassidy, also known as Michael Corrigan, and a woman. Cassidy, perhaps given to fantasy (he described himself as having been a General in the Mexican army), told a press photographer that he was going to marry the woman, and the photograph appeared above the words: 'Mr M. Corrigan, the race horse owner, and Miss [name omitted], whose engagement has been announced.' The action was brought by Mrs Cassidy, Cassidy's lawful wife. Although they lived apart Cassidy occasionally visited her. She argued that the words and picture were capable of meaning that 'Corrigan' was a single man and that, therefore, she was living in immoral cohabitation with him and only masquerading as his wife. At the trial, three of her acquaintances testified that they had in fact believed this on seeing the publication. The judge directed the jury to consider whether the publication was capable of conveying a meaning defamatory of the plaintiff to reasonably minded people who knew the circumstances. The jury returned a verdict for the plaintiff for £500. The defendants appealed.

Scrutton LJ

[T]he alleged libel does not mention the plaintiff, but I think it is clear that words published about A may indirectly be defamatory of B. For instance, 'A is illegitimate.' To persons who know the parents those words may be defamatory of the parents. Or again, 'A has given way to drink; it is unfortunately hereditary'; to persons who know A's parents these words may be defamatory. Or 'A holds a D. Litt. degree of the University at X, the only one awarded.' To persons who know B, who habitually describes himself (and rightly so) as 'D. Litt. of X,' these words may be capable of a defamatory meaning. Similarly, to say that A is a single man or a bachelor may be capable of a defamatory meaning if published to persons who know a lady who passes as Mrs A and whom A visits. . . .

In my view the words published were capable of the meaning 'Corrigan is a single man,' and were published to people who knew the plaintiff professed to be married to Corrigan; it was for the jury to say whether those people could reasonably draw the inference that the so-called Mrs Corrigan was in fact living in immoral cohabitation with Corrigan, and I do not think their finding should be interfered with.

But the second point taken was that the defendants could not be liable for the inference drawn, because they did not know the facts which enabled some persons to whom the libel was published, to draw an inference defamatory of the plaintiff. . . . In my view . . . it is impossible for the person publishing a statement which, to those who know certain facts, is capable of a defamatory meaning in regard to A, to defend himself by saying: 'I never heard of A and did not mean to injure him.' If he publishes words reasonably capable of being read as relating directly or indirectly to A and, to those who know the facts about A, capable of a defamatory meaning, he must take the consequences of the defamatory inferences reasonably drawn from his words.

It is said that this decision would seriously interfere with the reasonable conduct of newspapers. I do not agree. If publishers of newspapers, who have no more rights than private persons, publish statements which may be defamatory of other people, without inquiry as to their truth, in order to make their paper attractive, they must take the consequences, if on subsequent inquiry, their statements are found to be untrue or capable of defamatory and unjustifiable inferences. No one could contend that 'M. Corrigan, General in the Mexican Army,' was 'a source in whom we have full confidence.' To publish statements first and inquire into their truth afterwards, may seem attractive and up to date. Only to publish after inquiry may be slow, but at any rate it would lead to accuracy and reliability.

Russell LJ

Liability for libel does not depend on the intention of the defamer; but on the fact of defamation. . . . From a business point of view no doubt it may pay them [sc. the defendants] not to spend time or money in making inquiries, or verifying statements before publication; but if they had not made a false statement they would not now be suffering in damages. They are paying a price for their methods of business. . . .

> **Greer LJ** (dissenting)
>
> If the decision of my brethren in this case is right, it would be right to say that I could be successfully sued for damages for libel if, having been introduced to two apparently respectable people as persons engaged to be married, I repeated that statement in a letter to a friend, on the ground that my words meant that a lady totally unknown to me, who was in fact the wife of the man, was not his wife and was living in immoral intercourse with him. It seems to me wholly unreasonable to hold that my words could be construed as meaning anything of the kind, and wholly unjust that I should be made to pay damages because some unduly suspicious person drew an inference from the fact I stated, which was derogatory to the woman in question—and I am afraid that for the future people will have to walk with wary steps through life and hesitate a long time before they accept the assertion of any one whom they have known as a bachelor, that he is in truth a single man.
>
> *Appeal dismissed.*

COMMENTARY

The Court of Appeal regarded itself as bound by the decision of the House of Lords in *E Hulton & Co v Jones*, extracted later. In 1952, the Porter Committee (Cmd. 7536) considered that holding defendants liable in such circumstances, without regard to whether or not they had exercised reasonable care, was liable to produce injustice. It recommended the introduction of a new statutory defence in cases of 'unintentional defamation' where the defendant could prove that he had taken reasonable care not to defame the plaintiff. In the Committee's view, a defendant relying upon the defence should have to take steps to clear the plaintiff's reputation by publishing a correction and an apology, whose form, in the event of dispute, would be settled by the court. The defence was implemented, broadly in line with the Committee's recommendations, by Defamation Act 1952, s. 4. The most recent version of the defence appears in Defamation Act 1996, s. 2 (extracted in IV.5).

In *Baturina v Times Newspapers Ltd* [2011] 1 WLR 1526, the Court of Appeal rejected the argument that *Hulton v Jones* was incompatible with the right to freedom of expression (Article 10, ECHR) as incorporated in English law by the Human Rights Act 1998, and declined to limit liability in innuendo claims to cases where the defendant did not and could not reasonably have been expected to appreciate the innuendo meaning at the time of the statement. The defences available to the publisher already provide sufficient protection of the right.

It is worth observing, however, that the claim in *Cassidy*, and indeed in many of the other leading cases, would be unlikely to satisfy the 'serious harm' requirement introduced into the modern law (Defamation Act 2013, s. 1(1)).

2. The Statement must Refer to the Claimant

(a) General

'It is an essential element of the cause of action in defamation that the words complained of should be published "of the plaintiff"' (*Knuppfer v London Express* [1944] AC 116 at 120, per Viscount Simon LC). This is the requirement of reference to the claimant: the claimant must be identified as the person defamed. The claimant may be identified by name, description, pun (consider *Byrne v Deane*, extracted earlier) or any reasonable inference. It is not necessary that there should be any 'peg or pointer' in the defamatory words, but only that reasonable people might understand the words as referring to the claimant. Furthermore, 'words published about A may indirectly be defamatory of B' (*Cassidy v Daily Mirror Newspapers Ltd* [1929] 2 KB 331 at 338–9, per Scrutton LJ), so a statement that A is a single man or a bachelor may be capable of a defamatory meaning if published to persons who know a woman who passes as Mrs A and whom A visits (as in *Cassidy* itself). As with the question of defamatory meaning, it is not necessary that the defendant intended to refer to the claimant. The question is not who was *meant* but who was *hit* (*E Hulton & Co v Jones* [1910] AC 20 at 22, per Lord Loreburn LC, *arguendo*). It is irrelevant that the defendant did not intend to refer to any real person but was talking instead about a fictional character (see the following extract from *Hulton*) or even that he intended to refer to another person of whom the words were true (*Newstead v London Express Newspaper Ltd* [1940] 1 KB 377). To this extent, defamation is a tort of strict liability.

E. Hulton & Co v Jones [1910] AC 20

Artemus Jones, a barrister, brought an action against the defendants in respect of a newspaper article which he claimed referred to him; he had previously contributed pieces to the newspaper in question. The article referred to 'Artemus Jones' a church warden in Peckham and cast imputations on his moral behaviour at a motor festival in Dieppe ('There is Artemus Jones with a woman who is not his wife, who must be, you know—the other thing!'). The defendants argued they had never intended the article to refer to the 'real' Artemus Jones but instead had intended to create a fictitious character whom they had given a 'fancy name'. After the plaintiff had succeeded at trial, the defendants appealed to the Court of Appeal and then to the House of Lords.

Lord Loreburn

My Lords, I think this appeal must be dismissed. A question in regard to the law of libel has been raised which does not seem to me to be entitled to the support of your Lordships. Libel is a tortious act. What does the tort consist in? It consists in using language which others knowing the circumstances would reasonably think to be defamatory of the person complaining of and injured by it. A person charged with libel cannot defend himself by shewing that he intended in his own breast not to defame, or that he intended not to defame the plaintiff, if in fact he did both. He has none the less imputed something disgraceful and has none the less injured the plaintiff. A man in good faith may publish a libel believing it to be true, and it may be found by the jury that he acted in good faith believing it to be true, and reasonably believing it to be true, but that in fact the statement was false. Under those circumstances he has no defence to the action, however excellent his intention. If the intention of the writer be immaterial in considering whether the matter written is defamatory, I do not see why it need be relevant in considering whether it is defamatory of the plaintiff. The writing, according to the old form, must be malicious, and it must be of and concerning the plaintiff. Just as the defendant could not excuse himself from malice by proving that he wrote it in the most benevolent spirit, so he cannot shew that the libel was not of and concerning the plaintiff by proving that he never heard of the plaintiff. His intention in both respects equally is inferred from what he did. His remedy is to abstain from defamatory words . . .

The damages are certainly heavy, but I think your Lordships ought to remember . . . that the jury were entitled to think, in the absence of proof satisfactory to them (and they were the judges of it), that some ingredient of recklessness, or more than recklessness, entered into the writing and the publication of this article, especially as Mr Jones, the plaintiff, had been employed on this very newspaper, and his name was well known in the paper and also well known in the district in which the paper circulated.

Lord Atkinson, **Lord Gorell** and **Lord Shaw of Dunfermline** concurred.

Appeal dismissed.

COMMENTARY

Hulton has been described as 'the most famous case in the law of libel' and also 'the most controversial' (Lord Denning, *What Next in the Law* (London: Butterworths, 1982), p. 173). It would certainly seem very unfair that an author should be held liable in defamation just because a real-life person happened to share the name of one of the author's less attractive creations. However, this is unlikely to be the result of the decision. The jury must always be satisfied that the words could reasonably be understood as referring to the claimant. Perhaps what swayed the jury in this case was evidence revealed in cross-examination that the writer of the piece had actually had a previous run-in with the plaintiff, which substantially undermined his claim that his use of the name was pure coincidence (see Mitchell, 'Artemus Jones and the Press Club' (1999) 20 J Leg His 64). The damages award of £1,750—a 'staggering' £176,000 at 2015 values—certainly suggests as much (*Mitchell,* p. 154).

Negative Checking

In order to avoid liability under this principle, producers of film, television and radio fiction now habitually engage in a practice known as 'negative checking' by which attempts are made to ensure that characters cannot be coincidentally confused with real-life figures (see *Barendt*, pp. 114–15). During the making of a TV 'cop drama', for example, the programme-makers may check with the police force depicted to make sure there can be no confusion between real-life and fictional officers (p. 115n). *Barendt* comments (p. 195):

Arguably, it is bizarre to require broadcasters to go to the lengths they do to minimize the chance of liability for unintentional defamation. Negative checking of reference books and lists of addresses surely goes beyond the taking of reasonable precautions required in other areas of the law. Other media outlets do not have the time or the facilities to engage in this burdensome activity.

Bona Fide News Reports

The rule in *Hulton v Jones* was subsequently applied to bona fide news reporting (with what Lord Denning, *op. cit.*, considered 'an equally absurd result': p. 177). In *Morgan v Odhams Press Ltd* [1971] 1 WLR 1239, the defendants had published an article which stated that a certain woman had been kidnapped by a dog-doping gang. The woman had in fact been staying voluntarily with the plaintiff around this time. At trial, the plaintiff produced several witnesses who said that they thought that the article referred to him, and the jury returned a verdict in his favour. By a majority, the House of Lords held that the trial judge had been correct to leave the matter to the jury. It was immaterial that a close reading of the article would have made it clear that it could not refer to the plaintiff, as the ordinary reader does not read a newspaper article with the care with which a lawyer would read an important legal document, but may read it quickly in order to get a general impression.

Words True of their Intended Target

The difficulty facing news editors and other publishers is compounded by the rule that words true of their intended target may nevertheless be—wholly unforeseeably—defamatory of another. In *Newstead v London Express Newspaper Ltd* [1940] 1 KB 377, the *Daily Express* had described the prisoner in a trial for bigamy as 'Harold Newstead, thirty-year-old Camberwell man'. The plaintiff coincidentally fitted that description and successfully claimed for libel. The Court of Appeal applied *Hulton*, and held that the fact that the defendant had taken all due care was quite irrelevant. However, although Newstead won on the law before the Court of Appeal, the court declined to interfere with the jury's assessment of damages at a mere one farthing, perhaps 'an indication that the law had gone too far' (*Mitchell, op. cit.*, 158).

Ability to Make Offer of Amends

In cases of this type, as in cases of unknown defamatory meaning (discussed previously), defendants may be able protect themselves by making an offer of amends under Defamation Act 1996, s. 2. This applies, inter alia, to publications in which the defendant neither knew nor had reason to know that the statement referred to the claimant or was likely to be so understood. The provision requires defendants to offer to print a correction and apology, and to pay such compensation and costs as are agreed or determined by the court. An advantage for defendants is that such compensation is assessed, in default of agreement, by a judge rather than a jury, though the latter's diminishing role makes that less significant than before. See further in IV.5.

Effect of the Human Rights Act

In *O'Shea v MGN Ltd* [2001] EMLR 40, the claimant complained of an advertisement appearing in the *Sunday Mirror* on behalf of an adult internet service. The advertisement included a photograph of a glamour model who closely resembled the claimant. The claimant alleged that the advertisement meant that she was appearing or performing on a highly pornographic website containing material of an explicit, indecent and lewd nature and had shamelessly agreed to promote the website and her appearance on it in a national newspaper. The claimant pleaded that a number of persons had identified her with the photograph. The defendant applied for summary judgment. Morland J accepted that a jury might reasonably have concluded that the claimant was the person referred to in the publication, but granted the application on the basis that it would be contrary to Article 10 of the ECHR to impose strict liability for inadvertent defamatory reference to a claimant as a result of identification from a photograph of somebody else of similar appearance. The strict liability rule represented an interference with the Convention right to freedom of expression, and there was no pressing social need for such interference such as would justify it under Article 10(2):

> 45. The fact that in over a century no claim has been made in respect of a libel in respect of a 'look-alike' picture is an indication that there is no pressing social need for the application of the strict liability principle for the protection of the reputation of the 'look-alike' . . .
>
> 47. [M]y judgment is that the strict liability principle should not cover the 'look-alike' situation. To allow it to do so would be an unjustifiable interference with the vital right of freedom of expression disproportionate to the legitimate aim of protecting the reputations of 'look-alikes' and contrary to Article 10 of the Convention.

Morland J noted, at [33], that Defamation Act 1996, s. 2 did not substantially mitigate the strictness of the liability because it did not create a 'true' defence, for '[t]he blameless publisher has not only to make and publish a correction and apology but also to offer compensation'.

The *O'Shea* case indicates the potentially transformative effect of the Human Rights Act on the law of defamation, though it must be questioned whether the potential will ever be fully realised. When the Court of Appeal was asked to reappraise the basic rule in *Hulton v Jones* in the light of the Human Rights Act, it declined to restrict liability to cases where the defendant did not and could not reasonably have been expected to appreciate the innuendo meaning at the time of the statement (*Baturina v Times Newspapers Ltd* [2011] 1 WLR 1526). However, Lord Neuberger MR indicated, at [29]f, that he was inclined to think that *O'Shea* was correctly decided—perhaps as a small extension of the defence then known as media privilege (see IV.4).

(b) Group Defamation

Where words are spoken of a group of people, proof that the article refers to an individual member of that group is likely to be difficult. The classic example is the statement that 'all lawyers are thieves', which it has been said gives rise to no cause of action on the part of any individual lawyer (*Eastwood v Holmes* (1858) 1 F & F 347). However, there is no special rule precluding liability in all cases of group or class defamation.

Knuppfer v London Express Newspapers [1944] AC 116

The case arose out of a newspaper article, published at the time of World War II. The article claimed that a political party formed by émigrés from the Soviet Union, the 'Young Russians', consisted of 'quislings' with whom Hitler intended to establish a pro-German movement within the Soviet Union. The party, which the article stated was established in France and the United States, was alleged to be 'a minute body professing a pure Fascist ideology'; the article also claimed that 'Hitler intends to nominate a puppet fuehrer from their ranks to replace the Soviet national leaders of the Kremlin, and establish a reactionary totalitarian serf State . . . '. It concluded: 'The vast majority of Russian emigrés repudiate these people, but Hitler is accustomed to find instruments among the despised dregs of every community.' The plaintiff, a Russian resident in London who was head of the British branch of the Young Russia party, brought an action against the defendants for damages for libel, setting out the above words in his statement of claim, and alleging that they had been falsely and maliciously published of him by the defendants. The defendants denied that the words were reasonably capable of being understood to refer to the plaintiff. The total membership of the Young Russia Party worldwide was about 2,000 but the British branch comprised only twenty-four members. Four witnesses who were acquainted with the plaintiff testified that they thought of him when they read the article. The plaintiff won at trial, but lost before the Court of Appeal. He appealed to the House of Lords.

Viscount Simon LC

In the words complained of in this case there is no specific mention of the appellant from beginning to end, and the only countries in which it is stated that this group of emigrés is established are France and the United States. . . . The words make allegations of a defamatory character about a body of persons—some thousands in number—who belong to a society whose members are to be found in many countries . . .

Where the plaintiff is not named, the test which decides whether the words used refer to him is the question whether the words are such as would reasonably lead persons acquainted with the plaintiff to believe that he was the person referred to. There are cases in which the language used in reference to a limited class may be reasonably understood to refer to every member of the class, in which case every member may have a cause of action. A good example is *Browne v DC Thomson & Co*, 1912 SC 359, where a newspaper article stated in Queenstown 'instructions were issued by the Roman Catholic religious authorities that all Protestant shop assistants were to be discharged,' and where seven pursuers who averred that they were the sole persons who exercised religious authority in the name and on behalf of the Roman Catholic Church in Queenstown were held entitled to sue for libel as being individually defamed. . . . In the present case, however, the appellant rejected the view that every member of the Young Russia Group could bring his own action on the words complained of, and relied on his own prominence or representative character in the movement as establishing that the words referred to himself. There is, however, nothing in the words which refers to one member of the group rather than another. *Le Fanu v Malcolmson* (1848) 1 HLC 637 was, it is true, a decision of this House in which Lord Cottenham LC and Lord Campbell held that the verdict of a jury awarding damages to the owners of a factory in the county of Waterford against the proprietor of a newspaper published in that county could be upheld notwithstanding that the letterpress, in the course of denouncing the alleged cruelty with which factory operatives were treated, did not specifically refer to the plaintiff's factory. It appears, however, in that case that there were circumstances, such as the location of the factory, which enabled the jurors to identify the plaintiff's factory as the factory pointed at. . . . It will be observed that *Le Fanu v Malcolmson* was a case where there were facts pointing to the particular factory which was meant to be referred to though the article spoke in more general terms of a factory in Waterford. In the present case the statement complained of is not made concerning a particular individual, whether named or unnamed, but concerning a group of people spread over several countries and including considerable numbers. No facts were proved in evidence which could identify the appellant as the person individually referred to. Witnesses called for the appellant were asked the carefully framed question: 'To whom did your mind go when you read that article?' and they not unnaturally replied by pointing to the appellant himself, but that is because they happened to know the appellant as the leading member of the society in this country and not because there is anything in the article itself which ought to suggest even to his friends that he is referred to as an individual.

Lord Atkin in a short concurring opinion, warned against over-complicating the law in this area:

I venture to think that it is a mistake to lay down a rule as to libel on a class, and then qualify it with exceptions. The only relevant rule is that in order to be actionable the defamatory words must be understood to be published of and concerning the plaintiff. It is irrelevant that the words are published of two or more persons if they are proved to be published of him, and it is irrelevant that the two or more persons are called by some generic or class name. There can be no law that a defamatory statement made of a firm, or trustees, or the tenants of a particular building is not actionable, if the words would reasonably be understood as published of each member of the firm or each trustee or each tenant. The reason why a libel published of a large or indeterminate number of persons described by some general name generally fails to be actionable is the difficulty of establishing that the plaintiff was, in fact, included in the defamatory statement, for the habit of making unfounded generalizations is ingrained in ill-educated or vulgar minds, or the words are occasionally intended to be a facetious exaggeration. Even in such cases words may be used which enable the plaintiff to prove that the words complained of were intended to be published of each member of the group, or, at any rate, of himself.

Lord Thankerton and **Lord Russell of Killowen** concurred.

Appeal dismissed.

COMMENTARY

Mitchell, pp. 43–4, notes that the interpretative standard here is not that of the actual reader—the evidence of the four readers who believed the article referred to the plaintiff not being decisive—but 'an idealized, discriminating reader'. He questions whether this is a realistic approach in the context of modern political rhetoric. Nevertheless, the principles set out by Viscount Simon LC are now well established. In *Aspro Travel Ltd v Owners Abroad Group* [1996] 1 WLR 132 the Court of Appeal accepted, for the purposes of determining a preliminary issue, that a defamatory statement about the conduct of the affairs of a small family company could be understood as referring to each of the company directors. See also *Riches v News Group Newspapers* [1986] QB 256 (eleven members of 'the Banbury CID' defamed individually). In which of Viscount Simon's two categories did these cases fall? Cf. *Tilbrook v Parr* [2012] EWHC 1946 (QB), where Tugendhat J ruled that a statement that a political party was racist could not reasonably be understood as referring personally to its chairman, who was not named or otherwise identified in the statement.

How was it that the plaintiff was able to succeed in *Le Fanu v Malcolmson*, mentioned by Viscount Simon in the extract, even though the allegations did not refer to each and every member of the class mentioned in the offending newspaper article (factory-owners in the county of Waterford)?

3. The Statement must be Published

The law of defamation is concerned with the protection of people's reputation in the eyes of their fellows. Accordingly, it is a requirement of an action in defamation that the words complained of be published to a person other than the person impugned. 'Publication' here means no more than 'communication', even to a single person, and a publisher is any person who communicates a defamatory meaning to a third party. A statement may be published in an almost infinite variety of ways, for example in the course of a conversation, by letter, in a newspaper or book, in an email, 'tweet' or blog post or by broadcast transmission. Publication may also be by omission, for example a failure to remove graffiti scrawled on the walls of one's property (cf. *Byrne v Deane* [1937] 1 KB 818; unless removing the graffiti would require great trouble and expense: see p. 838, per Greene LJ), and in some circumstances a person may by conduct impliedly associate themselves with words which cannot be shown to have been written or uttered by them (*Hird v Wood* (1894) 38 Sol J 234: man's sitting near placard and pointing at it with his finger held to be a publication). It has long been established, by exception to the general rule, that communication to the defendant's spouse is no publication (*Wennhak v Morgan* (1880) 20 QBD 637), though communication to *the claimant's* spouse *can* give rise to liability (*Theaker v Richardson* [1962] 1 WLR 151).

Traditionally, every repetition of a defamatory statement is a new publication and creates a fresh cause of action in the person defamed (the 'multiple publication' rule). The publication must be made to a person capable of understanding the defamatory meaning. Where, for example, the statement is not defamatory on its face, but only when considered in the light of extrinsic evidence, the hearer must know of the extrinsic facts which make the statement defamatory (see *Cassidy*, extracted earlier). Similarly, if a defamatory statement is written in a foreign language the recipient must be able to understand it. It is not necessary for the claimant to prove that the publication was intentionally made, but only that it was the natural and probable consequence of their actions.

Huth v Huth [1915] 3 KB 32

A man sent to his wife a letter which was defamatory of her and their children. It was opened and read by the butler. At the time, a wife was unable to sue her husband in tort, so the action was brought by the children. At first instance, the jury returned a verdict in favour of the defendant. The plaintiffs appealed to the Court of Appeal, which considered the question whether evidence that the butler had opened and read the letter was evidence of publication to a third party.

Lord Reading CJ

[I]t is no part of a butler's duty to open letters that come to the house of his master or mistress addressed to the master or mistress. . . . No one can help a man's curiosity being excited, but it does not justify him in opening a letter, and it could not make the defendant liable for the publication to the butler of the contents of the envelope . . .

Swinfen Eady LJ and **Bray J** agreed.

Appeal dismissed.

COMMENTARY

In *Huth v Huth*, the correspondence was contained in an (unsealed) envelope. It appears that a different rule applies where it is conveyed by way of a postcard which is not enclosed in an envelope. According to the so-called 'postcard rule', the words are presumed to be published as soon as the card is sent through the post: see *Sadgrove v Hole* [1901] 2 KB 1 at 4–5 per A. L. Smith MR.

In *Theaker v Richardson* [1962] 1 WLR 151 the defendant wrote a defamatory letter to the plaintiff who was a married woman. The letter, which was addressed to the plaintiff, was contained in a manila envelope similar to the kind used for distributing election addresses. The plaintiff's husband opened the envelope thinking (he said) that it was an election address. At the trial the jury found there had been a publication of a defamatory statement and awarded damages to the plaintiff. On appeal to the Court of Appeal, Pearson LJ stated (at 161) that the question that should be asked was, '[Was] his (i.e. the recipient's) conduct so unusual, out of the ordinary and not reasonably to be anticipated, or was it something which could quite easily and naturally happen in the ordinary course of events?' This was pre eminently a jury question and as the jury had decided that the opening of the letter by the husband was something that could quite easily happen in the ordinary course of events the Court of Appeal would not interfere with their decision.

By Defamation Act 1996, s. 1, a special defence now applies to mere *distributors* of defamatory material, provided certain conditions are met. See further IV.6.

Repetition of Defamatory Statements

The originator of a defamatory statement may be liable not only for its republication with his authorisation, which gives rise to a second cause of action against him, but also for a third party's unauthorised but foreseeable repetition of allegations contained within the original publication (sometimes known as 'the grapevine effect'). Here, there is only one cause of action, and the repetition of the allegations by the third party goes only to the question of damages. In *Slipper v British Broadcasting Corporation* [1991] 1 QB 283, the plaintiff, a retired police officer, had been the subject of a television programme about attempts to bring the escaped 'Great Train Robber', Ronnie Biggs, back to Britain from Brazil. The plaintiff alleged that the programme portrayed him as an 'incompetent buffoon'. The defendant television company had shown a preview of the programme to an audience of the press and television journalists prior to its broadcast to the public at large. As a result of the preview a number of reviews appeared in newspapers and magazines repeating the defamatory sting of the programme. The plaintiff claimed that passages from several specified newspaper reviews which repeated the allegedly defamatory sting of the film should be taken into account in the assessment of general damages. The defendants applied to have the parts of the claim based on the repetition of the libel struck out. They argued that defendants in a libel action are not liable for the repetition of the libel by a third party who was not their agent unless the third party was authorised to do so, it was intended that the third party do so or the third party was morally bound to do so. The Court of Appeal rejected the defendant's argument that the repetition of a libel was only actionable in these limited circumstances, Slade LJ adopting a test of whether the repetition was reasonably foreseeable.

In *McManus v Beckham* [2002] 1 WLR 2982 Waller LJ thought that the use of the term 'reasonable foreseeability' was 'dangerous' and that there could be situations where the originator of a defamatory statement would not be liable for its foreseeable repetition. But he conceded that it might not be necessary to show that the defendant was actually aware of the risk of repetition, provided a reasonable person would have recognised the risk as significant.

The Court of Appeal was there concerned with an action for slander against the pop-star, Victoria Beckham, wife of the footballer, David Beckham. Whilst in the claimants' shop, which sold celebrity memorabilia, she claimed that an autograph that purported to be her husband's was a fake and said to customers in the shop: 'Excuse me but do not buy any autographs from this shop, they are all fakes. This is not my husband's signature out there.' The incident was later described in a number of press reports. In a preliminary hearing, the question for the Court of Appeal was whether to strike out that part of the statement of claim relating to the stories in the press and the loss which the claimants alleged their business had suffered as a result of the stories. The court denied the striking-out application. Although Waller LJ stated that it was best in such cases not to use a test of foreseeability, Laws LJ considered that this was still the underlying issue, though he conceded that the term might usefully be avoided in the interests of clarity and the jury instructed in more explicit terms. Clarke LJ stated that he saw no disagreement between his two colleagues and concurred with them both.

With new information technologies, the capacity for information to spread rapidly and uncontrollably has increased immeasurably, and the Court of Appeal has ruled that the potential for defamatory statements to 'go viral' on the internet is a legitimate factor to be taken into account in assessing the scope of publication and the damages to which the claimant is entitled (*Cairns v Modi* [2013] 1 WLR 1015 at [27], in the context of liability for a message posted on the Twitter micro-blogging site).

Publication on the Internet: ISPs, Websites and Search Engines

A question that has assumed increasing practical importance in recent times is: who is the publisher of defamatory material posted on the internet? The author, of course—but what about the internet service provider (ISP) hosting the website, or the moderator of a bulletin board or chat room? In *Bunt v Tilley* [2007] 1 WLR 1243 at [23] and [36], Eady J stated:

> [F]or a person to be held responsible there must be knowing involvement in the process of publication of the relevant words. It is not enough that a person merely plays a passive instrumental role in the process . . . [A]n ISP which performs no more than a passive role in facilitating postings on the Internet cannot be deemed to be a publisher at common law.

To the judge, an ISP was no more the publisher of defamatory material passing through its server without its knowledge than a telephone company would be the publisher of a defamatory call, or the postal services of a defamatory letter. In the usual case, 'ISPs do not participate in the process of publication as such but merely act as facilitators . . . They provide a means of transmitting communications without in any way participating in them' (at [9]). Exceptionally, however, the ISP could be held liable at common law if it had been notified of a defamatory posting and so rendered responsible for publication from that moment onwards (see, e.g., *Godfrey v Demon Internet Ltd* [2001] QB 201). In such a case, the ISP might be able to rely upon a defence as a mere 'distributor' of the material in question (see IV.6), but a 'facilitator' is not a publisher at all, and so has no need of a defence.

Since August 2002, the ISP has also been entitled to rely on the defences that it was the 'mere conduit' for the transmission of the defamatory material, that the transmission of the material resulted from automatic 'caching' and that it was merely hosting material which it did not know, and had no reason to know, was unlawful (Electronic Commerce (EC Directive) Regulations 2002, regs. 17–19).

The position of internet search engines is similar but not completely analogous. In *Metropolitan International Schools Ltd v Designtechnica Corp* [2011] 1 WLR 1743 Google was sued in respect of allegedly defamatory statements returned as search results in searches using the claimant's trading name. Like other search engines, Google uses automatic programmes to monitor the internet and to identify and index publicly accessible web pages ('web crawling'). When a user searches for a particular term, the 'hits' are ranked and displayed with a hyperlink to each webpage identified and a 'snippet' of text drawn from it. In the case under discussion, the claimant complained of text shown in snippets drawn from a thread started by a user in a forum on a website hosted by another defendant in the same proceedings. Rejecting the claim, Eady J extended his own analysis in *Bunt v Tilley*: it was unrealistic to attribute responsibility for the publication to Google because, when a web user initiates a search, the results that are posted are entirely the work of the automated web-crawling programme, and there is no human intervention in the process at all (at [50]–[53]). Though Google might have been liable had it failed to take adequate steps once informed of the defamatory snippets, Eady J considered that its 'take down' policy and its efforts to block URLs that were the source of the defamatory material were sufficient to negate any suggestion that it had acquiesced in the material's continued publication (at [54]–[64]).

Cf. *Tamiz v Google Inc* [2013] 1 WLR 2151, where the Court of Appeal ruled that Google's web-log hosting service, Blogger, does not play a purely passive role in the publication of material posted on the blogs it hosts, but is actively involved in such publication. On the facts, however, liability was denied on other grounds: see further in IV.6.

On these issues, see further Oster, 'Communication, defamation and liability of intermediaries' (2015) 35 LS 348.

Criticism and Reform of the Multiple Publication Rule

Under the common law, a fresh publication would occur every time already published material was accessed, but this 'multiple publication' rule attracted considerable criticism. In *Loutchansky v Times Newspapers Ltd (No. 2)* [2002] QB 783, the defendant newspaper argued that the court should abandon the traditional rule and adopt the 'single publication' approach that applies in several jurisdictions in the United States. Consequently, an article stored in an archive would be published once and for all at the time of its initial posting, and would give rise to only one cause of action no matter how many times it was accessed. Any claim brought more than a year after an article was put in the archive would presumptively fall outside the one-year limitation period prescribed for defamation claims. In support of its contention, the defendant newspaper relied on Article 10, ECHR as incorporated in English law by the Human Rights Act 1998. Rejecting the argument, the Court of Appeal found there was no inconsistency between the 'multiple publication' rule and the Convention right to freedom of expression. The traditional rule did not have a 'chilling effect' going beyond what was necessary and proportionate in a democratic society for the protection of reputation. Although the maintenance of archives, whether in hard copy or on the internet, had some social utility, it represented a comparatively insignificant aspect of freedom of expression. In any case, the law of defamation would not necessarily inhibit the responsible maintenance of archives, because attaching an appropriate notice to archive material which was or could be defamatory, so as to warn against treating it as the truth, would normally remove any defamatory sting. The court accepted that permitting an action to be based on the accessing of archive material long after its general publication could be seen to be at odds with some of the reasons for the introduction of a twelve-month limitation period for defamation, but it considered that the scale of the new publication and the injury resulting from it was likely to be modest when compared with the original publication. There was therefore no warrant for radically changing the law of defamation in the manner suggested.

In *Times Newspapers Ltd v United Kingdom* [2009] EMLR 14, the European Court of Human Rights (ECtHR) found no breach of Article 10 of the Convention (freedom of expression) in the *Loutchansky* decision. Agreeing with the Court of Appeal, the ECtHR stated, at [47], that the requirement to publish an appropriate qualification to the archived article where libel proceedings were initiated in respect of the version in print was not a disproportionate interference with the right to freedom of expression. The ECtHR ruled, at [48], that no question of a potentially ceaseless liability for defamation arose on the facts, as the libel claim regarding the archive was brought while proceedings regarding the print version were underway, but it cautioned that 'libel proceedings brought against a newspaper after a significant lapse of time may well, in the absence of exceptional circumstances, give rise to a disproportionate interference with press freedom under Article 10.'

The multiple publication rule was subsequently addressed in a Ministry of Justice consultation paper (Ministry of Justice, *Defamation and the internet: the multiple publication rule*, CP20/09, 2009). One option considered, as an alternative to introducing a single-publication rule, was to extend the defence of qualified privilege to publications in online archives outside the one-year limitation period for the initial publication, unless the publisher refuses or neglects to update the electronic version, on request, with a reasonable letter or statement by the claimant by way of explanation or contradiction. The following year, a Parliamentary committee recommended the introduction of a one-year limitation period on actions brought in respect of publications on the internet (House of Commons Culture, Media and Sport Committee, *Press Standards, Privacy and Libel*, HC (2009–10)

362-I, para. 230). The committee proposed that the limitation period should be extended if the claimant could not reasonably have been aware of the publication's existence. After the expiry of the limitation period, the claimant would be debarred from recovering damages in respect of the publication but would be entitled to obtain a court order to correct any defamatory statement.

The government subsequently decided to adopt the proposal of a single-publication rule (Ministry of Justice, *Draft Defamation Bill Consultation* (Cm. 8020, 2011), para. 70ff). Implementing this reform, s. 8 of the Defamation Act 2013 now provides:

8 Single publication rule

(1) This section applies if a person—(a) publishes a statement to the public ('the first publication'), and (b) subsequently publishes (whether or not to the public) that statement or a statement which is substantially the same.
(2) In subsection (1) 'publication to the public' includes publication to a section of the public.
(3) For the purposes of section 4A of the Limitation Act 1980 (time limit for actions for defamation etc) any cause of action against the person for defamation in respect of the subsequent publication is to be treated as having accrued on the date of the first publication.
(4) This section does not apply in relation to the subsequent publication if the manner of that publication is materially different from the manner of the first publication.
(5) In determining whether the manner of a subsequent publication is materially different from the manner of the first publication, the matters to which the court may have regard include (amongst other matters)—
　(a) the level of prominence that a statement is given;
　(b) the extent of the subsequent publication. . . .

Do you agree with the government that a reform of this nature was preferable to the alternative of maintaining the multiple-publication rule but providing the publisher with a defence of non-culpable republication where the claim is brought more than a year after the initial publication? Under s. 8, what incentive is there for the publisher of an archive to correct factually wrong and defamatory statements in the archived material? For criticism of the reform and advocacy of the alternative approach see Mullis and Scott, 'Worth the Candle? The Government's Draft Defamation Bill' (2011) 3 J Media L 1 at 13–15; *id.*, 'Tilting at Windmills: the Defamation Act 2013' (2014) 77 MLR 87 at 102–4.

iv. Defamation: Defences

A number of the general defences to liability in tort also apply in relation to actions in defamation (e.g. consent, on which see *Monson v Tussauds Ltd* [1894] 1 QB 671) but here the focus is upon those defences which are peculiar to that cause of action: (1) truth, (2) honest opinion, (3) privilege (both absolute and qualified), (4) publication on matter of public interest, (5) offer of amends and (6) innocent dissemination.

For a classification of the defences according to whether they (i) exclude unlawfulness (e.g. truth and honest opinion), (ii) exclude blameworthiness (e.g. publication on matter of public interest and innocent dissemination), or (iii) operate despite the injury being unlawful and blameworthy (e.g. qualified privilege, which the author considers anomalous and thinks should be abolished), see Descheemaeker, 'Mapping Defamation Defences' (2015) 78 MLR 641.

1. Truth

A defendant may 'justify' a defamatory allegation by proving its truth in all material respects. Defamatory statements are presumed to be false and the burden of proving their truth lies on the defendant, contrary to the law's general approach of placing the burden of establishing the principal elements of the cause of action on the claimant. Truth is an absolute defence whatever the defendant's motive, save where publication is contrary to the Rehabilitation of Offenders Act 1974 (considered later in this section). It is immaterial that the defendant acted maliciously in a deliberate effort to harm the claimant. Conversely, if the statement should turn out to be false, it is no defence that the defendant took all reasonable steps to establish its veracity. It is equally irrelevant whether or not the publication was in the public interest, for the English law of defamation is concerned only with false imputations against a person's reputation, not with unwarranted invasions of privacy.

Traditionally, these principles were embodied in the common law defence of 'justification', but this was replaced in 2013 by a new statutory defence of 'truth'.

Defamation Act 2013

2 Truth

(1) It is a defence to an action for defamation for the defendant to show that the imputation conveyed by the statement complained of is substantially true.

(2) Subsection (3) applies in an action for defamation if the statement complained of conveys two or more distinct imputations.

(3) If one or more of the imputations is not shown to be substantially true, the defence under this section does not fail if, having regard to the imputations which are shown to be substantially true, the imputations which are not shown to be substantially true do not seriously harm the claimant's reputation.

(4) The common law defence of justification is abolished and, accordingly, section 5 of the Defamation Act 1952 (justification) is repealed.

COMMENTARY

At common law, the test was whether the allegation was 'true in substance and in fact' (*Sutherland v Stopes* [1925] AC 47); minor inaccuracies would not preclude the defence. Section 2 of the 2013 Act was intended broadly to reflect the common law position, and the statutory phrase 'substantially true' bears the same meaning as the words had at common law (*Serafin v Malkiewicz* [2017] EWHC 2992 (QB) at [183], per Jay J). The Act renames the defence in the interests of transparency and clarifies certain aspects where problems have arisen.

According to the classic dictum of Burrough J in *Edwards v Bell* (1824) 1 Bing 403 at 409:

> It is sufficient if the substance of the libellous statement be justified . . . As much must be justified as meets the sting of the charge, and if anything be contained in a charge which does not add to the sting of it, that need not be justified.

Whether a defendant draws the sting of an allegation depends on what the court considers the allegation's 'gravamen' or 'real thrust'. Every case turns on its own facts. In *Alexander v North Eastern Railway Co* (1865) 6 B & S 340, 122 ER 1221, the defendants had published at their stations a notice which stated that the plaintiff had been caught riding without a valid ticket and had refused to pay the fare, and had subsequently been convicted by the magistrates, who sentenced him to pay a fine of £1 (plus costs) or suffer three weeks' imprisonment. In fact, the plaintiff had only been sentenced to fourteen days' imprisonment in default of payment of the fine. The plaintiff complained of the overstatement whose effect, he argued, was to make his offence appear more reprehensible than the justices had deemed it. The jury found for the defendants. But there was a different conclusion in a rather similar case decided shortly afterwards. In *Gwynn v SE Railway* (1868) 18 LT 738, the statement was that the plaintiff was sentenced to a fine of 1s or to three days' imprisonment with hard labour in default for travelling without a ticket. In fact, the allegation of hard labour was false. The jury found for the plaintiff and awarded damages of £250. It seems that the words must, in the opinion of the jury, have produced a wholly false impression of the gravity of the offence committed (see *Gatley*, para. 11.8n). See also *Weaver v Lloyd* (1824) 1 B & C 678, 130 ER 162 (allegations of various acts of cruelty to a horse; the Court of King's Bench stated that 'the statement that [the plaintiff] knocked out the horse's eye imputed a much greater degree of cruelty than a charge of beating him on other parts of the body' (at 679)).

A more modern example is provided by *Grobbelaar v News Group Newspapers Ltd* [2002] 1 WLR 3024, involving a well-known footballer who played in goal for Liverpool and then Southampton for several years in the 1980s and 1990s. In 1994, one of his associates told a journalist working for the defendants' newspaper, *The Sun*, that Grobbelaar had received money from a betting syndicate in South East Asia for fixing the result of matches in which he was playing. Seeking corroboration, *The Sun* covertly video-and sound-recorded a series of meetings between Grobbelaar and their informant. During these meetings, Grobbelaar confessed to having taken money for losing matches in the past and took money offered by the informant in return for fixing matches in the future. But subsequently, on being confronted by *The Sun* with the allegations of match-fixing, he denied any wrongdoing. The next day, the newspaper printed a front-page exclusive under the headline 'Grobbelaar took bribes to fix games', following this up with relentless coverage in the following days. Soon afterwards, Grobbelaar issued a writ against the defendant publishers, claiming damages for defamation. Before his action could proceed, however, Grobbelaar was arrested by the police in connection with the allegations made by *The Sun* and charged with criminal conspiracy and acceptance of a bribe. He stood trial twice on these charges, was found not guilty of conspiracy by a jury, and was acquitted of the count of bribe-taking after two juries were split on the issue and the prosecution declined to pursue the charge further. Subsequently, Grobbelaar pleaded guilty to a disciplinary charge of assisting in betting brought against him by the Football Association.

In his resumed defamation action, Grobbelaar succeeded in establishing liability at trial and was awarded £85,000 in compensatory damages. The defendants' main defence was justification (truth), which they pursued on appeal to the Court of Appeal, then the House of Lords. Before the Law Lords, it was agreed that there were two aspects of the defamatory allegations *The Sun* had made: first, that Grobbelaar had taken bribes (which could not be disputed); secondly, that he had fixed or attempted to fix the results of games in which he played (which could not be proved). The main dispute between the parties was which of these aspects conveyed the sting of the statements. Ruling in favour of Grobbelaar, a majority of the House of Lords held that the jury could not be criticised for taking the view that the sting was the accusation of match fixing. Lord Hobhouse commented (at 3043):

Even standing alone, it was a very serious accusation to make against a professional footballer and, if true, completely destructive of his reputation as a professional footballer. A goalkeeper who deliberately lets in goals is betraying the fans and reducing the game to a sham. For myself, I would have been surprised if the jury had come to any other verdict on the justification issue.

However, Grobbelaar's victory was somewhat pyrrhic as the Lords, taking account of the damage done to his reputation by the admitted wrongdoing, reduced the damages to £1, and awarded costs against him too.

Multiple Allegations

In the 2013 Act, s. 2(2) and (3) address the situation where the defendant makes two or more *distinct* imputations against the claimant (in contrast with *Grobbelaar*, where there was *one* imputation albeit with different aspects, and it was left to the jury to determine where exactly the 'sting' lay). In cases of distinct imputations, the common law originally required that, to succeed in a defence of justification, the defendant had to prove the truth of each of the meanings attributed to the words by the judge or jury. However, s. 5 of the Defamation Act 1952 introduced a statutory analogue to the common law's 'sting' doctrine (which applies only to a single defamatory charge) and this has now been reiterated in s. 2(2) and (3). The new Act updates the 1952 terminology but does not effect any substantive change in the law, whose operation may be illustrated by the case of *Robson v News Group Newspapers* [1996] CLY 5660: an unproven allegation that the defendant had defrauded the Department of Social Security was held there not to materially injure the plaintiff's reputation having regard to the effect of the distinct true allegation that he had been convicted of a £4 million mortgage fraud.

Specific Instances of General Misconduct

Allegations of general bad conduct are not justified by proof of a single instance of bad behaviour, so to call a person a 'libellous journalist' is not substantiated by a libel verdict against him on a single occasion (*Wakley v Cooke* (1849) 4 Exch 511). Conversely, a defamatory statement alleging that the claimant did a specific thing cannot be justified by evidence of other misconduct on their part. In *Bookbinder v Tebbit* [1989] 1 WLR 640 where the defendant, chairman of the Conservative Party, had alleged at a public meeting that the plaintiff, leader of a Labour-controlled council, had squandered £50,000 of public money in printing the caption 'Support Nuclear Free Zones' on all its school stationery, the Court of Appeal held that it was not possible to justify that allegation by pointing to other alleged instances of squandering public funds. But in *Williams v Reason* [1988] 1 WLR 96 a newspaper article containing an allegation that the plaintiff had, in breach of the code of conduct governing amateur rugby players, written a book for financial gain was held capable of bearing the wider meaning of a charge of 'shamateurism', and evidence that he had accepted 'boot money' was admissible by way of justification (i.e. truth). In such matters, it is not possible to give any guidance more specific than that the meaning of the words complained of must always be assessed in the light of the publication as a whole, and the precise context and circumstances of its communication.

A further complication, however, is that specific allegations contained in the same publication may share a common sting, rather than conveying distinct imputations. In such a case, s. 2(3) will not apply but it seems that the common sting may still be justified notwithstanding the defendant's failure to prove the truth of every specific allegation. Indeed the defendant may be able to make out a defence of truth by proving the veracity of allegations contained in the publication even if these are not mentioned in the claimant's particulars of claim, which focus only on allegations that the defendant cannot prove (*Polly Peck (Holdings) plc v Trelford* [1986] 1 QB 1000). The principle was applied in *Khashoggi v IPC Magazines Ltd* [1986] 1 WLR 1412. The claimant was featured in an article in *Woman's Own* headed 'What makes you divorce the richest man in the world'. The article contained what was described in the Court of Appeal as a highly coloured account of her marriage to an international arms dealer which was 'capable of carrying the meaning that she was a lady of considerable sexual enthusiasm'. In the article was an allegation that the last straw for her husband was an affair that she was having with a friend, the unnamed President of a nation state. At an interim hearing, the Court of Appeal held that the defendants were entitled to raise a '*Polly Peck* form of justification' on the basis that the sting of the article was promiscuity generally and it was not in the circumstances more defamatory to allege an extra-marital affair with one person rather than another; the defendants might therefore adduce evidence to justify that common sting even though they might not be able to prove the particular affair complained of. (The immediate significance of this ruling was that the defendants, simply by pleading a possible defence of justification, were able to resist the plaintiff's attempt to win an interim injunction against publication under the rule in *Bonnard v Perryman* [1891] 2 Ch 269: see V.2(b).)

A useful summary of the—rather complicated—principles applicable in this context was provided by Laws LJ in *Rothschild v Associated Newspapers Ltd* [2013] EMLR 18 at [24]:

These authorities establish a series of interlocking principles. They are: (1) A justification defence will run if the defendant shows that what he has alleged is substantially true. This general rule is given more concrete effect by the other principles. Thus it is limited by principle (2): a libel cannot be justified by proof of obliquity on the claimant's part which is unconnected with the accusation complained of. (3) However a defendant is entitled to justify a common sting derived from parts of a publication, taken as a whole – but there must be a common sting. (4) An instance of (3) arises where a general charge is justified by proved examples, even where the published example is unproved. But (5) in such a case the sting of the instance or instances which are proved must in essence be as sharp as the published, unproved libel: so that the claimant has no more reputation to lose by force only of the published, false accusation.

The 'Repetition Rule'

Section 2(1) attempts to encapsulate the common law's 'repetition rule' by requiring a focus on *the imputation* conveyed by the defendant's statement rather than its literal meaning. Where the defendant reports another person's beliefs or suspicions, their words may be treated as direct statements relating to the subject-matter to which the other was referring, in which case they can rely upon the defence of truth only if they show that the underlying facts are true ('*Truth' (NZ) Ltd v Holloway* [1960] 1 WLR 997). It is no defence that the defendant was merely repeating what they had been told (*Stern v Piper* [1997] QB 123 at 128, per Hirst LJ), for '[i]f one repeats a rumour one adds one's own authority to it and implies that it is well founded, that is to say, that it is true' (*Lewis v Daily Telegraph* [1964] AC 234 at 275, per Lord Hodson). Nevertheless, in *Aspro Travel Ltd v Owners Abroad Group* [1996] 1 WLR 132 the Court of Appeal accepted that there might be 'circumstances in which the existence of a rumour entitles a person to repeat that rumour even before he satisfies himself that the rumour is true and that in such circumstances it is possible to plead in justification that there were in truth such rumours' (at 140, per Schiemann LJ). In what circumstances might this be so? If the question is whether the circumstances warranted repetition of the rumour, would it be better to treat this as a matter of qualified privilege so that the defendant's motives can be taken into account? (See IV.3(b)).

The key question in all such cases is how the imputation conveyed by the defendant's words is to be construed. A statement that a person is under suspicion is not necessarily an affirmation of their guilt, but it usually implies that there are reasonable grounds for suspicion (*Lewis v Daily Telegraph* [1964] AC 234 at 275, per Lord Hodson), corresponding to 'Chase level 3' as described earlier in III.1(d). If so, the defendant can rely on truth only if they can prove that the claimant in fact acted in such a way as to cause a reasonable observer to be suspicious (*Shah v Standard Chartered Bank* [1999] QB 241). Where the defendant reports the issuing of a writ against the claimant, indicating what the claimant is alleged to have done wrong, the court must ascertain the report's true meaning before it can be determined whether or not the issuing of the writ itself establishes the defence (*Cadam v Beaverbrook Newspapers Ltd* [1959] 1 QB 413). In *Stern v Piper* [1997] QB 123, however, the Court of Appeal struck out a defence of truth where the defendant's newspaper had quoted from a witness statement which was to be relied upon in debt proceedings against the plaintiff. It was not enough that the allegations in question had indeed been taken from a witness statement as they were still essentially hearsay. The court attached particular importance to the one-sidedness of the report and the undesirability of private court documents being disseminated to the public at large. It may be noted that, in such a case, alternative defences may be available, including the statutory privilege applying to certain reports of court proceedings (Defamation Act 1996, ss. 14–15; see further IV.3(a) and IV.3(c)) and the recently recognised defence of 'reportage' (discussed later in IV.4).

Allegations of Criminal Conduct

If the charge is that the claimant is guilty of a criminal offence, the defendant need only point to the fact of the claimant's conviction for the offence by way of justification: conviction is conclusive evidence that the claimant has in fact committed it (Civil Evidence Act 1968, s. 13). However, the public interest in the rehabilitation of offenders has led to the introduction of a statutory provision to the effect that one who maliciously publishes details of a 'spent' conviction cannot rely upon the defence of justification (Rehabilitation of Offenders Act 1974, s. 8; a conviction becomes spent, except in the case of very serious criminal conduct, by the lapse of a period of time whose length is determined by the heaviness of the sentence imposed). The potential liability of the person who maliciously publishes true details of a spent conviction is the one (rather limited) exception to the rule that truth is a total defence to an action in defamation.

Do you agree with Descheemaeker, '"Veritas non est defamatio"? Truth as a Defence in the Law of Defamation' (2011) 31 LS 1 at 17 that this exception should be abolished because the correct cause of action in such a case should be the interference with privacy, not defamation?

2. Honest Opinion

Like truth, the defence of honest opinion, previously known as 'fair comment', is a complete defence to an action for defamation. According to Scott LJ, 'the right of "fair comment" . . . is one of the fundamental rights of free speech and writing which are so dear to the British nation, and it is of vital importance to the rule of law on which we depend for our personal freedom that the courts should preserve the right of "fair comment" undiminished and unimpaired' (*Lyon v Daily Telegraph* [1943] KB 746 at 753). In contrast with the defence of (qualified) privilege, the defence is not limited to those who have a duty to publish the imputations in question or an interest in so doing; any person is at liberty to express an opinion. However, the defence applies only to expressions of opinion, and not to statements of fact.

In 2013, the defence was renamed and placed on a new statutory footing.

Defamation Act 2013

3 Honest opinion

(1) It is a defence to an action for defamation for the defendant to show that the following conditions are met.

(2) The first condition is that the statement complained of was a statement of opinion.

(3) The second condition is that the statement complained of indicated, whether in general or specific terms, the basis of the opinion.

(4) The third condition is that an honest person could have held the opinion on the basis of—
   (a) any fact which existed at the time the statement complained of was published;
   (b) anything asserted to be a fact in a privileged statement published before the statement complained of.

(5) The defence is defeated if the claimant shows that the defendant did not hold the opinion.

(6) Subsection (5) does not apply in a case where the statement complained of was published by the defendant but made by another person ('the author'); and in such a case the defence is defeated if the claimant shows that the defendant knew or ought to have known that the author did not hold the opinion.

(7) For the purposes of subsection (4)(b) a statement is a 'privileged statement' if the person responsible for its publication would have one or more of the following defences if an action for defamation were brought in respect of it—
   (a) a defence under section 4 (publication on matter of public interest);
   (b) a defence under section 6 (peer-reviewed statement in scientific or academic journal);
   (c) a defence under section 14 of the Defamation Act 1996 (reports of court proceedings protected by absolute privilege);
   (d) a defence under section 15 of that Act (other reports protected by qualified privilege).

(8) The common law defence of fair comment is abolished and, accordingly, section 6 of the Defamation Act 1952 (fair comment) is repealed.

COMMENTARY

The three conditions for the application of the defence as set out in the Act (s. 3(2)-(4)) are not exactly those proposed by the Ministry of Justice in its prior Consultation Paper (*Draft Defamation Bill Consultation*, Cm 8020, March 2011, paras 33ff). The most notable change in the Act is to dispense with the traditional common law requirement that the opinion or comment be on a matter of public interest. In the Ministry's draft Bill, sub-cl. (3) originally read: 'Condition 2 is that the opinion is on a matter of public interest.' In its Consultation Paper, the Ministry explained its thinking at the time:

41. **Condition 2** reflects the current law by providing that the matter in respect of which the opinion is expressed must be a matter of public interest. However, in *Spiller [Joseph v Spiller* [2011] 1 AC 852] the Supreme Court suggested that there may be a case for widening the scope of the defence by removing this requirement. The arguments on this are finely balanced. On the one hand, the view could be taken that people should be free to express an opinion, without risk of liability, on any matter and not only things confined to subjects of public interest. We also understand that the question of whether a matter is of public interest or not is rarely an issue in practice, and that the definition has been substantially broadened in recent years. There is also the potential for confusion in the light of the proposed introduction of a new public interest defence, as the role of the public interest and the consideration involved may be different in the two contexts.

42. Set against this, removal of the public interest requirement would widen the defence so that it would protect expressions of opinion on matters which are private in nature and, while of interest to the public, could not be justified as being of public benefit to be aired (for example a criticism of how a person is bringing up their children). Care would also be needed to ensure Article 8 rights would not be infringed. In addition, the fact that the definition of what is in the public interest has been widely interpreted means that it is not obvious that the current position represents an inappropriate restriction on freedom of speech. On balance, a provision requiring the opinion to be on a matter of public interest has been included in the draft clause . . .

Do you agree that the defence of honest opinion should be available even for matters that are not of public interest?

Condition 1: A Statement of Opinion rather than Fact

Under the Act, as under the previous common law, the defendant's allegations must appear as an opinion rather than as a statement of fact. The distinction turns on not just the content of the allegations but also their context (see *Telnikoff v Matusevich* [1991] 2 AC 343), as well as the manner of their expression (e.g. whether they are prefaced by words like 'it seems' or 'in my opinion').

Allegations of specific wrongdoing, or even that there are reasonable grounds to suspect such wrongdoing, will usually fall on the side of fact rather than opinion (*Wasserman v Freilich* [2016] EWHC 312 (QB) at [22], per Eady J). But the courts have sometimes adopted a rather expansive approach to what constitutes opinion or comment. This may include, for example, an inference drawn in circumstances where it is clear that the publisher was not in a position to know, or to establish definitively, that it represented the true position and so could only be speculating (*ibid.*, at [21], citing *Branson v Bower* [2002] QB 737). The boundary was pushed to its limit in *British Chiropractic Association v Singh* [2011] 1 WLR 133, where the claimant sued a scientist who wrote a highly sceptical newspaper article about the alleged health benefits of chiropractics, stating that there was 'not a jot of evidence' to support the claimant's advocacy of its techniques. The Court of Appeal ruled that this was a comment, not a statement of fact. In context, the words asserted only a lack of worthwhile or reliable evidence, and thus expressed a value judgement. The outcome seems desirable, because it is surely in the general interest for the public to be informed about genuine scientific concerns relating to alternative therapies. But one feels that the court manipulated the fact/opinion distinction in order to reach the result it desired, which can now be achieved more transparently through the s. 4 defence of publication on matter of public interest.

Condition 2: Indication of the Basis of the Opinion

Condition 2, in its final form, restates a requirement of the common law defence that was recognised in *Kemsley v Foot* [1952] AC 345 and reconsidered in *Joseph v Spiller* [2011] 1 AC 852. In the latter case, Lord Phillips summarised the arguments in favour of the requirement:

> 101. There are a number of reasons why the subject matter of the comment must be identified by the comment, at least in general terms. The underlying justification for the creation of the fair comment exception was the desirability that a person should be entitled to express his view freely about a matter of public interest. That remains a justification for the defence, albeit that the concept of public interest has been greatly widened. If the subject matter of the comment is not apparent from the comment this justification for the defence will be lacking. The defamatory comment will be wholly unfocused.
>
> 102. It is a requirement of the defence that it should be based on facts that are true. This requirement is better enforced if the comment has to identify, at least in general terms, the matters on which it is based. The same is true of the requirement that the defendant's comment should be honestly founded on facts that are true.
>
> 103. More fundamentally, even if it is not practicable to require that those reading criticism should be able to evaluate the criticism, it may be thought desirable that the commentator should be required to identify at least the general nature of the facts that have led him to make the criticism. If he states that a barrister is 'a disgrace to his profession' he should make it clear whether this is because he does not deal honestly with the court, or does not read his papers thoroughly, or refuses to accept legally aided work, or is constantly late for court, or wears dirty collars and bands.

In the same case, the Supreme Court rejected the imposition of the further requirement that the indication of the basis for the opinion should be sufficient to enable it to be evaluated by those to whom it is communicated. The Court considered that a limitation of that nature would rob the defence of much of its efficiency. As Lord Phillips noted, at [99], '[t]oday the internet has made it possible for the man in the street to make public comment about others in a manner that did not exist when the principles of the law of fair comment were developed, and millions take advantage of that opportunity'. In his view, shared by the other Justices, it would be wrong to make the defence unavailable to the poster of a derogatory comment who failed to append a detailed explanation of the facts on which it was based so as to enable readers to evaluate it (*ibid.*; see also at [131], per Lord Walker).

In the Ministry of Justice's draft Bill, there was no requirement that the statement should indicate the basis of the opinion expressed, even if only in general terms. Instead, the defence was to be limited to matters of public interest. As already noted, the public interest requirement was later dropped, and the new formulation of Condition 2 may be seen—in loose terms—as the trade-off. Its inclusion seems a desirable safeguard that imposes and encourages a minimum standard of reasoned debate (Mullis and Scott (2011) 3 J Media L 1 at 11), while discouraging gratuitous vilification.

Condition 3: A Basis in Fact

At common law, the defendant was required to establish the truth of every factual matter upon which the publication purported to comment. But s. 6 of the Defamation Act 1952 relieved the defendant from having to substantiate each factual allegation individually, so long as such allegations as were proved to be true formed a sufficient basis for his comment. The new Defamation Act of 2013 seeks only to consolidate and simplify this approach (Consultation Paper, para. 43). In this respect, it is notable that the factual basis that must be indicated to satisfy Condition 2 need not be the same as the fact ultimately relied on to satisfy Condition 3, which the defendant need not have known at the time of the publication, provided that it existed at that time.

Section 3(4)(b) covers the case where the defendant expresses an opinion about a prior statement that is itself covered by an absolute or qualified privilege (e.g. a report of judicial or legislative proceedings: see IV.3, immediately following) but cannot demonstrate the truth of facts asserted in that statement. One difficulty that may arise in practice is that the defendant may not be able to tell from the report itself whether or not the conditions that attach to the exercise of the privilege (e.g. absence of malice) have been satisfied. It seems undesirable for the honest opinion defence to turn on factors beyond the defendant's control that he cannot reasonably be expected to know of.

The Act encapsulates the common law's requirement that the comment should be 'fair' by imposing the condition that an honest person could have held the opinion expressed on the basis of the existing or asserted fact relied upon. In truth, the adjective 'fair' added little to the common law defence. The test of fairness was simply: 'would any honest man, however prejudiced he might be, or however exaggerated or obstinate his views, have written this criticism' (*Turner v Metro-Goldwyn-Mayer* [1950] 1 All ER 449 at 461, per Lord Porter). The defence has always protected the 'crank' as well as those commenting intelligently on matters of public concern. In *Reynolds v Times Newspapers Ltd* [2001] 2 AC 127 at 193, Lord Nicholls noted that the latitude applied in determining whether a comment was fair was so extensive that 'time has come to recognise that in this context the epithet "fair" is now meaningless and misleading'. Do you think that the reference to 'an honest person' in s. 4 of the new Act provides a test that is any more meaningful?

Defence Defeated if Opinion not Actually Held

The common law defence was defeated by 'malice', a word whose interpretation gave rise to considerable difficulties. Over time, the courts accepted that the meaning of the term was to be construed more narrowly in this context than in the defence of qualified privilege: 'the only touchstone is that of honesty' and malice was not established by evidence that the defendant was prompted by the dominant motive of injuring the claimant (*Branson v Bower* [2002] QB 737 at [7]–[8], per Eady J). Section 3(5) confirms honesty as the test and avoids the potentially misleading reference to malice. Section 3(6) adapts the test where the defendant has quoted an opinion expressed by another person: in such a case, it is immaterial whether the defendant shared the same opinion, and relevant only whether he knew or ought to have known that the author did not hold the opinion.

3. Privilege

In certain situations, the law's concern for free discourse outweighs the need to protect personal reputations. An *absolute privilege* arises where the occasion demands utter freedom in the communication of views and information (e.g. in Parliament or in a court of law). A *qualified privilege* arises where the need for such freedom is not quite so great but nevertheless warrants some protection from the threat of litigation that is not allowed on non-privileged occasions. The reason why the privilege is described as qualified in these situations is that its effectiveness is conditional upon its bona fide exercise in the absence of malice: if the claimant can prove that the defendant was actuated by malice, the privilege is withdrawn. By way of contrast, an absolute privilege is effective no matter what the defendant's motivation.

(a) Absolute Privilege

The principal examples of absolute privilege are:

(i) Statements in Parliament, Art IX of the Bill of Rights 1688 stating '[t]hat the Freedome of Speech and Debates or Proceedings in Parlyament ought not to be impeached or questioned in any Court or Place out of Parlyament.' According to the Privy Council, 'the basic concept underlying Article 9 . . . [is] the need to ensure so far as possible that a member of the legislature and witnesses before Committees of the House can speak freely without fear that what they say will later be held against them in the courts' (*Prebble v Television New Zealand Ltd* [1995] 1 AC 321 at 334, per Lord Browne-Wilkinson).

(ii) Reports, etc., ordered to be published by Parliament (Parliamentary Papers Act 1840 s. 1).

(iii) Statements made in the course of, or for the purpose of, judicial proceedings (including proceedings before tribunals), extending to the initial complaint made by a purported victim of crime to the police, even if no prosecution ensues: see *Westcott v Westcott* [2009] QB 407. Where prosecution does ensue, however, there may be liability in the separate tort of malicious prosecution—provided the complainant was actively instrumental in setting the law in motion against the claimant and acted with malice.

(iv) Fair and accurate contemporaneous reports of court proceedings in the United Kingdom, in the courts of another country or territory, or in an international court or tribunal set up by the UN Security Council or by international agreement (Defamation Act 1996, s. 14, as amended by Defamation Act 2013, s. 7(1), which extends the privilege to reports of court proceedings in all countries and territories). The provision does not apply to a report published subsequently, but this may be covered by the qualified privilege under s. 15 of the 1996 Act (discussed later).

(v) Communications made by a minister or other officer of state to another in the course of their official duty (*Chatterton v Secretary of State for India* [1895] 2 QB 189).

In *A v United Kingdom* (2003) 36 EHRR 51, the European Court of Human Rights rejected a challenge to the absolute privilege applying to statements in Parliament. The privilege violated neither the right to respect to private life (Article 8) of the applicant, named in Parliament by her MP as a 'neighbour from hell', nor her right of access to a court (Article 6). It pursued the legitimate aim of protecting free parliamentary speech and could not be regarded as a disproportionate restriction on the applicant's rights.

(b) Qualified Privilege at Common Law

Reynolds v Times Newspapers Ltd [2001] 2 AC 127

Lord Nicholls of Birkenhead

There are occasions when the person to whom a statement is made has a special interest in learning the honestly held views of another person, even if those views are defamatory of someone else and cannot be proved to be true. When the interest is of sufficient importance to outweigh the need to protect reputation, the occasion is regarded as privileged. Sometimes the need for uninhibited expression is of such a high order that the occasion attracts absolute privilege, as with statements made by judges or advocates or witnesses in the course of judicial proceedings. More usually, the privilege is qualified in that it can be defeated if the plaintiff proves the defendant was actuated by malice . . .

Over the years the courts have held that many common form situations are privileged. Classic instances are employment references, and complaints made or information given to the police or appropriate authorities regarding suspected crimes. The courts have always emphasised that the categories established by the authorities are not exhaustive. The list is not closed. The established categories are no more than applications, in particular circumstances, of the underlying principle of public policy. The underlying principle is conventionally stated in words to the effect that there must exist between the maker of the statement and the recipient some duty or interest in the making of the communication. Lord Atkinson's dictum, in *Adam v Ward* [1917] AC 309, 334, is much quoted:

> a privileged occasion is . . . an occasion where the person who makes a communication has an interest or a duty, legal, social, or moral, to make it to the person to whom it is made, and the person to whom it is so made has a corresponding interest or duty to receive it. This reciprocity is essential.

The requirement that both the maker of the statement and the recipient must have an interest or duty draws attention to the need to have regard to the position of both parties when deciding whether an occasion is privileged. But this should not be allowed to obscure the rationale of the underlying public interest on which privilege is founded. The essence of this defence lies in the law's recognition of the need, in the public interest, for a particular recipient to receive frank and uninhibited communication of particular information from a particular source. That is the end the law is concerned to attain. The protection afforded to the maker of the statement is the means by which the law seeks to achieve that end. Thus the court has to assess whether, in the public interest, the publication should be protected in the absence of malice.

In determining whether an occasion is regarded as privileged the court has regard to all the circumstances: see, for example, the explicit statement of Lord Buckmaster LC in *London Association for Protection of Trade v Greenlands Ltd* [1916] 2 AC 15, 23 ('every circumstance associated with the origin and publication of the defamatory matter'). And circumstances must be viewed with today's eyes. The circumstances in which the public interest requires a communication to be protected in the absence of malice depend upon current social conditions. The requirements at the close of the twentieth century may not be the same as those of earlier centuries or earlier decades of this century.

COMMENTARY

Lord Nicholls here summarises the traditional common law approach to privilege—in the course of a decision whose chief significance was to recognise a new form of qualified privilege for media reports on matters of public concern, subject to a test of 'responsible publication'. This '*Reynolds* defence' has now been placed on an independent statutory basis (see IV.4). The traditional common law form of qualified privilege, based on a reciprocity of duty or interest as between the maker of the statement and the recipient, remains untouched by this reform.

Reciprocity of Duty or Interest

For the common law defence, the determination of whether a duty to communicate exists is solely for the judge. The opinion of the maker of the statement is not relevant: honest belief in the existence of a duty cannot create a duty to communicate. The duty need not be legal; a moral or social duty will suffice. The classic statement of the relevant principles is that of Lindley LJ in *Stuart v Bell* [1891] 2 QB 341 at 350:

> [T]he question of moral or social duty being for the judge, each judge must decide it as best he can for himself. I take moral or social duty to mean a duty recognized by English people of ordinary intelligence and moral principle, but at the same time not a duty enforceable by legal proceedings, whether civil or criminal.

A duty to communicate may arise from another person's request for information, at least where that person has an interest in the matter under consideration (e.g. in the case of an employment reference). But a request is not necessary, and it has been found for instance that a close relative is justified in writing an unsolicited letter of warning to a widow who is engaged to be married to a man he considers an unprincipled trickster, provided he acts in good faith (*Todd v Hawkins* (1837) 8 C & P 88).

It is well established that the existence of an *interest* in communicating may also be sufficient to raise the privilege. For instance, it is enough that the defendant is responding reasonably after being subjected to a verbal attack. As Lord Oaksey explained in *Turner v Metro-Goldwyn-Mayer Pictures Ltd* [1950] 1 All ER 449 at 470:

> [T]here is . . . an analogy between the criminal law of self defence and a man's right to defend himself against written or verbal [sic] attacks. In both cases he is entitled . . . to defend himself effectively, and he only loses the protection of the law if he goes beyond defence and proceeds to offence.

Accordingly, a person defamed in a newspaper has a right to respond via the letters' page, even if this involves impugning the reputation of the person making the attack or a third party with whom the claimant has been confused (see *Watts v Times Newspapers Ltd* [1997] QB 650).

It is also considered that officers of a company have a common interest in communicating to each other information about matters affecting the company's business (see *Watt v Longsdon* [1930] 1 KB 130, noted later in this commentary).

Excess of Privilege

For the common law defence, even if a reciprocal duty or interest arises, publication beyond the class of interested parties will be regarded as being in excess of privilege. Complaints, grievances and allegations of wrongdoing must be addressed to the proper authorities (e.g., in the case of complaints against a firm of solicitors, the Law Society or Ministry of Justice: see *Beach v Freeson* [1972] 1 QB 14) and must generally be investigated before being circulated to a wider class of person. In *De Buse v McCarthy* [1942] 1 KB 156, it was accepted that a local council had an interest in receiving a report from one of its committees which stated that certain council employees were suspected of the theft of petrol from a council depot. But the privilege did not extend to the publication of the employees' names and the suspicions against them in notices setting out the agenda for the meeting which were sent to and posted in public libraries. Ratepayers could not be regarded as interested in the domestic deliberations of the council before they had resulted in practical action or resolution; nor could the council have a duty or interest to tell ratepayers of their mere suspicions.

In the celebrated case of *Watt v Longsdon* [1930] 1 KB 130, the defendant, the director of a company, received a letter from an employee making allegations of immorality, drunkenness and dishonesty on the part of the plaintiff, who was the managing director of the company abroad. Without obtaining any corroboration of the contents of the letter, and without communicating with the plaintiff, the defendant showed the letter first to the chairman of the board of directors and then to the plaintiff's wife. The allegations in the letter were unfounded, but the defendant believed them to be true. The Court of Appeal held that the communication to the chairman of the board of directors was privileged but that the communication to the wife was not. The court emphasised that there was no general rule applicable in such cases, Scrutton LJ commenting (at 150):

It cannot, on the one hand, be the duty even of a friend to communicate all the gossip the friend hears at men's clubs or women's bridge parties to one of the spouses affected. On the other hand, most men would hold that it was the moral duty of a doctor who attended his sister in law, and believed her to be suffering from a miscarriage, for which an absent husband could not be responsible, to communicate that fact to his wife and the husband.

In what circumstances (if any) do you think you would benefit from qualified privilege in telling the spouse of your business colleague about your colleague's suspected infidelity?

Communications by Public Authorities

Where the defendant is a public authority, the application of these principles is made more complex by the requirements of the Human Rights Act 1998. If a statement made by a public authority violates the claimant's right to reputation—which is an aspect of the right to respect for private and family life under Article 8 of the European Convention—that precludes its assertion of a duty to publish, and so excludes the defence of qualified privilege. The issue arose in *Clift v Slough BC* [2011] 1 WLR 1774, where the claimant had got into an angry dispute with a council official, against whom she threatened violence, and the council had responded by placing her on its violent persons register which was circulated amongst council employees. In the claimant's subsequent action for defamation, the council pleaded the defence of qualified privilege. However, the Court of Appeal ruled that the publication interfered with the claimant's Article 8 right and, though it pursued a legitimate aim, it was disproportionate insofar as it extended to persons who were not likely to be directly approached by the claimant and were not at risk of harm from her. This violation of the Convention right meant that the foundation of the claim for qualified privilege—namely a duty to communicate—fell away. The court noted (at [46] per Ward LJ) that an alternative claim could have been brought under the HRA itself, but damages in a defamation action are bound to exceed any damages awarded under the Act, and the availability of the freestanding claim for breach of human rights provided no reason to ignore the implications of the Convention right for the claim in defamation.

(c) Qualified Privilege under Statute

In addition to qualified privilege at common law, the defence may also arise under statute. The Defamation Act 1996 accords a qualified privilege to the reporting, for example by newspapers or on the television or radio news, of various matters of record, including foreign parliamentary or judicial proceedings, statements issued on behalf of government departments and the conduct of public meetings.

Defamation Act 1996

15. Reports, &c, protected by qualified privilege

(1) The publication of any report or other statement mentioned in Schedule 1 to this Act is privileged unless the publication is shown to be made with malice, subject as follows.

(2) In defamation proceedings in respect of the publication of a report or other statement mentioned in Part II of that Schedule, there is no defence under this section if the plaintiff shows that the defendant—

    (a) was requested by him to publish in a suitable manner a reasonable letter or statement by way of explanation or contradiction, and

    (b) refused or neglected to do so.

For this purpose 'in a suitable manner' means in the same manner as the publication complained of or in a manner that is adequate and reasonable in the circumstances.

(3) This section does not apply to the publication to the public, or a section of the public, of matter which is not of public interest and the publication of which is not for the public benefit.

(4) Nothing in this section shall be construed

    (a) as protecting the publication of matter the publication of which is prohibited by law, or

    (b) as limiting or abridging any privilege subsisting apart from this section.

COMMENTARY

This provision of the Defamation Act 1996 (as amended by s. 7 of the Defamation Act 2013) is the latest restatement of statutory principles governing qualified privilege which date back to the Law of Libel Amendment Act 1888. Under the 1996 Act, the defence is no longer limited to *newspaper* reports (cf. Defamation Act 1952, s. 7).

Schedule 1 to the Act lists the reports and statements referred to in s. 15(1) under two headings. In Part I, there are various statements having 'qualified privilege without explanation or contradiction', meaning that there is no obligation on a defendant wishing to rely upon this defence to publish an explanation or qualification of the words in question if requested to do so by the claimant. The most important examples of such statements are fair and accurate reports of the proceedings of legislatures, courts, governmental inquiries and international organisations held in public anywhere in the world. Part I also applies to fair and accurate copies of or extracts from matter published by or on the authority of a government, legislature, international organisation or international conference anywhere in the world. The statements covered by Part II are 'privileged subject to explanation or contradiction'. If a defendant fails to publish in a suitable manner a reasonable letter or statement by way of explanation or contradiction of the defamatory words, as requested by the claimant, then the privilege is lost (s. 15(2)). Amongst the most important examples under this heading are fair and accurate reports of the proceedings of public meetings, general meetings of listed companies, decisions by associations in the fields of the arts and sciences, religion and charity, trade and industry, and games and sports, and public sittings of tribunals, boards, committees, etc., acting under statutory powers. The Defamation Act 2013 extends the range of application of the defence by removing from Part II previous limitations to the UK and EU member states so that the defence can now be raised in respect of fair and accurate reports of relevant proceedings anywhere in the world (s. 7). The Act also makes specific provision for reports of press conferences discussing matters of public interest (which previously might have been considered public meetings: *McCarten Turkington Breen v Times Newspapers* [2001] 2 AC 277) and the proceedings of scientific or academic conferences.

The same section of the Act further extends the ambit of the statutory defence by amending s. 15(3) so that it applies to publications of matter which is of 'public interest' rather than 'public concern', the latter being a potentially narrower category.

Additionally, s. 6 of the 2013 Act establishes a distinct new category of privilege applying to peer-reviewed publications in scientific or academic journals:

6 Peer-reviewed statement in scientific or academic journal etc

(1) The publication of a statement in a scientific or academic journal (whether published in electronic form or otherwise) is privileged if the following conditions are met.
(2) The first condition is that the statement relates to a scientific or academic matter.
(3) The second condition is that before the statement was published in the journal an independent review of the statement's scientific or academic merit was carried out by—
   (a) the editor of the journal, and
   (b) one or more persons with expertise in the scientific or academic matter concerned.

. . .

(6) A publication is not privileged by virtue of this section if it is shown to be made with malice. . . .

The provision responds to concerns expressed in the scientific and academic communities that the threat of defamation proceedings was stifling legitimate criticism and debate, and complements the privilege introduced for reports of scientific and academic conferences. However, two academics (Mullis and Scott (2014) 77 MLR 87 at 98–9) have questioned whether academic speech is worthy of greater protection than other forms of public interest speech, and—conversely—whether it is only peer-reviewed journal articles, and not books, blogs and press releases that merit such protection.

(d) Malice

In both its common law and statutory forms, the defence of qualified privilege is defeated by proof that the statement was made with malice (which also defeated the erstwhile common law defence of fair comment). Malice is not, however, to be equated with hostility or ill-will; a lack of honest belief in the truth of what is being said will suffice, or the use of a privileged occasion for any improper purpose, which may include—but is not limited to—the intention to cause the claimant injury.

Horrocks v Lowe [1975] AC 135

The facts are not necessary for present purposes.

Lord Diplock

The public interest that the law should provide an effective means whereby a man can vindicate his reputation against calumny has nevertheless to be accommodated to the competing public interest in permitting men to communicate frankly and freely with one another about matters in respect of which the law recognises that they have a duty to perform or an interest to protect in doing so. What is published in good faith on matters of these kinds is published on a privileged occasion. It is not actionable even though it be defamatory and turns out to be untrue. With some exceptions which are irrelevant to the instant appeal, the privilege is not absolute but qualified. It is lost if the occasion which gives rise to it is misused. For in all cases of qualified privilege there is some special reason of public policy why the law accords immunity from suit—the existence of some public or private duty, whether legal or moral, on the part of the maker of the defamatory statement which justifies his communicating it or of some interest of his own which he is entitled to protect by doing so. If he uses the occasion for some other reason he loses the protection of the privilege.

So, the motive with which the defendant on a privileged occasion made a statement defamatory of the plaintiff becomes crucial. The protection might, however, be illusory if the onus lay on him to prove that he was actuated solely by a sense of the relevant duty or a desire to protect the relevant interest. So he is entitled to be protected by the privilege unless some other dominant and improper motive on his part is proved. 'Express malice' is the term of art descriptive of such a motive. Broadly speaking, it means malice in the popular sense of a desire to injure the person who is defamed and this is generally the motive which the plaintiff sets out to prove. But to destroy the privilege the desire to injure must be the dominant motive for the defamatory publication; knowledge that it will have that effect is not enough if the defendant is nevertheless acting in accordance with a sense of duty or in bona fide protection of his own legitimate interests.

The motive with which a person published defamatory matter can only be inferred from what he did or said or knew. If it be proved that he did not believe that what he published was true this is generally conclusive evidence of express malice, for no sense of duty or desire to protect his own legitimate interests can justify a man in telling deliberate and injurious falsehoods about another, save in the exceptional case where a person may be under a duty to pass on, without endorsing, defamatory reports made by some other person.

Apart from those exceptional cases, what is required on the part of the defamer to entitle him to the protection of the privilege is positive belief in the truth of what he published or, as it is generally though tautologously termed, 'honest belief.' If he publishes untrue defamatory matter recklessly, without considering or caring whether it be true or not, he is in this, as in other branches of the law, treated as if he knew it to be false. But indifference to the truth of what he publishes is not to be equated with carelessness, impulsiveness or irrationality in arriving at a positive belief that it is true. The freedom of speech protected by the law of qualified privilege may be availed of by all sorts and conditions of men. In affording to them immunity from suit if they have acted in good faith in compliance with a legal or moral duty or in protection of a legitimate interest the law must take them as it finds them. In ordinary life it is rare indeed for people to form their beliefs by a process of logical deduction from facts ascertained by a rigorous search for all available evidence and a judicious assessment of its probative value. In greater or in less degree according to their temperaments, their training, their intelligence, they are swayed by prejudice, rely on intuition instead of reasoning, leap to conclusions on inadequate evidence and fail to recognise the cogency of material which might cast doubt on the validity of the conclusions they reach. But despite the imperfection of the mental process by which the belief is arrived at it may still be 'honest,' that is, a positive belief that the conclusions they have reached are true. The law demands no more.

Even a positive belief in the truth of what is published on a privileged occasion—which is presumed unless the contrary is proved—may not be sufficient to negative express malice if it can be proved that the defendant misused the occasion for some purpose other than that for which the privilege is accorded by the law. The commonest case is where the dominant motive which actuates the defendant is not a desire to perform the relevant duty or to protect the relevant interest, but to give vent to his personal spite or ill will towards the person he defames. If this be proved, then even positive belief in the truth of what is published will not enable the defamer to avail himself of the protection of the privilege to which he would otherwise have been entitled. There may be instances of improper motives which destroy the privilege apart from personal spite. A defendant's dominant motive may have been to obtain some private advantage unconnected with the duty or the interest which constitutes the reason for the privilege. If so, he loses the benefit of the privilege despite his positive belief that what he said or wrote was true.

Judges and juries should, however, be very slow to draw the inference that a defendant was so far actuated by improper motives as to deprive him of the protection of the privilege unless they are satisfied that he did not believe that what he said or wrote was true or that he was indifferent to its truth or falsity. The motives with which human beings act are mixed. They find it difficult to hate the sin but love the sinner. Qualified privilege would be illusory, and the public interest that it is meant to serve defeated, if the protection which it affords were lost merely because a person, although acting in compliance with a duty or in protection of a legitimate interest, disliked the person whom he defamed or was indignant at what he believed to be that person's conduct and welcomed the opportunity of exposing it. It is only where his desire to comply with the relevant duty or to protect the relevant interest plays no significant part in his motives for publishing what he believes to be true that 'express malice' can properly be found. . . .

COMMENTARY

In the Court of Appeal [1972] 1 WLR 1625 at 1630, Lord Denning MR summarised his approach in the following maxim: 'So long as they are honest, they go clear.' Is this an adequate statement of the law?

In the extract, Lord Diplock provides the classic statement of the principles governing the role of malice where there is a defence of qualified privilege. In short, malice can be established either by the defendant's lack of honest belief in the truth of the defamatory statement or by the presence of a dominant improper motive on the defendant's part (e.g. a desire to injure the claimant). In a case where the defendant positively believes in the truth of the defamatory statement, the courts will be slow to find that they were predominantly actuated by an improper motive. As Lord Diplock notes in a passage omitted from the extract, evidence of improper motive may be derived from either the defendant's conduct on other occasions or their incorporation of irrelevant defamatory matter in the communication in question. Irrelevant material might logically be said to fall altogether outside the privilege, but the law recognises that ordinary persons vary in their ability to identify what is logically relevant, and therefore that 'the protection afforded by the privilege would be illusory if it were lost in respect of any defamatory matter which upon logical analysis could be shown to be irrelevant to the fulfilment of a duty or the protection of the right upon which the privilege was founded' (at 151).

Because they normally involve allegations of dishonesty, pleas of malice should not be introduced lightly, and findings of malice in defamation trials are very rare (*MA v St George's Healthcare NHS Trust* [2015] EWHC 1866 (QB) at [55], per Sir David Eady).

Effect of Malice by a Co-Defendant

Where there are several co-defendants, proof of malice against one does not deprive others who did not themselves act maliciously of the defence: *Eggar v Viscount Chelmsford* [1965] 1 QB 248.

4. Publication on Matter of Public Interest

The roots of the defence of publication on a matter of public interest lie in the decision of the House of Lords in *Reynolds v Times Newspapers Ltd* [2001] 2 AC 127. That decision recognised a qualified privilege attaching to media reports on matters of public concern, subject to a test of 'responsible journalism'. As explained later in this section, there was a lack of certainty over how the *Reynolds* defence should be applied outside the context of mainstream journalism, and concern that this might create a chilling effect on freedom of expression. The Defamation Act 2013 consequently sought to rationalise the defence and put it on an independent statutory basis.

Reynolds v Times Newspapers Ltd [2001] 2 AC 127

Lord Nicholls of Birkenhead

[T]he common law has recognised there are occasions when the public interest requires that publication to the world at large should be privileged. In *Cox v Feeney* (1863) 4 F&F 13, 19, Cockburn CJ approved an earlier statement by Lord Tenterden CJ that 'a man has a right to publish, for the purpose of giving the public information, that which it is proper for the public to know'. Whether the public interest so requires depends upon an evaluation of the particular information in the circumstances of its publication . . . This solution has the merit of elasticity . . . It can be applied appropriately to all information published by a newspaper, whatever its source or origin.

Hand in hand with this advantage goes the disadvantage of an element of unpredictability and uncertainty. The outcome of a court decision, it was suggested, cannot always be predicted with certainty when the newspaper is deciding whether to publish a story. To an extent this is a valid criticism. A degree of uncertainty in borderline cases is inevitable. This uncertainty, coupled with the expense of court proceedings, may 'chill' the publication of true statements of fact as well as those which are untrue. The chill factor is perhaps felt more keenly by the regional press, book publishers and broadcasters than the national press. However, the extent of this uncertainty should not be exaggerated. With the enunciation of some guidelines by the court, any practical problems should be manageable. The common law does not seek to set a higher standard than that of responsible journalism, a standard the media themselves espouse. An incursion into press freedom which goes no further than this would not seem to be excessive or disproportionate . . .

Depending on the circumstances, the matters to be taken into account include the following. The comments are illustrative only.

1. The seriousness of the allegation. The more serious the charge, the more the public is misinformed and the individual harmed, if the allegation is not true.

2. The nature of the information, and the extent to which the subject-matter is a matter of public concern.

3. The source of the information. Some informants have no direct knowledge of the events. Some have their own axes to grind, or are being paid for their stories.

4. The steps taken to verify the information.

5. The status of the information. The allegation may have already been the subject of an investigation which commands respect.

6. The urgency of the matter. News is often a perishable commodity.

7. Whether comment was sought from the plaintiff. He may have information others do not possess or have not disclosed. An approach to the plaintiff will not always be necessary.

8. Whether the article contained the gist of the plaintiff's side of the story.

9. The tone of the article. A newspaper can raise queries or call for an investigation. It need not adopt allegations as statements of fact.

10. The circumstances of the publication, including the timing.

This list is not exhaustive. The weight to be given to these and any other relevant factors will vary from case to case . . .

[I]t should always be remembered that journalists act without the benefit of the clear light of hindsight. Matters which are obvious in retrospect may have been far from clear in the heat of the moment. Above all, the court should have particular regard to the importance of freedom of expression. The press discharges vital functions as a bloodhound as well as a watchdog. The court should be slow to conclude that a publication was not in the public interest and, therefore, the public had no right to know, especially when the information is in the field of political discussion. Any lingering doubts should be resolved in favour of publication.

Ministry of Justice, Draft Defamation Bill Consultation, CP 3/11, Cm. 8020 (March 2011)

Responsible publication on matter of public interest

8. A common law defence has been developed by the courts in this area in recent years, initially in the case of *Reynolds v Times Newspapers* [1999] 4 All ER 609. However, concerns have been expressed by NGOs, the scientific community and others that there is a lack of certainty over how the *Reynolds* defence applies outside the context of mainstream journalism, and that this creates a chilling effect on freedom of expression and reporting. They have indicated that the current common law provisions in *Reynolds* are difficult to rely on, and that this has led to a situation where legal advice given to them on running the defence is extremely cautious and discouraging, and so the defence is seldom used. They believe that a statutory defence would help small organisations to be more robust in reaching decisions in favour of publication.

9. The media and publishers also expressed concerns about the way in which *Reynolds* operates in practice, and have found the defence very complicated and expensive to run. From an opposing perspective, some lawyers working in the field expressed the view that the courts have already made clear that the *Reynolds* defence applies more widely than just to mainstream journalism, and that there is a risk that any statutory provision would complicate the law rather than clarify it.

10. There are clearly limits on the extent to which any statutory provisions could provide clarity and certainty in what is a complex area of the law, and inevitably any provisions would be subject to interpretation and development by the courts in individual cases. There is also a need to ensure that the right balance is struck between statute and the common law so that problems are not created as a result of legislating in areas where the common law is well established and the subject of extensive case law . . . However, the development of a common law defence relating to responsible publications on matters of public interest is quite recent so case law directly on the issue is relatively limited.

11. On balance, we consider that there is merit in providing a statutory defence which is clearer and more readily applicable outside the context of mainstream journalism, and that this would be helpful in ensuring that publications on matters of public interest are sufficiently protected so that responsible journalism can flourish and investigative journalism and the work of NGOs are not unjustifiably impeded by the threat of defamation proceedings.

Defamation Act 2013

4 Publication on matter of public interest

(1) It is a defence to an action for defamation for the defendant to show that—

    (a) the statement complained of was, or formed part of, a statement on a matter of public interest; and

    (b) the defendant reasonably believed that publishing the statement complained of was in the public interest.

(2) Subject to subsections (3) and (4), in determining whether the defendant has shown the matters mentioned in subsection (1), the court must have regard to all the circumstances of the case.

(3) If the statement complained of was, or formed part of, an accurate and impartial account of a dispute to which the claimant was a party, the court must in determining whether it was reasonable for the defendant to believe that publishing the statement was in the public interest disregard any omission of the defendant to take steps to verify the truth of the imputation conveyed by it.

(4) In determining whether it was reasonable for the defendant to believe that publishing the statement complained of was in the public interest, the court must make such allowance for editorial judgement as it considers appropriate.

(5) For the avoidance of doubt, the defence under this section may be relied upon irrespective of whether the statement complained of is a statement of fact or a statement of opinion.

(6) The common law defence known as the Reynolds defence is abolished.

COMMENTARY

The defence recognised by the House of Lords in the *Reynolds* case was expressed as an extension of the common law defence of qualified privilege, though it was subsequently observed that the term 'privilege' was misleading and the defence was more accurately described as a 'public interest defence' (*Flood v Times Newspapers Ltd* [2012] 2 AC 273 at [27], per Lord Phillips). This categorisation of the defence as distinct from the common law defence of qualified privilege is confirmed by s. 4 of the Defamation Act 2013, which presents the public interest defence as entirely independent, even if s. 3(7) provides that a statement is 'privileged' if it would attract the s. 4 defence. The Act as ultimately passed, though, makes a significant departure from the *Reynolds* approach—and from that initially proposed by the Ministry of Justice and incorporated in the Bill as introduced to the House of Commons in May 2012—in replacing the requirement for the defendant to show that they acted responsibly in publishing the statement complained of with a requirement for them to show that they reasonably believed that publishing the statement complained of was in the public interest (s. 4(1)(b)).

Abolition of the Requirement of Responsible Publication

The House of Lords in *Reynolds* rejected the defendant newspaper's argument that all political information should be recognised as privileged subject-matter whose publication could not give rise to liability unless shown to have been malicious. To the Law Lords, such an approach would provide insufficient protection of the right to reputation, which is an integral and important part of the dignity of the individual. Consequently, they preferred an approach in which the newspaper's defence was subject to a test of 'responsible journalism', which was to be applied with reference to the ten factors listed by Lord Nicholls in the preceding extract.

The test of responsible journalism was subsequently considered judicially on a number of occasions, most notably in *Jameel v Wall Street Journal Europe Sprl* [2007] 1 AC 359. There, an article in the defendant's newspaper described investigations into terrorist funding conducted by the banking authorities in Saudi Arabia at the request of US law enforcement agencies, and suggested (at a minimum) that there were reasonable grounds to investigate the involvement of the claimants' companies in the witting or unwitting funnelling of funds to terrorist organisations. The article stated that the companies 'couldn't be reached for comment'; in fact, the author had spoken to an employee the day before publication, but the employee had no authority to make a statement and asked for publication to be delayed for twenty-four hours so that the first claimant, who was overseas, could be contacted. The journalist declined the request. The House of Lords ruled the newspaper's failure to include the claimant's side of the story (Lord Nicholls' eighth factor) was not fatal to its defence of qualified privilege, even though delaying publication by twenty-four hours would have given the claimant the opportunity to comment. The newspaper had taken adequate steps to verify its story, and it was unlikely that the claimant would have made any comment that would have made a difference to what was published. It was the very nature of covert surveillance that its target was unaware of what was going on. The Law Lords emphasised that the standard of responsible journalism should not be raised too high. Lord Nicholls' ten factors were not tests which each allegation contained in a journalistic story had to pass, but only illustrative of the considerations relevant in determining, by reference to the story as a whole, whether or not the journalism was responsible. They were to be treated merely as 'pointers' and not as 'a series of hurdles to be negotiated by a publisher before he could successfully rely on qualified privilege' (at [33] per Lord Bingham).

This flexible approach was further reinforced by the decision of the Supreme Court in *Flood v Times Newspapers Ltd* [2012] 2 AC 273. The Law Lords emphasised that, in the words of Lord Phillips, '[n]ot all the items in Lord Nicholls's list in the *Reynolds* case . . . were intended to be requirements of responsible journalism in every case'.

Seeking to put the defence on a statutory basis, the Ministry of Justice initially proposed to maintain the requirement of 'responsible publication' (as it was renamed) and to incorporate a list of relevant factors based explicitly on those listed by Lord Nicholls in the leading case, albeit in a somewhat revised form. These were reflected in the Bill introduced to the House of Commons in May 2012 (cl. 4(2)). But concerns expressed during the Parliamentary debates led the government to propose amendments to the Bill so as to replace the test of responsible publication with a new test of reasonable belief that the publication was in the public interest. In putting forward the amendments, the government minister (Lord McNally) explained (HL Deb. 19 December 2012, col. 534f GC):

Consideration of whether a publication was 'responsible' involved both subjective and objective elements. 'Reasonable belief' also does this, but we believe that it brings out more clearly the subjective element in the test—what the defendant believed at the time rather than what a judge believes some weeks or months later—while retaining the objective element of whether the belief was a reasonable one for the defendant to hold. The courts will need to look at the conduct of the publisher in deciding that question . . .

[A further amendment] removes the list of factors which the clause currently invites the court to consider. This is a difficult issue. Although we do not believe that the courts would apply the list of factors, based on those in *Reynolds*, as a checklist, we have responded to strongly expressed concerns that the use of a list may be likely to lead in practice to litigants and practitioners adopting a risk-averse approach and gathering detailed evidence on all the factors listed, in case the court were ultimately to consider them relevant.

We recognise that in the short term removing the list may lead to some uncertainty as the courts consider how the new defence should be interpreted and applied. However, in the longer term, the position will clarify as case law develops and, on balance, we consider that it is preferable for there to be greater flexibility than a statutory list might provide. At the same time, in determining whether in all the circumstances the test is met, we would expect the courts to look at many of the same sorts of considerations as they have done before. We believe that these amendments improve the Bill and avoid an overly prescriptive approach, while at the same time maintaining an appropriate balance between the interests of claimants and defendants.

In the Act as passed, then, the list of relevant factors has been removed and s. 4(2) now contains a rather anodyne requirement for the court simply to 'have regard to all the circumstances of the case'. Though the government initially questioned whether this was necessary at all, it ultimately came to accept that it was 'helpful to send a signal to the courts and practitioners to make clear the wish of Parliament that the new defence should be applied in as flexible a way as possible in light of the circumstances' (Hansard, HL vol. 743. col. 198, 5 February 2013 (Lord McNally)).

It is important to note that the new test of reasonable belief refers to the *publishing* of the statement complained of (s. 4(1)(b)). The defendant must show that they believed, and that it was reasonable to believe, that publishing the statement was in the public interest, and it is not enough simply to show that they reasonably believed the statement was true. A court might well find that publishing the statement was not in the public interest if, though the defendant reasonably believed in its truth, they failed to ask the claimant for their response to allegations made or to include such a response in the published story. It may therefore be doubted that the new section will make much difference to how the courts apply the public interest defence in practice. Indeed, Lord McNally himself expressly foresaw that the courts would continue to look at many of the same sorts of considerations as before (see also Mullis and Scott (2014) 77 MLR 87 at 89–91; Descheemaeker, 'Three Errors in the Defamation Act 2013' (2015) 6 JETL 24 at 40).

In *Serafin v Malkiewicz* [2020] 1 WLR 2455, the Supreme Court reiterated that the *Reynolds* factors should not now be addressed one by one as a type of checklist, underlined that the issue is not whether the defendant acted 'responsibly' and criticised the Court of Appeal for speaking of a 'requirement' to offer the subject of a publication the opportunity to present their side of the story. Lord Wilson, delivering the judgment of the court, stated at [76]:

A failure to invite comment from the claimant prior to publication will no doubt always at least be the subject of consideration under subsection (1)(b) and may contribute to, perhaps even form the basis of, a conclusion that the defendant has not established that element of the defence. But it is, with respect, too strong to describe the prior invitation to comment as a 'requirement'. It was never a 'requirement' of the common law defence . . . and so to describe it would be to put a gloss on subsections (1)(b) and (2) of the section.

Does the new statutory formula allow a defendant to publish *irresponsibly* provided he has a reasonable belief that publication is in the public interest?

Reportage

In an important common law adaptation of the *Reynolds* defence, the courts came to apply it to the neutral reporting of the existence of a dispute between two parties without embellishment or subscribing to the truth of allegations made by either side (see *Al-Fagih v HH Saudi Research and Marketing (UK) Ltd* [2002] EMLR 215; *Roberts v Gable* [2008] QB 502). In this context, the defence came commonly to be known as 'reportage'. The Defamation Act 2013 has now put the defence on a statutory basis (s. 4(3)).

In *Flood v Times Newspapers* [2012] 2 AC 273, Lord Phillips explained the nature of the defence as it came to be recognised at common law:

> 77. . . . Reportage is a special, and relatively rare, form of *Reynolds* privilege. It arises where it is not the content of a reported allegation that is of public interest, but the fact that the allegation has been made. It protects the publisher if he has taken proper steps to verify the making of the allegation and provided that he does not adopt it. . . .
>
> 78. The position is quite different where the public interest in the allegation that is reported lies in its content. In such a case the public interest in learning of the allegation lies in the fact that it is, or may be, true. It is in this situation that the responsible journalist must give consideration to the likelihood that the allegation is true. *Reynolds* privilege absolves the publisher from the need to justify his defamatory publication, but the privilege will normally only be earned where the publisher has taken reasonable steps to satisfy himself that the allegation is true before he publishes it. Lord Hoffmann put his finger on this distinction in *Jameel*'s case [2007] 1 AC 359, para 62 when he said
>
>> In most cases the *Reynolds* defence will not get off the ground unless the journalist honestly and reasonably believed that the statement was true, but there are cases ('reportage') in which the public interest lies simply in the fact that the statement was made, when it may be clear that the publisher does not subscribe to any belief in its truth.

The 2013 Act deals with reportage in s. 4(3), prescribing that—if the statement complained of was an accurate and impartial account of a dispute to which the claimant was a party—the court must disregard any omission of the defendant to take steps to verify the truth of the imputation conveyed when it decides whether it was reasonable for the defendant to believe that publishing the statement was in the public interest. Though there were hints in *Flood* that the common law reportage defence might cover a 'spectrum' of situations, with an obligation of verification in at least some cases (see especially at [158], per Lord Mance), the statutory language seems to rule out such a requirement altogether if the reporting of the dispute is accurate and impartial.

5. Offers of Amends

At common law, liability in defamation is in most respects strict. It is no defence that the defendant did not intend to defame the claimant, nor even that they had no cause reasonably to foresee that the words published might defame the claimant (see, e.g., *Cassidy v Daily Mirror Newspapers Ltd* [1929] 2 KB 331, extracted in III.1). The harshness of these principles has been mitigated by statute, which provides a mechanism for a defendant who has 'innocently' defamed another person to make an offer of amends which, in certain circumstances, acts as a defence against defamation proceedings.

Defamation Act 1996

2. Offer to make amends

(1) A person who has published a statement alleged to be defamatory of another may offer to make amends under this section.

(2) The offer may be in relation to the statement generally or in relation to a specific defamatory meaning which the person making the offer accepts that the statement conveys ('a qualified offer').

(3) An offer to make amends—
  (a) must be in writing,
  (b) must be expressed to be an offer to make amends under section 2 of the Defamation Act 1996, and
  (c) must state whether it is a qualified offer and, if so, set out the defamatory meaning in relation to which it is made.

(4) An offer to make amends under this section is an offer—
  (a) to make a suitable correction of the statement complained of and a sufficient apology to the aggrieved party,
  (b) to publish the correction and apology in a manner that is reasonable and practicable in the circumstances, and
  (c) to pay to the aggrieved party such compensation (if any), and such costs, as may be agreed or determined to be payable.

The fact that the offer is accompanied by an offer to take specific steps does not affect the fact that an offer to make amends under this section is an offer to do all the things mentioned in paragraphs (a) to (c). . . .

3. Accepting an offer to make amends

(1) If an offer to make amends under section 2 is accepted by the aggrieved party, the following provisions apply.

(2) The party accepting the offer may not bring or continue defamation proceedings in respect of the publication concerned against the person making the offer, but he is entitled to enforce the offer to make amends, as follows.

(3) If the parties agree on the steps to be taken in fulfilment of the offer, the aggrieved party may apply to the court for an order that the other party fulfil his offer by taking the steps agreed.

(4) If the parties do not agree on the steps to be taken by way of correction, apology and publication, the party who made the offer may take such steps as he thinks appropriate, and may in particular—
  (a) make the correction and apology by a statement in open court in terms approved by the court, and
  (b) give an undertaking to the court as to the manner of their publication.

(5) If the parties do not agree on the amount to be paid by way of compensation, it shall be determined by the court on the same principles as damages in defamation proceedings. The court shall take account of any steps taken in fulfilment of the offer and (so far as not agreed between the parties) of the suitability of the correction, the sufficiency of the apology and whether the manner of their publication was reasonable in the circumstances, and may reduce or increase the amount of compensation accordingly.

(6) If the parties do not agree on the amount to be paid by way of costs, it shall be determined by the court on the same principles as costs awarded in court proceedings. . . .

(10) Proceedings under this section shall be heard and determined without a jury.

4. Failure to accept offer to make amends

(1) If an offer to make amends under section 2, duly made and not withdrawn, is not accepted by the aggrieved party, the following provisions apply.

(2) The fact that the offer was made is a defence (subject to subsection (3)) to defamation proceedings in respect of the publication in question by that party against the person making the offer. A qualified offer is only a defence in respect of the meaning to which the offer related.

(3) There is no such defence if the person by whom the offer was made knew or had reason to believe that the statement complained of—

(a) referred to the aggrieved party or was likely to be understood as referring to him, and
(b) was both false and defamatory of that party; but it shall be presumed until the contrary is shown that he did not know and had no reason to believe that was the case.

(4) The person who made the offer need not rely on it by way of defence, but if he does he may not rely on any other defence. If the offer was a qualified offer, this applies only in respect of the meaning to which the offer related.

(5) The offer may be relied on in mitigation of damages whether or not it was relied on as a defence.

COMMENTARY

These provisions replace those which previously regulated the defence of offer of amends under Defamation Act 1952, s. 4. The earlier provisions were very rarely used as they were unattractive to defendants—being complex, limited in scope and difficult to comply with—and to plaintiffs, to whom they gave no right to compensation. The Neill Committee—in whose *Report on Practice and Procedure in Defamation* (1991) the provisions of the new Act originate—stated (at para. VII.17) that it was:

unsatisfactory that defendants should have a defence available, based on their reasonable behaviour after publication, which would leave the plaintiff with no compensation at all, in respect of hurt feelings or injury to reputation, to take account of what was *ex hypothesi* a defamation . . . [W]e see no overriding public interest in depriving plaintiffs of all compensation merely because the defendants have seen the error of their ways.

Does this beg the question of whether the person whose reputation has been injured by an innocent statement has truly been defamed? If the defendant is 'innocent', could it be said that the claimant has suffered *damnum absque iniuria* (harm but no legal injury)?

The effect of the provisions is (1) to create a formal mechanism for the consensual resolution of defamation disputes, with provision for judicial determination of appropriate compensation, etc., in default of agreement between the parties, and (2) to allow a defence to an 'innocent' defamer whose offer of amends is rejected by the person defamed. Defamation claimants lose the right to compensation if they reject a valid offer of amends, unless they are able to prove that the publication was culpable in the sense that the defendant knew or had reason to know that the statement both referred to the claimant or was likely to be so understood, and was false and defamatory of the claimant (s. 4(3)). There is no culpability in this sense unless the defendant is at least aware of facts from which he ought to have formed the relevant knowledge; negligent ignorance of such facts is not enough (*Milne v Express Newspapers Ltd* [2005] 1 WLR 772). If the offer of amends is validly made, the claimant should therefore accept it; it then falls to determine what steps should be taken in fulfilment of the offer. As regards this latter matter, the offer of amends commits the defendant to make a suitable correction and a sufficient apology, and to publish the correction and apology in a reasonable and practicable manner. It also commits the defendant to pay compensation and legal costs.

In the first instance, it is for the parties to agree the amount of compensation and costs to be paid. If they do not do so, the task falls to the court, which asks first what would be fair compensation in defamation proceedings generally, and then ordinarily applies a discount of between 25 and 50 per cent to reflect the defendant's mitigation of the reputational damage by offering amends, having regard to the sufficiency of the apology etc (s. 3(5)). For a recent illustration see *Undre v Harrow LBC* [2017] EMLR 8, where Sir David Eady noted that a defendant making an offer of amends is now obliged to concede that the statement passes the 'serious harm' test in s. 1 of the 2013 Act and so faces difficulty in arguing that the award should be nominal or even small.

6. Innocent Dissemination

Every person responsible for the publication of a defamatory statement is at risk of liability. An action may be brought, for instance, not only against the author of a defamatory newspaper article, but also against the paper's editor and proprietor, and even its printer and distributor, and the retail outlets in which it is sold. At common law, a defence developed— termed 'innocent dissemination'—in respect of those who merely played a subsidiary part in the publication of defamatory material, provided they did not know, and had no reason to believe, that the publication in question contained any defamatory material at all (see *Vizetelly v Mudie's Select Library Ltd* [1900] 2 QB 170; in fact, the defence failed on the facts of this case because the defendants, a circulating library, had overlooked a publisher's request that the offending newspaper be returned in view of its defamatory contents). The defence has now been put in statutory form in Defamation Act 1996, s. 1, though without abolishing the common law defence.

Defamation Act 1996

1. Responsibility for publication

(1) In defamation proceedings a person has a defence if he shows that—

   (a) he was not the author, editor or publisher of the statement complained of,
   (b) he took reasonable care in relation to its publication, and
   (c) he did not know, and had no reason to believe, that what he did caused or contributed to the publication of a defamatory statement.

(2) For this purpose 'author', 'editor' and 'publisher' have the following meanings, which are further explained in subsection (3)—

   'author' means the originator of the statement, but does not include a person who did not intend that his statement be published at all;

   'editor' means a person having editorial or equivalent responsibility for the content of the statement or the decision to publish it; and

   'publisher' means a commercial publisher, that is, a person whose business is issuing material to the public, or a section of the public, who issues material containing the statement in the course of that business.

(3) A person shall not be considered the author, editor or publisher of a statement if he is only involved—

   (a) in printing, producing, distributing or selling printed material containing the statement;
   (b) in processing, making copies of, distributing, exhibiting or selling a film or sound recording (as defined in Part I of the Copyright, Designs and Patents Act 1988) containing the statement;
   (c) in processing, making copies of, distributing or selling any electronic medium in or on which the statement is recorded, or in operating or providing any equipment, system or service by means of which the statement is retrieved, copied, distributed or made available in electronic form;
   (d) as the broadcaster of a live programme containing the statement in circumstances in which he has no effective control over the maker of the statement;
   (e) as the operator of or provider of access to a communications system by means of which the statement is transmitted, or made available, by a person over whom he has no effective control. In a case not within paragraphs (a) to (e) the court may have regard to those provisions by way of analogy in deciding whether a person is to be considered the author, editor or publisher of a statement.

(4) Employees or agents of an author, editor or publisher are in the same position as their employer or principal to the extent that they are responsible for the content of the statement or the decision to publish it.

(5) In determining for the purposes of this section whether a person took reasonable care, or had reason to believe that what he did caused or contributed to the publication of a defamatory statement, regard shall be had to—

   (a) the extent of his responsibility for the content of the statement or the decision to publish it,
   (b) the nature or circumstances of the publication, and
   (c) the previous conduct or character of the author, editor or publisher.

Defamation Act 2013

10. Action against a person who was not the author, editor etc

(1) A court does not have jurisdiction to hear and determine an action for defamation brought against a person who was not the author, editor or publisher of the statement complained of unless the court is satisfied that it is not reasonably practicable for an action to be brought against the author, editor or publisher.

(2) In this section 'author', 'editor' and 'publisher' have the same meaning as in section 1 of the Defamation Act 1996.

COMMENTARY

The object of s. 1 of the Act of 1996 is to allow a defence to the merely mechanical distributors of defamatory material, provided that they have no reason to believe that their conduct might contribute to the publication of a defamatory statement. The defence applies to those other than the 'author, editor or [commercial] publisher' of the statement. It covers those involved only in the printing, distributing and selling of printed material, and the broadcaster of a live programme where there is no 'effective control' over what is said. A party who acts merely as the passive medium for publication (e.g. the postal service) is not a publisher at all and so, strictly speaking, has no need of a specific defence (see *Bunt v Tilley* [2007] 1 WLR 1243, considered in III.3).

The s. 1 defence's principal limitation is that, perhaps unlike the common law defence, it does not operate where the disseminator knows the material is defamatory but reasonably believes that it is true (see Milmo (1996) NLJ 222; cf. *Metropolitan International Schools Ltd v Designtechnica Corp* [2011] 1 WLR 1743 at [69]–[70], where Eady J expressed doubt that the common law defence was wider in this respect). In fact, the practice has developed of putting distributors, etc., 'on notice' of the risk that defamatory material may be contained in certain publications and requesting that the 'offending' publications be withdrawn. This has proved to be a very effective tactic to be deployed on the part of those anxious to prevent the widespread circulation of defamatory allegations about themselves. As *Barendt* remarks (p. 9): 'in comparison with writers and editors, committed to the truth of their book or paper and freedom of expression, distributors are much less likely to attempt to defend libel actions for reasons of principle.' If a distributor, etc., should continue to publish defamatory material after being given due warning of its content, they lose the benefit of the defence under s. 1.

Operators of websites

The application of the s. 1 defence to the operator of a website was considered in *Godfrey v Demon Internet Ltd* [2001] QB 201, where Morland J ruled that the defence could not be relied on where an internet service provider had failed to remove a defamatory posting from its newsgroup after being informed of its defamatory content and requested to take it down. Cf. *Tamiz v Google Inc* [2013] 1 WLR 2151, dealing with Google's blog-hosting service Blogger, where the Court of Appeal ruled that the period (if any) for which Blogger was responsible for a comment appearing on one of its blogs—subsequently taken down—was too short for it to have been accessed by significant numbers of readers and that any damage suffered by the claimant was too trivial to allow a claim for damages to proceed.

In light of continuing concerns about the uncertain scope of liability in respect of internet publications (see Ministry of Justice, *Draft Defamation Bill Consultation*, Cm. 8020, 2011, para. 101ff), the Defamation Act 2013 introduces an additional defence for the benefit of operators of websites:

5 Operators of websites

(1) This section applies where an action for defamation is brought against the operator of a website in respect of a statement posted on the website.
(2) It is a defence for the operator to show that it was not the operator who posted the statement on the website.
(3) The defence is defeated if the claimant shows that—
   (a) it was not possible for the claimant to identify the person who posted the statement,
   (b) the claimant gave the operator a notice of complaint in relation to the statement, and
   (c) the operator failed to respond to the notice of complaint in accordance with any provision contained in regulations.
(4) For the purposes of subsection (3)(a), it is possible for a claimant to 'identify' a person only if the claimant has sufficient information to bring proceedings against the person. . . .

The section continues by making provision as to the form in which a notice of complaint should be made (s. 5(6)).

Further Reform

The Defamation Act 2013 does not effect any change to the terms of the s. 1 defence (cf. paras 116ff of the preceding Consultation Paper), but s. 10 of the Act buttresses the protection for publishers other than authors, editors and commercial publishers by erecting a procedural bar to claims being brought against them except where it is not reasonably practicable to sue an author, editor or commercial publisher. The two provisions were considered by Warby J in *Brett Wilson LLP v Person(s) Unknown* [2016] 1 All ER 1006, an action by a law firm against the unidentified operator(s) of the website www.solicitorsfromhell.co.uk, on which the firm was listed, along with a letter of complaint by a dissatisfied (and also unknown) client. The judge found that the defendant(s) fell within the definition of 'editor' applying under both provisions, so neither could be relied upon on the facts. He granted the firm the injunctions it requested, requiring amongst other things the removal of the defamatory material from the website, and awarded damages against the person(s) unknown (in case subsequently identified).

The superimposition of the new procedural bar adds further complexity to an area of the law which is already fiendishly complicated, and it is to be regretted that the Act did not seek to consolidate in one legislative provision the common law principles on who constitutes a publisher (see III.3), the statutory rules on responsibility for publication, the specific defences provided to ISPs by the Electronic Commerce Regulations (also in III.3) and the new provisions added by the Act itself.

v. Remedies

1. Damages

In the case of libel and slander actionable *per se*, injury to reputation is presumed to flow from the publication of defamatory material and the claimant is entitled to damages 'at large'. This signifies that the assessment of damages depends almost entirely on the facts of the individual case; unlike the law of personal injury, the sheer variety of circumstances arising in different cases has precluded the development of a tariff-based system for the valuation of losses of reputation. The award reflects not only the claimant's loss of reputation but also injury to their feelings; like loss of reputation, this is generally presumed to result from the defamation and need not be specially pleaded. The element in respect of injury to feelings formerly had particular importance where the claimant's loss of reputation was insignificant, for example, because no one believed the defendant's allegations (see *Fielding v Variety Incorporated* [1967] 2 QB 841). But the new 'serious harm' requirement introduced by s. 1 of the Defamation Act 2013 is concerned only with harm to reputation, so injury to feelings alone, however grave, will not found a claim (*Theedom v Nourish Trading (t/a CSP Recruitment)* [2016] EMLR 10 at [15], per HH Judge Moloney QC).

Where the defamatory allegations relate to the claimant's business activities, an award may also be made for general loss of business profits or specific losses arising from particular contracts. Every award should reflect the seriousness of the charge, the extent of the publication and the nature of the defendant's conduct both in publishing the defamation and subsequently.

An apology and retraction will generally be taken into account in mitigation of damages, but they do not necessarily preclude the award of substantial compensation. Conversely the defendant's persistence in an unfounded defence of truth may serve to increase the distress suffered by the claimant as a result of the defamation and hence the size of the award. The award of damages will also reflect the nature of the claimant's reputation, as well as other features of the claimant's conduct (e.g. whether they were guilty of provocation: see *Watts v Fraser* (1835) 1 M & Rob 449).

Defamation is one of the few areas of law in which awards of exemplary (or punitive) damages are able to be pursued, but their role is now somewhat different following implementation of reforms proposed in the Leveson Report (*Leveson*, Part J, ch. 3, para. 5.12). In the case of liability for the commercial publication of 'news-related material' which is 'subject to editorial control', exemplary damages are now available as a mechanism for punishing the defendant for 'a deliberate or reckless disregard of an outrageous nature for the claimant's rights'—a wider test than applies at common law (see further Ch. 15. II.3). However, defendants signing up voluntarily to an approved system of self-regulation will prima facie be immune from exemplary damages (Crime and Courts Act 2013, ss. 34–8, 41–2).

John v MGN Ltd [1997] QB 586

Sir Thomas Bingham MR delivered the judgment of the Court of Appeal

The principles of law relating to damages in defamation

Introduction

It is standard practice for plaintiffs in defamation actions to claim damages and also an injunction against repetition of the publication complained of. If the action is compromised, the defendant ordinarily undertakes not to repeat the publication. If the action goes to trial and the plaintiff wins and recovers damages, the defendant ordinarily undertakes not to repeat the publication and if he is unwilling to give that undertaking an injunction restraining him from further publication will usually be granted. But it is the award of damages, not the grant of an injunction (in lieu of an undertaking), which is the primary remedy which the law provides on proof of this tort, both because, save in exceptional cases, the grant of an injunction in practice follows and is dependent on success in recovering damages, and also because an injunction, while giving the plaintiff protection against repetition in future, gives him no redress for what has happened in the past. It is to an award of damages that a plaintiff must look for redress, and the principles governing awards of damages are accordingly of fundamental importance in ensuring that justice is done to plaintiffs and defendants and that account is taken of such public interests as may be involved.

Compensatory damages

The successful plaintiff in a defamation action is entitled to recover, as general compensatory damages, such sum as will compensate him for the wrong he has suffered. That sum must compensate him for the damage to his reputation; vindicate his good name; and take account of the distress, hurt and humiliation which the defamatory publication has caused. In assessing the appropriate damages for injury to reputation the most important factor is the gravity of the libel; the more closely it touches the plaintiff's personal integrity, professional reputation, honour, courage, loyalty and the core attributes of his personality, the more serious it is likely to be. The extent of publication is also very relevant: a libel published to millions has a greater potential to cause damage than a libel published to a handful of people. A successful plaintiff may properly look to an award of damages to vindicate his reputation: but the significance of this is much greater in a case where the defendant asserts the truth of the libel and refuses any retraction or apology than in a case where the defendant acknowledges the falsity of what was published and publicly expresses regret that the libellous publication took place. It is well established that compensatory damages may and should compensate for additional injury caused to the plaintiff's feelings by the defendant's conduct of the action, as when he persists in an unfounded assertion that the publication was true, or refuses to apologise, or cross-examines the plaintiff in a wounding or insulting way. Although the plaintiff has been referred to as 'he' all this of course applies to women just as much as men.

There could never be any precise, arithmetical formula to govern the assessment of general damages in defamation, but if such cases were routinely tried by judges sitting alone there would no doubt emerge a more or less coherent framework of awards which would, while recognising the particular features of particular cases, ensure that broadly comparable cases led to broadly comparable awards. This is what has happened in the field of personal injuries since these ceased to be the subject of trial by jury and became in practice the exclusive preserve of judges. There may be even greater factual diversity in defamation than in personal injury cases, but this is something of which the framework would take account.

The survival of jury trial in defamation actions has inhibited a similar development in this field.

Barron v Vines [2016] EWHC 1226 (QB)

Warby J quoted from the judgment of Sir Thomas Bingham in *John v MGN Ltd*, and then made some additional points about the assessment of damages in defamation claims (at [21]):

(1) The initial measure of damages is the amount that would restore the claimant to the position he would have enjoyed had he not been defamed: *Steel and Morris v United Kingdom* (2004) 41 EHRR 22 [37], [45].

(2) The existence and scale of any harm to reputation may be established by evidence or inferred. Often, the process is one of inference, but evidence that tends to show that as a matter of fact a person was shunned, avoided, or taunted will be relevant. So may evidence that a person was treated as well or better by others after the libel than before it.

(3) The impact of a libel on a person's reputation can be affected by:
   (a) Their role in society. The libel of Esther Rantzen [see *Rantzen v Mirror Group Newspapers (1986) Ltd* [1994] QB 670] was more damaging because she was a prominent child protection campaigner.
   (b) The extent to which the publisher(s) of the defamatory imputation are authoritative and credible. The person making the allegations may be someone apparently well-placed to know the facts, or they may appear to be an unreliable source.
   (c) The identities of the publishees. Publication of a libel to family, friends or work colleagues may be more harmful and hurtful than if it is circulated amongst strangers. On the other hand, those close to a claimant may have knowledge or viewpoints that make them less likely to believe what is alleged.
   (d) The propensity of defamatory statements to percolate through underground channels and contaminate hidden springs, a problem made worse by the internet and social networking sites, particularly for claimants in the public eye: *C v MGN Ltd* (reported with *Cairns v Modi* [2013] 1 WLR 1015) [27]).

(4) It is often said that damages may be aggravated if the defendant acts maliciously. The harm for which compensation would be due in that event is injury to feelings.

(5) A person who has been libelled is compensated only for injury to the reputation they actually had at the time of publication. If it is shown that the person already had a bad reputation in the relevant sector of their life, that will reduce the harm, and therefore moderate any damages. But it is not permissible to seek, in mitigation of damages, to prove specific acts of misconduct by the claimant, or rumours or reports to the effect that he has done the things alleged in the libel complained of: *Scott v Sampson* (1882) QBD 491, on which I will expand a little. Attempts to achieve this may aggravate damages . . .

(6) Factors other than bad reputation that may moderate or mitigate damages, on some of which I will also elaborate below, include the following:
   (a) 'Directly relevant background context' within the meaning of *Burstein v Times Newspapers Ltd* [2001] 1 WLR 579 and subsequent authorities. This may qualify the rules at (5) above.
   (b) Publications by others to the same effect as the libel complained of if (but only if) the claimants have sued over these in another defamation claim, or if it is necessary to consider them in order to isolate the damage caused by the publication complained of.
   (c) An offer of amends pursuant to the Defamation Act 1996.
   (d) A reasoned judgment, though the impact of this will vary according to the facts and nature of the case.

(7) In arriving at a figure it is proper to have regard to (a) Jury awards approved by the Court of Appeal: *Rantzen*, 694, *John*, 612; (b) the scale of damages awarded in personal injury actions: *John*, 615; (c) previous awards by a judge sitting without a jury: see *John*, 608.

(8) Any award needs to be no more than is justified by the legitimate aim of protecting reputation, necessary in a democratic society in pursuit of that aim, and proportionate to that need: *Rantzen v Mirror Group Newspapers (1986) Ltd* [1994] QB 670. This limit is nowadays statutory, via the Human Rights Act 1998.

COMMENTARY

The presumption of jury trial in defamation claims was reversed by s. 11 of the Defamation Act 2013, which greatly reduces the importance of the practical question addressed by the Court of Appeal in *John v MGN*, namely the extent to which the judge may offer guidance to the jury on the assessment of damages. In passages of his judgment that are not extracted here, Sir Thomas Bingham stated that juries should not be informed of jury awards in other cases unless they had been approved by the Court of Appeal, but should be referred to conventional levels of award for personal injuries as a check on the reasonableness of what they might be minded to award for the defamation. In his list of additional points in *Barron v Vines*, Warby J effectively adapts the same approach for the purposes of the judicial assessment of damages, adding uncontroversially that reference can also be made to previous awards by a judge sitting without a jury (proposition (7)).

Notwithstanding Sir Thomas Bingham's optimism, in the extracted text, that making judges assess the damages would lead to broadly comparable awards in broadly comparable cases, in a Hong Kong Final Court of Appeal decision Lord Neuberger has more recently conceded that a significant degree of inconsistency remains inevitable (*Blakeney-Williams v Cathay Pacific Airways Ltd* [2013] EMLR 6 at [93]):

> It is inevitable that many people will consider that there is a significant degree of inconsistency in the amount of general damages awarded in defamation cases, because: (i) there is an inevitable degree of subjectivity in an area where there is so little logical or principled correlation between the damage suffered and money; (ii) opinions as to the seriousness of particular libels will legitimately vary; and (iii) the factual circumstances in which a defamatory statement is made, and the particular effect of a libel, will vary from plaintiff to plaintiff.

Evidence of Bad Reputation

As Warby J notes in the extract from *Barron v Vines* (proposition (5)), damages can be reduced if the claimant already has a bad reputation. Evidence of general reputation is admissible in court, though not evidence of rumours or suspicions about particular conduct (*Scott v Sampson* (1882) 8 QBD 491). The latter prohibition is subject to qualification, however, regarding (i) matter introduced in support of a properly pleaded defence of truth or honest opinion and (ii) matter that is directly relevant background context.

(i) Evidence Supporting a Defence of Truth or Honest Opinion

A defendant pleading truth or honest opinion must introduce factual evidence to make good the defence. Even if the defence fails, such facts as are proven may still be taken into account in the assessment of damages. In *Pamplin v Express Newspapers Ltd (No. 2)* [1988] 1 WLR 116 the allegation against the claimant was that he was a 'slippery unscrupulous spiv'. At trial, the defendant newspaper sought to demonstrate the truth of its statement and introduced evidence that forced the claimant to concede that he was indeed slippery and unscrupulous, but he successfully maintained that the newspaper had not shown he was a spiv. The Court of Appeal ruled that, in setting the level of damages, the jury was entitled to take into account both that the claimant's reputation was already low as a result of widespread press coverage of his activities (general evidence of bad reputation), and the evidence showing that his conduct had been slippery and unscrupulous on specific occasions, which could be regarded as 'partial justification' for the defamatory words. Another case of partial justification is *Grobbelaar v News Group Newspapers Ltd*, noted in IV.1, where the House of Lords awarded the claimant damages of only £1 in view of the proven allegations of corruption made against him by the defendant newspaper.

(ii) Directly Relevant Background Context

A further inroad on the basic prohibition against evidence of specific conduct was made by the Court of Appeal in *Burstein v Times Newspapers Ltd* [2001] 1 WLR 579. The claimant, a composer of tonal classical musical, was accused of having organised hecklers to wreck performances of modernist atonal music. In fact, though he had been a member of a group called 'The Hecklers' which opposed modernist atonal music, he had only ever booed (on a single occasion) after the end of the performance. There was therefore no plausible defence of truth, and fair comment was not available either as the relevant statement was clearly one of fact. The trial judge ruled that evidence of the claimant's membership of The Hecklers and his booing of a performance was inadmissible, even in mitigation of damages, and the jury awarded the claimant £8,000. The Court of Appeal found that the evidence should have been admitted in court, rather than leaving the jury to assess the damages 'in blinkers'. Though there should be no 'roving inquiry' into the claimant's life, the jury ought to be able to hear 'directly relevant background context'. On the facts, however, the Court of Appeal was not satisfied that the jury, even if it had heard the further evidence, would have assessed damages at any less than £8,000, and affirmed the initial award.

The rule seems clear enough, though it may be a difficult matter in individual cases to draw the line between directly relevant and irrelevant (or only indirectly relevant) background. A subsequent decision, *Turner v News Group Newspapers* [2006] 1 WLR 3469, illustrates the breadth of the principles. The claimant complained of the (untrue) allegation that he had pressurised his then wife into having sex with strangers at a 'swingers' club. The defendant sought to introduce evidence in mitigation of damages, and raised a '*Burstein* plea' which the Court of Appeal accepted in respect of (1) evidence that the claimant and his then wife had visited a private-members club on 'fetish nights' (relevant to the assessment of the claimant's injury to feelings) and (2) evidence that the claimant had previously publicised the failure of his marriage to her—'a page 3 model'—in the tabloid press (relevant to the assessment of his distress at the defendant's infringement of his privacy). It was immaterial that the evidence related not to the defamatory allegation itself but to the injury the claimant alleged that it had caused. The court also ruled in favour of the admissibility of evidence that the claimant had acted as his then wife's agent in arranging for her to be photographed in pornographic poses with a view to publication in 'top shelf' magazines: this fact was widely known within the circle of those who would have understood the defamatory reference to him, and was therefore a matter of 'general reputation' which was admissible irrespective of *Burstein*.

2. Injunctions

(a) General

Although the jurisdiction to grant the claimant an injunction to prevent the publication or republication of a libel arose some considerable time after the courts established the liability of a defamer to pay damages, in certain respects it can be regarded as the more important remedy, for it serves to preserve the claimant's reputation intact, not merely to compensate for its loss (but cf. the view of Sir Thomas Bingham MR in *John v MGN Ltd*, extracted earlier). Injunctions can be awarded not only to prevent the republication of a defamation that has previously been published, but also in advance of publication, in order to prevent an anticipated publication. In the latter circumstances, the injunction is described as *quia timet* ('because he or she fears [sc. the publication of defamatory material]').

Where the defendant has already published the defamatory words, the court will normally grant an injunction wherever it is satisfied that the words are injurious to the claimant and there is reason to fear further publication. Where the defendant has not yet published the defamation, it seems that (according to general principle) a *quia timet* injunction may be awarded if there is 'a very strong probability' that the defendant will cause 'grave damage' to the claimant in the future (*Morris v Redland Bricks Ltd* [1970] AC 652).

At common law, the courts had no power to order a defendant to issue an apology or correction, but statutory exceptions to this basic rule have now been admitted, first in respect of summary judgments for the claimant (Defamation Act 1996, ss. 8–9) and subsequently in respect of other judgments in the claimant's favour (Defamation Act 2013, s. 12; see further *Draft Defamation Bill Consultation*, para. 134f). Under the 2013 Act, the court may order the defendant to publish a summary of its judgment, the content of which, and the time, manner, form and place of its publication, is left for the parties to agree; if the parties cannot agree, the court may specify the wording of the summary and order its publication in a specified way. The corresponding provisions of the 1996 Act are broadly equivalent in effect.

It may be added here that a failure to publish a reasonable letter or statement by way of explanation or contradiction of a defamatory allegation may, subject to conditions, preclude reliance on a statutory defence of qualified privilege (Defamation Act 1996, s. 15: see IV.3(c)). Conversely, an 'offer of amends' incorporating a suitable correction and apology acts as a defence against liability if not accepted, and in any event may be relied on in mitigation of damages (see IV.5).

(b) Interim Injunctions

In the general law, the question whether an interim (previously, 'interlocutory') injunction should be awarded is determined according to the principles laid down by the House of Lords in *American Cyanamid Co v Ethicon Ltd* [1975] AC 396. But the particular considerations raised by the law of defamation have long been held to warrant the special treatment of cases in which the claimant seeks to prevent the defendant from publishing defamatory allegations about them pending full trial in front of a jury (see *Bonnard v Perryman*, extracted here).

Bonnard v Perryman [1891] 2 Ch 269

Lord Coleridge CJ read the following judgment, in which **Lord Esher MR** and **Lindley, Bowen** and **Lopes LJJ** concurred:

[I]t is obvious that the subject-matter of an action for defamation is so special as to require exceptional caution in exercising the jurisdiction to interfere by injunction before the trial of an action to prevent an anticipated wrong. The right of free speech is one which it is for the public interest that individuals should possess, and, indeed, that they should exercise without impediment, so long as no wrongful act is done; and, unless an alleged libel is untrue, there is no wrong committed; but, on the contrary, often a very wholesome act is performed in the publication and repetition of an alleged libel. Until it is clear that an alleged libel is untrue, it is not clear that any right at all has been infringed; and the importance of leaving free speech unfettered is a strong reason in cases of libel for dealing most cautiously and warily with the granting of interim injunctions. We entirely approve of, and desire to adopt as our own, the language of Lord Esher MR, in *Coulson (William) & Sons v James Coulson & Co* (1887) 3 TLR 846:

> To justify the Court in granting an interim injunction it must come to a decision upon the question of libel or no libel, before the jury have decided whether it was a libel or not. Therefore the jurisdiction was of a delicate nature. It ought only to be exercised in the clearest cases, where any jury would say that the matter complained of was libellous, and where, if the jury did not so find, the Court would set aside the verdict as unreasonable.

COMMENTARY

The special rules applicable in defamation should be contrasted with the rules generally applicable elsewhere in the law. Under the *American Cyanamid* principles, an interim injunction will be awarded where the claimant proves that (1) there is a serious question to be tried (but not necessarily a prima facie case) and (2) the balance of convenience favours the award of an injunction. However, the claimant may have to make an 'undertaking to pay damages to the defendant for any loss sustained by reason of the injunction if it should be held at the trial that the plaintiff had not been entitled to restrain the defendant from doing what he was threatening to do' (see [1975] AC 396 at 406, per Lord Diplock).

It has been held that the restatement by the House of Lords of the principles governing the award of interim injunctions in the *American Cyanamid* case did not affect the continued application of the rule of *Bonnard v Perryman*: see *J Trevor & Sons v Solomon* (1977) 248 EG 779; *Herbage v Pressdram Ltd* [1984] 1 WLR 1160. The rule against the award of an interim injunction also applies where the defendant pleads some other defence—see *Quartz Hill Consolidated Mining Co v Beal* (1882) 20 Ch D 501 (qualified privilege); *Fraser v Evans* [1969] 1 QB 349 at 360, per Lord Denning MR (fair comment, now the defence of honest opinion)—unless the defendant was clearly actuated by malice (*Harakas v Baltic Mercantile and Shipping Exchange Ltd* [1982] 1 WLR 958 at 960, per Lord Denning MR). Do you think that the rule in *Bonnard v Perryman* adequately acknowledges the claimant's interest in an unsullied reputation, given especially the prevalence of the sentiment 'no smoke without fire'?

The jurisdiction to award an interim injunction 'ought only to be exercised in the clearest cases' (*Coulson (William) & Sons v James Coulson & Co* (1887) 3 TLR 846). Hence it must be 'unarguable' that the statement is defamatory: see further *Kaye v Robertson* [1991] FSR 62 (inference that a well-known actor had given an 'exclusive' interview to a very low-brow newspaper was perhaps capable of being defamatory, but it was not unarguably defamatory).

Section 12 of the Human Rights Act directs the court to have regard to the Convention right to freedom of speech when considering the grant of any relief that might affect its exercise. Section 12(3) further specifies that, where injunctive relief is sought so as to restrain publication before trial, it is not to be granted 'unless the court is satisfied that the applicant is likely to establish that publication should not be allowed'. The 'likely' criterion was intended to set a minimum requirement for the grant of interim injunctive relief where questions of free speech are at issue, whatever the cause of action, but does not water down the more substantial protection already provided in defamation actions by the rule in *Bonnard v Perryman* (*Greene v Associated Newspapers Ltd* [2005] QB 972).

VI. Defamation, Free Speech and the Press

The question of whether English law strikes the correct balance between concerns of free speech and the protection of reputation may now be considered. Although English law traditionally did not allow direct reliance on the European Convention of Human Rights, judges sometimes addressed the question whether the law of defamation accorded with the rights recognised therein, for example in respect of the unqualified right to criticise a political body (see *Derbyshire County Council v Times Newspapers* [1993] AC 534, extracted in this section). With the implementation of the Human Rights Act 1998, however, the courts now have a positive obligation to take regard of the Convention rights in developing the common law (see *Flood v Times Newspapers* [2012] 2 AC 273 at [46], per Lord Phillips).

In *Reynolds v Times Newspapers* [2001] 2 AC 127 (extracted earlier), the House of Lords considered whether, with the coming into effect of this legislation imminent, it was appropriate to recognise a new defence to defamation liability related to the 'public figure' defence developed by the US Supreme Court in its decision in *New York Times Co v Sullivan*, 376 US 254 (1964), extracted later in this section. A relevant consideration in addressing such questions is the extent of the 'chilling effect' of the law of defamation on the reporting of the news by different segments of the media (see the following extract).

E. Barendt et al., *Libel and the Media: The Chilling Effect*
(Oxford: Clarendon Press, 1997)

[The book considers whether defamation law has had a 'chilling effect' on the media, with the result that there is undue restriction on the media's freedom to publish material of real public interest. After a survey involving consultation with in-house media lawyers, media lawyers in independent practice, and journalists, broadcasters, etc., the authors conclude:]

We believe that our investigation of the impact of defamation law on various media has demonstrated clearly that the chilling effect in this area genuinely does exist and significantly restricts what the public is able to read and hear . . . [H]owever, our findings have led us to the conclusion that, whilst the idea of the chilling effect is entirely valid, it requires some reformulation to reflect fully the complexity of the ways in which its pernicious effects are actually brought about.

The most obvious manifestation, which may be called the direct chilling effect, occurs when articles, books or programmes are specifically changed in the light of legal considerations. Most often perhaps this takes the form of omission of material the author believes to be true but cannot establish to the extent judged sufficient to avoid an unacceptable risk of legal action and an award of damages. This produces the attitude exemplified by most magazine editors and publishers . . . : 'if in doubt, strike it out'. 'Doubt' here, it should be emphasized, relates to their ability to present a legally sustainable defence, not to the editor's view of the validity of the story . . . [T]he impact of the directly chilling effect is not at all uniform. Different media experience it with notably different force . . . [I]t bears far more heavily on book publishers, broadcasters, and the regional press than on the national press, where its impact seems relatively minor.

However, there is another, deeper, and subtler way in which libel inhibits media publication. This may be called the structural [or indirect] chilling effect. It is not manifest through alteration or cancellation of a specific article, programme or book. Rather it functions in a preventive manner: preventing the creation of certain material. Particular organisations and individuals are considered taboo because of the libel risk; certain subjects are treated as off-limits, minefields into which it is too dangerous to stray.

[Amongst the 'no-go areas' the authors identify are: investigations of deaths in police custody, exploitative employment practices by various large companies operating in the United Kingdom and bribery or other corrupt practices by British companies bidding for overseas contracts.]

Nothing is edited to lessen libel risk because nothing is written in the first place . . . [I]n this respect, unlike the direct chilling effect, there is no indication that the national press is any less affected. . . .

A secondary form of structural chilling effect may be discerned, if less clearly. It is best encapsulated by the remark of a journalist on a national broadsheet . . . who suggested that the libel laws had made the British press more 'polemical'—by which he meant the antithesis of factually-orientated—than it otherwise might be. If true, this is a good example of the functional application of legal rules as understood by those who operate under them. The key point is that, whilst the defence of justification in effect requires proof of the truth of any seriously discreditable allegation, that of fair comment is a little more generous from the point of view of the media . . .

COMMENTARY

Clearly, the so-called 'chilling effect' is unobjectionable in so far as it protects deserved reputations against unwarranted attack. But concern has been expressed for a number of years that the English law of defamation is too harsh in its operation—and that it costs too much to defend a claim even when a good defence is available—with the result that it unduly interferes with the reporting of the news by the media, and acts as a shield which can be manipulated by the rich and powerful in order to deflect attention away from shady business deals and intrigue. The passage of the Human Rights Act 1998, which requires the courts in appropriate cases to have regard to the right to free speech in the European Convention of Human Rights, may serve to redress the balance to some degree, as may the specific reforms effected by the Defamation Act 2013, which had that specific aim in mind.

European Convention for the Protection of Human Rights and Fundamental Freedoms

Article 10

Freedom of Expression

(1) Everyone has the right to freedom of expression. This right shall include freedom to hold opinions and to receive and impart information and ideas without interference by public authority and regardless of frontiers. This article shall not prevent States from requiring the licensing of broadcasting, television or cinema enterprises.

(2) The exercise of these freedoms, since it carries with it duties and responsibilities, may be subject to such formalities, conditions, restrictions or penalties as are prescribed by law and are necessary in a democratic society, in the interests of national security, territorial integrity or public safety, for the prevention of disorder or crime, for the protection

of health or morals, for the protection of the reputation or rights of others, for preventing the disclosure of information received in confidence, or for maintaining the authority and impartiality of the judiciary.

COMMENTARY

The Convention allows restrictions on the right to free speech which are 'prescribed by law' and 'necessary in a democratic society'. As regards the latter requirement, a pressing 'social need' must be 'convincingly established' (*Weber v Switzerland* (1990) 12 EHRR 508). In the leading case of *Lingens v Austria* (1986) 8 EHRR 407, the European Court of Human Rights ruled that Austrian law violated Article 10 by allowing the Austrian Chancellor to bring a private prosecution for criminal defamation against a magazine publisher who had published allegations that the Chancellor had protected former members of the Nazi SS for political reasons. The court stated, at [41]:

Whilst the press must not overstep the bounds set, *inter alia*, for the 'protection of the reputation of others', it is nevertheless incumbent on it to impart information and ideas on political issues just as on those in other areas of public interest. Not only does the press have the task of imparting such information and ideas: the public also has a right to receive them . . . More generally, freedom of political debate is at the very core of the concept of a democratic society which prevails throughout the Convention. The limits of acceptable criticism are accordingly wider as such than as regards a private individual.

However, the Court has stressed that freedom of expression carries with it duties and responsibilities which assume especial significance when the reputation of a named individual is attacked. Journalists are required to act in good faith and to provide accurate and reliable information in accordance with the ethics of journalism. In principle, it is not incompatible with Article 10 to place on a defendant in defamation proceedings the onus of proving on the balance of probabilities that the defamatory statements were substantially true. See *Europapress Holding d.o.o. v Croatia* (2011) 53 EHRR 27 at [58] and [63].

The Convention is also important in areas not directly raising questions of press freedom. In *Tolstoy Miloslavsky v United Kingdom* (1995) 20 EHRR 442, the court accepted that jury awards of damages for defamation were 'prescribed by law' as required by Article 10, and that the need for flexibility in individual cases was reason enough for the lack of any requirement to give reasons for such awards. But the court found that the award of £1.5 million in damages in that case, in conjunction with the Court of Appeal's inability at the time to review disproportionately large awards, constituted breaches of Article 10 (but see now Courts and Legal Services Act 1990, s. 8). The award was the highest ever in a defamation action in this country. (The defendant had accused the plaintiff of a war crime.)

Derbyshire County Council v Times Newspapers [1993] AC 534

The Sunday Times printed articles in successive editions concerning share deals involving the superannuation fund of Derbyshire County Council. The articles were headed 'Revealed: Socialist tycoon's deals with a Labour chief . . . Bizarre deals of a council leader and the media tycoon' and 'Council share deals under scrutiny'. The articles questioned the propriety of certain investments made by the council of money in its superannuation fund in various deals with the tycoon or companies controlled by him. Following the publication, actions of damages for libel were brought against the publishers of *The Sunday Times*, its editor, and the two journalists who wrote the articles, by Derbyshire County Council and its leader. (Another action brought by the tycoon was settled by an apology and the payment of damages and costs.)

Lord Keith

There are . . . features of a local authority which may be regarded as distinguishing it from other types of corporation, whether trading or non-trading. The most important of these features is that it is a governmental body. Further, it is a democratically elected body, the electoral process nowadays being conducted almost exclusively on party political lines. It is of the highest public importance that a democratically elected governmental body, or indeed any governmental body, should be open to uninhibited public criticism. The threat of a civil action for defamation must inevitably have an inhibiting effect on freedom of speech. In *City of Chicago v Tribune Co* (1923) 139 NE 86 the Supreme Court of Illinois held that the city could not maintain an action of damages for libel. Thompson CJ said, at p. 90:

> The fundamental right of freedom of speech is involved in this litigation, and not merely the right of liberty of the press. If this action can be maintained against a newspaper it can be maintained against every private citizen who ventures to criticise the ministers who are temporarily conducting the affairs of his government. Where any person by speech or writing seeks to persuade others to violate existing law or to overthrow by force or other unlawful means the existing government, he may be punished . . . but all other utterances or publications against the government must be considered absolutely privileged. While in the early history of the struggle for freedom of speech the restrictions were enforced by criminal prosecutions, it is clear that a civil action is as great, if not a greater, restriction than a criminal prosecution. If the right to criticise the government is a privilege which, with the exceptions above enumerated, cannot be restricted, then all civil as well as criminal actions are forbidden. A despotic or corrupt government can more easily stifle opposition by a series of civil actions than by criminal prosecutions . . .

After giving a number of reasons for this, he said, at p. 90:

> It follows, therefore, that every citizen has a right to criticise an inefficient or corrupt government without fear of civil as well as criminal prosecution. This absolute privilege is founded on the principle that it is advantageous for the public interest that the citizen should not be in any way fettered in his statements, and where the public service or due administration of justice is involved he shall have the right to speak his mind freely.

These propositions were endorsed by the Supreme Court of the United States in *New York Times Co v Sullivan* (1964) 376 US 254, 277. While these decisions were related most directly to the provisions of the American Constitution concerned with securing freedom of speech, the public interest considerations which underlaid them are no less valid in this country. What has been described as 'the chilling effect' induced by the threat of civil actions for libel is very important. Quite often the facts which would justify a defamatory publication are known to be true, but admissible evidence capable of proving those facts is not available. This may prevent the publication of matters which it is very desirable to make public . . .

I regard it as right for this House to lay down that not only is there no public interest favouring the right of organs of government, whether central or local, to sue for libel, but that it is contrary to the public interest that they should have it. It is contrary to the public interest because to admit such actions would place an undesirable fetter on freedom of speech . . .

> In the case of a local authority temporarily under the control of one political party or another it is difficult to say that the local authority as such has any reputation of its own. Reputation in the eyes of the public is more likely to attach itself to the controlling political party, and with a change in that party the reputation itself will change. A publication attacking the activities of the authority will necessarily be an attack on the body of councillors which represents the controlling party, or on the executives who carry on the day to day management of its affairs. If the individual reputation of any of these is wrongly impaired by the publication any of these can himself bring proceedings for defamation. Further, it is open to the controlling body to defend itself by public utterances and in debate in the council chamber.
>
> The conclusion must be, in my opinion, that under the common law of England a local authority does not have the right to maintain an action of damages for defamation. That was the conclusion reached by the Court of Appeal, which did so principally by reference to Article 10 of the European Convention for the Protection of Human Rights and Fundamental Freedoms (1953) (Cmd 8969), to which the United Kingdom has adhered but which has not been enacted into domestic law . . .
>
> My Lords, I have reached my conclusion upon the common law of England without finding any need to rely upon the European Convention. My noble and learned friend, Lord Goff of Chieveley, in *Attorney General v Guardian Newspapers Ltd (No. 2)* [1990] 1 AC 109, 283–4, expressed the opinion that in the field of freedom of speech there was no difference in principle between English law on the subject and Article 10 of the Convention. I agree, and can only add that I find it satisfactory to be able to conclude that the common law of England is consistent with the obligations assumed by the Crown under the Treaty in this particular field.
>
> For these reasons I would dismiss the appeal . . .
>
> **Lord Griffiths, Lord Goff, Lord Browne-Wilkinson** and **Lord Woolf** concurred with Lord Keith.
>
> *Appeal dismissed.*

COMMENTARY

In *British Coal Corporation v National Union of Mineworkers*, unreported, QBD, 28 June 1996 the plaintiff, British Coal (previously the National Coal Board), sued over allegations in the magazine *Yorkshire Miner* that they had 'stolen' £450 million from the mineworkers' pension fund. French J held that the *Derbyshire* reasoning was not confined to democratically elected governmental bodies. His Lordship found that it was equally applicable to the case before him, commenting: 'the provisions of the relevant statues show how close is the control exerted by or on behalf of the minister, himself a member of a democratically elected government, over the activities of . . . the British Coal Corporation'. The same principle has also been applied to a political party (*Goldsmith v Bhoyrul* [1998] QB 459), but a university—even if publicly funded—is not an organ of government and therefore remains able to sue in respect of damage to its reputation caused by defamatory statements (*Duke v University of Salford* [2013] EWHC 196 (QB)).

The House of Lords' decision in the *Derbyshire* case came before the passage of the Human Rights Act 1998, although their Lordships were satisfied that the relevant provisions of English law were entirely consistent with the requirements of the European Convention of Human Rights (see also the *John* and *Reynolds* cases). It may therefore be questioned whether the implementation of the Act will produce any significant changes in the law in this area. Arguments have been addressed to the courts on numerous occasions to the effect that a particular rule of the law of defamation is inconsistent with the Convention right to free speech (see, e.g., *Loutchansky v Times Newspapers Ltd (No. 2)*, noted in III.3), but there are only very few examples of a court departing from established defamation principle on the basis of arguments under the HRA (see, e.g., *O'Shea v MGN Ltd*, noted in III.2; *Culnane v Morris* [2006] 1 WLR 2880). Nevertheless, one of the authors of the present book, after reviewing the relevant authorities, has concluded:

[O]f those rare cases in which reliance on the Convention rights can be said to have contributed to a change or development of defamation law, all were cases in which freedom of expression trumped the right to reputation, rather than vice versa. To that extent, the implementation of the HRA may be said to have effected a small shift in the law of defamation's centre of gravity.

(Oliphant, 'Defamation', in D. Hoffman (ed.), *The Impact of the UK Human Rights Act on Private Law* (Cambridge: CUP, 2011), p. 205.)

In *Jameel v Wall Street Journal Europe Sprl* (HL), noted in IV.4, one of the arguments before the House of Lords was that the HRA required a modification to the established approach to libel actions brought by trading corporations so as to introduce a requirement of actual, as opposed to presumed, damage. The argument attracted support from Lord Hoffmann and Lady Hale, the latter stating, at [158]:

[S]uch a requirement would achieve a proper balance between the right of a company to protect its reputation and the right of the press and public to be critical of it. These days, the dividing line between governmental and non-governmental organisations is increasingly difficult to draw. The power wielded by the major multi-national corporations is enormous and growing. The freedom to criticise them may be at least as important in a democratic society as the freedom to criticise the government.

But a majority of the House of Lords took a different view, finding that the established approach was not inconsistent with the Convention right to freedom of expression because (at [19], per Lord Bingham):

[A]s the text of article 10 itself makes plain, the right guaranteed by the article is not unqualified. The right may be circumscribed by restrictions prescribed by law and necessary and proportionate if directed to certain ends, one of which is the protection of the reputation or rights of others. Thus a national libel law may, consistently with article 10, restrain the publication of defamatory material.

Lord Bingham stated, at [21], that he considered the chilling effect of the existing rule to have been exaggerated, noting that a company's directors and individuals would in any case be free to sue as personal claimants, and the additional chilling effect resulting from the possibility of a claim by the company was therefore unlikely to be significant.

Though the Defamation Act 2013 in its original draft form did not address the position of trading corporations, a new clause inserted by the House of Lords—and ultimately accepted by the Commons—denies an action in defamation to anybody that trades for profit except where the defamatory publication causes the body serious financial loss (see now s. 1(2) of the Act; cf. Howarth, 'Libel: Its Purpose and Reform' (2011) 74 MLR 845, arguing that defamation law should not protect purely economic reputation at all, and that corporations should be unable to sue in defamation in any type of case).

The gradual development of English law to protect free speech may be contrasted with the greater boldness shown by the courts in the United States, as exemplified by the decision of the Supreme Court in the famous case of *New York Times v Sullivan*, extracted here.

New York Times Co v Sullivan, 376 US 254 (1964), United States Supreme Court

The *New York Times* published a full-page advertisement on behalf of the Committee to Defend Martin Luther King. At the bottom of the advertisement appeared the names of a number of alleged signatories, including those of the *New York Times*'s co-defendants. The advertisement protested at a 'wave of terror' against persons of colour involved in peaceful human rights demonstrations in the South of the United States, and detailed, inter alia, a number of incidents which had occurred in Montgomery, the capital of Alabama. The plaintiff was one of three elected commissioners in the city and was in charge of the city police department. He sued for defamation. The question for the Court was whether defamation law in Alabama was consistent with the Constitutional right to free speech.

Brennan J

Under Alabama law as applied in this case, a publication is 'libelous *per se*' if the words 'tend to injure a person . . . in his reputation'. . . . The question before us is whether this rule of liability, as applied to an action brought by a public official against critics of his official conduct, abridges the freedom of speech and of the press that is guaranteed by the First and Fourteenth Amendments.

Respondent relied heavily . . . on statements of this Court to the effect that the Constitution does not protect libelous publications. Those statements do not foreclose our inquiry here. None of the cases sustained the use of libel laws to impose sanctions upon expression critical of the official conduct of public officials . . . [L]ibel can claim no talismanic immunity from constitutional limitations. It must be measured by standards that satisfy the First Amendment.

The general proposition that freedom of expression upon public questions is secured by the First Amendment has long been settled by our decisions. . . . Thus we consider this case against the background of a profound national commitment to the principle that debate on public issues should be uninhibited, robust and wide-open, and that it may well include vehement, caustic, and sometime unpleasantly sharp attacks on government and public officials. . . . The present advertisement, as an expression of grievance and protest on one of the major public issues of our time, would seem clearly to qualify for the constitutional protection. The question is whether it forfeits that protection by the falsity of some of its factual statements and by its alleged defamation of respondent . . .

The constitutional guarantees require, we think, a federal rule that prohibits a public official from recovering damages for a defamatory falsehood relating to his official conduct unless he proves that the statement was made with 'actual malice'—that is, with knowledge that it was false or with reckless disregard of whether it was false or not.

COMMENTARY

In the United States (unlike England) it is generally necessary for a defamation claimant to prove fault on the part of the defendant. In *Sullivan*, the court substituted a requirement of 'actual malice' for the normal requirement of fault in cases involving the conduct of public figures. It went on to hold that there was insufficient evidence of such malice on the part of any of the defendants to support a judgment for the plaintiff-respondent. The burden of proof was to demonstrate malice with 'convincing clarity'. It was subsequently held that a defendant's 'serious doubts as to the truth of his publication' would be regarded as a species of malice (*St Amant v Thompson*, 390 US 727 (1968)). For a detailed account of the background to and impact of *Sullivan*, see A. Lewis, *Make No Law* (New York: Vintage Books, 1991).

The question whether a rule similar to that of *New York Times v Sullivan* should be introduced into English law was considered by both the Faulks and Neill Committees on Defamation (see *Report on Defamation*, Cmnd. 5909, 1975; *Report on Practice and Procedure in Defamation*, 1991). On both occasions, such a reform was considered undesirable. The Neill Committee commented (at 164–5):

> Standards of care and accuracy in the press are, in our view, not such as to give any confidence that a '*Sullivan*' defence would be treated responsibly. It would mean, in effect, that newspapers could publish more or less what they liked, provided they were honest, if their subject happened to be within the definition of a 'public figure'. We think this would lead to great injustice. Furthermore, it would be quite contrary to the tradition of our common law that citizens are not divided into different classes. What matters is the subject matter of the publication and how it is treated, rather than who happens to be the subject of the allegations. In our view the media are adequately protected by the defences of justification and fair comment at the moment, and it is salutary that these defences are available to them only if they have got their facts substantially correct.

In *Reynolds v Times Newspapers* (extracted in IV.3(b) and IV.4), the House of Lords indicated that it did not consider the *Sullivan* defence suited to English conditions (though it was not required to rule on the question).

With the recognition in *Reynolds* of an adapted public interest defence, and the broadening of the defence of honest opinion (see IV.2), plus the further reforms effected by the Defamation Act 2013, the distance between English and US law becomes much closer. However, it seems that English law will still allow liability to arise in respect of inadequately verified allegations of fact made against a public figure in circumstances in which liability under US law would be excluded by *Sullivan*. In your opinion, which legal system better balances the competing interests in reputation and freedom of expression in this context?

13 PRIVACY

1. Introduction

> **European Convention for the Protection of Human Rights and Fundamental Freedoms**
>
> **Article 8**
>
> Right to respect for private and family life
>
> (1) Everyone has the right to respect for his private and family life, his home and his correspondence.
>
> (2) There shall be no interference by a public authority with the exercise of this right except such as is in accordance with law and is necessary in a democratic society in the interests of national security, public safety, or the economic well-being of the country, for the prevention of disorder or crime, for the protection of health or morals, or for the protection of the rights and freedoms of others.

The right of privacy under Article 8 of the European Convention was incorporated into English law by the Human Rights Act 1998, but English law as yet recognises no tort of invasion of privacy as such. Admittedly, a number of specific torts protect particular aspects of privacy, but this protection may be regarded as haphazard, incidental and incomplete. Indeed the courts have adopted something of a scatter-gun approach, well-illustrated by *Kaye v Robertson* [1991] FSR 62 (extracted later), whereby a number of causes of action are fired at a problematic case in the hope that one might hit the target. The English judiciary has been almost entirely immune to the persuasive advocacy of a general privacy tort by judges and commentators in the United States, notably Warren and Brandeis in a famous article in the *Harvard Law Review* (see the next extract). Recent decades, however, have seen substantial developments in the protection given to particular privacy interests, above all by adapting the law of breach of confidence to provide a remedy against the unauthorised disclosure of personal information (see II).

> **S. Warren and L. Brandeis, 'The Right to Privacy'**
> (1890) 4 Harv L Rev 193
>
> That the individual shall have full protection in person and in property is a principle as old as the common law; but it has been found necessary from time to time to define anew the exact nature and extent of such protection. Political, social, and economic changes entail

the recognition of new rights, and the common law, in its eternal youth, grows to meet the demands of society. Thus, in very early times, the law gave a remedy only for physical interference with life and property, for trespasses *vi et armis*. Then the 'right to life' served only to protect the subject from battery in its various forms; liberty meant freedom from actual restraint; and the right to property secured to the individual his lands and his cattle. Later, there came a recognition of man's spiritual nature, of his feelings and his intellect. Gradually the scope of these legal rights broadened; and now the right to life has come to mean the right to enjoy life—the right to be let alone; the right to liberty secures the exercise of extensive civil privileges; and the term 'property' has grown to comprise every form of possession—intangible as well as tangible . . .

Recent inventions and business methods call attention to the next step which must be taken for the protection of the person, and for securing to the individual what Judge Cooley calls the right 'to be let alone' (*Cooley on Torts*, 2nd edn (1888), p. 29). Instantaneous photographs and newspaper enterprise have invaded the sacred precincts of private and domestic life; and numerous mechanical devices threaten to make good the prediction that 'what is whispered in the closet shall be proclaimed from the house-tops.' For years there has been a feeling that the law must afford some remedy for the unauthorized circulation of portraits of private persons; and the evil of the invasion of privacy by newspapers, long keenly felt, has been but recently discussed . . .

Of the desirability—indeed of the necessity—of some such protection, there can, it is believed, be no doubt. The press is overstepping in every direction the obvious bounds of propriety and of decency. Gossip is no longer the resource of the idle and of the vicious, but has become a trade, which is pursued with industry as well as effrontery. . . . The intensity and complexity of life, attendant upon advancing civilization, have rendered necessary some retreat from the world, and man, under the refining influence of culture, has become more sensitive to publicity, so that solitude and privacy have become more essential to the individual; but modern enterprise and invention have, through invasions upon his privacy, subjected him to mental pain and distress, far greater than could be inflicted by mere bodily injury. . . . It is our purpose to consider whether the existing law affords a principle which can properly be invoked to protect the privacy of the individual; and, if it does, what the nature and extent of such protection is . . .

[Having considered, and rejected, the possibility that the law of defamation might provide such a principle, the authors continue:]

[T]he legal doctrines relating to infractions of what is ordinarily termed the common-law right to intellectual and artistic property are, it is believed, but instances and applications of a general right to privacy, which properly understood afford a remedy for the evils under consideration.

The common law secures to each individual the right of determining, ordinarily, to what extent his thoughts, sentiments, and emotions shall be communicated to others. . . . The existence of this right does not depend upon the particular method of expression adopted. It is immaterial whether it be by word or by signs, in painting, by sculpture, or in music. Neither does the existence of the right depend upon the nature or value of the thought or emotion, nor upon the excellence of the means of expression. The same protection is accorded to a casual letter or an entry in a diary and to the most valuable poem or essay, to a botch or daub and a masterpiece. In every such case the individual is entitled to decide whether that which is his shall be given to the public. No other has the right to publish his productions in any form, without his consent. . . . The right is lost only when the author himself communicates his production to the public—in other words, publishes it. It is entirely independent of the copyright laws, and their extension into the domain of art. The aim of those statutes is to secure to the author, composer, or artist the entire profits arising from his publication; but the common-law protection enables him to control absolutely the act of publication, and in the exercise of his own discretion, to decide whether there shall be any publication at all . . .

What is the nature, the basis of this right to prevent the publication of manuscripts or works of art? It is stated to be the enforcement of a right of property; and no difficulty arises in accepting this view, so long as we have only to deal with the reproduction of literary and artistic compositions. They certainly possess many of the attributes of ordinary property: they are transferable; they have a value; and publication or reproduction is a use by which that value is realized. But where the value of the production is found not in the right to take the profits arising from publication, but in peace of mind or the relief afforded by the ability to prevent any publication at all, it is difficult to regard the right as one of property, in the common acceptation of that term. A man records in a letter to his son, or in his diary, that he did not dine with his wife on a certain day. No one into whose hands those papers fall could publish them to the world, even if possession of the documents had been obtained rightfully; and the prohibition would not be confined to the publication of a copy of a letter itself, or of the diary entry; the restraint extends also to a publication of the contents. What is the thing protected? Surely, not the intellectual act of recording the fact that the husband did not dine with his wife, but that fact itself. It is not the intellectual product, but the domestic occurrence . . .

Although the courts have asserted that they rested their decisions on the narrow grounds of protection to property, yet there are recognitions of a more liberal doctrine. Thus in the case of *Prince Albert v Strange* (1849) 1 McN & G 23 . . . the opinions of both the Vice-Chancellor and of the Lord Chancellor, on appeal, show a more or less clearly defined perception of a principle broader than those which were mainly discussed, and on which they both placed their chief reliance . . .

These considerations lead to the conclusion that the protection afforded to thoughts, sentiments, and emotions, expressed through the medium of writing or of the arts, so far as it consists in preventing publication, is merely an instance of the enforcement of the more general right of the individual to be let alone. It is like the right not to be assaulted or beaten, the right not to be imprisoned, the right not to be maliciously prosecuted, the right not to be defamed. In each of these rights, as indeed in all other rights recognised by the law, there inheres the quality of being owned or possessed—and (as that is the distinguishing attribute of property) there may be some propriety in speaking of those rights as property. But, obviously, they bear little resemblance to what is ordinarily comprehended under that term. The principle which protects personal writings and all other personal productions, not against theft and physical appropriation, but against publication in any form, is in reality not the principle of private property, but that of an inviolate personality . . .

It should be stated that, in some instances where protection has been afforded against wrongful publication, the jurisdiction has been asserted, not on the ground of property, or at least not wholly on that ground, but upon the grounds of an alleged breach of an implied contract or of a trust or confidence . . .

[T]he courts, in searching for some principle upon which the publication of private letters could be enjoined, naturally came upon the ideas of breach of confidence, and of an implied contract; but it required little consideration to discern that this would not support the court in granting a remedy against a stranger; and so the theory of property in the contents of letters was adopted . . .

We must . . . conclude that the rights, so protected, whatever their exact nature, are not rights arising from contract or from special trust, but are rights against the world; and, as above stated, the principle which has been applied to protect these rights is in reality not the principle of private property, unless that word be used in an extended and unusual sense.

> The principle which protects personal writings and any other productions of the intellect or of the emotions, is the right to privacy, and the law has no new principle to formulate when it extends this protection to the personal appearance, sayings, acts and to personal relations, domestic or otherwise.

COMMENTARY

No later writers have pleaded the case for a right to privacy and a remedy for its violation more eloquently than Warren and Brandeis. Their advocacy was instrumental in the development of liability for breach of privacy throughout the United States; and all on the basis of a creative interpretation of *English* authorities, notably *Albert v Strange* (1849) 1 McN & G 23.

Albert v Strange

Albert v Strange involved the unauthorised copying of etchings made by Queen Victoria and her husband for their private amusement. The etchings, which represented Victoria and Albert's children and other subjects of personal interest, had been kept privately by the Royal Family, although a few copies had been given to friends. The plates of the etchings were entrusted to a printer in Windsor for him to make further impressions. One of his employees made unauthorised copies which were sold to the defendant. The defendant proposed to exhibit them and publish a catalogue with their descriptions, but Prince Albert succeeded in getting an injunction to prevent both the exhibition and the publication of the catalogue. Lord Cottenham LC accepted that it was justified on the grounds of both the enforcement of the Prince's property right and the employee's breach of confidence.

In their article, Warren and Brandeis argue that the real basis of the decision in *Albert v Strange* was not the enforcement of property rights (as stated by the court) but the protection of privacy. In their view, there could be no other explanation for the fact that the rule prevented not only the reproduction of the etchings made by the plaintiff and Queen Victoria but also the publication of any description of them: the former would be a copyright infringement under the law of intellectual property, but the latter is only explicable as the protection of the right to privacy. On this basis Warren and Brandeis argued that the right to privacy was already recognised in the common law and could therefore be applied by analogy to novel situations without the need for (judicial) legislation. The English courts, however, were resistant to the idea that there was a general right to privacy whose invasion was actionable in damages, and continued to look on an ad-hoc basis for established causes of action that might provide incidental protection against intrusions into the claimant's private sphere, as in the next extract.

Kaye v Robertson [1991] FSR 62

The well-known actor Gorden Kaye, star of the television series *Allo!, Allo!*, was injured whilst driving his car when a piece of wood was detached from an advertising hoarding by gale-force winds and smashed through the vehicle's windscreen. He suffered very serious injuries to his head and brain and was taken to hospital, where he was put on a life-support machine and then in intensive care; he subsequently recovered sufficiently to be moved into a private room. At a time at which the actor was still in no fit condition to be interviewed, a journalist and photographer from the *Sunday Sport* newspaper gained access to Kaye's private room, ignoring notices which made it clear that they were not allowed to be there, and attempted to conduct an interview with him. The photographer took pictures which showed, inter alia, the substantial scarring on the actor's head. An interim application was made on the actor's behalf for injunctions to prevent the *Sunday Sport* from publishing an article, of which the actor's advisers had seen a draft, which claimed that Kaye had agreed to give an exclusive interview to the paper. Injunctions in the terms requested were granted by Potter J. The defendants, editor and publishers of the paper, appealed to the Court of Appeal.

Glidewell LJ

It is well-known that in English law there is no right to privacy, and accordingly there is no right of action for breach of a person's privacy. The facts of the present case are a graphic illustration of the desirability of Parliament considering whether and in what circumstances statutory provision can be made to protect the privacy of individuals.

In the absence of such a right, the plaintiff's advisers have sought to base their claim to injunctions upon other well-established rights of action. These are:

1. Libel

2. Malicious falsehood

3. Trespass to the person

4. Passing off.

The appeal canvassed all four rights of action, and it is necessary to deal with each in turn.

1. Libel

The basis of the plaintiff's case under this head is that the article as originally written clearly implied that Mr Kaye consented to give the first 'exclusive' interview to *Sunday Sport*, and to be photographed by their photographer. This was untrue: Mr Kaye was in no fit condition to give any informed consent, and such consent as he may appear to have given was, and should have been known by *Sunday Sport*'s representative to be, of no effect. The implication in the article would have the effect of lowering Mr Kaye in the esteem of right-thinking people, and was thus defamatory.

The plaintiff's case is based on the well-known decision in *Tolley v J S Fry & Sons Ltd* [1931] AC 333. Mr Tolley was a well-known amateur golfer. Without his consent, Fry published an advertisement which consisted of a caricature of the plaintiff with a caddie, each with a packet of Fry's chocolate protruding from his pocket. The caricature was accompanied by doggerel verse which used Mr Tolley's name and extolled the virtues of the chocolate. The plaintiff alleged that the advertisement implied that he had received payment for the advertisement, which would damage his reputation as an amateur player. The judge at the trial ruled that the advertisement was capable of being defamatory, and on appeal the House of Lords upheld this ruling.

It seems that an analogy with *Tolley v Fry* was the main plank of Potter J's decision to grant injunctions in this case.

Mr Milmo for the defendants submits that, assuming that the article was capable of having the meaning alleged, this would not be a sufficient basis for interlocutory relief. In *Coulson (William) & Sons v James Coulson & Co* [recte, (1887) 3 TLR 46], this court held that, though the High Court has jurisdiction to grant an interim injunction before the trial of a libel action, it is a jurisdiction to be exercised only sparingly. . . . This is still the rule in actions for defamation, despite the decision of the House of Lords in *American Cyanamid Co v Ethicon Ltd* [1975] AC 396 in relation to interim injunctions generally . . .

Mr Milmo submits that on the evidence we cannot be confident that any jury would inevitably decide that the implication that Mr Kaye had consented to give his first interview to *Sunday Sport* was libellous. Accordingly, we ought not to grant interlocutory relief on this ground. It is in my view certainly arguable that the intended article would be libellous, on the authority of *Tolley v Fry*. I think that a jury would probably find that Mr Kaye had been libelled, but I cannot say that such a conclusion is inevitable. It follows that I agree with Mr Milmo's submission and in this respect I disagree with the learned judge; I therefore would not base an injunction on a right of action for libel.

2. Malicious Falsehood

The essentials of this tort are that the defendant has published about the plaintiff words which are false, that they were published maliciously, and that special damage has followed as the direct and natural result of their publication. As to special damage, the effect of section 3(1) of the Defamation Act 1952 is that it is sufficient if the words published in writing are calculated to cause pecuniary damage to the plaintiff. Malice will be inferred if it be proved that the words were calculated to produce damage and that the defendant knew when he published the words that they were false or was reckless as to whether they were false or not.

The test in *Coulson (William) & Sons v James Coulson & Co (supra)* applies to interlocutory injunctions in actions for malicious falsehood as it does in actions for defamation. However, in relation to this action, the test applies only to the requirement that the plaintiff must show that the words were false. In the present case I have no doubt that any jury which did not find that the clear implication from the words contained in the defendants' draft article were false would be making a totally unreasonable finding. Thus the test is satisfied in relation to this cause of action.

As to malice I equally have no doubt from the evidence, including the transcript of the tape-recording of the 'interview' with Mr Kaye in his hospital room which we have read, that it was quite apparent to the reporter and photographer from *Sunday Sport* that Mr Kaye was in no condition to give any informed consent to their interviewing or photographing him. Moreover, even if the journalists had been in any doubt about Mr Kaye's fitness to give his consent, Mr Robertson could not have entertained any such doubt after he read the affidavit sworn on behalf of Mr Kaye in these proceedings. Any subsequent publication of the falsehood would therefore inevitably be malicious.

As to damage, I have already recorded that Mr Robertson appreciated that Mr Kaye's story was one for which other newspapers would be willing to pay 'large sums of money.' It needs little imagination to appreciate that whichever journal secured the first interview with Mr Kaye would be willing to pay the most. Mr Kaye thus has a potentially valuable right to sell the story of his accident and his recovery when he is fit enough to tell it. If the defendants are able to publish the article they proposed, or one anything like it, the value of this right would in my view be seriously lessened, and Mr Kaye's story thereafter be worth much less to him.

I have considered whether damages would be an adequate remedy in these circumstances. They would inevitably be difficult to calculate, would also follow some time after the event, and in my view would in no way be adequate. It thus follows that in my opinion all the preconditions to the grant of an interlocutory injunction in respect of this cause of action are made out. I will return later to what I consider to be the appropriate form of injunction.

3. Trespass to the Person

It is strictly unnecessary to consider this cause of action in the light of the view I have expressed about malicious falsehood. However, I will set out my view shortly. The plaintiff's case in relation to this cause of action is that the taking of the flashlight photographs may well have caused distress to Mr Kaye and set back his recovery, and thus caused him injury. In this sense it can be said to be a battery. Mr Caldecott, for Mr Kaye, could not refer us to any authority in which the taking of a photograph or indeed the flashing of a light had been held to be a battery. Nevertheless I am prepared to accept that it may well be the case that if a bright light is deliberately shone into another person's eyes and injures his sight, or damages him in some other way, this may be in law a battery. But in my view the necessary effects are not established by the evidence in this case. Though there must have been an obvious risk that any disturbance to Mr Kaye would set back his recovery, there is no evidence that the taking of the photographs did in fact cause him any damage. Moreover, the injunction sought in relation to this head of action would not be intended to prevent another anticipated battery, since none was anticipated. The intention here is to prevent the defendants from profiting from the taking of the photographs, i.e. from their own trespass. Attractive though this argument may appear to be, I cannot find as a matter of law that an injunction should be granted in these circumstances. Accordingly I would not base an injunction on this cause of action.

4. Passing Off

Mr Caldecott submits (though in this case not with any great vigour) that the essentials of the tort of passing off, as laid down by the speeches in the House of Lords in *E Warnink BV v J Townend & Sons (Hull) Ltd* [1979] AC 731, are satisfied here. I only need say shortly that in my view they are not. I think that the plaintiff is not in the position of a trader in relation to his interest in his story about his accident and his recovery, and thus fails from the start to have a right of action under this head.

Bingham LJ

This case . . . highlights, yet again, the failure of both the common law of England and statute to protect in an effective way the personal privacy of individual citizen. . . . If ever a person has a right to be let alone by strangers with no public interest to pursue, it must surely be when he lies in a hospital bed recovering from brain surgery and in no more than partial command of his faculties. It is this invasion of privacy which underlies the plaintiff's complaint. Yet it alone, however gross, does not entitle him to relief in English law . . .

[A] cause of action in malicious falsehood exists, but even that obliges us to limit the relief we can grant in a way which would not bind us if the plaintiff's cause of action arose from the invasion of privacy of which, fundamentally, he complains. We cannot give the plaintiff the breadth of protection which I would, for my part, wish.

Leggatt LJ

We do not need a First Amendment to preserve the freedom of the press, but the abuse of that freedom can be ensured only by the enforcement of a right to privacy. This right has so long been disregarded here that it can be recognised now only by the legislature. Especially since there is available in the United States a wealth of experience of the enforcement of this right both at common law and also under statute, it is to be hoped that the making good of this signal shortcoming in our law will not be long delayed.

Appeal allowed in part. Injunctions varied.

COMMENTARY

Kaye was granted an injunction to restrain publication of the malicious falsehood. Note the limited utility of this remedy (remarked upon by Bingham LJ): it allowed the publication of the story and certain less objectionable photographs provided that it was not claimed that the plaintiff had given his consent. The story eventually ran with a photograph of the actor lying asleep in bed.

What was the interest that the plaintiff was seeking to protect? Surely it was his interest in keeping his personal space inviolate and the details of his personal circumstances out of the public eye. By allowing him a remedy only in the tort of malicious falsehood, however, the law of the day made it appear that his principal concern was in the commercial exploitation of his situation.

Cf. the American case of *Barber v Time Inc*, 159 SW 2d 291 (1942), where the publication of the plaintiff's photograph, taken without consent whilst she was confined to a hospital bed, was held to be an invasion of a private right for which she was entitled to damages.

Subsequent Developments in English Law

After *Kaye v Robertson*, English law has changed very significantly, and readers should come back to the case after reading to the end of this chapter so as to consider whether the result reached by the Court of Appeal in 1991 would still be the outcome of such a case if brought today.

An initial question to be addressed is whether, as contemplated by the Court of Appeal, English law should recognise a new tortious cause of action for invasion of privacy. The case for a new tort was first given official consideration in England by the Younger Committee in 1972 (*Report on Privacy*, Cmnd. 5012). In fact, the committee came out against the recognition of a general right to privacy, regarding such a concept as 'ill-defined and unstable'. But it did recommend the creation of a set of new criminal offences and tortious liabilities (amongst the latter were a tort of unlawful surveillance by means of a technical device and a tort of disclosure or other use of information unlawfully acquired). The proposed new tortious liabilities were not implemented. Subsequently, Sir David Calcutt in his *Review of Press Self-Regulation* (1993, Cmnd. 2135) recommended that the case for a new statutory tort be reconsidered. Though the (Conservative) government of the day declined to do this, the Labour government elected in 1997 had the right to privacy very much in the forefront of its mind when it brought forward the legislation that became the Human Rights Act 1998. As already noted, the right to private life is one of the Convention rights (Article 8, ECHR) incorporated into English law under the Act. *Kaye v Robertson* was decided before the Act's implementation, and it fell to the House of Lords in *Wainwright v Home Office* [2004] 2 AC 406 (HL), extracted here, to determine the Act's effect on the judicial remedies available for the invasion of privacy.

Wainwright v Home Office [2004] 2 AC 406 (HL)

The claimants, a mother and her son, were subjected to strip searches on a prison visit to see the first claimant's son and the second claimant's half-brother, O'Neill. The prison authorities suspected that O'Neill was dealing in drugs in the prison and required all visitors who wanted an open visit with him to submit to a strip search. It was subsequently found that the searches of the claimants were conducted in breach of the prison's own rules. The claimants sought damages for (amongst other things) the invasion of their privacy, and succeeded in the County Court. The Court of Appeal allowed the defendant's appeal, and the claimants took their case to the House of Lords. (Other aspects of the decision are considered in Ch. 2.V.)

Lord Hoffmann

15. My Lords, let us first consider the proposed tort of invasion of privacy. Since the famous article by Warren and Brandeis ('The Right to Privacy' (1890) 4 Harvard LR 193) the question

of whether such a tort exists, or should exist, has been much debated in common law jurisdictions. Warren and Brandeis suggested that one could generalise certain cases on defamation, breach of copyright in unpublished letters, trade secrets and breach of confidence as all based upon the protection of a common value which they called privacy or, following Judge Cooley (*Cooley on Torts*, 2nd edn (1888), p. 29) 'the right to be let alone'. They said that identifying this common element should enable the courts to declare the existence of a general principle which protected a person's appearance, sayings, acts and personal relations from being exposed in public.

16. Courts in the United States were receptive to this proposal and a jurisprudence of privacy began to develop. It became apparent, however, that the developments could not be contained within a single principle; not, at any rate, one with greater explanatory power than the proposition that it was based upon the protection of a value which could be described as privacy. Dean Prosser, in his work on *The Law of Torts*, 4th edn (1971), p. 804, said that:

> What has emerged is no very simple matter . . . it is not one tort, but a complex of four. To date the law of privacy comprises four distinct kinds of invasion of four different interests of the plaintiff, which are tied together by the common name, but otherwise have almost nothing in common except that each represents an interference with the right of the plaintiff 'to be let alone'.

17. Dean Prosser's taxonomy divided the subject into (1) intrusion upon the plaintiff's physical solitude or seclusion (including unlawful searches, telephone tapping, long-distance photography and telephone harassment) (2) public disclosure of private facts and (3) publicity putting the plaintiff in a false light and (4) appropriation, for the defendant's advantage, of the plaintiff's name or likeness. These, he said, at p. 814, had different elements and were subject to different defences.

18. The need in the United States to break down the concept of 'invasion of privacy' into a number of loosely-linked torts must cast doubt upon the value of any high-level generalisation which can perform a useful function in enabling one to deduce the rule to be applied in a concrete case. English law has so far been unwilling, perhaps unable, to formulate any such high-level principle. There are a number of common law and statutory remedies of which it may be said that one at least of the underlying values they protect is a right of privacy . . . Common law torts include trespass, nuisance, defamation and malicious falsehood; there is the equitable action for breach of confidence and statutory remedies under the Protection from Harassment Act 1997 and the Data Protection Act 1998. There are also extra-legal remedies under Codes of Practice applicable to broadcasters and newspapers. But there are gaps; cases in which the courts have considered that an invasion of privacy deserves a remedy which the existing law does not offer. Sometimes the perceived gap can be filled by judicious development of an existing principle. The law of breach of confidence has in recent years undergone such a process . . . On the other hand, an attempt to create a tort of telephone harassment by a radical change in the basis of the action for private nuisance in *Khorasandjian v Bush* [1993] QB 727 was held by the House of Lords in *Hunter v Canary Wharf Ltd* [1997] AC 655 (HL) to be a step too far. The gap was filled by the 1997 Act.

19. What the courts have so far refused to do is to formulate a general principle of 'invasion of privacy' (I use the quotation marks to signify doubt about what in such a context the expression would mean) from which the conditions of liability in the particular case can be deduced . . .

31. There seems to me a great difference between identifying privacy as a value which underlies the existence of a rule of law (and may point the direction in which the law should develop) and privacy as a principle of law in itself. The English common law is familiar with the

notion of underlying values—principles only in the broadest sense—which direct its development. A famous example is *Derbyshire County Council v Times Newspapers Ltd* [1993] AC 534, in which freedom of speech was the underlying value which supported the decision to lay down the specific rule that a local authority could not sue for libel. But no one has suggested that freedom of speech is in itself a legal principle which is capable of sufficient definition to enable one to deduce specific rules to be applied in concrete cases. That is not the way the common law works.

32. Nor is there anything in the jurisprudence of the European Court of Human Rights which suggests that the adoption of some high level principle of privacy is necessary to comply with article 8 of the Convention. The European Court is concerned only with whether English law provides an adequate remedy in a specific case in which it considers that there has been an invasion of privacy contrary to article 8(1) and not justifiable under article 8(2). So in *Earl Spencer v United Kingdom* (1998) 25 EHRR CD105 it was satisfied that the action for breach of confidence provided an adequate remedy for the Spencers' complaint and looked no further into the rest of the armoury of remedies available to the victims of other invasions of privacy. Likewise, in *Peck v United Kingdom* Application No 44647/98 (2003) 36 EHRR 41 the court expressed some impatience, at paragraph 103, at being given a tour d'horizon of the remedies provided and to be provided by English law to deal with every imaginable kind of invasion of privacy. It was concerned with whether Mr Peck (who had been filmed in embarrassing circumstances by a CCTV camera) had an adequate remedy when the film was widely published by the media. It came to the conclusion that he did not.

33. Counsel for the Wainwrights relied upon *Peck's* case as demonstrating the need for a general tort of invasion of privacy. But in my opinion it shows no more than the need, in English law, for a system of control of the use of film from CCTV cameras which shows greater sensitivity to the feelings of people who happen to have been caught by the lens . . . [T]his is an area which requires a detailed approach which can be achieved only by legislation rather than the broad brush of common law principle.

34. Furthermore, the coming into force of the Human Rights Act 1998 weakens the argument for saying that a general tort of invasion of privacy is needed to fill gaps in the existing remedies. Sections 6 and 7 of the Act are in themselves substantial gap fillers; if it is indeed the case that a person's rights under article 8 have been infringed by a public authority, he will have a statutory remedy. The creation of a general tort will . . . pre-empt the controversial question of the extent, if any, to which the Convention requires the state to provide remedies for invasions of privacy by persons who are not public authorities . . .

[Lord Hoffmann proceeded to consider, and reject, a possible liability under *Wilkinson v Downton* (see the extract in Ch. 2.V), before returning to the matter of the claimants' Convention rights;]

48. Counsel for the Wainwrights submit that unless the law is extended to create a tort which covers the facts of the present case, it is inevitable that the European Court of Human Rights will find that the United Kingdom was in breach of its Convention obligation to provide a remedy for infringements of Convention rights. In addition to a breach of article 8, they say that the prison officers infringed their Convention right under article 3 not to be subjected to degrading treatment.

49. I have no doubt that there was no infringement of article 3. The conduct of the searches came nowhere near the degree of humiliation which has been held by the European Court of Human Rights to be degrading treatment . . .

50. In the present case, the judge found that the prison officers acted in good faith and that there had been no more than 'sloppiness' in the failures to comply with the rules. The prison officers did not wish to humiliate the claimants . . .

51. Article 8 is more difficult. Buxton LJ thought [2002] QB 1334 at [62], that the Wainwrights would have had a strong case for relief under section 7 if the 1998 Act had been in force. Speaking for myself, I am not so sure. Although article 8 guarantees a right of privacy, I do not think that it treats that right as having been invaded and requiring a remedy in damages, irrespective of whether the defendant acted intentionally, negligently or accidentally. It is one thing to wander carelessly into the wrong hotel bedroom and another to hide in the wardrobe to take photographs. Article 8 may justify a monetary remedy for an intentional invasion of privacy by a public authority, even if no damage is suffered other than distress for which damages are not ordinarily recoverable. It does not follow that a merely negligent act should, contrary to general principle, give rise to a claim for damages for distress because it affects privacy rather than some other interest like bodily safety: compare *Hicks v Chief Constable of South Yorkshire Police* [1992] 2 All ER 65.

52. Be that as it may, a finding that there was a breach of article 8 will only demonstrate that there was a gap in the English remedies for invasion of privacy which has since been filled by sections 6 and 7 of the 1998 Act. It does not require that the courts should provide an alternative remedy which distorts the principles of the common law.

53. I would therefore dismiss the appeal.

Lord Bingham, **Lord Hope**, **Lord Hutton** and **Lord Scott** concurred.

Appeal dismissed.

COMMENTARY

For Lord Hoffmann, the right of privacy was a *value* underlying the law but not a *principle* susceptible of direct application to individual claims. His antipathy towards a 'high level' privacy principle has been shared by a number of commentators, e.g. Wacks, who has argued: '"Privacy" has become as nebulous a concept as "happiness" or "security". Except as a general abstraction of an underlying value, it should not be used as a means to describe a legal right . . .' ('The Poverty of "Privacy"' (1980) 96 LQR 73).

As Lord Hoffmann noted, even in the United States, where the right to privacy is accepted as a principle, liability for invasion of privacy has to be broken down into a set of loosely linked and much narrower torts to provide adequate guidance on specific facts. The four types of invasion of privacy identified by Prosser, summarised by Lord Hoffmann in the extract, are now to be found in the US *Restatement of the Law of Torts*, 2d, 1977, § 652A. Reviewing the protection of the four distinct privacy interests in English law, Hartshorne finds that two receive protection comparable to that in the United States (disclosure of private facts and 'false light'), that the protection of name and likeness lags behind that across the Atlantic, though justifiably as the interest is more proprietary than personal, and that the major area of continuing concern is the lack of current protection against intrusion upon solitude or seclusion ('The Protection of Prosser's Privacy Categories within English Tort Law' (2014) 22 TLJ 37; see also Moreham, 'Beyond Information: Physical Privacy in English Law' [2014] CLJ 350). At present, the victim of voyeuristic spying or non-consensual filming during intimate moments generally has no remedy in English law as the gist of the wrong done is not the disclosure or even the misuse of *information* but the fact of *intrusion* into the private realm.

Do you agree with Hartshorne and Moreham that the law should extend its protection from informational to what the latter calls 'physical' privacy?

Protection of Privacy Interests by Way of Specific Torts

Pending any such development, English law remains committed to the 'scatter-gun' approach exemplified by *Kaye v Robertson*, and requires the claimant to make up for the lack of any general privacy tort by pleading as many specific torts as might plausibly provide a remedy on the facts. The protection offered by a selection of different torts is considered briefly in the following text (see also Seipp, 'English Judicial Recognition of a Right to Privacy' (1983) 3 OJLS 325), before we turn in the succeeding section of this chapter to the recent emergence of a new cause of action relating specifically to the disclosure of private information.

(I) Trespass to the Person and the Rule in *Wilkinson v Downton*

Various torts protect against the intentional infringement of rights over one's body. Assault and battery protect bodily integrity; false imprisonment protects personal liberty. The rule in *Wilkinson v Downton* [1897] 2 QB 57 has been invoked as a remedy against harassment (see *Khorasandjian v Bush* [1993] QB 727), although Parliament has gone further still by introducing a statutory liability under the Protection from Harassment Act 1997. The Act allows the imposition of liability where the claimant merely suffers upset, humiliation, alarm or distress, but it is doubtful that the common law liability goes so far. In *Wainwright*, at [46], Lord Hoffmann suggested that the Act's requirement of 'a course of conduct' demonstrated Parliament's desire to adopt a cautious approach in this area, and that the common law might be advised to show similar caution, but the matter did not arise for final decision because the claimants could not show intention on the facts. The matter is given further consideration in Chapter 2.V and is not pursued further here.

(II) Trespass to Land and Nuisance

'An Englishman's home is his castle', and the torts of trespass to land and nuisance provide substantial protection of every person's interest in being left alone while on their land. A *trespass to land* is an unauthorised entry onto land possessed by another person. Photographers hiding in the bushes of one's land commit the tort of trespass, as does a voyeur who hides in someone's bathroom to watch them shower. However, the protection provided by the tort of trespass to land suffers from two major limitations. First, it only applies to physical invasions of land possessed by the claimant, not to physical invasions of land not possessed but only used by them (see *White v Bayley* (1861) 10 CB (NS) 227). Hence, no claim in trespass can be brought by a lodger living in another's house, a guest staying in a hotel bedroom or a patient in a hospital ward. Secondly, trespass does not apply to simple spying upon the claimant's land from neighbouring property or indeed from the skies. In *Baron Bernstein of Leigh v Skyviews Ltd* [1978] QB 479, Griffiths J held that an aeroplane used to take aerial photographs of the estate of Lord Bernstein of Leigh, former owner of the Granada TV channel, did not trespass on his land; the judge ruled that a landowner's rights are limited 'to such a height as is necessary for the ordinary use and enjoyment of his land'. (Cf. *Anchor Brewhouse Developments Ltd v Berkley House (Docklands Developments) Ltd* (1987) 38 BLR 82.)

A number of cases falling outside the scope of trespass may nevertheless give rise to liability in the tort of *private nuisance*. Private nuisance covers a number of interferences with a person's use or enjoyment of land, ranging from persistent telephoning (*Khorasandjian v Bush*, above) to 'watching and besetting' (*Thomas v NUM* [1986] Ch 20; could this perhaps cover the encampment of journalists outside the claimant's house?). Though there is no right in private nuisance not to be overlooked on one's land, even in one's home (*Fearn v Board of Trustees of the Tate Gallery* [2020] Ch 621), these examples show that the tort is capable of remedying at least some types of intrusion into the peaceful enjoyment of one's property. Another possible example was considered in *Baron Bernstein of Leigh v Skyviews Ltd*, where Griffiths J considered the potential liability in private nuisance of those photographing activities on neighbouring land (at 489):

[N]o court would regard the taking of a single photograph as an actionable nuisance. But if the circumstances were such that a plaintiff was subjected to the harassment of constant surveillance of his house from the air, accompanied by the photographing of his every activity, I am far from saying that the court would not regard such a monstrous invasion of his privacy as an actionable nuisance for which they would give relief.

A very significant limitation on the protection provided by this tort is that private nuisance is actionable only by a person with an interest in the land affected (*Hunter v Canary Wharf* [1997] AC 655), and not by that person's spouse, children or house guests. It has been suggested that this rule may be inconsistent with the European Convention on Human Rights, but as yet it remains the law (see further in Ch. 11.II.4).

(III) Defamation

Although the tort of defamation protects an interest in 'personality', the interest that it protects (reputation) is very different from the interest in privacy. Under defamation law, a defendant has a complete defence of truth if the imputation in question is shown to be substantially correct; there is no need to demonstrate that its publication was in the public interest. This effectively undermines any potential that the law of defamation might have had for ensuring the secrecy of private information. The tort of defamation does, it must be admitted, provide some protection of privacy where the claimant is portrayed in a 'false light' (as in *Tolley v J S Fry & Sons Ltd*, discussed in the extract from *Kaye v Robertson*; for the wider context, see *Mitchell*, pp. 177–9), and to that extent prevents others from appropriating a person's name, image or likeness (which is one of the privacy interests listed by Prosser and in the US *Restatement of Torts*, 2d: see earlier). But it is arguable that this is primarily a public commercial matter, not a matter of personal privacy, for in many cases the complaint is that the defendant's conduct has served to reduce the claimant's market value and thereby prevented the claimant from themselves profiting to the utmost extent from the commercial exploitation of their name, image or likeness.

II. Misuse of Private Information

Notwithstanding the diversity of privacy interests addressed in the preceding section of this chapter, when people talk of privacy they are usually talking about what the Younger Committee termed 'privacy of information, that is the right to determine for oneself how and to what extent information about oneself is communicated to others' (*Report of the Committee on Privacy*, 1972, Cmnd. 5012, p. 10). Although the courts have been unwilling to develop a new, general privacy tort, the law of liability for the unauthorised disclosure of private information has moved forward very rapidly in recent years. Strikingly, the courts have expanded the frontiers of liability here with little express reliance upon the Human Rights Act 1998, which has tended to be used as a supporting reason for the changes, rather than their primary cause, and have preferred to present the process as the natural development of existing principles of the law of confidence.

Campbell v MGN Ltd [2004] 2 AC 457

Naomi Campbell, the famous fashion model, brought proceedings for damages against the defendant newspaper which she alleged had, acting on a tip-off, unlawfully published confidential information about her drug addiction and the therapy she had undergone for it with Narcotics Anonymous, with photographs of her in the street as she left a therapy session. The newspaper defended the action on the basis that it was in the public interest for it to correct the claimant's own untruthful public statements that she did not take drugs. The claimant conceded that the newspaper was entitled to publish the fact that she was a drug addict and receiving treatment for her addiction, but claimed damages in respect of further information the paper disclosed about her therapy sessions as well as the photographs it published. She succeeded before Morland J, but the Court of Appeal [2003] QB 633 ruled that the public interest which entitled the newspaper to inform its readers about the claimant's drug addiction and its treatment extended to its publication of details of her treatment. That information was justified by the need to give the story credibility, and journalists had to be given 'reasonable latitude' as to the manner in which they disclosed information in which the public was legitimately interested. Furthermore, the supporting photographs were of the claimant in the street as she was leaving a therapy session and did not convey information that was confidential. The claimant appealed to the House of Lords.

Lord Nicholls (dissenting)

Breach of Confidence: Misuse of Private Information

11. In this country, unlike the United States of America, there is no over-arching, all-embracing cause of action for 'invasion of privacy': see *Wainwright v Home Office* [2004] AC 406 (HL). But protection of various aspects of privacy is a fast developing area of the law . . . In this country development of the law has been spurred by enactment of the Human Rights Act 1998.

12. The present case concerns one aspect of invasion of privacy: wrongful disclosure of private information. The case involves the familiar competition between freedom of expression and respect for an individual's privacy. Both are vitally important rights. Neither has precedence over the other. The importance of freedom of expression has been stressed often and eloquently, the importance of privacy less so. But it, too, lies at the heart of liberty in a modern state. A proper degree of privacy is essential for the well-being and development of an individual. And restraints imposed on government to pry into the lives of the citizen go to the essence of a democratic state: see La Forest J in *R v Dyment* [1988] 2 SCR 417, 426.

13. The common law or, more precisely, courts of equity have long afforded protection to the wrongful use of private information by means of the cause of action which became known as breach of confidence. A breach of confidence was restrained as a form of unconscionable conduct, akin to a breach of trust. Today this nomenclature is misleading. The breach of confidence label harks back to the time when the cause of action was based on improper use of information disclosed by one person to another in confidence. To attract protection the information had to be of a confidential nature. But the gist of the cause of action was that information of this character had been disclosed by one person to another in circumstances 'importing an obligation of confidence' even though no contract of non-disclosure existed: see the classic exposition by Megarry J in *Coco v A N Clark (Engineers) Ltd* [1969] RPC 41, 47–8. The confidence referred to in the phrase 'breach of confidence' was the confidence arising out of a confidential relationship.

14. This cause of action has now firmly shaken off the limiting constraint of the need for an initial confidential relationship. In doing so it has changed its nature. In this country this development was recognised clearly in the judgment of Lord Goff of Chieveley in *Attorney General v*

Guardian Newspapers Ltd (No. 2) [1990] 1 AC 109, 281. Now the law imposes a 'duty of confidence' whenever a person receives information he knows or ought to know is fairly and reasonably to be regarded as confidential. Even this formulation is awkward. The continuing use of the phrase 'duty of confidence' and the description of the information as 'confidential' is not altogether comfortable. Information about an individual's private life would not, in ordinary usage, be called 'confidential'. The more natural description today is that such information is private. The essence of the tort is better encapsulated now as misuse of private information.

15. In the case of individuals this tort, however labelled, affords respect for one aspect of an individual's privacy. That is the value underlying this cause of action. An individual's privacy can be invaded in ways not involving publication of information. Strip searches are an example. The extent to which the common law as developed thus far in this country protects other forms of invasion of privacy is not a matter arising in the present case. It does not arise because, although pleaded more widely, Miss Campbell's common law claim was throughout presented in court exclusively on the basis of breach of confidence, that is, the wrongful *publication* by the 'Mirror' of private *information*.

16. The European Convention on Human Rights, and the Strasbourg jurisprudence, have undoubtedly had a significant influence in this area of the common law for some years. The provisions of article 8, concerning respect for private and family life, and article 10, concerning freedom of expression, and the interaction of these two articles, have prompted the courts of this country to identify more clearly the different factors involved in cases where one or other of these two interests is present. Where both are present the courts are increasingly explicit in evaluating the competing considerations involved. When identifying and evaluating these factors the courts, including your Lordships' House, have tested the common law against the values encapsulated in these two articles. The development of the common law has been in harmony with these articles of the Convention: see, for instance, *Reynolds v Times Newspapers Ltd* [2001] 2 AC 127, 203–4.

17. The time has come to recognise that the values enshrined in articles 8 and 10 are now part of the cause of action for breach of confidence. As Lord Woolf CJ has said, the courts have been able to achieve this result by absorbing the rights protected by articles 8 and 10 into this cause of action: *A v B plc* [2003] QB 195 at [4]. Further, it should now be recognised that for this purpose these values are of general application. The values embodied in articles 8 and 10 are as much applicable in disputes between individuals or between an individual and a non-governmental body such as a newspaper as they are in disputes between individuals and a public authority.

18. In reaching this conclusion it is not necessary to pursue the controversial question whether the European Convention itself has this wider effect. Nor is it necessary to decide whether the duty imposed on courts by section 6 of the Human Rights Act 1998 extends to questions of substantive law as distinct from questions of practice and procedure. It is sufficient to recognise that the values underlying articles 8 and 10 are not confined to disputes between individuals and public authorities. This approach has been adopted by the courts in several recent decisions, reported and unreported, where individuals have complained of press intrusion . . .

19. In applying this approach, and giving effect to the values protected by article 8, courts will often be aided by adopting the structure of article 8 in the same way as they now habitually apply the Strasbourg court's approach to article 10 when resolving questions concerning freedom of expression. Articles 8 and 10 call for a more explicit analysis of competing considerations than the three traditional requirements of the cause of action for breach of confidence identified in *Coco v A N Clark (Engineers) Ltd* [1969] RPC 41.

20. I should take this a little further on one point. Article 8(1) recognises the need to respect private and family life. Article 8(2) recognises there are occasions when intrusion into

private and family life may be justified. One of these is where the intrusion is necessary for the protection of the rights and freedoms of others. Article 10(1) recognises the importance of freedom of expression. But article 10(2), like article 8(2), recognises there are occasions when protection of the rights of others may make it necessary for freedom of expression to give way. When both these articles are engaged a difficult question of proportionality may arise. This question is distinct from the initial question of whether the published information engaged article 8 at all by being within the sphere of the complainant's private or family life.

21. Accordingly, in deciding what was the ambit of an individual's 'private life' in particular circumstances courts need to be on guard against using as a touchstone a test which brings into account considerations which should more properly be considered at the later stage of proportionality. Essentially the touchstone of private life is whether in respect of the disclosed facts the person in question had a reasonable expectation of privacy.

22. Different forms of words, usually to much the same effect, have been suggested from time to time. The *American Law Institute, Restatement of the Law, Torts*, 2d (1977), section 652D, uses the formulation of disclosure of matter which 'would be highly offensive to a reasonable person'. In *Australian Broadcasting Corpn v Lenah Game Meats Pty Ltd* (2001) 208 CLR 199 at [42], Gleeson CJ used words, widely quoted, having a similar meaning. This particular formulation should be used with care, for two reasons. First, the 'highly offensive' phrase is suggestive of a stricter test of private information than a reasonable expectation of privacy. Second, the 'highly offensive' formulation can all too easily bring into account, when deciding whether the disclosed information was private, considerations which go more properly to issues of proportionality; for instance, the degree of intrusion into private life, and the extent to which publication was a matter of proper public concern. This could be a recipe for confusion.

The Present Case

23. I turn to the present case and consider first whether the information whose disclosure is in dispute was private. Mr Caldecott [for the claimant] placed the information published by the newspaper into five categories: (1) the fact of Miss Campbell's drug addiction; (2) the fact that she was receiving treatment; (3) the fact that she was receiving treatment at Narcotics Anonymous; (4) the details of the treatment—how long she had been attending meetings, how often she went, how she was treated within the sessions themselves, the extent of her commitment, and the nature of her entrance on the specific occasion; and (5) the visual portrayal of her leaving a specific meeting with other addicts.

24. It was common ground between the parties that in the ordinary course the information in all five categories would attract the protection of article 8. But Mr Caldecott recognised that, as he put it, Miss Campbell's 'public lies' precluded her from claiming protection for categories (1) and (2). When talking to the media Miss Campbell went out of her way to say that, unlike many fashion models, she did not take drugs. By repeatedly making these assertions in public Miss Campbell could no longer have a reasonable expectation that this aspect of her life should be private. Public disclosure that, contrary to her assertions, she did in fact take drugs and had a serious drug problem for which she was being treated was not disclosure of private information. As the Court of Appeal noted, where a public figure chooses to present a false image and make untrue pronouncements about his or her life, the press will normally be entitled to put the record straight: [2003] QB 633, 658. Thus the area of dispute at the trial concerned the other three categories of information.

25. Of these three categories I shall consider first the information in categories (3) and (4), concerning Miss Campbell's attendance at Narcotics Anonymous meetings. In this regard it is important to note this is a highly unusual case. On any view of the matter, this information

related closely to the fact, which admittedly could be published, that Miss Campbell was receiving treatment for drug addiction. Thus when considering whether Miss Campbell had a reasonable expectation of privacy in respect of information relating to her attendance at Narcotics Anonymous meetings the relevant question can be framed along the following lines: Miss Campbell having put her addiction and treatment into the public domain, did the further information relating to her attendance at Narcotics Anonymous meetings retain its character of private information sufficiently to engage the protection afforded by article 8?

26. I doubt whether it did. Treatment by attendance at Narcotics Anonymous meetings is a form of therapy for drug addiction which is well known, widely used and much respected. Disclosure that Miss Campbell had opted for this form of treatment was not a disclosure of any more significance than saying that a person who has fractured a limb has his limb in plaster or that a person suffering from cancer is undergoing a course of chemotherapy. Given the extent of the information, otherwise of a highly private character, which admittedly could properly be disclosed, the additional information was of such an unremarkable and consequential nature that to divide the one from the other would be to apply altogether too fine a toothcomb. Human rights are concerned with substance, not with such fine distinctions.

27. For the same reason I doubt whether the brief details of how long Miss Campbell had been undergoing treatment, and how often she attended meetings, stand differently. The brief reference to the way she was treated at the meetings did no more than spell out and apply to Miss Campbell common knowledge of how Narcotics Anonymous meetings are conducted.

28. But I would not wish to found my conclusion solely on this point. I prefer to proceed to the next stage and consider how the tension between privacy and freedom of expression should be resolved in this case, on the assumption that the information regarding Miss Campbell's attendance at Narcotics Anonymous meetings retained its private character. At this stage I consider Miss Campbell's claim must fail. I can state my reason very shortly. On the one hand, publication of this information in the unusual circumstances of this case represents, at most, an intrusion into Miss Campbell's private life to a comparatively minor degree. On the other hand, non-publication of this information would have robbed a legitimate and sympathetic newspaper story of attendant detail which added colour and conviction. This information was published in order to demonstrate Miss Campbell's commitment to tackling her drug problem. The balance ought not to be held at a point which would preclude, in this case, a degree of journalistic latitude in respect of information published for this purpose.

29. It is at this point I respectfully consider Morland J fell into error. Having held that the details of Miss Campbell's attendance at Narcotics Anonymous had the necessary quality of confidentiality, the judge seems to have put nothing into the scales under article 10 when striking the balance between articles 8 and 10. This was a misdirection. The need to be free to disseminate information regarding Miss Campbell's drug addiction is of a lower order than the need for freedom to disseminate information on some other subjects such as political information. The degree of latitude reasonably to be accorded to journalists is correspondingly reduced, but it is not excluded altogether.

30. There remains category (5): the photographs taken covertly of Miss Campbell in the road outside the building she was attending for a meeting of Narcotics Anonymous. I say at once that I wholly understand why Miss Campbell felt she was being hounded by the 'Mirror'. I understand also that this could be deeply distressing, even damaging, to a person whose health was still fragile. But this is not the subject of complaint. Miss Campbell, expressly, makes no complaint about the taking of the photographs. She does not assert that the taking of the photographs was itself an invasion of privacy which attracts a legal remedy. The complaint regarding the photographs is of precisely the same character as the nature of the complaints regarding the text of the articles: the information conveyed by the photographs

was private information. Thus the fact that the photographs were taken surreptitiously adds nothing to the only complaint being made.

31. In general photographs of people contain more information than textual description. That is why they are more vivid. That is why they are worth a thousand words. But the pictorial information in the photographs illustrating the offending article of 1 February 2001 added nothing of an essentially private nature. They showed nothing untoward. They conveyed no private information beyond that discussed in the article. The group photograph showed Miss Campbell in the street exchanging warm greetings with others on the doorstep of a building. There was nothing undignified or distrait about her appearance. The same is true of the smaller picture on the front page. Until spotted by counsel in the course of preparing the case for oral argument in your Lordships' House no one seems to have noticed that a sharp eye could just about make out the name of the café on the advertising board on the pavement.

32. For these reasons and those given by my noble and learned friend, Lord Hoffmann, I agree with the Court of Appeal that Miss Campbell's claim fails . . .

Lord Hoffmann (dissenting)

36. My Lords, the House is divided as to the outcome of this appeal, but the difference of opinion relates to a very narrow point which arises on the unusual facts of this case. The facts are unusual because the plaintiff is a public figure who had made very public false statements about a matter in respect of which even a public figure would ordinarily be entitled to privacy, namely her use of drugs. It was these falsehoods which, as was conceded, made it justifiable, for a newspaper to report the fact that she was addicted. The division of opinion is whether in doing so the newspaper went too far in publishing associated facts about her private life. But the importance of this case lies in the statements of general principle on the way in which the law should strike a balance between the right to privacy and the right to freedom of expression, on which the House is unanimous. The principles are expressed in varying language but speaking for myself I can see no significant differences . . .

49. . . . Until the Human Rights Act 1998 came into force, there was no equivalent in English domestic law of article 8 of the European Convention or the equivalent articles in other international human rights instruments which guarantee rights of privacy. So the courts of the United Kingdom did not have to decide what such guarantees meant. Even now that the equivalent of article 8 has been enacted as part of English law, it is not directly concerned with the protection of privacy against private persons or corporations. It is, by virtue of section 6 of the 1998 Act, a guarantee of privacy only against public authorities. Although the Convention, as an international instrument, may impose upon the United Kingdom an obligation to take some steps (whether by statute or otherwise) to protect rights of privacy against invasion by private individuals, it does not follow that such an obligation would have any counterpart in domestic law.

50. What human rights law has done is to identify private information as something worth protecting as an aspect of human autonomy and dignity. And this recognition has raised inescapably the question of why it should be worth protecting against the state but not against a private person. There may of course be justifications for the publication of private information by private persons which would not be available to the state—I have particularly in mind the position of the media, to which I shall return in a moment—but I can see no logical ground for saying that a person should have less protection against a private individual than he would have against the state for the publication of personal information for which there is no justification. Nor, it appears, have any of the other judges who have considered the matter.

51. The result of these developments has been a shift in the centre of gravity of the action for breach of confidence when it is used as a remedy for the unjustified publication of personal

information. It recognises that the incremental changes to which I have referred do not merely extend the duties arising traditionally from a relationship of trust and confidence to a wider range of people. As Sedley LJ observed in a perceptive passage in his judgment in *Douglas v Hello! Ltd* [2001] QB 967 at 1001, the new approach takes a different view of the underlying value which the law protects. Instead of the cause of action being based upon the duty of good faith applicable to confidential personal information and trade secrets alike, it focuses upon the protection of human autonomy and dignity—the right to control the dissemination of information about one's private life and the right to the esteem and respect of other people.

[Lord Hoffmann agreed with Lord Nicholls that the appeal should be dismissed, giving similar reasons.]

Baroness Hale

147. I start . . . from the fact—indeed, it is common ground—that all of the information about Miss Campbell's addiction and attendance at NA which was revealed in the 'Daily Mirror' article was both private and confidential, because it related to an important aspect of Miss Campbell's physical and mental health and the treatment she was receiving for it. It had also been received from an insider in breach of confidence. That simple fact has been obscured by the concession properly made on her behalf that the newspaper's countervailing freedom of expression did serve to justify the publication of some of this information. But the starting point must be that it was all private and its publication required specific justification.

148. What was the nature of the freedom of expression which was being asserted on the other side? There are undoubtedly different types of speech, just as there are different types of private information, some of which are more deserving of protection in a democratic society than others. Top of the list is political speech. The free exchange of information and ideas on matters relevant to the organisation of the economic, social and political life of the country is crucial to any democracy. Without this, it can scarcely be called a democracy at all. This includes revealing information about public figures, especially those in elective office, which would otherwise be private but is relevant to their participation in public life. Intellectual and educational speech and expression are also important in a democracy, not least because they enable the development of individuals' potential to play a full part in society and in our democratic life. Artistic speech and expression is important for similar reasons, in fostering both individual originality and creativity and the free-thinking and dynamic society we so much value. No doubt there are other kinds of speech and expression for which similar claims can be made.

149. But it is difficult to make such claims on behalf of the publication with which we are concerned here. The political and social life of the community, and the intellectual, artistic or personal development of individuals, are not obviously assisted by pouring over the intimate details of a fashion model's private life. However, there is one way in which the article could be said to be educational. The editor had considered running a highly critical piece, adding the new information to the not inconsiderable list of Miss Campbell's faults and follies detailed in the article, emphasising the lies and hypocrisy it revealed. Instead he chose to run a sympathetic piece, still listing her faults and follies, but setting them in the context of her now-revealed addiction and her even more important efforts to overcome it. Newspaper and magazines often carry such pieces and they may well have a beneficial educational effect.

150. The crucial difference here is that such pieces are normally run with the co-operation of those involved. Private people are not identified without their consent. It is taken for granted that this is otherwise confidential information. The editor did offer Miss Campbell the

opportunity of being involved with the story but this was refused. Her evidence suggests that she was concerned for the other people in the group. What entitled him to reveal this private information about her without her consent?

151. The answer which she herself accepts is that she had presented herself to the public as someone who was not involved in drugs. It would have been a very good thing if she were not. If other young women do see her as someone to be admired and emulated, then it is all to the good if she is not addicted to narcotic substances. It might be questioned why, if a role model has adopted a stance which all would agree is beneficial rather than detrimental to society, it is so important to reveal that she has feet of clay. But the possession and use of illegal drugs is a criminal offence and a matter of serious public concern. The press must be free to expose the truth and put the record straight.

152. That consideration justified the publication of the fact that, contrary to her previous statements, Miss Campbell had been involved with illegal drugs. It also justified publication of the fact that she was trying to do something about it by seeking treatment. It was not necessary for those purposes to publish any further information, especially if this might jeopardise the continued success of that treatment.

153. The further information includes the fact that she was attending Narcotics Anonymous meetings, the fact that she had been doing so for some time, and with some regularity, and the photographs of her either arriving at or leaving the premises where meetings took place. All of these things are inter-related with one another and with the effect which revealing them might have upon her. Revealing that she was attending Narcotics Anonymous enabled the paper to print the headline 'Naomi: I am a drug addict', not because she had said so to the paper but because it could assume that she had said this or something like it in a meeting. It also enabled the paper to talk about the meetings and how she was treated there, in a way which made it look as if the information came from someone who had been there with her, even if it simply came from general knowledge of how these meetings work. This all contributed to the sense of betrayal by someone close to her of which she spoke and which destroyed the value of Narcotics Anonymous as a safe haven for her.

154. Publishing the photographs contributed both to the revelation and to the harm that it might do. By themselves, they are not objectionable. Unlike France and Quebec, in this country we do not recognise a right to one's own image: cf *Aubry v Éditions Vice-Versa Inc* [1998] 1 SCR 591. We have not so far held that the mere fact of covert photography is sufficient to make the information contained in the photograph confidential. The activity photographed must be private. If this had been, and had been presented as, a picture of Naomi Campbell going about her business in a public street, there could have been no complaint. She makes a substantial part of her living out of being photographed looking stunning in designer clothing. Readers will obviously be interested to see how she looks if and when she pops out to the shops for a bottle of milk. There is nothing essentially private about that information nor can it be expected to damage her private life. It may not be a high order of freedom of speech but there is nothing to justify interfering with it . . .

155. But here the accompanying text made it plain that these photographs were different. They showed her coming either to or from the NA meeting. They showed her in the company of others, some of whom were undoubtedly part of the group. They showed the place where the meeting was taking place, which will have been entirely recognisable to anyone who knew the locality. A picture is 'worth a thousand words' because it adds to the impact of what the words convey; but it also adds to the information given in those words. If nothing else, it tells the reader what everyone looked like; in this case it also told the reader what the place looked like. In context, it also added to the potential harm, by making her think that she was being followed or betrayed, and deterring her from going back to the same place again.

156. There was no need to do this. The editor accepted that even without the photographs, it would have been a front page story. He had his basic information and he had his quotes. There is no shortage of photographs with which to illustrate and brighten up a story about Naomi Campbell. No doubt some of those available are less flattering than others, so that if he had wanted to run a hostile piece he could have done so. The fact that it was a sympathetic story is neither here nor there. The way in which he chose to present the information he was entitled to reveal was entirely a matter for him. The photographs would have been useful in proving the truth of the story had this been challenged, but there was no need to publish them for this purpose. The credibility of the story with the public would stand or fall with the credibility of 'Mirror' stories generally.

157. The weight to be attached to these various considerations is a matter of fact and degree. Not every statement about a person's health will carry the badge of confidentiality or risk doing harm to that person's physical or moral integrity. The privacy interest in the fact that a public figure has a cold or a broken leg is unlikely to be strong enough to justify restricting the press's freedom to report it. What harm could it possibly do? Sometimes there will be other justifications for publishing, especially where the information is relevant to the capacity of a public figure to do the job. But that is not this case and in this case there was, as the judge found, a risk that publication would do harm. The risk of harm is what matters at this stage, rather than the proof that actual harm has occurred. People trying to recover from drug addiction need considerable dedication and commitment, along with constant reinforcement from those around them. That is why organisations like Narcotics Anonymous were set up and why they can do so much good. Blundering in when matters are acknowledged to be at a 'fragile' stage may do great harm.

158. The trial judge was well placed to assess these matters. He could tell whether the impact of the story on her was serious or trivial. The fact that the story had been published at all was bound to cause distress and possibly interfere with her progress. But he was best placed to judge whether the additional information and the photographs had added significantly both to the distress and the potential harm. He accepted her evidence that it had done so. He could also tell how serious an interference with press freedom it would have been to publish the essential parts of the story without the additional material and how difficult a decision this would have been for an editor who had been told that it was a medical matter and that it would be morally wrong to publish it.

159. The judge was also obliged by section 12(4)(b) of the 1998 Act, not only to have particular regard to the importance of the Convention right to freedom of expression, but also to any relevant privacy code. The Press Complaints Commission Code of Practice supports rather than undermines the conclusion he reached:

3. *Privacy
(i) Everyone is entitled to respect for his or her private and family life, home, health and correspondence. A publication will be expected to justify intrusions into any individual's private life without consent. (ii) The use of long lens photography to take pictures of people in private places without their consent is unacceptable. Note—Private places are public or private property where there is a reasonable expectation of privacy.

The public interest
There may be exceptions to the clauses marked * where they can be demonstrated to be in the public interest.
   1. The public interest includes: (i) Detecting or exposing crime or a serious misdemeanour. (ii) Protecting public health and safety. (iii) Preventing the public from being misled by some statement or action of an individual or organisation . . .

> This would appear to expect almost exactly the exercise conducted above and to lead to the same conclusion as the judge.
>
> 160. I would therefore allow this appeal and restore the order of the judge.
>
> **Lord Hope** and **Lord Carswell** delivered separate opinions allowing the appeal for reasons similar to Baroness Hale's.
>
> Appeal allowed.

COMMENTARY

This was the first occasion on which the House of Lords provided explicit protection for a claimant's right to informational privacy, and it did so by adapting the established equitable remedy for breach of confidence. The development was widely anticipated (see, e.g., Phillipson, 'Transforming Breach of Confidence? Towards a Common Law Right of Privacy under the Human Rights Act' (2003) 66 MLR 726) and all members of the House accepted that the remedy could be employed to protect private information even when it had not been acquired in the course of a confidential relationship. Lord Nicholls and Lord Hoffmann dissented on the ultimate disposition of the appeal, but their opinions contain some of the most useful analysis of the general principles to be applied. Significantly, Lord Nicholls had no qualms about describing the liability as a species of 'tort', despite its origins in equity, though he was the only member of the House of Lords to use that terminology. The tort terminology has been picked up, however, in more recent cases (see, e.g., *McKennitt v Ash* [2008] QB 73; *Imerman v Tchenguiz* [2011] Fam 116 at [65] per Lord Neuberger; *PJS v News Group Newspapers Ltd* [2016] AC 1081 at [32] per Lord Mance; *HRH Duchess of Sussex v Associated Newspapers Ltd* [2021] EWCA Civ 1810 at [34] per Vos MR).

Do you think that the gist of the claimant's complaint was the information published about her or the fact that the newspaper was hounding her when she needed to be left alone to recover? If the latter, does the decision of the House of Lords mark a step in the direction of greater protection for privacy in general rather than just private information?

Privacy or Confidence?

Legal obligations of confidentiality have been recognised since at least the early nineteenth century (see, e.g., *Abernethy v Hutchinson* (1824) 1 H & Tw 28; *Prince Albert v Strange* (1849) 1 McN & G 23). In the modern law, three requirements must be satisfied if an action for breach of confidence is to succeed (see *Coco v A N Clark (Engineers) Ltd* [1969] RPC 41): (1) the information must 'have the necessary element of confidence about it' (i.e. it must not be in the public domain); (2) the defendant must be under 'an obligation of confidence'; and (3) the defendant must make 'unauthorised use' of the information. Many of the cases involve trade or government secrets, but the availability of this action in respect of personal confidences was never in question (see, e.g., *Duchess of Argyll v Duke of Argyll* [1967] Ch 302: marital secrets). The key requirement of an obligation of confidence was traditionally thought to entail some form of relationship between the parties, e.g. doctor/patient, solicitor/client, or at least an acceptance of the information on the (explicit or implicit) basis that it would be kept secret. Gradually the requirement was watered down. An obligation of confidence could be found to arise on the basis that improper means were employed in order to acquire the information in question, e.g. where a person trespassed to place a 'bug' in the claimant's home (*Francome v News Group Newspapers Ltd* [1984] 1 WLR 892). In a well-known dictum, Lord Goff went further, suggesting that an obligation of confidence might arise purely on the basis of the confidential character of the information, irrespective of the means by which it was acquired, e.g. in 'certain situations, beloved of law teachers, where an obviously confidential document is wafted by an electric fan out of a window into a crowded street, or where an obviously confidential document, such as a private diary, is dropped in a public place, and is then picked up by a passer-by' (*AG v Guardian Newspapers (No. 2)* [1990] 1 AC 109 at 282).

In *Campbell v MGN Ltd*, the House of Lords confirmed this development, made clear that the fundamental question was whether the information was 'private' rather than 'confidential', and established a different framework for dealing with the private information cases, which was to proceed by direct reference to the rights under Articles 8 and 10, ECHR rather than the three requirements laid down by *Coco v Clark*. In effect, there are now two torts where previously there was one: one dealing with confidences (especially commercial confidences), in which the three requirements in *Coco v Clark* are applied; the other dealing with private information through the framework of the Convention rights. However, the two torts can on occasion be entangled. Information can be both private and subject to an obligation of confidence. In such a case, it seems unlikely that the court would embark upon two separate analyses—one in terms of the three requirements in *Coco v Clark*, the other in terms of the Convention rights—rather than simply treating the relationship of confidence as relevant to the claimant's expectation of privacy. Whether information is private depends on 'an interdependent amalgam of circumstances', including, for example, 'the nature of the information, the form in which it is conveyed and the fact that the person disclosing it was in a confidential relationship with the person to whom it relates' (*HRH Prince of Wales v Associated Newspapers Ltd* [2008] Ch 57 at [36], per Lord Phillips MR; see further *McKennitt v Ash* [2008] QB 73 and *Browne v Associated Newspapers Ltd* [2008] QB 103). However, the fact that the law of confidentiality was extended in *Campbell* to provide a remedy for the misuse of private information does not mean that restrictions on the new cause of action should also apply to 'old fashioned confidence' cases (*Imerman v Tchenguiz* [2011] Fam 116 at [67] and [71], where the Court of Appeal ruled that 'misuse' was not a precondition of liability for breach of confidence).

A further complication is that what is private to one person may have commercial value as a secret to another. The long-running legal saga of celebrity couple, Michael Douglas and Catharine Zeta-Jones, and *Hello!* magazine provides an illuminating case in point. The film stars sold *OK!* magazine the exclusive right to publish photographs of their wedding for a fee of £1 million, retaining a right of veto. They undertook to use their best efforts to ensure that no other media had access to the wedding and to prevent guests or anyone else present from taking photographs. All guests received with their invitation a separate notice stating, 'We would appreciate no photography or video devices at the ceremony or reception', and were visually checked for cameras on arrival, and all staff for the wedding were engaged on terms that no photographs be taken. A couple of days after the wedding, it came to the claimants' attention that *Hello!* magazine was planning to publish photographs of the wedding which, it later transpired, had been taken by a freelance photographer who had infiltrated the reception and taken pictures surreptitiously. The claimants failed in their application for an interim injunction to prevent the publication until trial of their action for breach of confidence, on the basis that they had been willing to trade their privacy for financial reward anyway (*Douglas v Hello! Ltd* [2001] 1 FLR 982), but they succeeded in their claim for damages at the subsequent trial (*Douglas v Hello! Ltd* [2003] 3 All ER 996). The photographs had interfered with their residual area of privacy, i.e. that which they retained even after selling the photographic rights to the wedding to *OK!* magazine, though this reduced the damages they were entitled to recover (£15,000). Their co-claimants, *OK!*, were awarded in excess of £1 million for loss of profit resulting from *Hello!*'s 'spoiler'. The Court of Appeal overturned the award in favour of *OK!* on the basis that the magazine had no rights over the Douglases' residual area of privacy (*Douglas v Hello! Ltd (No. 3)* [2006] QB 125) but the House of Lords subsequently restored the trial judge's decision (*sub nom. OBG Ltd v Allan* [2008] 1 AC 1). *OK!* had no claim to privacy under Article 8, ECHR; neither could it make a claim that was parasitic upon the Douglases' right to privacy. But that was irrelevant. *OK!*'s claim was for the wrongful disclosure of commercially confidential information which was controlled by the Douglases and which the Douglases had licensed *OK!* to use. The magazine had paid £1 million for the benefit of the obligation of confidence imposed on the wedding guests and there was no reason of principle or policy why it should not be entitled to enforce that obligation. The decision shows that rights over information may arise, independently but simultaneously, on account of both its private and its confidential character. The right to keep information private cannot be sold on, as it is by its nature personal, but this does not preclude the commercial sale of the right to enforce a confidence.

'A Reasonable Expectation of Privacy'

According to Lord Nicholls, the test of whether information is private is—somewhat circularly—whether its subject has a reasonable expectation of privacy. Lord Nicholls preferred this formulation to the alternatives he considered at [22], e.g. whether disclosure of the information would be considered 'highly offensive' (the latter adopted only by Lord Hope of the Law Lords sitting in *Campbell*: see [92]). The test of substantial offence tended to blur the distinction between two distinct questions: what is private and when is publication of private facts wrongful?

Whether a claimant has a reasonable expectation that the information be kept private is a binary question (*HRH Duchess of Sussex v Associated Newspapers Ltd* [2021] EWCA Civ 1810 at [84] per Vos MR). The answer can only be yes or no. But different claimants may have different reasonable expectations about information of the same type. What is private in respect of an ordinary member of the public, who has never courted publicity, might well not be private in respect of a contestant in a Big Brother-style reality TV show who knowingly submits to 24-hour-a-day surveillance. Lord Nicholls' version of the test—whether *the claimant* had a reasonable expectation of privacy—differs from that advanced elsewhere, e.g. in Lady Hale's speech at [134] (not extracted) where the test is whether *the person publishing the information* knows or ought to know there is a reasonable expectation of privacy (or confidence). Moreham ('Privacy in the Common Law: A Doctrinal and Theoretical Analysis' (2005) 121 LQR 628 at 648) prefers the latter version of the test, mainly because it would be too harsh to hold a person liable for the disclosure of apparently innocuous information about which they could not be expected to know that the claimant was unusually sensitive. But do such concerns not go to the separate question of whether the interference with the claimant's privacy was wrongful on the facts, rather than to the matter of privacy in itself? It seems unnecessarily complicated to adopt a rule which would allow information about A to be classified as private when B seeks to publish it, but not when C seeks to do so. In any case, it is Lord Nicholls' claimant-centred version of the test that has been adopted in subsequent authorities (see, e.g., *Murray v Express Newspapers plc* [2009] Ch 481 at [35], though the Court of Appeal also stated at [28] that Lady Hale's approach was 'the same' as Lord Nicholls').

Moreham further argues that an analysis in terms of *desires* is preferable to one based on *expectations* (p. 647):

[E]xpectations . . . suggests that liability depends on whether privacy is likely to be respected in a particular situation, rather than on whether it should be respected in that situation . . . On this approach (which could easily be adopted on the current formulation of the English 'reasonable expectation' test), whether or not there is a breach of privacy is determined by reference to the practices of privacy interferers *themselves*—once an intrusive practice becomes sufficiently widespread . . . then claimants will have no action for breach of privacy if it occurs. There therefore seems to be a strong argument for shifting the focus of the English privacy action away from the claimant's *expectations* of privacy and on to his or her *desires*.

We agree with the underlying sentiment, but the terminology 'reasonable expectation of privacy' now seems firmly established in the case law, which should be unproblematic so long as it is remembered that the question is what degree of privacy the claimant is entitled to expect that the law will protect, not whether they reasonably expect others in fact to respect their privacy.

ZXC v Bloomberg LP [2022] UKSC 5

The facts are summarised in the commentary that follows the extract, which provides useful guidance on the application of the two-stage approach now adopted by the courts in determining whether there has been a misuse of private information.

Lord Hamblen and Lord Stephens (with whom Lord Reed, Lord Lloyd-Jones and Lord Sales agreed)

47. As stated by Simon LJ at para 42 of his judgment in the present case [[2021] QB 28], at stage one, the question is whether the claimant has a reasonable expectation of privacy in the relevant information; if so, at stage two, the question is whether that expectation is outweighed by the countervailing interest of the publisher's right to freedom of expression. This two stage test is now well established.

Stage 1

48. In relation to both stage one and stage two, general guidance can be found in the growing body of domestic legal precedent and also the jurisprudence of the European Court of Human Rights ('ECtHR') on articles 8 and 10 which the court must take into account. Under section 12(4) of the HRA, where the proceedings relate to material 'which the respondent claims, or which appears to the court, to be journalistic, literary or artistic material (or to conduct connected with such material)' then the court 'must have particular regard' to 'any relevant privacy code.' In relation to newspapers and magazines the relevant privacy code is the Editors' Code of Practice, established by the Editors' Code of Practice Committee and overseen by the Independent Press Standards Organisation—see *Sicri v Associated Newspapers Ltd* [2020] EWHC 3541 (QB) . . .

49. Whether there is a reasonable expectation of privacy is an objective question. The expectation is that of a reasonable person of ordinary sensibilities placed in the same position as the claimant and faced with the same publicity—see *Campbell* at para 99 per Lord Hope of Craighead; *Murray* [*Murray v Express Newspapers plc* [2009] Ch 481] at para 35.

50. As stated in *Murray* at para 36, 'the question whether there is a reasonable expectation of privacy is a broad one, which takes account of all the circumstances of the case'. Such

circumstances are likely to include, but are not limited to, the circumstances identified at para 36 in *Murray* - the so-called 'Murray factors'. These are:

(1) the attributes of the claimant;
(2) the nature of the activity in which the claimant was engaged;
(3) the place at which it was happening;
(4) the nature and purpose of the intrusion;
(5) the absence of consent and whether it was known or could be inferred;
(6) the effect on the claimant; and
(7) the circumstances in which and the purposes for which the information came into the hands of the publisher.

51. Although the *Murray* factors are not exhaustive, and the significance of individual factors will vary from case to case, they have been regularly considered and applied by the courts by way of guidance and the appropriateness of so doing was affirmed by the majority of the Supreme Court in *In re JR38* [2016] AC 1131 . . .

52. Whilst all the circumstances of each case must be considered, *Gatley on Libel and Slander*, (12th ed) at para 22.5 suggests that there are certain types of information which will normally, but not invariably, be regarded as giving rise to a reasonable expectation of privacy so as to be characterised as being private in character. These are the state of a person's physical or mental health or condition; a person's physical characteristics (nudity); a person's racial or ethnic characteristics; a person's emotional state (in particular in the context of distress, injury or bereavement); the generality of personal and family relationships; a person's sexual orientation; the intimate details of personal relationships; information conveyed in the course of personal relationships; a person's political opinions and affiliations; a person's religious commitment; personal financial and tax related information; personal communications and correspondence; matters pertaining to the home; past involvement in criminal behaviour; involvement in civil litigation concerning private affairs; and involvement in crime as a victim or a witness . . .

53. *Gatley* also suggests that there are some types of information which will normally not be regarded as giving rise to a reasonable expectation of privacy so as not to be characterised as being private in character, namely: corporate information, a person's physical location, involvement in current criminal activity, a person's misperformance of a public role, information deriving from a hearing of a criminal case conducted in public, and the identity of an author. . . .

54. A relevant circumstance will be the extent to which the information is in the public domain. Information that was private may become so well known that it is no longer private. Whether this is so is a matter of fact and degree—see *K v News Group Newspapers Ltd* [2011] 1 WLR 1827, para 10(3). In relation to journalistic, literary or artistic material, section 12(4) of the HRA requires the court to have particular regard to 'the extent to which the material has, or is about to, become available to the public'.

55. The effect on the claimant must attain a sufficient level of seriousness for article 8 to be engaged—see *R (Wood) v Comr of Police of the Metropolis* [2010] 1 WLR 123 per Laws LJ at para 22; *In re JR38* at para 87. In general, there will be no reasonable expectation of privacy in trivial or anodyne information.

Stage 2

56. Stage 2 involves a balancing of the claimant's article 8 right to privacy and the publisher's article 10 right to freedom of expression in order to determine which should prevail in the particular circumstances of the case—the so-called 'balancing exercise'.

57. As Lord Hoffmann explained in *Campbell* at para 55:

> Both [rights] reflect important civilised values, but, as often happens, neither can be given effect in full measure without restricting the other. How are they to be reconciled in a

particular case? There is in my view no question of automatic priority. Nor is there a presumption in favour of one rather than the other. The question is rather the extent to which it is necessary to qualify the one right in order to protect the underlying value which is protected by the other. And the extent of the qualification must be proportionate to the need . . .

58. In *In re S (A Child) (Identification: Restrictions on Publication)* [2005] 1 AC 593, at para 17 Lord Steyn confirmed that neither right has precedence over the other and identified the following considerations as being of particular importance in carrying out the balancing exercise:

(1) 'an intense focus on the comparative importance of the specific rights being claimed in the individual case';
(2) 'the justifications for interfering with or restricting each right'; and
(3) 'the proportionality' of the respective interference or restriction.

59. Under section 12(4) of the HRA the court must have particular regard 'to the importance of the Convention right to freedom of expression'. As stated by Lord Nicholls in *Reynolds v Times Newspapers Ltd* [2001] 2 AC 127, 205:

. . . the court should have particular regard to the importance of freedom of expression. The press discharges vital functions as a bloodhound as well as a watchdog. The court should be slow to conclude that a publication was not in the public interest and, therefore, the public had no right to know, especially when the information is in the field of political discussion.'

60. The ECtHR jurisprudence is to similar effect. As stated in *Axel Springer AG v Germany* (Application No 39954/08) [2012] EMLR 15, para 79:

The Court has also repeatedly emphasised the essential role played by the press in a democratic society. Although the press must not overstep certain bounds, regarding in particular protection of the reputation and rights of others, its duty is nevertheless to impart - in a manner consistent with its obligations and responsibilities - information and ideas on all matters of public interest. Not only does the press have the task of imparting such information and ideas; the public also has a right to receive them. Were it otherwise, the press would be unable to play its vital role of 'public watchdog' (see *Bladet Tromsø and Stensaas v Norway* 29 EHRR 125, paras 59 and 62, and *Pedersen v Denmark* 42 EHRR 24, para 71).

61. The extent to which publication is in the public interest is of central importance. This is reflected in section 12(4) of the HRA under which, in relation to journalistic, literary or artistic material, the court is required to have particular regard to the extent to which 'it is, or would be, in the public interest for the material to be published'.

62. In considering the public interest in publication, the contribution that publication will make to a debate of general interest is a factor of particular importance. In *Von Hannover v Germany* (Application No 59329/00) [2004] EMLR 21, para 76 it was said by the ECtHR that it should be 'the decisive factor in balancing the protection of private life against freedom of expression'. In *Axel Springer* it was said to be an 'initial essential criterion'. Other factors of likely relevance identified in that case are:

(1) how well-known is the person concerned and what is the subject of the report;
(2) the prior conduct of the person concerned;
(3) the method of obtaining the information and its veracity;
(4) the content, form and consequences of publication; and
(5) the severity of the restriction or interference and its proportionality with the exercise of the freedom of expression.

COMMENTARY

The structure of the Convention right to privacy (Article 8, ECHR) makes clear that intrusions into a person's private life may sometimes be justified. It is therefore conducive to clarity to adopt a two-stage process of reasoning by which one asks, first, whether the claimant has a reasonable expectation of privacy in the relevant information, and, secondly, whether that expectation is outweighed by the countervailing interest of the publisher's right to freedom of expression. Stage 2 thus requires a balancing of the competing rights under Articles 8 and 10 of the Convention. Neither right has priority over the other. 'The question', as Lord Hoffmann put it, *Campbell* at [55], 'is rather the extent to which it is *necessary* to qualify the one right in order to protect the underlying value which is protected by the other. And the extent of the qualification must be proportionate to the need.' See also *PJS v News Group Newspapers Ltd* [2016] AC 1081 at [20], per Lord Mance.

This two-stage analysis dispenses with the need to apply the specific defences that have been recognised in the law of breach of confidence (e.g. immorality or other iniquity, and public interest), further demonstrating the independent nature of the cause of action for wrongful disclosure of private information. However, although the structure of the inquiry may be different, the underlying issues of substance are the same. In *X v Y* [1988] 2 All ER 648, for example, the issue was whether the newspaper publication of the names of NHS doctors who had contracted AIDS fell under the public interest defence recognised in the law of breach of confidence. The court was required to weigh the public interests in a free press and an informed public debate against that in the confidentiality of hospital records, especially those concerning the victims of AIDS. On the facts, the latter prevailed, Rose J attaching importance to the consideration that there was already a wide-ranging debate about AIDS generally and its effect on doctors, which would not be materially advanced by disclosure of the doctors' identities. Like *Campbell*, the case involved the disclosure of personal medical history. But Lady Hale said in *Campbell*, at [157] (quoted earlier), that the fact that someone was suffering from a cold or had a broken leg was unlikely to be considered to be so private that the press would be unable to report it. What is the difference between AIDS and a drug dependency, on the one hand, and a cold and a broken leg, on the other?

In the new law of privacy, as under the old law of confidence, the exposure of iniquity can justify what would otherwise be an unlawful intrusion into personal affairs. In *Campbell*, it was accepted that the newspaper had the right, in the wider public interest, to correct the claimant's misrepresentations about her past drug use. The divergence of view as between majority and minority Law Lords was over the extent of the latitude given to the newspaper in so doing, and in particular whether it should be able to support its story with a picture of the claimant in the street on leaving her Narcotics Anonymous therapy session. For Lord Hope, at [121], it was the photographs that tipped the balance in the claimant's favour.

In a suitable case, a person may be justified in revealing private information about another to correct a misrepresentation about themselves. That was accepted by the Court of Appeal in *HRH Duchess of Sussex v Associated Newspapers Ltd* [2021] EWCA Civ 1810, but the defendant's newspaper went too far in publishing a private letter by Meghan, Duchess of Sussex to her father as, while quoting a small part of the letter might have been a reasonable way of correcting inaccurate statements about him in the media, disclosing the full contents in a sensationalised scoop was disproportionate.

Reporting of Police Investigations

What expectation of privacy does a person have where they are under police investigation for a possible criminal offence? If the media are free to publicise the fact of the investigation, that could be seen to conflict with the presumption of innocence, and for that reason the lower courts have accepted in recent years that a suspect in a police investigation generally has a reasonable expectation of privacy about it up to the point of charge (see *Richard v BBC* [2019] Ch 169, *Sicri v Associated Newspapers Ltd* [2020] EWHC 1541 (QB)). The matter came before the Supreme Court for the first time in the extracted case, *ZXC v Bloomberg LP*, which confirms the approach of the lower courts. The defendant's financial news service published an article about a company for which the claimant was regional chief executive, relating to its activities in a country in that region. These activities had been the subject of a criminal investigation by a UK law enforcement body and the information in the article was almost exclusively drawn from a confidential letter of request sent by that body to the foreign state. The claimant argued that he had a reasonable expectation of privacy in information published in the article and in particular the details of the investigation into him and the law enforcement body's belief that he had committed specified criminal offences, which it was seeking to evidence. He sought damages and an injunction for misuse of his private information. At trial, the High Court upheld his claim and awarded damages of £25,000. The defendant's appeal was dismissed by the Court of Appeal and, in the extracted decision, by the Supreme Court. The Court rejected the defendant's argument that the general rule applied by the lower courts was unsound inasmuch as it significantly overstated the capacity of publication of the information to cause reputational and other damage to the claimant given the public's ability and propensity to observe the presumption of innocence. Lord Hamblen and Lord Stephens explained, at [108]:

> The presumption of innocence is a legal presumption applicable to criminal trials. In that context the presumption weighs heavily in the directions that a jury is given or in the self-directions that a judge sitting alone applies. However, the context here is different. In this context the question is how others, including a person's inner circle, their business or professional associates and the general public, will react to the publication of information that that person is under criminal investigation. All the material which we have set out [articulating concerns about the naming of persons suspected of criminal offences] . . . now admits to only one answer, consistent with judicial experience, namely that the person's reputation will ordinarily be adversely affected causing prejudice to personal enjoyment of the right to respect for private life such as the right to establish and develop relationships with other human beings.

For opposing arguments on the issue, published before the Supreme Court decision, see Moreham (2019) 11 JML 142 and (2020) 12 JML 1, and Craig and Phillipson (2021) 13 JML 153.

Sexual Morality

The issue of iniquity very frequently arises in the context of media exposés of celebrities' sexual indiscretions. In *Theakston v MGN Ltd* [2002] EMLR 22 at [60], Ouseley J suggested there was a spectrum of sexual relationships attracting different degrees of protection:

> Sexual relations within marriage at home would be at one end of the range or matrix of circumstances to be protected from most forms of disclosure; a one night stand with a recent acquaintance in a hotel bedroom might very well be protected from press publicity. A transitory engagement in a brothel is yet further away.

On the facts of the case before him, the judge declined to grant an injunction to prevent verbal descriptions of activities in which the claimant (a radio and television presenter) had engaged in a brothel, but awarded an injunction against the publication of photographs taken inside the premises as this would have been particularly intrusive and humiliating;

additionally, the photographs had been taken for the purposes of blackmail and printing them would constitute a breach of the Press Complaints Commission Code of Practice.

Ouseley J's dictum was approved by the Court of Appeal in *A v B plc* [2003] QB 195, where a Premiership footballer was found to be entitled to only a 'very modest' degree of confidentiality in respect of transient, extra-marital relationships he had pursued with two women, one of whom now wished to sell her story to the defendant newspaper. The footballer failed in his application for an interim injunction preventing publication of the story pending trial, and was left to his remedy (if any) in damages.

Subsequent developments, driven by the decision of the European Court of Human Rights in *von Hannover v Germany* (2005) 40 EHRR 1, discussed in the following section of commentary, mean that *A v B* would probably be decided differently today (E. Barendt, *Freedom of Speech*, 2nd edn (Oxford: OUP, 2007), p. 244). In *Mosley v News Group Newspapers Ltd* [2008] EMLR 20, without referring to *A v B* at all, Eady J found that a reasonable expectation of privacy arose in respect of a sado-masochistic sex party involving the claimant (the then president of the governing body of Formula One motor racing) and five professional dominatrices. On the facts, this expectation outweighed the defendant's interest in publishing the story, with accompanying photographs and video. The judge stated, at [127]: 'it is not ... for the media to expose sexual conduct which does not involve any significant breach of the criminal law'. It made no difference that the claimant's activities were adulterous and might be regarded by some as perverted.

Confirming this development in *PJS v News Group Newspapers Ltd* [2016] AC 1081 at [32], Lord Mance observed: 'the starting point is that (i) there is not, without more, any public interest in a legal sense in the disclosure or publication of purely private sexual encounters, even though they involve adultery or more than one person at the same time, (ii) any such disclosure or publication will on the face of it constitute the tort of invasion of privacy ... ' The main point in issue in that case was whether the claimant, a celebrity married to a well-known entertainer with whom he had two children, was entitled to an interim injunction to restrain the defendant from publishing in one of its national newspapers a story about his extra-marital sexual activities (widely reported as an 'olive oil bath threesome'), even though the story was already in the public domain, having been published in the United States and other countries, and being readily accessible by a simple internet search. The Supreme Court ruled in favour of the injunction by a majority of 4-1. The majority Justices underlined that there was a qualitative difference in the intrusiveness and distress resulting from the disclosures already made on the internet and that to be anticipated from the likely 'media storm' if the injunction were lifted, allowing unrestricted publication of intimate details of sexual activities in the print editions of English newspapers and on their own internet sites (*ibid.*, at [35], per Lord Mance; see also [63], per Lord Neuberger).

The *PJS* case provides an illustration of the controversial remedy popularly known as the 'super injunction', an injunction restricting publicity of the identity of the person who seeks the protection of the court (see also *CTB v News Group Newspapers Ltd* [2011] EWHC 1232 (QB); *H v News Group Newspapers Ltd* [2011] 1 WLR 1645). The practice has been seen by some as undermining the law's normal commitment to open justice (see, e.g., Zuckerman, 'Super Injunctions—Curiosity-Suppressant Orders Undermine the Rule of Law' (2010) 29 CJQ 131, referring at 138 to 'a Kafkaesque process that is inimical to the rule of law and contrary to democratic principles'). However, the Court of Appeal in *H v News Group* at [21] allayed at least some of these concerns by issuing guidelines to regulate the award of non-disclosure injunctions so as to minimise the extent of any encroachment on the open justice rule (see further *Practice Guidance (Interim Non-disclosure Orders)* [2012] 1 WLR 1003). A court making such an order should make public the fact that proceedings have taken place and the underlying court reasoning in support of its judgment, as well as stipulating for the review of its continued appropriateness. Of course, the court may yet find that there is a public interest in publication, as where the claimant—recently appointed England football captain—was shown to have been 'cheating' on his long-term partner while publicly maintaining that he was a 'reformed character' (*Ferdinand v MGN Ltd* [2011] EWHC 2454 (QB), Nicol J noting at [84] that even a 'kiss and paid for telling' story might be in the public interest notwithstanding the less-than-noble motives of the informant).

Where a sexual affair is part of the backdrop of an independently newsworthy story, the balance may tip the other way—in favour of publication—so as to place other events that occurred in context. In *Browne v Associated Newspapers Ltd* [2008] QB 103, the Court of Appeal upheld the *Mail on Sunday*'s right to publish details of a homosexual relationship involving the chief executive of the oil company BP because other allegations in the newspaper's story (e.g. that the executive had misused BP's resources to benefit his partner and had revealed business secrets to him) would make no sense without publication of the nature of the relationship. Conversely, in *K v News Group Newspapers Ltd* [2011] 1 WLR 1827, the Court of Appeal granted a non-disclosure injunction where a man who was well known in the entertainment industry had an extra-marital affair with a woman employed by the same organisation, and the woman lost her job shortly after the man had ended the affair. The story made no contribution to 'a debate of general interest'—which the ECtHR in *von Hannover*, at [76], had described as 'the decisive factor'—and its publication would be harmful to the man's children, who were still at school and would inevitably be exposed to playground ridicule as a result. The court emphasised, however, that the interests of a claimant's children should not be treated as a trump card preventing publicity in every case, but was merely an additional factor to be weighed in the scale.

In most of the preceding cases, the immediate issue for the court was whether to grant an interim injunction pending full trial of the action. Pursuant to s. 12(3) of the Human Rights Act 1998, the court should not make such an order unless it is satisfied that the claimant is likely (i.e. more likely than not) to obtain an injunction following a trial (see further *Practice Guidance (Interim Non-disclosure Orders)* [2012] 1 WLR 1003). However, failure to get an interim injunction does not mean that the claim for damages will necessarily fail at trial, while success in getting the interim order does not mean that the trial judge will ultimately rule in the claimant's favour.

Privacy in Public Places

A particularly interesting question is whether one can have a reasonable expectation of privacy in a public place (see Moreham, 'Privacy in Public Places' [2006] CLJ 606). In *von Hannover v Germany*, Application No. 59320/00 (2005) 40 EHRR 1, the ECtHR ruled that Princess Caroline of Hannover was entitled to protection against the publication of photographs showing her going about her daily life in public places. There was a zone of a person's interaction with others, even in a public context, that fell within the scope of 'private life' (para. 50). Even though the intrusion into this area, on the facts, was by non-state actors, Article 8 did not merely compel the state to abstain from arbitrary interference with individuals' private lives, but also to take positive measures to secure respect for private life even in the sphere of relations between individuals, e.g. by protecting a person's picture against abuse by others (para. 57). This protection of private life had to be balanced against the freedom of expression guaranteed by Article 10 of the Convention, and, in particular, the essential role played by the press in a democratic society (para. 58), but the sole purpose of the photographs in question was to satisfy the curiosity of a particular readership and their publication did not contribute to any debate of general interest to society (para. 65). 'In these conditions', said the Court, 'freedom of expression calls for a narrower interpretation' (para. 66). The Court concluded:

> [T]he public does not have a legitimate interest in knowing where the applicant is and how she behaves generally in her private life even if she appears in places that cannot always be described as secluded and despite the fact that she is well known to the public. Even if such a public interest exists, as does a commercial interest of the magazines in publishing these photos and these articles, in the instant case those interests must, in the Court's view, yield to the applicant's right to the effective protection of her private life.

However, in subsequent proceedings brought by the same applicant and her husband, the Court upheld the conclusion of the German Constitutional Court that photographs depicting them in the middle of a street in a ski resort contained information related to an event of contemporary society which the media were entitled to report—the illness affecting Prince Rainier III, Caroline's father and at the time the reigning sovereign of the Principality of Monaco, and the conduct of the members of his family during that illness. The photographs supported and illustrated the information conveyed in the report and thus contributed to a debate of general interest (*von Hannover v Germany*, Application Nos 40660/08 and 60641/08 (2012) 55 EHRR 16).

In *Campbell v MGN*, at [154], Lady Hale commented that there might be public interest in photographs of Naomi Campbell as she was popping out for a pint of milk. In *John v Associated Newspapers* [2006] EWHC 1611, Eady J considered this dictum on an application for an interim injunction to prevent publication of an innocuous photograph taken of the pop star Elton John in the street. Refusing the application, the judge noted that the photograph revealed nothing about the claimant's health or his social or sexual relationships, and it was not taken in circumstances involving harassment; the case was therefore akin to the Naomi Campbell pint of milk example. In *Murray v Express Newspapers plc* [2009] Ch 481, however, the Court of Appeal refused to strike out a claim for damages brought on behalf of the 19-month-old child of *Harry Potter* author, J. K. Rowling, in respect of the publication of a photograph of the child accompanied by its parents in a public street. The Court of Appeal rejected the proposition that routine acts such a visit to a shop or a ride on a bus could not attract a reasonable expectation of privacy. In its view, everything depended on the circumstances. In the case at hand, the claimant's age was decisive; it was the courts' responsibility to protect children from intrusive media attention. Likewise, in *Weller v Associated Newspapers Ltd* [2016] 1 WLR 1541, where the Court of Appeal upheld the award of damages and an injunction to the children of musician Paul Weller regarding photographs of them shopping and in a café, Lord Dyson MR stated (at [61]): 'The family element of the activity distinguishes it from Naomi Campbell's popping out to the shops for a bottle of milk and Sir Elton John standing with his driver in a London street, outside the gate to his home wearing a baseball cap and tracksuit.'

What if the claimant is not a celebrity? In *Peck v United Kingdom*, Application No. 44647/98 (2003) 36 EHRR 41, the applicant, suffering from depression, was filmed by closed circuit television (CCTV) cameras as he walked around his local town centre with a large kitchen knife in his hands; still on camera, he then attempted suicide by cutting his wrists. The police, notified by the CCTV operator, arrived shortly afterwards and gave him medical assistance. Some time later, the council, which owned the footage, included still images from it in a press release about the ways in which CCTV could help the police to prevent crime. The images were printed in local newspapers. The council also provided footage of the incident to local and national TV stations, which broadcast it with the applicant still recognisable even though his face was masked. On these facts, the ECtHR found that the council's disclosure of the film and images from it constituted an interference with the applicant's private life. Though it pursued the legitimate aim of public safety, the prevention of disorder and crime and the protection of the rights of others, the disclosure entailed a disproportionate interference with the applicant's private life and was therefore unjustified. The Court also found that the lack of an effective remedy for the interference against the newspapers and TV stations constituted a further violation of the Convention, under Article 13. At the relevant time (pre-*Campbell*), it was unlikely that a claim of breach of confidence would succeed, as the images seemed to lack the necessary quality of confidence and there seemed to be no circumstances importing an obligation of confidence.

After *Campbell*, do you think that the English courts would be able to find that, on such facts, there had been a wrongful disclosure of private information sounding in damages? Consider also what remedies might be available, against whom, under the Human Rights Act 1998 (passed only after the events in *Peck* had taken place).

The Human Rights Act and the European Convention

Under the Human Rights Act 1998, s. 2(1) the courts are required to have regard to relevant decisions of the ECtHR in determining any question arising in connection with a Convention right. But they are not bound by decisions of that court. Furthermore, even though the Act has, in one sense, incorporated the Convention rights into English law, it only provides an express remedy in the case of their violation by a public authority (see, e.g., Lord Hoffmann in *Campbell* at [49], quoted earlier). So it is not immediately apparent how the Convention rights, including the right to privacy and indeed the right to freedom of expression, are relevant in actions between private parties.

One possible answer is that the Human Rights Act has a 'horizontal' effect because the courts, as they fall under the definition of public authority in s. 6(3) of the Act, are subject to the basic obligation to act compatibly with the Convention rights that is imposed on public authorities by s. 6(1). But in *Campbell*, Lord Nicholls said, at [18] (also quoted earlier), that he was not going to deal with the question whether the obligation on the courts extended to matters of substantive law as distinct from questions of practice and procedure, while Lord Hoffmann, at [49]–[51] (quoted earlier) thought that the Act's 'subtle' effect was to make the courts question why privacy should be worth protection against the state and not a private person, and then embark on the development of existing (general) principles so as to address that anomaly. In fact, only Lady Hale seems to have positively embraced the argument of horizontal effect, stating in [132], not quoted earlier, that '[t]he 1998 Act does not create any new cause of action between private persons. But if there is a relevant cause of action applicable, the court as a public authority must act compatibly with both parties' Convention rights.' Whether this view will command majority acceptance in future is uncertain. For now, there remains considerable force in Morgan's criticism ((2004) 120 LQR 563 at 564) that the 'persistent judicial failure to engage with the horizontal effect issue' is 'the fundamental problem with the privacy case law since October 2000' (the date on which the Human Rights Act came into force). Cf. Phillipson, 'Privacy', in D. Hoffman (ed.), *The Impact of the UK Human Rights Act on Private Law* (Cambridge: CUP, 2011), ch. 7.

An alternative explanation is that English law has always recognised the fundamental values of privacy and free speech, and now just happens to find it convenient to address questions relating to them by reference to Articles 8 and 10 of the European Convention. On this view, the passage of the Human Rights Act is essentially coincidental.

What do you think is the best explanation of why the English courts have, in recent years, radically remoulded the established action for breach of confidence so as to provide a remedy for the wrongful disclosure of private information? Do you think they have struck an appropriate balance between the right of the individual to keep personal information private and the right of the press to publish matters of public interest? For discussion see Culture, Media and Sport Committee, *Press Standards, Privacy and Libel*, HC (2009–10) 362-I, which found that '[t]he high costs of litigation combined with the legal uncertainty, owing to the small amount of case law, undoubtedly discourages the media from contesting privacy cases' (para. 62), but concluded that 'for now matters relating to privacy should continue to be determined according to common law, and the flexibility that permits, rather than set down in statute' (para. 67). This was also the conclusion of the Leveson Inquiry into the culture, practices and ethics of the press, which observed that 'the way in which the common law has addressed . . . [issues of privacy] has allowed flexibility of approach and a sensible enunciation of the relevant factors to be taken into account when balancing the competing issues in fact sensitive cases . . . It does not appear that legislative intervention will do other than generate further litigation as attempts are made to discover the extent to which the new framework matches the developing law' (*Leveson*, Part J, para. 4.2; as to the damages awards arising out of the 'phone hacking scandal' that led to the Inquiry see *Gulati v MGN Ltd* [2017] QB 149).

By contrast, a statutory cause of action for invasion of privacy has been proposed in Australia (see Australian Law Reform Commission, *For Your Information: Australian Privacy Law and Practice*, Report No. 108 (2008), ch. 74: 'serious invasion of privacy'; Australian Law Reform Commission, *Serious Invasions of Privacy in the Digital Era*, Report No. 123 (2014)). Cf. New Zealand Law Commission, *Invasion of Privacy: Penalties and Remedies*, Report 113 (2010), ch. 7, recommending that the tort of invasion of privacy should be left to develop at common law.

14 VICARIOUS LIABILITY

This chapter is concerned with vicarious liability and the related concept of the non-delegable duty of care. Vicarious liability has been described as 'the only true exception' to the principle that liability in tort depends on the breach of a duty owed by the defendant to the claimant (*Armes v Nottinghamshire County Council* [2018] AC 355 at [30], per Lord Reed). Rather than being based on the breach of a personal duty owed to the claimant, vicarious liability rests on two pillars: a particular kind of relationship between the tortfeasor and the defendant, and a sufficient connection between that relationship and the tort. Typically, the law of vicarious liability operates so as to impose liability on an employer (in older authorities, the 'master') in respect of the torts of an employee ('servant'), although a form of vicarious liability also attaches to vehicle owners, and more importantly the scope of the doctrine has now been extended to relationships 'akin to employment'. As for the second pillar, in the classic case where the relationship is one of employment, the employer is liable only for torts of the employee which are sufficiently closely connected to the employment relationship (and hence 'in the course of employment'). The vicarious liability of the employer is additional to—rather than a substitute for—the primary liability of the employee, and the employer may be entitled to an indemnity from the employee for any vicarious liability that arises (see further, *Winfield & Jolowicz*, paras 21-038–21-040).

By contrast, liability based on a non-delegable duty of care is liability for the breach of a personal duty owed to the claimant by the defendant, and so is a form of primary (as opposed to vicarious) liability. Unlike vicarious liability, this primary liability arises irrespective of whether there was any employer–employee relationship present on the facts. What distinguishes a non-delegable duty of care from an ordinary duty of care is the fact that a defendant who owes such a duty is liable not only for their own negligence, but also for the negligence of an employee or contractor to whom the defendant has entrusted the task which is the subject of the duty. For this reason, the primary significance of the non-delegable duty of care concept is that by this means an employer can be held liable for the negligent conduct of an independent contractor. Vicarious liability should also be distinguished from what is often called 'accessory liability', whereby, for example, primary liability attaches to someone who instructs another person to commit a tort (see IV.1).

The doctrines explored in this chapter have undergone major changes since the turn of the present century, which are scrutinised in three recent monographs: P. Giliker, *Vicarious Liability in Tort: A Comparative Perspective* (Cambridge: CUP, 2010); A. Gray, *Vicarious Liability: Critique and Reform* (Oxford: Hart, 2018); C. Beuermann, *Reconceptualising Strict Liability for the Tort of Another* (Oxford: Hart, 2019).

1. Development of and Justification for Vicarious Liability

> **Reedie v The London & North Western Railway Company** (1849) 4 Exch 244, 154 ER 1201
>
> The facts are not relevant to the extract.
>
> **Rolfe B**
>
> The liability of anyone, other than the party actually guilty of any wrongful act, proceeds on the maxim *'Qui facit per alium facit per se'* [He who does anything by another does it by himself]. The party employing has the selection of the party employed, and it is reasonable that he who has made choice of an unskilful or careless person to execute his orders, should be responsible for any injury resulting from the want of skill or want of care of the person employed; but neither the principle of the rule, nor the rule itself, can apply to a case where the party sought to be charged does not stand in the character of employer to the party by whose negligent act the injury has been occasioned.
>
> If the defendants had employed a contractor, carrying on an independent business, to repair their engines or carriages, and the contractor's workmen had negligently caused a heavy piece of iron to fall on a bystander, it would appear a strange doctrine to hold that the defendants were responsible.

> **R. Stevens, 'A Servant of Two Masters'** (2006) 122 LQR 201
>
> At one time, the dominant view was that where one person speaks or acts through another, their words or actions are attributed to the other, as reflected in the maxim *qui facit per alium facit per se* . . . If the words or acts amount to a tort, the person to whom they are attributed is a tortfeasor. The 'Master's Tort' theory is nowadays usually dismissed as misleading. If a law tutor punches a student on the nose in frustration, it is said to be fictional to say that the university which employs the tutor is also delivering the blow. However, in everyday life we attribute one person's actions to another without considering this to be fictional. An analogy may be drawn with the rules of a game. In the 1966 World Cup Final the person whose physical actions caused the last goal to be scored was Geoff Hurst. However, the rules of the game also attribute his physical actions to his team, England. Both Geoff Hurst and England scored the goal. Beyond the selection and training of the players, it is not possible for either team's manager to control the conduct of the game once the players step out on to the pitch. If a player kicks the ball into his own team's net, this will be considered to be an own goal. It does not matter that he was acting contrary to the express instructions of his team manager, nor does it matter if he did so deliberately in a fit of anger.

COMMENTARY

The dominant view today is that the employer's liability for the tort of an employee is truly vicarious and does not rest on any primary liability (see *Winfield & Jolowicz*, para. 21–001; *Salmond & Heuston*, pp. 431–4). This is the 'servant's tort' theory. The maxim quoted by Rolfe B, *qui facit per alium facit per se*, lies at the heart of the rival 'master's tort' theory, according to which the employer breaches their own duty through the act of their employee, a theory which was more influential in past times (see Swain, 'A Historical Examination of Vicarious Liability' [2019] CLJ 640). The key conceptual distinction between the two theories is that according to the former it is the *tort* of the employee that is attributed to the employer, while according to the latter it is their *act* which is attributed (though there are not now many situations where the choice of analysis makes a practical difference). The master's tort theory garnered some judicial support in the twentieth century (see, e.g., *Twine v Bean's Express Ltd* (1946) 175 LT 131), but has now been 'firmly discarded' by the courts (*Majrowski v Guy's and Thomas's NHS Trust* [2007] 1 AC 224 at [15], per Lord Nicholls), though it still has some academic adherents, as the extract from Stevens shows (for a fuller version of his position, see *Stevens*, ch. 11), and provides a straightforward explanation for the rule that an employer is not vicariously liable for the tort of an independent contractor. One criticism that has been made of the master's tort theory, however, is that in itself it gives no guidance as to where the boundaries of vicarious liability should lie. According to *McBride & Bagshaw*, p. 856, for example, while this theory seeks to explain what is happening in cases of vicarious liability, 'it tells us nothing about when we *should* attribute an employee's actions to his employer and when not'.

But if, applying the rival servant's tort theory, it is the employee's tort for which the employer is held liable, what is the justification for this? The next three extracts consider this question.

G. Williams, 'Vicarious Liability and the Master's Indemnity'
(1957) 20 MLR 220

Then there is the idea . . . that the master is a cause of the mischief, or has set a noxious instrument in motion. In itself this is true. The master is a cause in the factual sense, for if he had not employed the servant to do the particular work the harm would not have happened. The servant might have been doing mischief elsewhere and to some other victim. However, it is a very primitive notion that a person must be responsible for harm merely because he is its cause. Causation plus fault is accepted to be enough, but not causation alone. What element in the master-servant situation is there to replace personal fault as an intelligible ground of liability?

[After considering and dismissing other possible justifications for vicarious liability, he continued:]

What other theory is there? Well, there is the purely cynical theory that the master is liable because he has a purse worth opening. The master is frequently rich, and he is usually insured—two arguments that might be used by any burglar, if he ever troubled to justify his thefts. The strange thing is to find them put forward by judges of eminence. . . . Whatever (one may ask) can have put this extraordinary idea into judges' heads, that the mere possession of wealth is enough to justify the imposition of legal liability for a wrong? Obviously there is something missing from the dicta. There must be some fact to create liability, and not merely the fact of being a master. If so, we have another unprovable principle of natural justice: that masters ought to pay because they belong to the class of masters. One can manufacture eternal principles of natural justice of this sort without limit . . .

However distasteful the theory may be, we have to admit that vicarious liability owes its explanation, if not its justification, to the search for a solvent defendant.

P. S. Atiyah, *Vicarious Liability* (London: Butterworths, 1967)

[I]t seems that in general the policy of placing the liability for the torts of servants on their employers is broadly a sound one. It is sound simply because, by and large, it is the most convenient and efficient way of ensuring that persons injured in the course of business enterprises do not go uncompensated. Of course if all workmen insured themselves against third-party risks, and if wages and salaries were slightly increased in order to enable workmen to do this, we could get on pretty well without vicarious liability at all. But this would not be so efficient or convenient a way of doing things simply because it would involve an enormous number of insurance policies instead of relatively few, with a consequent increase in insurance costs. Further, there would inevitably be a number of defaulters, even if such insurance were made compulsory by law—and this itself would of course cost money in enforcement.

Whether this is the most equitable way of distributing the risks created by business enterprises is a different and more difficult question which in the last resort depends on value judgments . . .

Bazley v Curry (1999) 174 DLR (4th) 45 (Supreme Court of Canada)

The defendant, a non-profit organisation, operated two residential care facilities for the treatment of emotionally troubled children. As it acted in place of the children's parents, it was responsible for all aspects of life for the children it cared for, from general supervision to intimate duties like bathing and tucking in at bedtime. Unknown to the defendant and without carelessness on its part, it hired a paedophile as an employee to work in one of its homes. It was later discovered that the employee in question had sexually abused some of the children, and an action was brought against the defendant alleging that it was vicariously liable for the damage caused to the children as a result of the actions of the employee.

McLachlin J

Fleming [*The Law of Torts* (9th edn, 1998)] has identified [the] policies lying at the heart of vicarious liability. In his view, two fundamental concerns underlie the imposition of vicarious liability: (1) provision of a just and practical remedy for the harm; and (2) deterrence of future harm. While different formulations of the policy interests at stake may be made (for example, loss internalization is a hybrid of the two), I believe that these two ideas usefully embrace the main policy considerations that have been advanced.

First and foremost is the concern to provide a just and practical remedy to people who suffer as a consequence of wrongs perpetrated by an employee. Fleming expresses this succinctly (at p. 410): 'a person who employs others to advance his own economic interest should in fairness be placed under a corresponding liability for losses incurred in the course of the enterprise'. The idea that the person who introduces a risk incurs a duty to those who may be injured lies at the heart of tort law. . . . This principle of fairness applies to the employment enterprise and hence to the issue of vicarious liability. While charitable enterprises may not employ people to advance their economic interests, other factors, discussed below, make it fair that they should bear the burden of providing a just and practical remedy for wrongs perpetrated by their employees. This policy interest embraces a number of subsidiary goals. The first is the goal of effective compensation. 'One of the most important social goals served by vicarious liability is victim compensation. Vicarious liability improves the chances that the victim can recover the judgment from a solvent defendant' (B. Feldthusen, 'Vicarious Liability for Sexual Torts', in *Torts Tomorrow* (1998), 221, p. 224.) Or to quote Fleming, the master is 'a more promising source of recompense than his servant who is apt to be a man of straw' (p. 410).

However, effective compensation must also be fair, in the sense that it must seem just to place liability for the wrong on the employer. Vicarious liability is arguably fair in this sense. The employer puts in the community an enterprise which carries with it certain risks. When those risks materialize and cause injury to a member of the public despite the employer's reasonable efforts, it is fair that the person or organization that creates the enterprise and hence the risk should bear the loss. This accords with the notion that it is right and just that the person who creates a risk bears the loss when the risk ripens into harm. While the fairness of this proposition is capable of standing alone, it is buttressed by the fact that the employer is often in the best position to spread the losses through mechanisms like insurance and higher prices, thus minimizing the dislocative effect of the tort within society. 'Vicarious liability has the broader function of transferring to the enterprise itself the risks created by the activity performed by its agents' (*London Drugs*, per La Forest J, at 339).

The second major policy consideration underlying vicarious liability is deterrence of future harm. Fixing the employer with responsibility for the employee's wrongful act, even where the employer is not negligent, may have a deterrent effect. Employers are often in a position to reduce accidents and intentional wrongs by efficient organisation and supervision. Failure to take such measures may not suffice to establish a case of tortious negligence directly against the employer. Perhaps the harm cannot be shown to have been foreseeable under negligence law. Perhaps the employer can avail itself of the defence of compliance with the industry standard. Or perhaps the employer, while complying with the standard of reasonable care, was not as scrupulously diligent as it might feasibly have been. As Wilkinson J. explained in the companion appeal's trial judgment:

> If the scourge of sexual predation is to be stamped out, or at least controlled, there must be powerful motivation acting upon those who control institutions engaged in the care, protection and nurturing of children. That motivation will not in my view be sufficiently supplied by the likelihood of liability in negligence. In many cases evidence will be lacking or have long since disappeared. The proof of appropriate standards is a difficult and uneven matter.

I agree. Beyond the narrow band of employer conduct that attracts direct liability in negligence lies a vast area where imaginative and efficient administration and supervision can reduce the risk that the employer has introduced into the community. Holding the employer vicariously liable for the wrongs of its employee may encourage the employer to take such steps, and hence, reduce the risk of future harm. A related consideration raised by Fleming is that by holding the employer liable, 'the law furnishes an incentive to discipline servants guilty of wrongdoing' (p. 410).

The policy grounds supporting the imposition of vicarious liability—fair compensation and deterrence—are related. The policy consideration of deterrence is linked to the policy consideration of fair compensation based on the employer's introduction or enhancement of a risk. The introduction of the enterprise into the community with its attendant risk, in turn, implies the possibility of managing the risk to minimize the costs of the harm that may flow from it. Policy considerations relating to the fair allocation of loss to risk-creating enterprises and the deterrence of harms tend to support the imposition of vicarious liability on employers. But, as Fleming notes, there often exists a countervailing concern. At one time the law held masters responsible for *all* wrongs committed by servants. Later, that policy was abandoned as too harsh in a complex commercial society where masters might not be in a position to supervise their servants closely. Servants may commit acts, even on working premises and during working hours, which are so unconnected with the employment that it would seem unreasonable to fix an employer with responsibility for them. For example, if a man assaults his wife's lover (who coincidentally happens to be a co-worker) in the employees' lounge at work, few would argue that the employer should be held responsible. Similarly, an employer would not be liable for the harm caused by a security guard who decides to commit arson for his own amusement: see, e.g., *Plains Engineering Ltd v Barnes Security Services Ltd* (1987) 43 CCLT 129 (Alta QB). On further analysis, however, this apparently negative policy consideration of when liability would be appropriate is revealed as nothing more than the absence of the twin policies of fair compensation and deterrence that justify vicarious liability. A wrong that is only coincidentally linked to the activity of the employer and duties of the employee cannot justify the imposition of vicarious liability on the employer. To impose vicarious liability on the employer for such a wrong does not respond to common sense notions of fairness. Nor does it serve to deter future harms. Because the wrong is essentially independent of the employment situation, there is little the employer could have done to prevent it. Where vicarious liability is not closely and materially related to a risk introduced or enhanced by the employer, it serves no deterrent purpose, and relegates the employer to the status of an involuntary insurer. I conclude that a meaningful articulation of when vicarious liability should follow in new situations ought to be animated by the twin policy goals of fair compensation and deterrence that underlie the doctrine, rather than by artificial or semantic distinctions.

COMMENTARY

According to the High Court of Australia, a 'fully satisfactory rationale for the imposition of vicarious liability' has been 'slow to appear in the case law' (*Prince Alfred College Inc v ADC* (2016) 258 CLR 134 at [39]), and the editors of *Winfield & Jolowicz* (para. 21–006) argue that 'the absence of a convincing rationale for vicarious liability has undoubtedly contributed to the difficulties the courts have faced in trying to construct an analytical framework that provides certainty and consistency in this area of tort law'.

Some of the traditional justifications for vicarious liability are listed by Atiyah in his book: (1) control of the employee by the employer; (2) as the employer benefits from the employee's work the employer should also bear any burdens from that work; and (3) the employer chooses the employee. These three, along with other possible rationales, are rejected in favour of the economic rationale for vicarious liability set out in the extract above. Glanville Williams (extracted earlier) described this form of loss distribution as a form of social insurance and argued it was the most persuasive justification for vicarious liability, and the one that best fitted the existing law (in 1957).

In *Various Claimants v Catholic Child Welfare Society* [2013] 2 AC 1 (hereafter '*Christian Brothers*'), Lord Phillips seemed to endorse the loss distribution argument when he stated that the policy underlying vicarious liability 'is to ensure, so far as it is fair, just and reasonable, that liability for a tortious wrong is borne by a defendant with the means to compensate the victim' (at [34]). However, Williams' dismissal of this 'deep pockets' argument (the employer is liable because the employer can more easily meet the liability) has been echoed in recent remarks of judges at the highest level (see, e.g., *Cox v Ministry of Justice* [2016] AC 660 at [20], where Lord Reed said that '[t]he mere possession of wealth is not in itself any ground for imposing liability'; and *Armes v Nottinghamshire County Council* [2018] AC 355 at [77], per Lord Hughes).

Instead, the courts have in recent decisions favoured the 'enterprise risk' argument put forward by the Supreme Court of Canada in *Bazley v Curry* (described by Lord Reed as 'the most influential idea in modern times' in *Armes v Nottinghamshire County Council* [2018] AC 355 at [67]). According to this theory, because the employer stands to benefit from the work of the employee undertaken on the employer's behalf, they should also shoulder the burden of the risks generated by that work. As Rix LJ put it in *Viasystems (Tyneside) Ltd v Thermal Transfer (Northern) Ltd* [2006] QB 510 at 529, liability is imposed on the employer on the basis that 'those who set in motion and profit from the activities of their employees should compensate those who are injured by such activities' when they are performed negligently. (How different is this rationale from the causation justification dismissed by Williams?) Academic proponents of this theory include Deakin (2003) 32 Ind LJ 97 and D. Brodie, *Enterprise Liability and the Common Law* (Cambridge: CUP, 2010), who argues that the courts' invocation of enterprise liability reflects contemporary concerns over the proper extent of corporate social responsibility. This rationale has, however, been questioned by other commentators who have pointed out the difficulties of squaring an argument based on the internalisation of the costs of the employer's enterprise with the fact that the employer's vicarious liability is typically contingent on the fault of the employee (after all, '*a* [social] loss caused without negligence is just as much a loss as one caused by negligence': Williams, *op. cit.*, 442), and who have queried whether the rationale extends to non-profit undertakings such as public authorities and charities, which have been the target of much of the recent litigation in this area (see, e.g., Nolan's review of Brodie's book (2012) 41 Ind LJ 370). It is also unclear to what extent on this theory the risks created by a particular undertaking should be weighed against the risks it eliminates or reduces: in *Bazley*, for example, the 'enterprise' was a charity which had taken the plaintiffs into its care, thereby presumably reducing many risks of harm to which they would otherwise have been subject. Finally, can the rationale explain why it is that the employee themself remains personally liable for the tort, or vicarious liability for omissions, where the defendant is sued not for creating a risk, but for failing to protect the claimant against a risk which has arisen in some other way? (For a thoroughgoing critique of the theory, see Gray, *op. cit.*, ch. 6.)

In *Bazley v Curry*, vicarious liability was also justified on deterrence grounds. As the employer creates a risk by conducting their enterprise and employing the employee, vicarious liability promotes conduct which minimises these risks. Of course, it might be argued that this is exactly what the law of negligence does, but McLachlin J considered that the requirement to exercise reasonable care might not provide the desired level of risk management, particularly when it came to the taking of precautions at a systemic or organisational level. The idea here is that the threat of vicarious liability encourages employers to take measures—such as providing training—that will have a positive effect on the behaviour of their employees, who would otherwise have little incentive to take care since they themselves are rarely worth suing. And while in theory the failure to take these measures could amount to negligence on the employer's part it would be hard to establish this (and harder still to demonstrate a causal connection between such a failure and a particular incident of employee fault). However, note that this argument is not necessarily limited to the employment context, and could also be used to justify, for example, imposing vicarious liability on parents for the fault of their children, which English law does not do.

Are you convinced by these rationales? If not, is there a better one, or is vicarious liability a doctrine incapable of justification? (See further J. Morgan, 'Vicarious Liability for Independent Contractors?' (2015) 31 PN 235 at 247–58.)

As Swain points out (*op. cit.*, 659), '[d]espite the struggle to find a coherent justification, vicarious liability has proved to be remarkably resilient'. And regardless of its rationale, there is no doubt that the doctrine is a fundamental building block of modern tort law, and little prospect of that changing for the foreseeable future. Indeed, in the first two decades of the present century the scope of the doctrine has been considerably expanded, as part of an ongoing process of development of which Lord Toulson said this in *Mohamud v Wm Morrison Supermarkets plc* [2016] AC 677 at [10]:

The development of the doctrine of vicarious liability can be traced to a number of factors; in part to legal theories, of which there have been several; in part to changes in the structure and size of economic and other (e.g., charitable) enterprises; and in part to changes in social attitudes and the courts' sense of justice and fairness, particularly when faced with new problems such as cases of sexual abuse of children by people in a position of authority.

The interaction of those factors, and the process of development of which Lord Toulson spoke, will be readily apparent to the student from the cases extracted in the remainder of this chapter.

II. Relationships Triggering Vicarious Liability

As noted earlier, a prerequisite of vicarious liability is that there is a relationship between the tortfeasor and the defendant that is capable of giving rise to such liability. Where, as is usually the case, these two parties are in a contractual relationship, the question is whether the tortfeasor is employed under a contract of service (employee) or a contract for services (independent contractor). In cases that do not fit this dichotomy—sometimes because one person is working for another in the absence of any kind of contract—the courts have in recent years been prepared to base vicarious liability on a relationship 'akin to employment'. Particular issues arise when a worker is loaned by one company to another, as where a crane is hired out with its driver, while a distinct form of vicarious liability (often styled as a form of 'agency') is recognised in cases where the tortfeasor is driving a vehicle on some business of the vehicle's owner. In this section these four questions are considered in turn.

1. Employee or Independent Contractor?

The question of whether one person is working for another as an employee or a contractor is significant in a range of legal contexts, including employment law, tax law and social security law. It used to be the case that little distinction was drawn between these different contexts, but more recently the courts have moved away from this formalist approach, and recognised that a worker may be an employee for the purposes of vicarious liability even though they would not be so classified for other purposes. As Ward LJ put it in *E v English Province of Our Lady of Charity* [2013] QB 722 at [59], the 'fluid concept of vicarious liability' should not 'be confined by the concrete demands of statutory construction arising in a wholly different context' (see also *Cox v Ministry of Justice* [2016] AC 660 at [11], per Lord Reed). After all, the concerns that underlie decisions over whether a person is an employee for other purposes may not be as pertinent when it comes to asking whether that person's tort should give rise to vicarious liability. (See further J. Prassl, *The Concept of the Employer* (Oxford: OUP, 2015), criticising what he calls, at p. 10, 'the received unitary concept of the employer, where the employer has come to be defined as a single entity, substantively identical in all circumstances and domains of employment law and beyond', and advocating a more functional approach to the employer concept 'which identifies the party, or indeed parties, exercising the relevant employer functions' in a particular context; for a prescient earlier argument to the same effect, see McKendrick, 'Vicarious Liability and Independent Contractors: A Re-examination' (1990) 53 MLR 770.) Having said that, many of the leading authorities on the employee/contractor distinction are not tort cases, and yet these still provide valuable guidance on the issue for the purposes of vicarious liability. One such authority is the next extracted case.

Market Investigations v Minister of Social Security [1969] 2 QB 173

The issue for the court was whether, for the purposes of assessing national insurance contributions, a person (a Mrs Irving) employed on a series of short-term contracts by a company to carry out interviews was an employee or an independent contractor. The relevant government department had decided that she was an employee. The contracts provided that, in consideration for a fixed remuneration, Mrs Irving would provide her own work and skill in the performance of a service for the company. The company could specify who was to be interviewed, the questions to be asked, the order in which questions should be asked and recorded, how answers were to be recorded and how she should probe for answers. She could be required to attend at the company's office for a short period to see a supervisor. Within the period specified for completion of a survey, however, she was normally free to choose when to work, could undertake similar work for other organisations, and could not be moved by the company from the area in which she had agreed to work. When working in the field the supervisor would have no means of getting in touch with her, and the company's officers were of the opinion that she could not be dismissed in the middle of a survey. No provision was made in the agreements for time off, sick pay or holidays.

Cooke J

I begin by pointing out that the first condition which must be fulfilled in order that a contract may be classified as a contract of service is that stated by MacKenna J in the *Ready Mixed Concrete* case, namely that A agrees that, in consideration of some form of remuneration, he will provide his own work and skill in the performance of some service for B. The fact that this condition is fulfilled is not, however, sufficient. Further tests must be applied to determine whether the nature and provisions of the contract as a whole are consistent or inconsistent with its being a contract of service.

I think it is fair to say that there was at one time a school of thought according to which the extent and degree of the control which B was entitled to exercise over A in the performance of the work would be a decisive factor. However, it has for long been apparent that an analysis of the extent and degree of such control is not in itself decisive. . . .

The inadequacy of this test was pointed out by Somervell LJ in *Cassidy v Ministry of Health* [1951] 2 KB 343 at 352 when he referred to the case of a certified master of a ship. The master may be employed by the owners under what is clearly a contract of service, and yet the owners have no power to tell him how to navigate his ship. As Lord Parker CJ pointed out in *Morren v Swinton and Pendlebury Borough Council* [1965] 1 WLR 576 at 582, when one is dealing with a professional man, or a man of some particular skill and experience, there can be no question of an employer telling him how to do the work; therefore the absence of control and direction in that sense can be of little, if any, use as a test.

Cases such as *Morren's* case ([1965] 1 WLR 576) illustrate how a contract of service may exist even though the control does not extend to prescribing how the work shall be done. On the other hand, there may be cases when one who engages another to do work may reserve to himself full control over how the work is to be done, but nevertheless the contract is not a contract of service. A good example is *Queensland Stations Pty v Federal Comr of Taxation* (1945), 70 CLR 539 at p 552, the 'drover' case, when Dixon J said:

> In considering the facts it is a mistake to treat as decisive a reservation of control over the manner in which the droving is performed and the cattle are handled. For instance, in the present case the circumstance that the drover agrees to obey and carry out all lawful instructions cannot outweigh the countervailing considerations which are found in the employment by him of servants of his own, the provision of horses, equipment, plant, rations, and a remuneration at a rate per head delivered.

If control is not a decisive test, what then are the other considerations which are relevant? No comprehensive answer has been given to this question, but assistance is to be found in a number of cases.

[Cooke J considered *Montreal Locomotive Works v Montreal and A-G for Canada* [1947] 1 DLR 161, *Bank voor Handel en Scheepvaart NV v Slatford* [1953] 1 QB 248, and *US v Silk* (1946) 331 US 704 and continued:]

The observations [in these cases] suggest that the fundamental test to be applied is this: 'Is the person who has engaged himself to perform these services performing them as a person in business on his own account?'. If the answer to that question is 'yes', then the contract is a contract for services. If the answer is 'no' then the contract is a contract of service. No exhaustive list has been compiled and perhaps no exhaustive list can be compiled of considerations which are relevant in determining that question, nor can strict rules be laid down as to the relative weight which the various considerations should carry in particular cases. The most that can be said is that control will no doubt always have to be considered, although it can no longer be regarded as the sole determining factor; and that factors, which may be of importance, are such matters as whether the man performing the services provides his own equipment, whether he hires his own helpers, what degree of financial risk he takes, what degree of responsibility for investment and management he has, and whether and how far he has an opportunity of profiting from sound management in the performance of his task. The application of the general test may be easier in a case where the person who engages himself to perform the services does so in the course of an already established business of his own; but this factor is not decisive, and a person who engages himself to perform services for another may well be an independent contractor even though he has not entered into the contract in the course of an existing business carried on by him . . .

[Cooke J considered the contract in question and continued:]

It is apparent that the control which the company had the right to exercise in this case was very extensive indeed. It was in my view so extensive as to be entirely consistent with Mrs Irving's being employed under a contract of service. The fact that Mrs Irving had a limited discretion when she should do the work was not in my view inconsistent with the existence of a contract of service. Nor is there anything inconsistent with the existence of a contract of service in the fact that Mrs Irving was free to work for others during the relevant period. It is by no means a necessary incident of a contract of service that the servant is prohibited from serving any other employer. Again, there is nothing inconsistent with the existence of a contract of service in the master having no right to alter the place or area within which the servant has agreed to work. So far as concerns practical limitations on a master's power to give instructions to his servant, there must be many cases when such practical limitations exist. For example, a chauffeur in the service of a car hire company may, in the absence of radio communication, be out of reach of instructions for long periods . . .

[Cooke J went on to hold that there were no provisions of the contract, which, when considered as a whole, were inconsistent with a contract of service.]

Appeal dismissed.

R. Kidner, 'Vicarious Liability: For Whom Should the "Employer" be Liable?' (1995) 15 LS 47

It is suggested that the following in some mix or other are appropriate for the question [who is an employer] in so far as it relates to vicarious liability.

(1) Control by the 'employer' of the 'employee'. Traditionally this has meant asking whether the employer can control not only what is done but also how it is done. This makes little sense and the variant of asking whether the employer has the legal right to control is merely circular. Rather this factor should look at the degree of managerial control which is exercised over the activity and this may depend on how far a person is integrated into the organisation of the enterprise. At the one end of the spectrum a contractor will merely be asked to achieve an end result, or more ambiguously the specification of that end result may be so detailed as to amount to detailed control over how that result is to be achieved. At the other end of the spectrum is the person who is actually controlled in every detail of how things are to be done. Another way to look at the control test is to examine the degree to which the 'employee' is accountable to the employer: in other words to what extent is he subject to the managerial procedures of the employer in relation to such matters as quality of work, performance, productivity etc?

(2) Control by the contractor of himself. This is not about the Mr Newall who took no orders from anybody [see *Mersey Docks and Harbour Board v Coggins & Griffith* [1947] AC 1] but is rather an element of the entrepreneur test and involves looking at how the contractor arranges his work, his use of assets, his payment etc.

(3) The organisation test (in the first sense of how central the activity is to the enterprise). This involves the question, how far the activity is a central part of the employer's business from the point of view of the objectives of that business. This element flows from the need to establish who it is that is engaging in the activity and the more relevant the activity is to the fundamental objectives of the business the more appropriate it is to apply the risk to the business.

(4) The integration test (i.e. organisation test in the second sense of whether the activity is integrated into the organisational structure of the enterprise). This also looks at the traditional test of whether the function is being provided for the business or by the business and is also part of the entrepreneur test for it asks whether the activity is part of the enterprise's organisation or of some other organisation. A service may be absolutely essential to the business or wholly peripheral to it, but if it is being provided by what is in effect a separate business it would be inappropriate to apply the risk to the enterprise. It is a factor of both who is engaging in the activity and also who stands to gain or lose from it.

(5) Is the person in business on his own account (the entrepreneur test)? This is not really a separate test as it is intimately involved in the other four, but it needs to be highlighted so that the burden of proof is right. For the purposes of vicarious liability a person should not be regarded as an independent contractor simply because according to the technical requirements of employment law he is not an employee. Rather it needs to be established that he is actually behaving as an entrepreneur and is taking the appropriate risks and has the possibility of resulting profits. Thus even if a person's activity is peripheral to the enterprise and even if he is not for managerial purposes regarded as part of the organisation, a person could still be regarded as an employee if it is clear that in relation to that business he is not acting as an entrepreneur. Agency workers would be an example.

The function of this article has been to argue that those for whom an 'employer' should be vicariously liable should not be restricted by recent approaches in employment law and tort law needs to be able to take account of new forms of employment. The point is not that the relationship between employer and employee should be defined totally differently in the two areas of law, but that because of the objectives to be achieved the emphasis needs to be different . . .

The change can only be achieved if it is admitted that the term 'employee' can have different meanings for different purposes: however it is not being argued that vicarious liability should jettison the concept of employment as the governing relationship, but rather that the core of the concept should remain, subject to different interpretation and emphasis in light of different objectives. In looking at these objectives vicarious liability should have greater regard for the role of the 'contractor' within the organisation and less regard for the nature of the contractual arrangements. The contract of employment rarely reflects what actually happens and tort always looks more to what the parties do than to what they are entitled to do . . .

COMMENTARY

In the early stages of the development of vicarious liability 'control' by the employer was the determining test, but this came to be criticised on the ground that it was an outdated approach. This critique was summarised by Kahn-Freud, 'Servants and Independent-Contractors' (1951) 14 MLR 504:

This distinction was based upon the social conditions of an earlier age: it assumed that the employer of labour was able to direct and instruct the labourer as to the technical methods he should use in performing his work. . . . The technical and economic developments of all industrial societies have nullified these assumptions. . . . To say of the captain of a ship, the pilot of an aeroplane, the driver of a railway engine, of a motor vehicle, of a crane, that the employer 'controls' the performance of the work is unrealistic and almost grotesque. If in such a case the employee relied on the employer's instructions 'how to do his work' he would be breaking his contract and possibly be liable to summary dismissal for having misrepresented his skill. . . .

The assumption that in this context 'control' means the ability to tell the employee how to do their job is, however, contested by Watts (2019) 135 LQR 7, who defends the use of control in the vicarious liability context (see also P. Morgan (2013) 129 LQR 139). According to Watts (at 9):

> The concept of control in this context has (at least) two meanings, both of which have some role to play, depending on the facts. The most important of these by far is its use as a shorthand for the duties of obedience and loyalty that an employee implicitly undertakes to an employer . . . The existence of these duties, and their scope . . . turns on agreement, albeit objectively determined . . . The other meaning of control refers to the giving of precise directions as to how a person must or must not act in order to achieve the stipulated end. The absence of this type of control, which might be called 'micro-control', is not important in determining whether vicarious liability should be imposed. But if there is a right to micro-control, or such control is assumed, then that can be a significant factor in finding that an employment relationship exists.

Might the use of a control-based approach to the distinction between employees and independent contractors have implications for the status of workers in the 'gig' economy, such as Uber drivers, whom the companies that rely on them style as contractors while simultaneously using technology to micro-manage their working lives?

In the extracted case Cooke J emphasised that control is now only one of the factors that the courts look to in deciding whether a relationship of employer–employee existed, and considered some of the other factors that might assist in the determination. Before we consider those factors, the point should be made that the courts look to the actual relationship rather than to form, so that the characterisation of the contract by the parties to it is not necessarily determinative, and may even be entirely irrelevant (compare *Dacas v Brook Street Bureau (UK) Ltd* [2004] ICR 1436, where the Court of Appeal regarded it as a factor to be considered, with the view of the majority of the same court in *Ferguson v John Dawson & Partners (Contractors) Ltd* [1976] 1 WLR 1213 that a mere expression of intention as to what the legal relationship between the parties should be could not in any way influence the conclusion of the law as to what the relationship was).

As far as the substantive analysis of the nature of the relationship is concerned, a good example of the relevant factors being weighed is *Hall (Inspector of Taxes) v Lorimer* [1994] 1 All ER 250, a case concerned with the appropriate tax schedule for a taxpayer. The taxpayer was trained and employed as a vision mixer, a skilled editing job in the television industry, and went 'freelance' in 1985. In the next four year he worked 800 days. He hired no staff but did provide replacements to his employers if he was unavailable. All work was carried out at the studios of the production company who employed him, and the equipment was also provided by those companies. He did not contribute to the cost of production nor was he exposed to profits/loss made by the production company, but he could lose money if a client of that company became insolvent or did not pay. He was assessed for taxation purposes as an employee, but the Court of Appeal affirmed earlier judgments overturning that assessment and holding that he was a contractor. Particular attention was paid to the fact that the risk of bad debts and outstanding invoices was not usually associated with a contract of service. It was also significant that the taxpayer had worked for a large number of separate employers for a short period (usually one day).

This case can be contrasted with *Lee Ting Sang v Chung Chi-Keung* [1990] 2 AC 374. The applicant was a stonemason who worked mainly for one subcontractor on short-term contracts. He was paid a piece-work rate (so much for finishing a job) or a daily rate. If he finished early he assisted the subcontractor in sharpening tools. Although he sometimes worked for others, he gave preference to the urgent work of the subcontractor, advising those for whom he was working at that time to replace him. Allowing an appeal from the Court of Appeal of Hong Kong, the Privy Council held him to be an employee. He provided no equipment, did not hire any helpers to assist him, had no responsibility for the management of the job, and did not 'price' the job. He was simply told to turn up for work and was told what to do (although, as a skilled worker, not how to do it). In short (at 384), '[t]he applicant ran no risk whatever save that of being unable to find employment which is, of course, a risk faced by casual employees who move from one job to another . . .'.

The approach adopted in *Market Investigations* to the employee/contractor distinction was recently followed in *Various Claimants v Barclays Bank plc* [2020] AC 973 (extracted in II.3), where the Supreme Court held that a doctor who carried out medical assessments of prospective employees for a bank was a contractor rather than an employee. In reaching the conclusion that the doctor was 'in business on his own account as a medical practitioner with a portfolio of patients and clients' (*ibid.*, at [28]), Lady Hale attached significance to the fact that the doctor was paid a fee for each report that he completed, but not a retainer which might have obliged him to accept a certain number of referrals from the bank. Other examples of vicarious liability cases in which this approach has been adopted include *E v English Province of Our Lady of Charity* [2013] QB 722 at [70], where Ward LJ said that an 'independent contractor works in and for his own business at his risk of profit or loss'; and *Kafagi v JBW Group Ltd* [2018] EWCA Civ 1157, where it was held that a bailiff who collected debts for a judicial services company was an independent contractor because he could turn down work or share it with others, worked for other clients, was free to collect debts as he wished, without control from the company, and maintained his own indemnity insurance.

For recent academic commentary on the employment relationship, see Bomball, 'Vicarious Liability, Entrepreneurship and the Concept of Employment at Common Law' (2021) 43 Syd L Rev 83 (who defends 'entrepreneurship' as an organising principle when distinguishing employees from independent contractors), and Deakin, 'Decoding Employment Status' (2020) 31 KLJ 180 (who seeks to take the abstraction out of 'employment' status and to break the relationship down into its component parts).

2. Lending of Employees

What if an employee of one employer is hired to someone else? Which employer is vicariously liable for the torts of the employee? This issue was considered by the Court of Appeal in the following extract.

Viasystems (Tyneside) Ltd v Thermal Transfer (Northern) Ltd
[2006] QB 510

The claimant engaged contractors to install air conditioning in their factory. These contractors subcontracted ducting work to A Ltd and labour for this work was supplied to A Ltd by B Ltd. The factory was flooded due to the negligence of one Darren Strang, a fitter's mate supplied by B Ltd to A Ltd. At the time of the accident, Mr Strang was working under the supervision of a Mr Horsley, A Ltd's foreman, and a Mr Megson, a fitter supplied by B Ltd. In an action by the factory owner, the trial judge found that only B Ltd was vicariously liable for Mr Strang's negligence. When B Ltd appealed, the Court of Appeal sought submissions on the permissibility of finding both A Ltd and B Ltd vicariously liable.

May LJ

18. The relevant negligent act was Darren Strang crawling through the duct. This was a foolish mistake on the spur of the moment. . . . [T]he core question . . . is who was entitled, and in theory, if they had had the opportunity, obliged, so to control Darren as to stop him crawling through the duct. In my judgment, the only sensible answer to that question in this case is that both Mr Megson and Mr Horsley were entitled, and in theory obliged, to stop Darren's foolishness. Mr Megson was the fitter in charge of Darren. Mr Horsley was the foreman on the spot. They were both entitled and obliged to control Darren's work, including the act which was his negligence. The second defendants, through Mr Horsley, would, I think, have qualified for vicarious liability, if it had been Mr Megson who foolishly crawled through the duct. It makes no difference to a sensible analysis that it was Darren who was negligent, and that Mr Megson in some respects was interposed. But neither is there any good sense in saying that, because Mr Horsley was relevantly entitled to control Darren, Mr Megson was not: and vice versa . . .

Rix LJ

76. In my judgment, there is no doubt that there has been a long standing assumption that dual vicarious liability is not possible, and in such a situation it is necessary to pause carefully to consider the weight of that tradition. However, in truth, the issue has never been properly considered. There appears to be a number of possible strands to the assumption . . . [these include] the formal principle that a servant cannot have two masters; and the policy against multiplicity of actions. As for the first, even if it be granted that an employee cannot have contracts of employment with two separate employers at the same time and for the same period and purposes—and yet it seems plain that a person can (a) have two jobs with separate employers at the same time, provided they are compatible with one another; or (b) be employed by a consortium of several employers acting jointly—nevertheless that does not prevent the employee of a general employer being lent to a temporary employer. As was so clearly exposed in *Denham*'s case [*Denham v Midland Employers' Mutual Assurance Ltd* [1955] 2 QB 437], it is an inaccurate metaphor to say that the employment or the employee has been transferred: it is rather that the services of the employee have been lent or hired out, or borrowed or bought in, in circumstances where the temporary employer becomes responsible, under the doctrine of vicarious liability (*respondeat superior*), for the employee's negligence, and does so even though the formal contract or relationship of employment has not been transferred. That demonstrates that the doctrine of vicarious liability may properly be invoked against an employer who is not really, in law, the employee's employer; and that the use of the expression 'transfer' is potentially misleading. As for the policy against multiplicity of actions: no doubt the law does not favour unnecessary complexity which may lead to the suing of unnecessary defendants. But such a policy, while it may inform the formulation of doctrine, cannot determine it; and, in any event, the history of this jurisprudence has demonstrated clearly that it is not safe for a claimant to assume that he can sue one employer only. . . .

77. In my judgment, if consideration is given to the function and purposes of the doctrine of vicarious liability, then the possibility of dual responsibility provides a coherent solution to the problem of the borrowed employee. Both employers are using the employee for the purposes of their business. Both have a general responsibility to select their personnel with care and to encourage and control the careful execution of their employees' duties, and both fall within the practical policy of the law which looks in general to the employer to organise his affairs in such a way as to make it fair, just and convenient for him to bear the risk of his employees' negligence. I am here using the expression 'employee' in the extended sense used in the authorities relating to the borrowed employee. The functional basis of the doctrine of vicarious

liability has become increasingly clear over the years. The Civil Liability (Contribution) Act 1978 now provides a clear and fair statutory basis for the assessment of contribution between the two employers. In my judgment, the existence of the possibility of dual responsibility will be fairer and will also enable cases to be settled more easily.

78. The remaining question is to attempt to define the circumstances in which the liability should be dual. It is possible that where the right to control the method of performance of the employee's duties lies solely on the one side or the other, then the responsibility similarly lies on the same side. . . . If so, then it will only be where the right of control is shared that vicarious liability can be dual. I would agree that the balance of authority is in favour of this solution. On this basis, I agree with May LJ's analysis of the facts in this case as demonstrating a situation of shared control. I would go further and say that it is a situation of shared control where it is just for both employers to share a dual vicarious liability. The relevant employee, Darren, was both part of the temporary employer's team, under the supervision of Mr Horsley, and part of the general employer's small hired squad, under the supervision of its Mr Megson.

79. However, I am a little sceptical that the doctrine of dual vicarious liability is to be wholly equated with the question of control. I can see that, where the assumption is that liability has to fall wholly and solely on the one side or the other, then a test of sole right of control has force to it. Even the *Mersey Docks* case [*Mersey Docks and Harbour Board v Coggins & Griffith (Liverpool) Ltd* [1947] AC 1], however, does not make the control test wholly determinative. Once, however, a doctrine of dual responsibility becomes possible, I am less clear that either the existence of sole right of control or the existence of something less than entire and absolute control necessarily either excludes or respectively invokes the doctrine. Even in the establishment of a formal employer/employee relationship, the right of control has not retained the critical significance it once did. I would prefer to say that I anticipate that subsequent cases may, in various factual circumstances, refine the circumstances in which dual vicarious liability may be imposed. I would hazard, however, the view that what one is looking for is a situation where the employee in question, at any rate for relevant purposes, is so much a part of the work, business or organisation of both employers that it is just to make both employers answer for his negligence. What has to be recalled is that the vicarious liability in question is one which involves no fault on the part of the employer. It is a doctrine designed for the sake of the claimant imposing a liability incurred without fault because the employer is treated by the law as picking up the burden of an organisational or business relationship which he has undertaken for his own benefit.

80. One is looking therefore for practical and structural considerations. Is the employee, in context, still recognisable as the employee of his general employer and, in addition, to be treated as though he was the employee of the temporary employer as well? Thus in the *Mersey Docks* situation, it is tempting to think that liability will not be shared: the employee is used, for a limited time, in his general employer's own sphere of operations, operating his general employer's crane, exercising his own discretion as a crane driver. Even if the right of control were to some extent shared, as in practice it is almost bound to be, one would hesitate to say that it is a case for dual vicarious liability. One could contrast the situation where the employee is contracted-out labour: he is selected and possibly trained by his general employer, hired out by that employer as an integral part of his business, but employed at the temporary employer's site or his customer's site, using the temporary employer's equipment, and subject to the temporary employer's directions.

In such a situation, responsibility is likely to be shared. A third situation, where an employee is seconded for a substantial period of time to the temporary employer, to perform a role embedded in that employer's organisation, is likely to result in the sole responsibility of that employer . . .

COMMENTARY

The two-member Court of Appeal in *Viasystems* held that both A Ltd and B Ltd were vicariously liable for Mr Strang's negligence, with equal contribution between them under the Civil Liability (Contribution) Act 1978. For comment on the decision, see Stevens (2006) 122 LQR 201.

Part and parcel of the functional conception of the employer proposed by Prassl (*op. cit.*) is the view that more than one entity can perform core employer functions for a single worker at the same time. In his words (Prassl, 'The Nature of the Employer' (2013) 129 LQR 380 at 389): 'There is nothing to suggest that all employer functions ought necessarily to be exercised by the same entity: they can be exercised jointly by several parties, or parcelled out between different *loci* of control.' Furthermore, he argues (*ibid.*, at 389–90) that there is nothing in the tests for the existence of an employment relationship 'that suggests that the various aspects ... need to be concentrated in a single party'. The control test, for example, does not '[demand] a unitary notion of the employer'; on the contrary, 'it often instinctively leads to a multilateral analysis'. Similarly, the test of economic or business reality 'is workable with single or multiple employing entities'. If Prassl is right, then it follows that the recognition of the possibility of dual vicarious liability should be welcomed. But is he correct to assume that this result sits as easily with an 'organisational integration' test of the kind favoured by Rix LJ as it does with the control-based approach of May LJ? One can readily appreciate that (as in *Viasystems*) there will be situations of dual control, but does not the test of organisational integration more obviously lend itself to an all-or-nothing answer?

The Court of Appeal in *Viasystems* considered that no binding authority prevented recognition of dual vicarious liability. One relevant case was *Mersey Docks and Harbour Board v Coggins & Griffiths (Liverpool) Ltd* [1947] AC 1, where, by and large applying the control test, the House of Lords held that a crane driver hired out with a crane remained the employee of the permanent (or general) employer and that more generally there was a heavy onus on the permanent employer to establish that a borrowed worker had become the employee of the temporary employer. Both May and Rix LJJ thought that in this case—as in the others they considered—it had been assumed rather than decided that dual vicarious liability was not possible. Their Lordships also agreed that, on its facts, *Mersey Docks* was not a case where dual vicarious liability would have been appropriate; the control exercised by the permanent employer was not sufficiently altered by the terms on which the employee was lent to change the identity of the employer for the purposes of vicarious liability (see also *Biffa Waste Services Ltd v Maschinenfabrik Ernst Hese GMBH* [2009] QB 725, applying the *Mersey Docks* presumption; cf. *Hawley v Luminar Leisure Ltd* [2006] IRLR 817, where a nightclub was held to be the sole employer for the purposes of vicarious liability of a doorman supplied to it on a long-term basis by a security services firm).

How frequently is dual vicarious liability likely to be found? May LJ (at [46]) said that in most cases 'a proper application' of the control-based approach would not yield joint vicarious liability, but Rix LJ's analysis seems more likely to produce this result. In *Christian Brothers* (see later) one issue for the Supreme Court was whether a religious order could be held liable for the torts of one of its members. The members of the religious order taught in a school that was run by a different organisation, that organisation having already been found to be vicariously liable for the tort of the member of the religious order it employed as a teacher. The Court accepted that dual vicarious liability was possible if, applying the approach of Rix LJ in *Viasystems* (which Lord Phillips said was to be preferred), the relationship of the tortfeasor with each defendant satisfied the requirement for vicarious liability, as indeed was held to be the case on the facts.

If dual vicarious liability exists, what should the division of responsibility be between the two employers in contribution proceedings? In a case of fault-based liability the court would generally consider the relative causative potency and blameworthiness of the defendants when deciding the amount of recoverable contribution, but in *Viasystems* the Court of Appeal held that, provided neither employer was in fact at fault, the division could only be 50/50 (this was described by May LJ, at [50], as 'close to a logical necessity'). By contrast, the Supreme Court of Canada in *Blackwater v Plint* [2005] 3 SCR 3 apportioned responsibility 75/25 between the two employers. Can this be correct? (See Neyers (2006) 122 LQR 195 at 199, arguing that the effect of *Plint* is that 'someone who was held liable without fault, could be more at fault than another person who was held liable without fault'.)

3. Relationships 'Akin to Employment'

As we have seen, the traditional dichotomy between employees and independent contractors was premised on the existence of a contract between the parties, with the central question being expressed as: 'Is the worker employed under a contract *of service* (employee) or a contract *for services* (independent contractor)?' However, in recent years the necessity for a contract between tortfeasor and defendant for vicarious liability to arise has come under challenge, with *Viasystems* being a good example, as there was no contract between the employee and the temporary employer in that case. There are also a number of other situations where it may seem appropriate to impose vicarious liability even though there is no conventional employer–employee relationship between the parties, for fear that otherwise the ambit of vicarious liability will come to rest on 'arbitrary distinctions between different categories of workers' (Giliker (2016) 7 UKSC Yearbook 152 at 156). After all, there is no 'conceptual necessity' for confining vicarious liability to employment relationships and 'elsewhere the equivalent concept' is not so limited (Bell, '"Double, Double Toil and Trouble": Recent Movements in Vicarious Liability' [2018] JPIL 235 at 236).

The seminal case in this regard was *E v English Province of Our Lady of Charity* [2013] QB 722 (hereafter '*E*'), where a majority of the Court of Appeal held that a trust which stood in the place of the diocesan Roman Catholic bishop was vicariously liable for sexual abuse of the claimants carried out by a parish priest, even though the priest was not an employee of the bishop, the rationale being that the relationship between the two was so akin to a relationship of employment that it was fair and just for vicarious liability to attach to it. According to Ward LJ (at [73]), the time had come 'emphatically to announce that the law of vicarious liability has moved beyond the confines of a contract of service'. By recognising a general category of relationships that could give rise to vicarious liability in the absence of such a contract, the decision in *E* brought about an important change to the law.

This new category of relationships akin to employment was further developed by the Supreme Court in *Catholic Child Welfare Society v Institute of the Brothers of the Christian Schools* [2013] 2 AC 1 (hereafter '*Christian Brothers*'), where it was used to justify imposing vicarious liability on a religious institute for abuse carried out by teachers who were brothers of the institute. According to Lord Phillips, it was appropriate to impose vicarious liability on the facts because: (1) the institute conducted its activities as if it were a corporate body; (2) the teaching activities of the members of the institute (the brothers) were undertaken because the institute directed them; (3) the teaching activities of the brothers furthered the institute's mission; and (4) the manner in which the brother teachers were obliged to conduct themselves was dictated by the institute. That the bond between the institute and its members was by vow rather than contract, and that the institute did not pay the brothers for the teaching (any earnings were in fact transferred *to* the institute), were not considered material; indeed 'they rendered the relationship between the brothers and the institute closer than that of an employer and its employees' (at [57]). Whether it was 'fair, just and reasonable' to recognise a relationship as one akin to employment depended on the extent to which it was characterised by the five features which made it appropriate to impose such liability on an employer, namely that (at [35]):

> (i) [T]he employer is more likely to have the means to compensate the victim than the employee and can be expected to have insured against that liability; (ii) the tort will have been committed as a result of activity being taken by the employee on behalf of the employer; (iii) the employee's activity is likely to be part of the business activity of the employer; (iv) the employer, by employing the employee to carry on the activity will have created the risk of the tort committed by the employee; (v) the employee will, to a greater or lesser degree, have been under the control of the employer.

In *E*, Ward LJ considered both the level of control over the tortfeasor and the extent to which that person (a priest) was integrated into the organisation of the party sought to be made vicariously liable (the bishop in whose diocese the priest worked). These are the conventional factors used to determine whether a contractual employment relationship is a contract of service or a contract for services (see *Market Investigations*, extracted in II.1), and if these are the factors that determine whether the relationship is 'akin to employment', the main effect of adopting the test will be to extend vicarious liability to persons who are *de facto*, if not *de jure* (because there is no contract between the parties) employees. If this is correct, it may not solve the difficulty that modern employment practices can make the classification of a worker as an employee or an independent contractor a difficult, and perhaps artificial, task. In *Dacas v Brook Street Bureau (UK) Ltd* [2004] ICR 1436 Mummery LJ noted that as yet 'unclassified' contracts of employment may best describe the relationship between the parties, such as a 'semi-dependent worker's contract' or 'quasi-dependent worker's contract'. If the traditional indicia for determining an employee relationship are used to determine what is 'akin to employment', the new test will provide little assistance where the binary divide between employee and independent contractor itself is being challenged, particularly since in *Various Claimants v Barclays Bank plc* [2020] AC 973 (extracted later in this section) the Supreme Court has recently upheld that divide, with the result that the 'akin to employment' category is limited to a grey area where the wrongdoer is neither an employee nor a contractor of the defendant.

Bell [2013] CLJ 17 welcomes the extension of vicarious liability beyond employees to all persons who are 'put out into the world to be the presence of the enterprise in the situation where harm was caused' (at 19). P. Morgan (2013) 129 LQR 139 at 143–4 also regards the extension of vicarious liability beyond employment relationships as a positive development 'insofar as it recognises the changing nature of occupation, and the range of occupational activities between the statuses of employee and independent contractors', but he warns that there is 'a risk that there will be overexpansion of the doctrine in the context of unincorporated associations of the loosest and most temporary kind'. He expands on this final point in 'Vicarious Liability and the Beautiful Game: Liability for Professional and Amateur Footballers?' (2018) 38 LS 242, where he argues that the extension of the doctrine may expose members of amateur sporting organisations such as pub football teams to liabilities that could be executed against their personal assets. For other academic commentary on the cases adopting the 'akin to employment' test, see Tan (2013) 129 LQR 30 and (2013) 21 TLJ 43; and Giliker (2013) 4 JETL 306.

Commenting on these cases extra-judicially, Lord Hope cautioned that the doctrine of vicarious liability is not 'infinitely extendable' ('Tailoring the Law on Vicarious Liability'

(2013) 129 LQR 514 at 525), but the scope of the phrase 'akin to employment' has been said to be 'not capable of precise definition' (*Blackpool Football Club Ltd v DSN* [2021] EWCA Civ 1352 at [100], per Stuart-Smith LJ), and it is not yet clear what the boundaries are to the types of relationship that can be considered to qualify. 'Quasi-employees' (i.e. those that have a relationship 'akin to employment' with the party sought to be made vicariously liable) could include agency workers who work primarily for one end-user (agency workers generally have a contract only with the agency and not with the end-user where the worker is deployed), unpaid volunteers working for charitable organisations and non-executive directors of companies. However, as P. Morgan, 'Recasting Vicarious Liability' [2012] CLJ 615 comments, it is unlikely that extending vicarious liability to relationships that are 'akin to employment' will cover every type of relationship where the imposition of vicarious liability is thought desirable. He argues (at 641–8) that whether a relationship attracts vicarious liability depends on the level of control by, and association with, the party sought to be made liable in the course of carrying out some activity for the benefit of or to achieve the objectives of that party. Under this approach, Morgan admits that there would be a 'limited expansion' of the relationships that attract vicarious liability, including in some cases those of franchisor–franchisee and university–PhD student. (What about the relationship between a parent company and an employee of a subsidiary? See C. Witting, *Liability of Corporate Groups and Networks* (Cambridge: CUP, 2018, ch.12.) Further guidance on the potential scope of the 'akin to employment' concept came in the following extracted case.

Cox v Ministry of Justice [2016] AC 660

The claimant, Mrs Cox, worked as a prison catering manager. On the day in question, she was working in the prison kitchen with a catering assistant and a number of prisoners. While moving some supplies to the kitchen stores, one of the prisoners, Mr Inder, lost his balance and dropped a sack of rice on the claimant's back, injuring her. The prison service was legally required to offer work to prisoners, and it was government policy that working prisoners be paid a nominal wage. However, since prisoners worked under compulsion, and not pursuant to contracts of employment, they were not employees of the prison service. The claimant brought proceedings against the defendant, which was responsible for the prison service. It was conceded that Mr Inder had been negligent, but the trial judge held that his relationship with the prison service was not 'akin to employment' for the purposes of vicarious liability. The Court of Appeal overturned the trial judge's decision on that question. The defendant appealed to the Supreme Court.

Lord Reed

1. 'The law of vicarious liability is on the move.' So Lord Phillips of Worth Matravers PSC said, in the last judgment which he delivered as President of this court, in *Various Claimants v Catholic Child Welfare Society* [2013] 2 AC 1, para 19 ('the "Christian Brothers" case'). It has not yet come to a stop. This appeal, and the companion appeal in *Mohamud v Wm Morrison Supermarkets plc* [2016] AC 677, provide an opportunity to take stock of where it has got to so far.

2. The scope of vicarious liability depends upon the answers to two questions. First, what sort of relationship has to exist between an individual and a defendant before the defendant can be made vicariously liable in tort for the conduct of that individual? Secondly, in what

manner does the conduct of that individual have to be related to that relationship, in order for vicarious liability to be imposed on the defendant? Although the answers to those questions are inter-connected, the present appeal is concerned with the first question, and approaches it principally in the light of the judgment in the 'Christian Brothers' case, where the same issue was considered. The appeal in *Mohamud v Wm Morrison Supermarkets plc* is concerned with the second question, and approaches it principally in the light of the historical development of this branch of the law. As will appear, the present judgment also seeks to relate the approach adopted to the first question to ideas which have long been present in the law. The two judgments are intended to be complementary.

3. The first question arises in this case in relation to a public authority performing statutory functions for the public benefit, on the one hand, and an individual whose activities form part of the means by which the authority performs its functions, on the other hand. Specifically, the question is whether the prison service, which is an executive agency of the appellant defendant, the Ministry of Justice, is vicariously liable for the act of a prisoner in the course of his work in a prison kitchen, where the act is negligent and causes injury to a member of the prison staff.

The 'Christian Brothers' case [2013] 2 AC 1

16. It has . . . long been recognised that a relationship can give rise to vicarious liability even in the absence of a contract of employment. For example, where an employer lends his employee to a third party, the third party may be treated as the employer for the purposes of vicarious liability. In recent years, the courts have sought to explain more generally the basis on which vicarious liability can arise out of a relationship other than that of employer and employee.

[His Lordship referred to the facts and decision in the *Christian Brothers* case and continued:]

20. The five factors which Lord Phillips PSC mentioned in para 35 are not all equally significant. The first—that the defendant is more likely than the tortfeasor to have the means to compensate the victim, and can be expected to have insured against vicarious liability—did not feature in the remainder of the judgment, and is unlikely to be of independent significance in most cases. It is, of course, true that where an individual is employed under a contract of employment, his employer is likely to have a deeper pocket, and can in any event be expected to have insured against vicarious liability. Neither of these, however, is a principled justification for imposing vicarious liability. The mere possession of wealth is not in itself any ground for imposing liability. As for insurance, employers insure themselves because they are liable: they are not liable because they have insured themselves. On the other hand, given the infinite variety of circumstances in which the question of vicarious liability might arise, it cannot be ruled out that there might be circumstances in which the absence or unavailability of insurance, or other means of meeting a potential liability, might be a relevant consideration.

21. The fifth of the factors—that the tortfeasor will, to a greater or lesser degree, have been under the control of the defendant—no longer has the significance that it was sometimes considered to have in the past, as Lord Phillips PSC immediately made clear. As he explained at para 36, the ability to direct how an individual did his work was sometimes regarded as an important test of the existence of a relationship of master and servant, and came to be treated at times as the test for the imposition of vicarious liability. But it is not realistic in modern life to look for a right to direct how an employee should perform his duties as a necessary element in the relationship between employer and employee; nor indeed was it in times gone by, if one thinks for example of the degree of control which the owner of a ship could have exercised over the master while the ship was at sea. Accordingly, as Lord Phillips PSC stated,

the significance of control is that the defendant can direct what the tortfeasor does, not how he does it. So understood, it is a factor which is unlikely to be of independent significance in most cases. On the other hand, the absence of even that vestigial degree of control would be liable to negative the imposition of vicarious liability.

22. The remaining factors listed by Lord Phillips PSC were that (1) the tort will have been committed as a result of activity being taken by the tortfeasor on behalf of the defendant, (2) the tortfeasor's activity is likely to be part of the business activity of the defendant, and (3) the defendant, by employing the tortfeasor to carry on the activity, will have created the risk of the tort committed by the tortfeasor.

23. These three factors are inter-related. The first has been reflected historically in explanations of the vicarious liability of employers based on deemed authorisation or delegation . . . The second, that the tortfeasor's activity is likely to be an integral part of the business activity of the defendant, has long been regarded as a justification for the imposition of vicarious liability on employers, on the basis that, since the employee's activities are undertaken as part of the activities of the employer and for its benefit, it is appropriate that the employer should bear the cost of harm wrongfully done by the employee within the field of activities assigned to him . . . The third factor, that the defendant, by employing the tortfeasor to carry on the activities, will have created the risk of the tort committed by the tortfeasor, is very closely related to the second: since the risk of an individual behaving negligently, or indeed committing an intentional wrong, is a fact of life, anyone who employs others to carry out activities is likely to create the risk of their behaving tortiously within the field of activities assigned to them. The essential idea is that the defendant should be liable for torts that may fairly be regarded as risks of his business activities, whether they are committed for the purpose of furthering those activities or not . . .

24. Lord Phillips PSC's analysis in the 'Christian Brothers' case [2013] 2 AC 1 wove together these related ideas so as to develop a modern theory of vicarious liability. The result of this approach is that a relationship other than one of employment is in principle capable of giving rise to vicarious liability where harm is wrongfully done by an individual who carries on activities as an integral part of the business activities carried on by a defendant and for its benefit (rather than his activities being entirely attributable to the conduct of a recognisably independent business of his own or of a third party), and where the commission of the wrongful act is a risk created by the defendant by assigning those activities to the individual in question.

28. . . . It may be said that the criteria are insufficiently precise to make their application to borderline cases plain and straightforward: a criticism which might, of course, also be made of other general principles of the law of tort. As Lord Nicholls observed in *Dubai Aluminium Co Ltd v Salaam* [2003] 2 AC 366, para 26, a lack of precision is inevitable, given the infinite range of circumstances where the issue arises. The court has to make a judgment, assisted by previous judicial decisions in the same or analogous contexts. Such decisions may enable the criteria to be refined in particular contexts, as Lord Phillips PSC suggested in the 'Christian Brothers' case, at para 83.

29. It is important, however, to understand that the general approach which Lord Phillips PSC described is not confined to some special category of cases, such as the sexual abuse of children. It is intended to provide a basis for identifying the circumstances in which vicarious liability may in principle be imposed outside relationships of employment. By focusing upon the business activities carried on by the defendant and their attendant risks, it directs attention to the issues which are likely to be relevant in the context of modern workplaces, where workers may in reality be part of the workforce of an organisation without having a contract of employment with it, and also reflects prevailing ideas about the responsibility of businesses for the risks which are created by their activities. It results in an extension of the

scope of vicarious liability beyond the responsibility of an employer for the acts and omissions of its employees in the course of their employment, but not to the extent of imposing such liability where a tortfeasor's activities are entirely attributable to the conduct of a recognisably independent business of his own or of a third party. An important consequence of that extension is to enable the law to maintain previous levels of protection for the victims of torts, notwithstanding changes in the legal relationships between enterprises and members of their workforces which may be motivated by factors which have nothing to do with the nature of the enterprises' activities or the attendant risks.

30. It is also important not to be misled by a narrow focus on semantics: for example, by words such as 'business', 'benefit', and 'enterprise'. The defendant need not be carrying on activities of a commercial nature: that is apparent not only from *E v English Province of Our Lady of Charity* [2013] QB 722 and the 'Christian Brothers' case [2013] 2 AC 1 but also from the long established application of vicarious liability to public authorities and hospitals. It need not therefore be a business or enterprise in any ordinary sense. Nor need the benefit which it derives from the tortfeasor's activities take the form of a profit. It is sufficient that there is a defendant which is carrying on activities in the furtherance of its own interests. The individual for whose conduct it may be vicariously liable must carry on activities assigned to him by the defendant as an integral part of its operation and for its benefit. The defendant must, by assigning those activities to him, have created a risk of his committing the tort. As the cases of *Viasystems (Tyneside) Ltd v Thermal Transfer (Northern) Ltd* [2006] QB 510, *E v English Province of Our Lady of Charity* and the 'Christian Brothers' show, a wide range of circumstances can satisfy those requirements.

31. The other lesson to be drawn from [those three cases] is that defendants cannot avoid vicarious liability on the basis of technical arguments about the employment status of the individual who committed the tort. As Professor John Bell noted in his article, 'The Basis of Vicarious Liability' [2013] CLJ 17, what weighed with the courts in *E v English Province of Our Lady of Charity* and the 'Christian Brothers' case was that the abusers were placed by the organisations in question, as part of their mission, in a position in which they committed a tort whose commission was a risk inherent in the activities assigned to them.

The present case

32. In the present case, the requirements laid down in the 'Christian Brothers' case [2013] 2 AC 1 are met. The prison service carries on activities in furtherance of its aims. The fact that those aims are not commercially motivated, but serve the public interest, is no bar to the imposition of vicarious liability. Prisoners working in the prison kitchens, such as Mr Inder, are integrated into the operation of the prison, so that the activities assigned to them by the prison service form an integral part of the activities which it carries on in the furtherance of its aims: in particular, the activity of providing meals for prisoners. They are placed by the prison service in a position where there is a risk that they may commit a variety of negligent acts within the field of activities assigned to them. That is recognised by the health and safety training which they receive. Furthermore, they work under the direction of prison staff. Mrs Cox was injured as a result of negligence by Mr Inder in carrying on the activities assigned to him. The prison service is therefore vicariously liable to her. . . .

Lord Neuberger, **Baroness Hale**, **Lord Dyson MR** and **Lord Toulson** agreed with Lord Reed.

Appeal dismissed.

COMMENTARY

For commentary on the *Cox* case, see Bell (2016) 32 PN 153; Giliker (2016) 7 UKSC Yearbook 152; P. Morgan [2016] CLJ 202; and Plunkett (2016) 132 LQR 556. Morgan (*op. cit.*, at 204) considers that the decision to make the Ministry of Justice vicariously liable was clearly correct, since Mr Inder's work was 'an integral part of the prison activities, carried out for its benefit'. *Cox* shows, he points out, that the 'akin to employment' concept is not limited to the child abuse context, 'and that it applies to new and emerging forms of enterprise and employment' (at 203). Bell also welcomes the decision, commending Lord Reed's judgment (*op. cit.*, at 155) as 'an admirably explicit and pragmatic response to a world where employment relationships are increasingly complex and variable, and not least the likes of Uber are unsettling the waters in even mundane and everyday transactions' (see also Giliker, *op. cit.*, at 163). Nevertheless, it is questionable whether the changing nature of 'modern workplaces' (see *Cox* at [29], per Lord Reed) has really been the prime motivation for the extension of vicarious liability beyond employment relationships of the traditional kind. After all, there is nothing particularly new about religious orders or working prisoners.

Cox is also significant for the more general observations that Lord Reed makes about the 'five factors' identified by Lord Phillips in *Christian Brothers*. Morgan (*op. cit.*, at 203) welcomes the downplaying of deep-pocket and insurance justifications (factor one) for vicarious liability, but not the dismissal of control (factor five) as a significant consideration in identifying relationships that give rise to such liability:

With respect, control is relevant: one has the power to direct exactly how employees carry out work (even if it is not exercised), something professionals in our increasingly managerial culture are discovering, whereas there is no such right over independent contractors unless it features in the contract.

In *Armes v Nottinghamshire County Council* [2018] AC 355, the Supreme Court held that the 'akin to employment' category extended to the relationship between a local authority and foster parents who had contracted with the council to undertake the care of a young girl. Applying his own test in *Cox*, Lord Reed said (at [60]) that the foster parents provided care to the girl 'as an integral part' of the authority's organisation of its child care services. Furthermore, by placing children with foster parents and thereby creating a 'relationship of authority and trust' between the two, the authority rendered the children 'particularly vulnerable to abuse' (at [61]). And while it was true that the authority did not exercise day-to-day control over foster parents, it retained powers of 'approval, inspection, supervision and removal' (at [62]), so an element of control was nevertheless a feature of its relationship with them. Finally, foster parents were unlikely to be able to satisfy an award of substantial damages, and local authorities were better placed to do so. Lord Hughes dissented in *Armes*, arguing that, if a business model was to be used, then foster parents looked a great deal more like independent contractors than employees, and citing policy objections to vicarious liability in this context, for example that it would inhibit the practice of placing children with members of their own family and would result in undesirable litigation of family activity. According to Dickinson ((2018) 134 LQR 359 at 361), Lord Reed's characterisation of foster parents 'as an integral part' of the authority's organisation of its child care services is difficult to reconcile with one of his main reasons for rejecting the claimant's argument that the authority had owed her a non-delegable duty of care (see IV.3), namely that the authority's duty was not to provide day-to-day care to the claimant, but to arrange for its provision by others. Dickinson also highlights the tension between Lord Reed's downplaying of *Christian Brothers* factors one and five in *Cox* and his reliance on those same factors to justify the imposition of vicarious liability in *Armes* (as regards control, see also *Blackpool Football Club Ltd v DSN* [2021] EWCA Civ 1352 at [78], where Stuart-Smith LJ reiterates the importance of the presence and more especially the *absence* of control in this context). Stephen Todd regrets the rehabilitation of factor one—the relative resources consideration—which seems 'to lead to nowhere save the depth of the defendant's pocket' ([2018] NZ L Rev 131 at 178; for criticism of the *way in which* Lord Reed relies on factor one, see Bell, '"Double, Double Toil and Trouble": Recent Movements in Vicarious Liability' [2018] JPIL 235 at 239–40). The majority in *Armes* seemed to accept that the outcome would probably have been different had the authority entrusted the claimant to the care of her own parents, or (perhaps) other family members, but then that raises the question of how the different treatment of a natural parent and a foster parent can be justified (see Todd, *op. cit.*; but for a defence of the distinction, see Beuermann, 'Up in *Armes*: The Need for a Map of Strict Liability for the Wrongdoing of Another in Tort' (2018) 25 Torts LJ 1 at 15–19). Bell (*op. cit.,* at 238) is also critical of the extension of the akin to employment category to fostering, which he says 'is very different from employed roles which might be said to approximate it most closely' (such as childminding), since it seeks to provide, as far as possible, a 'normal family life' to the child; indeed, its closest analogy—namely general, non-foster, parenting—is, he argues, not an *employment* task at all.

Not everyone will agree with Giliker [2018] CLJ 506 at 534, that *Armes* was 'a step too far', but there is no doubt that the decision did push the boundary of the akin to employment category, and in *Various Claimants v Barclays Bank plc* [2020] AC 973 at [23], Lady Hale described it as 'perhaps the most difficult' of the relevant authorities. Those difficulties are illustrated by the contrasting decisions of the New Zealand Court of Appeal in *S v Attorney General* [2003] 3 NZLR 450 (imposing vicarious liability on a public authority for the torts of foster parents) and the Supreme Court of Canada in *KLB v British Columbia* [2003] 2 SCR 403 (refusing to impose such liability). In an extended analysis of *Armes*, Beuermann, *op. cit.*, acknowledges the difficulties, but argues that the solution lies in focusing more explicitly on the particular relationship (whether foster child/local authority or foster parent/local authority) that could ground strict liability on the facts, and then determining whether strict liability should be imposed by reference to the features of that relationship.

In cases such as *E*, *Christian Brothers* and *Cox* there was no contract of any kind between the tortfeasor and the defendant, so there was no question of the former being an independent contractor of the latter. Rather, it seemed that the 'akin to employment' category was designed for cases in which the tortfeasor was neither an employee nor a contractor. However, in the aftermath of the *Cox* and *Armes* decisions, the longstanding rule that an employer could not be vicariously liable for the torts of an independent contractor came under attack, with reliance being placed on the 'akin to employment' cases, and especially on Lord Phillips' five factors from *Christian Brothers*. The issue came to a head in the next extracted case.

Various Claimants v Barclays Bank plc [2020] AC 973

Between 1968 and about 1984 the defendant bank had instructed a doctor (Dr Bates) to carry out medical examinations of prospective employees, many of whom were applying for their first job. The bank arranged the appointment with Dr Bates, told the job applicant when to report to his home (where the examinations took place) and provided Dr Bates with a pro forma report for him to complete. Dr Bates had what was described as a 'portfolio practice', consisting mostly of medical examinations and some hospital work, of which the assessments for the bank were a relatively minor component. The claimants alleged that during their examination Dr Bates had sexually assaulted them, and following the doctor's death they claimed damages from the bank on the basis that it was vicariously liable for the alleged assaults. At the trial of a preliminary issue, the judge held that the bank was vicariously liable for any torts proven to have been committed, and the Court of Appeal dismissed the bank's appeal. The bank appealed to the Supreme Court.

Baroness Hale

The parties' cases

7. The parties' respective positions can be simply put. As Lord Bridge of Harwich stated in *D & F Estates Ltd v Church Comrs for England* [1989] AC 177, 208 (echoing the words of Widgery LJ in *Salsbury v Woodland* [1970] 1 QB 324, 336), 'It is trite law that the employer of an independent contractor is, in general, not liable for the negligence or other torts committed by the contractor in the course of the execution of the work'. The bank argues that, although recent decisions have expanded the categories of relationship which can give rise to vicarious liability beyond a contract of employment, they have not so expanded it as to destroy this trite proposition of law, which has been with us since at least the decision of Baron Parke in *Quarman v Burnett* (1840) 6 M & W 499.

8. The claimants, on the other hand, argue that the recent Supreme Court cases of *Christian Brothers* [2013] 2 AC 1, *Cox v Ministry of Justice* [2016] AC 660 and *Armes v Nottinghamshire County Council* [2018] AC 355 have replaced that trite proposition with a more nuanced multifactorial approach in which a range of incidents are considered in deciding whether it is 'fair, just and reasonable' to impose vicarious liability upon this person for the torts of another person who is not his employee. That was the approach adopted both by the trial judge and the Court of Appeal in this case.

The recent decisions

[Baroness Hale considered the authorities and continued:]

24. There is nothing, therefore, in [the decisions in *Christian Brothers*, *Cox* and *Armes*] to suggest that the classic distinction between employment and relationships akin or analogous to employment, on the one hand, and the relationship with an independent contractor, on the other hand, has been eroded. . . .

27. The question therefore is, as it has always been, whether the tortfeasor is carrying on business on his own account or whether he is in a relationship akin to employment with the defendant. In doubtful cases, the five 'incidents' identified by Lord Phillips [in *Christian Brothers*] may be helpful in identifying a relationship which is sufficiently analogous to employment to make it fair, just and reasonable to impose vicarious liability. Although they were enunciated in the context of non-commercial enterprises, they may be relevant in deciding whether workers who may be technically self-employed or agency workers are effectively part and parcel of the employer's business. But the key, as it was in *Christian Brothers* [2013] 2 AC 1, *Cox* [2016] AC 660 and *Armes* [2018] AC 355, will usually lie in understanding the details of the relationship. Where it is clear that the tortfeasor is carrying on his own independent business it is not necessary to consider the five incidents.

Application in this case

28. Clearly, although Dr Bates was a part-time employee of the health service, he was not at any time an employee of the bank. Nor, viewed objectively, was he anything close to an employee. He did, of course, do work for the bank. The bank made the arrangements for

the examinations and sent him the forms to fill in. It therefore chose the questions to which it wanted answers. But the same would be true of many other people who did work for the bank but were clearly independent contractors, ranging from the company hired to clean its windows to the auditors hired to audit its books. Dr Bates was not paid a retainer which might have obliged him to accept a certain number of referrals from the bank. He was paid a fee for each report. He was free to refuse an offered examination should he wish to do so. He no doubt carried his own medical liability insurance, although this may not have covered him from liability for deliberate wrongdoing. He was in business on his own account as a medical practitioner with a portfolio of patients and clients. One of those clients was the bank.

Conclusion

30. I would allow this appeal and hold that the bank is not vicariously liable for any wrongdoing of Dr Bates in the course of the medical examinations he carried out for the bank.

Lord Reed, Lord Hodge, Lord Kerr and Lord Lloyd-Jones agreed with Baroness Hale.

Appeal allowed.

COMMENTARY

Silink (2018) 34 PN 46 at 46 said of the Court of Appeal's decision in *Barclays* that it was 'difficult not to conclude that the wall around vicarious liability for independent contractors' had been breached (see also the critical note on that decision by Watts (2019) 135 LQR 7). In the Supreme Court Lady Hale was at pains to repair that breach and to make it clear that, rather than subverting the employer/contractor dichotomy, the 'akin to employment' classification supplements it by extending vicarious liability to various *sui generis* relationships which it does not encompass.

The reaffirmation of the longstanding principle that no vicarious liability attaches to the torts of an independent contractor was perhaps unsurprising. After all, Lord Reed in *Cox* (at [29]) had specifically excluded from the ambit of vicarious liability cases where the activities of the tortfeasor were attributable to the conduct of 'a recognisably independent business of his own or a third party', while in *Armes* his Lordship (at [59]) had attached significance to the fact that the foster parents could not 'be regarded as carrying on an independent business of their own'. The continued relevance of the distinction between employees and independent contractors was also affirmed in *Kafagi v JBW Group Ltd* [2018] EWCA Civ 1157, where the Court of Appeal held that a judicial services company was not vicariously liable for the alleged torts of a bailiff to whom it had subcontracted the collection of council tax debts because the bailiff 'ran his own business' (see also the decision of the Singapore Court of Appeal in *Ng Huat Seng v Munib Mohammad Madni* [2017] 2 SLR 1074). Furthermore, as Todd ([2018] NZ L Rev 131 at 178) points out, the suggestion that Dr Bates was in a relationship akin to employment with the bank was difficult to square with the earlier cases on the 'akin to employment' category, where the wrongdoer 'held a position which was functionally analogous to employment, for example as regards the wrongdoer's accountability to the relevant organisation, integration into its structure, and performance of duties aimed at pursuing its fundamental aims and objectives on its behalf'.

As regards the 'akin to employment' category itself, Lady Hale cited with apparent approval the statement in *Ng Huat Seng v Munib Mohammad Madni* [2017] 2 SLR 1074 at [63] that this represents a 'fine-tuning' of the existing vicarious liability framework 'so as to accommodate the more diverse range of relationships which might be encountered in today's context', and that when 'whittled down to their essence', these relationships 'possess the same fundamental qualities as those which inhere in employer-employee relationships'. When it came to identifying relationships of this kind, her Ladyship moved the focus from Lord Phillips' five factors in *Christian Brothers* towards the details of the relationship between the tortfeasor and the defendant and its similarity to employment. It had never been intended that the five factors 'were the only criteria by which to judge the question' (at [18]), and while they might be relevant in borderline cases, it would not be necessary to consider them where it was clear that the tortfeasor was carrying on their own independent business.

The *Barclays* approach to this issue was applied in *JXJ v The Province of Great Britain of the Institute of Brothers of the Christian Schools* [2020] ELR 579, which concerned the same religious institute as the *Christian Brothers* case. The difference in *JXJ* was that the tortfeasor was not one of the institute's brothers but a lay person who was employed as a gardener and nightwatchman in a school managed by third parties but over which the institute exercised considerable control. Chamberlain J held that the relationship between the gardener and the institute was not akin to employment because there were no reciprocal obligations between the two; he was integrated into the work, business and organisation of the school, but not the institute; and (unlike the brothers of the institute) he was not engaged with the institute in the common enterprise of providing a Christian education to boys. There was no legal principle imposing vicarious liability on an undertaking for the torts of all those indispensable to the furthering of its mission, and nor had the law developed to the point where anyone who exercised influence over the operation of a business was vicariously liable for the torts of an employee of the business with whom it had no direct relationship. *Barclays* was also applied in two cases in which it was held that the relationship between a professional football club and a person who acted as a volunteer 'scout' and manager of unofficial 'feeder' teams was not akin to employment (*Blackpool Football Club Ltd v DSN* [2021] EWCA Civ 1352 and *TVZ v Manchester City Football Club Ltd* [2022] EWHC 7 (QB)). It was emphasised in both cases that the scout/manager had not been subject to directions by the club as to what he should do or how he should do it, and in *TVZ* that he was not subject to any disciplinary control short of the ultimate sanction of termination of the relationship. According to Stuart-Smith LJ in *DSN*, it was seldom sufficient for vicarious liability to arise that the tortfeasor could be described as 'doing something for, or for the benefit of, the "employer" or their enterprise', and the case law on relationships akin to employment suggested that 'what one should look for is not merely a beneficial involvement with (or for) the "employer's" enterprise but a real degree of integration of the primary tortfeasor into the employer's business or relevant activity' (at [102]–[103]). (For other post-*Barclays* cases on the akin to employment concept, see *The Trustees of the Barry Congregation of Jehovah's Witnesses v BXB* [2021] 4 WLR 42, holding that the relationship between a congregation of Jehovah's Witnesses and one of its elders was capable of giving rise to vicarious liability for the elder's rape of a member of the congregation; and *SKX v Manchester City Council* [2021] 4 WLR 56, holding that vicarious liability would not arise in respect of the torts of a person working for an independent contractor, in this case a private children's home to which the claimant had been entrusted by the defendant local authority.)

Nolan (2020) 49 ILJ 609 is broadly welcoming of the decision in *Barclays*, arguing that it restores 'some much needed certainty to the first stage of the vicarious liability analysis' (at 618; see also Bell (2020) 36 PN 150 and Gracie (2021) 26 Torts LJ 269). By contrast, Buxton [2020] CLJ 217 is critical, commenting (at 219–20) that the refusal to modify what he calls 'the independent contractor rule' means that the law of vicarious liability 'departs from the realities of modern life' in a world where 'operations intrinsic to a business enterprise are routinely performed by independent contractors, over long periods, accompanied by precise obligations and high levels of control'. As Purshouse (2020) 28 Med L Rev 794 at 800 points out, the decision 'avoids the potential pitfalls of extending vicarious liability to independent contractors in a haphazard fashion' but is likely to shift the focus to other mechanisms by which the law of tort can respond to 'vertical disintegration' of the enterprise (by outsourcing etc.), such as adjusting the dividing line between employees and contractors and expanding the scope of the doctrine of non-delegable duty (indeed, he argues that the claimants in *Barclays* may be able to establish that the defendant owed them a non-delegable duty which would have been breached by the alleged assaults). This chimes with an earlier analysis of J. Morgan, 'Vicarious Liability for Independent Contractors?' (2015) 31 PN 235 at 247, according to whom '[t]he problem is less whether to impose liability for truly independent contractors, more whether workers under new patterns of employment should be seen as independent at all'. Hence, while as a matter of practice, *Barclays* 'is a vital clarification', it does not 'tell us anything about how to resolve the conceptual tensions which led many to believe that the category of independent contractors had (to have) fallen' (Bell, *op. cit.*, at 152; see also Gracie, *op. cit.*, at 278, expressing surprise at Lady Hale's failure to engage with these broader issues).

Returning to the facts of *Barclays*, do you think that claimants who (often as teenagers straight out of school) were required by a prospective employer to attend unchaperoned medical examinations at the home of a particular doctor should be entitled to compensation from that employer if they were sexually assaulted by the doctor in the course of the examinations?

4. Vehicle Drivers

In addition to relationships of or akin to employment, vicarious liability (or a similar agency-based doctrine) is also capable of arising in respect of the negligent driving of a vehicle by a person using the vehicle with the defendant owner's permission, and in the performance of a task or duty delegated to them by the owner. An example of this form of vicarious liability is *Ormrod v Crosville Motor Services Ltd* [1953] 1 WLR 1120, in which the owner of a car asked a friend to drive it from Liverpool to Monte Carlo, where they were to begin a holiday together, and the friend negligently collided with a bus on the way, injuring the friend's wife, who was a passenger in the car. An attempt to extend this principle was rejected by the House of Lords in *Morgans v Launchbury* [1973] AC 127, where it was argued that a friend of the defendant's husband was her agent for the purpose of driving her husband (who was intoxicated) in a car of which she was the registered owner. The agency argument was unsuccessful as it was held that the car was not being used for the defendant's purposes, under delegation of a task or duty, at the time of the accident caused by the friend's negligent driving. As for the somewhat confusing use of the language of agency in this context, Lord Wilberforce said (at 135) that:

> I accept entirely that 'agency' in contexts such as these is merely a concept, the meaning and purpose of which is to say 'is vicariously liable' and that either expression reflects a judgment of value—*respondeat superior* is the law saying that the owner ought to pay.

Similarly, in the Court of Appeal, Lord Denning MR commented that '[t]he words principal and agent are not used here in the connotation which they have in the law of contract...

They are used as a shorthand to denote the circumstances in which vicarious liability is imposed' (*Launchbury v Morgans* [1971] 2 QB 245 at 255). The utility of using a concept that has an established meaning in another branch of the law (that of contract) for the purpose of imposing vicarious liability is doubtful (see Reynolds (2001) 117 LQR 180; Handford (2001) 9 Tort L Rev 97; Del Pont, 'Agency: Definitional Challenges Through the Law of Tort' (2003) 11 TLJ 68; P. Morgan, 'Recasting Vicarious Liability' [2012] CLJ 615 at 625–8).

The principle under discussion is specific to motor vehicles and there is no general rule that someone who performs a task at the request and for the benefit of another is the latter's agent such that the latter is liable for a tort committed by the former in the performance of the task. While there has clearly been an extension of the relationships that can attract vicarious liability beyond employees (see II.3) it is difficult to see why a mere request from A to B to perform a task on A's behalf should as a general rule make A vicariously liable for B's torts while carrying it out. There is therefore much to be said for the view that the cases involving motor vehicles are best seen as pragmatic attempts to ensure that victims of road accidents receive compensation from an insured party, although in practice the circumstances in which it will be necessary to resort to the owner of the vehicle as opposed to the driver are likely to be rare (*Winfield & Jolowicz*, para. 21–017; P. Giliker, *Vicarious Liability in Tort*, pp. 110–16). This view of the rule was taken by the High Court of Australia in *Scott v Davis* (2000) 204 CLR 333, where the majority refused to extend the doctrine to an aeroplane in circumstances where it appeared that the owner of the plane did not have insurance cover for the accident in respect of which the plaintiff claimed and was not required to have it by law (cf. the application of the doctrine to a boat in *The Thelma (Owners) v The Endymion (Owners)* [1953] 2 Lloyd's Rep 613). For comment on *Scott*, see Reynolds (2001) 117 LQR 180, and Handford (2001) 9 Tort L Rev 97. The absurdity of extending the principle to its logical conclusion is shown by the Irish case of *Moynihan v Moynihan* [1975] IR 192, where the owner of a teapot was held vicariously liable for her daughter's negligence in pouring tea.

III. The Course of Employment

An employer is not liable for every wrongful act of an employee, but only for acts done 'in the course of employment'. This concept is not free from difficulty but it 'remains a touchstone of liability' (*Prince Alfred College Inc v ADC* (2016) 258 CLR 134 at [41]), although it has recently been suggested that this concept no longer governs the question of vicarious liability in child sexual abuse cases (see III.4), and a *sui generis* approach is also adopted where the claimant seeks to make the employer liable for the fraud of an employee (see on this, *Winfield & Jolowicz*, paras 21-036–21-037). Finally, whether an employee's act is within the course of employment may vary in statutory contexts. In *Jones v Tower Boot Co* [1997] 2 All ER 395 the complainant sued for damages under the Race Relations Act 1976, which made the employers liable for racial abuse by their employees carried out in the course of employment (see now Equality Act 2010, s. 109). The Court of Appeal held that, as a matter of statutory construction, and in the light of the purpose of the 1976 Act, the phrase 'the course of employment' in the Act bore a wider meaning than the same phrase as used in the common law of vicarious liability.

In the discussion that follows, we begin by considering the course of employment concept in general terms, before turning to its application in three specific contexts: careless acts of the employee; cases involving an employee's use of vehicles on unauthorised journeys; and criminal acts of the employee.

1. The Close Connection Test

Historically, the resolution of the 'course of employment' issue came to depend on whether the employee's wrongful act fell within the implied authority conferred on them by the employer, with the result that the key question was thought to be whether the act of the employee was either a wrongful act authorised by the employer or a wrongful and unauthorised mode of doing some act authorised by the employer (this test was known as the '*Salmond*' test, as it was first put forward in J. W. Salmond, *Law of Torts* (London: Stevens & Haynes, 1907), p. 83). However, doubts arose as to the suitability of the *Salmond* test as a universal formula to be employed in all cases, as Lord Toulson explained in *Mohamud v Wm Morrison Supermarkets plc* [2016] AC 677 at [26]:

> Salmond's formula . . . was cited and applied in many cases, sometimes by stretching it artificially; but, even with stretching, it was not universally satisfactory. The difficulties in its application were particularly evident in cases of injury to persons or property caused by an employee's deliberate act of misconduct.

Those difficulties came to a head in the next extracted case.

Lister v Hesley Hall Ltd [2002] 1 AC 215

The defendants owned and managed a school for boys with emotional and behavioural difficulties. They employed G as warden of the school's boarding annex (Axeholme House). G sexually abused the claimants while they were resident at the school. The claimants sued the defendants, contending, inter alia, that they were vicariously liable for the personal injuries inflicted by G. The judge held that the defendants were not vicariously liable for the warden's torts but that they were vicariously liable for the warden's failure to report to them his intentions to commit acts of abuse and the harmful consequences to the claimants of those acts. The Court of Appeal allowed an appeal by the defendants, holding that G's acts could not be regarded as an unauthorised mode of carrying out his authorised duties and so were not within the course of his employment.

Lord Steyn

Since the decision in the Court of Appeal the law reports of two landmark decisions in the Canadian Supreme Court, which deal with vicarious liability of employers for sexual abuse of children, have become available: *Bazley v Curry* (1999) 174 DLR (4th) 45; *Jacobi v Griffiths* (1999) 174 DLR (4th) 71. Enunciating a principle of 'close connection' the Supreme Court unanimously held liability established in *Bazley's case* and by a four to three majority came to the opposite conclusion in *Jacobi's case*. The Supreme Court judgments examine in detail the circumstances in which, though an employer is not 'at fault', it may still be 'fair' that it should bear responsibility for the tortious conduct of its employees. These decisions have been described as 'a genuine advance on the unauthorised conduct/unauthorised mode distinction': Peter Cane, 'Vicarious Liability for Sexual Abuse' (2000) 116 LQR 21, 24. Counsel for the appellants invited your Lordships to apply the test developed in *Bazley's case* and in *Jacobi's case* and to conclude that the employers are vicariously liable for the sexual torts of their employee. . . .

For nearly a century English judges have adopted Salmond's statement of the applicable test as correct. Salmond said that a wrongful act is deemed to be done by a 'servant' in the course of his employment if 'it is either (a) a wrongful act authorised by the master, or (b) a wrongful and unauthorised *mode* of doing some act authorised by the master' . . . Situation (a) causes no problems. The difficulty arises in respect of cases under (b). Salmond did, however, offer an explanation which has sometimes been overlooked. He said (*Salmond on Torts*, 1st edn, pp. 83–4) that 'a master . . . is liable even for acts which he has not authorised, provided they are *so connected* with acts which he has authorised, that they may rightly *be regarded* as modes—although improper modes—of doing them' (my emphasis) . . . Salmond's explanation is the germ of the close connection test adumbrated by the Canadian Supreme Court in *Bazley v Curry* and *Jacobi v Griffiths*.

It is not necessary to embark on a detailed examination of the development of the modern principle of vicarious liability. But it is necessary to face up to the way in which the law of vicarious liability sometimes may embrace intentional wrongdoing by an employee. If one mechanically applies Salmond's test, the result might at first glance be thought to be that a bank is not liable to a customer where a bank employee defrauds a customer by giving him only half the foreign exchange which he paid for, the employee pocketing the difference. A preoccupation with conceptualistic reasoning may lead to the absurd conclusion that there can only be vicarious liability if the bank carries on business in defrauding its customers. Ideas divorced from reality have never held much attraction for judges steeped in the tradition that their task is to deliver principled but practical justice . . .

Our law no longer struggles with the concept of vicarious liability for intentional wrongdoing. . . . It remains, however, to consider how vicarious liability for intentional wrongdoing fits in with Salmond's formulation. The answer is that it does not cope ideally with such cases. It must, however, be remembered that the great tort writer did not attempt to enunciate precise propositions of law on vicarious liability. At most he propounded a broad test which deems as within the course of employment 'a wrongful and unauthorised mode of doing some act authorised by the master'. And he emphasised the connection between the authorised acts and the 'improper modes' of doing them. In reality it is simply a practical test serving as a dividing line between cases where it is or is not just to impose vicarious liability. The usefulness of the Salmond formulation is, however, crucially dependent on focusing on the right act of the employee . . .

[After considering *Rose v Plenty*, extracted in III.2, his Lordship continued:]

If this approach to the nature of employment is adopted, it is not necessary to ask the simplistic question whether in the cases under consideration the acts of sexual abuse were modes of doing authorised acts. It becomes possible to consider the question of vicarious liability on the basis that the employer undertook to care for the boys through the services of the warden and that there is a very close connection between the torts of the warden and his employment. After all, they were committed in the time and on the premises of the employers while the warden was also busy caring for the children. . . .

My Lords, I have been greatly assisted by the luminous and illuminating judgments of the Canadian Supreme Court in *Bazley v Curry* and *Jacobi v Griffiths*. Wherever such problems are considered in future in the common law world these judgments will be the starting point. On the other hand, it is unnecessary to express views on the full range of policy considerations examined in those decisions.

Employing the traditional methodology of English law, I am satisfied that in the case of the appeals under consideration the evidence showed that the employers entrusted the care of the children in Axeholme House to the warden. The question is whether the warden's torts were so closely connected with his employment that it would be fair and just to hold the employers vicariously liable. On the facts of the case the answer is yes. After all, the sexual abuse was inextricably interwoven with the carrying out by the warden of his duties in Axeholme House. Matters of degree arise. But the present cases clearly fall on the side of vicarious liability . . .

Lord Hobhouse of Woodborough

My Lords, the correct approach to answering the question whether the tortious act of the servant falls within or without the scope of the servant's employment for the purposes of the principle of vicarious liability is to ask what was the duty of the servant towards the plaintiff which was broken by the servant and what was the contractual duty of the servant towards his employer. The second limb of the classic Salmond test is a convenient rule of thumb which provides the answer in very many cases but does not represent the fundamental criterion which is the comparison of the duties respectively owed by the servant to the plaintiff and to his employer. Similarly, I do not believe that it is appropriate to follow the lead given by the Supreme Court of Canada in *Bazley v Curry*. The judgments contain a useful and impressive discussion of the social and economic reasons for having a principle of vicarious liability as part of the law of tort which extends to embrace acts of child abuse. But an exposition of the policy reasons for a rule (or even a description) is not the same as defining the criteria for its application. Legal rules have to have a greater degree of clarity and definition than is provided by simply explaining the reasons for the existence of the rule and the social need for it, instructive though that may be . . .

Lord Millett

Vicarious liability is a species of strict liability. It is not premised on any culpable act or omission on the part of the employer; an employer who is not personally at fault is made legally answerable for the fault of his employee. It is best understood as a loss-distribution device . . . The theoretical underpinning of the doctrine is unclear. Glanville Williams wrote ('Vicarious Liability and the Master's Indemnity' (1957) 20 MLR 220, 231):

> Vicarious liability is the creation of many judges who have had different ideas of its justification or social policy, or no idea at all. Some judges may have extended the rule more widely, or confined it more narrowly than its true rationale would allow; yet the rationale, if we can discover it, will remain valid so far as it extends.

Fleming observed (The *Law of Torts*, 9th ed, p 410) that the doctrine cannot parade as a deduction from legalistic premises. He indicated that it should be frankly recognised as having its basis in a combination of policy considerations, and continued: 'Most important of these is the belief that a person who employs others to advance his own economic interest should in fairness be placed under a corresponding liability for losses incurred in the course of the enterprise . . . ' Atiyah, *Vicarious Liability in the Law of Torts* wrote to the same effect. He suggested, at p 171: 'The master ought to be liable for all those torts which can fairly be regarded as reasonably incidental risks to the type of business he carries on.' These passages are not to be read as confining the doctrine to cases where the employer is carrying on business for profit. They are based on the more general idea that a person who employs another for his own ends inevitably creates a risk that the employee will commit a legal wrong. If the employer's objectives cannot be achieved without a serious risk of the employee committing the kind of wrong which he has in fact committed, the employer ought to be liable. The fact that his employment gave the employee the opportunity to commit the wrong is not enough to make the employer liable. He is liable only if the risk is one which experience shows is inherent in the nature of the business.

While this proposition has never, so far as I am aware, been adopted in so many words as a test of vicarious liability in any of the decided cases, it does I think form the unspoken rationale of the principle that the employer's liability is confined to torts committed by an employee in the course of his employment. The problem is that, as Townshend-Smith has observed ((2000) 8 Tort L Rev 108, 111), none of the various tests which have been proposed to determine this essentially factual question is either intellectually satisfying or effective to enable the outcome of a particular case to be predicted. The danger is that in borderline situations, and especially in cases of intentional wrongdoing, recourse to a rigid and possibly inappropriate formula as a test of liability may lead the court to abandon the search for legal principle.

[His Lordship set out the '*Salmond*' test, cited earlier, and continued:]

This passage has stood the test of time. It has survived unchanged for 21 editions, and has probably been cited more often than any other single passage in a legal textbook. Yet it is not without blemish. As has often been observed, the first of the two alternatives is not an example of vicarious liability at all. Its presence (and the word 'deemed') may be an echo of the discredited theory of implied authority. More pertinently, the second is not happily expressed if it is to serve as a test of vicarious liability for intentional wrongdoing.

In the present case the warden was employed to look after the boys in his care and secure their welfare. It is stretching language to breaking-point to describe the series of deliberate sexual assaults on them on which he embarked as merely a wrongful and unauthorised mode of performing that duty . . .

In a passage which is unfortunately less often cited, however, Sir John Salmond (Salmond, *Law of Torts*, 1st ed (1907)) continued his exposition as follows, at pp. 83–4:

> But a master, as opposed to the employer of an independent contractor, is liable even for acts which he has not authorised, provided they are so connected with acts which he has authorised, that they may rightly be regarded as modes—although improper modes—of doing them.

One of these steps in this analysis could, I think, usefully be elided to impose vicarious liability where the unauthorised acts of the employee are so connected with acts which the employer has authorised that they may properly be regarded as being within the scope of his employment. Such a formulation would have the advantage of dispensing with the awkward reference to 'improper modes' of carrying out the employee's duties; and by focusing attention on the connection between the employee's duties and his wrongdoing it would accord with the underlying rationale of the doctrine and be applicable without straining the language to accommodate cases of intentional wrongdoing.

But the precise terminology is not critical. The Salmond test, in either formulation, is not a statutory definition of the circumstances which give rise to liability, but a guide to the principled application of the law to diverse factual situations. What is critical is that attention should be directed to the closeness of the connection between the employee's duties and his wrongdoing and not to verbal formulae. This is the principle on which the Supreme Court of Canada recently decided the important cases of *Bazley v Curry* 174 DLR (4th) 45 and *Jacobi v Griffiths* 174 DLR (4th) 71 which provide many helpful insights into this branch of the law and from which I have derived much assistance . . .

> In the present case the warden's duties provided him with the opportunity to commit indecent assaults on the boys for his own sexual gratification, but that in itself is not enough to make the school liable. The same would be true of the groundsman or the school porter. But there was far more to it than that. The school was responsible for the care and welfare of the boys. It entrusted that responsibility to the warden. He was employed to discharge the school's responsibility to the boys. For this purpose the school entrusted them to his care. He did not merely take advantage of the opportunity which employment at a residential school gave him. He abused the special position in which the school had placed him to enable it to discharge its own responsibilities, with the result that the assaults were committed by the very employee to whom the school had entrusted the care of the boys. It is not necessary to conduct the detailed dissection of the warden's duties of the kind on which the Supreme Court of Canada embarked in *Bazley v Curry* and *Jacobi v Griffiths*. I would hold the school liable.
>
> I would regard this as in accordance not only with ordinary principle deducible from the authorities but with the underlying rationale of vicarious liability. Experience shows that in the case of boarding schools, prisons, nursing homes, old people's homes, geriatric wards, and other residential homes for the young or vulnerable, there is an inherent risk that indecent assaults on the residents will be committed by those placed in authority over them, particularly if they are in close proximity to them and occupying a position of trust . . .
>
> **Lord Clyde** delivered a separate speech agreeing that the appeal should be allowed. **Lord Hutton** agreed with Lord Steyn.
>
> *Appeal allowed.*

COMMENTARY

In *Lister* '[t]he Salmond formula was stretched to breaking point', since 'even on its most elastic interpretation, the sexual abuse of the children could not be described as a mode, albeit an improper mode, of caring for them' (*Mohamud v Wm Morrison Supermarkets plc* [2016] AC 677 at [39], per Lord Toulson). This was shown by *Trotman v North Yorkshire County Council* [1999] LGR 584, where the Court of Appeal refused to hold a special school vicariously liable for the sexual abuse by a teacher of a child with a learning disability. Relying on the *Salmond* test, Butler-Sloss LJ considered that the teacher's conduct was a negation of the authorised task of caring for the child, not an unauthorised mode of carrying out that task. The result was that in *Lister* the House of Lords was faced with the choice of denying the claims of the abused children or of abandoning (or at least radically modifying) the *Salmond* formula. They chose the latter option, overruling *Trotman*, and holding that if it could be said that the wrongful act of the employee had a sufficiently close connection with the employment this would be enough for vicarious liability to arise. By choosing to replace the *Salmond* formula with a test of close connection their Lordships brought about a revolution in the law of vicarious liability, the full implications of which are still being worked out two decades later. Why the revolution occurred when it did is explored by P. Giliker, 'A Revolution in Vicarious Liability: *Lister*, the *Catholic Child Welfare Society Case* and Beyond', in S. Worthington and G. Virgo (eds), *Revolution and Evolution in Private Law* (Oxford: Hart, 2018), who points out that it came in the aftermath of revelations of widespread physical and sexual abuse of children in care during the 1970s and 1980s. She also makes the important observation that although the claimants in intentional tort cases like *Lister* may be entitled to compensation under the Criminal Injuries Compensation Scheme (see Ch.17.II.2), awards under that scheme are often lower than tort damages, and may be withheld or reduced if the applicant has themselves committed criminal offences (with such behaviour sadly being a not uncommon consequence of childhood abuse: see, e.g., *SKX v Manchester City Council* [2021] 4 WLR 56, where the claimant had been refused compensation under the scheme on account of his unspent criminal convictions).

According to Lord Clyde in *Lister* (at [46]), it would be relatively easy to demonstrate a sufficient connection between the tortious act of the employee and the employment where the employer had been entrusted with the safekeeping or the care of some thing or some person and had then delegated that duty to the employee. One such case was *Morris v CW Martin & Sons Ltd* [1966] 1 QB 716, where an employee stole a fur entrusted to his employer. The facts of *Lister* itself also fell within this category, as the obligation to look after the boys had been entrusted to the defendants, and they had then delegated it to the warden. Lord Hobhouse employed similar reasoning, arguing (at [54]) that the situation was one where the employer had 'assumed a relationship to the plaintiff which imposes specific duties in tort upon the employer and the role of the employee is that he is the person to whom the employer has entrusted the performance of that duty'. In such cases, the motive of the employee and the fact that they were doing something expressly forbidden did not negative vicarious liability. A difficulty with this reasoning, however, is that it seems to blur the boundary between vicarious liability and primary liability for breach of a non-delegable duty. Lord Hobhouse's analysis in particular seems to rest entirely on the latter concept, but whereas breach by an employee of a non-delegable duty is generally considered to entail primary liability of the employer (see IV), his Lordship clearly stated that the liability he had in mind was vicarious in nature. The other members of the House of Lords also attached considerable significance to the fact the defendants had been entrusted with the care of the claimants and had delegated that duty to the warden, but they also failed to address the point that this reasoning has generally been associated with primary liability via the non-delegable duty concept.

In *Lister*, the time and place at which the tortious act took place were considered relevant, but not necessarily conclusive. Hence the fact that an act was performed outside working hours, or away from the workplace, might point to it being outside the scope of employment, though it did not follow that all tortious conduct occurring at the workplace in working hours gave rise to vicarious liability (see at [44], per Lord Clyde). The subsequent case law on the close connection test confirms that it may have a temporal and geographical component: see, e.g., *Maga v Birmingham Roman Catholic Archdiocese Trustees* [2010] 1 WLR 1441, where one reason why the defendant was held vicariously liable for sexual abuse by one of its priests was that some of the abuse took place on church premises. This is only one consideration, however (see, e.g., *Bellman v Northampton Recruitment Ltd* [2019] 1 All ER 1133, where vicarious liability was imposed for a work-related assault which took place away from the workplace and outside working hours) and much may depend on the context: if, for example, the employee travels as part of their job it is hard to see how location could be a decisive factor.

In *Prince Alfred College Inc v ADC* (2016) 258 CLR 134, the High Court of Australia refused to adopt the close connection test for the course of employment enquiry, observing, at [68], that 'a test of connection does not seem to add much to an understanding of the basis for an employers' liability' unless supplemented by a further requirement that it be 'fair and just' to impose liability, a requirement that 'imports a value judgment on the part of the primary judge which . . . will not proceed on any principled basis or by reference to previous decisions'. For commentary on the *Prince Alfred College* case, see Ryan [2017] CLJ 14; Beuermann (2017) 33 PN 179; Goudkamp and Plunkett (2017) 17 OUCLJ 162. According to Ryan (*op. cit.*, at 16), the High Court's assumption that the close connection test is supplemented by a separate enquiry of this kind was mistaken. This, he argues, would be 'tautologous and confusing', with the result that:

> Attempts at elevating those two (or three) epithets ['fair and just', or 'fair, just and reasonable'] to the status of an additional prong in the *Lister* test are, accordingly, undesirable. No such additional prong exists. If the connection is sufficiently close, then it will be fair and just to impose vicarious liability.

(For similar observations as to the utility of a separate enquiry into 'fair, just and reasonableness' at stage one of the vicarious liability enquiry, see *Cox v Ministry of Justice* at [41], per Lord Reed.)

As Lord Phillips noted in *Christian Brothers* (at [21]), the close connection test requires an evaluation of the connection between the relationship of the tortfeasor and the defendant, and the former's act or omission. Where the employee acts negligently in doing something that they are required or requested to do pursuant to their relationship with the defendant employer, the close connection test is likely to be satisfied. But in cases of criminal conduct, such as child sexual abuse, the application of the test has given rise to more difficulty (see III.4), as shown by the next extracted case.

Mohamud v Wm Morrison Supermarkets plc [2016] AC 677

The claimant went to the sales kiosk of one of the defendant's petrol stations and asked one of the employees on duty, a Mr Khan, if it was possible to print off some documents from a USB stick. Mr Khan refused the request in an offensive manner and subsequently directed racist abuse at the claimant and asked him to leave. He then followed the claimant back to his car on the station forecourt, and, having told him never to come back, subjected him to an unprovoked physical assault, ignoring his supervisor's order to stop. The claimant brought proceedings against the defendant, on the footing that it was vicariously liable for the assault. The judge dismissed the claim on the ground that there was not a sufficiently close connection between what Mr Khan was employed to do and his tortious conduct for vicarious liability to arise. The Court of Appeal upheld that decision. The claimant appealed to the Supreme Court.

Lord Toulson

1. Vicarious liability in tort requires, first, a relationship between the defendant and the wrongdoer and, secondly, a connection between that relationship and the wrongdoer's act or default, such as to make it just that the defendant should be held legally responsible to the claimant for the consequences of the wrongdoer's conduct. In this case the wrongdoer was employed by the defendant, and so there is no issue about the first requirement. The issue in the appeal is whether there was sufficient connection between the wrongdoer's employment and his conduct towards the claimant to make the defendant legally responsible. . . .

2. The question in this appeal concerns an employer's vicarious liability in tort for an assault carried out by an employee. It is a subject which has troubled the courts on numerous occasions and the case law is not entirely consistent. In addressing the issues which it

raises, it will be necessary to examine how the law in this area has developed, what stage it has reached and whether it is in need of significant change . . .

The present law

44. In the simplest terms, the court has to consider two matters. The first question is what functions or 'field of activities' have been entrusted by the employer to the employee, or, in everyday language, what was the nature of his job. As has been emphasised in several cases, this question must be addressed broadly . . .

45. Secondly, the court must decide whether there was sufficient connection between the position in which he was employed and his wrongful conduct to make it right for the employer to be held liable under the principle of social justice which goes back to Holt CJ [in *Boson v Sandford* (1691) 2 Salk 440; *Turberville v Stampe* (1698) 1 Ld Raym 264; and *Hern v Nichols* (1708) 1 Salk 289]. To try to measure the closeness of connection, as it were, on a scale of 1 to 10, would be a forlorn exercise and, what is more, it would miss the point. The cases in which the necessary connection has been found for Holt CJ's principle to be applied are cases in which the employee used or misused the position entrusted to him in a way which injured the third party . . .

46. Contrary to the primary submission advanced on the claimant's behalf, I am not persuaded that there is anything wrong with the *Lister* approach as such. It has been affirmed many times and I do not see that the law would now be improved by a change of vocabulary . . .

The present case

47. In the present case it was Mr Khan's job to attend to customers and to respond to their inquiries. His conduct in answering the claimant's request in a foul-mouthed way and ordering him to leave was inexcusable but within the 'field of activities' assigned to him. What happened thereafter was an unbroken sequence of events. It was argued by the respondent and accepted by the judge that there ceased to be any significant connection between Mr Khan's employment and his behaviour towards the claimant when he came out from behind the counter and followed the claimant onto the forecourt. I disagree for two reasons. First, I do not consider that it is right to regard him as having metaphorically taken off his uniform the moment he stepped from behind the counter. He was following up on what he had said to the claimant. It was a seamless episode. Secondly, when Mr Khan followed the claimant back to his car and opened the front passenger door, he again told the claimant in threatening words that he was never to come back to [the] petrol station. This was not something personal between them; it was an order to keep away from his employer's premises, which he reinforced by violence. In giving such an order he was purporting to act about his employer's business. It was a gross abuse of his position, but it was in connection with the business in which he was employed to serve customers. His employers entrusted him with that position and it is just that as between them and the claimant, they should be held responsible for their employee's abuse of it.

48. Mr Khan's motive is irrelevant. It looks obvious that he was motivated by personal racism rather than a desire to benefit his employer's business, but that is neither here nor there.

49. I would allow the appeal.

Lord Dyson MR agreed with Lord Toulson and delivered a short concurring judgment. **Lord Neuberger**, **Baroness Hale** and **Lord Reed** agreed with Lord Toulson.

Appeal allowed.

COMMENTARY

In *Lister*, the House of Lords had sought to maintain some continuity with the previous approach to the course of employment question. Lord Millett, in particular, merely warned (at [74]) against the 'excessively literal' application of the *Salmond* test, and sought to adapt that formula to incorporate the 'close connection' idea, rather than abandoning it altogether. Shortly after *Lister*, a version of Lord Millett's revised test was adopted in *Dubai Aluminium Co Ltd v Salaam* [2003] 2 AC 366, where Lord Nicholls emphasised the assistance that could be derived from earlier authorities in this context (at [26]). This relatively conservative approach can be contrasted with the two-part test for the course of employment put forward by Lord Toulson in *Mohamud* at [44]–[45], whereby the court first considers what functions or 'field of activities' were entrusted by the employer to the employee (a question to be addressed broadly), and then goes on to ask whether there was a sufficient connection between the position in which the employee was employed and their wrongful conduct to make it right for the employer to be held liable as a matter of social justice. Unlike Lord Millett's formula, this test entails the complete abandonment of the concept of 'authority' underlying the *Salmond* formula, while the result of its application on the facts of *Mohamud* suggested that it was likely to have a significant expansionary effect on the boundaries of vicarious liability, over and above the effect of *Lister* itself (for other examples of its application, see *Bellman v Northampton Recruitment Ltd* [2019] 1 All ER 1133; *Group Seven Ltd v Notable Services LLP* [2019] PNLR 22; and *Shelbourne v Cancer Research UK* [2019] PIQR P16).

In *Mohamud*, Lord Toulson described Mr Khan's job, at [3], as 'to see that the petrol pumps and the kiosk were kept in good running order and to serve customers', and (according to Treacy LJ in the Court of Appeal in the case) Mr Khan's 'instructions were not to engage in any form of confrontation with a customer, even an angry one' ([2014] 2 All ER 990 at [35]). In his consideration of the close connection issue in *Mohamud*, Lord Toulson focused not on these aspects of Mr Khan's employment, but on the fact that he had told the claimant never to come back to the petrol station. However, his Lordship's claim, at [47], that in giving this order 'he was purporting to act about his employer's business' is questionable. This instruction was in fact entirely contrary to his employer's interests, and is surely best understood as a manifestation of the employee's apparently racist personal antipathy towards the claimant.

It is also hard to square the decision in *Mohamud* with one of the central underlying themes of the approach to the course of employment question adopted in *Bazley v Curry* and *Lister*, namely that (in the words of McLachlin J in *Bazley* at [41]) vicarious liability 'is generally appropriate where there is a significant connection between the creation or enhancement of a risk and the wrong that accrues therefrom'. Is the risk of a racist assault created or enhanced by the employment of a petrol station attendant (see Plunkett (2016) 132 LQR 556 at 561)? Interestingly, McLachlin J in *Bazley*, at [42], specifically used as an example of a situation where it would *not* be justifiable to hold an employer vicariously liable, 'an incidental or random attack by an employee that merely happens to take place on the employer's premises', arguably an apt description of the facts of *Mohamud*. For critical commentary on *Mohamud*, see Plunkett (*op. cit.*); Bell (2016) 32 PN 153; P. Morgan [2016] CLJ 202; and Giliker (2016) 7 UKSC Yearbook 152 (arguing, at 159, that the decision 'seems to take the course of employment test to its absolute limits'); see also the critical remarks in *Prince Alfred College Inc v ADC* (2016) 258 CLR 134, especially at [83]. In a section of his judgment which is not extracted here, Lord Toulson conducted a thorough survey of the case law on the course of employment issue, and based his approach to the issue on an alleged 'principle of social justice' identified by Holt CJ around the turn of the eighteenth century. For a critique of this aspect of Lord Toulson's analysis, see Bell, 'Scope of Employment: Connecting Closely with the Past' (2021) 137 LQR 254, who argues that Holt CJ's reasoning in the cases concerned was in fact organised around much narrower and more precise grounds for identifying the act of a servant with his master, with the result that the historical foundation on which the *Mohamud* decision rests falls away.

A possible downside of the close connection test that now determines whether conduct was in the course of employment is the unpredictability of the outcome when the test is applied. According to Brodie (*op. cit.*, p. 24), the close connection standard 'fails to provide a meaningful test', although in his view the proper extent of the employer's responsibility is 'very much a matter of policy', with the result that the result in any particular case will largely be driven by 'the judicial assessment and ordering of policy considerations'. Giliker observes (*op. cit.*, 165) that the approach adopted in the *Mohamud* case in particular 'seems to leave key value judgments with the trial judge', a view also taken by Bell (*op. cit.*, 256), who says that while *Lister* 'left open multiple potential positions on assessing closeness [of relationship] . . . *Mohamud* disguises any and all positions under an unstructured policy decision'. In his concurring judgment in *Mohamud*, Lord Dyson MR accepted, at [54], that the close connection test was imprecise, but said that this was an area of law in which imprecision was inevitable: 'To search for certainty and precision in vicarious liability is to undertake a quest for a chimaera.' On the other hand, there are degrees of certainty and precision, and it is difficult to escape the conclusion that the law in this area is now less certain and less precise than it was before *Lister*. Whether that is a cause for concern is of course another question. According to Giliker, 'Vicarious Liability "On the Move": The English Supreme Court and Enterprise Liability' (2013) 4 JETL 306 at 313, in this area of law 'the common law has some distance to travel before the law provides the level of certainty common lawyers expect'. Do you agree?

The concerns to which the decision and reasoning in *Mohamud* gave rise must now be seen in the light of the approach taken by the Supreme Court in the following case.

Various Claimants v Wm Morrison Supermarkets plc [2020] AC 989

Andrew Skelton, an internal auditor employed by the defendant supermarket chain, harboured a grudge against his employer. In November 2013, he was tasked with collating and transmitting payroll data for the defendant's workforce to its external auditors, KPMG. Having done so, he secretly copied the data onto a personal USB stick and a few months later he uploaded it from a pay-as-you-go mobile phone to a publicly accessible file-sharing website. This conduct, which was intended to harm the defendant, amounted to the wrongs of misuse of private information, breach of confidence and breach of statutory duty (under the Data Protection Act 1998). Proceedings were brought against the defendant on behalf of over 9,000 of the employees whose personal information had been published, in part on the basis that it was vicariously liable for Skelton's wrongdoing. The trial judge held that Skelton's conduct had been sufficiently connected to his employment for vicarious liability to arise. The Court of Appeal applied the two-stage test from *Mohamud* and dismissed the defendant's appeal. The defendant appealed to the Supreme Court.

Lord Reed

1. This appeal is primarily concerned with the circumstances in which an employer is vicariously liable for the conduct of its employees, and provides the court with an opportunity to address the misunderstandings which have arisen since its decision in *Mohamud v Wm Morrison Supermarkets plc* [2016] AC 677. . . .

(I) Whether Morrisons is vicariously liable for Skelton's conduct

The Mohamud decision

16. The courts below applied what they understood to be the reasoning of Lord Toulson JSC in *Mohamud* [2016] AC 677. They treated as critical, in particular, his reference in para 45 of his judgment to 'the principle of social justice which goes back to Holt CJ', his references in para 47 to the connection between the employee's conduct in that case and his employment ('an unbroken sequence of events', or 'a seamless episode'), which they appear to have regarded as referring to an unbroken temporal or causal chain of events, and his statement in para 48 that 'Mr Khan's motive is irrelevant', Mr Khan being the employee whose conduct was in question in that case. The resultant approach, if correct, would constitute a major change in the law.

17. Lord Toulson JSC's judgment was not intended to effect a change in the law of vicarious liability: quite the contrary. That becomes clear if the judgment is read as a whole, as I shall explain. . . .

22. The 'close connection' approach to vicarious liability was considered . . . by the House of Lords in *Dubai Aluminium Co Ltd v Salaam* [2003] 2 AC 366, a case of commercial fraud committed by one of the partners in a firm. In a passage which is of particular importance, and which Lord Toulson JSC cited in *Mohamud*, at para 41, Lord Nicholls of Birkenhead (with whom Lord Slynn of Hadley and Lord Hutton agreed) said:

> 22. . . . it is a fact of life, and therefore to be expected by those who carry on businesses, that sometimes their agents may exceed the bounds of their authority or even defy express instructions. It is fair to allocate risk of losses thus arising to the businesses rather than leave those wronged with the sole remedy, of doubtful value, against the individual employee who committed the wrong. To this end, the law has given the concept of 'ordinary course of employment' an extended scope.
>
> 23. If, then, authority is not the touchstone, what is? . . . Perhaps the best general answer is that the wrongful conduct must be so closely connected with acts the partner or employee was authorised to do that, for the purpose of the liability of the firm or the employer to third parties, the wrongful conduct *may fairly and properly be regarded* as done by the partner while acting in the ordinary course of the firm's business or the employee's employment. Lord Millett said as much in *Lister v Hesley Hall Ltd* . . .
>
> 25. This 'close connection' test focuses attention in the right direction. But it affords no guidance on the type or degree of connection which will normally be regarded as sufficiently close to prompt the legal conclusion that the risk of the wrongful act occurring, and any loss flowing from the wrongful act, should fall on the firm or employer rather than the third party who was wronged . . .
>
> 26. This lack of precision is inevitable, given the infinite range of circumstances where the issue arises. The crucial feature or features, either producing or negativing vicarious liability, vary widely from one case or type of case to the next. Essentially the court makes an evaluative judgment in each case, having regard to all the circumstances and, importantly, having regard also to the assistance provided by previous court decisions. In this field the latter form of assistance is particularly valuable. (Original emphasis.)

23. In that passage, Lord Nicholls identified the general principle ('the best general answer', as he said at para 23) applicable to vicarious liability arising out of a relationship of employment: the wrongful conduct must be so closely connected with acts the employee was authorised to do that, for the purposes of the liability of the employer to third parties, it may fairly and properly be regarded as done by the employee while acting in the ordinary course of his employment. That test was repeated in later cases such as *Bernard v Attorney General of Jamaica* [2005] IRLR 398, *Brown v Robinson* (2004) 65 WIR 258 and *Majrowski v Guy's and St Thomas's NHS Trust* [2007] 1 AC 224. As Lord Phillips noted in [*Christian Brothers*], paras 83 and 85, the close connection test has been applied differently in cases concerned with the sexual abuse of children, which cannot be regarded as something done by the employee while acting in the ordinary course of his employment. Instead, the courts have emphasised the importance of criteria that are particularly relevant to that form of wrongdoing, such as the employer's conferral of authority on the employee over the victims, which he has abused.

24. The general principle set out by Lord Nicholls in *Dubai Aluminium*, like many other principles of the law of tort, has to be applied with regard to the circumstances of the case before the court and the assistance provided by previous court decisions. The words 'fairly and properly' are not, therefore, intended as an invitation to judges to decide cases according to their personal sense of justice, but require them to consider how the guidance derived from decided cases furnishes a solution to the case before the court. Judges should therefore identify from the decided cases the factors or principles which point towards or away from vicarious liability in the case before the court, and which explain why it should or should not be imposed. Following that approach, cases can be decided on a basis which is principled and consistent.

25. Having explained how the close connection case was expressed in *Lister* and elaborated in *Dubai Aluminium*, and having also explained that it had been applied in a number of subsequent cases at the highest level, Lord Toulson JSC summarised the present law in paras 44–46 of his judgment in *Mohamud* [2016] AC 677. 'In the simplest terms', he said, the court had to consider two matters. The first question was what functions or 'field of activities' had been entrusted by the employer to the employee. In other words, as Lord Nicholls put it in *Dubai Aluminium*, at para 23, it is necessary to identify the 'acts the . . . employee was authorised to do'. Secondly, Lord Toulson JSC said at para 45, 'the court must decide whether there was sufficient connection between the position in which he was employed and his wrongful conduct to make it right for the employer to be held liable under the principle of social justice which goes back to Holt CJ'. That statement, expressly put in the simplest terms, was more fully stated by Lord Nicholls in *Dubai Aluminium* [2003] 2 AC 366, para 23: in a case concerned with vicarious liability arising out of a relationship of employment, the court generally has to decide whether the wrongful conduct was so closely connected with acts the employee was authorised to do that, for the purposes of the liability of his employer, it may fairly and properly be regarded as done by the employee while acting in the ordinary course of his employment. That statement of the law, endorsed in *Mohamud* and in several other decisions at the highest level, is authoritative.

26. Lord Toulson JSC was not suggesting any departure from the approach adopted in *Lister* and *Dubai Aluminium*. His position was the exact opposite. Nor was he suggesting that all that was involved in determining whether an employer was vicariously liable was for the court to consider whether there was a temporal or causal connection between the employment and the wrongdoing, and whether it was right for the employer to be held liable as a matter of social justice. Plainly, the close connection test is not merely a question of timing or causation, and the passage which Lord Toulson JSC cited from *Dubai Aluminium* makes it clear that vicarious liability for wrongdoing by an employee is not determined according to individual judges' sense of social justice. It is decided by orthodox common law reasoning, generally based on

the application to the case before the court of the principle set out by Lord Nicholls at para 23 of *Dubai Aluminium*, in the light of the guidance to be derived from decided cases. In some cases, the answer may be clear. In others, inevitably, a finer judgment will be called for. . . .

28. Read in context, Lord Toulson JSC's comments [on the facts of *Mohamud*] that there was 'an unbroken sequence of events', and that it was 'a seamless episode', were not directed towards the temporal or causal connection between the various events, but towards the capacity in which Mr Khan was acting when those events took place. Lord Toulson JSC was explaining why, in his view, Mr Khan was acting throughout the entire episode in the course of his employment. When he followed the motorist out of the kiosk and on to the forecourt, he was following up on what he had said to the motorist in the kiosk. He ordered the motorist to keep away from his employer's premises, and reinforced that order by committing the tort. In doing so, he was 'purporting to act about his employer's business'. As Lord Toulson JSC said, 'this was not something personal'.

29. . . . Read in isolation, [Lord Toulson JSC's statement in *Mohamud*] that 'motive is irrelevant' would be misleading. Lord Toulson JSC had just said, in the preceding paragraph, that one of his reasons for finding that there was a close connection was that Mr Khan was purporting to act about his employer's business, and that his conduct towards the customer was not, therefore, 'something personal'. So the question whether Mr Khan was acting, albeit wrongly, on his employer's business, or was acting for personal reasons, was plainly important.

30. When Lord Toulson JSC said that Mr Khan's motive was irrelevant, he was addressing a point which the judge had mentioned, namely that the reasons why Mr Khan had become violent were unclear. As just mentioned, Lord Toulson JSC had already concluded that Mr Khan was going, albeit wrongly, about his employer's business, rather than pursuing his private ends, and had treated that fact as supporting the existence of a close connection between his field of activities and the commission of the tort. Having reached that conclusion, the reason why Mr Khan had become so enraged as to assault the motorist could not make a material difference. That is all, I believe, that the remark that 'Mr Khan's motive is irrelevant' was intended to convey.

Vicarious liability in the present case

31. It follows from the foregoing that the judge and the Court of Appeal misunderstood the principles governing vicarious liability in a number of relevant respects, of which the following were particularly important. First, the disclosure of the data on the internet did not form part of Skelton's functions or field of activities, in the sense in which those words were used by Lord Toulson JSC: it was not an act which he was authorised to do, as Lord Nicholls put it. Secondly, the fact that the five factors listed by Lord Phillips in [*Christian Brothers*], para 35 were all present was nothing to the point. Those factors were not concerned with the question whether the wrongdoing in question was so connected with the employment that vicarious liability ought to be imposed, but with the distinct question whether, in the case of wrongdoing committed by someone who was not an employee, the relationship between the wrongdoer and the defendant was sufficiently akin to employment as to be one to which the doctrine of vicarious liability should apply. Thirdly, although there was a close temporal link and an unbroken chain of causation linking the provision of the data to Skelton for the purpose of transmitting it to KPMG and his disclosing it on the internet, a temporal or causal connection does not in itself satisfy the close connection test. Fourthly, the reason why Skelton acted wrongfully was not irrelevant: on the contrary, whether he was acting on his employer's business or for purely personal reasons was highly material.

32. The question whether Morrisons is vicariously liable for Skelton's wrongdoing must therefore be considered afresh. Applying the general test laid down by Lord Nicholls in *Dubai Aluminium* [2003] 2 AC 366, para 23, the question is whether Skelton's disclosure of the data was so closely connected with acts he was authorised to do that, for the purposes of

the liability of his employer to third parties, his wrongful disclosure may fairly and properly be regarded as done by him while acting in the ordinary course of his employment.

33. Considering first the acts which Skelton was authorised to do, so far as relevant, he was given the task of collating and transmitting payroll data to KPMG. He performed that task on a date between 15 and 21 November 2013. The remaining question is whether Skelton's wrongful disclosure of the data was so closely connected with the collation and transmission of the data to KPMG that, for the purposes of the liability of his employer to third parties, the disclosure may fairly and properly be regarded as made by him while acting in the ordinary course of his employment.

34. The connecting factor between what Skelton was authorised to do and the disclosure is that he could not have made the disclosure if he had not been given the task of collating the data and transmitting it to KPMG. It was the provision of the data to him, so that he could perform that task, that enabled him to make a private copy of the data on 18 November 2013, which he subsequently used to make the disclosure on 12 January 2014.

35. Clearly, the mere fact that Skelton's employment gave him the opportunity to commit the wrongful act would not be sufficient to warrant the imposition of vicarious liability: see, for example, *Morris v C W Martin & Sons Ltd* [1966] 1 QB 716, 737 and *Lister* [2002] 1 AC 215, paras 25, 45, 50, 59, 65, 75, and 81–82. . . .

36. As already explained, in applying the close connection test it is necessary to have regard to the assistance provided by previous court decisions. Perhaps unsurprisingly, there does not appear to be any previous case in which it has been argued that an employer might be vicariously liable for wrongdoing which was designed specifically to harm the employer. The decided cases which are most closely comparable to the present case are those which have concerned vicarious liability for deliberate wrongdoing intended to inflict harm on a third party for personal reasons of the employee (leaving aside sexual abuse cases, where, as explained in para 23 above, a more tailored version of the close connection test is applied). . . .

[His Lordship considered various authorities on 'independent personal ventures' and assaults by employees and continued:]

47. All these examples illustrate the distinction drawn by Lord Nicholls in *Dubai Aluminium* [2003] 2 AC 366, para 32 between 'cases . . . where the employee was engaged, however misguidedly, in furthering his employer's business, and cases where the employee is engaged solely in pursuing his own interests: on a "frolic of his own", in the language of the time-honoured catch phrase'. In the present case, it is abundantly clear that Skelton was not engaged in furthering his employer's business when he committed the wrongdoing in question. On the contrary, he was pursuing a personal vendetta, seeking vengeance for the disciplinary proceedings some months earlier. In those circumstances, applying the test laid down by Lord Nicholls in *Dubai Aluminium* in the light of the circumstances of the case and the relevant precedents, Skelton's wrongful conduct was not so closely connected with acts which he was authorised to do that, for the purposes of Morrisons' liability to third parties, it can fairly and properly be regarded as done by him while acting in the ordinary course of his employment. . . .

Conclusion

56. For the reasons explained above, the circumstances in which Skelton committed wrongs against the claimants were not such as to result in the imposition of vicarious liability upon his employer. Morrisons cannot therefore be held liable for Skelton's conduct. It follows that the appeal must be allowed.

Lord Hodge, Lord Kerr, Lord Lloyd-Jones and Baroness Hale agreed with Lord Reed.

Appeal allowed.

COMMENTARY

Writing before the decision of the Supreme Court in the extracted case, Giliker, 'Analysing Institutional Liability for Child Abuse in England and Wales and Australia: Vicarious Liability, Non-delegable Duties and Statutory Intervention' [2018] CLJ 506 at 532–3 argued that the broad test for vicarious liability developed by the UK courts lacked 'definitional certainty' and 'a clear theoretical underpinning', and was 'expanding from case to case'. In her view, the courts needed 'to move towards a more structured and coherent framework', particularly at stage two of the analysis. While there is little sign in *Morrison Supermarkets* of a clearer theoretical framework for the doctrine, Lord Reed in his judgment does seem to be trying to place clearer limits on the scope of the doctrine and to provide greater predictability in its application. Whether these attempts are successful remains to be seen (compare Gordon [2020] CLJ 401 at 404, who is cautiously optimistic, commenting that the case 'moves us some steps further towards clarity' in the application of the stage two enquiry, with Bell (2020) 36 PN 150 at 155, who argues that a test of what 'may fairly and properly be regarded' as within the course of employment 'does not give any more guidance' than the *Mohamud* approach). But the decision does in any case bear out Lord Steyn's comment that, notwithstanding its recent expansion, the doctrine of vicarious liability is not 'infinitely extendable' (*Bernard v Attorney General of Jamaica* [2005] IRLR 398 at [23]).

In another article published before *Morrison Supermarkets*, Bell, '"Double, Double Toil and Trouble": Recent Movements in Vicarious Liability' [2018] JPIL 235 at 247, expressed the hope that *Mohamud* could be 'sidelined and confined to its facts'. Is that, do you think, the probable fate of the case following its 'clarification' by Lord Reed? According to Bell (*op. cit.*, at 243), Lord Toulson's judgment in *Mohamud* was seen 'first and foremost' as an attempt 'to replace the original form of the close connection test with a causal concept', in which the court asked whether the tortious conduct of the employee was the culmination of an unbroken sequence of events beginning with conduct that clearly fell four square within the employee's role (in *Mohamud*, the employee's responding to a customer request). As Bell points out, this idea of a continuous causal thread had also been relied upon in the earlier case of *Mattis v Pollock* [2003] 1 WLR 2158, where an assault by a doorman on a nightclub patron was described by Judge LJ (at [32]) as the 'virtual culmination' of an earlier incident in the club in which the employee had clearly been acting in the course of his employment, 'and could not fairly and justly be treated in isolation' from those events. Similar reasoning was employed by the Court of Appeal in *Morrison Supermarkets* to justify imposing vicarious liability on the defendant for Skelton's actions (see [2019] QB 772 at [74]), but in the Supreme Court Lord Reed decisively rejected this approach, arguing (at [28]) that the references in *Mohamud* to an 'unbroken sequence of events' which formed a 'seamless episode' were 'not directed towards the temporal or causal connection between the various events, but towards the capacity in which Mr Kahn was acting when those events took place', and stating that 'a temporal or causal connection does not in itself satisfy the close connection test' (at [31]). (See similarly *Chell v Tarmac Cement and Lime Ltd* [2020] EWHC 2613 (QB) at [36].) Lee (2020) 136 LQR 553 at 557 welcomes this abandonment of a temporal/causal approach, commenting tellingly that the problem with it is that 'time itself is a seamless and continuous sequence of events: any story can be told in a way that meets this test'. However, Lee is one of a number of commentators who find Lord Reed's claim that the Supreme

Court was addressing 'misunderstandings' which had arisen about the *Mohamud* decision somewhat implausible (*op. cit.*, at 558):

> The Supreme Court implies that their conclusions on the facts of [*Barclays Bank* and *Morrison Supermarkets*] followed inexorably from reasoning in the previous decisions . . . An alternative, more viable reading is that, having promoted an expansive approach that encouraged the breaking down of traditional limitations, the Justices have belatedly recognised that some parameters are necessary.

(See also Nolan (2020) 49 ILJ 609 at 620, arguing that despite his protestations to the contrary, 'Lord Reed's analysis amounts to an abandonment of the broad and open-ended approach to the course of employment question endorsed in *Mohamud* in favour of a more bounded and precedent-led enquiry'.)

Morrison Supermarkets is not a complete break with *Mohamud* as in both cases the starting off point of the analysis is the definitions that are given of the employee's role and of the wrongful act. And as Bell (2020) 36 PN 150 at 155 points out, the way in which these are characterised is vitally important:

> In *Mohamud* a key manoeuvre was defining everything from the initial conversation with the victim to the physical assault as a singular 'response to the customer', where 'responding to the customer' is the role. . . . In [*Morrison Supermarkets*], defining the role as collating and transmitting the data to the proper recipient showed it to be fairly clearly separate from transmitting it wrongfully over the internet. If the emphasis were more general, instead placed on eg looking after the data and controlling its disclosure, the connection might begin to look different.

Conversely, one respect in which *Morrison Supermarkets* clearly parts ways with *Mohamud* is the emphasis Lord Reed placed on Skelton's motivation for acting as he did; it was, his Lordship said (at [31]), 'highly material' whether in publishing the payroll data he was acting to further his employer's business or for purely personal reasons. The facts of the case were particularly striking in this respect, since not only was Skelton not seeking to further his employer's interests, he was actively attempting to inflict the maximum damage on the firm pursuant to a personal vendetta, not against a third party (as in previous cases) but against the employer itself. In emphasising the significance of the employee's motive in cases of this kind, Lord Reed relied on earlier authorities involving criminal conduct of the employee in which this distinction was also drawn (see further, III.4), and this aspect of Lord Reed's analysis was in turn relied on in *Ali v Luton BC* [2022] EWHC 132 (QB), where it was held that a leak by a local authority employee of confidential information concerning the wife and children of a man with whom the employee was having an affair was not in the course of her employment since she 'was engaged solely in pursuing her own agenda'.

Lord Reed's reliance on earlier case law on the employee's motivation, including many pre-*Lister* decisions, chimed with his emphasis on the importance in this context of precedent and reasoning by analogy from earlier cases, a theme also evident in his landmark judgment in *Robinson v Chief Constable of West Yorkshire Police* [2018] AC 736 (extracted in Ch. 3.II.4) on the duty of care in negligence. (On the importance of previous decisions in deciding whether vicarious liability arises, particularly at the second stage of the enquiry, see Beuermann, 'Vicarious Liability: A Case Study in the Failure of General Principles?' (2017) 33 PN 179.)

2. Carelessness of the Employee

In *Century Insurance Company Limited v Northern Ireland Transport Board* [1942] AC 509, a fire at a petrol station had been caused by the negligence of a petrol delivery driver who threw a lighted match onto the floor after using it to light a cigarette. On the assumption that the driver was an employee of the defendant delivery company, the House of Lords held that his conduct was within the course of his employment. According to Viscount Simon LC, the driver's actions in starting smoking and in throwing away a lighted match were plainly negligence in the discharge of the duties on which he was employed by the defendant. In Lord Wright's view, it was important to consider those acts, not in isolation, but in the context of the task on which the driver had been engaged. Furthermore, Lord Wright argued, it was immaterial that those acts had been done for the driver's own comfort and convenience and not for the benefit of his employer.

That the focus in cases of careless conduct of the employee is on the strength of the connection between the tortious conduct and the task the employee is employed to do is also shown by *Kay v ITW Ltd* [1968] 1 QB 140, where the employee's job consisted of driving trucks and small vans around his employer's worksite. Whilst driving a fork-lift truck, the employee found that the only entry to a warehouse where he wanted to go was blocked by a lorry not belonging to his employer. Although he had no right to move the lorry, the employee attempted to do so, and in the course of this attempt he negligently injured the plaintiff. The Court of Appeal held that the act was within the scope of his employment, because he was attempting to return the fork-lift truck to the defendant's warehouse, which was part and parcel of the job he was employed to do, and his misconduct was not so gross and extreme as to take it outside the scope of his employment.

Furthermore, in cases of this kind the fact that the employee's conduct was specifically prohibited will not necessarily take it outside the course of their employment, as the next extracted case demonstrates.

Rose v Plenty [1976] 1 WLR 141

The plaintiff was a 13-year-old child who had been employed by a milkman, Mr Plenty, to help deliver milk. This was contrary to a notice that Mr Plenty's employer had exhibited at the depot expressly prohibiting milkmen from using children to assist them in the performance of their duties and from giving lifts on the milk float. The plaintiff fell off the milk float as a result of Mr Plenty's negligent driving. He brought an action for damages for negligence against Mr Plenty and his employer, obtaining judgment against Mr Plenty, but failing against his employer on the ground that Mr Plenty had been acting outside the scope of his employment in employing the plaintiff and carrying him on the milk float contrary to the employer's instructions. The plaintiff appealed.

Lord Denning MR

In considering whether a prohibited act was within the course of the employment, it depends very much on the purpose for which it is done. If it is done for his employers' business, it is usually done in the course of his employment, even though it is a prohibited act. . . . But if it is done for some purpose other than his master's business, as, for instance, giving a lift to a hitchhiker, such an act, if prohibited, may not be within the course of his employment. . . . In the present case it seems to me that the course of Mr Plenty's employment was to distribute the milk, collect the money and to bring back the bottles to the van. He got or allowed this young boy, Leslie Rose, to do part of that business which was the employers' business.

It seems to me that although prohibited, it was conduct which was within the course of the employment; and on this ground I think the judge was in error. I agree it is a nice point in these cases on which side of the line the case falls; but, as I understand the authorities, this case falls within those in which the prohibition affects only the conduct within the sphere of the employment and did not take the conduct outside the sphere altogether. I would hold this conduct of Christopher Plenty to be within the course of his employment and the master is liable accordingly, and I would allow the appeal.

Scarman LJ

[The question of whether the employer should shoulder the liability for compensating the person injured by the tort] has to be answered by directing attention to what [Mr Plenty] was employed to do when he committed the tort that has caused damage to the plaintiff. The first defendant was, of course, employed at the time of the accident to do a whole number of operations. He was certainly not employed to give the plaintiff a lift, and if one confines one's analysis of the facts to the incident of injury to the plaintiff, then no doubt one would say that carrying the plaintiff on the float—giving him a lift—was not in the course of the first defendant's employment. But in *Ilkiw v Samuels* [1963] 1 WLR [991] at 1004 Diplock LJ indicated that the proper approach to the nature of the servant's employment is a broad one. He said:

> As each of these nouns implies [he is referring to the nouns used to describe course of employment, sphere, scope and so forth] the matter must be looked at broadly, not dissecting the servant's task into its component activities—such as driving, loading, sheeting and the like—by asking: What was the job on which he was engaged for his employer? and answering that question as a jury would.

Applying those words to the employment of [Mr Plenty], I think it is clear from the evidence that he was employed as a roundsman to drive his float round his round and to deliver milk, to collect empties and to obtain payment. That was his job. He was under an express prohibition—a matter to which I shall refer later—not to enlist the help of anyone doing that work. And he was also under an express prohibition not to give lifts on the float to anyone. How did he choose to carry out the task which I have analysed? He chose to disregard the prohibition and to enlist the assistance of the plaintiff. As a matter of common sense, that does seem to me to be a mode, albeit a prohibited mode, of doing the job with which he was entrusted. Why was the plaintiff being carried on the float when the accident occurred? Because it was necessary to take him from point to point so that he could assist in delivering milk, collecting empties and, on occasions, obtaining payment. The plaintiff was there because it was necessary that he should be there in order that he could assist, albeit in a way prohibited by the employers, in the job entrusted to [Mr Plenty] by his employers . . .

Now there was nothing of that sort [a prohibition on the sphere of employment] in the prohibition in this case. The prohibition is twofold: (1) that [Mr Plenty] was not to give lifts on his float; and (2) that he was not to employ others to help him in delivering the milk and so forth. There was nothing in those prohibitions which defined or limited the sphere of his employment. The sphere of his employment remained precisely the same after as before the prohibitions were brought to his notice. The sphere was as a roundsman to go round the rounds delivering milk, collecting empties and obtaining payment. Contrary to instructions, this roundsman chose to do what he was employed to do in an improper way. But the sphere of his employment was in no way affected by his express instructions . . .

Lawton LJ dissented.

Appeal allowed.

COMMENTARY

Where the employee acts contrary to an express prohibition by the employer, whether this takes them outside the course of their employment was traditionally said to depend upon the construction of the prohibition: 'there are prohibitions which limit the sphere of employment, and prohibitions which only deal with conduct within the sphere of employment' (*Plumb v Cobden Flour Mills Co Ltd* [1914] AC 62 at 67, per Lord Dunedin). The extracted case deals with the latter situation, but two earlier cases, distinguished by the majority, represent the former. In *Twine v Bean's Express Ltd* (1946) 175 LT 131, an employee driver was prohibited from allowing anyone to travel with him in his employer's van, but in breach of this prohibition gave a lift to T, who was killed as result of the driver's negligence. The Court of Appeal held that the employer was not liable for the negligence of its employee. Even though driving the van was clearly within the course of employment, giving a lift to another was equally clearly outside it. The second case is *Conway v George Wimpey & Co Ltd* [1951] 2 KB 266. The employee drove his employer's vehicle but with the express provision that it should only be used to provide transport for the employer's employees. However, it was common practice for other workers at the site to be given lifts by the drivers, although the employer did not know of this practice. Applying *Twine*, the Court of Appeal refused to hold the employer vicariously liable.

The line between some of these cases appears fine. In *Iqbal v London Transport Executive, The Times*, 6 June 1973, a bus conductor attempted to move a bus that was blocking the way of his bus, contrary to an express instruction that conductors should not drive buses. This action was held to fall outside his course of employment (see also *Beard v London General Omnibus Company* [1900] 2 QB 530). However, in *Ilkiw v Samuels* [1963] 1 WLR 991 a lorry driver had strict instructions from his employer not to allow the lorry to be driven by anybody else. The lorry had to be moved to make room for another lorry, and, notwithstanding his instructions, the driver allowed a workman to move it. The workman drove the lorry carelessly and the plaintiff was injured. The Court of Appeal held that the lorry driver had been negligent in allowing the workman to drive, and that this negligence arose in the course of his employment. He was employed to have charge and control of the lorry while engaged on the task, and the prohibition on allowing anyone else to drive was merely a prohibition on the mode of doing his job, disregard of which did not take the negligent act of driving outside the course of his employment. Would it have made any difference in *Iqbal* if, instead of acting of his own volition, the conductor had been asked by the driver to move the bus?

Although it is no longer required that the employee be acting for his employer's benefit to make the employer vicariously liable, the purpose of the employee's act is not irrelevant. As Lord Denning MR suggests in the extracted case, if the act is done for the employer's business it is usually done in the course of employment. But what is the 'master's benefit' in this context? The driver in *Conway v George Wimpey* (see earlier) was driving his lorry from one place to another for the benefit of his employer and would undoubtedly have been acting in the course of employment if his negligence had injured a pedestrian; yet he was held not to be acting in the course of employment *vis-à-vis* the unauthorised passenger who was injured. Conversely, in *Limpus v London General Omnibus Co* (1862) 1 H & C 526, 158 ER 993, an omnibus driver who obstructed a rival omnibus in contravention of his employer's stated wishes was nonetheless held to be acting for his employer's benefit (although the intense rivalry between omnibus companies at the time suggests that there may be more to the decision than meets the eye, especially as the London General Omnibus Company, founded as a French-controlled company, was perceived as being a foreign invader—for a fascinating account, see T. C. Barker and M. Robbins, *History of London Transport*, vol. 1 (London: Allen & Unwin, 1963), pp. 69–98). More generally, how can an act be for the employer's benefit if it has been expressly prohibited by the employer? Perhaps all that can be said is that, at various times and in various circumstances, judicial policy has pulled judges in different directions; hence the divergence in the case law. On the one hand, it seems unfair to hold an employer to what is effectively absolute liability where the employee acts contrary to instructions. On the other, as Willes J (at 539) noted in *Limpus*:

> It is well known that there is virtually no remedy against the driver of an omnibus, and therefore it is necessary that, for injury resulting from an act done by him in the course of his master's service, the master should be responsible; for there ought to be a remedy against some person capable of paying damages to those injured by improper driving . . .

Is this reasoning persuasive in the modern context of compulsory third party motor vehicle insurance?

Would the application of the 'close connection' test lead to different results in the above cases?

3. Employee's Use of Vehicles on Unauthorised Journeys

Smith v Stages [1989] AC 928

An employee was employed by the second defendant as a peripatetic lagger to install insulation at power stations. In August 1977 he was working on a power station in the English Midlands when he was taken off that job and sent with another employee, a Mr Stages, to carry out an urgent job on a power station in Wales. The two employees were paid eight hours' pay for the travelling time to Wales and eight hours' pay for the journey back, as well as the equivalent of the rail fare for the journey, although no stipulation was made as to the mode of travel. They travelled to Wales in Mr Stage's car and stayed there a week. At the end of the job, after working for twenty-four hours without a break in order to finish the job, they decided to drive straight back to the Midlands. On the way back the car, driven by Mr Stages, left the road and crashed through a brick wall. The employee was seriously injured and he brought an action against Mr Stages, who was uninsured, as well as the second defendant, whom he alleged was vicariously liable for Mr Stage's negligence. The employee subsequently died from unrelated causes and his widow continued the action on behalf of his estate. The trial judge held that the second defendant was not vicariously liable as Mr Stages had not been acting in the course of his employment when the accident happened, but this decision was reversed by the Court of Appeal. The second defendant appealed to the House of Lords.

Lord Goff

There are, however, circumstances in which, when a man is travelling to (or from) a place where he is doing a job for his employer, he will be held to be acting in the course of his employment. . . . So, if a man is employed to do jobs for his employer at various places during the day, such as a man who goes from door to door canvassing for business, or who distributes goods to customers, or who services equipment like washing machines or dishwashers, he will ordinarily be held to be acting in the course of his employment when travelling from one destination to another, and may also be held to do so when travelling from his home to his first destination and home again after his last. Again, it has been held that, in certain circumstances, a man who is called out from his home at night to deal with an emergency may be acting in the course of his employment when travelling from his home to his place of work to deal with the emergency: see *Blee v London and North Eastern Rly Co* [1938] AC 126. There are many other cases.

But how do we distinguish the cases in this category in which a man is acting in the course of his employment from those in which he is not? The answer is, I fear, that everything depends on the circumstances . . .

I approach the matter as follows. I do not regard this case as an ordinary case of travelling to work. It would be more accurate to describe it as a case where an employee, who has for a short time to work for his employers at a different place of work some distance away from his usual place of work, has to move from his ordinary base to a temporary base (here lodgings in Pembroke) from which he will travel to work at the temporary place of work each day. For the purpose of moving base, a normal working day was set aside for Mr Stages's journey, for which he was paid as for an eight-hour day. In addition to his day's pay he was given a travel allowance for his journey, and an allowance for his lodgings at his temporary base in Pembroke. In my opinion, in all the circumstances of the case, Mr Stages was required by the employers to make this journey, so as to make himself available to do his work at the Pembroke power station, and it would be proper to describe him as having been employed to do so. The fact that he was not required by his employer to make the journey by any particular means, nor even required to make it on the particular working day made available to him, does not detract from the proposition that he was employed to make the journey. Had Mr Stages wished, he could have driven down on the afternoon of Sunday 21 August, and have devoted the Monday to (for example) visiting friends near Pembroke. In such circumstances it could, I suppose, be said that Stages was not travelling 'in his employers' time'. But this would not matter; for the fact remains that the Monday, a normal working day, was made available for the journey, with full pay for that day to perform a task which he was required by the employers to perform.

I have it very much in mind that Mr Machin and Mr Stages were described by counsel for the employers as peripatetic laggers working at such sites as were available. This may well be an accurate description of their work. If so, their contracts of service may have provided at least an indication as to how far they would be acting in the course of their employment when changing from one power station to another. Indeed, accepting the description as correct, it is difficult to know how much weight to give to it in the absence of their contracts of service. However, the present case can in any event be differentiated on the basis that it was a departure from the norm in that it was concerned with a move to a temporary base to deal with an emergency, on the terms I have described.

I turn to Mr Stages's journey back. Another ordinary working day, Tuesday 30 August, was made available for the journey, with the same pay, to enable him to return to his base in the Midlands to be ready to travel to work on the Wednesday morning. In my opinion, he was employed to make the journey back, just as he was employed to make the journey out to Pembroke.

If he had chosen to go to sleep on the Monday morning and afternoon for eight hours or so, and then to drive home on the Monday evening so that he could have Tuesday free . . . that would not have detracted from the proposition that his journey was in the course of his employment. For this purpose, it was irrelevant that Monday was a bank holiday. Of course, it was wrong for him to succumb to the temptation of driving home on the Monday morning, just after he had completed so long a spell of work; but once again that cannot alter the fact that his journey was made in the course of his employment.

For these reasons, I would dismiss the appeal.

Lord Lowry

The paramount rule is that an employee travelling on the highway will be acting in the course of his employment if, and only if, he is at the material time going about his employer's business. One must not confuse the duty to turn up for one's work with the concept of already being 'on duty' while travelling to it.

It is impossible to provide for every eventuality and foolish, without the benefit of argument, to make the attempt, but some prima facie propositions may be stated with reasonable confidence.

(1) An employee travelling from his ordinary residence to his regular place of work, whatever the means of transport and even if it is provided by the employer, is not on duty and is not acting in the course of his employment, but, if he is obliged by his contract of service to use the employer's transport, he will normally, in the absence of an express condition to the contrary, be regarded as acting in the course of his employment while doing so.

(2) Travelling in the employer's time between workplaces (one of which may be the regular workplace) or in the course of a peripatetic occupation, whether accompanied by goods or tools or simply in order to reach a succession of workplaces (as an inspector of gas meters might do), will be in the course of the employment.

(3) Receipt of wages (though not receipt of a travelling allowance) will indicate that the employee is travelling in the employer's time and for his benefit and is acting in the course of his employment, and in such a case the fact that the employee may have discretion as to the mode and time of travelling will not take the journey out of the course of his employment.

(4) An employee travelling in the employer's time from his ordinary residence to a workplace other than this regular workplace or in the course of a peripatetic occupation or to the scene of an emergency (such as a fire, an accident or a mechanical breakdown of plant) will be acting in the course of his employment.

(5) A deviation from or interruption of a journey undertaken in the course of employment (unless the deviation or interruption is merely incidental to the journey) will for the time being (which may include an overnight interruption) take the employee out of the course of his employment.

(6) Return journeys are to be treated on the same footing as outward journeys.

All the foregoing propositions are subject to any express arrangements between the employer and the employee or those representing his interests. They are not, I would add, intended to define the position of salaried employees, with regard to whom the touchstone of payment made in the employer's time is not generally significant. . . .

Lord Keith, **Lord Brandon** and **Lord Griffiths** agreed with Lord Goff and Lord Lowry.

Appeal dismissed.

COMMENTARY

Particular problems have arisen in relation to passengers or bystanders injured by an employee driving a form of transport provided by the employer where the accident occurred in the course of an unauthorised detour taken by the employee. Although the cases are difficult to reconcile, whether the employer will be liable depends on the extent of the deviation from the authorised journey. As Parke B stated in *Joel v Morison* (1834) 6 C & P 501 at 503:

If he [the employee] was going out of his way, against his master's implied commands, when driving on his master's business, he will make his master liable; but if he was going on a frolic of his own, without being at all on his master's business, the master will not be liable . . .

The difference between a departure from the employer's implied command so as to make the employer liable and a 'frolic of one's own' is hard to identify, to say the least, and the cases only show how difficult it is to draw this distinction in practice (compare *Harvey v R G O'Dell* [1958] 2 QB 78—journey by workmen to get a meal during working hours was 'fairly incidental' to their work—with *Hilton v Burton (Rhodes) Ltd* [1961] 1 WLR 705—journey of the employees was seven or eight miles from their work site for tea after they had returned from lunch in a public house and the accident occurred on the return trip from the café; held not in the course of employment). See also *Nottingham v Aldridge* [1971] 2 QB 739.

4. Criminal Acts of the Employee

We saw previously in III.1 that cases of deliberate criminal conduct on the part of the employee raise particular difficulties when it comes to identifying the ambit of the employee's course of employment for the purposes of vicarious liability. Although the leading cases on this question (*Lister*, *Mohamud* and *Morrison Supermarkets*) are extracted and discussed in that section, there are many other cases on the issue, most of which concern assaults or sexual abuse by the employee.

In *Christian Brothers*, after analysing the cases where vicarious liability for sexual abuse was in issue, Lord Phillips said (at [86]):

> Vicarious liability is imposed where a defendant, whose relationship with the abuser put it in a position to use the abuser to carry on its business or to further its own interests, has done so in a manner which has created or significantly enhanced the risk that the victim or victims would suffer the relevant abuse.

In both *Lister* and *Christian Brothers* this idea of 'enterprise risk' (discussed in I) was identified as an important consideration when it came to the imposition of vicarious liability for deliberate wrongdoing, and the courts have attached much significance to it in recent cases, such as *Brayshaw v Partners of Apsley Surgery* [2019] 2 All ER 997, where it was held that a GP surgery was not vicariously liable for a locum GP having imposed his religious views on a patient (according to Martin Spencer J (at [69]) religious proselytization could not 'fairly be regarded as a reasonably incidental risk' of operating a doctors' surgery). Other possible factors to be taken into account when deciding whether deliberate wrongdoing is in the course of employment were suggested in *Bazley v Curry* (1999) 174 DLR (4th) 45 as being the extent to which the tort may have furthered the aims of the employer's enterprise; the extent to which friction, confrontation or intimacy between employees and the potential victims of their torts was inherent in the enterprise; the amount of power which employees had over potential victims by reason of their employment; and the level of vulnerability of potential victims to that power. Even with guidelines, however, it may be doubted whether the outcomes of cases can be predicted with any certainty. For example, in the companion case to *Bazley*, *Jacobi v Griffiths* (1999) 174 DLR (4th) 71, a majority of the Supreme Court of Canada refused to hold an employer, who ran a non-profit organisation which provided behaviour guidance and promoted the health and social, educational, vocational and character development of boys and girls, vicariously liable for the acts of its employee. Unlike in *Bazley*, where the sexual abuse had taken place in the home run by the employer, the sexual assaults took place outside working hours and working premises, so that the temporal and geographical aspects of the close connection test (see further in III.1) told against vicarious liability.

Prior to *Lister*, employers had generally been held vicariously liable for assaults by their employees only when the assault had been intended to promote the employer's interests, as opposed to being an act of personal vengeance (compare *Poland v John Parr* [1927] 1 KB 236 with *Warren v Henlys Ltd* [1948] 2 All ER 932). However, in the post-*Lister* case of *Mattis v Pollock* [2003] 1 WLR 2158 the Court of Appeal held that an employer was liable for an assault by a nightclub doorman on a patron, despite the fact that the doorman had gone home to pick up a knife before returning to the club to avenge an earlier altercation, so that his conduct was clearly a private act of vengeance which was not motivated by a desire to serve his employer's interests. The same was true in *Mohamud*, where Lord Toulson said, at [48], that Mr Khan's motives were 'neither here nor there'. These cases suggest that private acts of vengeance may now fall within the course of employment provided there is a close enough connection between the tortious conduct and the employment, although it remains to be seen whether this more expansive approach survives the decision in *Morrison Supermarkets*, where Lord Reed described the employee's motive as 'highly material' (at [31]) and cited with approval Lord Nicholls' distinction between an employee who was 'engaged, however misguidedly, in furthering his employer's business' and an employee who was 'engaged solely in pursuing his own interests' (*Dubai Aluminium Co Ltd v Salaam* [2003] 2 AC 366 at [32]). (On the application of these principles to assaults by police officers, see *Winfield & Jolowicz*, para. 21–034.)

In *Mattis v Pollock* and in *Gravil v Carroll* [2008] ICR 1222, where a rugby club was held vicariously liable for a punch by one of its players which caused serious injury to a member of the opposing team, it can be argued that the close connection test was satisfied because 'the use of reasonable force or the existence of friction [was] inherent in the nature of the employment': *Graham v Commercial Bodyworks Ltd* [2015] ICR 665 at [16], per Longmore LJ. (For another example, see *Brown v Robinson* [2004] UKPC 56, involving a security guard at a football stadium; and on vicarious liability in the sporting context, see generally P. Morgan, 'Vicarious Liability and the Beautiful Game: Liability for Professional and Amateur Footballers?' (2018) 38 LS 242.) But this was not the case in *Mohamud*, where Lord Toulson described Mr Khan's job, at [3], as 'to see that the petrol pumps and the kiosk were kept in good running order and to serve customers', and where (according to Treacy LJ in the Court of Appeal in the case) Mr Khan's 'instructions were not to engage in any form of confrontation with a customer, even an angry one' ([2014] 2 All ER 990 at [35]). In his consideration of the close connection issue in *Mohamud*, Lord Toulson instead focused on the fact that Mr Khan had told the claimant never to come back to the petrol station, but as we have seen, it is hard to accept his Lordship's claim, at [47], that in giving this order 'he was purporting to act about his employer's business'.

The operation of the close connection test in cases of intentional assaults by co-workers has produced mixed results, though in most such cases—both north and south of the border—vicarious liability has not been imposed: see *Wilson v Exel UK Ltd* 2010 SLT 671 (no vicarious liability for action of a male supervisor who pulled a female employee's ponytail in horseplay); *Weddall v Barchester Healthcare Ltd* [2012] IRLR 307 (different results reached on the close connection test in two appeals involving assaults on co-workers); *Vaickuviene v J Sainsbury plc* 2014 SC 147 (no vicarious liability for racist murder of a co-employee during working hours); cf. *Bellman v Northampton Recruitment Ltd* [2019] 1 All ER 1133, where vicarious liability was imposed for an assault by the defendant company's managing director on the claimant employee during late night drinks following the company's Christmas party, it being considered significant that the trigger for the attack was a comment of the claimant during a discussion of work matters in which the assailant had sought to assert his authority over the employees present. (However, Irwin LJ was at pains to emphasise, at [37], how unusual the facts of *Bellman* were, and how limited the parallels to the case would be.) Vicarious liability is also unlikely to arise where a prank played on a co-worker goes wrong: see, e.g., *Graham v Commercial Bodyworks Ltd* [2015] ICR 665; *Chell v Tarmac Cement and Lime Ltd* [2022] EWCA Civ 7.

Many of the leading cases on vicarious liability in recent times concern child abuse, and considerable guidance as to the operation of the close connection test in this context is provided by the *Lister* decision (extracted in III.1) in particular. *Lister* suggests that it will generally be straightforward to demonstrate a sufficient connection between child abuse and employment where the employer was entrusted with the care of the child and delegated that duty to the employee who perpetrated the abuse (see in particular [2002] 1 AC 215 at [45], per Lord Clyde). This was indeed the fact pattern in *Lister* itself, and also in *Armes v Nottinghamshire County Council* [2018] AC 355 (see II.3), where it was conceded that there was a close connection between abuse of a child in care by foster parents and the relationship between the foster parents and the local authority which had entrusted them with the child's care. Even when this fact pattern is not precisely replicated, vicarious liability may arise if the abuser was placed in a position of authority over the victim of abuse, as in the *Christian Brothers* case (see II.3), concerning the relationship between teaching members of a religious order and their pupils. Another case along these lines is *Maga v Birmingham Roman Catholic Archdiocese Trustees* [2010] 1 WLR 1441, where the defendant Roman Catholic archdiocese was held liable for the sexual abuse of the claimant by one of its priests. Although neither the claimant nor his parents were Catholics, he had met the priest at events that were organised by the priest and open to non-Catholics, and the Court of Appeal considered that the priest's pastoral duties, which included youth work in the general community, were sufficient for him to be considered equivalent to a parent or carer for those who attended these events. *Maga* was arguably a borderline case, and the decision is criticised by Giliker (2010) 126 LQR 521. See also *The Trustees of the Barry Congregation of Jehovah's Witnesses v BXB* [2021] 4 WLR 42 (hereafter '*BXB*'), where a religious organisation's conferral of authority on one of its elders sufficed to make it vicariously liable when he abused that authority by raping an adult member of his congregation.

It was made clear in *Lister* that the mere fact that the employment gave the employee the opportunity to carry out the abuse is not sufficient to establish the requisite close connection, so that, for example, one would not ordinarily expect vicarious liability to arise in respect of abuse by a gardener or cook working in a school or care home, even if resident in the institution (see also *Morrison Supermarkets* at [35]; cf. the surprising concession to the contrary in *JXJ v The Province of Great Britain of the Institute of Brothers of the Christian Schools* [2020] ELR 579, which concerned abuse of boys in a boarding school by a gardener/nightwatchman). In *Prince Alfred College Inc v ADC* (2016) 258 CLR 134 at [81], the High Court of Australia drew upon this analysis to propound a distinction between cases where the employment relationship provided the 'occasion' for the commission of the tort and those where it merely provided the 'opportunity' for it:

> [T]he relevant approach is to consider any special role that the employer has assigned to the employee and the position in which the employee is thereby placed vis-à-vis the victim. In determining whether the apparent performance of such a role may be said to give the 'occasion' for the wrongful act, particular features may be taken into account. They include authority, power, trust, control and the ability to achieve intimacy with the victim.

On the relevance of the role in which the employee is placed to the question of vicarious liability for criminal acts, see further Giliker, 'Making the Right Connection: Vicarious Liability and Institutional Philosophy' (2009) 17 TLJ 35.

In *Morrison Supermarkets* Lord Reed said that in cases concerning the sexual abuse of children 'a more tailored version of the close connection test' than the general course of employment test has been used, and that the courts have emphasised the importance of factors particularly relevant to this form of wrongdoing, 'such as the employer's conferral of authority on the employee over the victims, which he has abused' (at [23]). If his Lordship was suggesting that in this context vicarious liability may arise even though the tort is not within the course of employment then that is hard to square with *Lister*, where that was clearly still considered to be the governing concept. Brodie (2020) 24 Edin L Rev 389 at 393 questions whether any rigid bifurcation between abuse cases and other cases is desirable, and hazards that 'some very tricky demarcation issues will arise'. Would, for example, a special approach adopted for sexual abuse of children also encompass non-sexual physical abuse or psychological abuse, and might it also apply to sexual abuse of an adult? (For an affirmative answer to the last question, see *BXB*, though note the caveat at [96].) Nevertheless, there is no denying that in child abuse cases the courts have emphasised 'the importance of criteria that are particularly relevant to this form of wrong' (*Christian Brothers* [2013] 2 AC 1 at [83], per Lord Phillips) and, for example, the distinction employed in other types of case between conduct in furtherance of the employer's interests and purely self-interested conduct is not drawn in this context, where its effect would be to prevent vicarious liability from ever arising.

IV. Non-delegable Duty of Care

1. Introduction

In certain circumstances a person who employs another to do a task may be held personally, not vicariously, liable for the negligent performance of the task by that other person. Personal liability of this kind is usually based on the imposition of a non-delegable duty of care on the employer in respect of the activity in question, and arises irrespective of whether the person employed to carry out the task is an employee or an independent contractor. A duty of this kind is not just a duty to take care, but a duty *to ensure that care is taken* (see the decision of the Court of Appeal in *Woodland v Swimming Teachers Association* [2014] AC 537 at [5], per Laws LJ). This offers a significant advantage to claimants injured in, for example, a hospital setting, since they need show only that someone involved in their care was negligent for liability to attach to the hospital authorities: it is not necessary for them to establish who that person was.

Duties of this kind are described as 'non-delegable' because although the performance of the task to which the duty of care attaches can be delegated to a third party, the duty itself cannot, with the result that the employer is liable if the task is not properly performed by the third party, even if he exercised reasonable care in selecting that person. As Lord Wright stated in *Wilsons and Clyde Coal Co Ltd v English* [1938] AC 57 at 81, '[i]t is the obligation which is personal to him, and not the performance'. The result is that the person under the non-delegable duty takes the risk of negligence on the part of employees, or even independent contractors, whom they appoint to perform the task subject to the duty.

One critic of the non-delegable duty concept called it 'a disguised form of vicarious liability' (*Fleming*, p. 433), and J. Morgan, 'Vicarious Liability for Independent Contractors?' (2015)

31 PN 235 at 235 has described the two concepts as 'functionally identical'. That being so, Morgan argues, it may be better to call a spade a spade, and to replace the non-delegable duty concept with open recognition of the application of vicarious liability to independent contractors, though he concludes that whether this is appropriate may well depend on the particular context (see also J. Morgan, 'Liability for Independent Contractors in Contract and Tort' [2015] CLJ 109 at 133–7; and Plunkett, 'Taking Stock of Vicarious Liability' (2016) 132 LQR 556 at 559–60). A possible objection to such an extension of vicarious liability is that the non-delegable duty analysis latches on to a particular task that is assigned by the employer (or should we, following *Weir*, p. 315, say 'the customer'?) to the contractor, and the 'course of employment' criterion used to delineate the extent of an employer's vicarious liability may not work as well in a case of this kind. Then again, there is authority that a non-delegable duty only extends to negligence by the independent contractor in carrying out the task entrusted to them, and does not extend to 'collateral negligence' (see, e.g., *Woodland* at [23], per Lord Sumption), a rule which, as *Salmond & Heuston* (p. 466) point out, may simply be an obscure way of saying that an employer is liable only for acts which are within the 'scope of the contractor's authority', a concept with obvious echoes of the 'course of employment' requirement.

Other commentators have emphasised the differences between vicarious liability and liability for non-delegable duties. For example, liability for a non-delegable duty does not require that the person to whom the task has been delegated commit a tort (only that they are at fault), while vicarious liability does not require the employer to owe an independent duty of care to the victim (see R. Stevens, 'Non-Delegable Duties and Vicarious Liability' and J. Murphy, 'Juridical Foundations of Common Law Non-Delegable Duties', both in J. Neyers, E. Chamberlain and S. Pitel (eds), *Emerging Issues in Tort Law* (Oxford: Hart, 2007)). And certainly the conventional view of vicarious liability and non-delegable duty is that they are separate concepts, as reflected in Lord Reed's remark in *Armes v Nottinghamshire County Council* [2018] AC 355 at [50] that they are 'two distinct legal doctrines with different incidents and different rationales'.

Non-delegable duty must be distinguished from accessory liability, another form of primary liability, which extends to those who conspire with, procure, authorise or induce another to commit a tort, and also to those who have joined in a common design pursuant to which the tort was committed (*Crédit Lyonnais Bank Nederland NV v Export Credit Guarantee Corporation* [2000] 1 AC 486; Carty (1999) 19 LS 489). An example of the 'common design' form of accessory liability is *Brooke v Bool* [1928] 2 KB 578, where the defendant requested M to help him search for a gas leak. M did this by illuminating a gas pipe with a naked flame, causing an explosion. The defendant had previously searched a lower part of the pipe in this way. One ground on which the defendant was held liable was that M's tortious negligence was committed as part of a joint enterprise with the defendant. The leading case on 'common design' is now *Fish & Fish Ltd v Sea Shepherd UK* [2015] AC 1229. For further discussion of accessory liability in tort, see P. S. Davies, *Accessory Liability* (Oxford: Hart, 2015), ch. 6; J. Dietrich and P. Ridge, *Accessories in Private Law* (Cambridge: CUP, 2015), ch. 5.

2. Traditional Categories of Non-delegable Duty

'Tortious liabilities based not on personal fault but on a duty to ensure that care is taken are exceptional, and have to be kept within reasonable limits' (*Armes* at [32], per Lord Reed). One historically significant category of non-delegable duty case relates to the performance of extra-hazardous activities. Writing in 1956, Williams described this category as follows ('Liability for Independent Contractors' [1956] CLJ 180 at 186):

> [T]here is now vicarious liability wherever a contractor is employed to perform what Slesser LJ in *Honeywill & Stein v Larkin Bros* [1934] 1 KB 102 called 'extra-hazardous or dangerous operations'. The liability was held in that case to exist where a photographer was employed to take a flashlight picture in a theatre, the magnesium flash causing a fire in which the theatre suffered damage. It seems rather remarkable to regard the taking of an indoor photograph, even with magnesium powder, as 'extra-hazardous or dangerous'; of course it would be dangerous if performed negligently, but is that fact sufficient to create liability for contractors? The equation of 'extra-hazardous' and 'dangerous' is also worthy of remark. One would think that 'hazardous' and 'dangerous' are synonyms; if so, 'extra-hazardous' must mean something specially dangerous. Even if one goes so far as to say that the use of flashlight powder is 'dangerous', it is hyperbolical to describe it as 'extra-hazardous'. If this is extra-hazardous, we are left with no language to describe really dangerous conduct . . .

Williams was highly critical of the concept of 'extra-hazardous acts', which he argued 'was not a suitable one for legal rules'. The unsatisfactory nature of a non-delegable duty for extra-hazardous activities led the Court of Appeal in *Biffa Waste Services Ltd v Maschinenfabrik Ernst Hese GMBH* [2009] QB 725 to hold that its application should be kept as narrow as possible and applied only to activities that are exceptionally dangerous whatever precautions are taken (a test which the Singapore Court of Appeal said in *Ng Huat Seng v Munib Mohammad Madni* [2017] 2 SLR 1074 did not encompass minor demolition works, but which might be satisfied where explosives or extremely hazardous chemicals were used for some legitimate purpose). Furthermore, in the leading modern authority on non-delegable duties, *Woodland v Swimming Teachers Association* [2014] AC 537 (extracted in the next section), Lord Sumption, at [6], was markedly unenthusiastic about the extra-hazardous activity category, saying that many of the decisions were 'founded on arbitrary distinctions between ordinary and extraordinary hazards which may be ripe for re-examination' (cf. *Ng Huat Seng*, where the Singapore Court of Appeal defended the category as narrowly defined in the *Biffa Waste Services* case). Commenting on *Biffa Waste Services*, Stanton (2009) 17 Tort L Rev 9 at 12 noted:

> *Honeywill* is confined to the rare (and probably non-existent) category of cases in relation to which proper precautions fail to reduce the risk below that of being 'exceptionally dangerous'. It thus becomes arguable that, to take an extreme example, conducting maintenance work on a nuclear reactor is not an extra-hazardous activity such as would invoke the *Honeywill* principle because proper precautions can be taken which eliminate or minimize the risks. In essence, *Honeywill* has been distinguished out of existence rather than being overruled.

A less controversial application of non-delegable duties relates to fires. As long ago as 1401 it was held that the occupier of land was responsible for a fire lit by themselves, their servants or their guests (see Ch 11.III.5). *Baker* postulates that the standard of liability may well have varied from one type of case to another, observing that '[f]ire was particularly feared in a world of timber-framed buildings' (p. 435). Whether the reasons for the rule still apply is arguable, but it was affirmed, at least implicitly, by the Court of Appeal in *Gore v Stannard (t/a Wyvern Tyres)* [2014] QB 1. In *Balfour v Barty King* [1957] 1 QB 496 the defendant employed independent contractors to unfreeze some pipes, but they did so negligently with the result that a fire was started which damaged the plaintiff's adjoining premises. Even though the contractors were not employed to light a fire (indeed the negligence consisted in using a blow-torch in close proximity to flammable material), the Court of Appeal held the defendant liable for the contractor's negligence in starting a fire. Would the same result have been reached if, in attempting to unfreeze the pipes, the contractors had negligently caused them to burst, flooding the claimant's property. If so, why?

The most important category of non-delegable duty in modern times is the non-delegable duty owed by an employer in respect of the safety of his employees. This form of non-delegable duty arose as a way of avoiding the harsh consequences of the 'common employment' rule, according to which an employer was not in general vicariously liable to one employee for damage resulting from the negligence of another. That rule was abolished by statute in 1948 (Law Reform (Personal Injuries) Act 1948, s. 1; see *Mitchell*, ch. 8), but the idea of the employer's personal and non-delegable duty remains.

Although the employer's duty of care is non-delegable, it is limited to the tasks that attract the non-delegable duty in the first place, such as the provision of work equipment. In *Davie v New Merton Board Mills Ltd* [1959] AC 604, the plaintiff maintenance fitter suffered an eye injury because a tool which had been provided for his use by his employers (the defendants), although apparently in good condition, was of excessive hardness and therefore dangerous. The tool (called a 'drift', and similar to a chisel) had been negligently manufactured by reputable makers, who had sold it in turn to a reputable firm of suppliers; they had sold it to the employers, whose system of maintenance and inspection was not at fault. The plaintiff claimed damages for negligence against his employers on the ground that they had supplied him with a defective tool. He succeeded at trial, but that decision was reversed by the Court of Appeal, and an appeal from that decision was dismissed by the House of Lords. According to Viscount Simonds ([1959] AC 604 at 625):

> The employer, it was said, was under a duty to take reasonable care to supply his workmen with proper plant and machinery. It was assumed that this included tools such as drifts, and I, too, will, without deciding it, assume it. It was then said that the employer could not escape responsibility by employing a third party, however expert, to do his duty for him. So far, so good . . . But then comes the next step—but I would rather call it a jump, and a jump that would unhorse any rider. Therefore, it was said, the employer is responsible for the defect in goods that he buys in the market, if it can be shown that that defect was due to the want of skill or care on the part of anyone who was concerned in its manufacture. But, my Lords, by what use or misuse of language can the manufacturer be said to be a person to whom the employer delegated a duty which it was for him to perform? How can it be said that it was as the delegate or agent of the employer that the manufacturer failed to exhibit due skill and care? It is, to my mind, clear that he cannot . . .

Davie may be contrasted with the decision in *Taylor v Rover Co Ltd* [1966] 1 WLR 1491, where the employer was held liable for failure to withdraw a tool (a chisel) after it had become broken and dangerous. What is the material difference between the two cases? (Note that the narrow *ratio decidendi* of the House of Lords in *Davie* was effectively reversed by the Employer's Liability (Defective Equipment) Act 1969, which deems an employer to be personally at fault where an employee suffers personal injury in the course of their employment as a result of a defect in equipment provided by their employer for the purposes of the employer's business, and the defect is attributable wholly or partly to the fault of a third party; see further on the 1969 Act, Lang (1984) 47 MLR 48.)

In *Sumner v William Henderson & Sons Ltd* [1964] 1 QB 450 (reversed on different grounds at [1963] 1 WLR 823), the plaintiff's wife had been killed in a fire in the department store in which she worked; the store was undergoing extension and modernisation, and it appeared that the fire resulted from a fault in the electrical cable that had been laid down. Addressing certain preliminary questions raised by the case, Phillimore J held (following *Davie*) that the employers could not be held liable for any fault on the part of the manufacturers of the cable, but (distinguishing *Davie*) that they could be held liable for the negligence of those supervising or carrying out the work, including the electrical contractors engaged to install the wiring; the contractors were acting as the employers' delegates. The case would have been decided differently if the fault had been in the cable they were installing rather than in their execution of that task.

The issue of the employer's non-delegable duty of care was considered in the following case.

McDermid v Nash Dredging & Reclamation Co Ltd [1987] AC 906

The plaintiff lost his leg while working on a tug (the *Ina*) owned by Stevin, the Dutch parent company of the defendants, Nash. The plaintiff was an employee of Nash, which had instructed him to work on the *Ina*. The accident occurred when, as the plaintiff tried to untie the *Ina* from its mooring alongside a dredger, the tug's master, a Captain Sas, moved the vessel without waiting for the plaintiff to give the agreed signal by knocking twice on the side of the wheelhouse to indicate that the ropes were safely on board (the 'double knock system'). The plaintiff's leg was caught up in the ropes, resulting in his injuries.

Lord Hailsham of St Marylebone

The plaintiff's claim in the proceedings was based on the allegation, *inter alia*, of a 'non-delegable' duty resting on his employers to take reasonable care to provide a 'safe system of work'. . . . The defendants did not, and could not, dispute the existence of such a duty of care, nor that it was 'non-delegable' in the special sense in which the phrase is used in this connection . . . Equally the defendants could not and did not attempt to dispute that it would be a central and crucial feature of any safe system on the instant facts that it would prevent so far as possible the occurrence of such an accident as actually happened, *viz.* injury to the plaintiff as the result of the use of the *Ina*'s engine so as to move the *Ina* before both the ropes were clear of the dredger and stowed safely inboard and the plaintiff was in a position of safety.

Since such a system could easily have been designed and put in operation at the time of the accident in about half-a-dozen different ways, and since it is quite obvious that such a system would have prevented the accident had it been in operation, and since the duty to provide it was 'non-delegable' in the sense that the defendants cannot escape liability by claiming to have delegated performance of their duty, it is a little difficult to see what possible defence there could ever have been to these proceedings . . .

Although the duty of providing a safe system of work was 'non-delegable' in the special sense I have described, it had in fact been delegated on alternate shifts to Captain Sas and Captain Clifford in the circumstances I have described. In both cases the delegation covered, so far as can be ascertained, the whole operation of the *Ina*, the orders to the deckhand, the system of work to be followed and, since the skipper was at the wheel, the operation of the engine . . . [T]he defendants had delegated their duty to the plaintiff to Captain Sas, the duty had not been performed, and the defendants must pay for the breach of their 'non-delegable' obligation.

Lord Brandon of Oakbrook

A statement of the relevant principle of law can be divided into three parts. First, an employer owes to his employee a duty to exercise reasonable care to ensure that the system of work provided for him is a safe one. Secondly, the provision of a safe system of work has two aspects: (a) the devising of such a system and (b) the operation of it. Thirdly, the duty concerned has been described alternatively as either personal or non-delegable. The meaning of these expressions is not self-evident and needs explaining. The essential characteristic of the duty is that, if it is not performed, it is no defence for the employer to show that he delegated its performance to a person, whether his servant or not his servant, whom he reasonably believed to be competent to perform it. Despite such delegation the employer is liable for the non-performance of the duty.

In the present case the relevant system of work in relation to the plaintiff was the system for unmooring the tug *Ina*. In the events which occurred the defendants delegated both the devising and the operating of such system to Captain Sas, who was not their servant. An essential feature of such system, if it was to be a safe one, was that Captain Sas would not work the tug's engines ahead or astern until he knew that the plaintiff had completed his work of unmooring the tug. The system which Captain Sas devised was one under which the plaintiff would let him know that he had completed that work by giving two knocks on the outside of the wheelhouse . . . [O]n the occasion of the plaintiff's accident, Captain Sas did not operate that system. He negligently failed to operate it in that he put the tug's engines astern at a time when the plaintiff had not given, and he, Captain Sas, could not therefore have heard, the prescribed signal of two knocks by the plaintiff on the outside of the wheelhouse. For this failure by Captain Sas to operate the system which he had devised, the defendants, as the plaintiff's employers, are personally, not vicariously, liable to him.

Lord Bridge, **Lord Mackay** and **Lord Ackner** concurred.

Defendant's appeal dismissed.

COMMENTARY

Liability here was based on the employer's non-delegable duty to provide a safe system of work. The decision broke new ground by imposing liability on the employer where there was a failure to use a system that was supposed to be used, rather than a failure to adopt any system at all (see McKendrick (1990) 53 MLR 770 at 773–4, questioning this extension on the ground that it is easier for the employer to control the provision of a system than its operation). A plausible explanation of the decision is that, as the master of the tug was in charge of the plaintiff's workplace, he could for that reason be regarded as the employer's delegate. *McDermid* was followed in *Johnson v Coventry Churchill International Ltd* [1992] 3 All ER 14, where the plaintiff had been sent to work in West Germany by the defendant employers, an agency which recruited British personnel to work worldwide. While engaged on a construction site, the plaintiff suffered injury when a rotten plank gave way under his weight as he entered the site by means of a makeshift bridge. Deputy Judge J. W. Kay QC held that there was a clear failure to provide a safe means of access to the plaintiff's place of employment as no adequate system of inspection was in place. He stated (at 22): 'I do not think that it is necessary for me to find that there was something that the defendants could have done themselves about it since the onus is on them to ensure a safe means of access and no steps were taken by them to that end.' A reason for placing a non-delegable duty on the employer was that 'the plaintiff . . . had, and could have had, no means of judging in advance the measure of safety in force at the place where he was sent to work. It was, therefore, incumbent on the defendants as his employers to ensure a safe system of work' (*ibid.*).

3. A General Principle?

The courts have struggled to identify a common thread or explanation for the various circumstances in which a non-delegable duty of care has been held to exist. The most recent, and most comprehensive, attempt to provide such a judicial rationalisation came in the next extracted case.

Woodland v Swimming Teachers Association [2014] AC 537

The claimant was a girl of 10 who had suffered a serious brain injury during a swimming class. Although the claimant attended the class as part of her school programme, during normal school hours, the class was not provided by her school but by a Mrs Stopford, an independent contractor who had contracted with the local education authority to provide swimming lessons to the school's pupils. The only persons on the premises who were responsible for the conduct of the class (a swimming teacher, Ms Burlinson, and a lifeguard, Ms Maxwell) were not employees of the school, but (probably) of Mrs Stopford. One way in which the claimant attempted to make the school liable was to allege that the school was under a non-delegable duty of care to ensure her safety while at the pool, and that this duty had been breached by virtue of the negligence of Ms Burlinson and Ms Maxwell. This part of the claim was struck out as unarguable by the trial judge [2011] EWHC 2631 (QB), and the Court of Appeal (Laws LJ dissenting) upheld the decision of the trial judge on this issue: [2014] AC 537. The claimant appealed to the Supreme Court.

Lord Sumption

Non-delegable duties

3. In principle, liability in tort depends on proof of a personal breach of duty. To that principle, there is at common law only one true exception, namely vicarious liability. Where a defendant is vicariously liable for the tort of another, he commits no tort himself and may not even owe the relevant duty, but is held liable as a matter of public policy for the tort of the other: *Majrowski v Guy's* and *St Thomas's NHS Hospital Trust* [2007] 1 AC 224. The boundaries of vicarious liability have been expanded by recent decisions of the courts to embrace tortfeasors who are not employees of the defendant, but stand in a relationship which is sufficiently analogous to employment: *Various Claimants v Catholic Child Welfare Society* [2013] 2 AC 1. But it has never extended to the negligence of those who are truly independent contractors, such as Mrs Stopford appears to have been in this case.

4. The issue on this appeal is, however, nothing to do with vicarious liability, except in the sense that it only arises because there is none. On the footing that the local authority was not vicariously liable for the negligence of Mrs Stopford, Ms Burlinson or Ms Maxwell, the question is what was the scope of the authority's duty to pupils in its care. Was it a duty to take reasonable care in the performance of the functions entrusted to it, so far as it performed those functions itself, through its own employees? Or was it a duty to procure that reasonable care was taken in their performance by whomever it might get to perform them? On either view, any liability of the education authority for breach of it is personal, not vicarious.

5. The law of negligence is generally fault-based. Generally speaking, a defendant is personally liable only for doing negligently that which he does at all, or for omissions which are in reality a negligent way of doing that which he does at all. The law does not in the ordinary course impose personal (as opposed to vicarious) liability for what others do or fail to do . . .

The expression 'non-delegable duty' has become the conventional way of describing those cases in which the ordinary principle is displaced and the duty extends beyond being careful, to procuring the careful performance of work delegated to others.

6. English law has long recognised that non-delegable duties exist, but it does not have a single theory to explain when or why. There are, however, two broad categories of case in which such a duty has been held to arise. The first is a large, varied and anomalous class of cases in which the defendant employs an independent contractor to perform some function which is either inherently hazardous or liable to become so in the course of his work . . . Many of these decisions are founded on arbitrary distinctions between ordinary and extraordinary hazards which may be ripe for re-examination. Their justification, if there is one, should probably be found in a special public policy for operations involving exceptional danger to the public. But their difficulties do not need to be considered further on these appeals, because teaching children to swim, while it unquestionably involves risks and calls for precautions, is not on any view an 'extra-hazardous' activity . . .

7. The second category of non-delegable duty is, however, directly in point. It comprises cases where the common law imposes a duty on the defendant which has three critical characteristics. First, it arises not from the negligent character of the act itself but because of an antecedent relationship between the defendant and the claimant. Second, the duty is a positive or affirmative duty to protect a particular class of persons against a particular class of risks, and not simply a duty to refrain from acting in a way that foreseeably causes injury. Third, the duty is by virtue of that relationship personal to the defendant. The work required to perform such a duty may well be delegable, and usually is. But the duty itself remains the defendant's. Its delegation makes no difference to his legal responsibility for the proper performance of a duty which is in law his own. In these cases, the defendant is assuming a liability analogous to that assumed by a person who contracts to do work carefully. The contracting party will normally be taken to contract that the work will be done carefully by whomever he may get to do it: see *Photo Production Ltd v Securicor Transport Ltd* [1980] AC 827, 848 (Lord Diplock). The analogy with public services is often close, especially in the domain of hospital treatment in the National Health Service or education at a local education authority school, where only the absence of consideration distinguishes them from the private hospital or the fee-paying school performing the same functions under contract . . .

Assumption of responsibility

11. The duty to which Lord Blackburn was referring [in *Hughes v Percival* (1883) 8 App Cas 443 at 445–6] would today be regarded as arising from an assumption of responsibility imputed to the defendant by virtue of the special character of his relationship with the claimant. The concept of an assumption of responsibility is usually relevant in the law of negligence as a tool for determining whether a duty of care is owed to protect against a purely economic loss. There is no doubt in this case that the education authority owed a duty of care to its pupils to protect them from injury. But the concept of assumption of responsibility is relevant to determine its scope, whether the potential loss is economic or physical. The circumstances must be such that the defendant can be taken not just to have assumed a positive duty, but to have assumed responsibility for the exercise of due care by anyone to whom he may delegate its performance. This is a markedly more onerous obligation. What are the circumstances in which a person may be taken to have assumed it? They have been considered in a number of cases involving injuries sustained by employees, hospital patients, school pupils and invitees, at the hands of persons working for the defendant for whom the defendant was not vicariously liable.

12. There are a number of situations where by virtue of some special relationship the defendant is held to assume positive duties . . . It does not, however, follow from the mere

existence of a positive duty that it is personal to the defendant so as to make it non-delegable. In the nuisance or quasi-nuisance cases, the personal character of the duty results, as I have pointed out, from the fact it arises from the defendant's occupation of the land from which the hazard originates. In other cases, the personal character of the duty must be derived from something else. Both principle and authority suggest that the relevant factors are the vulnerability of the claimant, the existence of a relationship between the claimant and the defendant by virtue of which the latter has a degree of protective custody over him, and the delegation of that custody to another person . . .

In what circumstances will a non-delegable duty arise?
22. The main problem about this area of the law is to prevent the exception from eating up the rule. Non-delegable duties of care are inconsistent with the fault-based principles on which the law of negligence is based, and are therefore exceptional. The difference between an ordinary duty of care and a non-delegable duty must therefore be more than a question of degree. In particular, the question cannot depend simply on the degree of risk involved in the relevant activity. The ordinary principles of tortious liability are perfectly capable of answering the question what duty is an appropriate response to a given level of risk.

23. . . . If the highway and hazard cases are put to one side, the remaining cases are characterised by the following defining features: (1) The claimant is a patient or a child, or for some other reason is especially vulnerable or dependent on the protection of the defendant against the risk of injury. Other examples are likely to be prisoners and residents in care homes. (2) There is an antecedent relationship between the claimant and the defendant, independent of the negligent act or omission itself, (i) which places the claimant in the actual custody, charge or care of the defendant, and (ii) from which it is possible to impute to the defendant the assumption of a positive duty to protect the claimant from harm, and not just a duty to refrain from conduct which will foreseeably damage the claimant. It is characteristic of such relationships that they involve an element of control over the claimant, which varies in intensity from one situation to another, but is clearly very substantial in the case of schoolchildren. (3) The claimant has no control over how the defendant chooses to perform those obligations, ie whether personally or through employees or through third parties. (4) The defendant has delegated to a third party some function which is an integral part of the positive duty which he has assumed towards the claimant; and the third party is exercising, for the purpose of the function thus delegated to him, the defendant's custody or care of the claimant and the element of control that goes with it. (5) The third party has been negligent not in some collateral respect but in the performance of the very function assumed by the defendant and delegated by the defendant to him.

24. In *A (A Child) v Ministry of Defence* [2005] QB 183, para 47 Lord Phillips of Worth Matravers MR, delivering the leading judgment in the Court of Appeal, suggested that 'hitherto a non-delegable duty has only been found in a situation where the claimant suffers an injury while in an environment over which the defendant has control.' This is undoubtedly a fundamental feature of those cases where, in the absence of a relevant antecedent relationship, the defendant has been held liable for inherently hazardous operations or dangers on the public highway. But I respectfully disagree with the view that control of the environment in which injury is caused is an essential element in the kind of case with which we are presently concerned. The defendant is not usually in control of the environment in which injury is caused by an independent contractor. That is why as a general rule he is not liable for the contractor's negligence. Where a non-delegable duty arises, the defendant is liable not because he has control but in spite of the fact that he may have none. The essential element in my view is not control of the environment in which the claimant is injured, but control over the claimant for the purpose of performing a function for which the defendant has assumed responsibility . . .

25. The courts should be sensitive about imposing unreasonable financial burdens on those providing critical public services. A non-delegable duty of care should be imputed to schools only so far as it would be fair, just and reasonable to do so. But I do not accept that any unreasonable burden would be cast on them by recognising the existence of a non-delegable duty on the criteria which I have summarised above. My reasons are as follows.

(1) The criteria themselves are consistent with the long-standing policy of the law, apparent notably in the employment cases, to protect those who are both inherently vulnerable and highly dependent on the observance of proper standards of care by those with a significant degree of control over their lives. Schools are employed to educate children, which they can do only if they are allowed authority over them. That authority confers on them a significant degree of control. When the school's own control is delegated to someone else for the purpose of performing part of the school's own educational function, it is wholly reasonable that the school should be answerable for the careful exercise of its control by the delegate.

(2) Parents are required by law to entrust their child to a school. They do so in reliance on the school's ability to look after them, and generally have no knowledge of or influence over the arrangements that the school may make to delegate specialised functions, or the basis on which they do so, or the competence of the delegates, all of which are matters about which only the school is in a position to satisfy itself.

(3) This is not an open-ended liability, for there are important limitations on the range of matters for which a school or education authority assumes non-delegable duties. They are liable for the negligence of independent contractors only if and so far as the latter are performing functions which the school has assumed for itself a duty to perform, generally in school hours and on school premises (or at other times or places where the school may carry out its educational functions). In the absence of negligence of their own, for example in the selection of contractors, they will not be liable for the negligence of independent contractors where on analysis their own duty is not to perform the relevant function but only to arrange for its performance. They will not be liable for the defaults of independent contractors providing extra-curricular activities outside school hours, such as school trips in the holidays. Nor will they be liable for the negligence of those to whom no control over the child has been delegated, such as bus drivers or the theatres, zoos or museums to which children may be taken by school staff in school hours, to take some of the examples canvassed in argument and by Laws LJ in his dissenting judgment.

(4) It is important to bear in mind that until relatively recently, most of the functions now routinely delegated by schools to independent contractors would have been performed by staff for whom the authority would have been vicariously liable. The recognition of limited non-delegable duties has become more significant as a result of the growing scale on which the educational and supervisory functions of schools are outsourced, but in a longer historical perspective, it does not significantly increase the potential liability of education authorities.

(5) The responsibilities of fee-paying schools are already non-delegable because they are contractual, and the possibility of contracting out of them is limited by legislation. In this particular context, there seems to be no rational reason why the mere absence of consideration should lead to an entirely different result when comparable services are provided by a public authority. A similar point can be made about the technical distinctions that would otherwise arise between privately funded and NHS hospital treatment.

(6) It can fairly be said that the recognition of a non-delegable duty of care owed by schools involves imputing to them a greater responsibility than any which the law presently

recognises as being owed by parents. Parents would not normally incur personal liability for the negligence of (say) a swimming instructor to whom they had handed custody of a child. The claimants' pleaded allegation that the school stood in loco parentis may not therefore assist their case. The position of parents is very different to that of schools. Schools provide a service either by contract or pursuant to a statutory obligation, and while local education authority schools do not receive fees, their staff and contractors are paid professionals. By comparison, the custody and control which parents exercise over their children is not only gratuitous, but based on an intimate relationship not readily analysable in legal terms. For this reason, the common law has always been extremely cautious about recognising legally enforceable duties owed by parents on the same basis as those owed by institutional carers: see *Surtees v Kingston-upon-Thames Borough Council* [1992] PIQR P101, P121 (Beldam LJ); *Barrett v Enfield London Borough Council* [2001] 2 AC 550, 588 (Lord Hutton).

Application to the present case

26. In my opinion, on the limited facts pleaded or admitted, the respondent education authority assumed a duty to ensure that the claimant's swimming lessons were carefully conducted and supervised, by whomever they might get to perform these functions. The claimant was entrusted to the school for certain essential purposes, which included teaching and supervision. The swimming lessons were an integral part of the school's teaching function. They did not occur on school premises, but they occurred in school hours in a place where the school chose to carry out this part of its functions. The teaching and the supervisory functions of the school, and the control of the child that went with them, were delegated by the school to Mrs Stopford and through her to Ms Burlinson, and probably to Ms Maxwell as well, to the extent necessary to enable them to give swimming lessons. The alleged negligence occurred in the course of the very functions which the school assumed an obligation to perform and delegated to its contractors. It must follow that if the latter were negligent in performing those functions and the child was injured as a result, the educational authority is in breach of duty . . .

Baroness Hale delivered a concurring judgment. **Lord Clarke, Lord Wilson** and **Lord Toulson** agreed with Lord Sumption and Baroness Hale.

Appeal allowed.

COMMENTARY

According to the editors of *Winfield & Jolowicz* (para. 21–043), '[i]t seems clear that Lord Sumption did not intend to suggest that every instance of a non-delegable duty could be said to fall within' the two broad categories he identifies in his judgment in *Woodland*, which do not, for example, encompass the 'highway' cases he mentions at [25] (for discussion of these cases, see *Winfield & Jolowicz*, para. 21–050). Nevertheless, as Coulson J said in *GB v Home Office* [2015] EWHC 819 (QB) at [18], Lord Sumption's judgment 'provided a much-needed clarification of the law in this area'. Although his Lordship commented, at [25], that a non-delegable duty of care should be imposed on schools only if it would be fair, just and reasonable to do so, in a later Supreme Court case, *Armes v Nottinghamshire County Council*

[2018] AC 355 at [36], Lord Reed denied that this was an independent requirement of the imposition of a non-delegable duty, over and above Lord Sumption's dual criteria; not only would a separate inquiry into this issue be 'unnecessarily duplicative', it would also be 'apt to give rise to uncertainty and inconsistency'. As for Lord Sumption's use of the assumption of responsibility concept to explain the circumstances in which a non-delegable duty will arise, this echoes prior academic commentary to similar effect (see Stevens, *op. cit.*, and Murphy, *op. cit.*; and see also Mason J in *Kondis v State Transport Authority* (1984) 154 CLR 672 at 687), but has been criticised by J. Morgan, 'Liability for Independent Contractors in Contract and Tort' [2015] CLJ 109, who argues (at 128) that '"assumption of responsibility" provides no test at all, and no answers—it simply poses the same questions in a disguised form'. For other commentary on *Woodland*, see George (2014) 130 LQR 534; and Giliker (2015) 31 PN 259.

Paradigm instances of non-delegable duties within Lord Sumption's second category are those where there is a prior relationship between the parties characterised by the vulnerability of the claimant and the control of the defendant. These include the employment cases (see earlier), the school–pupil relationship exemplified by *Woodland* itself, and the non-delegable duty owed by a hospital to its patients (and by a dental practice to its NHS patients: *Hughes v Rattan* [2021] EWHC 2032 (QB)). In *Farraj v King's Healthcare NHS Trust* [2010] 1 WLR 2139, Dyson LJ (with whom Smith LJ agreed) held that this last duty did not extend to work carried out for patients outside of the hospital by an independent laboratory. Do you think that this decision is compatible with *Woodland*? Lord Sumption suggested in *Woodland*, at [23], that a prisoner would probably also be owed non-delegable duties on the same vulnerability/control basis, so it is no surprise that in *GB v Home Office* Coulson J held that the Home Office owed a non-delegable duty to an immigration detainee in respect of the provision of medical care at the immigration removal centre where she was detained (see also *Razumas v Ministry of Justice* [2018] PIQR P10, where Cockerill J accepted that the prison service owed prisoners a non-delegable duty of care in respect of matters arising out of their custody). Conversely, the pre-*Woodland* decision in *Harrison v Jagged Globe (Alpine) Ltd* [2012] EWCA Civ 835 that a travel company which arranged an overseas expedition did not owe a non-delegable duty in relation to the local guides it employed as independent contractors also looks to be consistent with Lord Sumption's reasoning, since on the facts the criteria of vulnerability and control would appear not to have been satisfied. It was also said obiter in *Armes v Nottinghamshire County Council* [2018] AC 355 at [41]–[43], that parents (or those with analogous responsibilities) do not owe a non-delegable duty of care to their children, as this might interfere with ordinary aspects of family life which were often in the interests of children themselves, such as stays with friends and relatives and the use of nurseries and childminders.

In *Woodland*, Lord Sumption said, at [25], that a school would be liable for the negligence of independent contractors only if and so far as the latter were 'performing functions which the school has assumed for itself a duty to perform, generally in school hours and on school premises (or at other times or places where the school may carry out its educational functions)'. In his dissenting judgment in the Court of Appeal in *Woodland*, Laws LJ had argued, at [30], that a school or hospital should owe 'a non-delegable duty to see that care is taken for the safety of a child or patient who (a) is generally in its care, and (b) is receiving a service which is part of the institution's mainstream function of education or tending to the sick'. According to one of the majority judges in the Court of Appeal, Tomlinson LJ (at [57]), this formulation would mean that if a child on an outing to a zoo as part of a school's regular schedule of educational visits was bitten by an animal as a result of the negligence of the zoo's staff, then the educational authority would be liable, unless (which Tomlinson LJ doubted) the trip could be regarded as not part of the school's mainstream function of education. His Lordship went on to express concern that the imposition of such liability would be likely 'to have a chilling effect on the willingness of education authorities to provide valuable educational experiences for their pupils'. In the Supreme Court, Lord Sumption responded to this concern, at [25], by saying that a school would not 'be liable for the negligence of those to whom no control over the child has been delegated', instancing as examples 'bus drivers or the theatres, zoos or museums to which children may be taken by school staff in school hours'. According to Lady Hale, at [39]:

> [The defining features of Lord Sumption's second category] clearly apply to the delegation of the conduct of swimming lessons to the swimming teacher, Mrs Burlinson, and (subject to any factual matters of which we are unaware) to the lifeguard, Ms Maxwell. Taking care to keep the children safe is an essential part of any swimming lesson and of the responsibility which the school undertakes towards its pupils. That is what the life-guard is for. These features clearly would not apply to . . . [a] zoo-keeper. They would not normally apply to the bus driver but they might do so if the school had undertaken to provide transport and placed the pupils in his charge rather than that of a teacher.

Do you detect a tension between the approaches of Lord Sumption and Lady Hale on this question? In any case, might a zoo-keeper not in some circumstances be given a degree of control over schoolchildren visiting a zoo, or be responsible for taking care to keep the children safe? As Giliker says (*op. cit.*, at 272), where an independent contractor is 'performing duties which are part of the school's integral duties to its pupils, i.e. core teaching, then there should be no difficulty in finding a non-delegable duty', but there 'remains a question mark over how to deal with situations where the independent contractor is involved in the provision of services of educational benefit to the child, but which are (arguably) not core duties'. Doubtless Lady Hale was wise to counsel, at [38]–[39], against treating judicial statements 'as if they were statutes', and to say that the exact boundaries of Lord Sumption's test would 'have to be worked out on a case-by-case basis' (see also *Armes v Nottinghamshire County Council* [2018] AC 355 at [36], per Lord Reed, arguing that Lord Sumption's criteria 'may need to be re-considered, and possibly refined, in particular contexts').

In *Woodland* Lord Sumption made it clear, at [25], that there would be no liability for the negligence of a contractor in its performance of a given function where the defendant's duty was not to perform that function itself, but 'only to arrange for its performance'. This may require close consideration of what precisely it was that the defendant assumed responsibility for, which, in the case of a statutory function, may turn on the wording of the relevant legislation. In *Armes*, the Supreme Court held that a local authority had not owed a non-delegable duty to a child physically and sexually abused by foster parents the authority had entrusted with her care, since on the proper interpretation of the relevant legislation the authority's statutory function was to arrange for day-to-day care to be provided to children, and to monitor its provision, rather than to provide such care itself. (The Court was also concerned about the implications of a non-delegable duty in this context, in particular that it might discourage local authorities from allowing children in care to stay with their families and friends, for fear of liability arising out of negligence on the part of those persons.) Similarly, in *Hopkins v Akramy* [2021] QB 564, because the governing statutory framework gave a Primary Care Trust (PCT) the option of either providing primary medical services to those in its area itself or of making suitable arrangements for such provision by a third party, it did not owe a non-delegable duty of care such that it became liable for deficiencies in the care provided by such third parties. This means that a PCT will not generally be liable for the negligence of a GP working in a surgery providing services pursuant to a contract with the PCT. The importance of the governing legislative framework is also shown by the contrasting decisions in *GB v Home Office* and *Razumas v Ministry of Justice* (mentioned earlier): in the former, it was held that the Home Office had owed a non-delegable duty to an immigration detainee in respect of healthcare provision, whereas in the latter no such duty was owed by the Ministry of Justice to a prisoner, since the statutory responsibility for providing medical care to prisoners lay with the NHS. (See also *SKX v Manchester City Council* [2021] 4 WLR 56: applying *Armes*, there was no non-delegable duty where a local authority placed a child in the care of a privately run residential home.)

Arguably one of the most powerful arguments Lord Sumption and Lady Hale put forward for imposing a non-delegable duty in *Woodland* was that otherwise a pupil's ability to bring a claim against their school in such a case might depend on whether the task had been contracted-out by the local education authority, or on whether the pupil was at a state school or a private school (since in the latter case, there would likely be a non-delegable contractual duty). (For an example by Lady Hale highlighting this issue, see *Woodland* at [30].) However, not everyone is convinced. According to J. Morgan, 'Vicarious Liability for Independent Contractors?' (2015) 31 PN 235 at 245–6:

> That different local authorities bear different (vicarious) liabilities according to their decision to outsource services or to provide them by council employees is a natural consequence (according to legal orthodoxy) of their employment relationship with the ultimate tortfeasor. It is no more surprising than the fact that companies are liable for negligent driving by their own (in-house) delivery drivers, but not for the negligence of independent courier firms (or indeed, the Royal Mail), in delivering on their behalf . . .
>
> [As for] the 'parity with contract' argument (ie seeking to avoid supposedly invidious distinctions with private pupils, patients etc) . . . [i]t proves far too much. In various respects, those suing under contracts enjoy advantages over those suing in tort for similar harms in a similar context. But nowhere else has it been suggested that tort ought therefore to incorporate all the advantageous features of contractual liability–in particular (and pertinently here) contract's strict liability. It is a trite point that parties to a contract can and do structure it to give all sorts of advantageous rights to a service recipient against the provider, limited only by their imaginations and bargaining power. How can tort possibly track such a set of obligations and–moreover–what would be the justification for doing so? To a considerable degree the whole point of *paying for contractual obligations* is to enhance what the background law (ie tort) provides to everyone for free. So the fact that if the parties had had a contract the claimant would have been better off cannot of itself provide compelling grounds for imposing the same obligations (through tort), when no contract existed.

(For a fuller version of the same argument, see J. Morgan, 'Liability for Independent Contractors in Contract and Tort' [2015] CLJ 109 at 111–18, where he describes the position taken on this issue in *Woodland* as 'ideological'.) Morgan nevertheless concedes that the court in *Woodland* may have been right to perceive that public opinion would find it hard to accept that a private school pupil could recover damages from their school in such a case, whereas a state school pupil could not. Do you agree? Would *you* find such a distinction acceptable?

15 DAMAGES FOR PERSONAL INJURY

I. Introduction

The tortious infliction of injury to another person is remedied through the award of damages by way of compensation. Damages are not the only weapon to be found in the law's remedial armoury, but in the tort context they are the principal remedy (although in some circumstances, e.g. a continuing nuisance or a threatened defamation, the award of an injunction may be of greater significance: see Ch. 11.II.5 and Ch. 12.V.2 respectively). The normal measure of damages is the compensatory measure, but other types of damages may also be awarded.

II. Different Types of Damages

1. Compensatory Damages

According to Lord Scarman, 'the principle of the law is that compensation should as nearly as possible put the party who has suffered in the same position as he would have been in if he had not sustained the wrong' (*Lim v Camden & Islington Area Health Authority* [1980] AC 174 at 187). The law's object here is sometimes described using the Latin phrase *restitutio in integrum* (indicating an attempt to restore the claimant to their pre-existing 'whole' state), but this risks obscuring the important distinction between compensation, which seeks to replace something that the claimant has lost, and restitution, which forces the defendant to give up something gained at the claimant's expense (see the following subsection). Compensatory damages focus upon the claimant's loss rather than the defendant's gain.

2. Restitutionary Damages

Restitutionary damages, by way of contrast, *do* focus on the defendant's gain. They oblige the defendant to give up some benefit—an 'unjust enrichment'—which they have derived at the expense of the claimant. The most notable examples of the law of tort awarding damages of a restitutionary nature are the torts of trespass to land and conversion (not covered in this book). Thus, if a person steals a car from its owner (an act which would constitute the tort of conversion by the thief) and uses it to conduct a mini-cab business, the owner would be able to claim damages based on the profits made by the thief in using the car rather than having to prove they had suffered any loss from being deprived of it. However, the scope for the award of restitutionary damages in the modern law of tort is a matter of some debate that is beyond the scope of this book (see further Law Commission, *Aggravated, Exemplary and Restitutionary Damages* (Law Com. No. 247, 1997); J. Edelman, *Gain-Based Damages* (Oxford: OUP, 2002); Rotherham, 'Gain-Based Relief in Tort After *AG v Blake*' (2010) 126 LQR 102).

3. Exemplary or Punitive Damages

Although the award of damages in the law of tort serves a primarily compensatory purpose, the court may exceptionally seek to punish (or make an example of) the defendant by the award of exemplary or punitive damages. The jurisdiction to award such damages dates back at least to the eighteenth century (and possibly earlier: see Taliadoros, 'Thirteenth-Century Origins of Punitive or Exemplary Damages' (2018) 39 J Leg Hist 278). Two cases arising out of the printing of a radical newspaper provide noteworthy examples (see *Wilkes v Wood* (1763) Lofft 1; *Huckle v Money* (1763) 2 Wils 205). The award of exemplary damages against agents of the state served to reinforce the courts' affirmation of the rule of law in the course of the same saga (*Entick v Carrington* (1765) 19 State Tr 1029). The old authorities were analysed and categorised in the influential speech of Lord Devlin in *Rookes v Barnard*, extracted next. This is the starting point for any discussion of the availability of exemplary damages in the modern law.

(a) The Current Law

Rookes v Barnard [1964] AC 1129

The facts of this case—which arose out of an industrial dispute—are not relevant for present purposes.

Lord Devlin

[T]here are certain categories of cases in which an award of exemplary damages can serve a useful purpose in vindicating the strength of the law and thus affording a practical justification for admitting into the civil law a principle which ought logically to belong to the criminal. I propose to state what these two categories are; and I propose also to state three general considerations which, in my opinion, should always be borne in mind when awards of exemplary damages are being made. I am well aware that what I am about to say will, if accepted, impose limits not hitherto expressed on such awards and that there is powerful, though not compelling, authority for allowing them a wider range . . .

The first category is oppressive, arbitrary or unconstitutional action by the servants of the government. I should not extend this category—I say this with particular reference to the facts of this case—to oppressive action by private corporations or individuals. Where one man is more powerful than another, it is inevitable that he will try to use his power to gain his ends; and if his power is much greater than the other's, he might, perhaps, be said to be using it oppressively. If he uses his power illegally, he must of course pay for his illegality in the ordinary way; but he is not to be punished simply because he is the more powerful. In the case of the government it is different, for the servants of the government are also the servants of the people and the use of their power must always be subordinate to their duty of service. It is true that there is something repugnant about a big man bullying a small man and, very likely, the bullying will be a source of humiliation that makes the case one for aggravated damages, but it is not, in my opinion, punishable by damages.

Cases in the second category are those in which the defendant's conduct has been calculated by him to make a profit for himself which may well exceed the compensation payable to the plaintiff. It is a factor that is taken into account in damages for libel; one man should not be allowed to sell another man's reputation for profit. Where a defendant with a cynical disregard for a plaintiff's rights has calculated that the money to be made out of his wrongdoing will probably exceed the damages at risk, it is necessary for the law to show that it cannot be broken with impunity. This category is not confined to moneymaking in the strict sense. It extends to cases in which the defendant is seeking to gain at the expense of the plaintiff some object—perhaps some property which he covets—which either he could not obtain at all or not obtain except at a price greater than he wants to put down. Exemplary damages can properly be awarded whenever it is necessary to teach a wrongdoer that tort does not pay.

To these two categories which are established as part of the common law there must of course be added any category in which exemplary damages are expressly authorised by statute.

I wish now to express three considerations which I think should always be borne in mind when awards of exemplary damages are being considered. First, the plaintiff cannot recover exemplary damages unless he is the victim of the punishable behaviour. The anomaly inherent in exemplary damages would become an absurdity if a plaintiff totally unaffected by some oppressive conduct which the jury wished to punish obtained a windfall in consequence.

Secondly, the power to award exemplary damages constitutes a weapon that, while it can be used in defence of liberty can also be used against liberty. Some of the awards that juries have made in the past seem to me to amount to a greater punishment than would be likely to be incurred if the conduct were criminal; and, moreover, a punishment imposed without the safeguard which the criminal law gives to an offender. I should not allow the respect which is traditionally paid to an assessment of damages by a jury to prevent me from seeing that the weapon is used with restraint. It may even be that the House may find it necessary to place some arbitrary limit on awards of damages that are made by way of punishment. Exhortations to be moderate may not be enough.

Thirdly, the means of the parties, irrelevant in the assessment of compensation, are material in the assessment of exemplary damages. Everything which aggravates or mitigates the defendant's conduct is relevant.

Thus a case for exemplary damages must be presented quite differently from one for compensatory damages; and the judge should not allow it to be left to the jury unless he is satisfied that it can be brought within the categories I have specified. But the fact that the two sorts of damage differ essentially does not necessarily mean that there should be two awards. In a case in which exemplary damages are appropriate, a jury should be directed that if, but only if, the sum which they have in mind to award as compensation (which may, of course, be a sum aggravated by the way in which the defendant has behaved to the plaintiff) is inadequate to punish him for his outrageous conduct, to mark their disapproval of such conduct and to deter him from repeating it, then it can award some larger sum. If a verdict given on such direction has to be reviewed upon appeal, the appellate court will first consider whether the award can be justified as compensation and if it can, there is nothing further to be said. If it cannot, the court must consider whether or not the punishment is, in all the circumstances, excessive.

> There may be cases in which it is difficult for a judge to say whether or not he ought to leave to the jury a claim for exemplary damages. In such circumstances, and in order to save the possible expense of a new trial, I see no objection to his inviting the jury to say what sum they would fix as compensation and what additional sum, if any, they would award if they were entitled to give exemplary damages.

COMMENTARY

Oppressive, Arbitrary or Unconstitutional Action by the Servants of the Government

A classic example of Lord Devlin's first category would be wrongful arrest by a police officer. According to Lord Reid, 'the category was never intended to be limited to Crown servants. The contrast is between "the government" and private individuals. Local government is as much government as national government, and the police and many other persons are exercising governmental functions' (*Cassell v Broome* [1972] AC 1027 at 1088). The category does not extend to the commercial activities of nationalised enterprises (*AB v South West Services Ltd* [1993] QB 507), though it has been questioned whether companies—especially large international concerns capable of exercising considerable power—should always be immune from exemplary damages (*Kuddus v Chief Constable of Leicestershire* [2002] 2 AC 122 at [66], per Lord Nicholls).

Conduct Calculated to Make a Profit in Excess of any Compensation Payable

The classic example here is of a newspaper that prints a libellous story in order to boost its circulation, though in future exemplary damages relating to the publication of news-related material will be governed by statute (as set out later in this commentary). In fact, however, the most common exemplary awards under this head have been in respect of wrongful eviction of tenants by landlords (where the latter commit the tort of trespass). Exemplary damages have also been awarded in this category in respect of the unlawful imprisonment and sexual exploitation of foreign women coerced into prostitution in the United Kingdom with a view to making profits for the defendants: *AT v Dulghieru* [2009] EWHC 225, noted by Keren-Paz (2010) 18 TLJ 87. Such damages are awarded not merely to reverse the defendant's unjust enrichment (the function of restitutionary damages), but—in Lord Devlin's words—'to teach a wrongdoer that tort does not pay'. If the award were only to reverse the defendant's gain, then the defendant would have 'nothing to lose' by going ahead with the tortious conduct. However, in *Kuddus v Chief Constable of Leicestershire* [2002] 2 AC 122, both Lord Nicholls, at [67], and Lord Scott, at [109], queried whether this category was necessary as the circumstances in which restitutionary damages could be awarded had increased and in most cases the profit of the wrongdoer could be disgorged in this way. Does this meet the criticism that the defendant is insufficiently deterred by an award of restitutionary damages?

For analysis of the situations in which exemplary damages have in fact been awarded, see Goudkamp and Katsampouka, 'An Empirical Study of Punitive Damages' (2018) 38 OJLS 90.

Exemplary Damages Limited to Certain Causes of Action

In *AB v South West Water Services Ltd* [1993] QB 507, the Court of Appeal introduced a 'cause of action' test for the award of exemplary damages. It took the view that the development of the law had been frozen into a rigid posture by *Rookes v Barnard* and that exemplary damages could only be awarded in relation to tortious causes of action in which such damages had been awarded prior to that case. Accordingly, inhabitants of Camelford in Cornwall who alleged that they were ill as a result of drinking contaminated water supplied by the defendant failed in their bid for exemplary damages. The causes of action they relied upon (negligence, nuisance and the rule in *Rylands v Fletcher*) did not allow the award of such damages. The decision was subjected to considerable academic criticism (see, e.g., Pipe (1994) 57 MLR 91) and was subsequently overruled by the House of Lords in *Kuddus v Chief Constable of Leicestershire* [2002] 2 AC 122. It does not follow, however, that a claimant need now prove only that their case falls into one of Lord Devlin's categories to be able to ask for exemplary damages. *Kuddus* does not preclude the courts adopting a revised 'cause of action' test based on a reasoned analysis of which torts should permit exemplary damages and which should not, rather than on the accidents of litigation prior to *Rookes v Barnard*. In *Kuddus*, only Lord Scott adverted to this possibility, at [122], stating that he preferred 'a pragmatic solution' whereby exemplary damages would be allowed in respect of all torts except negligence, nuisance, breach of statutory duty (in the absence of express statutory authorisation), and all torts of strict liability. It is not clear where this would leave defamation, often thought of as a tort of strict liability, but also a tort which is strongly associated historically with awards of exemplary damages. It is doubtful that Lord Scott intended to change this well-established position.

Exemplary Damages and the Media

A few years after *Kuddus*, in *Mosley v News Group Newspapers Ltd* [2008] EMLR 679 (noted in Ch. 13.II), at [172]–[211], Eady J was obliged to consider whether exemplary damages were available for the unlawful disclosure of private information. He ruled that they were not. He found that there was no authority for such an extension (is this aspect of Eady J's argument consistent with *Kuddus*?) and thought in any case that it would be undesirable for exemplary damages to be available in an area governed to so large an extent by the Convention rights to privacy and freedom of expressions (Articles 8 and 10, ECHR) when the idea of punitive or exemplary damages is alien to the Strasbourg court.

Subsequently, in 2012, the Leveson Report (*Leveson*, Part J, ch. 3, para. 5.12) recommended that exemplary damages should be available in actions for breach of privacy, breach of confidence and similar media torts, as well as for libel and slander. The reform was implemented by s. 34 of the Crime and Courts Act 2013, which makes exemplary damages available where the defendant incurs liability in respect of 'the publication of news-related material' (s. 34(1) (c)). The basic test to be applied in such cases is set out in s. 34(6):

Exemplary damages may be awarded under this section only if the court is satisfied that—

(a) the defendant's conduct has shown a deliberate or reckless disregard of an outrageous nature for the claimant's rights,
(b) the conduct is such that the court should punish the defendant for it, and
(c) other remedies would not be adequate to punish that conduct.

It should be noted that exemplary damages made under this provision are not confined to Lord Devlin's two categories; a wider test of 'outrageous disregard' is employed instead. See further in II.3(b) and Chapter 12.V.I.

Limits on the Award of Exemplary Damages

In *Thompson v Commissioner of Police of the Metropolis* [1998] QB 498 at 514–17, in the context of an action against the police for false imprisonment and malicious prosecution, the

Court of Appeal gave general guidance on the award of exemplary damages against public authorities:

(i) an award of exemplary damages will rarely be less than £5,000, otherwise it is probably not justified;

(ii) conduct has to be particularly deserving of condemnation for an award of £25,000, and £50,000 is the absolute maximum (in police cases, reserved for conduct directly involving officers of at least the rank of superintendent);

(iii) a rough upper-limit guide is three times the total of compensatory and aggravated damages (see II.4) except where basic damages are modest.

The *Thompson* guidelines were recognised as having significance outside the context of claims against the police in *Muuse v Secretary of State for the Home Department* [2010] EWCA Civ 45, where the claimant was unlawfully imprisoned pending deportation in circumstances where there was no right to deport. The amounts need to be adjusted for inflation and appear to be intended for single claimant cases, and thus do not preclude a larger award in excess of the 'absolute maximum' where it has to be shared between two or more claimants (*Rees v Commissioner of Police of the Metropolis* [2021] EWCA Civ 49: award of £150,000 to be shared between three claimants; it was accepted that the £50,000 in *Thompson* was worth an inflation-adjusted sum of around £91,500).

(b) Analysis

Whether an award of exemplary damages can be justified has been a matter of continued debate, with the House of Lords returning to the matter in *Cassell v Broome*, and more recently in *Kuddus v Chief Constable of Leicestershire* [2002] 2 AC 122, both extracted here. The Law Commission also issued a report on exemplary damages in 1997.

Cassell v Broome [1972] AC 1027

The facts of this case are not relevant for present purposes.

Lord Reid

That [sc. an award of exemplary damages] meant that the plaintiff, by being given more than on any view could be justified as compensation, was being given a pure and undeserved windfall at the expense of the defendant, and that in so far as the defendant was being required to pay more than could possibly be regarded as compensation he was being subjected to pure punishment.

I thought and still think that that is highly anomalous. It is confusing the function of the civil law which is to compensate with the function of the criminal law which is to inflict deterrent and punitive penalties . . .

I think that the objections to allowing juries to go beyond compensatory damages are overwhelming. To allow pure punishment in this way contravenes almost every principle which has been evolved for the protection of offenders. There is no definition of the offence except that the conduct punished must be oppressive, high-handed, malicious, wanton or its like—terms far too vague to be admitted to any criminal code worthy of the name. There is no limit to the punishment except that it must not be unreasonable. The punishment is not inflicted by a judge who has experience and at least tries not to be influenced by emotion; it is inflicted by a jury without experience of law or punishment and often swayed by considerations which every judge would put out of his mind. And there is no effective appeal against sentence. All that a reviewing court can do is to quash the jury's decision if it thinks the punishment awarded is more than any 12 reasonable men could award. The court cannot substitute its own award. The punishment must then be decided by another jury and if they too award heavy punishment the court is virtually powerless. It is no excuse to say that we need not waste sympathy on people who behave outrageously. Are we wasting sympathy on vicious criminals when we insist on proper legal safeguards for them? The right to give punitive damages in certain cases is so firmly embedded in our law that only Parliament can remove it. But I must say that I am surprised by the enthusiasm of Lord Devlin's critics in supporting this form of palm tree justice.

Lord Wilberforce

It cannot lightly be taken for granted, even as a matter of theory, that the purpose of the law of tort is compensation, still less that it ought to be, an issue of large social import, or that there is something inappropriate or illogical or anomalous (a question-begging word) in including a punitive element in civil damages, or, conversely that the criminal law, rather than the civil law is in these cases the better instrument for conveying social disapproval, or for redressing a wrong to the social fabric, or that damages in any case can be broken down into the two separate elements. As a matter of practice English law has not committed itself to any of these theories; it may have been wiser than it knew.

Kuddus v Chief Constable of Leicestershire [2002] 2 AC 122

The question for the House of Lords was whether the tort of misfeasance in public office was one in which exemplary damages could be awarded. Both parties argued the case on the basis that *Rookes v Barnard* and *Cassell v Broome* [1972] AC 1027 represented the law, and the specific issue was the correctness of the Court of Appeal decision in *AB v South West Water* (see earlier). However, several of their Lordships commented more generally on whether there was a role for exemplary damages in the modern law.

Lord Nicholls

The availability of exemplary damages has played a significant role in buttressing civil liberties, in claims for false imprisonment and wrongful arrest. From time to time cases do arise where awards of compensatory damages are perceived as inadequate to achieve a just result between the parties. The nature of the defendant's conduct calls for a further response from the courts. On occasion conscious wrongdoing by the defendant is so outrageous, his disregard of the plaintiff's rights so contumelious, that something more is needed to show that the law will not tolerate such behaviour. Without an award of exemplary damages, justice will not have been done. Exemplary damages, as a remedy of last resort, fill what would otherwise be a regrettable lacuna . . .

In *Rookes v Barnard* Lord Devlin drew a distinction between oppressive acts by government officials and similar acts by companies or individuals. He considered that exemplary damages should not be available in the case of non-governmental oppression or bullying. Whatever may have been the position 40 years ago, I am respectfully inclined to doubt the soundness of this distinction today. National and international companies can exercise enormous power. So do some individuals. I am not sure it would be right to draw a hard and fast line which would always exclude such companies and persons from the reach of exemplary damages. Indeed, the validity of the dividing line drawn by Lord Devlin when formulating his first category is somewhat undermined by his second category, where the defendants are not confined to, and normally would not be, government officials or the like . . .

Lord Scott

The law regarding exemplary damages did not become fossilised and set in stone when Lord Devlin pronounced in 1964 . . . or when the seven members of the House pronounced in 1972 . . . Since then the common law has flowed on. One of the great developments of the common law since the time of *Rookes v Barnard* has been in the area of public law and judicial review to which Lord Diplock [in *Cassell v Broome*] referred. Oppressive, arbitrary and unconstitutional acts by members of the executive can be remedied through civil proceedings brought in the High Court. The remedies the court can provide include awards of damages, declarations of right and, in most cases, injunctions. The developments since Lord Diplock's remarks in *Broome v Cassell* have transformed the ability of the ordinary citizen to obtain redress. The continuing need in the year 2001 for exemplary damages as a civil remedy in order to control, deter and punish acts falling within Lord Devlin's first category is not in the least obvious.

My noble and learned friend, Lord Hutton, has referred, as examples, to two cases in Northern Ireland where in his view the award of exemplary damages served a valuable purpose in restraining the arbitrary and outrageous use of executive power and in vindicating the strength of the law. In one case (*Lavery v Ministry of Defence* [1984] NI 99) a soldier was the wrongdoer. The Ministry of Defence was the defendant. In the other case (*Pettigrew v Northern Ireland Office* [1990] NI 179) prison officers were the wrongdoers. The Northern Ireland Office was the defendant. In each case the conduct of the wrongdoer, or wrongdoers, was outrageous and fell squarely within Lord Devlin's first category. But I do not follow why an appropriate award of aggravated damages [see II.4] would not have served to vindicate the law just as effectively as the fairly moderate awards of exemplary damages that were made. The condemnation of the trial judge of the conduct in question would have been expressed no differently. As to deterrence, in a case where the defendant is not the wrongdoer, and the damages are in any event going to be met out of public funds, how can it be supposed that the award of exemplary damages adds anything at all to the deterrent effect of the trial judge's finding of fact in favour of the injured person and his condemnation of the conduct in question? The proposition that exemplary damage awards against such defendants as the Ministry of Defence or the Northern Ireland Office, or, for that matter, the Chief Constable of Leicestershire Constabulary, can have a deterrent effect is, in my respectful opinion, fanciful . . .

My Lords, I view the prospect of any increase in the cases in which exemplary damages can be claimed with regret. I have explained already why I regard the remedy as no longer serving any useful function in our jurisprudence. Victims of tortious conduct should receive due compensation, not windfalls at public expense.

COMMENTARY

As the extracts from the two cases illustrate, judicial opinion on the desirability of awards of exemplary damages is radically polarised. In *Kuddus* their Lordships clearly felt that the underlying justifications for exemplary damages *should* have been argued before them, but the parties (no doubt for reasons of cost) limited the dispute to a narrow point. Nonetheless, two of the three Law Lords who proffered (obiter) comments on exemplary damages were broadly in favour, although Lord Nicholls thought Lord Devlin's categories in *Rookes v Barnard* did not represent a satisfactory basis on which to make such awards. Conversely, the speeches of Lord Reid in *Cassell* and Lord Scott in *Kuddus* reflect a reluctance to admit such awards into civil law, albeit for different reasons.

It may be noted that, when the issue of exemplary damages subsequently came before a panel of Law Lords wearing their other hats as members of the Judicial Committee of the Privy Council, a majority of them took an expansive view of the circumstances in which exemplary damages could be awarded under the common law of New Zealand: their award was not to be limited to cases where the defendant intended to cause the harm or was consciously reckless as to the risks involved, but extended to cases of negligence amounting to outrageous conduct (*A v Bottrill* [2003] 1 AC 449). Given continued divergences of judicial opinion, it cannot be said that the decision provides any real indication of how the UK Supreme Court might approach the issue in English law should it be invited to overrule *Rookes v Barnard*. But it may be noted that, following New Zealand's abolition of appeals to the Privy Council, its new Supreme Court proceeded to reinstate the requirement of advertent wrongdoing (*Couch v Attorney-General* [2010] NZSC 27).

When the question of exemplary damages was considered by the Law Commission (*Aggravated, Exemplary and Restitutionary Damages* (Law Com. No. 247, 1997)), it recommended that punitive damages should be retained though placed on a clear, principled, but tightly controlled, footing. It concluded that 'civil punishment can be adequately distinguished from criminal punishment, and has an important and distinctive role to play . . . The argument of principle for retaining exemplary damages is content . . . with a "fuzzy" line [sc. between the civil law and the criminal law], with a range of punishments from civil punishment, through criminal fines, to imprisonment' (para. 5.25).

The Law Commission proposed a statutory scheme, the core elements of which it summarised as follows:

(i) Punitive damages should be available for a legal wrong (other than breach of contract) if the defendant has deliberately and outrageously disregarded the claimant's rights. (The 'cause of action' and 'categories' tests should be abolished.)

(ii) The decision to award punitive damages, and their amount, should be matters for judges to decide; even where a civil trial is otherwise by jury, these matters should never be decided by a jury.

(iii) Punitive damages should be a 'last resort' remedy, which should not be awarded where the defendant has been convicted of a criminal offence for the same conduct, or where another available remedy is adequate punishment.

The government subsequently indicated that, because of the diversity of opinion displayed during the consultation period for the report, it did not intend to introduce legislation to give effect to these recommendations (Hansard, HC vol. 337 col. 502, 9 November 1999 WA). See further Department of Constitutional Affairs, *The Law on Damages* (CP 9/07, 2007), paras 196–9. However, as part of the reforms introduced in consequence of the Leveson Report into press practices, the Law Commission's proposal has now effectively been adopted as regards liability for the publication of news-related material (Crime and Courts Act 2013, s. 34, adopting a test of whether the defendant's conduct showed 'a deliberate or reckless disregard of an outrageous nature for the claimant's rights'; see the preceding discussion in II.3(a) for further details). For an argument that exemplary damages are inconsistent with the nature of private law and should be abolished, see Beever, 'The structure of aggravated and exemplary damages' (2003) 23 OJLS 87. Cf. Englard, 'Punitive damages – a modern conundrum of ancient origin' (2012) 3 JETL 1 (arguing that they may be complementary to compensatory damages and should be available in exceptional cases); Goudkamp and Katsampouka, 'Punitive Damages and the Place of Punishment in Private Law' (2021) 84 MLR 1257 (denying that punishment is alien to private law, with reference to other remedial rules that have or may have a punitive function).

Relevance of Criminal Conviction

If one purpose of exemplary damages is to punish, should their award be precluded if a criminal sanction has already been imposed? The Law Commission, as noted earlier, thought they should. The issue seems not to have arisen for decision in English law, but in *Gray v Motor Accident Commission* (1998) 196 CLR 1 a majority of the Australian High Court held, at [40], that '[w]here . . . the criminal law has been brought to bear upon the wrongdoer and substantial punishment inflicted, we consider that exemplary damages may not be awarded'. Callinan J agreed with the result on the facts, but advocated a more flexible approach (at [143]):

A court would also be entitled to take into account that lesser punishments may have been, or might be imposed as a consequence of the acceptance of a lesser plea, the availability (for what might be sound policy reasons in and for the purposes of the criminal law) of a small penalty only, the desirability of the less condemnatory process by way of civil rather than criminal proceedings, the need to encourage compliance with the law, and the fact that the possibility of any criminal sanction is illusory.

Do you think that judges and juries should have some discretion to award exemplary damages even if a criminal sanction has been imposed?

Exemplary Damages and Vicarious Liability

In a passage of his opinion in *Kuddus* not extracted earlier, Lord Scott stated that an award of exemplary damages against a defendant whose liability is merely vicarious was contrary to principle. Of the remaining members of the House, only Lord Hutton considered this issue. He took the contrary view that exemplary awards made against such a defendant could be supported on grounds of their deterrent effect, a position that appealed to the High Court of Australia in *New South Wales v Ibbett* (2006) 229 CLR 638. Lord Hutton felt that this was particularly so where the individual at fault could not be identified but it was known the wrongdoer was one of a number of people employed by the defendant. The issue came for decision by the Court of Appeal in *Rowlands v Chief Constable of Merseyside Police* [2007] 1 WLR 1065, the court ruling that exemplary damages should indeed be available even when the defendant's liability was vicarious. On the facts, the question was a chief constable of police's liability for one of his officers. Moore-Bick LJ, with whom Richards and Ward LJJ agreed, stated (at [47]):

[S]ince the power to award exemplary damages rests on policy rather than principle, it seems to me that the question whether awards can be made against persons whose liability is vicarious only must also be answered by resort to considerations of policy rather than strict principle. While the common law continues to recognise a power to award exemplary damages in respect of wrongdoing by servants of the government of a kind that has a direct effect on civil liberties, which for my own part I think it should, I think that it is desirable as a matter of policy that the courts should be able to make punitive awards against those who are vicariously liable for the conduct of their subordinates without being constrained by the financial means of those who committed the wrongful acts in question. Only by this means can awards of an adequate amount be made against those who bear public responsibility for the conduct of the officers concerned.

Do you agree that vicarious liability for exemplary damages, though contrary to principle, can be justified on grounds of public policy? For the opposing view, see Todd, 'Vicarious Liability, Personal Liability and Exemplary Damages', in S. Degeling, J. Edelman and J. Goudkamp (eds), *Torts in Commercial Law* (Pyrmont, New South Wales: Thomson Reuters Australia, 2011).

Punitive Damages in the United States

In the United States, the attachment to punitive damages (as they tend to be known) is very strong in some sectors of society, where they are seen as 'the only practical method of exercising social control over economically formidable offenders . . . because criminal penalties are no substitute' (Galanter and Luban, 'Poetic Justice: Punitive Damages and Legal Pluralism' (1993) 42 Am U L Rev 1393 at 1440). Law enforcement agencies, it is argued, cannot be relied upon to identify and prosecute egregious corporate wrongdoing. The punitive damages system is necessary to give injured parties and their lawyers the incentive to carry out necessary investigative work themselves so as to bring the wrongdoer to justice. See also S. Daniels and J. Martin, *Civil Juries and the Politics of Reform* (Evanston: Northwestern University Press, 1995), pp. 202ff; Sebok, 'Punitive Damages: From Myth to Theory' (2007) 92 Iowa L Rev 957.

Of course, these arguments are controversial. It has been argued on the other side of the debate that jury awards of punitive damages are erratic, arbitrary and unpredictable (Sunstein et al., 'Assessing Punitive Damages' (1998) 107 Yale LJ 2071), that it is unconstitutional to give private actors the power to exercise the power to punish as they are inevitably motivated by their own narrow interests rather than the public interest (Redish and Mathews, 'Why Punitive Damages are Unconstitutional' (2004) 53 Emory LJ 1), and that they cause economic harm because they discourage risk assessment based on the explicit balancing of costs and benefits (which could be thought offensive by jurors), and promote counterproductive spending and wasteful precautions that may lead to increased risk and discourage innovation (Viscusi, 'The Social Costs of Punitive Damages against Corporations in Environmental and Safety Torts' (1998) 87 Georgetown LJ 285).

The arguments against punitive damages have prevailed to some extent in several US states (see Magnus, 'Why is US Tort Law so Different?' (2010) 1 JETL 102, 105). Some have abolished punitive damages, some have introduced caps to limit their amount and others require the successful claimant to pay a proportion of any punitive award to the state. Additionally, the US Supreme Court has enunciated a constitutional principle that punitive damages must be proportional to the loss for which compensatory damages are available. Punitive awards that exceed compensatory damages by a ratio of more than 10:1 are now regularly found to be excessive and must be reduced on challenge. In the leading case of *BMW of North America Inc v Gore*, 116 S Ct 1589 (1996) BMW had a policy of not advising its dealers, and hence their customers, of pre-delivery damage to new cars when the cost of repair did not exceed 3 per cent of the car's suggested retail price. Gore bought such a car and later discovered it had been damaged. He successfully sued the car manufacturer for fraud. The jury awarded compensatory damages of $4,000, and $4 million in punitive damages, reduced to $2 million on appeal. On further appeal to the US Supreme Court the award of punitive damages was overturned as infringing the rights of due process guaranteed to the defendant by the fourteenth amendment to the US Constitution. One ground for the decision was that the ratio of compensatory damages to punitive damages was excessive (1:500); another was the lack of equivalence between the criminal sanction for the manufacturer's conduct ($2,000) and the punitive award. See also *State Farm v Campbell*, 538 US 408 (2003). Despite the previously mentioned restrictions, however, most US states still allow punitive damages in one form or another.

4. Aggravated Damages

In some cases, the manner in which the defendant acts may cause additional injury to the claimant. Aggravated damages compensate the claimant for the additional loss they have suffered because of the defendant's reprehensible conduct. They are of limited scope: in *Kralj v McGrath* [1986] 1 All ER 54, it was held that aggravated damages are never appropriate in actions in negligence even if the negligence is 'crass'. Aggravated damages occupy a murky middle ground between normal compensatory damages and exemplary damages. They are designed to compensate the claimant for any hurt to their feelings and dignity occasioned by the manner in which the defendant committed the tort or by the manner of the defendant's conduct of the litigation. Aggravated damages therefore serve a compensatory function, as was emphasised by Lord Devlin in *Rookes v Barnard* [1964] AC 1129. But they are not normal compensatory damages, for they allow compensation for matters that would not fall under the head of pain and suffering attributable to the tortious injury itself (e.g. the distress suffered as a result of a hostile cross-examination at trial). Furthermore, aggravated damages have a punitive aspect, as it is a traditional requirement that the defendant should be guilty of some exceptional misconduct if aggravated damages are to be awarded. It cannot yet be said that the tension between the compensatory and punitive elements of aggravated damages has been entirely resolved.

A more principled approach was advanced by the Law Commission in its report *Aggravated, Exemplary and Restitutionary Damages* (Law Com. No 247, 1997). This recommended that aggravated damages should be viewed as purely compensatory and assessed with reference to what is necessary to compensate the loss suffered by the claimant. They should not be assessed with reference to what is necessary to punish a defendant for their conduct. The Commission was not persuaded that legislative abolition of aggravated damages (and, with it, the exceptional conduct requirement) was desirable, because it might tend to limit the availability of damages for mental distress. It was not the case that losses which would be compensated by an award of aggravated damages could always be compensated under another, already recognised, head of damages for a particular tort. Some losses might only be compensated once it was found that the defendant had acted in a particularly bad manner; abolishing aggravated damages would prevent recovery for such losses. Accordingly, the Commission recommended legislation which clarified the true role of aggravated damages (see paras 2.39–2.42). However, in 2007, the government announced that subsequent decisions had introduced sufficient clarity to the law to obviate the need for a statutory definition so as to clarify that the purpose of aggravated damages is compensatory and not punitive (Department of Constitutional Affairs, *The Law of Damages* (2007), para. 205; cf. *Leveson*, Part J, ch. 3, para. 5.8).

In *Thompson v Commissioner of Police of the Metropolis* [1998] QB 498, giving general guidance on the award of aggravated damages against a public authority, the Court of Appeal indicated that, if it is appropriate to make such an award, it should rarely be less than £1,000 (around £2,000 in today's money) but should not normally amount to twice the basic compensatory damages unless the latter were modest.

In any case, where distress, humiliation and injury to feelings are already addressed through the basic compensatory award, there should be no further award for the same intangible injuries under the head of aggravated damages as this would give the claimant double recovery (*Rowlands v Chief Constable of Merseyside Police* [2007] 1 WLR 1065 at [26], per Moore-Bick LJ).

See further Murphy, 'The Nature and Domain of Aggravated Damages' [2010] CLJ 353; Tilbury, 'Aggravated Damages' (2018) 71 CLP 215.

5. Nominal Damages

Where a tort is actionable *per se*, the award of nominal damages denotes that the claimant's rights have been infringed by the defendant's tortious conduct even though the claimant has suffered no loss as a result of the tort. The claimant having suffered no loss is entitled to no substantial compensation, and is awarded no more than a few pounds, although the successful claimant will normally obtain a costs order in their favour. The award nevertheless performs the important function of vindicating the claimant's rights.

There has recently been some support—both judicial and academic—for the award of *substantial* 'vindicatory damages' to signal more emphatically that the infringement of the claimant's right should not have occurred (see *Attorney General of Trinidad and Tobago v Ramanoop* [2006] 1 AC 328 (Privy Council); *Ashley v Chief Constable of Sussex Police* [2008] 1 AC 962 at [22]–[23] and [29], per Lord Scott; *Stevens*, pp. 59ff; Witzleb and Carroll, 'The Role of Vindication in Tort Damages' (2009) 17 Tort L Rev 16). However, in *R (on the application of Lumba) v Secretary of State for the Home Department* [2012] 1 AC 245, a 6–3 majority of the Supreme Court ruled that vindicatory damages as such do not exist in English law. Expressing the majority reasoning, Lord Dyson JSC conceded that vindicatory damages might be appropriate in Commonwealth counties where the state can be liable for violating the Constitution, but rejected the application of the underlying reasoning to English law:

> 100 It is one thing to say that the award of compensatory damages, whether substantial or nominal, serves a vindicatory purpose: in addition to compensating a claimant's loss, it vindicates the right that has been infringed. It is another to award a claimant an additional award, not in order to punish the wrongdoer, but to reflect the special nature of the wrong. As Lord Nicholls made clear in *Ramanoop*, discretionary vindicatory damages may be awarded for breach of the Constitution of Trinidad and Tobago in order to reflect the sense of public outrage, emphasise the importance of the constitutional right and the gravity of the breach and deter further breaches. It is a big leap to apply this reasoning to any private claim against the executive . . .
>
> 101 The implications of awarding vindicatory damages in the present case would be far reaching. Undesirable uncertainty would result. If they were awarded here, then they could in principle be awarded in any case involving a battery or false imprisonment by an arm of the state. Indeed, why limit it to such torts? And why limit it to torts committed by the state? I see no justification for letting such an unruly horse loose on our law . . .

For comment, see Steel (2011) 127 LQR 527; Wilcox (2012) 3 JETL 390. For further discussion see Barker, 'Private and Public: The Mixed Concept of Vindication in Torts and Private law', *Challenging Orthodoxy*, ch. 3; Edelman, 'Vindicatory Damages', *Private Law in the 21st Century*, ch. 17; Varuhas, 'The Concept of "Vindication" in the Law of Torts. Rights, Interests and Damages' (2014) 34 OJLS 253. Rejecting the recognition of vindicatory damages in Australia: *Lewis v Australian Capital Territory* (2020) 381 ALR 375.

6. Contemptuous Damages

These are damages of a very small amount—very often the coin of lowest denomination in current circulation—which are designed to express contempt for the claimant's conduct, notwithstanding their (technical) victory on the law. They are very rarely awarded other than in defamation actions. In cases where contemptuous damages are awarded the successful claimant may not obtain a costs order in their favour. An example is provided by the case of the former Liverpool goalkeeper Bruce Grobbelaar, who sued *The Sun* over allegations that he had accepted bribes to let in goals from the opposition. After protracted legal proceedings the House of Lords in October 2002 reinstated the jury's original verdict in favour of Grobbelaar but reduced the damages from £85,000 to just £1 (*Grobbelaar v News Group Newspapers Ltd* [2002] 1 WLR 3024). Although *The Sun* had technically defamed Grobbelaar, because it had not demonstrated that he had sought to influence the result of any game in which he had played, other evidence showed that he had acted 'in a way in which no decent or honest footballer would act and in a way which could, if not exposed and stamped on, undermine the integrity of a game which earns the loyalty and support of millions': [2002] 1 WLR 3024 at 3036, per Lord Bingham. The following month their Lordships ordered Grobbelaar to pay two-thirds of *The Sun*'s legal costs—about £1m (*Guardian*, 27 November 2002). Although the winner in civil proceedings normally has their costs paid by the loser, the making of a purely contemptuous award justifies a change from the usual rule. As Lord Steyn explained in the October decision [2002] 1 WLR 3024 at 3038: 'By recovering only derisory damages Mr Grobbelaar has (effectively) lost the action to clear his name.' See further in Chapter 12.IV.1.

III. Lump Sums and Periodical Payments

Traditionally damages were recoverable once only and awarded as a lump sum. Where the loss was continuing, the court had to anticipate all that the future held in store for the claimant and adjust the lump sum accordingly. In a personal injury case, the greater the chance of recovery, the smaller the lump sum; the greater the chance of long-term disability, the larger the payment.

Lump sums are still the general rule. The payment made to the claimant includes compensation for both losses already suffered and those which are expected in the future. Each requires special adjustment in the light of a number of factors. Compensation for past losses must reflect the lapse of time between the date the losses were sustained and the date at which damages are awarded. As claimants are entitled to damages from the moment the loss is sustained, they are deprived of money that is rightfully theirs when they have to wait until trial to be paid. They lose the opportunity to use the money to their own advantage and see its real value diminish because of inflation. To make up for this, defendants are required to pay interest on top of the sum assessed as compensation for the claimant's pre-trial losses.

Where compensation for future losses is included in a lump sum award, it attracts no award of interest but does require adjustment to take into account the fact that the claimant's receipt of money is accelerated (the 'acceleration element'). Additionally, an adjustment must be made in respect of uncertainty as to what the future holds in store (the 'vicissitudes of life'). In *Lim Poh Choo v Camden & Islington Area Health Authority* [1980] AC 174 at 182–3, Lord Scarman summarised the 'insuperable problems' arising from the lump-sum rule in compensating for personal injuries:

> The award, which covers past, present and future injury and loss, must, under our law, be of a lump sum assessed at the conclusion of the legal process. The award is final; it is not susceptible to review as the future unfolds, substituting fact for estimate. Knowledge of the

future being denied to mankind, so much of the award as is to be attributed to future loss and suffering (in many cases the major part of the award) will almost surely be wrong. There is really only one certainty: the future will prove the award to be either too high or too low.

Lord Scarman emphasises that claimants cannot bring a second action on the same facts simply because their injuries turn out to be worse than was originally thought. As damages are usually assessed on a once-and-for-all basis, the court must make a guess as to how long the claimant's losses will continue into the future and how serious they will be. If the claimant's condition deteriorates or improves unexpectedly, that is of no significance (see *Fetter v Beal* (1701) 1 Ld Raym 339). As Lord Scarman observed, '[t]he award is final'.

The lump-sum, once-and-for-all rule was criticised by the *Pearson Commission* (1978), which considered that in cases of death or serious and lasting injury a system of periodic payments should be introduced, but this did not attract political support at the time. However, the Administration of Justice Act 1982, s. 6 made a slight inroad on the lump-sum rule by allowing for the award of so-called 'provisional damages'. Section 32A of the Senior Courts Act 1981 (as inserted; see also County Courts Act 1984, s. 51) provides:

(1) This section applies to an action for damages for personal injuries in which there is proved or admitted to be a chance that at some definite or indefinite time in the future the injured person will, as a result of the act or omission which gave rise to the cause of action, develop some serious disease or suffer some serious deterioration in his physical or mental condition.

(2) Subject to [minor exceptions] . . . as regards any action for damages to which this section applies in which a judgment is given in the High Court, provision may be made by rules of court for enabling the court, in such circumstances as may be prescribed, to award the injured person—

   (a) damages assessed on the assumption that the injured person will not develop the disease or suffer the deterioration in his condition; and

   (b) further damages at a future date if he develops the disease or suffers the deterioration.

The scheme consequently established (see CPR r. 41.2, 3 and Practice Direction 41) may be invoked by a person who has already suffered an injury, and fears a further disease or deterioration in future (e.g. epilepsy following a head injury), but not by a person for whom the risk of injury is entirely prospective: see *Rothwell v Chemical & Insulating Co Ltd* [2008] 1 AC 281. The procedure has the severe limitation that only one application for further damages can be made in respect of the type of injury or disease specified in the original action (CPR r. 41.3(2)). Awards of provisional damages are rare and one commentator has described the procedure as 'a backwater of personal injury litigation' (Lewis (1997) 60 MLR 230 at 237).

Another attempt to get around the problems created by the lump-sum, once and-for-all rule is the 'structured settlement' in which the parties agree that a portion of the damages is used to buy the claimant a life-assurance policy assuring a regular flow of income until the claimant's death or some other suitable date (see Law Commission, *Structured Settlements and Interim and Provisional Damages* (Law Com. No. 224, Cm. 2646, 1994), and R. Lewis, *Structured Settlements: The Law and Practice* (London: Sweet & Maxwell, 1993)). The big limitation of structured settlements was that they depended on the voluntary agreement of the parties: there was no judicial power to compel the parties to accept a 'structure'. Whether such a power should be introduced was considered in a governmental Consultation Paper in 2002, extracted here, which paved the way for the legislative introduction of 'periodical payment orders' (PPOs) by the Courts Act 2003.

Lord Chancellor's Department, *Damages for Future Loss: Giving the Courts the Power to Order Periodical Payments for Future Loss and Care Costs in Personal Injury Cases*, Consultation Paper (March 2002)

Lump Sums or Periodical Payments?

14. When successful claimants are awarded a lump sum they are paid for all past and future losses at once. However carefully the claimant's likely future losses and needs are estimated, they can never be known with certainty in advance. An underestimate will cause the claimant to suffer; an overestimate will unfairly penalise the defendant. We consider that greater use of periodical payments offers scope to reflect claimants' actual needs and losses more closely than is possible with lump sums.

15. The most significant area of uncertainty is the future life expectancy of the claimant. Unless claimants live for exactly the number of years expected, they will invariably be either over-or under-compensated by a lump sum. Periodical payments, on the other hand, continue for the actual lifetime of a permanently injured claimant, and cease on the claimant's death (unless the terms of a particular order or annuity provide otherwise).

16. The issue of life expectancy, and whether a lump sum will run out because they might live longer than expected, can be of concern to claimants. In particular, this concern can result in an overly cautious approach being adopted to spending money, leading to seriously injured or disabled claimants not receiving the required level of care or full benefits intended by the award. If the money runs out, either because they live for longer than expected, or they dissipate their award, claimants may need to fall back upon the State, causing an additional burden to the Government purse and the taxpayer.

17. If a claimant dies much earlier than expected, a lump sum award will provide a windfall for the heirs of that claimant, and it will be they who benefit most from the award. It is sometimes argued that this does not matter because the lump sum payment still serves to penalise the defendant. But the purpose of tort law in these cases is to compensate claimants for loss, in particular by restoring them, so far as possible, to the financial position they enjoyed before the accident: it is not to punish defendants or provide heirs of the deceased with a financial gain beyond any compensation that was awarded to them by the court. And the cost of any 'windfall' or 'profit' is ultimately borne, for example, by other insurance premium payers or by users of the NHS.

18. Lump sum compensation for future financial losses is a crude mechanism for restoring the claimant's position. Care costs are incurred over time, not all at once. Similarly, damages for lost earnings are intended to compensate for a stream of income that would have been earned in the future, not for the loss of an existing fortune. For these reasons, lump sums can place inappropriate pressures on claimants. There is a risk that claimants will be overawed by the amount awarded or that receipt of a very large sum may encourage a false sense of security. Claimants may also come under pressure from family or friends to spend the award inappropriately, for example by using money intended for their future care to help out someone in financial difficulties or to invest in a risky business venture. Although most adult claimants are free to spend their money as they choose, the system should not rely on a form of payment that enables, and arguably encourages, claimants to use their awards inappropriately.

19. Lump sums also impose on claimants the burden of investing the award (assuming they choose to do so) in a way that will enable them to purchase the care they require and to restore the income they have foregone because of the accident. It would be difficult for anyone to manage an entire lifetime's income so that it lasted until the day they died. That is why large awards often include provision for financial advice. But claimants may not seek or receive sound financial advice—lump sums can be difficult to manage, but easy to spend.

This difficulty is magnified when accident victims have to cope with the stress of ongoing disabilities and usually the knowledge that they have no alternative source of income.

20. Periodical payments, on the other hand, provide a guaranteed income and claimants will know exactly how much they are going to receive and when, without the need for expensive investment advice. They will know that they can spend the money on immediate needs, without the risk of depletion or worries about investment. Instead, periodical payments require the defendant or the defendant insurer to provide funds or invest in a manner that ensures successful claimants receive certain and ongoing streams of payments for the remainder of their lives. This places the risk associated with investment where it belongs, namely on the negligent party. And, in most cases, where that risk can be more effectively managed, namely on an insurance company or other large organisation. For example, insurance companies should be able to invest to meet their liabilities across a large portfolio of annuities or claims, with much lower overall expenditure on financial advice and other administrative costs compared to individuals each investing a single lump sum. Public sector defendants, in particular the NHS, will be better placed to manage their budgets effectively, because the total amounts paid out in damages in any given year will be more predictable. So periodical payments could offer advantages over lump sums for defendants, defendant insurers, and the NHS and its users, as well as for claimants.

21. It is sometimes argued that an advantage of lump sums is that they provide a clean break between the claimant and the defendant, putting an end to adversarial contact. The desire for a clean break is understandable. But where the defendant is insured, or is uninsured but has purchased an annuity, it will be a general insurer or life office making the stream of payments to the claimant, not the defendant. Similarly, with most clinical negligence cases, it is not the doctor or medical team that pay the compensation, but rather the NHS Litigation Authority. There is rarely an ongoing relationship with the negligent party in person. Moreover, facilities for electronic transfer of money can remove any personal element to the transaction. A more pertinent point concerning the clean break issue is . . . whether it should be possible to review awards of periodical payments.

22. To sum up, we consider that in most circumstances periodical payments are, in principle, the more appropriate means for paying compensation for significant future financial losses. They better reflect the purpose of compensation which is to restore the claimant's prior position. They place the risks associated with life expectancy and investment on defendants rather than claimants. This ensures that claimants who live longer than expected enjoy the quality of life they are entitled to, and do not have fall back on social security when the money runs out. It should also benefit defendants by allowing awards to be managed more cost-effectively. Lump sums invariably penalise one of the parties whereas periodical payments can provide better justice for both.

Damages Act 1996 (as amended by Courts Act 2003, s. 100)

Section 2: periodical payments

(1) A court awarding damages for future pecuniary loss in respect of personal injury—
   (a) may order that the damages are wholly or partly to take the form of periodical payments, and
   (b) shall consider whether to make that order.

(2) A court awarding other damages in respect of personal injury may, if the parties consent, order that the damages are wholly or partly to take the form of periodical payments.

(3) A court may not make an order for periodical payments unless satisfied that the continuity of payment under the order is reasonably secure . . .

(8) An order for periodical payments shall be treated as providing for the amount of payments to vary by reference to the retail prices index . . . at such times, and in such a manner, as may be determined by or in accordance with Civil Procedure Rules.

(9) But an order for periodical payments may include provision—
    (a) disapplying subsection (8), or
    (b) modifying the effect of subsection (8).

Damages (Variation of Periodical Payments) Order 2005, SI 2005/841

Article 1: Citation, commencement, interpretation and extent

. . . (2) In this Order—
    (a) 'the Act' means the Damages Act 1996;
    (b) 'agreement' means an agreement by parties to a claim or action for damages which settles the claim or action and which provides for periodical payments;
    (c) 'damages' means damages for future pecuniary loss in respect of personal injury . . .
    (f) 'variable order' means an order for periodical payments which contains a provision referred to in Article 2 . . .

Article 2: Power to make variable orders

If there is proved or admitted to be a chance that at some definite or indefinite time in the future the claimant will—

(a) as a result of the act or omission which gave rise to the cause of action, develop some serious disease or suffer some serious deterioration, or

(b) enjoy some significant improvement, in his physical or mental condition, where that condition had been adversely affected as a result of that act or omission, the court may, on the application of a party, with the agreement of all the parties, or of its own initiative, provide in an order for periodical payments that it may be varied . . .

Article 5: Contents of variable order

Where the court makes a variable order—

(a) the damages must be assessed or agreed on the assumption that the disease, deterioration or improvement will not occur;

(b) the order must specify the disease or type of deterioration or improvement;

(c) the order may specify a period within which an application for it to be varied may be made;

(d) the order may specify more than one disease or type of deterioration or improvement and may, in respect of each, specify a different period within which an application for it to be varied may be made;

(e) the order must provide that a party must obtain the court's permission to apply for it to be varied, unless the court otherwise orders . . .

> **Article 7: Limit on number of applications to vary**
>
> A party may make only one application to vary a variable order in respect of each specified disease or type of deterioration or improvement.

COMMENTARY

The Courts Act 2003, amending s. 2 of the Damages Act 1996, introduced a new judicial power to make a periodical payment order (PPO) with or without the consent of the parties. The court's coercive power is limited to damages for future pecuniary loss (s. 2(1)), although it may make an order for periodical payments in respect of other heads of damage with the consent of the parties (s. 2(2)). As was the case with structured settlements, the court must be convinced that the continuity of the payments is reasonably secure (s. 2(3)), e.g. because it is protected by a ministerial guarantee, covered by the statutory scheme providing an indemnity in the event of an insurer's insolvency, or to be paid by a government or health service body (s. 2(4), omitted from the extract). From the claimant's perspective, PPOs may be attractive not just because they protect against the risk that the compensation monies will run out, but also because (like structured settlements before them) they are accorded tax-free status.

The criteria to be used, and the procedure to be adopted, in determining whether to make a PPO are set out in Part 41 of the Civil Procedure Rules (as amended). Rule 41.7 states that the court must have regard to the form of award that best meets the claimant's needs. Further elaboration is to be found in a Practice Direction (PD41B), which states that the court must have regard to (amongst other things) the reasons for both the claimant's and defendant's preferences as to the form of award. Of course, it is not necessarily the case that the claimant will prefer a PPO (see Lush, 'Damages for Personal Injury: Why some claimants prefer a conventional lump sum to periodical payments' (2005) 1 London L Rev 187), and there has been judicial recognition that a PPO may not be appropriate where there is contributory negligence and the annual sum, reduced accordingly, would not fully cover the claimant's continuing care and other needs (*Rowe v Dolman* [2008] EWCA Civ 1040). For most claimants, a further key concern will be to ensure a sufficient contingency fund—whether instead of or in addition to periodical payments—to meet unexpected needs.

According to the official guidance (Department of Constitutional Affairs, *Guidance on Periodical Payments*, 2005, para. 8) the calculation of the periodical sum is to be effected by a 'bottom-up' approach:

> An important principle underlying the introduction of the power to order periodical payments was that it should lead to a fundamental change in the way in which these payments are calculated. Instead of the traditional 'top-down' approach used for structured settlements, requiring uncertain assumptions about life expectancy and investment, it is intended that where a periodical payments order is made or agreed, a 'bottom-up' approach will be adopted, which focuses instead on calculating the annual future needs of the claimant . . . Moving from a 'top-down' to a 'bottom-up' approach means that the claimant should no longer need financial advice on how to 'structure' the payments or on the best priced annuity available to meet his or her needs. The 'bottom-up' approach places the onus on the defendant to decide how to meet the terms of the court order or settlement.

The Guidance states that a top-down approach would preserve many of the disadvantages associated with lump sums, and—after the application of multipliers to allow for inflation, life expectancy and a discount rate—would produce payments which were unlikely to match the original assessment of the claimant's annual needs (paras 24–5).

By the Damages (Variation of Periodical Payments) Order 2005, a court may make a 'variable order' where there is a chance that the claimant will in future develop some serious disease or suffer some serious deterioration in their condition as a result of the tortious conduct, or that they will enjoy some significant improvement in his condition (Article 2). There is also provision for parties to a structured settlement to make it a 'variable agreement' in like circumstances (Article 9). But there can be no variation of a PPO or structured settlement except where the initial order or agreement was specified to be variable. The scope of the current provisions is thus the same as that governing the award of provisional lump sum damages (see the start of this section), except that they allow for the significant improvement of the claimant's condition, not just its deterioration. The Order follows the Lord Chancellor's Department's earlier recommendation that the power of variation should be limited to cases where the change in condition was foreseen and specified because allowing variation in respect of unforeseen medical changes would introduce unacceptably high levels of uncertainty and potential cost for both parties (*Damages for Future Loss*, 2002, para. 58). But the Order does not adopt the LCD's associated recommendation (paras 67–71) that variation should be allowed in other cases of significant unforeseen change (e.g. the death of a carer).

Independently of the 'variable order' procedure, the court may provide that the PPO may take the form of a 'stepped' order by stipulating in advance that the annual payment should increase or decrease in anticipation of changes in the claimant's condition or other significant changes of circumstances (e.g. when the claimant reaches the age of 18). (See CPR r. 41.8(3).)

The claimant is not allowed to assign or charge the right to receive periodical payments without the approval of the court and any attempt to do so is void (s. 2(6)). Thus the claimant may not foil the order of the court by selling their right to periodical payments in return for a lump sum. However, this presupposes that there has in fact been a judicial order for periodical payments. An important limitation on the court's power to override the wishes of the parties is that the vast majority of damages claims—even for very serious personal injuries—never reach the court at all but are the subject of out-of-court settlement. (See Ch. 17.I.3.) Except in cases involving children or 'patients' unable to manage their own affairs, there is no judicial control over the form of the settlement agreed by the parties. One commentator (Lewis (2006) 69 MLR 418 at 425) has accordingly concluded that lump sums will likely predominate even in serious injury cases, but he notes that the reform will still affect such cases because 'the possibility of imposing a PPO substantially influences the bargaining position of the parties' (e.g. because one side may be able to exploit the other's preference for a lump sum).

The PPO regime was strongly supported by claimants' organisations, but received a more guarded response from the liability insurance sector which feared that it would cost substantially more to fund a PPO than a traditional lump sum. However, it is too simplistic to describe the reform as a victory for claimants over liability insurers. As Lewis suggests, in the following extract, the short-term interests of the government in its management of public finances arguably provided the crucial impetus.

R. Lewis, 'The Politics and Economics of Tort Law: Judicially Imposed Periodical Payments of Damages' (2006) 69 MLR 418

[T]he catalysts for reform lay within Government itself . . . Claimants' interests were very much secondary to those involving public finance and the demands of the NHS. Far from being what they appear on the surface, the reforms in fact were politically driven.

The political and economic advantages to Government of periodical payments are as follows. In contrast to the problems faced by liability insurers, Government bodies such as the Ministry of Defence and especially the NHS will make immediate gains. This is because their budgets will no longer be denuded by the loss of large capital sums paid as damages. Their cash-flow will be improved because they can self-fund the periodical payments and they are not required to enter the expensive annuity market. It was forecast that in the first year of the new regime the NHS could save as much as £245 million out of the £330 million they would otherwise have to pay for the larger claims. This cash-flow saving will continue at a diminishing rate for 24 years until the accumulated liabilities reach, and thereafter outgrow, what would have been the capital sums needed to dispose of the claims entirely . . .

No matter what the short-term gains for the Treasury and the NHS, ultimately the taxpayer will have to pick up the total damages bill. There are at least two reasons to be concerned about this. First, the payments eventually are likely to be higher than they would have been if the traditional lump sums had continued to be used. This is because the move towards bottom-up assessments irrespective of the capital cost of providing the index-linked periodical payments drives up the ultimate cost of an award, and this will have an effect even upon those able to self-fund. Moreover, the tax and benefits savings made by the claimant in receiving payments in this way also occurs at a cost to the Exchequer. Secondly, the deferring of payments accumulates a debt which eventually will have to be met. The projection is that after 24 years the impact upon the cash-flow will be negative. That is, at that time not only will the good times come to an end and have to be paid for, but also there will be a real and increasing additional cost to the public purse. This cost may be relatively small in relation to the entire NHS budget, but Government finances should beware of these contingent liabilities, especially in the light of current concern about whether we should be paying more to fund future pensions in general. In effect, it will be our children who will have to find the money to pay for the full cost of today's medical negligence . . .

COMMENTARY

In Lewis's view, the reform can be considered amongst others in recent decades that effect a transfer of the rising cost of tort damages from the public to the private sphere (e.g. to liability insurers). Other reforms that may be mentioned here include the state's recoupment of social security benefits paid to successful claimants (see IV.4(b)), and the costs of their NHS treatment (see IV.3(b)). Of course, these costs are further dispersed throughout the private sphere. As Lewis observes (p. 441), 'the transfer results in a "stealth tax" which all premium payers and, ultimately, society at large must pay'. This brings us back—yet again—to one of the fundamental questions for all students of tort law: who is it that *really* pays the costs of the tort system?

IV. Damages for Personal Injury

A successful claimant is entitled to recover all losses—pecuniary or non-pecuniary (i.e. financial or non-financial)—that flow from the defendant's tort. Financial losses (e.g. loss of earnings or medical expenses) incurred up to the date of trial can be added up accurately and are termed 'special damages'. The sums claimed must be specified in the claimant's initial schedule of damages. Damages for financial losses that the claimant expects to incur in the future cannot be specified accurately and together with damages for non-pecuniary loss are termed 'general damages'.

For each head of loss the claimant is also entitled to the payment of interest as compensation for the diminution of the real value of money in the pre-trial period. Interest is normally awarded on special damages at half the special investment rate for money paid into court, from the date of the accident to the date of the trial (*Cookson v Knowles* [1979] AC 556; Law Commission, *Damages for Personal Injury: Medical, Nursing and Other Expenses; Collateral Benefits* (Law Com. No. 262, 1999), paras 7.1–7.16) and on non-pecuniary loss at a rate of 2 per cent, from date of service of the writ to the date of the trial (*Wright v British Railways Board* [1983] 2 AC 773; Law Commission, *Damages for Personal Injury: Non-Pecuniary Loss* (Law Com. No. 257, 1999), paras 2.29–2.58).

1. Non-Pecuniary Losses

(a) General

No amount of money can fully compensate for the loss of a limb or for extreme pain. Indeed, the assessment of damages for non-pecuniary losses has been described as an 'intrinsically impossible task' (*Cassell v Broome* [1972] AC 1027 at 1070, per Lord Hailsham LC). Nevertheless, 'slowly and painfully English law has evolved ways of assessing the incalculable' (*West v Shephard* [1964] AC 326 at 359, per Lord Devlin).

> **Royal Commission on Civil Liability and Compensation for Personal Injury, Chairman: Lord Pearson, *Report*** Cmnd 7054 (1978)
>
> **The function of damages for non-pecuniary loss**
>
> 359 By definition, money cannot make good a non-pecuniary loss. Yet damages for non-pecuniary loss are recoverable in both English law and, as *solatium*, in Scots law. Indeed they are recoverable in some form in almost all tort systems.
>
> 360 What, then, is the purpose of an award for non-pecuniary loss? Clearly it cannot provide full compensation—no amount of money can drive away pain and suffering, or restore a lost limb. But at least three functions may be suggested. First, a conventional award may serve as a palliative. Pain and suffering and loss of amenity are real enough, at least for the seriously injured plaintiff; and he may well feel entitled to some reparation where these misfortunes befall him because of an injury for which someone else is liable. Secondly, an award for non-pecuniary loss may enable the plaintiff to purchase alternative sources of satisfaction to replace those he has lost. Thirdly, it may help to meet hidden expenses caused by his injury. Although in theory all expenses resulting from injury are recoverable as pecuniary loss, in practice some of them may well be unquantifiable or unforeseen.

Heil v Rankin [2001] QB 272

The facts are not relevant to the extract.

Lord Woolf MR

25 In the case of pecuniary loss, the courts have progressively been prepared to adopt ever more sophisticated calculations in order to establish the extent of a claimant's loss. . . . In the case of non-pecuniary damages, the scale of damages has remained a 'jury question'. This is the position notwithstanding section 6 of the Administration of Justice (Miscellaneous Provisions) Act 1933, as a result of which the use of a jury to try personal injury cases became discretionary. In practice, since the 1960s the assessment of damages has been carried out primarily by the judiciary. The assessment requires the judge to make a value judgment. That value judgment has been increasingly constrained by the desire to achieve consistency between the decisions of different judges. Consistency is important, because it assists in achieving justice by facilitating settlements. The courts have become increasingly aware that this is in the interests of the litigants and society as a whole, particularly in the personal injury field. Delay in resolving claims can be a source of great injustice as well as the cause for expense to the parties and the justice system. It is for this reason that the introduction by the Judicial Studies Board ('JSB') in 1992 of its *Guidelines for the Assessment of General Damages in Personal Injury Cases* was such a welcome development . . .

27 Excessive importance must not, however, be attached to consistency. Care must be exercised not to freeze the compensation for non-pecuniary loss at a level which the passage of time and changes in circumstances make inadequate. The compensation must remain fair, reasonable and just. Fair compensation for the injured person. The level also must not result in injustice to the defendant, and it must not be out of accord with what society as a whole would perceive as being reasonable.

28 Whilst recognising the dangers which can arise from too rigid an application of tariffs, it has been the continuous responsibility of the courts not only to set tariffs for damages for non-pecuniary loss in the case of personal injuries, but also, having done so, to keep the tariffs up to date. The courts sought to achieve this by deciding guideline cases and subsequently making allowance for inflation, that is, the depreciation in the value of money, since the guideline was laid down. This usually involved doing no more than applying the guideline decision the appropriate difference between the RPI [Retail Price Index] at the date on which the guideline case was decided and the RPI at the date on which the guideline was applied.

29 However, the changes which take place in society are not confined to changes in the RPI. Other changes in society can result in a level of damages which was previously acceptable no longer providing fair, reasonable and just compensation, taking into account the interests of the claimants, the defendants and society as a whole. For this reason, it is clearly desirable for the courts at appropriate intervals to review the level of damages so as to consider whether what was previously acceptable remains appropriate.

COMMENTARY

It is now generally accepted that the most the law can do is provide for an award that is 'fair'. As is indicated in the extract, fairness is achieved in part through consistency in the level of awards, and this is ensured by awarding 'conventional' sums for non-financial losses, assessed after comparison with awards made in like cases in the past. Details of recent awards appear in the practitioners' work *Kemp & Kemp: Quantum of Damages*, and, as noted in the extract, further guidance is provided by what is now the Judicial College (*Guidelines for the*

Assessment of General Damages in Personal Injury Cases, 15th edn (2019)). Some illustrative 'brackets' indicated in the *Guidelines* may be cited by way of example: tetraplegia—£304,630 to £379,100; loss of both arms—£205,420 to £255,930; total blindness—in the region of £252,180; total deafness and loss of speech—£102,890 to £132,040; loss of smell—£23,460 to £30,870; total impotence and loss of sexual function and sterility in the case of a young man—in the region of £139,210; a woman's infertility with severe depression and anxiety, pain and scarring—£107,810 to £158,970 (the awards are much smaller for men and women who have already had children); severe post-traumatic stress disorder—£56,180 to £94,470; loss of or serious damage to several front teeth—£8,200 to £10,710. What criteria do you think are employed in assessing the guideline figures? Do you think that the law attaches *the right* value to these very different injuries? (For an attempt to value non-pecuniary losses objectively—with concepts borrowed from the field of health economics—see Karapanou and Visscher, 'Towards a Better Assessment of Pain and Suffering Damages' (2010) 1 JETL 48.)

The figures cited in the preceding text reflect an across-the-board increase in damages for non-pecuniary loss effected by the courts as part of a package of measures implementing proposals in the Review of Civil Litigation Costs led by Jackson LJ (the *Jackson Report* of 2009). The increase, intended to offset the effects of statutory changes in litigation funding and costs introduced by the Legal Aid, Sentencing and Punishment of Offenders Act 2012 (see Ch. 17.I.2), was announced by the Court of Appeal in *Simmons v Castle (Note)* [2013] 1 WLR 1239 and (subject to transitional arrangements) took effect from April 2013. The increase did not require legislation as it is the task of the Court of Appeal to set the tariffs for damages and keep them up to date.

Legislation in 2018 made a small but significant alteration to the common law approach by providing for a new statutory tariff to apply to whiplash injuries, meaning soft-tissue injuries in the neck, back or shoulder that are not connected to other injuries, where their actual or expected duration is less than two years (Civil Liability Act 2018, ss. 1 and 3). The Whiplash Injury Regulations 2021 establish an ascending scale of fixed sum payments banded by reference to duration (reg. 2), ranging from £240 for injuries of not more than three months (£260 if accompanied by minor psychological injury), to £4,215 for injuries of more than eighteen months but not more than twenty-four months (£4,345 if accompanied by minor psychological injury). An uplift of up to 20 per cent is allowed in exceptional circumstances where the judge finds either that the whiplash injury is exceptionally severe or that the injured person's exceptional circumstances increase the pain, suffering or loss of amenity caused (reg. 3). The reform was intended both to reduce the damages for whiplash injury below the levels of the Judicial College guidelines (which provide for damages of £1,290 to £2,300 for minor injuries where there is a complete recovery within three months) and to make it easier for litigants in person to identify the correct level of damages when bringing a claim in the small claims court (see further Ch. 17.I).

Should there be damages for non-pecuniary loss at all?

Whether tort law should compensate at all for non-pecuniary loss has been disputed. As *Atiyah* points out (p. 395), few compensation systems other than tort provide compensation as a palliative measure or to pay for alternative sources of satisfaction, and the reality is that the tort system is largely financed by insurance premiums paid by a substantial section of the public: 'one is forced to ask whether there are not other claims on society's resources which deserve priority . . . It is hard to justify compensation for mental distress and deprivation of pleasure when many disabled people receive little or no compensation even for income losses.' The *Pearson Commission* reached a similar conclusion:

382 We were struck by the high cost of compensation for non-pecuniary loss. It accounts for more than half of all tort compensation for personal injury, and for a particularly high proportion of small payments.

383 We think it likely that payments for minor non-pecuniary loss represent, in part, the price of a settlement. It may well be in the interests of the defendant's insurance company to offer more than a court would award as compensation for the plaintiff's pain and suffering and loss of amenity, in order to avoid the expense of continuing argument and possible litigation. We think this is wasteful.

384 Most of us find it hard to justify payments for minor or transient non-pecuniary losses, such as may equally be incurred through sickness or some everyday mishap. We find it impossible to justify their use as bargaining counters. The emphasis in compensation for non-pecuniary loss should in our view be on serious and continuing losses, especially loss of faculty.

The Commission recommended, by a majority, that no damages should be recoverable for non-pecuniary loss suffered during the first three months after the date of injury (para. 388). It estimated that this would produce a saving in the cost of tort compensation of about one-fifth of all awards for personal injury. The proposal was specifically rejected by the Law Commission, which took the view that it lacked any principled basis (*Damages for Personal Injury: Non-Pecuniary Loss* (Law Com. No. 257, 1999), paras 2.25–2.28), and has not been implemented.

Cf. the position in Australia, where most jurisdictions have eliminated claims for non-pecuniary loss for minor injury; see, e.g., Civil Liability Act 2002 (NSW), s. 16.

(b) Two Forms of Non-Financial Loss

Two categories of non-financial loss must be distinguished: pain and suffering, on the one hand, and loss of amenities, on the other. As Lord Scarman observed in *Lim Poh Choo v Camden & Islington AHA* [1980] AC 174 at 188:

> [The authorities] draw a clear distinction between damages for pain and suffering and damages for loss of amenities. The former depend on the plaintiff's personal awareness of pain, her capacity for suffering. But the latter are awarded for the fact of deprivation, a substantial loss, whether the plaintiff is aware of it or not.

Pain and suffering, then, is assessed subjectively: the damages measure the degree of pain actually felt by the claimant (and reflect therefore their capacity for suffering). Under this head, the claimant may recover damages to represent the trauma of knowing that their life expectancy has been shortened by the accident (Administration of Justice Act 1982, s. 1(1)(b); see *Kadir v Mistry* [2014] EWCA Civ 1177). Note that the previous, objectively assessed and conventional figure awarded for loss of expectation of life (see *Benham v Gambling* [1941] AC 157) was abolished by the Administration of Justice Act 1982, s. 1(1)(a).

Loss of amenities by contrast is assessed objectively. The sum awarded depends on the degree of deprivation—that is, the extent to which the victim is unable to do those things which but for the injury they would have been able to do (cf. Law Commission, *Damages for Personal Injury: Non-Pecuniary Loss* (Consultation Paper No. 140, 1995), para. 2.10). The claimant's lifestyle will be crucial here. As Lord Pearce has remarked, '[i]f there is loss of amenity apart from the obvious and normal loss inherent in the deprivation of the limb—for instance, the claimant's main interest in life was some sport or hobby from which he will in future be debarred, that . . . increases the assessment' (*West v Shephard*, extracted next, at 365).

The English approach to damages for non-pecuniary loss represents, then, a compromise between subjective and objective approaches, with the former applying to the calculation of damages for pain and suffering, and the latter to the award for loss of amenities. The competing merits of the two approaches were debated in a succession of cases dealing with claimants who were left with impaired consciousness as a result of the tortious conduct in question: *Wise v Kay* [1962] 1 QB 638; *H. West & Son Ltd v Shephard* [1964] AC 326 and *Lim Poh Choo v Camden and Islington Area Health Authority* [1980] AC 174. The present approach was decisively adopted by the House of Lords in *West v Shephard* (confirmed by the subsequent decision of the House of Lords in *Lim*).

H West & Son Ltd v Shephard [1964] AC 326

The plaintiff, a 41-year-old woman, sustained very severe injuries in a motor vehicle accident caused by the negligence of the defendant driver. She was left with cerebral atrophy on her right side and paralysis of all four limbs. As a result, she was no longer able to speak, and such communications as she was able to make were limited to movements of the eyes, face and right hand. She showed a very limited ability to understand what was said to her and might, to some extent, have been able to appreciate the condition she was in, but she suffered from a severe degree of dementia and there was no prospect of further improvement. She was unable to feed herself and required full-time hospital nursing care. At the date of the trial, some two years after the accident, her life expectancy was assessed at five years.

The House of Lords was obliged to rule on the correctness of the decision of the Court of Appeal in *Wise v Kay* [1962] 1 QB 638 to the effect that substantial damages may be awarded for loss of amenity even to a plaintiff who is unconscious.

Lord Morris

My Lords, the damages which are to be awarded for a tort are those which 'so far as money can compensate, will give the injured party reparation for the wrongful act and for all the natural and direct consequences of the wrongful act' (*Admiralty Comrs v Susquehanna (Owners), The Susquehanna* [1926] AC 655 at 661 per Viscount Dunedin). The words 'so far as money can compensate' point to the impossibility of equating money with human suffering or personal deprivations. A money award can be calculated so as to make good a financial loss. Money may be awarded so that something tangible may be procured to replace something else of like nature which has been destroyed or lost. But money cannot renew a physical frame that has been battered and shattered. All that judges and courts can do is to award sums which must be regarded as giving reasonable compensation. In the process there must be the endeavour to secure some uniformity in the general method of approach. By common assent awards must be reasonable and must be assessed with moderation. Furthermore, it is eminently desirable that so far as possible comparable injuries should be compensated by comparable awards. When all this is said it still must be that amounts which are awarded are to a considerable extent conventional.

In the process of assessing damages judges endeavour to take into account all the relevant changes in a claimant's circumstances which have been caused by the tortfeasor. These are often conveniently described as 'heads of damage' . . . If there has been some serious physical injury which, as the result of skilled medical attention, has happily not necessitated the enduring of pain, then it will follow that there will be no question of including in an award any sum as compensation for the enduring of pain. If someone has been made unconscious so that pain is not felt the like result will follow. Damages are awarded as a fair compensation for that which has in fact happened and will not arise in respect of anything that has not happened . . .

Certain particular questions have been raised. How are general damages affected, if at all, by the fact that the sufferer is unconscious? How are they affected, if at all, if it be the fact that the sufferer will not be able to make use of any money which is awarded?

The first of these questions may be largely answered if it is remembered that damages are designed to compensate for such results as have actually been caused. If someone has been caused pain then damages to compensate for the enduring of it may be awarded. If, however, by reason of an injury someone is made unconscious either for a short or for a prolonged period with the result that he does not feel pain then he needs no monetary compensation in respect of pain because he will not have suffered it. Apart from actual physical pain it may often be that some physical injury causes distress or fear or anxiety. If, for example, personal injuries include the loss of a leg, there may be much physical suffering, there will be the actual loss of the leg (a loss the gravity of which will depend on the particular circumstances of the particular case) and there may be (depending on particular circumstances) elements of consequential worry and anxiety. One part of the affliction (again depending on particular circumstances) may be an inevitable and constant awareness of the deprivations which the loss of the leg entails. These are all matters which judges take into account. In this connexion also the length of the period of life during which the deprivations will continue will be a relevant factor (see *Rose v Ford* [1937] AC 826). To the extent to which any of these last-mentioned matters depend for their existence on an awareness in the victim it must follow that they will not exist and will not call for compensation if the victim is unconscious. An unconscious person will be spared pain and suffering and will not experience the mental anguish which may result from knowledge of what has in life been lost or from knowledge that life has been shortened. The fact of unconsciousness is therefore relevant in respect of, and will eliminate, those heads or elements of damage which can only exist by being felt or thought or experienced. The fact of unconsciousness does not, however, eliminate the actuality of the deprivations of the ordinary experiences and amenities of life which may be the inevitable result of some physical injury.

If damages are awarded to a plaintiff on a correct basis, it seems to me that it can be of no concern to the court to consider any question as to the use that will thereafter be made of the money awarded. If follows that if damages are assessed on a correct basis, there should not then be a paring down of the award because of some thought that a particular plaintiff will not be able to use the money. In assessing damages there may be items which will only be awarded if certain needs of a claimant are established. A particular plaintiff may have provision made for some future form of transport: a particular plaintiff may have to have provision made for some special future attention or some special treatment or medication. If, however, some reasonable sum is awarded to a plaintiff as compensation for pain endured or for the loss of past or future earnings or for ruined years of life or lost years of life, the use to which a plaintiff puts such sum is a matter for the plaintiff alone. A rich man, merely because he is rich and is not in need, is not to be denied proper compensation: nor is a thrifty man merely because he may keep and not spend . . .

Lord Pearce

The loss of happiness of the individual plaintiff is not, in my opinion, a practicable or correct guide to reasonable compensation in cases of personal injury to a living plaintiff. A man of fortitude is not made less happy because he loses a limb. It may alter the scope of his activities and force him to seek his happiness in other directions. The cripple by the fireside reading or talking with friends may achieve happiness as great as that which, but for the accident, he would have achieved playing golf in the fresh air of the links. To some ancient philosophers the former kind of happiness might even have seemed of a higher nature than the latter, provided that the book or the talk were such as they would approve. Some less robust persons on the other hand are prepared to attribute a great loss of happiness to a quite trivial event. It would be lamentable if the trial of a personal injury claim put a premium on protestations of misery and if a long face was the only safe passport to a large award. Under the present practice there is no call for a parade of personal unhappiness. A plaintiff who cheerfully admits that he is as happy as he was, may yet receive a large award as reasonable compensation for the grave injury and loss of amenity over which he has managed to triumph.

Lord Reid (dissenting)

What is the basis on which damages for serious injuries are awarded? The determination of that question in the ordinary case where the injured person is fully conscious of his disability will go far to decide how to deal with a case like *Wise v Kaye* where the injured person was wholly unconscious with no prospect of ever regaining consciousness or like the present case where the respondent is only conscious to a slight extent.

In the ordinary case of a man losing a leg or sustaining a permanent internal injury, he is entitled to recover in respect of his pain and suffering: if he is fortunate in suffering little pain, he must get a smaller award. So it is not disputed that where an injured person does not suffer at all because of unconsciousness he gets no award under this head. Nothing was awarded in *Wise's* case and nothing has been awarded in this case. On the other hand no one doubts that damages must be awarded irrespective of the man's mental condition or the extent of his suffering where there is financial loss. That will cover the cost of treatment or alleviation of his condition just as much as it covers the cost of repairing or renewing his property. And it will cover loss of earning power: there may be a question whether some deduction should be made where his outgoings will be less than they would have been if there had been no accident, so as to reach his net financial loss, but that does not arise in the present case. The difficulty is in connexion with what is often called loss of amenity and with curtailment of his expectation of life. If there had been no curtailment of his expectation of life, the man whose injuries are permanent has to look forward to a life of frustration and handicap and he must be compensated, so far as money can do it, for that and for the mental strain and anxiety which results. But I would agree with Sellers LJ in *Wise's* case that a brave man who makes light of his disabilities and finds other outlets to replace activities no longer open to him must not receive less compensation on that account.

There are two views about the true basis for this kind of compensation. One is that the man is simply being compensated for the loss of his leg or the impairment of his digestion. The other is that his real loss is not so much his physical injury as the loss of those opportunities to lead a full and normal life which are now denied to him by his physical condition—for the multitude of deprivations and even petty annoyances which he must tolerate. Unless I am prevented by authority I would think that the ordinary man is, at least after the first few months, far less concerned about his physical injury than about the dislocation of his normal life. So I would think that compensation should be based much less on the nature of the injuries than on the extent of the injured man's consequential difficulties in his daily life. It is true that in practice one tends to look at the matter objectively and to regard the physical loss of an eye or a limb as the subject for compensation. But I think that is because the consequences of such a loss are very much the same for all normal people. If one takes the case of injury to an internal organ, I think that the true view becomes apparent. It is more difficult to say there that the plaintiff is being paid for the physical damage done to his liver or stomach or even his brain, and much more reasonable to say that he is being paid for the extent to which that injury will prevent him from living a full and normal life and for what he will suffer from being unable to do so.

If that is so, then I think it must follow that if a man's injuries make him wholly unconscious so that he suffers none of these daily frustrations or inconveniences, he ought to get less than the man who is every day acutely conscious of what he suffers and what he has lost. I do not say that he should get nothing. This is not a question that can be decided logically. I think that there are two elements, what he has lost and what he must feel about it, and of the two I think the latter is generally the more important to the injured man. To my mind there is something unreal in saying that a man who knows and feels nothing should get the same as a man who has to live with and put up with his disabilities, merely because they have sustained comparable physical injuries. It is no more possible to compensate an unconscious man than it is to compensate a dead man. The fact that the damages can give no benefit or satisfaction to the injured man and can only go to those who inherit the dead man's estate would not be a good reason for withholding damages which are legally due. But it is, in my view, a powerful argument against the view that there is no analogy between a dead man and a man who is unconscious and that a man who is unconscious ought to be treated as if he were fully conscious . . .

Lord Tucker concurred with Lord Morris. **Lord Devlin** delivered a separate dissenting opinion.

Appeal dismissed.

COMMENTARY

In *Lim Poh Choo v Camden and Islington Area Health Authority* [1980] AC 174, the House of Lords rejected a challenge to the authority of *West*. The plaintiff, a 36-year-old senior psychiatric registrar employed by the NHS, suffered serious injuries when she had a minor operation at the defendant's hospital. Following the operation her breathing stopped and she suffered a cardiac arrest, leaving her 'the wreck of a human being . . . only intermittently, and then barely, sentient and totally dependent on others' (at 182, per Lord Scarman). Although she was a helpless invalid needing total care, her life expectancy remained substantially as it had been before the accident. At trial, she was awarded £20,000 plus interest in respect of pain, suffering and loss of amenities (in addition to various sums awarded in respect of pecuniary losses). This award was upheld by the House of Lords, Lord Scarman, who delivered the leading speech, stated (at 188):

[I]t would be wrong now to reverse by judicial decision the two rules which were laid down by the majority of the House in *H. West & Son Ltd v Shephard*, namely (1) that the fact of unconsciousness does not eliminate the actuality of the deprivation of the ordinary experiences and amenities . . . and (2) that, if damages are awarded on a correct basis, it is of no concern to the court to consider any question as to the use that will thereafter be made of the money awarded.

A Functional Approach to the Assessment of Damages for Non-Pecuniary Loss?

English law, as the extract demonstrates, ignores the use to which an injured claimant may be expected to put any damages recovered (but cf. Lord Reid's dissent). A different view prevails in Canada where what is known as a 'functional' approach has been adopted (see *Andrews v Grand & Toy Alberta Ltd* (1978) 83 DLR (3d) 452, *Thornton v Board of School Trustees of*

School District No 57 (1978) 83 DLR (3d) 480 and *Arnold v Teno* (1978) 83 DLR (3d) 609). It was described in the following terms by Dickson J in *Andrews* (at 476–7):

> The . . . 'functional' approach . . . attempts to assess the compensation required to provide the injured person 'with reasonable solace for his misfortune'. 'Solace' in this sense is taken to mean physical arrangements which can make his life more endurable rather than 'solace' in the sense of sympathy. To my mind, this . . . approach has much to commend it, as it provides a rationale as to why money is considered compensation for non-pecuniary losses such as loss of amenities, pain and suffering, and loss of expectation of life. Money is awarded because it will serve a useful function in making up for what has been lost in the only way possible, accepting that what has been lost is incapable of being replaced in any direct way . . . If damages for non-pecuniary loss are viewed from a functional perspective, it is reasonable that large amounts should not be awarded once a person is properly provided for in terms of future care for his injuries and disabilities. The money for future care is to provide physical arrangements for assistance, equipment and facilities directly related to the injuries. Additional money to make life more endurable should then be seen as providing more general physical arrangements above and beyond those relating directly to the injuries. The result is a co-ordinated and interlocking basis for compensation, and a more rational justification for non-pecuniary loss compensation.

The functional approach has twice been rejected by the Law Commission (*Personal Injuries Litigation: Assessment of Damages* (Law Com. No. 56, 1973), para. 31; *Damages for Personal Injury: Non-Pecuniary Loss* (Law Com. No. 257, 1999), para. 2.7). One of the Commission's particular concerns (expressed in *Damages for Personal Injury: Non-Pecuniary Loss* (Consultation Paper No. 149, 1995), para. 4.09) was that 'it is unrealistic to assume that substitute pleasures can provide full solace to a plaintiff . . . Even if one thinks in terms of some of the damages being used to provide substitute pleasures, a sum would still seem to be required to make up for the loss of capacity to enjoy life that inevitably remains after "substitutes" have been bought.' Additionally, the Commission feared that awarding damages according to the uses to which a particular claimant could be expected to put the money would leave too much to the circumstances of the individual case, entail the abandonment of the tariff system and result in inconsistency in awards (*ibid.*).

Effect of Unconsciousness on Award of Damages for Non-Pecuniary Loss

Although the Law Commission rejected the functional approach of the Canadian courts, it did not regard the English 'diminution in value' approach as entirely satisfactory either. Considering the situation of the unconscious claimant, it stated (*ibid.*, para. 4.14):

> [W]e are attracted by the view that non-pecuniary loss should be rationalised in terms of the mental suffering and loss of happiness caused to the plaintiff. If the plaintiff is so badly injured that he or she is incapable of suffering, then we consider it strongly arguable that, just as if the plaintiff had been instantly killed, the plaintiff should be regarded as incurring no non-pecuniary loss at all; that, in other words, all non-pecuniary loss should be assessed subjectively (through the plaintiff's awareness of it) and not objectively (irrespective of the plaintiff's awareness of it).

The Commission indicated that this approach—which it termed 'the personal approach'—did not entail that claimants who made light of their injury would receive lower damages than others who failed to come to terms with their condition (para. 4.15). Why should this not follow?

The Commission rejected three possible objections to its approach:

(i) to the objection that the award of substantial damages to an unconscious claimant is necessary because it can never be certain that they are not suffering, the Commission replied that medical science is indeed capable of determining whether an individual patient is sentient of their condition (para. 4.16);

(ii) against the argument that the Commission's approach would produce the perverse result that it is cheaper to injure someone more seriously than less seriously, the Commission responded that 'this begs the question as to what are the relevant criteria for determining the seriousness of an injury: the basis of the "personal" approach is that the plaintiff who cannot feel anything is in a better position than someone who experiences pain and suffering' (para. 4.17);

(iii) in response to the concern that the introduction of a nil award for loss of amenity in such cases would produce a lacuna in the rights of a claimant's dependants, the Commission maintained that the rights of dependants should be addressed directly, and that an award in respect of their distress should not be disguised through an award to the injured claimant (para. 4.18).

After receiving responses from consultees, however, the final recommendation of the Commission was that no change in the law was required (*Damages for Personal Injury: Non-Pecuniary Loss* (Law Com. No. 257, 1999), para. 2.19). Arguments in favour of the present position included the fear that a subjective approach would lead to a lower award for non-pecuniary loss in respect of catastrophic injuries than for less serious ones. Further, consultees were not convinced by the Commission's previous responses to possible arguments: many expressed the concern that an allegedly unconscious claimant may have some level of awareness (para. 2.14), and some feared that the failure to award damages for loss of amenity to an unconscious claimant would in fact result in the dependants being deprived of compensation (para. 2.15). Which arguments do you find convincing here?

See further Ogus, 'Damages for Lost Amenities: for a Foot, a Feeling or a Function?' (1972) 35 MLR 1, and cf. *Skelton v Collins* (1966) 115 CLR 94.

2. Loss of Earnings

In cases of serious and lasting injury, the sum awarded for loss of earnings may be the most significant element of the damages. For a young employed adult claiming in respect of practically the whole of their working life, the damages for loss of earnings can easily run to hundreds of thousands of pounds, and awards of over a million pounds are increasingly common. As we have seen, damages for loss of earnings up to the date of trial fall under the head of 'special damages' as they can be assessed accurately and without undue difficulty; to the extent that the claimant has been 'kept out of their money' by being made to wait for receipt of this sum, the courts take account of this by the award of interest. It is in respect of future losses (i.e. those after the date of trial) that real difficulties arise.

(a) Future Losses

Only in a very small minority of claims (5.5 per cent, according to *Pearson*, vol. 2, para. 44) does a tort damages payment include compensation for future loss of earnings. But the injuries in such cases are likely to be among the most serious, and it is therefore necessary to take particular care to ensure the award is adequate. Where the loss is expected to continue for a period of years, there are two ways of calculating the appropriate award, depending on whether the claimant is to receive a lump sum or a periodical payment. Both methods may also be applied to other financial losses, for example medical costs, that are expected to continue into the future.

The traditional approach is the 'multiplier method' used for lump-sum compensation. The sum awarded is the product of two figures. The multiplicand is the annual loss (net of deductions) that the court expects the claimant to suffer. The multiplier reflects the number of years that the court estimates the loss will continue, adjusted to take account of the 'vicissitudes of life' and the fact of accelerated payment (the claimant receives a lump sum immediately and is therefore given investment opportunities that would not otherwise have presented themselves). The multiplier thus reflects a 'discount rate' derived from tables prepared on behalf of the government Actuary's Department (*Actuarial Tables with Explanatory Notes for Use in Personal Injury and Fatal Accident Cases*, 8th edn, updated 2021; commonly known as 'the Ogden Tables' after the judge who supervised the first edition). The tables give estimated life expectancies for men and women of different ages, and indicate how these should be adjusted in respect of projected retirement age, contingencies other than death (e.g. redundancy or inability to work because of sickness) and the assumed rate of return on investment ('the discount rate').

Setting the discount rate has proved particularly controversial, because it inevitably involves a certain amount of guesswork yet can have a very significant impact on the damages recoverable. Prior to *Wells v Wells* [1999] 1 AC 345, a discount rate of 4.5 per cent was conventionally applied, but the House of Lords found that this was unrealistically high in the prevailing economic circumstances and thus unduly depressed the value of court awards of damages. The Law Lords therefore adopted a lower rate of 3 per cent. Subsequently, exercising a power derived from the Damages Act 1996, s. 1, the Lord Chancellor intervened to set the presumptive rate at 2.5 per cent (Damages (Personal Injury) Order 2001, SI 2001/2301). Changed economic circumstances following the global financial crisis of 2008 meant that investments struggled to generate the returns presupposed even by this lower discount rate, and could in fact lose value relative to earnings. The problem was recognised by the government in consultations conducted in 2012 and 2013 (Ministry of Justice, 'Damages Act 1996: The Discount Rate: How Should it be Set?' (2012); Ministry of Justice, 'Damages Act 1996: The Discount Rate – Review of the Legal Framework' (2013)) but the actual change in the discount rate had to wait until the Damages (Personal Injury) Order 2017, setting the presumed rate of return on the investment of damages at *minus* 0.75 per cent, in recognition that damages could be expected to lose value over time even with prudent investment. Because of concern about the additional costs this would impose on businesses and consumers purchasing liability insurance, and on the public sector, the Ministry of Justice launched a new consultation in March 2017 to see whether the way in which the discount rate is set might be changed, departing from the *Wells v Wells* assumption of risk-free investment, so as to avoid not just under- but also over-compensation of injured persons (Ministry of Justice/Scottish Government, 'The Personal Injury Discount Rate: How It Should Be Set in Future', 2017). The outcome was s. 10 of the Civil Liability Act 2018, changing the basis of the actuarial assessment of the discount rate from *very low risk* to merely *less than ordinary risk* investments (amending the Damages Act 1995). This paved the way for the further revision of the discount rate to minus 0.25 per cent by the Damages (Personal Injury) Order 2019, reflecting the changed basis of assessment.

In recent years, the courts have been able to avoid the difficulties associated with the multiplier method by making a periodical payment order (PPO) instead of a lump sum award. A PPO is 'a wholly different creature . . . [T]here is neither a multiplicand nor a multiplier' (*Thompstone v Tameside and Glossop Acute Services NHS Trust* [2008] 1 WLR 2207 at [61], per Waller LJ). The court simply prescribes an annual amount that is to be paid at specified intervals for a stated period of time (e.g. until the claimant reaches a particular age or the claimant's death). A crucial advantage of the PPO is that it takes away the risk that the claimant's investment strategy might not provide sufficient protection against the effects of inflation, as explained further in the following extracts.

Flora v Wakom (Heathrow) Ltd [2007] 1 WLR 482

In a judgment with which the rest of the Court of Appeal agreed, Brooke LJ briefly reviewed the earlier developments summarised in the preceding text, and then proceeded to contrast the established approach to lump sums with the approach to be taken in respect of periodical payments, which were introduced by the Courts Act 2003, amending s. 2 of the Damages Act 1996.

Brooke LJ

27 This brief summary of the recent history of the discount rate used for the purpose of calculating lump sum awards for future pecuniary loss is sufficient to show that an award of a lump sum is entirely different in character from an award of periodical payments as a mechanism for compensating for such loss. When setting the appropriate discount rate in the context of a lump sum award the House of Lords or the Lord Chancellor had to guess the future and to hope that prudent investment policy would enable a seriously injured claimant to benefit fully from the award for the whole of the period for which it was designed to provide him/her with appropriate compensation.

28 A periodical payments order is quite different. This risk is taken away from the claimant. The award will provide him or her year by year with appropriate compensation, and the use of an appropriate index will protect him/her from the effects of future inflation. If he or she dies early the defendant will benefit because payments will then cease. It is unnecessary in the context of this statutory scheme to make the kind of guesses that were needed in the context of setting a discount rate. The fact that these two quite different mechanisms now sit side by side in the same Act of Parliament does not in my judgment mean that the problems that infected the operation of the one should be allowed to infect the operation of the other. There is nothing in the statute to indicate that in implementing section 2 of the 1996 Act (as substituted) Parliament intended the courts to depart from what Lord Steyn described in *Wells v Wells* [1999] 1 AC 345, 382–3 as the '100% principle', namely that a victim of a tort was entitled to be compensated as nearly as possible in full for all pecuniary losses . . .

R. Lewis, 'The Indexation of Periodical Payments of Damages in Tort: The Future Assured?' (2010) 30 LS 391

The key distinguishing feature of a PPO is that . . . there is no need to calculate any lump sum in order to work out what periodical payments must be made. Instead, using a 'bottom-up' approach, the court assesses the periodical payments the claimant needs for the future, irrespective of their capital cost. These annual payments do not have to be adjusted to take account of speculative estimates of the claimant's life expectancy; nor do returns have to be forecast of the income that arises upon investment of the damages: the lump sum is not there to invest. Instead, the defendant must comply with the order to make the specified regular payments no matter how the market performs and even if the claimant lives longer than forecast. In contrast to the traditional lump sum system, therefore, it is the defendant rather than the claimant who is exposed to an uncertain financial future by being burdened with the twin risks of investment return and mortality.

This can be explained further by noting that in the calculations needed for a PPO there is no place for the 'Ogden Tables'. That is, multipliers and discount rates are not used: no multiplier is required to reflect the period of years of the loss in order to convert it into an immediate capital amount; and no discount rate is needed to convert the future stream of financial losses into a capital sum representing present day values. The discount rate, in particular, continues to operate very harshly against claimants negotiating lump sums. This is because it expects claimants to obtain an unrealistic rate of return on their damages award. However, when PPOs are being considered, defendants cannot take advantage of the artificially high estimate of investment return embedded in the discount rate for lump sums. Instead, they can be ordered to provide annual payments irrespective of what this might cost as an equivalent capital sum. Furthermore, the order extends for an uncertain period—the rest of the claimant's life. The risks of uncertainty traditionally run by claimants have thus been transferred to defendants.

The Indexation Issue and the Potential Shortfall in Payments

In spite of the considerable advantages offered by PPOs as a result of this transfer of the mortality and investment risks, there was still concern that the new form of payment might not be widely used. For almost 3 years after the Courts Act 2003 came into force, it was thought that the lump sum might be more flexible, and better able to deal with the claimant's needs. This argument succeeded in a number of cases with the result that, although PPOs were being considered, ultimately they were often rejected. Why were claimants' lawyers and courts having doubts about the efficacy of judicial 'bottom-up' assessments which transferred the above risks? The answer lay in concern about exposing the claimant to another risk: this was that the periodical payments would not offer sufficient protection against anticipated increases in care costs because these were more affected by wage rates rather than prices. Although protection against price increases could be guaranteed, protection against wage increases could not. Whether it could be achieved depended on how payments were to be indexed. This was crucial to the future use of periodical payments.

Periodical payments have the advantage of providing certainty of provision for life. However, unless they are linked to an appropriate index the certainty they achieve may become the certainty of under-provision. The concern was that, even if periodical payments were tied to increases in the RPI, they would be insufficient to meet the claimant's future needs. This is because home care costs make up only about one tenth of 1 per cent of the RPI, and they have only a limited relationship with increases in the price of those consumer goods and services which dominate the index. Most future losses of personal injury claimants are directly or indirectly related not to price increases but to earnings. In particular, a very large element of future care costs is dependent upon the earnings of those workers who provide the care . . . Historically, on average, for the past 70 years the earnings of the population at large has risen about 2 per cent more each year than prices. Claimants and their advisors therefore feared that if this general trend were also to apply to care workers, then any award of periodical payments based on the RPI would prove insufficient to meet long-term care needs.

COMMENTARY

Flora v Wakom was the first major landmark in the 'indexation litigation' whose background is described in the extract from Lewis's article. At issue were the presumptive linking of payments under a PPO with the retail prices index (s. 2(8) of the Damages Act 1996 (as amended)) and the court's power to disapply that linking in an appropriate case (s. 2(9) of the Act). The claimant sought a PPO under which the sums payable would vary by reference to average earnings, not prices, as the main heads of his claim were future loss of earnings (necessarily wage-related) and the cost of future care (largely, if not entirely, wage-related). The Court of Appeal rejected the defendant's application to strike out this part of the claim, noting that there was nothing to limit s. 2(9) to exceptional cases. In *Thompstone v Tameside and Glossop Acute Services NHS Trust* [2008] 1 WLR 2207, the Court of Appeal rejected a challenge to its *Flora* decision and for the first time exercised the s. 2(9) power, accepting after an exhaustive review that it was appropriate to index future care costs on the basis of the Annual Survey of Hours and Earnings (ASHE), which tracks pay-rates by occupational category (here, care assistants and home carers).

In the conclusion of his article (not extracted here), Lewis praises the Court of Appeal for providing significantly greater security to claimants with serious long-term injuries. Of course, the increase in awards does not come cost-free, but the Court of Appeal stated clearly that it was not for the courts to consider questions of affordability once liability has been established and damages are being assessed (*Flora v Wakom*, at [29] per Brooke LJ; *Thompstone*, at [47]ff per Waller LJ).

Child Claimants

The calculation of damages for future pecuniary loss is especially tricky where the claimant is a child. The main difficulty is that there may be very little evidence as to what the child's earnings would be in later life. The courts therefore tend to take average national earnings as the starting-point (*Croke v Wiseman* [1982] 1 WLR 71), but a deviation from the average figure might be appropriate if the child were nearing the end of a job training scheme or embarking on a university law degree or had enjoyed a career as a child TV star. More controversially, the courts have also on occasion taken genetic inheritance and family circumstances into consideration. In one—surely very exceptional—case, the Court of Appeal approved an annual figure of almost 2.5 times national average earnings even though the claimant was injured at birth and was only 8 at the time of the trial (*Cassel v Riverside Health Authority* [1992] PIQR Q168). The court took account of the claimant's favourable family circumstances (caring, close-knit, happy and well-to-do) and heredity—several of his forebears had achieved success in commerce, the arts and the professions, including an uncle, grandfather and great grandfather who all became Queen's Counsel, his parents both achieved several 'O' and 'A' Levels at school, and his father had increased his assets by prudent investment in property, as others in the family had done in the past. The claimant therefore likely possessed 'legal ... artistic and entrepreneurial genes': [1992] PIQR Q1 at Q15 per Rose J. He would also have had as good an education as money could buy, having been put down for Eton (the famous private school) at or before birth. All things considered, it was reasonable to assume that he would have enjoyed earnings equivalent to the salary of a partner in a medium-sized City law firm. Do you think it is justified to compensate for loss of a career that the claimant could not even have embarked on for another dozen years or more?

In cases of significant uncertainty as to what the claimant would have earned in the absence of the tortious act, the courts have sometimes calculated the damages as a single global sum (see *Clarke v Devon County Council* [2005] 2 FLR 747, a case of failure to diagnose and treat dyslexia, where it was uncertain what the claimant would have earned if he had received special education). By contrast, where an annual figure can be estimated with greater confidence, it has been possible to apply the multiplier method sketched out earlier, but with an additional reduction in the multiplier, over and above that made in the case of an adult claimant. The greater reduction is required so as to reflect the passage of time before the child reaches working age, which both increases the uncertainties in comparison with an adult claimant, as many things could happen before the child was old enough to seek employment, and accelerates the payment the child receives (so a child claimant has longer to invest the money and a greater return can therefore be expected). These considerations led in the past to the adoption of very low multipliers for future economic loss in claims brought by children. In *Croke v Wiseman* [1982] 1 WLR 71, for example, a multiplier of five was adopted after the plaintiff, aged 21 months at the time of his accident and 7 years at the time of his trial, had suffered severe brain damage that rendered him incapable of working and reduced his life expectancy so that he was expected to live only until 40. In such a case, it is clear that the lump sum awarded will fall far short of what the claimant ought in justice to receive if he fulfils or surpasses his life expectancy. The advantages of periodical payment orders in this context are obvious, as the payment can continue for as long as the claimant survives and, as noted earlier (in III), it is possible to make a 'stepped' order whereby the amount paid each year is increased on the claimant attaining working age.

(b) The Lost Years

Where a person's life expectancy is reduced by an accident, do damages for loss of future earnings reflect the pre-or post-accident life expectancy? If the former, they may be styled 'wages in heaven', that is, they will compensate for a period in which the claimant is now expected to be dead. Lord Denning has described the problem as follows (*What Next in the Law* (London: Butterworths, 1982), p. 146):

> Take a man of thirty. If he had not been injured, he would have expected to live, say, till seventy-five. But owing to his injury, he will probably die at fifty. No doubt he should get damages for his loss of earnings from age thirty to age fifty. But is he to get damages for loss of earnings from age fifty to age sixty-five when he would have retired? Those fifteen years from fifty to sixty-five are 'lost years'—lost to him by reason of the accident. Ought damages be awarded for the 'lost years'?

The conclusion reached by the House of Lords in *Pickett v British Rail Engineering* [1980] AC 136 was that damages should indeed be awarded for the lost years. These would be calculated by taking the annual amount appropriate for the time during which, but for the accident, the claimant would have been alive and deducting from it the money the claimant would save by being dead, that is, their living expenses. Alternatively, the court may now make a PPO, providing for the payment of the full annual loss until the claimant dies, and then a reduced amount to the claimant's dependants until a specified date (e.g. when the claimant would have reached retirement age). But the same basic principle applies whether the award is in the form of a lump sum or a PPO: the damages extend to the lost years.

Pickett v British Rail Engineering Ltd [1980] AC 136

The deceased contracted the asbestos-related cancer, mesothelioma, while working for the defendant and as a result of the defendant's admitted negligence. Before his death, he issued a writ against the defendant claiming damages for personal injuries. The defendant contested the quantum of liability. The judge awarded the deceased damages under various heads, including a sum in respect of loss of earnings which covered only the one year from the date of trial for which the deceased was expected to survive (here the trial judge was bound by the previous Court of Appeal decision in *Oliver v Ashman* [1962] 2 QB 210). The deceased's estate appealed, arguing that damages for loss of future earnings should cover the whole period of the deceased's pre-tort working life expectancy.

Lord Wilberforce

In 1974, when his symptoms became acute, the deceased was a man of 51 with an excellent physical record. He was a champion cyclist of Olympic standard, he kept himself very fit and was a non-smoker. He was leading an active life and cycled to work every day. He had a wife and two children. There was medical evidence at the trial as to his condition and prospects, which put his then expectation of life at one year: this the judge accepted. There can be no doubt that but for his exposure to asbestos dust in his employment he could have looked forward to a normal period of continued employment up to retiring age. That exposure, for which the defendant accepts liability, has resulted in this period being shortened to one year. It seems, therefore, strange and unjust that his claim for loss of earnings should be limited to that one year (the survival period) and that he should recover nothing in respect of the years of which he has been deprived (the lost years). But this is the result of authority binding on the judge and the Court of Appeal, *Oliver v Ashman*. The present is, in effect, an appeal against that decision.

Oliver v Ashman is part of a complex of law which has developed piecemeal and which is neither logical nor consistent. Judges do their best to make do with it but from time to time cases appear, like the present, which do not appeal to a sense of justice. I shall not review in any detail the state of the authorities for this was admirably done by Holroyd Pearce LJ in *Oliver v Ashman*. The main strands in the law as it then stood were: (1) the Law Reform (Miscellaneous Provisions) Act 1934 abolished the old rule *actio personalis moritur cum persona* and provided for the survival of causes of action in tort for the benefit of the victim's estate; (2) the decision of this House in *Rose v Ford* [1937] AC 826 that a claim for loss of expectation of life survived under the 1934 Act, and was not a claim for damages based on the death of a person and so barred at common law (cf. *Admiralty Comrs v Owners of Steamship Amerika* [1917] AC 38); (3) the decision of this House in *Benham v Gambling* [1941] AC 157 that damages for loss of expectation of life could only be given up to a conventional figure, then fixed at £200; (4) the Fatal Accidents Acts under which proceedings may be brought for the benefit of dependants to recover the loss caused to those dependants by the death of the breadwinner; the amount of this loss is related to the probable future earnings which would have been made by the deceased during 'lost years'.

This creates a difficulty. It is assumed in the present case, and the assumption is supported by authority, that if an action for damages is brought by the victim during his lifetime, and either proceeds to judgment or is settled, further proceedings cannot be brought after his death under the Fatal Accidents Acts. If this assumption is correct, it provides a basis, in logic and justice, for allowing the victim to recover for earnings lost during his lost years.

This assumption is based on the wording of s. 1 of the 1846 Act (now s. 1 of the Fatal Accidents Act 1976) and is not supported by any decision of this House. It cannot however be challenged in this appeal, since there is before us no claim under the Fatal Accident Acts. I think therefore, that we must for present purposes act on the basis that it is well founded, and that if the present claim, in respect of earnings during the lost years, fails it will not be possible for a fresh action to be brought by the deceased's dependants in relation to them.

With this background, *Oliver v Ashman* may now be considered. I shall deal with it on authority and on principle . . .

[Having considered whether the decision in *Oliver v Ashman* was justified by the authorities, and found that it was not, his Lordship proceeded:]

As to principle, the passage which best summarises the underlying reasons for the decision in *Oliver v Ashman* is the following (at 240, per Willmer LJ):

> . . . what has been lost by the person assumed to be dead is the opportunity to enjoy what he would have earned, whether by spending it or saving it. Earnings themselves strike me as being of no significance without reference to the way in which they are used. To inquire what would have been the value to a person in the position of this plaintiff of any earnings which he might have made after the date when ex hypothesi he will be dead strikes me as a hopeless task.

Or as Holroyd Pearce LJ put it ([1962] 2 QB 210 at 230): 'What is lost is an expectation, not the thing itself.'

My Lords, I think that these are instinctual sentences, not logical propositions or syllogisms, none the worse for that because we are not in the field of pure logic. It may not be unfair to paraphrase them as saying: 'Nothing is of value except to a man who is there to spend or save it. The plaintiff will not be there when these earnings hypothetically accrue: so they have no value to him.' Perhaps there are additional strands, one which indeed Willmer LJ had earlier made explicit, that the whole process of assessment is too speculative for the courts to undertake; another that the only loss is a subjective one, an emotion of distress. But if so I would disagree with them. Assumptions, chances, hypotheses enter into most assessments, and juries had, we must suppose, no difficulties with them; the judicial approach, however less robust, can manage too. And to say that what calls for compensation is injured feelings does not provide an answer to the vital question which is whether, in addition to this subjective element, there is something objective which has been lost.

But is the main line of reasoning acceptable? Does it not ignore the fact that a particular man, in good health, and sound earning, has in these two things an asset of present value quite separate and distinct from the expectation of life which every man possesses? Compare him with a man in poor health and out of a job. Is he not, and not only in the immediate present, a richer man? Is he not entitled to say, at one moment I am a man with existing capability to earn well for 14 years, the next moment I can only earn less well for one year? And why should he be compensated only for the immediate reduction in his earnings and not for the loss of the whole period for which he has been deprived of his ability to earn them? To the argument that 'they are of no value because you will not be there to enjoy them' can he not reply, 'Yes they are; what is of value to me is not only my opportunity to spend them enjoyably, but to use such part of them as I do not need for my dependants, or for other persons or causes which I wish to support. If I cannot do this, I have been deprived of something on which a value, a present value, can be placed'?

I do not think that the problem can be solved by describing what has been lost as an 'opportunity' or a 'prospect' or an 'expectation'. Indeed these words are invoked both ways, by the Lords Justices as denying a right to recover (on grounds of remoteness, intangibility or speculation), by those supporting the appellant's argument as demonstrating the loss of some real asset of true value. The fact is that the law sometimes allows damages to be given for the loss of things so described (e.g. *Chaplin v Hicks* [1911] 2 KB 786), sometimes it does not. It always has to answer a question which in the end can hardly be more accurately framed than as: 'Is the loss of this something for which the claimant should and reasonably can be compensated?'

The defendant, in an impressive argument, urged on us that the real loss in such cases as the present was to the victim's dependants and that the right way in which to compensate them was to change the law (by statute; judicially it would be impossible) so as to enable the dependants to recover their loss independently of any action by the victim. There is much force in this, and no doubt the law could be changed in this way. But I think that the argument fails because it does not take account, as in an action for damages account must be taken, of the interest of the victim. Future earnings are of value to him in order that he may satisfy legitimate desires, but these may not correspond with the allocation which the law makes of money recovered by dependants on account of his loss. He may wish to benefit some dependants more than, or to the exclusion of, others; this (subject to family inheritance legislation) he is entitled to do. He may not have dependants, but he may have others, or causes, whom he would wish to benefit, for whom he might even regard himself as working. One cannot make a distinction, for the purposes of assessing damages, between men in different family situations.

There is another argument, in the opposite sense—that which appealed to Streatfeild J in *Pope v D. Murphy & Son Ltd* [1961] 1 QB 222. Why, he asked, should the tortfeasor benefit from the fact that as well as reducing his victim's earning capacity he has shortened his victim's life? Good advocacy but unsound principle, for damages are to compensate the victim not to reflect what the wrongdoer ought to pay.

My Lords, in the case of the adult wage earner with or without dependants who sues for damages during his lifetime, I am convinced that a rule which enables the 'lost years' to be taken into account comes closer to the ordinary man's expectations than one which limits his interest to his shortened span of life. The interest which such a man has in the earnings he might hope to make over a normal life, if not saleable in a market, has a value which can be assessed. A man who receives that assessed value would surely consider himself and be considered compensated; a man denied it would not. And I do not think that to act in this way creates insoluble problems of assessment in other cases. In that of a young child (cf. *Benham v Gambling*) neither present nor future earnings could enter into the matter; in the more difficult case of adolescents just embarking on the process of earning (cf. *Skelton v Collins* (1966) 115 CLR 94) the value of 'lost' earnings might be real but would probably be assessable as small.

There will remain some difficulties. In cases, probably the normal, where a man's actual dependants coincide with those for whom he provides out of the damages he receives, whatever they obtain by inheritance will simply be set off against their own claim. If on the other hand this coincidence is lacking, there might be duplication of recovery. To that extent injustice may be caused to the wrongdoer. But if there is a choice between taking a view of the law which mitigates a clear and recognised injustice in cases of normal occurrence, at the cost of the possibility in fewer cases of excess payments being made, or leaving the law as it is, I think that our duty is clear. We should carry the judicial process of seeking a just principle as far as we can, confident that a wise legislator will correct resultant anomalies.

Lord Salmon, **Lord Edmund-Davies** and **Lord Scarman** delivered separate concurring speeches. **Lord Russell of Killowen** dissented on the question of the 'lost years'.

Appeal allowed.

COMMENTARY

The question of the appropriate deduction in respect of living expenses under the rule in *Pickett* was considered by the Court of Appeal in *Harris v Empress Motors* [1984] 1 WLR 212. It held that the court should only deduct those sums spent by the plaintiff exclusively on themselves; money that was spent on dependants should not be deducted even if it could be regarded as benefiting the plaintiff too (e.g. paying the bills for a common residence). Compare the position with regard to such sums under the Fatal Accidents Act 1976 (see Ch. 16).

As Lord Wilberforce intimated, child claimants again raise special problems. The general position of the courts here—exemplified by the decision of the Court of Appeal in *Croke v Wiseman* (see earlier)—has been to regard earnings in the lost years as too speculative to make any award under this heading, although in the case of a child claimant with an established earning capacity an award might be justified (see Lord Scarman's example of a 5-year-old child TV star in *Gammell v Wilson* [1982] AC 27). It would also be unfair to ignore the lost years where their number is very large—as in the case of a child claimant whose post-accident life expectancy only just reaches adulthood—and in such a case they may be compensated through a small adjustment in the multiplier applied to the basic multiplicand, rather than by a separate calculation (*Neale v Queen Mary's Sidcup NHS Trust* [2003] EWHC 1471; see further *Housecroft v Burnett* [1986] 1 All ER 332 at 345, per O'Connor LJ). Limitation periods run against a claimant injured as a child only when they attain the age of majority, and if the claimant has indeed reached adulthood, the position changes and the lost years claim should be recognised (*JR v Sheffield Teaching Hospitals NHS Foundation Trust* [2017] 1 WLR 4847). The element of speculation in such a case is much less than where the claimant is still a young child.

For criticism of the *Croke* approach excluding lost years' claims by young children, see *Iqbal v Whipps Cross University Hospital NHS Trust* [2008] PIQR P9 at [45]f and [64] where Gage LJ considered the automatic exclusion to be inconsistent with *Pickett* and *Gammell*, but binding on the Court of Appeal. He was unwilling to accept that such claims were always so speculative that a court could not make a reasonable estimate of the loss.

In *Pickett* Lord Wilberforce expressed the generally held view that, once a claimant had successfully brought an action for their injuries while they were alive, this prevented their dependants from suing for loss of dependency under the fatal accidents legislation, even if the death was the result of the original tort. The solution reached in *Pickett* was to allow the living claimant a claim for 'lost years' but in *Gregg v Scott* [2005] 2 AC 176 at [182] Lord Phillips stated that a better solution would be to allow the dependants a claim even if the deceased had already successfully brought an action during his lifetime. From the dependants' point of view, using the lost years claim as a means of providing for them after the claimant's premature death carries two risks—at least where the claimant's damages are awarded in a lump sum. First, the claimant may spend the lost years component of the award before they die, with the result that there is nothing left for the dependants on the claimant's death. Secondly, even if the claimant has not dissipated this portion of their award by their death, whatever is left over will fall to be distributed under their will. Whilst the dependants may well be beneficiaries under the will, they do not have to be—and if they are not none of the lost years award will filter down to them. Given that one reason given in *Pickett* for allowing the lost years award was to provide for the dependants, do you agree with Lord Phillips' assessment that the protection of their interests by an award for the lost years is 'a poor substitute' for a direct claim for loss of dependency under the Fatal Accidents

Act 1976? Note, however, that the court now has power to make a periodic payment order in cases where damages for lost years are awarded (see CPR r. 41.8(2)). The order may provide, for example, for the payment of the full annual loss to the claimant until they die, and then a reduced amount to their dependants until a specified date (e.g. for the period during which the claimant would have been alive and providing financial support). Such an order would provide far greater protection for the dependants' interests than a lump sum awarded to the claimant, but not as much as an independent claim under the Fatal Accidents Act (where the amount of the award is calculated more generously than in a lost years claim: see Ch. 16.III).

3. Medical Care

(a) General

The cost of medical care is recovered in the same way as any other form of financial loss. In the case of future medical care, the courts again have a choice between the traditional multiplier method and a PPO. In both cases, the period of loss may be longer than that for the loss of earnings, because the victim's care needs may continue past retirement age.

One issue that arises here, and has been touched on earlier, is that 'inflation-proofing' the award by reference to movements in the retail price index may be inadequate, because care costs have historically risen faster than the RPI (see *Wells v Wells* [1999] 1 AC 345 at 369, per Lord Lloyd). The courts have already addressed this concern in respect of PPOs by opting to link the annual amount awarded for future medical care to average earnings, rather than prices (see in IV.2(a)). This contrasts with the approach taken to the award of lump sum damages, where no adjustment to either multiplier or multiplicand has yet been permitted. In *Cooke v United Bristol Healthcare NHS Trust* [2004] 1 WLR 251 the Court of Appeal ruled that the Lord Chancellor in setting the standard discount rate under the Damages Act 1996, s. 1 had plainly intended it to apply to care costs, not just lost earnings. His aim was to prescribe a single discount rate even at the expense of a somewhat 'rough and ready' approach to future pecuniary losses. There was no warrant for treating claims where future care costs were likely to be very high as 'exceptional' under s. 1 (2) and applying a different discount rate to them (see further *Warriner v Warriner* [2002] 1 WLR 1703, ruling that a departure from the stipulated rate could only be justified if there were special features of the case which had not been considered by the Lord Chancellor in setting the rate). Nor was it permissible to allow for future rises in care costs by stepped increases in the multiplicand, as this would be an illicit attempt to subvert the Lord Chancellor's order indirectly. Do you think it is justifiable to take a different approach to the inflation-proofing of future care costs depending on whether the award is made by PPO or lump sum?

A particular problem arises where the claimant is spared certain expenses as an incidental by-product of medical care. Where the claimant is in hospital, many of their day-to-day needs may be satisfied by the hospital. Thus, for example, there may be no need to spend money on meals as food is provided. If the claimant is being treated on the NHS, the position is governed by s. 5 of the Administration of Justice Act 1982. This section seeks to avoid double recovery by providing that maintenance at the public expense is to be taken into account by way of a set-off to damages awarded for lost earnings. If the claimant elects for private treatment, then the courts will deduct a 'domestic element' from the cost of the treatment so as to avoid overlap with that proportion of the claimant's lost earnings that would have gone on living expenses (per Lord Scarman in *Lim* at 191). In *Lim*, Lord Scarman concluded that the plaintiff was entitled to recover a sum representing her loss of earnings and her cost of care, but an amount reflecting the domestic element was deducted from the latter head of damages.

(b) Mitigation of Loss and the State Provision of Care

There is no duty to mitigate by seeking treatment on the NHS rather than privately. Law Reform (Personal Injuries) Act 1948, s. 2(4) provides:

> In an action for damages for personal injuries (including any such action arising out of a contract), there shall be disregarded, in determining the reasonableness of any expenses, the possibility of avoiding those expenses or part of them by taking advantage of facilities available under the National Health Service Act 2006 . . .

A claimant is therefore quite free to opt for private medical care instead of that which is offered free by the state, and cannot be accused of failing to mitigate in exercising that option. The subsection does not apply to the provision of care and assistance by local authorities, but a claimant who wishes to 'go private' in preference to reliance on statutory care or assistance provided by a local authority is also entitled to damages for the cost as of right: *Peters v East Midlands Strategic Health Authority* [2010] QB 48. Of course, if the claimant has in fact received state care they cannot claim for private treatment. As regards future medical treatment, if the claimant's needs cannot fully be met in the private sector, so that at some stage they will have to rely on the state, then a claim for the cost of private medical care will be reduced, and if the only way that treatment can be provided is through the NHS no claim for private treatment will be allowed (see *Housecroft v Burnett* [1986] 1 All ER 332; *Woodrup v Nicol* [1993] PIQR Q104). The prospect of the claimant claiming for the cost of future private medical care but in fact using the NHS prompted the *Pearson Commission* to recommend the repeal of s. 2(4) (para. 342) but the Law Commission recommended the section be retained, considering it unlikely that problems would arise in practice (*Damages for Personal Injury: Medical, Nursing, and Other Expenses* (Consultation Paper No. 144, 1996), paras 3.10–3.13, 3.18; *Damages for Personal Injury: Medical, Nursing and Other Expenses: Collateral Benefits* (Law Com. No. 262, 1999), para 3.18; see also Department of Constitutional Affairs, *The Law on Damages* (2007), paras 146–63).

In a related development, the government in 2001 requested that the Chief Medical Officer (CMO)—in a review of clinical negligence law and practice—consider whether the care costs element of NHS compensation payments should continue to be based on the costs of private rather than NHS care. In his subsequent report (*Making Amends*, 2003), the CMO noted concern expressed by claimant and patient groups at the NHS's capacity to provide care in accident cases currently handled in the private sector, and at the range of treatments and services the NHS was able to provide (para. 4.32). He also accepted that empirical investigation of how claimants used their damages did not support the contention that claimants who received damages reflecting the cost of private treatment in fact made frequent use of NHS services to provide their care (para. 4.30). Nevertheless, he submitted that the NHS was in a different position from other defendants, and recommended that clinical negligence claims arising from NHS treatment should be exempted from s. 2(4) (recommendation 17). In response to obvious concerns about the equity of exempting a state defendant from a responsibility imposed on defendants generally, the proposal was substantially watered down. The NHS Redress Act 2006 now provides for the creation of a scheme enabling redress to be provided to the victims of NHS negligence without recourse to civil proceedings, with 'redress' expressly extended beyond financial compensation to cover contracts to provide care or treatment (s. 3(3)(a)). In other words, the redress scheme would be able to offer the aggrieved party a special NHS care package—perhaps equivalent to private health care—in addition to financial compensation, making it less likely that the latter would opt for private care and seek to recover the costs in ordinary civil proceedings. What the impact would be on ordinary NHS care, and whether it is desirable to have a two-tier NHS, are large questions which we cannot address here. At the time of writing, sixteen years after it was enacted, the statute had still not been brought into force in England, though implementing regulations were passed in Wales in 2011 (Wales (National Health Service (Concerns, Complaints and Redress Arrangements) (Wales) Regulations 2011, SI 2011/704 (W.108)).

If the claimant does opt for state care, can the NHS (or whatever public body provides the care) pursue the tortfeasor for its own consequential costs? Such claims are for purely economic loss, and at common law are caught by the general exclusion of such claims from the tort of negligence (*Islington LBC v University College London Hospital NHS Trust* [2006] PIQR P3). But the position is of course different where there is express statutory provision, such as has applied for some considerable time in cases of hospital treatment following a road traffic accident. Successive Road Traffic Acts have accorded the provider of hospital treatment the right to recover expenses from the vehicle owner or the insurer where compensation has been paid in respect of death or injury arising out of a road accident, though the amount recoverable is capped at a relatively low level—£2,949 for each person treated as an in-patient (see Road Traffic Act 1988, s. 157, as amended). (Further small sums may be recovered by a practitioner giving emergency treatment to a traffic accident victim: ss. 158 and 159.) For many years, responsibility for seeking recovery was left with the individual hospital, but the Road Traffic (NHS Charges) Act 1999 shifted responsibility for collecting these sums, in respect of NHS hospitals, to the same central department (the Compensation Recovery Unit) that is responsible for recouping social security benefits using a similar procedure (see IV.4(b)). The Act also increased the charges recoverable to reflect more closely actual costs. (See further Lewis, 'Recovery of NHS Accident Costs' (1999) 62 MLR 903.) Subsequently, the scheme was extended beyond road traffic cases to all personal injury (but not disease) claims by the Health and Social Care (Community Health and Standards) Act 2003, which repealed the relevant provisions of the 1999 Act.

Health and Social Care (Community Health and Standards) Act 2003

Section 150: liability to pay NHS charges

(1) This section applies if—
   (a) a person makes a compensation payment to or in respect of any other person (the 'injured person') in consequence of any injury, whether physical or psychological, suffered by the injured person, and
   (b) the injured person has—
      (i) received NHS treatment at a health service hospital as a result of the injury.
      (ii) been provided with NHS ambulance services as a result of the injury for the purpose of taking him to a health service hospital for NHS treatment (unless he was dead on arrival at that hospital), or
      (iii) received treatment as mentioned in sub-paragraph (i) and been provided with ambulance services as mentioned in sub-paragraph (ii).

(2) The person making the compensation payment is liable to pay the relevant NHS charges—
   (a) in respect of—
      (i) the treatment, in so far as received at a hospital in England or Wales,
      (ii) the ambulance services, in so far as provided to take the injured person to such a hospital, to the Secretary of State . . .

(3) 'Compensation payment' means a payment, including a payment in money's worth, made—
   (a) by or on behalf of a person who is, or is alleged to be, liable to any extent in respect of the injury, or
   (b) in pursuance of a compensation scheme for motor accidents, but does not include a payment mentioned in Schedule 10.

(4) Subsection (1)(a) applies—
   (a) to a payment made—
      (i) voluntarily, or in pursuance of a court order or an agreement, or otherwise, and
      (ii) in the United Kingdom or elsewhere, and
   (b) if more than one payment is made, to each payment.

(5) 'Injury' does not include any disease.

(6) Nothing in subsection (5) prevents this Part from applying to—
   (a) treatment received as a result of any disease suffered by the injured person, or
   (b) ambulance services provided as a result of any disease suffered by him, if the disease in question is attributable to the injury suffered by the injured person (and accordingly that treatment is received or those services are provided as a result of the injury) . . .

COMMENTARY

The scheme came into force on 29 January 2007. The across-the-board recovery of NHS hospital charges accords with the recommendation of the Law Commission in its report, *Damages for Personal Injury: Medical, Nursing and Other Expenses; Collateral Benefits* (Law Com. No. 262 (1999), para. 3.43), and with subsequent Department of Health consultations. The government's Regulatory Impact Assessment (RIA) estimated that the scheme could allow the NHS to augment the sums recovered under the previous road traffic accident (RTA) scheme by up to 165 per cent per year (the additional sums being the cost of treating non-RTA personal injury cases), causing a 1.5 per cent increase in insurance premiums for businesses (RIA, para. 5.36). The 'fundamental principle' underlying the scheme is that 'the NHS, and therefore the taxpayer, should not have to subsidise those responsible for causing injury to others' (para. 11.2). The reform can be seen as an aspect of a broader transfer of the costs of accidental injury from the public to the private sector (see further in III). It is also expected that the scheme will contribute to better accident prevention (para. 2.3). The costs of primary NHS care (e.g. GPs' services), however, do not fall within the scheme and the NHS's 'subsidy' of tort defendants will therefore remain to that extent, with a consequent distortion of the incentives for accident prevention.

Schedule 10, mentioned in s. 150(3) cited earlier, provides for certain 'exempted payments' including payments under compensation orders made against convicted persons by the criminal courts, payments by the claimant's own (first-party) insurer and payments under the Fatal Accidents Act 1976 (i.e. damages for loss of dependency and bereavement), so there is no recovery of NHS costs where the primary victim's family brings a claim consequent on their death. As the dependants' claim under the 1976 Act does not extend to any medical expenses incurred by the deceased prior to their death, the tortfeasor's payment *to them* cannot reflect any benefit the tortfeasor may have gained by the deceased using NHS services before death; hence the exclusion of such payments.

The reference in s. 150(3)(b) to 'a compensation scheme for motor accidents' makes it clear that the recovery scheme extends to payments by the Motor Insurers Bureau in respect of road traffic accidents caused by uninsured or untraceable drivers (see further in Ch. 17. II.2(a)).

Compensation payments in respect of disease are excluded by s. 150(5), though sub-s. (6) qualifies this to a limited extent. If the claimant is injured and the injury itself triggers a disease (e.g. by infection), the costs of treating the disease are recoverable under the scheme. But if the claimant suffers a free-standing disease for which they receive compensation (e.g. employment-related asbestosis), all consequent NHS treatment falls outside the scheme. One concern was that the difficulties inherent in calculating treatment costs in disease cases might result in a burden on NHS information systems outweighing the benefits of the scheme, especially where the patient is suffering from other illnesses too (see Department of Health, *The Recovery of National Health Service Costs in Cases Involving Personal Injury Compensation: A Consultation* (2002), paras 5.2 and 5.3, also noting that many of the costs are likely to occur within the primary care sector and so be unrecoverable). Insurers and business also objected to the inclusion of disease claims because many cases would have retrospective costs (Department of Health, *The Recovery of National Health Service Costs in Cases Involving Personal Injury Compensation: Consultation Summary of Outcome*, September 2003, para. 5.16).

The recoverable charges are specified in the Personal Injuries (NHS Charges) (Amounts) Regulations 2015, reg. 2 and Sch. 1 (as amended): £225 for each ambulance journey, £744 for treatment as an outpatient and £915 per day where the claimant is admitted to hospital, subject to a maximum of £54,682. The amounts are reduced to the extent of any contributory negligence by the injured person (s. 153(3)).

(c) Gratuitous Provision of Care

A problem which all legal systems have to consider concerns care given gratuitously (e.g. by a relative) to the claimant because of injuries attributable to the defendant's negligence.

Hunt v Severs [1994] 2 AC 350

The plaintiff was seriously injured in a road accident whilst riding on the pillion of a motorcycle driven by the defendant, who admitted negligence. The plaintiff, aged 22 at the time of the accident, suffered paraplegia as a result and subsequently spent long periods in various hospitals. Whenever she was not in hospital, she and the defendant lived together and five years after the accident they were married. At trial, the plaintiff was awarded damages under various heads. Included in the award of special damages was a sum of £17,000 representing the value of the past services rendered by the defendant in caring for the plaintiff when she was at home. Included in the award for future loss was a sum of £60,000 representing the estimated value of the services which would be rendered by the defendant in caring for the plaintiff in future. The defendant appealed against a number of heads of damages awarded to the plaintiff, including the award of the two sums specified.

Lord Bridge

My Lords, a plaintiff who establishes a claim for damages for personal injury is entitled in English law to recover as part of those damages the reasonable value of services rendered to him gratuitously by a relative or friend in the provision of nursing care or domestic assistance of the kind rendered necessary by the injuries the plaintiff has suffered. The major issue which arises for determination in this appeal is whether the law will sustain such a claim in respect of gratuitous services in the case where the voluntary carer is the tortfeasor himself . . .

The law with respect to the services of a third party who provides voluntary care for a tortiously injured plaintiff has developed somewhat erratically in England. The voluntary carer has no cause of action of his own against the tortfeasor. The justice of allowing the injured plaintiff to recover the value of the services so that he may recompense the voluntary carer has been generally recognised, but there has been difficulty in articulating a consistent juridical principle to justify this result . . .

In *Cunningham v Harrison* [1973] QB 942 and *Donnelly v Joyce* [1974] QB 454 judgments were delivered by different divisions of the Court of Appeal on successive days. In *Cunningham* the wife of a severely disabled plaintiff, who had initially looked after him, had died before the trial. Lord Denning MR said, at pp 951–2:

> Before dealing with [the claim for future nursing expenses] I would like to consider what the position would have been if the wife had not died and had continued to look after her husband, as she had been doing. The plaintiff's advisers seem to have thought that a husband could not claim for the nursing services rendered by a wife unless the husband was legally bound to pay her for them. So, on their advice on 11 July 1972, an agreement was signed whereby the husband agreed to pay his wife £2,000 per annum in respect of her nursing services. We were told that such advice is often given by counsel in such cases as these when advising on evidence. I know the reason why such advice is given. It is because it has been said in some cases that a plaintiff can only recover for services rendered to him when he was legally liable to pay for them . . . But, I think that view is much too narrow. It seems to me that when a husband is grievously injured—and is entitled to damages—then it is only right and just that, if his wife renders services to him, instead of a nurse, he should recover compensation for the value of the services that his wife has rendered. It should not be necessary to draw up a legal agreement for them. On recovering such an amount, the husband should hold it on trust for her and pay it over to her. She cannot herself sue the wrongdoer . . . but she has rendered services necessitated by the wrongdoing, and should be compensated for it. If she had given up paid work to look after him, he would clearly have been entitled to recover on her behalf; because the family income would have dropped by so much: see *Wattson v Port of London Authority* [1969] 1 Lloyd's Rep 95, 102, per Megaw J. Even though she had not been doing paid work but only domestic duties in the house, nevertheless all extra attendance on him certainly calls for compensation.

In *Donnelly v Joyce* [1974] QB 454, the injured plaintiff was a boy of six. His mother gave up her work for a period to provide necessary care for him and the disputed item in his claim related to the mother's loss of wages. The judgment of the court delivered by Megaw LJ contains a lengthy review of the authorities, but the key passage relied on by the trial judge and the Court of Appeal in the instant case is at pp 461–2, and reads:

> We do not agree with the proposition, inherent in Mr. Hamilton's submission, that the plaintiff's claim, in circumstances such as the present, is properly to be regarded as being, to use his phrase, 'in relation to someone else's loss,' merely because someone else has provided to, or for the benefit of, the plaintiff—the injured person—the money, or the services to be valued as money, to provide for needs of the plaintiff directly caused by the defendant's wrongdoing. The loss is the plaintiff's loss. The question from what source the plaintiff's needs have been met, the question who has paid the money or given the services, the question whether or not the plaintiff is or is not under a legal or moral liability to repay, are, so far as the defendant and his liability are concerned, all irrelevant. The plaintiff's loss, to take this present case, is not the expenditure of money to buy the special boots or to pay for the nursing attention. His loss is the existence of the need for those special boots or for those nursing services, the value of which for purposes of damages—for the purpose of the ascertainment of the amount of his loss—is the proper and reasonable cost of supplying those needs. That, in our judgment, is the key to the problem. So far as the defendant is concerned, the loss is not someone else's loss. It is the plaintiff's loss.

Hence it does not matter, so far as the defendant's liability to the plaintiff is concerned, whether the needs have been supplied by the plaintiff out of his own pocket or by a charitable contribution to him from some other person whom we shall call the 'provider'; it does not matter, for that purpose, whether the plaintiff has a legal liability, absolute or conditional, to repay to the provider what he has received, because of the general law or because of some private agreement between himself and the provider; it does not matter whether he has a moral obligation, however ascertained or defined, so to do. The question of legal liability to reimburse the provider may be very relevant to the question of the legal right of the provider to recover from the plaintiff. That may depend on the nature of the liability imposed by the general law or the particular agreement. But it is not a matter which affects the right of the plaintiff against the wrongdoer.

With respect, I do not find this reasoning convincing. I accept that the basis of a plaintiff's claim for damages may consist in his need for services but I cannot accept that the question from what source that need has been met is irrelevant. If an injured plaintiff is treated in hospital as a private patient he is entitled to recover the cost of that treatment. But if he receives free treatment under the National Health Service, his need has been met without cost to him and he cannot claim the cost of the treatment from the tortfeasor. So it cannot, I think, be right to say that in all cases the plaintiff's loss is 'for the purpose of damages . . . the proper and reasonable cost of supplying [his] needs' . . .

[I]t is . . . important to recognise that the underlying rationale of the English law, as all the cases before *Donnelly v Joyce* [1974] QB 454 demonstrate, is to enable the voluntary carer to receive proper recompense for his or her services and I would think it appropriate for the House to take the opportunity . . . [to adopt] the view of Lord Denning MR in *Cunningham v Harrison* [1973] QB 942 that . . . the injured plaintiff who recovers damages under this head should hold them on trust for the voluntary carer.

By concentrating on the plaintiff's need and the plaintiff's loss as the basis of an award in respect of voluntary care received by the plaintiff, the reasoning in *Donnelly v Joyce* diverts attention from the award's central objective of compensating the voluntary carer. Once this is recognised it becomes evident that there can be no ground in public policy or otherwise for requiring the tortfeasor to pay to the plaintiff, in respect of the services which he himself has rendered, a sum of money which the plaintiff must then repay to him . . .

[B]efore your Lordships Mr McGregor [for the plaintiff], recognising the difficulty of formulating any principle of public policy which could justify recovery against the tortfeasor who has to pay out of his own pocket, advanced the bold proposition that such a policy could be founded on the liability of insurers to meet the claim. Exploration of the implications of this proposition in argument revealed the many difficulties which it encounters. But I do not think it necessary to examine these in detail. The short answer, in my judgment, to Mr McGregor's contention is that its acceptance would represent a novel and radical departure in the law of a kind which only the legislature may properly effect. At common law the circumstance that a defendant is contractually indemnified by a third party against a particular legal liability can have no relevance whatever to the measure of that liability . . .

Lord Keith, **Lord Jauncey**, **Lord Browne-Wilkinson** and **Lord Nolan** agreed with Lord Bridge.

Appeal allowed.

COMMENTARY

This decision met with a chorus of disapproval. For analysis, see Kemp (1994) 110 LQR 524, and Matthews and Lunney, 'A Tortfeasor's Lot is Not a Happy One' (1995) 58 MLR 395, and note the Australian High Court's preference for the former 'claimant need' approach in *Kars v Kars* (1996) 187 CLR 354 (noted by Lunney (1997–8) 8 KCLJ 115). One problem highlighted by Matthews and Lunney is the failure of the House of Lords to distinguish between pre-trial and post-trial caring services. Whilst it might have been justifiable to make no award in respect of pre-trial services—although the authors argue otherwise—different considerations apply to post-trial services because the defendant tortfeasor may become incapable of providing the same services in future; in such a case, the *Hunt v Severs* approach provides the claimant with no financial means to purchase alternative care. There are also several problems with the Law Lords' view that, in the normal case of gratuitous care rendered by a third party, the notional care costs should be held on trust for the carer, for example because the latter will receive an undeserved windfall if the victim dies unexpectedly.

For these and other reasons, the Law Commission (*Damages for Personal Injury: Medical, Nursing and Other Expenses; Collateral Benefits* (Law Com. No. 262, 1999), paras 3.62, 3.76) subsequently recommended legislation to reverse the result in *Hunt v Severs* in so far as it concerned gratuitous care rendered by the defendant. In all cases, the claimant would have a personal obligation to account to the carer (whether the tortfeasor or not) for pre-trial care, rather than an obligation under a trust. There would be no obligation to account to the carer for post-trial gratuitous care. The government accepted that reform was necessary (see Department of Constitutional Affairs, *The Law on Damages* (2007), paras 114–20) and included the following clause in its draft Civil Law Reform Bill presented in December 2009:

7 **Damages for gratuitous services**
(1) Subsection (2) applies if, on a claim for damages for personal injury, a court awards damages to the injured person in respect of a gratuitous provision of services to that person.
(2) The injured person must account to—
 (a) such persons as provided the services before the date of the award, and
 (b) such persons as provided the services on or after that date.

(3) A court must not refuse to award damages in respect of a gratuitous provision of services merely because the person providing the services is the defendant.

(4) But a court may not award damages in respect of a gratuitous provision of services by the defendant to the injured person for any period before the date of the award (and accordingly subsection (2)(a) does not apply) . . .

However, it was subsequently announced in Parliament that the government had decided not to proceed with the Bill (Hansard, HC vol. 521, col. 8WS, 10 January 2011). If adopted, would this provision have implemented the Law Commission's proposals? How would it have been applied on the facts of *Hunt v Severs* itself?

It may be noted that the *Hunt v Severs* analysis applies even when the gratuitous case is not provided by a family member or friend. See *Drake v Foster Wheeler Ltd* [2011] 1 All ER 63, where the deceased, suffering from mesothelioma, received palliative care for the last weeks of his life in a charitable hospice, his family being no longer able to cope. The deceased's estate was entitled to recover damages, to be paid on to the hospice, for the reasonable notional costs of such care.

For an argument that the basis of the carer's entitlement to compensation lies in the law of unjust enrichment rather than tort, see S. Degeling, *Restitutionary Rights to Share in Damages: Carers' Claims* (Cambridge: CUP, 2003). Degeling argues that the law should afford the carer, like an insurer exercising a right of subrogation, the power to compel the victim to sue. Do you think it is desirable that the law should intrude on private relations in such a way?

What if the defendant's tort, rather than necessitating the provision of gratuitous services *to the claimant*, prevents the claimant from providing gratuitous services *for others*? Can the claimant claim for the value of these services they can no longer provide? In *Daly v General Steam Navigation Ltd* [1981] 1 WLR 120 it was held that the plaintiff could recover the substitute value of unpaid household services which she could no longer perform as a result of the tort. As a dependant can recover for the value of the household services gratuitously provided before their death by the deceased under the Fatal Accidents Act 1976 (see Ch. 16.III), the decision in *Daly* ensures that damages are also recovered where the services cannot be provided as a result of the tortfeasor injuring rather than killing the gratuitous provider of the services (although they are recovered by the claimant rather than by the claimant's dependants). The limits of these claims, however, are more difficult to determine: they extend to gratuitous household services that the claimant provided for themselves (e.g. mowing the lawn) but would the cost of hiring a substitute dog walker be included? These and other difficulties led the High Court of Australia in *CSR v Eddy* (2005) 226 CLR 1 to reject any such awards, even in respect of household services: the failure to provide services to another simply reflected a change in the ability of the plaintiff to live her life in the way that she had previously lived, and there was no justification for taking this one aspect of loss of amenity—loss of the ability to provide caring services to others—and to compensate that aspect by reference to the pecuniary value of the services to the recipient. Such a loss was compensated as part of an award of general damages for loss of amenity. Do you agree? (Note that some jurisdictions in Australia have now introduced legislation allowing the value of gratuitous domestic services provided to dependants to be recovered, e.g. Civil Liability Act 2002 (NSW), s. 15B.)

For a comparative survey, see E. Karner and K. Oliphant (eds), *Loss of Housekeeping Capacity* (Berlin: de Gruyter, 2012).

4. Deductions

The aim of compensation is to replace what the claimant has lost. Hence lost income is assessed net of tax (*BTC v Gourley* [1956] AC 185). Furthermore, the court must inquire whether the claimant has taken up alternative, perhaps less demanding, employment after the accident and will award only the difference between the level of earnings if the accident had not occurred and that which the claimant will now earn.

In addition, various saved expenses must be taken into account, for example where the claimant is saved substantial costs incurred in going to work (see *Dews v National Coal Board* [1988] AC 1 at 12–13, per Lord Griffiths). We have already noted that a similar problem arises where the claimant is spared certain expenses as a result of receiving medical treatment.

In order to avoid double compensation, it may be necessary to deduct from the damages the amount of benefits received as a result of the accident from other sources ('collateral benefits'). Hence, where an employee receives sick pay after an accident has rendered them unfit for work, this is generally deducted from the amount of damages received. But the law here is not straightforward, as the following section reveals.

(a) Collateral Benefits: General Principles

In *Hussain v New Taplow Paper Mills Ltd* [1988] AC 514 at 527, the House of Lords recognised two exceptions to the rule requiring full deduction of collateral benefits (per Lord Bridge):

> [T]o the prima facie rule there are two well-established exceptions. First, where a plaintiff recovers under an insurance policy for which he has paid the premiums, the insurance moneys are not deductible from damages payable by the tortfeasor . . . Second, when the plaintiff receives money from the benevolence of third parties prompted by sympathy for his misfortune, as in the case of a beneficiary from a disaster fund, the amount received is again to be disregarded . . .

Tricky questions arise as to whether certain benefits received by the claimant from her employer as a result of her injury are appropriately regarded as 'insurance' payments which are non-deductible. Disability pensions and employers' sickness benefit schemes, for example, might be regarded as insurance schemes taken out by the employer on the employee's behalf and paid for by the employee whose wages are reduced as a consequence. In *Hussain*, Lord Bridge drew a distinction between:

(i) benefits which represent a partial substitute for earnings, such as sick pay, and

(ii) benefits ('pensions') which are only payable after employment ceases.

In his view, only the latter could be regarded as the fruits of insurance.

On the facts of the case before him, Lord Bridge held that an occupational long-term sickness benefit scheme was a substitute for earnings rather than the fruits of insurance. Under the scheme benefits were paid to employees incapacitated from work for the duration of the incapacity (until death or retirement age) so long as the employee remained in employment with the employer. This can be contrasted with the decision in *Parry v Cleaver* [1970] AC 1, where the House of Lords held that an occupational disability pension, whether contributory or non-contributory, was not deductible, because a pension is analogous to private insurance. Whether there should be a difference between occupational sick pay and occupational disability pensions is another matter; as Lord Morris pointed out, in his dissenting opinion in *Parry* (at 32):

> If under the terms of a contract of employment the time comes when instead of having full pay or half pay or sick pay a person retires with a pension, the loss which he suffers is the difference between the amount of his pay and the amount of his pension. If it is said that a pension is neither pay nor insurance benefit then I would say that where there is no discretionary element and where the arrangements leading to a pension are an essential part of the contract of employment then the pension payments are very much more akin to pay than to anything else.

Note that *Parry* was upheld in *Smoker v London Fire & Civil Defence Authority* [1991] 2 AC 502 on the basis that pension benefits were the fruits of money set aside in respect of past work and the defendant was not entitled to reduce his liability by appropriating these amounts. See also *Longden v British Coal Corporation* [1998] AC 653.

The reason for the exception of insurance payments from the normal rule of deductibility of collateral benefits was classically stated by Pigott B in *Bradburn v Great Western Railway Co* (1874) LR 10 Exch 1 at 3:

> [T]here is no reason or justice in setting off what the plaintiff has entitled himself to under a contract with third persons, by which he has bargained for the payment of a sum of money in the event of an accident happening to him. He does not receive that sum of money because of the accident, but because he has made a contract providing for the contingency; an accident must occur to entitle him to it, but it is not the accident, but his contract, which is the cause of his receiving it.

The reason charitable payments are not deducted was clearly stated by Lord Reid in *Parry v Cleaver* [1970] AC 1 at 14:

> It would be revolting to the ordinary man's sense of justice, and therefore contrary to public policy, that the sufferer should have his damages reduced so that he would gain nothing from the benevolence of his friends or relatives or of the public at large, and that the only gainer would be the wrongdoer.

The Law Commission found in 1999 that there was no need for statutory reform of the common law approach (*Damages for Personal Injury: Medical, Nursing and Other Expenses; Collateral Benefits* (Law Com. No. 262, 1999), para. 11.53). Subsequently, the government endorsed the principal exceptions to the general rule of deductibility but proposed that the claimant should, wherever practicable, be compensated at the expense of the tortfeasor rather than the collateral benefit payer (Department of Constitutional Affairs, *The Law on Damages*, (2007), paras 103 and 107). Collateral benefits should be disregarded in the assessment of damages—bringing the law into line with the treatment of Fatal Accidents Act claims (see further in Ch. 16.III.2)—with benefits already paid being refunded by the claimant from the damages, while the obligation to provide further benefits would be extinguished (para. 108). This proposal was not, however, included in the government's draft Civil Law Reform Bill of 2009 (which was never enacted anyway).

For general discussion of these issues, see Lewis, 'Deducting Collateral Benefits from Damages: Principle and Policy' (1998) 18 LS 15.

(b) Social Security Benefits

Special statutory rules apply to the deduction of social security benefits. The basic provisions are now set out in the Social Security (Recovery of Benefits) Act 1997. A particular area of controversy at that time had been the introduction in 1989 of a 'recoupment' regime, whereby the state was able to 'claw back' from the defendant certain benefits paid to the claimant under the social security system. Concern that this regime was unduly diminishing the compensation monies paid to tortiously injured persons led to the 1997 reform of the rules.

Social Security (Recovery of Benefits) Act 1997

Section 1: Cases in which this Act applies

(1) This Act applies in cases where—

    (a) a person makes a payment (whether on his own behalf or not) to or in respect of any other person in consequence of any accident, injury or disease suffered by the other, and

    (b) any listed benefits have been, or are likely to be, paid to or for the other during the relevant period in respect of the accident, injury or disease.

(2) The reference above to a payment in consequence of any accident, injury or disease is to a payment made—

    (a) by or on behalf of a person who is, or is alleged to be, liable to any extent in respect of the accident, injury or disease . . . but does not include a payment mentioned in Part I of Schedule 1.

(3) Subsection (1)(a) applies to a payment made—

    (a) voluntarily, or in pursuance of a court order or an agreement, or otherwise, and

    (b) in the United Kingdom or elsewhere.

(4) In a case where this Act applies—

    (a) the 'injured person' is the person who suffered the accident, injury or disease,

    (b) the 'compensation payment' is the payment within subsection (1)(a), and

    (c) 'recoverable benefit' is any listed benefit which has been or is likely to be paid as mentioned in subsection (1)(b) . . .

Section 3: 'The relevant period'

(1) In relation to a person ('the claimant') who has suffered any accident, injury or disease, 'the relevant period' has the meaning given by the following subsections.

(2) Subject to subsection (4), if it is a case of accident or injury, the relevant period is the period of five years immediately following the day on which the accident or injury in question occurred.

(3) Subject to subsection (4), if it is a case of disease, the relevant period is the period of five years beginning with the date on which the claimant first claims a listed benefit in consequence of the disease.

(4) If at any time before the end of the period referred to in subsection (2) or (3)—

    (a) a person makes a compensation payment in final discharge of any claim made by or in respect of the claimant and arising out of the accident, injury or disease, or

    (b) an agreement is made under which an earlier compensation payment is treated as having been made in final discharge of any such claim,

the relevant period ends at that time.

Section 4: Applications for certificates of recoverable benefits

(1) Before a person ('the compensator') makes a compensation payment he must apply to the Secretary of State for a certificate of recoverable benefits . . .

Section 6: Liability to pay Secretary of State amount of benefits

(1) A person who makes a compensation payment in any case is liable to pay to the Secretary of State an amount equal to the total amount of the recoverable benefits . . .

Section 8: Reduction of compensation payment

(1) This section applies in a case where, in relation to any head of compensation listed in column 1 of Schedule 2—

    (a) any of the compensation payment is attributable to that head, and
    (b) any recoverable benefit is shown against that head in column 2 of the Schedule.

(2) In such a case, any claim of a person to receive the compensation payment is to be treated for all purposes as discharged if—

    (a) he is paid the amount (if any) of the compensation payment calculated in accordance with this section, and
    (b) if the amount of the compensation payment so calculated is nil, he is given a statement saying so by the person who (apart from this section) would have paid the gross amount of the compensation payment.

(3) For each head of compensation listed in column 1 of the Schedule for which paragraphs (a) and (b) of subsection (1) are met, so much of the gross amount of the compensation payment as is attributable to that head is to be reduced (to nil, if necessary) by deducting the amount of the recoverable benefit or, as the case may be, the aggregate amount of the recoverable benefits shown against it.

(4) Subsection (3) is to have effect as if a requirement to reduce a payment by deducting an amount which exceeds that payment were a requirement to reduce that payment to nil.

(5) The amount of the compensation payment calculated in accordance with this section is—

    (a) the gross amount of the compensation payment, less
    (b) the sum of the reductions made under subsection (3), (and, accordingly, the amount may be nil).

Schedule 2: Calculation of compensation payment

(1) Head of compensation	(2) Benefit
1. Compensation for earnings lost during the relevant period.	Universal credit; Disablement pension . . . ; Employment and support allowance; Incapacity benefit; Income support; Invalidity pension and allowance; Jobseeker's allowance; Reduced earnings allowance; Severe disablement allowance; Sickness benefit; Statutory sick pay; Unemployability supplement; Unemployment benefit.
2. Compensation for cost of care incurred during the relevant period.	Attendance allowance; Daily living component of personal independence payment; Care component of disability living allowance; Disablement pension increase . . .
3. Compensation for loss of mobility during the relevant period.	Mobility allowance; Mobility component of personal independence payment; Mobility component of disability living allowance.

COMMENTARY

This statutory scheme, created in largely its present form in 1989, replaced the previous scheme implemented by s. 2(1) of the Law Reform (Personal Injuries) Act 1948. The essence of the earlier scheme was a 50 per cent rule, whereby the defendant was entitled to offset half of any specified benefits received or to be received, for five years from the date the cause of action accrued. After this period, the question of deduction was left to the common law, which adopted a principle of no deduction in many cases (e.g. in relation to the state retirement pension: *Hewson v Downs* [1970] 1 QB 73). There was no provision for the state to 'claw back' any of the benefits paid to the claimant.

The current law regarding the deduction of social security benefits can be summarised in the following (somewhat simplified) propositions:

(i) Under s. 8, the compensation received by the victim is reduced by the full value of specified benefits (defined in Sch. 2, col. 2) received during the relevant period. The deduction only applies to heads of compensation with which the particular benefit is matched (explained further later in the section).

(ii) The relevant period (defined in s. 3) is five years from the injury, or, in the case of a disease, five years from the date of the first claim for benefit as a result of the disease. However, a payment in final discharge of the claim brings the relevant period to an end.

(iii) No deduction at all is made in respect of benefits falling outside the relevant period, i.e. after the lapse of five years or the date of settlement, whichever is earlier (because s. 8 allows reduction of the compensation payment only in respect of 'recoverable benefits', which are defined in terms of 'the relevant period': s. 1(1)(b) and (4)(c)).

(iv) The 'compensator' (normally the tortfeasor or their insurer) is liable to pay the amount deducted from the compensation to the Secretary of State for Work and

Pensions (s. 6). The compensator must apply for a 'certificate of recoverable benefit' before making any compensation payment (s. 4(1)). This should normally be granted within twenty-eight days, after which the compensator has fourteen days in which to pay (ss. 4, 6, relevant subsections not extracted).

The original scheme of 1989 allowed for the deduction of recoverable benefits from the total amount of compensation payable, rather than from particular heads of claim. This was perceived to be unfair, especially because it could result in a nil award even though there was substantial pain and suffering, which social security benefits are not designed to compensate. The 1997 Act aimed to address this concern by dividing the award of damages into the components listed in column 1 of Sch. 2, extracted here, for the purpose of deduction. No deduction may be made against awards for pain and suffering, whilst only specified benefits may be deducted against awards for loss of earnings, cost of care and loss of mobility. One important change made by the 1997 Act related to where the amount of recoverable benefit is greater than the amount that can be deducted from the damages award. The compensator must, in every case, pay the Secretary of State the full amount of recoverable benefit (s. 6(1)), even if this results in a total payment in excess of the original damages award. For example, if the claimant receives an award of £10,000 (£5,000 for pain and suffering, £5,000 for loss of earnings) and the relevant benefit payable is £8,000, the result will be as follows. Assuming the relevant benefit is one that can be deducted against loss of earnings, the claimant's compensation for loss of earnings will be reduced to zero. This still leaves £3,000 of relevant benefit which cannot be deducted (because no deductions can be made against damages for pain and suffering). The result will be that the compensator will pay £5,000 to the claimant and £8,000 to the Secretary of State (a total of £13,000), even though the original damages award was only £10,000.

Another change from before 1997 was the abolition of an exemption in respect of small payments, being payments of less than £2,500, though the Act provides for regulations to restore the exemption if this is deemed necessary (see s. 1(2) and Sch. 1).

The Scheme is operated by a government agency, the Compensation Recovery Unit, whose website provides additional information: https://www.gov.uk/government/collections/cru. (The same agency now works with NHS bodies to recover treatment costs arising from accidental personal injury: see earlier.) See further R. Lewis, *Deducting Benefits from Damages for Personal Injury* (Oxford: OUP, 1999), chs 12 17; R. Lewis, 'Recovery of State Benefits from Tort Damages: Legislating For or Against the Welfare State?', *Tort Law and the Legislature*, ch. 14.

16 DEATH AND DAMAGES

The death of a person raises two questions in respect of liability in the law of tort. First, does the death of one of the parties to a tort action extinguish that action? At common law the general rule for a tort claim was that it did, but this has now been changed by statute (Law Reform (Miscellaneous Provisions) Act 1934, extracted in the next section). Death here does not create the cause of action; the question is what effect it has on an existing cause of action, and the person who brings any action under this Act does so as representative of the deceased. The second question is whether the death of another as a result of a tort gives rise to a new cause of action in those who have suffered damage as a result of the death. In this situation death is the factor that creates the cause of action, and the claimant in such an action sues for a loss suffered personally. Again, the common law frowned on such actions (*Baker v Bolton* (1808) 1 Camp 493), but a statutory cause of action was created in 1846, although both the plaintiffs and the damage for which they could sue were limited, and remain so in the modern version of the 1846 legislation (Fatal Accidents Act 1976).

1. The Effect of Death on Existing Causes of Action

> **Law Reform (Miscellaneous Provisions) Act 1934**
>
> **1. Effect of death on certain causes of action**
>
> (1) Subject to the provisions of this section, on the death of any person after the commencement of this Act all causes of action subsisting against or vested in him shall survive against, or, as the case may be, for the benefit of, his estate. Provided that this subsection shall not apply to causes of action for defamation . . .
>
> (1A) The right of a person to claim under section 1A of the Fatal Accidents Act 1976 (bereavement) shall not survive for the benefit of his estate on his death.
>
> (2) Where a cause of action survives as aforesaid for the benefit of the estate of a deceased person, the damages recoverable for the benefit of the estate of that person—
>
>   (a) shall not include—
>
>   (i) any exemplary damages;
>   (ii) any damages for loss of income in respect of any period after that person's death; . . .
>
>   (b) . . .

(c) where the death of that person has been caused by the act or omission which gives rise to the cause of action, shall be calculated without reference to any loss or gain to his estate consequent on his death, except that a sum in respect of funeral expenses may be included . . .

(4) Where damage has been suffered by reason of any act or omission in respect of which a cause of action would have subsisted against any person if that person had not died before or at the same time as the damage was suffered, there shall be deemed, for the purposes of this Act, to have been subsisting against him before his death such cause of action in respect of that act or omission as would have subsisted if he had died after the damage was suffered.

(5) The rights conferred by this Act for the benefit of the estates of deceased persons shall be in addition to and not in derogation of any rights conferred on the dependants of deceased persons by the Fatal Accidents Acts 1846 to 1976 . . . and so much of this Act as relates to causes of action against the estates of deceased persons shall apply in relation to causes of action under the said Acts as it applies in relation to other causes of action not expressly excepted from the operation of subsection (1) of this section.

Hicks v Chief Constable of the South Yorkshire Police
[1992] 2 All ER 65

The two deceased, spectators at the Hillsborough football stadium at the time of the tragic events there of April 1989, were killed when they and many others were crushed to death by the press of people in the pens at one end of the ground as a result of the defendant's negligence. Each suffered traumatic asphyxia which deprived them of their ability to breathe, and the medical evidence was that once the asphyxia had set in, unconsciousness would have followed within seconds and death would have occurred within five minutes. There was no indication in the post-mortem reports on either of the deceased of physical injuries attributable to anything other than the fatal crushing which caused the asphyxia, save for some superficial bruising in respect of one of the deceased which could have occurred either before or after loss of consciousness. The plaintiffs, administrators of the deceased's estates, brought actions for the benefit of the estates under s. 1(1) of the Law Reform (Miscellaneous Provisions) Act 1934, claiming damages from the defendant for the deceased's pre-death pain and suffering caused by the injury, including suffering from the awareness of impending death, that being a recoverable head of damage by virtue of s. 1(1)(b) of the Administration of Justice Act 1982. The trial judge and Court of Appeal dismissed the claim.

Lord Bridge of Harwich

My Lords, the appellants are the parents of two girls, Sarah and Victoria Hicks, who died in the disaster at Hillsborough Football Stadium on 15 April 1989 when they were respectively 19 and 15 years of age. In this action they claim damages under the Law Reform (Miscellaneous Provisions) Act 1934 for the benefit of the estate of each daughter of which they are in each case the administrators. The respondent is the Chief Constable of the South Yorkshire Police who does not contest his liability to persons who suffered damage in the disaster. The basis of the claim advanced here is that at the moment of death Sarah and Victoria each had an accrued cause of action for injuries suffered prior to death which survived for the benefit of their respective estates. . . .

The evidence here showed that both girls died from traumatic asphyxia. They were in the pens at one end of the Hillsborough Stadium to which access was through a tunnel some

23 metres in length. When the pens were already seriously overcrowded a great number of additional spectators, anxious to see the football match which was about to start, were admitted through the turnstiles and surged through the tunnel causing the dreadful crush in the pens in which 95 people died. Medical evidence which the judge accepted was to the effect that in cases of death from traumatic asphyxia caused by crushing the victim would lose consciousness within a matter of seconds from the crushing of the chest which cut off the ability to breathe and would die within five minutes. There was no indication in the post-mortem reports on either girl of physical injuries attributable to anything other than the fatal crushing which caused the asphyxia, save, in the case of Sarah, some superficial bruising which, on the evidence, could have occurred either before or after loss of consciousness. Hidden J was not satisfied that any physical injury had been sustained before what he described as the 'swift and sudden [death] as shown by the medical evidence'. Unless the law were to distinguish between death within seconds of injury and unconsciousness within seconds of injury followed by death within minutes, which I do not understand to be suggested, these findings, as Hidden J himself said 'with regret', made it impossible for him to award any damages.

Mr Hytner sought to persuade your Lordships, as he sought to persuade the Court of Appeal, that on the whole of the evidence the judge ought to have found on a balance of probabilities that there was a gradual build-up of pressure on the bodies of the two girls causing increasing breathlessness, discomfort and pain from which they suffered for some 20 minutes before the final crushing injury which produced unconsciousness. This should have led, he submitted, to the conclusion that they sustained injuries which caused considerable pain and suffering while they were still conscious and which should attract a substantial award of damages. The Court of Appeal, in a judgment delivered by Parker LJ with which both Stocker and Nolan LJJ agreed, carefully reviewed the evidence and concluded, in agreement with Hidden J, that it did not establish that any physical injury was caused before the fatal crushing injury. I do not intend myself to embark on a detailed review of the evidence. In the circumstances I think it sufficient to say that, in my opinion, the conclusion of fact reached by Hidden J and the Court of Appeal was fairly open to them and it is impossible to say that they were wrong.

A good deal of argument in the courts below and before your Lordships was addressed to the question whether damages for physical injuries should be increased on account of the terrifying circumstances in which they were inflicted. This may depend on difficult questions of causation. But on the facts found in this case the question does not arise for decision. It is perfectly clear law that fear by itself, of whatever degree, is a normal human emotion for which no damages can be awarded. Those trapped in the crush at Hillsborough who were fortunate enough to escape without injury have no claim in respect of the distress they suffered in what must have been a truly terrifying experience. It follows that fear of impending death felt by the victim of a fatal injury before that injury is inflicted cannot by itself give rise to a cause of action which survives for the benefit of the victim's estate.

Lords Goff, Browne-Wilkinson, Griffiths and **Templeman** agreed with Lord Bridge.

Appeal dismissed.

COMMENTARY

The case illustrates the anomaly that, in the English law of tort, it may be cheaper to kill than to maim. The practical outcome on the facts was that the estates of the deceased, sisters aged 15 and 19, recovered nothing in respect of their fear of impending death and nothing for their pain, suffering and loss of amenity in the time between injury and death. Neither could the estates recover for the sisters' loss of expectation of life, as this is not a recoverable head of damages under English law (Administration of Justice Act 1982, s. 1(1)(a)). The parents could recover funeral expenses and they had a statutory claim for bereavement damages, then worth £3,500, under s. 1A of the Fatal Accidents Act 1976 (discussed later in this chapter), but this arose only in respect of their younger daughter as the death of an adult child is not covered. Add to this the rejection in separate proceedings of the Hillsborough relatives' personal claims for post-traumatic stress (see Ch. 7.II). Do you think that the law's response to the sisters' tragic loss of life and their parents' consequent grief was really adequate? See also *Rothwell v Chemical & Insulating Co Ltd* [2008] 1 AC 281, where the House of Lords affirmed the gist of *Hicks*, holding that a living claimant has no claim for anxiety at the prospect of future injury. (But cf. the possible remedies now available under the HRA, considered later in this chapter.)

What damages are recoverable by the estate under the 1934 Act? The simple answer is all damages that the deceased could have claimed up to and including the date of death (with the addition of funeral expenses—s. 1(2)(c)). This will include any expenses incurred by the deceased from the date of the tort until the date of the death as well as loss of earnings during that time. In *Pickett v British Engineering Ltd* [1980] AC 136 the House of Lords held that a living plaintiff could recover damages for the loss of earnings during the period which, as a result of the tort, they would now be dead, and this claim was held to survive for the benefit of the deceased's estate under the 1934 Act in *Gammell v Wilson* [1982] AC 27. One reason for their Lordships' decision in *Pickett* was to provide benefits for the dependants of the plaintiff, for once the living plaintiff had been awarded damages the dependants could not bring a later claim against the defendant in respect of the same tort (see III.1). Thus if the (living) plaintiff did not receive any damages for the loss of earnings during the lost years the dependants would be uncompensated for the loss of dependency during those years. However, this policy ground did not apply where the victim of the tort died before bringing a claim, because in this case the dependants had an independent right to sue under the fatal accidents legislation (see the discussion later in this chapter). There was concern that if the lost years claim continued to survive for the benefit of the estate, the tortfeasor might in certain circumstances have to pay out twice to compensate for the same loss (the lost years claim to the estate and loss of dependency to the dependants). The 1934 Act was accordingly amended by the Administration of Justice Act 1982, s. 4. However, in *Gregg v Scott* [2005] 2 AC 176 at [182], Lord Phillips suggested that the preferable solution would be to disallow the claim of the living claimant for loss of earnings during the lost years but to allow an action under the Fatal Accidents Act to the dependants if the claimant later died, even though the claimant had brought a successful action during their lifetime. If the reason for allowing the claim for lost years was to benefit the dependants of the claimant, his Lordship argued that the *Pickett* claim was a 'poor substitute' for allowing the dependants their own action under the Fatal Accidents Act. His Lordship thought that this result could be achieved by a 'purposive interpretation' of s. 1(1) of the Fatal Accidents Act. (Cf. *Thompson v Arnold* [2008] PIQR P1.) Note, however, that one concern with using the lost years claim as a means of providing for dependants after the claimant's death—that the claimant might spend the lost years award during their own shortened life so that there is nothing left for dependants at their death—can be avoided by use of a periodical payment order (see in III.1).

Section 1(1)(a) of the 1982 Act abolished the claim for 'loss of expectation of life' that had been available to a living plaintiff whose life expectancy had been reduced as a result of the tort. The value of that claim had already been limited to the standardised amount of £200 since *Benham v Gambling* [1941] AC 157. However, s. 1(1)(b) allows for an award of pain and suffering damages to be increased to reflect the fact that a victim may suffer increased distress from the knowledge that their life-span is now reduced. But when can damages for pain and suffering be awarded in the first place? It is trite law that a claimant who has suffered physical injury can recover damages for the pain and suffering associated with that injury, but a physical injury there must be. In *Hicks*, the House of Lords affirmed that the short period of pain between the commencement of the crushing and unconsciousness or death did not amount to a physical injury for the purposes of awarding damages for the associated pain and suffering of that injury. This seems to apply a *de minimis* requirement: the gap between the commencement of the injury and death must be sufficiently long so that the court can find that the claimant suffered, as a matter of law, a 'physical' injury for which pain and suffering damages can be awarded (Cf. *Amin v Imran Khan & Partners* [2011] EWHC 2958 (QB) where it was assumed that a short period of 'intense and horrifying conscious pain' could justify an award.) Do you agree with P. Handford, *Tort Liability for Mental Harm*, 3rd edn (Sydney: Law Book Co, 2016), para. 6.180, that the duration of the discomfort 'has been afforded an undeserved prominence'? For example, would it be fair to deny pre-death pain and suffering damages to the estate of an air crash victim depending on the length of time it takes the plane to crash? For a discussion of US cases where recovery of these damages by the estate has been allowed see Handford, *op. cit.*, para. 6.180.

Defamation

Section 1 of the 1934 Act provides generally for the survival of actions in tort, with the exception of defamation (and now also bereavement damages under the Fatal Accidents Act 1976). Given that the defamation exception applies to both claimants and defendants, it might seem curious that a defendant should be excused from liability by the fortuitous death of the claimant. The Faulks Committee on Defamation, Cmnd 5909 (1975) explained the exception of the cause of action in defamation on the basis of a wish to avoid controversial areas and a desire to expedite the introduction of legislation to deal with the problem of deaths in road accidents. The Committee recommended survival of claims against the estate of a deceased defamer as well as a right of action in the personal representatives of a person defamed to seek an injunction and damages for pecuniary loss. A further right in relatives to seek a declaration, an injunction against publication and costs in respect of defamation of a deceased person within five years of the death was also proposed, but none of these proposals found favour with the Supreme Court Committee in its report on 'Practice and Procedure in Defamation' (1991, the 'Neill Report').

II. Death as a Cause of Action

1. Common Law

Clark v London General Omnibus Company Limited [1906] 2 KB 648

The plaintiff's daughter was killed as a result of an accident with one of the defendant's omnibuses. At trial the plaintiff recovered for, amongst other things, the cost of her burial. The Court of Appeal allowed an appeal against this head of damage both under Lord Campbell's Act (the predecessor of the current Fatal Accidents Act) and at common law. The extract is concerned with the common law position.

Lord Alvertsone CJ

But on the main question, if it was intended in *Baker v Bolton* (1808) 1 Camp 493 to enunciate the proposition that no action lies in respect of death apart from statutory enactment, it would, of course, be an authority in favour of the present defendants. What right can be said to be infringed? What is the *injuria* which has caused the *damnum*? The father has no right of property in the child in the sense that he can recover if his property is injured. In this case it seems to me that there is no duty towards the father which has been broken. There is no property of the father which has been injured, and no contract with the father which has been broken. Some breach of duty must be made out, and I can see no ground for any suggestion that there is any duty to the father that has been infringed, or any property of the father which has been injured. It seems to me that this case falls within that class to which reference is made in the notes to *Ashby v White* (1703) 2 Ld Raym 938, where there are certain wrongful acts which may place persons in the position of spending money and yet will not involve a legal liability to make that expenditure good. I am therefore of opinion that the plaintiff's action fails at common law. . . .

W. S. Holdsworth, 'The Origin of the Rule in *Baker v Bolton*'
(1916) 32 LQR 431

In 1808 Lord Ellenborough decided [in *Baker v Bolton*] that 'in a civil court the death of a human being could not be complained of as an injury'. . . . The principle as laid down by Lord Ellenborough is very wide and admits of two perfectly distinct applications. Firstly, it covers part of the ground covered by the maxim *actio personalis moritur cum persona*—the representative of a deceased victim of a tort, which has caused his (the victim's) death cannot sue in his representative capacity. Secondly, it makes it impossible for a plaintiff to sue a defendant for a wrong committed by the defendant to the plaintiff, when that wrong consists in damage causing the death of a person in the continuance of whose life the plaintiff had an interest. It is clear that the second application of the principle has nothing to do with the maxim *actio personalis, &c.*, as both plaintiff and defendant are still alive. The death is simply an element of the cause of action . . .

It is probable that the origin of the second application of this principle is to be found in the rule that, if a cause of action in tort disclosed a felony, the right of action in tort was affected [either by being suspended or lost] . . .

[After considering the cases on this rule, Holdsworth continued:]

It would seem to follow, therefore, that the mere fact that a felonious tort to the person results in death should not debar a person, who has suffered loss by the death, from suing in tort for such damages as he can prove that he has sustained, provided that the felony has been prosecuted. *A fortiori* he ought to be able to sue if the tortious act causing death does not amount to a felony. . . . But logic has been disregarded; and in cases where the tort results in death a right of action is denied. What, then, is the reason for a rule which, even on technical grounds, seems to be illogical. . . .

In the great majority of cases in which death ensues as a result of a tort felony has been committed. In a large number of cases also the persons damaged by the tort are the deceased's near relatives. I would like to suggest, therefore, that the rule based upon the maxim *actio personalis, &c.*, became confused with the rule based upon the fact that the tortious act was a felony . . . I should like to suggest, therefore, that when Lord Ellenborough gave his ruling in *Baker v Bolton* he was the victim of the same confusion of ideas.

COMMENTARY

The reason the felony might affect the tort claim was that the lesser wrong 'drowned' in the more serious felony: *Higgins v Butcher* (1607) Yelv 89, 80 ER 61; Dyson, 'The Timing of Tortious and Criminal Actions for the Same Wrong' [2012] CLJ 86.

Although it was common for felony to be prosecuted on indictment, there also existed a process known as an 'appeal of felony' which was 'essentially an oral accusation of crime made by someone closely affected' (*Baker*, p. 543). As felonies were particularly serious crimes a successful prosecution resulted in the death of the accused and forfeiture of their property. Although this did not provide compensation for the relatives, Holdsworth argues that the threat of an appeal of felony by the relatives against the tortfeasor might in practice have encouraged the tortfeasor to provide them with some compensation for the death. This possibility was eliminated when appeals of felony were abolished in 1819.

Whatever the historical explanation, a more modern rationale of the rule that death gives rise to no cause of action can be provided. The common law has never been keen to allow claims for 'relational' loss, that is, a loss caused as a consequence of an injury to someone else. Generally such claims are for pure economic loss and are subject to the restrictive rules applicable to that type of loss (*Cattle v Stockton Waterworks* (1875) LR 10 QB 453). So where the defendant's tort results in another's death the claim of those financially dependent upon them is relational (related to the death) and is for pure economic loss—hence the reluctance of the common law to allow a claim. See further Chapter 8.I.2. The problem with this approach, as applied to torts causing death, was twofold. First, the defendant who killed the victim rather than merely injuring them might face a liability in a merely negligible amount—potentially much less than in a non-fatal case. Secondly, the death of a husband often resulted in the immediate family being deprived of their 'breadwinner' and hence their means of support. These two factors were influential in convincing Parliament that statutory change was necessary.

2. The Background to Statutory Reform

R. Kostal, *English Law and Railway Capitalism*
(Oxford: OUP, 1994)

At the same time [by 1845], however, some prominent politicians and law reformers led by Lord John Campbell recognised that the revival of deodands [see commentary] by coroner's juries had not been sheer whimsy; it was a symptom of growing public anxiety about railway safety. Jurors had deliberately conscripted the deodand to the cause of punishing and deterring railway company negligence. They had done so because statutory and common law were seen as ineffective sources of safety regulation and financial compensation. Mindful of the need to maintain a legal deterrent to negligence, Lord Campbell introduced a bill to Parliament in 1845 designed to modify the common law principles concerning the right to sue in the case of a fatal accident. The bill enabled the immediate relatives of the deceased to bring an action for 'such damages . . . proportioned to the injury resulting from such death'. If enacted, the legislation instantly stood to give many accidental deaths monetary values. Although the railway industry appears to have offered some resistance to Lord Campbell's bill, its attention was greatly distracted by the railway promotional mania and subsequent stock market crash.

The fact that the fate of the Deodands Abolition Bill was linked to Lord Campbell's bill appears also to have diminished opposition to the measure. Both bills were passed into law in August 1846. This was a major turning-point in the history of English personal injury litigation.

W. Cornish et al, *Law and Society in England 1750–1950*
(2nd edn, Oxford: Hart, 2019)

One complaint which the Select Committee on Railway Labourers [1846] endorsed was the lack of protection or assistance offered to dependants of those who were killed. Even before that Committee's Report, Lord Campbell had taken up the cause, but could not be persuaded to do more than seek a remedy for this small part of the whole injustice. Accordingly two bills became law. One abolished deodands, the other gave dependants certain opportunities to claim compensation by civil action. The latter statute, although in many respects obscure, was nonetheless drawn with a degree of cunning. For it did not give the dependants of the deceased their own right of action, as would have followed from the Scots example of the *solatium* [see further III.3]. Instead, the personal representatives of the deceased person were permitted to maintain an action in any case where, if he had not died, he himself might have sued. Nevertheless the damages were to compensate those dependants who fell within a limited range—wife, husband, parent or child of the deceased . . .

Any defence that would have been open to the defendant against the deceased ran equally against a claim by his estate on his dependant's behalf; not only contributory negligence, but also common employment, were to prevent claims from succeeding under the Act. In 1846 *Priestley v Fowler* [the case which introduced the defence of common employment] was still a unique precedent standing against a wholly unfamiliar type of action and it was certainly assumed by some employers that they were being made vicariously liable to dead employees' relatives under the new Act. Yet the first case to reiterate the *Priestley v Fowler* rule refused relief under the Fatal Accidents Act 1846 to the widow of a deceased railwayman who, as administratrix, sought to make her husband's employers vicariously liable for the negligence of a fellow-worker. In the mines, where colliers died in their hundreds each year, the position was the same . . .

The families of deceased passengers did gain some benefit from the Act—indeed verdicts of £13,000 in 1871 and £16,000 in 1880 are recorded. But even they found that the courts interpreted the Act cautiously. Thus the judges refused to allow that the 'injury' suffered by the dependants could include their distress as well as their financial loss. The Scots precedent of the *solatium* was rejected, Coleridge J pointing out [in *Blake v Midland Railway Company* (1852) 18 QB 93 at 111] that the Act applied 'not only to great railway companies but to little tradesmen who sent out a horse and cart in the care of an apprentice'.

COMMENTARY

'The basic idea of the deodand was that if an animal or inanimate object caused or occasioned the accidental death of a human being, often by moving to the death, it would be confiscated' (Sutton, 'The Deodand and Responsibility for Death' (1997) 18 J Leg His 44). To get the confiscated item back, the owner would have to pay. A reason why railway companies may have been prepared to accept Lord Campbell's bill in return for abolishing deodands, suggested by Sutton, is that there was a revival in the use of deodands in the first half of the nineteenth century whereby deodands, often for extremely large sums of money, were imposed on steam engines and other new forms of transport which caused death. However, the use of this medieval remedy based on pre-modern notions of responsibility was ultimately an unsatisfactory way of dealing with fatal accidents (see Nolan, 'The Fatal Accidents Act 1846', *Tort Law and the Legislature*, ch. 7, who points out that the immediate catalyst for the Bill that became the 1846 Act was not—as is often assumed—accidents on the railways, but mining accidents).

The new way of dealing with fatal accidents was provided by Lord Campbell's Act of 1846, and the basic principle of giving the dependants a derivative, as opposed to an independent, action has been retained in all subsequent legislation dealing with tort liability for fatal accidents. This approach has been criticised by Waddams, 'Damages for Wrongful Death: Has Lord Campbell's Act Outlived its Usefulness?' (1984) 47 MLR 437, but is defended by Nolan, *op. cit.*, at pp. 156–7, who commends it as a 'sophisticated and appropriate' response to the question of damages for death.

III. Current Legislation

1. Loss of Dependency

Fatal Accidents Act 1976

1. Right of action for wrongful act causing death

(1) If death is caused by any wrongful act, neglect or default which is such as would (if death had not ensued) have entitled the person injured to maintain an action and recover damages in respect thereof, the person who would have been liable if death had not ensued shall be liable to an action for damages, notwithstanding the death of the person injured.

(2) Subject to section 1A(2) below, every such action shall be for the benefit of the dependants of the person ('the deceased') whose death has been so caused.

(3) In this Act 'dependant' means—
   (a) the wife or husband or former wife or husband of the deceased;
   (aa) the civil partner or former civil partner of the deceased;
   (b) any person who—
      (i) was living with the deceased in the same household immediately before the date of the death; and
      (ii) had been living with the deceased in the same household for at least two years before that date; and
      (iii) was living during the whole of that period as the husband or wife or civil partner of the deceased;
   (c) any parent or other ascendant of the deceased;
   (d) any person who was treated by the deceased as his parent;
   (e) any child or other descendant of the deceased;
   (f) any person (not being a child of the deceased) who, in the case of any marriage to which the deceased was at any time a party, was treated by the deceased as a child of the family in relation to that marriage;

(fa) any person (not being a child of the deceased) who, in the case of any civil partnership in which the deceased was at any time a civil partner, was treated by the deceased as a child of the family in relation to that civil partnership;

(g) any person who is, or is the issue of, a brother, sister, uncle or aunt of the deceased.

(4) The reference to the former wife or husband of the deceased in subsection (3)(a) above includes a reference to a person whose marriage to the deceased has been annulled or declared void as well as a person whose marriage to the deceased has been dissolved.

(4A) The reference to the former civil partner of the deceased in subsection (3)(aa) above includes a reference to a person whose civil partnership with the deceased has been annulled as well as a person whose civil partnership with the deceased has been dissolved.

(5) In deducing any relationship for the purposes of subsection (3) above—
(a) any relationship by marriage or civil partnership shall be treated as a relationship by consanguinity, any relationship of the half blood as a relationship of the whole blood, and the stepchild of any person as his child; and
(b) an illegitimate person shall be treated as—
  (i) the legitimate child of his mother and reputed father, or
  (ii) in the case of a person who has a female parent by virtue of section 43 of the Human Fertilisation and Embryology Act 2008, the legitimate child of his mother and that female parent.

(6) Any reference in this Act to injury includes any disease and any impairment of a person's physical or mental condition.

2. Persons entitled to bring the action

(1) The action shall be brought by and in the name of the executor or administrator of the deceased.

(2) If—
(a) there is no executor or administrator of the deceased, or
(b) no action is brought within six months after the death by and in the name of an executor or administrator of the deceased

the action may be brought by and in the name of all or any of the persons for whose benefit an executor or administrator could have brought it.

(3) Not more than one action shall lie for and in respect of the same subject matter of complaint.

(4) The plaintiff in the action shall be required to deliver to the defendant or his solicitor full particulars of the persons for whom and on whose behalf the action is brought and of the nature of the claim in respect of which damages are sought to be recovered.

3. Assessment of damages

(1) In the action such damages, other than damages for bereavement, may be awarded as are proportioned to the injury resulting from the death to the dependants respectively.

(2) After deducting the costs not recovered from the defendant any amount recovered otherwise than as damages for bereavement shall be divided among the dependants in such shares as may be directed.

(3) In an action under this Act where there fall to be assessed damages payable to a widow in respect of the death of her husband there shall not be taken account the re-marriage of the widow or her prospects of re-marriage.

(4) In an action under this Act where there fall to be assessed damages payable to a person who is a dependant by virtue of section 1(3)(b) above in respect of the death of the person with whom the dependant was living as husband or wife or civil partner there shall be taken into account (together with any other matter that appears to the court to be relevant to the action) the fact that the dependant had no enforceable right to financial support by the deceased as a result of their living together.

(5) If the dependants have incurred funeral expenses in respect of the deceased, damages may be awarded in respect of those expenses

(6) Money paid into court in satisfaction of a cause of action under this Act may be in one sum without specifying any person's share.

4. Assessment of damages: disregard of benefits

In assessing damages in respect of a person's death in an action under this Act, benefits which have accrued or will or may accrue to any person from his estate or otherwise as a result of his death shall be disregarded.

5. Contributory negligence

Where any person dies as the result partly of his own fault and partly of the fault of any other person or persons, and accordingly if an action were brought for the benefit of the estate under the Law Reform (Miscellaneous Provisions) Act 1934 the damages recoverable would be reduced under section 1(1) of the Law Reform (Contributory Negligence) Act 1945, any damages recoverable in an action . . . under this Act shall be reduced to a proportionate extent.

COMMENTARY

Under s. 1(1) if the deceased, had they not died, would have had an action against the defendant for damages, then the dependants (as defined) have a right of action under the Act. As noted earlier, the claim of the dependants is derivative, not independent, with the result that any defence available against the deceased would also be available under the Fatal Accidents Act. As Cornish et al. point out, this was problematic where the defence was common employment or contributory negligence. The former, a now-abolished defence absolving employers of liability for the negligence of an injured or deceased worker's fellow employee, involved no fault on the part of the victim and the latter only some degree of fault. The result was that one arbitrary restriction replaced another: the fate of the dependants rested on whether the tort was caused by a fellow employee or the presence of some carelessness of the deceased, rather than on whether the tort killed the victim or not. (Whether this should be seen as a failure of the 1846 Act or in subsequent developments in the law is open to question: see Nolan, *op. cit.*) However, with apportionment of damages for contributory negligence introduced in 1945 and the defence of common employment abolished in 1948, the lot of the dependants became more secure.

Nonetheless, contributory negligence of the deceased will still reduce the award to the dependants (s. 5). Also any contributory negligence of a dependant will reduce that dependant's award and may even eliminate it if the dependant was wholly responsible for the death, although the contributory negligence of one dependant has no effect on the claims of the others (see *Mulholland v McCrea* [1961] NI 135; *Dodds v Dodds* [1978] QB 543).

The derivative nature of the fatal accidents claim means that the dependants have no right of action where the deceased settled the case or obtained judgment before death. As noted earlier, this approach was questioned by Lord Phillips in *Gregg v Scott* [2005] 2 AC 176. In *Thompson v Arnold* [2008] PIQR P1 Langstaff J explained (at [86]) that the right of suit given to the dependants under s. 1(1) 'deals with the case in which a victim has not had the opportunity of obtaining funds which, indirectly, might benefit those for whom the victim cares, and those who depend upon his income'. Under the current law, this prevents the defendant from being liable twice over. This is because some of the settlement or judgment damages awarded to a living claimant (for example, loss of future earnings during the lost years) would go towards maintaining dependants, and it would be anomalous if, once the claimant died, the dependants could bring a further claim for damages in respect of a loss for which the defendant had already paid compensation. Of course, it would not be anomalous if, as Lord Phillips suggested, a living claimant could not claim damages for loss of earnings during the lost years. No doubt his Lordship's suggestion for reform was based on the fact that damages for loss of dependency under the Fatal Accidents Act are calculated more generously than damages for loss of earnings in the lost years (see *Thompson v Arnold* [2008] PIQR P1 at [22]–[25]). As the primary rationale for allowing the lost years claim to a living claimant is to provide for the dependants after the claimant's death, this difference is difficult to justify, although it would clearly require an amendment to the Fatal Accidents Act for Lord Phillips's suggestions to be implemented.

Although the dependant's claim is derivative, it is not *the same* claim as the deceased could have brought had he lived. In *Gray v Barr* [1971] 2 QB 554 Lord Denning explained:

> If [the deceased] had lived, i.e., only been injured and not died, and living would have been entitled to maintain an action and recover damages—then his widow and children can do so. They stand in his shoes in regard to liability, but not as to damages.

2. Who May Claim and for What?

Who is entitled to the benefit of an action under the Act? Section 1(2) provides that the action is for the benefit of 'dependants' and provides an exhaustive list of persons who qualify as such. The list has been updated over time and currently includes cohabitees in both heterosexual and same-sex relationships. However, the legislation retains the restrictions on claims by cohabitees that were imposed when such claims were first recognised by amending legislation in 1982: the person must have been living with the deceased in the same household as husband, wife or civil partner at the time of the death and for two years previously. In *Swift v Secretary of State for Justice* [2014] QB 373 the Court of Appeal rejected an argument that this two-year minimum period of cohabitation was incompatible with the Convention rights of cohabitees. Assuming without deciding that the facts were within the ambit of Article 8 so as to engage Article 14 ECHR, the court found that the two-year requirement was a proportionate means of pursuing the legitimate aim of confining the right to dependency damages to those who had relationships of some degree of permanence and constancy with the deceased, as could be presumed in the case of married couples.

It has from time to time been suggested that the list be extended to include those who cohabit without being in any kind of relationship (e.g. house-sharers). Indeed, a Civil Law Reform Bill in 2009 proposed the addition to the list of dependants of a residual category of people wholly or partly maintained by the deceased immediately before the death (Ministry of Justice, Civil Law Reform Bill Consultation Paper (CP53/09, 2009), Draft Bill cl. 1(2)). However, the then coalition government subsequently decided not to take forward this part of the Bill (Ministry of Justice, Civil Law Reform Bill, Response to Consultation CP(R) CP 53/09).

If such a change was implemented, would it mean that a person who received lifts to work or birthday presents from the deceased was 'partly dependent' and hence entitled to claim? See Law Commission, *Claims for Wrongful Death* (Consultation Paper No. 148, 1997), para. 3.31.

How much is each qualifying dependant able to claim? The following extracted case deals with this issue.

Franklin v South Eastern Railway (1858) 3 H & N 211, 157 ER 448

The issue for the court was the assessment of damages under Lord Campbell's Act.

Pollock CB

The statute does not in terms say on what principle the action it gives is to be maintainable, nor on what principle the damages are to be assessed . . .

It has been held that these damages are not to be given as a *solatium*; but are to be given in reference to a pecuniary loss. That was so decided for the first time in banc, in *Blake v The Midland Railway Co* (1852) 18 QB 93. That case was tried before Parke B, who told the jury that the Lord Chief Baron had frequently ruled . . . without objection, that the claim for damage must be founded on pecuniary loss, actual or expected, and that mere injury to feelings could not be considered. It is also clear that damages are not to be given merely in reference to the loss of a legal right, for they are to be distributed among relations only, and not to all individuals sustaining a loss. . . . If then the damages are not to be calculated on either of these principles, nothing remains except that they should be calculated in reference to a reasonable expectation of pecuniary benefit, as of right or otherwise, from the continuance of the life.

COMMENTARY

Although this case represents the general principle, 'pecuniary benefit' should not be read too strictly: it is well established that a dependant may claim for loss of services provided by the deceased (e.g. the caring services provided by a parent to a child—discussed later). There are limits, however, on what can be claimed. In *Burns v Edman* [1970] QB 541 Crichton J disallowed the claim by a widow and her children in respect of her husband's death: although it had been caused by the defendant's negligence, the support the husband provided was from the proceeds of his criminal activity and hence the *ex turpi causa* maxim (see Ch. 6.V) barred the widow's claim.

Although the dependency will normally result from a dependence upon the deceased's own earnings, this is not a necessary condition for a claim under the Act. In *Cox v Hockenhull* [2000] 1 WLR 750 it was held that a dependency could be founded on the state benefits payable to the deceased, although it was accepted that in the majority of such cases the dependant would suffer no loss as the level of support would be the same even if the amount was reduced to reflect the fact that one less adult was being supported. Cf. *Hunter v Butler* [1996] RTR 396, where the dependency was partly the product of benefits fraud.

What amounts to a reasonable expectation of pecuniary benefit is a question of fact but not of past fact. The court is asking what would have happened if the deceased had lived. In *Davies v Taylor* [1974] AC 207 the widow, who had been having an adulterous affair for the previous two years, had left her spouse five weeks before his death and, as Lord Reid put it (at 212), 'there was no immediate prospect of her returning to him'. Following his death she had an *ex post mortem* burst of affection for him and attempted to convince the courts that she might have returned to him (despite telling him shortly before his death that she would not do so). The House of Lords rejected the proposition that she had to show, on the balance of probability, that she would have returned to her husband. As long as there was a not insubstantial chance that she might return, the court could evaluate that chance, although on the facts the widow did not satisfy this requirement.

Even where no such complicating factors arise, the court is still faced with the task of valuing the dependency. As in the case of personal injury actions, there are now two methods of calculation: the multiplier approach and periodical payments. When the multiplier approach is used, the annual value of the dependency is calculated and is multiplied by a multiplier based on the length of time the dependency will last, but discounted to reflect the fact that the dependant is getting a lump sum and the possibility that the dependency would have ended for other reasons. The uncertainty is even greater here than in the assessment of a claimant's loss of future earnings; there is not only the possibility that the deceased may have died anyway but also that the dependant may die before the anticipated period of dependency has expired. The normal practice is to calculate a single multiplicand (representing the value of the dependency for all dependants) and to then apply a single multiplier, apportioning the total arrived at between the dependants (see CPR Part 41.3A), although separate multiplicands and multipliers can be calculated for each dependant (*Creswell v Eaton* [1991] 1 WLR 1113). Where the issue is the value of the services provided by the deceased, the Court of Appeal in *Spittle v Bunney* [1988] 1 WLR 847 stressed that a court must consider the decreasing need for those services in the case of a child dependant; as the child grows older the need for the services decreases and the ultimate award to the dependant should reflect this.

Until recently, the courts calculated the multiplier from the date of the deceased person's death rather than the date of trial (*Cookson v Knowles* [1979] AC 556). But the Supreme Court accepted in *Knauer v Ministry of Justice* [2016] AC 908 that this meant that the claimant would suffer a discount for early receipt of the money when in fact the money would not be received until after trial. The Court ruled that the correct date at which to assess the multiplier should therefore be the date of trial.

Periodical payments may also be ordered in actions under the Fatal Accidents Act (Damages Act 1996, ss. 2, 7). The method of calculating the value of the periodical payment is the same as in personal injury actions by a living claimant (see in Ch. 15.III) with the exception that the annual loss on which the periodical payment is based is the value of the dependency to each dependant.

Section 3(5) allows for the dependants to recover funeral expenses, although the estate of the deceased can also recover such expenses. It will be preferable for the estate to claim these expenses where the dependant's award will be reduced because of their own contributory negligence, because such negligence will not affect the estate's claim (Law Commission Consultation Paper, *op. cit.*, para. 2.61). Where the dependant's award will be reduced because of *the deceased's* contributory negligence, it does not matter who brings the claim as both are affected by the contributory negligence.

Benefits Arising from the Death

Although the death of the deceased may cause loss to the dependants, it may also cause benefits to accrue to them that they would not otherwise have received. For example, a dependant may be a beneficiary under the deceased's will or under a life insurance policy. Are these benefits to be taken into account?

One benefit is dealt with specifically in s. 3(3)—the remarriage of a widow or prospects of remarriage are not to be taken into account in assessing the widow's claim. The *Pearson Commission* described the failure to take into account the actual remarriage of a widow as a 'manifest absurdity' (para. 411). Conversely, a majority of the High Court of Australia has held that no separate discount for the prospects of remarriage should be made in an award to the surviving spouse; the general discount for vicissitudes would cover the possibility of re-partnering and there was no reason for selecting one contingency—re-partnering—and treating it differently from the myriad of other contingencies that might possibly affect the award (*De Sales v Ingrilli* (2002) 212 CLR 338). The Law Commission Consultation Paper, *op. cit.*, noted that the rationale behind the section was that 'taking into account widows' prospects of remarriage exposed the widows to distressing cross-examination and consideration by the judiciary of their appearance' (para. 3.57). However, as the Commission noted, the section does not prevent this kind of questioning in relation to a child dependant's claim (the possible remarriage of the widow being relevant to her ability to provide for the child), nor does it prevent a court considering benefits received by the widow from her partner in a de facto relationship. A number of alternative reforms were suggested, including taking into account the fact of the widow's remarriage and applying a presumption as to the prospects of remarriage based on objective statistical probability, which might be rebutted in a case where, for example, a widow was engaged to be married at the date of the trial and so would have a much greater likelihood of remarriage than one who was unattached (para. 365f). In its final report the Commission recommended the abolition of s. 3(3) in favour of taking into account future marriage only where the claimant had in fact remarried or was engaged to be married (*Claims for Wrongful Death* (Law Com. No. 263, 1999), para. 4.53). Although an amendment effecting that change was drafted (Ministry of Justice, Civil Law Reform Bill Consultation Paper (CP53/09, 2009), Draft Bill cl. 2), the then coalition government announced in 2011 that it would not be taken forward.

What does it tell you about the law's tacit assumptions regarding male and female employment that s. 3(3) of the 1976 act applies only to widows and not to widowers?

If prospects of remarriage are not taken into account it might be thought that neither should the prospects of divorce. However, the Court of Appeal in *Owen v Martin* [1992] PIQR Q151 took the view that this possibility did in fact have to be taken into account (while recognising that divorce might not end the other party's entitlement to financial support). Despite support for change in consultations by the Law Commission and the Department of Constitutional Affairs (now the Ministry of Justice), the then coalition government decided not to go ahead with proposed legislation to effect the change (Ministry of Justice, Civil Law Reform Bill Consultation Paper (CP53/09, 2009), Draft Bill cl. 3).

More generally, benefits arising from the deceased's death are dealt with in s. 4—any benefits which have accrued or may accrue to the dependant as a result of the death must be disregarded. This provision was introduced by amendment to the 1976 Act in 1982, changing the way in which benefits were dealt with, as previously the relevant section had merely specified a list of benefits which were not to be taken into account. Difficulties have arisen in relation to the gratuitous provision of services to a dependant after the deceased's death. If those services are equal to or an improvement on what the dependant was in fact receiving from the deceased, must the court nonetheless disregard the replacement services and award the dependant damages for the value of the deceased's services? In *Stanley v Saddique* [1992] QB 1 a child's parents were estranged at the time when he was born, and he lived with his mother. When his mother died in a road traffic accident the child was taken in by his father, who shortly afterwards met and married a young woman who accepted the boy as a member of their new family and provided services to the child that were at least as good as those provided by the deceased. The Court of Appeal held that on its proper construction the word 'benefit' in s. 4 of the 1976 Act was not restricted to direct pecuniary benefit but included the benefit accruing to the plaintiff as a result of his absorption into a new family unit consisting of his father, stepmother and siblings, and was thus to be disregarded. However, in *Hayden v Hayden* [1992] 1 WLR 986 a differently constituted Court of Appeal (although with Sir David Croom-Johnson sitting on both panels) decided that the replacement services provided to the deceased's children by her partner, the children's father, who was also the tortfeasor, could be taken into account in assessing the award that should be made to the child dependant. These two cases are considered in the following extract.

R v Criminal Injuries Compensation Board, ex p. K [1999] QB 1131

The issue for the Divisional Court was how substituted caring services provided by the aunt and uncle of the deceased to the deceased's children should be taken into account in assessing the children's claim under the Criminal Injuries Compensation Scheme (which for this purpose required the court to consider the position under the Fatal Accidents Act 1976).

Brooke LJ

In September 1989 a mother was murdered by her husband. Her three young children, then aged 3, 2 and 1 years old, were taken into the family of her husband's brother and his wife, and have lived there ever since. They have been very well looked after. In July 1993 a single member of the Criminal Injuries Compensation Board, Mr Conrad Seagroatt QC, awarded them £35,000 in respect of the loss of their mother's services, based on a multiplier of seven and an annual loss of £5,000. The Official Solicitor, who represented them, sought an oral hearing because he considered that the multiplier was too low. On 3 February 1997 a panel of the Board (Sir Jonathan Clarke and Mr Roderick Macdonald QC) reduced the award to £9,000. They did so because they considered themselves bound by the majority decision of the Court of Appeal in *Hayden v Hayden* [1992] 1 WLR 986 to hold that the general parental services provided by their uncle and aunt were at least as good as those provided by their mother before her death, so that the children had suffered no loss, and that those substituted services should not be disregarded by reason of the operation of section 4 of the Fatal Accidents Act 1976 (as substituted by section 3(1) of the Administration of Justice Act 1982) . . .

[S]ection 4 of the Fatal Accidents Act 1976, as substituted by section 3(1) of the Administration of Justice Act 1982, now reads:

> In assessing damages in respect of a person's death in an action under this Act, benefits which have accrued or will or may accrue to any person from his estate or otherwise as a result of his death shall be disregarded.

In *Stanley v Saddique (Mohammed)* [1992] QB 1 the Court of Appeal unanimously held that this wide wording was not to be cut down by reason of its juxtaposition to section 3 of the Act of 1976, as amended. In that case a child's parents were estranged at the time when he was born, and he lived with his mother, but when his mother died in a road traffic accident the boy, then three months old, was taken in by his father, who shortly afterwards met and then married a young woman who accepted the boy as a member of their new family. The Court of Appeal held that on its proper construction the word 'benefit' in section 4 of the Act of 1976, as amended, was not restricted to direct pecuniary benefit but included the benefit accruing to the plaintiff as a result of his absorption into a new family unit consisting of his father, stepmother and siblings. In those circumstances, by virtue of section 4, that benefit was to be wholly disregarded for the purposes of assessing damages for loss of dependency. . . .

If that decision had stood alone, there would not have been the slightest difficulty about the present case. The benefit conferred on the applicants by their uncle and aunt taking them into their own home would fall to be disregarded, and the applicants would be entitled to recover for the loss of their mother's services, however those might be valued. The difficulty arises from the decision of the Court of Appeal in *Hayden v Hayden* [1992] 1 WLR 986, and it is important, in my judgment, to see what that case was all about, and what it appears to have decided. . . .

It is necessary to avoid thinking that *Hayden v Hayden* sets out any principles of law of general application to the valuation of children's claims for three reasons. The first is that the assessment of damages is a jury question and the Court of Appeal had no power to interfere with the judge's award of £20,000 unless it was plainly too high or too low. The second is that in that case the father was the tortfeasor who was liable to pay the damages for the benefit of his child. The third was that there was no third party who stepped in to look after the orphaned child, like the grandmother in *Hay v Hughes* [1975] QB 790, the estranged father's new wife in *Stanley v Saddique* [1992] QB 1, or the uncle and aunt in the present case: it was the father himself who expanded the scope of his parental duties towards his daughter in the home they shared.

Both McCowan LJ (who dissented) and Sir David Croom-Johnson said that the court was bound by the earlier decision in *Stanley v Saddique*. . . .

What divided Sir David Croom-Johnson from McCowan LJ was their application of the law, as explained in *Stanley v Saddique*, to the particular facts of the case before them. Sir David Croom-Johnson considered that the court should first ask itself: 'Has the plaintiff suffered any loss at all?' and then: 'Are there any benefits which accrued to the child as a result of the death which are to be disregarded?'

The judge did not reveal the process by which he arrived at his figure of £20,000. Sir David Croom-Johnson said that he had plainly included in his award an element of financial benefit from the mother's earnings, but he was not persuaded that the judge distinguished the element in respect of the loss of services provided by the mother which were replaced by the defendant from the element in respect of the loss of those which were not. He rejected the proposition that a jury would have valued the lost services by reference to the cost of a 'notional nanny'. It would simply have gone on the established facts of what had happened in the past and was likely to happen in the future. He said [1992] 1 WLR 986, 998:

> If the result of making an allowance for the fact that the defendant has himself continued to act as a loving father means that his ultimate financial liability to the plaintiff is smaller, there is nothing wrong or objectionable in that. Emotive phrases like allowing the defendant 'to profit from his wrongdoing' are beside the point. It is preferable to say that what he had done has had, as one result, the reduction of his liability. Mr Crowther has submitted that to award any damages under his heading (i) [for the loss of services provided by the deceased which were replaced by the defendant] was wrong in law, but I do not think it was. There must be a claim for loss of the mother's services, in the special circumstances

of this case, over and above what the defendant has been able to replace. The judge has included it, and rightly so, although he has not particularised the amount.

This, then, was what Sir David Croom-Johnson held the child had lost in the particular context of a case in which she had remained at home and her father had replaced the mother's services to a certain extent. He then went on to consider whether at the second stage of the exercise there were any benefits which had to be disregarded under section 4 of the Act of 1976. He said, at pp. 999–1000:

> The facts in the instant case, however, are wholly different from those in *Stanley v Saddique* [1992] QB 1. The plaintiff remained in the family home with her father and, for a time, with her older brothers and sisters until they left home. She continued to be looked after by him. No reasonable judge or jury would regard the defendant, in doing what he did, as doing other than discharge his parental duties, many of which he had been carrying out in any event, and would be expected to continue to do. The reasoning of the trial judge in the instant case seems to be that he was making the first of Diplock LJ's two estimates, that is, of the initial loss to the plaintiff caused by the death of the mother. Whether that is so or not, the continuing services of the father are not a benefit which has accrued as a result of the death. In the end, what is a 'benefit' must be a question of fact.

It follows that both Sir David Croom-Johnson and McCowan LJ agreed that they were bound by *Stanley v Saddique* [1992] QB 1 but were unable to agree on the way in which the principles established in that case were to be applied to the facts in *Hayden v Hayden* [1992] 1 WLR 986; for McCowan LJ's dissenting view, see p. 993.

Parker LJ, for his part, adopted a rather different approach. He started his judgment, at p. 1000, by saying that when faced with claims by dependent children under the Fatal Accidents Act 1976 the court was faced with the task of quantifying in money that which in reality could not be so quantified, even in cases without complications. The facts of the case in *Hayden v Hayden* were such that the difficulties of reaching a just solution were greatly increased. After summarising the rival contentions he added:

> For the defendant it is pointed out that if his services are to be disregarded he will in effect be paying damages three times over. First he will be providing replacement services free of charge, secondly, he will be paying for the services which he has so provided, and thirdly he will have lost his employment in order to provide such services. This is true and on the face of it appears not to be in accordance with justice. Furthermore in cases in which it is shown that the services of the father are in every respect as good as, or even better than the services previously provided by the mother it is, again on the face of it, difficult to see that the child has suffered a recoverable loss. He will or she will of course have been deprived of the mother's love and affection but it is not and could not be suggested that this loss sounds in damages.

This passage shows that Parker LJ was concentrating his mind on the way to find a just solution in an unusual case where the father in a united family was not only providing the replacement services given by the mother, but was also the defendant tortfeasor from whom compensation was being sought.

Parker LJ, at pp. 1001–1003, reviewed the authorities and concluded that the court was entitled to prefer *Hay v Hughes* [1975] QB 790 to *Stanley v Saddique* [1992] QB 1, and to hold that the gratuitous services of a relative do not constitute a benefit resulting from the death of the deceased. I have already explained why, in my judgment, this court is bound to follow the decision in *Stanley v Saddique*, buttressed as it is by the opinion of two members of the Court of Appeal in *Hayden v Hayden* [1992] 1 WLR 986 . . .

[W]e are bound by *Stanley v Saddique* [1992] QB 1 to hold that in so far as the value of the replacement services formed a benefit resulting from the death (like the stepmother's services in that case) we must disregard them when assessing damages. In other words at the first stage of the inquiry we cannot say that the children have suffered no loss because the only way in which we could do so would be to take into account something which we are not allowed to take into account. The factual position is quite different from the factual position in *Hayden v Hayden* [1992] 1 WLR 986, in which the majority of the Court of Appeal held that the value of the tortfeasor father's replacement services was not to be disregarded under section 4(1) [in its original form], whether because section 4(1) did not apply at all (Parker LJ) or because this situation was totally different from a case in which the replacement services are voluntarily provided by a third party (Sir David Croom-Johnson). . . .

The effect of this judgment will enable the Board to revert to compensating child claimants for the most part as they used to do before this panel of the Board thought that the decision of the Court of Appeal in *Hayden v Hayden* [1992] 1 WLR 986 had made a much more radical change in the law. The correct way to resolve a claim by a child whose needs are met after its mother's death by someone who already owed parental duties to it before the death will have to be resolved by the courts on another occasion. . . .

Rougier J

The affidavit of Mr Macdonald QC does not suggest that the Board progressed beyond the first question—namely whether or not the children had suffered any loss. But if and in so far as they had considered section 4, it seems to me that they could only have reached a conclusion adverse to the applicants in reliance on a further obiter remark by Parker LJ in *Hayden v Hayden* [1992] 1 WLR 986, where, having quoted the judgment of Purchas LJ in *Stanley v Saddique*, Parker LJ said, at p. 1003:

> It is thus clear that he regarded the services of the stepmother as being a benefit resulting from the death of the deceased which is directly contrary to the decision in *Hay v Hughes* [1975] QB 790. On the point of construction Ralph Gibson LJ with hesitation agreed with Purchas LJ and Croom-Johnson LJ agreed with both judgments. With conflicting decisions on the point whether the gratuitous services of a relative do or do not result from the death of a mother I for my part have no hesitation in following *Hay v Hughes* [1975] QB 790 rather than *Stanley v Saddique* [1992] QB 1 and if this is right section 4 does not apply.

It seems to me that if and in so far as the Board may have been relying on this observation in support of a decision that section 4 does not apply, they were overlooking two factors. First, the majority of the court in *Hayden v Hayden* [1992] 1 WLR 986 declared that *Stanley v Saddique* [1992] QB 1 was binding upon them. Secondly, they were able to distinguish *Hayden v Hayden* on two specific differences of fact: (1) that the defendant himself was the tortfeasor who was continuing to provide the services, so that to make him pay for them would effectively be awarding triple damages, and (2) that the defendant, as the father of the children, had been providing services before the death by reason of no more than parental duty, so that the services he provided after death could not be said to arise as a result of the death.

To my mind the facts of the present case, in so far as they deal with the quality of substituted care, are far more akin to those of *Stanley v Saddique* [1992] QB 1 and there is no effective comparison to be drawn with the facts of *Hayden v Hayden* [1992] 1 WLR 986. For those reasons I think this application succeeds and the matter should be remitted to the Board for the purposes suggested by Brooke LJ.

Application granted.

COMMENTARY

Can the services provided by a parent to a child ever be replaced? Commenting on Parker LJ's reasoning in *Hayden* that the provision of the replacement services meant it was at least arguable that the child had suffered no loss, Kemp (1993) 109 LQR 173 notes (at p. 175): 'The child undoubtedly lost her mother's services. That is a loss.' Do you agree? Compare Parker LJ's reasoning in *Hayden* with that of Sir David Croom-Johnson, who rejected an argument that it was wrong to award *any* damages for the loss of the services of a parent which were replaced by the surviving parent, holding that '[t]here must be a claim for loss of the mother's services, in the special circumstances of the case, over and above what the defendant has been able to replace'.

The Divisional Court preferred *Stanley v Saddique* on the facts of the case before them, distinguishing *Hayden* on the grounds that: (1) the duties that the father took on after the mother's death were simply an extension of the existing parental duties of the father and hence did not arise as a result of the death; and (2) the provider of the substituted services was the tortfeasor. The result of these three decisions appears to be that, where the substituted caring services provided to the dependant are provided by a third party and are equivalent to or better than those provided by the deceased, such a benefit results from the death and, as a result of s. 4, is disregarded when calculating the value of the dependency.

The position is more complicated where a surviving parent provides the substituted services. In *H v S* [2003] QB 965 it was held by the Court of Appeal that if, at the time of death, the surviving parent was providing no support or caring services and there was no prospect of such services being provided in the future, any support or services provided by the surviving parent after the death fell within s. 4 and were to be disregarded. Although the Court did not explicitly say so, this seems to be the ground for distinguishing *Hayden*, where the surviving parent had been providing services prior to the death. This suggests that, if the parents of the child had been living together at the time of the death, or one parent had a legal obligation to support the child financially, substituted services provided by the surviving parent may be taken into account, as such services are the result of ordinary parental duties and do not result from the death. Thus the dependant child's award is reduced, either because the dependant suffers no loss or because the substituted services do not fall within s. 4. This result appears odd, because a surviving parent who provides support for the children that was previously provided by the deceased is clearly doing substantially more than simply performing ordinary parental responsibilities. The current situation also results in the paradox that, in terms of a dependency award under the Fatal Accidents Act 1976, it may be better to be a child of a single parent rather than of cohabiting parents who both care for the child. In the former case, if the surviving parent does provide substitute services after the death they will be disregarded, but in the latter the services will be considered as an extension of parental duties and taken into account, with the result that (1) the surviving parent and child have lost a partner and parent; and (2) the family income is doubly reduced because no damages are awarded for the substituted services and because the surviving parent may have given up remunerative work to perform the services. Can this be justified?

It should be noted further that *Hayden* can also be distinguished even where the surviving parent takes on additional parental duties after the death. The Court of Appeal in *Hayden* was clearly influenced by the fact that the *tortfeasor* was the provider of the substituted services, because in that case the tortfeasor was also the surviving parent. In light of the criticism in the previous paragraph, if the tortfeasor was not the surviving parent, it may be wondered whether the award to the dependant would be reduced if the surviving parent provided substituted services; that is, would the court hold that the latter was only acting out of an existing parental duty and hence the benefit was not caught by s. 4 and could be taken into account?

It will be remembered that the House of Lords in *Hunt v Severs* [1994] 2 AC 350 held that damages paid to a living claimant in respect of gratuitously provided caring services were held on trust for the carer (except where, as in that case, the carer was the tortfeasor). Despite criticism of that decision by academics and the recommendation of an alternative approach to compensating the carer by the Law Commission (see *Claims for Wrongful Death* (Law Com. No. 263, 1999), paras 7.22–7.23), the Court of Appeal has held that the same rule applies to the gratuitous provision of substituted caring services in claims under the Fatal Accidents Act. In *H v S* [2003] QB 965 it was held that the only basis on which such damages could be awarded was that they were used to reimburse the voluntary carer for services already rendered and were available to pay for such services in the future. Such amounts were to be held on trust, the trust being legally enforceable by the carer beneficiaries (cf. *Bordin v St Mary's NHS Trust* [2000] Lloyd's Rep Med 287, where the judge thought that the trust was not enforceable in the courts). Apart from the inappropriateness of the trust in this setting (demonstrated in this case by the appointment as trustees of the two eldest child claimants and their uncle), the consequences of giving the carer a proprietary right to the fund may be seen as undesirable. Should those who take on the responsibility of caring for another's children as part of the relationship with one of the parents expect financial remuneration for it? What if the services provided are poorer than those provided by the deceased, but better than nothing? Should the temporary partner of the surviving parent have a claim for substituted services actually provided, even if such services have ceased to be provided by the time of the trial because they have run off with someone else, leaving the surviving parent destitute? For comment on *H v S* see Lunney (2002) 13 KCLJ 219.

After considering the views of the Law Commission and the responses to its own consultation paper, the then Labour government proposed changes to how awards of damages for the provision of gratuitous services under the Fatal Accidents Act should be made. In the draft legislation (Ministry of Justice, Civil Law Reform Bill Consultation Paper (CP53/09, 2009), Draft Bill cl. 8) damages were to be awarded in respect of gratuitous services provided to a dependant that replaced the deceased's services, but the dependant was to be under a personal obligation to account to the gratuitous service provider. It also stipulated that the fact that the provider of the replacement services was the tortfeasor did not prevent the dependant from claiming for the value of those services but limited the claim to services to be provided post-trial. A similar amendment was proposed for damages awarded for gratuitous services to a claimant in a personal injury action (cl. 7: see further in Ch. 15.IV), the effect of which would have been that awards in respect of gratuitously provided services would be made on the same basis in both personal injury actions and in claims by dependants under the Fatal Accidents Act. Although the reform proposal was subsequently dropped, do you think these changes would have been preferable to the 'trust' solution?

3. Bereavement Damages

Fatal Accidents Act 1976

1A. Bereavement

(1) An action under this Act may consist of or include a claim for damages for bereavement.

(2) A claim for damages for bereavement shall only be for the benefit—

    (a) of the wife or husband or civil partner of the deceased;
    (aa) of the cohabiting partner of the deceased; and
    (b) where the deceased was a minor who was never married or a civil partner—
        (i) of his parents, if he was legitimate; and
        (ii) of his mother, if he was illegitimate.

(2A) In subsection (2) 'cohabiting partner' means any person who—

    (a) was living with the deceased in the same household immediately before the date of the death; and
    (b) had been living with the deceased in the same household for at least two years before that date; and
    (c) was living during the whole of that period as the wife or husband or civil partner of the deceased.

(3) Subject to subsection (5) below, the sum to be awarded as damages under this section shall be £15,120.

(4) Where there is a claim for damages under subsection (2)(a) and (aa), or under subsection (2)(b), for the benefit of more than one person, the sum awarded shall be divided equally between them (subject to any deduction falling to be made in respect of costs not recovered from the defendant).

(5) The Lord Chancellor may by order made by statutory instrument, subject to annulment in pursuance of a resolution of either House of Parliament, amend this section by varying the sum for the time being specified in subsection (3) above.

COMMENTARY

Under the civil law of Scotland a pursuer is allowed to claim a moderate sum—known as *solatium*—in acknowledgement of the grief and sorrow felt at a relative's death (see now Damages (Scotland) Act 2011 (asp 7) s. 4). No such claim was known to the common law and this did not initially change under the fatal accidents legislation. But the Administration of Justice Act 1982, s. 3 introduced a new section, s. 1A, into the Fatal Accidents Act 1976, creating a statutory right for a limited class of dependants to claim a fixed sum for bereavement, originally £3,500, but rising over time, and most recently increased to £15,120 for causes of action accruing after 1 May 2020 (Damages for Bereavement (Variation of Sum) (England and Wales) Order 2020/316).

The class who may claim for bereavement is currently much more limited than the general class of dependants in s. 1(2) and is somewhat anomalous: allowing the claim of the mother but not the father of an illegitimate child seems difficult to defend (Law Commission Consultation Paper, *op. cit.*, para. 3.144). However, two significant additions to the class of potential claimants have been made since the initial introduction of bereavement damages. The first was civil partners—on the passing of the Civil Partnership Act 2004. The second addition was cohabiting partners, but only after a rather tortuous process.

After much consultation (see, e.g., *Claims for Wrongful Death* (Law Com. No. 263, 1999), paras 6.31, 6.34 and 6.41), the then Labour government proposed in 2009 to extend the class of eligible claimants to include the father of an illegitimate child, children of the deceased under the age of 18 years (who would receive half the amount specified in s. 1(3)) and persons who had been living with the deceased as the deceased's husband or wife or civil partner for a period of at least two years ending with the date of the death (Ministry of Justice, Civil Law Reform Bill Consultation Paper (CP53/09), Draft Bill cl. 5(2)). However, the incoming coalition government decided not to take forward this part of the Bill. In *Smith v Lancashire Teaching Hospitals NHS Trust* [2018] QB 804 the Court of Appeal ruled that the unavailability of bereavement damages to a 'two year +' cohabitee of a tortiously killed deceased was incompatible with Article 14 of the ECHR (prohibition of discrimination) read with Article 8 (right to respect for private and family life) and that the relevant legislative provision could not be interpreted as though it extended to unmarried cohabitees. Exercising its power under s. 4 of the Human Rights Act 1998, the Court issued a declaration that s. 1A of the 1976 Act was incompatible with the claimant's Convention rights. This induced the now Conservative government to bring forward a remedial order to remove the incompatibility (Fatal Accidents Act 1976 (Remedial) Order 2020, SI 2020/1023), amending the statute so as to extend the entitlement to bereavement damages beyond wives, husbands and civil partners of a deceased to include a 'cohabiting partner' (s. 1A(2)(aa)) subject to the definitional requirements that the latter was living with the deceased in the same household immediately before the date of the death, had been living with the deceased in the same household for at least two years before that date and was living during the whole of that period as the wife or husband or civil partner of the deceased (s. 1(2A)).

Although the class of claimants who can claim for bereavement under the Fatal Accidents Act is limited, a wider class is eligible to claim a similar remedy if the death arises from a breach of Article 2 of the ECHR. In *Rabone v Pennine Care NHS Trust* [2012] 2 AC 72, the Supreme Court held that an effective remedy for breach of Article 2 requires 'victims' as defined under the Convention to have access to a claim in damages that should extend to non-pecuniary loss, including anxiety and distress caused by the death. Shortly afterwards, the ECtHR affirmed this interpretation of the Convention in *Reynolds v United Kingdom* (2012) 55 EHRR 35. As the HRA allows for such claims to be brought against public authorities in domestic legal proceedings (ss. 7–8), as long as the claimant is a victim of the unlawful act (s. 7(1), (7)) there will effectively be an alternative claim for bereavement to that under the Fatal Accidents Act. It remains to be seen what sort of ties with the deceased will enable such a claim to be brought, but it is clear that the class of victims—described by Tettenborn as an 'ill-defined class' ((2012) 128 LQR 327 at 331)—is much wider than that eligible to claim for bereavement under the 1976 Act. That was precisely why the HRA claim was brought in *Rabone*: see Lady Hale at [92], noting that 'the ordinary law of tort does not recognise or compensate the anguish suffered by parents who are deprived of the life of their adult child'. There is a further lack of clarity about the levels of compensation that should be awarded in an action under the HRA, not least because the damages are to be calculated taking into account the principles applied by the ECtHR in awarding compensation under Article 41 of the Convention. The Strasbourg Court has not stipulated a fixed sum to be awarded in this context and there has in fact been significant variation in the awards it has made: in the cases cited in *Rabone*, the amounts ranged from £4,200 to £50,000. At the higher end, this clearly exceeds the sum that is payable for bereavement under the Fatal Accidents Act, though the actual awards in *Rabone* were a rather modest £5,000 for each parent of the deceased.

Given the statutory remedy for breach of Article 2 under the HRA and the reluctance of the courts to adapt the common law of negligence to provide a remedy for breach of the ECHR (see Ch. 3.III.2), it is unlikely that the availability of this remedy will force the courts—in accordance with s. 3 of the HRA—to interpret the class of claimants in s. 1A more widely in order to comply with the ECHR (cf. *Swift v Secretary of State for Justice* [2014] QB 373, considered earlier). However, the result is that there may be different classes of claimants with different claims for bereavement, and potentially different amounts of damages, depending on whether the death results from a tort or from breach of Article 2. Is this a defensible distinction? See further Tettenborn, *op. cit.*, who argues that whenever a fatal accident claim is made against a state entity or public authority, the court must now decide as a preliminary matter whether the claim could also have been brought under Article 2 and, if so, determine eligibility for bereavement compensation accordingly.

17 HOW TORT WORKS

This chapter focuses on the role played by the law of tort in the compensation and prevention of personal injuries. The question addressed is how tort works, both at a descriptive and an evaluative level (i.e. both how does it in fact work and also how well does it work). We begin, in the first section, by examining the way that tort operates in practice: when are claims for compensation actually made; how are claims brought and how are they resolved; how much does it cost to bring a claim; is the compensation paid adequate; and who pays for it? A question of recurring importance here is whether recent rises in the numbers and costs of tort personal injury (PI) claims support the contention that a 'compensation culture' has developed. In the second section of this chapter we turn to evaluation, and focus upon the 'fault principle' that is enshrined in the law of tort, that is, the principle that compensation should only be paid to a person injured by another's fault. In this section, we shall consider how the law might depart from the fault principle by the development of strict liability or no-fault compensation, concluding with an examination of radical reform options involving the abolition of tort as a means of compensating for personal injuries.

I. Tort Law in Operation

1. When are Claims for Compensation Made?

D. Harris et al., *Compensation and Support for Illness and Injury* (Oxford: OUP, 1984)

[The extract summarises some of the findings of an empirical study conducted by the Oxford Centre for Socio-Legal Studies in 1976–7 ('the Oxford survey'). The researchers obtained general information about the incidence of illness, injury and handicap from a large-scale household survey and follow-up interviews with individuals incapacitated by illness or accident. The extract focuses upon the research team's analysis of the factors associated with claiming and obtaining damages (written up by Hazel Genn) and of accident victims' perspectives on fault and liability (written up by Sally Lloyd-Bostock).]

The survey showed that only a small minority of all accident victims initiate legal claims and obtain damages for the losses they have suffered. . . . For all types of accident taken together, the figure is 12 per cent of cases, but there are important differences in the success rates between different categories of accident. While fewer than one in three of road accident victims, and one in five of work accident victims obtained damages, fewer than one in fifty of all other types of accident victims obtained damages, despite the fact that this represented the largest category of accidents suffered by victims in the sample. Although the chances of obtaining damages were very high once there had been contact with a solicitor about the possibility of making a claim, the vast majority of victims either never considered the question of claiming compensation, or if they did so, failed to take any positive steps to make a definite claim.

Elderly victims and young victims appeared on the whole to be reluctant to claim damages, irrespective of the type of accident suffered, and, for elderly victims at least, irrespective of the degree of residual disability suffered as a result of the accident. Women suffering work accidents claimed less often than men suffering work accidents, although for road and other accidents the proportions were similar. In general, accident victims in full-or part-time employment were considerably more likely to claim damages than those not in employment. Contrary to our expectations, accident victims in lower status socio-economic groups were proportionately more likely to obtain damages than victims in professional or managerial groups. The seriousness of injury in both physical terms and the amount of time taken off work was not consistently associated with the likelihood that damages would be obtained, underlining the fact that the tort system is based on the cause of accidents rather than on the consequences.

Detailed analysis of what steps were involved in actually perceiving an accident as a problem for which legal advice should be sought indicated that women and the elderly were both less likely to consider the question of compensation, and having done so, were less likely than other groups actually to seek legal advice. For those accident victims who did succeed in obtaining damages it was clear that advice obtained before getting in touch with a solicitor was very important in providing or reinforcing the incentive to claim damages. More than two-thirds of those people in contact with a solicitor claimed that the idea of obtaining legal advice first came from another person. For victims who have accidents on the road or at work there are normally certain procedures for reporting the accident which have to be followed and during which advice about claiming may spontaneously be offered. For victims who have accidents elsewhere there are no such procedures and the people who disproportionately suffer these types of accidents—women, the elderly, children—are more isolated than those at work from networks of information and advice. Trade union activity in pressing claims for damages provides an important example of both the value of immediate advice and easy access to the legal system.

The reasons given for not proceeding with a claim by those people who had at some time considered the possibility indicate that lack of claims-consciousness, problems about providing evidence, and fear of the legal costs involved in making a claim represent important constraints . . .

Our data showed that it was not victims' attributions of fault which motivated them to make a damages claim . . . Fault was not always seen as appropriate grounds for compensation, nor was it necessarily seen as a precondition if a claim was to be made. In only half those cases where the victim took steps to initiate a claim for damages had he also attributed fault to the person against whom the claim would be made. Only about half of those who said their accident was someone else's fault said they had at any time thought that that person should compensate them. Moreover, the pattern of responses for different types of accidents suggested that even in those cases where attributions of fault did coincide with the initiation of a claim, the attribution of fault was a justification rather than a reason for the claim, and that, without the prospect of a possible damages award, fault might have been attributed differently, if at all.

The question of fault was certainly not unimportant to the victims. In particular, holding someone to blame was clearly seen as threatening to a relationship. However, the factors determining whether or not fault was attributed to someone else, and if so how, were extremely complex, and included many factors besides the causes and circumstances of the accident. Rather than the law reflecting the ordinary man's view of fault and liability, the victims' attributions of fault and liability reflected legal norms and the likelihood of a successful damages claim. The findings also confirmed that the attribution of fault in the context of a particular damages claim is very much a function of that context. It cannot be assumed that the type of attribution of fault generated by the tort system will be appropriate also for purposes of deterrence or accident prevention, where it may be far more effective to focus on quite different causal factors.

COMMENTARY

The survey is now rather out of date, but no more recent survey has collected data on the same range of issues, and it remains the best evidence we have of the reasons why some people claim for their injuries while others do not. The findings are broadly consistent with those of other empirical studies of the tort system in operation, but it must be noted that the numbers of injured persons who sue in tort for damages have increased very significantly in the interim. This factor has impacted on road traffic accidents claims in particular: the annual number of claims per year now exceeds the number of recorded injuries in such accidents. See further in the following extracts.

Another valuable—though also dated—source of information about the workings of the system is the Pearson Report (Royal Commission on Civil Liability and Compensation for Personal Injury, Chairman: Lord Pearson, *Report*, Cmnd 7054, 1978). Combining data from interviews with victims of accidental injury or work-related illness in the years up to 1973 with figures derived from analyses of court records, a survey carried out by the insurance industry, and other publicly available information, the *Pearson Commission* found that, of some three million people injured in the United Kingdom every year, only about 250,000 brought an action for damages, of whom only about 215,000 obtained tort compensation (*Pearson*, vol. 2, paras 50 and 59). This figure, which corresponds to a finding that tort damages are recovered by only about 6.5 per cent of those suffering personal injury, is even more striking than that obtained by the Oxford Survey, in whose study 12 per cent recovered damages; the difference is explicable on the basis that the latter considered only those injuries which prevented the victims from carrying out their normal activities for a period of two weeks or more.

As noted earlier, more recent studies indicate that the number of claims has risen substantially since the Pearson survey. In 1988, the annual number of claims was estimated by the Civil Justice Review to be 340,000 (*Report of the Review Body on Civil Justice*, Cm. 394, London: HMSO, 1988, para. 391). Only since 2000, however, has there been an accurate annual count of the number of tort personal injury claims. The relevant data are collected by the Compensation Recovery Unit (CRU), established in 1990 to administer the 'claw back' of social security benefits paid to those subsequently receiving tort compensation for the same injury. Initially small compensation claims (under £2,500) were excluded, but the claw-back regime now applies to personal injury claims of all sizes. Anyone receiving a claim—whether they accept liability or not—must report it to CRU, and in the overwhelming majority of cases this is done through the automated systems of liability insurers. We can therefore have a high degree of confidence in the reliability of the following reported figures.

Compensation Recovery Unit: Tort Personal Injury Claims Statistics

Number of cases registered to Compensation Recovery Unit

	Clinical Negligence	Employer	Motor	Other	Public	Not known	Total
2000/01	10,901	219,183	401,757	3,120	95,883	5,087	735,931
2001/02	9,779	170,554	400,445	1,953	100,989	4,595	688,315
2002/03	7,977	183,342	398,892	2,290	109,782	4,414	706,697
2003/04	7,121	291,210	374,761	2,069	91,453	3,629	770,243
2004/05	7,205	253,502	402,924	2,459	87,247	2,538	755,875
2005/06	9,321	118,692	460,097	3,232	81,615	1,465	674,422
2006/07	8,575	98,478	518,821	3,522	79,841	1,547	710,784
2007/08	8,876	87,198	551,905	3,449	79,472	1,850	732,750
2008/09	9,880	86,957	625,072	3,415	86,164	860	812,348
2009/10	10,308	78,744	674,997	2,806	91,025	3,445	861,325
2010/11	13,022	81,470	790,999	3,855	94,872	3,163	987,381
2011/12	13,517	87,350	828,489	4,435	104,863	2,496	1,041,150
2012/13	16,006	91,115	818,334	17,695	102,984	2,175	1,048,309
2013/14	18,499	105,291	772,843	14,467	103,578	2,123	1,016,801
2014/15	18,258	103,401	761,878	12,972	100,072	1,778	998,359
2015/16	17,895	86,495	770,791	11,388	92,709	2,046	981,324
2016/17	17,894	73,355	780,324	20,047	85,504	1,692	978,816
2017/18	17,400	69,230	650,019	19,172	96,067	1,727	853,615
2018/19	16,809	89,461	660,608	7,614	85,472	2,392	862,356
2019/20	15,845	79,027	653,052	7,086	72,587	1,655	829,252
2020/21	14,485	45,687	446,976	4,577	51,286	1,348	564,359

COMMENTARY

The last year's recorded figures show a significant fall in the number of claims that is surely attributable to the national lockdown in response to the COVID-19 pandemic. But comparison of the CRU data generally with the *Pearson Commission's* estimates from the 1970s shows a very striking increase in total claims numbers in recent decades: from a quarter of a million in 1973 to over a million from 2011 to 2014, albeit with a notable tailing back from that time on. Unfortunately there is no reliable data source which tracks the increase from year to year since the 1970s, and therefore no means of determining whether it proceeded by steady increments or in fits and starts as a result of particular causative factors. The figures have been relied upon by those who allege that recent decades have seen the emergence in the United Kingdom of a damaging 'compensation culture' (see Ch. 1.III.3), but it must be emphasised in response that a simple rise in claims numbers is insufficient to justify the frequent insinuation that significant percentages of claims are fraudulent, exaggerated or otherwise lacking in merit. The rise in claims numbers from the 1970s is equally consistent with there having been significant under-claiming at that time, with the subsequent increase being attributable to a greater propensity to take legal action by those who have genuine claims.

As the table shows, motor claims are now by far the biggest single category of personal injury claiming, having grown considerably since the CRU started reporting data in 2001. Almost all the overall increase in the number of personal injury claims is attributable to this phenomenon, which is said to have caused a substantial rise in motor insurance premiums (House of Commons Transport Committee, *The Cost of Motor Insurance*, Fourth Report of Session 2010–2011, HC 591, 2011, and various follow-up reports). Lewis and Morris ('Tort Law Culture in the United Kingdom: Image and Reality in Personal Injury Compensation' (2012) 3 JETL 230 at 260–2) suggest that three interrelated factors may be at play: the sophisticated systems introduced by claims management companies to discover the names and contact details of those involved in road accidents so they can be encouraged to claim; the routinisation and streamlining of claims-handling processes in this context; and the financial attractiveness of motor claims to 'no win no fee' providers of legal services. Morris explains in a subsequent article that, because motor claims are typically quick and easy to bring, they are particularly attractive to lawyers working on a conditional fee: 'they have a high rate of success, so that the risk of "no-fee" is very low, but their legal and factual simplicity means that they require only low investment and they are resolved quickly, thereby minimising problems with cash flow' (Morris, 'Tort and Neo-Liberalism', *Private Law in the 21st Century*, ch. 25, p. 511).

Conversely, the number of employers' liability claims has dropped quite substantially over the same period. Employment-related claims, in particular, have reduced very considerably in number since the time of the *Pearson Commission's* survey, when they constituted the largest category of claim (47 per cent of the total: *Pearson*, vol. II table 11). The reduction in numbers probably reflects changes in the nature of the UK economy and workforce, and improvements in workplace health and safety, but one more specific factor may also be highlighted: in the years up to 2004–05, the number of employers' liability claims was artificially inflated for a number of years by the Coal Health Compensation schemes that were established following successful High Court test cases in the late 1990s by former miners. The schemes processed a very large backlog of claims relating to work-related respiratory disease and 'vibration white finger', potentially dating back as far as 1954. In total, some 750,000 coal health claims were registered from 1999 to 2004 (the cut-off date for registration). See further Committee of Public Accounts, 'Coal Health Compensation Schemes', HC (2007–08) 350.

For other categories of claim, the CRU statistics provide no clear evidence of any trend in either direction. After motor claims, the second most numerous category is now public liability, covering such things as occupiers' liability and product liability: the word 'public' reflects insurance industry terminology, and does not indicate that the defendant is a public body, though 'tripping and slipping' and many other claims against local authorities do fall in this category. The number of clinical negligence claims is still relatively low compared with other categories, though it is very much higher than the *Pearson Commission's* estimate of 500 claims per year in the early 1970s, and these claims undoubtedly have an importance in public debates that outstrips their numerical representation.

Propensity to sue

Why some injured people sue, and others do not, may be explained by a number of factors. The *Pearson Commission* found that the most common reasons given by injured persons for not bringing a claim were that they did not consider the injury serious enough, that they did not know that they could claim or how to do so, that they considered it 'just an accident' and that they thought suing would be too much trouble or too upsetting, or 'did not want to make a fuss' (*Pearson*, vol. 2, table 84).

The process by which an injury is 'transformed' into an action for damages is described in a famous sociological analysis by Felstiner, Abel and Sarat, 'The Emergence and Transformation of Disputes: Naming, Blaming and Claiming' (1981) 15 L & Soc Rev 631. They identify the following three stages in the emergence of legal disputes (pp. 635–6):

> [The] first transformation—saying to oneself that a particular experience has been injurious—we call naming . . . For instance, asbestosis only became an acknowledged 'disease' and the basis of a claim for compensation when shipyard workers stopped taking for granted that they would have trouble breathing after ten years of installing insulation and came to view their condition as a problem. The next step is the transformation of a perceived injurious experience into a grievance. This occurs when a person attributes an injury to the fault of another individual or social entity . . . We call the transformation from perceived injurious experience to grievance blaming: our diseased shipyard worker makes this transformation when he holds his employer or the manufacturer of asbestos insulation responsible for his asbestosis. The third transformation occurs when someone with a grievance voices it to the person or entity believed to be responsible and asks for some remedy. We call this communication claiming. A claim is transformed into a dispute when it is rejected in whole or in part.

In an important contribution to the ongoing debate about compensation culture Annette Morris has applied this transformational account to an analysis of the factors that are alleged to have increased the general propensity to sue for personal injury ('Spiralling or Stabilising? The "Compensation Culture" and our Propensity to Claim Damages for Personal Injury' (2007) 70 MLR 349). 'Levels of claiming depend', she says (p. 373), 'on the prevalence of external factors and conditions which affect our ability and willingness to transform injuries into claims. It also depends on legal consciousness shaping perceptions of the ability and informing the willingness to claim.' Her particular focus is the influence of 'no win no fee' advertising by solicitors and claims management companies, which may be said to have increased our *ability* to name, blame and claim, because previously many injured people did not know they had a potential claim or how to pursue it, and our *willingness* to do so, especially by raising our awareness of the availability of compensation. Advertising also 'seeks to legitimise and normalise claiming by portraying the claims process as routine and administrative' (p. 374), and to suppress concerns about claiming by portraying the process as consumer-friendly, stress-free and costless. However, Morris also points out that, although people may now be more aware of their rights than in the past, the influence of the adverts may also be offset by the 'dampening' effect of the compensation culture debate itself (p. 376). Negative publicity about tort claims may have had the paradoxical outcome of dissuading the genuinely injured from bringing well-founded actions at the same time as encouraging a small 'have a go' minority to exaggerate or fabricate claims. See also Morris, 'Tort and Neo-Liberalism', pp. 504–13.

This analysis may usefully be compared with the final paragraph of the extract from the Oxford survey, cited earlier, reporting empirical evidence that it was rarely the defendant's fault, rather than the likelihood of winning damages, that motivated victims to make a claim.

Claims numbers, and what types of injury are claimed for, may also be influenced by the behaviour of the institutional actors involved in the claims process, as highlighted in the following extract.

R. Lewis, 'Structural Factors Affecting the Number and Cost of Personal Injury Claims in the Tort System', in E. Quill and R. J. Friel, *Damages and Compensation Culture: Comparative Perspectives* (Oxford: Hart, 2016)

Liability Insurers

... [T]he average payment of damages is less than £5,000. As a result, it is unusual for insurers to contest liability ... Because insurers make some payment in this great majority of cases, in effect, they encourage claims to be made.

Insurers also encourage claims by giving claimants ready access to a lawyer: they provide legal expenses insurance as an extra benefit in the motor and home policies they sell. Not only do insurers profit from this by including an additional cost in the premiums charged, but they also used to receive a referral fee from solicitors for each personal injury case they forwarded to their associated law firm. Referrals earned insurers about £700 per case and constituted a substantial income ... A related practice of insurers was to collect information about all potential claimants in an accident and again sell those details to law firms. The result was the development of an ultimately flawed business practice: profit was sought from these individual cases but in doing so a more febrile claims atmosphere resulted ...

[O]ne tactic still used today is 'third-party capture'. This is where the insurer makes a direct approach to any injured party who is not their own insured. They may do so either before or after they have contacted a solicitor. Insurers seek a quick settlement of the potential claim before any legal costs can be incurred. This has resulted in many people with only very minor injury from the accident in which they were involved (or often no injury at all) being offered sums to settle cases which they had no previous intention of bringing! ...

A similar insurer tactic employed to reduce legal costs which has also had the unintended effect of encouraging claims has been for insurers to make 'pre-med offers'. These are offers made to the claimants' solicitors very early in the proceedings, often immediately on receiving notice of a claim, and before any medical report has been obtained. They are pitched at a low level, usually less than £1,500, and are aimed at removing the nuisance value of a small claim together with its potentially disproportionate legal and disbursement costs. For example, until recently a quick offer could save an insurer paying up to £700 (now reduced to a maximum of £180) for the cost of a medical report even though these are often standard form and can be produced by a mere GP. Commonly made in whiplash cases, these pre-med offers have been heavily criticised on the one hand as attempts to buy off claims for derisory amounts and, on the other hand, as encouraging claims where injury is non-existent and thus feeding the compensation culture.

Claims Management Companies

Claims management companies (CMCs) first emerged about twenty years ago. They made money by trawling for accident victims and seeking quick settlements from which they extracted high fees from claimants. Alternatively, they passed on their clients to solicitors and received a referral fee in return. Today they also offer services such as vehicle repair and credit hire, and some can arrange accident reports and evidence from medical experts. To recruit clients, CMCs have used a variety of tactics from mass media advertising to direct approaches to individuals in the street. Over three-quarters of the population have reported being contacted about making a claim.

The growth of CMCs was fuelled especially by the removal of legal aid in 2000 which led to the more extensive use of conditional fee agreements. Under these agreements claimant lawyers could secure an increase in their fees in each case that they won . . . This potential for increased profit added to the incentives to obtain referrals. One problem solicitors faced was that conduct rules prevented them from paying CMCs for these claims. However, these rules were flouted on such a regular basis that the ban on referral payments was eventually lifted in 2004 . . .

The number of CMCs . . . [reached] a peak in late 2011 when there were 2,553 companies operating in the personal injury claims sector. However, following increased regulation and, in particular, the banning of referral fees in 2013 they have been halved in number . . .

Claimant Personal Injury Law Firms

Initially solicitors' firms were very reluctant to become involved with what was considered the distasteful business of claims gathering. By the late 1990s, however, following the relaxation of the rules on advertising, specialist personal injury firms were actively seeking clients. They still avoided the brash techniques of CMCs but many were prepared to pay referral fees to these companies; they were content to 'turn a blind eye' in order to secure a regular flow of work. Eventually more law firms recognised that the work being done by CMCs could be replicated by them. A few firms even adopted certain tactics which matched some of the excesses of the CMCs. For example, some offered inducements to sue including free iPads, shopping vouchers or cash promises of up to £2,000. CMCs were banned from making such gifts but solicitors continued to be able to do so until 2015. Although only a minority offered such inducements, the aggressive claims gathering of the profession has now resulted in solicitors supplanting many CMCs.

Further changes have occurred following the relaxation of the rules relating to the ability of law firms to form business relationships with other enterprises. Since 2011 non-lawyers have been able to own and manage legal practices as part of an 'alternative business structure' (ABS) which can involve a multidisciplinary partnership . . . The ABS is a particularly attractive vehicle for conducting personal injury work. The wider organisation can include within it, for example, a medical reporting agency that is able to give evidence on claims, or a financial department that gives advice on how a damages award should be invested. For present purposes, however, the significant advantage of an ABS is that it enables personal injury firms to avoid the difficulties caused by the prohibition of referral fees by making such payments 'in house'. As a result we have seen leading personal injury firms merge with CMCs or insurance companies . . .

[There has also been] a drive for efficiency in order to deal with the mass of small claims which dominate the system. Largely because of funding constraints, much of the work involving smaller run-of-the-mill claims in these firms is now being carried out by unqualified or paralegal personnel. They are working in what has been identified in the US as 'settlement mills' where the assembly line resolution of claims 'represents quite a departure from the intimate, individualized, and fact-intensive process thought to underlie the traditional process of tort' [Engstrom (2011) 86 NYU L Rev 805 at 810]. The legal process has been de-skilled and depersonalised in these factories which have direct comparators in the UK.

COMMENTARY

The extract highlights some of the changes in the market for legal services that have resulted from the deregulation of recent years. A major factor has been the introduction of conditional fee agreements (CFAs: see further I.3) whereby lawyers were able to take on claims on a 'no win, no fee' basis, as part of a general transfer of responsibility for the funding of PI claims from the public purse to the market. The effects have been profound. As Morris observes, 'government policy on the liberalisation of legal services and the commercialisation of funding, combined with the relaxation of rules on advertising, encouraged the commodification of claims, the growth of a claims market and a corresponding increase in claims' ('Tort and Neo-Liberalism', *op. cit.*, p. 523).

The new claims environment was reflected in changes in the organisation and practices of claimant law firms. A recent report found that, out of some 10,300 law firms in the United Kingdom, 833 are specialist PI firms (defined as PI accounting for more than 50 per cent of turnover) and another around 2,000 firms also engage in PI work to some extent (ICF, *An Assessment of the Market for Personal Injury: A Final Report for the Solicitors Regulation Authority*, October 2016, para. 7.1.2). The report explained further (*ibid*):

> The structure of the PI industry is changing and there is a growing gap between the smaller practices and larger firms. In terms of the industry structure, small firms still dominate in numerical terms (some 91 per cent are sole practitioners or firms with between 2-4 partners), but there has been a growth in the number of larger firms together with a noticeable market consolidation (solicitor firms coming together); Alternative Business Structures are now a reality. These were originally solicitor firms changing their business structures but increasingly there have been new entrants from firms that are new to the market (including Co-Op, BT, Saga and Tesco Law).
>
> Research by the Legal Services Board [*Evaluation: Changes in competition in different legal markets*, 2013, fig. 4] estimated that a quarter of the PI market in terms of value could be accounted for by ten firms, and the percentage has probably grown subsequently.

The internal organisation of law firms also changed to fit a business model based on the rapid turnaround of large numbers of low-value claims. In a process of de-skilling and de-personalisation, sizeable cohorts of non-professionally-qualified staff are now taken on to work in 'claims factories'—or 'settlement mills' as they have been dubbed in the United States (see Engstrom, 'Sunlight and Settlement Mills' (2011) 86 NYU L Rev 805). They work under supervision and according to prescribed procedures, often guided by computerised case-management systems: 'Aided by developments in information technology, lawyers have increasingly adopted standardised and routinised procedures over the years to handle low-value claims... [including] case management systems involving scripting and standardised letters and documents' (Morris, 'Tort and Neo-Liberalism', *op. cit.*, pp. 519, 520).

Another of the most striking effects of the deregulation of the claims market was the rise of new entities known as claims management companies (CMCs) that quickly gained a reputation for their aggressive pursuit of potential claimants, typified by the use of pressure sales techniques. Their incentive was the referral fee they would get for passing a claim on to a law firm. There thus developed a market in claims, which were effectively treated as commodities to be bought and sold. This operated not just at the level of individual claims, through the referral fee system, but also at a macro level as large firms acquired the entire PI claims business of smaller rivals. The use of referral fees was banned by ss. 56–60 of the Legal Aid, Sentencing and Punishment of Offenders Act 2012 (LASPO), but the extract explains how the claims sector has found ways of getting around the ban by exploiting the possibilities of the new organisational form known as an 'alternative business structure' (ABS), first allowed under the Legal Services Act 2007, Part V.

The ways in which liability insurers have responded to these changes have also had a profound effect on the claims market. Note in particular what Lewis says in the extract about the controversial practices of 'third-party capture' and 'pre-med offers' (the latter now abolished by statute: see later in this section).

Whiplash and the Issue of Fraudulent Claims

The changes described in the preceding paragraphs have raised concerns about the development of a 'compensation culture' in which fraudulent, exaggerated and undeserving claims are commonplace (see further Ch. 1.III.3). One has to be careful about the use of such language, however, as it is not entirely clear what criteria should be used to assess whether a claim is 'deserving', nor that 'undeserving' claimants should be bracketed together with those engaging in fraud. Further, the coupling of fraud with exaggeration blurs the line between what is criminal and what may only be an optimistic estimate of the strength of a claim.

In recent years, much of the public concern has been directed at 'whiplash claims'. A narrative emerged in which whiplash was identified as a category that is ripe for exploitation by those willing to engage in fraud and exaggeration, and the deregulated litigation environment facilitated that process by inducing institutional actors in the civil justice system to become complicit with dishonest claimants. Lawyers were provided with financial incentives through the CFA regime to take on routine whiplash claims despite their low value—and to do so without looking too closely at the veracity of their clients and the reality of the injury alleged or its effects. Doctors compliantly certified whiplash injuries out of sympathy for their own patients or, when acting as independent experts, to ensure their continued engagement in that role. And insurers were willing to settle claims without adequate evidence of the injuries alleged or their effects, or even before any medical evidence had been submitted at all, because they saw economic advantage in closing their files as quickly as possible.

According to Morris and Oliphant ('England and Wales', in E. Karner and B. C. Steininger (eds), *European Tort Law 2018* (Berlin: de Gruyter, 2019), no. 8):

Four inter-related factors fuelled these concerns. First, whiplash is a soft tissue injury and so does not show up on an X-ray or MRI scan. Instead, diagnosis usually depends on the self-reporting of symptoms leaving much room for subjectivity or, some would say, abuse. Second, whiplash claims are financially attractive to the claims market because they are quick, easy and cheap to resolve and so it became extremely pro-active in seeking them out, some would say, regardless of quality . . . Third, with the claims market making it so easy to claim, it is feared that people have been tempted into 'having a go' in the hope of a quick pay-out. Finally, Insurers have frequently settled rather than investigated these lower-value claims on commercial grounds – often without consulting the claimant's medical records.

A series of reforms ensued. In 2015, a system of independent medical panels, backed up by an accreditation scheme, was introduced with a view to establishing a more robust system of medical reporting and scrutiny for whiplash claims. Claims may now only proceed with an approved medical report from an accredited expert, for which a fixed fee of £180 is prescribed (CPR r. 45.19(2A)). Separately, a new internet platform, www.askCUE.co.uk, was created to allow claimant law firms to check records held on a database of reported incidents of personal injury before submitting a claim. This 'know your client' check must be done before the claim is notified to the defendant, who is able to access the search results to check for patterns of suspicious claiming.

A further attempt to counter fraudulent and exaggerated claims was made with the introduction, also in 2015, of a statutory requirement that a court must dismiss any personal injury claim in which it finds that the claimant was fundamentally dishonest, unless it is satisfied that the claimant would suffer substantial injustice if the claim were dismissed. Section 57 of the Criminal Justice and Courts Act 2015 now provides:

Section 57. Personal injury claims: cases of fundamental dishonesty

(1) This section applies where, in proceedings on a claim for damages in respect of personal injury ('the primary claim')—
    (a) the court finds that the claimant is entitled to damages in respect of the claim, but
    (b) on an application by the defendant for the dismissal of the claim under this section, the court is satisfied on the balance of probabilities that the claimant has been fundamentally dishonest in relation to the primary claim or a related claim.
(2) The court must dismiss the primary claim, unless it is satisfied that the claimant would suffer substantial injustice if the claim were dismissed.
(3) The duty under subsection (2) includes the dismissal of any element of the primary claim in respect of which the claimant has not been dishonest.
(4) The court's order dismissing the claim must record the amount of damages that the court would have awarded to the claimant in respect of the primary claim but for the dismissal of the claim.
(5) When assessing costs in the proceedings, a court which dismisses a claim under this section must deduct the amount recorded in accordance with subsection (4) from the amount which it would otherwise order the claimant to pay in respect of costs incurred by the defendant.

For an application of this provision, see *Sinfield v London Organising Committee of the Olympic and Paralympic Games* [2018] PIQR P8, where the claimant, having broken his arm while serving as a volunteer at the 2012 London Olympic and Paralympic Games, claimed some £14,000 for gardening expenses without revealing that his gardener had worked the same hours for him before his accident. Applying s. 57, the High Court dismissed his claim in its entirety. The claim for special damages was for over £33,000 but the mere fact that it included genuine damages did not trigger the 'substantial injustice' exception in s. 57(2) (at [89], per Julian Knowles J).

Further Reform

These initiatives did not sate the government's appetite for reform. In late 2015 it announced its intention, in light of continuing concern at the number and cost of whiplash claims, to raise the small claims limit from £1,000 to £5,000 for the non-pecuniary loss component of personal injury claims in general and to remove the right to claim non-pecuniary damages for minor whiplash injuries. Following consultation, it stepped back slightly from this initial proposal, responding to concern that, as legal costs are not recoverable from the losing party in the small claims track, the higher limit would increase the numbers of litigants in person who might encounter difficulties in running their own claim without legal representation, which could cause delays, require increased judicial resource and prevent access to justice, as well as creating inequality of arms insofar as insurers would still have legal representation (Ministry of Justice, *Part 1 of the Government Response to: Reforming the Soft Tissue Injury ('whiplash') Claims Process: A Consultation on Arrangements Concerning Personal Injury Claims in England and Wales*, Cm 9422, February 2017, para. 88). In the ensuing reform, effective from 31 May 2021, the £5,000 limit was applied only to road traffic accident (RTA) claims, amongst which whiplash claims predominate, with exceptions for specific vulnerable claimants for whom the limit remains at £1,000 (e.g. children, pedestrians, horse riders and bicycle or motor cycle users or passengers. For non-RTA claims the limit is raised only to £1,500. See CPR, r. 26.6(1)ff, Practice Direction 27B and Pre-Action Protocol for Personal Injury Claims below the Small Claims Limit in Road Traffic Accidents ('The RTA Small Claims Protocol')).

The government also resolved not to remove altogether the right to claim general damages for minor whiplash injuries, but only to introduce a new statutory tariff setting the compensation for minor pain and suffering and loss of amenity (Ministry of Justice, *op. cit.*, paras 63 and 110–12). This was effected by the Civil Liability Act 2018 and the Whiplash Injury Regulations 2021, considered further in Chapter 15.IV(1)(a), providing for an ascending scale of fixed sum payments from £240 to £4,215, banded by reference to duration.

A further aspect of the reform to note is the new prohibition on insurance companies and other regulated persons settling a whiplash claim without first seeing appropriate evidence of whiplash injury—for example, in the medical report the claimant is required to obtain (Civil Liability Act 2018, s. 6). The aim was to stop insurers making 'pre-med offers'. Breach of the prohibition is not a criminal offence, nor does it make the settlement agreement void or unenforceable, but it may trigger regulatory action against the regulated person (ss. 7–8).

For criticism of the way in which the public debate about whiplash claims has been conducted, and in particular that the focus on fraudulent and exaggerated claims has diverted attention from those who have genuine claims, and how they may be affected by the various reforms, see Oliphant, '"The Whiplash Capital of the World": Genealogy of a Compensation Myth', *Damages and Compensation Culture*, ch. 1.

2. The Personal Injury Claims Process

A. Morris, 'Deconstructing Policy on Costs and the Compensation Culture', in E. Quill and R. J. Friel, *Damages and Compensation Culture: Comparative Perspectives* (Oxford: Hart, 2016)

The turn of the millennium saw significant changes in the personal injury claims process. In April 1999, a new civil justice system was introduced with the implementation of the Woolf reforms. Lord Woolf had found that litigation was too often seen as a 'battlefield' where no rules applied and where questions of expense and delay had only low priority. Whilst the majority of claims settled, they did so often after the issue of proceedings, if not at the door of the court, and after much expense had been incurred. Parties controlled the conduct and pace of litigation and pursued their claims and defences in isolation, using partisan experts who only added to the problem. Woolf's reforms, implemented through the Civil Procedure Rules 1998 (CPR) were designed to reduce cost, delay and complexity through a reduction of adversarialism and a commitment to the policy of proportionality. In other words, the achievement of the right result was to be balanced against the expenditure of time and money needed to achieve that result.

The reforms sought to achieve proportionality in three main ways. First, the rules encourage parties to settle their claims without the need to issue proceedings, either through negotiation or alternative dispute resolution. Parties follow pre-action protocols which encourage pre-action contact, the early exchange of information and pre-action investigation by both sides. Second, if claims cannot be settled, then they proceed to litigation but are subject to rationed procedures and judicial case management. Claims are allocated to one of three tracks which give parties access to procedure proportionate to the value and complexity of the claim:

- The small claims track . . . provides a quick and cheap process involving a short, informal hearing where the rules of evidence are relaxed. There is generally no provision for the recovery of costs on the small claims track as it is expected that parties can represent themselves.
- Claims of up to £25,000 are generally allocated to the fast track. Such claims are subject to judicial case management but generally involve standardised directions. Parties are expected to use single joint experts and are subject to fixed timetables. Trials, for example, are expected to take place within 30 weeks of allocation.
- Claims above £25,000 and/or claims involving complex or important issues are allocated to the multi-track. Such claims are allowed access to more procedure but are still subject to judicial management of the timetable for the case, provisions for disclosure and the use of factual and expert evidence.

Finally, successful parties are only able to recover proportionate costs from their opponent under the loser pays principle. This means that unless lawyers charge clients directly, limits are placed on the amount of work that can be undertaken to progress a claim.

Shortly after the introduction of the Woolf reforms, the operation of conditional fee (or so-called 'no win no fee') agreements (CFAs) was reformed. In April 2000, the then Labour government abolished legal aid for the majority of personal injury claims on the assumption that they could be funded through the CFA market instead. However, it introduced the concept of recoverability as a corollary which operated in conjunction with the loser pays principle. Unsuccessful claimants paid their own lawyer 'no fee' and used an after-the-event (ATE) insurance policy to pay the other side's legal costs whilst successful claimants could recover the success fee payable under the CFA and the cost of the ATE policy in addition to their normal legal costs. In allowing claimants to obtain legal assistance regardless of their financial capacity, recoverability was 'an interesting attempt to squeeze public provision into a private model approach' [Moorhead (2002) 55 NILQ 153 at 154]. It effectively transferred the costs of claiming from claimants and/or the state to the market or rather, as the majority of personal injury claims are successful, to insurers. Lawyers were permitted to charge success fees of up to 100 per cent of the normal legal costs though recoverability was subject to reasonableness. The idea was that CFAs would work on a swings and roundabout basis. Success fees recovered in successful cases would absorb the cost of unsuccessful cases and also help fund other claims until their conclusion. CFAs altered both the economics and dynamics of the claims market. Lawyers reported that the way to make money out of CFAs was to have 'a regular throughput of small, easy cases' [T. Goriely, R. Moorhead and P. Abrams, *More Civil Justice? The Impact of the Woolf Reforms on Pre-Action Behaviour* (London: Law Society and Civil Justice Council, 2002)]. This encouraged claims advertising and aided the proliferation of claims management companies which farmed claims through mass advertising and direct marketing and then sold them on to lawyers for a referral fee.

Despite the Woolf reforms, concerns about the cost of resolving claims continued and indeed escalated during the 2000s . . . Reform was seen to be necessary. In 2008, and with the support of the Ministry of Justice, the Master of the Rolls asked Lord Justice Jackson to undertake a review of civil litigation costs. Jackson published an extensive final report in December 2009 and the majority of his recommendations were accepted . . . The reforms were introduced in April 2013 through the Legal Aid, Sentencing and Punishment of Offenders Act 2012 (LASPO) and amendments to the CPR. They were wide-ranging and pursued the policy of proportionality with renewed rigour. The controversial practice of paying for the referral of claims was abolished, as was the concept of recoverability associated with CFAs. Recoverability was seen as a major driver of 'excessive' costs which the claimant, with no financial stake in the claim, had no interest in controlling. The new regime now operates in conjunction with 'qualified one-way costs shifting'. Unsuccessful claimants do not have to pay the defendants' legal costs except in exceptional circumstances. This is intended to remove the need for ATE insurance in the majority of claims. Those wanting ATE insurance must now pay for it themselves. Whilst successful claimants can still recover their legal costs from insurers, they can no longer recover the success fee. This must instead be met directly by claimants, usually from their damages. To ameliorate the effects of this reform for claimants, damages for pain, suffering and loss of amenity have been increased by 10 per cent [*Simmons v Castle* [2013] 1 WLR 1239]. Also, whilst lawyers are still permitted to charge success fees of up to 100 per cent, they are not permitted to recover success fees in excess of 25 per cent of claimants' damages, excluding damages for future care and loss. For lawyers, however, the reforms have led to a substantial reduction in their returns on CFA work. . . .

Significant restrictions have also been placed on the recovery of legal costs. Fast-track claims, which had previously involved some fixed costs, are now subject to a full fixed cost regime. In addition, the rule governing the recovery of costs has been reformulated. Whilst the Woolf reforms required costs to be assessed with reference to proportionality, the decision in *Lownds v Home Office* [[2002] 1 WLR 2450] meant that successful parties could recover costs disproportionate to the damages if they were deemed to be necessary and reasonable. Jackson felt this conflicted with the underlying purpose of the CPR and proposed that, having assessed each item of cost in relation to reasonableness, judges should consider whether the global figure is proportionate and reduce appropriately if not. The result is that successful parties may not be able to recover the actual costs they have incurred in preparing and advancing their claim even if those costs have been reasonably or necessarily incurred.

Alongside the implementation of the Jackson reforms, the Coalition [in government 2010–15] extended the streamlined procedure that had been introduced for road traffic accident (RTA) claims between £1,000 and £10,000 in April 2010. The scheme now applies to RTA, employers' liability (EL) and public liability (PL) claims between £1,000 and £25,000—the majority of all claims. The streamlined procedure, which utilises an online portal, has three stages. The first stage requires early notification of claims with only basic information. Defendants are then given short time frames on which to respond on liability (15 days in RTA claims, 30 in EL claims and 40 in PL claims). If liability is admitted, claims proceed to the second stage where the claimant gathers supporting evidence for the claim and completes a settlement pack with an offer of damages. Defendants then have 15 days in which to accept or reject the offer and, where relevant, to make a counter offer. If the parties cannot settle within 20 days, the claim proceeds to the third stage and is referred to the court for a decision on quantum. The court can assess damages on the papers though the parties may request, or the court may order, a court hearing. Pre-action protocols introduced as part of the Woolf reforms were seen to aid settlement but to lead to the frontloading of costs as both parties investigated liability and quantum before engaging in negotiations. The new process provides a quick and cheap process for claims to be resolved where liability is not in dispute. If the insurer denies liability, admits liability but alleges contributory negligence or does not respond within specified time limits, the claim falls out of the streamlined and into the normal process. Each stage is subject to fixed costs and the fixed costs that were already in place for RTA claims have been significantly reduced.

Unsurprisingly, the reforms proved extremely controversial. Critics have argued that it is wrong in principle that damages, awarded to provide full compensation following wrongdoing, should be used to pay legal costs. In addition, significant concerns have been raised in relation to access. In combination, the abolition of recoverability, the extension of fixed fees and the tighter restrictions placed on the recovery of legal costs in successful claims have significantly reduced the profitability of personal injury work. The concern is that this will tighten the squeeze on the swings and roundabouts principle and make it more difficult for lawyers to take new cases on a CFA basis.

Concerns have also been raised in relation to under-settlement. Claimant lawyers have argued that streamlined procedures are unsuitable for more complex and higher value claims involving issues of law. . . . [E]ven outside the streamlined procedure, the extension of fixed costs and restrictions on the ability to cover actual costs incurred in pursuing a claim, will constrain lawyers in the amount of work they can undertake on a claim and still make a profit. This will, in turn, constrain their ability to establish liability on behalf of their injured clients and ensure that they recover the compensation to which they are legally entitled. It will also further impede their ability to have their case heard in court. As insurers will not be operating under the same financial constraints, there are concerns about inequality of bargaining power. In sum, it is argued that the reforms will undermine the claims process by reducing both access and justice. Rather than re-balancing the system, it is feared the reforms will skew it in favour of defendants and their insurers.

COMMENTARY

The excessive costs of litigation have been a regular target of critics of the legal system. According to the *Pearson Commission* (*Pearson*, vol. I, para. 83):

[T]he operating costs of the tort system amount to about 85 per cent of the value of tort compensation payments, or about 45 per cent of the combined total of compensation and operating costs. Of these operating costs, about 40 per cent is accounted for by the costs of insurers in handling claims and on general administration. The remaining elements are the commissions paid by insurers to brokers and agents, claimants' legal fees, and profit. Each represents about a fifth. On small claims, the expenses can be greater than the damages paid.

More recent evidence suggests that the cost overhead of processing tort claims remains at broadly the same level. Sources considered by Lewis, Morris and Oliphant ('Tort Personal Injury Claims Statistics: Is There a Compensation Culture in the United Kingdom?', *op. cit.*, p. 174) suggest that legal costs alone (excluding insurers' costs) amount to approximately 30 per cent of the total costs of a tort claim, a significant proportion even if it is not perhaps sufficient to warrant Lord Woolf's conclusion, in his landmark report on civil justice, that 'the present system provides higher benefits to lawyers than to their clients' (*Access to Justice: Final Report*, s. II, ch. 1, para. 11). Still, costs of this magnitude suggest that litigants get poor value for money from the legal system and risk putting the courts beyond the reach of ordinary individuals. (See also *Jackson Report*, ch. 2.)

Concern about costs was a very significant reason for the adoption in 1998 of a new set of Civil Procedure Rules (CPR), which now regulate every stage of the claims process. The reform followed recommendations in Lord Woolf's report (*Access to Justice: Final Report*, 1996), which highlighted a number of defects in the civil justice system of the day (*ibid.*, s. I, para. 2):

[O]ur present system . . . is too expensive in that the costs often exceed the value of the claim; too slow in bringing cases to a conclusion and too unequal: there is a lack of equality between the powerful, wealthy litigant and the under-resourced litigant. It is too uncertain: the difficulty of forecasting what litigation will cost and how long it will last induces the fear of the unknown; and it is incomprehensible to many litigants. Above all it is too fragmented in the way it is organised since there is no one with clear overall responsibility for the administration of civil justice; and too adversarial as cases are run by the parties, not by the courts and the rules of court, all too often, are ignored by the parties and not enforced by the court.

Woolf's response was to urge a move away from the traditional approach to civil litigation, which applied the policy that 'time and money are no object'. In his view, it was important to balance the achievement of the right result against the expenditure of time and money needed to achieve that result, and the means of the parties. In some cases, a 'no-frills' approach would be more appropriate. As Morris highlights, 'proportionality' was thus a key element of the reforms introduced, as manifested by the 'rationing' of procedure according to the value of the claim. This was effected mostly clearly through the three-track system that Morris describes.

It was in the creation of the new 'fast track' (CPR r. 28) that Woolf's ambition to move away from the 'time and money are no object' approach of the past is most obvious. Its key features are:

(i) *Limited procedures*, e.g. in relation to disclosure and inspection of documents, governed where appropriate by standard directions.

(ii) *Fixed timetables*. A period of no more than thirty weeks will usually be stipulated between allocation of the claim to the fast track and trial, with interim deadlines for the exchange of witness statements, expert reports, etc.

(iii) *Limited trials*. The trial should normally be concluded on one day, and the judge will specify the time allowed for cross-examination of witnesses (on the basis of written witness statements) and legal submissions by each side.

(iv) *Fixed costs*. The legal costs recoverable from a losing opponent should be fixed at sums specified in advance, and not on the basis of the hourly rate for the work done. See further later in this commentary.

In the years after the Woolf reforms, it became apparent that—though successful on a number of levels—they were not achieving their primary aim of reducing cost (see Goriely, Moorhead and Abrams, *op. cit.*; J. Peysner and M. Seneviratne, *The Management of Civil Cases: The Courts and the Post-Woolf Landscape* (DCA, 2005); J. Sorabji, *English Civil Justice after the Woolf and Jackson Reforms: A Critical Analysis* (Cambridge: CUP, 2014)). There was especial concern that the Woolf-inspired system was unable to constrain the costs inflation that was produced by changes in the way that personal injury claims were funded.

The Funding of Personal Injury Claims

Traditionally, public financing has played a very significant role in the funding of civil litigation in the form of legal aid. However, over several decades legal aid was cut back very substantially in an effort to control public expenditure, and now it is practically irrelevant in tort claims. At the same time, government attempted to shift the burden of providing the necessary finance from the public to the private sector, especially by the introduction and promotion of conditional fee agreements (CFAs). Under these arrangements, it is solicitors who provide the necessary up-front funding for litigation and who bear the risk of loss, as they take on cases on the basis that their client pays no fee if the litigation is unsuccessful. In exchange, they are entitled to a 'success fee' in the event their client wins (as explained in Lord Chancellor's Department, *Access to Justice with Conditional Fees*, Consultation Paper (4 March 1998) para. 2.1):

Conditional fee agreements, also known as no-win-no-fee agreements, allow a lawyer to agree to take a case on the understanding that if the case is lost, he will not charge his client for the work he has done. If, however, the case is won, the lawyer is entitled to charge a success fee calculated as a percentage of his normal costs, to recompense him for the risk he has run of not being paid. Clients sometimes have to pay for the expenses, known as disbursements (medical or other expert reports, court fees or enquiry agent's fees) that the lawyer has had to pay, although in some cases the lawyer may agree to fund these costs as well as part of the agreement. Conditional fees allow lawyers and clients to share the risk of litigation. The success fee is set according to the risk the lawyer is taking. The higher the chance of winning, the lower the success fee should be set, and vice versa. . . .

CFAs were first introduced by statutory instrument in 1995. In 1998, the then Labour government announced that it planned to abolish legal aid for personal injury litigation almost completely and to place near exclusive reliance on CFAs as the means of ensuring access to justice. This was effected by the Access to Justice Act 1999, which ended legal aid for most cases of personal injury (other than clinical negligence), at the same time as increasing very considerably the number of cases in which CFAs are permitted (s. 27). An explicit aim was to limit the call on legal aid funds by providing an alternative means of access to justice for which the state did not have to pay. Crucially, the Act promoted the CFA system by providing that, if the claim was successful, the legal costs recoverable from the defendant would include both the solicitor's success fee and the premium for the 'after-the-event' (ATE) insurance that claimants commonly took out to eliminate the risk of being ordered to pay the defendant's costs if the claim should fail.

Following this reform, CFAs came to be employed in the overwhelming majority of personal injury claims other than for clinical negligence, including 93 per cent of claims referred to solicitors by claims management companies (CMCs), 99 per cent of trade union cases, 91 per cent of claims covered by legal expenses insurance and 86 per cent of the 'other' caseload (P. Fenn et al., *The Funding of Personal Injury Litigation: Comparisons Over Time and Across Jurisdictions*, DCA Research Series 2/06 (2006), para. 5.1). In the early years of the new century, funding of clinical negligence claims was split in roughly equal shares between CFAs, legal aid and private hourly fee (*ibid.*, para. 5.2, but note that most legal aid funding for clinical negligence has now been removed: see later).

Despite or perhaps because of their popularity, CFAs have proved very controversial. Shortly after their introduction, liability insurers began a series of legal challenges to costs orders against them, alleging that success fees agreed by claimants and their solicitors were unreasonable (see, e.g., *Callery v Gray* [2002] 1 WLR 2000, where a majority of the House of Lords affirmed the Court of Appeal's reduction of the success fee from 60 per cent to 20 per cent). This 'costs war', as it was styled, was temporarily brought to an end by the Civil Justice Council's negotiation of agreements between the representatives of the main insurance and solicitors' organisations and the Bar. The agreements covered the success fees to be charged in employers' liability and road traffic accident claims by both solicitors and barristers (e.g. a standard 25 per cent of solicitors' costs for employers' liability accident claims settled without trial (12.5 per cent in road traffic accident claims) rising to 100 per cent if there was a trial).

Hostilities were re-opened with the publication of the *Jackson Report* in December 2009. The Report stated that 'the CFA regime has emerged as one of the major drivers of excessive costs' in the civil justice system (para. 4.3.26), and highlighted what Jackson conceived as its major flaws:

10.4.12 The first flaw in the recoverability regime is that it is unfocused. There is no eligibility test for entering into a CFA, provided that a willing solicitor can be found.

10.4.13 The second flaw is that the party with a CFA generally has no interest in the level of costs being incurred in his or her name. Whether the case is won or lost, the client will usually pay nothing. If the case is lost, the solicitors waive their costs and pay the disbursements, in so far as not covered by ATE insurance. If the case is won, the lawyers will recover whatever they can from the other side either (a) by detailed or summary assessment or (b) by negotiation based upon the likely outcome of such an assessment.

10.4.14 This circumstance means that the client exerts no control . . . over costs when they are being incurred. The entire burden falls upon the judge who assesses costs retrospectively at the end of the case, when it is too late to 'control' what is spent.

10.4.15 The third flaw in the recoverability regime is that the costs burden placed upon opposing parties is excessive and sometimes amounts to a denial of justice . . .

10.4.16 If the opposing party contests a case to trial (possibly quite reasonably) and then loses, its costs liability becomes grossly disproportionate. Indeed the costs consequences of the recoverability rules can be so extreme as to drive opposing parties to settle at an early stage, despite having good prospects of a successful defence. This effect is sometimes described as 'blackmail', even though the claimant is using the recoverability rules in a perfectly lawful way . . .

10.4.19 . . . [I]t is a [fourth] flaw of the recoverability regime that it presents an opportunity to lawyers substantially to increase their earnings by cherry picking [i.e. taking on only the most potentially lucrative cases and rejecting others]. This is a feature which tends to demean the profession in the eyes of the public.

Jackson consequently recommended abolition of recoverability as regards success fees and ATE premiums (para. 10.4.20). In return, so as to prevent personal injury claimants being left worse off, he made two countervailing proposals. First, because successful claimants must now pay their lawyers' success fee out of the damages they recover, Jackson recommended a one-off and across-the-board increase in the level of general damages for pain, suffering and loss of amenity of 10 per cent, as well as a cap on the amount of success fee that lawyers may deduct at 25 per cent of damages, excluding damages for future economic losses (paras 10.5.3ff). The same increase would apply to general damages for nuisance, defamation and any other tort which causes suffering to individuals (para. 10.5.6). Secondly, a 'qualified one way costs shifting rule' should apply in PI claims, meaning that losing claimants normally have no liability to pay the successful defendant's costs, thereby obviating the need for ATE insurance. In Jackson's view, this bold reform was justified because injured persons might otherwise be deterred from bringing claims for compensation:

19.1.2 *Important features of personal injuries litigation.* There are two important features of personal injuries litigation. First and self-evidently, the claimant is an individual. For the vast majority of individuals it would be prohibitively expensive to meet an adverse costs order in fully-contested litigation. The most recent *Social Trends* report shows that 73% of all households have savings (made up of securities, shares, currency and deposits) of less than £10,000. Defence costs can easily be many times higher than £10,000 in fully-contested litigation. This would mean that for three quarters of households their other financial assets (their own home in most cases) would be at risk from an adverse costs order. Secondly, the defendant is almost invariably either insured or self insured. By 'self insured', I mean that the defendant is a large organisation which has adopted the policy of paying out on personal injury claims as and when they arise, rather than paying substantial liability insurance premiums every year.

19.1.3 *Factors pointing towards one way costs shifting.* The factors which make one way costs shifting a serious candidate for consideration in relation to personal injuries litigation are the following:

(i) Claimants are successful in the majority of personal injury claims. Defendants seldom recover costs, so they derive little benefit from two way costs shifting.
(ii) Personal injuries litigation is the paradigm instance of litigation in which the parties are in an asymmetric relationship . . . [This is a reference to the inequality of bargaining power between the claimant and the defendant's insurer.]
(iii) The principal objective of recoverable ATE insurance premiums is to protect claimants against adverse costs orders. One way costs shifting would be a less expensive method of achieving the same objective.
(iv) One way costs shifting is not a novel concept in personal injuries litigation. Between 1949 and 2000, the vast majority of personal injury claims proceeded under a one way costs shifting regime, namely the legal aid 'shield' [whereby costs ordered against a legally-aided individual were not to exceed the amount which was a reasonable one to pay having regard to all the circumstances, including the financial resources of the parties to the proceedings, and their conduct in connection with the dispute] . . .

The Jackson proposals were adopted as a package by government and enacted over the course of 2012 and 2013 by a mixture of legislative and non-legislative measures. The Legal Aid, Sentencing and Punishment of Offenders Act (LASPOA) 2012, ss. 44 and 46 provide respectively for the non-recoverability of success fees and ATE premiums by amending the Courts and Legal Services Act 1990 (CLSA) (see CLSA 1990, ss. 58, 58A and 58C). Qualified one-way costs shifting was introduced in personal injury claims by amendments to the CPR effected by the Civil Procedure (Amendment) Rules 2013/262 (see CPR r. 44.14(1)). The 10 per cent increase in damages for pain, suffering and loss of amenity was implemented by the Court of Appeal, which has responsibility for keeping damages awards up to date, in *Simmons v Castle* [2013] 1 WLR 1239. The reforms were coordinated to come into effect together on 1 April 2013.

Concurrently, LASPOA further curtailed the already very limited availability of legal aid in actions for damages. This is now available only in claims of clinical negligence in respect of severe disability from neurological injury sustained prior to, during or immediately after birth, and for claims relating to human trafficking or the violation of human rights for which legal aid is required under international conventions, including claims to the European Court of Human Rights but not claims in domestic courts under the Human Rights Act (s. 9 and Sch. 1).

For critical analysis, see McIvor, 'The Impact of the Jackson Reforms on Access to Justice in Personal Injury Litigation' (2011) 30 CJQ 411. For the government's assessment of the impact of the reforms, see Ministry of Justice, *Post-Implementation Review of Part 2 of the Legal Aid, Sentencing and Punishment of Offenders Act 2012 (LASPO): Civil Litigation Funding and Costs*, CP38, February 2019.

Who do you think stands to gain the most from the reforms? Who will lose the most? Consider in particular who will end up having to subsidise the cost of *unsuccessful* claims.

Damages-Based Agreements (DBAs)

A further aspect of the Jackson reforms was the removal of the prohibition of the use in court-based proceedings of US-style contingency fees, to be known in the United Kingdom as 'damages-based agreements' (DBAs). This is where the lawyer takes a percentage of the damages rather than an uplift on the regular fee; in personal injury cases, the lawyer's 'cut' is subject to the same limit as applies to success fees—25 per cent of damages, excluding damages for future economic losses (*Jackson*, paras 12.4.11 and 5.1). Reviewing the use of DBAs in the employment tribunals (where they have never been prohibited), Moorhead concludes that, though DBAs have not led to the explosion of litigation feared by some, they constitute a rather weak mechanism for promoting access to justice because practitioners struggle to make DBA claims profitable and may therefore be disinclined to take them on ('An American Future? Contingency Fees, Claims Explosions and Evidence from Employment Tribunals' (2010) 73 MLR 752). DBAs were introduced for court-based proceedings by LASPOA, s. 45, which repeals former restrictions on their use (CSLA, s. 58AA), allowing them to be generally available as an alternative to a CFA. However, in line with Moorhead's prediction and perhaps for the reasons he suggests, they have not yet proved popular in the funding of PI claims (Morris, 'Deconstructing Policy', *op. cit.*, p. 131).

Fixed Costs

An area where reform is still ongoing is in the move away from a system in which lawyers bill by the hour to one based on fixed costs. The *Jackson Report* (ch. 15) repeated Lord Woolf's earlier call for a fixed-costs system to be introduced in all fast-track cases, with a pre-determined tariff applying to PI claims and an overall limit in non-PI cases. Such a reform enables parties to anticipate their potential liabilities in advance, removes the need for taxation of costs and allows solicitors to work to a known budget (Woolf, *Access to Justice: Final Report*, 1996, p. 45). The Woolf proposal was strongly resisted by claimant PI lawyers and, because it proved to be so controversial, it was implemented only in stages. Initial steps included the application of tariffs of 'fixed recoverable costs' (FRCs) to advocates appearing in fast-track trials (CPR Part 45, Section VI) and to all legal expenses incurred in low-value road traffic accident claims (CPR Part 45, Section III, initially applying to claims of up to £10,000). In 2013, the approach was extended to employers' liability (EL) and public liability (PL) and to claim values of up to £25,000.

In 2021, the Ministry of Justice announced the government's intention to extend FRCs to all civil cases in the fast track, up to a value of £25,000, as well as to a new category of 'simpler' intermediate-value claims of between £25,000 to £100,000—to be effected by an expansion of the fast-track's scope (Ministry of Justice, *Extending Fixed Recoverable Costs in Civil Cases: The Government Response*, September 2021). This broadly followed recommendations made by Sir Rupert Jackson in a 2017 report commissioned by the Judiciary of England and Wales (Lord Justice Jackson, *Review of Civil Litigation Costs: Supplemental Report. Fixed Recoverable Costs*, July 2017), which were put out to public consultation in 2019 (Ministry of Justice, *Extending Fixed Recoverable Costs in Civil Cases: Implementing Sir Rupert Jackson's Proposals*, March 2019). The introduction of a bespoke regime of FRCs in lower value clinical negligence claims has been pursued separately in a parallel initiative led by the Department of Health & Social Care (Department of Health & Social Care, *Fixed Recoverable Costs in Lower Value Clinical Negligence Claims: A Consultation*, January 2022).

Small Claims

The small claims track was established in 1999 in line with the recommendation in Lord Woolf's influential report, *Access to Justice* (1996). Building upon the previous county court arbitration scheme introduced in 1973, its simplified and informal procedures are intended to be suitable for litigants in person and legal representation is discouraged inasmuch as, by way of exception to the usual 'loser pays' rule, a successful litigant cannot recover their legal costs from the other side. The small claims track applies to claims of up to £10,000, but until recently that was subject in personal injury cases to a maximum of £1,000 in respect of damages for pain, suffering and loss of amenity (PSLA). At the end of May 2021, addressing continuing concerns about whiplash claims arising from road traffic accidents (RTAs, discussed earlier in I.2), the PSLA limit was raised to £5,000 in RTA claims, with exceptions for specific vulnerable claimants, and to £1,500 in non-RTA cases. See CPR r. 26.6(1)ff, Practice Direction 27B and Pre-Action Protocol for Personal Injury Claims below the Small Claims Limit in Road Traffic Accidents ('The RTA Small Claims Protocol'). The reform means that greater numbers of RTA personal injury claims will be brought by claimants without the benefit of expert legal advice—a deficit that is meant to be addressed by the creation of a new online portal, officialinjuryclaim.org.uk, providing step-by-step assistance to litigants in person bringing low-value RTA personal injury claims.

How do you think the raising of the small claims limit in RTA cases will impact on the way that claims are brought, the role of lawyers in them and the justice of the outcomes achieved in practice?

3. The Settlement of Personal Injury Claims

Most claims brought to solicitors are settled without any judicial determination of their merit. The Oxford survey found that in only 2.7 per cent of accident claims in which compensation was paid was there a court hearing. Far from being regarded as unsatisfactory, this situation may actually be beneficial to the proper resolution of claims, and the promotion of out-of-court settlements has in fact long been a major theme underlying reforms of the civil justice system. In 1996, the Woolf Report on the civil justice system stated that it was part of its purpose 'to develop measures which will encourage reasonable and early settlement of proceedings'. Lord Woolf noted the paradox that, although most claims end in settlement, the existing rules of the court were mainly directed towards preparation for trial: 'My aim', he responded, 'is to increase the emphasis on resolution otherwise than by trial' (*Access to Justice*, p. 194).

D. Harris, D. Campbell and R. Halson, *Remedies in Contract and Tort*, 2nd edn (London: Butterworths, 2000)

[Drawing upon earlier empirical studies (see especially the Oxford survey cited earlier, and H. Genn, *Hard Bargaining: Out of Court Settlement in Personal Injury Actions* (Oxford: OUP, 1987)) Harris et al. explain how the damages system works in practice. They examine, in particular, the out-of-court settlement process by which the vast majority of claims are resolved.]

The Damages System in Practice . . .

Nearly all claims are settled out of court as the result of negotiations between the parties' representatives (usually between C's solicitor and a claims inspector from D's insurance company). In these negotiations there are many pressures on claimants to accept sums which heavily discount the amount which a judge would award if he found D 'fully' liable, viz. if he decided every disputed question in C's favour. There will be a discount for every risk or uncertainty facing C: the risk that he does not have adequate evidence to prove C's fault (C can only guess the strength of the evidence available to D); that he might be found to have been partly at fault himself; that the medical reports on his side about his prognosis may not be accepted by the judge; that his evidence about his future employment prospects may not be accepted.

Added to these are the uncertainties about how much further delay there would be in waiting for a court hearing; about how much the legal costs might amount to and whether part or all of them might fall on P himself; and about how much the judge might award for intangible losses, such as pain and suffering and loss of amenity. Every one of these risks or uncertainties is a negotiating weapon in the hands of D's insurance representative . . .

The impact of these risks and uncertainties on the parties differs greatly, because there is a structural imbalance between them which puts C into an unequal bargaining position. First, insurance companies have the resources to collect all the available evidence as soon as possible, and to arrange for experts to report on the accident. Even while P is on his way to hospital, D will often be reporting the accident to his insurance company, which can then immediately arrange for assessors to take photographs of the scene and to seek out witnesses. . . . Secondly, insurance companies are . . . 'repeat players' to whom any particular case is merely one of many. They can afford to take a detached, neutral view of C's individual case, because they are concerned with the overall results of all the cases they handle. They can 'average' or spread their risks over them all and so can be risk-neutral in their attitude to the individual case. But what is routine to the insurance man is unique to C. He is . . . a 'one-shotter' who is almost invariably risk-averse: if he is seriously injured the case is of crucial importance to him and the risk of losing it is a powerful incentive on him to compromise for a smaller sum than he could hope to win in court on the basis of 'full' liability. He cannot spread his risk and is also likely to be under financial and psychological pressure. If he is not back at work he may be in urgent need of money . . .

Insurance companies obviously try to settle claims as cheaply as possible; they operate within the existing fault-based system, and their principal responsibility is to their premium payers (and shareholders), not to protect the interests of accident victims. . . . They consider it legitimate to take advantage of any rule, whether of substance or procedure, which will assist them in minimising their expenditure. They search for and then expose any weakness in C's case . . .

[I]n a personal injury claim C is almost completely dependent on his solicitor's advice at all stages of the claim and particularly in regard to the amount he could expect to recover. The process of bringing a claim is so complicated, and the formal rules create such uncertainty, that C has no option except to give his solicitor effective control over all the crucial decisions—whether to go to court, to settle (and if to settle, for which amount), or to abandon the claim. The large number of uncertainties surrounding the claim has the effect of nearly always protecting the solicitor from criticism, no matter what advice he gives. Almost no case is so certain in regard to the amount of damages to be expected that his advice can be shown to be negligent; in practice, he can be held negligent only if he flagrantly fails to take a necessary step in the litigation procedure or fails to meet a specified time limit . . .

COMMENTARY

The *Pearson Commission* found that only 1 per cent of claims actually reach a court: the rest are settled informally by the parties (*Pearson*, vol. I, para. 79). As Harris et al. note, even experienced solicitors will advise their clients to settle out of court if there is a reasonable offer on the table. Conversely, it is economically rational for insurers to make an offer of settlement, even if it is uncertain that the claimant would succeed in establishing liability if the case were eventually to come to trial. The practice in such cases is to make a discount for settlement, that is, a reduction to reflect the possibility of failure before a court. The amount of the discount will of course vary according to the extent of the uncertainties surrounding the claimant's case, and in particular whether the defendant is contesting liability or only the quantum of damages. In fact, although the emphasis in most tort books is on the elements of liability, liability issues are comparatively rare in practice. One survey found, for example, that there was no or no significant dispute over liability in 78 per cent of personal injury claims conducted under a CFA other than those for clinical negligence (P. Fenn et al., *op. cit.*, para. 5.1.2).

A number of reasons can be advanced as to why claims are settled out of court (see further Harris et al., *op. cit.*, pp. 12–14):

(i) *Cost.* It is cheaper to settle than to fight it out in court. Out-of-court settlements save the parties the expenditure of legal fees, time and inconvenience. These savings represent a 'bonus' that can be split between the parties if they can agree a settlement. And there is also a saving of societal resources (to the extent that court fees do not cover the full cost of court proceedings).

(ii) *Flexibility.* Outcomes are more varied than the all-or-nothing solution imposed by the court; the parties can agree a compromise. Furthermore, an out-of-court settlement allows the parties to impose conditions on each other that could not be ordered in court, e.g. as to publicity or to prevent the claimant's solicitors from acting for other clients in subsequent cases arising out of the same circumstances.

(iii) *Harmful effects of litigation on continuing relationships.* Litigation can be damaging to the health of a continuing relationship, and tends to be viewed as a parting shot (e.g. where an employee is injured at work, the working relationship is more likely to be preserved if there is a negotiated agreement).

(iv) *Harmful effects of litigation on individuals.* Litigation may result in psychological pressure on individuals involved in it, perhaps leading to what is known as 'compensation neurosis'.

(v) *Uncertainty of litigation.* Settlement ends the inevitable uncertainty as to the outcome of litigation and enables parties to organise their affairs without having to bear in mind the risk of winning or losing in subsequent court proceedings.

Inequality of Bargaining Power and the Role of the Solicitor

It has been said that 'tort law in action is differentiated from the formal law by its greater simplicity, liberality and inequity' (H. L. Ross, *Settled Out of Court: The Social Process of Insurance Claims Adjustment*, 2nd edn (New York: Aldine, 1980), p. 237). Tort law in action is simpler than the law in the books because it involves the routine processing of claims on the basis of rules of thumb (see further Halliday, Ilan and Scott, 'Street-Level Tort Law: The Bureaucratic Justice of Liability Decision Making' (2012) 75 MLR 347), more liberal because claims may be paid out even when it is doubtful that the claimant can prove fault (e.g. because of their nuisance value) and liable to cause inequity because it rewards those who get effective legal representation, while those who do not lose out. Further possible inequity results from the 'structural imbalance', or inequality of bargaining power, that Harris, Campbell and Halson explain in the extract. Insurance claims adjusters can—entirely within the law—exploit the relative weakness of the other side, for whom the difference between winning and losing may be overwhelming.

Claimants must rely upon the legal expertise of their solicitors to redress this imbalance, but they may be let down for a number of reasons. First, there is inexperience. In the past, claimants often went to a generalist high-street practice lacking experience in personal injury work (see Genn, *op. cit.*, pp. 40–50). Such lawyers tended to take a conciliatory approach and to assume the insurer would act reasonably. With the current proliferation of specialist firms, this is much less likely to be a factor today. Secondly, there may be a conflict of interest between solicitor and client. Solicitors might want to settle quickly in order to increase their turnover, recognising that further expense or effort might be disproportionate to the benefit gained. They may also want to settle to ensure that their costs are met, as insurers generally pay costs in addition to compensation. Naturally, this point should not be overstated: a solicitor who prefers their own interests to those of their client is in breach of their fiduciary duty to the client. But the fact remains that there are a number of factors that may limit the effectiveness of the solicitor's representation, and these are aggravated by the lack of any practical way for clients to monitor their solicitor's performance.

There is a tendency in some quarters to view defendants and their insurers as the somewhat ruthless 'bad guys' in the settlement process. Genn, for example, states: 'Defendants adopt a theoretically uncompromising approach which includes taking advantage of whatever opportunities may be presented for avoiding or minimizing expenditure on claims' (p. 53). But a later study by Dingwall et al. ('Firm Handling: The Litigation Strategies of Defence Lawyers in Personal Injury Cases' (2000) 20 LS 1) draws a more nuanced picture, on the basis of data derived from (inter alia) interviews with various parties involved in the asbestos disease litigation of the late 1980s. The authors conclude (p. 17):

> Where Genn sees homogeneity among defendants, we have shown that they are also a diverse group with diverse interests. In the asbestos study, large general insurers, small regional insurers, self-insured companies, government agencies, and Lloyds brokers were all reported as behaving in rather different ways. Even within these categories, different enterprises had different traditions and cultures . . . Their responses [to claims] were mediated in different ways through their legal representatives, from enthusiastic hired guns dedicated to winning to cooler professionals who saw their job as properly testing the victims' claims and requiring justification for spending their client's money rather than minimising pay-outs by every available means. A category like 'repeat players' occludes these differences. In PI work, defendants are indeed almost all repeat players but this structural location does not indicate a uniform strategy . . .

The authors also criticise the tendency to regard 'hard bargaining' (aggressive and uncooperative negotiating) as invariably the best strategy for claimant solicitors to adopt. In fact, it is their view that '[h]ard bargaining . . . is not particularly effective *as a universal strategy* because of the amount of variation among both plaintiffs and defendants . . . The real skill for lawyers *on either side* is to produce a correct analysis of the other's position and to develop a litigation strategy appropriate to it. Sometimes this may be adversarial, sometimes it may be co-operative, often it may be some combination' (p. 16).

R. Lewis, 'Tort Tactics' (2017) 37 LS 162

[R]eform of the various ways in which the claims industry is funded has led to a considerable increase in the number of actions brought and has changed the way in which law firms and insurance companies are structured. This has affected the way in which they negotiate. They have had to devise techniques to deal efficiently with large numbers of claims. In addition, consolidation in the industry has led to the breakdown of traditional relationships between negotiators: dealing with familiar local representatives of the other side is less common. By contrast, the reputation of a law firm or insurance company now features more prominently and greater care is taken to safeguard this during negotiation. Similarly, the standing of opponents is now tracked much more carefully and tactics have been tailored to deal with a much wider range of firms and types of claim compared to when the previous studies were published.

A major factor affecting the tactics used is whether costs are recoverable. Defendants complained of claimants frontloading work in order to claim disproportionate rewards. They also thought that the value of claims was being manipulated in order to avoid the fixed cost limits, which played no part in the past. Litigators recognised that renewed emphasis on costs being proportionate to the value of claim limited their room to manoeuvre. They suggested that cases now were less well prepared and that they were less familiar with the details especially where minor injuries were involved. Where low-value claims were made that fell within the 'claims portal', there might be little investigation of the accident at all. By contrast, in more serious claims the need to present a strong evidential case remained as important as ever.

Contrary to previous studies, there was evidence in the survey that it was claimants who enjoyed the initial tactical advantage. This was because they were able to prepare their cases thoroughly before giving defendants first notice of the claim. Although there was much support for the traditional view that it was for defendants to make the first offer, it was suggested that this culture is beginning to change, partly because claimants are now expected to take the initiative in smaller claims. Earlier studies emphasised that defendants could take advantage of various weaknesses in both claimants and their lawyers and this was further illustrated here. There has always been disagreement concerning the appropriate level at which an offer should first be made. However, the earlier studies did not discuss two types of offer now being made by defendants: the 'pre-med' attempt to dispose of a claim at a very early stage; and the combined offer, which does not differentiate costs from damages . . .

Although the traditional defence tactic of delay was noted in the survey as part of a strategy to wear down the other side, it did not figure prominently. More widely recognised was the need to dispose of claims quickly and at low cost. Harrying the other side into a favourable settlement where it is suspected that they are already under pressure of work is a traditional strategy. However, there may now be more opportunity to use this tactic because of increasing pressures resulting from the need to process bulk claims. When considering whether it was better to adopt such a combative approach or to be more conciliatory, there was evidence in the survey to support Dingwall's view that experienced litigators are selective in the techniques they employ. Interviewees discussed the difficulties that could be caused by the more aggressive approach advocated by Genn.

Overall, the experience of those in practice clearly reveals that the resolution of claims is not determined only by the rules of tort but is affected by many other factors and, among these, the tactical skill of the litigator can be key. In response to the changing structure of personal injury litigation, these negotiation tactics continue to develop. They are an integral component of a bureaucratic institutional regime presently dominated by concerns about costs and efficiency.

COMMENTARY

The survey evidence Lewis relies on provides support for the Dingwall view that PI litigators need to be flexible in the strategies they adopt rather than invariably engaging in 'hard bargaining'. The techniques they employ reflect the claims landscape in which they act, in particular the business imperative of dealing with large numbers of claims as economically as possible. Practices adopted by the rival sides—frontloading of costs by claimant lawyers; third-party capture and pre-med offers (discussed earlier) by insurers, etc.—are regularly criticised by opponents. 'Combined offers', whereby the insurer offers a single sum by way of settlement, to cover both the claimant's damages and the lawyer's costs, are especially worrying because they place the lawyer in an obvious conflict of interests.

Offers to Settle

A further tactic that is open to either side to employ is to make a formal 'offer to settle' under provisions contained in CPR Part 36. If the claimant makes an offer to settle at a particular figure, and this is rejected by the defendant, then the defendant bears the risk of being held responsible for unnecessarily prolonging the litigation. If the judge ultimately awards the claimant a sum that is more than the claimant had offered to accept (say, the judge awards £10,000 but the claimant had offered to settle at £5,000) then the defendant can be penalised. Until recently, the penalty took the form of an increase in the costs the defendant had to bear over their normal amount. The *Jackson Report* thought this did not go far enough in terms of incentivising defendants to accept offers made by claimants and, to provide greater incentives for defendants to accept settlement offers, recommended that where a defendant fails to beat a claimant's offer, the claimant's damages should be increased by 10 per cent. This was enacted through LASPOA, s. 55 and the Civil Procedure (Amendment) Rules 2013/262 (see now CPR r. 36.17). The 10 per cent increase applies to damages awards of up to £500,000; if the award exceeds that figure, 5 per cent of the excess is added to the penalty, up to a maximum penalty of £75,000.

Where it is the claimant who fails to do better than the defendant's offer, they will be held liable as before for the defendant's costs incurred after the period for acceptance expires unless the court considers that this would be unjust. This constitutes an exception to the one-way costs shifting rule applying to PI claims since 2013: Part 36 trumps qualified one-way costs shifting inasmuch as a costs order made against a claimant under Part 36 may be enforced to the amount of any orders for damages and interest made in the claimant's favour (CPR r. 44.14). Under the Part 36 regime, then, claimants may lose all their damages in paying costs, even if the claim succeeds, but are not supposed to be left out of pocket. This may, however, be the practical outcome once their own legal fees and disbursements (court fees, medical reports, etc.) are taken into account.

Since their introduction in 1999, offers to settle have been seen as a valuable feature of the litigation landscape. In research carried out for the Law Society and Civil Justice Council (Goriely, Moorhead and Abrams, *More Civil Justice? The Impact of the Woolf Reforms on Pre-action Behaviour* (London: Law Society, 2002)) the reform was praised by both claimants, who saw offers to settle as a useful way of obtaining a response from the defendant, and defendants, who appreciated them for setting an upper limit to the bargaining range. Prior to 1999, it was only the defendant who could make a formal offer of settlement, which had to be backed by payment of the amount of the offer into a court-administered account, but this was felt to offend against the principle of equality (see Woolf, *Access to Justice: Interim Report*, 1995, ch. 24) and the current procedure strikes a better balance between the interests of the rival parties.

4. The Cost and Adequacy of Tort Damages

Law Commission, *Personal Injury Compensation: How Much is Enough? (A study of the compensation experiences of victims of personal injury)* (Law Com. No. 225, 1994)

[As part of its review of the law of damages, the Law Commission commissioned a survey of the adequacy of tort compensation in the light of the subsequent experiences of recipients. The survey, which was conducted by Professor Hazel Genn, considered claims at every level from the small to the very large, dividing them into a number of 'settlement ranges', but it focused upon cases involving the payment of more than £50,000 by way of compensation, typically involving serious and long-lasting injury, and sampled disproportionately fewer awards under this figure. The evidence suggested that even large awards of damages often proved inadequate, especially in view of the unexpectedly large proportion of accident victims who did not return permanently to work after their accident.]

The Failure to Return to Work and Adequacy of Damages

A particular concern is the high proportion of accident victims in all settlement ranges who did not return to work at all after their accident, or who returned for a period and were then forced to leave work as a result of the continuing effects of their injuries. For many of these victims, the amount of damages received did not cover their past losses and will not cover their future loss of earnings and the extra expenses resulting from their injury. It is notable that many accident victims fail to realise, in the period after settlement, just how little they have received, relative to their potential losses, and for how long they are likely to be affected by their injuries. Accident victims are often not aware of the extent to which they will be dependent on their damages in the future. In this respect, victims of catastrophic injury may be in a more favourable position because their permanent inability to carry out normal work is evident at the time of settlement. For many others, however, it appears that at the time of settlement their own expectations of their ability to return to work in the future are unrealistic. It is not entirely clear whether this is because experts fail to anticipate the extent of future incapacity, or whether the effect of a prolonged recovery period reduces the chances of finding work, or whether appropriate work is unavailable. What is clear, however, is that many respondents are unprepared for the impact of their injuries on their long-term capacity for work.

This problem is reflected most clearly in respondents' changing perceptions of the value of damages. Although most respondents are satisfied at settlement when presented with what appears to be a very substantial sum of money, this sense of satisfaction alters dramatically over time as accident victims are faced with the reality of long-term ill-effects of their injuries and a reduced capacity for work.

COMMENTARY

The Law Commission's finding that, in high value claims involving serious and long-lasting injury, the amount of damages awarded is prone to fall short of what is necessary to compensate fully for the claimant's losses is corroborated by empirical evidence about the operation of the labour market collated by Lewis et al., 'Court Awards of Damages for Loss of Future Earnings' (2002) 29 JLS 406. They argue that the courts have tended to make insufficient allowance for two factors in particular: first, the extent to which the claimant's earnings might have increased progressively with age, perhaps partly because of economy-wide earnings growth; and, secondly, the extent of the disadvantage the claimant will now suffer in the market for jobs as a result of the disability.

In the extracted study, the Law Commission noted that the difficulties of calculating the lump sum were particularly significant in so far as compensation for future needs was concerned, for example because there was virtually no possibility of the award being modified at a later stage because of deterioration or improvement in the claimant's condition or circumstances (para. 1.2). Do you think that the replacement of lump sum awards with periodic payment will improve the chances of achieving full compensation for the victims of serious long-term injuries? (See further Ch. 15.III.)

Increases in Damages

The introduction of periodical payment orders (PPOs) is just one of several recent reforms or developments intended to ensure that claimants receive full compensation for their injuries. The result has been a considerable increase in the level of damages. The unavoidable corollary has been an increase in the costs that defendants and/or their insurers have to bear.

A number of developments may be highlighted (see generally Lewis, Morris and Oliphant, 'Tort Personal Injury Claims Statistics: Is There a Compensation Culture in the United Kingdom?' (2006) 14 TLJ 158 at 172–74; Lewis, 'Structural Factors', *op. cit.*, pp. 51–59). First, the introduction of PPOs has itself been a factor in increasing the financial burden of compensation for personal injury. Although their use is limited to the small percentage of cases involving future pecuniary loss, such cases are responsible for a substantial proportion of the overall damages bill: insurers have estimated that the top 1 per cent of cases by value account for almost a third of the total paid to claimants (Lewis, 'Structural Factors', *op. cit.*, p. 52). Moving to PPOs in such cases increases the amount the insurer has to pay because insurers usually fund the payments by purchasing an annuity, which can prove much more expensive than paying lump sum damages because of a lack of competition in supplying the annuities required (*ibid.*).

Secondly, increases in the tariffs used for the compensation of non-pecuniary loss have served to further increase the burden on compensators (see Ch. 15.IV.1(a)). The decision in *Heil v Rankin* [2001] QB 272 sought to protect the value of non-pecuniary damages against the effects of inflation through a one-third increase in awards of £150,000 or more, and tapered increases for awards of between £10,000 and £150,000. Awards of up to £10,000, probably accounting for the majority of personal injury claims, were not increased. Subsequently, a further increase of 10 per cent was made to all non-pecuniary damages as part of the package of reforms recommended in the *Jackson Report* (*Simmons v Castle* [2013] 1 WLR 1239).

Thirdly, changes in the calculation of damages for pecuniary loss have also played a role (see Ch. 15.IV.2(a)). The courts now make use of actuarial forecasts of mortality and other relevant contingencies, contained in the 'Ogden Tables' (see now *Actuarial Tables with Explanatory Notes for use in Personal Injury and Fatal Accident Cases*, 8th edn updated 2021), rather than relying on historical data as to life expectancy, etc. As estimated life expectancy has increased, so too has the cost of paying compensation for injuries expected to endure until death. Where future care costs are to be compensated, the courts also now take into account that these will rise in line with earnings, rather than retail prices, which also exerts an upwards influence on the value of awards as real earnings growth has historically exceeded price inflation by almost 2 per cent a year. Another factor has been successive reductions made in the discount rate applied to future pecuniary losses, which makes allowance for the anticipated investment return on damages. For thirty years prior to 1998 the rate was 4.5 per cent but this was then reduced by the House of Lords in *Wells v Wells* [1999] 1 AC 345 to 3 per cent and then by the Lord Chancellor, using new statutory powers, to 2.5 per cent. The discount rate remained at that level for sixteen years, in the face of evidence that returns on the risk-free investments envisaged had fallen significantly, ultimately to negative values. In February 2017, the rate was finally amended—to *minus* 0.75 per cent, a figure that caused alarm in the insurance industry, which raised concerns about the additional costs that it will entail. Ensuing consultation resulted in a revision of the methodology for setting the rate and this resulted in the adoption of a new rate of minus 0.25 per cent from 2019 on.

A final burden that has fallen on compensators in recent times has been to reimburse the state for welfare benefits paid to the claimant and NHS hospital charges. This curtails a hidden subsidy of tortfeasance out of tax revenues, but means that the cost will now have to be borne by the defendant and/or insurer, and then no doubt passed on to customers or premium payers.

Evidence about the Cost of Compensation

Evidence that compensation costs per claim have increased over time may be derived from a number of different sources (see further Lewis, Morris and Oliphant, *op. cit.*, 159–68). One that should be mentioned here is the *UK Bodily Injury Awards Studies* (1997, 1999, 2003 and 2007), which provide insurance industry figures in respect of personal injury claims arising from motor accidents between 1991 and 2006. The most recent of the studies shows an increase in the total costs of bodily injury claims paid out by UK motor insurers of 9.5 per cent per annum between 1996 and 2006, compared with an increase in national average earnings of 4.3 per cent per annum. The average value of claims increased at an annual rate of 6.5 per cent in the period, with higher claims inflation in larger value claims. Annual increases of on average nearly 3 per cent in the number of claims also contributed to the rise in the overall costs.

Another useful source of statistical information here is the National Health Service Litigation Authority (NHSLA), renamed NHS Resolution, which has responsibility for the defence of all compensation claims against the NHS. The earliest year for which reliable information about NHS clinical negligence compensation costs is available is 1990–91, in which they were put at £53.2 million. For 2020–21, the figure was £2,209.3 million. (See *NHS Resolution Annual Report and Accounts 2020/21*, HC387, p. 15.) It will be apparent that this rise is massively higher than both price and earnings inflation in the period in question.

No-one has yet succeeded in making a reliable estimate of the total annual costs of the tort system in the United Kingdom or its constituent nations. The figure of £10 billion, or just over 1 per cent of GDP, advanced by an Institute of Actuaries working party in 2002 ('The Cost of Compensation Culture', www.actuaries.org.uk/documents/cost-compensation-culture-working-party-report) relied to a very large extent on guesswork. In 2005, the American insurance consultants, Tillinghast Towers Perrin, estimated that total tort costs in the United Kingdom, covering compensation payments, legal costs and administrative expenses, were 0.69 per cent of GDP in 2003, having risen from 0.53 per cent in 2000 (*US Tort Costs and Cross-Border Perspectives: 2005 Update* (2005), 13). Compared with the other countries surveyed, the costs for 2003 were lower than in Belgium, France, Germany, Italy, Japan,

Spain and Switzerland (and, of course, the United States), and higher only than Denmark and Poland. The report notes, however, that the data available outside the United States was limited and that the figures 'should not be overanalysed'. By contrast, the US Chamber Institute for Legal Reform was more confident of the information it presented in its *International Comparison of Litigation Costs* (2013), which extrapolated from data provided by insurance brokers on the costs of liability insurance purchased in different countries. The Institute estimated that the UK's total liability costs as a proportion of GDP were 1.05 per cent in 2011, behind the United States (1.66 per cent) and Canada (1.19 per cent), but ahead of nine other European countries in the same study (citing a Eurozone average of 0.63 per cent).

5. Who Pays Damages?

P. S. Atiyah, *The Damages Lottery* (Oxford: Hart, 1997)

The Guilty Parties Do Not Pay . . .

[I]n serious cases the wrongdoers never pay. In fact the only kind of case where the wrongdoers—the negligent parties—commonly pay are in very minor road accidents where a car is slightly damaged but no injuries are caused. In these cases, reasonable motorists will often admit their fault and pay out of their own pockets to save claiming against their insurance, with consequent loss of no-claims bonus. But in more serious cases, and in virtually all injury claims, the parties guilty of negligence will not pay. In fact solicitors acting for a plaintiff will not usually bother to claim against them. They will simply extract the name of the defendant's insurance company and address their claim straight to the insurers. From then on, the whole procedure will be dealt with by the insurers on the defendant's side, and the plaintiff's solicitor on his side. The insurers will decide whether to admit blame, whether to settle, how much to offer, how to fight the case if it goes to trial, what barrister to brief, whether to appeal if they lose, and so on, all without troubling to consult the nominal defendant . . . Insurers may even choose to settle a case against the wishes of the insured who might prefer to defend it . . .

Some might think that, at least where damages are awarded against companies, the companies themselves are often seriously to blame and it is fair therefore that they should pay for their own faults. This is a very popular viewpoint . . . But this is one of those areas where the popular viewpoint and the legal viewpoint both seem founded on misconceptions. A company or a government department or other public body is an abstraction. It is real people not abstractions who commit acts of negligence. Generally speaking, the liability of a company involves no imputation at all against the company itself—it is just legally liable for the negligence of its employees . . .

Paradoxically, there is actually one group of negligent people who do, in a peculiar sense, pay for their own negligence, and these are accident victims themselves. Whenever an accident victim who makes a claim has his damages scaled down because of his own contributory negligence he is paying, in a rather special sense, for his own negligence. People do not insure against the effects of their own contributory negligence so they 'pay' for it themselves . . .

The Public Pays

If the actual wrongdoers don't pay for the damages, who does? The answer . . . is that, in a broad sense, the whole public pays . . . It is actually very much like taxation . . . First, it is clear that businesses have to pay a large part of the cost of damages in the first instance. All large businesses insure against this sort of liability, and indeed, it is legally compulsory for them to insure against their liability to pay damages to their own employees. So in a sense, the damages will actually be paid by insurance companies rather than the businesses themselves. But of course insurance companies have to collect premiums, and the business concerns who insure against this kind of risk have to provide these premiums. Where do they get the money from to pay the premiums? The answer is that finding the money is just an overhead cost of the business, like the rent paid for the premises, or the cost of heating the premises.

The business has to charge—its customers—enough money to cover its overheads, so some small part of what we pay for all the goods and services we buy in the market is actually going to fund this kind of insurance, and ultimately to pay the damages which the insurance companies have to pay out. If the business is unable to pass on the whole cost to its customers for competitive reasons then the shareholders (rather than, or as well as, the customers) will pay. So damages premiums are just like a bit more VAT levied on businesses, and passed onto the public.

There is a simpler, more direct payment route, with regard to private motorists. As everybody knows, an ordinary motorist is legally obliged to insure against third party risks—he has to buy insurance to cover the risk of being held liable to pay damages through use of his car on the road. So here again, the money is paid through insurance companies, but is levied in effect as a charge on the motorist. Since it is compulsory the resemblance to a tax is stronger still . . . In other cases the route through which the money moves is even simpler, but the ultimate result is much the same. For instance, whenever the government (or a government department) is held liable to pay damages, there is no insurance because the central government never insures, but the money is just paid out of taxes. So here, it is even more clear that damages are just like any other government expenditure which has to be paid from taxes. If the government wants to pay social security benefits, it has to raise taxes to pay for the benefits, and if it is willing to pay damages, it has to do the same.

The Consequence of Recognising that the Public Pays

The fact that damages are ultimately paid for like this, by members of the public, is critically important . . . [I]t means that sympathy for accident victims comes with a price label attached if we want to do anything about it. Sympathy itself is cheap; but if we want to translate that sympathy into more compensation or higher damages, then we, the public, will have to pay more. Some people may be willing to do this; others, looking at the huge damages awarded sometimes awarded for relatively minor injuries, or in dubious circumstances, may feel less sure . . . The public perception of these matters appears still to be that damages are somehow paid by wrongdoers, negligent and blameworthy parties, and this perception fuels demand for more and higher damages. It is time that the public understood that they themselves are paying for these damages awards.

COMMENTARY

Atiyah proceeds to argue that the fact that tort damages are really, albeit indirectly, paid by the public at large 'makes nonsense of the whole fault principle' (p. 115). This matter is considered further in the following section (II.1).

We have already noted the very extensive influence that insurers have over the day-to-day operation of the tort system, and their increasing input into matters of policy (see Ch. 1.III.1). One point raised in the earlier discussion was that an action ostensibly between private individuals may be, in reality, between their insurance companies. In cases of property damage, in particular, the action is often brought by the claimant's (first-party) insurer who, having paid out under the policy of insurance, may exercise a right of subrogation and bring an action—in the claimant's name but for the insurer's sole benefit—against the liability insurer lying behind the nominal defendant. The result is that tort law becomes nothing more than a mechanism for shifting risks between different classes of insurers. The financial burden on members of the public—many of whom are comprehensively insured, i.e. pay both first-party and liability insurance premiums—remains substantially the same. It was an acceptance that there was nothing to be gained from expensive litigation as to which of two insurance companies should bear the costs of compensation that led to the development of so-called 'knock-for-knock' agreements between insurers in respect of collisions between comprehensively insured motorists. Insurers offering comprehensive policies calculated that it would be cheaper for them in the long run if they entered into bilateral agreements whereby, after a collision between vehicles insured by the contracting parties, each would pay compensation to its own insured irrespective of which of the two motorists was actually at fault (i.e. they agreed not to exercise their rights of subrogation). Over time, the number of occasions on which they paid up 'unnecessarily' would balance against the number of occasions on which they were saved having to discharge the liabilities incurred by their insureds (see further Atiyah, p. 224f). In recent years, however, knock-for-knock agreements have fallen into disuse, partly as a result of a growth in the number of insurers targeting groups of motorists perceived to be safe drivers. Such insurers could only lose out if required to pay the costs of accidents caused by 'dangerous' drivers insured elsewhere.

The 'Tort Tax'

Atiyah was prescient in highlighting motor insurance as resembling a tax on motorists. This has in fact become a persistent refrain in modern discussion of the liability system, especially by those who bemoan the growth of a 'compensation culture'. The matter received detailed and repeated attention from the House of Commons Transport Committee in a series of reports, beginning with *The Cost of Motor Insurance*, Fourth Report of Session 2010–2011 (HC 591, 2011). In submissions to the committee and via other channels, insurers and their representative bodies argued that fraudulent, exaggerated or trivial claims, especially for whiplash injury, were adding substantially to the price of motor insurance: the Association of British Insurers submitted that whiplash claims alone cost insurers £2.2 billion in 2011, equivalent to about £90 of the average motor insurance premium (House of Commons Transport Committee, *Cost of Motor Insurance: Whiplash*, Fourth Report of Session 2013–2014 (HC 117, 2013), vol. I Ev 67). Whether savings resulting from reforms designed to reduce the number and cost of whiplash claims will ultimately be passed on to motorists remains, however, to be seen.

The perception of tort liability as a form of taxation on the general public is shared by a number of other writers. The American commentator, Peter Huber, coined the phrase 'the tort tax' to describe the phenomenon (*Liability: The Legal Revolution and its Consequences* (New York: Basic Books, 1988), p. 4). But the tax is not like other forms of taxation, such as income tax (at least in the United Kingdom), because it is regressive in effect. It produces a system in which the rich get larger awards than the poor—because their income losses are greater, or their damaged property more valuable, or because they are more likely to opt for expensive (and non-deductible) private medical treatment for their injuries—without this being necessarily or adequately reflected in the amounts of money they pay into the tort system by way of liability insurance premiums. As Abel writes ('Tort', in D. Kairys (ed.), *The Politics of Law*, 3rd edn (New York: Basic Books, 1998), p. 454):

> Damages deliberately reproduce the existing distribution of wealth and income . . . [T]he cost of preserving privilege is borne by everyone buying liability insurance, purchasing products and services, and paying taxes. Thus, all insured car owners pay the cost of compensating the privileged few who drive Rolls-Royces or earn a million dollars a year. They also pay for the superior medical care consumed by victims from higher socioeconomic strata.
>
> In effect, then, 'a regressive subsidy . . . is hidden in the operation of the damages system' as average and low earners subsidise the rich (Harris, Campbell and Halson, *op. cit.*, p. 425).

II. Tort and the Fault Principle Evaluated

In the modern law of tort, liability is premised upon fault, which usually takes the form of the intention to injure another or negligence. The so-called 'fault principle' appears to have taken a hold in the law of tort in the late eighteenth or early nineteenth century, though how this evolution is accounted for is a matter of dispute: some view it as a response to pressure from newly formed industrial concerns who were anxious to stave off the threat of strict liability (i.e. liability without fault) in respect of statistically inevitable accidents; some as an intellectual attempt to group together a number of disparate liabilities of more limited scope as part of a process of rationalising and developing the law (see further Ch. 1.I.6). It may be doubted whether a principle of strict liability was ever widely espoused in the pre-industrial law, but it did have a few proponents in the nineteenth century, as the famous decision of *Rylands v Fletcher* demonstrates (see Ch. 11.III). Nevertheless, strict liability is somewhat exceptional in the modern law in which tort liability is predominantly fault-based.

1. The Moral Basis of the Fault Principle

The fault principle has intuitive appeal: to many, fault is simply the natural standard of liability. It seems to be morally right that a person who injures another through fault should have to pay compensation. Nevertheless, the moral basis of the fault principle may be disputed.

> **P. Cane and J. Goudkamp, *Atiyah's Accidents, Compensation and the Law*, 9th edn** (Cambridge: CUP, 2018)
>
> [Patrick Atiyah's path-finding work on accidents, compensation and the law was first published in 1970. Inaugurating the well-known *Law in Context* series, Atiyah took the rules of the law of tort and considered them in the light of the accident compensation system as a whole, dealing not only with tort but also with social security, insurance and other sources of compensation. Atiyah's criticisms of the tort system were encapsulated in the book in his celebrated 'indictment' of the fault principle (headed more neutrally an 'appraisal' of the fault principle in the most recent editions, prepared by Peter Cane and—from the 9th edition—James Goudkamp). The following are the most important counts on Atiyah's indictment.]

The Compensation Bears No Relation to the Degree of Fault . . .

Fault is like a magic talisman: once it is established, all shall be given to the injured party. It is generally immaterial whether the fault was gross or trivial, or whether the consequences of the fault were catastrophic or minor. A degree of fault on the part of someone results in the injured person being compensated for all the losses suffered, provided the claimant was in no way personally at fault. Yet the seriousness of the consequences of a negligent action often bears no relation to the degree of fault which gave rise to it. A piece of momentary thoughtlessness on the road may cost someone their life and cause great loss to their family; but similar acts of thoughtlessness – or much more serious acts of negligence – may be committed by scores of others every day with only minor or even no adverse consequences . . .

[I]t may seem inequitable that the few whose negligence results in injury or loss to others should be required to bear this burden while the majority of negligent people go free . . .

The Compensation Bears No Relation to the Means of the Tortfeasor

In tort law, the tortfeasor's wealth or financial means are usually irrelevant to liability. At least in principle, the fact that a tortfeasor is rich is no ground for imposing liability, and the fact that they are poor is no ground for not imposing liability. Most people would probably accept this position of equality before the law regardless of wealth, which is implicit in the fault principle, as morally right. But, when we take into account the fact that, once liability is imposed, the compensation payable will bear no relationship to the means of the tortfeasor, we may begin to doubt whether it really is fair to ignore their financial position . . . No criminal court would think of imposing a fine for culpable conduct of the amounts that civil courts award as damages every day, at least not without serious inquiry into the ability of the defendant to pay . . .

A Harm-Doer May be Held Legally Liable Without Being Morally Culpable and Vice Versa . . .

The traditional justification [of the fault principle] is that the legal concept of liability for fault embodies a moral principle to the effect that, if a person, by blameworthy conduct, causes damage or loss to an innocent person, the former should compensate the latter for that damage or loss. But there are at least two grounds on which people have questioned whether tort law actually does embody such a moral principle. In the first place, it is said, if tort law were based on fault it would prohibit liability insurance, vicarious liability and other loss distribution devices by which the burden of paying compensation can be shifted from a party at fault to another party not at fault. . . .

A second ground on which tort law's adherence to a moral principle of responsibility for fault has been questioned is this: if the law really reflected morality, it would not adopt an objective definition of fault which, on the whole, ignores the personal qualities of the individuals involved and which does not require that the harm-doer should have had any consciousness of moral wrongdoing, or even of the risk they were creating or the dangerousness of their conduct . . .

But even if the law is out of step with morality, it does not follow that this is a bad thing. . . . [I]f we think that the main purpose of the law is to compensate injured persons, there is no reason why moral fault should be the criterion of liability to pay compensation. Indeed, if this is our aim, the criterion of whether a person is entitled to compensation ought to be whether they have been injured, regardless of how they were injured. From this point of view, the chief shortcoming of the tort system is not that it sometimes compensates people whose injuries were not the result of moral fault, but that it fails to compensate very many other people who have suffered injuries in circumstances that do not fall within the tort system at all. . . .

COMMENTARY

The extract covers the principal counts on Atiyah's indictment of the fault principle; additional counts not set out in the extract include: the fault principle pays little attention to the conduct or needs of the victim; justice may require the payment of compensation without fault; and, lastly, reliance on fault is open to the pragmatic objections that the concept is too abstract and fact-sensitive to act as a useful guide to conduct, and can be difficult to prove after the event.

Fault and the Objective Standard of Care

In the extract, Atiyah distinguished moral fault from the objective notion of fault adopted by the law of tort. This is perhaps most evident in the rule that lack of skill or experience is no defence to a claim of tortious liability (see *Nettleship v Weston*, extracted in Ch. 4.IV.1). But it is perhaps necessary to separate out the question whether the defendant has been guilty of moral wrongdoing from the question whether it is morally right to make the defendant pay compensation to the claimant. A line of argument dating from the nineteenth century suggests that the imposition of liability on one who is in breach of the law's objective standard of care, but not morally at fault, can be justified on the basis that it serves to maintain general standards of safety and personal security across society as a whole (see, e.g., Oliver Wendell Holmes, *The Common Law* (1881)). Some may object that the individual defendant ought not to be sacrificed to this utilitarian concern when they are not morally culpable. In an attempt to answer this objection, Tony Honoré developed a theory of 'outcome responsibility' in which he maintained that the imposition of liability without moral fault may be justifiable as a means of reinforcing the moral responsibility of the individual for their actions and their outcomes; to accept a plea of 'lack of skill' or 'lack of experience' would undermine the legal subject's status as a morally responsible agent, as it would mean that the ability to take reasonable care of the interests of others could no longer be regarded as an essential aspect of legal personality (see 'Responsibility and Luck' (1988) 104 LQR 530).

Deterrence

A counter-argument against Atiyah's scepticism as to the fault principle's value is that, by setting an objective standard of care and imposing a liability in damages for its breach, the law provides incentives to respect the safety of others and thereby contributes to the important public goal of accident prevention. Whether it in practice has this effect has, however, been doubted—bearing in mind that the incentives provided by tort law are dampened by liability insurance and in any case are to some extent duplicative of health and safety regulation, personal morals and even our desire to avoid injury to ourselves.

Empirical evidence of the effectiveness of tort law in providing appropriate incentives to guard against accidents is difficult to assess, but seems to support the view that tort's deterrent effect varies from sector to sector. In a major survey of the existing literature, Dewees and Trebilcock, 'The Efficiency of the Tort System and its Alternatives: A Review of the Empirical Evidence' (1992) 30 Osgoode Hall LJ 57, studied the deterrent effects of tort law relative to regulation in the context of five different categories of accidents: automobile accidents, medical malpractice, product-related accidents, environmental injuries and workplace injuries. The authors' assessment was that the deterrent effects of tort law are hard to gauge but appear strongest in relation to automobile accidents and weakest in relation to environmental injuries; in other contexts, the deterrent effects of tort law are variable. Although they also found that the evidence about the effectiveness of regulation is 'decidedly mixed', the authors nevertheless concluded (p. 137):

In the final analysis, our review of the empirical evidence leads us to a relatively bleak judgment about the properties of the tort system as a deterrent mechanism . . . In most of the accident contexts that we have reviewed, regulatory alternatives seem to hold out more promise than the tort system from the deterrence perspective.

See also the fuller account provided in D. Dewees, D. Duff and M. Trebilcock, *Exploring the Domain of Accident Law: Taking the Facts Seriously* (New York: OUP, 1996).

Strict Liability

As mentioned, Atiyah criticised the fault principle inasmuch as justice may sometimes require the payment of compensation without fault. One mechanism for doing so is strict liability. Under strict liability, it is not necessary for the claimant to prove that their injury was attributable to the defendant's fault; it is enough that the defendant has caused the claimant's injury in prescribed circumstances. Strict liability is exceptional in the modern law. The recognition of a new rule of strict liability in the classic case of *Rylands v Fletcher* was followed shortly afterwards by an effort to restrict greatly its scope (see Ch. 11.III). But, although the common law has not developed any practically significant example of strict liability—at least in so far as personal injury is concerned—a number of statutes do impose liabilities of this nature. Under the Nuclear Installations Act 1965 there is strict liability for death, personal injury or damage to property arising from (inter alia) emissions of radiation from nuclear installations (subject to certain statutory maxima). The Civil Aviation Act 1982, s. 76(2) imposes strict liability in respect of loss or damage to persons or property on land or water caused by a civil aircraft while in flight. By virtue of the Gas Act 1965, s. 14, strict liability applies to the underground storage of gas. And the Animals Act 1971, s. 2 subjects the keeper of a dangerous animal to strict liability as well. It should also be noted that in the area of industrial safety a number of duties laid down by statute are strict; however, for the most part, their presumed actionability in tort was reversed by s. 69 of the Enterprise and Regulatory Reform Act 2013 (see further in Ch. 10.III.1).

See also Lord Sumption, 'Abolishing personal injuries law—a project' (2018) 34 PN 113, endorsing the Atiyah critique of the fault principle and making the case for the abolition of fault-based liability for personal injuries, which could be replaced by a strict liability for causing damage to another person, thereby avoiding the costs and uncertainties inherent in the requirement of fault. For discussion, see J. Morgan, 'Abolishing Personal Injuries Law? A Response to Lord Sumption' (2018) 34 PN 122.

Proposals for Further Strict Liability Regimes

The *Pearson Commission* in its report of 1978 recommended the introduction of new strict liability regimes in a number of areas: rail transport, defective products and vaccine damage. It also proposed that strict liability in respect of personal injury caused by dangerous things and activities should be put on a statutory footing (vol. 1, para. 1643). In advocating strict liability in these areas, the Commission's guiding concerns were the insurability of the risk in question ('Can those who may cause an injury take out insurance more conveniently and cheaply than those who may be injured?') and 'whether the victim is likely to experience particular difficulty in proving fault', as in the case of defective products (para. 316).

Although the Commission's proposals were not directly implemented—a special scheme was, however, set up to provide fixed lump-sum payments to the victims of vaccine damage—a statutory regime of strict products liability was ultimately introduced as a result of European Community Directive 85/374 (see further Ch. 10.II).

Generally speaking, other European legal systems are much more willing to countenance tortious liability for damage without proof of fault—or, more accurately, a range of liabilities that are progressively stricter than the ordinary liability for fault. See B. A. Koch and H. Koziol (eds), *Unification of Tort Law: Strict Liability* (Kluwer, 2002).

Arguments For and Against Strict Liability

What are the arguments in favour of strict liability? A classic American exposition of the case for strict liability, in the context of products liability, was given in the California Supreme Court by Traynor J in *Escola v Coca Cola Bottling Co of Fresno*, 150 P 2d 436 (1944) (later approved by the entire court in *Greenman v Yuba Power Products, Inc*, 377 P 2d 897 (1963)):

> I believe the manufacturer's negligence should no longer be singled out as the basis of a plaintiff's right to recover in cases like the present one. . . . Even if there is no negligence . . . public policy demands that responsibility be fixed wherever it will most effectively reduce the hazards to life and health inherent in defective products that reach the market. . . . The cost of an injury and the loss of time or health may be an overwhelming misfortune to the person injured, and a needless one, for the risk of injury can be insured by the manufacturer and distributed among the public as a cost of doing business.

Traynor J's suggestion that strict liability is simply 'a cost of doing business' suggests a 'licence fee' rationale for strict liability (or 'enterprise liability' as it is often called in this context): the cost of compensating the victims of defective products can be regarded as a licence fee exacted from manufacturers who, after all, are in business in the pursuit of profit. The question for the manufacturer will be whether the profits to be derived from a particular product outweigh the cost of paying compensation claims (see further V. Nolan and E. Ursin, *Understanding Enterprise Liability: Rethinking Tort Reform for the Twenty-first Century* (Philadelphia: Temple University Press, 1995)).

Strict liability has attracted a number of significant opponents. For Oliver Wendell Holmes, '[a]s action cannot be avoided, and tends to the public good, there is obviously no policy in throwing the hazard of what is at once desirable and inevitable upon the actor . . . [The state's] cumbrous and expensive machinery ought not to be set in motion unless some clear benefit is to be derived from disturbing the *status quo*. State interference is an evil, where it cannot be shown to be a good . . .' (*The Common Law*, p. 77). Holmes also seems to have viewed it as simply 'unfair' that liability should be imposed in the absence of fault, and many people intuitively sympathise with this point of view. For further criticisms, see Priest, 'The Invention of Enterprise Liability: A Critical History of the Intellectual Foundations of Modern Tort Law' (1985) 14 J Leg Stud 461.

Given the criticisms of the fault principle listed in the preceding text, do you think that strict liability is any more unfair than liability based on *legal* fault?

2. Alternatives to Tort Law

We have already considered some options for minor reform of the tort system. But if the criticisms made of the tort system by Atiyah and others are taken seriously, more radical reform— perhaps even the replacement of the law of tort—is needed. Reform proposals of this nature are not currently on the table in the United Kingdom, but Lord Woolf warned more than a quarter of a century ago that, if his attempts to reduce the cost of personal injury litigation prove unsuccessful, '[m]ore fundamental measures, possibly involving the removal of at least moderate-sized injury claims from the litigation system, would have to be envisaged' (*Access to Justice: Interim Report*, 1995, ch. 7, paras 24–5). This final section considers two radical reform options: the introduction of 'no-fault' compensation alongside or in place of the law of tort; and the abolition of tortious liability for personal injuries in order to encourage an increase in self-reliance through the acquisition of first-party insurance.

(a) No-Fault Compensation: General

Royal Commission on Civil Liability and Compensation for Personal Injury, Chairman: Lord Pearson, *Report,* Cmnd 7054 (1978)

[T]he term 'no-fault' . . . refer[s] to compensation which is obtainable without proving fault and is provided outside the tort system. No-fault compensation is a system of obtaining payment from a fund instead of proceeding against the person responsible for the injury . . . The relationship between tort compensation and no-fault compensation is a central theme of our report . . .

[W]e have found a widespread ignorance of the fact that in this country we already have a considerable element of no-fault provisions . . . [W]e have had no-fault provision on quite a considerable scale since the 1897 Workmen's Compensation Act. Now, as well as the contributory benefits of the social security scheme, we have non-contributory no-fault benefits available to disabled people, the medical benefits of the National Health Service, and local authority social services provision of various kinds.

In some respects, this no-fault provision for the whole population already exceeds that provided by the no-fault schemes of limited scope which have been introduced in other countries. For example, medical and hospital cover under the National Health Service is open ended, whereas most United States no-fault schemes for road accidents provide only limited medical and hospital cover. Additional no-fault schemes for those injured in accidents in the United Kingdom would for most of them be a matter of building on to the no-fault provision which already exists . . .

A Look Overseas . . .

For centuries, tort was the only means of obtaining compensation for personal injury. In most countries, compensation is now provided from a variety of no-fault sources, in addition to tort or in partial or total replacement of it . . .

The break away from tort started in Germany in the nineteenth century with Bismarck's scheme of industrial accident insurance. No-fault provision has since spread all over the world. In many countries, including Canada, Australia and the USA, workmen's compensation has virtually replaced tort as a source of compensation for work injuries.

The twentieth century has seen the introduction of no-fault provision for road injuries. By the middle of the century, as motor cars multiplied and became more powerful and to some extent more lethal, thoughts turned to special provision for victims of road accidents. This time the movement started in North America . . .

Our Strategy . . .

The fundamental problem with which we were faced was the balance between no-fault and tort. The extreme options might be thought of as exclusive reliance on one or the other. A total dependence on the tort system, however, would be unrealistic—there could be no question of sweeping away the growing structure of social security provision. On the other hand, the possibility of relying exclusively on no-fault required more careful consideration . . . asking two main questions—how far no-fault should be extended; and whether tort should be abolished . . .

[L]eaving aside the merits of the issue and the matter of cost, our terms of reference precluded us from considering whether to recommend a no-fault scheme covering all injuries . . . We therefore came of necessity to ask ourselves whether there were persuasive reasons for extending no-fault compensation for particular categories of injury, and whether any new no-fault schemes could be satisfactorily financed.

Our decision to approach the extension of no-fault in this manner had an obvious bearing on the question whether tort should be abolished. It was clear to us that social security should be regarded as the primary method of providing compensation—it is quick, certain and inexpensive to administer, and it already covers a majority of the injured. But, in the absence of a no-fault scheme covering all injuries, the abolition of tort for personal injury would deprive many injured people of a potential source of compensation, without putting anything in its place. We concluded that tort must be retained; and most of us saw good reason for keeping tort even where all injuries in a given category are covered by a no-fault scheme . . .

We reached three main conclusions on the extension and improvement of no-fault provision. These were that the structure of the industrial injuries scheme should remain basically unchanged, albeit with some improvements; that a new scheme should be introduced for road injuries; and that a new social security benefit should be introduced for severely handicapped children.

We considered the introduction of new no-fault schemes for other categories covered by our terms of reference, but, in broad terms, we thought that the case for such schemes was less compelling; that our proposals as they stood would be enough, for the present at any rate, for the administrative system to absorb; and that the miscellaneous circumstances of accidents would make it difficult, and sometimes impracticable, to construct and finance schemes other than those covered by our main conclusions.

COMMENTARY

Under a no-fault system, compensation is paid out of a centrally controlled fund to victims of accidents (and perhaps illness) regardless of whether their injuries were the result of anyone else's fault. Although the social security system provides benefits on a no-fault basis, the value of these benefits is limited and they cannot be regarded as full compensation for losses sustained by the claimant. Accordingly, no-fault compensation is normally understood to refer to particular schemes falling outside both the tort and social security systems that aim at compensation at more than bare subsistence levels. Workers' compensation, which could formerly be regarded as a no-fault scheme in this sense, is now more appropriately regarded as part of the social security system. Now known as the Industrial Injuries Scheme, it no longer offers benefits on an earnings-related basis, and the task of dealing with short-term injuries now falls to statutory sick pay (which is not limited to those injured in the course of their employment and pays only flat-rate benefits). Where incapacity lasts more than fifteen weeks, industrial injuries disablement benefit can still be claimed, but this reflects only the claimant's degree of disablement, not their pre-accident earnings. At the time of writing, the maximum level of benefit was £188.60 per week (cf. £99.35 for statutory sick pay).

Severely Disabled Children

One of the principal impetuses for the setting up of the *Pearson Commission* was the public outcry at the Thalidomide tragedy of the 1960s (see *The Thalidomide Children and the Law: A Report by the Sunday Times* (London: André Deutsch, 1973), p. 8; H. Teff and C. Munro, *Thalidomide: The Legal Aftermath* (Farnborough: Saxon House, 1976), p. 18). Thalidomide, a pharmaceutical drug given to pregnant women suffering from morning sickness, was withdrawn from the British market in 1961 having been found to have been the cause of very serious congenital injuries suffered by some 10,000 children across the world (many of them born without arms or without legs, some with no limbs at all). Some 400 claims for damages were made against Distillers Co (Biochemicals) Ltd which made and sold the drug in Britain. In view of legal advice warning that such claims were very speculative—given especially the likely difficulty of proving negligence on the part of Distillers and the legal uncertainty as to whether an unborn child could be owed a duty of care—in 1968 an initial group of plaintiffs settled out of court at 40 per cent of the total to which they would have been entitled if the company had been found liable; the average award was £16,129 and the total payment was about £1 million. Subsequently, in 1974 (twelve years after the issue of the first writ) another settlement was reached with the remaining plaintiffs by which Distillers paid a total of £20 million, from which immediate cash payments averaging £54,000 were made to each of the children, with the balance of some £14 million going into a charitable trust fund (see Teff and Munro, *op. cit.*, pp. 12, 20). According to Teff and Munro, the litigation 'highlighted some fundamental shortcomings of the tort system', in particular 'the fact that the consumer has to prove negligence to succeed against the manufacturer, and the defects of the procedural framework within which the parties operate' (p. 129).

The litigation stimulated legal change, notably the statutory recognition of the right to sue in respect of congenital disabilities (Congenital Disabilities (Civil Liability) Act 1976). But the *Pearson Commission's* recommendation of a new (no-fault) social security benefit for severely disabled children was not acted upon. However, children are eligible for disability living allowance, paid to their parents to provide help with personal care and/or mobility (up to a maximum £156.90 per week at present rates), while a parent caring for a disabled child may be entitled to a carer's allowance (currently £69.70 per week). The issue of redress for those suffering serious birth injuries returned to the political agenda with a new Department of Health consultation in March 2017 (*A Rapid Resolution and Redress Scheme for Severe Avoidable Birth Injury: a Consultation*), the consultation document asking whether the ordinary negligence standard (reasonable care) or the higher standard of 'an experienced specialist' should be preferred. Though the views on that question were divided, the government announced at the end of 2017 that it was committed to introducing a new scheme (Department of Health, *A Rapid Resolution and Redress Scheme for Severe Avoidable Birth Injury: Government Summary Consultation Response*, November 2017), but at the time of writing no concrete proposal had been advanced.

No-Fault Compensation for Road Accidents

A *Pearson Commission* proposal that wholly awaits implementation is its recommendation of a no-fault compensation scheme for the victims of road accidents (see further Bartrip, 'No-fault Compensation on the Roads in Twentieth Century Britain' [2010] CLJ 263, placing the proposal in wider historical context). The Commission found that the fault principle operated with 'particular capriciousness' in motor cases, and was impressed also with the fact that '[r]oad accidents are numerous, particularly likely to be the cause of serious injury, and an unavoidable hazard for most of the population' (vol. 1, paras 286–7). No action was taken to implement the proposal at the time, but a consultation paper, *Compensation for Road Accidents*, published by the Lord Chancellor's Department in 1991 proposed that a person suffering personal injuries as a result of a road accident should be able to recover compensation up to a maximum of £2,500 without having to prove that another person was at fault. Compensation was to be assessed according to normal principles of the law of damages, as any reduction in the level of damages (justified, for example, by the speedier disposal of claims and the more certain entitlement to compensation) might encourage victims to abandon the scheme in favour of ordinary tort litigation. The LCD believed that the range of road accident victims eligible for compensation would be wider than under the tort system, and that disputes over liability for minor injuries would be greatly reduced. The scheme was to be funded and operated by the insurance industry, which would have had to increase the level of premiums accordingly, and would not therefore impose any additional costs on public funds.

The LCD proposal appears to have died a quiet death, and may in any case be criticised for preferring those suffering minor injuries, who do not have to prove fault, over the seriously injured, who must do so. It is also unclear whether it would in fact result in any savings in resources, as the scheme would only cover personal injury, leaving accident victims to pursue separate proceedings through the courts in respect of any damage sustained to their property.

A more general question is whether it is justifiable to give preferential treatment to the victims of road accidents as compared with the victims of accidents in general, on which see Lewis, 'No-Fault Compensation for Victims of Road Accidents: Can it be Justified?' (1981) 10 J Soc Pol 161.

The Motor Insurers' Bureau

In this context, a brief mention is warranted of the Motor Insurers' Bureau (MIB), which was set up by the insurance industry in 1946 in response to pressure from the then Minister of Transport. The idea was that insurers should contribute, *pro rata* to the amount of their motor business, to a fund from which compensation would be paid to victims of uninsured drivers. Uninsured Drivers Agreements between successive Ministers of Transport and the MIB have provided a legal basis for the compensation payments. Since 1968, a separate set of agreements has safeguarded the victims of hit-and-run or otherwise untraceable drivers (the Untraced Drivers Agreements). The most recent agreements are 3 July 2015 and 28 February 2017 respectively, though both have been or may be expected to be amended by later supplementary agreements. The purpose of the agreements is to provide compensation where none would be recovered by means of ordinary tort litigation, but the scheme does not provide for no-fault compensation in the strict sense, as the claimant must still show that the injuries were suffered as a result of the tort of an uninsured or untraced driver. In 2020, the MIB paid a total of £277.5 million in compensation under the two schemes (source: *MIB Annual Report and Accounts 2020*). For further details see *Atiyah*, pp. 241–5.

Criminal Injuries Compensation

Outside the social security system, the Criminal Injuries Compensation Scheme (introduced in 1964) is perhaps the best example in English law of state-provided compensation in respect of personal injury. It may perhaps be regarded as problematic to regard this as an example of 'no fault', because by definition the compensation is only paid in respect of criminally inflicted injuries. Nevertheless, the state assumes the obligation to pay compensation in respect of such injuries as a matter of social responsibility, and not as a matter of fault on its part.

The current scheme, operated under the terms of the Criminal Injuries Compensation Act 1995, has been effective since 2012 and is administered by the Criminal Injuries Compensation Authority (CICA). It provides compensation to defined classes of claimants who have been the victim of a 'crime of violence' or other specified criminal injury (CICA, *The Criminal Injuries Compensation Scheme 2012* (amended 2019), paras 4–7). There are eligibility conditions that must be satisfied before an award can be made (*ibid.*, paras 10ff), and awards can be reduced or withheld on grounds of the applicant's unreasonable conduct (*ibid.*, paras 22ff). Until 1996, awards were assessed in accordance with the rules of assessment for common law damages, but since then there has been a statutory 'tariff' which now consists of twenty different levels of compensation for physical and mental injury, with separate tariffs for sexual and physical abuse; the maximum tariff-sum payable is £250,000. Loss of earnings (beyond the first twenty-eight weeks) and 'special expenses' may also be compensated under the scheme; the rules for calculating these awards are similar to but less generous than those at common law (*ibid.*, paras 42ff). The maximum total amount payable in respect of a single injury is £500,000 (*ibid.*, para. 31). In 2020–21, the scheme resolved 27,669 applications (10,478 were disallowed) and paid out tariff compensation totalling over £153 million to victims of crime (CICA, *Annual Report and Accounts 2020–21* (HC395, 2021)). The number of applications was impacted by the COVID-19 pandemic and was 20 per cent below the five-year average of 34,467 (*ibid.*, 18).

For a discussion of the background to the 1995 Act, and the controversy caused by its adoption, see Ganz, 'Criminal Injuries Compensation: The Constitutional Issue' (1996) 59 MLR 95. For further discussion, see *Atiyah*, ch. 12.

After the 7/7 terrorist attacks on London in 2005, there were calls to treat the victims of terrorist violence as a special case, and to restore to them the full compensation entitlements enjoyed by ordinary tort claimants. Initially, the government was strongly opposed, reiterating the longstanding policy of treating payments under the scheme as akin to charity rather than the discharge of a liability, though it did take steps in 2012 to extend compensation entitlements to the victims of acts of terrorism abroad (*Victims of Overseas Terrorism Compensation Scheme 2012*). Following further domestic terrorism incidents, however, there was another public consultation (Ministry of Justice, *Criminal Injuries Compensation Scheme Review 2020*, CP277, July 2020) and the government announced its intention to create a new standalone scheme for victims of both domestic and overseas terrorism. Amongst other proposals contained in the review is the removal of the 'same roof' rule that currently prevents the award of criminal injuries compensation if, at the time of the injury, the applicant and assailant were adults living together and they continue to do so. The rule is considered to disadvantage the female victims of domestic violence in particular. In June 2019, the scope of the rule had already been narrowed to exclude children from its application (Criminal Injuries Compensation Scheme 2012 (Amendment) Instrument 2019), following a Court of Appeal ruling that this was discriminatory against them on account of their age (*JT v First-Tier Tribunal* [2019] 1 WLR 1313).

Is it fair that victims of criminal violence should receive less compensation than those awarded tort damages for comparable injuries? Is it fair that they should receive more than accident victims who have to rely upon social security?

A No-Fault Scheme for Victims of Medical Misadventure?

The idea of a no-fault scheme for the victims of medical misadventure (including, but going beyond, medical negligence) has been on and off the political agenda for the last couple of decades. No-fault schemes were twice proposed in Private Members' Bills put before Parliament in the early 1990s, though nothing came of either initiative through lack of government support. Notwithstanding this lack of success, the British Medical Association campaigned for many years for the introduction of 'no fault', and remains a vociferous critic of the current clinical negligence regime. The matter returned to the political agenda, largely as a result of recommendations in the report of Sir Ian Kennedy's inquiry into infant deaths in the cardiac unit at the Bristol Royal Infirmary (Bristol Royal Infirmary Inquiry, *Learning from Bristol: The Report of the Public Inquiry into Children's Heart Surgery at the Bristol Royal Infirmary 1984–1995*, CM 5207(1), 2001: http://www.bristol-inquiry.org.uk/final_report/the_report.pdf). The report recommended the abolition of the clinical negligence system, which acts as a disincentive to open reporting and the discussion of adverse events and near misses, and its replacement with 'an alternative system for compensating those patients who suffer harm arising out of treatment from the NHS' (para. 119). However, a subsequent report by the Chief Medical Officer (*Making Amends: A Consultation Paper Setting Out Proposals for Reforming the Approach to Clinical Negligence in the NHS* (Department of Health, 2003)) rejected the Kennedy recommendation because it believed that a true no-fault scheme could potentially lead to huge increases in claims numbers and costs, might alternatively offer only limited compensation not meeting the needs of the victim and might reduce incentives on health professionals to take reasonable care. Notwithstanding these concerns, the report thought that there was a case for no-fault compensation to be paid in respect of birth injuries resulting in severe neurological impairment, but this was not taken up in the subsequent Act, whose main purpose was to establish a scheme for the resolution of low-value clinical negligence claims against the NHS without recourse to civil proceedings (NHS Redress Act 2006). One of the aims of the reform was to safeguard public funds by persuading victims of clinical negligence to accept (at their discretion) special care packages offered by the NHS rather than seeking private care, the costs of which would in principle be recoverable from the NHS in an action in tort (see further in Ch. 15.IV.3(b)). Notwithstanding the considerable passage of time, the regulations required to implement the scheme have not yet been forthcoming in England, though it has already been established in Wales (National Health Service (Concerns, Complaints and Redress Arrangements) (Wales) Regulations 2011, SI 2011/704 (W.108)).

(b) Universal No-Fault Compensation

Compared with the piecemeal and secondary approach to no-fault compensation that has so far prevailed in the United Kingdom, a more radical approach would be to introduce no-fault compensation *in place of* liability for personal injuries in the law of tort. The *Pearson Commission* declined to take such a radical step—construing its terms of reference narrowly so as to preclude a comprehensive reform of this nature—and indicated that the fault principle was still of intuitive appeal to some of its members. In New Zealand, by contrast, this bold reform had already been implemented. In 1974, following a path-finding report by a Royal Commission of Inquiry, the right to recover compensatory damages for personal injury was abolished, and its place taken by a claim under a state-organised, no-fault compensation scheme.

Royal Commission of Inquiry (Chairman: The Honourable Mr Justice Woodhouse), *Compensation for Personal Injury in New Zealand* (Wellington, NZ: Government Printer, 1967)

The toll of personal injury is one of the disastrous incidents of social progress, and the statistically inevitable victims are entitled to receive a coordinated response from the nation as a whole. They receive this only from the health service. For financial relief they must turn to three entirely different remedies, and frequently they are aided by none.

The negligence action is a form of lottery. In the case of industrial accidents it provides inconsistent solutions for less than one victim in every hundred. The Workers' Compensation Act provides meagre compensation for workers, but only if their injury occurred at their work. The Social Security Act will assist with the pressing needs of those who remain, provided they can meet the means test. All others are left to fend for themselves.

Such a fragmented and capricious response to a social problem which cries out for coordinated and comprehensive treatment cannot be good enough. No economic reason justifies it. It is a situation which needs to be changed . . .

We have made recommendations which recognise the inevitability of two fundamental principles.

First, no satisfactory system of injury insurance can be organised except on a basis of community responsibility;

Second, wisdom, logic, and justice all require that every citizen who is injured must be included, and equal losses must be given equal treatment. There must be comprehensive entitlement. Moreover, always accepting the obvious need to produce something which the country can afford, it seemed necessary to lay down three further rules which, taken together with the two fundamental matters, would provide the framework for the new system. There must be complete rehabilitation. There must be real compensation—income-related benefits for income losses, payment throughout the whole period of incapacity, recognition of permanent bodily impairment as a loss in itself. And there must be administrative efficiency . . .

Community Responsibility—If the well-being of the work force is neglected, the economy must suffer injury. For this reason the nation has not merely a clear duty but also a vested interest in urging forward the physical and economic rehabilitation of every adult citizen whose activities bear upon the general welfare. This is the plain answer to any who might query the responsibility of the community in the matter. Of course, the injured worker himself has a moral claim, and further a more material claim based upon his earlier contribution, or his readiness to contribute to the national product. But the whole community has a very real stake in the matter . . .

Injury, not Cause, is the Issue—Once the principle of community responsibility is recognised the principle of comprehensive entitlement follows automatically. Few would attempt to argue that injured workers should be treated by society in different ways depending upon the cause of injury. Unless economic reasons demanded it the protection and remedy society might have to offer could not in justice be concentrated upon a single type of accident to the exclusion of others. With the admirable exception of the health services this has occurred in the past. There has been such concentration upon the risks faced by men during the working day that the considerable hazards they must face during the rest of each 24 hours (particularly on every road in the country) have been virtually disregarded. But workers do not change their status at 5 p.m., and if injured on the highway or at home they are the same men, and their needs and their country's needs of them are unchanged.

COMMENTARY

The Woodhouse Commission envisaged that the scheme it proposed would be financed by the abolition of tort liability for personal injuries and the application of the funds thereby saved to the new system. The institution of the new no-fault system would make tort law simply 'irrelevant' (para. 280).

New Zealand's Accident Compensation Scheme came into operation on 1 April 1974, enacting—with a few notable exceptions—the proposals of the Woodhouse Committee. In what was viewed as a 'social contract' between the state and the people of New Zealand, the right to sue for compensation for personal injury was abolished in return for the introduction of a system of no-fault compensation. The essential elements of the scheme as introduced can be summarised as follows:

(i) Coverage was dependent upon the suffering of a 'personal injury by accident'. It was not necessary to prove that this was occasioned by another's breach of duty: effectively, the requirement of 'fault' was replaced by that of 'accident'.

(ii) Compensation was offered for loss of earnings ('earnings-related compensation', paid on a periodic basis at 80 per cent of pre-accident earnings, at least in so far as these did not exceed a fixed 'cap'); non-pecuniary loss (originally paid in the form of lump sums); medical costs and adjustment expenses; and loss of dependency.

(iii) Levies on employers, motor vehicle licence holders and others provided the principal source of finance for the scheme, with the balance being met out of general taxation.

Reform of the Scheme

The scheme has been subjected to significant reforms on several occasions. In 1992, a number of changes were made to it in an effort to reverse the steady 'cost creep' and resultant financial problems which had afflicted the scheme in the 1980s (see Accident Rehabilitation and Compensation Insurance Act 1992). First, a new and more rigid definition of compensatable personal injury was introduced in order to prevent incremental expansions in the scope of coverage that were thought to have resulted from reliance upon the largely undefined notion of 'personal injury by accident'. Secondly, the benefits payable under the scheme were limited in a number of respects, notably by replacing the right to lump-sum compensation for non-pecuniary loss with an entitlement, in cases of residual disability only, to an independence allowance. Lastly, the funding basis of the scheme was altered in an attempt to impose a greater degree of individual responsibility upon those actually responsible for accidents (especially by providing for experience-rating in the setting of individual levies).

Then, in 1998, new legislation provided for the opening up of workplace injury insurance to a competitive market (Accident Insurance Act 1998). The legislation imposed a requirement on all employers to purchase private accident insurance for work-related personal injuries suffered by their employees, although the state was to continue to provide personal injury insurance cover for injuries not occurring in the workplace. In addition, self-employed persons could opt to continue within the state-run scheme.

A change of government in 2000 heralded an additional round of changes. Undoing many of the previous reforms, the partial privatisation of the scheme set out in the preceding text was ended and the state again became responsible for its running (Accident Compensation Act 2001). Another reversion to the past was the re-introduction of lump sum compensation for permanent impairment in place of the independence allowance introduced in 1992. These changes returned the scheme to something close to its form at the time of its establishment in 1974, and it broadly retains this form notwithstanding further legislative intervention since.

Views of the Scheme

According to Sir Geoffrey Palmer, one of the architects of the scheme and subsequently New Zealand's Prime Minister, the no-fault regime 'signal[led] the achievement of real security upon which a better society can be built' (*Compensation for Incapacity* (Wellington, New Zealand: OUP, 1979), p. 407). The secret of the new scheme's success lay in its very moderate administrative costs—approximately 15 cents per New Zealand dollar of compensation (cf. the administrative costs of tort compensation in I.2)—which enabled it to spread its net of compensation far wider than tort for the same total expenditure. Yet, although the scheme has been held up as a model of enlightened reform by critics of the tort system in other jurisdictions, no other jurisdiction in the Anglo-American legal world has followed its lead. In contrast, the 'social insurance' systems of some civilian jurisdictions, e.g. Sweden, achieve much the same results and can be regarded as comparable initiatives.

The following extract summarises some common criticisms of the New Zealand scheme.

J. Henderson, 'The New Zealand Accident Compensation Reform' (1981) 48 U Chi L Rev 781

[In a review of G. Palmer, *Compensation for Incapacity*, Henderson sets out a series of arguments in an effort to undermine the claims made for the New Zealand scheme by Palmer and other supporters.]

A. The Failure to Compensate Some Accident Victims Was Not a Significant Social Problem

One who believes that accident victims who recover little or nothing through the tort system present a significant social problem probably is thinking of the relatively few instances in which serious and permanent injuries cause great financial hardship for the victims and their families. Such cases do occur, and some are tragic. But there was no strong correlation between suffering accidental injury and experiencing financial hardship. Only a small percentage of accident victims encountered significant financial hardship, because of the availability of free medical care and, for many accident victims, of other benefits, including public welfare and personal savings. (Studies of automobile accident cases in the United States, for example, indicate that a small percentage (no more than five percent) of accident victims suffer significant dislocation costs . . . It seems reasonable to assume that in New Zealand, with its greater public welfare programs, the percentage was no higher, and probably lower.) To the unfortunate few who fell into the hardship category, of course, the problems were significant. But it would seem more realistic to view this minority as part of the problem of poverty than as part of the problem of uncompensated accident victims . . . Thus, the New Zealand compensation system can be justified on the basis of social welfare principles only if those principles are expanded to include welfare for those not in particular financial need . . . [T]his is, in essence, a social welfare system for the middle and upper-classes . . .

B. The Common Law Tort System Never Purported to Address All Unexpected Financial Hardships of Individuals . . .

The reformers [in New Zealand] understood that the expanded no-fault compensation system could become a reality only if it replaced the tort system, because otherwise the need for new funding would be so great as to render unattractive any expanded commitment to compensation. Thus, there had to be an 'utterly devastating' attack on the common law. If the reformers had focused on the true objectives of tort law—the enhancement of social utility and the promotion of shared notions of fairness—the attack would have fallen short. The reformers possessed no empirical data to support conclusions that the tort system had failed to achieve either of these objectives, so the focus of attention had to be shifted to the compensation objective for the attack to succeed. Indeed, once the compensation objective is considered paramount, it is self-evident that a system promising 'integrated and comprehensive . . . compensation that is usually swift and sure' is preferable to one that offers only '[u]ncertain, uncoordinated, and capricious remedies.'

Thus, the strategy of reform that led to the Act was to attack the tort system for failing to achieve an objective that it never purported to recognize and then to belittle as tangential and ineffective its efforts to enhance utility and fairness . . .

C. The New Zealand System is an Inadequate Solution to the Problem of Financial Disruptions . . .

[T]here is no reason why victims of misfortunes other than accidents should not have equally valid claims to compensation as accident victims. Why, for example, should the working person whose leg must be amputated because of cancer be denied benefits because he lost his leg through disease rather than by accident? Diseases such as cancer may often cause more significant disruptions in people's lives than accidents . . . If the New Zealand system is not expanded, what will have emerged from the reforms is a system that violates the principle of compensating victims of unexpected misfortune even as it purports to embody that principle. One may wonder whether the critics who spoke of the 'false morality' of tort law will be able to appreciate the hypocrisy reflected in the system they helped create . . .

D. The New Zealand System is Likely to have Negative Effects on Allocative Efficiency and Fairness

The tort system's objectives include the enhancement of allocative efficiency and the promotion of shared notions of fairness. The former objective is accomplished by deterring unacceptably risky conduct, the latter by providing private remedies against those who commit wrongs. The tort system does fail to compensate some accident victims who have suffered loss, but it must neglect the compensation objective if it is accomplish the others. Replacing the tort system with a compensation system may well generate benefits only at the cost of detracting from efficiency and fairness . . .

Generally, if actors are not required to pay a fair share of the costs of their activities, including the accident costs, they will tend to overengage in those activities whose costs they can most successfully escape from paying. Thus, if everyone were required to pay into a universal accident compensation fund on a flat-rate, per capita basis, those who engaged in comparatively safe activities would pay more than their share of the total accident costs generated by all activities, and those who engaged in relatively risky activities would pay less. The resulting wealth transfers would encourage actors at the margin (those indifferent to which sort of activities to engage in) to switch from safe to risky activities. Not everyone would switch, but enough would to cause the overall accident costs in the society to increase over what they would have been if those engaging in relatively safe activities had not been required to subsidize their risk-preferring fellow citizens. Resources would be misallocated to relatively risky activities; the increase in accident costs would constitute social waste.

The solution to this problem of waste, one that to a limited extent was incorporated in the New Zealand scheme, is to require contribution to the compensation fund in proportion to the risk of accidents created by the actor. If the amount contributed is appropriate, the proper

> balance between safe and risky activities will be achieved. The tort system consciously aims at attaching the appropriate price tags to risky conduct, but there is no reason in theory why a system providing universal compensation could not do the same thing . . .
>
> [Henderson finds, however, that in practice there is 'little likelihood of achieving adequate safety incentives under the New Zealand scheme', mainly because of the very high administrative costs involved in ascertaining the riskiness of different activities and in imposing differential levies on the basis of that information; p. 669.]
>
> In addition to considering the potentially negative effects on allocative efficiency of moving to a compensation system such as the one adopted in New Zealand, such a move must be assessed from the standpoint of shared notions of fairness. A New Zealand-type system can be criticized on several fairness grounds. First, citizens would no longer have some of the traditional methods of vindicating individual rights in our legal system. A person intentionally struck by another, for example, would no longer be entitled to a legal judgment that his right to personal integrity had been violated. Second, the anomalies created by the Act are open to attack. For example, distinctions drawn between illness and accidental injury under the system cause persons similarly disadvantaged to be treated differently. Third, the measures of recovery include a number of arbitrary limits that cause persons dissimilarly disadvantaged to receive essentially the same benefits. Finally, the procedures under the compensation system reflect a willingness to sacrifice the interests of the individual to the greater good.

COMMENTARY

The New Zealand experience is relied upon by both proponents and opponents of no-fault compensation. It remains an open question whether no-fault is desirable in principle and feasible in practice. It is, however, notable that New Zealand's accident compensation scheme has maintained very broad cross-party political support, as well as the support of the unions, (some) employers' organisations and legal and medical professional bodies in that country.

For further comment, see Miller, 'The Future of New Zealand's Accident Compensation Scheme' (1989) 11 Hawaii L Rev 1; Palmer, 'New Zealand's Accident Compensation Scheme: Twenty Years On' (1994) U of Toronto LJ 223; Gaskins, 'Regulating private law: Socio-legal perspectives on the New Zealand Accident Compensation Scheme' (2009) 17 TLJ 12; Todd, 'Forty Years of Accident Compensation in New Zealand' (2011) 28 TM Cooley L Rev 189; Palmer, 'A Retrospective on the Woodhouse Report: The Vision, the Performance and the Future' (2019) 50 VUWLR 401. For a proposal to introduce comprehensive no-fault compensation in the United States see S. Sugarman, *Doing Away with Personal Injury Law* (New York: Quorum, 1989).

(c) Compensation for Incapacity to be Exclusively a Matter of Private Insurance

In his classic work, *The Common Law*, Oliver Wendell Holmes rejected the idea of a state-run mutual insurance scheme of the type subsequently introduced in New Zealand on the basis that '[s]tate interference is an evil'. In his view, '[u]niversal insurance, if desired, can be better and more cheaply accomplished by private enterprise' (p. 77). Holmes did not consider the possibility that tort compensation for personal injury might be abolished with a view to letting private insurance provision take its place, but this option has in more recent times been advocated by Patrick Atiyah in his book, *The Damages Lottery* (1997). Some time previously, Atiyah had been a well-known proponent of the type of reform adopted in New Zealand in the 1970s, namely, the introduction of a no-fault compensation scheme in place of tort compensation. Indeed, Atiyah actually sat on the Australian Woodhouse Commission that recommended a similar (in fact, more extensive) reform for that country a few years later. (A change of government meant that the reform never took place.) The 'early Atiyah' made his name with his book *Accidents, Compensation and the Law*, which survives in something like its original state in the most recent edition by Peter Cane and James Goudkamp. Atiyah meanwhile has moved on: from 'woolly liberal', with a belief in the capacity of the state to protect individual welfare, to supporter of the free market, with a deep antipathy to state interference and a preference for individual responsibility. The 'late-period Atiyah' is to be found in his subsequent book, *The Damages Lottery*, which decries the extent to which both tort law and no-fault compensation schemes encourage a so-called 'blame culture'. In the following extract, Atiyah presents his new vision for reform.

P. S. Atiyah, *The Damages Lottery* (Oxford: Hart, 1997)

The action for damages for personal injuries should simply be abolished, and first-party insurance should be left to the free market. This proposal might seem at first little short of revolutionary, but closer examination shows that it is a perfectly natural development of current trends.

For a start, it should not be assumed that the action for damages for personal injuries is in any sense a real cornerstone of our legal system. This type of legal liability is of quite recent origin in the history of modern legal systems. In fact it is little more than a century old, and its rise closely parallels the rise of third-party liability insurance . . . Unfortunately, the law got onto the wrong track from the very outset, developing and encouraging third-party insurance instead of first-party insurance. So to abolish the action for damages for personal injuries today would only be to put the law back onto the right lines from which it diverged a hundred years ago. Many countries have already abolished the action for damages for special kinds of injuries, such as road accidents and workers' compensation injuries. There is no evidence that this causes any sense of grievance or public outrage, provided that some kind of alternative insurance system is put in its place . . . [I]f the case for abolition of the present system is once agreed to be made out [sic], the only really practical alternative today . . . seems to be to leave the matter largely to the free market. If we don't do this, we shall probably end up with a whole collection of special compensation schemes, one for road accidents, one for workers' compensation, one perhaps for medical injuries, one for sporting injuries and so on. The compensation payable for all these kinds of injuries will doubtless differ from case to case, with just as many anomalies and absurdities as we have today. Only if we allow people the free choice to make their own decisions as to what kind of insurance they want, will these variations become acceptable.

Of course, a transitional period of several years would be needed before such a change could be implemented, and in the interim it would be necessary for the insurance industry, with pressure from the government, to come up with some sensible proposals for first-party insurance schemes to be established which would cover the most ordinary forms of accident. People would in this way be encouraged to insure themselves and their families against these risks. No doubt this would not be done on an individual policy basis—groups of people would be encouraged to take out policies together. For example, schools should take out policies to cover their children against sporting injuries on a no-fault basis (actually this is already beginning). Employers and trade unions should be encouraged to co-operate in taking out policies to cover the workers against industrial accidents. Homeowners' insurance policies should cover people against accidents in the home on a no-fault basis. Pregnant women should be encouraged to insure against the risk of having a disabled baby. And so on . . .

[T]he basic point must be the gradual encouragement of first-party insurance by more and more people, with the state simply acting as a fall-back protection for those who have no insurance of their own. There would be enormous advantages in this course. First, we should get rid of all the wasteful legal and administrative costs associated with claims for damages and third-party insurance . . . Secondly, it will vastly improve the coverage which most people have against a large variety of risks. Instead of being offered a small, often a minuscule chance of recovering enormous damages for some injuries, people will have a much better chance of obtaining reasonable compensation for all, or anyhow, most injuries. What is more, the compensation will be obtainable on a much fairer basis than the present lottery—broadly, you will get what you choose to pay for. Third, this reform would begin the job of getting rid of the artificial distinctions embodied in the present law and practice between accidental injuries and disabilities from other causes . . .

Fourth, the shift to a free market in insurance would introduce a great deal of consumer choice in an area where it is significantly absent today . . . [I]t could enable people to decide what level of income they want to insure, whether they want life insurance and so on. For this reason, also, it will distribute more equitably the burden of many accidents, where at present the third-party system favours the more highly-paid and discriminates against the low-paid, the unemployed and the retired. It means that the right people would be paying for the insurance cover for their own possible income losses . . .

Some may object that this idea is all very well for those who can afford to insure themselves, but what about those who can't? But the answer to this is that almost everybody will actually save more money by abolishing the present system than they will need to pay for their new first-party insurance. The poorest people, especially, will actually save on their motor insurance policies, which should become substantially cheaper for those on low incomes, or for the pensioners who don't need income-loss protection or life insurance cover. And even those who don't have cars will save on the price of goods and services, as businesses will no longer have to pay huge premiums to cover the risk of damages claims. Of course some state social security safety net will still be needed for those who are not otherwise covered at all.

This would indeed be a reform worth striving for.

COMMENTARY

Do you agree with Atiyah that the time has now come to abolish the tort system for compensating personal injuries? Is it satisfactory to leave compensation to the free market, via first-party insurance policies, especially for those on low incomes? (Consider Kalven's comment: 'If the poor were not quite so poor, we could decently ask them to provide their own accident insurance' ((1955) 33 Texas L Rev 778 at 782).)

In fact, Atiyah does suggest one very significant qualification to his proposed turn to the free market: there should be compulsory first-party insurance in respect of road accidents. He seems to view the abolition of tort liability on the roads, and its replacement with such a scheme, as a first step towards the complete abolition of tort. For 'purely pragmatic reasons', namely, 'too many people would probably end up without any cover' if this new kind of insurance were entirely voluntary (p. 187), Atiyah proposes that there should be a compulsory element to it. He suggests, however, that the compulsory element could be limited (e.g. allowing for only modest levels of income replacement) and that it should be possible to acquire 'top up' policies on a voluntary basis.

Why should compulsory first party insurance be limited to the road traffic context? Does the risk that 'too many people would probably end up without any cover' arise in other contexts too? Do you think that there should be a compulsory basic level of insurance protection for everyone, albeit of course with the ability to purchase 'top up' protection as well? Should this reform be pursued wholly outside the social security system, or is there a case for integrating at least the compulsory elements of any reformed system of accident or disability compensation within the social security system?

Following Atiyah, Smillie, 'The Future of Negligence' (2007) 15 TLJ 300 also advocates the abolition of the tort of negligence and its replacement with 'nothing', though he would favour higher levels of state income protection than envisaged by Atiyah. For criticism of Atiyah's approach, see Ripstein, 'Some Recent Obituaries of Tort Law' (1998) 48 UTLJ 561; Conaghan and Mansell, 'From the Permissive to the Dismissive Society: Patrick Atiyah's Accidents, Compensation and the Market' (1998) 25 JLS 284.

INDEX

actions on the case 7–8, 625, 664
aims of tort law 18–22
  see also justice
  appeasement 18, 20
  compensation 19
  deterrence 19, 20–1
apportionment
  contributory
    negligence 312–20
arrest and detention 81–5
  citizen's arrest 81
  police 81
  reasonableness 105
  rule of law 81
  use of reasonable force 81
assault
  conditional assault 52
  consent 88
  criminal offence of assault 51
  definition 49
  immediacy or imminence requirement 49–52
  intention 52–3
  reasonableness of apprehension of force 52–3
  silent telephone calls 50–3
  threats 50–1
  trespass to the person 31
  words 50–1
assumpsit 5–6, 8, 10, 106

battery
  consent 87–8
  definition 53–5
  horseplay 53–5
  hostility 55
  implied consent 55
  intention 53
  medical treatment 100
  necessity 100
  police 56
  touching 53–5
  trespass 8, 31, 57
breach of duty 171–226
  see also fault
  clinical negligence 194–5
  common practice 215–21
  cost of precautions 185–8
  dangerous substances 196
  defective products 118–19, 196
  defendant's standpoint, negligence from the 194–9

exclusion of liability 296, 543, 553
experience 202–5
foreseeability 171–4, 181–5, 196
negligence, definition of 173
precautions 171–7, 185–8, 196
precedential value of decisions 176
probability of harm 171–4, 181–5
questions of fact and law 175–6
reasonableness 543
recklessness 198–9
res ipsa loquitur 221–6
Social Action, Responsibility and Heroism Act 2015 191–2
sport 193, 196–9
temporal dimension 194–8
terminology of special and general duties 176
utility of defendant's conduct 188–94
breach of statutory duty 601–24
  common employment defence 607–8
  common law 602
  development 602–7
  distinguished from other statutory liabilities 601–2
  foreseeability 619
  parliamentary intent, indicators of 607–17
  prisons, segregation of 612–13
  reform 619–24
  relevance 601
  scope of protection 617–19
  strict liability 601
burden of proof
  defamation 738
  material contribution 249–51
  res ipsa loquitur 221–6
  trespass to the person 43–4
but-for test *see* causation

capacity *see* consent
care
  see also damages for personal injury
  damages 955–60
  gratuitous services 929–33, 955–60

household services 933
substituted services 955–60
case, trespass on the 5–6, 7–9, 44–5, 102
causation 227–83
  see also intervening acts; scope of liability
  but-for test 227–65
  contribution 281–3
  contributory negligence 307–12
  epidemiological evidence 259–60
  factual causation 227–73
  indeterminate defendant 263–4
  loss of a chance 241–2
  material contribution 242–65
  multiple sufficient causes 265–73
  remoteness 227, 283–9
  rescuers 283
  third parties 281–3, 491–523
  uncertainty 262–3
children
  allurements 526
  birth injuries 1006
  capacity to consent 88
  congenital disabilities 130–4
  contributory negligence 315–20
  foreseeability of injury 210–13
  Gillick competency 100
  occupiers' liability 526, 537–8
  severely disabled children 1003
  standard of care 201, 210–13
Civil Justice Review 966
civil procedure
  see also costs
  criticisms 978
  damages-based agreements 982–3
  funding of personal injury claims 979–82
  offers to settle 989
  process of making claim 975–84
  road traffic accidents 995–6
  small claims 983–4
  Woolf reforms 978–9, 984
classification of obligations 9–12

clinical negligence *see* **breach of duty; professional negligence**
collateral benefits, deductions of *see* **damages for personal injury**
compensation culture 19–20, 24–41, 968
  Better Regulation Task Force 34–6, 39, 40, 192
  claims management companies 34, 38
  Compensation Act 2006 39–40, 191–4
  deterrence 33, 39, 192
  individual responsibility 32–4
  insurance 28
  legislative intervention 38–41
  McDonald's coffee case 37–8
  media 35, 192–3
  risk assessment 36
  tort reform in other countries 40–1
  volunteers, deterrence of 39
Compensation Recovery Unit (CRU) 939, 966–7
congenital disabilities 130–4, 1003
consent
  see also **volenti non fit injuria**
  advance consent to sexual contact 88
  assault 88
  battery 55, 87–8
  capacity 88
  children, capacity of 88
  contraceptive treatment 88
  duress 87
  false imprisonment 88–91
  fraud 87–8
  HIV status, failure to disclose 88
  identity of person, mistake as to 87
  implied consent 55
  intentional interference with the person 86–92
  knowledge 86
  medical treatment 86–7, 88
  mental disabilities, capacity of persons with 88
  public policy 88
  revocation 88–92
  sado-masochistic acts 88
  sexual assault, fraud and 87
  sports 88
  trespass to the person 86
contract
  concurrent liability in contract and tort 24, 450–2
  consideration 426

employment contracts 817, 823–9
exemption clauses 320–6
privity of contract 114
unfair contract terms 296, 320–6
contributory negligence 307–12
  apportionment 312–20
  breach of duty 181
  causation 307, 312–20
  children 315–20
  crime, involvement in 79–80
  defective products 120–1
  discount 319–20
  discretion 319
  drink driving 299–302
  fault 308–12
  foreseeability 311
  historical background 307–8
  intervening acts 279–81
  last clear chance doctrine 309
  Law Reform (Contributory Negligence) Act 1945 308–12
  mistake 104
  volenti non fit injuria 299–302
costs
  damages-based agreements 982–3
  fixed costs 983
  funding of personal injury claims 979–82
  Part 36 offers and payments 989
  road traffic accidents 995–6
criminal injuries compensation
  assessment 1005
  eligibility 1005
  loss of earnings 1005
  no-fault compensation 1004–5
  tariff 1005
  terrorism, victims of 1005

damage 123–6
damages
  see also **damages and death; damages for personal injury; exemplary or punitive damages; no-fault compensation**
  adequacy 990–3
  aggravated damages 896
  Civil Justice Review 966
  Compensation Act 2006 39–40, 192–4, 253
  compensatory damages 19, 20, 885, 891, 896
  contemptuous damages 897–8

defamation 698, 734, 766–71, 775
deterrence function 19, 20–1
dishonest claims 973–5
empirical studies 964–75
exemplary or punitive damages 698, 767, 886–95
fraudulent claims 973–4
justice function 18–19, 21–2
knock-for-knock agreements 995
nominal damages 897
propensity to sue 969–73
proportional damages 244–8, 260–1
purpose of damages 885
reform 974–5
responsibility for payment 993–5
restitutionary damages 885–6, 888
settlements 984–9
statistics 967–8
trespass to land 885
types of damages 885–98
unjust enrichment 885, 888
when claims are made 964–75
whiplash claims 973–4
who makes claim 964–75
damages and death 940–63
  apportionment 950, 953
  benefits arising from death 950, 954–60
  bereavement damages 943, 949, 961–3
  caring services 955–60
  cause of action, death as 944–8
  Civil Law Reform Bill 952, 955, 960
  civil partnerships 951
  cohabitees 951
  common law 944–6
  contributory negligence 947, 950, 954
  dependants 942–3, 946, 948–60
  divorce, prospects of 954
  expenses 943
  Fatal Accidents Act 1976 940, 943, 948–60
  funeral expenses 943, 953
  Law Reform (Miscellaneous Provisions) Act 1934 940–3
  loss of expectation of life 943–4
  pain and suffering 940, 943–4
  pecuniary losses 953
  periodical payments 953

personal representatives 947
relational loss 946
remarriage 954
survival of actions 944
**damages for personal
  injury** 885–98
  acceleration element in lump
    sum awards 898
  care costs 905, 925–33
  children 919–20
  collateral benefits, deduction
    of 934–6
  Compensation Recovery
    Unit 939
  deductions 934–5
  discount rate 916
  function 885, 906
  functional approach 913
  future care 904
  future losses 898, 915–25
  general damages 906–9
  guidelines 907–8
  indexation 917–18
  inflation 898, 907
  insurance 908, 934
  interest 898, 906
  life expectancy 913, 920–5
  loss of amenity 909–15
  loss of earnings 920, 934, 939
  lost years 920–5
  lump sums 898–905, 916–17
  medical care 906, 925–33
  mitigation of loss 926–9
  multiplicands 916–17
  multipliers 916–17
  non-pecuniary losses 906–15
  Ogden Tables 916
  pain and suffering
    909–15, 939
  periodical payment orders
    (PPOs) 902–4, 916
  periodical payments 898–905,
    916, 917–18
  provisional damages 899
  sick pay, deduction of 934
  social security benefits,
    recoupment of 905, 934,
    936–9
  special damages 906
  stepped orders 904
  structured settlements
    899, 903
  unconsciousness, effect
    of 914–15
  variable orders 904
  variable PPOs 902–4
**damages-based
  agreements** 982–3
death *see* **damages and death**
deceit 421
defamation 698–781
  see also **privilege**
  amends, offers of 729

apologies 726, 767
archival material 736–7
assessment of
  damages 766–71
bulletin boards or chat
  rooms 734–5
burden of proof 738
business, imputation of
  unfitness in 703
caching 735
causes of action, elements
  of 704–37
chilling effect 736, 774–5
'common sting' 739, 740
correction, duty to
  publish 766
criminal conduct, imputation
  of 702–3, 707, 742
damages 698, 734, 766–71,
  775, 889, 944
Defamation Act 2013 702,
  738, 743
defamatory
  hatred, contempt and
    ridicule 705–6
  homosexuality,
    imputations of 707
  insults and jokes 706–7
  sexual behaviour 703, 707
  standards of opinion 713–15
  threshold of
    seriousness 708–13
  unchastity 703
defences 698, 737–66
  honest opinion 698, 742–6
  innocent
    dissemination 760–3
  mere conduit defence 735
  offers of amends 729,
    760–3
  publication on matter of
    public interest 698, 737,
    755–60
  reportage 760
  responsible journalism,
    former defence of 755,
    758–60
  truth 698, 702, 724,
    738–42, 794
  unintentional defamation,
    defence of 726
directly relevant background
  context 771
distributors 734, 763–6
evidence of bad
  reputation 770
exemplary damages 698,
  767, 889
'false light' 794
Faulks Committee 702, 944
freedom of expression 32,
  698, 726, 729–30, 736,
  775–81

grapevine effect 733
group defamation 730–2
historical origins 699
honest opinion 698, 742–6,
  770–1
Human Rights Act 1998 31–2,
  698, 729, 736, 775–81
identification of
  claimant 726–30
injunctions 698, 772–3
innuendo 715–26, 724
insolvency 707
interim injunctions 698,
  772–3
internet 734–5
justification 698, 702, 738–42,
  794
knowledge of defamatory
  meaning 724–6
libel 698, 699–700, 786
  distinguished from
    slander 699–700
malice 699, 701, 752–4
meaning, questions
  of 715–26
multiple allegations 740
negative checking 728
Neill Committee 762, 944
news reports 728
newspapers
  archives 736
  freedom of
    expression 775–81
  qualified privilege 746
  reportage 760
  responsible
    journalism 755, 758–60
operators of websites 765–6
pictures 706
Porter Commission 702, 726
postcard rule 733
press 736, 760, 775–81
privilege 746–54
  absolute privilege 747
  common law 747–50
  duty to communicate 749
  excess of privilege 749–50
  interest in
    communicating 749
  media 747–54
  public authorities 750
  qualified privilege 737,
    747–52
public authorities 776–9
publication 727, 732–7
  multiple publication
    rule 736–7
  single publication
    rule 736–7
refer to claimant, statement
  must 726–30
references from
  employers 449

defamation (*cont.*)
remedies 698, 766–73
repetition 732, 733–4, 741–2
reputation 726, 732, 766–73
shun or avoid 708
single publication rule 736–7
slander 698, 700–3
business, imputation of unfitness in 703
criminal conduct, imputation of 702–3
diseases, imputation of certain contagious 703
special damage 699, 700–3
unchastity, imputation of 703
special damage 699, 700–3
specific instances of general misconduct 740–1
spouse, communication to 732
statements must be defamatory 704–26
'sting' 739, 740
substantial harm, requirement of 708–13
tendency to defame 705–6, 707–8
time limits 736–7
truth
defence 698, 724, 738–42, 770–1
evidence 201
unintentional defamation 726
defective goods/buildings
economic loss 403–21
defective products
see also **strict liability**
breach of duty 118–19, 196
Brexit 562
causation 120–1, 585–6
Consumer Protection Act 1987 555–92
blood products 571–4
Brexit 562
causation 585–6
damage 565–6, 584–5
defective, meaning of 564, 571–80
defences 564–5, 586–91
deterrence 556
development risks defence 586–91
effectiveness 591–2
EU law 562, 568
instructions 584
interpretation 563, 567
liability 563–4
manufacturers 555–92
medical products 574–80
misuse or abuse of products 584

non-standard products 581–2
product, definition of 570–1
Product Liability Directive 555, 586–91
purpose of Act 563
standard products 582–3
strict liability 118, 570–1, 586
suppliers 567
warnings 584
contractual liability 119
duty of care 108–10, 117–21
electric vehicles 597–601
EU law 562, 568
extension of liability 118
fault 119
future of 592–601
instructions 584
manufacturers 117–21, 555–92
rationale for strict liability 556–62
volenti non fit injuria 120
warnings 584
dependants, damages for *see* **damages and death**
direct/indirect distinction 8–9
duty of care 106–66
see also **omissions; pure economic loss; psychiatric injury; public authorities**
actionable damage 123–6
assumpsit 102
assumption of responsibility 154–6
contractual duties 107
corrective justice 142
dangerous articles 108–10, 112–14
deconstruction 121
defective products 108–10, 117–21
fair, just and reasonable test 140
floodgates argument 108, 140
foreseeability 126–34
general duty, formulation of 106–21
historical background 106–10
legal profession 142
modern law 121–57
morality 108, 115
nature of duties 121–2
neighbour principle 110–15, 134, 135–7
notional duty 122–6
overkill argument 145–6
police 141, 143–57
policy 134, 137, 142, 151–3
privity of contract 114

property, defence of 104
protected interests 122
proximity 112, 138–9
rights, correlation to 123
Robinson case 143–57
role 121, 122
three-stage *Caparo* test 134–42, 452–5

EC law *see* **EU law**
economic analysis of law 20–1, 182, 464–7
economic loss *see* **pure economic loss**
egg-shell skull rule 185
see also **remoteness of damage**
emergency services
omissions 477–82
employers' liability
compulsory insurance 39
references 449
statistics 967–8
stress at work 378–83
volenti non fit injuria 302–5
EU law
defective products 555, 562, 568
European Convention on Human Rights
fair hearings 31
freedom of expression 32, 78, 698, 729–30, 736, 775–81, 889
Human Rights Act 1998 28–32
defamation 31–2, 698, 729, 736, 775–81
false imprisonment 85
negligence 31, 166–70
omissions 477
private nuisance 626, 664, 671
public authorities 30
trespass to the person 31
liberty and security, right to 31, 85
life, right to 31
private and family life, right to respect for 664–5, 782, 789, 791, 803–4, 814–15
ex turpi causa **rule** *see* **illegality (*ex turpi causa* rule)**
exclusion of liability
exemption clauses 321–6
statutory controls 296, 321–6, 543, 553
warning notices 320–1
exemplary or punitive damages 886–95
cause of action test 888–9
civil law systems 895

conduct calculated to make a
profit 888
defamation 698, 767, 889, 893
deterrence 895
government servants 888
historical background 886
juries 887, 893
limitations 889–90
media 889
proportionality 895
public authorities, limits
on awards against
the 889–90
United States 895
vicarious liability 894–5
extra-hazardous activities 686

fair comment *see* **defamation**
**fair, just and reasonableness
test** *see* **duty of care**
false imprisonment
consent 88–92
curfews 59–60
damage 60
deportation 59–60
directness 62–5
elements 58–62
Human Rights Act 1998 85
imprisonment, meaning
of 58–9
intention 58–65
jury trial 61
knowledge 61–2
lawful authority defence 85
liberty and security, right
to 31, 85
malicious prosecution 62–5
prison, restrictions of liberty
in 81–5
protestors 60
rape 61
solitary confinement in
prison 81
fatal accidents *see* **damages and
death**
fault 996–1014
see also **breach of duty**
attribution 965
contributory
negligence 308–12
development of fault-based
liability 7–8
moral basis 996–1000
negligence 7–8, 15
no-fault compensation 1000–6
objective standard 998
role of 7
strict liability 14, 176, 996,
998–1000
fire
Rylands v Fletcher, rule
in 694–6
strict liability 694–6

floodgates argument *see* **duty
of care**
force of arms (*vi et armis*) 3–5,
7, 8–9, 13, 42, 43, 57
foreseeability
breach of statutory duty 617
characteristics of
claimants 127–30
children 210–13
congenital disabilities
caused by pre-natal
injuries 130–4
contributory negligence 311
defamation 733
duty of care 126–34
intervening acts 273–8
negligent misstatements 441,
452–4
nuisance 649–51
remoteness 283–9, 289–95
Rylands v Fletcher, rule
in 686, 693
third parties 492, 496, 497
forms of action 2–6
abolition 2, 9–11
actions on the case 7–8, 625,
664
assumpsit 5–6, 8, 10, 102
case, trespass on the 5–6,
44–5
classification of obligations 9
direct/indirect
distinction 8–9
eighteenth-century
developments 8
form of writs 7
Judicature Acts 2, 3, 9–11
nuisance 625
trespass, writs of 2–5, 43,
44–5, 57, 102
writs 2–6
fraud
consent 87–8
negligent
misstatements 421–2
sexual assault 87
freedom of expression *see*
defamation

harassment
course of conduct 79, 792
criminal offence, as 78
definition 76, 77–8
freedom of expression 78
injunctions 658
nuisance 658
prohibition 76–9
health and safety *see* **employers'
liability**
human rights *see* **European
Convention on Human
Rights; Human Rights
Act 1998**

Human Rights Act 1998 28–32
defamation 31–2, 698,
729–30, 736, 775–81
false imprisonment 85
horizontal/vertical effect 167
negligence 31, 166–70
omissions, liability for 477
private nuisance 626, 664–5,
671
public authorities 30
trespass to the person 31

**illegality (*ex turpi causa*
rule)** 326–47
causation 326–47
Henderson case 336–47
joint illegal enterprises 330–2
own criminal acts, recovery for
consequences of 330–4
Patel case 334–6
policy 326–9
professional
negligence 345–7
public policy 334–47
rationale 347–8
seriousness of criminal
conduct 333–4
volenti non fit injuria 296–7
independent contractors
insurance 543
occupiers' liability 540–3
injunctions
defamation 698, 772–3
harassment 658
nuisance 625–6, 649–51, 666,
670–81
privacy 785–9
super injunctions 811–12
insurance 24–8, 966, 987
see also **motor insurance**
compensation culture 28, 39
distribution of loss 25–8
employers' liability compulsory
insurance 39
liability insurance 15–16,
24–8
loss insurance 26
intention
ALI Restatement 47–8
assault 52–3
battery 53
false imprisonment 62
interference with the
person 65–8
negligence, contrasted
with 46–9
trespass to the person 47–9,
65–8
**intentional interference
with the person** *see*
**assault; battery;
false imprisonment;
*Wilkinson v Downton***

INDEX

intervening acts 274–83
see also **causation; scope of liability**
  claimants, acts of 279–81
  contribution 282
  contributory negligence 279–81
  foreseeability 273–8
  joint and several liability 281
  last opportunity test 279
  medical treatment 282
  reasonableness 273–8, 280
  rescuers 273–8
  third parties 273–8, 491
  wrongful acts, intervention by deliberately 279

joint and several liability 281
juries
  exemplary or punitive damages 887, 893
  when jury trial available 13, 61
justice 18–19, 21–2
  corrective justice 21–2
  distributive justice 21
justiciability *see* **public authorities**

landlord and tenant
  omissions 598
libel *see* **defamation**
limitation periods (time limits) 44–6, 132, 416, 445, 585–6, 736–7
loss of amenity, damages for *see* **damages for personal injury**
loss of a chance
  see also **causation**
  but-for test 229–42
  clinical negligence 229–42
  control mechanisms 236
  economic loss 241–2
loss of earnings, damages for *see* **damages for personal injury**
loss of expectation of life, damages for *see* **damages for personal injury**
lost years, damages for *see* **damages for personal injury**

malice
  defamation 699, 701, 752–4
  malicious falsehood 787
  malicious prosecution 64–5
material contribution
  see also **causation**
  asbestosis 249–52, 253–62
  burden of proof 249–51

but-for test 242, 249–52
Compensation Act 2006 253
cumulative contribution 243–4
divisible injuries 244–8
indeterminate defendants 263–4
medical evidence 248–9
proportionality 260–1
risk, contribution to 248–65
single agent 261–2
medical care and damages *see* **damages for personal injury**
mental disabilities
  capacity 88
  false imprisonment 61–2
  Mental Capacity Act 2005 61, 95–101
  standard of care 201, 206–20
misfeasance in public office 84–5, 891–2
Motor Insurers' Bureau 1004
multiple sufficient causes *see* **causation**

necessity 92–105
  autonomy 95–101
  best interests 98–101
  caesareans, consent to 99
  capacity 92–105, 98–101
  conjoined twins 98
  emergencies 93–5
  Gillick competency 100
  medical treatment 93–5, 99–100
  prisoners 98–9
  refusal of treatment 99–100
  self-defence 104
  sterilisation of persons with mental disabilities 93–5
negligence
  see also **breach of duty; causation; contributory negligence; duty of care; fault; omissions; negligent misstatements; professional negligence; pure economic loss; psychiatric illness, duty of care and; public authorities; standard of care**
  actions on the case 7–8
  communitarianism 12–13
  definition 173
  development 8–17
  Human Rights Act 1998 31, 166–70
  individualism 12–13, 15, 17
  modern pre-eminence 12–17

neighbour principle 11–12, 15
public authorities
  alternative remedies 163
  discretion 160–1
  equality principle 157–9
  irrationality 160–1
  justiciability 162–3
  policy/operational dichotomy 162–3
  public law controls 159–63
  reform 164–6
  ultra vires 160–1
  transformative factors 12–13
  trespass to the person and 43–6, 65–8
negligent misstatements
  auditors and accountants 436–45
  care and skill 431–2
  concurrent liability in tort and contract 450–2
  contract 421–2, 428–31, 445–8, 450–2
  deceit 421
  detrimental reliance 421–64
  floodgates argument 466
  foreseeability 441, 452–4
  fraud 421
  friends 430
  Hedley Byrne exception 421–64
  profession or business, in course of 431–52
  proximity 422–8, 434–5, 436–45, 452–4
  public authorities 430
  social context, advice in 431
  special relationships 422, 427
  supply of information 431–52, 464–5
  third parties 431–45
  three-stage *Caparo* test 452–5
  voluntary assumption of responsibility 421, 422–8, 432–4, 440, 445–8
  websites 431
  wills 456–64
negligent provision of services 445–8
nervous shock *see* **psychiatric illness**
New Zealand, no-fault compensation scheme in 1006–14
no-fault compensation 1000–6
non-delegable duty of care
  accessory liability distinguished 872
  categories 872–6
  general principle 877–84
  meaning 871
  vicarious liability distinguished 872

novus actus interveniens see
  intervening acts
nuisance 625–81
  see also **private nuisance**;
    public nuisance

occupiers' liability 524–55
  allurements 526
  callings, special
    risks associated
      with particular
      callings 538–9
  children 526, 537–8
  common duty of care 537–40
  common humanity, duty of 544
  contractual entrants 525, 530
  contributory negligence 538
  Countryside and Rights of
    Way Act 2000 554–5
  dangerous activities 535
  definition of occupiers
    530–4, 546
  exclusion of liability 543, 553
  independent
    contractors 540–3
  insurance 543
  invitees 525, 531
  licensees 527, 531
  Occupiers' Liability Act 1957
    position before Act 525–6
    provisions 527–43
  parental responsibility 537–8
  standard of care 551–2
  trespassers 525, 526, 544–55
  visitors 525, 531, 535–6,
    547–55
  volenti non fit injuria 543, 552
  warnings 537–8, 544, 552–3
Occupiers' Liability Act 1984
  position before Act 525–6
  provisions 545–7
omissions 472–90
  acts and omissions,
    distinction
    between 474–5
  affirmative action duties 477,
    504–5
  assumption of
    responsibility 477, 485,
    486–90
  control and
    responsibility 496–7
  danger, creation of 474
  emergency services 474–80,
    477–82
  Human Rights Act 1998 474
  landlord and tenant 498
  occupiers' liability 488–9
  office or position, occupation
    of 477, 489–90
  parent companies 499–504
  parents and children 477, 490
  police 508–15

prison, suicide and self-harm
  in 490
private nuisance 505
psychiatric patients 497–8
public authorities 477
reliance 482–6
rescuers 472–3
third parties, failure to
  control 491–23
trespassers 505
trespassers, dangers created
  by 489

**pain and suffering, damages
  for** see **damages for
    personal injury**
periodical payments see
  damages and death;
    **damages for personal
      injury**
planning permission
  private nuisance 641–5
police
  aggravated damages 896
  arrest and detention 81–5
  damages 889–90, 896
  exemplary or punitive
    damages 889–90
  false imprisonment 62–5
  investigative immunity 31
  omissions 508–15
**post-traumatic stress disorder
  (PTSD)** see **psychiatric
    injury**
prisons
  after-release care 614–17
  false imprisonment 81–5
  liberty and security, right to 85
  misfeasance in public
    office 84–5
  restrictions on liberty 81–5
  segregation 612–13
  strip searches 789–92
  suicide and self-harm 490
privacy 782–815
  claimant-centred test 805
  correcting
    misrepresentations 809
  damages 889
  development of right 782–3
  freedom of expression 794–815,
    803, 809
  freedom of the press 788
  Human Rights Act 1998 782,
    789, 791, 794, 803–4,
    814–15
  informational privacy 802–3
  nuisance 793–4
  passing off 788
  police investigations 809–10
  public authorities 814
  public places, privacy
    in 812–14

publication in public
  interest 794, 805–12
reasonable expectation of
  privacy 805–9, 813
sensitive claimants 805
sexual relationships 810–12
strip searches 789–92
surveillance 803–4
trespass 793
trespass to land 793–4
trespass to the person 787–8,
  793
two-stage approach 806–9
Wilkinson v Downton, rule
  in 793
private nuisance 629–81
  amenity interests 639, 656,
    661–3
  authorisation 655
  claimants 658–65
  'coming to the
    nuisance' 665–70
  continuing nuisance 651–6
  damages in lieu of an
    injunction 674
  damages for loss of
    amenity 673
  defences 665–70
  definition and
    nature 658–65
  foreseeability 649–51
  gravity of the
    interference 636–8
  Human Rights Act 1998 626,
    664–5, 671
  injunctions 649–51, 666,
    670–81
  locality principle 638–45
  material injury to
    property 638–45, 660
  nature, acts of 656–8
  negligence 649–51, 657, 666
  personal discomfort and
    inconvenience 638–45,
    660, 664
  personal injury 663–5
  planning permission 641–5
  prescription 670
  property tort, as 664
  proprietary interests
    658–65
  public benefit 647–9, 676
  public nuisance
    distinguished 626–7
  reasonableness of defendant's
    conduct 645–7
  regulatory
    compliance 670–3
  remedies 673–81
  statutory authority 671
  third parties 651–6
  unreasonable interference
    625, 635–49, 650, 665

INDEX

privilege, defamation and *see* **defamation**
procedure 4–5
product liability *see* **defective products**
professional negligence 216–21
  see also **clinical negligence**
proximity *see* **duty of care**
psychiatric illness, duty of care and 349–93
  aftermath doctrine 365, 367–70, 370–1
  assumption of responsibility 383–4
  communication of distressing news, liability for 376–7
  contractual obligations at work 383
  criticism of current law 386–9
  fear of developing physical illness 384–5
  floodgates argument 386, 390–1
  foreseeability 127–30, 134–5, 185, 387, 389–93
  love and affection, relationships of 387, 391
  occupational stress 378–83
  perception, proximity of 373–4
  primary victims 375–6, 393
  recognised psychiatric illness requirement 367–70
  reform 389–93
  secondary victims 185, 363–77, 389–93
  shock requirement 374–5, 392
  time and space, proximity in 371–3
  witnesses 349–77, 389–93
public authorities
  creation of a source of danger 515–21
  Human Rights Act 1998 30, 522–3
  local authorities 515–21
  negligence
    alternative remedies 163
    discretion 160–1
    equality principle 157–9
    irrationality 160–1
    justiciability 162–3
    policy/operational dichotomy 162–3
    public law controls 159–63
    reform 164–6
    ultra vires 160–1
  omissions 489
  police 508–15
public nuisance
  civil liability 626–7
  criminal offence 625, 626–7

definition 626–7
private nuisance
  distinguished 626–7
special damage 625, 626–9
punitive damages *see* **exemplary or punitive damages**
pure economic loss
  allocation of risk 400–3
  assumption of responsibility 394
  complex structure theory 410–11, 413, 414, 415
  critical evaluation 467–71
  dangerous defects 409–10, 417–21
  defective goods/buildings 403–21
  defective premises 410
  defective premises legislation 415–17
  economic analysis 464–7
  exclusionary rule 394–403
  floodgates argument 399
  health and safety 411
  Hedley Byrne exception 421–64
  latent defects 416, 419–21
  negligent misstatements 421–64, 464–71
  negligent provision of services 446–52
  policy 464, 467–71
  preventive damages 400
  proximity 409, 411
  quality, defects of 409–10
  relational loss 399–400
  wills 456–64

recklessness
  breach of duty 198–9
remoteness of damage 283–9
  see also **intervening acts**; **scope of liability**
  causation 227, 283–4
  direct or natural consequence of act 287
  foreseeability 283–9, 289–95
  policy 289–95
  scope of duty approach 289–95
  scope of risk approach 284–9
  third parties 493–4
  valuations 293
res ipsa loquitur
  application of maxim 223–6
  burden of proof 221–6
  definition 221
  evidence 221–4
  future 226
  purpose and effect 220–1
rescuers
  causation 283

  intervening acts 276–8
  omissions 472–3
  scope of liability 532
***Rylands v Fletcher*, rule in** 681–96
  consequential loss 686
  damages 686
  dangerous things 681, 694
  dangerousness 687
  defences 693–4
  escape 686–7
  extra-hazardous activities 686
  fire 694–6
  foreseeability 686, 693
  non-natural use of land 688–92
  nuisance 652, 681–96
  reform 696–7
  strict liability 694–6

scope of liability 227
  intervening acts 274–83
    claimant 279–81
    deliberate wrongdoers 279
    negligent third parties 281–3
    rescuers 283
  remoteness of damage 284–9
  scope of duty approach 289–95
  Wagon Mound approach 284–9
self-defence and related defences 101–5
  lethal force, use of 101–4
  mistake 101–3
  reasonableness 101–3
  trespass to the person 104–5
settlements 984–9
  cost and delay 986
  flexibility 986
  hard bargaining 987
  inequality of bargaining power 984, 986–7
  offers 989
  reasons for settlement 986
  solicitors, role of 986–7
  strategy 987–8
  structured settlements 899, 903
  uncertainty of litigation 986
slander *see* **defamation**
social security
  Compensation Recovery Unit 939, 966–7
  damages for personal injury 905, 934, 936–9
  deduction of benefits from damages 936–9
  no-fault compensation 1002
standard of care
  see also **breach of duty**
  age 210–13

alternative medicine 205–6
children 201, 210–13
clinical negligence 204–6
common industrial
    practice 215–16
experience 202–6
first-aiders 215
learner drivers 202–4, 214
mental disabilities 201,
    206–10
objectivity 200–14, 998
physical disability 206–10
professional
    standards 216–21
special skills 213–15, 220–1
sport 199, 206
strict liability 200

strict liability
  see also **breach of statutory
    duty; defective
    products**
  arguments for and
    against 1000
  Motor Insurers' Bureau 1004
  road accidents 1003–4
  Rylands v Fletcher, rule
    in 694–6
  vaccine damage 999

theories of tort 17–24
  aims of tort law 18–22
  doctrinal classifications 23–4
thin skull rule *see* **egg-shell
    skull rule**
trespass to the person
  see also **assault; battery; false
    imprisonment**
  burden of proof 43–4
  consent 86
  defences 104–5
  fault 43–6
  Human Rights Act 1998 31
  indirect harm 65–8
  intention 47–9
  liberty and security, right
    to 31
  life, right to 31

medical treatment 86
negligence 43–6, 65–8
privacy 787–8
recklessness 47–8
time limits 44–6, 45–6
writ of trespass 2–5, 43, 44–5

unfair contract terms
  Consumer Rights Act
    2015 323–6

vicarious liability 816–84
  carelessness of
    employee 862–5
  close connection test 846–61
  course of employment
    carelessness of
      employee 862–5
    close connection
      test 846–61
    criminal acts of
      employee 868–71
    meaning 845
    vehicles used on
      unauthorised
      journeys 865–8
  criminal acts of
    employee 868–71
  deterrence 822–3
  employer–employee
    relationship 823–9
  enterprise risk 822
  exemplary or punitive
    damages 894–5
  historical
    development 817–23
  independent contractors 818
  justification for vicarious
    liability 817–23
  lending employees 829–33
  loss distribution 821–2
  master's tort theory 817,
    818–19
  non-delegable duty of
    care 871–84
  vicarious liability
    distinguished 872

policy 819–21
relationships akin to
    employment 833–44
relationships triggering
    liability
  employment
    relationships 823–9
  generally 823
  lending employees 829–33
  relationships akin to
    employment 833–44
  vehicle drivers 844–5
servant's tort theory 818
vehicle drivers 844–5
vehicles used on unauthorised
    journeys 865–8
volenti non fit injuria 296–307
  contributory
    negligence 299–302
  employers 298
  employers' liability 302–5
  evaluation 305–7
  express assumption of
    risk 297
  implied assumption of
    risk 297, 299–307
  knowledge of risk 296–7
  operation of defence
    298–305
  warnings 552

warnings
  defective products 584
  exclusion of liability 20,
    320–1
  occupiers' liability 537–8,
    544, 552–3
  omissions 485
  volenti non fit injuria 552
Wilkinson v Downton, rule in
  42–3, 65–75, 77, 793
wills
  delays by solicitor in drawing
    up will 456–65
writ of trespass 2–5, 7
**wrongful birth and wrongful
    life** 133